Buddhist Studies

Buddhist Studies

by

J. W. de Jong

edited by

Gregory Schopen

ASIAN HUMANITIES PRESS

A Division of

LANCASTER-MILLER PUBLISHERS

Berkeley, California

A Note to the Reader

Because of the exceptional importance of Professor de Jong's work, the Publishers have desired to make these articles—hitherto scattered throughout a number of difficult-to-obtain scholarly journals—more readily available both to scholars and to the interested public. Due to the prohibitively high cost of retypesetting a work of this magnitude and complexity, it has been prepared as a facsimile edition, in which the original pagination is preserved. It is hoped that this book will be found useful to all those who are working in the field of Buddhist studies.

ISBN 0-89581-002-6

PRINTED IN THE REPUBLIC OF CHINA

Table of Contents

Preface

The publication of the present volume requires very little justification. It reprints all the major articles and reviews of J. W. de Jong which are primarily concerned with Buddhism in India, and thus makes available in a single volume any number of publications which are essential to any serious student of Buddhist literature in India. It is impossible, for example, to read with profit the original text of either the *Rāṣṭrapālaparipṛcchā* or the *Karuṇāpuṇḍārika* without constant reference to the corrections and emendations to these two texts which Prof. de Jong has published. It is impossible now to refer to Śāntideva without referring to his "La Légende de Śantideva," or to use Roerich's Biography of Dharmasvāmin without consulting Prof. de Jong's complete review. This same pattern, in fact, occurs over and over.

As noted above, the present volume reprints Prof. de Jong's articles and reviews which deal primarily with Indian Buddhism and therefore leaves aside almost entirely those specifically devoted to China, Tibet and Mongolia. The nature and number of those publications which were omitted on this basis can be easily determined by consulting the complete—up to September 1977—bibliography of Prof. de Jong's publications which is to be found at the end of this book.*For the selection of those which were included I am, in the end, responsible.

*It should be noted that one item is here reprinted which does not occur in the bibliography and was published anonymously. This is the Appendice to the *Indo-Iranian Reprints* edition of L. Finot, *Rāṣṭrapālaparipṛcchā.*

I made my selection primarily on the basis of the degree to which the individual publications made a significant contribution—lexical, historical, bibliographical, or text-critical—to the work or works under consideration. Such a criterion is of couse largely subjective, and others would undoubtedly have made other choices. To compensate for this admittedly subjective process of selection I then also tried to select items which would fully reflect the full range of Prof. de Jong's writings. This resulted in the seven categories under which I came to group the material: I. General Studies; II. Buddhist Authors; III. Pali Literature; IV. Sanskrit Hīnayāna Literature; V. Mahāyāna Sūtra Literature; VI. Śāstra Literature; and VII. Tantric Literature. I can only hope that this process has not distorted the overall picture of Prof. de Jong's total production to date.

The index for this volume required some difficult decisions. As would be obvious to anyone familiar with the material, a full word-index would have required a small volume in itself and therefore was out of the question. Since the great majority of the publications dealt with problems in specific texts, and since these problems were almost always treated in the order in which they occurred in their respective texts, a text-title index seemed a good compromise. To these text titles were then added a few personal names, notable words (many corrections, additions, etc., to Edgerton's *Buddhist Hybrid Sanskrit Grammar and Dictionary* are indexed under the latter's name), etc. In short, the index is not complete and should be approached accordingly. It should also be noted that a short list of errata has been appended to the volume. This corrects only obvious printing errors, etc. Apart from this, all the items are reprinted exactly as they first appeared.

The table of contents also requires a few words. The titles which occur there, especially of reviews, are often abbreviated. Before each title is added a number. This number refers to the number of the particular item in the complete bibliography of Prof. de Jong's publications which will be found at the end of the book. There all the bibliographical information concerning any particular item—full title, original place of publication, etc. —will be found. Although new, consecutive pagination has been added, to facilitate references, the original pagination has also been retained in all cases.

In the preparation of this volume I have received a great deal of help: Prof. de Jong has had an active hand in it from the beginning; the index is in fact a joint production of myself, my colleague Paul Harrison, who also helped in many other ways, and Betty Kat, who in addition did all the typing—some of it several times—and in general made my task much easier. Sigrid Loofs carefully checked the index and table of contents. To all of these go my thanks. I would also like to thank Prof. Edward Conze and Dr. Akira Yuyama for lending me their personal copies of a number of Prof. de Jong's articles and reviews otherwise unavailable to me; and all the publishers who graciously gave their permission to reprint material which first appeared in their publications.

Gregory Schopen
Canberra, September 28, 1977.

I
General Studies

J. W. DE JONG, CANBERRA

THE STUDY OF BUDDHISM. PROBLEMS AND PERSPECTIVES*

The first chair for the study of Sanskrit in Europe was created in 1814 at the Collège de France in Paris for Antoine-Léonard de Chézy (1773-1832). He was succeeded by Eugène Burnouf (1801-1852) who occupied the chair for twenty years (1832-1852). It is not necessary to dwell upon the importance of Burnouf's contribution to Buddhist studies. Even today the student of Buddhism makes frequent use of his monumental works: *Introduction à l'histoire du Buddhisme indien* (Paris, 1844) and *Le Lotus de la bonne loi* (Paris, 1852). Since Burnouf, many distinguished scholars have studied Buddhist scriptures in Pāli, Sanskrit, Chinese, Tibetan and Mongolian. Buddhist studies have developed into an important branch of Orientalism. However, until recently no special chairs for Buddhist studies existed in European universities. It was only in 1926 that a chair for "philologie bouddhique" was created in Paris for Jean Przyluski (1885-1944). A second chair was established in the University of Leiden in 1956.[1] The creation of these chairs has been prompted by the awareness of the fact that Buddhist studies cannot be undertaken as a subsidiary subject by a professor of Sanskrit, Chinese or Mongolian. This becomes obvious when one takes into account the various fields associated with the study of Buddhism. By analysing some of the more important problems encountered in the past and at present, it is possible to find some indications as to the future perspectives of the study of Buddhism.

As is well-known, Buddhism originated in the Eastern part of India, spread over the Indian continent and subsequently over a great part of South, Central and East Asia. However, the history of Buddhism outside India will

* The original Dutch version of this paper was read as an inaugural lecture in the University of Leiden on the 28th September 1956. It was published in the same year by Mouton & Co., The Hague, under the title *De Studie van het Boeddhisme. Problemen en Perspectieven.* Apart from a few minor changes and corrections, the English version is identical with the Dutch version. The author is much obliged to Miss E. J. J. C. Kat and Professor O. Berkelbach van der Sprenkel for their help in preparing the English translation.

[1] Since 1956 chairs of Buddhist studies have been established at the universities of Hamburg and Vienna.

not be taken into consideration, at any rate in so far as it does not assist the study of Buddhism in India. Indian Buddhism can be divided into three so-called vehicles, the Little Vehicle, the Great Vehicle and the Diamond Vehicle, terms which were used by the Buddhists themselves. The Little Vehicle comprises the schools, traditionally 18 in number, that developed in the centuries preceding our era. Around the beginning of our era the Great Vehicle emerges and finally after about five centuries the Diamond Vehicle appears. Each of these vehicles has produced a rich literature. Undoubtedly, this literature is the most important source of knowledge of Buddhism. Buddhist art, inscriptions and coins have supplied us with useful data, but generally they cannot be fully understood without the support given by the texts. Consequently, the study of Buddhism needs first of all to be concentrated on the texts which have been transmitted; and, indeed, it only made good progress after Buddhist philology had been established on a sound basis. Therefore, when discussing the problems of the study of Buddhism one has to take as a starting point the particular difficulties which have been encountered, and are still being encountered, in the field of Buddhist philology: difficulties arising from the way Buddhist literature developed and was transmitted over the centuries.

The Buddha preached his message of salvation to all of those who came flocking to hear his words; he addressed himself not only to those belonging to the highest classes, as did the brahmans (who were loath to impart their knowledge to others) but to all who wished to hear. The Buddha preached in the local dialect; the brahmans used Sanskrit, which was unintelligible to the lower classes of the people. He desired to share with everyone the Awakening he had obtained under the bodhi-tree, whereas the brahmans instructed their pupils only in the traditionally transmitted texts. The Buddha's teaching did not consist of a number of dogmas, which he tried to inculcate in the minds of his followers. He endeavoured to call forth in others the desire to try to obtain Awakening through their own efforts; the brahmans, on the contrary, taught their pupils to recite the sacred Vedic texts without the slightest variation of a single word or even a single accent. In these circumstances it is understandable that the Buddhavacanam, the word of the Buddha, spread over the whole of India and was preached everywhere in the local dialect. After the Buddha's death the schools of the Little Vehicle gradually developed, each having its own canon of sacred texts, each differing in content and language. For centuries these texts were transmitted orally. Were all these texts, in the course of time, committed to writing in the various languages in which they had been transmitted from one generation to the next? It is difficult to answer this question since, as a result of the almost total disappearance of Buddhism from the continent of India, very few manuscripts of Buddhist texts have survived in India. However, one of the schools, that of "the Elders", spread to Ceylon before our era, according to the tradition, already during the time of Asoka in the third century B. C. The canon of this school, written in Pāli, a middle-Indo-Aryan language, was put down in writing and its manuscripts have been preserved. Ceylonese tradition has it that Pāli is identical with Māgadhī, i. e. the language of the country of Magadha, where Buddhism originated and that therefore the Pāli-canon contains the word of the Buddha in the very language used by him. This tradition has been overthrown by modern scholarship. At present it is generally agreed that Pāli is neither the language of Magadha, nor one of the languages spoken at the time anywhere in India, but a literary language containing elements derived from more than one local dialect. Attempts to discover the origin of Pāli, or the main dialect on which it is based, have been fruitless. It has been established that, linguistically, the Pāli-canon consists of various strata, and that at least parts of it are translated from texts in another language, designated by Sylvain Lévi as 'langue précanonique du bouddhisme'[2] and by Lüders as Māgadhī or old-Ardhamāgadhī[3]. The latter scholar is of the opinion that the Buddhist texts in Pāli and Sanskrit are based on an original canon in Māgadhī. This assertion is not borne out conclusively, or indeed made plausible, by the results of his research. In the first place there is no evidence whatsoever of the existence of an original canon established either in oral form or in writing. It seems more reasonable to assume that only a small number of texts, above all verses and stereotyped dogmatic formulas, at an early stage attained a definite form, and that they were subsequently translated into Pāli and other middle-Indo-Aryan languages. But it is difficult to believe that the extensive Pāli-canon with its various linguistic strata—not to mention the Buddhist Sanskrit texts—was translated in its entirety from an original canon. Secondly, it has by no means been proved by Lüders that Māgadhī was the language of this original canon. Contemporary texts in Māgadhī are totally lacking, and the earliest inscriptions at our disposal date from the time of Asoka, the middle of the third century B. C., or later. It is impossible to determine to what extent the language of these inscriptions reflects the spoken Māgadhī of that period. It is quite conceivable that Asoka's chancellery used a *lingua franca* in which Māgadhī probably dominated, as may

[2] "Observations sur une langue précanonique du bouddhisme", *JA*, 1912, II, pp. 495-514.

[3] *Beobachtungen über die Sprache des buddhistischen Urkanons* (Berlin, 1954), p. 8.

be deduced from the fact that inscriptions far beyond the borders of Magadha were also couched in the same language as the inscriptions in Magadha itself. Literary texts in Māgadhī appear only after the beginning of our era in a few scarce fragments of Buddhist plays, and not until much later more fully in classical dramas. The artificial character of the so-called theatre-Māgadhī is well-known. Consequently, neither the inscriptions nor the texts provide sufficient material to give a clear insight into the development of the language of Magadha. Even with the best will in the world it would still be impossible to draw from this scanty material enough evidence to allow the conclusion that the original canon was written in Māgadhī.

In view of these facts, the most reliable method would seem to be to scrutinize closely the Pāli texts and parallel texts in other languages; thus to try to discover where these texts go back to a precanonic text, and then to try to determine the character of the language of this text. Lüders has done much valuable work in this direction, and it is a task for the future to continue research in the way indicated by him, avoiding rash theories, which can only hinder progress. As to the languages in which the canons of the other schools of the Little Vehicle were written, only suppositions can be advanced, since such indications as the Buddhist tradition has to offer with regard to this point are completely useless, and no other texts in a middle-Indo-Aryan language have come down to us—with the exception of one text written in a language of the north-west of India: the Gāndhārī Dharmapada. Unfortunately it is impossible to be certain whether this text formed part of an existing canon.[4] In Kashmir, Afghanistan and Central Asia fragments in Sanskrit have been found of texts belonging to two schools of the Little Vehicle, the Sarvāstivāda and Mūlasarvāstivāda schools, and it is generally held that these schools made use of Sanskrit in writing down their canon. If we bear in mind the results obtained from the study of the Pāli canon, we ought to be extremely wary in drawing any such conclusion. It has been ascertained that this canon was written in a literary language and not in a dialect. On the other hand the oldest layers of the Pāli canon already show a Sanskrit influence, an influence which is increasingly apparent in the later strata. According to tradition,

[4] John Brough believes that the Gāndhārī Dharmapada [MS Dutreuil de Rhins] belongs to the canon of a school and declares that the Dharmaguptakas and Kāśyapīyas must be considered as eligible, but that still other possibilities cannot be ruled out; cf. *The Gāndhārī Dharmapada* (London, 1962), pp. 43-45. Franz Bernhard decides in favour of the Dharmaguptakas, cf. "Gāndhārī and the Buddhist Mission in Central Asia", *Añjali. A Felicitation Volume Presented to O.H. de Alwis Wijesekera* (Peradeniya, 1970), pp. 55-62.

which on this point has some evidential support, the writing down of the Pāli-canon took place in Ceylon several decades before the beginning of our era. Since then the manuscripts have for centuries been subjected to a process of normalization at the hands of commentators and grammarians who have replaced ancient readings by others more agreeable to Pāli-grammar[5]. Traces of the influence of Sanskrit were in all probability greatly reduced in this way. If then the Pāli-texts in India had already been strongly marked by Sanskrit influence well before the Christian era, would it then be too bold an assumption to make that they escaped a process of ever-increasing Sanskritization precisely because of the fact that they had so early been committed to writing in Ceylon? The canons of the schools in India must have experienced the influence of Sanskrit to an ever increasing degree. It is therefore not at all improbable, that the canons, of which only fragments in Sanskrit have survived, were also originally transmitted in a middle Indo-Aryan language. This hypothesis is supported by the linguistic aspect of the fragments, the language of which is not pure Sanskrit, but Sanskrit mixed with middle-Indo-Aryan forms. Moreover, the oldest manuscripts do not date back further than to the 5th or 6th century. The process of Sanskritization is clearly visible in the scriptures of another school, the Mahāsāṃghikas. To this school belongs an extensive text, written in Buddhist Hybrid Sanskrit, and transmitted in Nepalese manuscripts. A linguistic analysis of this text, the Mahāvastu, has proven the presence of different linguistic strata. The language of the oldest strata deviates much more from classical Sanskrit than does that of the later strata. Undoubtedly, the oldest parts go back to a text in middle Indo-Aryan. More uniform in character is the language of the recently published Vinaya texts of the same school.[6] These texts must originally have been composed in a middle-Indo-Aryan language but Prakrit forms have been replaced to a large degree by Sanskrit forms.

The above considerations justify the preliminary conclusion that the texts of the Little Vehicle have been subject to a process of Sanskritization to an ever-increasing degree. It is difficult to establish in detail the course of this process and the period of time involved, for the texts, handed down to us in

---

[5] Cf. H. Smith, *Saddanīti, la grammaire palie d'Aggavamsa*, vol. I (Lund, 1928), pp v-vi; vol. IV (1949), p. 1139.

[6] The *Prātimokṣa-sūtra of the Mahāsāṅghikas.* Edited by W. Pachow and Ramakantha Mishra, *Journal of the Ganganatha Jha Research Institute*, IX (1952), pp. 239-260; X (1952-1953), app. pp. 1-48; XI-XII (1953-1955), pp. 243-248; *Abhisamācārika.* Edited by B. Jinananda. Patna, 1969; *Bhikṣuṇī-vinaya.* Edited by Gustav Roth. Patna, 1970.

manuscripts, reveal only the final stage of the development. However, by taking into account the history of Indian languages, it is possible to obtain a better insight into this problem. Epigraphy is here of great importance, since inscriptions which can be reliably dated, are available to us. The oldest Indian inscriptions are those of Asoka, dating back to the middle of the third century B. C., and are in middle-Indian. The earliest inscription in Sanskrit probably dates from the end of the first century B. C. After the middle of the second century A. D. the use of Sanskrit increased, with the result that inscriptions in middle-Indian are hardly to be found at all in North India after the third century, or in South India after the fourth century. Sanskrit influence on inscriptions in middle-Indo-Aryan is noticeable in varying degrees. It is a task for the future to study the epigraphic materials and to try to trace how far the linguistic characteristics can be explained by historical, geographical, political, social and religious factors. It is to be hoped that in this way new light may be shed not only on the history of Indian languages, but also on the Sanskritization of Buddhist texts.

In discussing the linguistic problems of the transmission of Buddhist texts we have limited ourselves so far to the literature of the Little Vehicle. However, it is necessary to study in the same way the literature of the Great Vehicle; and also the history of both Vehicles, because after the rise of the Great Vehicle in India, the schools of the Little Vehicle did not disappear but continued to transmit their texts. The surviving texts of the Great Vehicle in Indian languages can be divided into those in pure Sanskrit, and those in the so-called Buddhist Hybrid Sanskrit mentioned earlier. This last is a Sanskrit which, as shown by the extant texts, has been interspersed to a greater or lesser degree with middle-Indo-Aryan forms, words and constructions. In past years the question has been much discussed, whether these texts were originally composed in one or more middle-Indo-Aryan dialects, or in a *lingua franca* derived from several middle-Indo-Aryan languages. The second solution gives rise to the question whether this language was generally spoken; or was a religious language only, in which case one may also inquire whether this language was spoken amongst the Buddhist or used only for writing down texts and/or for recitation. Finally, the question was raised, whether those texts, whose language is almost completely free of middle-Indian influence, were written directly in this language or, alternatively, should be seen as the end product of a long process of Sanskritization. It is not my intention to discuss these problems in detail. From the discussions one often gains the impression that one is inclined too soon to have an answer and an explanation ready without a careful study of all available material. First and foremost attention needs to be drawn to a very important source of material, which has so far hardly been made use of: namely the translations of Indian Buddhist texts into other languages. Only a small amount of the Buddhist literature that once existed in Indian languages has survived—though we must add that, in the past seventy years especially, important finds have been made in Central Asia, Kashmir and Tibet. Nevertheless, this amounts to only a very small quantity compared to the thousands of texts which have come down to us in Chinese and Tibetan translation. Buddhism came to China in the first century A.D. and to Tibet in the seventh or eighth century. The Chinese translations, collected in the Chinese Buddhist canon, were almost all made between the second and the twelfth centuries. The Tibetan translations collected in two canons, the Kanjur and the Tanjur, were completed between the eighth and seventeenth centuries. Being exceptionally literal, they are of the greatest importance for textual criticism; though only of secondary importance as far as the history of the texts is concerned, since for the most part they came into being in a period when Buddhism in India had passed its peak, and when most of the texts had already received their definitive form. The Chinese translations, on the other hand, though much less exact and (especially in the earliest period), often very poorly translated, are of incalculable value for the history of Buddhist texts. Chinese translations of many texts exist from various periods. They thus enable us to see how the texts in question gradually developed. It appears for instance that some texts of the Little Vehicle, by reason of changes and additions, were transformed into texts of the Great Vehicle. With the aid of the Chinese translations the various layers of a text can often be determined. It is obvious how important this is for the study of texts in Buddhist Hybrid Sanskrit. For the problem of the middle-Indian original text can only be properly posed when the original nucleus has been extracted from the text. Moreover, from a careful study of Chinese transcriptions of proper names it is possible to reconstruct their original form. However, before making use of Chinese translations one needs to determine when they were translated and to what extent the present text is identical with the original text of the translation.

The Chinese, with their predilection for bibliography, already in early times began to compile catalogues of Buddhist texts. The data contained in these catalogues need to be critically analyzed by comparing one catalogue with another, and confronting the results with data supplied by the biographies of the translators. Finally, the texts themselves must be analyzed critically. The translations were often improved and changed, or wrongly attributed. Such critical analysis has recently been carried out quite excellently, mainly by Japanese scholars, and has already yielded important results. Up till now the work of Japanese scholars in this field, as also in other fields of Buddhist studies, has been insufficiently studied by non-Japanese scholars. This has been either because of inadequate knowledge of the Japanese language, or because of the absence of Japanese publications in University libraries. Today one can see a noticeable change: for, in addition to Sanskrit, Pāli, Tibetan and Chinese, more and more attention is being paid by non-Japanese scholars to work in Japanese. And, as well, there is a growing tendency in Japan to give more general currency to the work of Japanese scholars by translations into English or French, or by summaries in these languages.

From the foregoing it will be clear that the study of Chinese translations is essential for a better understanding of Indian Buddhist literature. A critical scrutiny of these translations cannot be made without studying the history of Chinese Buddhism. In the same way it can be shown that the study of Buddhism in the other countries to which it spread is also necessary for the understanding of Indian Buddhism. In particular, it is of great importance to study Buddhism in those countries where it is still flourishing today, and where an uninterrupted tradition extends back to Indian Buddhism. For the Great Vehicle, Tibet and Japan are of particular interest; and for the Little Vehicle, Ceylon, Burma, Siam and Cambodia. This is not only because texts of Indian origin have been transmitted, translated, explained and analyzed in those countries ever since the introduction of Buddhism, but even more so because the study of present-day Buddhism, and the direct contact with the Buddhist mentality which these countries afford, can contribute to a deepening of our understanding. The study of Buddhism in Europe has been mainly concerned with its philological aspects. Since, in the field of Asian studies, university chairs were established only for Asian languages, it was often a Sanskritist or a Sinologist who specialized in this study.

Here we may find the answer to our question, why the need of special chairs for Buddhism has hardly made itself felt up till now. It was only the realization of the scope of the task of Buddhist philology which led to the creation in Paris of a chair for "philologie bouddhique". It is hardly surprising therefore, that excellent work was done in the field of philology. Furthermore, we must not overlook the important progress that the study of Buddhism has made in India and Japan since the 'twenties', through the adoption of the methods of Western philology there, especially as developed by the French school under the guidance of Sylvain Lévi.

Activities in Europe were by no means restricted to editing, translating and studying the texts. The number of books and articles attempting to explain the teaching and history of Buddhism, are as numerous as the grains of sand on the banks of the Ganges. However, if one considers how effective these publications have been in providing a better insight into the essence of Buddhism, the results appear to be disappointing. It is necessary to examine in what ways, and for what reasons, this has been so, if the mistakes of the past are to be avoided in the future.

In order to give a clear example of the difficulties encountered in understanding Buddhism as a religion, I would like to draw attention to the various concepts which are to be found in the works of Western scholars concerning the figure of the Buddha. On the analogy of the term Christology, it would be possible to designate this branch of Buddhist studies by the term Buddhology. However, it may be better to avoid this term in order to prevent any assumption of an analogy between the problems in those two fields of study.

Burnouf, the brilliant founder of the study of Buddhism, occupied himself only incidentally with the figure of the Buddha. In his *Introduction à l'histoire du Buddhisme indien,* published in 1844, he gave a systematic description of the Buddhist Sanskrit manuscripts which Hodgson had sent to Paris from Nepal. With remarkable intuition Burnouf divided these texts into three groups,[7] corresponding to the three Vehicles mentioned above. Basing himself on the texts of the first group, Burnouf regarded the teachings of the Buddha as dominated by ethical doctrines.[8] He was of the opinion that the Buddha, during his life-time, had always been a human being even for his most ardent followers.[9] We hear quite a different sound in the *Essai sur la lègende du Buddha* by Senart, which appeared in 1875. The story of the Buddha's life contained in the texts, as he interprets them, is the story of a sun-hero. As a god of light the Buddha descends in the cloud-womb ("le sein nuageux") of his mother, who perishes after his birth in the blaze of his rays.[10] In this way Senart explains the legend of the Buddha, from beginning to end, as a naturalistic myth. He regards the non-mythic elements in the legend as of secondary importance, as later additions to the myth, which has gradually been transformed into a divine legend and subsequently into a hero-legend, having in the process assumed more realistic elements.[11] Seven years later, in his *Geschiedenis*

---

[7] *Op. cit.*, p. 581.

[8] *Op. cit.*, p. 126, 152, 335.

[9] *Op. cit.*, p. 340.

[10] *Op. cit.*, 2nd ed. (1882), p. 433.

[11] *Op. cit.*, p. 435, 445.

van het Buddhisme in Indië [History of Buddhism in India], Kern carried this method of interpretation even further. Even Buddha's preaching becomes a manifestation of a sun-god. As an example I quote what Kern says about the first sermon of the Buddha: "The first sermon falls on the day of midsummer, and therefore according to all rules of mythology, the Buddha was not allowed to preach about anything else but the text which nature offered him: he recommended the middle way. Seldom has the golden middle way been commended in a more trivial way, surely, but then this recommendation of a generally acknowledged, praiseworthy principle was not the main consideration."[12]

The mythological explanations of Senart and Kern found little approval. Naturalistic mythology had already passed its peak; although, for example, in the field of the Veda, its influence would continue to be felt for a long time. Moreover, more attention was soon given to the oldest Buddhism and to the Pāli texts, of which only a few had so far been published and translated. Schayer has pointed out that the study of Buddhism has been greatly influenced by the view that in the history of a religion only the original is real, all that comes later being more or less a degeneration. Just as protestant theologians tried to reveal true evangelical Christianity, so one wanted to get to know "the wonderful figure of the Buddha" and "the original world of ideas" on the basis of the Pāli-texts.[13] To this observation by Schayer can be added the fact that the influence of 19th century ideas about Christianity is also noticeable in the attempt now made to regard the Buddha as a teacher of humanity, preaching a sublime morality. While on the one hand one tried to point out similarities between Buddhist and Christian morality, on the other, there was no lack of emphasis on the fact that the oldest Buddhism was a religion without a god. Although undoubtedly such views were more prominent in the more popular literature about Buddhism, one cannot ignore their influence on the work of scholars. All these factors contributed to the wide response given to Oldenberg's work: *Buddha, sein Leben, seine Lehre, seine Gemeinde*, published in 1881. However, it was certainly the masterly way in which Oldenberg presented his views which turned the scale. Regularly reprinted for more than 80 years, this book, as no other, has left its mark on the way Buddhism has been understood in the West. Oldenberg reproved Senart for having made use of texts dating from a time in which the memory of the Buddha had become overgrown by legendary and mythological elements. According to him, one should first and foremost turn to the Pāli-texts, most of which were already compiled

[12] *Op. cit.*, Vol. I (1882), p. 240.

[13] *Ausgewählte Kapitel aus der Prasannapadā* (Krakau, 1931), p. ix.

during the century following the Nirvāṇa of the Buddha.[14] Legendary traditions about Buddha's life in these texts should be ignored. Once these non-historical elements have been eliminated, there remains a series of positive facts which are, historically, completely reliable.[15] With a sound philological knowledge, and always with references to his sources, Oldenberg carried out this programme. Up to the present his method has found many followers who, however, frequently did not observe the same caution and carefulness shown by Oldenberg himself, and therefore often went much further than he in their search for historical facts in the texts.

In the long run, however, a reaction against Oldenberg's viewpoint was bound to come. This was caused, in the first place, by a change in the evaluation of the Pāli texts. It appeared more and more impossible to date the texts as early as Oldenberg had done. At the same time, more emphasis was placed on the fact that the Pāli canon embodied the tradition of one school only of the Little Vehicle and consequently could not be regarded as fully representative of original Buddhism. It was gradually realized that the legendary elements in the Pāli texts were not to be so easily put aside. They both appeared in the oldest strata and were closely interwoven with the other elements. Moreover, from the study of the inscriptions and of archaeological remains it became apparent that already at an early stage the legendary element played a great role. All this resulted in a more careful approach toward determining the historical element in the texts. Some scholars even gave it as their opinion that no adequate criterion existed for distinguishing between historical and non-historical elements. This view has been advanced very forcefully in an extremely interesting article[16] by Lamotte in which he surveys the study of the legend of the Buddha and analyzes its sources on the basis of texts in Pāli, Sanskrit and Chinese. In this article he shows that the legendary element already formed an integral part of the oldest documents, and has played an ever increasing role as time went on. It appears, moreover, that it took almost ten centuries to write a complete biography of the Buddha, as the oldest texts only relate some episodes from his life, while other episodes were added later on. According to Lamotte every attempt to discover an historical kernel in the legend of the Buddha is doomed to failure; one can only endeavour to trace the growth of the legend, and if possible to explain this process by means of a critical study

[14] *Op. cit.*, p. 77.

[15] *Op. cit.*, p. 92.

[16] "La légende du Buddha", *Revue de l'histoire des religions*, t. CXXXIV (1947-48), pp. 37-71.

of the texts and the archaeological monuments.

Following Lamotte, one can distinguish three different tendencies in the views of Western scholars. Firstly, the mythological explanation, as given by Senart and Kern, then the rationalistic explanation with Oldenberg as its most important representative; and finally the pragmatic attitude, which has been formulated most clearly by Lamotte himself. Adherents of the first view tried completely to reduce the Buddha to a god by eliminating all historical or pseudo-historical elements; whereas, contrariwise, those adopting the second view wanted to emphasize Buddha as a human being by eliminating all that pertains to the legend. In both cases too great a reliance was placed on the method used. Each school, by assuming either the mythological or the historical element to be the "original" one, thought themselves able to prove their thesis by critically sifting the sources. The mythological explanation failed to pay attention to the Buddha as founder of Buddhism. His very existence was doubted by Kern, who claimed that "the Buddha of the legend is a mythical figure, who no longer bears the marks of the historical founder of the school, even if he existed."[17]

Senart was much more careful on this point, and stated emphatically that it was not his intention to prove that the Buddha never existed.[18] He even considered it possible that memories of true events were interwoven with the legend; but he believed that the historicity of these elements could not be proven. With the rationalistic explanation, on the other hand, there was no doubt about the possibility of eventually revealing an historic kernel in the legend of the Buddha. There was, however, a difference of opinion about the question whether to his immediate followers the Buddha had been a human or a supernatural being. It was not fully realized that this is the fundamental question—the question which needs to be put at the very beginning of the enquiry. This is because, to form an opinion as to the historic value of the sources regarding the Buddha, it is necessary first to trace the ideas with regard to the Buddha which are found in the sources themselves. Reading the oldest Pāli texts, it becomes clear that the alternative man/god does not apply to the Buddha. For the Buddhists, gods were beings who as a result of their merits in a previous existence, enjoyed a state of bliss in heaven. With the passage of time, however, their existence as gods ends. Although in many respects the life of these gods is more pleasant than that of human beings, only human beings are able to hear Buddha's sermons, to obtain salvation

[17] *Op. cit.*, vol. I, p. 233.
[18] *Op. cit.*, p. 452.

from the cycle of rebirth and to become free from all impurities—impurities from which the gods cannot be completely free. How possibly could Buddha's followers ever have regarded him as a god? Only an outsider could ask himself this question. A famous text[19] narrates how a brahman asks the Buddha whether he is a god, a demi-god, a demon or a human. The Buddha replies that the impurities which could have made him one of these beings had been rooted out:

> "Just as a lotus, born in the water, rises above it without being soiled by it, so have I, born in the world, overcome the world and remain in it without being soiled by it. Realize, brahman, that I am a Buddha."

How evident it is from this passage, to which numerous others could be added, that the Buddha must be regarded as a being *sui generis*—as a unique being. No matter how, in later texts, the concept of the Buddha changes and the miraculous and supernatural become more prominent, he nevertheless always remains the Buddha. This must be the starting-point in the study of Buddhist literature. Its authors are not historians in the sense which a modern European scholar would ascribe to this word. Their history of the Buddha, his birth, his Awakening and his death, is a history of salvation. In the same way, what has been written by the schools of the Little and the Great Vehicle is religious history. From the texts one can learn the Buddhists' point of view about the Buddha, and learn which traditional beliefs existed in the various schools. The actual historical truth can only be found if one resorts to other, non-Buddhist sources. If they confirm the Buddhist tradition on a particular point, then one may assume, according to the rules of historical criticism, that this point is an historical fact. Too often another method is followed by scholars who seek to find the historical truth by establishing an agreement in the traditions of the various Buddhist schools. Some years ago, in connection with a work in which this method was used, Demiéville once again clearly pointed out that in this way one can only show that in so far as the various traditions of different schools agree, a common tradition underlies them; but this affords no ground for assuming this common tradition to be a reflection of historical reality.[20] Undoubtedly, if this method is rejected, only very few historical facts can be established: for the number of cases in which different, independent sources relate the same facts is extremely limited in the history of Indian Buddhism. The establishment of historical facts, however, requires a rigorously critical

---

[19] *Aṅg Nik.*, vol. II, pp. 38-39.

[20] "A propos du concile de Vaiśālī", *T'oung Pao*, XL (1951), pp. 269-270.

approach, and one cannot rest content with traditions simply for lack of historically reliable sources. No matter how carefully one tries to free 'traditions' from all miraculous elements, and reduces them to their common source, they stubbornly resist transformation into historical documents. Using such a method, one falls inevitably into a way of history-writing which is in direct conflict with the character of the sources.

In the past European Orientalists have applied themselves especially to the history of Buddhism, as has recently been underlined by Eliade.[21] Educated in the historical tradition of the nineteenth century, scholars believed they could learn all about Buddhism by studying its history. In the first place they tried to obtain a knowledge of the facts and data in order to form a picture of the development of the Buddhist ideas. This method is doomed to failure because in the spiritual life of India the historical dimension is of much less importance than it is in Western civilization. The most important task for the student of Buddhism is the study of the Buddhist mentality. That is why contact with present-day Buddhism is so important, for this will guard us against seeing the texts purely as philological material and forgetting that for the Buddhist they are sacred texts which proclaim a message of salvation.

[21] "Le bouddhisme et l'occident", *Le Figaro*, 6 August 1952.

The Background of Early Buddhism

J. W. de Jong (University of Leiden)

How and why a religion comes into being is one of the most difficult problems facing the student of religious phenomena. In many cases no answer can be given at all for the simple reason that the origins of many religions are buried in an ancient past, which has not left any historical data. Buddhism, however, like Christianity and Islam, made its appearance in Historical times. No one today will deny that its founder lived in India some centuries before the beginning of the Christian era. The period preceding the Buddha's activities brought forth an extensive literature, the Vedic literature, the beginning of which can be traced back to the 2nd. millennium B. C., when the Aryans entered India from the North West. Excavations have brought to light the remains of a past even more remote, so that since 1921 we are certain of the existence of a flourishing culture in the West of India in the third millenium B. C. Hence, it might easily be concluded that abundant evidence is available which can be used to determine the causes leading to the rise of Buddhism. As a matter of fact, since the beginning of the 19 th century this question has occupied many eminent men of learning. Yet, when studying the wellnigh too voluminous literature on the subject, one can hardly state that the question has been satisfactorily answered. For this reason a renewed effort to arrive at an answer to this question and to take a closer look at some of its aspects would not be superfluous.

Critical studies of the birth of Buddhism in particular and of the first stage of its development were first embarked upon by Western scolars during the 19 th century. Precisely the earliest period of Buddhism has received most attention in critical research since that time to the relative neglect of later developments; only recently more attention has been afforded to the later stadia. Schayer has remarked, quite rightly, that this almost exclusive interest in the "astounding person of the Buddha" and in the "original realm of Buddhist thought" can be traced back to the 19th century Protestant conception of true, evangelical Christianity, which was applied to Buddhism. Undoubtedly, this has been, consciously or unconsciously, an important factor in the predilection for Buddhism in its oldest forms. Other factors such as rationalism and a liberal humanism, both characteristic of the mentality of 19th century scholars, played an important role, too. These schools of thought were particularly attracted by the image of the Buddha given by such scholars as Rhys Davids and Oldenberg on the basis of the canonical texts of the Little Vehicle, the *Hīnayāna*. Both Rhys Davids and Oldenberg made a considerable contribution to a better knowledge of this literature by means of the publication of these texts and their translation. They looked upon these texts as the most important source for understanding original, true Buddhism, which had not yet been distorted by mythological fantasies, but which retained the memory of the sublime Buddha, the great teacher of suffering mankind, who accomplished his blessed labour in preaching and dialogue, possessed of a socratic calm and irony. The almost exclusive concentration on the philosophical aspect of Buddhism was typical of this 19th century conception. The religious aspect, which cannot be separated from it, was much less an object of study and consideration. Here again contemporary trends go far to explain this lack of interest. Christianity had been reduced to an ethic, expounded by a noble teacher, in the work of many theologians. Others, in a revulsion from traditional beliefs, sought a spiritual home in irreligious or anti-religious rational systems of philosophy. Both trends discovered in Buddhism a belief which denied the god of creation or of revelation, but possessed an ethic, which could be said to be based on reason.

Although this image of the Buddha, which in the last quarter of the 19th century became more and more clearly outlined, is no longer being accepted in its totality by any scholar, it cannot be ignored, since even today it is still quite influential. To a large extent this can be explained by the impact of the towering figure of Oldenberg, who in a superb and fascinating manner poured this image of Buddhism into a classical mould in his book which was first published in 1881. For countless numbers this book—of which the 13 th reprint appeared in 1958—has been the fountain-head of wisdom. It offered a very carefully documented and reliable conception of Buddhism which was rooted in the best traditions of the last century. This is not the place to enter into a full discussion of Oldenberg's work. Since its publication it has been subject to many attacks. Hardly any feature of Oldenberg's picture of Buddhism is nowadays accepted. Yet, no new and different picture has been construed which can carry as much conviction for students and specialists. Research has been carried on and former insights and conceptions have been revised in many respects. Yet, the results of all this work have not yet been coordinated into a reliable synthesis. A partial explanation may be found in the progress of research, which steadily grows in scope and volume, so that a complete survey becomes more difficult as the years go by. The most important cause, however, must be sought elsewhere. In spite of many apparent contradictions the second half of the 19 th century revealed a considerable consensus of opinion as to the world conception of scholars. This offered a favourable climate for fruitful scholarly research. Our age has lost this degree of homogeneity; the result is ever growing specialization. There is an increasing inability to acquaint oneself with new conceptions, approaches and methods which are being developed in other fields of research. This is particularly noticeable in those fields whose scholars are few in number, e. g. the field of Buddhist studies. Although the picture of Buddhism as conceived during the last century no longer prevails, there is an insufficient awareness of the need to apply new methods and insights. What progress has been achieved is due to the study of the ever-increasing source material by applying the methods of former days. Hence, we can also say as regards the study of the origin of Buddhism that the problem is still being handled with the methods of Oldenberg, i. e. there is still the attempt to explain the ideas of earliest Buddhism from the pre-Buddhist world of thought.

Although it has long been recognized in many fields of research that a philosophy or religion cannot be studied outside the framework of the society in which it was born, Indologists have shown themselves insufficiently open to this approach. In far too many cases it is felt that political history, economics, sociology, religion and philosophy should be studied in isolation. There is also too strong an attachment to antiquated conceptions of history, which took their cue from the natural sciences in emphasizing the quest for causes. The only scholar since Oldenberg, who approached the study of Buddhism in an entirely new manner, was a non-specialist, the great German sociologist Max Weber, who attempted a systematic study of the connection between religion and society in the second volume of his collected essays on the sociology of religion and in his principal work "Wirtschaft und Gesellschaft". Although these studies of Weber were published over 40 years ago, almost no reference to his work can be found in the publications of specialists, let alone critical discussions. It is difficult to find more striking proof of the one-sided approach and interest of these scholars, whose excellent philological training cannot be doubted.

Admittedly, Max Weber used a relatively limited number of sources for his analysis of Buddhism; yet, we must concede that he showed excellent insight into many, important facets. Several of his ideas have been confirmed by the research of scholars who were not acquainted with his work. It is, of course, not very well possible to accept the results of his studies as definite. It will be necessary to scrutinize his theories by means of further studies of much more extensive source material than that used by Weber. He did not confine his studies to Buddhism in India, but also included later developments in Ceylon, Burma, Indo-China, China, Korea, Japan and Tibet. Within the limits of one hundred pages he could not do more than mention many things in passing. Many of his hypotheses were not founded upon extensive research and argument. In evaluating his work, we should emphasize his method rather than his theories, even though these theories were both valuable and fruitful.

It is certainly to be hoped that further studies of Buddhism and other

Indian religions will continue Weber's work. As to the earliest period of Buddhism one can surely achieve new results, as many new sources have been discovered and studied in the century behind us. Present-day studies of early Buddhism no longer concentrate exclusively upon the Pāli-canon. Texts which had perished in India, but have been preserved in Chinese and Tibetan translations are more and more being consulted. Hence, it is now possible to evaluate the Pāli-tradition by means of independent literary sources. Furthermore, a considerable amount of new material has been found in the course of archaeological excavation. Until recently very little was known about the period beginning with the eclipse of the prehistoric Harappa culture until the third century B. C. Recent excavations have contributed much to a better knowledge of this period. It is to be expected that future excavations will throw further light upon the period between 800 and 200 B. C., the period of the birth of Buddhism and its subsequent spread in large parts of India. Undoubtedly excavations have until now uncovered but little of the immense amount of evidence hidden in the soil of India.

On the basis of this new evidence and of earlier known data it is now possible to obtain a more correct picture of India as it was in the Buddha's days. During this era the centre of political developments shifted to the East, the area around Benares and Patna. The seat of Brahman culture, situated near present-day Delhi in the West of India appears to have lost most of its former power. It is quite clear that in this area, the old domain of the Āryan tribes which had invaded India from the North West, new trends met with more resistance than in the East, where Āryan kings and Brahman priests were but the thin upper crust imposed upon a predominantly non-Āryan population. In the East, a completely new pattern of political power was beginning to take shape in this period. The power of the feudal, landowning nobility was steadily waning, the former small states and kingdoms were being swallowed by ambitious warrior-kings, who strove to establish large, well-organized kingdoms. In the days of the Buddha the states of Kosala and Magadha in particular steadily extended their borders. These states were ruled by hereditary dynasties, who did not even belong to the old Kṣatriya nobility as exemplified in the ruler of Kosala. These states were fundamentally different from the old small states which were ruled by an oligarchy of the nobility or by a king, who might be primus inter pares, but whose function did not automatically devolve upon his descendants. Some of these small states still existed in the days of the Buddha, e. g. his own country of birth, the small kingdom of the Śākya's at the foot of the Himālaya. But they owed suzerainty to the ruler of Kosala and shortly afterwards lost their independence. Other small oligarchic states, e. g. the Malla and the Licchavi, were ruled by oligarchies of non-Āryan clans. It was their fate, too, to be conquered by their more powerful neighbours. The emergence of large, centralized states in the East of India brought also the establishment of big cities, which grew into centres of royal power and mercantile wealth. Excavations have shown that iron was first used in India in the 8 th century B. C. The introduction of iron made the art of warfare much more effective and was also of great importance in the clearance of forests for agriculture. In his "Introduction to the study of Indian history" Kosambi correctly stresses the far-reaching consequences of the introduction of iron in the history of the Ganges plains. Iron implements made it possible to claim for agriculture the swamps and forests covering this region. In the days of the Buddha rice was grown on a large scale. This humid, tropical rice-growing country was markedly different from the old Āryan region in the West, which relied mainly on animal husbandry and the cultivation of wheat. The cultivation of the soil along the banks of the Ganges also had important effects upon trade and the emergence of cities. Rājagṛha, the old capital of Magadha, which rapidly became the most powerful state of India, was situated 40 miles south of the Ganges in hilly country. The new capital, Pāṭaliputra arose on the banks of the Ganges near modern Patna. The Ganges, which was easily navigable, stimulated mercantile traffic by water and this probably caused the shifting of the site of the capital. Buddhist texts furnish clear evidence of the growing importance of shipping in this period, although the old trade routes overland retained their importance, as shipping could only serve those towns and villages which were situated along the navigable rivers. In those days trade assumed ever growing importance. Caravans and ships traversed great distances to transport goods from one place to another. Trade goods consisted predominantly of luxury articles, e. g. cosmetics, perfumes, fine linens, salt, precious stones, sandalwood etc., since trade in other goods was not profitable on account of the high costs of transport and the levying of many duties. It is self-evident that the emergence of strong and powerful states offered favourable conditions for the expansion of trade, which was no longer trammeled by the many levies imposed by local potentates. In the wake of trade came a growing need for money and many cities started minting their own coinage. Finds of coins in places far removed from the centres where they had been minted amply prove the territorial expansion of trade and the enormous distances traveled.

These profound changes in the political and social field were paralleled by considerable religious ferment. In the hands of the Brahmans the old Vedic religion had by this time been reduced to an extremely formalized ritualism, emphasizing rigid observance of the rules prescribed for the performance of the sacrificial rites. In Eastern India, however, the influence of Brahmanism was limited. People sought other ways by which to attain deliverance. Buddhist texts tell us about śramaṇa's, hermits, who retreated into the forests. Many religio-philosophical groups sprang up, too. They were led by wandering teachers, who preached all sorts of doctrines, ranging from the sublime to crass materialism. The majority of these sects were short-lived. The names of their teachers and doctrines are known to us from Buddhist and Jain texts. Three religious leaders, however, attained lasting fame, i. e. the founders of Buddhism, Jainism and the system of the Ājīvika's. These three religions sprang up almost simultaneously in Eastern India and spread over the larger part of India. With the exception of Jainism, which is still alive today, especially in the Bombay area and in a few other places in Western India, they finally disappeared from the Indian continent.

No other period of India's history witnessed as much mental and spiritual activity as the 6 th and 5 th centuries B. C. The enormous political and social changes taking place in Eastern India during this period furnish a partial explanation. Another factor was the meeting of two cultures, the brahman culture of the Āryan conquerors and the culture of the autochthonous peoples, which influenced and fructified each other. In the absence of concrete data we are hardly able to form an idea of the character of the culture of the non-Āryan peoples. Many speculative theories have been put forward, which assumed too easily that anything which was not explicitly mentioned in Vedic literature should be classified as non-Āryan. However, this argument ought to be used cautiously. Notwithstanding the large volume of Vedic literature, we cannot possibly derive from it a complete image of the Āryan thought world. There is a danger that we ascribe too much to the non-Āryan, autochthonous peoples; yet, we must also beware of underestimating the contribution of the original population of India. It should be borne in mind that Vedic literature sprang up and flourished on Indian soil in the course of many centuries. It has been demonstrated that the oldest portion of the Ṛgveda contains traces of non-Āryan influence. Although we should exercise great restraint in determining Āryan and non-Āryan elements, we can still attempt an acceptable sketch as long as the structural differences between the Āryan and non-Āryan societies are taken into account. Moreover, the many new trends emerging in this period contain so many new elements which are alien to Vedic literature, that we must make considerable allowances for the influence of autochthonous ideas.

It is, indeed, not feasible to enumerate all new ideas encountered during this period. The extant texts reveal such proliferation of ideas, that one is left with the impression that every thinkable or unthinkable proposition was experimented with. A few ideas, however, predominated and were expounded in several religio-philosophical systems. The doctrine of *ahiṃsā*, i. e. the avoidance of harm to all life, gained general acceptance.

We should not be amazed that the rice-growing East of India gave birth to this doctrine instead of the Āryan motherland, where animal husbandry was one of the main props of the economy and animal sacrifices formed an integral part of brahman ritual. The doctrine of *karman*, which holds that actions committed in this life have their reward in future reincarnations, also gained general recognition during this period. The doctrine of *karman* was equally acceptable to those who recognized a Self, an *ātman*, as it was to the Buddhists who rejected the conception of *ātman*. This doctrine which had already penetrated the youngest strata of Vedic literature, is undoubtedly rooted in non-Āryan conceptions, which are found among many agricultural peoples. Buddhist literature reveals a preference for metaphors derived from agriculture. The act is compared to the seed, the outcome of the act with the fruit. The alms given to a monk are likened to the seeds sown in a fertile field. Systematic study of the metaphors used by the Buddha to clarify his ideas might help us in gaining a more profound grasp of the essence of Buddhism and in understanding its origin. Buddhist concepts have far too often been detached from their original form. In this respect, too, it would be commendable to come down to earth from the heaven of abstract notions. It should not be forgotten that the Buddha was not a philosopher, who composed tracts in the quiet of his study. He was a preacher, who taught his doctrines to all who were willing to listen.

Buddhism adopted and developed both the doctrine of the *ahiṃsā* and of the *karman*. But it rejected asceticism, which was widely practised in those days. Scholars differ widely on the origins of asceticism in India. According to some, asceticism occurs even in the oldest Vedic document, the Ṛgveda. All later developments derived from this. Others hold that asceticism is a non-Āryan principle and essentially alien to Vedic culture, although Vedic culture underwent its influence in early times. The problem is further complicated by the fact that many are inclined to weld asceticism, yoga and shamanism together into one complex of notions and ideas. To do so is to bedevil the problem to such an extent that it becomes impossible to make any headway whatever. In order to extricate ourselves from this impasse it is necessary to distinguish clearly between the various forms of asceticism which are found in the texts. According to Vedic literature the aim of asceticism is the generation of *tapas*, i. e. heat, energy, which enables the ascetic to possess himself of supernatural powers and ecstasies. The ritualistic texts, the Brāhmaṇa's repeatedly describe Prajāpati's creation of the world and of man by means of *tapas*. Eliade has pointed out that this notion of the equivalence of power and heat can also be found among other Indo-European peoples. However, this conception is so deeply rooted in an archaic mentality that the non-Āryan peoples of India can hardly be assumed not to have been acquainted with the idea, even though we cannot adduce positive proof. The form of asceticism which we encounter in the days of the Buddha is, however, totally different. It is most extensively described in the texts of the Jains, who were the greatest competitors of the Buddhists. For the Jains asceticism is not primarily a means to power, but a method of purification from the tarnishing substance of sin. Carried to its ultimate consequences the Jains commit ritual suicide through prolonged fasting. It is quite evident that Jain asceticism is utterly different in its nature and purpose, although its techniques do not deviate from those used in Vedic asceticism. It curiously resembles the techniques of the blacksmith, who purifies and forges his iron in fire. The resemblance is even more pronounced if one takes into consideration that the Jains viewed all matter as animated and did not distinguish between physiological and psychological processes. Nor should it be forgotten that in those days, when the manipulation of iron had only recently been discovered, the blacksmith must have been a person possessed with great magical power. In other cultures, and even today among several tribes in India, we meet with similar attitudes.

According to the legend the Buddha also practised asceticism until he recognized that asceticism would not lead to deliverance. The Buddha's rejection of asceticism cannot be separated from his conception of sin as the result of the passions and of ignorance, whereas the Jains thought of sin as a material substance. Buddhist thought catalogues deeds as deeds of the body, of the word and of the mind. The core of each category of deeds is not the deed itself, but the intention which motivates it. Such a system of intentionalist ethics had no room for asceticism, but it could admit yoga techniques. The Buddhists did take over these techniques, although not without thoroughly changing their character. One has to try to extract from the Buddhist texts a clear understanding of the yoga techniques as practised by the non-Buddhists, if one wants to gain a correct insight into Buddhist yoga. The yoga technique of the non-Buddhist was aimed at attaining a cataleptic condition in which all conscious activity was completely suspended. The Buddha taught that ignorance is the root of all evil and suffering. Hence, he could not see the attainment of catalepsis as desirable in itself, and he transformed yoga from a purely physiological technique into a method inducing a state of mental concentration, in which supreme insight into the nature of suffering is realized. Enlightenment acquired in this manner is not theoretical knowledge, but deliverance from suffering.

Buddhist yoga is characteristic of the ways in which Buddhism adopted and transformed autochthonous conceptions. The doctrine of *karman* acquired in a similar way the peculiar imprint of Buddhism. This doctrine, which originally may have been a belief in the rebirth of man, rooted in totemist notions, was rationalized by means of the law of cause and effect. The same thing happened in the field of ethics. In ethical matters the intention is the determining factor, which stands in sharp contrast with Jainism. This rationalization superimposed on spiritualization, which is so clearly discernible in Buddhism, most certainly owes much to Brahmanic culture, whose rationalistic approach is unmistakable; we need only think of the ritualistic sacrificial theory and the sacral ancillary disciplines such as phonetics and grammar. Both Brahmanism and Buddhism set high store by correct thinking and correct acting. To the Brahmanic mind both are indispensable for a successful performance of the sacrificial rite. To the Buddhist correct thinking and acting are part of the path leading to deliverance from suffering. Buddhism changes the ritualistic precepts of Brahmanism into a means to attain deliverance. Thus Āryan and non-Āryan conceptions achieve in Buddhism a synthesis of which it can be said that a substratum of non-Āryan conceptions has been purified and further developed under the influence of Āryan rationalism.

That Buddhism attained so much success must be ascribed to its ability to weld together the most valuable elements of the two cultures at a time when they first established intensive contacts into a harmonious doctrine which accorded with the spirit of the age. We cannot, of course, assume that large numbers of people left everything in order to follow the Buddha. Most adherents of Buddhism were laymen who provided the monks with food and clothing and listened to the teachings of the Buddha, who promised heaven and deliverance in a future life as the reward of their good deeds in the present. Religiously speaking, the laymen were not important to Buddhism. As the providers of the economic foundation of the community of the monks they were, however, most valuable. To follow the difficult path as taught by the Buddha is not possible for the layman. How can he cut all links with his life in the world, as is required from the monk? If we wish to gain a better understanding of early Buddhism, we should try to ascertain who were the persons courageous enough to take the decisive step and find an explanation for their decision. Unfortunately, no statistical research on the social origins of the monks has been undertaken, although it should be possible to adduce statistical data from the information contained in the earliest Buddhist texts. It cannot, however, be doubted that the majority of the monks belonged to the upper strata of society, the castes of the brahman's, the kṣatriya's and the rich merchants. It should, of course, be remembered that conversions among the upper classes usually attract more attention. But in the case of Buddhism it can safely be assumed that the information given by the texts faithfully records the true facts. For Buddhism is an aristocratic doctrine of deliverance, making high ethical and intellectual demands. The Buddha emphatically states that he only shows the path, but that each and every one attains bodhi through his own efforts. The aim of Buddhism, deliverance from suffering by attaining the undefinable state of Nirvāṇa, would have a greater appeal for those who have come to know the vanity of worldly pleasures than for them who are not so privileged and hope for compensation in some kind of paradise. Finally, Buddhism is an individualistic doctrine. Emotional elements are utterly alien to it. To enter the community of monks is a juridical act, devoid of initiation rites in the form of a magical act, as for instance baptism. Buddhism fights shy of ritual and, unlike Brahmanism, does not make use of an esoteric language, comprehensible to priests only. The Buddha preaches in the vernacular, not in order to descend to the common people, but because the listeners should attain enlightenment. Western scholars have said that the Buddha was a cold realist. This is utterly untrue. His compassion for mankind is clearly evinced from his desire to deliver man from suffering by showing him the path. Buddhism is sustained by anaristocratic, distant love for mankind, deriving from a truly aristocratic attitude of mind. There is no trace of attempts at coercion by means of emotionalism or magic ritual.

The intellectualistic character of the Buddhist doctrine of deliverance is in accordance with an age which saw the emergence of large kingdoms requiring a more rational organization of the state. The enhanced power of the ruler undermined the position of the aristocratic landowning nobility, who were deprived of their former prestige. The absolute ruler stood in need of officials, who owed their positions to him alone. Naturally, such officials were more easily found outside the caste of the kṣatriya's. In these circumstances the aristocratic doctrine of deliverance of the Buddha was capable of giving new meaning to the life of the kṣatriya who had lost his old security and privileges. The brahmans found themselves in a similar position. A few found employment as priest at the royal court. But for most of them life became much more insecure because of the decline of their former employers and protectors, the kṣatriya's. Brahmanism itself was not flexible enough to be capable of adaptation to new conditions. Buddhism offered them an opening as religious specialists in a new guise. The merchant class, which grew increasingly prominent, could not but feel attracted by a doctrine which offered them a position superior to the one accorded by Brahmanism, where brahmans and kṣatriya's predominated. Trade and commerce were not congenial to the brahman spirit with its emphasis on ritual purity, which might be endangered by distant travels. The intellectualistic features of Buddhism were also closer to a class which, in contrast to the landed nobility, was dependent on a monetary economy. Buddhist ethics emphasizing the acquisition of religious merit and the intention likewise earned the approval of merchants who urgently needed trust in each other for their transactions and a religious sanction for their acqyisitions. The Buddha taught that actions, not birth were important. A class which had gained its prominence by their own effort must have welcomed such teaching.

This may suffice as an inevitably incomplete sketch of the beginnings of Buddhism and its place in the society of that age. It may be superfluous to remark that no incontrovertible proofs can be given, since we are engaged in composing a jig-saw puzzle of which most of the pieces are lost.

THE ABSOLUTE IN BUDDHIST THOUGHT

J. W. de Jong

The Absolute has been the ultimate goal of mystics and philosophers throughout the ages. But perhaps no religion has been more preoccupied with this subject than Buddhism. Herein lies one of its most important contributions to philosophic thought and for this reason I believe that it will be not without interest to consider the Buddhist attitude with regard to the Absolute.

Buddhist thought is not mere speculation for the sake of knowledge only. Right knowledge is highly valued by the Buddhists, however, not as an aim in itself, but as a means to obtain deliverance. Scholars have often gone astray by trying to reduce Buddhist teaching to a coherent philosophical system. Consequently they have met great difficulties in understanding Nirvana, the fundamental concept of Buddhism. Misled by many utterances in the scriptures they have been tempted to consider Nirvana as a negative entity. A right understanding of Nirvana, however, teaches us that it is not a metaphysical concept, but a soteriological Absolute, the final aim for him who wants to obtain deliverance from this world. Nirvana cannot be understood by reasoning but must be experienced. Strictly speaking this experience of Nirvana cannot be communicated to others because no language can describe the merging of the individual into the Absolute. However, like all mystics the Buddhists have not abstained from speaking about the Absolute. Often Nirvana is being described in positive terms and this has been the cause of a wrong interpretation, directly contrary to the one above mentioned. For these positive terms are not meant to indicate that Nirvana is an ontological reality or even a kind of paradise as has been asserted sometimes.

In order to understand such terms as "highest bliss", "the other shore", "the refuge", "the goal", which terms with many others have been used to indicate Nirvana, one has to realize the problem which the mystic has to face when desiring to speak of the Absolute. His experience is of such an overwhelming intensity that he feels himself completely transformed by it. In comparison everything else dwindles to nothing. He cannot but remember continually this supreme moment. How great is his desire to tell others of the felicity which he has felt! He knows that no words are capable of describing the ineffable content of his experience, for language is bound to the earth, to human existence. Therefore the mystic makes use of an indirect way of expression. He cannot say what the Absolute is, but he can say what it is not. Its most essential characteristic is its fundamental difference from all things mundane. In this world everybody is subject to death: Nirvana, however, is said to be the immortal place (*amatapadam* or *amatam padam*, Dhammapada 21, Udanavarga IV.1, etc.). From birth to death life is suffering (*dukkha*); Nirvana on the contrary is supreme bliss (*paramam sukham*, Majj. Nik. I.508, Dhammapada 203-204, Udanavarga XXVI, 6-7), free from birth and becoming (*ajāta*, *abhūta*, Ud. 80, Itiv. 37). Empirical life offers no shelter, no refuge; Nirvana is called the island (*dīpa*, Samy. Nik. IV, 372), the shelter (*leṇa*, ibid.), the protection (*tāṇa*, ibid.), the refuge (*saraṇa*, ibid.) and the goal (*parāyana*, Saṁy. Nik. IV, 373). Life is impurity; Nirvana is purity (*suddhi*, Samy. Nik. IV, 372). Many other terms are used in connection with Nirvana, but not one of these words contains a description or definition of Nirvana. They only point to the other shore (*pāra*, Samy. Nik. IV, 369). If we subject these terms to a careful examination, we see that they convey either an antithesis to the conditions of *saṁsāra* or a negation of these. For instance, bliss is the antithesis of suffering. In human life or even in a heavenly paradise no bliss exists, because in these states no everlasting bliss is possible and according to the Buddhists everything that has an end is suffering. On earth the immortal and the unborn are unthinkable because here below one perceives the universality of birth and death. Bliss, immortality and the unborn are words that do not correspond to real things which a human being can know or see. The mystic who has experienced the state of Nirvana makes use of these words exactly for this reason. However inadequate they may be, they are the only means which language can offer him to express that which essentially cannot be put into words because words are only capable of denoting the realities of empirical life.

Scholars have noticed the fact that Nirvana is often called a place or a sphere (*dhātu*). The Dhammapada (225) speaks of the unchangeable place (*accutam hānam*) and the Suttanipata (204) of the unchangeable place of Nirvana (*nibbānapadam accutam*). Also in several places Nirvana is said to be the stable (*dhuva*, Samy. Nik. IV, 370). These texts have been put forward as an argument to support the theory that the Buddhists consider Nirvana to be a place or an abode of bliss. But words like *pada* and *thāna* do not have such definite a meaning that they have to be understood as indicating a place or an abode in which the mystic resides. *Nibbānapadam* is undoubtedly used as a synonym of Nirvana and *nibbānadhātu* is clearly a term coined with the object of distinguishing Nirvana as a fourth sphere from the three spheres of desire, form and formlessness (*kāmādhātu*, *rūpadhātu* and *arūpadhātu*) of which the world consists. To the Buddhist the sphere of Nirvana never had the slightest resemblance to the three others. As in all the preceding examples this term only denotes the fact that Nirvana does not belong to our world and lies absolutely outside the field of ordinary experience.

Human language is unfit to describe the content of mystical experience; the conditions necessary to attain the desired goal, on the contrary, are much more easily susceptible to linguistic expression. This is the principal reason why mystics always deal at greater length with the *via mystica* than with the *unio mystica*. Therefore the specific nature of Buddhism can only become clear through an examination of its mystic way. During the whole history of Buddhism the way to Nirvana has been the core of the doctrine. Progress on the Way is to be brought about through a special technique. Every school of mysticism has developed a technique which enables the mystic to attain his final goal. At the time of the Buddha the technique of yoga was practised by many recluses who devoted themselves to yoga exercises in solitary retirement. Not much is known about their doctrines and the goal towards which they directed their efforts. Most probably at that time yoga was nothing more than a technique and many centuries had still to elapse before it grew into a philosophical system. This untheoretical character of yoga made its adaptation to many different purposes possible. After repudiation of mortification the Buddha applied the technique of yoga and with its help succeeded in attaining the Awakening. Many texts tell us how the Buddha passed through many stages of meditation before reaching the final insight. With the example of the Buddha before their eyes his followers could not but be always aware of the primary importance of yoga. Buddhist literature treats yoga technique at great length and manifests clearly the tendency to an increasing systematization and refinement of yoga exercises. It is impossible to decide which was the original form of yoga adopted by primitive Buddhism, but the description of it in the oldest texts makes it probable that the goal of non-Buddhist yoga must have been the attainment of a state of absolute unconsciousness. Many texts describe a series of nine consecutive stages of contemplation. According to the Buddhists the heretics knew the eighth stage, the stage of neither consciousness nor unconsciousness (*naivasamjñānāsamjñāyatana*) but did not know the ninth stage in which consciousness and sensation are abolished (*samjñāvedayitanirodha*, or *nirodhasamāpatti*, the attainment of cessation). The Buddhists carefully distinguished this stage from the attainment of unconsciousness (*asamjñisamāpatti*) which the heretics took as their final goal. It seems clear, however, that the attainment of cessation does not differ much from the methods of concentration used by the yogins. But the Buddhists could not content themselves with a mere cessation of consciousness and this accounts for the many theories which Buddhist scholasticism developed in order to incorporate the attainment of cessation into their soteriological system. According to the Theravadins, in the *nirodhasamāpatti* one touches Nirvana with one's body and in this way one comes to enjoy Nirvana in this world (*dṛṣṭa-dharmanirvāṇa*). The Sarvastivada school considered it as an entity similar to Nirvana. But both schools believed that for the final attainment of Nirvana an intuitive knowledge was required. Other schools claimed that in the state of the attainment of cessation some sort of consciousness continued to exist. Their opinions are discussed at great length by Vasubandhu in his Karmasiddhiprakarana.[1] These different theories about the attainment of cessation show clearly that the Buddhists specifically avoided to confuse Nirvana with a state of unconsciousness. From the outset Buddhism has been considered to consist of three parts : rules of conduct (*śīla*), concentration (*samādhi*) and insight (*prajñā*). The highest insight is the intuitive insight (*bhāvanāmayī*) which is produced by concentration. The importance which the Buddhists attached to insight can only be understood if we call to mind the nature of the Buddhist experience of Nirvana. We have tried to make it clear that the main characteristic of this experience was its complete otherness in regard to all the experiences of empirical life. In order to realize fully this otherness it is of essential importance to understand the nature of our world. The discovery that our world is suffering, evanescent and subject to dependent origination is inseparably bound up with the experience of Nirvana. If Nirvana only meant a state of unconsciousness as it was assumed by the yogins, it would not be necessary to analyse the laws which govern the world.

In later scholasticism Buddhism advocated the theory of the two ways, the way of vision (*darśanamārga*) and the way of meditation (*bhāvanāmārga*). The first way caused the destruction of the false views and the second that of the passions. But the germ of this theory can already be seen in primitive Buddhism. Vision of the supreme truth and eradication of the passions are both essential for attaining Nirvana. The history of Buddhist thought is closely interwoven with the interplay of these two elements. Never Buddhism has transformed itself either into a mere philosophical system or into a technique to attain a trance-like state of unconsciousness. This accounts for the great richness of Buddhist teaching which avoids both extremes. Knowledge may be stressed more than meditation and conversely; still, never one element succeeds in wholly supplanting the other. For knowledge is no theoretical knowledge, but intuitive knowledge born out of meditation. Consequently, it is not the opposite of meditation, but to the contrary coexistent with it. To a certain extent it may seem that in the schools, in which the *abhidharma*, the analysis of the elements of existence, plays a preponderant part, the mystic element has disappeared. But, nevertheless, these elaborate scholastic systems culminate in the attainment of Nirvana. They closely examine the elements produced by causes (*samskṛtadharma*) in order to obtain a clearer insight into the elements not produced by causes (*asamskṛtadharma*) to which latter Nirvana belongs.

Thus far we have confined ourselves to an examination of Hinayana Buddhism, and we have tried to point out the nature of the experience of Nirvana and of the way leading up to it. In the schools of Mahayana Buddhism the same themes have absorbed the interest of the Buddhists. However much their concepts may seem to be different from those current in the Hinayana schools, the main lines of thought show a remarkable affinity between both Vehicles. The doctrines of the Mahayana schools are foreshadowed in the texts of primitive Buddhism and they carry to a logical fulfilment ideas the germ of which is already clearly visible in the oldest texts. Among the Mahayana schools those most important from the point of view of philosophic thought are the Yogacara and the Madhyamika. The former advocates the theory of mind-only (*cittamātram*), and maintains that the Absolute is thought. In tracing back the origin of this theory many scholars among whom one must mention La Vallée Poussin[2], Sachayer[3], Frauwallner[4], and the Japanese scholars Kimura[5], Akanuma[6], Nishi[7] and Sakamoto[8] have drawn the attention to a passage in the Anguttara Nikaya (vol. I, p. 10) and in Vasumitra's Treatise on the Buddhist schools (cf. A. Bareau, Journal Asiatique, 1954, p. 244) saying : "Luminous is that thought, but it is defiled by adventitious defilements" (*pabhassaram idaṁ cittaṁ taṁ ca kho āgantukehi upakkilesehi upakkiliṭṭham*). Vidushekhara Bhattacharya has discovered in Jayaratha's commentary of Abhinavagupta's Tantraloka a verse which uses almost the same words in presenting the views of the Yogacaras : *prabhāsvaram idaṁ cittaṁ prakṛtyāgantavo malāḥ, teṣām apāye sarvārthaṁ taj jyotir avinaśvaram*[9]. How did the Yogacaras arrive at this concept of luminous thought being the true reality ? The text of the Anguttara Nikaya clearly refers to the way of the mystic who purifies himself from the defilements caused by the passions and the false views. The Yogacaras transferred to the Absolute this concept of a pure mind realized in the the course of the mystic way. The transition from the one concept to the other may probably be seen in the speculations of the Hinayana schools on the persistence of some kind of consciousness in the state of attainment of cessation to which we have referred. On the other hand already in the oldest texts there is mention of an invisible infinite consciousness radiating in all directions (*viññāṇam anidassanam anantam sabbato pabham*, Digha Nik. I, 223 ; Majjh. Nik. I, 329)[10]. It is clear that the Yogacaras, and already some of the later schools of Hinayana, have taken up again trends of speculation already existent though not preponderant in primitive Buddhism, and even earlier in Upanishadic speculations because this idea of an infinite consciousness reminds us of several passages in the Upanishads[11]. In a certain sense one can say that the Yogacaras with their theory of mind-only have done nothing else than develop the idea of the purification of mind which plays such an important role in early Buddhism as is testified by the well-known verse : "To abstain from all evil, to do good, and to purify one's mind, that is the teaching of the Buddhas" (*sabbapāpassa akaraṇaṁ kusalassa upasampadā sacittapariyodapanam etaṁ buddhāna sāsanam*, Dhammapada 183, Udanavarga XXVIII, 1, Digha Nik. II, 49, Mahavastu III, 420).

The doctrine of the Madhyamikas has often been misinterpreted as an absolute nihilism. But all the negative arguments in their texts only serve to make clear that the Absolute is ineffable and cannot be described by words. According to the Madhyamikas the highest reality can only be realized by silence. A famous aphorism says that from the night of Awakening till the night of his entrance into Nirvana everything spoken by the Buddha is true (*yañ ca rattiṁ tathāgato anuttaraṁ sammāsambodhiṁ abhisambujjhat, yañ ca rattiṁ anupādisesāya nibbānadhātuyā parinibbāyati, yaṁ etasimiṁ antare bhāsati lapati niddisati, sabbaṁ taṁ tath'eva hoti no aññathā*, Digha Nik. III, 135 ; Ang. Nik. II, 24 ; Itiv. 121). The Madhyamikas have changed this aphorism to the effect that between these two nights nothing has been spoken by the Buddha because he was constantly plunged in meditation (*yāṁ ca śāntamate rātriṁ tathāgato 'nuttarāṁ samyakasaṁbodhim abhisaṁbuddho yāṁ ca rātrim anupādāya parinirvāsyati, asminn antare tathāgatenaikākṣaram api nodāhṛtaṁ na pravyāhṛtaṁ nāpi pravyāhariṣyati, Prasannapadā* p. 366)[12] The Lankavatarasutra, a text quoted often by both the Madhyamikas and the the Yogacaras, explains that the word of the Buddha is wordless (*avacanaṁ buddhavacanam*) because on the one hand his mystic vision belongs to his own personal experience and is beyond words and concepts (*svapratyātmagatigocaraṁ vāgvikalparahitam*) whilst on the other hand his mystic experience deals with the unchangeable nature of things (*dharmatā dharmasthititā dharmaniyāmatā tathatā bhūtatā satyatā*[13] Lank. 142-144). This explanation shows clearly that the mystic experience is by its very nature ineffable because it is a personal experience and its aim the absolute nature of things. The importance the Madhyamikas attach to silence is sufficient evidence of the fact that their seemingly nihilistic reasonings are only meant to clear the way for their mystic experience.

La Vallée Poussin has defined Buddhism as Nirvanamysticism. No better definition can be given. The foregoing remarks try to illustrate some aspects of Buddhism from this point of view which, I believe, can help us greatly to understand the true nature of the teachings of the Buddha.

NOTES

[1] French translation by Et. Lamotte, Mélanges chinois et bouddhiques, IV, 1936, pp. 151-263; Japanese translation by S. Yamaguchi, Seshin no jogoron, Kyoto, 1951.

[2] Nirvana, Paris, 1925, p.64; l'Abhidharmakosa de Vasubandhu, chap. VI, Paris—Louvain, 1925, p.299; Vijnaptimatratasiddhi, Paris, 1928-1929, pp. 109-113, 215, 530.

[3] Precanonical Buddhism, Archiv Orientalni, VII, 1935, p.131.

[4] Beitrage zur indischen Philologie und Altertumskunde, Hamburg, 1951, p.152.

[5] Shojo Bukkyo Shisoron, Tokyo, 1937, p.400.

[6] Bukkyo Kyori no Kenkyu, Nagoya, 1939, p.210.

[7] Bukkyo Kenkyu, V, 2, 1941, p.20; Genshi Bukkyo ni okeru Hannya no Kenkyu, Yokohama, 1953, p.347.

[8] Indogaku Bukkyogaku Kenkyu, II, 1, 1953, p. 20.

[9] The Agamasastra of Gaudapada, Calcutta, 1943, p.70.

[10] Cf. N.Dutt, Aspects of Mahayana Buddhism, London, 1930, p.148; Schayer, op. cit., p.131; C.Regamey, Rocznik Orientalistyczny, XXI, 1957, p.48.

[11] Cf. H.Nakamura, Harvard Journal of Asiatic Studies, XVIII, 1955, pp. 78-79 and Chand. Up. VIII.4,2: *sakṛdvibhāto hy evaiṣa brahmalokaḥ.*

[12] Cf. Et. Lamotte, Le traîté de la grande vertu de sagesse, I, Louvain, 1944, p.30, n.2.

[13] For this often recurring formula see La Vallee Poussin, Mélanges chinois et bouddhiques, V, 1937, p.207, n.3.

J. W. DE JONG

THE PROBLEM OF THE ABSOLUTE IN THE MADHYAMAKA SCHOOL*

The problem of the absolute in the Madhyamaka school has given rise to numerous interpretations, not only divergent, but sometimes diametrically opposed. This lack of unanimity bears witness once again to the inherent difficulties which beset any attempt to understand the essence of a philosophy. These difficulties are even greater when we are dealing with a philosophy which is not based on one of the two great sources of western civilization: Greco-Latin antiquity and Christianity. One must beware of drawing too hasty conclusions about analogies and proximities with western thought, because one runs the risk of distorting Indian thought and failing to recognise that each philosophy is an organic whole. Neither can one expect to find ready-made answers in a philosophy. Thus, too often, in order to define the nature of the absolute of the Mādhyamikas, scholars are satisfied with searching for passages which could be quoted in support of a proposed interpretation. Isolated passages cannot be used to decide such questions.

The only way of arriving at a satisfactory and non-preconceived answer is to follow step by step the development of Madhyamaka thought. Only in this manner can enough data be gathered for an attempt to be made of finding a solution to the fundamental problem of this philosophy: the nature of the absolute. With this aim in mind, we will first examine the principal themes and leading ideas in the thought of Nāgārjuna. This philosophy is distinguished from all those which he attacks in that it excludes the possibility of establishing an ontology. He does not spare the Sāṃkhya doctrine, nor the Vaiśeṣika nor the Hīnayāna, but his criticism is aimed particularly at the Abhidharma of the Sarvāstivādins and the Vaibhāṣikas. The Sarvāstivādins had reduced the world to a limited number of ontological categories (*dharma*). Even though they considered the *dharmas* as real, they did not attribute any reality to the entities, made up of groups of *dharmas*. For them these entities were nothing but designations (*prajñapti*). Nāgārjuna is not satisfied with this reduction to ontological categories and points out that each *bhāva* (thing),

Journal of Indian Philosophy **2** (1972) 1–6. *All Rights Reserved*

each *dharma* is itself devoid of reality. The *bhāvas* are not real, because they cannot come into being. Nāgārjuna proves by *reductio ad absurdum* that 'a thing' does not originate from itself, nor from something else; it does not originate from itself and from something else, nor is it without cause. The idea of "production" therefore is false. But a thing which does not come into being cannot be real. Therefore, the things which the layman considers as real are not real. According to Nāgārjuna, a thing is real when it is endowed with *svabhāva*, a concept which is of great importance for the understanding of his thought. It is very difficult to know exactly what he wishes to express by this word every time, as it contains several notions.

Schayer has distinguished in it four meanings:

(1) *Svabhāva* means *svo bhāva*, the essence. Heat, for instance, is not the essence of water, but the essence of fire, because fire is always hot.

(2) *Svabhāva* is also the *svalakṣaṇa*, the individual character. In this form it is found in the doctrine of the Vaibhāṣikas, according to whom the world consists of a multitude of elements each having its individual character. The Vaibhāṣikas in fact make a distinction between individual and general character. Impermanency, for instance, is a general characteristic of all the *saṃskṛta* or conditioned elements. The *svalakṣaṇa*, on the other hand, only belongs to a single *saṃskṛta*, and distinguishes it from others.

(3) *Svabhāva* is the *āśraya* (basis) or *prakṛti* (nature), i.e. the unchanging substratum of each thing (*bhāva*).

(4) Finally, *svabhāva* is the *svato bhāva*, the absolute being, which is completely independent.

However, this fourfold distinction cannot be accepted because, for Nāgārjuna, the four concepts are directly linked one to the other and can be reduced to two. Let us take again the example of fire. Its origin depends on causes and conditions such as the sun, a lens, fuel etc. Heat, being the essence of fire, is dependent on the same causes and the same conditions. According to Nāgārjuna the real *svabhāva* is non-contingent and has no relation to anything whatsoever. Heat is thus not *svabhāva* and fire, not possessing *svabhāva*, has no 'own-being' or, as the *Mādhyamikas* say, is empty of 'own-being' (*śūnyaḥ svabhāvena*). All things, like fire, are born of causes (*pratītyasamutpanna*) and are empty of 'own-being' (*śūnya*). The Mādhyamikas in this way conclude that the concepts of *śūnya* and *pratītyasamutpanna* are equivalent.

Candrakīrti rejects the *svalakṣaṇa*, equating it with the *svo bhāva* which has already been eliminated. As a matter of fact, in his opinion, the layman attributes to things an individual character (*svalakṣaṇa*), because they believe in a plurality of real elements. Consequently, the *svo bhāva* and the *svalakṣaṇa*, the 'own-being' and the individual character have one and the same meaning.

On the other hand, for Candrakīrti, the unchanging basis (*āśraya*) is identical to the absolute being (*svato bhāva*). By no means does he distinguish, as Schayer leads us to believe, an *āśraya* or a *prakṛti* peculiar to each thing, but he gives a more extensive meaning to this concept: *āśraya* to him is the unchanging support of all things (*bhāva*) taken together. This support can only be non-contingent, because there is nothing outside of it. It becomes thus the *svato bhāva*. We may therefore conclude that for the Mādhyamikas the concept of *svabhāva* has only two meanings: (1) that of the 'own-being of each thing' (*svalakṣaṇa* or *svo bhāva*), which, incidentally, they consider unreal, and (2) that of the 'own-being of all things taken together' (*prakṛti* or *svato bhāva*).

Do the Mādhyamikas likewise reject the reality of this latter *svabhāva*, arriving in this way at a total nihilism which has often been attributed to them?

To answer such a question, one must proceed from the distinction made by the Mādhyamikas between *saṃvṛti* and *parāmartha*. *Saṃvṛti* is the 'apparent reality' of the world as seen by the layman. The laymen believe in the reality of things, they believe that everything is born and perishes. They believe in the reality of suffering, of transmigration and of deliverance obtained in Nirvāṇa. In fact, they accept all the views and the whole soteriological doctrine of the Hīnayāna. The Mādhyamikas, on the contrary, consider that the plurality of things and the categories of the Hīnayāna have no reality. They maintain that things are not real, that there is no real origination (*samutpāda*), but only origination dependent on causes (*pratītyasamutpāda*). On the level of *saṃvṛti*, things exist, but they do not exist on the level of *paramārtha*, 'the supreme meaning', 'the absolute'. The layman remains on the level of *saṃvṛti*, the Yogin is beyond it, on the level of *paramārtha*. He does not see that what is seen by the layman. Candrakīrti compares him to a healthy man whose eyes do not see the hairs which are perceived by the eyes of a man afflicted with ophthalmia (*taimirika*).

Is *paramārtha* then nothing but nothingness? Never has a direct and precise answer been given to the question "What is *paramārtha*?" *Paramārtha*, say the Mādhyamikas, cannot be reached by words. The duality between words and the things that they designate, just as the duality which exists between knowledge and its object, belongs to *saṃvṛti*, but does not exist in *paramārtha*. *Paramārtha* cannot be taught or known.

However, the Mādhyamikas have not refrained from talking about it. They resort to three methods which one finds again and again in the history of philosophy, when it is a question of expressing a concept which goes beyond the bounds of discursive knowledge.

The first is the method of negation, which consists in denying a series of attributes to *paramārtha*, yet without bestowing on it the contrary attributes. The second method bestows on it contradictory attributes. *Paramārtha* becomes at the same time a void and a non-void, *svabhāva* and *asvabhāva*, *śūnyatā* (voidness) and *svabhāva*. These two characteristics can also be simultaneously denied: *paramārtha* is neither being nor non-being, neither a void nor a non-void. Therefore, the logical rule that "what contradicts itself cannot exist" (*na vipratisiddhaṃ saṃbhavati*) is no longer applicable to *paramārtha*.

The third and last method makes use of metaphor. Expressions by which the absolute is indicated, such as *pratītyasamutpāda*, *śūnyatā*, *dharmatā*, *prakṛti*, *naiḥsvābhāvya*, *tathatā* etc. must be considered as metaphors in as much as the term "metaphor" is exact, because in each of these metaphors one of the terms is missing or rather escapes our knowledge.

Thus, making use of all the resources of philosophical dialectics the Mādhyamikas attempt to give an approximate idea of *paramārtha*. But *paramārtha* always remains beyond the comprehension of the layman. For it cannot be taught; it is only accessible, comprehensible to the saint (Yogin) who obtains deliverance.

We have seen the layman being compared to the man afflicted with ophthalmia seeing hairs which do not exist in reality. The Yogin might be able to convince the layman of his illusion, but cannot prevent him from seeing those hairs; this vision disappears only when the ophthalmic has regained normal sight. It is the same with *paramārtha*. Only that layman who by himself attains true self-knowledge – he has access to *paramārtha*. This knowledge, this "state", is dependent on mystical intuition, which dispels ignorance and so leads to deliverance. We are here beyond the realm of philosophical thought, where one proceeds with the aid of words and concepts, we are on the plane of individual experience, beyond all language and all thought.

There is no doubt that *paramārtha*, being the "supreme goal" of the believer, may be called 'the absolute'. But this absolute by its very nature is inaccessible to philosophical thought. One might try to approach it by indirect means, but all one could say or think about it would of necessity be false. It cannot be thought of as being or as nothingness. For the Mādhyamikas it is "the silence of the saints".

Schayer must rightly be credited with having emphasized the very important role of mystical intuition in the Mādhyamika school. But it is impossible to follow him when he attempts to identify *paramārtha* with the totality of being. According to Schayer the Mādhyamikas only accept as real the totality of being and consider the plurality of ontological entities as resulting from discursive and analytical thinking and consequently as unreal. This interpretation is wrong on two points. In the first place it is contrary and entirely alien to the spirit of Buddhist thought, which never at any stage visualizes unreal constituents forming a whole, which is real. To illustrate this we need only look at the simile of the chariot and its parts, a simile taken up by Candrakīrti. In opposition to the Hīnayānists, but in conformity with the doctrine of the Mādhyamikas, he not only considers the chariot as unreal, but moreover the parts which make up the chariot are for him just as unreal as the chariot itself. In the second place, by considering the absolute of the Mādhyamikas as the totality of being, Schayer replies in philosophical terms to a question which, as we have seen, can only be solved on the mystical level. It seems that Schayer has floundered on the hazards which exist for Western thought with regard to an absolute which is neither totality nor nothingness.

Stcherbatsky, for his part, has studied this same problem with a vast store of philological and philosophical knowledge, but the essential fault in his method consisted in looking for analogies with Western thinking. This often leads to a distortion of Buddhist thought, as is witnessed by his translation of *śūnya* by "relative". Stcherbatsky reasons: – Each element is a void because it is *pratītyasamutpanna*. Consequently, it can only be defined in relation to other elements. Each element thus becomes relative and "empty" therefore means "relative". The word "relative" has two meanings, "being in relation with" and "opposite of absolute". Stcherbatsky, in playing on those two meanings, introduces an interpretation which nowhere follows from the texts. Because of this initial error, all his subsequent interpretations of Nāgārjunian thinking are false. In his article on *The three directions of Buddhist philosophy* published in 1934, Stcherbatsky departs even more from the spirit of Nāgārjunian philosophy. Here, it is no longer a question of a "non-relative absolute", but of an "absolute truth", which he sets up as the sole principle of explanation of this world. The absolute, identified by him with *dharmakāya* (the body of the doctrine, the absolute) thus becomes an idea of dialectic reason. The attempt to elucidate the absolute of the Mādhyamikas by means of the transcendental dialectics of the critique of pure reason, seems to indicate a lack of understanding of the mystical and soteriological character of the philosophy of the Mādhyamikas.

We hope that we have succeeded in establishing that it is impossible to consider the absolute of the Mādhyamikas either as the totality of being or as nothingness. Such an alternative can only be put forward within the framework of western thought. The absolute has a completely different meaning for the Mādhyamikas. On a philosophical level, they refrain from any opinion whatsoever, but mystical experience leads them to the absolute by way of deliverance.

NOTE

* The original French version of this paper was read at the 21st Congress of Orientalists in Paris on 27 July 1948. It was published in the *Revue philosophique de la France et de l'étranger* under the title 'Le problème de l'absolu dans l'école Madhyamaka'. It contains several misprints due to the fact that no proofs were sent to the author. For instance Madhyamaka occurs twice as Mâdhyamaka! The author is much obliged to Miss E. J. J. C. Kat, Mrs L. A. Hercus and Professor O. Berkelbach van der Sprenkel for their help in preparing the English translation.

J. W. DE JONG

EMPTINESS*

Nāgārjuna's concept of "Emptiness" (*śūnyatā*) has been studied by many scholars. First of all Burnouf described Nāgārjuna's doctrine as a nihilistic scholasticism (*Introduction à l'histoire du Buddhisme indien*, Paris, 1844, p. 560). This interpretation was accepted by most scholars in the West in the second half of the nineteenth century and in the beginning of the twentieth century. In *The Conception of Nirvāṇa* (Leningrad, 1927) Stcherbatsky vigorously advocated a positive interpretation of the Mādhyamika absolute: "In Mahāyāna all parts or elements are unreal (*śūnya*), and only the whole, i.e. the Whole of the wholes (*dharmatā* = *dharma-kāya*), is real" (p. 41). According to him "the reality of the Buddha is the reality of the Universe" (p. 45) and the "real Buddha must be perceived directly by intuition" (p. 44). Stcherbatsky is not the first to have stressed the ontological nature of Nāgārjuna's teachings. Indian and Japanese scholars had already proposed similar interpretations.[1] Their opinion, however, did not have the same effect as Stcherbatsky's forceful statements. Schayer was greatly influenced by Stcherbatsky, although he did not accept all his philosophical conclusions. In the introduction to the *Ausgewählte Kapitel aus der Prasannapadā* (Kraków, 1931), Schayer writes that in the act of mystical intuition the Saint apprehends the absolute reality, the infinity, the totality (p. XXIX). At first de La Vallée Poussin was disinclined to accept this interpretation but in a short note, published after his death, he pronounced himself without ambiguity: "J'ai longtemps cru (divers articles de l'*Encyclopédie de HASTINGS, Nirvâṇa, Dogme et philosophie*) que le Madhyamaka était "nihiliste", niait l'Absolu, la chose en soi. Dans un mémoire "Madhyamaka" (*Mélanges chinois et bouddhiques, 2*), je glisse vers une solution moins catégorique. Enfin, dans la présente note, je me dispose à admettre que le Madhyamaka reconnaît un Absolu" (*HJAS*, III, 1938, p. 148). To complicate matters Stcherbatsky did not maintain his own interpretation. In a sharp attack on Schayer he rejected his own theory and maintained that the Madhyamaka denied the possibility of an Absolute Reality ('Die

Journal of Indian Philosophy **2** (1972) 7–15. *All Rights Reserved*

drei Richtungen in der Philosophie der Buddhismus', *RO*, X, 1934, pp. 1–37; cf. also *Madhyāntavibhāga*, Leningrad, 1936, pp. vi–vii). The Mādhyamika are monists, not in the sense of a unique monistic reality but in the sense of a unique principle of explanation, which excludes all real plurality. The absolute is now explained by him as an idea of the dialectic Reason. On the other hand, Schayer arrived at a more explicit explanation of the nature of the Mahāyāna absolute which he considered to be common to both Mādhyamikas and Yogācāras ('Das Mahāyānistische Absolutum nach der Lehre der Mādhyamikas', *OLZ*, 1935, Sp. 401–415). According to him the absolute is infinite, homogenous and undifferentiated; pure, not split into subject and object, inactive and non-fluctuating consciousness; transcending all words and concepts, inexpressible, beyond all predicates and communication. Moreover, infinity is spatial in nature and consciousness is a spiritual substance more subtle than all other substances. In order to substantiate this spiritual monism Schayer does not refer to the Mūlamadhyamakakārikās but to the Samādhirāja and other texts.

Besides the studies of Stcherbatsky, Schayer and de La Vallée Poussin, Poul Tuxen's *Indledende Bemaerkninger til buddhistik Relativism* (Copenhagen, 1936), containing a penetrating analysis of Nāgārjuna's Kārikās and Candrakīrti's *Prasannapadā*, also deserves mention here, although this work has not yet received the attention it merits. It is listed in May's bibliography (Candrakīrti, *Prasannapadā madhyamakavṛtti*, Paris, 1959, p. 43), but nowhere mentioned in the book itself. Streng remarks that it contains a general analysis depicting Nāgārjuna's dialectic as the negation of every particular entity in order to express the "whole" or "total" that is the source of all particulars (p. 243). Tuxen had a deep knowledge of Indian philosophies and religions, and his book on *Yoga* (Copenhagen, 1911) is certainly one of the best ever written on the philosophical Yoga system. Also written in Danish and almost completely unknown outside Denmark is his *Buddha* (Copenhagen, 1928), the fruit of a long sojourn in Siam and of a thorough study of Pāli texts. Tuxen keenly understood the value of Stcherbatsky's and Schayer's interpretations but he reproached them for not paying adequate attention to the religious aspect of Nāgārjuna's teachings. Stcherbatsky (in 1927) and Schayer (in 1931) opposed the unreality of particular phenomena to the reality of their totality. Tuxen shares their opinion that the Absolute can only be apprehended by the Yogin in a mystical intuition, but he does not consider the Absolute to be the totality of particular phenomena. If I am not mistaken, he uses the word totality (*Helhed*) only once but adds immediately that, as all other words, it is unfit to designate the highest, mystical Reality (p. 95).

After World War II the study of Nāgārjuna was taken up again by a new generation of scholars. One must mention here the names of André Bareau[2], Jacques May[3], T. R. V. Murti[4], Edward Conze[5] and Richard Robinson[6]. It is not possible to analyse their contributions to the study of the Mādhyamika system which, in various degrees, have greatly promoted a better understanding of this system and its basic concepts. Streng's book is the most recent study on the Mādhyamika system. Its importance lies in the fact that Streng examines Nāgārjuna's system from the point of view of a historian of religions. However Nāgārjuna's works, in particular his Kārikās, are interpreted, there is no doubt that Nāgārjuna is one of the most important religious thinkers and belongs to the common heritage of mankind. The study of his work ought not to be reserved to philologists and specialists of Indian philosophy. Streng shows himself well equipped for his difficult task. His knowledge of Sanskrit enables him to analyse Nāgārjuna's terminology without having to rely on translations made by other scholars. At the same time his reading in the works of Western scholars is extensive, as is shown by the annotated bibliography which contains an excellent systematic survey of the relevant literature (pp. 229–247). More important is the fact that Streng is a clear thinker who explains carefully the concepts he uses. His book makes no easy reading but this is due to Nāgārjuna himself and to the fact that Streng does not gloss over any difficulties.

It is not our intention to summarize section by section Streng's book because this would fail to do justice to his closely reasoned arguments. However, I would like to discuss a few points which are of particular importance for the understanding of Nāgārjuna. The central section of Streng's book is certainly the third part which is the basis for the fourth, dealing with the soteriological meaning of "emptiness", and which illuminates the arguments used in the preceding sections. Streng distinguishes three structures of religious apprehension in Indian thought: the mythical structure, the intuitive structure and Nāgārjuna's dialectical structure. The mythical structure of apprehension makes use of the paradigmatic force of words, forming the religious truth through the use of special words or a myth. The intuitive structure presumes an absolute essence or "universal" which can be known only through a unique means of perception unlimited by particular forms (p. 151). Elsewhere, Streng says that in the intuitive structure the "real" is apprehended as the totality of all particular phenomena, which requires a mode of apprehension different from mental apprehension (p. 106). Both the intuitive and mythical structures of apprehension use words in a descriptive way, for they presume that there is a referent having static ultimate ontological status as a correlate to the descriptive term (p. 105). Nāgārjuna's negative dialectic provides a positive apprehension, not of "a thing", but of the insight that there is no independent and absolute thing which exists externally, nor a "thing" which can be constructed (p. 148). In it the power of reason is an efficient force for realising Ultimate Truth (p. 149). In using the term "emptiness" together with his critical dialectic, Nāgārjuna expresses a religious vision which must be distinguished from the "intuition of Ultimate Reality" that denies the phenomenal world as real, and from the notion that there is Ultimate Reality which is activated to take material forms by the creative force of sacred words or sounds (p. 105).

Using Streng's own words we have tried to elucidate his conception of Nāgārjuna's negative dialectic as opposed to the mythical and intuitive apprehensions. Streng attributes to the negative dialectic the insight that there is no absolute reality. How is this insight, obtained through negative dialectic, related to the activity of "wisdom" (*prajñā*) and to intuition? Streng devotes a special chapter to the discussion of wisdom but does not deal specifically with intuition. In this chapter wisdom is described as a means to dissipate any absolute notion about something (p. 83). It seems therefore to fulfil the same function as the negative dialectic. However, elsewhere wisdom is said to be, in part, a concentrative exercise which dissolves the mental and emotional attachment of the apparent mind to "things" (including ideas and assertions), for it is the awareness that all "things" are empty (p. 91). Wisdom and negative dialectic are clearly separated in the following passage: "The dialectical activity of the Madhyamakakārikās, informed by the wisdom (*prajñā*) of indifference to logical proof or refutation, is reality-being-realized" (p. 156). One has the impression that Streng has not succeeded in explaining the difference between the functions of the negative dialectic and of wisdom. The same must be said with regard to his remarks on intuition in Nāgārjuna's system. Streng sharply distinguishes Nāgārjuna's negative dialectic from an intuition which apprehends an absolute essence, a "universal" or a totality. He refers explicitly to the theories of Murti and Schayer who see the Mādhyamika dialectic as only preparatory for the intuition of the reality behind the illusory phenomena (p. 76). As we have mentioned before, this theory was first proclaimed by Stcherbatsky in 1927. One must agree with Streng's rejection of the concept of an intuition which apprehends a totality. However, Streng does not consider intuition to be entirely absent from Nāgārjuna's system. He seems to admit that the Ultimate Truth can be manifested through logical reasoning as well as intuition (cf. pp. 94 and 147). According to him the difference between Nāgārjuna and Candrakīrti resides in the fact that the latter holds that mystical intuition is the only way of apprehending Ultimate Reality (p. 97). If I understand Streng correctly, he seems to be of the opinion that both reason (or logic or negative dialectic) and intuition can lead to the manifestation of Ultimate Truth but that wisdom transcends both. This seems to be clearly stated in the following passage, if one admits that the words "mysticism" and "mystical awareness" refer to mystical intuition: "The faculty of religious knowledge which transcends both logic and mysticism is wisdom (*prajñā*); at the same time, wisdom uses discursive mental structures together with a mystical awareness of the inadequacy of logical and empirical knowledge" (p. 159).

To determine exactly the relations between reason, intuition and wisdom in the Mādhyamika system is undoubtedly the crux of the problem. It seems to me that it is not possible to study this problem on the basis of Nāgārjuna's *Kārikās* and *Vigrahavyāvartanī* alone. Streng mentions in his foreword that he has used the Sanskrit texts attributed to Nāgārjuna. However, no reference whatsoever is made to the *Ratnāvalī*, of which the greater part has been preserved in Sanskrit (cf. G. Tucci, "The Ratnāvalī of Nāgārjuna', *JRAS*, 1934, pp. 307–325; 1936, pp. 237–252, 423–435), and to his Hymns. The Sanskrit text of two of Nāgārjuna's hymns (*Niraupamyastava*, *Paramārthastava*) has been published by Tucci (*JRAS*, 1932, pp. 309–325). It is not possible to study here the problem of the authenticity of the works attributed to Nāgārjuna, but one must point out that Candrakīrti in his *Madhyamakaśāstrastuti* (cf.

Oriens Extremus, IX, 1962, pp. 47–56) attributes the authorship of Hymns (*saṃstuti*) to Nāgārjuna. In his commentary on the *Bodhicaryāvatāra*. Prajñākaramati mentions a *Catustava*.[7] The question, which four *stava* are included in the *Catustava*, has been studied by de La Vallée Poussin, Patel, and Tucci (cf. Tucci, *Minor Buddhist Texts*, I, Roma, 1956, pp. 236–237). Recently Lamotte has proposed to identify the *saṃstuti*, mentioned by Candrakīrti, with these four hymns (*Le traité de la grande vertu de sagesse*, III, Louvain, 1970, p. XLIII). Lamotte rejects Tucci's theory, according to which the four *stava* are the *Lokātītastava*, the *Niraupamyastava*, the *Acintyastava* and the *Paramārthastava*. Following de La Vallée Poussin, he opts for the following four: *Niraumpamyastava*, *Lokātītastava*, *Cittavajrastava* and *Paramārthastava*. However this may be, both Prajñākaramati and the author of the *Catuḥstavasamāsa*, published by Tucci, are much later than Candrakīrti who does not limit the authorship of Nāgārjuna to a group of four Hymns. In any case, the Sanskrit materials are not limited to the *Kārikās* and the *Vigrahavyāvartanī*. However, even taking into account not only the abovementioned texts but also the texts attributed to Nāgārjuna by Candrakīrti and preserved only in Tibetan translation, it will probably still be extremely difficult to form a coherent picture of Nāgārjuna's doctrines. In order to understand such an author as Nāgārjuna it is absolutely necessary to consult the commentaries on his work and, in the first place, the commentaries on the *Kārikās*. It is only after having studied these commentaries and after having compared their different interpretations that one can try to distinguish the doctrine of Nāgārjuna from that of his commentators.

I would like to illustrate by one example how Streng has been led into error by the fact he did not consult the commentaries on the *Kārikās*, although three of them have been translated into Western languages (cf. Streng, pp. 239–240 for Walleser's two translations and the translations of the 27 chapters of the *Prasannapadā*. In xviii. 12 Nāgārjuna says: *saṃbuddhānām anutpāde śrāvakāṇāṃ punaḥ kṣaye / jñānaṃ pratyekabuddhānām asaṃsargāt pravartate //* which is rendered by Streng as follows: "If fully-completed Buddhas do not arise [in the world] and the disciples [of the Buddha] disappear, then, independently, the knowledge of the self-produced enlightened ones is produced." Streng comments: "The knowledge of 'emptiness' is not conceived as an expression of 'something';

it is not a proposition about something. Rather it is a power which spontaneously operated throughout existence (or nonexistence, both or neither)" (p. 83). For the correct interpretation of this verse one must consult the *Akutobhayā* and the *Prasannapadā*; both explain this verse in the same way. According to the *Prasannapadā* the knowledge of the Pratyekabuddhas arises *pūrvajanmāntaradharmatattvaśravaṇahetubalāt* "through the force of the cause consisting in the hearing of the true doctrine in former lives" (p. 378.9–10). This explanation is in complete agreement with the traditional Buddhist idea of the Pratyekabuddha. Consequently, this verse does not bear out Streng's interpretation. There are other cases in which Streng's translation or interpretation could have been more correct if he had taken into account the commentaries and the translations of the verses, embodied in the various translations of the 27 chapters of the *Prasannapadā* and in Walleser's translations.

More important, however, is the fact that the *Kārikās* do not contain any explicit reference to the nature of *prajñā*. The word *prajñā* is not mentioned even once in the *Kārikās* and the *Vigrahavyāvartanī*. These texts are extremely useful for the study of Nāgārjuna's negative dialectic as is obvious from the excellent chapters in which Streng studies Nāgārjuna's analysis of such basic Buddhist concepts as the *dharmas*, the *pratītyasamutpāda* and *Nirvāṇa*. The *Kārikās* and the *Vigrahavyāvartanī* are polemical works in which Nāgārjuna by means of negative dialectic shows the non-existence of all dharmas, but they do not deal with the nature of *prajñā* and intuition. Nāgārjuna's teachings can only be seen in the right perspective by taking into account not only all his works but also the commentaries on his works and the works of later Mādhyamikas such as Āryadeva, Buddhapālita, Bhāvaviveka and Śāntideva, who develop the ideas of Nāgārjuna and, in this way, help us to understand the implications of his teachings. This is, of course, not a task for a single scholar, but for several generations of scholars. Only when the main works of the Mādhyamikas have been translated and analysed, will it be possible to understand fully the place of each thinker within the Mādhyamika school.

Streng's book has great merits. Even though its textual basis is too narrow and the philological interpretation of Nāgārjuna's verses not always correct, his work is a very important contribution to the study of the religious meaning of Nāgārjuna's ideas. This is due to the fact that Streng has gone beyond the two short texts, taken as his basis, and has carefully and critically examined the most important scholarly works dealing with Buddhism and, in particular, with the Mādhyamika system. In many respects and above all with regard to the soteriological aspect of Nāgārjuna's teachings, he has been more perceptive than many specialists in the field of Buddhist studies. However, he has not been entirely successful in analysing the relations between reason, intuition and wisdom with regard to the attainment of Ultimate Truth. Let me conclude this review by briefly stating my own opinion which does not pretend to be more than an impression based upon the reading of only a few Mādhyamika texts. One of the fundamental ideas of Buddhism throughout its doctrinal history is that true insight is obtained through concentration of mind. First comes *śīla*, then *samādhi* and finally *prajñā*. The *prajñāpāramitā*, the last and highest of the *pāramitās*, is to be obtained after the *dhyānapāramitā*. In the Mādhyamika system the Ultimate Truth can only be apprehended by *prajñā* in the act of concentration. The Ultimate Truth cannot be described with words or concepts but the insight gained in concentration, enables the Yogin to use his dialectical reason on the plane of *saṃvṛti* in order to demonstrate the unsubstantiality of all dharmas, Nirvāṇa included. The negative dialectic does not lead to the understanding of the Ultimate Truth but prepares the ground for the true insight to be gained through concentration. *Prajñā* transcends reason and can only, if imperfectly, be described as a mystical intuition which sees by way of not seeing (*adarśanayogena*). From a philosophical point of view the Mādhyamika system is the culmination of a basic tendency in Buddhism which consists in the emptying of ontological categories. Early Buddhism denies the reality of the Self (*ātman*), the Mādhyamika system the reality of all dharmas. The Mādhyamikas have carried the Buddhist concept of the transitoriness of everything (*sarvaṃ kṣaṇikam*) to its ultimate conclusion (*sarvaṃ śūnyam*).

Our Western philosophy has its roots in Greek philosophy. Greek θεωρεῖν means not only "to see", but also "to think, to speculate, to theorize". The philosophy of Plato reaches its climax in the vision of that which is best in existence (ἡ τοῦ ἀρίστου ἐν τοῖς οὖσι θέα, Res publica VII, 532c). The Greek looks at the visible things and tries to penetrate into their essence. The mystic vision of the Indian yogin is turned away from the visible world towards the invisible world. I believe that this fundamental difference between the Greek and Indian spirit explains the difficulties one encounters in understanding Indian thought in its supreme manifestation.

NOTES

* Frederick J. Streng, *Emptiness. A Study in Religious Meaning.* A Depth Study of the Philosopher Nagarjuna and His Interpretation of Ultimate Reality. Including translations of Nagarjuna's "Fundamentals of the Middle Way" and "Averting the Arguments", Nashville, New York, Abingdon Press, 1967.

[1] See the references given by Schayer, *OLZ*, 1935, Sp. 401 and by de La Vallée Poussin, *MCB*, II, 1933, p. 36, n. 1.

[2] *L'absolu en philosophie bouddhique* (Paris, 1951), pp. 172–198, 294.

[3] 'Recherches sur un système de philosophie bouddhique', *Bulletin annuel de la Fondation Suisse*, III, 1954, pp. 21–33; 'La philosophie bouddhique de la vacuité', *Studia Philosophica*, XVIII, 1958, pp. 123–137; 'Kant et le Mādhyamika', *IIJ*, III, 1959, pp. 102–111; *Candrakīrti Prasannapadā madhyamakavṛtti* (Paris, 1959), pp. 5–22.

[4] *The Central Conception of Buddhism* (London, 1955).

[5] *Buddhist Thought in India* (London, 1962), pp. 238–249.

[6] *Early Mādhyamika in India and China* (Madison, Milwaukee and London, 1967), pp. 39–70.

[7] Prajñākaramati always uses the form *catustava*, not *catuḥstava*; cf. de La Vallée Poussin's edition of the *Bodhicaryāvatārapañjikā*, p. 533, n. 10.

ABBREVIATIONS

HJAS = Harvard Journal of Asian Studies.
IIJ = Indo-Iranian Journal.
JRAS = Journal of the Royal Asiatic Society.
MCB = Mélanges chinois et bouddhiques.
OLZ = Orientalistische Literaturzeitung.
RO = Rocznik Orientalistyczny.

BOOK REVIEW

Guy Richard Welbon, *The Buddhist Nirvāṇa and Its Western Interpreters*, The University of Chicago Press, 1968. XI+320 pp., $8.50.

The history of Buddhist studies in the West is a fascinating but rather neglected topic. Scholars have been more inclined to advance Buddhist studies than to trace their history. Windisch's *Geschichte der Sanskrit-Philologie und indischer Altertumskunde* (Berlin und Leipzig, 1917–20) contains relatively little concerning Buddhist studies. Raymond Schwab (*La Renaissance orientale*, Paris, 1950) and Henri de Lubac (*La rencontre du bouddhisme et de l'occident*, Paris, 1952) have made useful contributions but, as is obvious from the titles of their works, they are primarily interested in the reception of Indian and Buddhist ideas in the West. Welbon's study of the interpretation of Nirvāṇa by Western scholars is not only a history of philological and historical studies on Nirvāṇa. The author stresses in his preface his concern with the fact that the interpretations of the meaning of Nirvāṇa reflect the individual scholar's own personal commitment. At the same time his study is intended to be a contribution to the understanding of European intellectual history in the nineteenth and twentieth centuries, especially with regard to the encounter of European intellectuals with an alien tradition.

The execution of a programme of this scope presupposes three elements: knowledge of the philological and historical problems studied by Western scholars; understanding of their personal commitment; insight into the intellectual approach to religious studies in general in the nineteenth and twentieth centuries. If, in addition, like Welbon, one assumes that the response to the question of the meaning of Nirvāṇa is at the same time an answer more or less complete to all questions about Buddhism, it is obvious that it would be too optimistic to expect this study to be entirely satisfactory. Welbon has written this book with great enthusiasm. Many of his remarks are perceptive. Nevertheless, it cannot be recommended without reservations.

Journal of Indian Philosophy **1** (1972) 396–403. *All Rights Reserved*

The first chapters of Welbon's book are rather disappointing. Buddhist literature has only gradually become accessible to scholars. Even today only part of it has been studied by Western scholars, mainly the Pāli and Sanskrit texts but of the enormous mass of texts, preserved in Tibetan and Chinese translations, very few have been adequately translated and studied. The interpretation of the meaning of Nirvāṇa depends very much on the texts studied. Welbon does not always make this sufficiently clear. He remarks that Colebrooke in his essay on Buddhism does not quote any primary sources. It would have been necessary to pay more attention to the sources used by Colebrooke.[1] His main source is Śaṅkara's *Brahmasūtrabhāṣya* II.2.18–32 with the commentaries by Vācaspatimiśra, Govindānanda and Advaitānanda. Careful study of this passage would have prevented Welbon from stating that Colebrooke was not altogether secure as to what beliefs differentiated Buddhists from Jainas, that even today it is not always clear to what sect a given native critique is directed and that the polemicists themselves were by no means always sure of the distinctions which characterize various sects. It would also have been useful to emphasize the importance of Colebrooke's remarks on the 'succession of thought', quoted by Welbon on p. 29, in view of the later discussion of de La Vallée Poussin's study on the *vijñānasaṃtāna* theory (pp. 263 sq.). Louis de La Vallée Poussin fully realized the value of the texts, directed against the Buddhists, and he had studied them carefully (cf. *JA* (1902), **II**, p. 284, n. 3). It is also noteworthy to remark that in his *Le dogme et la philosophie du bouddhisme* (Paris, 1930, p. 51) de La Vallée Poussin quotes with approval the following passage from Colebrooke's essay: "The notion of nirvāṇa as of a happy condition seems to be derived from the experience of ecstacies, or from that of profound sleep, from which a person awakes refreshed."[2]

In the chapter on Csoma de Körös Welbon quotes an article by William Hunter. This article, which seems based on nothing else than Duka's *Life and Works of Alexander Csoma de Körös*, has been unhappily revived by an Indian publisher as an introduction to a reprint of two of Csoma's articles (*The Life and Teachings of the Buddha*, Calcutta, 1957). William Hunter, historian of the British raj in the nineteenth century, discusses Csoma's linguistic phantasies and contrasts them with Bopp's achievement. This induces Welbon to mention Bopp and to add a totally superfluous note, listing several publications on Bopp. Without adducing any proof Welbon states pedantically that "Csoma's methodological poverty does dim his analytical and commentatorial achievements". Anybody who knows Csoma's works and has some knowledge of Tibetan will read this statement with utter astonishment. Welbon quotes a long passage from one of Csoma's articles and adds: "Those compendious statements are so tantalizing!" (p. 48). Those statements would have been less tantalizing if Welbon had taken the trouble to consult Csoma's article 'Notices on the Different Systems of Buddhism, Extracted from the Tibetan Authorities' (*JASB* **VII**, 1 (1838), pp. 142–7; reprinted in *Tibetan Studies*, Calcutta, 1912, pp. 73–9), and not the extract given by Duka. From Csoma's article he would have learned that this passage is based upon Tsongkhapa's *Lam-rim chen-mo* (for literature on the *Lam-rim chen-mo* see Rudolf Kaschewsky, *Das Leben des lamaistischen Heiligen Tsongkhapa Blo-bzaṅ-grags-pa*, Bonn, 1967, p. 396, n. 963).[3]

Welbon seems to admire Jules Barthélemy Saint-Hilaire's knowledge of Sanskrit which, according to him was considerable (p. 71). In a note Welbon remarks that he translated the entire *Sāṃkhyakārikā* in his 'Premier mémoire sur le Sânkhya' (*Mémoires* etc. **VIII** (1852), pp. 107–560). Probably Welbon has never seen either the Sanskrit text of the *kārikā* or Barthélemy Saint-Hilaire's work which has been well characterized by Richard Garbe (cf. *Die Sâṃkhya-Philosophie*, 2e Auflage, Leipzig, 1917, p. 109). Welbon defends him against Schwab but does not mention de Lubac's pages on him (pp. 157–8). Henri de Lubac, a great Catholic scholar, is obviously even more embarrassed about him than Schwab to judge from his final paragraph: "Enfin dans une brochure de 1880, ce jugement définitif, qui compromet le christianisme plutôt qu'il ne l'exalte: "Le bouddhisme n'a rien de commun avec le christianisme, qui est autant au-dessus de lui que les sociétés européennes sont au-dessus des sociétés asiatiques"."

Welbon devotes a long and welcome chapter on James d'Alwis but it is much to be regretted that he has not tried to obtain more information on him. A note states briefly that "repeated inquiries have failed to disclose sufficient biographical details for even a brief sketch. For me at this writing, D'Alwis is his critical volume." (p. 130, n. 2). However, on the next page Welbon declares that D'Alwis was a long-time resident missionary and student in Ceylon and on p. 144 he becomes 'a distinguished missionary'. A glance in the catalogue of the British Museum would have been sufficient to bring to the notice of the author a book which contains much information on D'Alwis: *Memoirs and Desultory Writings of the late James d'Alwis* (Colombo, 1939). From it he would have learned that D'Alwis was not a missionary and a Western interpreter of Buddhist Nirvāṇa, but a Sinhalese scholar (1823–1878) who for many years was a member of the Legislative Council. His works on Sinhalese and Pāli grammar are well-known and, as recently as 1966, the long introduction to his translation of the *Sidat Sangarāva* was reprinted by the Department of National Museums, Ceylon (*A Survey of Sinhala Literature*).

Among the chapters which can be read with profit although not with entire approval, one must mention those dealing with the views of Oldenberg and de La Vallée Poussin, perhaps the most outstanding scholars of all those who have made important contributions to the study of the concept of Nirvāṇa. Welbon is right in maintaining against E. J. Thomas and H. Dumoulin that Oldenberg has not changed his ideas about Nirvāṇa in any essential point. One of the reasons is perhaps the fact that in later years Oldenberg was more occupied with Vedic studies. Nevertheless, he has carefully kept himself informed of the progress of Buddhist studies and each new edition of his famous *Buddha* has been revised by the author. Welbon compares the English translation (based on the first German edition of 1881) with the sixth German edition of 1914. It would have been interesting to compare the changes made by Oldenberg in the editions published during his lifetime, because they contain his reactions to criticisms and to new theories.[4] His discussion with de La Vallée Poussin is carried through till the seventh German edition of 1920, the last edition revised by Oldenberg. In his chapter on de La Vallée Poussin, Welbon does not mention at all Oldenberg's reactions.

Nobody has written more on Nirvāṇa than de La Vallée Poussin.[5] It was of course impossible for Welbon to discuss everything written on Nirvāṇa by de La Vallée Poussin. However, it would have been necessary to take into account his latest discussions in 'Une dernière note sur le Nirvāṇa' (*Études d'orientalisme*, publiées par le Musée Guimet à la mémoire de Raymonde Linossier, **II**, Paris, 1932, 329–54) and in the appendix to the second edition of *Indo-européens et Indo-ariens. L'Inde jusque vers 300 av. J.-C.* (Paris, 1936, 389–92). In his early writings de la Vallée Poussin reacted strongly against the defenders of the orthodoxy of Pāli Buddhism. Although his reaction has certainly been carried too far, the result has been of great importance to Buddhist studies. In 1902 de La Vallée Poussin concluded the first part of his article on 'Dogmatique bouddhique' (*JA* (1902), **II**, 237–306) with some methodological remarks on the necessity for a thorough study of Buddhist scholasticism. He stresses the importance of the *Kośa* to which he was to devote many years of study.[6] He concludes these remarks by pointing out that the dogmatics of the ancient *sūtras* must be studied in the light of the scholastic commentaries. The programme traced by de La Vallée Poussin in these remarks, has consequently been carried out by him. Therefore he was fully entitled to write in 1936 (*Indo-européens*, etc. p. 391) that the exegesis of Nirvāṇa had made decisive progress; "En ce qui concerne l'important problème du Nirvāṇa, notre exégèse a fait des progrès que je crois décisifs. Le point était de distinguer les temps, les écoles, et de lire les textes sans parti-pris" (p. 391). However, as to the doctrines of the old canonical texts almost everything still has to be done: "L'obscurité est encore profonde; l'analyse idéologique et chronologique de Canon est à peine commencée et présente de sérieuses difficultés" (p. 392). One cannot say that since 1936 much progress has been made along the lines indicated by de La Vallée Poussin.

In the above pages no mention has been made of the second and third part of the task which Welbon has set himself: the study of the personal commitment of the scholars discussed and of the relation of the study of Nirvāṇa to the intellectual history of the nineteenth and twentieth centuries. Undoubtedly, in most cases, the biographical information available is insufficient for an adequate study of the personal background of the scholars concerned. Welbon has been careful not to extrapolate the personal points of view of the authors from their writings, which, often, are the only sources at our disposal. One would, however, have welcomed a final chapter on the intellectual background, shared by most of the scholars. Only a few remarks can be made here. When one reads the work of such careful and meticulous scholars such as Oldenberg and de La Vallée Poussin, one is forcibly struck with their supercilious attitude towards the Indian mentality. It suffices to refer to the following passage of Oldenberg's *Buddha*: "Dem Inder aber sind die besten der Interessen und Ideale, die gesundes Volksleben in seinen Tiefen ergreifen, fremd .... (13th ed., 1959, p.15; see also p. 284: "In der schwülen Stille Indiens ....") and to the passage from de La Vallée Poussin's *The Way to Nirvāṇa*, quoted by Welbon (p. 272): "The historian has not to deal with Latin notions worked out by sober and clearsighted thinkers, but with Indian 'philosophumena' concocted by ascetics ... men exhausted by a severe diet and often stupified by the practice of ecstacy. Indians do not make a clear distinction between facts and ideas, between ideas and words, they never clearly recognized the principle of contradiction." In fairness to de La Vallée Poussin one must, however, draw attention to his confession in the preface of the fifth edition of his *Bouddhisme* (Paris, 1925): "Je dois le dire aussi, j'ai à la longue pris du Bouddhisme une singulière estime .... C'est faire grand tort au Bouddhisme de le baigner les eaux du Léman, de la Sprée ou de la Tamise" (p. VIII). These opinions of Oldenberg and de La Vallée Poussin are certainly to be explained by the intellectual climate of the second half of the nineteenth century in which they were brought up.

In a few places Welbon mentions the concern of nineteenth century scholars for 'origins'. In his introduction to his *Ausgewählte Kapitel aus der Prasannapadā* (Krakow, 1931, p. IX) Schayer remarks: "Die falsche Suggestion, dass in der Geschichte der Religion nur das Ursprüngliche echt, alles Jüngere dagegen mehr oder weniger eine 'Entartung' sei, hat von Anfang an den Gang der Studien, ihre Richtung und ihre Methode beeinflusst." He adds in a note: "Man errät leicht, woher diese Suggestion stammt: es ist die protestantische Auffassung des 'wahren, evangelischen Christentums' auf das Gebiet des Buddhismus übertragen." Schayer's remarks help us to understand de La Vallée Poussin's reaction to the concepts of the Pāli school. For a Catholic scholar, nurtured in the sacred tradition of the church, a religion is much more than the pure, unadulterated teachings of its founder. However, de La Vallée Poussin was quite aware of the necessity to distinguish older and younger strata in the Buddhist canon (cf. the passage quoted above, p. 400). Welbon states that "the so-called canonical collections in Pāli and Sanskrit Buddhism (*sic*) would not permit a clear distinction between actual statements of the Buddha and later interpretations without making use of the most recent methods of Formsgeschichte (*sic*) – methods which, for the most part, are still inaccessible to Buddhist scholars" (p. 116). Here again, one is rather annoyed to find a statement which is not elaborated and substantiated. Many Buddhist scholars are aware of the great problems which complicate the critical study of the Buddhist canon. A careful comparative study of the Buddhist canonical texts in Pāli, Sanskrit and Chinese would be helpful in determining the older layers of the Buddhist canon but one wonders how one has to proceed from there in order to distinguish between the words of the Buddha and those ascribed to him in later periods. If New Testament scholars have elaborated a method which could be applied to the Buddhist scriptures, Buddhist scholars would only be too glad to make use of it but this has to be shown in some detail. General statements of this kind are not really helpful.

The length of this review, which could easily be extended, is prompted by the interest of the topic studied by Welbon. One has to appreciate the courage of this scholar in undertaking such an ambitious piece of research. It is a pity that the value of Welbon's work is marred not only by many inaccuracies[7] but also by an insufficient knowledge of the problems inherent in the study of Buddhist literature. Horace's words in his *De arte poetica* have lost nothing of their value: *sumite materiam vestris, qui scribitis, aequam / viribus et versate diu, quid ferre recusent, / quid valeant umeri.* If Welbon heeds Horace's advice, we can look forward with confidence to his future publications.

J. W. DE JONG

A.N.U. Canberra

NOTES

[1] According to Welbon one of Colebrooke's sources was 'the *Sāṃkhya* (Kapila), one chapter on Bauddhas' (p. 26, n. 8). Colebrooke's essay was published originally in the *Transactions of the Asiatic Society of London*, volume I. It has been reprinted in the first (London, 1837) and second (London, 1873) editions of his *Miscellaneous Essays*. Only the first edition of his *Miscellaneous Essays* could be consulted by me. It contains the following passage: "The *Sánc'hya* of Capila devotes a whole chapter to controversy; and notices the sect of *Buddha*..." (vol. I, p. 380.).

[2] On p. 26, n. 9 Welbon writes that he cannot understand that Colebrooke has been overlooked as the scholar who unquestionably established that Buddhism was born in India and refers to de Lubac p. 112 (error for p. 115) and to Renan's 'Premiers travaux sur le bouddhisme'. However, as mentioned by de Lubac this discovery has been made long before 1827 by Ricci (de Lubac, p. 118). In fact, Renan does not say that Hodgson discovered the Indian origin of Buddhism, but that Hodgson by announcing the existence of Sanskrit Buddhist manuscripts set at rest all doubts which could perhaps be raised: "Tous les doutes furent levés quand M. Hodgson annonça aux Sociétés asiatiques de Calcutta, de Londres et de Paris l'existence dans les monastères du Népal d'une vaste collection de livres bouddhiques écrits en sanscrit et inconnus dans le reste de l'Inde." (*Oeuvres complètes de Ernest Renan*, Tome VII (1955), p. 748). One wonders whether Welbon has consulted this passage, referred to by de Lubac.

[3] According to Welbon Csoma studied the grammar and dictionary of Giorgi. This description of Giorgi's *Alphabetum Tibetanum* shows clearly that Welbon is not acquainted with the contents of this work (cf. Sylvain Lévi, *Le Népal* I, Paris, 1905, 117–8; L. Petech, *I Missionari italiani nel Tibet e nel Nepal* I, Roma, 1952, XCIX–CII).

[4] On p. 194, n. 1 Welbon states that revised editions of Oldenberg's *Buddha* appeared in 1890, ca. 1894, 1904, 1914 and–just after Oldenberg's death–in 1921. He adds that for much bibliographical assistance, he is indebted here and elsewhere to Shinsho Hanayama, *Bibliography on Buddhism*. Welbon seems not to be aware of the many inaccuracies of Hanayama's work. In his *Nachwort* to the 13th edition of Oldenberg's *Buddha* (Stuttgart, 1959, 457–8) Helmuth von Glasenapp has briefly studied the successive editions. Oldenberg has revised the second (1890), third (1897), fourth (1903), fifth (1906), sixth (1914) and seventh (1920) editions. On p. 209 Welbon mentions Oldenberg's excursus (*sic*) on the term *upādisesa* in the first edition. He makes a few suppositions to explain the fact that it is not reprinted in later editions (p. 213), but has not consulted the preface of the second edition in which Oldenberg explains why he has omitted the three excursus of the first edition (p. VIII).

[5] For biographical details Welbon seems to have consulted only Paul Masson-Oursel's obituary (*JA* (1938), 287–90). According to this source de La Vallée Poussin attended the University of Liège from 1881 to 1888 (from his twelfth to his nineteenth year). It was there that he was introduced to Sanskrit and Pāli by Charles de Harlez and Philippe Colinet. Ludo Rocher has already drawn attention to the unlikelihood of this information and adds: "We prefer to believe that he attended Liège university from 1888 until he went to Paris at the age of 22" (*JAOS* **90** (1970), p. 590). It is not clear on which source Rocher bases his belief. According to reliable sources of information de La Vallée Poussin studied from 1884 to 1888 at the University of Liège. From 1888 to 1890 he studied Sanskrit, Pāli and Avestan under the direction of Charles de Harlez and Philippe Colinet at the University of Louvain (cf. Marcelle Lalou et Jean Przyluski, 'Notice nécrologique de Louis de La Vallée Poussin', *Mélanges chinois et bouddhiques* VI (1939), 5–10; Étienne Lamotte, 'Notice sur Louis de La Vallée Poussin', *Annuaire de l'Académie royale de Belgique* (1965), 145–68).

[6] Curiously enough, Welbon does not mention at all de La Vallée Poussin's translation of the *Kośa*, undoubtedly his greatest contribution to Buddhist studies.

[7] Welbon is very careless in quoting French and German words, for instance 'trachenden' (p. 207), 'philosophumène' (p. 260, n. 28), 'besoin' for 'soin' (p. 283), 'Révue de l'Histoire des Religions' (p. 309).

Abbreviations:
JA – Journal Asiatique, Paris.
JAOS – Journal of American Oriental Society, New Haven.
JASB – Journal of the Asiatic Society of Bengal, Calcutta.

BUDDHA'S WORD IN CHINA

In the past, the general view of China has often been that of a country which existed for many centuries without change, free from all influence from foreign ideas. However, the study of China has shown that nothing could be further from the truth than this idea. In the long course of its history, China has undergone many foreign influences and continues to experience them even today. These influences have manifested themselves in many different fields. In that of religion, one can name six foreign faiths, all of which entered China during the first millennium of our era: Buddhism, Mazdaism, Manichaeism, Nestorianism, Islam, and Judaism. Of all these foreign religions, none has been more successful than Buddhism. There is no doubt that Buddhism existed already in China in the first century A.D. During its almost 2,000-year-long history there, Buddhism exerted a great influence on many different aspects of Chinese life. In the view of one of the leading scholars in the field of Chinese Buddhism, Paul Demiéville, Buddhism dominated Chinese philosophical thought from the fourth to the tenth century. During that period, it is in Buddhism that the key to all creative thought is to be found, whether such thought was inspired by Buddhist ideas, or, on the contrary, directed against them.[1] Not less important, perhaps, is the contribution Buddhism has made to Chinese art. The cave-temples of Yün-kang and Lung-men are a lasting testimony to the great period of Chinese Buddhist sculpture. In many other fields, too, the influence of Buddhism has been of great significance for Chinese culture. In order to understand the role played by Buddhism in China, it is necessary first to understand how Buddhism came there.

Buddhism is the oldest of the three universal religions. It arose more than five centuries before Christianity, and more than eleven before Islam. These three religions have some very important characteristics in common. They all go back to a founder whose life and actions were piously recorded by his followers. In the second place, all are universal religions. Their message is directed to everybody, without distinction of race or social status. Finally, they all possess sacred scriptures which contain their fundamental teachings. There is, however, a great difference between these religions in the way in which they spread from their original homeland to other countries and peoples. The propagation of Christianity and Islam was often associated with military conquest or commercial expansion. The spread of Buddhism, on the contrary, was mainly due to individual missionaries who were without any support from worldly powers. The main concern of these missionaries was to bring the message of the Buddha, as laid down in the sacred writings, to other peoples in order to deliver them from the sufferings of *saṃsāra*, or transmigration. These sacred scriptures of the Buddhists are very voluminous. They do not consist of a single volume like the Bible or the Koran. Both the Christians and the Moslems soon codified their scriptures into a canon. In Buddhism, however, only some of the older schools have established, in the course of time, a collection of texts with the status of a canon, and from only one of them, the school of the Sthaviras, the elders, has a complete canon been preserved. This collection contains, in its latest edition, no less than forty volumes.[2] However, the later Buddhism schools never arrived at establishing a well defined canon.

As I have already mentioned, Buddhism is the oldest of the universal religions. Never before in the history of mankind had it been so expressly stated that a doctrine was to be taught to everybody capable of understanding it. According to the Buddhist tradition, as soon as the Buddha had obtained a small number of followers he addressed them with the following words:

> O monks, I have been delivered from all bonds both divine and human. Monks, you are delivered from all bonds both divine and human. O monks, you must lead the religious life for the advantage of many people, for the happiness of many people, out of compassion for the world, for the benefit, the advantage and the happiness of Gods and men. Do not go alone, go together. Monks, teach the doctrine which is good at the beginning, good at the middle, good at the end, in the spirit and in the letter. Proclaim the pure conduct, complete in its entirety and purified. There are human beings who by nature have few passions. Through not hearing the doctrines they will perish. They will be the ones who will understand the doctrine.[3]

During the forty-five years which elapsed after the illumination of the Buddha until his *Nirvāṇa*, he himself untiringly taught the doctrine. When he was at the point of entering into *Nirvāṇa*, he said to his cherished disciple, Ānanda: 'O Ānanda, I have taught the doctrine without making any distinction between esoteric and exoteric'.[4] With these words the Buddha stressed the fact that the doctrine had been taught by him in its entirety. The Buddha told Ānanda that from now on the doctrine itself, the *Dharma*, was to be the only refuge for the followers of Buddha.[5]

After the Buddha's *Nirvāṇa*, his disciples continued the work of propagating the doctrine. More than a century after the *Nirvāṇa* of the Buddha, in the middle of the third century B.C., Buddhism was actively fostered by King Aśoka whose realm occupied almost the entire Indian sub-continent. From a doctrine known only to a few people in a small region, the present-day Bihar, Buddhism had become one of the major religions of India. Of particular importance for the expansion of Buddhism outside India is the fact that in the third, second, and first centuries B.C., northwestern India became a more and more important centre of Buddhism. The northwest has always played a significant part in ancient Indian history. From Alexander the Great, foreign invaders have always penetrated India through the passes in northwestern India. On the other hand, it was by this same route that Indian culture was able to spread its influence to Central Asia and to China. It is from the northwest, from Kashmir and Afghanistan, that Buddhism penetrated into Central Asia and from there into China. The earliest testimony concerning the existence of Buddhism in China dates from the year 65 A.D.[6] It is very likely that Buddhism had already penetrated into China by the first half of the first century A.D.

The first Buddhist missionaries did not come from far away India but from countries situated both west and east of the Pamir. The most important centre of Buddhism west of the Pamir was the country of the great Yüeh-chih. From here Buddhism spread east to Parthia and north to Sogdiana. To the east of the Pamir is the Tarim basin, bordered to the north by the T'ien-shan and to the south by the K'un-lun ranges. This country, which today is called East Turkestan, or Chinese Turkestan, has been the meeting place of the cultures of India and China. It is for this reason that the great discoverer, Sir Aurel Stein, gave the name Serindia to Chinese Turkestan. In this region existed a series of small states which played a great role in the transmission of Buddhism from India to China. These states are to be found in the northern and the southern parts of the Tarim basin. Through these northern and southern states led the two main routes which connected northwestern India and China. The southern route passed, travelling from east to west, through the states of Kashgar, Yarkand, Khotan, Lou-lan, and finally ended at Tun-huang in the extreme northwest of China. The northern route passed through Aksu, Kucha, Karashar, and Turfan and also ended at Tun-huang. It is in the old remains along these routes that very important discoveries have been made between the end of the nineteenth century and World War I. Scholars from Russia, England, Germany, Japan, and France discovered many Buddhist sites. Excavations brought to light the remains of Buddhist buildings in which many pieces of sculpture, wall paintings, and other works of art inspired by Buddhism were found. Above all, and of the greatest importance, were the great quantities of manuscripts found in several places. The great majority of these manuscripts were Buddhist texts written in various languages and different scripts. Many were written in Sanskrit or other Indian languages or in Chinese, but some were written in languages almost entirely or entirely unknown at the time of their discovery: Iranian languages such as Sogdian and Khotanese, and two languages of undetermined affiliation. In 1908 it was shown that these two languages belonged to the Indo-European family.[7] Some scholars thought that they were the languages of the Tokharians who are known to us from Greek sources as the inhabitants of ancient Bactria. For this reason these languages were called Tokharian A and Tokharian B, or West Tokharian and East Tokharian. Other scholars, however, have objected to the name Tokharian being given to these languages. They proved that the so-called Tokharian A was the indigenous language of Karashar, of which the old name is Agni; and that Tokharian B was the indigenous language of Kucha. They therefore proposed naming these languages Agnean and Kuchean.

The discovery of all these manuscripts opened up new fields of research for linguistic and Buddhist studies. They were also of great consequence—which is our concern here—for the history of Buddhism in China. It was already known from Chinese sources that missionaries had come from the countries west and east of the Pamir, countries collectively called the 'Western Regions' by the Chinese. Chinese Buddhists had also travelled to these regions. With these discoveries, however, concrete evidence of the importance of Buddhism in this part of the world has, for the first time, become available. As a result, there is today a plethora of material on the history of Buddhism in Central Asia.[8] It is to be hoped that in the future a scholar will write a comprehensive and up-to-date book on Central Asian Buddhism. At present the most detailed work in this field is a Japanese work published in 1914.[9] Although it contains much information, it is, of course, not up to date, and in the second place, it does not contain a critical examination of the traditions found in the different sources. Few expeditions by Western scholars have been undertaken since World War I[10] but the publication of the material already obtained continues and, if every document is to be studied in detail, will continue for quite some time. However, new material has been brought to light in a number of other areas. Very important results have been obtained by the excavations undertaken by the French in Afghanistan.[11] Also in more recent years, Russian scholars have been very actively digging in the Soviet Republics north of Iran, Afghanistan, and East Turkestan.[12] New discoveries can be expected at almost every moment. Nevertheless, if one takes into account the dates of the documents already obtained from Central Asia, it is not to be expected that much information will be forthcoming from this source concerning the period extending roughly from the beginning of our era to about 400 A.D. Most of the documents are of a later date. There are certainly some that go back to this period but they are almost entirely of a secular nature and do not give any information about Buddhism in Central Asia. For this reason we are still forced to rely mainly on Chinese sources.

These sources give much information about the first four centuries, but one must not forget the fact that most of them belong to a later period and the information which they contain has to be sifted critically before it can be used for the reconstruction of the history of Buddhism in Central Asia. One thing, however, is quite obvious. The main source from which Chinese Buddhism was nourished in the first centuries of its existence was Central Asia. According to a Chinese tradition, in the year 2 B.C. a Chinese named Ch'in Ching-hsien 秦景憲 was orally taught Buddhist *sūtras* by the envoy of the Prince of the Great Yüeh-chih, I Ts'un 伊存.[13] Modern scholars reject this story as apocryphal. The interesting point in it, however, is the fact that it refers to the explanation of Buddhist *sūtras*. As already remarked, Buddhism was brought to China by missionaries who came there as individuals. They went to China in the first place with the intention of explaining and preaching the Buddhist *sūtras*. In the propagation of Buddhism, the main stress was always put on the Buddhist scriptures. Of course, Buddhism contains many more elements than its sacred writings. Buddhism, as a religion, implies an organisation of monks, the building of monasteries and *stūpas*, the making of sculptures of Buddhas and Bodhisattvas, and the performance of rites and practices. The sacred texts are, however, the *conditio sine qua non* for the existence of Buddhism. Buddhism in China depended, above all, on a knowledge of the sacred scriptures.

Although it is probably not an historical fact that the envoy of the Prince of the Yüeh-chih was the first to bring the word of the Buddha to China, there is no doubt that in the early period of Chinese Buddhism it was mainly the missionaries from the Western Regions who were responsible for the spread of Buddhism to China. In his studies on Buddhism and the Western Regions, Liang Ch'i-ch'ao has brought together information from Chinese biographies of Buddhist monks concerning the origin of the monks who came to China in the first period of Chinese Buddhism up to the end of the period of the three kingdoms in 265 A.D.[14] It is evident from his lists that the great majority of foreign monks came from the Western Regions. In the following period, from 265 till the end of the (Liu) Sung dynasty in 479, most of the monks came from Kashmir in northwestern India. It is only in the period from 479 till the end of the Sui dynasty in 618 that most are found to have come from the sub-continent as a whole.

Chinese sources do not tell us only about foreign monks who came to China in order to spread the doctrine, but also about Chinese pilgrims who went to the Buddhist countries. Their motives were different: some went there to search for the sacred books; others hoped to be instructed in the sacred doctrine by monks in India; others again wanted to see the sacred places of Buddhism; some, finally, went to foreign countries in order to invite famous teachers to come to China.[15] Of all these motives, the most important seems to have been the first, the desire to obtain the sacred texts. According to the Chinese sources, in the early period the Chinese pilgrims mainly went to the Western Regions. The first Chinese pilgrim whose name is recorded is Chu Shih-hsing 竺士行, who in 260 A.D. travelled to Khotan in the southern part of the Tarim basin.[16] His example was followed by others. For the period until the middle of the fifth century, Chinese sources already mention many names of pilgrims who undertook long and arduous voyages.[17] In the beginning most of them went to the Western Regions but gradually they extended their travels to Kashmir, a famous centre of Buddhism. The first pilgrim who seems to have gone further is the famous Fa-hsien 法顯. In 399 A.D., when he was almost sixty years old, he left the capital, Ch'ang-an, and went via Tun-huang by the southern route to India. He stayed three years in Patna. On his return journey by ship, he visited Ceylon, where he remained for two years, and Java, where he stayed for five months. In 413 he arrived in Nanking after an absence of fourteen years from China.[18] We cannot here mention the names of the many Chinese pilgrims who went to India after Fa-hsien. I-ching 義淨, who at the end of the seventh century travelled by boat to India and Sumatra, at that time a famous centre of Buddhist studies, wrote a work in which he relates the voyages of sixty pilgrims during a period of only fifty years in the second half of the seventh century.[19] We must, however, name the most famous of all, Hsüan-tsang 玄奘, who left China in 629 and went to India by the northern route through Central Asia. He remained about twelve years in India and returned by way of Central Asia, this time by the southern route. He finally arrived back in 645 in Ch'ang-an where he was welcomed by a great crowd.[20]

When the Chinese first came into contact with Buddhism, Buddhist literature had already reached great proportions. As mentioned before, only some of the older schools had established a canonical collection of their sacred texts.[21] With the rise of the *Mahāyāna*, the Great Vehicle, Buddhist scriptures increased more and more, in both number and length, though without codification in one or more canonical collections. For the pious Buddhist, every Buddhist text was part of the Word of the Buddha, the

Buddhavacanam. Only the learned monks were interested in knowing whether a certain text contradicted the tenets of the school to which he belonged. In some cases they even rejected a text as apocryphal. Needless to say, such doctrinal subtleties were of no concern to Chinese Buddhists in the early period. To them, every Buddhist text, coming from India, the country of the Buddha, was sacred. All texts brought to China were received with great respect.

How did these Buddhist texts arrive in China? They were not always written texts. Some were brought from India and Central Asia by monks who had learned them by heart. One must not forget that in India sacred texts have always been handed down from master to pupil by oral tradition. The holy scriptures of India, the *Veda*, were transmitted orally for centuries before being committed to writing.[22] Even today it is still possible to find in India pandits who are able to recite these texts from memory. The importance of the oral tradition is due to the fact that only the spoken word of the teacher possesses authority. Another reason is that written texts can be communicated to persons belonging to impure castes, who are not entitled to hear the sacred teachings. This did not apply to Buddhism, which made no distinction between pure and impure castes. Nevertheless, the sanctity of the spoken word among Buddhists, too, was such that for many centuries the sacred texts were not committed to writing, although writing was certainly practised both by monks and nuns.[23] Only in the more recent texts of the *Mahāyāna* schools writing is recommended but, it seems, only in order to facilitate the committing to memory of the sacred texts.[24] In one of the most famous *Māhāyana sūtras*, the *Lotus Sūtra*, great merit is promised to those who will write down the text. Immediately after proclaiming the merit of writing, the Bodhisattva Samantabhadra declares: 'How much greater will be the mass of merit reaped by those who will preach and recite it, meditate and fix their mind on it'.[25]

There is no doubt that in later times Buddhist texts were written in India on the leaves of palm trees and, mainly in northwestern India, on the bark of birch trees. There is an interesting reference in a Buddhist text to ladies who at night were writing Buddhist texts on birch-bark with the help of ink and a writing-reed, called *kalamā* after Greek *kalamos.*[26] However, from Chinese sources—there are no Indian sources which give any information on this point—one gains the impression that even in the first centuries A.D. the number of manuscripts available in India was still very limited. Most of the Buddhist manuscripts mentioned in this period by Chinese sources seem to have come from Central Asia. We have already noted that in 260 a Chinese Buddhist, Chu Shih-hsing, went to Khotan to obtain a Buddhist text. It is in the neighbourhood of this same place that the oldest Indian manuscript actually known has been found. This manuscript, written on birch-bark, dates probably from the second century A.D.[27] However, it is not impossible that in the earlier periods some manuscripts had already been brought from India itself to China. For instance, according to Chinese sources (admittedly of much later date) a manuscript was brought by an Indian monk to the Chinese capital, Lo-yang, about the middle of the second century.[28] Half a century later a biography of the Buddha was translated into Chinese. The manuscript of the text translated is said to have come from Kapilavastu, the capital of the state of the Śākyas, where the father of the Buddha had reigned.[29] However, during this period the manuscripts generally came from Central Asia. Their number cannot have been very great. According to the sources available only one text, or at most a few, were brought at a time, although some of them were quite voluminous. It is not until the beginning of the fifth century that greater numbers of manuscripts are mentioned. Chih Fa-ling 支法領 brought back from his voyages more than two hundred *Mahāyāna sūtras* which he most probably had collected in Khotan.[30] It is only in the sixth century that reference is made to great masses of texts, or bundles, which were brought to China from India itself. They were called 'bundles' because they took the form of piles of palm leaves, or of writing material prepared from birch-bark, held together by a string passing through holes, one or sometimes two, pierced in the leaves. Each such bundle might consist of one or more texts, or if the text was very long, then of only part of it. The house of the Indian translator, Bodhiruci, who worked in the first half of the sixth century in Lo-yang and Yeh, is said to have contained 10,000 bundles.[31] Although this number is probably greatly exaggerated, there is no ground for doubting other references to several hundred texts or bundles.[32] The interest in Buddhist manuscripts was certainly considerable at that period. This is obvious from the fact that a Chinese military expedition to Lin-i 林邑, in present-day Vietnam, did not hesitate to bring back, as spoils of war, 564 bundles of Buddhist texts. In the next century, the seventh, Hsüan-tsang brought back from India 657 texts in 520 bundles, of which he himself translated 74.[33] However, while he was crossing the Indus, he lost a number of manuscripts. In 654, in reply to a letter from two Indian monks from the Mahābodhi monastery in Bodhgayā, Hsüan-tsang sent a list of the missing texts with a request that they should send them to him.[34] From what we can learn from Chinese sources, it seems evident that manuscripts did not arrive in great numbers from India before the sixth and seventh centuries. This can probably be explained by the existence in India at that time of great monasteries which were famous centres of learning, such as, for instance, Nālandā.

Chinese sources also make frequent references to the amazing memory of Indian monks who could recite by heart quite voluminous texts. To mention only a few examples: In 383 Saṃghadeva, a monk from Kashmir, translated from memory a text which, in the Chinese version, contained more than 380,000 characters. Prodigious though his memory was, it appears that he had forgotten a chapter. It was later added from recitation by another monk from Kashmir. In 407 two Indian monks wrote down a text which they knew by heart. It took them a full year, but it was not until six years later, in 414, that they had learned Chinese well enough to be able to translate the text into Chinese. We know of at least one instance in which the Chinese decided to put the memory of an Indian monk to the test. This was in 410 when Buddhayaśas was invited to learn by heart, in three days, forty pages of prescriptions and census registers. He was able to recite them without making any mistakes in the weight of a drug or a census figure. After having been tried in this way Buddhayaśas orally translated a text, which in Chinese ran to more than 630,000 characters.[35]

The Buddhist texts which arrived in China, whether in the form of manuscripts or by oral transmission, had to be translated into Chinese in order to become accessible to the Chinese. This is not as obvious as it seems to be at first. In the history of religions there are many examples of sacred scriptures which, in other countries, continued to be studied in their original language. Sometimes they are recited without being understood, as is the case, for instance, with the Sanskrit texts which are recited in Bali. With regard to Buddhism, it is sufficient to point out that in Ceylon and in Southeast Asia the Buddhist scriptures are studied in the first place in Pāli, a Middle-Indian language. Probably in Central Asia too the Buddhist scriptures were studied for centuries in their original languages. However, China did not have such close cultural contacts with India as did Central Asia. Moreover, the structure of the Chinese language is fundamentally different from that of Sanskrit, a highly developed analytical Indo-European language. For the Central Asian speakers of Indo-European languages it was, of course, much more easy than it was for the Chinese to study the Buddhist texts from India in their original languages.

In the past it was assumed that the Buddhist texts from India were all written in Sanskrit. Study of the Chinese translations, especially of the transcription of Indian names, and the linguistic analysis of Indian Buddhist texts have shown that, in India, Buddhist texts were also composed in Middle-Indian languages and in Buddhist Hybrid Sanskrit. The discovery at the beginning of this century of Buddhist texts in non-Indian languages has led to the supposition that Chinese Buddhist texts were sometimes even translated from Central Asian languages.[36] This has recently been affirmed again by van Gulik in his book on Siddham.[37] However, to my knowledge, it has not been proved that any specific Chinese text must necessarily have been translated from a text in a Central Asian language. Although many manuscripts containing Buddhist texts in different languages have been discovered in Central Asia, none of them is older than 500 A.D. In the opinion of specialists in these languages, the Tokharian manuscripts date from 500 to 700, the Khotanese documents from the seventh to the tenth centuries, and the Sogdian manuscripts mostly from the ninth and tenth centuries.[38] The Buddhist manuscripts of an earlier period that have been found in Central Asia are written in Sanskrit or other Indian languages. After 500 A.D., as we have seen, great numbers of manuscripts came from India to China. It is, of course, possible that an orally transmitted Buddhist literature in Central Asian languages existed already before 500 A.D., and that one or more Chinese texts go back to a Central Asian original. The available evidence is not sufficient to warrant such a conclusion.[39]

The work of translating Buddhist texts into Chinese was first undertaken in the middle of the second century and continued to the middle of the eleventh century. Thereafter only very few texts were translated. The task confronting the translators was extremely difficult. The texts which arrived in China belonged to different Buddhist schools. They were composed not only in Sanskrit but also in other Indian languages, languages greatly differing in structure from Chinese. Last, but not least, the Buddhist concepts were foreign to the Chinese mind. Nevertheless, the difficulties were overcome, although not always with complete success.

The number of translations increased rapidly, as appears from a catalogue of Chinese Buddhist texts compiled in 374 by the famous monk, Tao-an 道安. This catalogue has not been preserved, but has been reconstructed from a catalogue published in the beginning of the sixth century.[40] Tao-an's catalogue contained 611 texts, of which 561 were translations, the fifty others being apocryphal texts and commentaries. Tao-an carefully arranged these 561 translations under five heads. One: translations, where the author was known, listed in chronological order; two: translations of which the author was unknown; three: variant versions produced in Kansu; four: variant versions produced in Ch'ang-an; five: variant versions in archaic style. Tao-an's catalogue did not extend beyond the beginning of the fourth century and comprised a period of only little more than a century and a half. He lived in a time of war, when communications between the different parts of China were difficult. Therefore the number of existing translations must certainly have been greater than the 561 mentioned by Tao-an in his catalogue. After Tao-an, the volume of translations increased enormously.[41] It is difficult to know from the later catalogues how many translations were actually made, because these include a great number of lost translations of doubtful authenticity; the number must have been in the thousands. The most recent edition of the Chinese Buddhist Canon, the so-called Taishō edition, published from 1924 to 1934, contains about 1,700 translations.[42] This certainly represents only a part of all the translations which have been made in China. In the passage of centuries many texts have been lost and many manuscripts have yet to be published.

How were these texts translated into Chinese? There were no Sanskrit-Chinese dictionaries and no grammars. It is not until after 600 that manuals began to be compiled for students.[43] Even if we find a dictionary mentioned somewhere, it bears little resemblance to dictionaries as we know them. For instance, in 1035 there is a record of a dictionary of Indian words being presented to the Emperor, but this work does not contain anything more than an explanation of Indian sounds and syllables and their mystic meaning.[44] In the early period of Chinese Buddhism, as we have mentioned already, the Chinese did not go to India and Indians did not come to China. It was mainly men from Central Asia who were responsible for the introduction of Buddhism and for the translations of Indian texts. Living in Central Asia, in countries which were subjected to the influence of Chinese culture, or having settled in the Western Regions of China, they knew enough Chinese to be able to translate Indian texts into Chinese.

Translators did not work alone. With very few exceptions, all translations were the result of team-work. Chinese sources provide a great deal of information about the way in which these teams functioned, and these sources have been carefully studied by scholars, mainly Chinese and Japanese.[45] Most useful is an article published four years ago by Tso Sze-bong, bringing together information on translation techniques which can be found in such Chinese works as catalogues of Chinese translations, biographical works, and prefaces to translations.[46] It appears from these sources that already in the early period several persons were engaged in the making of a single translation. One man would hold the Indian text in his hand and read it, or recite it from memory; he was called the main translator, and in many cases only his name has been attached to the translation. A second person was charged with the translation from Sanskrit into Chinese. A third person, finally, wrote it down or 'received it with the pen' as the phrase goes in Chinese. The work of translating took place in public. The chief translator not only recited the text but also explained it. His explanations were written down by his disciples, who later compiled commentaries to the text. Sometimes many hundreds or thousands of people were present at these translation centres. Questions would be asked about difficult problems, and the answers of the chief translator were written down. These notes were later consulted for the verification of the translation. It does not seem likely that at these gatherings many people were able to ask questions about the meaning of the text, as Tso Sze-bong seems to imply.[47] For most of them the recitation and explanation of the Indian text by a famous translator must have been a sacred ceremony which they attended with religious devotion. Once the translation was written down, it was again revised and the style polished. Sometimes the meaning of the original was changed during this process. A famous example of stylistic improvement is to be found in the biography of the Chinese monk, Seng-jui 僧叡, a pupil of the famous translator, Kumārajīva (active about 400 A.D.).

When Kumārajīva was translating the famous *Lotus Sūtra*, he apparently consulted at the same time an older translation made by Dharmarakṣa. When they arrived at a passage where Dharmarakṣa had translated: 'The Gods see the men and the men see the Gods', Kumārajīva remarked that the translation was correct but the wording too coarse. Then Seng-jui proposed a translation: 'The men and the Gods are in mutual relation and see each other'. Kumārajīva gladly accepted this suggestion.[48]

It is obvious that these translations could not have been made without material support. To begin with this was given by lay followers, but soon, especially in the north where non-Chinese dynasties reigned, official patronage was extended to the work of translating. After the re-unification of China in 589, Buddhism received great support from the emperors. They also vigorously promoted the work of translating. Official supervisors were appointed to assist the translation centres. At the same time there was also an important change in the methods of translating. It now became entirely the work of specialists, each of whom was made responsible for a particular aspect of the work. Hsüan-tsang, who translated many texts, was assisted by a team of twenty-three specialists, as well as by a number of scribes.[49] He was one of the very few Chinese who had learnt Sanskrit exceptionally well, and was able to translate texts without the help of foreigners. Hsüan-tsang did not want to be bothered by intruders during his work. He therefore requested the Emperor to allow him to go to a quiet place away from noisy towns and villages, but the Emperor wanted to keep him in the capital, and built a special monastery for him.[50]

A study of the methods of translation can only indirectly throw light on the quality of the translations. In this respect much work remains to be done by scholars. Only very few Chinese translations have been critically compared with their Indian originals or with other translations from Indian languages; in particular, those in Tibetan. With very few exceptions, no systematic study has been undertaken of the terminology used by each translator, although this would be of great importance in helping to evaluate the translations and decide their attribution, which is often doubtful.[51] It is at present only possible to make a few general observations. In the beginning, the translators tried to use existing Chinese philosophical and religious terminology, especially Taoist terminology, in order to convey Buddhist concepts. Only gradually was a specific Chinese terminology for

Buddhist concepts worked out. At the time of Kumārajīva, special attention began to be paid to the style of the translation, and many of them from that period are very readable, though they do not always strictly adhere to the letter of the original, as we have seen in the passage from the *Lotus Sūtra* quoted earlier. The translations of Hsüan-tsang are probably the most accurate ever made in China, but Chinese Buddhists have usually preferred Kumārajīva's translations for the excellent Chinese in which they were written.

The Chinese translations vary greatly in quality. It is not always easy to understand their meaning, and in many cases it is clear that the translation only very imperfectly represents the original. Nevertheless, the value of these translations is considerable. Of the immense Buddhist literature which once existed in India, only a small part has been preserved in its original form. If one wants to study Buddhist literature, it is absolutely necessary to consult the translations. Only in two languages, Tibetan and Chinese, does there exist a great number of Buddhist texts translated from Indian originals. The Chinese Buddhist Canon contains many texts which were not translated into Tibetan. Although the Chinese translations are never as literal and precise as the Tibetan ones, for which a uniform terminology was soon created, the former possess nevertheless one important advantage over the latter. Chinese translations, almost all of them, date from the second to the eleventh centuries, while in Tibet the task of translating did not begin before the eighth century. Apart from their intrinsic value for the history of Buddhism in China, the Chinese translations therefore are also of great importance for the study of Indian Buddhism, particularly for the period before the eighth century. By studying them it is possible to learn of the existence of many Indian texts, of which no original has been preserved. The date of translation gives us the ***terminus ad quem*** of their composition. Finally, the contents and the form of the lost Indian originals, though not, of course, the exact wording, can be reconstructed from the Chinese versions. In the course of centuries many Indian Buddhist texts were gradually added to, and this process of expansion can in several cases be studied by means of successive Chinese translations. For these reasons, no student of Buddhism, even if he is interested only in Indian Buddhism, can neglect the enormous corpus of Chinese translations.

In India, by far the greater part of the texts which existed only in manuscript form were lost. Although after the middle of the eleventh century Buddhism declined in China, this did not happen there. Already at the end of the sixth century Chinese monks were anxious lest the Buddhist doctrine might disappear, for they had learned from Indian texts that three periods in the history of the Buddhist doctrine could be expected: the first, the period of the true doctrine, the *Saddharma*; the second, the period of the counterfeit doctrine; and the third, the period of the end of the doctrine, in Chinese *mo fa* 末法.[52] Texts relating to this theory were translated in the sixth century, but greater poignancy was given to their fears that the final period of the doctrine now confronted them by the fact that in 574 the faith was suffering persecution in Northern Chou, one of the kingdoms ruling in northern China.[53] Although this persecution continued for only a few years, it seems to have made a deep impression. In order to ensure the preservation of the texts of the scriptures for the future, when, after the disappearance of the doctrine, Buddhism would again revive, it was decided to engrave them on stone. At the end of the sixth century, in a number of different parts of China, this task was begun. The most important of these undertakings was due to a monk named Ching-wan 靜琬, who, early in the seventh century, conceived the idea of engraving the entire Buddhist Canon. He pursued this work until his death in 639, after which it was continued by five generations of his disciples. Only then was the work interrupted. However, in the eleventh century it was taken up again, and many new texts were added to those already engraved. This Mountain of the Stone *Sūtras*, as it is called in Chinese, is famous. Situated forty miles southwest of Peking, it was thoroughly studied by a group of Japanese scholars in 1934.[54] Even here, though, where a larger number of texts was engraved than anywhere else in China, still only a part of the entire Buddhist Canon is preserved.

It is a fortunate circumstance that the Buddhists did not have to rely on texts engraved in stone for the transmission of their Canon. With the growth of printing, a technique which the Buddhists had made a substantial contribution to develop, an entirely new situation arose. The Buddhists were among the first to use the new technique on a large scale. The oldest preserved book is indeed a Buddhist text printed in 868.[55] According to a very recent report, an even older book has been found in a Korean pagoda, and this is said to have been printed between 704 and 751. No scholarly confirmation has yet been published concerning this find.[56] The Buddhists did not hesitate to print even the entire Buddhist Canon, despite its massive size. From 971 to 983 this collection of texts was printed in southwestern China in an edition that contained no less than 5,048 chapters. The wooden blocks used for this edition numbered more than 130,000. This first edition of the Buddhist Canon, of which only a few fragments have been preserved, was followed by many other editions in China, Korea, and Japan. Of most of the older editions very little remains. Of great importance therefore was the discovery in 1931 of an almost complete set of the so-called Chi-sha edition printed in the thirteenth century in Su-chou.[57] A photolithographic facsimile of this edition was printed in Shanghai in an edition limited to 500 copies, of which very few were distributed outside China. A copy, however, is in the oriental collection of the Menzies Library. Mention must be made also of the Korean xylographic printing of the thirteenth century, for the only ancient edition of which the original blocks have been preserved.[58] At the present time this edition of the Canon is being reprinted from the original blocks, and the National Library of Australia is acquiring a copy of this beautiful work as the volumes appear.

Chinese Buddhism is the product of the meeting of the cultures of India and China. The interrelation of these two great cultures constitutes one of the most fascinating chapters in the history of mankind. Without the untiring efforts of so many Buddhist believers in India, Central Asia, and China, it would not have been possible to bring the word of the Buddha to China, to translate it into Chinese, and to spread it by writing and printing. We are deeply conscious of our debt to these men who were prompted by no other motive than the desire to spread the doctrine of the Buddha.

REFERENCES

I have not been able to consult a number of articles, mainly Japanese. For this reason some bibliographical references are incomplete or perhaps inaccurate. Nevertheless, I have thought it better to include them, rather than omit them altogether or delay publication unduly.

ABBREVIATIONS

Abh. Ak. d. Wiss., Berlin	*Abhandlungen der Preussischen Akademie der Wissenschaften*
BEFEO	*Bulletin de l'École française d'Extrême-Orient*
BSOAS	*Bulletin of the School of Oriental and African Studies*
JA	*Journal asiatique*
JRAS	*Journal of the Royal Asiatic Society*
SBPAW	*Sitzungsberichte der Preussischen Akademie der Wissenschaften. Philosophischhistorische Klasse*
T	*Taishō shinshū daizōkyō* 大正新脩大藏經
TP	*T'oung Pao*
ZDMG	*Zeitschrift der Deutschen Morgenländischen Gesellschaft.*

[1] Paul Demiéville, 'La pénétration du Bouddhisme dans la tradition philosophique chinoise', *Cahiers d'histoire mondiale*, Vol. 3 (1956), pp. 19-20.

[2] *The Tipiṭaka in the Approved Sixth Synod Edition*, Rangoon, 1956 (2nd ed. 1958). On this edition see Frank-Richard Hamm, 'Zu einigen neueren Ausgaben des Pali-Tipiṭaka', *ZDMG*, Vol. 112 (1962), pp. 353-78; see also ibid., p. 429.

[3] Vinaya, Mahāvagga, I.11.1, *The Vinaya Piṭaka*, ed. Herman Oldenberg, Vol. 1, London, 1879, pp. 20-1.

[4] Mahāparinibbānasuttanta, 2.25, *Dīgha Nikāya*, Vol. 2, Pali Text Society, London, 1903, p. 100.

[5] Mahāparinibbānasuttanta, 2.26; 6.1, ibid., pp. 100, 154.

[6] Éd. Chavannes, 'Les pays d'occident d'après le *Wei lio*', *TP*, Vol. 6 (1905), p. 550, n. 1. The relevant passage in the *Hou Han shu* has been studied by many scholars. For bibliographical references see E. Zürcher, *The Buddhist Conquest of China*, Leiden, 1959, p. 327, n. 47; Tsukamoto Zenryū 塚本善隆, *Gi-sho Shaku-Rō-shi no kenkyū* 魏書釋老志の研究, Kyoto, 1961, pp. 147-51.

[7] E. Sieg and W. Siegling, 'Tocharisch, die Sprache der Indoskythen. Vorläufige Bemerkungen über eine bisher unbekannte indogermanische Literatursprache', *SBPAW* (1908), pp. 915-32.

[8] For a bibliography of Central Asiatic studies see *Saiiki bunka kenkyū* 西域文化研究, Vol. 1, Kyoto, 1958, pp. 53-87; Vol. 2, Kyoto, 1959, pp. 1-27.

[9] Hatani Ryōtai 羽溪了諦, *Saiiki no bukkyō* 西域の佛教, Kyoto, 1914, translated into Chinese by Ho Ch'ang-ch'ün 賀昌群, *Hsi-yü chih fo-chiao* 西域之佛教, Shanghai, 1933 (2nd. ed. 1956).

[10] For the Sino-Swedish Expedition from 1927 to 1935 see *Reports from the Scientific Expedition to the North-western Provinces of China under the Leadership of Dr. Sven Hedin*, Stockholm, 1937 and later years.

[11] Cf. *Mémoires de la délégation française en Afghanistan*, Paris, 1928 and later years.

[12] For a recent survey of the results of these excavations see B. Ya. Stavisky, *Meždu Pamirom i Kaspiem (Srednyaya Aziya v drevnosti)*, Moscow, 1966.

[13] James R. Ware, 'Wei shou on Buddhism', *TP*, Vol. 30 (1933), p. 110. See also Zürcher, op. cit., pp. 24-5, p. 326, notes 32-4; Tsukamoto, op. cit., p. 86.

[14] Liang Ch'i-chao 梁啓超, *Fo-hsüeh yen-chiu shih-pa p'ien* 佛學研究十八篇 (3rd ed.); Shanghai, 1941, No. 5: 'Fo-chiao yü hsi-yü' 佛教與西域, pp. 5-8; No. 6: 'Yu fo-chiao yü hsi-yü' 又佛教與西域, pp. 8-13. See also John Brough, 'Comments on third-century Shan-shan and the history of Buddhism', *BSOAS*, Vol. 28 (1965), p. 587.

[15] T'ang Yung-t'ung 湯用彤, *Han Wei liang-Chin nan-pei-ch'ao fo-chiao shih* 漢魏兩晉南北朝佛教史 (2nd ed.), Peking, 1956, p. 378.

[16] Cf. P. Demiéville, 'Le Bouddhisme, les sources chinoises', Section 2048 in *l'Inde classique*, Vol. 2, Paris-Hanoi, 1953; Zürcher, op. cit., pp. 61-3.

[17] Cf. T'ang Yung-t'ung, op. cit., pp. 378-80.

[18] Fa-hsien's account of his travels was translated into French by Abel Rémusat (1836) and into English by Samuel Beal (1869, 1884), James Legge (1886), Herbert A. Giles (1877, 1923), and Li Yung-hsi (1957).

[19] Translated by Édouard Chavannes, *Mémoire composé à l'époque de la grande dynastie T'ang sur les religieux éminents qui allèrent chercher la loi dans les pays d'Occident*, Paris, 1894.

[20] For bibliographical information on Hsüan-tsang see Kenneth K. S. Ch'en, *Buddhism in China: A Historical Survey*, Princeton, 1964, p. 523.

[21] Cf. Ét. Lamotte, 'La formation du canon des écritures', *Histoire du bouddhisme indien*, Vol. 1, Louvain, 1958, pp. 154-210.

[22] In the seventh century the *Vedas* were still transmitted orally, cf. I-ching's *Record of the Buddhist religion*, trans. J. Takakusu, Oxford, 1896, pp. 182-3. Al-Bīrūnī, (973-1048) mentions that, not long before his time, Vasukra, a native from Kashmir, had committed the *Veda* to writing; cf. *Alberuni's India*, trans. Edward C. Sachau, London, 1888, Vol. 1, p. 126.

[23] Cf. M. Winternitz, *A History of Indian Literature*, Vol. 1, Calcutta, 1927, pp. 32-3. Winternitz's statement, that in the sacred books of Buddhism there is not to be found the least indication that the books themselves were copied or read, is only valid for the older Buddhist literature.

[24] Cf. *Vajracchedikā*, ed. E. Conze, Rome, 1957, p. 43, and Conze's translation, ibid., p. 79: 'What should we say of him who, after writing it [i.e. this discourse on *dharma*], would learn it, bear it in mind, recite it, study it, and illuminate it in full detail for others?'

[25] Cf. *Saddharmapuṇḍarika*, ed. H. Kern and Bunyiu Nanjio, St.-Pétersbourg, 1912, p. 478, ll. 3-7.

[26] *Divyāvadāna*, ed. E. B. Cowell and R. A. Neil, Cambridge, 1886, p. 532, ll. 9-11. S. Dutt (*Buddhist Monks and Monasteries of India*, London, 1962, p. 236, n. 3) states that this passage probably dates from the first century B.C. A considerably later date is much more likely.

[27] Cf. John Brough, *The Gāndhārī Dharmapada*, London, 1962, p. 56.

[28] Cf. Zürcher, op. cit., p. 332, n. 92.

[29] Cf. Tsukamoto Zenryū, *Shina bukkyōshi kenkyū*, *Hoku-Gi hen* 支那佛教史研究, 北魏篇, Tokyo, 1942, p. 54, n. 9; Zürcher, op. cit., p. 333, n. 99.

[30] Cf. *T* 1858, 155c 10-12; *T* 2145, 11c 9-10, 61a 1-2, 104a 19-20; *T* 2059, 335c 3-4, 359b 17-18; T'ang Yung-t'ung, op. cit., pp. 385-6; W. Liebenthal, *The Book of Chao*, Peking, 1948, p. 98; Tsukamoto Zenryū (ed.), *Jōron kenkyū* 肇論研究, Kyoto, 1955, pp. 43, 100, n. 126; Zürcher, op. cit., pp. 62, 246.

[31] See the references given by Satō Shingaku 佐藤心岳, 'Hoku-Sei bukkyōkai ni okeru bongo butten no jūshi' 北齊佛教界における梵語佛典の重視, *Indogaku bukkyōgaku kenkyū* 印度學佛教學研究, Vol. 12, No. 1 (1964), p. 201, n. 1.

[32] In 522 Hui-sheng 惠生 and Sung-yün 宋雲 brought back 170 works; cf. Éd. Chavannes, 'Voyage de Song Yun dans l'Udyāna et le Gandhāra (518-522 p. C.)', *BEFEO*, Vol. 3 (1903), pp. 379-80; James R. Ware, op. cit., p. 163; Tsukamoto Zenryū, *Gi-sho Shaku-Rō-shi no kenkyū*, pp. 270-2. In 556 Narendrayaśas arrived in Yeh. At that time there were more than 1,000 bundles of Indian texts in the Tripiṭaka Hall of the T'ien-p'ing temple, cf. *T* 2060, 432c 6, Éd. Chavannes, 'Jinagupta', *TP*, Vol. 6 (1905), pp. 349-51, n. 1. In 581 Pao-hsien 寶暹 and others brought back 260

texts; cf. Éd. Chavannes, ibid., p. 346. Paramārtha arrived in 548 in Nanking with 340 bundles, cf. *T* 2149, 266b 11-12; or with 240 bundles, cf. *T* 2034, 88b 3. (According to the *Hsü kao-seng chuan* (*T* 2060, 430b 23-24), 240 is the number of bundles left untranslated by Paramārtha. Ui supposes that 240 certainly refers to the number of bundles which he brought to China: cf. Ui Hakuju 宇井伯壽, *Indo tetsugaku kenkyū* 印度哲學研究, Vol. 6, Tokyo, 1930, pp. 48-9.)

[33] *T* 2053, 252c 11-12, 277a 1-2.

[34] *T* 2053, 261a 26-262a. Cf. P. C. Bagchi, *India and China* (2nd ed.), Bombay, 1950, pp. 80-5; Li Yung-hsi, *The Life of Hiuan-tsang*, Peking, 1959, pp. 234-40.

[35] Cf. P. Demiéville, 'A propos du concile de Vaiśālī', *TP*, Vol. 40 (1951), pp. 245-7, n. 1; T'ang Yung-t'ung, op. cit., p. 405.

[36] Cf. Haneda Tōru 羽田亨, 'Kanyaku no butten ni tsuite' 漢譯の佛典について, *Geibun* 藝文, Vol. 2, Pt. 2 (ge) (1911); reprinted in his *Ronbunshū*, Vol. 2, Kyoto, 1958, pp. 348-57. The first to advance this theory seems to have been Tsan-ning 贊寧 in his *Sung kao-seng chuan*, composed from 982 to 988, cf. *T* 2061, 723c (Haneda refers to this passage which was translated by Sylvain Lévi, *BEFEO*, Vol. 4 (1904), pp. 562-3). Tsan-ning uses the term *chung-i* 重譯, 're-translation', to indicate a Chinese translation which, via one or more Central Asian versions, goes back to an Indian original. It must be remarked that, since Tao-an, the term *chung-i* is regularly used in catalogues to indicate different translations of the same text. Japanese scholars use the term *chung-i (jūyaku)* in the sense in which it was first used by Tsan-ning. Tsan-ning (loc. cit.) gives the following examples of Central Asian words: Sanskrit *upādhyāya* = Kashgar *hu-shê* 鶻社, Khotan *ho-shang* 和尚; Kubera = *hu* 胡 (Central Asia) Vaiśramaṇa. Much has been written on *ho-shang;* cf. Paul Pelliot, *Notes on Marco Polo*, Vol. 1, Paris, 1959, pp. 211-14. H. W. Bailey interprets it as **vāźā*, from northwestern Prakrit **vǎjāya* (*BSOAS*, Vol. 13 (1949), p. 133). However, it has not been found in Khotanese texts. It is, of course, very possible that the Prakrit form reached China via Khotan without having been used in Khotanese. This would explain why it was considered to be a Khotanese word by Chinese scholars of later date, such as Hsüan-ying and Tsan-ning, who knew the correct Sanskrit form but were unable to relate to it the Prakrit form underlying *ho-shang*. Pelliot (loc. cit.) admits the possibility that *hu-shê* really represents a Kashgarian word. Nothing is known about the language of Kashgar apart from the fact that almost certainly it was an Iranian language (H. W. Bailey, *BSOAS*, Vol. 13 (1950), p. 651). The fact that Tsan-ning believes that *Vaiśramaṇa* is the Central Asian word for *Kubera* (which he transcribes as *chü-yün-lo* 拘均羅!) does not inspire much confidence in his knowledge and judgment. The association of *Vaiśramaṇa* with the north and hence with Central Asia and especially with Khotan (see *Hôbôgirin*, Tokyo-Paris, 1929-1937, p. 79) probably accounts for Tsan-ning's statement.

[37] R. H. van Gulik (*Siddham*, Nagpur, 1956, p. 47) refers to an article by Wogihara Unrai 荻原雲來, 'Kanyaku butten no gengo o ronzu' 漢譯佛典の原語を論ず

(*Mujintō* 無盡燈, Vol. 10 (1909), reprinted in *Wogihara Unrai bunshū* 荻原雲來文集, Tokyo, 1938, pp. 767-809). However, Wogihara does not examine Chinese translations of texts written in Central Asian languages, but of texts written in Indian languages other than Sanskrit. Only incidentally does he refer to translations from Central Asian languages; cf. *Bunshū*, pp. 769, 807-8.

[38] For Tokharian see W. Krause, *Tocharisch (Handbuch der Orientalistik)*, Leiden, 1955, p. 4; for Khotanese, H. W. Bailey in *Iranistik (Handbuch der Orientalistik)*, Leiden, 1958, p. 131; and for Sogdian, W. B. Henning, in ibid., p. 55.

[39] It is well known that the *Hsien-yü ching* 賢愚經 (*T* 202) is based upon tales told in the *hu* language in Khotan shortly before 445. Much has been written upon this text; cf. J. Takakusu, 'Tales of the Wise Man and the Fool, in Tibetan and Chinese', *JRAS* (1901), pp. 447-60, 'A comparative study of the Tripiṭaka and the Tibetan Dsaṅ-lun. The wise man and the fool', *Actes du XIIe Congrès des Orientalistes*, Vol. 2 (1902), pp. 11-32; P. Pelliot, *BEFEO*, Vol. 2 (1902), p. 299, ibid., Vol. 11 (1911), p. 466, 'Autour d'une traduction sanscrite du Tao-tö-king', *TP*, Vol. 13 (1912), pp. 355-6, 'Notes à propos d'un catalogue du Kanǰur', *JA* (1914, Vol. II), p. 139, 'La version ouigoure de l'histoire des princes Kalyānaṃkara et Pāpaṃkara', *TP*, Vol. 15 (1914), pp. 226-7, 'Neuf notes sur des questions d'Asie centrale', ibid., Vol. 26 (1929), pp. 256-63; B. Laufer, 'Loan-words in Tibetan', ibid., Vol. 17 (1916), pp. 415-22; F. W. K. Müller, 'Uigurica, III', *Abh. Ak. d. Wiss., Berlin*, 1922; Sylvain Lévi, 'Le Sūtra du Sage et du Fou dans la littérature de l'Asie centrale', *JA* (1925, Vol. II) pp. 305-22; H. W. Bailey, 'Kāñcanasāra', *B.C. Law Volume*, Vol. II, Poona, 1946, pp. 11-13; W. Baruch, 'Le cinquante-deuxième chapitre du *mJaṅs-blun*', *JA* (1955), pp. 339-66; Tsumaki Naoyoshi 妻木直良, 'Tonkō sekishitsu goshu butten no kaisetsu' 燉煌石室五種佛典の解說, *Tōyō gakuhō* 東洋學報, Vol. 1, No. 3 (1911), pp. 350-65; Matsumoto Bunzaburō 松本文三郎, 'Tonkō-bon Daiungyō to Kengukyō 燉煌本大雲經と賢愚經, II', *Geibun*, Vol. 3, Pt. I (jō) (1912), pp. 542-56; Fukui Rikichirō 福井利吉郎, 'Tōdaiji-bon Kengukyō' 東大寺本賢愚經, ibid., Pt. II (ge) (1912), pp. 463-83, 546-73; Hikata Ryūshō 干潟龍祥, *Honjō kyōrui no shisōshi-teki kenkyū* 本生經類の思想史的研究, Tokyo, 1954, pp. 129-30; supplementary volume (fuhen 附篇), pp. 67-71; Takahashi Moritaka 高橋盛孝, 'Kengukyō tansaki' 賢愚經探査記, *Nihon Chibetto gakkai kaihō* 日本西藏學會々報, Vol. 9 (1962), pp. 1-2, 'Kengukyō to Zan-run' 賢愚經とザン・ルン, *Tōhōgaku* 東方學, Vol. 26 (1963), pp. 47-55. Matsumoto is the only scholar who has tried to prove that the Chinese text was translated from the Khotanese by pointing out transcriptions which cannot have been derived from Sanskrit originals. However, he did not at all take into account the possibility that the original was not in Sanskrit but in Prakrit. In reconstructing the original forms of Kalyānaṃkara and Pāpaṃkara (*Kalyāṇṇagari; *Pābagari or *Pāvagari) Pelliot expressly states that these forms belong to a north-western Prakrit (*TP*, Vol. 15, p. 227). It must be left to specialists of Khotanese to come to a final conclusion on this matter. It is much to be desired that other Chinese texts also, which are known to have been translated from texts of Central Asian

origin, will be studied by specialists in Central Asian languages. Only a careful and systematic study of the transcription used in these Chinese translations can prove their derivation from Central Asian originals. References in Chinese sources alone are not conclusive.

[40] Cf. Tokiwa Daijō 常盤大定, *Go-Kan yori Sō-Sei ni itaru yakkyō sōroku* 後漢より宋齊に到る譯經総錄, Tokyo, 1938, pp. 159-81; Hayashiya Tomojirō 林屋友次郎, *Kyōroku kenkyū* 經錄研究, Tokyo, 1941, pp. 381-428.

[41] Cf. Tokiwa, op. cit., 'Yakkyōsū taishōhyō' 譯經數對照表, pp. 1-4; Hayashiya Tomojirō, *Iyaku kyōrui no kenkyū* 異譯經類の研究, Tokyo, 1945, pp. 1-2 of the English résumé; 'Ta-tsang sheng-chiao fa-pao piao-mu' 大藏聖教法寶標目, *Shōwa Hōbō sōmokuroku* 昭和法寶總目錄, Vol. 2, Tokyo, 1929, pp. 773b-4b. According to this catalogue, from 67 to 1306, 194 translators translated 1,440 texts in 5,586 chapters. Ono Gemmyō 小野玄妙 enumerates altogether 202 translators in chronological order; cf. *Bussho kaisetsu daijiten* 佛書解說大辭典, Vol. 12, Tokyo, 1936, pp. 1-188. For the translators see also Nanjio Bunyiu, *A Catalogue of the Chinese Translation of the Buddhist Tripiṭaka*, Oxford, 1883, Appendix II, pp. 381-458; P.C. Bagchi, *Le Canon bouddhique en Chine*, Vols. 1-2, Paris, 1927-1938, *India and China* (2nd ed.), Bombay, 1950, pp. 203-20; *Hôbôgirin, fascicule annexe. Tables du Taishô Issaikyô*, Tokyo, 1931, pp. 127-52; P. Demiéville, 'Le bouddhisme, les sources chinoises', Sections 2067-2100.

[42] The first 32 volumes of this edition contain 1,692 translations; cf. Demiéville, 'Le bouddhisme, les sources chinoises', Section 2046. Hayashiya (*Iyaku kyōrui no kenkyū*, p. 1 of the English résumé) mentions 1,711 translations without explaining how he arrives at this number.

[43] Cf. P. C. Bagchi, *Deux lexiques sanskrit-chinois*, Vols. 1-2, Paris, 1929-1937; van Gulik, op. cit., pp. 31-5.

[44] Mochizuki Shinkō 望月信亨, 'Tenjiku jigen' 天竺字源, *Bukkyō daijiten* 佛教大辭典, Vol. 4, Tokyo, 1936, pp. 3809a-10a; van Gulik, op. cit., pp. 91-6; Jan Yün-hua, 'Buddhist relations between Indian and Sung China', *History of Religions*, Vol. 6, 1966, p. 158.

[45] Cf. Walter Fuchs, 'Zur technischen Organisation der Übersetzungen buddhistischer Schriften ins Chinesische', *Asia Major*, Vol. 6 (1930), pp. 84-103; Liang Ch'i-chao, op. cit. (cf. n. 14), No. 10: 'Fo-tien chih fan-i' 佛典之翻譯; Ōchō Enichi 横超慧日, *Chūgoku bukkyō no kenkyū* 中國佛教の研究, Kyoto, 1958, pp. 219-55, 'Kumarajū no honyaku' 鳩摩羅什の翻譯, *Ōtani daigaku gakuhō* 大谷大學々報, Vol. 37, No. 4 (1958), pp. 1-25; Kenneth Ch'en, 'Some problems in the Translation of the Chinese Buddhist Canon', *Tsing-hua Journal of Chinese Studies*, N.S. Vol. 2, No. 1 (1960), pp. 178-86; T'ang Yung-t'ung, op. cit., pp. 402-14; Zürcher, op. cit., *passim;* Demiéville, 'Le Bouddhisme, les sources chinoises', Sections 2067-9.

[46] Tso Sze-bong 曹仕邦, 'Lun Chung-kuo fo-chiao i-ch'ang chih i-ching fang-shih yü ch'eng-hsü' 論中國佛教譯塲之譯經方式與程序, *Hsin Ya hsuēh-pao* 新亞學報, Vol. 5 (Hongkong, 1963), pp. 239-321.

[47] Ibid., p. 252; but see p. 292.

[48] Cf. *T* 2059, 364b 2-6; J. Nobel, 'Kumārajīva', *SBPAW* (1927), p. 232; Arthur F. Wright, 'Seng-jui alias Hui-jui', *Liebenthal Festschrift*, Santiniketan, 1957, p. 276; Kenneth Ch'en, *Tsing-hua Journal of Chinese Studies*, N.S. Vol. 2, No. 1 (1960), p. 180; Tso Sze-bong, op. cit., p. 291; K. K. S. Ch'en, *Buddhism in China*, Princeton, 1964, p. 368, n. 2; Richard H. Robinson, *Early Mādhyamika in India and China*, Madison, 1967, p. 80.

[49] *T* 2053, 253c 19-254a 6; Tso Sze-bong, op. cit., pp. 257-8.

[50] *T* 2053, 253c 1-8.

[51] Cf. Robinson's examination of Kumārajīva's translation of the first sixteen stanzas of the *Chung-lun* (*T* 1564, 1-3), op. cit., pp. 83-8; Hayashiya Tomojirō's study of An Shih-kao's terminology, 'Anseikō-yaku no Zōagon to Zōichiagon' 安世高譯の雜阿含と增壹阿含, *Bukkyō kenkyū* 佛教研究, Vol. 1, No. 2 (1937), pp. 11-50, esp. pp. 16-20, 29-32.

[52] Cf. Ét. Lamotte, *Histoire du Bouddhisme indien*, Vol. 1, Louvain, 1958, pp. 210-22; Tsukamoto Zenryū, 'Sekkyōzan Ungoji to sekkoku daizōkyō' 石經山雲居寺と石刻大藏經, *Tōhō gakuhō* 東方學報, Vol. 5 (supplement), Kyoto, 1935, pp. 36-47; some bibliographical references in Ch'en, *Buddhism in China*, p. 529.

[53] Cf. Tsukamoto Zenryū, 'Hoku-Shū no haibutsu ni tsuite' 北周の廢佛に就いて, *Tōhō gakuhō*, Kyoto, Vol. 16 (1948), pp. 29-101, Vol. 18 (1950), pp. 78-111, 'Hoku-Shū no shūkyō haiki seisaku no hōkai' 北周の宗教廢棄政策の崩壞, *Bukkyō shigaku* 佛教史學, Vol. 1 (1949), pp. 3-31. Both articles are reprinted in *Gi-sho Shaku-Rō-shi no kenkyū*, (Kyoto, 1961), pp. 357-544.

[54] *Bōzan Ungoji kenkyū* 房山雲居寺研究, Tōhō gakuhō, Vol. 5 (supplement), Kyoto, 1935.

[55] Cf. Th. F. Carter, *The Invention of Printing and its Spread Westward* (2nd ed.), New York, 1955, pp. 54-6; Paul Pelliot, *Les débuts de l'imprimerie en Chine*, Paris, 1953, pp. 47-8.

[56] According to a newspaper article (*Canberra Times*, 16 Feb. 1967) a scroll, printed from 12 wooden blocks, was found in the stonework of a South Korean pagoda built in 751. The scroll contains a text translated no later than 704.

[57] A second almost complete copy was discovered in August 1940 by Sakai Shirō in the monastery Ch'ung-shan in T'ai-yüan 太原 (Shansi); cf. Sakai Shirō 酒井紫朗, 'Sō Sekisaban daizōkyō ni tsuite' 宋磧砂版大藏經に就いて, *Piṭaka*, Vol. 8, No. 10 (1940); Yoshii Hōjun 吉井芳純, 'Taigen Sūzenji hakken no Sekisaban zōkyō ni tsuite' 太原崇善寺發見の磧砂版藏經に就いて, *Mikkyō kenkyū* 密教研究, Vol. 80

(1942), pp. 80-92. A third copy of the Chi-sha edition is in the Gest Library. It contains 2,330 volumes of the original edition, 868 volumes in various early Ming editions and 2,150 hand-copied volumes; cf. Hu Shih, 'The Gest Oriental Library at Princeton University', *The Princeton University Library Chronicle*, Vol. 15, No. 3 (1954), pp. 129-34. On this edition see further *Ying-yin Sung Chi-sha tsang-ching* 影印宋磧砂藏經, introductory volume in 2 parts *(shou-ts'e* 首冊*)*, Shanghai, 1936; P. Demiéville, *Bibliographie bouddhique*, Vols. 7-8, Paris, 1937, pp. 113-14, in Pelliot, *Les débuts de l'imprimerie en Chine*, Paris, 1953, pp. 133-4, 138, n. 4 and the literature quoted by him; Mochizuki Shinkō, 'Sekisaban daizōkyō' 磧砂版大藏經, *Bukkyō daijiten*, Vol. 8 (1958), pp. 152b-4a; Ogawa Kanichi 小川貫弌, *Daizōkyō* 大藏經, Kyoto, 1964, pp. 63-6. Mention should also be made of the twelfth-century Chin edition of which an incomplete copy was discovered in 1933; see P. Demiéville, *Bibliographie bouddhique*, Vols. 7-8, pp. 112-14; id., *Les débuts de l'imprimerie en Chine*, pp. 137-8; Tsukamoto Zenryū, 'Bukkyō shiryō toshite no kinkoku daizōkyō' 佛教史料としての金刻大藏經, *Tōhō gakuhō*, Vol. 6 (Kyoto, 1935), pp. 26–100; Mochizuki Shinkō, 'Kinzō' 金藏, *Bukkyō daijiten*, Vol. 8 (1958), pp. 76a-9a; Ogawa, op. cit., pp. 42-3. Of this edition 49 rare texts were reprinted in the *Sung-tsang i-chen* 宋藏遺珍 (Shanghai-Peking, 1934-5); cf. Mochizuki Shinkō, 'Sōzō-ichin' 宋藏遺珍, *Bukkyō daijiten*, Vol. 8 (1958), pp. 162a-3a. A copy of this reprint is also in the Menzies Library.

[58] On this edition see P. Demiéville, *BEFEO*, Vol. 24 (1924), pp. 198-9; Mochizuki Shinkō, 'Kōraizō' 高麗藏, *Bukkyō daijiten*, Vol. 2 (1932), pp. 1106-7; Ikeuchi Hiroshi 池內宏, 'Kōraichō no daizōkyō' 高麗朝の大藏經, *Tōyō gakuhō*, Vol. 13 (1923), pp. 307-62; Vol. 14 (1924), pp. 91-130, 546-58; Ōya Tokujō 大屋德城, 'Chōsen Kaiinji kyōhan-kō' 朝鮮海印寺經版攷, *Tōyō gakuhō*, Vol. 15 (1926), pp. 285–362; Ono Gemmyō, 'Kōrai daizōkyō chōin-kō' 高麗大藏經雕印考, *Butten kenkyū* 佛典研究, Vol. 4 (1929); Ōya Tokujō, 'Kōraizō no kyūchōhon to shinchōhon to no kōshō ni kansuru jisshō-teki kenkyū' 高麗藏の舊雕本と新雕本との考證に關する實證的研究, *Shina bukkyō shigaku* 支那佛教史學, Vol. 3, No. 1 (1939); Nak Choon Paik, "Tripiṭaka Koreana', *Transactions of the Korea Branch of the Royal Asiatic Society*, Vol. 32 (1951), pp. 62-78; Okamoto Keiji 岡本敬二. 'Kōrai daizōkyō-ban no kokusei' 高麗大藏經板の刻成, *Rekishigaku kenkyū* 歷史學研究, special issue (tokushūgō 特集號) (July 1953), pp. 14-23; Ogawa, op. cit., pp. 38-9.

J. W. DE JONG, CANBERRA

A BRIEF SURVEY OF CHINESE BUDDHIST HISTORIOGRAPHY

Buddhism has contributed more to Chinese culture than any other foreign religion. From the fourth century onwards, its influence gathered momentum and continued to increase. It reached its zenith during the Sui dynasty and the first half of the T'ang dynasty. Although after the middle of the eleventh century Buddhism slowly declined, it continued to be one of the formative factors of Chinese civilization. Chinese Buddhist monks and laymen have played an important role in the history of China. Chinese historians, however, have generally paid little attention to Buddhism, because their outlook was dominated by the Confucian ideology which rejected Buddhism as a foreign religion. Consequently, little information about the activities of Chinese Buddhists can be found in the works written by Chinese historians and scholars. Therefore it is absolutely necessary to study the works by the Buddhists themselves.

In India historical scholarship was almost entirely neglected in ancient times. There is perhaps more historical awareness in Buddhism than in other Indian religions, because the memory of the founder, the Buddha, always remained vivid. Nevertheless, the legendary and mythological elements predominate in the biographies of the Buddha and of the great Buddhist masters. Very little historical information can be gained from these sources. In China, however, Chinese Buddhists lived in a country rich in historical tradition and learning. In writing the lives of Buddhist monks and laymen and the history of Buddhism in China, they adopted the same methods as those applied by the non-Buddhist historians. The influence of the supernatural was admitted by both Buddhist and Confucian scholars. Proper to the Buddhist scholar was the belief in the law of karma which manifested itself in the events which he described.

The first important biographical works, which are preserved, were written at the beginning of the sixth century. The most famous is the *Kao-seng chuan* [I] "Lives of Eminent Monks" (T. 2059), written by Hui-chiao [II] (497-554).[1]

[1] As Hui-chiao's preface is dated 519 A. D., this year has generally been considered to be the date of completion of the work. Arthur Wright has argued that it was probably completed towards the end of the period 519-533 (see Bibliography no. 2, pp. 399-400). In the biography

It contains 257 main biographies and more than 200 biographical notices, and comprises the period from 67 to 519.[2] These biographies are grouped in ten categories of which the most important are the first two: the translators and the exegetes.[3] Hui-chiao has used a great number of sources, some of which are mentioned by him in his preface. Others, such as separate biographies (mostly written by pupils), inscriptions, doctrinal treatises, prefaces to translations and letters, are quoted in the work itself.[4] Of all these works, two are of particular importance for understanding the way in which Hui-chiao used his sources: the *Ch'u san-tsang chi-chi* [**III**] (T. 2145) by Seng-yu [**IV**] (445-518) and the *Ming-seng chuan* [**V**] by Pao-ch'ang [**VI**], a pupil of Seng-yu. The *Ch'u san-tsang chi-chi*, which was for the greater part compiled in the last quarter of the fifth century although not completed before 515 (some alterations were even made after the death of the author), contains an introduction, a catalogue of translations and a collection of prefaces and postfaces; as well as a biographical section in three chapters (chapters 13-15), which include principal biographies of twenty-one foreigners and eleven Chinese.[5] Biographies of all of them are also found in the *Kao-seng chuan*. In some cases Hui-chiao has literally copied Seng-yu's accounts, in others he has used only the basic data and supplemented them with information from other sources.[6] The *Ming-seng chuan*,

---

of Fa-hsien [**XXXV**], the theft of a Buddha tooth from the Superior Ting-ling temple in 522 is reported (T. 2059, ch. 13, p. 412, a2). Pelliot, who assumed 519 to be the date of completion, considered this passage a later interpolation (*TP* 32, pp 281-282, note).

[2] These subordinate biographies were appended to the main biographies. They treat of minor subjects linked to the major by the disciple-master relationship, by some common activity, or by geographical propinquity (Wright, *op. cit.*, p. 390). The number of the subordinate biographies varies according to the sources: more than 200 (Hui-chiao's preface), 243 (BD, p. 1067a), 259 (Wright, p. 387).

[3] Cf. Wright, *op. cit.*, pp. 386-7.

[4] Part IV of the index of the *Kao-seng chuan* compiled by Tsukamoto Zenryū [**XXXVI**], Iwai Tairyō [**XXXVII**] and Ryūchi Kiyoshi [**XXXVIII**]: *Ryō Kōsōden sakuin* [**XXXIX**] (*Shina Bukkyō shigaku* [**XL**] I, 1-II, 1, (1937-9) lists the titles of all the works mentioned by Hui-chiao.

[5] On the date of the *Ch'u san-tsang chi-chi*, see H. Maspero, *BEFEO* X (1910), p. 113; P. Pelliot, *TP* XII (1911), p. 674; *TP* XIX (1919), pp. 266-8; *JA* 1923, I, p. 162; P. Demiéville, *BEFEO* XXIV (1924), p. 4; Wright, *op. cit.*, p. 421; Naitō Ryūo [**XLI**] in *IBK* VII (1958), pp. 162-3. Chapter I has been translated by Arthur Link in *JAOS* 80 (1960), pp. 34-40; 81 (1961), pp. 87-103, 281-299.

[6] See the remarks made by Wright (*op. cit*, p. 422), Arthur Link (Bibliography No. 5) and Tso Sze-bong (Bibliography no. 1, part 1, p. 454). A detailed comparison of the 32 biographies by Seng-yu with the corresponding ones in the *Kao-seng chuan* is still a

written by Seng-yu's pupil Pao-ch'ang in the second decade of the sixth century, is lost, apart from a few extracts copied by a Japanese monk in 1235.[7] Most probably Hui-chiao made good use of it, although he expressed himself critically about its merits. In his preface Hui-chiao explains his reasons for recording the lives of "Eminent Monks" and not those of "Famous Monks", implicitly criticizing the title of Pao-ch'ang's work.[8] By including worthy monks and excluding unworthy ones, he followed the famous historical tradition of "Praise and Blame" although his inspiration was not derived from Confucian values but from his belief in the tenets of Buddhism, and especially in the importance of the rules of conduct laid down in the Vinaya section of the Buddhist Canon.[9] For Hui-chiao as a Chinese of the sixth century it was not possible to distinguish sharply between fact and fiction and between natural and supernatural events. According to a competent judge, however, he worked with all the care and judiciousness of superior Chinese historians of his day.[10]

Hui-chiao's work has been the example for later biographers. His work was continued by the founder of the Vinaya school, Tao-hsüan [**VII**] (596-667), the author of the *Hsü Kao-seng chuan* [**VIII**] (T. 2060). According to the preface, it was completed in 645 and contained 340 (331 in some editions) main biographies and 160 subordinate biographies.[11] Tao-hsüan seems to have himself written a supplement which was later incorporated into the work itself.[12] In the period between Hui-chiao and Tao-hsüan almost no collection of lives of monks was compiled. In his preface he mentions only the *Shih-te chi* [**IX**] or "Notes on the ten virtuous ones" by Shih Ling-yu [**X**]. However, Tao-hsüan made extensive enquiries, interrogated travellers, and consulted literary works and separate biographies. His work is the main source for the monks who lived during the period from the beginning of the Liang dynasty (502-556) to 665.

desideratum.

[7] Cf Wright, *op. cit.*. pp. 408-412.

[8] Cf. Wright, *op. cit*, pp. 408-9.

[9] Tso Sze-bong (Bibliography No. 1) has convincingly shown the reasons for the compilation of biographical works and catalogues by monks of the Vinaya school during the period 500-1000.

[10] Cf. Wright, *op. cit*, p 389.

[11] In the Korean edition, there are 414 main biographies and 201 subordinate biographies; in the "Three editions" (Sung, Yüan, Ming), 489 and 213 (cf BD, p. 3131a-b; 485 and 219 according to CY).

[12] Cf. BD, p. 3131a-b; Wu chi-yu, "A study of Han-shan. Appendix 4. The Authenticity of the Hou-chi Hsü Kao-seng chuan", *TP* 45 (1957), pp. 447-450.

The third biographical work written by a monk of the Vinaya school is the *Sung Kao-seng chuan* [**XI**] (T. 2061), compiled between 982 and 988 by Tsan-ning [**XII**] (919-1002).[13] It contains 531 main biographies and 124 subordinate biographies.[14] Tsan-ning also included lives of monks who were omitted in Tao-hsüan's work. Tsan-ning's work was officially commissioned by the Emperor. He lived in a period in which the state had taken almost complete control of the Buddhist church. Although outwardly still flourishing, Buddhism had lost the vigour it manifested at the time of Hui-chiao, when it was steadily increasing in strength, or at the time of Tao-hsüan when Buddhism had an almost dominating position. At the end of the tenth century, however, Buddhism had not recovered from the heavy blows received during the persecutions of 845 and 955. Many temples and steles had been destroyed, and valuable historical materials were lost. For this reason, Tsan-ning took great pains to show the reliability of the sources used by him.

Tsan-ning advocated a reconciliation among rival Buddhist schools and between the three religions of China: Buddhism, Taoism and Confucianism. He showed great respect towards the secular rulers who had become the main protectors of Buddhism. To eighty-seven lives, Tsan-ning added *hsi* [**XIII**] or appendices in which he discussed a great variety of topics. Tso Sze-bong has shown that in them Tsan-ning often explained Buddhist terms and customs. These explanations were necessary because his work was not in the first place meant for his co-religionists, as were the *Kao-seng chuan* and the *Hsü Kao-seng chuan*, but for the Emperor on whom the destiny of the Buddhist church depended.

Tsan-ning was a highly educated monk well versed in profane learning. As most historians, he did not exclude *hsiao-shuo* [**XIV**] "fiction" from his sources, although the distinction between history and fiction had already been made by Liu Chih-chi [**XV**] (661-721) in his *Shih-t'ung* [**XVI**]. However, he shows himself remarkably free from superstitious beliefs.

The three *Kao-seng chuan* are the major biographical works written before 1000 A. D. Although compiled by monks of the Vinaya school, they are not sectarian in their treatment and record the lives of monks belonging to all

---

[13] Most authors assume 1001 to be his date of death. However, Makita Tairyō has shown that the year 1002 is to be preferred (cf. Bibliography no. 8, p. 130). Tsan-ning was assisted by Chih-lun, cf. Jan Yün-hua, "Buddhist relations between India and China", *History of Religions* VI (1966), p. 30.

[14] According to BD, p. 3058b (CY 532 and 125; Jan Yün-hua, Bibliography no. 7, p. 363, 530 and 130; BK, II, p. 21c: 533 and 138).

Buddhist schools. Valuable historical material is also to be found in the catalogues of Buddhist translations (T. 2145-2158). Mention must also be made of the annalistic chronicle of the history of Buddhism up to 597, which constitutes the first part (chapters 1-3) of the *Li-tai san-pao chi* [**XVII**] (T. 2034), completed in 597 by Fei Ch'ang-fang [**XVIII**], and of the *Pi-ch'iu-ni chuan* [**XIX**] "Lives of the nuns" (T. 2063) by Pao-ch'ang. Historical information for the same period is also to be found in many other works such as separate biographies, histories of temples, local gazetteers and collections of miraculous stories.

Already during the T'ang dynasty monks of the Ch'an and T'ien-t'ai schools compiled collections of the lives of masters of their own schools, e. g. the *Pao-lin chuan* [**XX**], written in 801, and the *Hung-tsan fa-hua chuan* [**XXI**] (T. 2067).[15] The oldest hagiographical work of the Ch'an school is the *Tsu-t'ang chi* [**XXII**][16] written in 952 by Ching [**XXIII**] and Yün [**XXIV**]. It has served as an example for the biographical works on the transmission of the lamp written by Ch'an monks during the Sung dynasty beginning with the *Ching-te ch'uan-teng lu* [**XXV**] (T. 2076), completed in 1004 by Tao-yüan [**XXVI**]. This work contains the lives of 1071 Ch'an monks. Similar works were written by T'ien-t'ai and Ching-t'u monks.[17] Comprehensive histories of Buddhism were also written during this period. The most famous is the *Fo-tsu t'ung-chi* [**XXVII**] (T. 2035), written by the T'ien-t'ai monk, Chih-p'an, from 1258 to 1269. Chapters 34-48 contain a chronicle of the history of Buddhism. This part of Chih-p'an's work was inspired by Ssu-ma Kuang's *Tzu-chih t'ung-chien*, but the other parts are modelled on the example of the *Shih-chi*.[18]

---

[15] Of the ten chapters of this work only seven remain (cf. *Sung-tsang i-chen* [**XLII**]). It has been studied by Tokiwa Daijō [**XLIII**], "'Hōrinden' no kenkyū" [**XLIV**], *Zoku Shina Bukkyō no kenkyū* [**XLV**], Tokyo, 1941, pp. 203-326. The *Pao-lin chuan* is preceded by several works written in the eighth century: *Ch'uan-fa-pao chi* [**XLVI**] (T. 2838), *Leng-ch'ieh shih-tzu chi* [**XLVII**] (T. 2837), *Li-tai fa-pao chi* [**XLVIII**] (T. 2075); cf. Yokoi Shōzan [**XLIX**], "Tōshi no keifu" [**L**] *Nihon bukkyō gakkai nenpō* [**LI**], vol. 19, Tokyo, 1953, pp. 1-46. For the *Hung-tsang fa-hua chuan*, see BD, p. 661a-b.

[16] Cf. BD, vol IX, p. 565; Paul Demiéville, "Le Recueil de la Salle des patriarches (*Tsu-t'ang tsi*)", *TP* 56 (1970), pp. 262-286.

[17] On Buddhist historiography in the Sung dynasty, see Jan Yün-hua, Bibliography, no. 7

[18] Cf. Jan Yün-hua, Bibliography nos. 10, 11; Makita Tairyō [**LII**], "Sōdai ni okeru bukkyō shigaku no hatten" [**LIII**], *IBK* III (1957), pp 631-3; H Franke in *Historians of China and Japan*, London, 1961, pp 130-132; Tso Sze-bong, Bibliography no. 12. Franke (pp. 132-3) makes also a few remarks on the *Fo-tsu li-tai t'ung-tsai* [**LIV**] (T. 2036) by Nien-ch'ang [**LV**]

After the Sung dynasty, Buddhist authors continued to compose historical and biographical works, but their value cannot be compared with that of the works mentioned above.[19]

Important historical materials are also to be found in Tsan-ning's *Ta-Sung Seng-shih lüeh* [**XXVIII**] (T. 2126) which in 59 sections describes Buddhist institutions.[20] It was written at the request of the Emperor in the last quarter of the tenth century. The *Shih-shih yao-lan* [**XXIX**] (T. 2127) by Tao-ch'eng [**XXX**] contains excerpts from texts concerning matters of importance for the daily life of the monks.[21] It was completed in 1019.

The only foreign Buddhist sources are the diaries of Japanese priests who visited China. They contain very interesting observations on many aspects of Chinese society and culture. The most important are the diaries of Ennin [**XXXI**] (793-864) and of Jōjin [**XXXII**] (1011-1081) Ennin travelled in China between the years 838 and 847. His diary, entitled *Nittō guhō junrei gyōki* [**XXXIII**], has been translated by Edwin O. Reischauer (*Ennin's Diary*, New York, 1955).[22] Jōjin left Japan on the 6th April 1072. His diary, *San Tendai Godai san ki* [**XXXIV**], begins with the day of his departure and ends with the return of his companions from Ningpo on the 19th July, 1073. Jōjin himself never returned to Japan.[23]

Buddhist historiography is generally neglected by Sinologists, who are too much influenced by the Confucian outlook of the Chinese historians. It is not yet fully realized that a study of the Buddhist sources is of essential importance for the understanding of Chinese history and culture. Donald Holzman's recent article on the origin of the chair in China is only one example of the valuable evidence which can be gained from the study of Buddhist historical works.[24]

Postscript. The author is much obliged to Professors Paul Demiéville and Jan Yün-hua for reading a first draft of this paper. Their suggestions have been very helpful.

---

and the *Shih-shih chi-ku lüeh* [**LVI**] (T. 2037) by Chüeh-an [**LVII**]. Both works were compiled during the Yüan dynasty.

[19] Cf. CY, pp. 135-148; Tso Sze-bong, *op. cit.*, third part, p. 154.

[20] Cf. BD, p. 3319.

[21] Cf. BD, p. 2151.

[22] See also Edwin O. Reischauer, *Ennin's Travels in T'ang China*, New York, 1955.

[23] On Jōjin's diary, see P. Demiéville in P. Pelliot, *Les débuts de l'imprimerie en Chine*, Paris, 1952, pp. 126-131.

[24] "A propos de l'origine de la chaise en Chine", *TP* 53 (1967), pp. 279-292.

BIBLIOGRAPHICAL NOTE

The only monograph on Chinese Buddhist historiography is Ch'en Yüan [**LVIII**], *Chung-kuo fo-chiao shih-chi kai-lun* [**LIX**] Peking, 1955 (cf. P. Demiéville, *RBS*, I, no. 6). Jan Yün-hua, who has written several articles on this subject, has announced a book entitled *The Chinese Buddhist Historiography* (cf. *ZDMG* 114, (1964), p. 376, no. 60). Much information can be found in Japanese reference works such as Mochizuki Shinkō [**LX**], *Bukkyō daijiten* [**LXI**], 10 vols., Tokyo, 1932-1963; Ono Gemmyō [**LXII**], *Bussho kaisetsu daijiten* [**LXIII**], 12 vols., Tokyo, 1933-1936. In the following bibliography only a few publications can be mentioned. Most of them contain references to other works.

1. Tso Sze-bong [**LXIV**], "Chung-kuo fo-chiao shih-chuan yü mu-lu yüan-ch'u lü-hsüeh sha-men chih t'an-t'ao" [**LXV**], *Hsin Ya Hsüeh-pao* [**LXVI**] VI, 1 (1964), pp. 415-486; VII, 1 (1965), pp. 305-361; VII, 2 (1966), pp. 79-155.
2. Wright, Arthur F., "Biography and Hagiography, Hui-chiao's *Lives of Eminent Monks*", *Silver Jubilee Volume of the Zinbun-Kagaku-Kenkyusho Kyoto University*, Kyoto, 1954, pp. 383-432.
3. Shih, Robert, *Biographies des moines éminents* (*Kao seng tchouan*) *de Houei-kiao*, traduites et annotées. Première partie: Biographies des premiers traducteurs (*Bibliothèque du Muséon*, vol. 54), Louvain, 1968 (translation of chapters 1-3 of the *Kao-seng chuan*).
4. Link, Arthur E., "Shih Seng-yu and His Writings", *JAOS* 80 (1960), pp. 17-43.
5. Link, Arthur E., "Remarks on Shih Seng-yu's *Ch'u san-tsang chi-chi* as a Source for Hui-chiao's *Kao-seng chuan* as Evidenced in Two Versions of the Biography of Tao-an", *Oriens* 10 (1957), pp. 292-295.
6. Nogami Shunjō [**LXVII**], *Zoku kōsōden shikō* [**LXVIII**], Kyoto, 1959.
7. Jan Yün-hua, "Buddhist Historiography in Sung China", *ZDMG* 114 (1964) pp. 360-381.
8. Makita Tairyō [**LXIX**], "Sannei to sono jidai [**LXX**], *Chūgoku kinsei bukkyōshi kenkyū* [**LXXI**], Kyoto, 1957, pp. 96-133.
9. Makita Tairyō, "Chōsō bukkyōshi ni okeru Kaisū no tachiba [**LXXII**]", *ibid.*, pp. 134-168.
10. Jan Yün-hua, *A Chronicle of Buddhism in China, 581-960 A. D., Translated from Monk Chih-p'an's Fo-tsu T'ung-chi.* Visva-Bharati, Santiniketan, 1966.

11. Jan Yün-hua, "The Fo-tsu-t'ung-chi, a Biographical and Bibliographical Study", *OE* 10 (1963), pp. 61-82.
12. Tso Sze-bong, "Lun *Fo-tsu-t'ung-chi* tui chi-chuan t'i-ts'ai ti yün-yung" [**LXXIII**], *Hsin Ya hsüeh-pao*, IX, 1, 1969, pp. 121-180.

ABBREVIATIONS

BD	Mochizuki Shinkō, *Bukkyō daijiten*.
BEFEO	*Bulletin de l'École française d'Extrême-Orient*. 1901-
BK	Ono Gemmyō, *Bussho kaisetsu daijiten*.
CY	Ch'en Yüan, *Chung-kuo fo-chiao shih-chi kai-lun*.
IBK	*Indogaku Bukkyōgaku Kenkyū* [**LXXIV**], Tokyo. 1952-
JA	*Journal asiatique*. 1822-
JAOS	*Journal of the American Oriental Society*. 1851-
OE	*Oriens Extremus*. 1954-
RBS	*Revue bibliographique de Sinologie*. 1957-
T	*Taishō shinshū daizōkyō* [**LXXV**], Tokyo, 1924-1932.
TP	*T'oung Pao*. 1890-
ZDMG	*Zeitschrift der deutschen morgenländischen Gesellschaft*. 1847-

I	高僧傳	XXXI	圓仁
II	慧皎	XXXII	成尋
III	出三藏記集	XXXIII	入唐求法巡禮行記
IV	僧祐		
V	名僧傳	XXXIV	參天台五台山記
VI	寶唱	XXXV	法獻
VII	道宣		
VIII	續高僧傳	XXXVI	塚本善隆
IX	十德記	XXXVII	若井諦亮
X	釋靈祐	XXXVIII	龍池清
XI	宋高僧傳	XXXIX	梁高僧傳索引
XII	贊寧	XL	支那佛教史學
XIII	系	XLI	內藤龍雄
XIV	小説	XLII	宋藏遺珍
XV	劉知幾	XLIII	常盤大定
XVI	史通	XLIV	寶林傳の研究
XVII	歷代三寶記	XLV	續支那佛教の研究
XVIII	費長房		
XIX	比丘尼傳	XLVI	傳法寶記
XX	寶林傳	XLVII	楞伽師資記
XXI	弘贊法華傳	XLVIII	歷代法寶記
XXII	祖堂集	XLIX	橫井聖山
XXIII	靜	L	燈史の系譜
XXIV	筠	LI	日本佛教學會年報
XXV	景德傳燈錄		
XXVI	道源	LII	牧田諦亮
XXVII	佛祖統記	LIII	宋代における佛教史學の發展
XXVIII	大宋僧史略		
XXIX	釋氏要覽	LIV	佛祖歷代通載
XXX	道誠	LV	念常

LVI 釋氏稽古略

LVII 覺岸

LVIII 陳垣

LIX 中國佛教史籍概論

LX 望月信亨

LXI 佛教大辭典

LXII 小野玄妙

LXIII 佛書解說大辭典

LXIV 曹仕邦

LXV 中國佛教史傳與目錄源出律學沙門之探討

LXVI 新亞學報

LXVII 野上俊靜

LXVIII 續高僧傳私考

LXIX 牧田諦亮

LXX 贊寧とその時代

LXXI 中國近代佛教史研究

LXXII 趙宋佛教史における契嵩の立場

LXXIII 論佛祖統紀對紀傳體裁的運用

LXXIV 印度佛學教學研究

LXXV 大正新脩大藏經

II
Buddhist Authors

L'AUTEUR DE L'ABHIDHARMADĪPA

PAR

J. W. DE JONG

Nous devons à M. P. S. Jaini une excellente édition de *l'Abhidharmadīpa* [1]). Dans le commentaire, intitulé *Vibhāṣāvṛtti*, l'auteur est appelé *Dīpakāra*, „l'auteur du *Dīpa*". L'*Abhidharmadīpa* critique Vasubandhu du point de vue des Vaibhāṣika. Les *kārikā* et le commentaire ont dû être écrits par le même auteur. En dehors de l'*Abhidharmadīpa*, il a écrit un ouvrage intitulé *Tattvasaptati*, qui est cité une fois dans le commentaire (p. 225, l. 1). Dans son introduction, M. Jaini a étudié le problème que pose l'identité de l'auteur de l'*Abhidharmadīpa* (pp. 129-135). A titre d'hypothèse, il mentionne la possibilité de l'identifier avec Vimalamitra dont la légende est racontée par Hiuan-tsang dans le *Si-yu ki* [2]). Nous y apprenons que Vimalamitra est un maître Sarvāstivādin du Kaśmīr et qu'il vénère la mémoire de Saṃghabhadra, adversaire de Vasubandhu. Il jure d'écrire des traités afin que les savants du Jambudvīpa mettent fin au Grand Véhicule et abolissent le nom de Vasubandhu. Comme objection à cette hypothèse, j'ai déjà relevé le fait que l'*Abhidharmadīpa* ne se réfère jamais aux ouvrages de Saṃghabhadra. On pourrait ajouter que, d'après Hiuan-tsang, Vimalamitra s'en prenait à Vasubandhu le Mahāyāniste, et non à Vasubandhu l'auteur de l'*Abhidharmakośa*, dont les opinions Sautrāntika sont critiquées par l'*Abhidharmadīpa*. Toutefois, l'*Abhidharmadīpa* contient des références aux tendances mahāyānistes de l'ouvrage de Vasubandhu. Il se peut très bien que l'école Sautrāntika déjà était considérée comme étant au moins à mi-chemin du Mahāyāna.

L'hypothèse de M. Jaini garde sa valeur tant que l'on n'aura pas apporté des preuves décisives pour identifier l'auteur de l'*Abhidhar-*

---

[1]) *Abhidharmadīpa with Vibhāṣāprabhāvṛtti*, critically edited with notes and introduction by Padmanabh S. Jaini, *Tibetan Sanskrit Works Series*, IV, Patna, 1959. Cf. mon compte rendu dans l'*Indo-Iranian Journal*, VI (1962), pp. 173-175.

[2]) M. Jaini cite la traduction de Beal, *Buddhist Records of the Western World*, Vol. I (London, 1884), pp. 196-197. Cf. Taishō no. 2087, vol. LI, p. 892b3-22.

madīpa avec un autre maître bouddhiste. Pour le moment, ces preuves manquent et on en est réduit à des hypothèses. Le même *Si-yu ki* nous offre la possibilité d'en formuler une autre. Dans la section sur le Gandhāra, Hiuan-tsang s'occupe assez longuement de la ville de *Po-lou-cha* 跋虜沙 [1]). Il raconte qu'au Nord de cette ville il y a un stūpa en honneur du prince Sudāna, qui y avait fait don du grand éléphant de son père à un brahmane. Il continue: ,,A côté de ce stūpa se trouve un monastère avec plus de cinquante moines[2]) qui, tous, étudient le Petit Véhicule. Autrefois, le maître des *śāstra* I-che-fa-lo 伊濕伐邏 a écrit ici l'*A-p'i-ta-mo ming-teng louen* 阿毘達磨明燈論 ''(p. 881b10-12). I-che-fa-lo transcrit le sanskrit Īśvara, ce qui est confirmé par une glose du texte selon laquelle I-che-fa-lo est en chinois *tseu-tsai* 自在. *A-p'i-ta-mo ming-teng louen* a été reconstitué par Stanislas Julien en *Abhidharmaprakāśasādhana-śāstra*. Le texte utilisé par Julien et Beal (*op. cit.*, vol. I, p. 112) porte *ming-tcheng* 明證 au lieu de *ming-teng*. Déjà Watters (*op. cit.*, vol. I, p. 218) a indiqué que l'édition de Tōkyō (1880-1885) a *ming-teng* d'après l'édition coréenne. Le Taishō Issaikyō a également adopté cette dernière leçon, en mentionnant *ming-tcheng* comme une variante des ,,Trois éditions''. *Ming-teng* correspond exactement au sanskrit *dīpa*, ,,lampe, lumière'', et on peut reconstituer le titre original en *Abhidharmadīpaśāstra*. Malheureusement, Hiuan-tsang ne donne pas d'autres renseignements sur Īśvara et son *Abhidharmadīpaśāstra* qui permettraient d'identifier cet ouvrage avec l'*Abhidharmadīpa* édité par M. Jaini. La tradition tibétaine mentionne un maître Īśvarasena (*dBaṅ-phyug sde*), élève de Dignāga et maître de Dharmakīrti, auteur d'un sous-commentaire du *Pramāṇasamuccaya* [3]). Il n'est pas exclu qu'un élève de Dignāga ait pu écrire un ouvrage sur le *Kośa*, car le Tandjour contient un commentaire du *Kośa*, intitulé *Abhidharmakośamarmapradīpa*, qui est attribué à Dignāga.

---

[1]) Selon M. Ét. Lamotte (*Histoire du Bouddhisme indien, I*, Louvain, 1958, p. 829), Po-lou-cha est Varṣapura (Shāhbāzgaṛhī). Cette identification semble être empruntée aux travaux de Foucher mentionnés p. 366, n. 49.

[2]) Le texte chinois pourrait signifier qu'il y a plus de cinquante monastères. C'est ainsi que Julien a traduit. Beal (*op. cit.*, I, p. 112, n. 101) remarque que la présence de plus de cinquante monastères auprès d'un stūpa est improbable. Watters (*On Yuan Chwang's Travels in India*, Vol. I, London, 1904, p. 217) suit l'interprétation de Beal.

[3]) *History of Buddhism* (*Chos-ḥbyung*) *by Bu-ston*, translated by E. Obermiller, Part II (Heidelberg, 1932), p. 152. Cf. aussi *Târanâtha's Geschichte des Buddhismus in Indien*, übersetzt von Anton Schiefner (St. Petersburg, 1869), pp. 159 et 176.

Selon Obermiller, ce n'est qu'un abrégé du commentaire de Vasubandhu lui-même (*op. cit.*, Part II, p. 150. n. 1053).

Il n'est guère possible d'identifier l'Īśvara de Hiuan-tsang avec l'Īśvarasena de Bu-ston; mais, tant que l'on ne dispose pas d'autres données, il faut signaler toutes les possibilités. C'est pour cette raison que j'ai voulu attirer l'attention sur ce passage du *Si-yu ki*. Il est à espérer que des recherches dans les commentaires du *Kośa*, conservés en traduction tibétaine [1]), pourront mettre au jour des références plus précises à l'*Abhidharmadīpa* et à son auteur.

---

[1]) C'est surtout des volumineux commentaires de Sthiramati et de Pūrṇavardhana que l'on pourrait espérer tirer des renseignements intéressants.

LA LÉGENDE DE ŚĀNTIDEVA*

par
J. W. DE JONG
Canberra

L'ouvrage que Mlle Amalia Pezzali a consacré à Śāntideva est divisé en deux parties: I. La vie et les œuvres; II. La pensée. Comme le relève M. Olivier Lacombe dans sa préface le travail de Mlle Pezzali s'attache à synthétiser les connaissances critiques acquises par la bouddhologie sur la vie, les œuvres et la doctrine de Śāntideva. Des travaux de ce genre peuvent être très utiles, même si l'auteur n'apporte rien de neuf, à condition que l'information donnée soit exacte et complète. Malheureusement, l'ouvrage présent est loin de remplir ces deux conditions essentielles pour un travail de synthèse. On y trouve non seulement maintes inexactitudes, fautes d'impression, de lecture du sanskrit et du tibétain, etc., mais aussi des lacunes sérieuses dans l'information. Nous n'avons nullement l'intention de signaler toutes les erreurs dont ce livre fourmille.[1] Le lecteur averti sera capable de faire lui-même les corrections nécessaires. Il nous a paru utile d'examiner les documents concernant la vie de Śāntideva que Mlle Pezzali a réunis dans le premier chapitre de la première partie de son ouvrage (pp. 3-45).

La vie ou plutôt la légende de Śāntideva nous est racontée par trois historiens tibétains: Bu-ston (1290-1364), Tāranātha (1575- ?) et Sum-pa mkhan-po (1704-1788).[2] L'ouvrage de Bu-ston, "Histoire du bouddhis-

* A propos de Amalia Pezzali, *Śāntideva, mystique bouddhiste des VIIe et VIIIe siècles*, Firenze, Vallecchi Editore, 1968. USA $7.80.

[1] Il faudrait commencer par les abréviations (page XIII). Le catalogue de Cordier n'est pas en trois volumes mais en deux. Il faut corriger Hiuan-tsang en Hiouen-thsang et Stanislaus en Stanislas. La Prasannapadā ne fut pas publiée en 1913 mais de 1903 à 1913.

[2] Mlle Pezzali fait mourir Tāranātha en 1608 et Sum-pa mkhan-po en 1777. Tāranātha a écrit son "Histoire du Bouddhisme en Inde" en 1608 à l'âge de 34 ans (cf. *Târanâtha's Geschichte des Buddhismus in Indien.* Aus dem tibetischen uebersetzt von Anton Schiefner, St. Petersburg, 1869, p. VI). La date de sa mort semble être inconnue. Sum-pa mkhan-po est mort en 1788 (cf. J. W. de Jong, "Sum-pa mkhan-po [1704-1788] and his works", *HJAS*, 27 (1967), p. 209).

me" (chos-'byuṅ), fut écrit en 1322-1323.[3] Le passage de son ouvrage, relatif à Śāntideva, fut traduit par Obermiller: *Bu-ston, History of Buddhism*, II. Part (Heidelberg, 1932), pp. 161-166. Dans l'édition, utilisée par Obermiller, ce passage occupe les feuillets 126b-128b. Dans l'introduction à la première partie Stcherbatsky écrit que la traduction est faite d'après un vieux xylographe (Heidelberg, 1931), p. 4. Le texte tibétain que Mlle Pezzali reproduit a la même pagination que celle traduite par Obermiller. Il doit s'agir de l'édition de Bkra-śis lhun-po décrite par M. Yamaguchi Zuihō car on retrouve dans la traduction d'Obermiller la même pagination pour les trois premiers chapitres (la traduction s'arrête avant la fin du quatrième chapitre).[4] Cette édition qui contient 244 feuillets a été décrite aussi par Sakai Shirō et par A. I. Vostrikov.[5] M. Yamaguchi décrit deux autres éditions du Chos-'byuṅ: l'une en 190 feuillets (sans indication de lieu de publication) et l'autre, celle de Derge en 203 feuillets.[6] Il y a encore une autre édition du Chos-'byuṅ qui fait partie du Gsuṅ-'bum publié en 28 volumes à Lhasa en 1921.[7] Le Chos-'byuṅ occupe 212 feuillets dans le volume Ya.[8] La pagination des six chapitres est la suivante: I. ff. 1-2b7; II. ff. 2b7-34b6; III. ff. 34b6-122b5; IV. ff. 122b6-143a4; V. ff. 143a5-210a1; VI. ff. 210a1-212a1. L'histoire de Śāntideva se trouve aux feuillets 113b3-115b3. Au lieu de faire une édition critique de ce passage à l'aide des quatre éditions, signalées ci-dessus, Mlle Pezzali s'est contentée de reproduire le texte d'une seule édition. L'utilité de l'édition de ces feuillets est diminuée par le fait que le texte reproduit comporte plusieurs fautes de lectures comme on peut le constater aisément sans avoir recours au xylographe.[9] La traduction suit de près celle d'Obermiller qui est excellente. Mlle Pezzali en copie les rares

[3] Cf. R. A. Stein, *Recherches sur l'épopée et le barde au Tibet* (Paris, 1959) p. 33.
[4] *Catalogue of the Toyo Bunko Collection of Tibetan Works on History*, edited by Zuihō Yamaguchi, (Tokyo 1970), p. 95.
[5] Sakai Shirō, "Kazō Chibetto-zō-gai butten no oboegaki", *Nihon chibetto gakkai kaihō*, No. 3 (1956), p. 1; A. I. Vostrikov, *Tibetskaja istoričeskaja literatura* (Moskva, 1962), pp. 91 and 257.
[6] *Op. cit.*, pp. 94-96. L'édition en 190 feuillets fut utilisée par H. Hoffmann (cf. *Quellen zur Geschichte der tibetischen Bon-Religion*, (Wiesbaden, 1950), p. 272). Pour l'édition de Derge voir aussi Stein, *loc. cit.* et Lokesh Chandra, "Les imprimeries tibétaines de Drepung, Derge et Pepung", *JA* (1961), p. 511, no. 68.
[7] Cf. D. S. Ruegg, *The Life of Bu ston rin po che* (Roma, 1966), pp. 41-42, n. 3.
[8] *Catalogue of the Tohoku University Collection of Tibetan Works on Buddhism* (Sendai, 1953), p. 72, no. 5197. Les 28 volumes ont été réimprimés par l'International Academy of Indian Culture. Volume Ya a paru en 1971. Je dois à l'amabilité du professeur Lokesh Chandra un tiré-à-part de ce volume contenant le texte complet du Chos-'byuṅ.
[9] F. 126b3 bltams čas, lire bltams nas; 126b5 bras nas, lire bros nas; 126b6 rab-tu

erreurs.[10] Selon cette recension de la légende, Śāntideva naquit dans le Sud comme fils du roi Kalyāṇavarman du Surāṣṭra.[11] Il fut appelé Śāntivarman.

L'ouvrage de Tāranātha fut édité et traduit par Anton Schiefner.[12] Mlle Pezzali reproduit le texte de Schiefner, en y apportant quelques erreurs.[13] L'édition de Schiefner repose sur quatre manuscrits. Mlle Pezzali n'a consulté aucune édition tibétaine.[14] Dans sa traduction elle a essayé d'améliorer celle de Schiefner mais sans grand succès.[15] Le troisième texte, reproduit par Mlle Pezzali, est emprunté à l'édition du Dpag-bsam ljon-bzaṅ par S. C. Das. L'édition de Das est presque inutilisable à cause du grand nombre de fautes d'impression. Dans ce cas il aurait été absolument nécessaire de consulter le xylographe sur lequel M. R. A. Stein a donné des renseignements.[16] Ajoutons que l'ouvrage de Sum-pa mkhan-po date de 1748. Comme le dit Mlle Pezzali Sum-pa mkhan-po n'ajoute rien de neuf en ce qui concerne Śāntideva.

Le dernier document, présenté par Mlle Pezzali, est un manuscrit népalais que Haraprasād Śāstri a signalé pour la première fois dans un article sur Śāntideva.[17] Ensuite, il a décrit le manuscrit et a reproduit le

byuṅ ba'i byaṅ, lire rab tu byuṅ ba'i bya ba; 127a6 po ma šes pa, lire ṅo ma šes pa; 127b4 lhuṅ bzed gad, lire lhuṅ bzed gaṅ; 127b5 bru ba chabs nen te, lire bru ba cha bas nen te; 128a3 khru dam and 'khru dam, lire 'khrud ma.

[10] Ainsi f. 127a5 rjogs-par bton-te gšegs-so "il termina ainsi la récitation et il réapparut". Obermiller, p. 163: "And, after the recitation was completed, he appeared again". Il faut évidemment traduire: "Après avoir récité [le texte] complètement, il s'en alla".

[11] Mlle Pezzali traduit: "Dans la région méridionale de Surāṣṭra". Obermiller a: "In the southern country, of Saurāṣṭra". Le texte dit qu'il naquit comme le fils, appelé Śāntivarman, du roi, appelé Kalyāṇavarman, du Surāṣṭra dans le Sud.

[12] Cf. ci-dessus note 2; *Târanâthae de doctrinae buddhicae in India propagatione narratio.* Contextem Tibeticum e codicibus Petropolitanis edidit Antonius Schiefner. Petropoli, 1868. Texte et traduction furent réimprimés en 1963 à Tokyo par la Suzuki Research Foundation.

[13] P. 126, l.11 sdon, lire sṅon; p. 128, l.5 dge slon, lire dge sloṅ; p. 128, l.10 rtags por, lire rtags bor; p. 128, l.20 yin n'aṅ, lire yin na'aṅ; p. 128, l.21 yul gaṅ in, lire yul gaṅ yin.

[14] Pour une édition, imprimée à Derge, voir Stein, *op. cit.*, p. 41 et Lokesh Chandra, *JA* (1961), p. 509, no. 36.

[15] Voir p. 126, ll.10-11 (yi-dam-gyi phyag-mchan šiṅ-gi ral-gri gčig 'čhaṅ-gin yod), p. 126, l.15 (gnod-kyaṅ sla-yi; sla = bla, cf. Bu-ston f. 128a1), etc. A un seul endroit Mlle Pezzali améliore la traduction de Schiefner dans une certaine mesure: p. 126, l.13 ral-gri yaṅ šiṅ las med-do "son épée, qui est en bois, est inutile". Schiefner (p. 164): "sein Schwert nicht von Holz sei". Il faut traduire: "son épée n'est rien d'autre que du bois". Pour la valeur de *las* suivi d'une négation voir le dictionnaire de Jäschke, p. 546b; Michael Hahn, *Lehrbuch der klassischen tibetischen Schriftsprache* (Hamburg, 1971), p. 97.

[16] Cf. *JA*, 1952, pp. 91-92; J. W. de Jong, *op. cit.*, p. 210.

[17] "Śāntideva", *Indian Antiquary*, XLII (1913), pp. 49-52. Mlle Pezzali indique vol. XIII mais voir Winternitz, *A History of Indian Literature*, vol. 2 (Calcutta, 1933), p. 366,

texte dans le premier volume du catalogue des manuscrits sanskrits du gouvernement du Bengale.[18] D'après Haraprasād Śāstri l'écriture est la Newarī du 14e siècle. Le texte est assez corrompu. Les corrections, proposées par Haraprasād Śāstri, se limitent à l'addition de deux syllabes et d'un visarga.[19] Mlle Pezzali reproduit le texte tel qu'il a été publié en devanāgarī en caractères romains en ajoutant des fautes d'impression et de lecture. Elle signale en note quelques corrections dont une seule est valable (lire *antarikṣagataḥ* pour *antarīkṣagataḥ*). Des corrections évidentes n'ont pas été indiquées. Par exemple: il faut corriger *mātuvādeśaṃ* en *māturādeśaṃ* (ataḥ sa mātur ādeśaṃ śirasi nidhāya ...). Mlle Pezzali traduit: "Alors, lui, acceptant respectueusement le conseil de sa mère", mais ne mentionne pas que cette traduction implique la correction de *mātuv* en *mātur*.

Ni Haraprasād Śāstri ni Mlle Pezzali n'ont signalé le fait que le Tanjur tibétain contient un texte qui est très proche du texte sanskrit qu'ils ont publié. Ce texte tibétain se trouve au début d'un commentaire du Bodhicaryāvatāra écrit par Vibhūticandra: Byaṅ-chub-kyi spyod-pa la 'jug-pa'i dgoṅs-pa'i 'grel-pa khyad-par gsal-byed ces-bya-ba = Bodhicaryāvatāratātparyapañjikā viśeṣadyotanī nāma.[20] Dans un article sur les commentaires du Bodhicaryāvatāra Ejima Yasunari signale cette biographie de Śāntideva et ajoute que, si Vibhūticandra en est l'auteur, elle est antérieure au texte publié par Haraprasād Śāstri.[21] Selon M. Ejima le commentaire de Vibhūticandra date de la seconde moitié du douzième siècle ou du début du treizième siècle. M. Ejima n'a pas tenu compte du fait que le manuscrit date du quatorzième siècle (si l'on accepte la datation de Haraprasād Śāstri) mais que le texte même peut être beaucoup plus ancien. Il est évident que M. Ejima n'a pas comparé les textes sanskrit et tibétain car, dans ce cas, il aurait vu que le texte tibétain doit remonter au même texte original que le texte sanskrit. Les dates exactes de Vibhūticandra ne sont pas connues. Les historiens tibétains racontent qu'il est

n. 1. Je n'ai pas pu consulter cet article.

18 *A descriptive Catalogue of Sanskrit Manuscripts in the Government Collection under the care of the Asiatic Society of Bengal*, vol. I (Calcutta, 1917), no. 52 (pp. 51-53) MS. 9990.

19 Cf. ci-dessous sections VI, VIII et XV du texte sanskrit.

20 Cf. P. Cordier, *Catalogue du fonds tibétain de la Bibliothèque nationale*, III (Paris, 1915), p. 310 (Mdo-'grel XXVII.8). Pour le texte tibétain voir l'édition de Pékin, Dhu-ma, Śa ff. 229b6-231b5 = *The Tibetan Tripitaka*. Peking edition. Edited by Daisetz T. Suzuki, vol. 100 (Tokyo-Kyoto 1957), p. 236, 1.6-5.5. Je n'ai pas pu consulter d'autres éditions du Tanjur.

21 Ejima Yasunori, "*Nyūbodaigyōron* no chūshaku bunken ni tsuite", *Indogaku bukkyōgaku kenkyū*, XIV (1966), p. 646.

arrivé au Tibet en 1204. Il fut un des neufs jeunes pandits qui accompagnaient Śākyaśrībhadra.[22] D'après plusieurs colophons d'ouvrages, traduits par Vibhūticandra, il était originaire de Jagaddala dans l'Inde orientale.[23] C'est aussi à Jagaddala que Śākyaśrībhadra résidait avant de partir pour le Tibet.[24] Le colophon du commentaire de Vibhūticandra mentionne aussi le nom de Śākyaśrībhadra: slob-dpon 'phags-pa dpal źi-ba'i lha'i źabs-kyis(xyl. kyi)mdzad-pa byaṅ-chub sems-dpa'i spyod-pa la 'jug-pa'i dgoṅs-pa 'grel-pa khyad-par gsal-byed ces bya-ba rig-pa'i 'byuṅ-gnas dbus-'gyur-gyi śar-phyogs pa-rendrar rgyal-rigs las 'khruṅs-śiṅ / sa-bcu'i dbaṅ-phyug rje-btsun 'jam-pa'i dbyaṅs-kyis rjes-su bzuṅ-ba / rig-pa'i gnas rnam-pa lṅa la mkhas-śiṅ tshul-khrims dri-ma med-pa'i brgyan-gyis spras-pa / rim-pa gñis-kyi don-la rgyud legs-par sbyaṅs-pas lam-gyi rtogs-pa goṅ-nas goṅ-du cher (xyl. char)-'phel-ba / rtsod-pa'i dus-kyi (343a) thams-cad mkhyen-pa gñis-par grags-pa / ma-'oṅs-pa'i saṅs-rgyas kha-che'i paṇḍi-ta chen-po bsod-sñoms-pa śā-kya-śrī-bha-dra la sogs-pa paṇ-grub du-ma'i legs-bśad-kyis / thugs-kyi bum-pa legs-par bltams-pas phyogs phyi-naṅ-gi theg-pa ma-lus-pa la mṅa' brñed-śiṅ / sgra daṅ tshad-ma'i mig-gis śes-bya'i de-ñid gzigs-pa / rgya-gar śar-phyogs dza-ga-ta-la bi-ha-ra'i paṇḍi-ta chen-po śrī-mi(sic!)-bhū-ti-tsandras mdzad-pa rdzogs-so: "Fin du *Khyad-par gsal-byed* (Viśeṣadyotanī), commentaire [expliquant] le sens (*tātparyapañjikā*) du Bodhicaryāvatāra, ouvrage du noble Śrīśāntidevapāda. Le commentaire est écrit par Vibhūticandra, paṇḍita du vihāra Jagaddala dans l'Inde orientale, né de la famille royale de Varendra, région orientale du pays du Milieu[25], source de connaissances, lui, qui a reçu la grâce du vénérable Mañjughoṣa, le seigneur des dix terres, qui est expert dans les cinq sortes de connaissances (*vidyāsthāna*), qui est orné par l'ornement de la bonne conduite immaculée, qui, l'esprit bien exercé dans les deux sortes de buts (*svārtha*

[22] Cf. Bu-ston, *op. cit.*, II, p. 222; *The Blue Annals*, transl. by George N. Roerich, II (Calcutta, 1953), p. 600 et pp. 1063-1064. Selon ce dernier texte, Śākyaśrībhadra a vécu de 1127 à 1225, mais, selon d'autres sources, il aurait vécu de 1140 à 1238 ou de 1145 1243, cf. D. S. Ruegg, *op. cit.*, pp. 42-43, n. 1. Sur les activités de Śākyaśrībhadra au Tibet voir Hadano Hakuyū, "Kāśmīra-mahāpaṇḍita Śākyaśrībhadra", *Bunka*, 21 (1957), pp. 676 (1)-656 (21).

[23] Sur Jagaddala et sa location voir l'introduction de D. D. Kosambi au *Subhāṣitaratnakoṣa* (HOS, vol. 42) (Cambridge, Mass., 1957), p. xxxvii, n. 7.

[24] Cf. *The Blue Annals*, II, p. 1066.

[25] Le texte a *dbus-'gyur-gyi śar-phyogs* 'la région orientale qui se trouve au milieu' (?) ou 'la région orientale de ce qui se trouve au milieu (i.e. l'Inde)' (?). Cordier traduit *dbus-'gyur* par Magadha (*op. cit.*, II, p.20), mais le texte a *dbus-'gyur-tshal* (Rgyud-'grel. vol. Ṅa, f. 241a4). Le dictionnaire tibétain-mongol de Sumatiratna traduit *dbus-'gyur-tshal* par *Enedkeg-ün vačir-tu sayurin* = *Vajrāsana* (Bodhgayā), cf. Sumatiratna, vol. II, p. 300. D'habitude, dans les textes tibétains, Magadha est translittéré: ma-ga-dha.

et *parārtha*), a développé de plus en plus la compréhension du chemin (*margādhigama*), lui qui est connu comme le deuxième omniscient de l'époque Kali, lui dont la cruche de l'esprit a été remplie par les bonnes paroles de plusieurs savants tels que le moine mendiant Śākyaśrībhadra, le grand paṇḍita du Kaśmīr, le Buddha de l'avenir, lui qui connaît parfaitement tous les véhicules aussi bien ceux des hérétiques que ceux des bouddhistes, lui qui voit la vraie nature du connaissable avec la parole et l'œil de la connaissance."

Le colophon de la Viśeṣadyotanī ne mentionne que le nom de Vibhūticandra comme auteur et traducteur mais, tout au début du commentaire, Rnal-'byor zla-ba (Yogacandra?) est mentionné comme auteur: 'grel-pa mdzad-pa rnams-kyis kyaṅ // 'phags-pa'i dgoṅs-pa gsal-ma byas // de'i-phyir dgoṅs-pa'i 'grel-pa 'di // rnal-'byor zla-bas cuṅ-zad bri //: "Les auteurs de commentaires n'ont pas élucidé l'intention du vénérable. C'est pourquoi Rnal-'byor zla-ba a écrit tant soit peu ce commentaire [qui explique] le sens (*tātparyapañjikā*)."[26] Selon Cordier, Rnal-'byor zla-ba a traduit deux textes, l'un avec Vibhūticandra et l'autre avec 'Jam-dpal gźon-nu.[27] Le colophon du premier texte, la Guṇabharaṇī nāma ṣaḍaṅgayogaṭippaṇī, dit tout d'abord que le texte a été traduit par Vibhūticandra. Ensuite, à la demande de Chos-grags dpal-bzaṅ-po, Dpal-ldan Blo-gros brtan-pa de Dpaṅ a traduit et corrigé le texte (bsgyur-ciṅ źus-chen grub-pa'o). Le colophon se termine ainsi: pan-chen rnal-'byor-zla-ba'i raṅ-'gyur la // phyed-tsam ma-bsgyur 'ol-phyir mdzad-pa las // blo-gros brtan-pas sgra-don ji-bźin bsgyur. Ce passage est assez difficile à traduire. D'habitude, l'expression *raṅ-'gyur* 'traduit par soi-même' s'emploie pour une traduction faite par l'auteur même. Ainsi, par exemple, Bu-ston dit du commentaire du Bodhicaryāvatāra par Vibhūticandra: vi-bhu-ti-tsa-ndras mdzad-pa'i spyod-'jug-gi 'grel-pa de'i raṅ-'gyur "Le commentaire du Bodhicaryāvatāra, écrit par Vibhūticandra, et traduit par lui-même."[28] Toutefois, on rencontre aussi l'expression *sgra raṅ-'gyur* qui semble désigner une traduction faite oralement. Par exemple, le colophon du Ṣaḍaṅgayoga (Cordier, II, p. 21: Rgyud-'grel IV.22) dit: dpal śa-ba-ri-pa dbaṅ-phyug-gis paṇḍi-ta ma-hā-bi-bhū-ti-tsa-ndra la gsuṅs-pa'o // des sgra raṅ-'gyur-du bsgyur-nas gsuṅs-pa'o // "Récité par Śrī Śabarīśvara au paṇḍita Mahāvibhūticandra. Récité par lui après l'avoir traduit en traduction orale". Il se peut donc que l'expression

[26] Tanjur, Dbu-ma, Śa f. 229b5-6.

[27] P. Cordier, *op. cit.*, II (Paris, 1909), p. 24 (Rgyud-'grel IV.34) et III (Paris, 1915), p. 397 (Mdo-'grel LII.2).

[28] Chos-'byuṅ (édition de Lhasa), f. 159a5-6.

raṅ-'gyur soit une abréviation pour *sgra raṅ-'gyur*. Dans ce cas, la traduction, faite oralement par Rnal-'byor zla-ba, ne peut être que la traduction de Vibhūticandra. Ainsi Rnal-'byor zla-ba ne serait qu'un autre nom pour Vibhūticandra. C'est aux futures recherches de démontrer si cette hypothèse est valable ou non.

Mlle Pezzali écrit que des fragments de la Viśeṣadyotanī, appelée Bodhicaryāvatāraṭippanī, ont été conservés.[29] Elle ajoute que L. de La Vallée Poussin s'en est servi pour son édition.[30] Dans l'introduction à son édition de la Bodhicaryāvatārapañjikā (*Bibliotheca Indica*, 1901-1914) de La Vallée Poussin écrit: "Some help has been found in a little tract, of which some fragments only are preserved, called Bodhicaryāvatāraṭippanī; this MS. was discovered in the Durbar Library at Kathmandu by Professor Cecil Bendall and was copied for him. I refer to it as Ṭipp". De La Vallée Poussin ne dit pas que cette ṭippanī est identique à la Viśeṣadyotanī de Vibhūticandra. Je doute fort que Mlle Pezzali ait pu trouver ce renseignement dans le catalogue de la bibliothèque du Durbar par Haraprasād Śāstri que je n'ai pas pu consulter. Probablement elle a emprunté cette information à l'introduction de P. L. Vaidya à son édition du Bodhicaryāvatāra dans laquelle il écrit: "There is also a Tippaṇī called Viśeṣadyotanī by Vibhūticandra, fragments of which are found in the original Sanskrit and in Tanjur (T No. 3880) and they were used by Poussin".[31] De La Vallée Poussin donne le début de la ṭippanī que j'ai comparé avec le début de la Viśeṣadyotanī. Les textes n'ont rien de commun. Une comparaison du début de la ṭippanī avec les débuts d'autres commentaires, conservés en traduction tibétaine, a également livré un résultat négatif.

Ci-dessous je fais suivre le texte sanskrit tel qu'il a été édité par Haraprasād Śāstri dans le catalogue des manuscrits sanskrits du gouvernement du Bengale[32] et le texte tibétain d'après l'édition de Pékin. A.P. = Amalia Pezzali; H.S. = Haraprasād Śāstri; T. = la traduction tibétaine; P = l'édition de Pékin de la traduction tibétaine. La division en seize sections a été faite pour faciliter la comparaison des textes. La traduction qui suit est faite d'après le texte tibétain à fin de faciliter la comparaison des textes sanskrit et tibétain. Je tiens à exprimer mes remerciements au professeur Ōjihara Yutaka qui a eu l'amabilité de me donner des renseignements précieux sur l'étymologie du mot *ṛṣi* (cf. ci-dessous note 28).

[29] Cf. p. 55.
[30] Cf. p. 49.
[31] *Buddhist Sanskrit Texts*, No. 12 (Darbhanga, 1960), p. X.
[32] Je n'ai pas noté les consonnes géminées après *r*.

La légende de Śāntideva

Textes sanskrit et tibétain

Sanskrit	Tibétain
I. +++++++ nagare śrīmañjuvarmanāmno rājnaḥ putraḥ pūrvajinakṛtādhikāraḥ prāptamokṣabhāgīyakuśalamūlaḥ samyak mahāyānagotraḥ[1] sarvakalākuśalo yauvarājyābhiṣekasamaye kuliśayoṣinnirmāṇarūpayā[2] jananyā rājamahiṣyā abhitaptodakais tapyamānas tāpam asahamāna uktaḥ /	I. 'di-skad brgyud-pa las thos-te / lho'i phyogs-su dpal na-ga-ra la mi'i-rgyal-po 'jam-dpal go-cha'i bu-ru skyes / sṅon-gyi saṅs-rgyas la bya-ba byas-pa / thar-pa'i cha-mthun-gyi dge-ba'i rtsa-ba thob-pa / theg-pa chen-po'i rigs yaṅ-dag-pa / rgyu-rtsal thams-cad la mkhas-pa / rgyal-tshab-tu dbaṅ-bskur-ba'i dus-su rdo-rje-rnal-'byor-ma'i sprul-pa / rgyal-po'i btsun-mo chen-mo yum (P. yul)-gyis chu dron-pos khrus-byed-du bcug-pas / de'i drod mi-bzod-pa mthoṅ-nas / yum-gyis 'di-skad-du smras-te /
II. putra trayaḥ svargaṃ na gacchanti rājā citrakaraḥ kavir iti / nareśvarībhūya pāpaṃ kṛtvā mṛtasya nirayagatasya ato 'pi tīvrataraṃ duḥkhaṃ te bhaviṣyaty alam anena rājyena / gaccha vatsa buddhabodhisattvadeśaṃ[3] śrīmañjuvajrādhiṣṭhānaṃ tava bhadraṃ[4] bhaviṣyatīty	II. sñigs-ma'i dus-su rgyal-po byas-na ñon-moṅs-pa'i dbaṅ-gis sems-can sdug-tu (230a) bcug-la // śi-nas dmyal-bar 'di-bas kyaṅ drag-pa'i sdug-bsṅal myoṅ-bar 'gyur-bas rgyal-srid-kyis dgos-pa med-kyi bu khyod bhaṃ-ga-la'i yul-du soṅ / der khyod-la 'jam-pa'i dbyaṅs-kyis byin-gyis brlob-par 'gyur źes-so /
III. ataḥ sa mātuvādeśaṃ[5] śirasi nidhāyākuṭilahṛdayo haridaśvavaram abhiruhya calitaḥ / sa cānekadināny aniśaṃ gacchan bhojanapānādikaṃ manasy akurvan tadādeśaikatānamānasaḥ[6] kvacid[7] araṇye kanyāratnam apaśyat tayā vājinaṃ vivṛtyāsau[8] bhuvam avatāritaḥ //	III. de-nas yum-gyi bka' de spyi-bor bźag-nas / thugs draṅ-po rta-mchog ljaṅ-gu la źon-te gśegs-so / de yaṅ źag du-ma ñin-mtshan med-par 'gro-ste / bza'-btuṅ la sogs-pa yid-la mi-byed-par de'i-bka' gcig-po la rtse-gcig-par 'gro-ba la / bhaṃ-ga-la'i yul-gyi mtha'-mar nags-tshal-gyi naṅ-na bu-mo rin-po-che źig mthoṅ-ṅo // bu-mo des

IV. sa tṛṣārto jalaṃ dṛṣṭvā pātum udyataḥ / tayā viṣodakam etad ity uktvā nivāryānyad amṛtodakaṃ pāyito māṃsañ cāgninā dagdhvā bhojitaḥ /

V. svasthaḥ sa tām āha / kutas tvam āgatāsīti / sā prāha / ihāvaste sa mahākaruṇāruṇavipaṇaḥ[9] sadguṇagaṇābharaṇaḥ siddhaśrīmañjuvajrasamādhir asmadguruḥ tatsakāśād aham āgatāsmīty ukto labdharatna iva duḥkhito[10] janaḥ paramapramodaprāptaḥ

VI. tam eva darśayety uktvā tayādṛto[11] ghoṭakam ādāya gato guruguṇagaṇādhāradhīragambhīraṃ[12] śamadamathaprāptaṃ gurum ālokya turaṅgamam ātmānañ ca namaskṛtya gurave nityā[ni]tya[13] durantabhavaduḥkhābdher upadeśadānena māṃ ... ty adhīṣṭavān

VII. tena ca paripāṭīkramād[14] upadiṣṭo dvādaśavarṣās tatraiva samādhārya[15] mañjuvajram adhyakṣīkṛtya mañjuśrījñānaṃ labdhvā gaccha madhyadeśam iti guruṇā samādiṣṭo gatvā magadharājānaṃ sevate sma / rāututvena[16] acalasenanāmā devadārukhaḍgena koṣagatena rāutucaryayaḥ[17] dharmārā-

rta bzuṅ-nas de rta-las babs-so //

IV. de ni śin-tu skom-pas mdun-du chu mthoṅ-nas btuṅ-bar brtsams-so // bu-mos 'di ni dug-gi chu yin-pas ma-'thuṅ-źig ces smras-na / de-las bzlog-te bdud-rtsi'i chu 'thuṅ-du bcug-pa daṅ / śa bsregs-nas za-ru bcug-pas /

V. tshim-par gyur la bu-mo la smras-te / khyed gaṅ-nas 'oṅs źes-so // des smras-pa / nags-tshal chen-po 'di'i dbus-su yon-tan dam-pa'i tshogs-kyis brgyan-pa / thugs-rje-can dpal-'jam-pa'i rdo-rje tiṅ-ṅe-'dzin sgrub-pa bdag-gi bla-ma bźugs-te / de-nas 'oṅs źes-so // de thos-pa tsam-gyis bkren-pas rin-po-che thob-pa ltar dga'-bde chen-pos dbugs-phyuṅ-nas

VI. smras-te / kye de bdag-la ston-cig / bu-mos de 'bod-pa rta bzuṅ-ste gśegs-par gyur-to / der phyin-pas śin-tu zab-pa'i thugs daṅ-ldan-źiṅ // lus-ṅag źi-ba gser-gyi ri lta-bu bla-ma'i mchog mthoṅ-nas / bdag-ñid daṅ rta-mchog phul-nas gus-pas bla-ma de-la phyag-byas-te / 'jam-pa'i dbyaṅs-kyi tiṅ-ṅe-'dzin-gyis (230b) gdams-pas bdag rjes-su 'dzin-par 'tshal-to // źes gsol-to //

VII. bla-mas yaṅ de yoṅs-su smin-par mdzad-pa'i rim-pas gdams-par mdzad-do // des ni lo bcu-gñis der bźugs-la tiṅ-ṅe-'dzin-gyis 'jam-pa'i dbyaṅs mṅon-sum-du mdzad-ciṅ // de-rjes bla-mas yul-dbus-su 'gro-bar bka'-stsal-pas soṅ-ste / ma-ga-dha'i rgyal-po sten (P.rten)-ciṅ śiṅ-gi ral-gri śubs daṅ-bcas-pa mo[18] viharati sma /

VIII. kālāntareṇa tatsampattim asahamānair anyai rāutvai rājānaṃ vijñapya deva devadārukhaḍgena acalasya seveti yuddhakāle katham asau yudhyeta / tad deva nirūpayāsya khaḍgam iti adhṛṣyo[19] 'sau na śakyate niyoktum itīrṣyāśalyacitta[pī]ḍyamānamarmabhis tair militvā sarveṣāṃ khaḍgo draṣṭavya iti rājājñayā vyājena sarveṣāṃ karavālam ālokyācalasenasya nistriṃśadarśanam upajātaṃ /

IX. acalasena āha na me khaḍgo draṣṭuṃ yujyate tridhā nivāraṇe 'pi niścalāt[20] nṛpateṃ[21] cakṣur ekaṃ pidhāya tam eva paśyeti vijane darśite tatkhaḍgajvālayā[22] rājñaś cakṣur ekaṃ bhūmau patitaṃ / prabhāvadarśanād āvarjitaṃ nṛpaṃ vicintya ...... praśastaśilake nikṣipya (?) nirva 'rthīkṛtya[23] śrīnālandāmahāvihāraṃ gatvā veśāntareṇa pravrajitaḥ /

X. śāntidevanāmā praśāntatvāt piṭakatrayaṃ śrutvā dhyāyati sma / bhuñjāno 'pi prabhāsvaraṃ[24] supto 'pi kuṭiṃ gato 'pi tad eveti bhūsukusamādhisamāpannatvāt bhūsukunāmākhyātaṃ /

bzuṅ-pas rta-pa'i tshul mi-g.yo-ba'i-sde źes-pa'i miṅ-can rgyal-pos bkur-ba spyod-pa de-ñid-kyis chos kho-na yid-la byed-ciṅ bźugs-so //

VIII. dus gźan-źig-na rta-pa gźan-rnams-kyis de'i phun-sum-tshogs-pa mi-bzod(P.bzad)-pas rgyal-po la smras-te / mi-g.yo-ba'i-sde 'di ni śiṅ-gi ral-gris khyed bsten(P.brten)-pas 'khrug-pa'i dus-su dgra-la ji-ltar rdeg-par 'gyur // de-bas-na de'i ral-gri blta-bar 'tshal / de-ltar yin-yaṅ draṅ-por smra mi nus-pas rta-pa thams-cad-kyi ral-gri blta-bar bya'o // źes rgyal-pos bka'-stsal-pas kha-cig-gi (P.gis) ral-gri bltas-nas / mi-g.yo-ba'i-sde la yaṅ ral-gri blta'o źes bka'-stsal-to //

IX. des gsuṅs-pa / bdag-gi ral-gri khyed-kyis blta-bar mi 'os źes-so // rgyal-pos nan-tan-gyis yaṅ-daṅ-yaṅ-du źus-pas mi-g.yo-ba na-re cis-kyaṅ mthoṅ-bar 'dod-na phyogs dben-par khyed-raṅ kho-na lag-pas mig gcig bkab-ste / blta-bar gyis-śig de bltas-pas ral-gri'i gzi-brjid(xyl. bzid)-kyis rgyal-po'i mig ma bkab-pa ṅos(?) sa-la lhuṅ-ṅo // nus-pa de mthoṅ-nas rgyal-po śin-tu mos-par 'gyur-bar dgoṅs la mig-gi bu-gar mig bcug-ste / zug-rṅu med-par byas-la gtsug-lag-khaṅ chen-po nālandar gśegs-la / mi-g.yo-ba'i-sde rab-tu byuṅ-ste /

X. (231a) źi-ba daṅ-ldan-pas źi-ba'i lha źes miṅ-btags / der sde-snod gsum mñan(P.mñam)-pa'i rjes-la za-ruṅ ñal-ruṅ 'chags-ruṅ rgyun-tu 'od-gsal bsgom-pas bhu-su-ku źes tiṅ-ṅe-'dzin la gnas-pa'i phyir bhu-su-ku źes miṅ yoṅs-su grags-so //

XI. saṃghe 'pi kālāntareṇa kaiścid bālaiḥ kutūhalibhir ālocitaṃ / kim ayaṃ kiñcij jānāti na veti[25] nirūpyatāṃ tāvat / tatra ca pratyabdaṃ jyaiṣṭhamāsi[26] śukłapakṣe ṛddhiprātihāryaiḥ pūraṇaprabhṛtayaḥ śāstrā pūrvaṃ nirākṛtā iti tadanukāraya pāṭhaḥ kriyate tatraivāyaṃ nirūpyatāṃ ity ayam ādiṣṭaḥ nāhaṃ kiñcij jānāmīti tena punaḥ punaparihāre syadhīṣṭa(?)[27] tair vihārād bahiḥ pūrvottarasyāṃ vistīrṇāyāṃ dharmaśālāyāṃ mahāpaṇḍitamaṇḍalamadhye sa ca svayaṃ cintayati sma

XI. de-nas dus gźan (P. gźag)-źig-na dge-'dun-gyi naṅ-du ma-ruṅs-pa 'ga'-źig-gis / 'dis ni dge-'dun-gyi naṅ-du bya-ba gaṅ yaṅ ma-byas-par sgom-pa ltar gnas-te / ci-śes brtag-dgos źes bgros-la / daṅ-po cho-'phrul-gyi dus-su lo re-re-źiṅ chos 'don-pa yod-pas / 'di-la 'chol dgos źes bsams-nas / de-la źus-te-(P. de) gsuṅs-pa bdag-gis (P. gi) ci-yaṅ mi-śes-so // yaṅ-nas yaṅ-du bkag-kyaṅ de-dag-gis źus-śiṅ gtsug-lag-khaṅ-gi phyi-rol gyi dbaṅ-ldan-gyi phyogs-su sa-phyogs yaṅs-pa la mchod-pa'i rnam-pa du-ma bśams-te / skye-bo ma-lus-pa bos-nas seṅge'i khri śin-tu mthon-po bśams-te spyan-draṅs-so // des der bźugs-śiṅ bsams-te /

XII. pūrvakṛtaṃ sūtrasamuccayaṃ śikṣāsamuccayaṃ bodhicaryāvatārākhyaṃ granthatrayam astīti cetasi kṛtvā siṃhāsanagataḥ prāha kim ārṣaṃ paṭhāmi arthārṣaṃ vā //

XII. mdo-sde kun-las btus-pa daṅ / bslab-pa kun-las btus-pa daṅ / byaṅ-chub spyod-pa la 'jug-pa źes gźuṅ-gsum bdag-gis byas yod-do // de-la spyod-pa la 'jug-pa gdon-par 'os źes bsams-nas gsuṅs-te draṅ-soṅ-gis gsuṅs-pa 'am / de'i-rjes las byuṅ-ba gaṅ gdon /

XIII. tatra ṛṣiḥ paramārthajñānavān ṛṣa gatāv ity atra auṇādikaḥ kviḥ[28] ṛṣiṇā jinena proktam ārṣaṃ nanu prajñāpāramitādau subhūtyādideśitaṃ katham ārṣaṃ ity atrocyate yuvarājāryamaitreyeṇa //

yad arthavad dharmapadopasaṃhitaṃ
tridhātusaṃkleśanivarhaṇaṃ vacaḥ /
bhaved bhavacchāntyanuśaṃsadarśakaṃ[29]

XIII. don-dam rtog-pa ni draṅ-soṅ-ṅo // des mdzad-pa gsuṅ-rab-bo // de-la brten-nas gźan-gyi bya-ba de rjes-las byuṅ-ba'o // 'phags-pa byams-pas de gsuṅs-pa /

gaṅ-gi don-can chos-kyi tshig daṅ-ldan //
khams-gsum ñon-moṅs dag-par byed-pa'i tshig /
źi-ba'i phan-yon ston-par bved-pa de //

tadvat kramārṣaṃ[30] viparītam anyathā //

draṅ-sroṅ las byuṅ de-las bzlog-pa gźan // źes-so //

XIV. tadākṛṣṭam āryādyair[31] arthārṣaṃ subhūtyādideśanā tu bhagavadadhiṣṭhānād ity adoṣaḥ[32] //

XIV. des gaṅ 'chad-par 'gyur-ba le'u (231b) bcu-pa nas /
bdag kyaṅ 'jam-dbyaṅs bka'-drin-gyis /
sa rab-dga'-ba thob bar-du //
rab-tu tshe-rabs dran-pa daṅ /
rab-tu 'byuṅ-ba'aṅ thob-par śog // ces-pa de yaṅ rig-par 'gyur-ro /

XV. kutūhalāt tair uktaṃ arthārṣam eva tāvat paṭhyatām iti caryāvatāraṃ paṭhati sma // tatra ca pāṭhe /

yadā na bhāvo nābhāvo mateḥ santiṣṭhate puraḥ /
tadānyagatyabhāvena nirālamba[ḥ][33] praśāmyati //

ity atra śloke bhagavān mañjuśrīḥ pura āvirbhūtaḥ sa ca tenaiva sārdhaṃṃ antarīkṣagataḥ[34] kramād antarhitaḥ //

XV. de-dag-gi ṅo-mtshar skyes-nas smras-te / gźan-pa 'don-par źu 'tshal ces brjod-pa daṅ / des kyaṅ spyod-pa la 'jug-pa 'don-par brtsams-so //

de-la gaṅ-tshe dṅos daṅ dṅos-min dag //
blo-yi mdun-du mi gnas 'gyur //
de-tshe rnam-pa gźan med-par //
dmigs-pa med-par rab-tu źi //

źes bya-ba 'don-pa'i skabs-su de-la mthoṅ-lam mṅon-du gyur-ba daṅ / 'phags-pa 'jam-dpal mdun-gyi nam-mkha'-la snaṅ // de'i-rjes-la de-daṅ-bcas-pa skye-bo-rnams la mi snaṅ-bar gyur /

XVI. tataḥ bhadradarśanasaṃvignais[35] tallayanavicāre poḍhukuṭyāṃ[36] tatpustakatrayaṃ sūtrasamuccayādi labdhvā paṇḍitair loke pracāritam /

XVI. de-nas de ma-mthoṅ-bas 'gyod-par gyur-pa'i skye-bo rnams-kyis de'i braṅ-khaṅ-du bltas-pas / mdo-sde kun-las btus-pa la sogs-pa gsum blaṅs-te / mkhas-pa rnams kyis sgo-nas 'jig-rten-du grags-par byas-so //

(début du commentaire:) tatra sugatety ādivṛtteḥ /

(début du commentaire:) de-la / bde-gśegs sras-bcas chos-kyi sku daṅ-bcas //

Notes afférentes au texte sanskrit

1 Lire *samyaṅmahāyānagotraḥ.*
2 Lire *kuliśayoginīnirmāṇarūpayā*, cf. T.

3 T. *bhaṃgaladeśam.*

4 Lire *tatra*, cf. T. *der.*

5 Lire *mātur ādeśaṃ.*

6 A.P. lit *tadā deśai°* et traduit: "l'esprit uniquement tendu vers ce pays"!

7 A.P. *kkacid.*

8 Lire *vidhṛtyā°*? T. *bzuṅ* A.P. traduit: "A cause d'elle il détourna son cheval et mit pied à terre". Dans la traduction tibétaine *babs-so* ne correspond pas à *avatāritaḥ* mais à *avatīrṇaḥ*; probablement le traducteur a modifié la construction de la phrase.

9 A.P. traduit: "Ici habite notre maître, celui qui débite de la grande compassion". Le traducteur tibétain a dû lire quelque chose comme: iha mahāvana āste sa kāruṇikaḥ.

10 T. *daridro.*

11 Je ne comprends pas très bien le mot *'bod-pa* 'appeler, inviter' dans le passage tibétain correspondant. Est-ce que *'bod-pa* traduit *āhūto*?

12 Seul le mot *gaṃbhīra* est confirmé par T.

13 Corruption pour *niryātayati* ou *niryātayitvā*, Cf. T. *phul-nas.*

14 T. traduit 'par la méthode qui fait mûrir' (paripācana?). Probablement une traduction erronée de paripāṭīkrama.

15 A.P. traduit 'séjourné'. Je ne sais pas comment corriger *samādhārya.*

16 T. traduit *rāutu* par *rta-pa* 'chevalier'. A.P. lit *raututvena* et traduit: "en qualité de *rauta*".

17 La traduction mot-à-mot du passage tibétain correspondant est: "respecté par le roi avec la même conduite (*tayaiva caryayā*?)".

18 A.P. propose de lire: *rautacaryayā dharmarato.* Il faut évidemment garder *dharmārāmo.*

19 A.P. *adhraṣyo* et, en note, lire: *adhṛṣyo*? Le texte imprimé dans le Descriptive catalogue a *adhṛṣyo.*

20 T. *nirbandhāt*?

21 Lire *nṛpate.*

22 A.P. *tatkhaḍgaccālayā* et, en note, lire *khaḍgacalāyā.* Le texte imprimé dans le Descriptive catalogue a *°jvālayā.*

23 Lire *nirvraṇīkṛtya*? Cf. T.

24 Il y a probablement une lacune dans le texte, cf. T.

25 H.S. et A.P. *naveti.*

26 T.: "au temps des prodiges" (cho-'phrul-gyi dus). Au Tibet *cho-'phrul zla-ba* "le mois des prodiges" est le premier mois de l'année (cf. G. Tharchin, ed., *Yig-bskur rnam-gźag*, Kalimpong, 1956, p. 161). La tradition tibétaine attribue à Tsoṅ-kha-pa l'institution de la fête de la grande prière (*smon-lam chen-mo*) en 1409. Cette fête qui a lieu pendant la

première quinzaine du premier mois commémore les miracles faits par le Buddha, cf. George N. Roerich, *The Blue Annals*, II, Calcutta, 1953, p. 1077; Luciano Petech, *I Missionari Italiani nel Tibet e nel Nepal*, II, Roma, 1953, p. 262; Albert Grünwedel, *Die Tempel von Lhasa*, Heidelberg, 1919, p. 58; Rudolf Kaschwesky, *Das Leben des lamaistischen Heiligen Tsong-khapa Blo-bzaṅ-grags-pa*, I, Wiesbaden, 1971, p. 164 et p. 279, n. 36. Selon Claus Vogel le premier mois tibétain correspond au mois Magha ("On Tibetan Chronology", *CAJ*, IX, 1964, p. 230). Celà est confirmé par le colophon d'une traduction faite par Bu-ston (cf. J. W. de Jong, "Notes à propos des colophons du Kanjur", *Zentralasiatische Studien*, 6, 1972, p. 533, no. 485: *cho-'phrul chen-po rta*; mong.: *qubilγan mag sara*). Dans deux des colophons, publiés par Bacot, se rencontre le mois *cho-'phrul zla-ba* mais l'équivalent sanskrit n'y est pas mentionné ("Titres et colophons d'ouvrages non canoniques tibétains", *BEFEO*, XLIV, 1954, p. 294, no. 39 et p. 316, lignes 1-2). Dans l'Inde même les opinions des bouddhistes sur le début de l'année ont beaucoup varié (cf. Claus Vogel, "Die Jahreszeiten im Spiegel der altindischen Literatur", *ZDMG*, 121, 1971, pp. 296-303). Nous ne savons pas si, au treizième siècle, le "temps des prodiges" était un autre nom pour le "mois des prodiges" et quel mois indien était censé correspondre au "temps des prodiges".

27 A.P. *punaḥ puna*[*ḥ*] *parihāre syadhista*[*ḥ*].

28 Lire ṛṣī gatāv ity atra auṇādikaḥ kin. Note du professeur Ōjihara: Lire '(auṇādikaḥ) k-in', au lieu de '(...) kviḥ'. Uṇ. 4.119 (= 559, d'après la numérotation de la SK., Uṇādiprakaraṇa): – 'ig-upadhāt k-it' ('in', 4.117 = 557) – sū. qu'illustre la SK. par 'kṛṣiḥ / ṛṣiḥ / śuciḥ / lipiḥ //' Tattvabodhinī: – 'kṛṣa vilekhane, ṛṣī gatau, śuca śoke, lipa upadehe, ityāder ig-upadhād dhātor in syāt, sa ca k-it'. Même remarque chez les lexicographes. Ainsi "Ṭīkāsarvasva" ad Amara 2.7.43a ('ṛṣayaḥ satyavacasaḥ'): – 'jñānasya pāra-gamanād ṛṣiḥ / "ṛṣī gatau" / "ig-upadhāt kiḥ" iti kiḥ" (sic éd. Gaṇapati S., TSS LI, p. 37) – Lire ici aussi '... k-it" iti k-in', quoique la leçon 'kiḥ' ressemble bien plus à celle de Haraprasad S. 'kviḥ'; Śabdakalpadruma, s.v. ṛṣi: – 'ṛṣati prāpnoti sarvān mantrān, jñānena paśyati saṃsāra-pāraṃ vā, iti / ṛṣ + "ig-upadhāt k-it" iti uṇādisūtreṇa in / k-ic ca / jñāna-saṃsāra-yoḥ pāra-gantā //' Cf. Vācaspatyam, cité par MW (Dictionary, s.v. ṛṣi, init.): 'ṛṣati jñānena saṃsāra-pāram'. Etant donné la paraphrase de √ṛṣ- par pra-√āp-, ainsi que la mention pāragamana- ou °-gantṛ-, il paraît bien que les commentateurs indigènes ont compris 'ṛṣī gatau' (dh. 6.7) comme signifiant "√ṛṣ-, au sens de 'mouvement'." De cette même racine, le mot ṛkṣa- est censé dériver avec l'uṇ. -sa-: Uṇ. 3. 66 sq. (= 346 sq., SK.), d'abord nt. comme

synonyme de nakṣatra-, puis msc. "ours".

29 Lire *bhavec ca yacchānty°*. Cf. Ratnagotravibhāga V.18.

30 Lire *tad uktam ārṣaṃ*.

31 A.P. *āryyadvair*.

32 Le texte de T. est tout à fait différent. La stance citée est Bodhicaryāvatāra X.51.

33 Lire *nirālambā*. Cf. Bodhicaryāvatārapañjikā, ed. L. de La Vallée Poussin, p. 417.

34 A.P. *sārdham mantarīkṣsagatah* et, en note, lire *antarikṣagataḥ*.

35 Lire *tatas tadadarśanasaṃvignais*?

36 A.P. *poṭhukuṭhyāṃ* et, en note: *poṭhokuṭhyāṃ* pour *pothīkuṇḍyām*.

Traduction du texte tibétain

I. Ainsi est raconté par la tradition. Il naquit dans le Sud à Śrīnagara comme fils du roi Mañjuśrīvarman. Il avait servi les Buddha du passé et il avait obtenu des racines de bien conduisant à la libération. Il appartenait à la vraie lignée du Mahāyāna et était expert en tous les arts. Au moment de sa consécration comme prince héritier, sa mère, la reine principale, incarnation d'une kuliśayoginī, le fit baigner dans de l'eau chaude. Quand elle vit qu'il ne supportait pas la chaleur, elle lui dit:

II. "Si, à l'époque de la corruption (kaṣāyakāle), tu es roi, tu feras souffrir les êtres vivants par la force de la passion. Après la mort tu souffriras en enfer des souffrances encore plus terribles que celle (produite par l'eau chaude). Le royaume ne te servira à rien. Va au pays Bhaṃgala. Là tu obtiendras la bénédiction de Mañjughoṣa".

III. Alors, lui, acceptant respectueusement l'ordre de sa mère, droit d'esprit, s'en alla, monté sur un cheval bai. Jour et nuit, il continua son chemin pendant plusieurs jours sans penser ni à la boisson ni à la nourriture, l'esprit tout entier résolu à exécuter son ordre. A l'extrémité du pays Bhaṃgala il vit dans une forêt une belle fille. La fille retint son cheval et il descendit de son cheval.

IV. Extrêmement assoiffé et voyant de l'eau devant lui il fut sur le point de la boire. La fille lui dit: "C'est de l'eau empoisonnée. N'en bois pas!" L'en détournant, elle lui fit boire de l'eau ambroisique, cuisit de la viande et l'en nourrit.

V. Rassasié, il dit à la fille: "D'où viens-tu?" Elle répondit: "Au milieu de cette grande forêt vit mon maître; paré d'une masse de qualités excellentes et compatissant, il a accompli le samādhi de Śrī Mañjuvajra.

Je viens de chez lui". Rien qu'en entendant cela il fut réconforté par une grande joie comme un pauvre qui a obtenu un joyau.

VI. "Montre-le moi", dit-il et, invité (?) par la fille, il prit son cheval et partit. En arrivant il vit l'excellent maître à l'esprit très profond et au corps et à la parole apaisés, semblable à une montagne d'or. Faisant l'offrande de soi-même et de son cheval excellent, il vénéra le maître avec respect. Il lui dit: "Faites-moi la grâce de m'enseigner le samādhi de Mañjughoṣa".

VII. Le maître l'instruisit par la méthode systématique. Quand il eut séjourné là pendant douze ans, par la méditation il obtint une vision de Mañjughoṣa. Ensuite le maître lui ordonna d'aller au Madhyadeśa. Il y alla et entra au service du roi de Magadha, en qualité de chevalier sous le nom d'Acalasena, avec une épée en bois pourvue d'un fourreau. Respecté par le roi, il le servit, l'esprit uniquement occupé du dharma.

VIII. Après quelque temps les autres chevaliers ne supportant pas sa fortune dirent au roi: "Cet Acalasena vous sert avec une épée en bois. En temps de guerre comment pourrait-il frapper les ennemis? Veuillez examiner son épée". Puisqu'il ne pouvait pas dire la vérité le roi ordonna d'examiner les épées de tous les chevaliers. Ayant examiné l'épée de plusieurs, il dit à Acalasena: "Je désire voir ton épée".

IX. Il lui dit: "Mon épée ne doit pas être vue par vous". Quand le roi le demanda avec insistance à plusieurs reprises, Acalasena lui dit: "Si vous désirez la voir à tout prix, regardez-la dans un endroit solitaire après avoir couvert de la main un œil." Le roi regarda mais par l'éclat de l'épée l'œil du roi qui n'était pas couvert tomba à terre. Pensant que le roi était converti par la vue de sa puissance il mit l'œil dans son trou et il le guérit de sa souffrance. Il se rendit au grand vihāra de Nālandā. Acalasena devint religieux.

X. En raison de sa tranquillité on lui donna le nom Śāntideva. Ayant écouté les trois piṭaka, il méditait sur la lumière sans interruption en mangeant, en dormant et en marchant. Persistant ainsi dans le samādhi appelé bhusuku, il fut connu sous le nom de Bhusuku.

XI. Après quelque temps un homme très méchant dans la communauté réfléchit: "Lui, il ne fait rien dans la communauté et se comporte comme s'il médite. Il faut examiner ce qu'il sait". Il pensa: "Chaque année au temps des prodiges on récite le dharma. C'est alors qu'il faut l'examiner". Sur sa demande (de réciter le dharma) il lui dit: "Je ne sais rien". Bien qu'il refusa à plusieurs reprises, ils (continuèrent) à demander. Ensuite ils préparèrent plusieurs sortes d'offrandes dans un grand espace au nord-est en dehors du vihāra. Ils convoquèrent tout le monde et, ayant préparé un siège de lion élevé, l'invitèrent (à y prendre place). Il s'y assit et réfléchit:

XII. "J'ai composé trois livres, appelé Sūtrasamuccaya, Śikṣāsamuccaya et Bodhicaryāvatāra. Il convient de réciter le Bodhicaryāvatāra". Il dit: "Est-ce que je récite ce qui est dit par les ṛṣi ou ce qui est venu à la suite de cela?"

XIII. Le ṛṣi est celui qui comprend le sens suprême. C'est lui qui a composé les écritures sacrées. Ce qui est fait par d'autres en s'y basant est "ce qui est venu à la suite de cela". Le noble Maitreya a dit: "La parole qui est pourvue de sens, qui est en possession des paroles du Dharma, qui purifie les souillures du triple monde et qui montre les avantages de l'apaisement de l'existence, provient des ṛṣi. Toute autre (parole) en est l'opposé".

XIV. Il faut aussi savoir (le vers suivant) du dixième chapitre qui sera expliqué par lui:

"Puissé-je toujours me rappeler mes naissances et obtenir la sortie du monde jusqu'à ce que, par la grâce de Mañjughoṣa, j'obtienne la Terre Pramuditā".

XV. Étonnés, ils dirent: "Nous vous prions de réciter autre chose". Il commença de réciter le Bodhicaryāvatāra. Quand il récita: "Lorsque ni existence ni non-existence ne se présentent plus devant l'esprit, alors, n'ayant plus de champ (l'esprit) privé de point d'appui s'apaise", le noble Mañjuśrī apparut dans l'air devant lui dans son champ de vision. Ensuite il disparut avec lui de la vue des hommes.

XVI. Ne le voyant plus, les hommes, pleins de remords, examinèrent sa cellule. Ils en prirent les trois livres, Sūtrasamuccaya, etc., qui furent (ensuite) répandus dans le monde par les savants.

Il est évident que les textes sanskrit et tibétain doivent remonter au même texte original. Les différences entre les deux versions dans les sections XIII et XIV sont dûes à des additions. Le texte sanskrit a ajouté une phrase sur l'étymologie de ṛṣi (ṛṣī gatāv ity atra auṇādikaḥ kin) et une référence à l'enseignement de Subhūti: nanu prajñāpāramitādau subhūtyādideśitaṃ katham ārṣam "Comment ce qui a été enseigné par Subhūti dans la Prajñāpāramitā, etc. peut-il être *ārṣa*?"[33] Le passage précédent explique qu'*ārṣa* est ce qui est dit par le *ṛṣi*, i.e. le *jina*. Le texte tibétain est légèrement différent: des mdzad-pa gsuṅ-rab-bo = tatkṛtam pravacanam. Ensuite le texte tibétain continue en expliquant qu'*arthārṣa* (Tib.

[33] Mlle Pezzali traduit: "C'est ce qui, n'est-ce pas, a été, au début de la *Prajñāpāramitā*, montré à Subhūti et aux autres. 'Comment est l'*ārṣa*'?".

"ce qui est venu à la suite de cela") est ce qui est fait par d'autres en s'y basant: tadāśritam anyaiḥ kṛtam (?). Cette explication se trouve dans la section XIV du texte sanskrit: tadākṛṣṭam āryādyair arthārṣam (lire tadākṛṣṭam anyādyair arthārṣam?). Ensuite le texte sanskrit ajoute: subhūty° ... adoṣaḥ alors que la version tibétaine cite une stance du dixième chapitre du Bodhicaryāvatāra. Dans la section XIII Vibhūticandra, auteur de la légende de Śāntideva, cite une stance du Ratnagotravibhāga (V.18). Probablement, il a lu cette stance dans la Bodhicaryāvatārapañjikā de Prajñākaramati (éd. L. de La Vallée Poussin, p. 432.14-17) et non dans le Ratnagotravibhāga même. Vibhūticandra ne cite pas la stance suivante du Ratnagotravibhāga qui explique que pareil à *ārṣa* est tout ce qui est dit par des gens à l'esprit non-distrait en se référant au Jina comme le seul maître et ce qui est conforme au chemin de l'accumulation qui fait obtenir la délivrance:

yat syād avikṣiptamanobhir uktam
śāstāram ekaṃ jinam uddiśadbhiḥ
mokṣāptisaṃbhārapathānukūlaṃ
mūrdhnā tad apy ārṣam iva pratīcchet.

Le Ratnagotravibhāga ne fait pas de distinction entre *ārṣa* et *arthārṣa* (Tib. de-rjes las byuṅ-ba), mais dit que tout ce qui est dit en conformité avec certaines conditions est *ārṣam iva*. Pour *ārṣa* Mlle Pezzali renvoie à la Bodhisattvabhūmi (éd. Wogihara p. 385.17[34]) où le nirvāṇa est dit être *ārṣa*. Edgerton avait déjà remarqué qu'*ārṣa* est ici une corruption pour *ārṣabha*.[35] L'édition de la Bodhisattvabhūmi par Nalinaksha Dutt a, en effet, *ārṣabha* au lieu d'*ārṣa* (p. 266.6). Le mot *ārṣa* se rencontre dans le Mahāyānasūtrālaṃkāra (XVIII.31): *ārṣaś ca deśanādharmo*, mais le commentaire ne l'explique pas. Il se peut très bien que le mot *arthārṣa* soit corrompu mais la version tibétaine qui en donne une traduction libre ne permet pas de le corriger. On ne retrouve la distinction entre *ārṣa* et *arthārṣa* ni chez Bu-ston ni chez Tāranātha. Le premier parle de ce qui était connu autrefois (sṅar grags-pa) et ce qui ne l'est pas (ma grags-pa) et le dernier de ce qui existait autrefois (sṅar byuṅ-ba) et ce qui ne l'est pas (ma byuṅ-ba).[36] Pour conclure cette discussion signalons encore que, dans section XV, le texte sanskrit a *arthārṣam* mais la version tibétaine *gźan-pa* = *anyad*.

[34] Mlle Pezzali renvoie à p. 385, l.15.
[35] Buddhist Hybrid Sanskrit Dictionary, s.v. *ārṣa* et *ārṣabha*.
[36] Bu-ston, *Chos-'byuṅ*, éd. de Bkra-śis lhun-po f. 127a3 (A.P., p. 6); Tāranātha, éd. Schiefner, p. 127.8 (A.P., p. 14).

En dehors du passage sur *ārṣa* et *arthārṣa* la légende de Śāntideva contient plusieurs éléments qui mériteraient d'être étudiés pour comprendre l'origine et le développement de la légende. Il ne semble guère possible d'y découvrir un noyau historique qui permettrait de déterminer où et quand Sāntideva a vécu. En ce qui concerne les dates de Śāntideva il y a deux hypothèses. La première remonte à Bendall qui s'est servi de l'ouvrage de Tāranātha.[37] Bendall conclut que Śāntideva a vécu au milieu du VIIème siècle car, selon Tāranātha, il naquit pendant le règne d'un fils du roi Harṣa, nommé Śīla, qui aurait vécu pendant 140 ans et qui aurait régné presque cent ans. On ne peut pas avoir beaucoup confiance en ce que raconte Tāranātha car, comme le dit Bendall lui-même: "It is true that neither this 'Çīla' (if that be his real name) nor any other son of Çrīharṣa is known to either Indian or Chinese records" (pp. III-IV). Ajoutons que, si Śāntideva était né pendant le règne centenaire d'un fils de Harṣa, il aurait vécu plus tard qu'au milieu du VIIème siècle. Bendall signale aussi que, selon Tāranātha, Śāntideva a dû être un contemporain plus jeune de Dharmapāla (p. III, n. 3). Nous sommes assez bien renseignés sur Dharmapāla et Ui Hakuju a même essayé de calculer exactement ses dates (530-561).[38] Bendall pensait que Dharmapāla avait vécu au début du VIIème siècle comme l'avait dit Takakusu.[39] On voit donc que les renseignements, donnés par Tāranātha, sont contradictoires. Si Śāntideva naquit pendant le règne du fils de Harṣa, il a dû vivre pendant la deuxième moitié du VIIème siècle ou même plus tard. En tant que contemporain de Dharmapāla il n'a pas pu vivre plus tard que la deuxième moitié du VIème siècle. Signalons encore que Tāranātha ne semble pas être bien renseigné sur Dharmapāla car il le confond avec Dharmapāla de Suvarṇadvīpa, le maître d'Atīśa (982-1054).[40]

La deuxième hypothèse a été avancée pour la première fois par B. Bhattacharya en 1926.[41] Selon lui, Śāntideva a dû vivre après le départ de l'Inde d'I-tsing car ni I-tsing ni Hsüan-tsang mentionnent Śāntideva. D'autre part, il a dû vivre avant le départ de Śāntirakṣita pour le Tibet car ce dernier cite une stance du Bodhicaryāvatāra (I.10) dans un ouvrage,

[37] Çikshāsamuccaya (*Bibliotheca Buddhica*, I, 1897-1902), Introduction, pp. III-VI.

[38] *Indo tetsugaku kenkyū*, vol. V (Tokyo, 1929; réimprimé en 1965), pp. 128-132. Déjà, en 1911, Noël Peri avait écrit que Dharmapāla mourut vraisemblablement aux environs de l'année 560, "A propos de la date de Vasubandhu", *BEFEO*, XI (1911), p. 383.

[39] Cf. l'introduction à sa traduction d'I-tsing, *A Record of the Buddhist Religion* (Oxford, 1896), p. lviii.

[40] Cf. Tāranātha, trad. A. Schiefner, pp. 161-2.

[41] Cf. sa préface à l'édition du Tattvasaṃgraha (*Gaekwad Or. Ser.*, vol. XXX (Baroda,

intitulé Tattvasiddhi, que le colophon lui attribue. En rectifiant les dates, mentionnées par Bhattacharya, Mlle Pezzali conclut que la vie de Śāntideva, ou tout au moins la période productive de sa vie en tant que maître bouddhiste, se situe entre 685 et 763.[42] Ce raisonnement serait irréfutable si la Tattvasiddhi était, en effet, l'ouvrage de Śāntirakṣita et si, d'autre part, le fait qu'I-tsing ne mentionne pas Śāntideva, signifiait qu'il n'a pas pu vivre avant 685. Il faut attendre la publication de la Tattvasiddhi pour pouvoir vérifier l'exactitude de l'attribution de cet ouvrage à Śāntirakṣita. En ce qui concerne l'*argumentum ex silentio*, inutile de dire qu'il faut le manier avec circonspection. Pour autant que je sache, on n'a pas encore montré que Hsüan-tsang et I-tsing aient mentionné tous les maîtres bouddhistes de quelque importance qui ont vécu pendant ou avant leur séjour dans l'Inde.

Bendall avait déjà remarqué que la date de la traduction tibétaine du Śikṣāsamuccaya fournit le *terminus ad quem*. Selon lui, le *terminus ad quem* est l'année 800 (p. V). On arrive presque à la même date en tenant compte des dates des traducteurs du Bodhicaryāvatāra. Cet ouvrage a été traduit par Sarvajñadeva et Dpal-brtsegs d'un manuscrit provenant du Kaśmīr. Ensuite, la traduction a été corrigée à l'aide d'un manuscrit venant du Madhyadeśa par Dharmaśrībhadra, Rin-chen bzaṅ-po et Śā-kya blo-gros. Cette traduction fut révisée par Sumatikīrti et Blo-ldan śes-rab.[43] Dpal-brtsegs est un traducteur bien connu. Il a travaillé au début du neuvième siècle. Il est, en outre, un des compilateurs d'une liste de traductions existant dans le palais de Ldan-kar.[44] Cette liste indique après chaque titre le nombre total des śloka composant l'ouvrage. Mlle Lalou s'est demandée quel est le sens du mot śloka quand il s'agit d'ouvrages en prose et en vers ou uniquement en prose. Le même problème se poserait d'ailleurs si un ouvrage, écrit en vers, utilisait d'autres mètres

1926)), p. XXIII: "The evidence of Tattvasiddhi where Śāntarakṣita quotes a full śloka from the Bodhicaryāvatāra once for all settles the question (of Śānti Deva's date). It proves that Śānti Deva flourished in a period between the departure of I-Tsing from India in 695 and before Śāntarakṣita's first visit to Tibet in A.D. 743." (T. R. V. Murti, *The Central Philosophy of Buddhism* (London, 1955), p. 100, n. 6). Je cite ce passage d'après l'ouvrage de Murti car l'édition du Tattvasaṃgraha n'est pas à ma disposition.

[42] Kanakura que Mlle Pezzali ne mentionne pas arrive à une conclusion semblable. Selon lui Śāntideva naquit dans la deuxième moitié du VIIème siècle et exerça son activité aux environs de l'année 700 (Kanakura Enshō, *Satori ye no michi* (Tōkyō, 1957), pp. 232-3).

[43] Cf. Friedrich Weller, *Über den Quellenbezug eines mongolischen Tanjurtextes* (Berlin, 1950), p. 88.

[44] Marcelle Lalou, "Les textes bouddhiques au temps du roi Khri-sroṅ-lde-bcan", *JA* (1953), pp. 313-353. M. Tucci suppose que la liste a été compilée en 812, cf. G. Tucci, *Minor Buddhist Texts*, II (Roma, 1958,) pp. 46-8, n. 1.

que le śloka. Sans aucun doute, les compilateurs de cette liste ont suivi l'usage indien d'utiliser le śloka comme unité de mesure, le śloka désignant un texte contenant 32 syllables qu'il soit écrit en prose ou en vers. Selon la liste de Dpal-brtsegs, le Bodhicaryāvatāra contient 600 śloka et deux bam-po. Tāranātha mentionne trois recensions du Bodhicaryāvatāra, une recension kaśmīrienne en plus de 1000 śloka, une recension orientale en 700 śloka et une recension du Madhyadeśa en 1000 śloka. L. de La Vallée Poussin et Sylvain Lévi ont déjà étudié ce passage de Tāranātha.[45] La liste de Dpal-brtsegs leur était inconnue. Le fait que le traducteur même du Bodhicaryāvatāra indique que l'ouvrage ne contient que 700 śloka n'est pas dénué d'intérêt. L'ouvrage actuel contient 913 vers en dix chapitres. Selon Tāranātha, les orientaux supprimèrent les chapitres II et IX.[46] On arrive ainsi à un total de 679 vers. Le colophon de la traduction tibétaine dit que Dpal-brtsegs s'est servi d'un manuscrit kaśmīrien, mais, d'après Tāranātha, ce n'est pas la recension kaśmīrienne mais la recension orientale qui contient 700 śloka. Bu-ston s'est aussi occupé de ce problème dans un passage de son Chos-'byuṅ que Mlle Pezzali n'a pas signalé: byaṅ-chub sems-dpa'i spyod-'jug źi-ba lhas mdzad-pa rṅog-'gyur / 'di dkar-chag chen-mo gsum-gar śu-log drug-brgya bam-po gñis źes 'byuṅ mod-kyi śu-log stoṅ-du grags-so // spyod-'jug le'u dgu-pa blo-gros mi-zad-pas mdzad zer-ba de daṅ 'di mi-gcig ces smra-ba maṅ-yaṅ sdig-bśags-kyi le'u logs-su byas ma-byas-kyi khyad-par daṅ 'gyur sṅa-phyi'i khyad ma-gtogs-pa gcig-par kho-bo smra'o[47] – "Le Bodhicaryāvatāra, écrit par Śāntideva, et traduit par Rṅog (i.e. Blo-ldan śes-rab, cf. ci-

[45] L. de La Vallée Poussin, "Çāntideva et la composition du Bodhicaryāvatāra d'après Tāranātha", *Muséon*, XI (1892), p. 68 sq.; "Une version chinoise du Bodhicaryāvatāra", *Muséon*, n.s. IV (1903), p. 313 sq.; Sylvain Lévi, "Une version chinoise du Bodhicaryāvatāra", *BEFEO*, II (1902), pp. 253-255.

[46] Mlle Pezzali traduit: "Ils abrégèrent les chapitres sur la confession et sur la sagesse" (p. 14), mais *'chad-pa* ne signifie pas 'abréger' mais 'supprimer' (cf. Jäschke: *'chad-pa* 'to be cut off'). Schiefner traduit: "es fehlt der Abschnitt von dem Sündenbekenntniss, der Abschnitt von der Weisheit" (pp. 165-6).

[47] Éd. de Lhasa f. 159a2-4.

[48] Le catalogue du palais Ldan-dkar (dkar-chag ldan-dkar-ma) doit être un de ces trois grands catalogues. Bu-ston s'y réfère dans une énumération de catalogues (cf. Seyfort Ruegg, *op. cit.*, p. 19, n. 2). Le premier catalogue, mentionné par Bu-ston, est le catalogue du palais de Ldan-dkar: Pho-braṅ stod (xyl. stoṅ)-thaṅ ldan-dkar-gyi dkar-chag. Les deux autres catalogues sont probablement le catalogue du monastère 'Phaṅ-thaṅ-ka-med ('phaṅ-thaṅ-ka-med-kyi dkar-chag ou dkar-chag 'phaṅ-thaṅ-ma) et le catalogue de Mchims-phu près de Bsam-yas (bsam-yas mchims-phu'i dkar-chag). Sur Mchims-phu voir A. Ferrari, *Mk'yen brtse's Guide to the Holy Places of Central Tibet* (Roma, 1958), p. 115, n. 145. Les catalogues de Ldan-dkar et de 'Phaṅ-thaṅ-ka-med sont aussi mentionnés dans le dkar-chag du Kanjur d'Urga, cf. Lokesh Chandra, "A newly discovered Urga Edition of the Tibetan Kanjur", *IIJ*, 3 (1959), p. 181.

dessus). Il est dit dans les trois grands catalogues[48] qu'il contient 600 śloka et deux bam-po mais c'est un fait bien connu qu'il contient 1000 śloka. Il y en a beaucoup qui disent que le neuvième chapitre du Bodhicaryāvatāra a été écrit par Blo-gros mi-zad-pa (Akṣayamati) et qu'il [l'ouvrage en 600 vers?] n'est pas identique à celui-ci [l'ouvrage en 1000 vers?], mais je déclare qu'ils sont identiques, abstraction faite de la différence (résultant) de l'exclusion ou non du chapitre II et de la différence entre l'ancienne et la nouvelle traduction."[49]

On a beaucoup discuté du problème que pose l'attribution d'un Sūtrasamuccaya à Śāntideva.[50] Pour autant que je sache, on n'a pas signalé le fait que, dans la section des śāstra du Mahāyāna, la liste de Dpal-brtsegs énumère au début les cinq ouvrages suivants: (655) Śikṣāsamuccaya, (656) Jātakamālā, (657) Mdo-sde sna-tshogs-kyi mdo btus-pa (titre sanskrit reconstruit par Mlle Lalou: Viśvasūtrasamuccaya), (658) Sūtrasamuccaya, (659) Bodhicaryāvatāra. Le Sūtrasamuccaya désigne certainement l'ouvrage que le Tanjur attribue à Nāgārjuna. Tous les deux sont en cinq bam-po.[51] Le *Mdo-sde sna-tshogs-kyi mdo btus-pa* n'existe plus aujourd'hui et la possibilité n'est pas exclue que cet ouvrage soit identique au Sūtrasamuccaya que les commentateurs indiens du Bodhicaryāvatāra et les historiens tibétains attribuent à Śāntideva.

La monographie que Mlle Pezzali a consacrée à Śāntideva ne nous aide guère à avoir une idée exacte des recherches faites jusqu'alors.[52] Śāntideva est un des plus grands écrivains de l'Inde bouddhique. Il y a encore beaucoup de problèmes à résoudre en ce qui concerne sa vie et ses ouvrages et il faut espérer que la découverte de données nouvelles aideront à dissiper des obscurités qui sont encore plus épaisses qu'on ne le suppose généralement.

[49] Kanakura cite le début de ce passage, *op. cit.*, p. 238, n. 6.

[50] Aux indications bibliographiques, données par Mlle Pezzali (pp. 80-87) il faut ajouter: Sasaki Kōken, "Śikṣāsamuccaya, Sūtrasamuccaya no kankei ni tsuite", *Indogaku Bukkyōgaku kenkyū*, XIV (1965), pp. 180-3; Ichishima Masao, "Sūtrasamuccaya no sakusha ni tsuite", *id.*, XVI (1968), pp. 844-6; "Sūtra-samuccaya ni tsuite", *Tendai gakuhō*, 8 (1967), pp. 49-53; "Sūtra-samuccaya no bonbun danpen", *id.*, 14 (1972), pp. 165-169.

[51] Cf. Marcelle Lalou, *op. cit.*, p. 335; P. Cordier, *Catalogue*, III p. 323: Mdo-'grel XXX.29.

[52] Il paraît superflu de signaler toutes les fautes et erreurs commises par Mlle Pezzali mais il faut, au moins, signaler que la traduction mongole est indubitablement basée sur la version tibétaine. Selon Mlle Pezzali, M. Weller insiste sur l'impossibilité de préciser actuellement si la version mongole est basée sur la version tibétaine ou l'original sanscrit (p. 59). Citons M. Weller lui-même: "Bedürfte es dieses Beweises noch, dass Mo [i.e. la traduction mongole] aus dem Tibetischen übersetzt wurde, dann wäre er aus den beiden eben angestellten Betrachtungen schlüssig abzuleiten" (*op. cit.*, p. 2).

Biography of Dharmasvāmin (Chag lo-tsa-ba Chos-rje-dpal). A Tibetan Monk Pilgrim. Original Tibetan text deciphered and translated by George Roerich. With a historical and critical introduction by A. S. Altekar (= *K. P. Jayaswal Research Institute, Patna, Historical Research Series,* II), (Patna, 1959), xlv + 119 pp. Rs. 8/–

Parmi les textes, photographiés au Tibet par Rāhula Sāṅkṛityāyana, se trouve un manuscrit de la biographie (*rnam-t'ar*) de C'os-rje-dpal (1197–1264). L'intérêt principal de cette biographie réside dans la relation du voyage de C'os-rje-dpal dans l'Inde au moment où le Bouddhisme succombait aux attaques des conquérants islamites. Elle contient des descriptions détaillées de Bodhgayā et de Nālandā, des observations sur la situation religieuse et sociale et une peinture animée des dangers d'un voyage à cette époque troublée.

L'ouvrage, publié par le K. P. Jayaswal Research Institute comme deuxième volume de la *Historical Research Series*, est le produit de la collaboration de deux savants dont on déplore la disparution récente: A. S. Altekar (1898–1959) et G. Roerich (1902–1960). On doit au premier une longue introduction (pp.i-xxxviii) divisée en huit sections qui portent les titres suivants: I. Importance of the work; II. Indo-Tibetan intercourse; III. The life of Dharmasvāmin; IV. Reliability of the account; V. Light on the political history; VI. Effect of the Muslim conquest in Bihar; VII. Religious and social conditions; VIII. Light on geography and topography. Altekar met en lumière l'importance du témoignage de C'os-rje-dpal pour la connaissance de l'Inde de cette époque. Son excellent travail est d'un grand intérêt pour l'étude de l'histoire de l'Inde dans la première moitié du 13e siècle. Quelques petites erreurs sont à rectifier. Altekar écrit à plusieurs reprises que l'oncle de C'os-rje-dpal, C'ag lo-tsā-ba dGra-bcom (1153–1216), est mort dans l'Inde (pp.ii, v, xii) mais la biographie n'en dit rien. Elle raconte que, dans l'Inde, il fut le compagnon fidèle de dPyal lo-tsā-ba C'os-kyi-bzaṅ-po et qu'il mourut à l'âge de 64 ans (f.4b du texte tibétain). – C'os-rje-dpal participa à la traduction d'une trentaine de textes énumérés par Roerich (pp. xliii–xlv). Il n'en est pas l'auteur comme le dit Altekar (p.xi). – Enfin, la biographie ne mentionne pas la date de naissance de

C'os-rje-dpal (p.xi). Apparemment, le premier ouvrage qui l'indique est le *Deb-t'er sṅon-po* (trad. Roerich, p. 1057). La biographie ne contient que quelques dates: l'année *'brug* (43a); l'année *yos* (43a); l'année *rta* (44a); l'année *śiṅ-p'o-byi* (47b). La dernière date est celle de la mort de C'os-rje-dpal (1264). A l'exception de celle-ci, toutes les dates sont notées d'après le cycle duodénaire que l'on a dû employer encore longtemps après 1027. Nous avons déjà signalé que l'emploi de ce cycle explique la différence entre les dates de Milarépa d'après son *rnam-t'ar* et des ouvrages historiques: 1052–1135 et 1040–1123 (cf. *Mi la ras pa'i rnam thar*, 's-Gravenhage, 1959, pp. 11–12). Selon Roerich, gŹon-nu-dpal, l'auteur du Deb-t'er sṅon-po, a dû se servir de la biographie de C'os-rje-dpal pour l'esquisse de sa vie (trad. Roerich, pp. 1057–1059). Probablement gŹon-nu-dpal, qui attachait beaucoup d'importance à une chronologie exacte, a calculé la date de naissance de C'os-rje-dpal d'après un passage de sa biographie selon lequel il avait 61 ans dans l'année *rta* (1258).[1] Peut-être, c'est aussi sa biographie qui lui a fourni les dates de dGra-bcom, l'oncle de C'os-rje-dpal. Elle raconte qu'il exhorta C'os-rje-dpal à aller dans l'Inde quand celui-ci avait vingt ans. Immédiatement après il est fait mention de la mort de dGra-bcom à l'âge de 64 ans (4a-b). En supposant que ces deux événements aient eu lieu dans la même année – ce que la biographie ne dit pas -, on peut faire le calcul suivant: C'os-rje-dpal avait vingt ans en 1216, l'année de la mort de dGra-bcom; donc celui-ci naquit en 1153. Cet exemple peut nous montrer de quelle manière gŹon-nu-dpal a dû procéder souvent pour établir des dates. Il faut donc se garder d'avoir une trop grande confiance dans les dates mentionnées dans le Deb-t'er sṅon-po. Des sources, telles que la biographie de C'os-rje-dpal, ne se préoccupaient guère de problèmes chronologiques. Aussi, elles reposent souvent sur des traditions orales mises bout à bout pour faire un récit continu. Ainsi, C'os-dpal dar-dpyaṅ, l'auteur de la biographie de C'os-rje-dpal, cite partout les paroles de celui-ci. Celà ne prouve nullement qu'il ait écrit la biographie sous la dictée de C'os-rje-dpal comme le dit Roerich (p.xxxix). On ignore la date de C'os-dpal dar-dpyaṅ ainsi que celle de Śes-rab dbaṅ-p'yug qui l'a exhorté à écrire la biographie. D'après le colophon, C'os-dpal dar-dpyaṅ a composé son ouvrage à 'Ju-p'u, endroit où C'os-rje-dpal a posé ses pieds. Ce passage suggère plutôt que la biographie a été écrite après la mort de C'os-rje-dpal à un endroit où l'on avait gardé la mémoire de ses paroles.

De même que l'on doit déduire la date de naissance de C'os-rje-dpal des données que contient la biographie, de même la date de son voyage dans l'Inde ne peut être déterminée qu'indirectement d'après les indications suivantes: après la mort de dGra-bcom C'os-rje-dpal fait voeu d'aller à Bodhgayā (4b); ensuite il étudie pendant dix ans au gTsaṅ (5a); de là il part au Népal où il reste huit ans (7b); il séjourne pendant deux ans au Magadha (38a). Faisant ce calcul, Roerich arrive aux conclusions suivantes: en 1216 C'os-rje-dpal décide de partir; en 1226 il quitte gTsaṅ et en 1234 le Népal; donc c'est en 1234 ou environ qu'il part pour l'Inde (p.xli). La fragilité de ce calcul est évidente bien que, faute d'autres données, on soit bien obligé de l'adopter. Il faut tenir compte de la marge d'incertitude qui entoure la date du voyage de C'os-rje-dpal. On ne peut donc suivre Altekar quand il dit que la date de 1234 pour la rencontre de C'os-rje-dpal avec le roi Buddhasena est "quite definite" (p.xv,n.1), Il est certes vrai que, pour l'époque en question, la chronologie des sources tibétaines est beaucoup plus sûre que celle des sources indiennes mais il ne faut pas croire que les dates, empruntées aux sources tibétaines, soient inébranlables.

[1] D'après le système de calcul des Tibétains la date de naissance devrait être 1198 et non 1197. Le fait que C'os-rje-dpal est mort dans le mois Mārgaśīrṣa (f.47b) explique peut-être le calcul de gŹon-nu-dpal. Voir les remarques de M. R. A. Stein sur les difficultés que comporte la fixation de la date du Nouvel An (*JA*, 1952, p. 96).

Dans la section, consacrée à la géographie et à la topographie, Altekar essaie de déterminer la longueur d'une étape, mesure utilisée par C'os-rje-dpal pour indiquer des distances. Altekar écrit: "Vaiśālī to Bodha-Gayā is about 70 miles and Dharmasvāmin states that the distance was of eight 'stages'. This suggests that a 'stage' was about eight miles" (p.xxviii). Altekar se réfère au passage suivant de la biographie: *de-nas Yaṅs-pa-can-gyi mt'a'-nas rDo-rje-gdan-du lhor ñin-lam brgyad yod c'u-bo Gaṅgā yod* (11b). Roerich traduit: "Southwards from the border of Vaiśālī, at a distance of eight stages, lies Vajrāsana. There is also the river Gaṅgā" (p. 63). Notons d'abord qu'il y est question de la distance à partir de la *frontière* de Vaiśālī dont, d'après un autre passage de la biographie (10a; trad. p. 61), la plus grande longueur est de 20 étapes et la plus grande largeur de 8 étapes. En outre, il nous semble que, dans le texte tibétain, il faut rayer le premier *yod* et traduire: "Ensuite [en allant] de la frontière de Vaiśālī à Bodhgayā dans la direction du Sud le Gange se trouve à [une distance de] huit étapes." Plus loin, (p.xxxvii), Altekar reproche à C'os-rje-dpal d'avoir dit que Nālandā se trouve sur l'autre rive du Gange, et à une distance de deux jours au Sud-Ouest de Vajrāsana. Le texte dit: *de ni c'u-bo Gaṅgā'i p'ar-'gram-na ñin-gñis-sṅa-sleb-kyi sa-na rDo-rje-gdan-nas lho-nub-tu p'yin-pas gro-sṅa-sleb-kyi sa-na yod* (31a). Roerich traduit: "It was situated on the further bank of the Gaṅgā at a distance of about two days to the south-west (mistake for south-east) of Vajrāsana" (p. 90). Nous aimerions proposer une traduction différente: "Elle se trouve sur l'autre rive du Gange à un endroit, éloigné de deux jours et demi, et, en allant de Vajrāsana vers le Sud-Ouest, à un endroit éloigné d'un matin."[2] Si l'on corrigeait *p'ar-'gram-na* en *p'ar-'gram-nas*, le texte serait plus clair mais, en tout état de cause, il dit bien que Nālandā n'est pas sur la rive même mais à une distance de deux jours et demi du fleuve. Il est vrai que, en indiquant la direction dans laquelle se trouve Vajrāsana, C'os-rje-dpal se trompe à moins qu'il ne faille corriger *rDo-rje-gdan-nas* en *rDo-rje-gdan-du*.

A la liste des traductions auxquelles C'os-rje-dpal participa (pp.xliii-xlv) il faut ajouter le *Śrīvajraḍākasya stava daṇḍaka nāma* (Cordier, vol II, rGyud-'grel, XII, 23) et le *Guhyasamāja* (Ōtani Kanjur Catalogue, No. 81).

Avant de faire quelques remarques à propos de la traduction du texte tibétain il faut signaler le fait que cet ouvrage a été publié d'une manière extrêmement négligente. Le nombre des fautes d'impression est vraiment ahurissant. Une page entière du texte tibétain a disparu entre les pages 16 et 17 de l'édition. De toute évidence, la faute n'en incombe pas au traducteur. Pour un exemple évident de la négligence de l'éditeur de l'ouvrage renvoyons à un passage de la traduction où il est fait mention de "dried and raw sugar" (p. 104). Le texte tibétain a *ts'os daṅ bu-ram* et, en se référant à ce passage, Altekar mentionne "dyes and raw sugar" (p.ix). Le manuscrit du traducteur a donc dû contenir le mot "dyes" transformé en "dried" pendant l'impression. Peut-être ceci est un cas exceptionnel. Si, dans d'autres cas, les fautes d'impression du texte anglais le déparent sans l'altérer, elles constituent un vrai désastre en ce qui concerne le texte tibétain. A plusieurs endroits on y rencontre des mots incompréhensibles. Alors on a le choix entre quatre possibilités: A. C'est une faute d'impression; B. Le traducteur a mal déchiffré le manuscrit; C. L'erreur se trouvait déjà dans le manuscrit; D. Il s'agit d'un mot ou expression inconnus aux dictionnaires. S'il avait éliminé la première possibilité, l'éditeur de l'ouvrage aurait bien diminué les difficultés que l'on éprouve dans l'étude du texte tibétain.

La biographie est écrite dans un style simple probablement assez proche de la langue parlée de l'époque. Néanmoins, à plusieurs endroits, le texte est loin d'être facile à

[2] La traduction de *sṅa* et *gro-sṅa* n'est pas sûre. Très probablement ils signifient tous les deux "matin, marche d'un matin", cf. Jäschke, *A Tibetan-English Dictionary* (London, 1881), p. 78b sub voce *gro*: **do źig** W. a morning's march. On trouve dans les textes aussi bien *sṅa-gro* que *sṅa-dro* mais nous n'avons jamais rencontré *gro-sṅa*.

comprendre. Celà s'explique certainement par le fait qu'il s'agit d'un manuscrit qui n'a pas été revu en vue d'une impression. Il est probable que les Tibétains ont eu l'habitude de corriger soigneusement un texte avant de le livrer à l'impression. D'autre part, c'est justement l'emploi d'expressions, empruntées à la langue parlée, qui cause des difficultés car les dictionnaires tiennent davantage compte de la langue littéraire. A cet égard, la traduction de Roerich ne nous aide pas beaucoup car, à quelques exceptions près, il s'est abstenu d'ajouter des notes pour justifier et expliquer la traduction de mots et expressions inconnus. Souvent on est obligé de deviner les raisons qui ont motivé la traduction. Celà serait moins grave si l'on pouvait être sûr que la traduction soit digne de confiance. Malheureusement il faut constater qu'elle laisse beaucoup à désirer. Non seulement le traducteur a traduit trop librement et a sauté des mots et des bouts de phrase mais aussi il y a des passages où il s'est trompé gravement. Il nous semble qu'une nouvelle édition et traduction seraient souhaitables. Sans avoir l'intention d'anticiper sur un tel travail nous aimerions étudier ci-dessous plusieurs passages de la traduction afin d'en montrer la nécessité.

F.1b: *k'o-bo ni C'ags lo-tsā-ba dGra-bcom źes-pa rGya-gar rDo-rje-gdan-du bsṅugs-pa*; His *upādhyāya* (personal teacher) was Chag lo-tsā-ba dGra-bcom, who was sent to Vajrāsana in India (p. 48). – *K'o-bo* doit certainement être corrigé en *k'u-bo*; pour *bsṅugs* Roerich propose de lire *mṅags-'dug-pa* mais c'est peut-être simplement une erreur pour *bźugs*, car la suite de ce passage raconte ce qu'il faisait à Bodhgayā. Donc il faut traduire: "Son oncle paternel, qui s'appelait dGra-bcom le traducteur de C'ag, se trouvait à Vajrāsana."

F.2b: *rgyud-ris*; annals (p. 49). Jäschke qui a dû rencontrer cette expression dans le rGyal-rabs (éd. de sDe-dge f. 87a et plus loin) traduit par "Wall, panel (?)". Le sens en est indubitablement quelque chose comme "peinture murale".

F. 3a: *t'ag bzaṅ-ba*; well-shaped (p. 50). Cette épithète des dents est bien connue par la liste des 32 marques du Buddha. Elle traduit skt. *avirala* (Mahāvyutpatti, 234) ou *sahita* (Rāṣṭrapālaparipṛcchā p. 46.17, p. 50.17) qui signifient "sans séparation, serré".

F.4a: *nus-na rGya-gar rDo-rje-gdan-du gźud / rGya-gar-gyi-c'u 't'uṅ-ba tsam-gyis kyaṅ 'oṅ-ṅo / sgra-bzaṅ-la lce bde-bar 'gro*; If able, go to the Indian Vajrāsana. It will come about by the mere drinking of Indian water (i.e. he will get acclimatized and will be able to undertake a journey in India). Learned in Grammar, proceed with nimble tongue! (p. 51). – Si tu peux, va à Vajrāsana dans l'Inde. Même si tu ne fais que boire de l'eau indienne, ce sera bien. Tu deviendras réputé et éloquent. – Dans un autre passage Roerich a bien saisi le sens de *'oṅ-ba*: *gtugs-na 'oṅ-bar 'dug* (36a); it would be good to meet (him) (p. 95).

Ff. 6a-b contiennent une description vivante de la procession de Matsyendranātha nommé ici Avalokiteśvara. D'après la biographie son image se trouve dans le vihāra de Bu-k'am qui correspond à Bugma (variantes: Buṅgama, Buga, Bugama) mentionné par M. L. Petech (*Mediaeval History of Nepal*, Roma, 1958, pp. 30, 102, 108, 146).

F. 6a: *k'rus-źu daṅ bza' bgra-ka 'oṅ*; faut-il lire: *kr'us-c'u daṅ bza'-ba gñis-ka 'oṅ*? Cf. 18a: *k'rus-c'ab daṅ bza'-ba gñis-ka 'oṅ*.

F.7b: *g.yog-med-ciṅ rtsod-dus mi-rgod maṅ yaṅ*; when I had to struggle alone without attendant; even though wrld men were numerous (p. 57). – Bien que je fûs sans serviteur et que, dans le Kaliyuga, il y ait beaucoup de brigands.

F. 8b: *lo-skor-gcig-tu*: during the year (p. 58). – Pendant douze ans.

F. 10a: *ma-he'i Bod-skad-du g.yag-rgod ces-par ḅsgyur-ram gźan skad-dod med gsuṅ*; The Dharmasvāmin said that "ma-hes" meant wild yak in Tibetan, and that there was no corresponding word in another language (p. 60). – Le D. disait que "ma-he" se traduit en tibétain par yak sauvage et qu'il n'y a pas d'autre équivalent.

F. 10b: *Gar-log-gi dmag 'ur-c'e-bas*; because of rumours (about the arrival) of Turushka troops (p. 61). – Par le grand bruit de l'armée des Turuṣka. – *'Ur* ne s'emploie pas dans le sens de "rumeur".

F. 13b: *nam-żod-dus-su ñi-ma'i grib-ts'ad mi-gsal-ba'i ts'e*; early in the morning at sunrise (p. 66). – Dans la saison des pluies quand l'ombre du soleil n'est pas bien visible. – *Nam-żod* = *c'ar-pa'i dus* (cf. le dictionnaire de C'os-grags, p. 465b). Jäschke traduit par "in the morning" en renvoyant à Schmidt.

F. 14a: *pa-lcag-cig dkar ldem-me btsugs-pa k'o-na 'dra-ba-tsam mt'oṅ gsuṅ-ṅo* // *ri-med-pas ñi-ma śar-lugs kyaṅ sa'i steṅ-du p'ub btsugs-pa k'o-na 'dra-ba śar 'oṅ gsuṅ-ṅo*; The Dharmasvāmin said that its pinnacle of glittering white looked like a flame and that it shone like a shield placed flat on the ground in sunshine (p. 66). – Le D. disait que le pinacle blanc et vibrant ressemblait à un [ici un mot, probablement "pilier" a dû tomber] dressé. Il disait que, par l'absence de montagnes, le soleil en se levant ressemblait à un bouclier planté debout en terre (littéralement: Le D. disait que, par l'absence de montagnes, quant à la façon de se lever du soleil il se levait exactement comme un bouclier planté sur la terre). – Pour *ldem-me-ba* = *p'ar-ts'ur g.yo-ba* cf. C'os-grags, p. 449a. Le sens de *btsugs* est le contraire de "placed flat".

Ff. 15a-16a: La même légende se trouve dans le rGyal-rabs (éd. de sDe-dge ff. 8a–9a) où la mère demande d'ouvrir la porte après trois mois et deux jours, un jour trop tôt.

F. 15a: *lha dbaṅ-p'yug c'en-po dṅos yod-pas;* there is an image of the God Maheśvara (p. 67). – Le dieu Maheśvara s'y trouve en personne. Cf. f. 33b: *Saṅs-rgyas dṅos-kyi 'du-śes*; the notion that it is a real Buddha (p. 92).

F. 16b: *żag bdun-du gcig-gis ma-ts'aṅ-ba'i dus-su sgo p'ye zer-ba-cig byuṅ-ba-la żag gcig ma-ts'aṅ sgo mi-'byed byas-pa*; after seven days some one said that it should be opened before the indicated time. The mother said that it should not be opened before the indicated time (p. 69). – Un jour avant l'expiration du terme de sept jours quelqu'un vint et dit: "Ouvre la porte." Il (le fils le plus jeune) dit: "C'est un jour trop tôt. Je n'ouvrirai pas la porte."

F. 18a: *ts'ems de 'c'aṅ-bar bcaṅs-na yar-mar gñis-kar lhag-ge yoṅ-ba yod* (éd. *yed*) *gsuṅ-ṅo*; The Dharmasvāmin said that when the tooth was being carried, it used to increase (in size) from the top and from below (p. 71). – Le D. disait que, quand on portait la dent, elle brillait de haut en bas. – *Lhag-ge* est une variante de *lhaṅ-ṅe*, cf. Jäschke, p. 600b.

F. 18a: *sṅon yaṅ-dag-par rdzogs-pa'i Saṅs-rgyas-kyis ma-'oṅ-ba'i*(éd. *pa'i*)*-dus-su sems-can dbaṅ-po rnon-pas gsuṅ-rab mt'oṅ-bas kyaṅ śes-te dbaṅ-po rtul-po-rnams Saṅs-rgyas 'jig-rten-du byon-nam ma-byon sñam*(éd. *snam*)*-nas t'e-ts'om za-bar 'oṅ-bas*; Formerly, a thought occurred to the Fully Enlightened Buddha whether in future times those sentient beings of sharp intellect, who had mastered the Scriptures and disciplined their faculties, would be able, or not to appear as Buddha in the World?" and doubt was produced in his mind (p. 71) – Autrefois le Samyaksaṃbuddha eut cette pensée: "A l'avenir, les êtres d'intelligence vive sauront déjà par l'étude de l'Ecriture [que le Buddha est arrivé] mais les êtres de faible intelligence douteront si le Buddha est arrivé dans le monde ou non."

F. 19b: *Ñes-sdo-pa*; p. 18, n. 5: Read: *Ñan-t'os-pa*. – Lire *Ñan-t'os sde-pa*?

F. 22b: *la-la bde-ba-la bkod-de lha-daṅ-'dra / la-la dmag-'dren-ciṅ t'ab-rtsod byed-pas lha-min daṅ-'dra / la-la c'ad-pa bcad-pas dmyal-ba daṅ-'dra-żiṅ rigs-drug-gi spyod-pa ts'aṅ-bar yod-pa'i skabs-su*; Some he will establish in peace like a god; against others he will lead armies and wage wars, like an Asura; to some he will mete out punishments like hell. When the customs of the six kinds of sentient beings had become purified (pp. 77–78). – Comme un dieu, il établira quelques-uns dans le bonheur; pareil à un Asura, il conduira son armée et livrera bataille avec d'autres; pareil à un être de l'enfer, il infligera des punitions à d'autres encore. Quand il eût complètement accompli les actes propres aux six classes d'êtres.

F. 24b: *rgyal-po-la gtam bya-ba rin-po-c'e'i p'reṅ-ba'i le'u gsum-pa'i skabs daṅ ṅag-gi dbaṅ-p'yug grags-pa'i 'c'i-ba bslu-bar c'os-rgyal Mya-ṅan-med bżin-no*; The story is told in the third chapter about the precious garland of Rājā La-gtam and the chapter of the

Dharmarāja Aśoka, redeemed from death known as Vāgīśvara (p. 80). – *rgyal-po-la gtam bya-ba rin-po-c'e'i p'reṅ-ba* est la *Rājaparikathā Ratnāvalī* qui est citée plusieurs fois dans la biographie, Ṅag-gi dbaṅ-p'yug grags-pa est Vāgīśvarakīrti, l'auteur de plusieurs ouvrages sur la *Mṛtyuvañcanā* (*'C'i-ba bslu-ba*).

F. 25a–b: *mc'od-la k'ad-pa;* lire *mc'oṅ-la k'ad-pa.*

F. 25a-b: *p'yag ma-'ts'al zer-kyaṅ lha-gcig-la p'yag-'ts'al-bas lha de 'dar sig-sig 'dug-kyaṅ gas-su ma-btub-nas gzigs-pas de'i spyi-bo-na naṅ-pa'i lha sNaṅ-ba mt'a'-yas cig 'dug-nas de gsal-te p'yag-'ts'al-bas ts'al-par żags*; "When I was told to prostrate myself, I prostrated myself once before the god, and though the image shuddered, I was unable to split it. I then looked at the image, and saw clearly the image of the Buddha Amitābha on its head. When I prostrated myself again, the image split" (p. 82). – Bien qu'[une voix] me dit: "Ne te prosterne pas", je me prosternai devant le dieu. Le dieu trembla mais je fus incapable de le fendre. En regardant, je vis que sur sa tête se trouvait le dieu bouddhique Amitābha. Après l'avoir éloigné, je me prosternai et [l'image] se fendit en morceaux. – Il faut corriger *gsal* en *bsal* et *żags* en *'gas.*

F. 26b: *ts'e-'dir 'jig-rten-'di'i dṅos-grub*; the mastery of this World (p. 82). – Un pouvoir surnaturel qui appartient à cette vie-ci et à ce monde-ci.

F. 31b: *de-na dbu-rtse c'en-po bdun dbus-su bsgrigs-pa yod / gñis ma-gtogs-pa rgyal-pos bżeṅs gñis slob-dpon c'en-po gñis-kyis re-re bżeṅs-pa*; it had seven great pinnacles in its centre, two of which had been erected by the Rājā and two by two great Āchāryas, one each (p. 90). – Au milieu sept grands pinacles avaient été construits. A l'exception de deux ils avaient été érigés par le roi. Ces deux avaient été érigés par deux grand maîtres, par chacun un.

F. 34a: *sgo nub-tu blta-ba cig-na*; When one looks at the western gate (p. 93). – Près de la porte orientée à l'Ouest. Cf. f. 26a: *sgo śar-du blta-ba*; a gate, facing East (p. 82).

F. 35a: *k'yod dam-ts'ig-can 'or-c'e*; You are keeping your vow and great is your burden (p. 94). – Je vous suis reconnaissant d'observer votre voeu. Cf. C'os-grags, p. 786a: *'or-c'e-ba = drin-c'e-ba lta-bu.*

F. 40b: *gson-gśin p'yed-pa yin de'u raṅ śi-ste*; I almost died! One day I passed out (p. 101). – J'étais entre la vie et la mort et sur le point de mourir. Cf. C'os-grags, p. 401a: *de'u-śi-skad = śi-k'a-la slebs-pa, gsod-la k'ad, 'c'i-la k'ad.*

F. 41b: *gser-'bum*; a golden vase (p. 102). – La *Śatasāhasrikā* écrite en or. Cf. plus loin: *gser-gyi ñi-k'ri*; the *Pañchaviṃśatisāhasrikā* written in gold.

F. 42a: *yab-mes kun-gyis rGya-gar-du ma-btaṅ-bas lan sku-drin c'e-la c'uṅ-du byuṅ c'e-ste c'os daṅ loṅs-spyod daṅ ma-bral-ba mdzad / c'uṅ-ste rGya-gar-du ma-btaṅ*; my father and my grand-father did not allow me to go to India. As a result of which their grace diminished. At the best they did not make me abandon religion and wealth, at the worst they did not send (me) to India (p. 103). – Parce que mon père et mon grand-père ne m'ont pas envoyé dans l'Inde, ils m'ont rendu un bon et un mauvais service; un bon service en tant qu'ils ne m'ont pas séparé de la religion et de la richesse; un mauvais service en tant qu'ils ne m'ont pas envoyé dans l'Inde.

F. 42b: *żabs-kyis gaṅ-daṅ-gaṅ bcags-pa / bkra-śis lo-legs bde-skyid-ldan*; Those who were walking (on the road) said that it was an auspicious year full of peace (p. 104). – Partout où il posait ses pieds, la prospérité régnait et l'année était bonne et heureuse.

F. 43a: *dad-gus gżan-pas c'e*; others were filled with faith and devotion (p. 104). – Il lui témoignait plus de respect que les autres. Cf. f.4a: *dad-gus gżan-las c'e'o*; honoured him more than the others (p. 51).

F. 43b: *Hor-Bod-kyi mi-blo-can kun-gyis lam-du groṅ-na p'aṅs-par mt'oṅ / dpon Zin Śes-rab-skyabs-kyis Hor-Bod-kyi mi-sna kun bsags-te lam-du groṅ-pa-na rgyal-po yaṅ mi-mñes / Bod-du bżugs-na 'gro-ba kun-la p'an-k'ams c'e-bas Hor-Bod kun gros-kyis zer-ba-la brten-nas Hor-Bod kun-gyis Bod-du bżugs-par żus*; Mongol and Tibetan dignitaries deliberated, saying that if Mongol and Tibetan learned men were to die on the road, it would not be good; if all Tibetan and Mongol dignitaries summoned by the official Śes-rab-skyabs were to die on the road, the Great Khan would not be pleased; if the Dharmasvāmin were to stay in Tibet, great benefit would arise for sentient beings. They therefore requested the Dharmasvāmin to remain in Tibet (p. 105). – Tous les Mongols et Tibétains intelligents comprenaient que, s'il (le Dharmasvāmin) mourait en route, ce serait une grande perte. Le préfet Śes-rab-skyabs de Zin rassembla tous les représentants des Tibétains et des Mongols. Ils discutèrent et dirent que, s'il mourait en route, le roi serait mécontent mais que, s'il restait au Tibet, ce serait un grand bienfait pour tous les êtres. En raison de [cet avis] tous les Mongols et Tibétains lui demandèrent de rester au Tibet.

F. 43b: *dpon Śes-rab-skyabs-kyis žus-pa bla-ma paṇḍi-ta c'en-po bcu-gñis / Bod-du lo-tsā-ba bži mk'as-btsun ñi-śu-la c'os gsan-pa'i gsan-yig c'en-mo de mdzad-de gnaṅ*; the Dharmasvāmin addressed an epistle on the Doctrine to the twelve Paṇḍitas invited by the official Śes-rab-skyabs, to the four lo-tsā-bas of Tibet, and to twenty learned monks (p. 105). – Il écrivit à la demande du préfet Śes-rab-skyabs un mémoire sur les doctrines qu'il avait apprises de douze grands savants, de quatre traducteurs tibétains et de vingt moines savants et vénérables.

F. 47b: La biographie cite un passage du *Mahāyānasaṃgraha*. On en trouvera une meilleure traduction dans *La Somme du Grand Véhicule* par M. Ét. Lamotte (Tome II, Traduction et commentaire, fascicule 2, Louvain, 1939, pp. 341–342).

Leiden J. W. de Jong

De Jong, J. W. (Canberra)

NOTES À PROPOS DES COLOPHONS DU KANJUR

Introduction.

Les colophons des Kanjurs tibétain et mongol sont une source importante non seulement pour l'histoire des traductions tibétaines et mongoles mais aussi pour l'histoire du bouddhisme tibéto-mongol. Nombreux sont les renseignements qui y ont été empruntés mais, jusqu'à la parution de l'ouvrage de M. BISCHOFF[1], il n'y avait pas de traduction complète de ces colophons. Malheureusement, l'utilité de cet ouvrage est sérieusement diminuée par de nombreuses fautes de traduction dues à des connaissances insuffisantes du tibétain, du mongol et de la terminologie bouddhique. En outre, M. BISCHOFF n'a pas consulté plusieurs travaux qui se rapportent directement ou indirectement aux colophons du Kanjur.

La traduction des colophons est faite d'après le texte des colophons mongols qui, pour la plupart, consistent en deux parties, la première étant la traduction du colophon de la traduction tibétaine et la deuxième ayant trait à la traduction mongole. Pour la première partie des colophons M. BISCHOFF a consulté le texte original tibétain d'après la reproduction photomécanique du Kanjur de Pékin[2]. Pour chaque texte M. BISCHOFF donne des références au catalogue du Kanjur mongol par M. LIGETI[3], au catalogue du Kanjur manuscrit par BECKH[4], au catalogue de l'université Ōtani[5] et au volume de la réimpression japonaise du Kanjur de Pékin. Des références supplémentaires aux Kanjur de Narthang , Derge, Cone et Lhasa auraient facilité la comparaison du texte des colophons dans les différentes éditions du Kanjur. Cela n'aurait pas été difficile à faire grâce aux travaux suivants: Alexandre CSOMA DE KÖRÖS, Analyse du Kandjour (Annales du Musée Guimet, II, 1881, pp. 131-349, 379-489, 495-577); O.; A Complete Catalogue of the Tibetan Buddhist Canons, 2 vols., Sendai, 1934 (désormais : Derge); Taishun MIBU, A Comparative List of the Bkaḥ-ḥgyur Division in the Co-ne, Peking, Sde-dge and Snar-thaṅ Editions (Taishō Daigaku Kenkyū Kiyō, No. 44, 1959); Erik HAARH, A Comparative List of the Derge and Lhasa Editions of the Kanjur (Asia Major, IX, 2, 1958, pp. 179-205); TAKASAKI Jikidō, Rasa-ban Chibetto Daizōkyō sōmokuroku, Tōkyō, 1965. Les titres sanskrits et tibétains sont cités d'après le Kanjur mongol alors que M. LIGETI les a reproduits d'après O.[6]. On ne voit pas très bien l'utilité de la reproduction de ces titres défigurés. Puisque le travail de M. BISCHOFF ne peut être étudié sans le catalogue de M. LIGETI, il aurait été préférable d'omettre entièrement les titres sanskrits, tibétains et mongols et d'utiliser la place ainsi gagnée pour des références à d'autres éditions du Kanjur et pour la reproduction du texte tibétain des colophons.

Probablement M. BISCHOFF a choisi de traduire les colophons mongols parce qu'ils se rapportent aussi bien aux traductions tibétaines qu'aux traductions mongoles. La seule raison qui pourrait plaider en faveur de ce choix est le fait que les colophons mongols peuvent être facilement consultés grâce à l'ouvrage de M. LIGETI. Pour le reste, il ne comporte que des inconvénients. En traduisant les colophons du Kanjur tibétain d'après la traduction mongole, M. BISCHOFF répète les erreurs commises par les Mongols qui n'ont pas toujours bien interprété le texte tibétain. En outre, l'étude simultanée de l'histoire des traductions tibétaines et de celle des traductions mongoles n'est guère possible. Le fait que M. BISCHOFF ne distingue pas par un moyen typographique la première de la deuxième partie des colophons contribue à compliquer l'affaire. Ce qu'il nous faudrait en premier lieu, c'est une traduction des colophons tibétains faite d'après le texte tibétain. Avant d'entreprendre un tel travail il faudrait éditer le texte de ces colophons d'après une édition du Kanjur tibétain, en signalant soigneusement les variantes des autres éditions. C'est seulement après avoir édité et traduit les colophons du Kanjur tibétain que l'on pourra étudier les colophons du Kanjur mongol, en comparant tout d'abord la première partie de ceux-ci avec les colophons du Kanjur tibétain.

En comparant la traduction de plusieurs colophons par M. BISCHOFF avec les textes tibétain et mongol, on s'aperçoit vite des imperfections de son travail. On ne peut guère espérer voir bientôt paraître un autre travail sur ce même sujet[7]. C'est pourquoi il m'a paru nécessaire d'étudier le travail de M. BISCHOFF d'une manière assez détaillée. En premier lieu, les notes suivantes se rapportent à la traduction des colophons. N'étant pas mongolisant, je me suis abstenu d'étudier la deuxième partie des colophons mongols et les problèmes qu'ils posent pour l'histoire du Kanjur mongol. En ce qui concerne la première partie, je me suis reporté au texte tibétain. Puisque M. BISCHOFF a traduit cette partie des colophons d'après le texte mongol, j'ai dû citer aussi le texte mongol que je n'interprête pas toujours de la même façon que M. BISCHOFF. Je signale ces cas de désaccord, en laissant aux spécialistes la décision finale. La traduction des colophons tibétains n'est pas toujours aisée. Malheureusement, dans ces cas, la version mongole ne nous aide guère. J'ai signalé les passages des colophons tibétains que je n'ai pas bien compris. Le texte tibétain est cité d'après l'édition de Lhasa (désormais : Lh.) que j'ai pu consulter dans une excellente reproduction photocopiée que la bibliothèque de l'Australian National University a pu se procurer grâce aux bons soins de M. F.-R. HAMM, professeur à l'université de Bonn. La seule raison pour choisir cette édition était le fait qu'elle pouvait être facilement consultée. En outre, j'ai consulté la réimpression japonaise de l'édition de Pékin mais sans comparer systématiquement tous les colophons dans les éditions de Lhasa et de Pékin car un tel travail ne pourrait se faire qu'en comparant aussi d'autres éditions qui ne sont pas à ma disposition. Partout où je cite l'édition de Pékin, je l'ai indiqué en ajoutant P. entre parenthèses. D'autre part, dans ces notes, j'ai essayé de déterminer les dates des traducteurs mentionnés dans les colophons. Plusieurs traducteurs qui ont travaillé au début du neuvième siècle sont mentionnés dans l'introduction au Sgra-sbyor bam-po gñis-pa : les indiens Jinamitra, Surendrabodhi, Śīlendrabodhi, Dānaśīla, Bodhimitra ; les tibétains Ratnarakṣita, Dharmatāśīla, Jñānasena (Ye-śes sde), Jayarakṣita, Mañjuśrīvarman et Ratnendraśīla[8]. Un grand nombre de traducteurs sont contemporains de Rin-chen bzaṅ-po : Śraddhākaravarman, Padmākaravarman, Subhāṣita, Kamalagupta (ou Kamalarakṣita ou Kamalaguhya), Dharmaśrībhadra, Subhūtiśrībhadra, Śākya blo-gros (Śākyamati), Gaṅgādhara, Buddhabhadra, Vijayaśrīdhara, Janārdana, Buddhaśrīśānti, Vīryabhadra, Tathāgatarakṣita, Devākara, Kanakavarman, Atiśa, Tshul-khrims yon-tan, Bsod-nams rgyal-ba, Yon-tan śī-la (Guṇaśīla), Śāntibhadra, Tshul-khrims rgyal-ba (ou Nag-tsho), Śākya 'od (Śākyaprabha), Subhūtiśrīśānti, Dge-ba'i blo-gros, Lha-btsas[9]. Selon M. TUCCI, ils ont dû travailler pendant la deuxième moitié du dixième siècle et pendant les premiers trois quarts du onzième siècle. Pendant la deuxième moitié du onzième siècle travaillaient Jñānaśrībhadra, Rgyal-ba śes-rab, Śākya bśes-gñen, Byaṅ-chub śes-rab de Maṅ-'or. Rin-chen rdo-rje (Ratnavajra) fut le disciple de Gaṅgādhara, mentionné ci-dessus[10]. En suivant l'exemple de M. TUCCI j'ai tiré profit du fait que, dès que l'on sait les dates d'un traducteur, on peut déterminer les dates de tous ceux qui ont coopéré avec lui dans le travail de traduction. Le catalogue de CORDIER et le Répertoire de Mlle LALOU m'ont été très utiles[11]. D'autre part, je me suis servi de la traduction du Deb-ther sṅon-po par George N. ROERICH, puisque cet ouvrage est considéré digne de foi en ce qui concerne les indications chronologiques[12]. Evidemment, il n'était pas possible de résoudre tous les problèmes que pose la détermination des dates des traducteurs. Les indications, données dans les colophons de différentes éditions, ne s'accordent pas toujours. D'autre part, un même traducteur se rencontre sous des noms différents. Souvent on ne sait pas si l'on a à faire à un Tibétain ou un Indien, car un Tibétain peut être désigné par un nom sanskrit. Une étude de tous ces problèmes ne pourra se faire qu'en consultant les colophons non seulement du Kanjur mais aussi du Tanjur dans les différentes éditions et en étudiant les renseignements relatifs aux traductions et aux traducteurs qui sont fournis par d'autres auteurs tels que Bu-ston.

1. Selon le colophon de 1 (les numéros se réfèrent à la numérotation continue des textes dans L. et BK.) le patron de la traduction fut Bla-ma dam-pa Chos-kyi rgyal-po que M.BISCHOFF suggère d'identifier avec Atiśa en renvoyant au colophon de 3. Dans 3 Chos-kyi rgyal-po est dit être "orné de vertus excellentes et illimitées", yon-tan phul-tu byuṅ-la (P. ba) dpag-tu med-pas spras-pa'i Bla-ma dam-pa Chos-kyi rgyal-po ; iruγumal boluγsan čaγlasi ügei erdem-iyer čimegdegsen nom-un qaγan degedü blam-a ; BK.: "(auf Befehl) des Iruγumal boluγsan (Phul-tu byuṅ ba = Atiśa), des eminenten Lama, König der Lehre, welcher mit unendlichem Vorzug geziert worden war". Le texte tibétain montre l'impossibilité de cette interprétation. Comme l'avait déjà reconnu CORDIER, Bla-ma dam-pa Chos-kyi rgyal-po est une désignation du célèbre 'Phags-pa[13] qui a vécu de 1235 à 1280 d'après les sources tibétaines et de 1239 à 1279 ou 1280 d'après les sources chinoises[14]. Selon le colophon de 1, le traducteur fut Blo-gros brtan-pa, le deuxième ; rgyud-'di Blo-brtan gñis-pas legs-par bsgyur ; ene dandr-a-yi nögüge Blo-rtan sayitur orčiγulbai, "ce tantra a été bien traduit par Blo-rtan, le deuxième" ; BK. : "hat jedoch Blo rtan dieses Tantra als Zweiter trefflich übersetzt". Dans un compte rendu du catalogue de M. LIGETI W. BARUCH a remarqué à propos de ce colophon : "In the colophon of No. 1(1) it is said that Blo-gros rtan-pa translated and edited the work. Then it goes on : ertenü tedeger yeke kelemürčin ber: ene dandr-a-yi orčiγulun bügüde-dür aldarsiγulǰu amui-ǰ-a : 'those former great translators have distinguished themselves in the translation of this Tantra'. Thus that part of the colophon is missing in which the pandit Kamalagupta and the locava Rin-čhen bzaṅ-po are named as earlier translators"[15]. Le passage mongol, cité par BARUCH, signifie : "Ces grands traducteurs d'autrefois ont traduit ce tantra et l'ont fait connaître à tous", cf. le texte tibétain : sngon-gyi sgra-sgyur chen-po de-dag-gis // rgyud-'di bsgyur-ciṅ kun-la grags lags-mod, "Ces grands traducteurs d'autrefois ont traduit ce tantra, et [il] est bien connu de tous" ; BK.: "Sicher wird dieses Tantra, übersetzt von eben diesen grossen Übersetzern der Vergangenheit, überall berühmt werden". BARUCH supposait que M. LIGETI avait omis un passage qui se rapportait à la première traduction du texte par Kamalagupta et Rin-chen bzaṅ-po mais un tel passage ne se trouve ni dans P. ni dans Lh. Seul le catalogue du Kanjur de Derge dit que Kamalagupta et Rin-chen bzaṅ

po ont traduit le texte et que Śoṅ Blo-gros brtan-pa l'a révisé[16]. Cet exemple montre la nécessité de consulter différentes éditions du Kanjur et surtout les trois plus importantes, celles de Narthang, de Derge et de Pékin.

CORDIER énumère quatre Blo-gros brtan-pa. Les deux premiers sont Blo-gros brtan-pa de Dpaṅ et Blo-gros brtan-pa de Śoṅ. Les deux autres sont désignés comme le troisième et le quatrième (Rép. p. 200). Blo-gros brtan-pa de Dpaṅ a vécu de 1276 à 1342 et est donc exclu[17]. Il doit s'agir de Blo-gros brtan-pa de Śoṅ comme l'indique aussi le catalogue de Derge. Ceci est confirmé par le fait qu'il a traduit avec Dpal Sa-dbaṅ bzaṅ-po (Śrī Mahīndrabhadra) du Népal la Vibhaktikārikā. Cette traduction fut exécutée par ordre de 'Phags-pa[18]. Puisque les dates de 'Phags-pa sont bien déterminées, on sait donc que les traducteurs suivants ont travaillé dans la deuxième moitié du douzième siècle : Śoṅ Blo-gros brṭan-pa, Dpal Sa-dbaṅ bzaṅ-po et Lakṣmīkara. La traduction de 1 a eu lieu dans le monastère de la Méditation (bsam-gtan gliṅ et non bstan-gtan gliṅ comme dans BK.). Le colophon se termine par les lignes suivantes : zab-ciṅ rgya-che rdo-rje theg-pa yi // ṅes-don ye-śes don-gñer skyes-bu dag // chos daṅ don-la legs-par mi rton-par // gaṅ-zag 'tshig-'bru'i rjes-su ma-'braṅ-źig // ; gün narin aγui yeke včir-tu kölgen-ü : maγad udq-a-tu belge bilig-i kereglegči arad : nom kiged udq-a-dur sayitur sitüge edügüy-e : budgalis-un üges-ün qoyin-a-ača buu daγaγtun, "Hommes qui cherchez le sens définitif (nītārtha) et le savoir (jñāna) du Vajrayāna profond et étendu, vous ne devez pas ne pas vous fier à la doctrine (dharma) et au sens (artha) et suivre un homme (pudgala) et la lettre (vyañjana)" ; BK.: "Setze nicht in trefflicher Weise das Vertrauen in Leute denen die Weisheit um den tiefen Sinn des allertiefsten, allergrössten Vajra-Fahrzeuges fehlt, um die Lehre, um den Sinn ! Nimmer laufe Pudgala-Reden nach !" Le texte tibétain repose sur le Catuḥpratiśaraṇasūtra (Abhidharmakośavyākhyā, éd. U. WOGIHARA, p. 704. 20-22 ; cf. Ét. LAMOTTE, "La critique d'interprétation dans le bouddhisme", Annuaire de l'Institut de philologie et d'histoire Orientales et Slaves, t. IX, 1949, pp. 341-361). Le traducteur mongol n'a pas vu que ṅes-don ye-śes et gaṅ-zag 'tshig-'bru doivent être interprétés comme ṅes-don daṅ ye-śes et gaṅ-zag daṅ 'tshig-'bru. En suivant la version mongole au lieu du texte tibétain, on ne peut pas arriver à une interprétation correcte.

3. Le texte fut traduit pour la première fois par Somanātha et le moine de 'Bro, Śes-rab grags. Ces deux traducteurs ont vécu au onzième siècle[19]. La traduction fut corrigée par ordre de 'Phags-pa et du dpon-chen (BK.: blon chen-po "grosser Minister") Śā-kya bzaṅ-po. Celui-ci était le premier des dpon-chen chargés des

affaires politiques et militaires par les empereurs mongols[2o]. Kun-dga' bzaṅ-po, tué en 1281 lui succéda[21]. 'Phags-pa et le dpon-chen Śā-kya bzaṅ-po ont aussi donné l'ordre de traduire ou corriger les textes suivants : Vimalaprabhā (Rép. pp.199b, 213a)[22], Nāgānanda (CORDIER, Mdo XCII. 3), Bodhisattvāvadānakalpalatā (Mdo XCIII), Buddhacarita (Mdo XCIV. 1) et Kāvyādarśa (Mdo CXVII. 3). Ceux qui ont exhorté (bskul-te ; duradduγad) à réviser la traduction sont le maître de Źaṅ Mdo-sde dpal et le moine Tshul-khrims dar. La révision fut exécutée par le maître de Śoṅ (Śoṅ-ston = Rdo-rje rgyal-mtshan) qui "savait le traité de la grammaire de la langue sanskrite", legs-par sbyar-ba'i skad-kyi (Lh. et P. : kyis) brda-sprod-pa'i bstan-bcos rig-pa ; Sangrida-yin ayalγu-bar dokiyalduγulqui sastir (BK.:"Śastra von der Übereinstimmung mit der Sanskritsprache"). On trouve dans les colophons mongols différentes traductions pour brda-sprod-pa (skt. vyākaraṇa). Dans 87 legs-par sbyar-ba'i skad-kyi brda-sprod-pa est rendu par Sangrida-yin ayalγu dokiyan; BK.: "die Auslegung der Sanskrit-Laute(Sprache)". Dans 122 brda-sprod-pa "le grammairien" est rendu par dokiyalduγuluγči ; BK.: "Korrektor". Selon le dictionnaire de KOWALEWSKI (p. 1868b) brda-sprod-pa se traduit en mongol par dokiy-a taniγulqu. Selon le dictionnaire tibétain-mongol de SUMATIRATNA (Ulaan Baatar, 1959, vol. I, p. 1131) un autre équivalent mongol est dokiyan-i medegülkü. Plusieurs passages de ce colophon n'ont pas été bien compris dans BK. : don-gyi cha-la legs-par dpyad-ciṅ ; udqas-un qubi-yi sayitur sinǰileǰü, "ayant bien examiné le sens [litt. la partie du sens]", BK.: "haben .... die [einzelnen] Teile des Werkes trefflich durchforscht" ; gaṅ-gi thugs-dgoṅs rnam-par dag-pa yis // 'di-la bskul-źiṅ mthun-rkyen bsgrubs-pa ; ken-ü masi ariluγsan ǰoriγ sedkil-iyer : egün-i durad-qaǰu ǰokilduqui siltaγan-i bütügegsen, "Ceux d'esprit pur qui ont exhorté à [réviser] ce [texte] et qui ont réuni les fonds nécessaires" ; BK.: "Diejenigen deren Geist wohl gereinigt ist, und die, dieses [Tantra] überdenkend, das Notwendige vollbracht haben". Tib. bskul est rendu en mongol par duradqaqu au lieu de duradqu comme ci-dessus. Pour mthun-rkyen (ǰokilduqui siltaγan), cf. J. BACOT, "Titres et colophons d'ouvrages non canoniques tibétains", BEFEO, XLIV, 1954, p. 333 : mthun cha rkyen, ressources, fonds.

5. Dans ce colophon se rencontre l'expression źal-sha-nas : ... Śrī-bha-dra-bo-dhi'i źal-sha-nas daṅ / bod-kyi lo-tsā-ba Gyi-jo ban-dhe Zla-ba'i 'od-zer-gyis 'Bro dge-sloṅ-gis (P. et Lh. : gi) phyir bsgyur-ciṅ źus-te gtan-la phab-pa ; ... Śrībhadrabodhi-yin dergede : töbed-ün kelemürči Gyi-ǰo bande Saran gerel neretü-yin orčiγuluγsan-i 'Bro ayaγ-q-a tegimlig ǰiči orčiγuluγad nayiraγulǰu (la traduction mongole montre qu'il faut suppléer dans le texte tibétain bsgyur-te après Zla-ba'i 'od-

zer-gyis). A propos de la traduction de ce colophon par BECKH, LAUFER a fait remarquer que źal-sňa-nas ne signifie pas "en présence de" mais n'est rien de plus qu'une addition honorifique qui correspond à notre "Révérend" (JRAS, 1914, p. 1135)[23]. Il y a de nombreux cas où cette expression a certainement ce sens mais on peut se demander si źal-sňa-nas a toujours le sens que lui donne LAUFER. Il y a plusieurs colophons où après źal-sňa-nas le mot daṅ est omis, par exemple : 9 ... Ga-ya-dha-ra'i źal-sňa-nas bod-kyi lo-tstsha-ba dge-sloṅ Śā-kya ye-śes-kyis bsgyur...; 11. .... Dpal Śes-rab gsaṅ-ba'i źal-sňar Kaṃ Chos-kyi ye-śes daṅ / Phyug-mtshams Dgra-bcom-gyis.... bsgyur-ciṅ ; 15. Rin-chen bzaṅ-po yis // mkhas-pa Padma-ka-ra'i źal-sňar ni // rig-pa'i 'byuṅ-gnas Kha-che'i dpe-las bsgyur...... Grags-pa'i źal-sňar ni // sgra-sgyur dge-sloṅ Pra-dzñā-kī-rti daṅ // Mar-pa sgra-sgyur Chos-kyi dbaṅ-phyug-gis.....; 69. Ra-tna-śrī'i źal-sňa-nas / lo-tstsha-ba Grags-pa rgyal-mtshan-gyis.... bsgyur-ro ; 127..... U-pa-śma(?)-ra-ksi-ta'i źal-sňa-nas lo-tsā-ba Glaṅ dge-sloṅ Dha-rma blo-gros-kyis bsgyur-ciṅ ; 791. Ā-na-nda-śrī'i źal-sňa-nas / maṅ-du thos-pa'i lo-tstsha-ba Śā-kya'i dge-sloṅ Ñi-ma rgyal-mtshan dpal-bzaṅ-pos ..... bsgyur-ciṅ. Il n'est guère possible de supposer que, dans tous ces cas, daṅ ait été omis par erreur. Dans tous ces exemples źal-sňa-nas ne s'emploie qu'après les noms de maîtres indiens. C'est pourquoi je me demande si źal-sňa-nas ne pourrait pas signifier ici en présence du maître indien qui récite le texte. D'un colophon il ressort clairement que le traducteur tibétain écoute le maître indien réciter le texte : 18. ....Rgyal-ba'i-sde'i źal-sňa-nas daṅ / bod-kyi lo-tstsha-ba Śā-kya'i dge-sloṅ Dha-rma yon-tan-gyis mňan-ciṅ bsgyur-ba'o (la version mongole ne traduit pas daṅ : Ilaγuγsan-u ayimaγ-un aman-ača töbed-ün kelemürči ayaγ-q-a tegimlig Dharma erdem-tü sonusuγad), "l'entendant de Rgyal-ba'i sde, le traducteur tibétain, le moine bouddhique Dha-rma yon-tan, le traduisit". L'expression źal-sňa-nas semble avoir causé des difficultés aux traducteurs mongols qui l'ont rendue par dergede (5, 11), emün-e (9), emün-e-eče (74, 82), niγur-un nide-eče (104), niγur-ún emün-e niden (?) (105)[24], aman-ača (12, 18, 21, 93, 127, 424, 791) et pāda ou bhā-da (= skt. -pādāḥ) (15, 26, 69, 84).

Les traducteurs Śrībhadrabodhi et Zla-ba'i 'od-zer, seigneur de Gyi, ont vécu au onzième siècle[25].

8. Le colophon de 8 est le suivant : (P.) rgya-gar-gyi mkhan-po Smri-ti-dzñā-na-kir-ti ñid-kyis sgyur / yon-bdag bod-kyi mkhan-po Gźon-nu grags-pas źus-nas bśad-nas gtan-la phab-ciṅ źus; Enedkeg-ün ubadini Smṛtijñānakīrti böged orčiγulbai : öglige-yin eǰen kemebesü töbed-ün ubadini J̌alaγu aldarsiγsan neretü

nayiraγulǰu nomlaγad orusiγulbai, "Le savant indien Smṛtijñānakīrti l'a traduit lui-même ; le dānapati, le savant tibétain, Gźon-nu grags, après l'avoir corrigé et expliqué, l'a mis en ordre et l'a corrigé ". BK.: "Der indische Lehrer Smriti injan a kirti hat [dieses] selbst übersetzt. Weil ein Spendeherr [solches] erbat, hat der tibetische Lehrer, J̌alaγu aldarsiγsan genannt, [es] korrigiert, vorgetragen und ediert". Je ne crois pas que kemebesü peut signifier "Weil er erbat", cf. KOWALEWSKI, p. 2482b : kemebesü, quand on parle, s'il faut dire ; 2. par rapport à , quant à ; 3. par exemple ; 4. car, parce que. Ici kemebesü doit avoir le sens de "quant à ".

Selon le Deb-ther sṅon-po Smṛtijñānakīrti est arrivé au Khams quelque temps avant la naissance de Roṅ-zom Chos-kyi bzaṅ-po qui a vécu au onzième siè - cle(BA., pp. 160, 167).

11. Le maître indien Dpal Śes-rab gsaṅ-ba est mentionné aussi dans les colophons de 12, 13 et 14 . Dans les colophons du Tanjur nous trouvons les noms suivants qui semblent tous désigner le même maître indien : Śes-rab dpal gsaṅ-ba, Śes-rab dpal gsaṅ-źabs, Śes-rab gsaṅ-ba, Śes-rab gsaṅ-ba'i źabs, Gsaṅ-ba śes-rab, Prajñāśrīgupta (cf. Rép.). Selon ROERICH (BA. pp. 696-697) il aurait vécu au dixième siècle. Je ne sais pas à quelle source ROERICH a emprunté cette date. L'Arhat (Dgra-bcom) de Phyug-mtshams est mentionné dans un autre colophon (CORDIER, Rgyud XXII. 47) sous le nom de Dbaṅ-phyug rgya-mtsho de Phyug-mtshams. Dans le Kanjur mongol 11 a un long colophon à la louange de Ligdan dans lequel on trouve le passage suivant : erkin degedü šasin-i naran metü manduγuluγad, "Il a fait lever la doctrine suprême comme le soleil" ; BK.: "welcher, aufgegangen wie die Sonne über der höchsten Religion".

13. Le colophon tibétain se termine par la phrase suivante : slad-kyis Dpal Sa-skya'i dben-gnas-su źu-gtugs g. yar khral bgyis-so. Selon les dictionnaires g. yar-khral signifie "capitation" (cf. CHOS-GRAGS p. 807a ; DAS p. 1151b). Est-ce que źu-gtugs g. yar-khral désigne "la capitation pour payer la révision du texte" ? L'expression źus-gtugs g. yar-khral se retrouve dans le colophon de 80 dans un passage qui n'est pas traduit en mongol : Rgya-gar-gyi mkhan-po Śrī-dzñā-na-ka-ra pas bśad-nas / źu-chen-gyi lo-tstsha-ba 'Gos Lhas-btsas-kyis źus-gtugs g. yar-khral-du 'tshal-ba'o, "Quand le maître indien Śrījñānākara avait expliqué le texte, le traducteur et réviseur Lhas-btsas de 'Gos, désirait une capitation de révision"(?). Dans le colophon de 123 il y a źu-thug au lieu de źus-gtugs: (P.) 'grel-pa daṅ bstun-nas bcos-śiṅ źu-thug g. yar-khral-du blaṅs-nas / Bu-ston-gyis bgyis-pa'o ;

tayilbur-i-dur dokiyalduγulǰu ǰasaγad dokiyalduγul-un abču Bu-ston orusiγuluγsan bolai ; BK.: "Bu ston ... hat es ... mit dem Kommentar verglichen, verbessert und, solcher Art verbessert, ediert". Je ne sais pas très bien comment traduire le texte tibétain : "Le texte fut comparé avec le commentaire et il fut corrigé . Une capitation de révision fut levée. [Cela] fut fait par Bu-ston(?)". Dans 13 la version mongole traduit zu-gtugs g. yar-khral bgyis-so par : albatandan(?) neyilegülǰü toγtaγan üiledügsen bolai ; BK.:"[nochmals]... ? ...verglichen und in der richtigen Weise zusammengestellt". Je ne sais pas comment corriger albatandan, cf. KOWALEWSKI, p. 83a : alba(n), tribut , impôt ; 84a : albatu , sujet qui paye les impôts, tributaire.

15. Le texte fut traduit par Rin-chen bzaṅ-po et Padmākara et révisé par Rtogs-pa daṅ-ldan Grags-pa, Prajñākirti et le traducteur Chos-kyi dbaṅ-phyug de Mar. Je pense que Rtogs-pa daṅ-ldan Grags-pa désigne Sumatikīrti (Blo-gros bzaṅ-po grags-pa) qui a traduit de nombreux textes avec Mar-pa (cf. Derge 1434, 1435, 1437, 1443, 1444, 1448, 1568, 1569, 157o, 1571, 1572). Chos-kyi dbaṅ-phyug est appelé aussi Mar-pa Do-pa, l'homme de Mar dans le Do (BA., p. 383 ; CORDIER, Rgyud XLIII. 3). LAUFER a reproché à BECKH d'avoir rendu son nom comme "C'os-kyi dbaṅ-p'yug, der Übersetzer aus Mar" au lieu de "Mar-pa, le traducteur qui porte le titre de Dharmeśvara"(JRAS, 1914, p. 1135) mais le Deb-ther sṅon-po dit que son nom propre est Chos-kyi dbaṅ-phyug (BA. p. 383). Il doit être distingué de Mar-pa Lho-brag Chos-kyi blo-gros, le célèbre maître de Mi-la ras-pa. Chos-kyi blo-gros de Mar dans la province de Lhobrag a vécu de 1o12 à 1o97[26]. Selon le Deb-ther sṅon-po Chos-kyi dbaṅ-phyug naquit quand Mar-pa avait environ 31 ans (± 1o42) et mourut à l'âge de 95 ans (± 1136). Contemporains sont les traducteurs et correcteurs suivants : Sumatikīrti (CORDIER, Rgyud XII. 15), Kumārakalaśa (Rgyud XIII. 31), Kṛkara de l'Inde et Lha-btsas de 'Gos (Rgyud XIII. 52), Dīpaṃkararakṣita (Rgyud XIII. 53), Vāgīśvara du Népal (Rgyud XIII. 57), Vajrabodhi du Kaśmīr (Rgyud XIII. 56), Mahājana (alias Mahājñāna) (Rgyud XIV. 1o), Gźon-nu 'bar de Klog-skya (Rgyud XL. 16), Jayākara (Rgyud XLV. 8), Blo-ldan śes-rab (Rgyud LXVIII. 18), Muditāśrījñāna du Népal (Rgyud LXXIII. 12), Bhadrabodhi du Kaśmīr (Rgyud LXXXIII. 69), Darma grags (Mdo XXVI. 2) et Seṅ-rgyal de Źa-ma (Mdo XXXI. 5).

16. Le texte fut traduit par Atiśa et Rin-chen bzaṅ-po , révisé d'abord par Jñānaśrī et Chos-kyi brtson-'grus de Khyuṅ-po et ensuite par le paṇḍita Ānanda et le petit traducteur (lo-chuṅ). Jñānaśrī a vécu au onzième siècle (BA., p. 7o).

Contemporains de Chos-kyi brtson-'grus sont Kālacakra de l'Inde, Jñānagarbha du Tibet, Jo-sras de 'Brog (CORDIER, Rgyud LIX. 9) et Kumārakalaśa (Rgyud LXIII. 1). Le petit traducteur est Grags-'byor śes-rab (cf. CORDIER, Mdo XVII. 12). Ānanda ou Jayānanda (cf. CORDIER, Mdo XVII. 16) a vécu autour de l'an 1100 car il est contemporain de Śar-ba-pa (1070-1141 , cf. BA., pp. 271-272), de Ñi-ma grags-pa de la branche Pha-tshab des Ldoṅ et de Mdo-sde 'bar de Khu (CORDIER, Mdo. XXXII. 1). Contemporains de Grags-'byor śes-rab sont Sumatikīrti (CORDIER, Rgyud VII. 7), Śrī Bhairavadeva (Rgyud XIV. 15), Gzon-nu śes-rab (Mdo XVII. 12), Śrīratha du Kaśmīr (Mdo XXXIII. 92), Vināyaka du Kaśmīr (Mdo XCIV. 19) et Devendrabhadra (Mdo CXIV). Ñi-ma grags, né en 1055 selon le Re'u-mig (cf. sur lui BA., pp. 341-343), est contemporain de Tilaka (Bstod 28), Kanakavarman de l'Inde (Rgyud XXVI. 11), Tilakakalaśa de l'Inde (Rgyud XXXIII. 15), Alaṃkakalaśa de l'Inde (Rgyud XXXIII. 17), Muditāśrījñāna de l'Inde (Rgyud LXXII. 40), Sūkṣmajana de l'Inde (Mdo XVIII. 1), Mahāsumati de l'Inde (Mdo XXIII. 1) et de Bhavyarāja du Kaśmīr (Mdo CXII. 15). Mdo-sde 'bar est contemporain de Gźon-nu mchog et Dharma grags de Gñan (Mdo XVII. 4).

18. Le colophon dit de Jayasena qu'il touche la poussière des lotus que sont les pieds (skr. padāmbuja) de Śrī Vajravārahī, dpal rdo-rje phag-mo'i źabs-kyi chu-skyes-kyi rdul-la reg-pa ; čoγtu bajar varāhi-yin köl-ün usun-ača törügsen-ü toγusun-dur kürülčegsen, BK. : "der den Staub derer, die aus dem Wasser des Flusses der glanzvollen Bacar varāhi geboren sind, berührt". Je ne comprends pas très bien le passage suivant : phyis gaṅ-zag chos-kyi spyan-can dpal-mchog daṅ-po'i rdo-rje'i bka'i-tshul daṅ yaṅ bstun-te ; qoyina Nom-un nidüten budgalis degedü čoγtu-yin uridu včir-un ǰarliγ-un yosuγar ber dokiyalduγulǰu , "plus tard il comparait aussi avec la méthode de la parole de l'Ādivajra, l'éminent individu qui possède l'œil de la Loi"(?). Le passage suivant n'a pas été compris par BK. : mkha'-mñam bde-rdzogs sna-tshogs sprul-pa saṅs-rgyas-rnams-kyi sku // des gsuṅs dri-med sna-tshogs gdul-bya'i bsam-dbaṅ-gis // gsuṅ gcig-gis kyaṅ sna-tshogs don-maṅ ston-pas dpyad-pa dka' // ; oγtarγui-luγ-a sača amuγulang tegüsügsen eldeb qubilγ-a-tu burqad-un bey-e: tere ber kkir ügegüy-e nomlaγsan eldeb ǰüil nomuγad-qaqun-u sedkil-ün erke-ber : nigen ǰarliγ-iyar ču eldeb ǰüil udq-a-yi olan üǰügülüg-sen-ü tula uqaquy-a berke , "Le corps des Buddha est semblable à l'espace, complet en bonheur et [se manifeste] en toutes sortes de créations (nirmāṇa). Ses paroles pures sont difficiles à pénétrer car elles expriment avec un son unique des sens différents selon l'esprit des différents gens à convertir" (cf. Ét. LAMOTTE, Histoire du bouddhisme indien, I, Louvain, 1958, pp. 609-610) ; BK. : " O himmel-

weite Seligkeit, Leib der Buddha's, in vollkommener Weise verschiedentlich verwandelt! Für die Kraft des Geistes eines in jeder Weise Zuchtvollen, welcher in diesem [Sinne] fehlerlos gelehrt hat, ist es schwer in einem einzigen Wort die verschiedenen Bedeutungen wiederzugeben und vieles aufzuzeigen" .

Jayasena et Dha-rma yon-tan sont contemporains de Lha-rje Zla-ba'i 'od-zer qui a vécu de 1123 à 1182 (BA., pp. 229-232, 388) .

19.   Le Bande de Rgyus, Smon-lam grags n'est pas mentionné ailleurs. BK. fait de lui deux personnes :"der Bande Brgyus [und] Smon lam grags". Gźan-la phan-pa mtha'-yas est probablement identique à Gźan-la phan-pa (bzaṅ-po) ou Parahita(bhadra) qui est contemporain de 'Phags-pa śes-rab (Rgyud VII. 8), Śes-rab rgyal-mtshan de Nag-tsho (Rgyud XIV. 16), Gźon-nu mchog (Mdo XXIV. 5), Dga'-ba rdo-rje de Gzu (Mdo) XLIV. 3), et Blo-ldan śes-rab (Mdo CX. 1) qui a vécu de 1o59 à 11o9 (BA., p. 325). Le réviseur est le célèbre Gźon-nu dpal, l'auteur du Deb-ther sñon-po qui a vécu de 1392 à 1481 (BA., p. i.).

2o.   Si Yon-tan 'bar est identique à l'élève de 'Brom-ston: Ston-pa Yon-tan 'bar, il aura vécu au onzième siècle (cf. BA., p. 264). Le nom de sa place d'origine s'écrit de manières différentes : 'Chiṅs, Mchims, Chiṅs, La bciṅs, La chiṅs, La la chiṅs. Selon LAUFER, la forme correcte est Chiṅs (TP, IX, 19o8, p. 45 ; JRAS, 1914, p. 1139, n. 1).

21.   Le maître de Khu, Dṅos-grub, est probablement identique au maître de Khu, Brtson-'grus g. yuḥ-druṅ qui a vécu de 1o11 à 1o75 (BA., pp. 93-94). Dṅos-grub a traduit deux textes avec Atīśa (Rgyud LXXII. 7o ; LXXXIV. 16). Selon Alfonsa FERRARI, Khu-ston était un des trois élèves les plus éminents d'Atīśa au Tibet central[27]. Les textes auxquels elle renvoie (BA., pp. 93-94, 327 ; Kloṅ-rdol, Za f. 2a) ne disent pas qu'il était un élève d'Atīśa. Selon Kloṅ-rdol (Za f. 2a) 'Brom-ston, Rṅog-ston Śes-rab et Khu-ston Brtson-'grus g. yuḥ-druṅ s'appelaient les trois maîtres du Tibet : Bod-kyi ston-pa gsum. Dans un autre passage du Deb-ther sñon-po Khu-ston est mentionné parmi les élèves d'Atīśa (BA., p. 262). Selon FERRARI (n. 7) Atīśa traduisait beaucoup de textes à Bsam-yas avec Khu-ston mais le passage cité (BA., p. 257) dit qu'Atīśa traduisait des textes à Bsam-yas avec le traducteur (i. e. Nag-tsho) qui est né en 1o11 (BA., p. 88).

Jñānākara du Kaśmīr était un élève de Na-ro-pa. Après la mort d'Atīśa il traduisait des textes avec Nag-tsho (BA., pp. 26o-261 ; Rgyud XXXIII. 9 ; LXXII. 14,

15). Nag-tsho ou Tshul-khrims rgyal-ba a traduit un grand nombre de textes (cf. Rép. p. 2o5). Contemporains sont Krsnapandita de l'Inde (Bstod 1o), Samantabhadra de l'Inde (Rgyud XXII. 2), Śāntibhadra (Rgyud XLII. 2), Dānakīrti (Rgyud XLIII. 1), Vajrapāni de l'Inde (Rgyud XLVII. 37), Brtson seṅ-ge de Rgya (Rgyud LXVI. 6), Dharmapāla du Suvarnadvīpa (Mdo XXVII. 7) et Kamalaraksita (ibid.).

23. Le colophon commence par le passage suivant : dpal O-ddyā-na nas ṅes-par 'byuṅ-ba'i rnal-'byor-ma'i rgyud chen-po stoṅ-phrag bcu-gñis-pa las / 'jig-rten-pa daṅ / 'jig-rten las 'das-pa'i rgyal-po chen-po dpal Indra-bhū-ti'i žabs-kyis bkod-ciṅ gsal-bar mdzad-pa'o ; Čoγtu Indabina(?)-ača maγad γarqui yogini-yin yeke dandr-a arban qoyar mingγan toγatu-ača yirtinčü kiged yirtinčü-eče nögčigsen yeke qaγan čoγtu Indrabodhi bhada čoγuliduγad toda ǰokiyabai , "Le vénérable Indrabhūti, le grand roi, qui vit dans le monde (laukika) et le dépasse (lokottara) , l'a couché par écrit et l'a expliqué [après l'avoir extrait] du grand Yoginī tantra en 12.ooo [śloka] qui provient du glorieux Uddiyāna" ;BK."Das grosse Tantra von der Yoginī die aus dem glanzvollen Intabina sicher errettet, hat ein grosser König, der glanzvolle Indr a bodhi bhada, nachdem er von seinen mehr als zwölf tausend Laien [-untertanen] und aus der Welt gegangen war, geoffenbart und erläutert". Plus loin le colophon dit : slad-kyis de-ñid-kyi tshe pa-ndi-ta gñis la'ah gtugs-te ; ǰiči tegün-i čaγ-tur qoyar pandita-dur ber nayiraγulǰu, BK.: "Später, [aber noch] zu dessen Lebzeiten, haben zwei Pandite [es] korrigiert". Toutefois, selon les textes tibétain et mongol, il faudra traduire : "De nouveau, pendant sa vie même, il l'a aussi comparé à deux pandit". Est-ce que cela veut dire qu'il a comparé la traduction avec un texte récité par deux pandit? Dans les colophons tibétains "comparer avec" se dit la gtugs-pa ou dah gtugs-pa (cf. aussi ci-dessous 485).

26. Gayādhara est contemporain de Lhas-btsas du monastère de 'Gos et de la tribu Khug (17 ; CORDIER, Rgyud XII. 31). Lhas-btsas a vécu au onzième siècle (cf. 15). Gayādhara appartient à la caste des écrivains (kāyastha). M. BISCHOFF lui donne le nom Gayasatvaghayadhara. Il est mentionné dans de nombreux colophons : 9, 28-32, 34-35, 39, 41-46, 48, 5o-57, 6o, 63, 64-67. Son co-traducteur Śā-kya ye-śes est contemporain de la yoginī Candramālā de l'île Simhala (36-38, 4o, 47, 49), Ratnavajra (27 ; CORDIER, Rgyud IX. 3), Prajñendraruci (Rgyud XVII. 1), Ratnaśrīmitra (Rgyud XX. 13) et Ratnaśrījñāna de l'Inde (Rgyud XXI. 21). Le colophon dit : "Plus tard pour confondre ceux qui, après avoir fabriqué de petits changements dans les traductions d'autres traducteurs tibétains, inscrivent leur propre nom et effacent le nom des autres, et [pour confondre] les ignorants,

le moine Śā-kya ye-śes lui-même l'a comparé subséquemment à quatre tantra indiens" ; slad-nas kyaṅ bod-kyi lo-tstsha-ba gžan-rnams-kyis bsgyur-ba la zur mi – 'dra-bar bcos-nas raṅ-gi miṅ bcug-ciṅ / gžan-gyi miṅ 'phyi-ba de-dag daṅ / mi-śes-pa de-dag sun – dbyuṅ -ba'i phyir slad-nas kyaṅ rgya-gar-gyi rgyud-bži daṅ / dge-sloṅ Śā-kya ye-śes de-ñid-kyis gtugs-nas ; ǰiči basa busu töbed-ün kelemürčid busud-un orčiγuluγsan üges-i öber-e bolγan ǰasaǰu : öber-ün ner-e-ben oruγulǰu busud-un ner-e-yi arčiγči tedeger kiged : tedeger 'ülü medegčin-i oyudqaqu-yin tula ǰiči basa enedkeg-ün dörben dandr-a kiged : Šakyalig-ud-un ayaγ-q-a tegimlig Belge bilig-tü tere öber-iyen böged dokiyalduγûl-un. BK. : "Um solche Nichtswisser zu vernichten, welche Worte, die von anderen tibetischen Übersetzern anders übersetzt worden waren, nachträglich abändern und dann den Namen der anderen [Übersetzer] unterschlagen und ihren eigenen einsetzen, hat der Mönch vom Stamme der Śākya Belge bilig-tü hernach noch vier indische Tantren selbst verglichen".

BK. corrige oyudqaqu en oyadqaqu mais , dans 87 , tibétain sun-dbyuṅ-ba est rendu par moquγan γarγaqu. Il faut donc lire moquγaqu au lieu de oyudqaqu.

58. Colophon :(P.) Kha-che'i mkhan-po Dzñā-na-ba-dzras raṅ -'gyur-du mdzad-pa rdzogs-ste ; Kasmir-un ubadini Jñanabajar öber-ün yosuγar orčiγul-un üiledügsen tegüsbe ; BK. : "Der Lehrer Ñjan a bacar hat [dieses] auf seine Weise übersetzt und die Arbeit vollendet". Le texte tibétain dit que Jnanavajra a fait sa propre traduction du texte. Probablement cela veut dire qu'il en était aussi l'auteur. L'expression raṅ-'gyur se retrouve dans le colophon de 88 : (P.) Paṇḍi-ta mkhas-pa chen-po Smṛ-ti-dzñā-na-kīr-tis (P. tas) raṅ-'gyur byas-pa cig-kyaṅ yod-par gda'o, "Il y a aussi une traduction, faite par le pandit, le grand savant Smṛtijñānakīrti, lui-même ". Le traducteur mongol traduit ce passage ainsi : yeke mergen paṇḍita Smṛti-jñā-na-kīrti öber-iyen bolqui nigen üilen bui ; BK. : "Der grosse gelehrte Pandit Smriti ñjā na kirti hat [es mit einer Standartabschrift (sic!)] verglichen, indem er sagte : 'Diese eine Arbeit geht ganz von selbst!' (?)".

61. Abhayākaragupta est contemporain de Rma lo-tsā-ba qui a vécu de 1044 à 1089 (BA., pp. 219-222, 226). Il a donc vécu au onzième siècle ainsi que son co-traducteur 'Khor-lo grags de Khe'u (variante Khe)-rgad (cf. CORDIER, Rgyud LXX. 1). Les réviseurs Buddhakīrti et Śes-rab dpal de Ke-po ont vécu à la même époque car, d'après deux colophons (CORDIER, Rgyud XIII. 47 ; XLVIII. 142), ils ont traduit des textes avec Abhayākaragupta. D'après le colophon de Rgyud LXX. 1 la place

d'origine de Śes-rab dpal est le Khams mais, d'après celui de Mdo XI. 1, Kre-bo. Probablement Ke-po ou Kre-bo est un village ou monastère au Khams.

63. Jinapara et Lha(s)-btsas (cf. 15) ont vécu à l'époque de Chos-kyi dbaṅ-phyug de Mar (± 1o41 - ± 1135).

69. Un des deux traducteurs, Grags-pa rgyal-mtshan de Yar-luṅs, originaire de Śud-kye ou Śud-ke (cf. CORDIER, Rgyud XLIV, 43), est mentionné dans le colophon de 74. Ce dernier texte fut traduit grâce à l'exhortation de Byaṅ-chub rin-chen qui a vécu de 1158 à 1232 (BA., p. 277). Donc les traducteurs, mentionnés dans 69 et 74 : Ratnaśrī, Grags-pa rgyal-mtshan et Vimalaśrībhadra, ont vécu à cette même époque. Ceci est confirmé par le fait que Vimalaśrībhadra a traduit un texte avec Blo-brtan de Śoṅ (CORDIER, Rgyud XVI. 2) qui a traduit des textes par ordre de 'Phags-pa (cf. 1). BK. traduit brten-nas (sitüǰü) par "die Ehre erweisend" dans le passage suivant de 69 : Rin-chen rgyal-mtshan-gyi sku-drin la brten-nas / bla-ma dus-'khor-ba chen-po Śes-rab se-ṅges bskul-źiṅ sbyin-bdag mdzad-pa la brten-nas ; Ratnadhvaja-yin ači-dur sitüǰü blam-a yeke čaγ-un kürdün Prajña-siṁh-a duraddu γči öglige-yin eǰen-dür sitüǰü, "grâce à la faveur de Rin-chen rgyal-mtshan et grâce au guru Śes-rab se-ṅge, le grand spécialiste du Kālacakra, qui a exhorté et a été le dānapati ". BK. ne traduit pas bskul (duraddu γči) qui indique que Prajñāsiṁha a exhorté à traduire le texte (cf. ci-dessus 3).

7o. Atuladāsavajra est contemporain de Chos-kyi dbaṅ-phyug de Mar (cf. 15).

77. Sa-skya paṇḍita (1182-1251) a aussi traduit 123. Selon le colophon de 77 le texte fut traduit dans Sreg-źiṅ de Śaṅs. BK. pense que Saṅs est à corriger en Tsang (probablement erreur pour Gtsaṅ), mais le district Saṅs et le fleuve Śaṅs sont bien connus (cf. CORDIER, Rgyud LXXXII. 1o7 : Śaṅs-pa, secte de l'Ecole des Bka'-brgyud-pa, tirant son nom du district de Śaṅs, province de Gtsaṅ, au Nord de Bkra-śis lhun-po ; FERRARI, n. 6oo).

78. Je ne comprends pas le début du colophon : Ldaṅ-'phrul (P. 'bul)-gyi gtsug-lag-khaṅ chen-po Ra-sa Ra-mo-cher Pha-rgyal Khams-pas źus-pa'i don-du ; Ldaṅ-'bul-un yeke buqar keyid Ra-sa ra-mu-cir kemekü ečige ilaγuγsan orud či ber öčig-sen-ü tulada, "A la demande de Pha-rgyal de Khams dans le Ra-mo-che de Ra-sa, le monastère de Ldaṅ-'phrul(?)". BK. : "Weil ein Einwohner von 'Vatersieger', genannt Ra sa ra mu jir, aus dem grossen Kloster Ldaṅ 'bul, darum gebeten hatte(?)". Le texte fut traduit par Samantaśrī et Chos-rab que la traduction mongole restitue

en Dharmaprabha. CORDIER restitue Chos-rab en Dharmavara. En tous cas, il s'agit d'un tibétain. Chos-rab a traduit plusieurs textes avec Vāgīśvaragupta (CORDIER, Rgyud IV. 6, 7, 1o ; V. 5-7 ; XIV. 62, 63). Vāgīśvaragupta ou Vāgīśvara est contemporain de Chos-kyi dbaṅ-phyug de Mar (cf. 15). Vāgīśvara, Samantaśrī et Chos-rab sont donc des contemporains.

79. Tāksakagaṇa et Byaṅ-chub śes-rab de Maṅ-'or ont aussi traduit un texte du Tanjur (CORDIER, Mdo LXI. 14). Dans ce dernier colophon on trouve pour Tāksakagaṇa la variante Ks(v)elakagaṇa (Ksemagagaṇa dans Derge 4o83).

8o. Il y a des divergences considérables dans le texte de ce colophon selon les Kanjur de Pékin et de Lhasa et le Kanjur mongol. Tous s'accordent quant au début selon lequel le texte a été traduit par Śraddhākaravarman et Rin-chen bzaṅ-po. Ensuite P. continue : slad-kyis paṇ-ḍi-ta bla-ma rdo-rje 'dzin-pa chen-po rje-btsun Ñi-ma'i dbaṅ-po'i źal-sha-nas Chag lo-tsha-ba dge-sloṅ Chos-rje dpal-gyis gus-pas źus-śiṅ dag-par bcos-te gtan-la phab-pa. Ce passage se retrouve à la fin du colophon mongol, mais ne figure pas dans Lh. qui a le texte suivant : rgya-gar-gyi mkhan-po Śrī-dzñā-na-ka-ra pas bśad-nas / źu-chen-gyi lo-tstsha-ba 'Gos Lhas-btsas-kyis źus-gtugs g.yar-khral-du 'tshal-ba'o // 'dus-pa'i rtsa-rgyud la lo-chen-gyis bsgyur-ba maṅ-du snaṅ-na'aṅ / 'Gos-kyis 'gyur-bcos mdzad-pa ñuṅ-bar snaṅ-la / 'grel-pa'i bśad-pa 'Gos-'gyur-gyi steṅ-nas byed-pa la rgyud-kyi 'Gos-'gyur gal-che-bar mthoṅ-nas bris-pa'o, (pour le début cf. ci-dessus 13) "Bien que la traduction du Mūlatantra par le grand traducteur (i. e. Rin chen bzaṅ-po, cf. BA, p. 351) soit un grand [ouvrage] et la correction de la traduction par 'Gos un petit [travail], l'explication du commentaire (le Pradīpoddyotana, cf. CORDIER, Rgyud XXVIII. 1) est faite en plus de la traduction de 'Gos. Vu l'importance de la traduction de 'Gos, nous l'avons copiée". Si j'ai bien compris ce passage, Lhas-btsas a corrigé la traduction du texte à la lumière du commentaire. C'est le texte, corrigé par Lhas-btsas, qui fut substitué à la traduction de Rin-chen bzaṅ-po. Le colophon mongol contient un passage qui mentionne l'excellent arhat, le Chos-kyi rgyal-po, Grags-pa 'byuṅ-gnas-pa rgyal-mtshan dpal-bzaṅ-po (degedü arqad Nom-un qaγan Aldarsiγsan γarqu-yin orun čoγtu sayin ilaγuγsan čimeg), et Gźon-nu dpal (Jalaγu čoγtu). Ce passage qui fait défaut aux Kanjur de Pékin et de Lhasa pose des problèmes. Gźon-nu dpal a vécu de 1392-1481. Chag lo-tsa-ba Chos-rje-dpal qui est mentionné comme réviseur à la fin du colophon, a vécu de 1197 à 1265 (cf. BA., p. 1o47, n. 1). Je suppose que ce passage du colophon mongol résulte d'une confusion entre Lhas-btsas de 'Gos et

Gźon-nu dpal de 'Gos. Grags-pa 'byuṅ-gnas rgyal-mtshan dpal-bzaṅ-po est aussi mentionné dans le colophon de la traduction du Prakāśa nāma śrīhevajrasādhana par Śrī Vanaratna de l'Inde et Gźon-nu dpal (CORDIER, Rgyud XXI. 2o). Vanaratna a vécu de 1382 à 1468 (BA., pp. 797-8o5). Il a traduit des textes avec 'Jam-dpal ye-śes (CORDIER, Rgyud XXVI. 45), Bsod-nams rgya-mtsho'i sde de Byams-pa gliṅ (CORDIER, Bstod 63, Rgyud LXXIV. 15, 3o) qui a vécu de 1424 à 1482 (BA., pp. 8o5-837) et avec Roṅ-ston ou Śa-kya rgyal-mtshan (CORDIER, Mdo LXXXIX. 1) qui a vécu de 1367 à 1449 (BA., 1o8o-1o81).

81. Les colophons de P. et Lh. sont identiques mais le colophon mongol ajoute un passage qui mentionne Chos-kyi rgyal-po Grags-pa 'byuṅ-gnas-pa (Nom-un qaγan aldarsiqui boluγsan orun : L. a oyun qui est à corriger en orun ; BK. : "der als König der Lehre berühmt geworden ist") et Gźon-nu dpal. Pour pouvoir bien interpréter ce passage il faudrait en retrouver l'original tibétain qui est peut-être transmis dans une autre édition du Kanjur. Je pense que, dans le passage suivant, il faut corriger üǰeǰü en öčiǰü : Čoγtu ǰalaγu qoyar ündüsün aγui üliger-i öčiǰü , "Čoγtu ǰalaγu (Gźon-nu dpal) , après avoir corrigé le texte étendu des deux tantra (i. e. 8o et 81)"; BK., "Čoγtu ǰalaǰu ...., indem er die beiden Tantren, das hohe Gleichnis, studierte". Mongol üliger rend certainement tibétain dpe . Il est difficile de distinguer üǰe- et öči- dans l'écriture mongole. L'expression źu-chen "grand réviseur " est rendue par üǰegči yeke selon le catalogue de M. LIGETI (78) mais, dans 84 , il note : öčigči (!) yeke . Probablement il faut lire partout öčigči au lieu de üǰegči . Il y a en tibétain deux verbes źu-ba , l'un signifiant "demander", l'autre "corriger". En traduisant źu-chen les traducteurs mongols ont traduit machinalement źu-ba "demander" au lieu de źu-ba "corriger".

82. Le texte tibétain du début de ce colophon est le suivant : thugs-dam sa'i sñiṅ-po Tho-liṅ, "Tho-liṅ, le centre du pays du vœu". Le traducteur mongol a lu : thugs daṅ sa'i sñiṅ-po, ǰirüken kiged γaǰar-un ǰirüken. Dans 12o le texte tibétain de P. et Lh. a : thugs-dam pa'i sñiṅ-po, bisilγalčin-u ǰirüken. Tibétain pa est certainement une erreur pour sa. Dans un colophon du Tanjur (Mdo XLIV. 3) Tho-liṅ est appelé : thugs-dam sa Tho-liṅ, "Tho-liṅ, le pays du vœu".

Bk. fait deux personnes du sgra-sgyur-gyi lo-tstsha-ba chen-po bod-kyi Lha-btsan-po bla-ma dge-sloṅ Źi-ba'i 'od : "ein tibetischer Dolmetscher, unter Assistenz des grossen Lha bcan po Lama Mönch Amurlingγu-yin gerel". Cf. aussi 12o : sgra-sgyur-gyi lo-tstsha-ba Lha-btsan-po dge-sloṅ bla-ma'i Źi-ba'i 'od, BK.:

"der Dolmetscher-Übersetzer Lha bcan po [und] der Dge slon Lama Źi źi (?) va'i 'od". Il s'agit évidemment d'une seule personne : Źi-ba'i 'od, le frère du roi Byan-chub 'od qui régnait dans la deuxième moitié du onzième siècle[28].

84. Le colophon se termine par les vers suivants : Ye-śes rdo-rje kun-las btus // rnal-'byor chen-po'i gsal-byed yin // ye-śes ran-bźin 'khor ba dan // mya-han 'das-pa'i no-bo la // de-gñis dbyer-med rdo-rje ste // kun-'dir 'dus-pas kun-las btus // de ston-pa la der brtags-nas // gźun-la'an min-don 'tsham-pa yin //; Belge bilig-ün včir-i qamuγ-ača tegüküi : ma-hā yoga-yi geyigülügči bui : belge bilig-ün mön činar orčilang kiged : γasalang-ača nögčigsen-ü činar bolai : tere qoyar ilγal ügei včir buyu : qamuγ egün-dür quriyaγsan-iyar qamuγ-ača tegüküi teyin ber üjügülügči tede nereyidčü : yosun-dur ber ner-e udq-a-yin činegen bui, "Le Vajrajñāna-samuccaya éclaircit le mahāyoga. La nature propre du savoir est l'essence du Samsāra et du Nirvāṇa. Ces deux, qui ne sont pas séparés, sont le vajra. Parce que tout est ici réuni, [le texte s'appelle] réunion (samuccaya). Prenant en considération le fait que [l'ouvrage] montre cela (i. e. samuccaya), [on constate que] dans l'ouvrage, nom et sens s'accordent". BK.: "Der 'Zusammengedrängte Abschnitt von der Zauberwaffe des Wissens' ist eine Erläuterung zum Mahāyoga. (Es folgt die Übersetzung dreier siebensilbiger tibetischer Doppelverse frommen Inhalts)".

87. Le colophon commence par le passage suivant : mkhan-chen Thar-pa lo-tsā-ba'i phyag-dpe'i gseb-nas śog yar lha byun-ba śhar bsgyur-ba las // phyis Ñan-stod Smon-'gro'i gtsug-lag-khan-nas rgya-dpe lhag-ma rnams rñed-nas bsgyur-bar rtsom-pa na // dpal-dus-kyi 'khor-lo'i phyi-nan-gźan gsum-gyi tshul-la mi-'jigs-pa'i spobs-pa thob-pa'i bla-ma yan-dag-pa'i dge-ba'i bśes-gñen chen-po legs-par sbyar-ba'i skad-kyi brda-sprod-pa'i tshul-la blo-gros śin-tu byan-ba'i 'jig-rten-gyi mig Chos-grags-dpal bzan-po'i bkas bskul-źin sbyin-bdag mdzad-nas // Bu-ston-gyis bsgyur-ba'i yi-ge-pa ni dge-slon Rin-chen rgyal-mtshan-pa'o // Yeke ubadiy-a Tarba kelemürči bičig-ün dotur-a-ača tabun qaγudasu uridu orčiγuluγsan-ača : qoyin-a Ñan-stod smon-gro-yin buqar keyid-eče ülegsen enedkeg bičig-üd-i olǰu orčiγulun toγurbiqui-dur čoγtu čaγ-un kürdün-ü γadaγadu dotuγadu öber-e γurban yosun-dur ayul ügei sambaγ-a-yi oluγsan ünen maγad degedü yeke baγsi Sangrida-yin ayalγu dokiyan-u yosun-dur oyun-iyan masi bisiluγsan yirtinčü-yin γaγča kü nidün Čhos-grag dpal bzan-po öglige-yin eǰen duraduγsan-iyar Bu-ston orčiγulbai : bičigči dge-sloh Rin-čhen rgyal-mchan bolai, "Autrefois les cinq premiers feuillets, provenant des livres du grand savant Thar-pa, avaient

été traduits. Plus tard, quand on avait obtenu le reste du manuscrit tibétain du monastère Smon-'gro dans le Ñaṅ-stod, on a entrepris de le traduire. Bu-ston l'a traduit, après avoir été exhorté par la parole du dānapati Chos-grags dpal-bzaṅ-po qui avait obtenu une intelligence parfaite (litt. : sans crainte) dans la méthode des trois [divisions :] extérieure, intérieure et différente du Śrīkālacakra, le guru, le parfait et grand kalyāṇamitra, l'œil du monde (lokacakṣus) dont l'esprit était très savant dans la méthode de la grammaire de la langue sanskrite. Rin-chen rgyal-mtshan était le scribe". En traduisant śog yar lha par "les cinq premiers feuillets", je ne sais pas si j'ai bien compris le sens de yar. Les trois divisions du Kālacakra sont expliquées par Kloṅ-rdol (vol. ca). BK. : "Auf Ansuchen des Spendeherrn Čhos grag dpal bzaṅbo , welcher eine aller Ungewissheit bare Meisterschaft in jeder der vier inneren und äusseren Methoden des glanzvollen Kreises der Zeit erworben hatte, ein wahrhaft erhabener, grosser Meister, überaus bewandert in den Regeln der Auslegung der Sanskrit-Laute (Sprache) - kurz, ein Auge der Welt - welcher, nachdem er die ersten fünf Folien aus dem Exemplar des grossen Lehrers Tarba, des Übersetzers, übersetzt hatte, später die übrigen indischen Bücher aus dem Kloster Ñaṅstod smon gro erwarb damit ihre Übersetzung in Angriff genommen werde, [auf Ansuchen dieses Spendeherren, also] hat Bu ston [dieses] übersetzt. Der Schreiber war der Mönch Rinčhen rgyalmchan".

Il faut aussi corriger la traduction de deux autres passages du colophon : rgyud-min rgyud-ltar bcos-pa yi // chos-min sun-dbyuṅ-bya phyir daṅ //; dandr-a busu-yi dandr-a metü ǰasadaγ : nom busu-yi moquγan γarγaqu-yin tula ba, "Pour réfuter le mauvais dharma (adharma) [du tantra] qui fut fabriqué en tantra bien qu'il ne soit pas un tantra". Ceci se rapporte au texte 88 dont l'authenticité était mise en question par Bu ston[29]. BK. : "Um eine Tantra-ähnliche Verfälschung, die aber kein Tantra ist, und eine Afterlehre zum Schweigen zu bringen und auszumerzen". Plus loin le colophon dit : 'di-don 'byed-pa'i 'grel-pa daṅ // rgya-dpe'i dpe yaṅ (Lh. et Derge : dpaṅ) ma-rñed-ciṅ //; egün-ü udq-a-yi ilγaqu-yin tayilbur kiged : enedkeg-ün üliger bičig dokiyalduγulqu-yi ese oluγad, "N'ayant pas obtenu un commentaire qui en explique le sens et aussi un texte indien". J'ai traduit dpe'i dpe comme équivalent de dpe. Peut-être faut-il lire avec les Kanjur de Lhasa et de Derge rgya-dpe'i dpe-dpaṅ "un texte témoin [consistant en] un texte indien(?)"(cf. aussi ci-dessous 485). Dans la traduction mongole se trouvent les mots üliger et bičig qui, tous les deux, s'emploient pour rendre dpe. BK. : "Da ich weder einen Kommentar zum genauen Verständnis des Sinnes dieses [Tantras], noch eine Vergleichsmöglichkeit in Form einer indischen Standartabschrift(sic!) besass".

La fin du colophon mongol s'accorde avec la fin du colophon dans l'édition de Pékin : 'di-la dbu-nas śog-lto gcig ma tshaṅ-bas rñed-na bsgyur-bar bya'o // 'di-daṅ thun-moṅ ma-yin-pa'i gsaṅ-ba gcig-tu 'dod-pa yaṅ-dag-par 'khrul-bar snaṅ-ṅo // 'dis 'khor-ba sdug-bsṅal-gyi rgya-mtsho chen-po myur-du skems-par gyur-cig, "Ici au début le recto d'un feuillet manque. Si on l'obtient, il faudra le traduire. Désirer exclusivement un secret qui n'est pas semblable à celui-ci, est une erreur. Que, par cela (i.e. le mérite qui provient d'avoir traduit ce texte), le grand océan de douleur de la transmigration se dessèche vite!" Dans Lh. la fin du colophon est le suivant : 'di-daṅ... snaṅ-ṅo // rgya-dpe zubs-pa'i bar-skabs nas ma-tshaṅ-ba rnams-su dkyus-mchan re bkod-yod-pas śes-par bya'o, "Il faut savoir que des notes marginales ont été mises aux endroits où le texte n'est pas complet par le fait que le manuscrit sanskrit était effacé". Dans Derge le texte est identique à Lh. à l'exception des mots dkyus-mchan re qui ont été remplacés par sa-stoṅ. Ensuite suit un long passage qui traite de la traduction du début d'après la version chinoise par Mgon-po skyabs (cf. TP, LIV, 1968, pp. 183-185).

Kun-spaṅs Chos-grags dpal-bzaṅ-po fut un élève de Dol-po-pa qui a vécu de 1292 à 1361 (BA., p. 777 : D. S. RUEGG, op. cit., p. 123. n. 1).

88. Le colophon se termine ainsi : rgyud-'di U-rgyan-nas slob-dpon chen-po Dom-bi-he-ru-kas gdan-'draṅs gsuṅ-ṅo ; ene ündüsün-i Odiyan-a-ača ma-hā aciry-a Dombi-heruka-yi ǰalaǰu nomlabai, "Il est dit que ce tantra fut rapporté de l'Uḍḍiyāna par le grand maître Ḍombiheruka" ; BK.: "Ein mahācarya aus Oḍiyāna, Ḍombi heruka hat dieses Tantra eingeführt und gepredigt".

89. Je n'ai pas pu déterminer les dates des traducteurs : Devapūrnamati du Népal et Chos-kyi bzaṅ-po de 'Gar. Le premier a traduit un texte avec Vajradeva de Se'u (CORDIER, Rgyud LXIV. 72) ; le deuxième a traduit plusieurs textes avec Dharmaśrīmitra (CORDIER, Rgyud, LXI, 10-12, 14, 17-23).

92. Adayaśrīmati est contemporain de Chos-kyi dbaṅ-phyug grags qui doit être le même que Chos-kyi dbaṅ-phyug de Mar (cf. 15).

93. Le nom du traducteur s'écrit de plusieurs manières différentes: A-ba-yu-ga-ta, A-bi-ju-ga-ta, A-bhi'-jug-rta, A-ju-ga-ta-pa. La forme correcte est Abhiyukta (CORDIER, Rgyud XIV. 79 ; LXVIII. 196 ; LXXXII. 95, 106). Il a vécu

au onzième siècle car il est contemporain de Chos-kyi brtson-'grus (cf. 16).

94. Le traducteur tibétain s'appelle ici bla-ban Chos-kyi brtson-'grus. BK. écrit Balban et ajoute : "vielleicht verderbte Form von bal-po = Nepal?". Je n'ai pas trouvé l'expression bla-ban dans les dictionnaires mais je suppose que c'est une abréviation pour bla-ma ban-dhe.

97. Ratnakīrti et Khyuṅ-grags sont contemporains de Yon-tan 'bar (cf. 2o) qui a traduit plusieurs textes avec Ratnakīrti (CORDIER, Rgyud XL. 25, Mdo VIII. 4, LXI. 15). Khyuṅ-grags a traduit des textes avec Kiraṇākaravarman (CORDIER, Rgyud LXIII. 4) et Divākaracandra (Rgyud LXVIII. 155).

1oo. Dpal-brtsegs de Ska-ba et Klu'i rgyal-mtshan ont vécu au début du neuvième siècle car le dernier a traduit des textes avec Jinamitra, cf. Introduction (CORDIER, Mdo LXXVII. 1 ; LXXVIII. 2, 5 ; LXXX ; LXXXII. 1, 2 ; LXXXVI ; XC. 9, 1o). Il a aussi traduit un texte avec Jñānagarbha de l'Inde (CORDIER, Mdo XCIV. 3) qui a donc vécu à la même époque. Dpal-brtsegs est contemporain de Vidyākaraprabha (CORDIER, Bstod 51), Buddhaguhya (Rgyud LXVI. 17), Mañjuśrī de Dbas (Rgyud LXXII. 1), Muktikā de Bran-kha (ibid.), Vidyākarasiṃha (Mdo VIII. 3), Sarvajñadeva (Mdo XVIII. 2), Dānaśīla (Mdo XXXIV. 7), Mañjuśrīgarbha (Mdo XXXIV. 14), Prajñāvarman (ibid.), Jinamitra (Mdo XXXVII. 3), Śākyasiṃha de l'Inde (Mdo XXXVIII. 4), Viśuddhasiṃha (Mdo LVIII. 8), Devendrarakṣita de Rtsaṅs (ibid.). Rin-chen mchog et Dharmākara ont vécu à la même époque car ils ont traduit des textes avec Sarvajñadeva (Bstod 44) et Jñānagarbha (Mdo LXXII. 4).

1o4. Bha-ro phyag-rdum et Rdo-rje grags de Ra ont vécu au onzième siècle car le dernier a traduit un texte avec Dīpamkararakṣita (CORDIER, Rgyud XLIII. 67). Contemporains de Rdo-rje grags sont aussi Ānanda de l'Inde (CORDIER, Rgyud XLIII. 56), Amoghapāda (Rgyud XLIII. 65) et Mahākaruṇa (Rgyud XLIII. 127).

1o9. Le colophon du Kanjur de Pékin s'accorde avec le colophon mongol : Bla-ma Chos-kyi rgyal-po'i gsuṅ-gi 'od-zer daṅ / bho-ṭa pa-ṇḍi-ta'i gsuṅ daṅ / mi'i dbaṅ-po Kun-dga' bzaṅ-po'i gsuṅ daṅ / dpon Kun-gźon-gyis gser gnaṅ-ba la brten-nas / Śā-kya'i dge-sloṅ Tsan-dra-śrī'i źal-sha-nas źus-śiṅ / paṇ-ḍi-ta chen-po Tsan-dra-kī-rti daṅ / Yar-luṅs Grags-pa rgyal-mtshan-gyis Bal-yul Yam-bu'i groṅ-khyer-du bsgyur-ro. Je ne comprends pas très bien le sens de gsuṅ-gi 'od-zer ; ǰarliγ-un gerel ; BK. : "Im Lichte des Befehls". Faut-il comprendre 'od-zer comme une expression honorifique : "le lustre de sa parole", "sa parole glorieuse" ? Bla-ma Chos-kyi rgyal-po est 'Phags-pa et Kun-dga' bzaṅ-po est le deuxième dpon-chen (cf. ci-dessus 3). Le Bhoṭapaṇḍita est aussi mentionné dans trois colophons du Tanjur (CORDIER, Mdo CXVI. 6, CXXIII. 5, 34). Dans le premier les patrons de la traduction sont 'Phags-pa et le Bhoṭapaṇḍita[3o)], les traducteurs Dpal Sa-dbaṅ bzaṅ-po et Śoṅ Blo-brtan. Le colophon de Mdo CXXIII. 5 mentionne d'abord comme traducteurs Dharmadhara et Grags-pa rgyal-mtshan et continue ainsi : grub-pa kun-mkhyen Chos-rgyal-gyi / gsuṅ-gi 'od-zer snaṅ-bar brten / mkhan-chen bho-ṭa pa-ṇḍi-ta dam-chos / 'dzin-dag (lire : pa'i ?) gsuṅ brten-nas // Yar-luṅs Grags-pa rgyal-mtshan-gyis / Guṅ-thaṅ rgyal-sar legs-par bsgyur /, "Suivant l'éclat du lustre de la parole du siddha, l'omniscient Roi de la loi, et suivant la parole du grand savant, le Bhoṭapaṇḍita, le saddharmadhara, [le texte] a été bien traduit par Grags-pa rgyal-mtshan dans la capitale Guṅ-thaṅ ". Dans le dernier colophon le patron est le Mahāpiṭakadhara Mahābhoṭapaṇḍita et les traducteurs sont Dharmadhara et Grags-pa rgyal-mtshan de Spaṅs . Tous ces colophons confirment que le Bhoṭapaṇḍita a dû vivre à l'époque de 'Phags-pa et des traducteurs Dpal Sa-dbaṅ-bzaṅ-po, Śoṅ Blo-brtan, Dharmadhara et Grags-pa rgyal-mtshan mais ils n'ajoutent pas de détails qui permettraient de l'identifier. Je n'ai pas pu non plus identifier le dpon Kun-gźon. Candraśrī et Candrakīrti ont dû vivre au douzième siècle. Le colophon de ce texte dans l'édition de Derge semble être identique à celui de l'édition de Pékin car, selon Derge 474, le texte fut traduit par Candrakīrti et Grags-pa rgyal-mtshan. Dans l'édition de Lhasa les patrons sont 'Phags-pa et le dpon-chen Kun-dga' bzaṅ-po, les traducteurs Rāhulaśrībhadra et Blo-brtan. Le lieu de la traduction est le grand monastère des Sa-skya.

11o. Le colophon mentionne Jaganmitrānanda, Vajraśrīkhalarudra et Byams-pa'i dpal. Byams-pa'i dpal est né en 1172 ou 1173[31)]. Il a traduit des textes avec Buddhaśrījñāna (CORDIER, Rgyud XIII. 34 ; XIV, 67, etc.), Mitrānanda (Rgyud LXVIII. 164), Mitrayogin (Rgyud XLIV. 35, 38-4o, 47 ; XLVIII. 126-127), Śākyaśrībhadra (Rgyud XXVI. 6, 13, 39-4o, etc.), Sugataśrī (Rgyud XXVI. 38), Subhaśānti (Rgyud XLIV. 36), et Buddhaśrībhadra(jñāna) (Rgyud XIV. 67 ; XXII. 41 ; XLIV. 37 ; XLVIII. 123). Il y a des biographies de Mitrayogin et de Śākyaśrībhadra dans le Deb-ther sṅon-po (BA. pp. 1o3o-1o34 ; 1o63-1o71). Selon ce texte Śākyaśrībhadra a vécu de 1127 à 1225 et est arrivé au Tibet en 12o4. Selon une biographie, citée par M. TUCCI (Tibetan Painted Scrolls, pp. 335-336) il a vécu de 1145 à 1243 (cf. FERRARI, n. 53).

111.   Selon le colophon mongol le texte fut traduit par Brangdi ciny-a ragcidi(?).
Selon les Kanjur de Pékin et de Derge le traducteur fut Rin-chen bzaṅ-po .

112.   Le colophon se termine par le passage suivant : rgyud-dpe rṅiṅ-'gyur mi-
'dra-ba gsum bstun-te źus-dag bsgrubs-so ; adali bögesü γurban öber-e orčiγuluγsan qaγučin bičig-lüge dokiyalduγulǰu : orčiγulbai, "En comparant trois textes du
tantra [contenant] trois vieilles traductions différentes, ils ont établi [un texte] correct" ; BK.: "Und wenn dem so ist, hätten sie [es] mit drei alten Exemplaren welche
unabhängig von einander übersetzt worden waren, verglichen und [neu] übersetzt".

113.   Karmavajra et Gźon-nu tshul-khrims ont vécu au onzième siècle car le
dernier a traduit un texte avec Dipaṃkaraśrijñāna (CORDIER Mdo XC. 5). Il est aussi contemporain de Mañjuśrī (Rgyud XLIV. 73).

115.   Rin-chen mchog de Rma a vécu autour de l'an 8oo, car le Deb-ther shon-
po le mentionne dans une énumération de siddha qui ont vécu à l'époque du roi Khri-
sroṅ lde-btsan (mort en 797[32]) et de son fils (cf. aussi Paul DEMIÉVILLE, Le concile de Lhasa , Paris, 1952, p. 34 note). Contemporains sont Sarvajñadeva de l'Inde
(CORDIER, Bstod, 1, 4, 44-46 ; Mdo XXXIII. 96-1oo), Vajrahasa de l'Inde (Rgyud XXV.
1o, 15, 16), Śāntigarbha (Rgyud LXXII. 69), Jñānakumāra de Gñags (Rgyud LXXVI. 1)
et Vidyākaraprabha de l'Inde (Mdo XXXIII. 34 ; LXXI. 1 ; XCIV. 29) ; cf. aussi ci-
dessus 1oo pour Rin-chen mchog, Sarvajñadeva et Vidyākaraprabha.

117.   Devendradevapāda et Maṇikaśrijñāna ont vécu à l'époque de Chos-rje
dpal de Chag : 1197-1285 (cf. ci-dessus 8o). Chos-rje-dpal est contemporain de Ni-
ma'i dbaṅ-po'i 'od-zer (Ravīndraprabha), Ratnarakṣita de l'Inde et Rāhulaśrībhadra
(CORDIER, Rgyud LXX. 1). Ratnarakṣita est contemporain de Grub-pa dpal bzaṅ-
po du Źaṅ (Rgyud XIII. 46).

118.   Jñānavajra est contemporain de Śes-rab grags de 'Bro qui a vécu au onzième siècle (cf. ci-dessus 3).

12o.   Le colophon tibétain se termine ainsi : lo-tstsha chen-po Rin-chen bzaṅ-
po yis // Dpal mchog-daṅ-po'i rgyud 'di bsgyur-ba la // bar-bar dpe ma rñed-pas
ma-'gyur nas // bdag-gis 'bad-pas dpe-btsal rñed-pas bsgyur ; yeke kelemürči
Rin-čhen bzaṅ-po : čoγtu uridu degedü ene dandris-i orčiγulqui-daγan : ǰaγur-a-yin
üsüg-ün ese oluγsan-i öber-ün qataγučil-iyar eriǰü oluγad orčiγulbai bi, "Moi, le

grand traducteur Rin-chen bzaṅ-po, je me suis efforcé de chercher des textes et, après les avoir obtenus, j'ai traduit les passages qui ne furent pas traduits lors de la traduction de ce Śrīparamādyatantra parce que [les traducteurs] n'en avaient pas obtenu un texte". BK.: "Ich, der grosse Übersetzer Rin čhen bzaṅ po habe bei meiner [Neu-]übersetzung dieses glanzvollen, alten, erhabenen Tantras, diejenigen Lesungen welche [die vormaligen Übersetzer] nicht herausgefunden hatten, mit eigener Anstrengung gesucht, gefunden und übersetzt".

Mantrakalaśa a vécu à l'époque du roi Źi-ba'i 'od (cf. ci-dessus 82). Il est le fils de Tārakalaśa et le petit-fils de Kumārakalaśa (CORDIER, Rgyud XXVII. 1).

122. Sugataśrī a vécu à l'époque de Kun-dga' rgyal-mtshan ou Sa-skya paṇḍita (1182-1253). Le colophon tibétain a Kun-dga'-rgyal-mtshan, le colophon mongol : Kun-dga' rgyal-mchan dpal bsaṅ-po paṇḍita, "Kun-dga' rgyal-mtshan dpal bzaṅ-po , le paṇḍit " ; BK.: "Kundgā' rgyal mchan, ein dpal bsaṅ po Pandit".

123. Le texte tibétain mentionne le commentaire du maître Praśāntamitra: slob-dpon Rab-źi bśes-gñen ; Masi amurlingγui sayin nökür baγsi tayilbur-i ; BK.: "dem Kommentar des Masi amurlingγui, eines Meisters der Metaphysik". Sanskrit kalyāṇamitra est rendu en tibétain par dge-ba'i bśes-gñen et ne signifie pas "Meister der Metaphysik". Plus loin de colophon dit : mi-bcos-su mi-ruṅ-ba re-re tsam 'grel-pa daṅ bstun-nas bcos-śiṅ ; ǰasaqui ügei ülü bolqu : niǰeged niǰeged tedüi tayilbur-i-dur dokiyalduγulǰu ǰasaγad, "Chaque endroit qui ne pouvait pas ne pas être corrigé, fut comparé par lui avec le commentaire et corrigé" ; BK.: "Da es aber nicht unverbessert bleiben konnte, hat er es Stück für Stück mit dem Kommentar verglichen, verbessert".

125. Le début du colophon dit : dam-pa'i rgyud-'di gaṅs-can 'di-na shon // rnam-pa kun-tu bsgyur-ba ma rñed-nas // ; Ene degedü dandr-a urida ene Časutan-dur ǰüil bügüde-yi orčiγulqui ese olǰu, "n'ayant pas du tout obtenu une traduction de cet excellent tantra [faite] autrefois dans ce pays de neige" ; BK.: "Wir konnten keine irgendwie geartete frühere Übersetzung dieses erhabenen Tantras in dem Schneereichen [Lande] (Tibet) ausfindig machen".

127. Le nom du traducteur indien n'est pas bien fixé mais, probablement, la forme correcte est Upaśamarakṣita . Dha-rma blo-gros de Glan a traduit des textes avec Tathāgatarakṣita (CORDIER, Rgyud VII. 5 ; XII. 2 ; XXII. 43), Sādhurak-

ṣita (Rgyud XVIII goṅ), Vairocanarakṣita (Rgyud XXI. 31 ; XLIII. 54, 91, 92 ; LXXXIV. 7), Dānaśrī (Rgyud XXII. 6), Ye-śes-kyi mkha'-'gro-ma Ni-gu-ma (Rgyud XXII. 8 ; LXXIII. 3o, 31, 34, 35, 37, 39-41), Vairocana (Rgyud LXXI. 39o) et Grub-pa-can Rdo-rje gdan-pa (Rgyud LXXXIV. 8). Tathāgatarakṣita a traduit des textes avec Gźon-nu 'bar de Klog-skya (CORDIER, Rgyud XXXIII. 18) et Rin-chen bzaṅ-po (Rgyud XL. 27). Contemporains sont aussi Rin-chen grags de Ba-ri (Rgyud XII. 3), Mya-ṅan med-pa'i dpal de Cog-gru (Rgyud XXVI. 15-2o) et Atīśa (Rgyud XXXIV. 9). Tous ces traducteurs ont donc dû vivre au onzième siècle. Vairocanarakṣita de l'Inde et Vairocana de l'Inde sont probablement identiques(cf. CORDIER, Mdo XXVII. 3). Selon le colophon le moine Yon-tan rdo-rje a fait la demande [pour la traduction] : dge-sloṅ Yon-tan rdo-rjes gsol-ba btab-pa'o : Erdem-ün vcir ayaγ-ɨ-a tegimlig ber ǰalbarin öčibei ; BK. : "der Mönch Erdem-ün včir hat es betend rezitiert". On peut aussi interpréter cette phrase comme signifiant qu'il a fait une prière après l'achèvement de la traduction.

128. Ce-lu du Kaśmir et 'Phags-pa śes-rab ont vécu au onzième siècle car le dernier a traduit des textes avec Mahākaruṇa (CORDIER, Rgyud LIII), cf. ci-dessus 1o4 et Atuladāsa(Rgyud LXXXI. 8) qui est probablement identique à Atuladāsavajra (cf. ci-dessus 7o). Contemporains sont aussi Jñānaśrībhadra (Rgyud XXIII. 28), Parahita (Rgyud VII. 8 ; XII. 4), Śrījñāna (Rgyud LIX. 1), Tejadeva (Rgyud LXVIII. 2o2-2o6 ; LXXII. 25, 26, 29-31), Kumāraśrībhadra (Mdo C ; CVIII. 2 ; CXII. 4) et Seṅdkar de 'Bro ou Śā-kya 'od (ibid.).

129. Bya'i gdoṅ est contemporain d'Atīśa .

131. Kumāravajra et le traducteur Ra-byid ont traduit le texte par ordre du roi Khri-sroṅ lde-btsan (mort en 797, cf. ci-dessus 115).

132. Brtson-'grus seṅ-ge de Rgya est identique à Brtson seṅ-ge de Rgya (cf. ci-dessus 21).

138. Le colophon mentionne comme traducteurs Vidyāgarbhaprabha et Dpal-gyi lhun-po et comme réviseurs Vidyākaraprabha et Dpal-brtsegs. Vidyāgarbhaprabha est probablement une erreur pour Vidyākaraprabha qui a vécu dans la deuxième moitié du huitième siècle (cf. ci-dessus 1oo et 115).

162. Vimalamitra, Rin-chen sde et Nam-mkha' (skyoṅ) ont vécu à la fin du huitième siècle, car le premier a traduit des textes avec Rin-chen mchog de Rma

(CORDIER, Rgyud LXXVI. 1), Jñānakumāra de Gñags (ibid.), Surendrākaraprabha du Li (Mdo XVI. 6) et Jñānagarbha du Tibet (Mdo XVI. 8). Vimalamitra a écrit un texte avec Buddhaguhya et Līlāvajra (CORDIER, Rgyud LXXV. 23).

164. Le colophon mentionne le roi Byaṅ-chub 'od : dpal lha btsan-po lha btsun-pa Byaṅ-chub 'od ; cf. TUCCI, Indo-Tibetica, II, p. 24.

168. Klu'i dbaṅ-po a vécu à l'époque de Jnanagarbha de l'Inde (cf. ci-dessus 1oo).

176. Le colophon contient l'expression bcom-ldan-'das-kyi riṅ-lugs; ilaǰu tegüs nögčigsen-ü törü yosun-i bariǰu, "celui qui suit la doctrine du Tathāgata"; BK.: "die Anweisung des Siegreich Vollendeten beobachtend". L'expression riṅ-lugs a été étudiée par M. TUCCI, Minor Buddhist Texts, Part II, Roma, 1958, pp. 56-67, note 2 ; cf. Chos-grags riṅ-lugs - yun-riṅ-du gnas-pa'i lam-srol "coutumes qui existent depuis longtemps". Les traducteurs mongols ont rendu riṅ-lugs ou riṅ-lugs-pa ailleurs par qola-yin yosutu (375 ; BK. corrige qola en ꞏula = Skt. kula), öni yosun (379), yosutu (461) et öni yosutu (539). Chos-grub est bien connu, cf. Paul DEMIÉVILLE, Le concile de Lhasa, Paris, 1952, pp. 2o-21, n. 5 : "Un moine probablement tibétain, Čhos-grub, en chinois Fa-tch'eng 法成, en Sanskrit Dharmasiddhi, qui vécut à Touen-houang et à Kan-tcheou aux alentours de l'an 8oo, est l'auteur de nombreuses traductions tibéto-chinoises et sino-tibétaines" ; pour une excellente étude de sa vie et de ses travaux voir UEYAMA Daishun 上山大俊, Daibankoku daitoku sanzō hōshi shamon Hōjō no kenkyū 大蕃國大徳三藏法師沙門法成の研究, Tōhō gakuhō, 38, 1967, pp. 133-198; 39, 1968, pp. 119-222.

184. Amoghavajra, élève de Mitrayogin (cf. CORDIER, Rgyud LXXXIV. 9) est contemporain de Rin-chen grags de Ba-ri qui a vécu au onzième siècle (cf. ci-dessus 127). Amoghavajra a traduit des textes avec Śes-rab bla-ma de Cog-gru (CORDIER, Rgyud XLIII. 4), Chos-'bar de Mar (Rgyud LXXXI. 17). Rin-chen grags a traduit des textes avec Atulavajra (Rgyud VI. 3) qui doit être identique à Atula-dāsa ou Atuladāsavajra (cf. ci-dessus 7o et 128) et avec Mañjuśrī de l'Inde (Rgyud XIII. 23).

192. Le colophon dit : pa-ṇḍi-ta A-tu-la-dā-sa-ba-dzra la źus-nas bod-kyi lo-tstsha-ba Mar-pa Chos-kyi dbaṅ-phyug grags-pas bsgyur-ba'o; Atula-dasa-bajar paṇḍi-ta-dur öčiǰü : töbed kelemürči Marba Nom-un erketü aldarsiγsan

orčiγulbai, "Après avoir demandé au savant Atuladāsavajra [de réciter le texte], Chos-kyi dbaṅ-phyug grags-pa de Mar l'a traduit" ; BK. : "Mit dem gnädigen Einverständnis des Atula...".

2o4. Chos-kyi sde est contemporain de Rin-chen grags de Ba-ri (cf. ci-dessus 127) et de Nam-mkha' rdo-rje (CORDIER, Rgyud LXIX. 176).

2o5. Ne'u mkhan-po est nommé un excellent ascète (sdom-brtson dam-pa). Il est peut-être identique au sdom-brtson dam-pa dge-sloṅ Amogha qui est le patron de la traduction du Yogaśataka par Dpal Ñi-ma rgyal-mtshan dpal bzaṅ-ba. Ce dernier est contemporain de Buddhaśrījñāna (CORDIER, Mdo CXXIII. 13) qui a vécu autour de l'an 12oo (cf. ci-dessus 11o), Dpal Rgyal-ba'i sñan bzaṅ-po(Bstod 6), Gautamabhadra du Magadha (Rgyud XIV. 4o-42), Mañjuśrī du Népal (Rgyud XIV. 66), Jetakarṇa (ibid.), Puruṣottama (Rgyud LXIX. 115), Gautamaśrī (Mdo CXXIII. 15) et Rāma du Népal (ibid.).

2o8. Le colophon mongol a déformé le nom de Parahita en Prasantabadr-a, BK. : Parsanta padr a (Praśāntabhadra?). Dans le colophon d'une autre traduction mongole de ce texte ce nom est écrit d'une manière plus correcte : Prā hi da (cf. HEISSIG, op. cit., p. 72). Parahita (cf. ci-dessus 19 et 128) et Dga'-rdor de Zu ou Gzu (cf. CORDIER, Mdo XLIV. 3) ont vécu au onzième siècle.

21o. Mahājñāna ou Mahājana a vécu autour de l'an 11oo (cf. ci-dessus 15). Contemporains sont Gźon-nu 'od (CORDIER, Rgyud XXVI. 22), 'Phags-pa Śes-rab (Rgyud LIX. 1), Tshul-khrims gźon-nu (Rgyud LXI. 9), Blo-gros grags de Mal (Rgyud LXXXIII. 64) et Seṅge rgyal-mtshan (Mdo XVI. 15).

223. Vidyākarasiṃha a vécu autour de l'an 8oo (cf. 1oo). Dpal-gyi lhun-po'i sde doit être identique à Dpal-gyi lhun-po qui a vécu à la même époque(cf. ci-dessus 138). Dpal-gyi lhun-po'i sde est contemporain de Jñānaśānti de l'Inde (CORDIER, Bstod 36) ou du Zahor (Mdo CXXIII. 29) et Dharmaśrībhadra de l'Inde (Mdo XXXIII. 53 ; CXXXVI. 38).

289. Le colophon mongol contient le passage suivant : Tere boγda-yin nomlaγsan degedü ǰarliγ nom-ud-i ...... tayiming Činggis qaγan tal keleten mergedi orčiγul kemen duradduγsan-dur, "Quand, en disant 'Traduisez', le tayiming Činggis qaγan exprima le désir que ces paroles et dharma suprêmes, prêchés par ce Saint, furent traduits par des savants qui savaient les deux langues". BK. :"Als

... Tayiming Činggis qaγan ..... bedachte dass beider Sprachen kundige Gelehrte diese Schriften der erhabenen Worte des Heiligen, die da gelehrt worden sind, übersetzen sollten". Plus loin le colophon dit : eldeb ǰüil ene üiles-ün dandris sudurnuγud-i, "Ces caryātantra et sūtra de différentes sortes"; BK. : "diese Tantrabücher zu allerlei Zwecken".

335. Vajrapāni a vécu au onzième siècle (cf. ci-dessus 21). Contemporains sont Thos-pa dga' de Pa-reg (CORDIER, Rgyud XIII. 34), Chos-'bar de Rma (Rgyud XIII. 36), Ye-śes 'byuṅ-gnas de Mtshur (Rgyud XIV. 54 ; XLVI. 14) et le traducteur Dharmakīrti (Rgyud XLVI. 11). Contemporains de Chos-kyi śes-rab sont Vinayadeva de l'Inde (Rgyud XVIII 'og, 1), Dulo-pa ou Adulo-pa de l'Inde (Rgyud XXII. 59 ; LXXII. 56), Śuddhākarabhadra de l'Inde (Rgyud XXXIX. 9), Vinayacandra (Rgyud XLII. 3), Kanakaśrī du Népal (Rgyud XLVIII. 148), Munīndrabhadra (Rgyud LVII. 14), Subhadra de l'Inde (Rgyud LX. 1), Buddhākaravarman de l'Inde (Rgyud LXXI. 388), Kṛṣṇavara de l'Inde (Mdo XVIII. 6) et Abhiyuktaka Tāraśrīmitra (Mdo XXIX. 6).

344. Ce texte fut d'abord traduit à l'époque dans laquelle les rois et les ministres furent des bodhisattva : rgyal-blon byaṅ-chub-sems-dpa' rnams-kyi sku-riṅla ; Bodhi-satuva-yin qubilγan qad noyad-un üy-e-dür. Plus tard l'upāsaka Grags-pa rgyal-mtshan l'a comparé avec un texte indien et l'a très bien corrigé : dusphyis dge-bsñen Grags-pa rgyal-mtshan-gyis... rgya-dpe-la gtugs-nas śin-tu dag-par byas-pa'o ; Qoyin-a Grags-pa rgyal-mchan ubasi... enedkegčin-ü bičig-iyer dokiyalduγulǰu : masi ǰöb ariγun bolγabai. Ce texte ne permet pas d'identifier Grags-pa rgyal-mtshan avec un des nombreux Grags-pa rgyal-mtshan mentionnés dans le Deb-ther sṅon-po (cf. BA. p. 1152).

349. Phur-bu 'od de Du-gu luṅ (cf. CORDIER, Rgyud LXXXIII. 1) est contemporain d'Amoghavajra (cf. ci-dessus 184).

368. Punyasambhava est contemporain de Ñi-ma grags (cf. ci-dessus 16).

369. Somaśrībhavya et Tshul-khrims 'od-zer ne sont pas mentionnés dans d'autres colophons.

372. Mañjuśrīvarman a traduit un texte avec Buddhaguhya et Muti ou Muktikā (CORDIER, Rgyud LXIII. 9) qui ont vécu aux alentours de l'an 800 (cf. ci-dessus 100). Blo-ldan śes-rab ne peut donc être identique à Blo-ldan śes-ran de Rṅog qui a vécu de 1059 à 1109 (cf. ci-dessus 19).

374. Dans ce colophon ainsi que dans ceux de 375, 379, 538 et 539 rgya'i dpe signifie "texte chinois"(BK.: "indischen Buch ; indischen Oringinalausgabe" (sic!)). Ces traductions, faites du chinois en tibétain, ont été étudiées par UEYAMA Daishun, cf. l'article cité ci-dessus 176.

381. Jambhala est contemporain de Rin-chen grags de Ba-ri (cf. ci-dessus 127).

39o. Prajñākara est contemporain de Lha-btsas (cf. ci-dessus Introduction 15) de 'Gos et de la tribu Khug (cf. CORDIER, Rgyud XXIII. 6).

391. Rdo-rje sems-ma et Śes-rab 'byuṅ-gnas de 'Gar ne sont pas mentionnés dans d'autres colophons.

393. Śes-rab brtsegs de Klog-skya est contemporain de Vāgīśvara ou Vāgīśvaragupta qui a vécu dans la deuxième moitié du onzième siècle (cf. ci-dessus 15 et 78). Contemporains de Śes-rab brtsegs sont Devākaracandra (CORDIER, Rgyud LXI, 3) et Advayavajra (Rgyud LXXXI. 16).

4o9. Je ne comprends pas très bien la fin du colophon : Sa-'og 'khrul-'khor bde-legs rin-chen gter // gsaṅ-bdag rdo-rje 'dzin-pa dam-pa'i bka' // gaṅs-can 'gro-la phan-pa'i blo-gros-kyis // bsgyur-ba'i bsod-nams 'dzin-bcas rnams-la byin // ; badala-yin yandar engke amuγulang-tu erdeni-yin sang : niγučas-un ejen včir bariγči degedü-yin(?) jarliγ-iyar Časutu orun-u amitan-a tusatu oyun-iyar : orčiγuluγsan buyan-iyan bariγči selte-dür öggümüi ; BK.: "Das Badala-yin yandar (sa 'og) wird allen jenen einen Kleinodienschatz von Friede und Wohlstand schenken, welche das Tugendverdienst besitzen, auf des Vajraträgers, des Herren der Geheimnisse, erhabenen Befehl hin, in Einsich (sic!) des Vorteiles der Wesen des Schneelandes, dieses überetzt (sic!) zu haben". Le mot mongol yandar est probablement le mot sanskrit yantra (tib. 'khrul-'khor), mais quel est le sens de pātālayantra ? Comment faut-il interpréter 'dzin-bcas?

424. Skyo 'od-'byuṅ ('Od-'byuṅ de Skyo?) est contemporain d'Amoghavajra (cf. ci-dessus 184).

432. Līlāvajra (Sgeg-pa'i rdo-rje) ou Śrī Viśvarūpa ou Varabodhi (cf. CORDIER, Rgyud LVIII. 2) a vécu à la fin du huitième siècle (cf. ci-dessus 162).

438.   Dpal-'byor est contemporain de Dharmākara (cf. ci-dessus 1oo).

458.   Vairocana de Pa-gor est le célèbre élève de Padmasambhava (cf. COR-
DIER, Rgyud LXXVI. 27 ; LXXXIV. 18). Il a vécu dans la deuxième moitié du huitième siècle. Śrīsimha (Rgyud LXXXV. 6-9, 17) ou Śrīsiṃhaprabha (Mdo CXII. 6) a vécu à la même époque.

461.   Dharmabodhi, Dānaraksita et Che-btsan-skyes ne sont pas mentionnés
dans d'autres colophons.

467.   Le colophon mongol contient le passage suivant : egün-i büridken orčiγul
kemen puṇya maṅghalaṁ kemekü-yin erkin ǰarliγ-ača dabaquy-a berke-yin tula ;
BK. :"Da es schwehr (sic!) fällt, das höchste Gebot zu übertreten - es treisst puṇya
maṅghalam und lautet : 'Übersetze ihn [den Kanǰur,] zuende !' "   Puṇyamaṅgala
est le nom d'un moine, cf. le passage suivant de 791 : ayaγ-q-a tegimlig Puṇy-a-
maṅgalaṁ blam-a-yin : ariγun sayin ǰarliγ-ača dabaquy-a berke-yin tula ; BK. :
"Da es schwer fällt, [solch] einem reinen, schönen Befehl des Mönches Puṇiy a
maṅgalam (Puṇyamaṅgalam) zuwiderzuhandeln"

472.   Selon LAUFER (JRAS, 1914, p. 1137) le texte de ce colophon dans le
Kanjur manuscrit de Berlin est altéré et doit être comparé avec une autre édition.
Dans les éditions de Pékin et de Lhasa le texte semble être identique à celui du
Kanjur manuscrit de Berlin : rgya-gar-gyi lo-tsā-ba mkhas-par lobs-pa Bal-po
Śrī-kīr-tis gtan-la phab-ste skad-gsar-pas bsgyur-nas sog-po Mchog-gi-sñiṅ-po
daṅ / An-bkra-śis daṅ / Bal-mo Bzaṅ-bkra-śis-rgya-mtshos yon-bdag bgyis-nas
Maṅ-yul Byams-sprin-gyi gtsug-lag-khaṅ-gi ya-thog-gi dbu-rtser śin-tu gsaṅ-ste
skad gsal-bar bsgyur-ro //. Śrīkīrti n'est pas mentionné dans d'autres colophons.

485.   La traduction fut terminée le quinzième jour du mois Māghā (cho-'phrul
chen-po rta ; qubilγan mág sara) de l'année Plava ('Phar-ba ; čögebüri kemekü čaγan üker). Le traducteur fut Rin-chen grub ou Bu-ston (1290-1364). L'année Plava
est la trente-cinquième année du cycle sexagénaire. La traduction fut donc terminée
le quinze du premier mois de l'année 1361. Ce colophon prouve que le mois cho-'phrul
est le premier mois de l'année. La traduction mongole a čaγan üker au lieu de ča-
γaγčin üker . Le scribe fut Bsod-nams grub : yi-ge-pa ni ....Bsod-nams grub-kyis
bgyis-so ; BK. : "...Bsod nams grub ... hat [diesen Kolophon?] gemacht". Cette traduction est aussi mentionnée dans la biographie de Bu-ston, cf. D. S. RUEGG, op.
cit., pp. 149, 161 et 182. Le colophon se termine par le passage suivant : pa-ṇḍi-ta

la ma-gtugs-šiṅ // dpe-dpaṅ 'grel-pa ma rñed-pas // sgra-don log-par gyur srid-na // mkhas-pa rnams-kyis bcos-par gsol // ; mergen pandita-luγ-a ese dokiyal-duγuluγsan ger-e bičig-ün tayilburi ese oldaγsan-iyar : ayalγu udq-a-luγ-a alji-yan orčiγuluγsan bolbasu ele : mergen aran sayitur jasan suyurq-a, "Puisque le texte n'a pas été comparé à des pandit et que l'on n'a pas obtenu un commentaire comme texte-témoin, il est possible qu'il y ait des erreurs dans le sens des mots ; puissent les savants les corriger" ; BK. "Es fand sich kein Kommentar zu diesem Glanz-Buche [welches also] nicht, zusammen mit einem gelehrten Pandit, korrigiert wurde. Wenn daher der Übersetzer nicht die Übereinstimmung mit dem Wortlaut getroffen haben sollte, so mögen gnädigst gelehrte Männer [die Fehler] richtigstellen". À propos de l'expression pa-ṇḍi-ta la gtugs voir ci-dessus 23. Dans deux éditions du colophon de 87 se trouvait l'expression dpe-dpaṅ. Ce colophon prouve que le texte de ces deux éditions doit être préféré à celui de l'édition de Pékin qui a dpe yaṅ au lieu de dpe-dpaṅ.

533. Le colophon mongol a Jinagarbha qui est une erreur pour Jñānagarbha car ce texte est identique au texte 168, cf. O. 517 et O. 166.

538. Ce texte est identique aus texte 374, cf. O. 522 (dans le catalogue il faut corriger No. 399 en No. 369) et O. 369.

604. Ce texte est identique au texte 323, cf. O. 588 et O. 318. Dans le colophon mongol il faut donc corriger Dharmataši en Dharmašrimitra.

709. La relation de ce texte avec d'autres versions en chinois, tibétain et ouigour ne pourra être déterminée qu'après une comparaison détaillée des textes énumérés IIJ, III, 1959, pp. 76-78. Aux indications bibliographiques il faudra ajouter Walter SIMON, BSOAS, 21, 1958, pp. 335-336 et 341 ; Walther HEISSIG, Mongolische Handschriften, Blockdrucke, Landkarten, Wiesbaden, 1961, Nos. 206-213 ; Louis de LA VALLÉE POUSSIN, Catalogue of the Tibetan Manuscripts from Tun-huang in the India Office Library, London, 1962, Nos. 458-463. Les extraits des nos. 458 et 459 correspondent à des passages de Taishō no. 2897.

745. Le titre finit par les mots suivants : stod-na bla-ma rgyud-pa'i mtshan-'bum maṅ-po daṅ-bcas-pa ; ekin-dür ündüsün blam-a-nar-un olan laks-a ner-e-lüge nigen-e orusiba, "au début, pourvu de nombreux laksa (= 100.000) de noms de gurus tantriques" ; BK.:" [somit dieser] als erster die vielen Qualitäten der vor-

züglichsten unter den Tantren, in einem Bande zusammen[-gefasst], eingeführt hat". BK. ajoute dans une note à propos de Qualitäten : "liess(sic!) nar = maṅ po statt ner-e ; wenn ner-e, dann Tib. miṅ statt maṅ ". Évidemment, ner-e traduit mtshan "nom". Le texte énumère au début une série de noms de maîtres tantriques.

746. La traduction mongole contient un long colophon dont plusieurs passages ont déjà été traduits, cf. W. HEISSIG, Die Familien-und Kirchengeschichtsschreibung der Mongolen, I, Wiesbaden, 1959, pp. 45-46 ; W. HEISSIG, UAJ, 26, 1954, p. 1o9 ; F. W. CLEAVES, HJAS, 17, 1954, p. 127. C'est pourquoi je me borne à signaler quelques passages qui n'ont pas été examinés dans ces travaux. L'expression olan sonusuγsan se rencontre dans la qualification suivante de Siregetü : olan sonusuγsan erdem-ün čoγčas-iyar čimegsen,"le savant (tib. maṅ-du thos-pa ; skt. bahuśruta) orné d'une accumulation de vertus" ; BK.: "der mit Anhäufungen vielberühmter Vorzüge geschmückte". Plus loin le colophon dit : sasin nom-un naran anu ... delgeren manduqu boltuγai "Que le soleil de la doctrine et du dharma puisse s'accroître et se lever". BK.: "Möge ... die strahlende Sonne der ... Lehre und Religion ... stehen". Dans un autre passage le colophon dit que l'on a fait lever le soleil de la doctrine : sasin-u naran-i manduγulǰu ; BK.: "die [Mātṛkā] die Sonne ... entzündet hat". Tout ce colophon mérite d'être étudié et traduit par un mongolisant compétent.

758-761. Le colophon de la traduction mongole contient un passage qui se retrouve dans 11o2 : eremsin esergülegči dayisun-i emün-e-ben sögüdken kesegegči, "qui soumet en faisant s'agenouiller devant lui l'ennemi qui s'oppose de manière arrogante" ; BK. (758-761) : "(Auf Befehl des) glorreichen Streiters, ...des Siegers, der die Feinde vor sich in die Kniee zwingt", (11o2) : " des stolzen Streiters, des Siegers, der seine Feinde vor sich in die Kniee zwingt". Plus loin le colophon dit que Sam gtab sengge et le Pandit continuent la lignée de nombreux savants éminents : degedü olan merged-eče ündüsülen iregsen ; BK.: "hervorragend über viele grosse Gelehrte". Cette expression se retrouve aussi dans 11o2: degedü olan merged-ün ündüsülen iregsen gün narin bilig-tü : degüderel ügei tabun uqaγan-i tegüs medegči sambaγ-a-tu, "qui continuent la lignée de nombreux savants éminents, profondément savants, parfaitement versés dans les cinq sciences sans hésitation (degüderel = degüdegerel ?)aucune, pourvus d'une intelligence vive" ; BK.: "den mit der allertiefsten Weisheit, welche sich von vielen erhabenen Gelehrten herleitet, begabten, vollendeten Gelehrten in den fünf [Zweigen des] Wissens, den glänzenden (pratibhāna-stobs pa)".

765. BK. signale lui-même qu'un passage de ce colophon a été traduit par M. HEISSIG (UAJ., 26, 1954, pp. 1o9-11o). M. HEISSIG traduit ainsi le passage suivant : šasin qaγan nirvan-u qutuγ-i oluluγ-a : "erlangte der Glaubenskönig (dadurch) die Segnung des Nirwana" ; BK. : "Lasst uns den Segen des Nirvāna des Königs der Lehre erlangen !" Le colophon dit au début que le Buddha a établi le règne de la loi (nom-un törü ; tib. chos-srid) au pays Magadha. BK. rend nom-un törü par "Hierarchie". Ensuite le texte continue : ulamǰilan tendeče böged ulaγan qangsiyar-tu Časutu ulus-tur orčiγulǰu nom-un törü yosun-i : ülemǰi naran metü geyigülülüge "ensuite transmettant [la doctrine] , il tournait [la roue de la Loi] pour le peuple à la face rouge du pays des neiges et il faisait briller davantage la doctrine de la loi à l'instar du soleil ". BK. : "Hernach stiess dieser Heilige vor und übertrug die Hierarchie auf das rotgesichtige Schneevolk [Tibets] , welches er, gleich einer Sonne, überaus erleuchtete".

766. Śākyasena et Jnanasiddhi sont contemporains de Dharmatāśila (cf. Intr. [= Introduction]).

771. BK. traduit uγ uqaγan par "Ursache (rgyu rig = hetu)". Dans Mahāvyutpatti on trouve hetu = rgyu-rig(s), cf. éd. SAKAKI no. 8o18, mais hetu est ici la désignation d'un nombre élevé (cf. F. EDGERTON, Buddhist Hybrid Sanskrit Dictionary , p. 621b : hetu (3) a high number : hetuh Mvy 8o18). Je suppose qu'ici uγ uqaγan désigne la connaissance qui est la base de la transmigration, c.-à-d. la nescience (avidyā).

791. Ce colophon contient le passage suivant : (P.) byaṅ-chub-kyi sñiṅ-po rdo-rje'i gdan-las dpag-tshad brgya-tsam ; bodhi ǰirüken včir-tu saγurin-ača ǰaγun ber-e-yin tedüi, "à environ cent yojana de Vajrāsana (Bodhgayā), l'essence de la Bodhi" ; BK.: "etwa hundert Yojana weit von dem Sitze des Herzensvajra der Bodhi". Le colophon mentionne le Źa-lu-pa (P. źal-bu-pa) sku-źaṅ Grags-pa rgyal-mtshan qui a vécu à l'époque de l'empereur Ölǰeitü (1294-13o6), cf. TUCCI, Indo-Tibetica , IV, 1, p. 8o et RUEGG, op. cit., p. 1o (corriger ici 1284 en 1294 et Olǰäitü en Ölǰäitü) : Źa-lu-pa sku-źaṅ Grags-pa rgyal-mtshan du-dben-śa ; Saluba-yin naγaču Kirti-dhvaja uš-a-yin egem (?). Au sujet de sku źaṅ voir les références données par M. RUEGG, op. cit., p. 9, n. 2 ; du-dben-śa transcrit tu-yüan shuai 都元帥 , cf. TUCCI, Tibetan Painted Scrolls, p. 33 ; p. 696, n. 393.

Un des traducteurs fut Ānandaśrī dont le colophon dit : (P.) byaṅ-chub-kyi sñiṅ-po rdo-rje'i gdan-las lho-phyogs su-dpag-tshad drug-brgya tsam bgrod-pa'i gnas / Siṅ-ga-gliṅ-pa bram-ze'i rigs-las legs-par rab-tu byuṅ-źiṅ ; bodhi ǰirüken včir-tu saγurin-ača emün-e ǰüg-tür jirγuγan ǰaγun ber-e-yin tedüi kürbe-sü : Singgal-a-yin orun-a : qoyina-daki biraman-u iǰaγur-ača sayitur toyin bolu-γad , "originaire du Ceylan, un pays qui se trouve à environ six cents yojana au Sud de Vajrāsana, le centre de la Bodhi , définitivement sorti du monde, [lui, qui appar-tenait] à une famille brahmanique" ; BK.: "welcher, als er etwa hundert Yojana in südlicher Richtung von dem Sitze des Herzensvajra der Bodhi aus gelangt, trefflich zu einem Kleriker (toyin) der Brahmanenkaste der Insel Ceylon geworden war". Ānan-daśrī est aussi mentionné dans le colophon de 11o5 : yon-tan daṅ-ldan Siṅ-ga-gliṅ yul-gyi / stoṅ-phrag maṅ-po'i dge-'dun kun-gyi gtso / Mar-me-mdzad slob Rdo-rje-gdan bźugs-pa / paṇ-chen Ā-nan-da-śrī : erdem-lüge tegüsügsen Singga-la-yin töb-teki orun-u olan mingγan toγatan qamuγ quvaraγ-ud-un erkin Dibang-gar-a sin (?) tidsi včir-tu orun-dur saγuγsan : yeke bančen Ananda-sari, "le grand savant Ānandaśrī, qui séjourna comme élève de Dīpaṃkara à Vajrāsana (?), le chef de toute la congrégation de nombreux milliers [de moines] du pays Siṃha-ladvīpa , plein de vertus " ; BK.: "dem gewandten Jünger Dibanggar-a's, des Vor-stehers allen viel tausend[köpfigen] Klerus Ceylons, dem Lande der Mitte, [also, diesem Jünger,] der sich [seinerseits] auf den Vajra-Thron gesetzt hat , [nämlich] dem grossen Bančen Ananda-sari ". Je ne suis pas sûr d'avoir bien compris ce passage. Dans le texte mongol il faut probablement lire Dibanggar-a-yin tidsi. Si Ānandaśrī était en effet l'élève de Dīpaṃkara à Bodhgayā , le passage yon-tan ...gtso ne peut guère se rapporter à Dīpaṃkara bien que cela soit préférable du point de vue de la syntaxe tibétaine. Le Dīpaṃkara qui est mentionné ici ne peut être identique à Dīpaṃkaraśrījnana (=Atiśa), car Ānandaśrī a traduit 791 proba-blement dans la deuxième moitié du treizième siècle. Il a traduit 11o5 avec Kun-dga' rgyal-mtshan qui a vécu de 1182 à 1251. Atiśa mourut en 1o54.

794. Munivarman est contemporain de Jinamitra et Dānaśīla (cf. ci-dessus 1oo).

819. Le colophon se termine par un vœu à l'égard des : eǰed terigüten ečige eke amitan-u. BK. traduit : "die Herren, und vor allen derjenige, der Vater und Mutter der Wesen ist". Probablement amitan-u est une erreur car le vœu doit se rapporter aux seigneurs, etc., le père, la mère et les êtres vivants, cf. 878 :

eǰed qad kiged ečige eke terigüten yerünggei bükün, "tous, universellement, à commencer par les seigneurs, les rois, et mes parents" ; BK.: "allen Oberen, den Herrn Fürsten, Vater, Mutter, und so weiter". La traduction mongole fut faite dans l'année sira moγai (1629) pendant le règne du Ligdan Qaγan.

839. Kamalaśila a vécu dans la deuxième moitié du huitième siècle. Il est un des deux protagonistes dans la controverse sur le quiétisme, cf. Paul DEMIÉVILLE, Le Concile de Lhasa, I, Paris, 1952.

849. BK. traduit öčiǰü par "hat korrigiert". Les dictionnaires mongols ne donnent pas ce sens pour öčikü mais les traducteurs mongols ont traduit tibétain źus-te en confondant źu-ba "corriger" et źu-ba "demander", cf. ci-dessus 81. À d'autres endroits BK. rend öčiǰü et öčin par "ehrfurchtsvoll" (8o : öčiǰü ; źus-śiṅ) et "andächtig" (868 et 953 : öčin). Dans les colophons on rencontre quelques fois des formes du verbe üǰekü pour rendre tib. źu-ba . Il faudra probablement les corriger en formes du verbe öčikü , cf. 17 : üǰeǰü (BK. "durchstudiert") ; 81 : üǰeǰü (BK. "studierte") ; 465 : üǰegsen-dür (BK.: "geprüft") ; 953 : üǰen (BK.: "übersetzt").

Le colophon décrit le corps du Buddha : lagsan kiged sayin üliger-tü beye : "le corps pourvu des marques (skt. lakṣaṇa ; tib. mtshan) et sous-marques (skt. anuvyañjana ; tib. dpe-byad bzaṅ-po)" ; BK.: "des mit hundert tausend schönen Zierden begabten Leibes". Dans le colophon de 867 on lit : üliger lagšan-iyar čimegsen, "orné de sous-marques et marques" ; BK.: "mit dem Zeichen der Schönheit gezierten".

Dpal-gyi dbyaṅs est contemporain de Vidyākarasimha (cf. ci-dessus 1oo).

854. Ye-śes sñiṅ-po est contemporain de Prajñāvarman (cf. ci-dessus 1oo).

856. Legs-kyi sde est contemporain de Prajñāvarman (cf. ci-dessus 854).

863. Le traducteur mongol a rendu rgya'i slob-dpon Yen-hpi par: enedkegün baγsi Wenanhi. Ici rgya signifie "la Chine". Pour le commentaire de Yüan-hui et la traduction de Chos-grub voir le travail d'UEYAMA Daishun cité ci-dessus.

867 . Le colophon contient le passage suivant : üiles-i sedkigsen-ü yosuγar bütügegči dakinis-luγ-a, "avec les ḍakiṇī qui accomplissent des actes conformément à leurs pensées" ; BK.: zu den Dākinī's , den Vollenderinnen derer, die die

Werke (karma) durchschaut haben".

874-875-876. Dge-ba'i blo-gros (Sayin oyutu) qui est mentionné dans ce colophon n'est pas identique à Atiśa comme le dit BK. ; il est un élève de Rin-chen bzaṅ-po, cf. Intr. et. BA., p. 7o.

878. Le passage suivant du colophon contient quatre instrumentaux : egün-i orčiγuluγsan ab ali buyan-u küčün-iyer : eǰed qad kiged ečige eke terigüten yerüng-gei bükün-iyer egenegde böged edür söni ügegüy-e tegüs ǰirγal-iyar : egüride ǰir-γan atuγai delekei-dekin-nuγud-iyar, "Que par la force du mérite quel qu'il soit, [résultant du fait] d'avoir traduit ce [texte], tous, universellement, à commencer par les seigneurs, les rois, et mes parents jouissent avec le monde entier éternellement d'un bonheur parfait [qui dure] toujours aussi bien le jour que la nuit" ; BK.:"(?) Bei der Kraft jedweden aus dieser Übersetzung entstandenen Tugendverdienstes, - bei allen Oberen, den Herrn Fürsten, Vater, Mutter, und so weiter, - bei der immerwährenden Seligkeit, die weder Tag noch Nacht kennt, - bei den immerfrohen niederen Erdensöhnen". Ensuite le colophon continue : erkin degedü yeke bari-nir-van-u sudur-i : erkilen Šarang Čangsiu ..., "Šarang et Čangsiu qui ont préféré cet excellent Mahāparinirvāṇasūtra ..."; BK.: "wurde jedes der hocherhabenen Mahā-parinirvāṇa-Sūtren, welche vornehmlich von Šarang und von Čangšiu ...".

884. Ce texte ainsi que 893 et 894 est traduit en mongol par Sayin oyutu šasin-i bariγči mergen Tai kunda gusi . BK. traduit : "Sayin oyutu šasin-i bariγči [und der] Gelehrte Tai künda güsi (laut RAGHU VIRA, Mong.-Sk. Dict., p. 2o, No. 7 & 1o : 2 verschiedene Personen)". M. HEISSIG énumère parmi les trente-cinq traducteurs du Kanjur en 1628-1629 Günding güsi darqan blama et Sayin oyutu (Die Pekinger Lamaistischen Blockdrucke in mongolischer Sprache, Wiesbaden , 1954, p. 41, n. 4). Dans cette note M. HEISSIG renvoie au colophon du Kanjur mongol alors que, dans le passage auquel la note se rattache, il dit que trente-cinq noms de traducteurs peuvent être trouvés dans les colophons du Kanjur. Je n'ai pas trouvé cette liste de traducteurs dans le colophon du Kanjur tel qu'il est reproduit dans le catalogue de M. LIGETI. Les colophons de 885 et 113o mentionnent le tegünčilen ireg-sen Gundang gūsi nom-un qaγan ou tegünčilen Gunding gusi darqan blam-a qui doit être identique au Tai kunda gusi du colophon 884 (dans 893 et 894 son nom s'écrit Tai gunding gusi). Puisque Gundang gusi est nommé nom-un qaγan , RAGHU VIRA se trompe en disant que nom-un qaγan est une épithète exclusive de Kun-dga' 'od-

zer (op. cit., p. 17).

895. Le colophon de la traduction mongole contient le passage suivant : genedde učiraǰu ǰöb boluγsan bögesü : kesig ebedčin taqul : sayitur amurliqu boltuγai, "si, inopinément, il se trouve que [la traduction] soit correcte, puissent la goutte et la peste être bien guéries" ; BK. : "Sollte die Wahrheit zufällig auftauchen, so möge das Podagra sie tunlich zähmen! (scherhafte Vertauschung ; richtig : 'Sollte plötzlich Krankheit befallen, so möge Glück walten und sie wirklich ausheilen!')" . Il faut comparer la fin du colophon de 1o72 : genedde učiraǰu ǰöb boluγsan buyan-iyar : gegegen uqaγatan qad noyad qamuγ amitan-a : gem ügei törü šasin delgereged geyigülün ǰirγaǰu burqan-u qutuγ-tur kürkü boltuγai, "Que par le mérite [obtenu] s'il arrive que [la traduction] soit correcte, la loi et la doctrine parfaites se répandent et éclaircissent les rois et les officiers illustres et sages et tous les êtres vivants et que , heureux, ils arrivent à l'état de Buddha" ; BK. : "Durch glückhaft verwirklichtes Verdienst mögen die erhabenen, weisen Fürsten, Fürstinnen und alle Wesen - da Recht und Religion sich unermesslich ausbreiten - sich der Erleuchtung erfreuend, die Würde eines Buddhas erlangen !" Cf. aussi F. W. CLEAVES, HJAS, 28, 1968, p. 31, n. 133.

916. Kumārarakṣita est contemporain de Dharmatāśīla (cf. Intr.).

92o. Dge-ba dpal est contemporain de Viśuddhasiṃha (cf. ci-dessus 1oo).

936. Rin-chen mtsho est contemporain de Dharmatāśīla (cf. 988). Pour celui-ci voir ci-dessus Introduction.

952. Le mongol Ngagvang (BK. : Nggvang ?) est tib. Ṅag-dbaṅ .

959. Bzaṅ-skyoṅ est contemporain de Dharmākara (cf. ci-dessus 1oo).

972 . Le mongol Badaslan-yin udaki est une déformation de Vatsa-yin Udayana , cf. O. p. 338 note.

986. Le colophon de la traduction mongole se termine par le passage suivant : ali nigen tedüi dokiyalduγsan buyan-iyar : amitan-u bodhi ǰirüken-dür ǰorin iregesügei , "Je consacre le peu de mérite qui m'est échu au bodhicitta des êtres vivants"; BK. : "Möge ich, durch das einmalige Tugendverdienst [der Abschrift dieses Sūtra's],

indem ich zu dem Bodhiherzen strebe, [alle] Wesen (amitan-i) segnen! " Pour ǰorin iregekü, tib. yoṅs-su bsṅo ba, skt. pariṇāmayati voir KOWALEWSKI p. 24o2a ; PELLIOT, JA, 1914, II, p. 135 ; HAR DAYAL, The Bodhisattva Doctrine in Buddhist Sanskrit Literature, London, 1932, pp. 188-193.

996. Le Ho-śaṅ (ho-shang 和上) Zab-mo et Rnam-par mi-rtog-pa ont aussi traduit le Samādhipratipakṣavyavasthāna (CORDIER, Mdo XXX. 27). Sur Zab-mo et Rnam-par mi-rtog-pa qui ont dû vivre aux alentours de 8oo voir Paul DEMIÉVILLE, Le concile de Lhasa, p. 21 note, p. 228, n. 1 ; Giuseppe TUCCI, Minor Buddhist Texts, Part II, Roma, 1958, p. 47 note.

999. La traduction mongole attribue la traduction de ce texte à Chos-grub mais selon le Kanjur de Pékin les traducteurs furent Śīladharma et Rnam-par mi-rtog-pa, cf. P. PELLIOT, JA, 1914, II, pp. 135-137.

1o21. Les traducteurs mongols ont utilisé un texte imprimé à Pékin : Tayidu-yin darumal. Pour Tayidu = Ta-tu 大都 voir F. W. CLEAVES, HJAS, 12, 1949, p. 124, n. 198. Le colophon de 863 mentionne aussi un texte imprimé de Pékin (BK. : "von überall [hergeschafften] gedruckten Ausgaben"). Dans sa traduction de 183 et 1o21 BK. retient Tayidu sans donner aucune explication de ce nom. Le colophon se termine par le passage suivant : erkin qoyar čiγulγan-u liγad-i delgeregülǰü, "développant les lotus (lingquad) des deux accumulations suprêmes" ; BK. : "die erhabenen Lotuse beider Länder (?) zu erblühen bringen". Cf. 1o72 : "eldeb ǰüil-iyer qoyar čiγulγan dügürgeǰü, "complétant les deux accumulations par différents moyens" ; BK. : "vollendete die beiden Ansammlungen (chogs gñis : - des Lernens und des Tugendverdienstes) vermittels verschiedener diesbezüglicher Handlungen (rigs)". Les deux accumulations sont le puṇya- et le jñānasaṃbhāra[33].

1o47. BK. traduit seulement le début de ce colophon et renvoie à un troisième volume dont on ne trouve aucune mention dans la préface. Pour la traduction des colophons de 1139, 114o et 1143 il faudra aussi attendre la parution du troisième volume.

1o61. Dans le colophon se rencontre l'expression altan-uruγ que BK. traduit par "Familie Altan [qan's] ". Pour cette expression voir Louis LIGETI, "Notes sur le colophon du 'Yitikän Sudur' ", Asiatica, Leipzig, 1954, p. 399 : "descendance d'or ", "descendance impériale", "lignée de Gengis khan" ; H. SERRUYS, "Mongol Altan 'Gold' = 'Imperial' ", MS, 21, 1962, pp. 357-378. Dans 1123 BK. traduit altan uruγ par "Goldene Sippe".

Selon le colophon Činggis qaγan est né 3253 ans après le Nirvāṇa dans l'année sim morin (1162), cf. W. HEISSIG, Die Familien-und Kirchengeschichtsschreibung der Mongolen, I, Wiesbaden, 1959, p. 47. La demande de traduire le texte fut faite 453 ans après cette date dans une année takiy-a. Je ne sais pas à quelle année correspond cette date car 1614 et 1615 ne sont pas des années de la poule. Le texte fut traduit dans l'année sim γaqai qui correspond à 1623 selon M. HEISSIG, mais d'après la table de Pavel POUCHA (CAJ, vii, 1962, entre p. 196 et p. 197), 1623 est une année küi γaqai.

1o64. Jñānaśrīgupta est contemporain de Śākya blo-gros (cf. ci-dessus Intr.).

1o72. BK. traduit yerü qubi-tan amitan par "mit allerlei Schicksalen beladenen Wesen". Plus loin il l'omet : qubi-tan öber-ün öber-ün kelen-iyer, "für jeden in seiner eigenen Sprache". Dans 1124 BK. rend qubi-tan par "die Guten". Le sens de qubi-tu est "heureux", cf. tibétain skal-ldan ou skal-ba can qui rend skt. bhavya. Dans le passage suivant BK. ne traduit pas les mots orui deger-e-ben "au-dessus de la tête" : alaγan-u kumuda čečeg ümügürel-ten orui deger-e-ben : asuru qamtudqan : "in der Weise, dass er die Kumuda-Blüten [seiner] schutzreichen Handflächen fest aneinanderpresste". La traduction mongole a été notée dans l'année sir-a moγai (1629) pendant le règne de Liγdan qaγan.

1o98. Selon le colophon le texte fut traduit du sanskrit en chinois par Hsüan-tsang et (du chinois?) en tibétain par Lha-btsun Chos-kyi rin-chen. Les mêmes sont mentionnés dans le colophon de la traduction du Nyāyapraveśa (CORDIER, Mdo XCV. 8).

11o2. BK. traduit nom-un činar par "wahre Natur (dharmatva - chos ñid)", mais cette expression correspond à dharmatā "l'absolu", cf. Louis de LA VALLÉE POUSSIN, La Siddhi de Hiuan-tsang, II, Paris, 1929, pp. 743-761.

11o3. Plusieurs passages du colophon de la traduction mongole ne sont pas bien interprétés par BK. : degedüs-ün qutuγ-i ünen maγad-iyar eriǰü bör-ün, "avec une vraie détermination il chercha à obtenir l'état des [hommes] suprêmes" ; BK.: "da er wahrhaftig die Würde eines Erhabenen erlangt hatte" ; qarangγui mungqaγ oyutu amitan-i qangγaγul-un ǰokiyabai degedü qutuγ-tur, "il remplissait les désirs des êtres à l'esprit obscurci et les établissait dans l'état supérieur" ; BK.: "brachte die Erfüllung [aller Wünsche] über die in dunkler Unwissenheit [wandelnden] Wesen - durch die Macht seiner Heiligkeit" ; erdeni burqan baγsi-yin nomlaγsan : eldeb üliger-tü-yin sudur-i enedgek-ün kelen-eče ulamǰilan : endegürel ügei töbed-ün keleber : delgerenggüy-e sayitur orčiγulǰu bör-ün, "Ce sūtra [qui raconte] différentes paraboles fut prêché par l'illustre Buddha, le maître ; le transmettant de la langue de l'Inde , on l'a bien traduit en tout détail et sans faute en langue du Tibet" ; BK. : "als dieses Sūtra allerlei Geschichten, von dem Meister, dem Kleinodien-Buddha, gepredigt und in der indischen Sprache überliefert, in fehlerfreie tibetische Sprache wohl in extenso übersetzt worden war".

1105. La traduction de plusieurs passages de ce colophon doit être corrigée: dge-sloṅ luṅ-rigs 'dzin / skad-gñis smra-ba mchog-gi rjes-'jug-pa / Kun-dga' rgyal-mtshan thub-bstan dpal-bzaṅ-pos // ston-pa 'das-nas lo-stoṅ brgyad-brgya daṅ / lha-bcu lhag-pa'i zla-ba bcu 'das dus //; esi uqaγan-i bariγči ayaγ-q-a tegimlig : qoyar kelen-i ögülekü-yin manglai-yi daγan oruγči : śakyamuni-yin sayin čoγtu dhvaja burqan baγsi nirvan boluγsan qoyina mingγan naiman ǰaγun tabin od ilegüü arban sar-a önggeregsen čaγ-tur, "Après le dixième mois, le mois intercalaire, de l'an 1850 après le Nirvāṇa du Maître, le moine qui connaît la tradition (āgama) et la logique (yukti), qui suit le meilleur de ceux qui parlent les deux langues, Kun-dga' rgyal-mtshan thub-bstan dpal-bzaṅ-po" ; BK. : "hat der Mönch Esi uqaγan-i bariγči , der das Reden (liess : ögülekü-yi) in beiden Sprachen in seine Stirne eingepflanzt hatte, -- am Ende des Schaltmondes [nach dem] zehnten [Mond] des Jahres 1850 nach dem Nirvāṇa Śākyamunis , des hocherhabenen Dhvaja's, Buddhas des Meisters". Ici le traducteur mongol traduit luṅ-rigs par esi-uqaγan ; dans 1124 nous trouvons agam uqaγan : agam uqaγan-u činar-tu nom-un kürdün-ü, "la roue de la Loi qui a pour nature la tradition et la logique" ; BK. : "das Rad der Lehre, dessen Wesen das Āgama-Wissen ist ". Ce même passage a été étudié par M.F.W. CLEAVES qui traduit : " the wheel of the law which has the nature of the understanding of the agam (āgama) ", cf. HJAS, 17, 1954, p. 119, n. 306. Le nom de Kun-dga' rgyal-mtshan (1182-1251) est défiguré dans la traduction mongole. D'habitude, il est nommé Kun-dga' rgyal-mtshan ou Kun-dga' rgyal-mtshan dpal-bzaṅ-po. Il est encore mieux connu sous le nom de Sa-skya paṇ-chen. Le texte mongol traduit lhag-pa'i zla-ba bcu par ilegüü arban sar-a. Je suppose que le texte tibétain veut dire que le dixième mois est un mois intercalaire. L'expression usuelle pour mois intercalaire est zla-(b)śol , cf. CHOS-GRAGS : zla-bśol - zla-lhag, jun yüeh 閏月 . Le texte tibétain continue : chos-kyi rgyal-po Ha-śaṅ mña'-gsol tshe ; nom-un qaγan Qasang-un öčigsen čaγ-tur, "au moment autorisé (?) par le dharmarāja Ha-śaṅ ". Je ne sais pas comment interpréter cette phrase. L'expression sku-drin (mong. bey-e-yin ači) n'a pas été compris par BK. qui traduit :"Gnade des Leibes (Person, Bild, oder Reliquie ?)". Le mot sku est ajouté avant un mot pour former une expression honorifique, cf. A. CSOMA DE KÖRÖS, A Grammar of the Tibetan Language, Calcutta, 1834, p. 32 ; Ph. Éd. FOUCAUX, Grammaire de la langue tibétaine, Paris, 1858, pp. 126-128 ; JÄSCHKE, Tibetan Grammar, Addenda by A. H. FRANCKE, assisted by W. SIMON, Berlin-Leipzig, 1929, pp. 132-133 ; S. C. DAS, A Tibetan-English Dictionary, Calcutta, 1902, p. 88b (dans 69 sku-drin est traduit par ači). Plus loin le colophon contient le passage suivant : 'phags-nor rgyan-ldan skyes-bu dam-pa rnams // dam-chos rin-chen 'di-la gtsug-rgyan mdzod // ; qutuγ-tan-u ed-iyer tegüs čimeg-tü boγda sayid : ene degedü erdeni nom-i orui-yin čimeg bolγaγdaqui, "Les hommes excellents, ornés des richesses des saints, doivent faire du joyau de la vraie Loi (saddharma) un ornement de tête"; BK. :"Die heiligen Güter, völlig geschmückt mit den für Erlauchte geziemenden Dingen, [diese Güter, das heisst, also,] das erhabene Dharma-Kleinod zum Kopfschmuck zu machen". Pour les sept richesses du Saint voir Étienne LAMOTTE, L'Enseignement de Vimalakīrti, Louvain, 1962, p. 294, n. 27 ; MOCHIZUKI Shinkō, Bukkyō-daijiten, II, 1932, pp. 1893a-1894a. Ensuite le colophon contient le passage suivant : dge-ba 'di gźan ma-lus legs-bsdoms-te // bla-ma thub-dbaṅ Byams-pa mgon la-sogs // saṅs-rgyas kun mñes rnam-dag rgya-chen źiṅ // rnam-dag rab-bsgrubs bstan-pa mchog bsgrubs-nas // phyogs-bcu'i źiṅ-rdul sñed-kyi sprul-pa yis // sems-can thams-cad bstan-la dad byas-śiṅ // saṅs-rgyas bstan-pa rab-tu rgyas byas-te // saṅs-rgyas sku-gsum ye-śes myur thob-śog / ; ene buyan-iyar busud qočurli ügei sayitur batulaγad erketü čidaγči blam-a itegel mayidari terigüten : qamuγ burqan-a taγui yekede ariγun-a bayasqaγad ariγun-a sayitur bütügsen ülemji šasin-i bütügejü : arban jüg-ün toγusun-u toγatan qubilγan-iyar : qamuγ amitan-i šasin-dur süsülgeküi bolγaγad burqan-u šasin-i sayitur delgeregül-ün üiledčü : burqan-u γurban bey-e belge bilig-i darui-dur olqu boltuγai, "Que, par ce mérite, tous les autres soient bien retenus et que l'on réjouisse de manière pure et extensive tous les Buddha à commencer par le guru, le munīndra, Maitreya le protecteur ; que, quand la doctrine pure et achevée a été accomplie, des manifestations (nirmāṇa), [nombreuses comme] la poussière des champs des dix directions, inspirent à tous les êtres de la foi en la doctrine et répandent largement la doctrine du Buddha ; que [tous les êtres] obtiennent rapidement les trois corps du Buddha et le savoir !" BK. :"Durch dieses [Tugend-] Verdienst, mögen diejenigen welche an der herrlichen Verbreitung der Religion Buddhas arbeiten, alsogleich die Weisheit (Prajña) [, das ist] die Drei Leiber Buddhas erlangen, nachdem sie a) alle Anderen, ohne Ausnahme, gefestigt, b) sich an der überaus grossen Reinheit aller Buddhas (liess : burqan-u), vornehmlich Maitreyas, des mächtigen Heiligen, des Blama's, der Zuflucht, erfreut, [und] c) während dem sie, selbst trefflich zur Reinheit Vollendete, die höchste Religion vollenden, in Verwandlungen, zahlreich wie der Staub in den acht Richtungen, alle Wesen zur Verehrung der Religion gebracht haben !" Le colophon continue ainsi : śes-bya mtha'-yas rab-tu zab-phyir daṅ // ; medegdekün-i kiǰaγalasi ügei masi gün-ü tula, "Puisque les choses à savoir sont infinies et profondes" ; BK.: "Wegen der unendlichen Tiefe ihrer Gelehrsamkeit".

1123. Le texte du colophon tibétain a été publié et traduit par LAUFER d'après des éditions séparées (TP, VIII, 1907, pp. 391-409). Le texte manque dans les Kanjur de Narthang, Derge et Lhasa mais se trouve dans l'édition de Pékin et le Kanjur manuscrit de Berlin. Le texte du colophon est mal transmis dans l'édition de Berlin mais l'édition de LAUFER et la traduction mongole permettent d'établir un texte assez correct. Le colophon commence par le passage suivant : ston-pa rdzogs-pa'i saṅs-rgyas-kyis gsuṅs-pa rme-bdun źes-pa'i skar-ma'i mdo-sde 'di / brtan (P. brten auquel correspond mong. dulduyidču)-pa'i semskyis dran-źiṅ (P. dra cha nid ; mong. duradduγad) gaṅ mchod-pa / de-la phanpa 'byuṅ źes rab-śes nas // U-rug-bo-ga'i miṅ-can zu (P. bu)-gur-che // chuṅ-ṅu-i dus-nas rtag-par chos-'di la // yid-ches ldan-pas rgyun-du klog-ciṅ mchod / ; toγuluγsan burqan baγsi-yin nomlaγsan : doluγan ebügen neretü odun-u sudur : egün-i dulduyidču sedkil-iyer duradduγad ken takibasu : tusa ači inu : tegün-dür bolumui kemen sayitur medeged. Urus (!) boga neretü yeke sikür-tü aburida üčüken büküi-eče ene nom-tur : ariγun bisirel sedkil-iyer ürgülǰi ungsiǰu takiγad, "Il y aura bénéfice pour celui qui, avec un esprit ferme, médite et vénère ce sūtra de la constellation de la Grande Ourse qui a été prêché par le maître, le Samyaksambuddha. Sachant cela, le sügürči nommé Ürüg boγa[34] a depuis son enfance toujours eu confiance dans ce texte et l'a continuellement récité et vénéré ". Tib. zu-gur-che est une transcription du mongol sügürči (cf. M. LEWICKI, RO, 15, 1949, p. 240, n. 6 ; sur ce mot voir F. W. CLEAVES, HJAS, 20, 1957, pp. 438-440, n. 41). En traduisant le colophon tibétain en mongol le traducteur n'a pas vu que tib. che servait à transcrire -či. LAUFER avait pris zu-gur-che pour un nom propre. BK. traduit d'après le texte mongol : "mit dem grossen

[Königs-] Schirm" et ajoute dans une note : "yeke sikür-tü = Tib. gur čhe ; Tib. zu fehlt". Dans la deuxième partie du colophon Ürüg boγa est appelé : gim-rtse goṅ-lu ta'i (P. na'i)-hu'i g. yu'i-ši ta'i (P. tha'i)-hu (hu manque dans LAUFER). La première partie correspond au titre chin-tzŭ kuang-lu ta-fu 金紫光祿大夫 (cf. M. LEWICKI, ibid. ; sur ce titre voir F. W. CLEAVES, HJAS, 12, 1949, pp. 57-58, n. 191). Dans g. yu'i-ši LAUFER a voulu reconnaître yü-shih 御史 et dans ta'i le nom de famille T'ai 臺 . LEWICKI considérait g. yu'i-ši ta'i comme une transcription de yü-shih t'ai mais la leçon de P. est préférable: g. yu'i-ši ta'i-hu = yü-shih ta-fu 御史大夫 . Après klog-ciṅ mchod le texte continue ainsi : raṅ-gi go-'phaṅ tshol-žiṅ gsol-'debs-pas / 'thun-par spyod (LAUFER : skyob ; mong. ǰokilduqu)-pa'i bdag (P. de dag)-po bsod-nams can // grol-mdzad ston-pa saṅs-rgyas sprul-pa gaṅ // thog (manque dans le texte de LAUFER) the-mur rgyal-bu (P. rgya ba du) yun-du tshe-riṅ žiṅ / thug-can rgyal-po chen-por 'gyur-bar 'dod // ; asuru öber-ün qutuγ-i erijü ǰalbariγsan-u tulada : ǰokilduqu yabudal-un buyan-tu eǰen : tonilγan üileddügči burqan baγsi-yin qubilγan : Toγan temür-ün qaγan öni urtu nasulaγad : toγan-ača yeke qaγan bolqu-yi küsejü , "Désirant un rang élevé pour lui-même, il pria, exprimant le désir que le seigneur à la conduite conforme, plein de mérite, une manifestation du Buddha, le délivreur, le maître, le prince Tuγ temür deviendrait un grand roi qui vivrait longtemps et serait thug-can (?)". Cette interprétation s'écarte de celle donnée par LAUFER : "Kraft seines Strebens nach einer Würde und kraft seiner Gebete hat der friedlich regirende Herr, der verdienstreiche, der eine Verwandlung des die Erlösung bewirkenden Buddha ist, der Prinz Temur, den Wunsch gehegt, ein dereinst die Gefilde des langen Lebens erreichender grosser Fürst zu werden". LAUFER fait rapporter 'dod au prince Temür ce qui est grammaticalement possible mais improbable du point de vue du sens. LAUFER s'est trompé en traduisant žiṅ par "Gefilde" car il s'agit de la particule qui est jointe à des formes verbales. Je ne comprends pas l'expression thug-can que la traduction mongole rend par toγan-ača "au-dessus du nombre" (?) BK. traduit : "Da er sehr sehnlich eine Würde für sich wünschte, [wurde Orus boga in einer späteren Existenz] der verdienstreiche Herr des friedlichen Wandels, eine Verwandlung Buddhas, des Bewirkers der Befreiung, Toγan temür-ün qaγan. [Dieser,] nachdem er lange gelebt hatte, verlangte danach, [alle] Zahlen übersteigende Male grosser Qaγan zu werden". Le colophon continue avec le passage suivant : blo-ldan byaṅ-chub sems-dpa' bdag-po de / slob (LAUFER: bsleb ; mong. arγ-a bilig-i surču)-nas se-chen rgyal-po'i gdan-sar bžugs (P. da dugs) // bdag-gi yid-la 'dod-pa tshim (P. tshis) gyur-pas // the-tshom med-par chos-'dir ńes-śes skyes // yu (P. bu) -gur yi-ger chos-kyi mdo-sde 'di // snon-chad gźan-gyis bsgyur-ba med-pas na // mań-po'i hor-rnams dad-pas mchod-gyur ces // bdag-gis hor-gyi skad-du bsgyur-ba yin // ; ariγun uqaγ-a-tu bodhi-satuva eǰen tere böged : arγ-a bilig-i surču Sečen qaγan-u orun-dur saγubai : ali ba küsegsen anu öber-ün sedkil-tür bütügsen-iyer adqaγ sesig ügei ene nom-tur Uyiγur üsüg-iyer bisirel törügülügči: ene nom sudur-i urida busud orčiγuluγsan ügei bögetele olan mongγol irgen bisirel-iyer takituγai : kemen our mongγol-un kelen-iyer orčiγulbai bi, "(Ürüg boγa pensant :) Maintenant que ce seigneur, un sage bodhisatt-va, après avoir appris [ce qu'il devait apprendre] , se trouve sur le trône du roi Sečen, le désir [que j'éprouvais] dans mon esprit est satisfait et j'éprouve une con-fiance absolue, libre de doutes, dans ce texte. Ce sūtra de la Loi, écrite en lettres ouigoures, n'étant pas traduit auparavant par quelqu'un, je l'ai traduit en langue mongole [espérant que] beaucoup de Mongols le vénéreront pieusement". J'ai pré-féré la leçon slob qui est confirmée par la traduction mongole mais ce n'est pas sans hésitation. LAUFER a pris Blo-ldan Byań-chub sems-dpa' comme un nom propre et considère tout le passage comme étant prononcé par l'empereur : "Nach der An-kunft des bLo-ldan Byań - c'ub-sems-dpa bdag-po bestieg er den Tron des Kaisers Se-c'en (d. i. Kublai) und sagte : 'Meines Herzens Wünsche sind nun befriedigt. . ' ". BK. a la même interprétation puisqu'il pense que Ürüγ boγa s'est incarné dans l'empereur : " Nachdem er als jener Ariγun uqaγan-tu bodhi-satuva eǰen (Blo ldan byań čhub sems pa bdag po) Geschick und Weisheit erlernt hatte, setzte er sich auf den Thron des Sečen qaγan. 'Was auch immer ich mir im Geiste gewünscht habe , ist in Erfüllung gegangen : das ist ohne Zweifel ein Anlass zum Glauben an diese Schrift. Derzeit hat noch niemand dieses buddhistischen Sūtra , das auf Uigurisch [vorliegt] , übersetzt. Mögen die vielen Mongolen es gläubig verehren ! Hiermit [be-schliesse] ich [dieses Sūtra] in die Our-mongolische Sprache übersetzen [zu las - sen] '". BK. remarque à propos du mong. our : "wohl mong. Umschrift des Tib. hor, und nicht 'pur' KOWALEWSKI, p. 339 a ; cf. auch infra !" Au sujet de ce mot voir F. W. CLEAVES, HJAS, 17, 1954, pp. 18, 21 ; p. 35, n. 63 ; pp. 37-38, n. 82 ; Walther HEISSIG, Die mongolische Steininschrift-und Manuskriptfragmente aus Olon süme in der inneren Mongolei, Göttingen, 1966, p. 11, notes 3 et 4. Le texte mongol du passage suivant a été traduit par M. F. W. CLEAVES, cf. HJAS, 17, 1954, pp. 123-124, n. 323. Le texte mongol ne correspond pas entièrement au texte tibétain, cf. yun-du sku-tshe riń-źiń, "Puissent-ils vivre longtemps" ; erüsčü möngke ǰirγaγad ,

"Attaining [it], having been eternally happy" (trad. F. W. CLEAVES). BK. remarque dans une note : "erüscü = Tib. sku che". M. CLEAVES a aussi traduit le passage suivant (op. cit., p. 126, n. 336). Dans le texte mongol il faut corriger ende todqar en ada todqar (cf. aussi le colophon de 289 où il faut apporter la même correction). Pour cette expression voir F. W. CLEAVES, op. cit., pp. 123-124, n. 323 ; HJAS , 22, 1959, pp. 74-76, n. 138 ; Pentti AALTO, Prolegomena to an Edition of the Pañcarakṣā , Studia Orientalia, XIX : 12, Helsinki, 1954, p. 31 . Le texte tibétain de ce passage est le suivant : rgyal-khams dgra daṅ 'khrug-pa źi-ba daṅ / gdon daṅ bar-chad rims-med bde gyur-cig / char-rluṅ dus-'bab mu-ge med 'gyur-źiṅ // bdag-gis smras daṅ bsam-don 'grub gyur-cig /. LAUFER a correctement traduit ce passage mais n'a pas rendu le mot rims "épidemie" ("möge es sich wohl befinden, von bösen Geistern und Unfällen verschont") qu'il faut ajouter après "Unfällen". BK. :"Des Friedensreiches Feinde und [alle] Aufruhr mögen sich beruhigen ; Friede und Wohlstand ohne Schranken hier herrschen ; Regen und Wind zur rechten Zeit auftreten ; Hungersnot uns nicht behelligen -- und noch während dem ich [dieses] spreche und denke, diese Dinge sich vollenden !"

La deuxième partie du colophon dit que le texte a été imprimé dans le dixième mois de la première année, l'année dragon, de Teng-li (=T'ien-li 天曆) : then-li daṅ-po'i lo 'brug-gi zla-ba bcu-pa ; Teng-li terigün on-u luu-yin ǰil-un arban sar-a[35]. LAUFER traduit :"des zehnten Monats , eines Drachenmonats, des ersten Jahres der Periode T'ien-li" mais 'brug se rapporte à l'année. BK. suit LAUFER et remarque que le mois du dragon est le cinquième mois (cf. p. 551, n. h.). Plus loin le colophon contient l'expression rgya-chen-po'i yul "le pays étendu". LAUFER la traduit par "China" et BK. traduit la version mongole (erkin yosud-un orun) par "Lande von gigantischen Ausmassen". Je suppose que le traducteur mongol a pris rgya-chen-po comme signifiant "noble, illustre". Rgya-chen-po ou rgya-che-ba rendent aussi bien skt. vistīrṇa "étendu" que skt. udāra "noble, illustre",. cf. Mahāvyutpatti , éd. SAKAKI nos. 2352, 2687, 2688. Dans le passage suivant le traducteur mongol a rendu tib. rgyal-po chen-po'i blon-po "le ministre du grand roi" par yeke qaγan-u noyad tüsimed "les officiers et les ministres du grand roi". LAUFER a bien traduit le texte tibétain alors que BK. suit la traduction mongole. Vers la fin le colophon dit que ceux qui ont autrefois adhéré aux croyances des Sog-po sont entrés dans la Loi du Buddha, sont sortis du monde et jouissent des excellences de celle-ci (i. e. la Loi du Buddha) :

saṅs-rgyas-kyi chos-la žugs-śiṅ rab-tu byuṅ-ste / 'di'i yon-tan rnams ñams-su myoṅ-bar gyur-pa'o ; burqan-u nom-tur oruγad maγad γarču egün-ü erdem-üd-ün bisilγal-i tegsi amsabai. LAUFER n'a pas bien rendu 'di'i : "traten ... zur Religion des Buddha über, empfingen die Weihen und genossen deren Vortrefflichkeit". De même BK.: "traten ... zu(sic!) Lehre Buddhas über, erhielten die Weihen und genossen deren Vortrefflichkeit".

1124 . Ce colophon débute par trois phrases pour louer le Buddha, la Loi et la communauté des moines. J'aimerais proposer une traduction différente de la deuxième phrase : qan Śakyamuni böged esrun-u egesig-iyer : qamuγ nisvanis-i daruqui yerüdeg bolγan : qaγarqay-a Sangskirida-yin kelen-iyer nomlaγsan : γayiqamsiγ šasin nom-i kündelen takisuγai , "Respectueusement je vénérerai la merveilleuse doctrine, prêchée clairement en langue Sanskrite par le roi Śākyamuni avec sa voix brahmique comme antidote pour réprimer toutes les souillures (kleśa)". BK.: "Lasset uns tief verehren den König Śākyamuni und die wundervolle religiöse Lehre, welche er, indem er das Heilmittel zur Vernichtung aller Sünden hervorbrachte, mit Brahma's Stimme, in klarer Weise, in der Sanskritsprache gepredigt hat !" Cette interprétation résulte du fait que böged a été traduit par "und" mais ce mot est souvent employé pour mettre l'accent sur le mot qui précède, cf. dans le colophon précédent : ejen tere böged : arγ-a bilig-i surču "ce seigneur, ayant appris le moyen (upāya) et la sagesse (prajñā)". Dans les grammaires et dictionnaires du mongol à ma disposition je n'ai pas trouvé une analyse de cet emploi de böged . Plus loin le colophon dit que le Buddha a clairement prêché des légendes (avadāna) : domuγ-nuγud-iyan todurqay-a nomlaǰu. BK.:"predigte er in klarer Weise ... seinen eigenen Lebenslauf (avadāna)".

Index des traducteurs.

L'index contient les noms des traducteurs mentionnés dans l'introduction et l'étude des colophons. Les renvois se limitent aux passages qui se rapportent aux dates d'un traducteur.

Notes

1. F. A. BISCHOFF, Der Kanjur und seine Kolophone, Band I (Vol. 1-25 : Tantra), III + 3o7 pp.; Band II (Vol. 26-47 : Prajñāpāramitā , Vol. 48-53 : Ratnakūṭa, Vol. 54-59 : Avataṃsaka, Vol. 6o-92 : Sūtra , Vol. 93-1o8 : Vinaya), pp. 3o8-575. 1968, The Selbstverlag Press, P.O. Drawer 6o6, Bloomington , Indiana 474o1. $ 16.oo (désormais : BK). La même maison d'édition a publié un Index to F.D.LESSING's Lamaist Iconography of the Peking Temple, Yung-ho-kung, 31 pp. et un Analytical Index to the Tables of Contents of the CENTRAL ASIATIC JOURNAL , Volumes One through Ten, vi + 82 pp.

2. The Tibetan Tripitaka , Peking edition . Edited by Daisetz T. SUZUKI, 168 vols., Tokyo-Kyoto, 1955-1961 ; Bkaḥ-ḥgyur Vols. 1-45.

3. Louis LIGETI, Catalogue du Kanǰur mongol imprimé. Vol. I. Catalogue. Budapest, 1942-1944 (désormais : L.) .

4. Dr. Hermann BECKH, Verzeichnis der tibetischen Handschriften, Berlin, 1914 (Die Handschriftenverzeichnisse der Königlichen Bibliothek zu Berlin, XXIV). (désormais : B.).

5. A Comparative Analytical Catalogue of the Kanjur Division of the Tibetan Tripiṭaka, Kyōto, 193o-1932. (désormais : O.).

6. Cf. W. BARUCH, Asia Major , N. S. II, 1951, p. 126.

7. Un ouvrage annoncé en 1955 (Erik HAARH, Entstehungsgeschichte des tibetischen Tripiṭaka) n'a jamais paru.

8. Nils SIMONSSON, Indo-tibetische Studien. Die Methoden der tibetischen Übersetzer, untersucht im Hinblick auf die Bedeutung ihrer Übersetzungen für die Sanskritphilologie, I, Uppsala, 1957, p. 241. Beaucoup de tibétologues se sont référés à cette introduction en la désignant comme le colophon de la Mahāvyutpatti , cf. SIMONSSON, op. cit., p. 238, n. 2.

9. Giuseppe TUCCI, Indo-Tibetica, II. Rin c'en bzaṅ po e la rinascita del Buddhismo nel Tibet intorno al mille, Roma, 1933, pp. 49-51.

1o. TUCCI, loc. cit.

11. P.CORDIER, Catalogue du fonds tibétain de la Bibliothèque Nationale, deuxième partie et troisième partie, Paris, 19o9-1915 ; Marcelle LALOU, Répertoire du Tanjur d'après le catalogue de P. Cordier, Paris, 1933. (désormais : CORDIER et Rép.).

12. George N.ROERICH, The Blue Annals, two parts, Calcutta, 1949-1953. (désormais : BA.).

13. Rép. p. 158a : Matidhvajaśrībhadra (v. 'Phags-pa, Bla-ma dam-pa čhos-kyi° Blo-gros rgyal-mchan dpal bzaṅ-po).

14. Cf. G. TUCCI, Indo-Tibetica, IV, 1, Roma, 1941, p. 74 ; P.RATCHNEVSKY, "Die mongolischen Grosskhane und die buddhistische Kirche", Asiatica, Leipzig, 1954, p. 492, n. 29 ; p. 494, n. 45.

15. Op. cit., p. 127.

16. Derge 36o.

17. BA., pp. 785-787.

18. CORDIER, Mdo CXVI. 6

19. Cf. BA., pp. 72, 766 et 9o6-9o7.

2o. Cf.TUCCI, Indo-Tibetica, IV, 1, pp. 9o-91 ; Tibetan Painted Scrolls, p. 34.

21. Cf.TUCCI, Tibetan Painted Scrolls, p. 16.

22. Dans le catalogue même (cf. Rgyud I-II) CORDIER ne les mentionne pas. Le répertoire contient donc des données qui ne se trouvent pas dans le catalogue.

Dans la préface au répertoire Mlle LALOU ne signale pas cette différence entre le catalogue et le répertoire. Probablement CORDIER a inclus plus tard dans le répertoire des renseignements omis dans le catalogue. 'Phags-pa et Śā-kya bzaṅ-po sont mentionnés dans le colophon de la Vimalaprabhā d'après le catalogue du Tanjur de l'Université Ōtani : A Comparative Analytical Catalogue of the Tanjur Division of the Tibetan Tripitaka , I, 1, Tōkyō, 1965, p. 26.

23. Cf. BACOT, op. cit., p. 313, n. 4 : "źal-sṅa-nas. Expression laudative et très respectueuse ayant perdu son premier sens littéral : en présence de" ; HADANO Hakuyū, "Chibetto Daizōkyō engi", Suzuki gakujutsu zaidan kenkyū nenpō, 3, 1966, p. 46b : "źal-sṅa-nas , terme honorifique signifiant 'gozen, geika, kakka'".

24. Une version plus ancienne des colophons de 1o4 et 1o5 se trouve dans un manuscrit étudié par Walther HEISSIG, " Zur Entstehungsgeschichte der Mongolischen Kandjur-Redaktion der Ligdan Khan-Zeit (1628-1639)", Studia Altaica , Wiesbaden , 1957, pp. 71-87. Dans ce manuscrit źal-sṅa-nas est rendu par bida et bada (=skt. pādāḥ), cf. HEISSIG, p. 8o.

25. BA., p. 72. Selon LAUFER Gyi-jo signifie "the lord of Gyi"(JRAS, 1914, p. 1135). BECKH et CORDIER ont pris Gyi-jo (variante : Gyi-co) comme nom de lieu, B. p. 63, Rép. p. 225.

26. Cf. G. TUCCI, Tibetan Painted Scrolls , p. 257, n. 163. LAUFER s'est trompé en scindant Mar-pa Lho-brag Chos-kyi blo-gros en deux personnes : Chos-kyi blo-gros et Mar-pa de Lho-brag (JRAS, 1914, p. 1135).

27. Mk'yen brtse's Guide to the Holy Places of Central Tibet , Roma, 1958, n. 288 (désormais : FERRARI).

28. Cf. TUCCI, Indo-Tibetica, II, pp. 24, 5o.

29. Cf. BA., p. 417, note ; D. S. RUEGG, The Life of Bu ston rin po che , Roma, 1966, p. 123, n. 2 ; p. 181, n. 1.

3o. CORDIER dit que la traduction fut exécutée par ordre de Bla-ma dam-pa Chos-kyi rgyal et sur la demande de savants tibétains mais le colophon ne mentionne qu'un bhoṭapaṇḍita : bho-ṭa pa-ṇḍi-ta-yis bskul-ba bźin-du.

31. Cf. RUEGG, op. cit., p. 14, n. 1.

32. Cf. TUCCI, The Tombs of the Tibetan Kings, Roma, 195o, p. 2o.

33. Les deux accumulations sont aussi mentionnées dans le colophon du Bolor Erike, cf. F.W. CLEAVES, HJAS, 28, 1968, p. 35, n. 164.

34. Sur ce nom voir L. LIGETI, "Notes sur le colophon du 'Yitikän Sudur'", Asiatica, Leipzig, 1954, p. 4oo, n. 12; F.W. CLEAVES, HJAS, 2o, 1957, p. 441, n. 44. On trouvera une biographie d'Ürüγ boγa dans Yüan shih, ch. 145.

35. C'est l'année 1328, cf. L. LIGETI, "Les noms mongols de Wen-tsong des Yuan", TP, 27, 193o, p. 6o, n. 1.

III
Pāli Literature

The Elders' Verses, I: *Theragāthā*. Translated with an introduction and notes by K. R. Norman (*Pali Text Society Translation Series*, No. 38), London, published for the Pali Text Society, Luzac and Company, Ltd., 1969. lxiv + 319 pp. £ 5.5.—.

In 1933 the editors of the *Critical Pāli Dictionary* expressed their unreserved admiration for the *PTS Translation Series* (*CPD*, p. XXIX). Undoubtedly, they would have welcomed with great joy the most recent addition to this series, Mr. K. R. Norman's translation of the *Theragāthā* which supersedes the excellent translation published by Mrs. C. A. F. Rhys Davids in 1913. Mr. Norman's work consists of three parts: introduction (pp. xix-lxiv) preceded by a preface, a bibliography and list of abbreviations; translation (pp. 1-116) and notes (pp. 117-300). Three indexes conclude the work: one of parallel passages in Sanskrit, Prakrit and non-canonical prose (pp. 301-304), one of names (pp. 305-309) and one of words discussed or quoted in the notes (pp. 310-316). In this last index words or meanings, not given in *PED* (= *Pāli-English Dictionary*, PTS, 1925) are marked with an asterisk.

Mrs. Rhys Davids greatly relied on the commentary for the explanation of difficult words and expressions. Mr. Norman does not neglect the commentary which is copiously cited, but he adopts a more critical attitude towards it. No explanation, given by the commentary, is accepted without having been carefully examined. Mr. Norman proposes many emendations for the text of the *Theragāthā* (cf. the list of emendations in the second edition of the *Thera- and Therī-gāthā*, PTS, 1966, pp. 223-232). Not all of the emendations, listed in this edition, have been maintained by him because some of the readings found in other editions are due to later normalization. Mrs. Rhys Davids made only a few remarks on the metres of the *Theragāthā* (*Psalms of the Brethren*, p. LII). Her hope expressed there that a competent discussion of this subject would be undertaken in the future has been realized by Mr. Norman. In his introduction the metres of the text are listed and the metre of each pāda, except the ślokas, is analyzed. In a paragraph on metrical licence Mr. Norman lists the changes which would be required for regularizing unmetrical verses under the following headings: the unhistoric doubling of consonants, the simplification of consonant groups, the restoration of doubled consonants, the shortening of nasalized vowels, removal of syllables, lengthening of vowels and shortening of vowels. The last paragraph of the introduction discusses consonant groups not making position and svarabhakti vowels. Mr. Norman states that the metre is a great guide in deciding between alternative readings, but he is careful to remind us that it would be wrong to try to correct every metrical irregularity. He points out that the fact that the metre of a verse can be improved, is no evidence that it should be improved. In many instances irregular pādas seem incapable of improvement. Mr. Norman remarks: "Unless we assume that the text is hopelessly corrupt, we are forced to admit that the authors wrote unmetrical verses." Perhaps the authors of the verses are not always to blame but those who 'transposed' the original Eastern text into Pāli and who were unable to keep the metre of the original text.

In discussing the date of the *Theragāthā*, Mr. Norman expresses his disagreement with Winternitz's opinion that the two poems on the decline of the Dharma (920-48, 949-980) were later than the time of Aśoka.[1] It is difficult to adduce any convincing proof in support of either of these conflicting views.[2] Undoubtedly, evil monks must have existed already in the early period of Buddhism, but these vivid descriptions of the decline of the Dharma remind us of the numerous passages of a similar nature which

[1] Winternitz's view is shared by Nakamura Hajime, cf. "Genshi bukkyō seiten

are to be found in later Sanskrit and Chinese texts (cf. Et. Lamotte, *Histoire du bouddhisme indien*, I, Louvain, 1958, pp. 210-222). A careful study of Buddhist eschatological literature will perhaps lead to a better understanding of its historical background and development. Nakamura has pointed out that *Theragāthā* 234-236 and *Therīgāthā* 400 must have been composed at a time when Pāṭaliputta was flourishing. According to him these verses have been composed after Aśoka and before the time of king Khāravela and king Menander, i.e. between 223 and 160 B.C. (*op.cit.*, pp. 36-37). He also believes that 892-919 were composed during the Maurya period, because 914 mentions 'The lord of Jambusaṇḍa' (*op.cit.*, p. 32). However this may be, it is obvious that the *Theragāthā* cannot have been compiled before the time of Aśoka.

The *Theragāthā* belongs to the *Khuddakanikāya*, a *nikāya* which seems to have been compiled at a later date than the other four *nikāyas* (cf. Lamotte, *op.cit.*, pp. 167-181). Oldenberg was the first to point out that the *Sthaviragāthā*, mentioned in the *Divyāvadāna*, must be the Sanskrit equivalent of the *Theragāthā* (*ZDMG*, 52, 1898, p. 656). The recent publication of fragments of the *Sthaviragāthā* by Heinz Bechert (*Bruchstücke buddhistischer Verssammlungen aus zentralasiatischen Sanskrithandschriften*, I: *Die Anavataptagāthā und die Sthaviragāthā*, Berlin, 1961) proves the correctness of this hypothesis. At the same time the text of the *Anavataptagāthā* shows that the contents of the *Sthaviragāthā* are not identical with those of the *Theragāthā*. Several verses spoken by Anuruddha (910-919) are to be found in the *Anavataptagāthā*. Bechert's publication of these two texts, to which Mr. Norman does not refer, gives us some idea of the way in which authors, belonging to different Buddhist schools, compiled collections of verses attributed to famous monks. In view of the fact that many verses of the *Theragāthā* are to be found also in the *nikāyas* and in the parallel texts of the *āgamas*,[3] it is possible to assume that these authors combined verses, not collected in the *nikāyas*, with verses taken from them. Perhaps this process of compilation took place during a long period in which verses were continually added to an existing collection.

It is impossible to summarize the wealth of information on metrical, grammatical and lexicographical problems contained in the notes to the translation. The word index makes it easy to locate the discussion of individual words. There is however no index to the important grammatical remarks made by Mr. Norman. Mention must certainly be made of the following notes: 9. *sv* for *so*, a "mistranslation" of an Eastern *se* = *taṃ*; 22. *ṇamul*-gerunds; 36. passive past participles as action nouns; 42. split compounds; 49. confusion of *p* and *s*; 57. alternation between *-k-* and *-y-*, or *-k-* and *-t-*; 78. aorists ending on *-issaṃ*; 225. derivatives of *sma*; 405. *a*(*n*) before finite verbs (see also R. Otto Franke, *ZDMG*, 48, 1894, pp. 84-85); 527. future active participles in *-esin*.

Mr. Norman's excellent work shows clearly that the many problems in Pāli texts and especially in verses can only be solved by an exhaustive and thorough study of the metrical, grammatical and lexicographical particularities. It is with great pleasure that we look forward to Mr. Norman's translation of the *Therīgāthā* which has been announced in the last report of the Pali Text Society.

---

seiritsu kenkyū no kijun ni tsuite [On guiding principles in the study of the formation of the early Buddhist scriptures]", *Nihon bukkyō gakkai nenpō*, 21 (1955), pp. 52-53.

[2] The evidence quoted from the *Mahāvaṃsa*, composed in Ceylon near the end of the fifth century A. D. (cf. Wilhelm Geiger, *Culture of Ceylon in Mediaeval Times*, 1960, p. 71), does not carry too much weight.

[3] The Japanese translation of the *Theragāthā* by Masunaga Reihō (*Nanden daizōkyō*, vol. 25, Tokyo, 1936) gives references to the parallel verses in the Pāli *nikāyas* and the Chinese translations of the *āgamas*. They greatly facilitate the comparison of the Pāli and Chinese versions of these verses.

To conclude this review I venture to submit the following remarks which are meant at the same time as a tribute to Mr. Norman's fine scholarship and as a small contribution to the study of this important text.

The first pāda of 9 (=885a) has only seven syllables: *svāgataṃ nāpagataṃ*. *CPD* proposes to add a svarabhakti vowel (see s.v. *apagata*). Mr. Norman admits svarabhakti vowels in *dvāra* and *tvaṃ* (p. lxiv), but does not state his reasons for rejecting the same solution in this case.

Verse 16 speaks of a *bhaddo ājañño naṅgalāvattanī sikhī*. The commentary explains that *ājañña* can refer to a bull, a horse or an elephant. In this verse the commentary takes *ājañña* to be a bull. However, Mr. Norman remarks that *sikhin* does not apply to a bull. He proposes to solve this difficulty by assuming that the thoroughbred is a horse and that *naṅgala* means here 'tail' or is a mistake for *naṅgula*. However, according to the *Medinikośa śikhin* can also refer to a *balīvarda*. Perhaps, in this case, *śikhā* means the tuft on the belly of a bull. Mr. Norman always translates *ājañña* by 'thoroughbred'. I suppose that in 173 and 659 he takes it as referring to a bull. In both verses Mr. Norman translates *dhura* by 'load'; 173 *vahate dhuraṃ* 'draws its burden'; 659 *dhure yutto dhurassaho* 'yoked to a load, enduring a load'. According to *PED dhura* is used figuratively in the meaning of 'burden, load, charge, office, responsability'. This may be true or not but, in any case, it seems preferable to translate *dhura* in these two verses by 'yoke' (cf. also 359 *viriyadhuraniggahīto* where *dhura* is used figuratively: 'restrained by the yoke of energy').

In note 22 Mr. Norman suggests taking *jhāyaṃ* as a *ṇamul*-gerund. He quotes other examples of *ṇamul*-gerunds in Pāli. One of these: *jīva-gāhaṃ ca naṃ aggahesi* can better be taken as an example of a cognate accusative (cf. J. S. Speyer, *Sanskrit Syntax*, § 44; L. Renou, *Grammaire sanscrite*, p. 289). To these gerunds can be added *ālumpakāraṃ* which has to be read in *Dhp-a* II.55,22: *ubhohi hatthehi ālumpakāraṃ guthaṃ khādi*. Norman's edition has *ālumpākāragūthaṃ*, but one of his manuscripts (C) has the reading *ālumpakāragūthaṃ*. *CPD* quotes this passage under *ālumpakārakaṃ* but states wrongly that manuscript C reads *ālumpakārakaṃ gūthaṃ* and that Norman's edition has *ālumpakāragutham*.[4] *CPD* does not refer to BHS *alopakāraṃ* and *ālopakārakaṃ* both taken as gerunds by Edgerton (*BHS Grammar* 22.5, 35.3, 35.5; *Dictionary* ss.vv. *ālopa* and *-kārakam*). Cf. also Pāli *sannidhikārakaṃ*, BHS *saṃnidhikāraṃ* (*Mahāvastu* I.343.18).

In verse 55 a new interpretation for *āsandiṃ* is proposed by Mr. Norman who takes it as the 1st sg. aorist of a form *ā-sad-* showing a nasal infix. A Sanskrit version of this verse is to be found in the fragments of the *Sthaviragāthā* published by Heinz Bechert (*op.cit.*, p. 263). Instead of *āsandiṃ* this version has *āsannāṃ* which probably resulted from a misunderstanding of *āsandiṃ*. Mr. Norman remarks that in the first line of 55 a finite verb is missing. However, the second line is a cliché which occurs often in the *Theragāthā* (24, 66, 107, 108, 220, 224, 286, 562, 639, 886, 903). In two verses (117, 349) the first pāda has *tisso vijjā ajjhagamiṃ* for *tisso vijjā anuppattā*. If one replaces in 55c *anuppattā* by *ajjhagamiṃ*, a finite verb would not be required in the first line. The Sanskrit version of the second line is slightly different: *tisro vidyā mayā* (*prāptāḥ kṛtaṃ buddhasya śāsanam*). This shows that alternative readings existed in the second line.

In 104 *lahuko vata me kāyo phuṭṭho ca pītisukhena vipulena*, Alsdorf suggests reading *piti* m.c. and deleting *ca*, in order to restore the Āryā metre. However, instead of *phuṭṭho* the original reading must have been *phuṭo* 'suffused', cf. 383 *pītiyā phuṭasarīro*. Therefore *ca* has to be maintained.

In 305 *sugatavara* is rendered by 'the best of the well-farers'. The commentary gives

[4] *CPD* quotes variant readings from Norman's edition, using the same signs. This is likely to create confusion. For instance, according to the system of *CPD* S indicates a Siamese text whereas Norman's S refers to a Sinhalese print.

two explanations: *sugatassa varassa sugatesu ca varassa*. The first seems preferable. For this use of *vara* see *PED*. It seems unlikely that the Buddha would have been considered the best of the Buddhas. The expression *buddha-seṭṭha* occurs several times (175, 368, 1168-69). In the commentary on 175 two explanations are given: *Buddhassa sambuddhassa tato eva sabba-satt'uttamatāya seṭṭhassa Buddhānaṃ vā sāvaka-buddhādinaṃ seṭṭhassa*. Here again the first explanation is the more acceptable one. According to the second explanation *buddha* refers to the disciples. The same interpretation is proposed twice by the commentary for *tathāgata* (see Norman's note ad 1205). Miss Horner and Mr. Norman rightly reject this interpretation. I believe that *sugatavara* and *buddhaseṭṭha* have to be interpreted as equivalents of *varasugata* and *seṭṭhabuddha*. The position of *vara* and *seṭṭha* in compounds is discussed by the *Saddanīti* (ed. Helmer Smith, p. 924) according to which *vara* has to be used as second member of a compound; *seṭṭha* can be both first or second member: *pavara-varasaddesu pavarasaddo pubbanipāti, varasaddo pacchānipāti: pavararājā, rājavaro. Uttamādayo pubb'-uttaresu: uttamarājā — rājuttamo, seṭṭharāja — rājaseṭṭho icc ādi*. Another example of *vara* used in this way is *sabbākāravarūpeta* in 929 and 1046. For BHS *sarvākāravaropeta* see *BHS Dictionary*. The expression *pañcaseṭṭha* in 1275 is not clear, but I do not believe that it is possible to interpret it as meaning the best of the five Buddhas of the Buddhakappa.

In 386 Mr. Norman rejects Smith's suggestion to read *phassissaṃ* for *phusissaṃ*, because *phusissaṃ* seems essential to pick up *phusit'aggalaṃ* in 385. However, other texts have *phassita* (BHS *sparśita*, see *BHSD*) in this expression. Mr. Norman's rendering of *phusissaṃ catasso appamaññāyo* with 'I shall fasten on to the four illimitables' is probably caused by his translation of *phusit'aggalaṃ* by 'with its door fastened'. The idiomatic use of *phusita* in this expression makes it rather awkward to use the same English equivalent with regard to the four illimitables. In 725 *phusiṃsu* is rendered more appropriately by 'they attained' (see also 212, 980 and 1114).

In 419 *aññānamūlabhedāya* is explained by the commentary as *tassa* (i.e. *aññānamūlassa*) *bhedāya vajirūpama-ñāṇena bhindan'atthāya*. Mr. Norman translates: 'by breaking the root of ignorance', assuming a feminine *bhedā* which does not seem to be attested elsewhere.

Verse 511 is well interpreted by the commentary which explains that only an unlucky man would turn away with hands and feet the goddess of Fortune who had arrived at his couch. To such a man is compared somebody who after having pleased the Teacher, would displease him. Mr. Norman refers to Mrs. Rhys David's note according to which the commentary takes *siri* not as the goddess of luck but as the *sirisayana* or cathedra of a teacher. Mrs. Rhys Davids has certainly misread the commentary (*saviggahaṃ siriṃ, sayane upagataṃ*) which makes no mention whatsoever of a *sirisayana*. Mr. Norman remarks that *pāṇāmeyya* would seem to require an object and suggests reading *siraṃ* instead of *siriṃ*. His translation of *virādh-* by 'transgress, sin' does not render its meaning adequately. The word-play between *ārādh-* and *virādh-* is not on 'honour, worship' and 'transgress, sin', but on 'propitiate, please' and 'offend, displease', cf. *BHSD* ss.vv. *ārāgayati* and *virāgayati*. I see no difficulty in translating the text as it is: 'He who would turn away with his hands and feet the goddess of Fortune who has arrived, would after having pleased such a master displease him.'

In a note on 528 Mr. Norman remarks that *dumāni* could be an Eastern masculine accusative plural in *-āni*. However, *dumāni* in this verse is a nominative.

In 677-678 Mr. Norman translates *nibbindati* by 'becomes indifferent to' but gives no other examples for interpreting *nibbindati* in this way. I believe that this verb has here its usual meaning 'have enough of, turn away from, be disgusted with'. In 1207 Mr. Norman translates *Māra nibbinda buddhamhā* by 'Keep away from the Buddha, Māra', but *nibbinda* here means 'turn away (in disgust on account of the hopelessness of your attack on the Buddha)'.

In 695 the text reads *dhammakucchi samāvāso*. Mr. Norman suggests reading *kucchi dhamma-samāvāpo* 'his belly is the fireplace of the doctrine'. The parallel passage in Chinese (*Taishō*, No. 26, Vol. I, p. 608c11) has 'his belly is the retainer of the dharmas' which would correspond to *kucchi dhammasamāvāso*.

In 947 occurs the expression *pacchimo kālo* which Mr. Norman translates by 'the last hour'. The same expression is to be found in 977 where it is rendered by him as 'the last time'. Both 920-48 and 949-80 deal with prophecies of the decline of the dharma. I believe that the commentary on 947 is right in explaining *pacchimo kālo* as the *atita-satthuko carimo kālo*, cf. *paścime kāle* in the texts quoted by Lamotte, *Histoire du bouddhisme indien*, p. 215.

Mr. Norman has a long note on *pātālakhittaṃ* and *baḷavāmukhaṃ* in 1104. He points out that at *JA* iv. 141 *vaḷabhāmukha* occurs as the name of a sea and that Pātāla exists in BHS as the name of a locality (*BHS Dictionary* gives only one reference to the badly transmitted *Mahāmāyūrī*). However, in *JA* iv. 141 as in the corresponding story in the *Jātakamālā* (ed. H. Kern, p. 92.25) *vaḷabhāmukha* is both an imaginary geographical location and the gateway to hell. Both *pātāla* and *vaḍavāmukha* are to be found together in the following verse of the *Mahābhārata* in which there can be no question of geographical names: *antakaḥ śamano mṛtyuḥ pātālaṃ vaḍavāmukham / kṣuradhārā viṣaṃ sarpo vahnir ity ekataḥ striyaḥ* (Poona ed., XIII. 38.29).

In 1141 the mind is said to be *anissitaṃ sabbabhavesu hehisi*. Mr. Norman translates: 'you will be free from all existences'. In Pāli texts *anissita* is used in the meaning 'free from craving and view', cf. E. Conze, *The Large Sutra on Perfect Wisdom*, Part I (London, 1961), p. xli. The commentary explains: *sabbesu pi bhavesu taṇhādi-nissayehi anissitaṃ bhavissasi*. It seems to me that Mr. Norman is right in not following the commentary but one would have welcomed a note explaining his reasons.

In 1165 the interpretation given by the commentary seems more acceptable. It explains *sithilam ārabbha* by *sithilaṃ katvā, viriyaṃ akatvā*, cf. also *CPD* s.v. *ārabbha*. Mr. Norman translates the first *pāda* by 'This is not referring to a slack thing'. I suggest the following translation: 'It is not by slackness, it is not by a little effort that Nirvāṇa which releases all ties can be obtained.'

Australian National University J. W. de Jong

Ludwig Alsdorf, *Les études jaina. État présent et tâches futures.* Paris, Collège de France, 1965. iv + 96 pp. 10 N.F.
Ludwig Alsdorf, *Die Āryā-Strophen des Pāli-Kanons metrisch hergestellt und textgeschichtlich untersucht* (= *Akademie der Wissenschaften und der Literatur, Abh. d. Geistes- u. sozialw. Kl.*, Jahrgang 1967, Nr. 4). 89 pp. DM 14,—.

Les conférences, faites par M. Ludwig Alsdorf au printemps 1965 au Collège de France, sont d'un très grand intérêt, non seulement pour le cercle restreint des spécialistes du jainisme qui lisent le français mais aussi pour tous les indianistes. En particulier, les spécialistes du bouddhisme ont beaucoup à apprendre de cet exposé lucide où il est souvent question de problèmes de la philologie bouddhique. M. Alsdorf commence par souligner l'importance de la comparaison du bouddhisme et du jainisme, deux religions nées dans les mêmes conditions et à la même époque. Il montre à l'aide de quelques exemples — *phasu(ya)*, *āsava*, *mālavihāra*, *tāī* — que la même terminologie se retrouve dans les textes jainas et bouddhiques. Après avoir brièvement caractérisé la littérature jaina et sa contribution à la religion, la philosophie et la littérature de l'Inde, M. Alsdorf esquisse son importance pour l'étude du prākrit, de l'apabhraṃśa et des langues dravidiennes. Ensuite il examine le problème que pose la langue des textes anciens du canon et la possibilité de déceler les traces d'une langue pré-canonique, la 'véritable' ardhamāgadhī qui se caractérise par l'*s* occidental comme seule sifflante, *l* oriental pour *r* et *-e* au lieu de *-o* à partir de *-as*. Selon lui, la traduction ou l'adaptation linguistique des textes jainas en prākrit canonique a dû avoir lieu longtemps avant le concile de Valabhī au cinquième siècle, probablement à l'époque même où le canon bouddhique primitif était traduit en pāli. Le parallélisme avec les travaux de Lüders sur la langue du canon bouddhique primitif est évident. Comme Lüders, M. Alsdorf fait appel au témoignage des inscriptions d'Aśoka pour déterminer les caractéristiques des dialectes occidental et oriental. De même que Lüders avait découvert un abl. sing. en *-aṃ* en pāli, M. Alsdorf en démontre l'existence dans un texte canonique jaina: *Uttarādhyayana* 23,46.[1] Espérons que M. Alsdorf entreprendra lui-même d'écrire "Les considérations sur la langue du canon jaina primitif" qu'il considère comme une des tâches les plus importantes des études jaina.

En passant ensuite en revue les éditions des textes canoniques jainas dont on dispose à présent M. Alsdorf constate que, pour 21 des 48 textes canoniques, il existe des éditions de style européen mais que la plupart devraient être refaites. M. Alsdorf attire l'attention sur les éditions du canon publiées par les Sthānakvāsin, une secte réformatrice du début du dix-huitième siècle, et l'intérêt que présente le nombre et l'ordre des textes dans ces éditions. Il examine ensuite la valeur des commentaires en prākrit (*niryukti* et *cūrṇi*) et en sanskrit (*ṭīkā*) pour l'établissement d'éditions critiques. M. Alsdorf montre que des fautes métriques et des fausses sanskritisations témoignent du fait que, malgré une tradition orale et écrite ininterrompue, les textes canoniques n'ont pas été préservés de la déformation et de la corruption.[2] Selon lui, il faudrait manifester encore plus d'indépendance à leur égard que l'on a fait jusqu'à présent.

M. Alsdorf s'étend plus en détail sur l'importance de la métrique pour l'étude de la chronologie du canon jaina. C'est surtout l'*āryā* qui permet de déterminer l'âge relatif d'un texte ou d'un passage d'un texte: "les textes en āryā sont ipso facto récents, des āryās à l'intérieur de textes en mètres anciens, ou bien en vieille prose, sont des adjonc-

[1] M. John Brough fait remarquer que l'on peut aussi expliquer des formes pālies en *-aṃ* comme dues à une erreur graphique, le scribe ayant écrit *-aṃ* au lieu de *-ā* (*The Gāndhārī Dharmapada*, London, 1962, pp. 79-80). M. Alsdorf ne discute pas cette possibilité et s'appuie sur la tradition pour maintenir la forme *visabhakkhaṇaṃ* (*Uttarādhyayana* 23,46). Pourtant il n'hésite pas pour corriger ailleurs le texte de l'*Uttarādhyayana* à l'encontre de la tradition (cf. p. 41 où, dans *Utt.* 25,7, il propose de lire *janna-jaṭṭhā* au lieu de *jannaṭṭhā*).

[2] A propos du pāli *bhūnaha* ou *bhūnahu* M. Alsdorf remarque que Baburam Saksena a indiqué la bonne étymologie en 1936 (*BSOS*, VIII, p. 713). Déjà H. Kern avait proposé la même étymologie, cf. *Bijdrage tot de verklaring van eenige woorden in Pali-geschriften voorkomende* (Amsterdam, 1886), pp. 52-53; *Toevoegselen op 't woordenboek van Childers*, I (Amsterdam, 1916), pp. 5-6. Kern avait aussi déjà proposé de lire *muñcantu* au lieu de *pamuñcantu* dans *Jātaka* III, p. 179 (*Bijdrage*, p. 79; cf. L. Alsdorf, *Die Āryā-Strophen des Pāli-Kanons*, p. 24).

tions plus récentes ou des citations". M. Alsdorf décrit la forme classique de l'*āryā* ainsi qu'une forme archaïque qui ne se rencontre que dans trois chapitres des textes canoniques et une variante semi- prosaïque, le *veḍha.* Avant d'étudier l'*āryā* dans le canon jaina et, en particulier, dans l'*Uttarādhyayana,* M. Alsdorf examine l'emploi de l'*āryā* dans les textes pālis. L'*āryā* archaïque s'y rencontre surtout dans le *Suttanipāta* où elle avait été signalée déjà par Jacobi en 1895 (*Jaina Sutras,* Part 2, *SBE,* 45, p. 271, n. 2) et dans quelques autres textes. L'*āryā* classique se trouve dans six *jātaka* (Nos. 542, 525, 485, 479, 358 et 301). En étudiant ces *jātaka* M. Alsdorf montre que leur contenu confirme leur caractère récent par rapport à des *jātaka* dont les vers sont en *śloka* ou en *triṣṭubh.* Cette conclusion est corroborée par l'examen des *āryā* dans les *jātaka* du *Mahāvastu* et dans les *Therīgāthā.* Après les *jātaka* et les *Therīgāthā* c'est le début du *Mahāvagga* qui contient le plus grand nombre d'*āryā.* M. Alsdorf constate que "l'utilisation relativement fréquente et visiblement originale de l'āryā éloigne considérablement ce texte dans le temps du deuxième fragment ancien de biographie de Bouddha, le Mahaparinibbānasutta". Quelques *āryā* se trouvent encore dans les *Theragāthā,* le *Sagāthavagga,* le *Vimānavatthu,* le *Petavatthu* et l'*Apadāna.* Le nombre total des *āryā* archaïques s'élève à 46, celui des *āryā* classiques à environ 450. Alors que chez les jainas l'*āryā* prédomine dans la littérature postcanonique, le mètre normal de la littérature postcanonique en pāli est le *śloka.* M. Alsdorf constate deux exceptions: le *Nettipakaraṇa* et le *Peṭakopadesa* et les préfaces et les épilogues des commentaires de Buddhaghosa. Selon M. Alsdorf, ces exceptions s'expliquent par le fait que l'émigration du pāli au Ceylan a arrêté l'emploi de l'*āryā* dans la littérature pālie. Le *Nettipakaraṇa* a dû être écrit par un indien du nord de l'Inde dont Buddhaghosa est aussi originaire. Le *Peṭakopadesa* est une suite du *Nettipakaraṇa* et son auteur l'a pillé largement.

Après avoir étudié l'*āryā* dans la littérature pālie M. Alsdorf revient au canon jaina. Il démontre que l'*Uttarādhyayana* contient environ 129 *āryā* dont 109 se trouvent dans six chapitres du dernier tiers du texte. Plusieurs passages, écrits dans ce mètre, contiennent des développements scholastiques et dogmatiques d'origine plus récente. En outre, 45 de ces 109 *āryā* se retrouvent dans des textes canoniques récents. D'un intérêt particulier est un passage, rédigé en *āryā,* relatif au goût, à l'odeur et au toucher des *leśyā.* Ce passage témoigne d'une élaboration scholastique de la théorie karmanique des *leśyā* "couleurs de l'âme".

Dans la dernière partie de ce petit livre l'auteur mentionne comme une des tâches futures des études jaina la reprise du travail sur l'*Āvaśyaka* par Ernst Leumann et, en premier lieu, une édition critique de l'*Āvaśyakaniryukti.* Pour terminer M. Alsdorf attire l'attention sur la littérature des *digambara* et, en particulier, sur les problèmes que suscite la publication récente de textes anciens, le *Ṣaṭkhaṇḍāgama* et le *Kaṣāyaprābhṛta* avec les commentaires qui s'y rattachent. M. Alsdorf montre que ces textes contiennent des passages qui se retrouvent dans des textes des *śvetāmbara.* Le phénomène s'observe en plus grande mesure dans d'autres textes des *śvetāmbara*: le *Mūlācāra* de Vaṭṭakera et la *Mūlāradhanā* de Śivārya.

J'espère avoir réussi à montrer l'intérêt que présente l'ouvrage de M. Alsdorf pour tous ceux qui s'intéressent de loin ou de près aux études jaina. Espérons que de jeunes indianistes seront inspirés par les perspectives tracées, de manière magistrale, par l'auteur. Il constate avec regret une certaine récession des études jaina dans l'indologie du présent. Peut-être ce phénomène s'explique par le fait que les études jaina sont d'un accès assez difficile et se sont développées dans un certain isolement. M. Alsdorf montre bien que les difficultés ne sont pas insurmontables et que l'isolement doit être rompu dans l'intérêt aussi bien des études jaina mêmes, que d'autres branches de l'indianisme et surtout des études bouddhiques.

Sur un seul point l'argumentation de M. Alsdorf ne me paraît pas tout à fait convaincante. Il est hors de doute que l'*āryā* est un indice qui permet de dater un texte par rapport à d'autres textes. M. Alsdorf effectue le passage d'une chronologie à une chronologie absolue en adoptant comme *terminus ante quem* le milieu ou la deuxième moitié du troisième siècle avant J.-Chr.: "la suite de l'évolution de l'*āryā* en pāli est évidemment arrêtée par son émigration vers Ceylan, qui date du milieu ou de la deuxième moitié du IIIe siècle avant J.-Chr. Tout ce qu'il y a en fait d'āryās dans le canon pāli doit être plus ancien" (p. 70). C'est le même *terminus ante quem* que M. Alsdorf propose pour la traduction du canon bouddhique primitif en pāli: "Pour cette dernière, le sûr *terminus ante quem* est l'introduction de textes pālis au Ceylan, c'est-à-dire selon l'opinion courante au milieu du IIIe siècle avant J.-Chr." Je ne sais pas si c'est l'opinion courante mais, en tout cas, cette opinion doit se baser surtout sur la tradition singhalaise selon laquelle Mahinda, le fils d'Asoka, a introduit à Ceylan le canon pāli. M. Ét. Lamotte a bien montré l'invraisemblance de cette tradition (*Histoire du Bouddhisme Indien*, I, Louvain, 1958, p. 339). Un autre problème qui se pose est le suivant. Est-ce que des passages plus récents, rédigés en *āryā*, se sont déjà adjoints au canon primitif ou est-ce qu'ils se sont produits seulement après sa transposition en pāli? En ce qui concerne l'*āryā* archaïque la conclusion de M. Alsdorf est la suivante: "Que l'āryā ancienne n'apparaît nettement que dans des textes anciens du canon pāli, que la plupart des exemples se rencontrent dans un texte comme le Suttanipāta — cela correspond tout à fait au rôle qu'elle joue dans le canon jaina." Il y a dans le canon pāli aussi de nombreuses *āryā* qu'il faut considérer comme des formes de transition entre l'*āryā* archaïque et l'*āryā* classique (cf. p. 68). Malheureusement, M. Alsdorf ne donne pas un inventaire des passages qui contiennent de telles *āryā*. Ces formes de transition qui semblent être bien plus rares chez les jainas compliquent les problèmes chronologiques. Je ne peux que signaler ici ces problèmes qui méritent d'être étudiés plus en détail.

Dans *Die Āryā-Strophen des Pāli-Kanons metrisch hergestellt und textgeschichtlich untersucht* M. Alsdorf établit un texte correct du point de vue métrique pour toutes les *āryā* du canon pāli à l'exception de celles qui se trouvent dans les *Thera-* et *Therīgāthā*.[3] La première partie donne les textes en *āryā* archaïques. En ce qui concerne la louange du Buddha par Upāli (*MN* I 386,3-32) on s'étonne que l'auteur ne fasse pas mention du fragment de la recension sanskrite publiée par Hoernle (*Manuscript Remains*, pp. 27-35). La publication de Hoernle contient aussi une étude de la version chinoise par Watanabe. Ce dernier travail n'est pas exempt d'erreurs et il y aurait lieu d'étudier de nouveau les différentes recensions de ce texte en tenant compte des corrections que M. Alsdorf propose pour le texte pāli.

Parmi les textes en *āryā* classique le plus intéressant est sans doute le début du *Mahāvagga* dans lequel M. Alsdorf a retrouvé dix-neuf strophes écrites dans ce mètre.[4]

[3] Cf. *The Thera- and Therī-Gāthā*, ed. H. Oldenberg and R. Pischel. Second edition with Appendices by K. R. Norman and L. Alsdorf (London, Pali Text Society, 1966), pp. 233-250.

[4] Selon M. Alsdorf le grand nombre de strophes *āryā* dans ce texte n'a pas été pris en considération jusqu'à maintenant. Toutefois il faut faire remarquer que ces strophes ont retenu l'attention de plusieurs savants. Déjà Jacobi avait reconnu que la célèbre strophe *ye dhammā hetuppabhavā* ... (*Vin.* I, p. 40) était une *āryā* (*ZDMG*, 38, 1884, p. 602). M. Alsdorf rejette les corrections proposées par Jacobi (cf. p. 66) comme l'avait fait avant lui Helmer Smith dans un travail que M. Alsdorf ne mentionne pas (*Analecta Rhytmica*, *Studia Orientalia* XIX:7, Helsinki, 1954, p. 13). Remarquons en passant que Jacobi est le premier à avoir trouvé des strophes en *āryā* dans le *Suttanipāta* (*Jaina Sutras*, *SBE*, vol. 45, Oxford, 1895, p. 271, n. 2). En ce qui concerne les neuf strophes qui décrivent la victoire du Buddha sur le *nāga* (*Vin.* I, p. 25, 18-34) Oldenberg a bien reconnu que ce passage est écrit en vers, bien qu'il n'ait pas pu en déterminer le mètre (cf. le passage de "Zur Geschichte der indischen Prosa" cité par M. Alsdorf, pp. 56-57; plus loin M. Alsdorf dit: "Nur weil er die Verse nicht als solche erkannte,

M. Alsdorf ne se contente pas de rétablir un texte correct pour ces strophes mais il discute aussi en détail les problèmes qui résultent de la comparaison avec des textes parallèles en sanskrit et, avant tout, avec le *Catuṣpariṣatsūtra* (*CPS*). Il nous avertit que la relation de la version pāli avec les autres versions (M. Alsdorf parle de versions plus tardives) et, en premier lieu, le *CPS* ne peut être définitivement déterminée qu'après une comparaison détaillée des textes entiers. Toutefois, il lui semble vraisemblable que la version pāli est la plus ancienne qui soit conservée et aussi la source la plus importante des autres versions. Que la version pāli soit plus authentique que celle, représentée par le *CPS*, n'a pas de quoi nous surprendre, car celui-ci appartient au *Vinaya* des Mūlasarvāstivādin qui est "clos à une époque tardive" (Lamotte, *op. cit.*, p. 187). Il est regrettable que M. Alsdorf n'ait pas consulté les textes parallèles, traduits du chinois, par Ebbe Tuneld (*Recherches sur la valeur des traditions bouddhiques pālie et non-pālie*, Lund, 1915), M. André Migot, ("Un grand disciple du Buddha, Śāriputra", *BEFEO*, XLVI, 1954, pp. 405-554) et M. André Bareau (*Recherches sur la biographie du Buddha dans les Sūtrapiṭaka et les Vinayapiṭaka anciens*, Paris, 1963). Surtout ce dernier travail est de la plus haute importance pour l'étude du début du *Mahāvagga* car M. Bareau a traduit les passages parallèles des *Vinaya* des Mahīśāsaka et des Dharmaguptaka, Vinaya plus anciens que celui des Mūlasarvāstivādin.

Pour terminer qu'il me soit permis d'ajouter quelques remarques de détail à propos du *Mahāvagga*. M. Alsdorf constate que la phrase *anupahacca* .... (*Vin.* I, pp. 24-25) est empruntée au *Pāyāsi-suttanta* (corriger en D II 326.2 326 en 336). Il signale aussi que A. P. Buddhadatta a corrigé la traduction fautive de ce passage par Rhys Davids. Déjà Leumann avait bien interprété ce passage ("Beziehungen der Jaina-Literatur zu anderen Literaturkreisen", *Actes du sixième congrès international des orientalistes tenu en 1883 à Leide*, III, 2, Leide, 1885, p. 479) comme, après lui, Neumann (*Die Reden Gotamo Buddhos*, II, Zürich-Wien, 1957, pp. 760-761) et le *Critical Pāli Dictionary* (p. 198b).

La strophe *appaṃ vā bahuṃ*.... (*Vin.* I, p. 40, 24-25) se retrouve dans le *Mahāvastu* III, p. 60, 20-21) et le *CPS* (ed. E. Waldschmidt, p. 378). Dans ce dernier le texte sanskrit est très fragmentaire. D'après la traduction tibétaine, le premier pāda est rétabli par M. Waldschmidt comme *mahyam eva arthena kāryam*. M. Alsdorf remarque: "Das Tibetische hat in der Tat *kho bo la ni don dgos kyi*, aber allein sinnvoll wäre doch *mayham arthenaiva kāryam*! Irrtum oder Nachlässigkeit des tibetischen Übersetzers?" Remarquons que le tibétain ne traduit pas *eva* et que l'ordre des mots en tibétain n'est pas nécessairement le même qu'en sanskrit. C'est pourquoi je propose de rétablir: *arthena mahyaṃ kāryam* (cf. *Mahāvastu*: *arthena mahyaṃ kāriyaṃ*). Les trois autres pāda du *CPS* correspondent étroitement au texte pāli mais dans un ordre différent (les pāda a,b et d du pāli correspondent aux pāda c, d et b du *CPS*). On ne peut donc pas dire que la strophe du *CPS* correspond à la strophe du *Mahāvastu* où les pāda c et d sont tout à fait différents (cf. Alsdorf, p. 66).

Dans une strophe qui se retrouve deux fois dans le *CPS* M. Waldschmidt a rétabli *a(mara)m* (cf. Alsdorf, p. 67; *CPS*, pp. 380 et 384). Cette reconstruction ne repose pas sur la traduction tibétaine qui a *rjes-su rtogs* (*anugatam*?).

Dans deux strophes, corrigées par M. Alsdorf, il garde la forme *anupatte* à l'encontre

---

konnte Oldenberg..."!). Deux autres strophes en *āryā* (*Vin.* I, p. 40, 24-25 et 33-34; cf. Alsdorf, pp. 64-71) ont été signalées par E. J. Thomas (*The Life of Buddha*, London, 1927, p. 94, n. 1). C'est surtout Helmer Smith qui, à plusiers reprises, a étudié les strophes en *āryā* du *Mahāvagga* (*Saddanīti*, vol. IV, Lund, 1949, pp. 1161-1165; *Les deux prosodies du vers bouddhique*, Lund, 1950, pp. 38-40; *Analecta Rhytmica*, Helsinki, 1954, pp. 13-15). M. Alsdorf ne cite que le deuxième de ces trois travaux. Dans une note (p. 52, n. 2), il déclare que, à bien des égards, il ne partage pas les idées de Helmer Smith sur la métrique pāli et moyen-indienne. Espérons que M. Alsdorf trouvera l'occasion de les soumettre à un examen systématique.

de la tradition orientale et de la traduction tibétaine (*Vin.* I, p. 42, 33-37; Alsdorf, p. 69, n.2; p. 70, n. 2). M. Alsdorf traduit ces deux strophes de la manière suivante: "Als die beiden im Veḷuvana *angekommen* waren ... da prophezeite der Meister von ihnen: 'Hier *kommen* zwei Gefährten'". J'ai mis en italique les mots "angekommen" et "kommen" pour faire ressortir que la leçon *appatte* doit être préférée. Dans la traduction de la version tibétaine il vaudra mieux traduire *'gyur* par le futur: "Ces deux-là seront la meilleure paire de mes Auditeurs" (Alsdorf p. 70: "sind diese beiden das beste Paar meiner Hörer").

Australian National University J. W. de Jong

Oskar von Hinüber, *Studien zur Kasussyntax des Pāli, besonders des Vinaya-piṭaka* (= *Münchener Studien zur Sprachwissenschaft*, Beiheft, Neue Folge, 2). München, J. Kitzinger, 1968. 340 pp.

Dr. Oskar von Hinüber's study of the syntax of the cases in the *Vinaya-piṭaka* fills an important lacuna in the field of Pāli grammar. It is certainly the most important publication to appear since Hans Hendriksen's *Syntax of the infinite verb-forms of Pāli* (Copenhagen, 1944). The studies by H. O. de A. Wijesekera and A. Fahs, mentioned by von Hinüber in his introduction, are not easily accessible. No use has been made by him of A. K. Warder's *Introduction to Pāli* (London, 1963) which pays more attention to syntax than other grammars. The choice of the *Vinaya* with the exception of the *Parivāra* is an excellent one because it contains probably more ancient parts than other Tipiṭaka texts. Moreover, the interpretation of the *Vinaya-piṭaka* is often far from easy. Von Hinüber intended his work to be at the same time a syntactic commentary on the *Vinaya* and, as such, it is of great use for a better understanding of this often difficult text. Although it is mainly based upon the *Vinaya*, other Pāli texts are also taken into account especially with regard to more difficult problems of Pāli syntax. Von Hinüber critically examines the translations of the *Vinaya* by Rhys Davids and Oldenberg and by Miss Horner; in quite a few places he arrives at a better understanding of the text. His text emendations are generally convincing as for instance the emendation of *papato* and *patitā* into *papatā* (3 p. sg.aor.) cf. pp. 45-46. Lexicographical problems are also studied by him, as for instance the meaning of *cirāciram* 'rarely' (p. 95).

In a few places von Hinüber refers to the Sanskrit fragments of other *Vinayas* but they have not been of much help to him. Apart from the *Prātimokṣas* of the Sarvāstivādin, the Mūlasarvāstivādin and the Mahāsāṃghika (badly edited by Pachow and Mishra), only some fragments of the *Vibhaṅga* of one school, the Sarvāstivādin, are available. However, the Chinese canon contains complete versions of the *Vinayas* of five schools. In many cases, the *Vinaya* texts of the different schools have much in common. It must have been of particular importance to transmit the *Vinaya* rules as faithfully as possible. In studying the Pāli *Vinaya* it is not possible to leave the other *Vinayas* entirely out of consideration. Of course, the Chinese versions can offer but little help in the study of the syntax of the Pāli *Vinaya*. However, in places which are difficult to understand because the text is evidently corrupt or the meaning of a word not very well known, it may be useful to compare the Pāli text with parallel passages in the Chinese versions of the *Vinayas*. An interpretation of a Pāli passage, which is not confirmed by parallel passages in other *Vinayas* cannot be accepted without reservations. One must of course be aware of the fact that the Chinese translations must be handled with extreme caution. Their usefulness resides in the fact that one can compare the texts of four *Vinayas* (Mahīśāsaka, Mahāsāṃghika, Dharmaguptaka and Sarvāstivādin). The *Vinaya* of the Mūlasarvāstivādin is of lesser importance in this respect. Moreover, the Chinese versions, by the fact that they are translations, offer an interpretation of the text, which is quite often of greater value than the one to be found in Buddhaghosa's *Samantapāsādikā*.

In discussing the existence of an absolute nominative in Pāli, von Hinüber examines *Vin.* II.167.15ff. *vihāraggena gāhentā vihārā ussādiyiṃsu ... anujānāmi bhikkhave anubhāgaṃ pi dātuṃ* (pp. 28-30). Von Hinüber proposes to read *ussārayiṃsu* and to consider *vihārā* as a corruption for *vihāre*. His translation is as follows: "Nach der Zahl der Lager (die Mönche) ergreifen lassend, schicken sie (die Wohnplatzanweiser) (die Mönche) zu den Lagern weg." According to him *ussāreti* means 'vertreiben, wegschicken' (*Vin.* I.276.8) or 'auswerfen' (*Vin.* II.237.32). He assumes the same meaning 'wegschicken' for *Vin.* IV.99.9 *khādaniyaṃ ussādiyittha* "das Essen wurde weggeschickt". Von Hinüber remarks that the manuscript tradition confuses *ussād-* and *ussār-* and adds that, according to the lists of roots, both roots have the same meaning (*gati*, *gamana*). I do not think that the last argument is very strong because the *dhātupāṭhas* have the habit of explaining many roots by *gati*. In *Vin*. II.237.29-30 (*yaṃ hoti mahāsamudde mataṃ kuṇapaṃ taṃ khippaṃ ñeva tīraṃ vāheti thalaṃ ussāreti*) *ussāreti* seems preferable, cf. Thieme (*ZDMG*, 111, p. 116) who translates *samuddavīcīhi thale ussāritaṃ* by "was von den Wogen des Meers ans Festland geschnellt (geworfen) ist". Von Hinüber's translation of *Vin*. II.167.15ff. does not explain why, after the distribution of the *vihāras*, a supplementary portion (*anubhāga*) is distributed to the monks. As to his translation of *Vin*. IV.99.9 no *Vinaya* mentions the fact that the food is sent back. The food is being kept for Upananda and is not distributed to the other monks. In both places *ussād-* seems to have the meaning of 'to put aside' which corresponds quite well to Sanskrit *utsādayati*. Therefore I would like to suggest to read in *Vin*. II.167.18 *vihāre ussādayiṃsu* "they put aside *vihāras* (which were not distributed)", and to translate *khādaniyaṃ ussādiyittha* by "the food was put aside", rejecting Buddhaghosa's explanation, quoted by von Hinüber (p. 30, n.1).

Von Hinüber studies at length a difficult passage relating to the *pātimokkhuddesa*: *Vin*. I.112.11-12 *nidānaṃ uddisitvā avasesaṃ sutena sāvetabbaṃ* (pp. 176-177). It is not possible to explain *sutena*. In order to solve this difficulty von Hinüber reads *sute na* "der Rest ist nicht zu rezitieren, da er (bei früheren Uposatha-Feiern) gehört ist". The same passage occurs in the *Poṣadhavastu* of the *Mūlasarvāstivādavinaya* (*Gilgit Manuscripts*, III, 4, p. 94.10-11): *nidānam uddiśya avaśiṣṭaṃ śrutena śrāvayanti*. I have not consulted the Tibetan version which probably would only give a literal translation. However, one would expect a negation to have left traces in the Chinese versions of the *Vinaya*. In three of them (Mahīśāsaka, Mahāsāṃghika, Dharmaguptaka) the text has "the rest is always heard by the *saṃgha*"; the *Sarvāstivādavinaya* has "the rest was previously heard by the *saṃgha*". I am afraid that the Chinese versions do not help us to understand the Pāli text but, in any case, one must draw attention to the fact that none of them contains a negation.

For *taṃkhaṇikā* (*Vin*. III.139.9) von Hinüber proposes a new interpretation 'Augenblick' and rejects the traditional interpretation 'harlot, temporary wife, Hure' (pp. 194-196). Von Hinüber adds that probably already the Vibhaṅga commentary has misunderstood the word. The Pāli text mentions as the tenth of ten kinds of wives the *muhuttikā* (139.25) and explains *muhuttikā nāma taṃkhaṇikā vuccati* (140.7).[1] There seems therefore no doubt that the commentary has understood *taṃkhaṇikā* to mean 'a temporary wife'. This meaning certainly fits the context. In V.1 Udāyin acts as a go-between for two young girls. In V.2 he acts as go-between for a *vesiyā* and the rule adds to *jāyattane vā jārattane vā* the words *antamaso taṃkhaṇikāya pi*. In this episode the monks say: *kathaṃ hi nāma ayyo Udāyi taṃkhaṇikaṃ sañcarittaṃ samāpajjissati* (138.33). Von Hinüber translates: "Wie kann der Herr Udāyi in eine zeitweilige Vermittlung geraten." The word *taṃkhaṇikaṃ* is absent from the same formula in the previous episode: *kathaṃ hi nāma āyasmā Udāyi sañcarittaṃ samāpajjissati* (137.29-30). There seems no reason for the addition of a word, meaning 'temporary', in 138.33. However, this difficulty does not arise if one translates as Miss Horner: "How can the venerable Udāyin act as a go-between for a temporary wife?" Etymologically the meaning 'temporary wife' for *taṃkhaṇikā* 'one for that moment' is unobjectionable. Von Hinüber refers to *tatkṣaṇa-* in Buddhist Hybrid Sanskrit as meaning a shorter period than *kṣaṇa*. However, the text of the *Divyāvadāna* is certainly corrupt because, according to other Buddhist texts, 120 *kṣaṇa* make one *tatkṣaṇa* (cf. T. Watters, *On Yuang Chwang's Travels in India*, I, London, 1904, p. 143; L. de La Vallée Poussin,

[1] Seven kinds of wives are enumerated in the *Vinayas* of the Mūlasarvāstivādin and the Sarvāstivādin, cf. *Mahāvyutpatti* Nos. 9448-9454 and V. Rosen, *Der Vinayavibhaṅga zum Bhikṣuprātimokṣam der Sarvāstivādins* (1959) p. 61, n. 5, where one must omit *balena anupraskandya* and add *tatkṣaṇikā*.

L'Abhidharmakośa, III, Paris-Louvain, 1926, p. 179). Moreover *tatkṣaṇa* seems to occur only in enumerations of measures of time. The Chinese *Vinayas* render *tatkṣaṇikā* as 'a single meeting', 'a momentary one', etc. The text of the *Sarvāstivādavinaya* (*antatas tadkṣaṇam api*) is probably corrupt. In this case the *Mūlasarvāstivādavinaya* has clearly preserved the true reading — (*antatas tat*)*kṣaṇikāyām api*.

A last remark concerning *dassanāya* (von Hinüber, p. 224). According to von Hinüber a gen.obj. is used in the case of a pl., an acc. in the case of a sg. This rule is not confirmed by the texts, cf. *DN* II.140.12-13 *te mayam labhāma manobhāvanīye bhikkhū dassanāya*; *AN* III.317-319 *cha samayā manobhāvanīyassa bhikkhuno dassanāya upasaṃkamituṃ*. It would be possible to consider that, in the first example, the acc. depends on *labhāma* (cf. von Hinüber, p. 193), but it seems more probable to admit that the acc. depends on *dassanāya* as in other examples.

Von Hinüber's book contains a wealth of information. The above remarks are only meant to show how it stimulates discussion with the author in the rare cases in which one cannot completely agree with him. It is to be hoped that von Hinüber will also undertake a study of the syntax of late Pāli, the desirability of which is mentioned in his introduction.

Australian National University J. W. de Jong

Ria Kloppenborg, *The Paccekabuddha*. A Buddhist Ascetic. A study of the concept of the paccekabuddha in Pāli canonical and commentarial literature [= *Orientalia Rheno-Traiectina*, vol. 20]. Leiden, E. J. Brill, 1974. XIV + 135 pp. DGld. 40.-.

As the author remarks in her introduction the *paccekabuddha* has received little detailed attention. Louis de La Vallée Poussin's article in the *Encyclopaedia of Religion and Ethics* (vol. X, 1918, pp. 152–154) is based mainly on Sanskrit texts. According to him the *pratyekabuddha* embodies the old ideal of a solitary and silent life. R. K. remarks in the introduction that the concept of the *paccekabuddha* presented the opportunity to include pre-buddhist recluses and seers in Buddhism. This explains why *paccekabuddhas* are referred to by terms used to denote ascetics, e.g. *muni, isi, samaṇa, tāpasa, jaṭila*. La Vallée Poussin's theory has been accepted by many scholars both in the West and in Japan. However, it must be pointed out that an entirely different theory on the origin of the concept of the *paccekabuddha* was proposed by Ui Hakuju (1882–1963) in volume IV of his *Indo tetsugaku kenkyū* (Tōkyō, 1927). According to Ui this concept arose in connection with the tradition that the Buddha, after having obtained the *bodhi*, hesitated to preach the doctrine. The Buddha in obtaining the *bodhi* realised the truth of the doctrine of *pratītyasamutpāda*. Therefore the *pratyekabuddha* is considered to have obtained the *bodhi* by meditating on the *pratītyasamutpāda*. In his article on the origin of the *pratyekabuddha* Fujita Kōtatsu remarks that Ui's theory has been followed by other leading Japanese scholars such as Kimura Taiken in his *Shōjō bukkyō shisō ron* (Tōkyō, 1937) and Sakaino Kōyō ('Byakushibutsu ron', *Gendai bukkyō*, 1933).[1] However, Fujita shows clearly in his article that Ui's theory is not based upon early Buddhist texts and has to be rejected. According to him La Vallée Poussin's theory has been elaborated in Japan by Mochizuki Shinkō ('Engaku', *Bukkyōdaijiten*, vol. I, 1931) and Akanuma Chizen, (*Bukkyō kyōten shiron*, Nagoya, 1939). On the basis of a detailed study of early Buddhist texts in Pāli and Chinese, Fujita arrives at the same conclusion.

Ria Kloppenborg's work is based entirely upon Pāli texts. A study of this kind would certainly have been very useful if an attempt would have been made to trace the development of the concept of the *paccekabuddha* in the canonical texts and the commentaries. However, the author has not tried to differentiate between earlier and later texts. She remarks in the introduction: "The explanations of the commentary have simply been followed. To do otherwise would probably have proved an impossibility." (p. 12). It is difficult to imagine a more defeatist point of view. It is certainly impossible to maintain. The author herself, in discussing the importance of the verses of the Khaggavisāṇasutta of the Suttanipāta, is forced to remark that the term *paccekabuddha* is not used in these verses because at the time when they were composed, the concept of the *paccekabuddha* was not or had not yet developed within the Buddhist system (p. 11). It would certainly have been necessary to differentiate, not only between canonical texts and commentaries, but also between the earlier and later strata of the canonical writings as has been done, for example, by Sakurabe Hajime in an article on the *pratyekabuddha*.[2] Sakurabe draws attention to the fact that the word *paccekabuddha* is not to be found in texts which are considered to belong to the oldest stratum of Buddhist literature, such as the Suttanipāta, the Dhammapada, the Ittivuttaka, the Thera- and Therīgāthā, etc., whereas it is

[1] 'Sanjō no seiritsu ni tsuite. Byakushibutsu kigen kō', *Indogaku Bukkyōgaku Kenkyū*, V (1957), pp. 419–428. R. K. mentions Fujita's article as one of two Japanese publications about the concept of the *pratyekabuddha* and his position in the Mahāyāna schools which she has been unable to consult (p. 1, n. 1). This article does not deal at all with the concept of the *pratyekabuddha* in the Mahāyāna schools. As is indicated by the title itself Fujita studies the origin of the concept and its development in early Buddhism.

[2] 'Engaku kō', *Ōtani Gakuhō*, XXXVI, 3 (1956), pp. 40–51.

found in the Aṅguttaranikāya and more frequently in such younger texts as the Khuddakapāṭha, the Apadāna and the two Niddesas. The author limits herself to a systematic arrangement of the materials in three chapters: 1. The *paccekabuddha*; 2. The Way towards *paccekabodhi*; 3. The *paccekabuddha*'s way of life. Chapter four contains a translation of the 41 verses of the Khaggavisāṇasutta together with parts of the commentary. An appendix gives a translation of the Pratyekabuddhabhūmi. The author fails to make mention of the fact that this text is a chapter of Asaṅga's Yogācārabhūmi and that the Sanskrit text has been published by Alex Wayman in the *Journal of Indian and Buddhist Studies* (VIII, 1, 1960, pp. 376–375).

The author translates a number of passages from Pāli texts but their usefulness is greatly impaired by several serious blunders. A few examples may suffice. P. 19: "*paccekabuddhas* are born when no *buddhas* are found and in the time of the birth of a buddha"; Sn.A. p. 51: *paccekabuddhā buddhe appatvā buddhānaṃ uppajjanakāle yeva uppajjanti* "*paccekabuddhas* arise without having met *buddhas* and only at the time of the birth of *buddhas*". The author makes no comment on the fact that this passage mentions that *paccekabuddhas* exist at the time of the births of *buddhas* although in the following chapter she quotes a passage from the Sāratthappakāsinī according to which *paccekabuddhas* are said to exist only in periods when there are no *buddhas* (p. 37). Entirely misleading is the translation given of a passage twice quoted by the author (pp. 19 and 77). P. 19: "*paccekabuddhas* comprehend not the essence of the *dhamma*; because not causing (others) to ascend to the supra-mundane (i.e. *nibbāna*) they are able to teach the vague concept (*paññatti*)", cf. p. 77: "for, not causing to ascend to the supra-mundane state they are able to teach the notion (*paññatti*)"; Sn.A. p. 51: *na hi te lokuttaradhammaṃ paññattiṃ āropetvā desetuṃ sakkonti* "for they are unable to put the supra-mundane doctrine into verbal concepts and to teach it". Pāli *paññatti*, BHS *prajñapti* is not 'a vague concept' but 'a verbal designation or concept'. The author seems to have experienced considerable difficulties in translating the word *dassana* 'seeing, view'. One of the conditions for the resolve to set out on the way towards *paccekabodhi* is "the seeing of one who has destroyed evil influences" (*vigatāsavadassana*). The commentary explains that this refers to either a *buddha* or a *paccekabuddha* or a disciple (*buddhapaccekabuddhasāvakānaṃ yassa kassaci dassanan to*). R. K. translates *vigatāsavadassana* (Sn.A. p. 51) as "having the destruction of evil influences in view" and the explanation of the commentary as "whose view is (the same as the view) of *buddhas*, *paccekabuddhas* and disciples" (p. 39). On p. 114 R. K. translates *nāṭakadassanaṃ āgataṃ aññataraṃ kuṭumbikabhariyaṃ* (Sn.A. p. 115) "A certain landlord's wife who had come to see a dancer" as follows: "A certain landlord's wife, who resembled a dancer." The author is critical of the existing translations of the Suttanipāta but she does not hesitate to render *anaññaposi*(n) with 'not nourished by others' (p. 116), a translation based upon the explanation given in the commentary: *posetabbakasaddhivihārikādivirahita* (Sn.A. p. 118.10). According to R. K. this means: "without a co-resident etc. who has to (provide) the food"! It is certainly needless to continue this enumeration of elementary mistakes, but it is necessary to point out that the translation of the Pratyekabuddhabhūmi is, if possible, even worse. For instance, *kalpaśataṃ buddhotpādam ārāgayati* is rendered as "in a hundred kalpas (he) acquires the resolution to become a *buddha*". This expression has been explained by Edgerton in his dictionary s.v. *ārāgaṇa*: "*buddhotpādārāgaṇatā*, attainment of the production of Buddhas, i.e. the privilege of being born when a Buddha is born".[3] R. K. translates *asati ca buddhānām utpāde* with "without (having made) the resolution of the *buddhas*". Translations of this kind of course make nonsense of the text of the Pratyekabuddhabhūmi.

It is obvious that the author does not possess the required knowledge of Pāli and Sanskrit to translate the materials studied by her. This combined with the fact that no attempt has been made to arrange the materials in a historical perspective forces us to arrive at the sad conclusion

[3] Weller proposes two different interpretations: "Entzücken über das Erscheinen eines Buddha" or "Einen erscheinenden Buddha erfreuen", cf. *Zum Kāśyapaparivarta* (Berlin, 1965), p. 77, note 5.

that the author has been badly advised in publishing this book. A comprehensive and satisfactory study of the concept of the *paccekabuddha* is still outstanding. The best contribution published so far is undoubtedly the short article by Fujita mentioned above. An English translation would be very welcome.

Australian National University J. W. DE JONG

IV
Sanskrit Hīnayāna Literature

LES *SŪTRAPIṬAKA* DES SARVĀSTIVĀDIN ET DES MŪLASARVĀSTIVĀDIN

PAR

J. W. DE JONG

Le développement et la filiation des écoles bouddhiques est un des chapitres les plus difficiles des études bouddhiques. Les renseignements que fournissent des auteurs indiens, tibétains et chinois ne méritent pas une confiance absolue. Dans la plupart des cas, ils ont vécu longtemps après les événements qu'ils racontent. Avec raison, M. Lamotte nous met en garde contre les ' trésors d'imagination ' avec lesquels ils ont suppléé au manque d'informations dont ils disposaient[1]. Pour des informations, plus dignes de confiance, il faut s'adresser à d'autres sources telles que les inscriptions, les relations des pèlerins chinois et les renseignements fournis par les textes mêmes. Depuis le début de ce siècle la découverte de nombreux textes bouddhiques en Asie centrale a livré de nouveaux matériaux pour l'étude de l'histoire des écoles bouddhiques.

Par la relation de Hiuan-tsang nous savons que, dans le deuxième quart du VIIe siècle, les Sarvāstivādin étaient nombreux à Kučā et d'autres oasis de l'Asie centrale[2]. Houei-tch'ao, qui visita Kučā en 727, raconte qu'on y pratique le Hīnayāna. Il ajoute que des moines chinois y pratiquent le Mahāyāna (T. 2089, 979a27-29). La prédominance de l'école Sarvāstivāda a été confirmée par la découverte de fragments du *Vinaya* de cette école. Déjà, en 1911, Louis Finot publia trois feuillets des manuscrits Pelliot provenant de l'ancien temple de Duldur-âqur à Kučā (*JA*, 1911, II, 619-625)[3]. Du même

1. Ét. LAMOTTE, *Histoire du Bouddhisme indien*, I, Louvain, 1958, p. 584.
2. LAMOTTE, *op. cit.*, p. 598.
3. L'appartenance de ces fragments au Vinaya des Sarvāstivādin fut constatée plus tard, *JA*, 1913, II, p. 550. Cf. aussi HIRAKAWA Akira, *Ritsuzō no kenkyū*, Tōkyō, 1960, pp. 74-75. M. Hirakawa a examiné les fragments sanskrits du Vinaya du

endroit proviennent des manuscrits du *Prātimokṣasūtra* des Sarvāstivādin, publiés par Louis Finot avec la traduction française de la version chinoise de Kumārajīva par Édouard Huber (*JA*, 1913, II, pp. 465-547). De la région de Kučā viennent aussi des fragments du *Vinaya* des Sarvāstivādin publiés par Jean Filliozat et Hōryū Kuno (*JA*, 1938, pp. 21-64). En 1926, M. Ernst Waldschmidt publia des fragments du *Bhikṣuṇī-Prātimokṣa* et du *Vinayavibhaṅga* des Sarvāstivādin, en utilisant des manuscrits provenant de Qizil (36 km au nord-ouest de Kučā[1]), de Šorčuq à l'est de Kučā, de Sängim (36 km à l'est de Turfan[1]), et de Murtuq près de Turfan[2]. Dans tous ces cas, la comparaison avec la version chinoise du *Vinaya* des Sarvāstivādin suffit pour prouver l'appartenance des fragments sanskrits à cette école.

Le canon bouddhique chinois a conservé des versions des *Vinaya* de cinq écoles (Sarvāstivāda, Mahāsāṅghika, Dharmaguptaka, Mahīśāsaka et Mūlasarvāstivāda). Il n'en est pas de même en ce qui concerne le *Sūtrapiṭaka*. Le canon chinois contient quatre *Āgama* : le *Dirghāgama* (T. 1), le *Madhyamāgama* (T. 26), le *Saṃyuktāgama* (T. 99), l'*Ekottarāgama* (T. 125) et une version plus brève du *Saṃyuktāgama* (T. 100). Ce sont surtout des savants japonais qui ont essayé de déterminer les écoles auxquelles ces *Āgama* appartiennent[3]. La plupart d'entre eux sont d'opinion que le *Dīrghāgama* appartient à l'école Dharmaguptaka et que le *Madhyamāgama* et le *Saṃyuktāgama* (T. 99) appartiennent à l'école Sarvāstivāda, mais les preuves ne sont pas entièrement concluantes. On fera bien de tenir compte de l'avertissement donné par M. Demiéville : « On n'arrive guère à relever, ni en comparant entre elles les recensions chinoises, ni en les comparant avec la recension pāli, des témoignages nets d'appartenance à des écoles déterminées »[4]. C'est pour-

Sarvāstivāda, en les comparant avec la version chinoise, *op. cit.*, pp. 73-94. Nous y renvoyons pour les publications des fragments sanskrits du *Vinaya* du Sarvāstivāda par Louis Finot (*JA*, 1913, II, pp. 548-556), A. F. R. Hoernle (*Manuscript Remains of Buddhist Literature*, Oxford, 1916, pp. 4-16), Herbert Härtel (*Karmavācanā*, Berlin, 1956) et Valentina Rosen (*Der Vinayavibhaṅga zum Bhikṣuprātimokṣa der Sarvāstivādins*, Berlin, 1959).

1. Ces distances sont indiquées par Dieter Schlingloff, *Ein buddhistisches Yogalehrbuch*, Berlin, 1964, p. 9 et p. 10, n. 2.

2. Ernst Waldschmidt, *Bruchstücke des Bhikṣuṇī-Prātimokṣa der Sarvāstivādins*, Leipzig, 1926.

3. Cf. les ouvrages de Akanuma Chizen, *Bukkyō kyōten shiron*, Nagoya, 1939, pp. 29-52 et de Maeda Egaku, *Genshi bukkyō seiten no seiritsu-shi kenkyū*, Tōkyō, 1964, pp. 619-673 qui donnent beaucoup de références. Pour des références à des études sur le *Dīrghāgama* cf. Ét. Lamotte, *Le traité de la grande vertu de sagesse*, II, Louvain, 1949, p. 811, n. 1 et John Brough, *The Gāndhārī Dharmapada*, London, 1962, pp. 50-54.

4. *Inde classique*, II, Paris, 1953, § 2108.

quoi il n'est guère possible de savoir beaucoup sur les *Sūtrapiṭaka* des différentes écoles. A cet égard on peut espérer obtenir des renseignements dans les manuscrits sanskrits de sūtra découverts en Asie centrale. Les admirables publications récentes des manuscrits sanskrits de Turfan[1], rapportés par les expéditions allemandes, montrent la popularité en Asie centrale d'un groupe de sūtra consistant des textes suivants : *Daśottarasūtra*, *Saṅgītisūtra*, *Catuṣpariṣatsūtra*, *Mahāvadānasūtra* et *Mahāparinirvāṇasūtra* (y compris le *Mahāsudarśanasūtra*)[2]. M. Ernst Waldschmidt a comparé les trois derniers textes avec des textes parallèles et a montré qu'ils représentent la tradition des Sarvāstivādin ou Mūlasarvāstivādin. Il faut remarquer qu'il n'est pas possible de déterminer si ces textes appartiennent exclusivement à l'une ou l'autre de ces deux écoles[3]. On peut supposer que les Mūlasarvāstivādin aient adopté le *Sūtrapiṭaka* des Sarvāstivādin tant que l'on ne dispose pas de témoignages qui démontrent l'existence d'un *Sūtrapiṭaka* différent chez les Mūlasarvāstivādin. En ce qui concerne ce groupe de sūtra il y a des indices qui plaident en faveur d'une telle supposition. Le *Daśottarasūtra* est certainement un texte de l'école Sarvāstivāda. Le canon chinois contient une traduction séparée de ce texte due à Ngan Che-kao (T. 13)[4]. Dans l'ensemble, la traduction de Ngan Che-kao s'accorde parfaitement avec le texte des fragments sanskrits alors que, comme l'a montré M. Schlingloff pour les Nipāta IX et X, la version chinoise de ce sūtra dans le *Dīrghāgama*

1. L'emploi du nom de lieu Turfan dans les publications des manuscrits sanskrits remonte à Pischel (« Die Turfan-Recension des Dhammapada », *SPAW*, 1908, pp. 968-985). En réalité, les manuscrits proviennent de quatre régions différentes : Tumšuq, la région de Kučā, Šorčuq et l'oasis de Turfan, cf. Ernst Waldschmidt, *Sanskrithandschriften aus den Turfanfunden*, I, Wiesbaden, 1965, pp. v-vi. M. Schlingloff a attiré l'attention sur les relations entre les lieux d'origine des manuscrits et les écoles auxquelles elles appartiennent. A Qizil (près de Kučā) l'école des Sarvāstivādin domine. Ici aucun texte du Mahāyāna n'a été trouvé. Plus à l'Est à Šorčuq et dans la région de Turfan, en dehors des textes des Sarvāstivādin, des fragments de textes appartenant aux Mūlasarvāstivādin et au Mahāyāna furent découverts, *op. cit.*, p. 10.

2. Cf. Kusum Mittal, *Dogmatische Begriffsreihen im älteren Buddhismus*, I, Berlin, 1957, pp. 12-14.

3. D'habitude, les éditeurs de ces textes n'optent pas pour l'une ou l'autre de ces deux écoles. Seul M. Schlingloff, dans son édition des Nipāta IX-X du *Daśottarasūtra*, ne mentionne que les Sarvāstivādin, cf. *Dogmatische Begriffsreihen im älteren Buddhismus*. Ia. Daśottarasūtra IX-X, Berlin, 1962, p. 7.

4. L'attribution à Ngan Che-kao paraît bien assurée. La terminologie archaïque est celle qu'on trouve dans les quatre traductions (T. 14, 602, 603, 604) dont l'attribution est garantie par les préfaces que le *Tch'ou san tsang ki tsi* (T. 2145) a conservées, cf. Hayashiya Tomojirō, *Bukkyō kenkyū*, I, 2, 1937, pp. 16-20. Déjà, le catalogue de Tao-ngan qui date de 374 mentionne cette traduction (T. 2145, i, 6a 5). Je ne sais pas pourquoi M. Pauly dit que cette traduction doit être plus récente vers 350-400 de notre ère (*JA*, 1957, p. 286).

(T. 1, 10) ne s'accorde ni avec le texte pāli du *Dasuttarasuttanta* ni avec le texte sanskrit[1]. Dans Nipāta VII, 3 (ce passage n'est pas représenté dans les fragments du texte sanskrit) la version de Ngan Che-kao énumère les sept *bhava: narakabhava, tiryag-, preta-, manuṣya-, deva-, karma-* et *antarā-* (T. 13, 236b14-16). Saṃghabhadra, un Sarvāstivādin orthodoxe, cite ce texte, en disant « Le Sūtra dit » (T. 1562, xxiv, 475a26-27). Akanuma Chizen en conclut que la recension du *Daśottarasūtra*, traduite par Ngan Che-kao, appartient à l'école Sarvāstivāda (*Bukkyō kyōten shiron*, Nagoya, 1939, p. 63). On peut ajouter que Saṃghabhadra cite ce texte aussi sous le nom de *Saptabhavasūtra*, en énumérant les sept *bhava* (xxi, 459b27-28). Saṃghabhadra nous apprend encore que l'authenticité du *Saptabhavasūtra* est contestée par d'autres écoles (i, 330a28). La raison en est que celles-ci nient l'*antarābhava*[2].

Si le *Daśottarasūtra* appartient à l'école Sarvāstivāda, il devra en être de même pour les quatre autres sūtra. Mais ce groupe de sūtra était reconnu aussi par les Mūlasarvāstivādin. M. Waldschmidt a relevé que le *Bhaiṣajyavastu* du *Mūlasarvāstivādavinaya* (éd. N. Dutt, *Gilgit Manuscripts* III, Part I, p. 97, 13) renvoie au *Mahāsudarśanasūtra* dans le groupe de six sūtra du *Dīrghāgama: vistareṇa mahāsudarśanasūtre dīrghāgame ṣaṭsūtrakanipāte* (le texte de Dutt a *ṣaṭsūtrikanipāte*)[3]. Comme le remarque M. Waldschmidt, on ne sait pas si le *Mahāsudarśanasūtra* a été compté à part ou non. Je suis incliné à penser que le *Mahāsudarśanasūtra* n'était pas compté à part et qu'il faut chercher ailleurs pour trouver le sixième sūtra. Dans l'introduction à son édition des Nipāta IX et X du *Daśottarasūtra* M. Schlingloff remarque que, dans le manuscrit S 473, il y a une lacune d'un peu plus de quatre feuillets entre la fin du *Daśottarasūtra* et le début du *Saṅgītisūtra*. Cette lacune fait supposer l'existence d'un texte qui mesure un peu plus que le tiers du *Daśottarasūtra*. Il lui semble peu probable qu'un sūtra ait rempli cette

1. L'accord de la version de Ngan Che-kao avec les fragments du *Daśottarasūtra* dans le Fonds Pelliot sanskrit a été déjà constaté par M. Pauly qui attribue cette recension à l'école des Dharmaguptaka ou à celles des Mahīśāsaka ou des Kāśyapīya. Il exclut le Sarvāstivāda puisque l'ordre des termes est différent dans le *Saṅgītiparyāyaśāstra*, texte de l'école Sarvāstivāda (Cf. *JA*, 1957, pp. 285-287). Cela s'explique par le simple fait que ce texte est basé sur le *Saṅgītisūtra* et non sur le *Daśottarasūtra*. Dans un article, intitulé « The Daśottarasūtra » (*Indian and Buddhist Studies in Honour of Professor Kanakura*, Kyoto, 1966, pp. 3-25), j'ai comparé en détail les fragments du texte sanskrit avec la version de Ngan Che-kao, le *Dasuttarasuttanta* et la version incluse dans le *Dīrghāgama*.

2. Cf. de La Vallée Poussin, *Nirvāṇa*, Paris, 1925, p. 23, n. 1 b ; *Abhidharmakośa*, III, Paris-Louvain, 1926, p. 13, n. 2, p. 32, n. 1, p. 36, n. 2.

3. *Das Mahāparinirvāṇasūtra*, Berlin, 1950-1951, p. 101. Le passage correspondant de la version chinoise du *Bhaiṣajyavastu* porte « dans le *Dīrghāgama* dans le 63e groupe » (T. 1448, xiii, 57a23). Il doit s'agir d'une erreur du traducteur.

lacune. En signalant un fragment qui traite des treize dharma, il émet l'hypothèse que le *Daśottarasūtra* ait continué au-delà du dixième Nipāta.

Il me paraît difficile d'accepter cette hypothèse. Si le *Daśottarasūtra* contenait plus de dix Nipāta, il ne pourrait pas s'appeler *Daśottarasūtra*, titre qui est mentionné plusieurs fois dans les fragments du *Saṅgītisūtra*[1]. Un fragment contient la fin du *Daśottarasūtra* et le titre de l'ouvrage[2]. D'autre part, on n'a signalé nulle part dans les textes bouddhiques la mention d'un titre de sūtra qui correspondrait à un texte comportant plus de dix Nipāta. Mlle Mittal a attiré l'attention sur le fait que, dans les relations du premier concile dans les *Vinaya* des Mahīśāsaka et des Dharmaguptaka, le *Daśottarasūtra* et le *Saṅgītisūtra* sont mentionnés en relation avec un autre sūtra du même genre, l'*Ekottara*. En effet, la version chinoise du *Dīrghāgama* qui est attribuée aux Dharmaguptaka contient ce sūtra à la suite du *Daśottarasūtra*. Dans l'édition de Taishō le *Daśottarasūtra* du *Dīrghāgama* occupe 413 lignes, l'*Ekottarasūtra* 157 lignes. L'*Ekottarasūtra* se présente comme un extrait du *Daśottarasūtra*. Dans le dernier texte chaque Nipāta est divisé en 10 catégories. Dans l'*Ekottarasūtra* chacun des dix Nipāta est divisé en cinq catégories qui correspondent aux numéros 1, 2, 3, 4 et 10 du *Daśottarasūtra*. On ne voit pas très bien pourquoi le *Dīrghāgama* a inclus ce sūtra qui manque au *Dīghanikāya* pāli. En tout cas, aussi bien le *Dīrghāgama* des Dharmaguptaka que celui des Mahīśāsaka ont contenu ce sūtra. On peut supposer que le *Dīrghāgama* des Sarvāstivādin ait également contenu un *Ekottarasūtra*. Une citation d'un *Ekottarasūtra* dans la *Mahāvibhāṣā* (T. 1545, liii, 277c12, 16) que signale Akanuma (*op. cit.*, p. 51, n. 3) semble l'indiquer. Toutefois, il y a ici une difficulté, car la *Mahāvibhāṣā* cite ce texte à propos des cinq *pudgala*. Dans la recension du *Daśottarasūtra*, traduite par Ngan Che-kao, ces cinq *pudgala* ne sont pas mentionnés. Si l'*Ekottarasūtra* du Sarvāstivāda était construit comme celui du *Dīrghāgama*, il devrait contenir les catégories 1, 2, 3, 4 et 10 des dix Nipāta de la recension traduite par Ngan Che-kao. Il se peut que le traducteur du *Dīrghāgama* n'ait pas traduit le texte de l'*Ekottarasūtra* mais se soit contenté de reproduire partiellement le *Daśottarasūtra*. Les cinq *pudgala* sont mentionnés dans le *Saṅgītiparyāya* (T. 1536, xiv, 425c28 - 426a2) et ont dû se trouver dans le texte du *Saṅgītisūtra* des Sarvāstivādin. On pourrait donc aussi penser que l'auteur de la *Mahāvibhāṣā* se soit trompé, en citant l'*Ekottarasūtra* au lieu du *Saṅgītisūtra*.

1. Kusum Mittal, *op. cit.*, p. 12.
2. Schlingloff, *op. cit.*, p. 30.

Quoi qu'il en soit, il me paraît bien possible de supposer que le *Dīrghāgama* des Sarvāstivādin ait contenu un *Ekottarasūtra*[1]. Dans ce cas, il n'y a rien de surprenant à ce que, dans un groupe de six sūtra, l'*Ekottarasūtra* ait été placé entre le *Daśottarasūtra* et le *Saṅgītisūtra*.

J'ai signalé que le texte sanskrit du *Bhaiṣajyavastu* aussi bien que la traduction du Yi-tsing renvoient au groupe de six sūtra dans le *Dīrghāgama*. Le texte sanskrit contient aussi des renvois au *Saṃyuktāgama* (p. 19), à l'*Ekottarikāgama* (p. 45) et au *Madhyamāgama* (pp. 93, 98, 111, 112 et 217). On trouve les mêmes renvois dans la traduction de Yi-tsing à deux exceptions près. Le texte sanskrit renvoie au *Saṃyuktāgama* pour l'histoire d'Otalāyana (p. 19) mais la traduction de Yi-tsing donne le texte complet (T. 1448, x, 43c20-44a13). Le renvoi de la page 217 au *Madhyamāgama* ne se trouve pas dans la traduction de Yi-tsing car la fin du *Bhaiṣajyavastu* (pp. 220-288) n'a pas été traduite par lui. Tous les autres renvois se retrouvent dans la traduction chinoise : skt. p. 45 = T. 1448, xi, 48b2 ; p. 93 = xii, 56b11-12 ; p. 98 = xiii, 57b13-14 ; p. 111 = xiii, 58c1 ; p. 112 = xiii, 58c16. On peut en conclure que le texte sanskrit, traduit par Yi-tsing, a dû être très proche de celui des manuscrits de Gilgit. Il n'en est pas de même en ce qui concerne la traduction tibétaine car celle-ci ne contient pas les renvois que l'on trouve dans le texte sanskrit et la traduction chinoise. Dans chaque cas, la traduction tibétaine est plus développée et donne le texte complet des histoires sans mentionner les *Āgama* auxquels elles sont empruntées. Dans les traductions chinoise et tibétaine du *Bhaiṣajyavastu* on peut déceler deux états du *Vinaya* des Mūlasarvāstivādin. Le premier renvoie aux *Āgama* alors que le dernier les ignore. Il semble que le *Vinaya* des Mūlasarvāstivādin ait fini par absorber la substance des *Āgama*. Ceci se montre aussi dans le Kanjur tibétain qui ne contient pas une traduction des *Āgama* mais seulement plusieurs sūtra isolés qui correspondent à des sūtra dans les versions chinoises des Āgama.

Un siècle, à peine, sépare la traduction de Yi-tsing de la traduction tibétaine[2]. Il n'est pas absolument nécessaire de supposer que ce

1. Maeda (*op. cit.*, p. 636, n. 19) signale que, selon Minō Kōjun, l'*Ekottarasūtra* a dû faire partie de l'état primitif du *Dīghanikāya-Dīrghāgama* (« Kubunjūnibukyō no kenkyū », [Ōtani daigaku] *Bukkyō Kenkyū*, VII, 3, p. 110).

2. Yi-tsing est parti en 671 et est revenu en 695. Jusqu'à sa mort en 713 il s'est consacré à la traduction des manuscrits qu'il avait rapportés. La traduction tibétaine du *Vinayavastu* est due à Sarvajñadeva, Vidyākaraprabha, Dharmakara et dPal-gyis Lhun-po, et elle a été révisée par Vidyākaraprabha et dPal-brtsegs. Ce dernier a participé à la compilation du catalogue de lDan-kar qui a eu lieu dans l'année du Dragon. Plusieurs savants ont essayé de déterminer cette année. Yoshimura Shūki

développement du *Vinaya* des Mūlasarvāstivādin a dû avoir lieu dans cette période. Il est possible que, à l'époque de Yi-tsing, il y avait déjà des manuscrits plus développés que ceux qu'il a rapportés. En tout cas, il est évident que deux recensions différentes étaient à la base des traductions chinoise et tibétaine, la première plus brève précédant la seconde plus développée. La première recension renvoie au *Dīrghāgama* pour le groupe de six sūtra qui étaient des textes de l'école Sarvāstivāda. Cet exemple suggère que les *Āgama* auxquels le *Vinaya* des Mūlasarvāstivādin renvoie faisaient partie du *Sūtrapiṭaka* des Sarvāstivādin. Probablement ces *Āgama* n'auraient pas été absorbés par le *Vinaya* des Mūlasarvāstivādin si ces derniers avaient possédé leur propre *Sūtrapiṭaka*.

En comparant les versions chinoise et tibétaine du *Vinaya* des Mūlasarvāstivādin, on a souvent reproché à Yi-tsing d'avoir supprimé des passages. Les manuscrits de Gilgit prouvent qu'il a dû traduire une recension plus brève. Pour cette raison la version de Yi-tsing garde sa valeur par rapport à la version tibétaine et surtout pour les passages qui ne sont pas représentés dans les manuscrits de Gilgit. A propos du *Dīrghāgama* il faut signaler un de ces passages dans lequel se rencontre un renvoi à ce texte pour l'histoire d'Ambaṭṭha (T. 1448, viii, 35a3 ; cf. aussi T. 1451, xl, 413a23). Dans le *Dīghanikāya* le sutta d'Ambaṭṭha est le troisième des 13 sutta qui forment le *Sīlakkhandavagga*. Il est intéressant de voir que Yi-tsing renvoie au *Śīlaskandhavarga* (ou *Śīlaskandhanipāta*) du *Dīrghāgama* Dans le *Dīrghāgama* des Dharmaguptaka il n'y a pas de *Śīlaskandhavarga* et ce sūtra est le premier du troisième groupe de sūtra (nos. 20-29). Le *Dīrghāgama* des Sarvāstivādin a donc dû comporter un groupe de six sūtra et un autre, intitulé *Śīlaskandha* qui contenait le sūtra d'Ambaṭṭha.

Les collections de fragments sanskrits d'Asie centrale en Allemagne, Angleterre et France contiennent encore de nombreux textes inédits. On peut espérer qu'ils nous fourniront des renseignements précieux sur le développement des écoles bouddhiques et de leurs écritures. Avec l'aide de ces textes on pourra contrôler les données fournies par les pèlerins chinois et les traductions chinoises. Pour ne citer qu'un seul exemple. Ci-dessus j'ai signalé les témoignages de Hiuan-tsang et de Houei-tch'ao sur le bouddhisme à Kučā. De nombreux manuscrits proviennent de cet endroit mais

qui publiait une édition de ce catalogue (*The Denkarma*, Kyōto, 1950) opte pour 824, FRAUWALLNER pour 800 (*WZKSOA*, I, 1957, p. 103), TUCCI pour 812 (*Minor Buddhist Texts*, II, Roma, 1958, p. 48), SATŌ Hisashi (*Kodai Chibetto-shi Kenkyū*, II, Kyōto, 1959, p. 772) pour 788 et TAKAHASHI Moritaka pour 824 (*Tōhōgaku*, 26, 1963, p. 53). Voir aussi Marcelle LALOU, *JA*, 1953, p. 316 et Nils SIMONSSON, *Indo-tibetische Studien*, I, Uppsala, 1957, pp. 217-219.

l'étude paléographique n'est pas encore assez poussée pour pouvoir déterminer leur date dans des limites assez étroites[1]. Les résultats d'une telle étude pourraient confirmer ou infirmer les témoignages de Hiuan-tsang et de Houei-tch'ao. C'est ainsi du rapprochement des données, empruntées aux fragments sanskrits d'Asie centrale et aux sources chinoises, que l'on peut espérer apprendre beaucoup sur le bouddhisme en Asie centrale et le rôle qu'il a joué comme intermédiaire entre le bouddhisme indien et le bouddhisme chinois.

Canberra.

1. M. Waldschmidt a annoncé une étude paléographique des manuscrits sanskrits, rapportés par les expéditions allemandes, par Mlle Lore Holzmann (*Sanskrithandschriften aus den Turfanfunden*, I, p. XXXIII).

A PROPOS DU NIDĀNASAMYUKTA

PAR

J. W. DE JONG

Canberra

Dans un article, paru en 1957, M. Ernst Waldschmidt a identifié un manuscrit sanskrit de Tourfan qui contient des textes relatifs au *pratītyasamutpāda* (1). Il y montre que ce manuscrit (S 474) présente 25 sūtra qui correspondent aux sūtra 283-303 et 343-346 du Tsa-a-han king (T. 99), traduction chinoise du Saṃyuktāgama. Des textes parallèles de presque tous les sūtra se trouvant dans le Nidānasaṃyutta (Saṃyuttanikāya, éd. P.T.S., vol. 2, 1-133), M. E. W. intitule le texte sanskrit Nidānasaṃyukta. Dans l'article précité, il a publié les fragments des sūtra 1-3, un texte restauré de ces sūtra et une traduction de la version chinoise des sūtra 1-4. On lui doit également l'édition du sūtra 25, accompagnée d'une traduction anglaise de la version chinoise (*BSOAS*, XX, 1957, 569-579).

L'édition complète des 25 sūtra, due à M. Chandrabhāl Tripāṭhī, est arrangée comme les éditions précédentes des textes sanskrits de Tourfan (2). L'introduction est suivie par la première partie consacrée

Note additionnelle. — M. Murakami (autrefois Hirano) Shinkan a publié trois articles sur le Nagarasūtra : Innensōō no bonbun shiryō — Indo kotō shutsudo no renga meibun no naiyō hitei, *Indogaku bukkyōgaku kenkyū*, XII (1964), pp. 158-161 (cf. *IIJ*, X, 1967, pp. 198-199, n. 1) ; Engijōdōsetsu shiryō, *ibid.*, XIII (1965), pp. 187-191 ; Sansukuritto-bon Jōyūkyō (nagara) — Jisshi engi to jūni engi (sono ichi), *Bukkyō kenkyū*, 3 (1973), pp. 20-47. Le manuscrit de mon article fut envoyé à Paris en mars 1964. Pour cette raison les articles de M. Murakami ainsi que d'autres publications qui ont paru depuis n'y sont pas mentionnés.

(1) « Identifizierung einer Handschrift des Nidānasaṃyukta aus den Turfanfunden », *ZDMG*, 107, 1957, 372-401.

(2) *Fünfundzwanzig Sūtras des Nidānasaṃyukta*, D. Ak. d. W. z. Berlin, Inst. f. Orientf. Veröff. Nr. 56 = *Sanskrittexte aus den Turfanfunden* VIII (Berlin, Akademie-Verlag, 1962), 4°, 238 pp.

aux manuscrits : description des manuscrits, leurs particularités graphiques et linguistiques, édition des fragments, concordance des manuscrits et du texte restauré. La deuxième partie contient la « Textbearbeitung » dans laquelle l'éditeur s'est efforcé de combler les lacunes des manuscrits. M. Waldschmidt a expliqué que, pour restaurer le texte des sūtra 1-2, il s'est servi de quatre sources : 1. la version chinoise correspondante ; 2. des textes parallèles pālis et des expressions stéréotypées qui se trouvent ailleurs dans les écritures pālies ; 3. la structure analogue et les passages identiques des sūtra 1-2 ; 4. les répétitions qui se rencontrent dans les sūtra mêmes (*ZDMG*, 107, 1957, p. 383, n. 3). M. Tripāṭhī a employé le même procédé avec de légères différences. De la version chinoise il ne cite que quelques passages traduits pour lui par M. Waldschmidt. En citant des passages parallèles, il ne se limite pas aux écritures pālies mais tire aussi profit des textes sanskrits bouddhiques. La différence principale entre les travaux de M. Waldschmidt et de M. Tripāṭhī réside dans le fait que le premier se basait presqu'exclusivement sur le manuscrit S 474 alors que M. Tripāṭhī a utilisé également un grand nombre de fragments d'autres manuscrits. Il s'avère que le texte de ces manuscrits n'est pas partout identique à celui du manuscrit principal S 474. M. Waldschmidt avait déjà attiré l'attention sur l'existence de divergences entre le texte sanskrit tel qu'il est transmis par S 474 et la version chinoise (*op. cit.*, p. 375, n. 1 et n. 2). Dans sa préface M. C. T. signale que, par rapport au texte pāli, le manuscrit S 474 présente souvent un texte abrégé. Il n'y fait pas mention des différences entre ce manuscrit et d'autres manuscrits. Ce n'est qu'en étudiant attentivement la « Textbearbeitung » que l'on pourra se rendre compte de ce fait [1]. Il s'en suit que la situation est assez compliquée du fait qu'on peut distinguer au moins 4 textes (ou groupes de textes) : 1. la version chinoise ; 2. le manuscrit S 474 et les manuscrits qui présentent le même texte ; 3. le(s) manuscrit(s) qui présente(nt) un texte différent ; 4. les textes parallèles pālis. En outre, il ne faut pas exclure la possibilité que les manuscrits sanskrits ne contiennent pas que deux textes différents mais davantage. Pour ces raisons il est difficile de partager l'optimisme que M. C. T. manifeste à l'égard du texte établi par lui [2]. Ainsi, à titre d'exemple, il cite l'introduction du sūtra 6 qu'il croit pouvoir restaurer

---

[1] P. 86, n. 5 : « Sowohl die Haupt-Hs S 474 wie auch 401 und 500e, Frag. 1, scheinen hier starke Abkürzungen vorgenommen zu haben. Danach die abgekürzte Ergänzung bei Waldschmidt, « Identifizierung », p. 388. Das Manuskript 500e, Frag. 2 (= Hs 44.2-3) dagegen enthält Reste, die uns vermuten lassen, dass dort keine Abkürzung vorlag. »

[2] Cf. p. 13, § 9.

avec une certitude complète [1]. Cependant il est forcé de reconnaître que le texte restauré s'écarte de celui que le manuscrit a dû contenir [2].

Tout porte à croire que l'éditeur part de trois suppositions implicites que l'on pourra formuler ainsi : 1. les différentes versions du texte en sanskrit, chinois et pāli remontent à un et même texte ; 2. ce texte ne comporte pas d'abréviations ; 3. l'éditeur peut rétablir ce texte, en ayant recours à tous les matériaux à sa disposition. La conséquence en est que le choix des leçons et des restaurations n'est pas guidé par un principe cohérent. Pour ne citer que deux exemples. En ce qui concerne la restauration du texte de 1.10 (= sūtra 1, § 10), l'éditeur se fonde sur le manuscrit 500e (cf. p. 86, n. 5 citée ci-dessus n. 3) mais, pour la section suivante 1.11, il utilise le manuscrit 400 et mentionne les leçons de 500e en bas de page. Dans la restauration de 5.13-14, l'éditeur écarte expressément le témoignage de trois textes parallèles et se fonde sur le Lalitavistara pour établir un texte qu'aucun manuscrit ne corrobore [3]. Dans ce dernier cas, il faut signaler encore un autre texte dont l'éditeur n'a pas tenu compte. Une inscription sur des briques, trouvées à Gopālpur, nous livre un texte parallèle à Nidānasaṃyukta 5.10-27 et à Mahāvadānasūtra 9 b.9-c. 12 [4]. Une comparaison du passage 5.13-14,

---

(1) P. 106, n. 4 : « Der in der Hs S 474 fast gänzlich fehlende Wortlaut der Absätze 1-4 lässt sich nach Sūtra 23.1-4 mit voller Sicherheit ergänzen. »

(2) P. 107, n. 1 : « Ergänzt im Anschluss an das Pāli nach dem ähnlichen Wortlaut in Sūtra 23.3. Die Lücke in der Hs 3.2 ist an sich jedoch nicht gross genug, um die Einfügung des vollen Wortlauts der Abs. 3-4 zu gestatten. Dies lässt darauf schliessen, dass der Schreiber den Text dieser Absätze in irgendeiner Weise abgekürzt hat. »

(3) P. 97, n. 6 : « Im Pāli.......schlägt die Nidāna-Kette vom Bewusstsein *(vijñāna)* aus um ; ebenso in unserem Sūtra 6.10 und im MAV 9b.12-13. Unsere Ergänzungen können sich unter anderem auf LV., p. 347 stützen. » L'indication « unter anderem » ne suffit pas pour justifier les leçons adoptées.

(4) E. H. Johnston, « The Gopālpur Bricks », *JRAS*, 1938, 547-553. Dans les lignes 8-9 de la brique IIa Johnston a lu *pratya[yā]d āvartlate* qu'il faut corriger en *pratyudāvartlate*. Sur la photographie (Plate VIII) le *u* souscrit est clairement lisible. Voir aussi Mahāvadānasūtra 9b.13 où M. Waldschmidt lit *(p)r(a)tyu(dāvarta)* .. et Saṃyuttanikāya, II, 104.30 : *paccudāvattati*. Le texte, inscrit sur les briques de Gopālpur, peut être un fragment du sūtra 5 du Nidānasaṃyukta ou du Mahāvadānasūtra. La première possibilité est la plus vraisemblable pour les raisons suivantes. D'abord le Mahāvadānasūtra est beaucoup plus long que le Nidānasūtra. Ensuite, il est facile de voir que le Nidānasūtra entier aurait pu être inscrit sur quatre briques dont la première et la dernière ne sont pas conservées. En dernier lieu, on connaît déjà plusieurs inscriptions qui traitent du *pratītyasamutpāda*. La plus ancienne est une inscription en écriture kharoṣṭhī qui donne le texte de l'aspect *anuloma* du *pratītyasamutpāda*, cf. Pandit V. Natesa Aiyar, « An Inscribed Relic Casket from Kurram », *Ep. Ind.* XVIII, 1925-1926, 16-20 ; Sten Konow, « Remarks on a Kharoṣṭhī Inscription from the Kurram Valley », *Indian Studies in Honor of Charles Rockwell Lanman* (Cambridge, Mass., 1929), 53-67 et son édition de la même inscription dans le *Corpus inscr. Ind.* II, 1 (Calcutta, 1929). Très populaire a dû être un texte relatif aux deux aspects *anuloma*

restauré par l'éditeur, avec les passages parallèles de l'inscription de Gopālpur et du Mahāvadānasūtra suffit pour montrer la différence entre le texte restauré et les deux autres.

Inscription de Gopālpur	Mahāvadānasūtra	Nidānasaṃyukta
tasya mamaitad abhavat kasmin sati vijñānaṃ bhavati kiṃpratyayaṃ ca punar vvijñānaṃm iti tasya mama vijñānāt pratyudāvarttate mānasaṃ nātaḥ pareṇa vyativarttate ya[duta] vijñānapratyayaṃ nāmarūpaṃ nāmarūpapratyayaḥ....	9 b.12 tasyaitad abhavat/ kasmin (nu) sati vijñānaṃ bh(a)vati / kiṃpratyayaṃ ca puna(r vi)jñā(nam /) tasya y(o)n(i)ś(o) man(asi kurva)ta e(vaṃ) yathābhūtasyābhisamaya udapādi / nāmarū(p)e s(a)t(i) vijñānaṃ bha(vati /) nāmarūpapratyayañ ca punar vijñānam /	5.13 tasya mamaitad abhavat / kasmin (nu sati vijñānaṃ bhava)t(i) / kiṃpratyayañ ca punar vijñā(nam) / (tasya mama yoniśo mana)si kurvata evaṃ yathā(bhūtasyābhisamaya udapādi / saṃskāreṣu satsu vijñānaṃ bhavati / saṃskārapratyayañ ca punar vijñānam /)
	13 tasya vijñānā(t p)r(a)tyu(dāvarta) .. .. .. nāt(a)ḥ parato vyativartate /	14 (tasya mamaitad abhavat / kasmin nu sati saṃskārā bhavanti / kiṃpratyayāś ca punaḥ saṃskārāḥ /) (tasya mama yoniśo manasi kurvata evaṃ yathābhūtasyābhisamaya udapādi / avidyāyāṃ satyāṃ saṃskārā bhavanti / avidyāpratyayāś ca punaḥ saṃskārāḥ /)
	14 yad uta nāmarūpapratyayaṃ vijñānaṃ vijñānapratyayaṃ nāmarūpaṃ (nā)marū(pa)p(ra)tyayaṃ...	15 (ity avidyāpratyayāḥ saṃskārāḥ / saṃskārapratyayaṃ vijñānam / vijñānapratyayaṃ nāmarūpam / nāmarūpapratyayaṃ .....

Aussi la version chinoise du Nidānasaṃyukta (T. 99, vol. II, 80 c 3-4) ainsi que les trois versions chinoises de ce sūtra, traduites à part (T. 713-715, vol. XVI, 826 c 10, 828 a 4, 829 b 16), exposent la chaîne des *nidāna* jusqu'à *vijñāna* d'où elle retourne en sens inverse. Les deux textes

---

et *pratiloma* du *pratītyasamutpāda* qui y sont désignés par les termes *ācaya* et *apacaya*. Ce texte se trouve sur une brique, trouvée à Gopālpur, cf. V. A. Smith and W. Hoey, « Buddhist Sūtras Inscribed in Bricks found at Gōpālpur in the Gōrakhpur District », *Proc. ASB.*, 1896, July, 99-103 et E. H. Johnston, *op. cit.*, 547-550 ; sur une plaque de cuivre, trouvée à Kasiā, cf. F. E. Pargiter, « The Kasia Copper-plate », *A.S.I. Ann. Rep.*, 1910-1911, 73-77 et sur une brique, trouvée à Nālandā, cf. A. Ghosh, « An Inscribed Brick from Nalanda of the Year 197 », *Ep. Ind.* xxiv, 1937, 20-22 et Hirananda Sastri, *Nalanda and its Epigraphic Material* (Memoirs A.S.I. No. 66, 1942), p. 65. Selon Johnston, l'inscription de Gopālpur date d'environ 500 après J.-C. Pargiter place l'inscription de Kasiā environ 450-475. L'inscription de Nālandā date de 197 de l'ère Gupta = 516-517 après J.-C. Trois autres inscriptions, relatives au *pratītyasamutpāda*, seront mentionnées plus loin.

sanskrits, l'inscription de Gopālpur, le Mahāvadānasūtra et les quatre versions chinoises s'accordent donc sur le point essentiel. Les différences sont mineures. Le Mahāvadānasūtra contient un passage *(tasya yoniśo.......... ca punar vijñānam)* qui manque à l'inscription de Gopālpur mais ce même passage s'y trouve avec de légères variantes à propos d'autres membres de la chaîne, par exemple : *tasya mama yoniśomanasikurvvata evaṃ yathābhūtasyābhisamayo babhūva nāmarūpe sati ṣaḍāyatanaṃ bhavati nāmarūpapratyayaṃ ca punaḥ ṣaḍāyatanam*. Les quatre versions chinoises donnent ce passage et corroborent donc le texte du Mahāvadānasūtra.

L'édition des fragments sanskrits du Nidānasaṃyukta par M. Tripāṭhī montre la nécessité de se rendre compte comment les textes bouddhiques se sont transmis avant de fixer les règles qui doivent déterminer l'établissement critique des textes. Il est évident que les sūtra du Hīnayāna ont été transmis pendant longtemps oralement avant d'être couchés par écrit. Par conséquent, il est difficile de supposer que les différentes traditions écrites remontent toutes à un archétype d'autant plus que, pendant de longs siècles, on a continué de réciter les textes. L'histoire de la traduction des textes bouddhiques en Chine nous apprend que, très souvent, le texte fut récité par un moine indien qui le connaissait par cœur. Pendant des siècles, les manuscrits ont dû être très rares. Ce n'est peut-être qu'après la fondation de grands monastères comme Nālandā qu'il devint possible de faire copier les manuscrits en plus grand nombre. Ainsi, au VIIe siècle, Hiun-tsang pouvait emporter en Chine une grande collection de manuscrits. Avant cette époque, la difficulté de trouver des scribes qualifiés et des matériaux à écrire a dû empêcher la diffusion des manuscrits. D'autre part, il ne faut pas perdre de vue que, en Inde, la récitation de textes religieux jouissait d'un prestige sacré qui faisait défaut aux textes écrits. Plusieurs facteurs ont dû contribuer à faire changer cette situation. D'abord, la fondation de grands monastères, richement dotés, où il y avait assez de scribes pour satisfaire les demandes de manuscrits. Ensuite, la rédaction de grands traités philosophiques tels que la Yogācārabhūmi d'Asaṅga qui n'ont guère pu être composés oralement. A cette époque, le développement des écoles philosophiques du Mahāyāna a produit une littérature qui a dû s'adresser en premier lieu à des spécialistes, c'est-à-dire à des moines érudits qui, dans la tranquillité des monastères, disposaient du loisir et du savoir indispensables pour étudier des textes de ce genre. De tels ouvrages ne devaient pas être récités pour un public de laïcs par des moines ambulants. A leur intention, des textes de dévotion furent compilés. Ces deux groupes de textes ne se distinguaient pas seulement par leur contenu mais aussi par la langue dans laquelle ils furent composés. Les premiers furent écrits en sanskrit comme l'attestent les ouvrages de Nāgārjuna, Āryadeva, Vasubandhu, Asaṅga, etc., qui ont été conservés et transmis par des manuscrits alors que les autres ont été composés d'abord en prākrit ou en sanskrit bouddhique hybride. Ces derniers textes ont été sujets à un processus de sanskritisation progressive qui, probablement, a commencé à l'époque à laquelle ils furent notés pour la première fois. Les conditions sous lesquelles furent composés ces deux groupes de textes du Mahāyāna, les traités philosophiques *(śāstra)* et les textes de dévotion *(sūtra)* expliquent pourquoi le texte des premiers est beaucoup mieux transmis. Si, pour les sūtra, on a longtemps pu croire à une tradition uniforme et bien établie, c'est uniquement parce que les manuscrits tardifs dont on disposait descendaient d'un ancêtre commun qui ne remontait pas très loin dans le temps. La découverte de manuscrits plus anciens et la comparaison avec les versions chinoises et tibétaines a montré que la situation est beaucoup plus compliquée. Il s'est avéré que les différences entre les textes transmis d'un même sūtra n'étaient pas limitées à des variantes ou même à des particularités dialectales mais qu'il existait des recensions de longueur différente. Au cours des siècles, les sūtra se sont accrus en même temps que l'aspect linguistique a subi des transformations profondes à tel point que la diversité des recensions est plus grande pour les sūtra du Mahāyāna que pour ceux du Hīnayāna bien que ces derniers remontent à une époque plus ancienne.

Une comparaison des différentes versions du Nidānasaṃyukta montre bien l'impossibilité de reconstruire un texte commun dont elles dériveraient. Ces versions présentent des recensions qui sont le point d'aboutissement de lignées de transmission divergentes. Dans ces conditions, on doit essayer de déterminer quelles recensions sont plus proches l'une de l'autre. Ainsi, dans le cas actuel, il est évident que la recension, présentée par la version chinoise, est beaucoup plus proche de celle, conservée par les manuscrits sanskrits de Tourfan, que la recension pālie. Toutefois, il y a des différences qui ne sont pas négligeables. Par exemple, le manuscrit S 474 ne contient pas l'introduction détaillée à chaque sūtra que l'on trouve dans la version chinoise. Il faut se garder d'en conclure, comme le fait l'éditeur, que le scribe de ce manuscrit a dû omettre ou abréger ces introductions. Il est de fait que, par rapport au *nidāna*, l'exposition du lieu de l'action, la tradition est souvent beaucoup moins bien établie que par rapport au texte même. Rien ne prouve *a priori* que le texte de la version chinoise est plus digne de foi et authentique que celui du manuscrit sanskrit. Aussi sur d'autres points, il y a d'assez nombreuses différences entre la version chinoise et les manuscrits sanskrits comme l'a déjà indiqué M. Waldschmidt (*op. cit.*, p. 375, n. 1). Une traduction complète de la version chinoise aurait été très souhaitable pour faire ressortir clairement toutes ces différences.

Plus considérables sont les différences avec le texte pāli parallèle auquel l'éditeur fait appel avec une trop grande confiance. Non seulement il y a ainsi des divergences entre le texte sanskrit, la version chinoise et le texte pāli parallèle mais aussi les manuscrits sanskrits ne contiennent pas tous le même texte. Il aurait fallu étudier, de manière systématique, toutes les variantes que présentent ces manuscrits afin de savoir s'ils ont transmis des recensions différentes ou s'il s'agit de variantes d'importance secondaire. Quoique les manuscrits proviennent tous de Tourfan, il ne s'ensuit pas forcément qu'ils appartiennent à la même tradition écrite. Une telle supposition a obligé l'éditeur à admettre des abréviations, dûes au scribe, à tous les endroits où le texte de S 474 ou d'un autre manuscrit est plus bref par rapport à un texte plus développé qui se trouve ailleurs dans un des manuscrits. A ce propos, on ne peut pas non plus négliger le fait que l'écriture du manuscrit S 474 est plus ancienne que celle de tous les autres manuscrits [1]. D'ailleurs, les différences entre les manuscrits ne se limitent pas à l'absence ou la présence d'abréviations dans des passages stéréotypés. Par exemple, on trouve dans les manuscrits 41, 43 et 42 les mots *sparśa[kā]ma*, *(ta)ruṇasya koma[l](asya)* et *[u]pekṣāvataḥ* qui ne sont pas confirmés par les autres manuscrits (voir les notes de l'éditeur, p. 84, n. 2, p. 85, n. 2 et p. 88, n. 3).

L'inscription de Gopālpur montre que le cinquième sūtra du Nidānasaṃyukta était répandu à part. Ceci est confirmé par le fait que le canon chinois bouddhique a conservé trois traductions de ce sūtra. D'après le catalogue *K'ai-yuan che-kiao lou* deux traductions parurent déjà sous la dynastie des Han postérieurs [2]. Il s'en suit que ce sūtra a dû être répandu à part en Inde déjà au moins dans le deuxième siècle de notre ère. Un autre sūtra du Nidānasaṃyukta qui a dû jouir d'une grande popularité c'est le seizième intitulé *ādi-sūtra* dans l'édition de M. Tripāṭhī. Ce sūtra expose le *pratītyasamutpāda* dans l'aspect *anuloma* et explique ensuite un à un les douze *aṅga*. La première partie s'appelle *ādi*, la deuxième *vibhaṅga*. Ce sūtra est aussi connu par des inscriptions. Deux briques, trouvées à Nālandā en 1924, portent chacune le texte complet de ce sūtra. N. P. Chakravarti qui a publié cette inscription la date du sixième siècle (*Ep. Ind.*, XXI, 1931-1932, 193-199) [3].

---

(1) M. Tripāṭhī appelle l'écriture de S 474 « ältere zentralasiatische Brāhmī » et celle des autres manuscrits « spätere nordturkistanische Brāhmī », cf. p. 15, n. 2.

(2) Cf. Sylvain Lévi, *JA*, 1910, II, p. 436.

(3) Traduction allemande par M. Erich Frauwallner dans *Die Philosophie des Buddhismus*, 2. Aufl. (Berlin, 1958), 39-43. N. Aiyaswami Sastri a reconstruit le texte sanskrit avec l'aide de la traduction tibétaine, *Adyar Library Bulletin*, VIII, 1, February 1944, 21-24. Ensuite il a publié deux fois le texte de l'inscription de Nālandā, *Adyar Library Bulletin*, XI, 4, December 1947, 61-64 ; *Ārya Śālistamba Sūtra* (Adyar Library,

P. C. Bagchi a traduit la version chinoise de ce sūtra due à Hiuan-tsang (*ibid.*, 201-204). M. V. V. Gokhale a publié une inscription en écriture brāhmī trouvée sur un pilier près de Touen-houang [1]. Elle contient un fragment du sūtra. L'éditeur date l'inscription de la deuxième moitié du ve siècle. En 1946 on a trouvé dans le Musée de Djakarta onze plaques d'or dont les deux premières contiennent le même sūtra. L'éditeur, M. J. G. de Casparis, date l'inscription entre 650 et 800 ap. J.-C. [2]. Le fait que Vasubandhu mentionne ce sūtra dans son exposé du *pratītyasamutpāda* montre l'importance qu'il y attacha [3]. Le Pratītyasamutpādasūtra est mentionné plusieurs fois dans l'Abhidharmakośavyākhyā (cf. l'index où il faut ajouter p. 292.19). A un endroit Yaśomitra se réfère à l'explication de *nāmarūpa*, donnée dans le Pratītyasamutpādasūtra : *Pratītyasamutpādasūtre nāmarūpavibhaṃga evaṃ nirdeśāt*, et cite ensuite un passage qui se retrouve dans l'édition de M. Tripāṭhī 16.7 (Vyākhyā pp. 299.32-300.1). Yaśomitra ne cite pas seulement le Pratītyasamutpādasūtra mais aussi d'autres sūtra du Nidānasaṃyukta [4]. Le Pratītyasamutpādasūtra est le seul sūtra dont le titre soit mentionné par lui. Le titre Pratītyasamutpādasūtra ne se trouve pas dans les manuscrits du Nidānasaṃyukta où il est désigné par Pratītyasamut-

---

1950), 21-24. On lui doit également une édition de la traduction tibétaine d'après l'édition de Narthang, *Adyar Library Bulletin*, XI, 3, October 1947, 53-56 ; *Ārya Śālistamba Sūtra*, 65-69. Il n'a pas consulté la ṭīkā de Guṇamati.

(1) « A Brāhmī Stone Inscription from Tunhuang », *Sino-Indian Studies*, I, 1 (1944), 18-22.

(2) J. G. de Casparis, *Selected Inscriptions from the 7th to the 9th Century A.D.* II (Bandung, 1956), p. 52.

(3) L. de La Vallée Poussin, *L'Abhidharmakośa de Vasubandhu*, troisième chapitre (Paris-Louvain, 1926), pp. 70, 85. La Prasannapadā (éd. L. de La Vallée Poussin, p. 452.6-9) contient une citation qu'elle attribue au Pratītyasamutpāda(sūtra). Elle n'est pas empruntée à ce sūtra mais au Sahetusapratyayasanidānasūtra qui est mentionné deux fois dans l'Abhidharmakośavyākhyā (éd. U. Wogihara, pp. 288, 289). Dans la traduction chinoise du Saṃyuktāgama ce sūtra se trouve dans le chapitre 13, no. 334 (T. vol. II, 92b21-c11). Le texte sanskrit se laisse presqu'entièrement reconstruire à l'aide de trois citations dans l'Abhidharmakośavyākhyā, cf. p. 523.10-21 (ici le sūtra est intitulé Sahetusapratyayakramasūtra), p. 288.26-28 et p. 288.30. Le titre Sahetusapratyayasanidānasūtra est confirmé par la traduction chinoise qui le donne à deux reprises : 有因有緣有縛法經.

(4) Cf. pp. 286-300 qui contiennent des citations des sūtra 5, 6, 10, 14 et 16. Nous ne pouvons pas ici comparer ces citations avec les passages correspondants du Nidānasaṃyukta. Il faut relever une citation du sūtra 6.13 qui se trouve p. 668.2-6 car elle permet de remplir une lacune du Nidānasaṃyukta : *tadyathāyuṣman Śāriputra dve naḍakalāpāv* (l'édition de Wogihara a °*kalāpyāv*) *ākāśe ucchrite syātāṃ. te anyonyaniśrite anyonyaṃ niśritya tiṣṭheyātāṃ. tatra kaścid ekām apanayet. dvitīyā nipatet. dvitīyām apanayet. ekā nipatet. evam āyuṣman Śāriputra nāmaṃ ca rūpaṃ cānyonyaniśritaṃ. anyonyaṃ niśritya tiṣṭhatīti vistaraḥ. vijñānapratyayaṃ nāmarūpam iti vacanāt.*

pādavibhaṅgasūtra ou ādisūtra [1]. Le titre ādisutra est mentionné dans sūtra 23.15 b : *pūrvavad yathā ādisūtre*. Dans la traduction chinoise (T. vol. II, 95 a 18) il est dit : 如前分別經說 (*pūrvavad yathoktaṃ vibhaṅgasūtre*). Le texte de la traduction chinoise est plus correct car 23.15 b se réfère à un passage de la deuxième partie du sūtra qui contient le vibhaṅga, l'explication des aṅga. La version chinoise du Pratītyasamutpādasūtra, due à Hiuan-tsang (T. 124), s'appelle Yuan-k'i king, 緣起經 = Pratītyasamutpādasūtra. Le Pratītyasamutpādasūtra est traduit en tibétain, cf. *Otani Kanjur Catalogue*, No. 877 (éd. de Pékin, réimpression photomécanique, vol. 34, 306 d 1-307 b 3). Le titre en est : Rten-ciṅ 'brel-bar 'gyur-pa daṅ-po daṅ rnam-par dbye-ba bstan-pa ce qui correspond à Pratītyasamutpādādivibhaṅganirdeśa [2]. Le Tandjour contient un commentaire, dû à Vasubandhu, intitulé : Rten-ciṅ 'brel-bar 'byuṅ-ba daṅ-po daṅ rnam-par dbye-ba bśad-pa (éd. de Pékin, réimpression photomécanique, vol. 104, 277-306 d 8). D'après la traduction tibétaine elle-même le titre traduit Pratītyasamutpādādivibhaṅgayornirdeśa, mais les catalogues préfèrent Pratītyasamutpādādivibhaṅganirdeśa (cf. le catalogue de P. Cordier, *Mdo*, XXXVI, 1). Un fragment du texte sanskrit a été publié par M. Giuseppe Tucci (*JRAS*, 1930, 611-623) qui l'intitule Pratītyasamutpādavyākhyā puisque ce titre se trouve dans les colophons des chapitres mais ces colophons contiennent souvent des titres abrégés. Peut-être le titre était Pratītyasamutpādādivibhaṅgavyākhyā qui correspond mieux au titre tibétain et au titre du sūtra commenté. A son tour, l'ouvrage de Vasubandhu a été commenté par Guṇamati dans son Rten-ciṅ 'brel-bar 'byuṅ-ba daṅ-po daṅ rnam-par 'byed-pa bstan-pa'i rgya-cher bśad-pa = Pratītyasamutpādādivibhaṅganirdeśaṭīkā (éd. de Pékin, réimpression photomécanique, vol. 104, 306 e-vol. 105, 33 d 6). En ce qui concerne le titre du sūtra les témoignages, cités ci-dessus, suggèrent la solution suivante. Le titre complet a dû être Pratītyasamutpādādivibhaṅganirdeśa mais, dans l'usage courant, on le citait sous le titre de Pratītyasamutpādasūtra.

En guise de conclusion à ces remarques à propos du Nidānasaṃyukta nous faisons suivre ici la traduction tibétaine du Pratītyasamutpādādivibhaṅganirdeśa d'après l'édition de Pékin. Pour faciliter la comparaison avec le texte sanskrit, édité par M. Tripāṭhī, la traduction tibétaine est divisée également en 18 paragraphes. Le texte de base est la traduction du sūtra même. Les leçons, citées en bas de page, renvoient à la traduction

---

[1] Cf. p. 157, n. 2.

[2] Le titre sanskrit que l'on trouve au début de la traduction tibétaine est évidemment refait sur le titre tibétain par des érudits tibétains. L'*Otani Kanjur Catalogue* le corrige en Pratītyasamutpādādināvibhaṅganirdeśa mais °*ādinā*° n'est guère mieux que °*adinaca*°.

tibétaine (désignée par B) de la ṭīkā de Guṇamati qui cite presque le texte complet du sūtra (vol. 104, 310 c 4 - 311 a 6).

rgya-gar skad-du / pra-tī-tya-sa-ṅud-pā-da-a-di-na-tsa-bi-bhaṅ-ga-nir-de-śa nā-ma sū-tra / bod skad-du / rten-ciṅ 'brel-bar 'gyur-ba daṅ-po daṅ rnam-par dbye-ba bstan-pa źes-bya-ba'i mdo // dkon-mchog gsum-la phyag-'tshal-lo / 'di-skad bdag-gis thos-pa'i dus gcig-na / bcom-ldan-'das mñam-yod-na / rgyal-bu rgyal-byed-kyi tshal mgon-med-zas-sbyin-gyi kun-dga' ra-ba-na bźugs-so // de-nas bcom-ldan-'das-kyis dge-sloṅ rnams-la bka'-stsal-pa [1] /

1. dge-sloṅ-dag khyod-la rten-ciṅ 'brel-bar 'byuṅ-ba [2] daṅ-po daṅ rnam-par dbye-ba bstan-gyis / de legs-par rab-tu ñon-la [3] yid-la zuṅ-śig daṅ / bśad-do //

2. rten-ciṅ 'brel-bar 'byuṅ-ba [2] daṅ-po gaṅ że-na / 'di-lta-ste / 'di yod-na 'di-byuṅ / 'di skyes-pas 'di skye-ba ste / 'di-lta-ste / ma-rig-pa'i rkyen-gyis 'du-byed / 'du-byed-kyi rkyen-gyis rnam-par śes-pa / rnam-par śes-pa'i rkyen-gyis miṅ-daṅ-gzugs / miṅ-daṅ-gzugs-kyi rkyen-gyis skye-mched drug / skye-mched drug-gi rkyen-gyis reg-pa / reg-pa'i rkyen-gyis tshor-ba / tshor-ba'i rkyen-gyis sred-pa / sred-pa'i rkyen-gyis len-pa / len-pa'i rkyen-gyis srid-pa / srid-pa'i rkyen-gyis skye-ba / skye-ba'i rkyen-gyis rga-śi daṅ / mya-ṅan daṅ / smre-sṅags 'don-pa daṅ / sdug-bsṅal-ba daṅ / yid mi-bde-ba daṅ / 'khrug-pa rnams 'byuṅ-bar 'gyur-ro [4] // de-ltar na sdug-bsṅal-gyi phuṅ-po chen-po 'ba'-śig-po 'di'i [5] 'byuṅ-bar 'gyur-ro // 'di ni rten-ciṅ 'brel-bar 'byuṅ-ba daṅ-po [6] źes-bya'o //

3. rten-ciṅ 'brel-bar 'byuṅ-ba'i rnam-par dbye-ba gaṅ że-na /

4. ma-rig-pa'i rkyen-gyis 'du-byed ces-bya-ba'i [7] ma-rig-pa gaṅ że-na / gaṅ [8] sṅon-gyi mtha' mi-śes-pa daṅ / phyi-ma'i mtha' mi-śes-pa daṅ / sṅon daṅ phyi-ma'i mtha' mi-śes-pa daṅ / naṅ mi-śes-pa daṅ / phyi mi-śes-pa daṅ / naṅ daṅ phyi mi-śes-pa daṅ / las mi-śes-pa daṅ / rnam-par smin-pa mi-śes-pa daṅ / las daṅ rnam-par smin-pa mi-śes-pa daṅ / saṅs-rgyas mi-śes-pa daṅ / chos mi-śes-pa daṅ / dge-'dun [131 b] mi-śes-pa daṅ / sdug-bsṅal mi-śes-pa daṅ / kun-'byuṅ [9] daṅ / 'gog-pa daṅ / lam

---

(1) 'B commence ainsi : *gleṅ-gźi ni mñam-yod-na'o // der bcom-ldan-'das-kyis dge-sloṅ rnams-la bka'-stsal-pa /*

(2) *'brel-le 'byuṅ-ba'i.*

(3) Au lieu de *rab-tu ñon-la* B a *ñon-la śin-tu.*

(4) *'gyur-te.*

(5) Au lieu de *'ba'-śig-po 'di'i* B a *'di 'ba'-źig.*

(6) *daṅ-po'o.*

(7) *ces-bya-ba la.*

(8) *gaṅ de.*

(9) *kun-'byuṅ-ba mi-śes-pa.*

mi-śes-pa daṅ / rgyu mi-śes-pa daṅ / rgyu-las yaṅ-dag-par 'byuṅ-ba'i chos mi-śes-pa daṅ / dge-ba daṅ mi-dge-ba daṅ / kha-na ma-tho-ba daṅ-bcas-pa daṅ / kha-na ma-tho-ba med-pa daṅ / bsten-par bya-ba daṅ / bsten-par bya-ba ma-yin-pa daṅ / ṅan-pa daṅ / gya-nom-pa daṅ / nag-po daṅ / dkar-po daṅ / rnam-par dbye-ba daṅ-bcas-pa'i rten-ciṅ 'brel-bar 'byuṅ-ba daṅ / reg-pa'i skye-mched drug yaṅ-dag-pa ji-lta-ba bźin khoṅ-du mi chud-pa daṅ / gaṅ de-daṅ-der yaṅ-dag-pa ji-lta-ba bźin-du mi-śes-pa daṅ / ma-mthoṅ-ba daṅ / mṅon-par ma-rtogs-pa [1] daṅ / rmoṅs-pa daṅ kun-tu rmoṅs-pa daṅ / ma-rig-pa daṅ / mun-pa'i rnam-pa źes-bya-ba 'di ni ma-rig-pa źes-bya'o //

5. ma-rig-pa'i rkyen-gyis 'du-byed ces-bya-ba'i 'du-byed gaṅ że-na / 'du-byed ni rnam-pa gsum-ste [2] / gsum gaṅ że-na / lus-kyi 'du-byed daṅ / ṅag-gi 'du-byed daṅ / yid-kyi 'du-byed-do //

6. 'du-byed-kyi rkyen-gyis rnam-par śes-pa źes-bya-ba'i [3] rnam-par śes-pa gaṅ że-na / rnam-par śes-pa'i tshogs drug-ste / mig-gi rnam-par śes-pa daṅ / rna-ba'i rnam-par śes-pa daṅ [4] / sna daṅ / lce daṅ / luś daṅ yid-kyi rnam-par śes-pa'o //

7. rnam-par śes-pa'i rkyen-gyis miṅ-daṅ-gzugs źes-bya-ba-la miṅ gaṅ że-na / gzugs-can ma-yin-pa'i phuṅ-po bźi-ste / tshor-ba'i phuṅ-po daṅ / 'du-śes-kyi phuṅ-po daṅ / 'du-byed-kyi phuṅ-po daṅ / rnam-par śes-pa'i phuṅ-po'o // gzugs gaṅ że-na / gzugs gaṅ yin-pa ci-yaṅ ruṅ / de-dag [5] thams-cad 'byuṅ-ba chen-po bźi daṅ / 'byuṅ-ba chen-po bźi-dag rgyur byas-pa ste / gzugs 'di daṅ / sṅa-ma'i miṅ gñi-ga [6] gcig-tu mṅon-par bsdus-nas miṅ-daṅ-gzugs śes [7] -bya'o //

8. miṅ-daṅ-gzugs-kyi rkyen-gyis skye-mched drug ces-bya-ba'i skye-mched drug gaṅ że-na / naṅ-gi skye-mched drug-ste / mig naṅ-gi skye-mched daṅ / rna-ba daṅ / sna daṅ / lce daṅ / lus daṅ / yid naṅ-gi skye-mched-do //

9. skye-mched drug-gi rkyen-gyis reg-pa źes-bya-ba'i reg-pa gaṅ [132 a] że-na / reg-pa'i tshogs drug-ste / mig-gi 'dus-te reg-pa daṅ / rna-ba daṅ / sna daṅ / lce daṅ / lus daṅ / yid-kyi 'dus-te [8] reg-pa'o //

10. reg-pa'i rkyen-gyis tshor-ba źes-bya-ba'i [3] tshor-ba gaṅ że-na / tshor-ba ni gsum-ste / bde-ba daṅ sdug-bsṅal-ba daṅ / bde-ba yaṅ ma-yin / sdug-bsṅal-ba yaṅ ma-yin-pa'o //

---

(1) *ma-rtog-pa.*
(2) *gsum-mo.*
(3) *źes-bya-ba la.*
(4) *rna-ba daṅ.*
(5) B omet *dag.*
(6) *gñis.*
(7) *źes.*
(8) B omet *te.*

11. tshor-ba'i rkyen-gyis sred-pa źes-bya-ba'i (1) sred-pa gaṅ że-na / sred-pa ni gsum-ste / 'dod-pa'i sred-pa daṅ / gzugs-kyi sred-pa daṅ / gzugs-med-pa'i sred-pa'o //

12. sred-pa'i rkyen-gyis len-pa źes-bya-ba'i (1) len-pa gaṅ źe-na / len-pa ni bźi-ste / 'dod-pa ñe-bar len-pa daṅ / lta-ba ñe-bar len-pa daṅ / tshul-khrims daṅ brtul-żugs ñe-bar len-pa daṅ / bdag-tu smra-ba ñe-bar len-pa'o //

13. len-pa'i rkyen-gyis srid-pa źes-bya-ba'i (1) srid-pa gaṅ źe-na / srid-pa ni gsum-ste / 'dod-pa'i srid-pa daṅ / gzugs-kyi srid-pa daṅ / gzugs-med-pa'i srid-pa'o //

14. srid-pa'i rkyen-gyis skye-ba źes-bya-ba'i (1) gaṅ źe-na / (2) gaṅ sems-can de-daṅ de-dag-gi sems-can-gyi ris de-daṅ de-dag-tu gaṅ skye-ba daṅ (2) / śin-tu skye-ba daṅ / 'pho-ba daṅ / mṅon-par byuṅ-ba (3) daṅ/ rab-tu byuṅ-ba (4) daṅ / phuṅ-po so-sor thob-pa daṅ / khams so-sor thob-pa daṅ / skye-mched so-sor thob-pa daṅ / phuṅ-po rnams mṅon-par grub-pa daṅ / srog-gi dbaṅ-po rab-tu skyes-pa 'di ni skye-ba źes-bya'o //

15. skye-ba'i rkyen-gyis rga-śi źes-bya-ba'i (1) rga-śi (5) gaṅ źe-na / (6) gaṅ de'i spyi-ther daṅ / skra-dkar daṅ / gñer-ma tshogs-pa daṅ / rñis-pa daṅ / żum-pa daṅ / ba-laṅ chu 'thuṅ-ba ltar gug-pa daṅ / lus nag-po'i thig-les gaṅ-ba daṅ / lud-pa lu-żiṅ dbugs rgod-pa daṅ / mdun-du lus 'bug-pa ltar byed-pa daṅ / khar-ba la rten-pa daṅ / blun-pas moṅ rtul-ba-ñid daṅ / żan-pa-ñid daṅ / ñams-pa daṅ / yoṅs-su ñams-pa daṅ / dbaṅ-po rgud-pa daṅ / ñams-pa daṅ / 'du-byed rnams rñiṅs-pa daṅ / śin-tu rñiṅs-par gyur-pa ni 'di ni rga-ba źes-bya'o // (6)

16. 'chi-ba gaṅ źe-na / sems [132 b]-can gaṅ yin-pa de-daṅ de-dag sems-can-gyi ris de-daṅ de-dag-nas 'phos-pa (7) daṅ / 'pho-ba-ñid (8) daṅ / żig-pa (9) daṅ / naṅ ñams-pa (10) daṅ / tshe ñams-pa daṅ / drod

---

(1) *źes bya-ba la.*

(2) *sems-can rnams gaṅ yin-pa de-daṅ sems-can-gyi ris de-daṅ de-dag-tu skye-ba gaṅ yin-pa daṅ.*

(3) *'pho-ba.*

(4) *'byuṅ-ba.*

(5) B a *rga-ba* qui est la bonne leçon.

(6) Le texte de B est très différent : *gaṅ de'i spyi-cher daṅ / skra-dkar daṅ / gñer-ma'i tshigs-pa daṅ / 'khogs-pa daṅ / sgur-bo daṅ / rgu-bo daṅ / 'khyor-ba daṅ / śa gnags-pa daṅ / lud-pa lu-ba daṅ / dbugs rgod-pa daṅ / khar-ba la brlen-pa daṅ / moṅ rtul-ba daṅ / źan-pa daṅ / ñams-pa daṅ / yoṅs-su ñams-pa daṅ / dbaṅ-po rnams rgud-pa daṅ / mi gsal-ba daṅ / 'du-byed rnams rñiṅs-pa daṅ / 'jig-par ñe-ba 'di ni rga-ba źes-bya'o //.*

(7) *'chi-ba.*

(8) B omet *ñid.*

(9) *'jig-pa.*

(10) *rmugs-pa.*

yal-ba daṅ / srog-gi dbaṅ-po 'gags-pa daṅ / phuṅ-po rnams 'dor-ba daṅ / śi-ba daṅ / dus-byed-pa 'di ni śi-ba źes-bya-ste / śi-ba 'di daṅ sṅa-ma rga-ba gñis gcig-tu bsdus-nas rga-śi źes-bya-ste /

17. 'di ni rten-ciṅ 'brel-bar 'byuṅ-ba (1) rnam-par (2) dbye-ba yin-no (2) //

18. dge-sloṅ dag khyed-la rten-ciṅ 'brel-bar 'byuṅ-ba (1) daṅ-po daṅ rnam-par dbye-ba bśad-par bya'o źes (3) ṅas smras-pa gaṅ yin-pa de'i ched-du ṅas smras-pa 'di-dag yin-no (3) //

rten-ciṅ 'brel-bar 'byuṅ-ba daṅ-po daṅ / rnam-par dbye-ba bstan-pa źes-bya-ba'i mdo rdzogs-ste //

(1) *'byuṅ-ba'i.*

(2) *dbye-ba'o.*

(3) *ṅas gaṅ smras-pa de-dag ni ṅas smras-pa de-dag yin-no.* B et le texte sanskrit se terminent sur cette phrase.

The Daśottarasūtra

by

J.W. de Jong

A. N. U., Canberra

Abbreviations.

Note: References to Chinese Buddhist texts are to the Taishō edition; references to Pāli texts are to the editions of the Pāli Text Society. Roman numerals refer to the Nipātas, Arabic numerals to their subdivisions.

A = An Shih-kao's translation of the Daśottarasūtra, 長阿含十報法經 T. 13, 233 b–241 c.

AN = Aṅguttaranikāya

Behrsing = S. Behrsing, Das Chung-Tsi-King (衆集經) des chinesischen Dīrghāgama. Übersetzt und mit Anmerkungen versehen, *Asia Major*, VII, 1932, 1–149, 483; VIII, 1933, 277.

CPD = A Critical Pāli Dictionary, Copenhagen, 1924–

D = Dīrghāgama text of the Daśottarasūtra, T. 1 (10) 十上經, 52c–57b

MN = Majjhimanikāya

P = Pāli text of the Dasuttarasuttanta, Dīghanikāya, vol. III, 272–292.

S = Pāli text of the Saṅgītisuttanta, Dīghanikāya, vol. III, 207–271.

SA = Dīrghāgama text of the Saṅgītisūtra, T. 1(9), 衆集經, 49 b–52 c.

SB = 佛說大集法門經 T. 12, 226 c–233 b.

SN = Saṃyuttanikāya

Sn = Suttanipāta

SP = Saṅgītiparyāya, T. 1536, 367 a–453 b

SYM = The readings of the Sung, Yüan and Ming editions

T = The text of the Taishō edition

Vin = Vinayapiṭaka

Introduction

The Daśottarasūtra must have been one of the most popular of Buddhist sūtras. Both the Vinaya of the Mahīśāsakas and that of the Dharmaguptas mention this sūtra in their account of the recitation of the canon at the first council (T. 1421, 191 a; T. 1428, 968 b). The recension of the Dharmaguptas has been conserved in the Chinese translation of their Dīrghāgama (T. 1, sūtra nr. 10). In the Dīghanikāya of the Theravādins the Dasuttarasuttanta is the 34th text. A separate translation of the Daśottarasūtra by An Shih-kao belongs to the school of the Sarvāstivādins, as has been shown by Akanuma Chizen (see below commentary on Nipāta VII, 3). The German Turfan expeditions have brought back a great number of fragments of the Sanskrit text or the Daśottarasūtra. They have been very carefully edited by Miss Kusum Mittal and Dr. Dieter Schlingloff[1]. A comparison of the Sanskrit fragments with An Shih-*

1. Kusum Mittal, *Dogmatische Begriffsreihen im älteren Buddhismus.* I. Fragmente des Daśottarasūtra aus zentralasiatischen Sanskrit-Handschriften (=D. Ak. d. Wiss. zu Berlin, Inst. f. Orientf., Veröff. Nr. 34: Sanskrittexte aus den Turfanfunden, IV), Berlin, Akademie-Verlag, 1957; Dieter Schlingloff, *Dogmatische Begriffsreihen im älteren Buddhismus.* Ia. Daśottarasūtra IX-X (ibid., Veröff. Nr. 57: Sanskrittexte.........IVa), Berlin, 1961; a few fragments of the Daśottasūtra from the Pelliot Sanskrit collection have been edited by Bernard Pauly, *JA*, 1957, 281-292; 1959, 248-249.

Daśottarasūtra T. 13

Nipāta I

1. (apramādaḥ kuśale)ṣu dharmeṣu	1. id. 但守行
2. kāyagatā s(mṛt)i(ḥ śātasaha gatā)	2. id. kāyagatā smṛtiḥ 意不離身

*kao's translation, the Dīrghāgama text of the Daśottarasūtra and the Dasuttarasuttanta shows clearly that An Shih-kao's translation and the Sanskrit fragments give the same text with very minor differences.

Several of the categories of the Daśottarasūtra occur also in the Saṅgītiparyāya, the Sarvāstivāda commentary on the Saṅgitisūtra of the Sarvāstivādins. The agreements between the Saṅgītiparyāya and the Daśottarasūtra as represented by An Shih-kao's translation and the Sanskrit fragments confirm the Sarvāstivāda character of the last two texts. For the greater parts the Dasuttarasuttanta and the Daśottarasūtra of the Dharmaguptas correspond, but the differences show that they do not go back to the same original text.

The following synoptic table gives the categories of the four texts of the Daśottarasūtra; 1. The Sanskrit fragments, 2. An Shih-kao's translation; 3. The Dasuttarasuttanta; 4. The Daśottarasūtra of the Dīrghāgama. The commentary discusses the differences between the texts and gives references to other Pāli texts and Chinese translations. Only a few references are given because many categories occur very often in the Buddhist canon.

Dasuttarasuttanta	T. 1(10)
Nipāta I	
1. id.	1. id.
2. id. kāyagatā sati sātasahagatā	2. id. kāyagatā smṛtiḥ sātatā ? 常自念身

3. s(pa)rśaḥ sāsrava (upādānīyaḥ)	3. id. sparśaḥ sāsravaḥ 世間麁細
4. asmimānaḥ	4. id. 憍慢
5. ayoni(śo manasikāraḥ)	5. ? 意本觀
6. yoniśo manasikāraḥ	6. id. 本觀
7. (ānanta)ryac(e)t(aḥ)samādhiḥ	7. id. 不中止定
8. asāmayikī..............	8. ? 意止
9. sarvasattvā āhārasthitayaḥ	9. id. 一切人在食
10. akopyā cetovimuktiḥ	10. id. ? 意莫疑

Nipāta II

1. smṛtiś ca saṃprajanyaṃ ca	1. id. 當有意亦當念
2. (śamathaś ca vipaśya)nā ca	2. id. 止亦觀
3. nāmaṃ ca rūpaṃ ca	3. id. 名字
4. avidyā ca bhavatṛṣṇā ca	4. id. 癡亦世間愛
5. āhrīkyam anavatrāpyaṃ ca	5. id. 不愧不慚
6. hriś ca vyavatrāpyaṃ ca	6. ? 兩法當不爾爾
7. sthānaṃ ca sthānato duṣprativedham asthānaṃ cāsthānataḥ	7. ? 當不爾爾
8. kṣayajñānam anutpādajñānañ ca	8. id. 盡黠。不復生黠
9. yaś ca hetur yaḥ pratyayaḥ sattvānāṃ saṃkleśāya/yaś ca hetur yaḥ pratyayaḥ sattvānāṃ viśuddhaye	9. id. 人本何因緣在世間得苦。亦當知何因緣得度世

3. id. phasso sāsavo upādānīyo	3. id. sparśaḥ sāsravaḥ 有漏觸
4. id.	4. id.
5. id.	5. śubhā bhāvanā? 不惡露觀 (SYN no 不)
6. id.	6. aśubhā bhāvanā 惡露觀 (SYM adds 不)
7. id.	7. id.
8. akuppaṃ ñāṇaṃ	8. sāsravā vimuktiḥ 有漏解脫
9. id.	9. id.
10. id.	10. asaṅgā cetovimuktiḥ? 無礙心解脫

Nipata II

1. id.	1. hrīś ca vyapatrāpyaṃ ca (Skt. 6) 知慚，知愧
2. id.	2. id.
3. id.	3. id.
4. id.	4. id.
5. dovacassatā ca pāpamittatā ca	5. sīlavipatti, diṭṭhivipatti (S II, 27) 毀戒，破見
6. sovacassatā ca kalyāṇamittatā ca	6. sīlasampadā, diṭṭhisampadā (S II, 26) 戒具，見具
7. yo ca hetu yo ca paccayo sattānaṃ saṃkilesāya, yo ca hetu yo ca paccayo sattānaṃ visuddhiyā (Skt. 9)	7. =P 7
8. id.	8. id.
9. dve dhātuyo	9. sthānaṃ cāsthānaṃ ca? (cf. Skt. 7) 處非處

10. vidyā ca vimuktiś ca	10. id. 慧亦解脫
Nipāta III	
1. sa(t)pu(ruṣasaṃsevaḥ sad-dharma)śravaṇaṃ yoniśo manasikāraḥ	1. id. 事慧者。亦聞法經。亦當觀本
2. trayaḥ samādhayaḥ	2. id. 欲念定。不欲但念。亦不欲亦不念
3. trayo bhavāḥ	3. id. 欲有。色有。不色有
4. tisras tṛṣṇāḥ	4. id. 欲愛。色愛。不色愛
5. trīṇy akuśalamūlāni	5. id. 本三惡(!)
6. trīṇi kuśalamūlāni	6. id. 無有貪欲本。無有瞋恚本。無有愚癡本
7. trīṇi nimittāni	7. id. (三)相
8. trīṇi vimokṣamukhāni	8. id. 三活句
9. tisro vedanāḥ	9. id. 三痛
10. tisro 'śaikṣyo vidyāḥ	10. id. 不復學
Nipāta IV	
1. catvāri devamanuṣyānāṃ cakrāṇi	1. id. (四)天人輪
2. (catvāri smṛtyupasthā)nāni	2. id. 四意止

10. id.	10. id.

Nipāta III

1. a+b id. c dhammānudhammapaṭipatti	1. T=P 1 ; SYM c śubhā bhāvanā ? (cf. I, 5) 非惡露觀
2. id.	2. SYM id. ; T suññato samādhi, animitto samādhi, appaṇihito samādhi (S III, 51)
3. tisso vedanā	3. T=P 3 ; SYM id.
4. id.	4. id.
5. id.	5. id.
6. id.	6. id.
7. tisso nissāraṇiyā dhātuyo	7. SYM id. ; T āryaduṣprativedhaḥ, saddharmaśravaṇaduṣprativedhaḥ, tathāgataduṣprativedhaḥ ? 賢聖難解，聞法一一，如來一一
8. tiṇi ñāṇāni	8. SYN id. ; T tiṇi nimittāni. samathanimittaṃ, paggāhanimittaṃ, upekkhānimittaṃ (cf. SA III, 24) 三相：息止相，精進一，捨離一
9. tisso dhātuyo	9. SYM id. ; T=P 7
10. id.	10. a+c id.; b dibbacakkhuñāṇaṃ 天眼智

Nipāta IV

1. id.	1. id.
2. id.	2. id.

3. (catvāra āhārāḥ)	3. id. 四飯
4. catv(āry upādānāni)	4. id. 四蟻(SYM 𢷾)
5. catasro vipattayaḥ	5. id. 四失
6. (catasro saṃpattayaḥ)	6. id. 四成
7. catvāry āryasatyāni	7. id. 四諦
8. catvāri jñānāni	8. id. 四黠(SYM 點)
9. (catasraḥ saṃjñāḥ)	9. id. 四相識
10. (catvāraḥ sākṣīkaraṇīyā dharmāḥ)	10. id. (四當知法)法身當知，一意一一，一眼一一，一慧一一

Nipāta V

1. (pañca prādhānikasyāṅgāni)	1. id. 五種斷意
2. ——	2. pañca dhyānāni 五種定
3. pañcopādānaskandhāḥ	3. id. (五受種)色受種，痛一一，想一一，行一一，識一一
4. (pañca nīvaraṇāni)	4. id. 五蓋
5. (pañca cetaḥkhilāḥ)	5. id. 五心意釘
6. pañce(nd)r(iyāṇi)	6. id. 五根
7. (pañca) n(i)ḥsaraṇīyā dhātavaḥ	7. id. 五行得要出
8. āryaḥ pañcajñānikaḥ sam(yaksamā)dhi(ḥ)	8. id. 五慧定
9. pañca vimuktyāyatanāni	9. id. 五解脫
10. pa(ñ)ca (dharmas)kandhāḥ	10. id. 不學陰，一一戒，一一定，一一慧，一一度世解脫

Nipāta VI

1. ṣa(ṭ) saṃraṃjanīyā dharmāḥ	1. id. (六)不共取重
2. ṣaṭ sātatavihārāḥ	2. id. 六共居
3. ṣaḍ ādhyātmikāny āyatanāni	3. id. 六內入

3. id.	3. id.
4. cattāro oghā	4. id.
5. cattāro yoghā	5. =P 5
6. cattāro visaṃyogā	6. =P 6
7. cattāro samādhī	7. id.
8. cattāri ñāṇāni	8. SYM id.; T=P 8
9. cattāri ariyasaccāni (Skt. 7)	9. SYM id.; T catvāraḥ pratisaṃvidaḥ 四辯才
10. cattāri sāmaññaphalāni	10. SYM (?); T=P 10

Nipāta V

1. id.	1. id.
2. pañcaṅgiko sammāsamādhi	2. pañcendriyāṇi (Skt. 6) 五根
3. id.	3. id.
4. id.	4. id.
5. id.	5. id.
6. id.	6. 五喜本：悅，念，猗，樂，定
7. id.	7. pañca vimuktyāyatanāni (Skt. 9) 五解脫入
8. id.	8. id.
9. id.	9. pañca niḥsaraṇīyā dhātavaḥ (Skt. 7) 五出要界
10. id.	10. id.

Nipāta VI

1. id.	1. id.
2. cha anussatitṭṭhānāni (Skt. 8)	2. =P 2
3. id.	3. id.

4. ṣaṭ tṛṣṇākāyāḥ	4. id. 六愛
5. ṣaḍ agauravatāḥ	5. id. 六不恭敬
6. (ṣaḍ gauravatāḥ)	6. id. 六恭敬
7. (ṣaḍ niḥsaraṇīyā dhātavaḥ)	7. id. 六行度世
8. ——	8. ṣaḍ anusmṛtayaḥ 六念
9. ——	9. ṣaḍ anuttaryāni 六無有量
10. ——	10. ṣaḍ abhijñāḥ 六知

Nipāta VII

1. ——	1. sapta dhanāni 七寶
2. ——	2. sapta bodhyaṅgāni 七覺意
3. ——	3. sapta bhavāḥ 七有
4. ——	4. sapta anuśayāḥ 七結
5. ——	5. sapta asaddharmāḥ 惡人七法 (！)
6. ——	6. sapta saddharmāḥ 七慧者法
7. sapta vijñā(na)sthitayaḥ	7. id. 七識止處
8. sapta samādhipariṣkārāḥ	8. id. 直見，一念，一語，一法，一業，一方便，一意
9. sapta nirdoṣavastūni	9. id. 七現恩
10. ——	10. sapta satpuruṣadharmāḥ 有法，有解，知時，一足，一身，一衆，一人前後

Nipāta VIII

1. aṣṭau dharmapratyayāḥ	1. id. 八因緣
2. ā(ryo 'ṣṭaṅgo mārgaḥ)	2. id. 八種道
3. (aṣṭau lokadharmāḥ)	3. id. 八世間法

4. cha taṇhākāyā, rūpataṇhā, saddataṇhā, gandhataṇhā, rasataṇhā, phoṭṭhabbataṇhā, dhammataṇhā.	4. =P 4
5. id.	5. id.
6. id.	6. id.
7. id.	7. =Skt.+P 9
8. cha satatavihārā (Skt. 2)	8. =P 8
9. id.	9. =Skt.+P 7
10. id.	10. id.

Nipāta VII

1. id.	1. id.
2. id.	2. id.
3. satta viññāṇaṭṭhitiyo (Skt. 7)	3. =P 3
4. id.	4. id.
5. id.	5. id.
6. id.	6. id.
7. satta sappurisadhammā (Skt. 10)	7. =P 7
8. satta saññā	8. =P 8
9. id.	9. id.
10. satta khīṇāsavabalāni	10. =P 10

Nipāta VIII

1. id.	1. id.
2. id.	2. id.
3. id.	3. id.

4. aṣṭau mithyāṅgāni	4. id. 不直見，一一念，一一語，一一法，一一業，一一方便，一一意，一一定
5. aṣṭau kausīdyavastūn(i)	5. id. 八瞢瞢種
6. aṣṭau vīryārambhavastūni	6. id. 八精進方便道
7. aṣṭau vimokṣāḥ	7. id. 八解脱
8. aṣṭau mahapuruṣavitarkāḥ	8. id. 八大人念
9. aṣṭāv abhibhvāyatanāni	9. id.（八自在）
10. ——	10. aṣṭāv arhato bhikṣoḥ kṣīṇāsravasya balāni 八無有著行者力

Nipāta IX

1. (na)va vīrya(vitaraṇaviśuddhipūrvaṅgamā dharmāḥ)	1. 九意喜：聞法喜，念一，喜一，樂一，受猗一，安一，定一，止一，離一
2. (nava ce)tasaḥ prasā(dapūrvaṅga)mā dharmāḥ	2.（九）精進致淨：精進度致淨，意一一一，見一一一，疑一一一，道道致淨，慧見如淨，見慧愛斷度致，斷種，度世
3. (nava sattvāvāsāḥ)	3. id. 九神止處
4. ——	4. nava saṃyojanāni 九結
5. (navāghātavastūni)	5. id. 九惱本
6. (navāghātaprativinodanāni)	6. id. 除九意惱（！）
7. (nava...............)	7. nava apāśrayaṇāni？九依住
8. nav(ānupūrvavihārāḥ)	8. id. 九次定
9. ——	9. nava akṣaṇāḥ 九不應時
10. ——	10. nava nirodhāḥ 九（T. 無）滅

Nipāta X

1. daśa nāthakarak(ā dharmāḥ)	1. id. 十救法
2. d(aśa nirj)v(a)r(ava)stūni	2. id. 十種直

4. id.	4. id.
5. id.	5. id.
6. id.	6. id.
7. aṭṭh' akkhaṇā asamayā brahmacariyavāsāya	7. =P 7
8. id.	8. id.
9. id.	9. id.
10. aṭṭha vimokkhā	10. =P 10

Nipāta IX

1. nava yonisomanasikāramūlakā dhammā	1. =P 2
2. nava pārisuddhipadhāniyaṅgāni	2. =P 1
3. id.	3. id.
4. nava taṇhāmūlakā dhammā	4. =P 4
5. id.	5. id.
6. id.	6. id.
7. nava nānattā	7. nava brahmacaryāṇi 九梵行
8. nava saññā	8. =P 8
9. nava anupubbavihārā (Skt. 8)	9. =P 7
10. id. nava anupubbanirodhā	10. id.

Nipāta X

1. id.	1. id.
2. dasa kasiṇāyatanāni (Skt. 8)	2. dasa sammattā 十正行

3. (daśa rūp)iṇy āya(ta)nāni	3. id. 十內外色入
4. paṃca.......hyāni nī(varaṇ......	4. id. 十內外蓋
5. da(śākuśalāḥ) karmapa(thāḥ)	5. id. (十)惡行
6. daśa kuśalāḥ karmapathāḥ	6. id. 十淨行
7. (da)śāryāvāsāḥ	7. id. 十德道居
8. (daśa kṛtsnāyatanāni)	8. id. 十普定
9. daśa t(athāgatasya balāni)	9. id. 佛十力
10. (daśāśaikṣā dharmāḥ)	10. id. 十足學不復學

Commentary

Nipāta I

2. Skt. *śātasahasagatā* is supplied by the editor on the basis of Pāli *sātasahagatā*. D 常 and P *sātasahagatā* probably go back to a common original *sātatā* (cf. Skt. VI, 2) or *sātatyasahagatā*.

3. Here 麁細 must translate *sparśa*. Normally in An Shih-kao's translations it is used to translate *spraṣṭavya*, cf. T. 13, 240 c 25 麁細入 *spraṣṭavyāyatanam*; T. 607, 232 a 12, 身更麁細 'the body touches the *spraṣṭavya*'. Skt. *upādānīyaḥ* is supplied by the editor on the basis of the Pāli text. It is missing in both A and D.

4–5. To *ayoniśo manasikāraḥ* and *yoniśo manasikāraḥ* correspond in D 不惡露觀 and 惡露觀. The latter usually renders *aśubhā bhāvanā* and the former probably stands for *śubhā bhāvanā*. In Nipāta III, 1 c the SYM text of D has 非惡露觀 as against *yoniśo manasikāraḥ* of Skt. and A. Probably in all these places the text of D is corrupt. In A 意本觀 must probably be corrected in 非本觀. Cf. T. 31, 813 a 9–10 where An Shih-kao translates *yoniśo manasikāra* and *ayoniśo manasikāra* by 本觀 and 非本觀.*

3. id.	3. id.
4. dasa micchattā	4. =P 4
5. id.	5. id.
6. id.	6. id.
7. id.	7. id.
8. dasa saññā	8. dasa pāsaṃsāni ṭhānāni 十稱譽處
9. dasa nijjaravatthūni (Skt. 2)	9. =P 9
10. id.	10. =P 10

---

*8. Skt. is quoted in the Abhidharamakośavyākhyā p. 590. 18–19: *eko dharma utpādayitavyaḥ. katama ity āha. sāmayikī kāntā cetovimuktir iti.* See also Abhidharmakoṣa, transl. by L. de La Vallée Poussin, chapitre VI (Paris, Louvain, 1925), pp. 260–262 and Pāli *sāmā̊yikaṃ vā kantaṃ ceto-vimuttiṃ upasampajja viharissati asāmā̊yikaṃ vā akuppaṃ* MN III. 110. 30–32.

10. Skt. is quoted in the Adhidharmakośavyākhyā p. 590. 20–21: *eko dharmaḥ sākṣātkartavyaḥ. katama ity āha. akopyā cetovimuktir iti.* In Pāli the expression *akuppā cetovimutti* occurs often, cf. CPD s.v. *akuppa.*

Nipāta II

3. An Shih-kao translates *rūpa* by 字. Cf. T. 603, 174 c 10: 字爲色, 名爲四不色陰 "*tzŭ* is *rūpa*, *nāma* is the four immaterial *skandhas*'.

6. Probably Án Shih-kao's translation means: 'The reverse of the two dharmas (named above)'.

7. Cf. Pāli *aṭṭhānaṃ ca aṭṭhānato yathābhūtaṃ pajānāti*, SN V. 304. 13, AN III. 417. 18–19, 419. 5. The first of the 10 forces of the Buddha is the *sthānāsthānajñānabala*, cf. E. Waldschmidt, *MIO*, VI, 1958, p. 385, n. 18.

Nipāta III

7. The three *nimittas* of D (Taishō text) occur also in the Saṃgītisūtra of the Dīrghāgama. Behrsing (p. 5, XXIV) wrongly renders 止息相 by *samādhinimittam*. Cf. S II, 24.

8. The three *vimokṣamukhas* are identical with the three *samādhis* in D III, 2 (Taishō text) and S III, 51.

Nipāta IV

2. The description of the first *smṛtyupasthāna* is different in all four texts. Skt. is the shortest. P is more detailed. A is similar to P but adds 內外身觀=*ajjhatta-bahiddhā vā kāye kāyānupassī viharati* (cf. DN II. 292. 2-3). D has the most detailed text and is identical with IV, 11 of the Saṃgītisūtra of the Dīrghāgama, T. 1, viii, 50 c, 9-13, Behrsing pp. 8-9.

5. Pāli *sīlavipatti, ācāra-, diṭṭhi-, ājīva-* cf. Vin II. 242. 10-12.

6. A group of 4 *sampadās* does not occur in the Pāli texts. *Sīlasampadā* and *diṭṭhisampadā* are mentioned in S II, 26.

8. In Skt., A and D (SYM) the four knowledges are *duḥkha-jñānam, samudaya-, nirodha-* and *mārga-*. P had *dhamme ñāṇaṃ anvaye-, paricce-* (variant: *paricchede*) and *sammuti-*. To these four knowledges correspond in D (Taishō) 法智，未知一，等一，智他心一. They also occur in SP vii, 393 c 12, SA viii, 51 a 18 and SB 228 c 21-22. See Behrsing pp. 78-79, notes 179-182 for a discussion of the various Chinese translations of these four knowledges.

Nipāta V

1. The order of the five members is the same in Skt., A and SP. In P the order is 1, 3, 2, 4, 5. D has the same order as P but the wording of 4 is different, cf. Behrsing p 14. Cf. below VII, 9 (1).

2. The first four members of A describe the four *dhyānas*. The text is very similar to Sāmaññaphalasutta (DN I. 73-76), T. 22,

274 c–275 a and MN Nr. 77.

4. To Skt. 4 *auddhatyakaukṛtyam* and 5 *vicikitsa* correspond in A 戲樂 and 悔疑. Probably one must read 戲樂悔 and 疑.

6. The five joys in D are probably *pāmujjam, sati, passaddhi, sukham* and *samādhi*. With the exception of *smṛti* they occur also in Skt. V, 9 (1c) and in Skt. IX, 2 (IX, 1 in A and P). See also DN I. 73. 20–23 : ***samanupassato pāmujjaṃ jāyati, pamuditassa pīti jāyati pītimanassa kāyo passambhati, passaddhakāyo sukhaṃ vedeti, sukhino cittaṃ samādhiyati*** (cf. DN III. 241. 9–11 ; Vin I. 294. 4–7 ; AN III. 21).

7. Skt. contains a comparison with a cock's feather (Pāli ***kukkuṭapatta***) and a sinew-thong (Pāli ***nahāradaddula*** ; Skt. ***snāyudardula***) which is also found in A, SP (xiv, 427 b 24) and the Madhyamāgama (T. 26, xxi, 564 b 11–564 b 2) but is missing in P, D, S, SA and SB. In this passage of the Madhyamāgama 無欲 (564 b 22) and 己身 (565 a 13) correspond to ***naiṣkramya*** and ***satkāya***. These translations are based on a Prākrit original.

8. The order of the five members of ***samādhi*** is the same in Skt. and A. In P and D the order is 4, 1, 2, 3, 5.

9. The five ***vimuktyāyatanas*** occur also in the Adhidharmakośavyākhyā (pp. 54–55) and the Madhyamāgama (T. 26, xxi, 563 c 22–564 b 3). The text of the Abhidharmakośavyākhyā agrees with that of A and SP (xiii, 424 a 4–b 25). The Pāli text (P and S, DN III. 241. 3–243. 2) is much longer than D and SA (viii, 51 c 3–12). In the Abhidharmakośavyākhyā, A, SP, D, SA and SB (230 c 7–215 b 9) members two and three deal respectively with the recitation of the dharma and the proclamation of it to others. In the Pāli text two and three are reversed. In all texts the different items are essentially identical although the wording varies.

10. In D the five *dharmaskandhas* are called *aśaikṣāḥ skandhaḥ*. In A *aśaikṣāḥ skandhaḥ* has become the first *skandha* and the fifth (*vimuktijñānaskandha*) has been left out. The first four *skandhas*

occur in SP (vii, 394 b 16) and in S IV, 25.

Nipāta VI

1. The six *saṃramjaniyā dharmāh* occur also in the Mahāparinirvāṇasūtra (ed. by Waldschmidt, Berlin, 1950–1951, pp. 128–132). In DN (II. 80–81) they are called *aparihāniyā dhammā*. In AN III. 132. 9–20 1, 2, 3, 5 and 6 are given under the name *phāsuvihārā*.

4. A and SP (xv. 429 b 26–430 c 4) agree with Skt.

5. Skt. is fragmentary but seems to agree with A and SP (xv. 430 c 5–12). The first four items are the same in all the texts. In A and SP 5 and 6 are 'speaking bad words' and 'associating with bad friends', in P disrespect for *appamāda* and *paṭisanthāra*, in D disrespect for meditation and parents. P agrees with AN IV. 339 and Vin V. 92.

6. The six *gauravatās* are exactly the opposite of the six *agauravatās*.

7. The order of the six items is the same in Skt., P, SP (xv, 430 b 21–431 a 15) and SB (232 a 20–b 27). In A, D and SA (52 a 9–16) 5 and 6 are reversed. This is one of the rare cases in which A differs from Skt. and SP.

Nipāta VII

2. D is more detailed Cf. Behrsing, p. 107, n. 338 who refers to AN II. 16: *idha...bhikkhu satisambojjhaṅgaṃ bhāveti vivekanissitaṃ virāganissitaṃ nirodhanissitaṃ*.

3. The seven *bhavas* are *narakabhava, tiryag-, preta-, manuṣya-, deva-, karma-*, and *antara-*, cf. Mochizuki Shinkō's Bukkyōdaijiten, p. 1888 c, Abhidharmakośa, trad. L. de la Vallée Poussin, chapitre III (Paris-Louvain, 1926), p. 13, n. 2. Akanuma Chizen 赤沼智善 points out that the seven *bhavas* are quoted from the Daśottarasūtra by Saṃghabhadra in his 順正理論, xxiv, 475 a 26–27 (Akanuma refers also to p. 352 c but the seven *bhavas* are not mentioned here). The

use of the expression 'the sūtra says' proves that A is a Sarvāstivāda text (*Bukkyō kyōten shiron* 佛教經典史論, 1939, p. 63). The seven *bhavas* are enumerated by Saṃghabhadra in chapter xxi, 459 b 27–29.

4. In SP (xvii, 439 a 17–29) the seven *anuśayas* are: 1. *kāmarāga*; 2. *pratigha*; 3. *bhavarāga*; 4. *māna*; 5. *avidyā*; 6. *dṛṣṭi*; 7. *vicikitsā*. In A the order is 1, 2, 3, 4, 6, 5, 7; in P 1, 2, 6, 7, 4, 3, 5; in D 1, 3, 6, 4, 2, 5, 7.

5. In P, S and D the 7 *asaddhammas* are: 1. *asaddho*; 2. *ahiriko*; 3. *anottappī*; 4. *appasuto*; 5. *kusīto*; 6. *muṭṭhassati*; 7. *duppañño*. A and SP (xvii, 436 c 14–437 a 6) have 不定 *asamāhita* instead of *appassuta* and the order is 1,2, 3, 5, 6, 4 (=*asamāhita*), 7.

6. The *saddharmas* are exactly the opposite of the *asaddharmas*.

7. In A the third category is missing and 4, 5 and 6 have been numbered 3, 4 and 5.

9. SP (xvii, 439 b 1–17) and A differ much from P and D. In SP 1 is identical with the first of the *prādhānikasyāṅgāni* (422 b 15–18), cf. DN III 84. 18–20; SN V. 219. 2; MN I. 320. 17–20: *Tathāgate saddhā niviṭṭhā hoti mūlajātā patiṭṭhitā daḷhā asaṃhāriyā samaṇena vā brāhmaṇena vā devena vā Mārena vā Brahmunā vā kenaci vā lokasmiṃ*. 2 is identical with P VIII, 1(4) and S and P X, 1(1). 3 is associating with good friends, cf. S and P X, 1 (3). 4: 'He rejoices in meditation and possesses the two withdrawals, the withdrawal of the body and the withdrawal of the mind', cf. Skt. VIII, 1 (3): *dvayena vyāpakarṣeṇa samanvāgato bhavati/kāyavyāpakarṣeṇa ca cittavyāpakarṣeṇa ca*. 5 is identical with P V, 1 (4) and VIII, 1 (6) but omits '*akusalānaṃ dhammānaṃ pahānāya kusalānaṃ dhammānaṃ upasampadāya*. 6 is identical with P VIII. 1(7). 7 is identical with the fifth *prādhānikasyāṅga*, cf. P V, 1(5) and SP xiii, 422 b 27–c 1. For the differences of P and S with D and SA see Behrsing, p. 106, n. 332.

10. In SP (xvii, 437 b 18–20) and A the order of the categories

is the same. In D, P and S (VII, 5) the order is 1, 2, 5, 4, 3, 6, 7. In the Pāli texts 7 is *puggalaññū* but the Sinhalese manuscripts read *puggalaparovaraññu* which is confirmed by SP 知補特伽羅有勝有劣 and A 知人前後.

Nipāta VIII

1. Skt. is very fragmentary but A seems to agree with it, with the exception of the fifth category which in A is identical with the seventh of P. In many respects P differs from Skt. and A. D agrees with P with the exception of 4 and 7. D 4 is AN IV. 153. 7-9: *saṅghagato kho pana anānākathiko hoti atiracchānakathiko, sāmaṃ vā dhammaṃ bhāsati, paraṃ vā ajjhesati, ariyaṃ vā tuṇhībhāvaṃ nātimaññati.* D 7 is P V. 1(5).

3. In SP (xviii. 442 c 28-29), D and SA (52 b 11-12) the order is 1. *lābha*; 2. *alābha*; 3. *nindā*; 4. *praśaṃsā*; 5. *yaśas*; 6. *ayaśas*, 7. *sukham*; 8. *duḥkham*. In A the order is 1, 2, 5, 6, 3, 4, 7, 8; in P 1, 2, 6, 5, 3, 4, 7, 8.

5. The order of the categories is different in Skt. and SP (xviii, 441c8-442a21). SP and D have the same order 2, 1, 4, 3, 6, 5, 7, 8. In A the order is probably 2, 1, 5, 6, 3, 4, 7, 8, but the text of 5, 6, 3 and 4 is not very clear and does not allow us to identify these categories. In P the order is 3, 4, 5, 6, 2, 1, 7, 8. In all the texts 1 follows 2. The Skt. text is very fragmentary and perhaps is the same as in the other texts. Also in the fragment from Duldur-Aqur (cf. *JA*, 1957, p. 291) 1 follows 2.

6. As in 5 the Skt. categories are arranged in SP (xviii, 442 a 22-c 4) and D in the following order 2, 1, 4, 3, 6, 5, 7, 8. In A the order is 2, 1, 5, 6, 3, 4, 7, 8.

7. A replaces the first *vimokṣa* by the first *abhibhvāyatana*, cf. Skt. VIII, 9(1); DN II. 110.7-10.

9. The second *abhibhvāyatana* has been wrongly reconstructed by the editor; *adhyatmam arūpasaṃjñī bahirdhā rūpāṇi paśyati*

paritrāṇi...Read *adhyātmaṃ rūpasaṃjñī* (cf. MS 87. 5) *bahirdhā rūpāṇi paśyati adhimātrāṇi* (cf. MS 62. 6)......, cf. Abhidharmakośavyākhyā, p. 690. 22–23 (in lines 26–28 the words *tathā......abhibhv' āyatanaṃ* have to be deleted).

10. For the eight *balas* of A see Abhidharmakosavyākhyā, p. 591. 29–33 ; Abhidharmakośa, transl. L. de La Vallée Poussin, chapitre 6 (Paris-Louvain, 1925), p. 265, n. 1 ; T. 99, xxvi, 188 b 21–27 ; AN IV. 224–225. See also Schlingloff's edition of Daśottarasūtra IX-X, p. 10, n. 4.

Nipāta IX

1. Skt. corresponds to A IX. 2. A IX. 2 (1) is *vīryavitaraṇaviśuddhi.* A 2-4 agree with P but A has everywhere *vitaraṇaviśuddhi* instead of *viśuddhi*. A 5 and A 9 are probably also identical with P but A 6-8 are difficult to understand. In general D agrees with P with the exception of 7 除浄滅 and 8 無欲. In regard to these categories A seems to agree with D.

2. Skt. corresponds to A IX, 1, P IX, 1 and D IX, 2 but the differences between the texts are considerable.

4. In SP (xix, 446 a 25–28) and the Abhidharmakośa, chapitre 5, pp. 81–82 the nine *saṃyojanas* are 1. *anunaya* ; 2. *pratigha* ; 3. *māna* ; 4. *avidyā* ; 5. *dṛṣṭi* ; 6. *parāmarśa* ; 7. *vicikitsā* ; 8. *īrṣyā* ; 9. *mātsarya*. In A 6 is 疑 *vicikitsā* and 7 貪 *rāga*.

5-6. D agrees with P. A is more detailed and probably agrees with Skt.

7. The editor has placed *akuśalaṃ prajahāti* in 1 and *kuśalaṃ bhāvayati* in 2. According to A both belong to 1. In A 7 is 'having rejected one dharma he understands one dharma', 8 'having understood one dharma he accepts one dharma' and 9 'having accepted one dharma he exercises one dharma'. In A the categories are called 依住 which probably translates *apaśrayaṇa*. 6-9 occur in Pāli under the name *apassena*, cf. DN III. 224. 20–22 ; 270. 1–4 ; MN I. 464.

13-15, cf. Mahāvyutpatti 430: *caturapāśrayaṇaḥ*.

9. The nine *akṣaṇas* of A do not agree with one of the lists of *akṣaṇas* given by Edgerton in his Buddhist Hybrid Sanskrit Dictionary s.v. *akṣaṇa*.

10. D agrees with P with the exception of 1: P *kāmasaññā*, D 聲 *śabda*? A seems to enumerate 9 members of the *pratītyasamutpāda*: 1. *nāmarūpanirodha*; 2. *ṣaḍāyatana-*; 3. *sparśa-*; 4. *vedanā-*; 5. *tṛṣṇā-*; 6. *upādāna-*; 7. *bhava-*; 8. *jāti-*; 9. *jarāmaraṇa-*.

Nipāta X

1. The first seven categories of A are identical with the 7 *nirdoṣavastus* in SP (xvii, 439 b 1-17) and A VII, 9. A8-10 agrees with Skt. A is followed by an *antaroddāna* as in Skt. after V, 8 and VIII, 1. For a comparison of Skt. and P see Schlingloff, p. 23, n. 4. D has the following order: 1. *śīlavān* (Skt. 2, P 1); 2. *kalyāṇamitraḥ* (Skt. 3, P 3); 3. *suvacaḥ* (Skt. 8, P 4); 4. *dharmakāmaḥ* (Skt. 9, P 6); 5. *analasaḥ* (Skt. 10, P 5); 6. *bahuśrutaḥ* (P 2); 7. *ārabdhavīryaḥ* (Skt. 5, P 8); 8. *smṛtimān* (Skt. 6, P 9); 9. *prajñāvān* (Skt. 7, P 10); 10. *pratisaṃlīnaḥ* (Skt. 4). D adds explanations to each category as in Skt.

2. For the 10 *sammattās* of D see AN V. 240. 6-10 where 9 and 10 are *sammāñāṇa* and *sammāvimutti*. In D 9 and 10 are reversed. A agrees with Skt. but the name of the categories corresponds to P *sammattā*.

4. In A 1 and 2 are *abhyantaraḥ kāmacchandaḥ* and *bāhyaḥ kāmacchandaḥ*; 3 and 4 are *pratigha* and *pratighanimitta*. In Skt. the editor reconstructs in 3 and 4 *vyāpāda* and *pratigha* but probably Skt. has to be reconstructed in agreement with A because *pratigha* and *pratighanimitta* constitute the *vyāpādanīvaraṇa*, cf. Abhidharmakośa, chapiter II, p. 158. A 5-10 correspond to Skt. but *auddhatya* and *kaukṛtya* have been very imperfectly rendered by 惱 and 疑.

7. The 10 *āryavāsas* occur also in AN V. 29, T. 125, xli, 775 c 18–21. The Chinese translations of categories 5 and 6 in A, D and T 125 differ considerably and it is impossible to reconstruct the Indian original which they render.

Stache-Rosen, Valentina: Dogmatische Begriffsreihen im älteren Buddhismus. II: Das Saṅgītisūtra und sein Kommentar Saṅgītiparyāya. Nach Vorarbeiten von Kusum Mittal bearbeitet. Berlin: Akademie-Verlag 1968. Teil I: 488 S., Teil II: 155 S. 4⁰ = Deutsche Akademie d. Wissenschaften zu Berlin, Institut f. Orientforschung, Veröff. Nr. 65/1–2: Sanskrittexte aus den Turfanfunden, hrsg. von E. Waldschmidt, IX. Kart. M 139,–. Bespr. von J. W. de Jong, Canberra A.C.T.

After publishing fragments of the Daśottarasūtra (Dogmatische Begriffsreihen im älteren Buddhismus. I: Fragmente des Daśottarasūtra aus zentralasiatischen Handschriften, Berlin, 1957) Dr Kusum Mittal untertook to publish the fragments of the Saṅgītisūtra. As she was unable to complete her task, Dr Stache-Rosen has continued with her work. A complete translation of the Saṅgītiparyāya and two glossaries of the Saṅgītisūtra (I. Sanskrit-Chinese-German; II. Chinese-Sanskrit-German) have been added by the new editor. The introduction to the Saṅgītisūtra was already edited and translated by Professor E. Waldschmidt (ZDMG, 105, 1955, pp. 298–318; Von Ceylon bis Turfan, Göttingen, 1967, pp. 258–278).

The edition of the fragments, the restoration and the translation of the Sanskrit text of the Saṅgītisūtra follow the example of the preceding publications in the series Sanskrittexte aus den Turfanfunden. Although the manuscripts contain many lacunae, the editor has been able to restore an almost complete text with the help of parallel texts. Both the restoration of the text and the translation are done with great care. Only in one instance a different restoration is necessary. The text of the second *abhibhvāyatana* (Teil I, p. 197) is: *paśyaty adhimātrāṇi suvarṇadurvarṇāni* as pointed out in my article on the Daśottarasūtra (p. 23) published in Kanakura Hakushi koki kinen: Indogaku Bukkyōgaku ronshū (Kyoto, 1966). The reading *adhimātrāṇi* is confirmed by MS. 62.6 which has ... *trāṇi*. Dr Mittal had read ... *ritrāṇi* but there are no traces of *ri* on the facsimilé of the manuscript (cf. Faksimile-Wiedergaben von Sanskrithandschriften aus den Berliner Turfanfunden I, The Hague, 1963, pl. CLXIX c).

The translation of the complete text of Hsüan-tsang's version of the Saṅgītiparyāya is a great achievement. No other Abhidharma text of such dimensions has been translated since Louis de La Vallée Poussin's translation of the Abhidharmakośabhāṣya. Dr Stache-Rosen has gone to great pains to render exactly the highly technical language, to point out parallel passages in Sanskrit and Pāli texts, to trace quotations, etc. Anybody who wants to undertake a thorough study of this text, which is of great importance for the study of the Abhidharma of the Sarvāstivādins, will be grateful to Dr Stache-Rosen for the considerable amount of work accomplished by her. In general she has been successful in translating this difficult work but, as is evident from the query-marks in the text and from the passages quoted in the notes, some places have remained obscure to her. In part, this is undoubtedly due to the fact that a translator of Chinese Buddhist texts disposes of far fewer aids than a translator of Tibetan texts who is able to consult a whole series of glossaries. Moreover, even such a conscientious translator as Hsüan-tsang is by no means as consistent in his terminology as the Tibetan translators. For this reason the glossaries of the Saṅgītisūtra, compiled by Dr Stache-Rosen, will be of great help to the student of Chinese Buddhist texts. The recent publication of the Sanskrit text of the Abhidharmakośabhāṣya by P. Pradhan (Patna, 1967) would make it possible to compile a very detailed Chinese-Sanskrit glossary.

I believe that Dr. Stache-Rosen could have greatly benefited from the work of Japanese scholars. In the first place one must mention in this respect the Japanese translation of the Saṅgītiparyāya by Watanabe Baiyū in the collection Kokuyaku issaikyō (Bidon vols. 1–2, Tōkyō, 1929). The translations in this collection are uneven in quality. However, Watanabe is one of the leading specialists in the Abhidharma of the Sarvāstivādin. His translation is excellent and accompanied by a great profusion of notes, which are extremely useful for the references to parallel texts and for the Sanskrit equivalents of technical terms. Watanabe's chief work is his Ubu Abidatsuma-ron no kenkyū (Tōkyō, 1954) which contains a long chapter dealing with the Saṅgītiparyāya (pp. 495–591). Watanabe has also written an article on the references to the Dharmaskandha in the Saṅgītiparyāya (cf. Hikata Hakushi koki kinen ronbunshū, Tōkyō, 1964, pp. 31–42). According to Takakusu the Dharmaskandha is anterior to the Saṅgītiparyāya because it is quoted in it (cf. Teil I, p. 12). Watanabe suggests that Hsüan-tsang who translated the Saṅgītiparyāya after having translated the Dharmaskandha could very well have referred to this work in order to avoid the repetition of identical passages. He also advances arguments in support of the posteriority of the Dharmaskandha with regard to the Saṅgītiparyāya.

Another Japanese publication which has not been used by Dr. Stache-Rosen is Akanuma Chizen's Comparative Catalogue of Chinese Āgamas and Pāli Nikāyas (Nagoya, 1929; reprint, Tōkyō, 1958). At the end of IV. 27 the Saṅgītiparyāya quotes seven stanzas (cf. p. 108). Dr. Stache-Rosen refers to five (1–4, 7) parallel stanzas in Pāli. All seven are to be found in the Chinese translation of the Madhyamāgama (Taishō, vol. I, pp. 722c–723a) as indicated by Akanuma (p. 171). Dr. Stache-Rosen translates the fifth stanza as follows: „Wer an Reifen und Frucht der Werke glaubt, der . . . Vater, Mutter, Dienerschaft usw. preisen den Wissenden". From the comparison of both Chinese versions it is obvious that one must translate this stanza differently: „Who believes in acts, fruits and ripening and gives that what he esteems himself to father, mother, servants, etc., him praise all the wise men". In the bibliography Dr. Stache-Rosen lists only Anesaki's Concordance which is entirely superseded by Akanuma's work.

Dr. Stache-Rosen has made great use of Louis de La Vallée Poussin's translation of the Abhidharmakośabhāṣya and of Wogihara's edition of the Abhidharmakośavyākhyā. In translating technical terms profit could have been derived from the Chinese index of the Kośa compiled by Funahashi Suisai and Funahashi Issai: Kandō-bon Kusharon sakuin (Kyōto, 1956). For instance *tseng-yü* 增語 translated as „Bezeichnung für Anhäufen" (p. 135), is regularly used by Hsüan-tsang as a rendering of *adhivacana* (cf. Taishō Nr. 1556, ch. 10, p. 52 c 6). This term is found in the following enumeration which occurs several times in the Saṅgītiparyāya (cf. Teil 2, p. 110, note 40): 異語，增語，想等，想，施設，言說. The Sanskrit equivalents are *paryāya*, *adhivacana*, *saṃjñā*, *samajñā*, *prajñapti*, *vyavahāra* (cf. Edgerton's Dictionary s. v. *samajñā*). The last four terms are explained by Haribhadra in his Abhisamayalaṃkārālokā Prajñāpāramitāvyākhyā (ed. U. Wogihara, p. 71). Not even Mochizuki Shinkō's well-known Bukkyō daijiten seems to have been used by Dr. Stache-Rosen. For instance on p. 121 she translates *lung-nao* 龍腦 as 'Betelnüsse' (Teil 1, p. 78) and adds in a note (Teil II, p. 49, note 121): wörtl. Drachenhirn für *nāgadeṇṭikā?*'. However, *lung-nao* renders *karpūra*, cf. Bukkyō daijiten s. v. *ryūnōko* (pp. 5002b–c). It is described by Hsüan-tsang in his Records of the Western Countries (tr. S. Beal, II, p. 232).

The fact that without making use of the above-mentioned publications Dr. Stache-Rosen has been able to make such a good translation of this difficult text bears witness to her excellent knowledge of Chinese. In a few places she has been misled by the wrong punctuation of the Taishō text. Sometimes she tends to translate disyllabic expressions as two separate words but this is partly due to a lack of familiarity with Hsüan-tsang's terminology. In order to illustrate my critical remarks on the translation I would like to discuss a few passages which have been misunderstood by Dr. Stache-Rosen but, before doing so, I must stress very strongly that her translation is an excellent piece of work. Few scholars would have had the courage to translate such a long and difficult work. The passages which are wrongly or imperfectly translated constitute only a small part of the whole text.

Teil 1, p. 66, l. 7: 'sie können den Glauben nicht erhalten' (cf. Teil 2, p. 33, n. 22) – 'they cannot be relied upon'. Teil 1, p. 66, l. 9: 'überdenkt man ihre Vernichtung: 'Dieser Pfad führt wirklich zur Entsagung' (cf. Teil 2, p. 33, n. 24) – 'one considers that their destruction is the true peace (śānti); one considers that this path is the true *naiṣkramya*'. Teil 1, p. 72, l. 7: 'Ferner leidvolle Empfindungen oder die damit zusammenhängenden Dinge oder beide' (cf. Teil 2, p. 42, n. 67) — 'Also painful sensations, dharmas associated (*saṃprayukta*) with them, dharmas coexistent (俱有 *sahabhū*) with them'. Teil 1, p. 81, l. 24: 'Verdienst bedeutet Reinheit des Lebenswandels in Beherrschung des Körpers und der Worte, der mit Spenden versehen ist. Tun bedeutet Wille zum Geben und Willenskraft ... Gegenstand bedeutet: der Gabenherr gibt [der Akt des Gebens] und der gespendete Gegenstand' (cf. Teil 2, p. 51, n. 137) — 'Restraint of the body (*kāyasaṃvara*), restraint of the word (*vāksaṃvara*) and purity of life (*ājīvapariśuddhi*) which accompany (俱行 *sahagata*) the gift are called merit. The volition (*cetanā*), the purpose (*saṃcetanā*) ... which accompany the gift are called action. The giver, the receiver and the given object are called object'. Teil 1, p. 104, l. 22: 'Wesen beruhen auf Nahrung, und es werden bei Bissen große und kleine graduell unterschieden [??]. Was ist die Grobheit und Feinheit in dieser Sache?' (cf. Teil 2, p. 78, n. 119 and n. 120) — 'According to the size of the beings to be fed and according to [the size] of the morsels in a corresponding ratio it is called coarse and fine. How is this?' Next the text mentions three aquatic monsters of decreasing size: *timiṅgilagila*, *timiṅgila timi*. These names are correctly transliterated in the quotation of this passage in the Mahāvibhāṣā (cf. Taishō nr. 1545, ch. 130, p. 675 c 6ff.). Teil 1, p. 108, l. 13: [Es folgt eine Erklärung, warum die Gabe vom Gebenden her rein ist und nicht vom Empfangenden her, die ich nicht verstehe]' (cf. Teil 2, p. 82, n. 160) — 'The giver possesses those members (*avayava*) and that equipment (*saṃbhāra*) which have to be cultivated and brought together by the giver but the receiver does not possess those members and that equipment which have to be cultivated and brought together by the receiver. Therefore the gift is pure as far as the giver is concerned but impure as far as the receiver is concerned'. By 'members' conditions or qualities are meant. Teil 1, p. 123, l. 7 (cf. Teil 2, p. 100, n. 301) — 'He refuses food, made specially for him (Pāli *uddissakata*), and spoiled food.' Teil 1, p. 124, l. 37: 'Sie nehmen Abstand von groben Worten, die Worte die sie sprechen, sind nicht grob, nicht heftig, nicht bitter, sie rufen kein Ärgernis hervor und sind auch nicht unangenehm, unerfreulich, unliebsam und unangebracht für viele Menschen.' (cf. Teil 2, p. 102, n. 308). — 'They refrain from coarse and bad words. The words spoken by them are not so coarse, so rude, so bitter that they provoke resentment from others, cause many people displeasure, distress, lack of joy and happiness, and obstruct the exercise of concentration (*samādhi*) by being concentrated (*samāhita*).' (cf. Teil 1, p. 127, l. 36). Teil 1, p. 145, l. 45: 'ist er wie ein Baum, dessen Wurzel abgehauen wird, oder ein Tālabaum, dessen Spitze abgeschlagen wird, der nicht wieder wachsen kann in späterer Zeit.' — Not the monk but the *āsravas* are compared to the palm-tree of which the roots have been cut off. For the comparison cf. Vinaya vol. III, p. 2, 1. 18: *pahīnā ucchinnamūlā tālāvatthukatā anabhāvaṃ gatā āyatiṃ anuppādadhammā*. Teil 1, p. 154, 1. 38: 'und in ihren Bemühungen nicht nachlassen.' (cf. Teil 2, p. 117, n. 152) — 'and without resting they cultivate the *prayogamārga*' (cf. Abhidharmakośa VI. 277). Teil 1, p. 157, 1. 20: 'er unterwirft die Aufsässigkeit' (cf. Teil 2, p. 119, n. 172) — 'he subdues and opposes (i. e. the pleasures)'. Teil 1, p. 171, l. 27: 'Wenn ein edler Schüler auf diese Weise des Buddhas gedenkt, dann hat er früher verwirklichter Kenntnisse wegen die rechte Ansicht. Denken, Gedenken, ... das wird Gedenken an den Buddha genannt.' (cf. Teil 2, p. 129, n. 85 and n. 86) — 'When a noble disciple reflects upon the Buddha as having these signs (*nimitta*), the thoughts (*smṛti*), reflections (*anusmṛti*) ... which are associated (*saṃprayukta*) with the realization, based on vision, are called reflection upon the Buddha (*buddhānusmṛti*).' Teil 1, p. 173, l. 34: '... es in Hinsicht auf diese Form Gier, Begierde, Haß oder Verblendung oder den einen oder anderen geistigen Faktor gibt, so entstehen die geringen Befleckungen.' (cf. Teil 2, p. 133, n. 103) — 'and with regard to these forms at the appropriate moment (literally 'at the time when they must arise') desire, passion, hate and illusion arise, or *upakleśas* which follow each of these mental states.' The *upakleśas* derive (*niṣyanda*) from the *kleśas* (cf. Abhidharmakośa V. 91). Teil 1, p. 175, l. 25: 'die ursprüngliche Disziplin' (cf. Teil 2, p. 134, n. 113) — 'the restraint of the senses (*indriyasaṃvara*)'. Teil 1, p. 183, l. 31: 'die fünf Arten des körperlichen Bewußtseins, die zu Geistbewußtsein führen, das beruht auf und verbunden ist mit Gestalt usw. und mannigfache Hindernisse für die Versenkung bildet, sind nicht vorhanden.' (cf. Teil 2, p. 141, n. 66) — 'the manifold notions (*saṃjñā*) which are produced by the five kinds of corporeal knowledge, which are associated with the *manovijñāna*, which take forms, etc. as their object and which obstruct concentration, do not exist.'

The Sūtra on the Foundation of the Buddhist Order (Catuṣpariṣatsūtra) translated by Ria Kloppenborg [= *Religious Texts Translation Series Nisaba*, volume one]. Leiden, E. J. Brill, 1973. XVI + 123 pp. DGld. 16.-.

The Catuṣpariṣatsūtra (henceforth abbreviated as CPS) is one of the most important Buddhist texts published in recent times. In 1951 Ernst Waldschmidt published a comparative analysis, followed in 1952 by a transcription of the Sanskrit fragments and in 1957 and 1962 by a synoptic edition of the Sanskrit text and parallel versions in Pāli, Tibetan and Chinese. The CPS contains the Sarvāstivāda version of the early history of the Buddhist order, beginning with the obtaining of the bodhi by the Buddha and ending with the conversion of his chief pupils Śāriputra and Maudgalyāyana.

Ria Kloppenborg's translation is meant to provide text-material for students of Buddhism who do not know Sanskrit and is therefore as literal as possible. On the whole the translation is accurate but in some places other interpretations can be suggested. Several passages present difficulties because the text is not well established. In the following notes references are made to the chapters and sections into which the text has been divided by the editor.

Introduction. Section 3. For a parallel passage see *Gilgit Manuscripts*, vol. III, part IV (Calcutta, 1950), p. 216.3–11. R. K. renders *jñānadarśana* with "insight into knowledge" but *jñānadarśana* has to be interpreted as a dvandva. For the explanation of the terms *jñāna* and *darśana* by the Abhidharmakośavyākhyā, and for references see L. de La Vallée Poussin, *Abhidharmakośa de Vasubandhu*, VIII, p. 193, n. 2.

I.7: "O Thou of whom all pride is gone." In a note R. K. explains that she translates *garvalopa* instead of *pūrṇalopa*. Waldschmidt's restoration *garvalopa* is based upon Tibetan *ṅa-rgyal bcom* but at p. 434, n. 16 he points out that the reading of the manuscript is more like *rṇ* than like *rva*. The Gilgit manuscript has *parṇalopa* and MS. 42.3 *rṇalopa*. It is not possible to read *garvalopa* since it is neither confirmed by the manuscripts nor attested elsewhere as far as I know. The parallel passages have been studied by Alsdorf, *Die Āryā-Strophen des Pāli-Kanons* (Wiesbaden, 1968), pp. 54–55. Alsdorf arrives at the following conclusion: "Ein Vergleich dieser Texte zeigt sofort, dass *pūrṇabhāra*, *pūrṇalopa*, *parṇalopa* and *prajñākāra* sämtlich Entstellungen von *pannabhāra* sind, das allein einen wirklich guten Sinn gibt."[1] It is not easy to see how *bhāra* could have been transformed into *lopa*, but perhaps this is due to the influence of Pāli *pannaloma*. Tib. *bcom* corresponds to *lopa* but Tib. *ṅa-rgyal* 'pride' is unexplainable.

3.12: "Furthermore, the gods belonging to the train of Māra, who form a danger are not able to harm the virtuous"; *parato ye upasargā devatā mārakāyikāḥ / na śaknuvanty antarāyaṃ kṛtapuṇyasya kartu vai //*. *Paratas* can mean 'further' or 'farther' but not 'furthermore'. Here it

[1] See also *Bhikṣuṇī-vinaya*, edited by Gustav Roth (Patna, 1970), p. 122.5–7: bahuśrutaṁ citrakathaṁ Buddhasya paricārakaṁ / parṇabhāravisaṁyuktaṁ. Read *parṇabhāraṁ* (= *pannabhāraṁ*) *visaṁyuktaṁ*, cf. bahussuto cittakathī buddhassa paricārako / pannabhāro visaññutto, Theragāthā 1021; pannabhāro visaṃyutto, Aṅguttaranikāya, vol. I, p. 162.21.

certainly means 'from others': "Those disasters (coming) from others (such as) the gods belonging to the train of Māra."

4.6: "capable of speaking for themselves (on the dharma) and well-acquainted (with the dharma)"; *alaṃ svasya vādasya paryavadātāro*: "capable of elucidating their own doctrine", cf. Tib. *raṅ-gi smra-ba gsal-bar byed-nus-pa'i.* See also Edgerton, *Buddhist Hybrid Sanskrit Dictionary* (henceforth abbreviated as BHSD) s.v. *paryavadāpayitar*: "one who purifies completely: *svasya vādasya paryavadāpayitāro* Divy. 202.13". Burnouf translates: "ils peuvent faire adopter aux autres tous leurs raisonnements" (*Introduction à l'histoire du Buddhisme indien*, Paris, 1844, p. 78).

4.7: "The ascetic Gautama will (not) enter complete extinction." In a note the translator remarks that perhaps a negation has been left out of this sentence. A negation is found in the Tibetan translation and must be accepted into the text even if it is absent in the Gilgit manuscript. Cf. CPS p. 438, n. 2, in which Waldschmidt refers to 16.12 where the negation is of course absent.

8.2: "The dharma obtained by me is profound, of deep splendour." "Of deep splendour" renders *gambhīrāvabhāso*. Here *avabhāsa* has the meaning 'appearance' as the corresponding Pāli *obhāsa* in the passage on the four pools (*udakarahada*) of which the first is said to be *uttāno gambhīrobhāso* (Aṅg. Nik., II, p. 105). Woodward translates: "The shallow which looks deep" (*Gradual Sayings*, II, p. 112).

10.8: "Conquerors like me who achieved the destruction of evil influences must be recognized"; *jinā hi mādṛśā jñeyā ye prāptā āsravakṣayam*: "Those like me who achieved the destruction of evil influences must be acknowledged as Jinas."

10.10: "For 'correct' people who know the ways of the world do not radiate": *na hi santaḥ prakāśante viditvā lokaparyayam*. In the corresponding verse of Udānavarga 21.7 Bernhard reads *prakāśyante*. The Tibetan translator seems also to have read *prakāśyante*: *skyes-bu dam-pa grags mi-srid* "They cannot be celebrated as excellent people."

11.7: "men of delusion"; *mohapuruṣaḥ* "stupid fellows", cf. BHSD s.v.

11.18: "The Tathāgata only ate in the morning at the proper time"; *tathāgata pratiyaty' eva kālabhojī*. In 16.2 R. K. translates *pratiyaty' eva* with 'immediately': "When his body was tired, he immediately went to sleep"; *śrāntakāyaḥ prāgbhāraḥ pratiyaty' eva middham avakrāntaḥ*. The expression *pratiyaty' eva* has given rise to different explanations and translations, cf. Jean Filliozat, 'Fragments du Vinaya des Sarvāstivādin', *JA*, 1938, p. 45, n. 3 [= *Laghu-prabandhāḥ*, Leiden, 1973, p. 103]: "On pourrait interpréter *pratiyaty* comme locatif absolu du participe présent *pratiyant-* et traduire "tout en répliquant"; Bernard Pauly, 'Fragments sanskrits de haute Asie', *JA*, 1957, p. 292: "le sens de "tout en répliquant" ne me semble pas absolument satisfaisant. On pourrait peut-être comprendre "tout en faisant cette réflexion" à moins qu'il ne s'agisse d'un sens temporel: "sur le champ, sans plus tarder"; Louis Renou, compte rendu de Kusum Mittal, *Dogmatische Begriffsreihen im älteren Buddhismus*, I, *JA*, 1959, p. 261: "On relèvera, d'après l'éditeur, la forme *pratiyaty eva*, qu'il rend tantôt par "rapidement", tantôt par "au plus haut degré": double traduction qui n'est pas sans trahir quelque embarras. La seconde interprétation peut s'appuyer sur la racine *yat-* "faire effort" avec une évolution de sens analogue à *sahasā* "avec force", d'où "tout-à-coup"." Renou's interpretation has been accepted by Luise Schwarzschild, cf. 'Notes on some words meaning "Immediately" in Middle Indo-Aryan', *JRAS*, 1961, p. 39, n. 3. Waldschmidt translated *pratiyat' eva* in the same context as CPS 16.2 with "schnell", cf. 'Zu einigen Bilinguen aus den Turfan-Funden', *NGAW*, 1955, p. 19 [= *Von Ceylon bis Turfan*, Göttingen, 1967, p. 256]. Waldschmidt pointed out that Pāli *paṭigacc' eva* or *paṭikacc' eva* corresponds to *pratiyaty' eva* (*ibid*., n. 138). Edgerton considered *pratyatya* 'in advance' to be a semi-Prakritic form of *pratikṛtya* and Pāli *paṭikacca* (or °*gacca*). According to him the meaning 'quickly' is a result of specialization or distortion of the meaning 'in advance' (Review of *Das Catuṣpariṣatsūtra*, *Language*, 39, 1963, p. 491). The form *pratiyatya* has been correctly explained by Brough who remarked that Buddhist Sanskrit has the form *pratikṛtya* which corresponds to Pāli *paṭikacca* or *paṭigacca* but that in addition it shows on occasion *pratiyatya* due to a misunderstanding of a Prakrit *paḍiyacca*. As to the meaning Brough said: "For *pratikṛtya* Edgerton gives the meaning 'in advance', and the word may indeed be translated in this way without undue distortion. In many places, however, it continues to carry the connotation of 'making preparations to meet a contingency'." (*The Gāndhārī Dharmapada*, London 1962, p. 278). The Tibetans translate *pratyaty' eva* with *myur-du* 'quickly' or with expressions meaning 'previously, before' (*sṅon-chad, goṅ-ma bźin-du*). From the meaning 'previously' (i.e. "sooner than usual", cf. Dines Andersen, *A Pāli Reader*, glossary s.v. *paṭigacca*) the meanings 'quickly, immediately' have developed. Apart from the places quoted see further Udānavarga (ed. F. Bernhard) 4.16: *pratiyatyeva tat kuryād, yaj jāned dhitam ātmanaḥ*; 27.8: *etat tu śalyaṃ pratiyatya paśyato, hy adhyavasitā yatra prajāḥ prasaktāḥ*; *Gilgit Manuscripts*, Vol. III, Part 2 (Srinagar, 1942), p. 86.10: *amuko bhikṣuḥ sa bhagavatā pratiyatyeva* (Ms. *pratipatyeva*; Dutt *pratipadyeva*!) *vyākṛtaḥ* (Dutt *vyākṛtāḥ*); p. 107.13: *pratiyatyevāsau* (Dutt *pratipattyevāsau*) *vihāraḥ śobhane viviktāsane ca bhūbhāge pratiṣṭhāpitaḥ*.

12.12: "I was not released . . . nor did I leave this or was I separated (from it), free (from it), nor far removed (from it), with undeluded mind." The translation uses five expressions to render four Sanskrit words: *mukto, nisṛto, visaṃyukto, vipramukto*. As to "undeluded mind" the translator refers to *aviparītena cittena* which Waldschmidt had restored on p. 150 but the Tibetan translation (*phyin-ci-log daṅ bral-ba'i sems-kyis*) shows clearly that *viparyāsāpagatena cetasā* is the correct reading.

25a.11: "method of the dharma"; *dharmavinaya*! Same mistake in 25b.9.

27b.10: "The man, hearing (this) from king Śraiṇya Biṃbasāra of Magadha, said: "Be it so, Your Majesty"; *evaṃ deveti sa puruṣo rājño māgadhasya śraiṇyasya biṃbasārasya pratiśrutya*. *Pratiśru-* means here of course 'to consent to, agree, acquiesce'.

27c.20: "They speak of food, drinks and tastes, of sensual desires and women. Seeing that these impurities tend to attachment, therefore I was not delighted with regard to sacrifice and oblation"; *annāni pānāni tathā rasāṃś ca, kāmāṃś ca strīś caiva vadanti haike / etāṃ malān upadhau saṃprapaśyaṃs, tasmān na yaṣṭe na hute rato 'ham*. In a note the translator remarks that 'they' refer to the sacrifices. The text has not 'they' but 'some here'. The manuscript reads *vadantīhaike* which Waldschmidt has changed to *vadanti haike* metri causa. It would be preferable to write *vadant' ihaike* (cf. Edgerton, *Buddhist Hybrid Sanskrit Grammar* § 4.25). In the second half the translation has to be corrected: "Seeing that in attachment there are these impurities."

27c.21: "If your mind is not delighted by that, by sensual desires, by food, drinks and tastes, then, in the world of gods and men where does your mind delight in?"; *kathan nu te devamanuṣyaloke rataṃ manaḥ* "How can your mind delight in the world of gods and men?"

27e.22: "The path (of worldly existence) being cut off, it does not proceed. Irreparably it comes to destruction." The translation of *apratisandhi* with 'irreparably' is based upon Waldschmidt's note but the meaning of Pāli *appaṭisandhiya* is 'not leading (or subject to) rebirth', cf. *Critical Pāli Dictionary* s.v.; Edgerton, *op. cit.*, p. 493: *apratisaṃdhi* (adv.) 'without rebirth'.

28b.3: "he was closely following the reverend Aśvajit"; *āyuṣmantam aśvajitam āgamayamānaḥ*; "he was waiting for the venerable Aśvajit".

27e.23: "In what is he who is completely released? In the opposite of suffering, the destruction of it . . ."; *tatra bhikṣavaḥ kaḥ parinirvṛtaḥ / anyatra duḥkhaṃ tan niruddhaṃ*. The text is not very well established, cf. CPS p. 362, n. 7. In the corresponding passage of the Nidānasaṃyukta (ed. Chandrabhāl Tripāṭhī, Berlin, 1962, p. 140) the editor reads *anyatra yad duḥkham*. He translates: "Wer hat in einem solchen Fall, ihr Mönche, das volle Nirvāṇa erlangt? Es ist nichts weiter als dass das, was leidvoll ist, vernichtet . . . ." In a note he refers to BHSD s.v. *anyatra* (2). I believe that this translation is correct but that it requires a negation which is found in the Gilgit manuscript: *tatra bhikṣavaḥ kaḥ parinirvṛto nānyatra yad duḥkham . . .*: "In this case, O monks, who is he who is completely released? There is nothing else except that suffering is destroyed . . . (literally: "not except that which is suffering is destroyed . . ."). The

Tibetan translation confirms this interpretation: *dge-sloṅ-dag de-la yoṅs-su mya-ṅan-las 'das-pa gaṅ źe-na / gźan med-kyi sdug-bsṅal 'gags-pa gaṅ yin-pa / de ni ñe-bar źi-ba /.*

28e.7: The Sanskrit text is missing and R. K. translates in a note the Tibetan translation: "The teacher . . . saw the friends Upatiṣya and Kolita coming to the Veṇuvana. Concerning those two, having come in this way in the middle of the excellent assembly, he taught with certainty: "Those two (will) become the best pair of my disciples in the doctrine"." Tib. *ston-pa . . . 'od-ma'i tshal-du ma phyin-par / de-ltar mchi-ba* (cf. p. 391, n. 5) *gzigs gyur-nas / tshogs mchog dbus-su de gñis ni / 'di gñis ṅa-yi ñan-thos-kyi / zuṅ-mchog 'gyur źes ṅes bstan-te /*, "The teacher . . . having seen the two friends Upatiṣya and Kolita, who had not yet arrived at the Veṇuvana, coming in this way, proclaimed: "In the excellent assembly these two, both of them, will be the best pair of my disciples", cf. Alsdorf, *op. cit.*, p. 70 and *IIJ*, XIII (1971), p. 212.

28g.1–3: "1. In the morning then many monks dressed and taking (their) bowls and robes, entered Rājagṛha to collect alms. 2. Then the people of Rājagṛha, seeing these monks, acted contemptuously towards the (former followers of the) heretical school of Sañjayin, who were admitted and ordinated, and they uttered the verse:". "The Buddha arrived in Rājagṛha, the capital of the people of Magadha. All are guided by Sānjayin. Whom else will you guide?" "; *atha saṃbahulā bhikṣavaḥ pūrvāhṇe nivasya pātracīvaram ādāya rājagṛhaṃ piṇḍāya prāviśan.* 2. *atha rājagṛhakā manuṣyāḥ saṃjayinā tīrthyāyatanena pravrājitenopasaṃpāditena tāṃs tān bhikṣūn dṛṣṭvā avaspandayamānā gāthāṃ bhāṣante.* 3. *prāpto rājagṛhe buddho magadhānāṃ purottame / sarve saṃjayino nītāḥ kiṃ nu bhūyo nayiṣyatha //.* The text in section two seems to be incomplete. According to the Tibetan translation the original text ran something like this: *atha ye rājagṛhakā manuṣyāḥ saṃjayinā tīrthyāyatanenācirapravrājitenopasaṃpāditenānāttamanaso 'nabhinandinas te tāṃs tān . . .* : "Then the people of Rājagṛha, furious and discontented because the (followers of the) heretical school of Sañjayin were recently admitted and ordained seeing all these monks . . . . Cf. Tib. *de-na rgyal-po'i khab-kyi mi gaṅ-dag yaṅ-dag rgyal-ba-can-gyi mu-stegs-can-gyi gnas rab-tu phyuṅ źiṅ bsñen-par rdsogs-nas riṅ-po ma lon-pas yi ma raṅs-śiṅ mṅon-par mi dga'-ba de-dag-gis dge-sloṅ de daṅ de-dag mthoṅ-nas.* In 3. *saṃjayino* designates the followers of Sañjayin: "All the followers of Sañjayin are lead (by the Buddha)", cf. Pāli *sabbe sañjaye netvāna* "Leading all Sañjaya's (followers)". (tr. I. B. Horner, *The Book of Discipline*, IV, p. 56). In 3d *nayiṣyatha* must be a mistake for *nayiṣyati* which is found in the Pāli and in the Mahāvastu: "What more will he lead?" The parallel texts have *kaṃ* instead of *kiṃ* but *kiṃ* is confirmed by the Tibetan translation (*ci-źig*) and may have been used to express more forcibly the contempt with which the people of Rājagṛha treated the monks.

The translator does not seem to have consulted Edgerton's review of Waldschmidt's edition in which he rejects, for instance, the spellings *kunmāsa* and *Yaṣṭivana*. Edgerton's suggestion to read *apratibhānamātraṃ* in 28f.12 and 28g.6 is very attractive.

Australian National University J. W. DE JONG

Sanskrit Wörterbuch der buddhistischen Texte aus den Turfan-Funden. Begonnen von Ernst Waldschmidt. Herausgegeben von der Akademie der Wissenschaften in Göttingen unter der Leitung von Heinz Bechert. 1. Lieferung: a-, an- / antar-vāsa. Göttingen, Vandenhoeck & Ruprecht, 1973. XVIII + 80 pp. DM. 42,–.

Dans une 'Vorbemerkung' de la troisième partie de son édition du Catuṣpariṣatsūtra M. Ernst Waldschmidt annonça la publication d'un dictionnaire des Catuṣpariṣat-, Mahāvadāna– et Mahāparinirvāṇasūtra. On doit se réjouir du fait que le plan se soit élargi afin d'inclure tous les textes bouddhiques, exception faite pour les textes du genre kāvya et les sūtra du Mahāyāna. En ce qui concerne ces derniers le dictionnaire inclut quelques fragments qui contiennent des variantes dignes d'intérêt, notamment des fragments de l'Aṣṭādaśa– et de la Śatasāhasrikā Prajñāpāramitā.

La préface de M. Heinz Bechert nous renseigne sur l'histoire et le plan du dictionnaire. Depuis 1953 plusieurs savants ont été occupés à réunir les matériaux pour ce dictionnaire. La rédaction en a été confiée à M. Georg von Simson qui a rédigé la plupart des articles de ce premier fascicule. Dans sa préface le rédacteur explique que le dictionnaire contient le vocabulaire complet et des citations détaillées de tous les passages. Une exception a été faite pour des mots très communs comme *bhagavat, bhikṣu* et la plupart des particules et pronoms. Dans ce cas un astérisque indique que tous les passages ne sont pas cités. Ainsi dans ce fascicule on trouvera un astérisque devant les mots *atha, atra* et *adas.* Le dictionnaire servira donc en même temps de concordance. Comme le remarque M. von Simson, le dictionnaire rendra de grands services en incorporant la phraséologie du sanskrit bouddhique des textes canoniques des Sarvāstivādin car la plupart des textes canoniques dans la collection de Turfan appartiennent à cette école.

Le travail lexicographique a été rendu plus difficile par l'état fragmentaire des textes. L'éditeur a souvent vérifié les leçons à l'aide de photocopies et, dans plusieurs cas, il a corrigé les leçons adoptées par l'éditeur du texte. Dans d'autres cas, il a proposé d'autres conjectures. Il n'était évidemment pas possible de se rapporter toujours aux manuscrits. Beaucoup de fragments ont été publiés en photocopie mais pour d'autres il faut faire foi aux éditeurs des textes. Il peut s'en suivre que le dictionnaire incorpore des leçons erronées. Ainsi on trouvera dans le lemma *adhiṣṭhā* une forme *adhiṣṭhamāno.* La leçon du MS. est mentionnée dans un article de M. Lambert Schmithausen que l'éditeur, probablement, n'a pas pu consulter à temps pour en tenir compte dans ce premier fascicule. Dans Udānavarga 15.2 Bernhard a lu: *nityaṃ smṛto bhikṣur adhiṣṭhamāno / labheta pūrvāparato viśeṣam.* Selon l'apparatus critique le MS. TTT. VIII. B a: *etāṃ smṛtiṃ yo hy-adhiṣṭhamāno*, mais M. Schmithausen signale que le MS. a *adhitiṣṭhamāno*[1].

[1] 'Zu den Rezensionen des Udānavargaḥ', *WZKSA* 14 (1970), 70; Annemarie von Gabain, *Türkische Turfan-Texte VIII* (Berlin, 1954), p. 24.

M. von Simson propose de lire: *etām smṛtiṃ bhikṣur adhiṣṭhamāno*. Le texte tibétain correspondant a: *dge-sloṅ dran-pa de legs-'jog-pa na*. M. Schmithausen remarque que la leçon *adhitiṣṭhamāno* fausse le mètre. Peut-être faudrait-il lire *adhiṣṭhihitvā*.

Le texte de l'Udānavarga pose beaucoup de problèmes par le grand nombre de variantes que l'on trouve dans les manuscrits et les textes parallèles. L'édition de Bernhard est un travail de premier ordre mais, comme le montre l'article de M. Schmithausen, tous les problèmes sont loin d'être résolus. Dans le deuxième volume de son édition Bernhard a donné des concordances des textes parallèles en langues indiennes. M. Schmithausen a découvert d'autres parallèles dans la Yogācārabhūmi. Un de ces parallèles confirme une conjecture proposée dans le dictionnaire s.v. *aṇḍa-saṃbhava* où l'éditeur suggère de lire *aṇḍasaṃbhavaḥ* au lieu de *aṇḍasaṃbhavam* (cf. Schmithausen, *op.cit.*, p.53). Bernhard avait l'intention de publier dans un autre volume des parallèles dans des langues non-indiennes. Il faut espérer que les matériaux de Bernhard seront publiés car l'étude de l'Udānavarga n'est pas possible sans consulter les parallèles et surtout ceux en tibétain et en chinois. Ne citons qu'un seul exemple. Pour Udānavarga 29.56d Bernhard ne cite aucun parallèle. Dans la Yogācārabhūmi on trouve: *caturyogāpagato na jātim eti* (Schmithausen, p. 53) ce qui correspond au pāli: *catuyogātigato na jātim eti* (Udānam. p. 71, l. 11). Le texte tibétain a: *rnal-'byor bźi dan-bral-ba skye-ba med*. Le texte chinois correspondant a: 'les quatre yoga et il ne reçoit pas la naissance' (T. no.212, p. 752c10). Le commentaire explique que les quatre yoga ont été coupés définitivement (p.752c21). Les textes pāli, tibétain et chinois correspondent bien au texte de la Yogācārabhūmi mais l'Udānavarga a: *yogāpetam attṛnasaṅgam eti*. M. von Simson a eu raison de mettre un point d'interrogation après le mot *attṛnasaṅgam* qui semble pourtant bien attesté par les manuscrits. Il s'agit sans doute d'une vieille corruption. On pourrait corriger ce pāda en lisant *yogāpetamatir na saṅgam eti* mais il est évident que les textes parallèles ne confirment pas cette conjecture.

Dans Udānavarga 27.13 le texte de Bernhard a: *etāv antāv anajñāya / tv atilīyanti bāliśaḥ* (que M. von Simson corrige en *bāliśāḥ*) / *apare tv atidhāvanti*. M. von Simson traduit *ati-lī* par 'allzusehr haften oder kleben (an der Sinnenwelt)', et en renvoyant au BHSD il ajoute entre parenthèses 'oder: schlaff, energielos sein?". La traduction, proposée par Edgerton, repose sur un seul passage du Vinaya des Mūlasarvāstivādin: *na ca dhāvasi nātilīyase* (I,9.12) qu'il faut citer ici car on y trouve un parallèle au vers de l'Udānavarga. Il en ressort que la traduction d'Edgerton n'est guère justifiée. Aussi la traduction tibétaine de l'Udānavarga confirme le sens donné par M. von Simson: *lhag-par źen-par byed*. Dans ce cas il aurait été utile de citer la traduction tibétaine bien que l'on ne puisse pas toujours faire confiance aux traductions tibétaines. Ainsi pour *atidhāvanti* la traduction tibétaine a *mṅon-par rgyug-par byed-ciṅ* que M. Schmithausen reconstruit en **abhidhāvanti*. Il est facile de confondre *bhi* et *ti* et la traduction tibétaine ne prouve aucunement que le manuscrit dût avoir *abhidhāvanti* ce qui ne correspondrait pas à *atilīyanti*. Dans tous les cas où le sens d'un mot n'est pas définitivement établi il serait opportun de citer la traduction tibétaine. Ainsi pour *aghādin* (?) où la traduction tibétaine a *sdig-pa byed-cin*.

Le fait que le dictionnaire cite tous les passages dans lesquels un mot se rencontre aidera beaucoup à vérifier les leçons des manuscrits et à déceler les fautes des scribes. Ainsi sub *ati-dūre* l'éditeur note que ce mot ne se rencontre qu'avec le génitif. Parmi les exemples cités un seul s'en écarte: *Vārāṇasyāṃ nagaryāṃ nātidūre* et il est donc vraisemblable qu'il s'agit d'une faute du scribe car c'est leur habitude d'être négligents dans la notation des *visarga* et des *anusvāra*.

Sub *anu-rakṣin* l'éditeur signale que *vācānurakṣin* peut contenir un instrumental *vācā* ou on thème vocalique en *–ā*. Il préfère la dernière solution puisque ce thème se retrouve dans l'Udānavarga. Ajoutons que l'on trouve aussi dans ce texte un thème en *–a* dans le titre du chapitre VIII Vācavarga et dans l'*uddāna* à la fin du chapitre X: *vācakarmaśraddhā*. Dans le titre du chapitre XII du Dharmasamuccaya le manuscrit, utilisé par Lin Li-kouang, a *cārāvarmo* (?). Lin avait corrigé en *vāgvargo* puisque l'*uddāna* à la fin du chapitre XX a *vāk*: *cittavākkarma*. L'autre manuscrit du Dharmasamuccaya a *vācāvaśo* et il faut certainement lire *vācāvargo* (et non *vācovargo* comme j'avais proposé dans les appendices du volume II, p. 24).

Sub *antar* l'éditeur mentionne le passage: *bahir ārāmasya* ... *antarārāme*. Ici il analyse *antarārāme* en *antar* (préposition avec loc.) et *ārāme* mais sub *antarā* il cite le même passage comme exemple pour *antarā* (préposition avec loc.), en ajoutant entre parenthèses: 'oder ist *antarārāme* als adv. zu verstehen? Vgl. CPD *antarārāmaṃ, antarā-bhatte, antarā-magge*'. Notons que la leçon *antarārāmaṃ* qui ne se trouve qu'une seule fois dans le canon pāli n'est pas du tout sûre et qu'il ne semble pas nécessaire d'interpréter *antarābhatte* et *antarāmagge* comme des adverbes (le CPD considère *antarabhatte* comme un locatif). En tout cas il paraît préférable d'analyser *antarārāme* en *antar-ārāme, antar* étant une préposition ou un adverbe.[2]

L'éditeur renvoie souvent au CPD et au BHSD comme on doit s'y attendre, mais il ne les mentionne pas à propos d'*anu-bhū* bien que son interprétation ne s'accorde pas avec celle que l'on trouve dans ces deux dictionnaires. L'éditeur donne le sens de 'erreichen, erzielen, hervorbringen (?)' à *anu-bhū* dans le passage suivant: *yā api tā lokasya lokāntarikā andhastamā ... yatremau sūryācandramasāv evammahardhikau mahānubhāvāv ābhayābh(āṃ nā)nubhavatas.* Le CPD, en citant un passage parallèle en pāli (DN II,12.13), suit les commentaires: *pabhāya na ppahonti*, Sv = *attano pabhāya obhāsituṁ an-abhisambhuṇanti*, pṭ. Le sens de 'to be equal to, to be able, to suffice' semble bien attesté dans les textes pālis et Edgerton s.v. *anubhavati* donne le sens suivant: 'suffices for, is sufficient to produce: *ābhayāpy ābhāṃ nānubhavato (candrasūryau)* SP 163.10.' C'est évidemment le bon droit de l'éditeur d'un dictionnaire de différer d'opinion avec ses devanciers mais il aurait été préférable d'en faire mention.

Pour terminer nous aimerions signaler quelques traductions qui ne semblent pas entièrement correctes. Pour *an-icchantika* l'éditeur donne 'frei von Wünschen' en renvoyant au BHSD: 'somehow based on pres. pple. of *icchati*'. Quelle que soit l'étymologie exacte de ce terme, il n'y a pas de doute que, dans les textes bouddhiques, *icchantika* signifie 'one destitute of Buddha-nature' (cf. BHSD) et il vaut certainement mieux traduire *an-icchantika* comme 'one not destitute of Buddha-nature'. Ajoutons aux références, données par Edgerton, G. Tucci, *Opera minora*, I (Roma, 1971), pp. 85–86, 236–238; Mochizuki Shinkō, *Bukkyōdaijiten*, vol. I, pp. 148c – 149c. Le terme *icchantika* se rencontre souvent dans le Mahāparinirvāṇasūtra mahāyāniste comme il ressort de l'index du Taishō Daizōkyō (vol. 4, Tōkyō, 1965, p. 132). Selon ce texte même les *icchantika* possèdent la nature de Buddha. Cette question était vivement discutée en Chine au début du cinquième siècle par Tao-sheng et ses adversaires (cf. Kenneth Ch'en, *Buddhism in China*, Princeton, 1964, pp. 115–116) Vour aussi sur *icchantika*: D. Seyfort Ruegg, *La théorie du Tathāgatagarbha et du Gotra* (Paris, 1969), index p. 520 s.v. *icchantika*; Takasaki Jikidō, *Nyoraizō shisō no keisei* (Tōkyō, 1974), p. 188, n. 37.

On trouvera dans ce premier fascicule quelques termes propres aux textes de la Prajñāpāramitā. L'éditeur traduit *an-upalambha* par 'unfassbar, unbegreiflich'. La traduction 'unbegreiflich' ne nous paraît guère acceptable car *an-upalambha* signifie 'ce qui est sans point d'appui'. 'Ungreifbar' aurait été préférable. Pour ce mot l'éditeur aurait pu citer les *Materials* de Conze qui cite de nombreux passages pour *an-upalambha*. S.v. *ajātaniryāta* l'éditeur traduit *a-niryāta* par 'nicht hinausgelangt (= vergangen?)' et renvoie à Waldschmidt, SHT T.III, S.269. Dans une note M. Waldschmidt renvoie à Edgerton s.v. *niryāta* et *niryāna*. Edgerton remarque que *niryāta* 'seems blended or confused in BHS with *nirjāta*'. Dans ce cas aussi il aurait été utile de renvoyer aux *Materials* de Conze qui s.v. *nirjāta* et s.v. *niryāta* cite de nombreux textes ainsi que les traductions tibétaines. Les matériaux, réunis par M. Conze, confirment pleinement la confusion entre *nirjāta* et *niryāta* sur laquelle Edgerton avaitattiré l'attention.

Les fautes d'impression sont extrêmement rares. Nous n'en avons rencontré que deux: p. 4b sub *a-kṛtānudharman*. Pour J.B. Horner lire I.B. Horner; p. 78b sub *antarākathā-samudāhāra* NidSa 22.18 *yāvad evābhūdaāyuṣmato*, lire ... *evābhūd āyuṣmato*.

Les remarques faites ci-dessus n'ont nullement l'intention de diminuer les mérites de ce dictionnaire. Il s'agit de points de détail sur lesquels on peut différer d'opinion. Ce

[2] Cf. PW s.v. *antar* 2) praep. a) mit folg. oder vorang. loc.: 'In dieser Verbindung met dem loc. ist *antar* streng genommen noch adv., das als nähere Bestimmung des vieldeutigen loc. auftritt'. CPD s.v. *anto* 2 c: 'forming adverbial compounds with nouns, generally in abl.'.

dictionnaire rendra des services éminents aux etudes bouddhiques par le soin avec lequel l'éditeur et ses collaborateurs ont réuni les matériaux et ont rédigé les articles. C'est un ouvrage dont l'importance ne peut être comparé qu'avec celle du Critical Pāli Dictionary et du Buddhist Hybrid Sanskrit Dictionary.[3] Les indianistes qui travaillent dans d'autres domaines de l'indianisme peuvent à bon droit envier aux spécialistes du bouddhisme ces magnifiques instruments de travail.

Australian National University J. W. DE JONG

John Brough, *The Gāndhārī Dharmapada. Edited with an Introduction and Commentary* (= *London Oriental Series*, vol. 7). London, 1962. xxvi + 319 pp., 24 pl. £ 5.5s.

En 1892 des fragments d'un manuscrit kharoṣṭhī, sur écorce de bouleau, furent acquis à Khotan par Dutreuil de Rhins et Grenard, d'une part, et par N. Th. Petrovskij, d'autre part. Cinq ans plus tard, ces fragments furent confiés à Senart et à Oldenburg qui ne tardèrent pas à voir qu'ils faisaient partie d'une recension prākrite du *Dhammapada*. Déjà en 1898, Senart publia le texte de tous les fragments, obtenus par Dutreuil de Rhins et Grenard, dans le *Journal Asiatique* (1898, II, pp. 193-308, 545-548). A titre de spécimen, Oldenburg publia en 1897 un des fragments, acquis par Petrosvkij, mais l'édition complète qu'il y annonça ne vit jamais le jour. Même ce fragment, publié dans une édition à tirage restreint, resta pratiquement inconnu jusqu'en 1943 quand Sten Konow en publia une nouvelle édition (*Acta Or.*, 19, 1943, pp. 7-20). C'est ainsi que, pendant longtemps, l'étude du *Dharmapada* prākrit reposait surtout sur la publication de Senart.

L'ouvrage de M. John Brough contient une édition de tous les fragments du manuscrit qui se trouvent à Leningrad et à Paris. Soixante-dix ans après la découverte du manuscrit, tous les fragments sont enfin réunis et édités dans une seule publication. L'édition du texte n'est qu'une partie de cet ouvrage. On y trouvera également une longue introduction (pp. 1-118) et un commentaire détaillé (pp. 177-282) qui sont d'une grande importance non seulement pour l'étude du texte mais aussi pour celle du bouddhisme, du prākrit et de la paléographie. Pour plusieurs raisons ce manuscrit mérite d'être étudié. Comme le dit l'auteur: "It [le Ms.] has generally been accepted to be the oldest manuscript now extant of any Indian text. It is the only literary text known which is written in the Kharoṣṭhī script, in the north-western dialect of the Gāndhāra region, the only Buddhist text (apart from a few minute fragments quoted in inscriptions and among the Niya documents) in this language – indeed, the only Buddhist text from the earlier period which has survived in any Indian language other than Pali and Sanskrit" (p. 1).

L'introduction comprend deux parties. La première qui s'intitule "The manuscript and

---

XII (Tokyo, 1964), pp. 158–161. M. Hirano a comparé la plupart des inscriptions, citées ci-dessus, avec le *Nidānasaṃyukta* et le *Tsa a-han king*. Il y rectifie aussi l'identification erronée d'un texte qui traite des deux aspects *anuloma* et *pratiloma* du *pratītyasamutpāda*, en les désignant par les termes *ācaya* et *apacaya* (cf. "A propos du Nidānasaṃyukta", n. 8). Les éditeurs du *Taishō shinshū daizōkyō* l'avaient identifié au sūtra 298 du *Tsa a-han king* (cf. vol. 2, p. 85, n. 3). M. Yamada Ryūjō a accepté cette identification (*Bonbun butten no shobunken*, Kyoto, 1959, p. 43). M. Hirano montre que ce texte est identique au sūtra 358 du *Tsa a-han king* (*T.* II, p. 100a12-19). A ce texte appartient probablement un fragment publié par M. Ernst Waldschmidt (*Sanskrithandschriften aus den Turfanfunden*, Teil I, Wiesbaden, 1965, No. 152f).

the text" est divisée en six sections: I. "Discovery of the manuscript and publication" raconte la découverte du manuscrit et énumère les publications qui s'y rapportent. L'auteur y souligne la grande valeur des travaux de Senart, Lüders, Franke, Konow et Bailey et le peu de mérite du livre de Barua et Mitra. II. "Extant parts and their arrangement" est consacrée à l'examen de l'arrangement des fragments conservés et à une estimation du nombre des chapitres et des stances du texte complet. L'auteur y arrive aux résultats suivants. Le texte a dû comprendre 26 chapitres et environ 540 stances dont 350 sont conservées. Les titres des treize premiers chapitres sont donnés par une stance *uddāna* mais ceux des autres chapitres doivent être déduits du contenu en tenant compte des titres des chapitres des recensions pālie et sanskrite. III. "General relationships with the Pali *Dhammapada* and the Udānavarga" examine les relations de la recension prākrite avec le *Dhammapada* pāli et l'*Udānavarga*. L'auteur montre que la recension prākrite est plus proche de la recension pālie qui a 423 stances que de l'*Udānavarga* qui en a presque 1000 et que les trois recensions ont environ 330 à 340 stances en commun. En ce qui concerne les titres des chapitres (26 dans les recensions pālie et prākrite, 33 dans l'*Udānavarga*), 16 sont identiques dans les trois recensions, 7 dans deux recensions alors que 17 ne se trouvent que dans une seule recension. Malgré le fait que les trois recensions ont beaucoup en commun, l'ordre des chapitres et des stances diffère trop d'une recension à l'autre pour que l'on puisse reconstruire un *Dharmapada* primitif. Selon l'auteur, au moment où les écoles ont commencé à établir leurs canons, elles ont dû avoir gardé la tradition d'un *Dharmapada* qui devait être inclus dans le canon. Quant aux stances communes aux trois recensions on ne peut pas prouver que l'une des trois recensions les ait conservées plus fidèlement que les autres. L'auteur attribue les différences entre les recensions pour une grande partie à une tradition orale nonchalante mais relève aussi le fait que le texte prākrit montre des traces d'une transmission par manuscrit. Il y a peut-être parmi les exemples, cités par l'auteur à l'appui de la thèse d'une transmission écrite, plusieurs qui pourraient aussi provenir des erreurs de la tradition orale – quiconque a entendu des enfants réciter des poèmes sait comme le résultat peut être surprenant et ceci dit sans vouloir assimiler des moines bouddhistes à des enfants européens! – mais, pris dans l'ensemble, ils justifient pleinement la conclusion de M. J.B.[1]

Une fois les différentes recensions établies, le texte ne reste pas inchangé comme le prouve l'*Udānavarga* dont il existe une recension plus proche des recensions pālie et prākrite – celle éditée par Chakravarti sur la base d'un manuscrit sur bois –, et une autre dont le sanskrit est plus correct.[2] La traduction tibétaine s'accorde tantôt avec l'une tantôt avec l'autre recension et quelquefois elle diffère des deux. On en trouvera plusieurs exemples dans le commentaire. Après la publication des fragments sanskrits par MM. Franz Bernhard et Bernard Pauly[3] il sera possible d'étudier de manière

[1] L'hypothèse d'une transmission par écrit à une époque assez reculée n'est peut-être pas tellement à l'encontre de l'opinion courante comme le suppose l'auteur page 218 (cf. J. Filliozat, *T'oung Pao*, XLIII, 1954, pp. 150-151; Heinz Bechert, *Bruchstücke buddhistischer Verssammlungen aus zentralasiatischen Sanskrithandschriften*, I, Berlin, 1961, pp. 41-42).

[2] Ajoutons qu'aussi les manuscrits de Berlin contiennent des recensions différentes, cf. R. Pischel, *SPAW*, 1908, p. 971.

[3] M. Bernard Pauly a publié 25 feuillets d'un manuscrit sanskrit de l'*Udānavarga* (*JA*, 1960, pp. 213-258; corrigé et réimprimé avec les fac-similés des 25 feuillets dans la collection *Manuscrits de Haute Asie conservés à la Bibliothèque Nationale*, fasc. IX, Paris, 1962) et une édition du 33e varga, le *Brāhmaṇavarga* (*JA*, 1961, pp. 333-410). M. Franz Bernhard vient de publier une édition de l'*Udānavarga* basée sur les manuscrits de Berlin, Londres et Paris: *Udānavarga*, Band I: *Einleitung, Beschreibung der Handschriften, Textausgabe, Bibliographie* (= *Sanskrittexte aus den Turfanfunden*, X, *Abh. d. Ak. d. Wiss. in Göttingen, phil.-hist. Kl.*, Dritte Folge, Nr. 54) (Göttingen, 1965).

systématique les différences entre les recensions sanskrites de l'*Udānavarga* et les traductions chinoises et tibétaine. IV. "Other Dharmapada texts" donne un aperçu des autres recensions du *Dharmapada*: l'*Udānavarga*, le *Dharmapada* cité dans le *Mahāvastu* et les quatre traductions chinoises. A propos du *Fa-kiu king* dont le noyau central correspond au *Dhammapada* pāli l'auteur donne quelques précisions sur les sources des autres parties.[4] L'auteur remarque que la préface du *Tch'ou-yao king* attribue la compilation de l'*Udānavarga* à Dharmatrāta mais qu'il n'est pas mentionné dans un passage du *Mahāprajñāpāramitāśāstra*.[5] Toutefois, déjà dans un passage de la *Mahāvibhāṣā* traduit par La Vallée Poussin (*Abhidharmakośa*, Introduction, Paris-Louvain, 1931, p. XXXII) et Lin Li-Kouang (*L'aide-mémoire de la vraie loi*, Paris, 1949, p. 314, n. 1), la compilation lui est attribuée. Lin Li-Kouang qui a longuement examiné le problème que pose l'existence de plusieurs *Dharmatrāta* (*op. cit.*, pp. 314-351), est d'opinion que le compilateur de l'*Udānavarga* est identique au Dharmatrāta de la *Mahāvibhāṣā*, un maître de l'école Dārṣṭāntika, branche dissidente de l'école Sarvāstivādin (pp. 332, 351). Indépendamment de lui, M. Mizuno est arrivé à la même conclusion (*op. cit.*, pp. 7-8).

Dans V. "Affiliation of the Gāndhārī Text" l'auteur étudie le problème à quelle école le *Dharmapada* prākrit peut être attribué. Il est d'opinion que l'existence de ce *Dharmapada* implique l'existence d'un canon qui n'est pas nécessairement rédigé entièrement en Gāndhārī. Le *Dharmapada* prākrit pourrait appartenir aux Dharmaguptaka ou aux Kāśyapīya qui, tous les deux, sont mentionnés dans les inscriptions en kharoṣṭhī du Nord-Ouest de l'Inde. En faveur des Dharmaguptaka on peut citer le fait que, d'après le *Vinaya* de cette école (*Taishō*, vol. XXII, p. 869b), ils avaient un *Kṣudrakapiṭaka* comprenant un *Dharmapada* (cf. Mizuno, *op. cit.*, p. 16, n. 2; Ét. Lamotte, *Histoire du Bouddhisme indien*, I, Louvain, 1958, p. 176). D'autres textes qui, probablement, appartiennent aussi à l'école des *Dharmaguptaka* mentionnent également un *Dharmapada*.[6] Un passage intéressant qui se trouve dans le *Vinaya* des Mulasarvāstivādin et les deux versions de l'*Aśokāvadāna* montre qu'un *Dharmapada* prākrit ou un *Dharmapada* traduit du prākrit en sanskrit était connu aux auteurs de ces ouvrages. L'auteur prouve que, très probablement, ce passage se réfère au *Dharmapada* gāndhārī.

Le gāndhārī est une langue moyen-indienne du Nord-Ouest de l'Inde. Le *Dharmapada*

[4] On trouvera des renseignements utiles sur les traductions chinoises du *Dharmapada* dans un article de Mizuno Kōgen, "Udāna to Hokku", *Komazawa daigaku gakuhō*, fukkan, 2, 1953, pp. 3-24.

[5] *Mahāprajñāpāramitopadeśa* est le titre le plus ancien, cf. P. Demiéville, *JA*, 1950, p. 375; Ét. Lamotte, *Histoire du Buddhisme indien*, I (Louvain, 1958), p. 841.

[6] Cf. le *Pie-yi tsa-a-han king* (*Taishō*, vol. II, p. 480c; Lamotte, *op. cit.*, p. 177). D'après Mizuno (*op. cit.*, p. 15) c'est probablement un texte de l'école Dharmaguptaka. Akanuma Chizen (*Bukkyō Kyōten shiron*, Nagoya, 1939, p. 49) opte pour l'école Kāśyapīya. Le *P'i-ni-mou king* (*Taishō*, vol. XXIV, p. 818a) mentionne aussi un *Dharmapada*. Depuis Przyluski (*Le Concile de Rājagṛha*, Paris, 1926-8, p. 316) beaucoup de savants l'attribuent à l'école Haimavata (cf., en dernier lieu, Kanakura Enshō, *Nihon Bukkyō gakkai nenpō*, XXV, 1959, pp. 129 sq.). Toutefois, Akanuma a attiré l'attention sur les ressemblances de ce texte avec le *Vinaya* des Dharmaguptaka (*op. cit.*, p. 26). La théorie de Przyluski repose sur une phrase du texte (p. 819a29-bl) qu'il traduit ainsi: "C'est ainsi que, (d'après l'École) des 'Montagnes Neigeuses' (Haimavata), les Corbeilles de la Loi ont été rassemblées par les cinq cents *bhikṣu*." C'est une traduction tendancieuse car le texte dit simplement: "C'est ainsi que, dans les montagnes neigeuses, les Corbeilles de la Loi ont été rassemblées par les cinq cents moines." Hirakawa Akira, enfin, préfère ne pas prendre parti mais promet de revenir plus tard sur cette question (*Ritsuzō no kenkyū*, Tokyo, 1960, p. 264).

prākrit est le seul texte écrit dans cette langue. C'est H. W. Bailey qui a proposé le nom de gāndhārī pour la désigner (*BSOAS*, XI, 1946, pp. 764-797). Une des sources les plus intéressantes pour la connaissance du gāndhārī est la version chinoise du *Dīrghāgama* qui se rattache à l'école Dharmaguptaka.[7] A la suite de H. W. Bailey l'auteur étudie le texte prākrit à la base de la version chinoise dans VI. "The Gāndhārī Language". Il arrive à la conclusion que "the original of these *Dīrghāgama* transcriptions was fundamentally the same language as that of the Dharmapada".[8] Cette conclusion montre l'importance de l'étude des transcriptions chinoises pour la connaissance du gāndhārī. Une étude systématique de ces transcriptions pourrait livrer des résultats intéressants. Le *Dīrghāgama* et le *Vinaya* des Dharmaguptaka sont des textes étendus qui offrent assez de matériaux à cet égard.

La deuxième partie de l'introduction est consacrée à l'étude de la paléographie et de la grammaire du texte. Avec raison, l'auteur remarque que la paléographie du kharoṣṭhī n'est pas encore née si l'on comprend paléographie dans le sens qu'on donne à ce mot par rapport à des documents européens. Son travail est sans aucun doute une contribution de première valeur à la création d'une telle paléographie. L'étude de la grammaire s'occupe surtout de la phonétique de la langue du texte qui est analysée de manière pénétrante.

L'édition du texte donne pour chaque stance le texte des parallèles pālis et des références aux stances de l'*Udānavarga* (pp. 119-175). L'édition du texte est suivie d'un commentaire étendu qui contient une foule d'observations aussi bien sur le texte gāndhārī que sur les parallèles pālis, sanskrits et tibétains (pp. 177-282). Quelque fois même, l'auteur cite les traductions chinoises. On ose espérer qu'il a réservé leur étude pour une autre publication. Le livre se termine par des concordances (I. Manuscript lines to verses: II. Pali Dhammapada; III. Udānavarga) et des index (I. Dharmapada; II. Index of words cited: III. Index of parallel gāthās).

Les concordances II et III permettent de voir quelles stances du *Dhammapada* pāli et de l'*Udānavarga* se retrouvent dans le texte gāndhārī.[9] L'index du *Dharmapada*

[7] L'appartenance du *Dīrghāgama* à l'école des Dharmaguptaka a été reconnu déjà en 1914 par Shiio Benkyō et a été accepté par la presque totalité des savants qui se sont occupés de cette question à l'exception de F. Weller et Ishikawa Kaijō. Pour des références à la littérature on peut renvoyer à Ét. Lamotte, *Le traité de la grande vertu de sagesse*, II (Louvain, 1949), p. 811, n. 1, P. Demiéville, *T'oung Pao*, XL (1951), p. 253, n. 1 et Maeda Egaku, *Genshi Bukkyō seiten no seiritshu-shi kenkyū* (Tokyo, 1964), p. 635, n. 2 et n. 3.

[8] Hiän-lin Dschi était arrivé à la même conclusion, cf. "Die Umwandlung der Endung *-aṃ* in *-o* und *-u* im Mittelindischen", *NGAW*, *Phil.-hist. Klasse*, 1944, pp. 142-144. Comme particularités de la langue du *Dīrghāgama* il relève la conservation du *r* après dentale et l'existence des trois sifflantes.

[9] Depuis W. W. Rockhill (*Udānavarga*, London, 1883, pp. 217 sq.) plusieurs concordances ont paru. Récemment M. Maeda Egaku (*op. cit.*, p. 746, n. 44) a souligné la nécessité d'une concordance des stances de toutes les recensions du *Dharmapada* et a énuméré les travaux partiels qui ont été faits pour telle ou telle recension. Il faut y ajouter l'article de L. de La Vallée Poussin, "Essai d'identification des *gāthās* et des *udānas* en prose de l'Udānavarga de Dharmatrāta", *JA*, 1912, I, pp. 311-330, et la publication récente de l'*Udānavarga* par M. Franz Bernhard (un deuxième volume contiendra des tableaux synoptiques et des concordances). Rappelons à ce propos que R. O. Franke avait entrepris la compilation de concordances des stances du canon pāli. Il a publié des concordances des stances du *Dīghanikāya*, du *Vinayapiṭaka*, du *Majjhimanikāya* et du *Suttanipāta* (voir les références données par F. Bernhard, *op. cit.*, pp. 520-521) et a laissé des matériaux considérables pour une concordance complète des stances pālies. Il est à craindre que ces matériaux se soient perdus pendant la guerre.

contient tous les mots du texte avec les équivalents pālis et sanskrits et des références aux numéros des stances et aux paragraphes de la deuxième partie de l'introduction. C'est un travail de précision qui rendra de grands services. Les fragments du texte sont reproduits sur 24 planches dont la clarté ne laisse rien à désirer—

L'ouvrage de M. John Brough est une mine inépuisable de richesses. Qu'il s'agit de problèmes paléographiques, linguistiques ou philologiques, la perspicacité et le savoir de l'auteur ne font jamais défaut. Pour le *Dharmapada* gāndhārī et toutes les questions qui s'y rattachent on ne s'adressera jamais à ce travail sans en tirer grand bénéfice.

A.N.U., Canberra J. W. de Jong

J. W. DE JONG

THE MAGIC WALL OF THE FORTRESS OF THE OGRESSES: APROPOS OF *āsīyati* (MAHĀVASTU III, 86.3)

The *Mahāvastu* contains two versions of the story of the 500 merchants and the island of the ogresses, one in prose (ed. Senart, III, 67.17-77.7) and the other in verse (*ibid.*, 77.8-90.10). The story tells how 500 merchants after having been shipwrecked reach the island of the Rākṣasīs who receive them very well, but warn them not to go along the way to the south. The leader of the group disobeys this order and discovers an iron city encircled by a copper wall: *ayomayaṃ nagaraṃ tāmraprākāraparikṣiptaṃ* (71.9). Climbing an acacia tree, he talks with the men inside who tell him that 250 of them and their children were eaten by the Rākṣasīs: *asmākaṃ paṃcānāṃ vāṇijaka-śatānāṃ aḍḍhātiyā vāṇijakaśatā ākhāyitā ye py asmākaṃ mūlāto dārakā jātā te pi sānaṃ khāyitā.* (72.11-13). J. J. Jones (*The Mahāvastu*, III, London, 1956, 76) translates: "Of our five hundred merchants two hundred and fifty, and those the younger ones among us, were devoured." However, the text says clearly that not only 250 of the 500 merchants were devoured but "also the children who were born from us". The metrical version has the following verses:

vāṇijānāṃ śatā paṃca ye sma etāhi uddhṛtā /
tato aḍḍhātiyā ettha avaśeṣā tu khāyitā //
ye pi maṃ putrakā āsi bālakā maṃjubhāṇino /
te pi khāyitā etāhi rasagṛddhāhi māriṣa // (84.16-19).

Jones' translation is as follows (*op. cit.*, 88):

"There were five hundred of us merchants who were rescued by them. Here are now but two hundred and fifty; the rest have been devoured.

Those of us who were sons, young and soft-voiced, have been devoured by these voracious women, my friend."

The translation of the second verse should be changed to: "Also our young and soft-voiced children have been devoured by these voracious women, my friend."

The merchants who have been spared by the ogresses tell the leader of the group that he must wait for the arrival of the king of horses, Keśin (called Valāha in the metrical version), who will carry him and the other merchants through the air to safety. At this point in the story the metrical version contains the following passage:

etha māriṣa yuṣme pi upetha hayasāhvayaṃ /
āyasaṃ nagaraṃ tāmraṃ laṃgetha rākṣasīpuraṃ /
86.1 *atha khanatha heṣṭhāto tato gaṃsatha svastinā* //
hanta mārṣa na jānāsi laṃghayante pi varddhati /
āsīyati khanante pi dṛḍhaṃ tāmramayaṃ puraṃ // (85.19-86.3)

The difficult word in this passage is *āsīyati*. Edgerton's *Buddhist Hybrid Sanskrit Dictionary* (New Haven, 1953, 111a) has the following entry: "*āsīyati* Mv iii. 86.3 (vs), apparently 3 sg. pass. of ās, impersonal, *it is sat, one sits*; but the passage is obscure to me." Jones translates the passage as follows (p. 89):

"The leader of the merchants said: 'Come, my friends, do you, too, repair to this horse of renown. Leap out of this iron stronghold, this gloomy fortress of the Sirens. Or else dig beneath it and escape to safety.'

'Ah, friend,' said they, 'you do not know that this coppery fort of the Sirens is too high to leap over and too firmly founded to dig beneath it.'"

Jones adds in a note (p. 89, n. 3) that *langhayante pi varddhati* means literally "is large (or high) when one leaps". Apropos of *āsīyati* he remarks: "*Asīyati*, from *ā* + *sī* (= *śī*). Cf. Pali *āsīyati*, and see *P.E.D.*, which prefers this derivation to Trenckner's *ā* + *śyā*, and cites *Miln.* 75, where it is said of the lotus *udake āsīyati*, 'is supported in the water'. Edgerton (*B.H.S.D.*) explains it as 3rd sg. pass. impersonal of *ās*, 'to sit' (p. 89, n. 4)." Neither Edgerton nor Jones gives an acceptable interpretation of *āsīyati*. Edgerton's explanation of *āsīyati* as 3 sg. pass. of *ās-* makes the passage incomprehensible. Jones' reference to Pāli *āsīyati* is not very helpful because the etymology and the meaning of this word, which seems to occur only once in the *Milindapañha* (p. 75: *kaddame jāyati, udake āsīyati*), are not clear as is evident from the various explanations quoted by the P.T.S. dictionary. Even if one assumes that the meaning given by the P.T.S. dictionary "to have one's home, one's abode or support in (loc.), to live in, thrive by means of, to depend on" applies both to Pali *āsīyati* and to BHSD *āsīyati*, it does not fit very well the above passage. This is obvious from the fact that Jones' literal translation of *varddhati* ("is large or high") and his rendering of *āsīyati* ("is too firmly founded") are clearly rather desperate attempts to obtain a satisfactory meaning of this passage. For this reason I propose a very small amendation, i.e. to change *āsīyati* into *osīyati* = Skt. *avasīdati*, Pāli *osīdati*. According to Edgerton's *Buddhist Hybrid Sanskrit Grammar*, §2.32, we find (rarely) *y* for an intervocalic stop (see also §32.23 for *khāyi* 'ate', based on a Prakritic **khāyati* = Skt. *khādati*; it occurs in *Mahāvastu* iii, 299.11 in a verse). With the reading *osīyati* in 86.3 the translation of this passage (86.2-3) presents no difficulties: "Ah, friend, you do not know that this solid coppery fortress increases when one leaps, but sinks down when one digs." Although the text speaks of the fortress (*puraṃ*) which increases and sinks down, it is of course only its wall which moves up and down.

In the prose version there is no word corresponding to *āsīyati*. When the leader of the newly arrived merchants says to the imprisoned merchants, "Leap over the walls of the stronghold, or else dig beneath them", they answer: "You do not know what the stronghold of the Sirens is like. We cannot leap out of it" (73.7-8; Jones, *op. cit.*, 76-77). This version does not explain why it is impossible to leap over the wall or to dig beneath it. Many parallel versions of the story of the ogresses are to be found in Buddhist literature. It is not necessary to enumerate here all these versions as it will be sufficient to indicate parallel passages in those versions in which the imprisoned merchants explain the impossibility of escaping from the fortress. In the version contained in the *Madhyamāgama* the imprisoned merchants reply: "Sir. We thought: 'Let us together make a hole in this wall and return to our country.' When we conceived this idea, this wall became twice as high as usual" (T. 26, ch. 34; I, 643 c 21-23). Another version is found in the *Fo pen hsing chi ching*, which was partially translated by Samuel Beal under the title *The Romantic Legend of Sâkya Buddha* (London, 1875).[1] It is well known that this text is closely related to the *Mahāvastu*. In this version the merchants reply: "When we intend to climb the wall, then the wall becomes longer. When we dig the earth and wish to escape, then the hole is closed again" (T. 190, ch. 49; III, 881 a 25-26). The story of the ogresses is alluded to in two verses of the *Udānavarga*, ch. XXI *Tathāgatavarga*, verses 14-15 (Franz Bernhard, *Udānavarga*, Göttingen, 1965, 282). The whole story is told in the prose commentary of the Chinese translation of the *Udānavarga* the *Ch'u-yao ching*. Here the imprisoned merchants say: "When we conceive the plan to return to Jambudvīpa, this iron wall becomes several times as thick and cannot be destroyed" (T. 212, ch. 21; IV, 719 b 8-10). Éd. Huber pointed out that the story of the ogresses occurs also in the Chinese translation of the *Vinayavibhaṅga* of the *Mūlasarvāstivādavinaya*. The compiler of the *Divyāvadāna* took the beginning of the story from the *Mūlasarvāstivādavinaya* and referred for the remaining part to the *Rākṣasīsūtra* (*Divyāvadāna* 524.19-20). This part is to be found in the Chinese translation of the *Vinayavibhaṅga* (T. 1442, ch. 47-48; XXIII, 888 a 4-889 c 19) and was summarized by Huber ("Études de littérature bouddhique", *BEFEO*, VI, 1906, 23). In this version the answer of the imprisoned merchants is more detailed than in the other versions (XXIII, 888 c 10-14). In the Tibetan translation of the *Vinayavibhaṅga* the text of this passage is as follows:

bzod-ldan kho-bo-cag-la ni gaṅ-gis bde-legs daṅ / bde-ba dag-tu 'dzam-bu'i (176b) gliṅ-du phyin-par 'gyur-ba'i thabs 'ga'-yaṅ med-do // de ci'i-phyir źe-na / bdag-cag-gis gal-te 'di-sñam-du kye-ma bdag-cag lcags-kyi groṅ-khyer 'di'i-'og brtol-te 'bros-so sñam-na / de-'og ñis-gyur sum-gyur-du skye-la / gal-te 'di-sñam-du kye-ma bdag-cag lcags-kyi groṅ-khyer 'di'i-steṅ-na rgal-te 'bros-so sñam-an / de'i-steṅ ñis-gyur sum-gyur-du skye-ba'i phyir-te / (Peking ed., Vol. Te, f. 167 a 8-167 b 2).

"Sir. We have no means whatsoever to arrive safely and easily in Jambudvīpa.

[1] The story of the ogresses is to be found on pp. 332-340 of Beal's translation; cf. C. Regamey, "Le Pseudo-Hapax *ratikara* et la lampe qui rit dans le «Sūtra des ogresses» bouddhique", *Etudes Asiatiques*, XVIII/XIX (1965), 179, n. 8. Beal's translation is not at my disposal.

Why? Because, if we think: 'Let us make a hole under [the wall of] this iron city and escape', then it becomes twice or thrice [as thick] and if we think: 'Let us climb over [the wall of] the iron city and escape', then it becomes twice or thrice [as high]."

The story of the ogresses also occurs elsewhere in the *Mūlasarvāstivādavinaya*, namely in the *Bhaiṣayjavastu*. The Chinese translation does not give the full text, but contains only a reference to the *Madhyamāgama* (T. 1448, ch. 15; XXIV, 69 b 7-9). However, the Tibetan translation gives the entire story. In this version the text of the reply of the imprisoned merchants is as follows:

kye naṅ-rje re-śig bdag-cag gaṅ-gis-na legs-pa daṅ / bde-bar 'dzam-bu'i gliṅ-du phyin-par 'gyur-ba'i thabs ni cuṅ-zad kho-bo-cag-la med-de / de ci'i-phyir źe-na / gal-te bdag-cag-gis 'di-sñam-du bdag-cag-gis lcags-kyi mkhar 'di-las rgal-te 'bros-so sñam-du bsams-na / de'i ñis-gyur ram de'i sum-gyur-gyis mthon-por 'gyur-ro // gal-te bdag-cag-gis 'di-sñam-du kye-ma bdag-cag-gis lcags-kyi mkhar 'di'i-glo phug-ste 'bros-so sñam-du bsams-na / de'i ñis-gyur ram / de'i sum-gyur gyis źeṅ-du skye-bar 'gyur-te / de-ltar re-śig bdag-cag legs-pa daṅ / bde-bar 'dzam-bu'i gliṅ-du phyin-par 'gyur-ba'i thabs bdag-cag la med-do // (Peking ed., Vol. Ge, f. 222 a 2-5).

"Oh, Sir. We have no means whatsoever to arrive safely and easily in Jambudvīpa. Why? If we think: 'Let us climb over the wall of this iron fortress and escape', then it becomes twice or thrice as high. If we think: 'Let us make a hole in the side of this iron fortress and escape', then it becomes twice or thrice as wide. Thus we have no means to arrive safely and easily in Jambudvīpa."

In all these versions of the story of the ogresses the impossibility of escaping from the fortress of the ogresses is explained by the fact that whenever the imprisoned merchants try to do so, the wall changes magically and makes escape impossible. The way in which the wall is transformed differs according to the versions. It is clear, however, that the theme of the magical transformation of the wall is common to these versions of the story of the ogresses. The fact that this theme so frequently recurs supports the emendation which has been proposed for *āsīyati*. As is well known, the text of the *Mahāvastu* is very corrupt and in spite of the efforts of Senart and Edgerton to establish a better text, many passages are still incomprehensible. There is always an element of the hypothetical in text emendations. As regards Buddhist Sanskrit texts corroborative evidence can often be obtained from Tibetan and Chinese translations. With the *Mahāvastu*, however, the only help to be found is from parallels which, fortunately, can, in many instances, be adduced.

CANBERRA

J.W. DE JONG

NOTES ON THE *BHIKṢUṆĪ-VINAYA* OF THE MAHĀSĀṂGHIKAS

In 1932 Sylvain Lévi published one leaf of the Vinaya of the Mahāsāṃghikas which had been found by Hackin in Bāmiyān in 1930.[1] In 1934 Rāhula Sāṅkṛtyāyana photographed in the Źva-lu Ri-phug monastery[2] many leaves of manuscripts belonging to the Mahāsāṃghika Vinaya. The Chinese Tripiṭaka contains the following Vinaya texts of the Mahāsāṃghikas: Taishō no. 1425 Mahāsāṃghika Vinaya (vol. XXII, pp. 227-549a); no. 1426 *Bhikṣu-prātimokṣa-sūtra* (pp. 549a-556a); no. 1427 *Bhikṣuṇī-prātimokṣa-sūtra* (pp. 556a-566). The Vinaya consists of the following sections: (a) *Bhikṣu-prātimokṣa-vibhaṅga* (pp. 227a-412b); (b) *Bhikṣu-prakīrṇaka-vinaya* (pp. 412b-499a); (c) *Bhikṣu-abhisamācārika-dharma-s* (pp. 499a-514a); (d) *Bhikṣuṇī-prātimokṣa-vibhaṅga* (pp. 514a-544c); (e) *Bhikṣuṇī-prakīrṇaka* (pp. 544c-549a). The texts, photographed by R. Sāṅkṛtyāyana, have been edited in three separate publications. The *Bhikṣu-prātimokṣa-sūtra* (44ff.) was published in 1956 by W. Pachow and Ramakanta Mishra.[3] The *Bhikṣu-abhisamācārika-dharma-s* (50ff.) was published in 1969 by B. Jinananda.[4] Roth's edition of the *Bhikṣuṇī-vinaya* (80ff.) includes the *Bhikṣuṇī-prakīrṇaka* and the uddānas of the *Bhikṣu-prakīrṇaka.*[5] The *Bhikṣuṇī-vinaya* consists of two parts: the Eight *guru-dharma* and the *Bhikṣuṇī-prātimokṣa-vibhaṅga.* The texts published by Roth correspond to the following sections of the Chinese version of the Mahāsāṃghika Vinaya: 1. Eight *guru-dharma* – Taishō vol. XXII, pp. 471a25-476b8; 2. *Bhikṣuṇī-prātimokṣa-vibhaṅga* – pp. 514a-544c; 3. *Bhikṣuṇī-prakīrṇaka* – pp. 544c-549a; 4. uddānas of the *Bhikṣu-prakīrṇaka* – cf. pp. 426b, 442b, 446c, 455b, 464b, 478b, 483b, 485c, 488b, 493c, 495b, 496c, 497b and 499a. In the Taishō edition the Vinaya texts of the Mahāsāṃghikas occupy 340 pages. The 174 leaves photographed by R. Sāṅkṛtyāyana correspond to 63 pages, almost one-fifth.

We must be grateful that these important texts have been published. However, the usefulness of two of the three publications is seriously diminished by the fact that the editors have been unable to reproduce the readings of the manuscript accurately. A comparison of the photocopy of f. 25a, reproduced in Pachow and Mishra's edition, with the text (pp. 21-22), shows that the editors have misread the manuscript in several places. It is to be hoped that the new edition of this text by N. Tatia, which has been announced, will be more adequate. Many sections of the *Prātimokṣasūtra* are to be found

L. Cousins et al. (eds.), Buddhist Studies in Honour of I.B. Horner, 63-70

in the notes of Roth's edition of the *Bhikṣuṇī-vinaya* (for f. 25a see Roth, pp. 187-188). Jinananda's edition of the *Abhisamācārikā* is also far from being satisfactory. Dr. Roth has kindly put at my disposal photocopies of the texts, edited by himself and Jinananda. This has enabled me to ascertain that Jinananda has often misread the manuscript. The fact that his corrections of manuscript readings cannot always be accepted is a lesser evil. For details I refer to my review of Jinananda's edition which will be published in the *Indo-Iranian Journal*. It is very regrettable that such important texts have been edited so unsatisfactorily. The publication of facsimile editions would be highly desirable.

Roth's edition of the *Bhikṣuṇī-vinaya*, on the other hand, deserves full praise. Although the photocopy of the manuscript is often difficult to decipher, Roth has spared no pains to reproduce as accurately as possible the readings of the manuscript. Abundant notes explain difficult words and expressions and contain numerous references to parallel texts. The index of words (pp. 335-403) gives exact references and greatly facilitates the study of the text. A lengthy introduction (pp. I-LXI) deals in great detail with many aspects of the text and problems connected with it. The *Bhikṣuṇī-vinaya* and the other Mahāsāṃghika Vinaya texts are written in a Prākrit which has been submitted to a process of Sanskritization. The introduction draws attention to some striking Prakritic features of the language of the text. More information on the language and the terminology is to be found in two separate articles, published by Roth in 1966 and 1968: 'Bhikṣuṇīvinaya and Bhikṣu-prakīrṇaka and Notes on the Language', *J. Bihar Res. Soc.* **LII** (1966) 29-51; 'Terminologisches aus dem Vinaya der Mahāsāṃghika-Lokottaravādin', *ZDMG* 118 (1968) 334-348.

The Chinese version of the *Bhikṣuṇī-vinaya* corresponds very closely to the Indian text. During his stay in Göttingen in 1960 Professor Hirakawa Akira translated the Chinese version of the eight *Guru-dharma*. Hirakawa is at present working on a complete translation of the Chinese version of the *Bhikṣuṇī-vinaya* which will be very helpful for the interpretation of the Indian text. Roth plans to publish a complete translation of the Indian text. These two translations will be of great importance for the study of the Vinaya in general and especially for the Mahāsāṃghika Vinaya.

As Roth points out in his introduction, the *Bhikṣuṇī-vinaya* belongs to the Vinaya of the Ārya-Mahāsāṃghika-Lokottaravādin (= Ma-L). The Chinese version belongs to the Mahāsāṃghika Vinaya. Roth remarks that the whole *Guru-Dharma* complex is placed before the *Bhikṣuṇī-prātimokṣa-vibhaṅga* whereas in the Chinese version of the Mahāsāṃghika Vinaya this section is to be found in the *Bhikṣu-prakīrṇaka-vinaya* (p. XXIX). Roth has also discovered influences of a later period in the text of the *Bhikṣuṇī-vinaya*. As an instance he refers to the use of the term *yogācārā bhikṣuṇī*. The parallel of this chinese passage (p. 541c2) does not render *yogācārā* and has only the word "good" (p. XLII). Consequently, the Ma-L *Bhikṣuṇi-vinaya* would differ from the Mahāsāṃghika *Bhikṣuṇī-vinaya* in two respects: the structure of the text and the use of terms belonging to a later period. However, these two facts do not inevitably point to such a conclusion. According to Roth's examination of the script the manuscript was written in the 11th or 12th century. A manuscript of that period does not necessarily reflect the structure of the original Ma-L *Bhikṣuṇī-vinaya*. It is quite well possible that the scribe was of the opinion that the *Bhikṣuṇī-vinaya* would be incomplete without the eight *guru-dharma*. As to the term *yogācāra*, it occurs quite often in the *Abhisamācārikā* (pp. 106.9, 107.14, 202.5, 213.3, 215.1, 217.8, 219.1). In most cases the corresponding Chinese text has "sitting in meditation" *(tso-ch'an*, Jap. *zazen)*. The Chinese version of the *Abhisamācārikā* does not correspond as closely to the Indian text as the Chinese version of the *Bhikṣuṇī-vinaya*. It seems to be often abridged and the arrangement of the sections in the fourth and fifth vargas differs. Nevertheless, a confessedly cursory perusal of the Chinese version does not show up any important divergences in terminology or in disciplinary matters. A detailed investigation would have to be undertaken but, at a first glance, it seems that the differences between the Chinese version and the Indian text of both the *Bhikṣuṇī-vinaya* and the *Abhisamācārikā* are not greater than can be expected in texts which have been transmitted in different circumstances and languages.

The Mahāsāṃghika Vinaya is of course of foremost importance for Vinaya studies. Of information on other matters two points deserve to be mentioned. The *Bhikṣuṇī-vinaya* (p. 314; Taishō XXII, p. 546c27) mentions festivals for the birth of the Buddha *(jātimahā)*, for his Awakening *(bodhimahā)*, for his Setting in motion of the Wheel of the Law *(dharmacakramahā)*, for Ānanda *(Ānandamahā)*, and for Rāhula *(Rāhulamahā)*. This probably indicates that Ānanda and Rāhula were held in high consideration by the Mahāsāṃghikas. The text also mentions the quinquennial gathering *(pañcavārṣika)*.[6]

In his *Buddhist India* (London 1902; 9th edition, Delhi, 1970, pp. 46ff.) T.W. Rhys Davids remarks that writing is mentioned in the Vinaya but that there is nowhere the least trace of any reference to books or manuscripts.[7] The *Divyāvadāna* contains a reference to ladies who at night were writing Buddhist texts on birch-bark with ink and a writing-reed (ed. by Cowell and Neil, p. 532, 9-11). The *Abhisamācārikā* not only mentions a written inventory (p. 50.10; Taishō XXII, p. 503a6) but also refers several times to *pusta-*

ka-s (p. 38.5,13 – Taishō XXII, p. 502a27, b6; p. 124.15-16 – Taishō XXII, p. 510b15). The Chinese text translates *pustaka* by *ching* which normally renders *sūtra*.

To conclude these few notes on the *Bhikṣuṇī-vinaya* I would like to draw attention to some passages where a different reading or an alternative interpretation may be suggested. All references are to page and line of Roth's edition. Reference to the Chinese version indicate page, column and line of the Taishō edition.

P. 6.8: *evam tu tāyi Bhagavato santike*. It is not possible to keep *tāyi*. Also a gen. *tāyino* is most unlikely because the word *tāyin* seems to have been used only in verses.[8] Probably one must read *tādi*, a reading mentioned as possible by Roth in his note.

P. 23.6: Roth corrects the MS reading *paribhavane* to *paribhavanena*. It would be better to read *paribhavena* as in the parallel passages mentioned in the note.

P. 52.14: *ahan tāyo ... brahmacaryāto yācayāmiti*. Read *cyāvayāmiti* for *yācayāmiti* ?

P. 61.15: *jyeṣṭha-paryāyatā karohīti*. Read *jyeṣṭha-parṣāya tāvat karohīti*. The *jyeṣṭha-parṣā* is the assembly of the monks (cf. p. 69.25). In the manuscript *ṣa* and *ya* are not easy to distinguish (cf. Roth p. 269, n. 4). In the *Bhikṣu-prātimokṣa-sūtra* (ed. by Pachow and Mishra) we find *bhikṣuparyāye* (p. 5.6) which must certainly be corrected to *bhikṣuparṣāye*. See also Roth p. 62.2, 10.

P. 81.4-6: *bhikṣuṇiyo gṛhiṇām upavasitehi vasanti / Rāṣṭrā nāma bhikṣuṇī / sā dāni aparasya Śākyasya udu-vasite vasati / sā dāni Rāṣṭrā tasya Śākiya-kumārasya uddiśati*. Roth explains *udu-vasita* as "water-residence". The Chinese translation does not mention water-residences and, as far as I know, they are not mentioned in other Vinaya texts. I believe that one must read *upavasite*. As to *uddiśati* Roth refers to a parallel passage which has *uddeśan dadāti* "gives a hint". In the Vinaya *uddesa* is used regularly as meaning 'recitation' (cf. I.B. Horner's translation, vol. V, London 1952, p. 308, n. 1). The Chinese version has "she teaches sūtras".

P. 117 verse 20c: *an-āpṛcchati vartante*. Read *anāpṛcchya nivartante*.

P. 119 verse 8: Cf. *Dhammapada* 150, *Gāndhārī Dharmapada* 284, *Udānavarga* XVI.23.

P. 138.1: *Mallā nāmā Mallakalyo nāma nigamo*. Read *Mallānām Āmallakalyo nāma nigamo*. Cf. p. 139.16 *Āmalakakalyato*.

P. 141.6: *keṣāñcit kiṭena vā kāliñjena vā veṭhayitvā dahyati*. Read *kaṭena vā kilañjena vā* ? Cf. p. 260.7.

P. 169.5: *bimboya-dhānasya*. Read *bimbopadhānasya*.

P. 170.17: *saṃghasya bhaktakāni samādāyeti.* Read *samādāpeti.*

P. 201.11: *ṛṣidhvajanena.* MS. *ṛṣidhvajena.* Cf. 201.23: *śramaṇa-cīvaran ti ṛṣi-dhvajaṃ.*

P. 204: Five devaputras have fallen in love with Bharaṇī and decide to compose verses in praise of her. The verses are introduced as follows: *yo 'tra sarva-suṣṭhu adhyavasito bhaviṣyati sa grahīṣyati.* Roth translates: "He, who will have been determined to be praised the best of all in this [in composing a verse], he will gain [Bharaṇī]". *Adhyavasita* has here the meaning "attached to, covetous" (cf. Edgerton s.v.): "He who most of all is in love with her will obtain her".

P. 214: Bhadrā cooks her own food and gives some to her nephews. The nephews find it delicious *(mṛṣṭaṃ)* and ask from where it comes. Bhadrā explains that it comes from their own house. They reply that in their house such delicious food is not cooked. This passage has been misunderstood by Roth (cf. n. 3).

P. 216, last two lines: *tāya tasya pānīya-mallakaṃ mastake āpiṭṭitaṃ.* Roth takes *āpiṭṭita* in the sense of *āpīḍita* "squeeze, press': "the water-pot was pressed upon his head by her". On p. 267, n. 6 Roth explains *pari-piṭṭita* by Pkt. *piṭṭiya, "pīṭā huā, tāḍita".* See also p.227.12: *ātmānaṃ khaṭa-capeṭa-mustakehi piṭṭāyati.* I believe that *āpiṭṭita* must have the same meaning: "the water-pot was thrown (lit. struck) at his head by her". The Chinese translation is of no help here: "she sprinkled his face with water" (p. 530a-24).

P. 221.4: *strīṇāṃ bastiṃ sthapeti / mūḍha-garbhāṃ cikitsati.* Roth explains *basti* or *vasti* as a medical barrack for the treatment of women. See, however, Jolly, *Medicin* (Strassburg, 1901), p. 26: *vasti* "Klystier, Klystierbeutel".

P. 223.22: *karmaṇy enāṃ rājā tena.* Read *karmaṇyenāṅgajātena* (cf. 269.7 and 308.5). Ibid. *parivāteti.* Read *paripāteti ?* Cf. p. 316.1-2: *so me devaro paripāteti.*

P. 224.1: Roth suggests translating *viṭṭālayati* as "to make impossible". The normal meaning "to make unclean, defile" (cf. 290.12 and 309.14) applies here.

P. 229.1: *na ca āghāta-vastūni.* Read *nava* etc.

P. 239, last line: add with MS after *pṛcchitavyā: atha dāni evaṃ pi na bhavati.*

P. 249.11: *asmākaṃ Bhagavatā daṇḍa-karma prajñaptaṃ / imā sāmoktikā.* Roth refers to Skt. Bhik. 130.22 (not 136.22), where the term *muktikā jñaptiḥ* occurs. According to him "*sāmoktikā* is a Vṛddhi-form of *samuktikā* designating a nun about whom a *sa-muktikā jñaptiḥ* has to be moved". I believe that one has to read *imāsāṃ muktikā* "but for them there is absolution". One may compare Bapat's translation of *vimokkha* in *saññāya abhāvena vimokkho* "getting absolved because of not knowing the precept" and of *mukti* in *naiva ajñānān muktiḥ* "ignorance of law is no excuse" (*Shan-Chien-P'i-P'o-Sha*, Poona, 1970, pp. LIV and 416, n. 11). The same expression occurs several times in the *Abhisamācārikā* but the manuscript readings vary greatly: p. 5.17-18: *asmākaṃ bhagavān daṇḍakarman dadāti dvitīyasthavirasya sontikā*; p. 6.2-3: *asmākaṃ bhagavāṃ daṇḍakarman deti / dvitīyasthavirasya sontikā*; p. 9.6: *asmākaṃ bhagavāṃ daṇḍakarman deti / eṣāṃ montiko*; p. 24.4-5: *asmākaṃ bhagavāṃ daṇḍakarman deti / dvitīyasthavirasya muntikā*; p. 24.14-15: *asmākaṃ bhagavān daṇḍakarma deti / dvitīyasthavirasya muttikā*; p.28.11: *asmākaṃ bhagavān daṇḍakarman deti / imeṣāṃ muktikā*; p. 29.2-3: *asmākaṃ bhagavān daṇḍakarman deti / imeṣāṃ mottikā*; p. 35.12: *asmākaṃ bhagavān daṇḍakarman deti / imeṣāṃ muktikā*; p. 41.9: *asmākaṃ bhagavā[n] daṇḍakarman deti / imeṣāṃ muktikā* (the readings are based on the manuscript and not on Jinananda's edition). It is sometimes difficult to distinguish *su* and *mu*. It seems probable that *muktikā* must be read everywhere.

P. 258.11: *anirmokāṃ*. Read with MS *upānāhāṃ anirmokāṃ*

P. 262.9: *aye hi strī*. Read *apehi strī*.

P. 263.11-14: *yadi viprakaṭā bhonti mṛttikā-karmeṇa vā iṣṭakā-karmeṇa vā / paliguddhā bhavanti vaktavyaṃ / āgametha tāvad bhaginīyo / tena te bhikṣū upasaṃkrāmitvā vaktavyāḥ / āyuṣmanto nivāsetha prāvaratha bhikṣuṇiyo praviśanti /*. Roth proposes to read *vāpaliguddhā*: "If they are not occupied one should say". I believe that one must maintain *paliguddhā* and understand: "If they are naked or if they are occupied with clay-work or with brickwork, he [i.e. the doorkeeper] must say: 'Wait a moment, sisters'. He must go to the monks and say to them: 'Sirs, be dressed, cover yourself; the nuns will enter'." The meaning "naked" for *viprakaṭa* is borne out by the Chinese version (p. 539a3) and by the words *nivāsetha prāvaratha*.

P. 277.17: *yadāvarti(ta) bhavati*. Read *yadā varti-bhavati*. Cf. Edgerton s.v. *vartti-bhavati*, p. 81.15 *(ārya evam eva vartā bhaviṣyāmi)* and p. 219.4 *(atha khu pratigupte pradeśe sthātavyaṃ yāvad varttā bhavati)*.

P. 287.6: *yatra śākhāni praveśayati*. Read *patraśākhāni*.

P. 287.8: *kim vikrīto*. Read with MS *kim mayā vikrīto*.

P. 306.5-6: *tathā prāvaritavyam yathā dāni stanāpiḍitā bhavanti*. Read *stanā piḍitā*.

P. 313.3: *stanāvaḍḍāś caṃkramantiya utpatanti*. Read *stanā vaḍḍāś* and not *stanā-āvaḍḍāś* as suggested by Roth in note 2. Both *vaḍa* and *vaḍḍa* are used as epithet of *stana*, cf. Index s.v. *vaḍa*.

P. 318.11-12: MS *na dāni kṣamati bhikṣuṇiya onaddhā varcakuṭī kārāpa-*

yituṃ. Roth corrects to *onaddha-varcakuṭiṃ*. More likely is *onaddhāṃ varcakuṭiṃ*.

P. 319.12-15: *taṃhi tadā nīyāḥ kṣiprasamāpattikāḥ / yāhi ca middham anokrāntaṃ tāḥ sratti vaihāyasam abhyudgatāḥ / yāvanta samāpattikā yāhi ca middham avakrāntaṃ tāyo kulaputrakehi gṛhya viheṭhitāḥ*. I suggest correcting *tadā nīyāh* to *tadāniṃ* (or *dāni) yāḥ* and *yāvanta samāpattikā* to *yā dandhasamāpattikā*. In Pāli texts *khippābhiññā* is opposed to *dandhābhiññā*.

P. 321.9: *saṃgho vāsati vastusmin nāśeti*. Read *vā sati*.

Australian National University,
Canberra

NOTES

1 *JA* CCXX (1932) 4-8. The text corresponds to Taishō no. 1425, vol. XXII, pp. 425c10-426a12. Roth mentions four palm-leaves (*Bhikṣuṇī-vinaya*, p. XIII) but Sylvain Lévi refers to only one leaf (notre feuillet) and does not say that it is a palm-leaf.

2 Cf. G. Roth, *Bhikṣuṇī-vinaya*, p. XIX. The Źva-lu Ri-phug hermitage is mentioned by Mkhyen-brtse who visited it in 1851, cf. Alfonsa Ferrari, *Mk'yen brtse's Guide to the Holy Places of Central Tibet*, Roma 1958, p. 60 and p. 143, n. 429.

3 *The Prātimokṣa-sūtra of the Mahāsaṅghikas*. Edited by W. Pachow and Ramakanta Mishra, Allahabad, 1956. Also published serially in the *Journal of the Ganganatha Jha Research Institute* IX (1952) 239-260, X (1952-1953), App. 1-48, XI-XII (1953-1955), 243-248.

4 *Abhisamācārikā* [Bhikṣuprakīrṇaka]. Edited by Dr. B. Jinananda. *Tibetan Sanskrit Works Series*, vol. IX. Patna, 1969.

5 *Bhikṣuṇī-vinaya* including Bhikṣuṇī-prakīrṇaka and a summary of the Bhikṣu-prakīrṇaka of the Ārya-Mahāsāṃghika-Lokottaravādin. Edited by Gustav Roth. *Tibetan Sanskrit Works Series*, volume XII. Patna, 1970.

6 For the quinquennial gathering see J. Przyluski, *La légende de l'empereur Açoka*, Paris 1923, 116-117; *Le concile de Rājagṛha*, Paris 1926-1938, 282-283; P. Pelliot in A. Godard, Y. Godard et J. Hackin, *Les Antiquités bouddhiques de Bāmiyān*, Paris 1928, 80-81; *T'oung Pao* 26 (1929) 184-185, *ibid.*, 28 (1931) 432-434; M.W. de Visser, *Ancient Buddhism in Japan*, I, Leiden 1935, 190-193; Edgerton, *Buddhist Hybrid Sanskrit Dictionary* s.v. *pañcavarṣika*; Arthur Link, 'Shi Seng-yu and his writings', *JAOS* 80 (1960) 23, n. 42; V.S. Agrawala, 'Some obscure words in the Divyāvadāna', *JAOS* 86 (1966) 73.

7 See also M. Winternitz, *A History of Indian Literature*, I, Calcutta, 1927, 32-33; J.W. de Jong, *Buddha's Word in China*, Canberra 1968, p. 8.

8 Cf. Edgerton's *Buddhist Hybrid Sanskrit Dictionary* s.v. *tāyin*. For *tāyin* and Pāli *tādin* see further E. Burnouf, *Introduction à l'histoire du Buddhisme indien*, Paris 1844, p. 227, n. 1; *Le lotus de la bonne loi*, Paris 1852, p. 337; H. Kern, *The Saddharma-puṇḍarika*, Oxford 1884, p. 25, n. 1; E. Hultzsch, 'A Buddhist Sanskrit inscription from Koṭa', *IA* 14 (1885), 46, lines 6 and 11; E. Senart, *Le Mahâvastu*, II, Paris 1890, p. 543; R. Morris, 'Notes and Queries', *JPTS* (1891-3), 53-55; Th. Zachariae, *Die indischen Wörterbücher*, Strassburg 1897, p. 24, n. 7; L. de la Vallée Poussin, *Bouddhisme, Études et matériaux*, London 1898, pp. 105 and 391; J.S. Speyer, 'Buddhas Todesjahr nach dem Avadānaśataka', *ZDMG* 53 (1899) 122-123; L. de La Vallée Poussin, *Bodhicaryāvatārapañjikā*, fasc. 1, Calcutta 1901, p. 75, n. 5; J.S. Speyer, 'Critical Remarks

on the text of the Divyāvadāna', *WZKM* **16** (1902) 349; F. Kielhorn, 'Nagpur Museum Inscription of Bhavadeva Raṇakesarin', *JRAS* (1905) 619 and 624; L. de La Vallée Poussin, *Introduction à la pratique des futurs Bouddhas*, Paris 1907, p. 18, n. 2; 'Vedānta and Buddhism', *JRAS* (1910) 139-140; Sylvain Lévi, 'L'Apramāda-varga', *JA* (1912) sept.-oct., 242-243; R. Otto Franke, *Dīghanikāya*, Göttingen-Leipzig 1913, p. 88, n. 2; E. Leumann, *Maitreya-samiti*, Strassburg 1919, p. 215; Vidhushekara Bhattacharya, 'The Gauḍapāda-kārikā on the Māṇḍukya Upaniṣad', *Proceedings and Transactions of the Second Oriental Conference*, Calcutta 1923, 449-451; Sylvain Lévi, 'Maitreya le consolateur', *Mélanges Linossier*, II, Paris 1932, 357-8; *Mahākarmavibhaṅga*, Paris 1932, p. 93.3; *Abhisamayālaṃkārāloka*, Tokyo 1932-1935, p. 37.14; *Abhidharmakośavyākhyā*, Tokyo 1932-1936, p. 374.10; L. Finot, 'Manuscrits sanskrits de sādhana's retrouvés en Chine', *JA* **CCXXV** (1934) 21; P.V. Bapat, 'Tāyin, tāyi, tādi', *D.K. Bhandarkar Volume*, Calcutta 1940, 249-258; *Samādhirājasūtra* (ed. by N. Dutt 1941-1954), pp. 28.14, 63.16, 178.17, 238.17, n. 13, 249, n. 8, 312.5, 407.15, 411.3, 416.6, 447.14, 449.9, 451.13, 613.2, cf. Murakami Shinkan, 'Samādhirājasūtra goi no kenkyū', *Hachinohe kōgyō kōtō senmon gakkō kiyō* **2** (1967) 88; Vidhushekhara Bhattacharyya, *The Āgamaśāstra of Gauḍapāda*, Calcutta, 1943, p. 212, n. 2; Lin-Li-kouang, *Dharmasamuccaya*, I, Paris 1946, pp. 82-3, n. 1; *L'aide-mémoire de la vraie loi*, Paris 1949, p. 163, n. 17; Ernst Waldschmidt, *Das Mahāparinirvāṇasūtra*, Berlin 1950-1951, pp. 190 and 400; D.R. Shackleton Bailey, *The Śatapañcāśatka of Mātṛceta*, Cambridge 1951, p. 152; J.J. Jones, *The Mahāvastu*, II, London 1952, p. 318, n. 2; III, London, 1956, p. 446, n. 5; Ernst Waldschmidt, *Das Mahāvadānasūtra*, Berlin 1943-1956, p. 72.2; Heinrich Lüders, *Beobachtungen über die Sprache des buddhistischen Urkanons*, Berlin 1954, pp. 92-94; H. Nakamura, *Vedānta tetsugaku no hatten*, Tokyo 1955, 500-501; V. Raghavan, Buddhist Sanskrit, *Indian Linguistics* **16** (1955) 320; W. Pachow and Ramakanta Mishra, *The Prātimokṣa-sūtra of the Mahāsāṅghikas*, Allahabad 1956, p. 1: buddhena lokānucareṇa tāyinā-m-udeśitaṃ prātimokṣaṃ vidunā; Jakob Wackernagel – Albert Debrunner, *Altindische Grammatik. Nachträge zu Band I*, Göttingen 1957, p. 115; Bernard Pauly, 'Fragments sanskrits de Haute Asie', *JA* **CCXLVII** (1959) 245 and 247; N.G. Narahari, 'On the Word "Tāyin" ', *Indian Linguistics* **21** (1960) 108-111; H. Bechert, *Bruchstücke buddhistischer Verssammlungen*, I, Berlin 1961, p. 84.9; John Brough, *The Gāndhārī Dharmapada*, London 1962, p. 265; L. Alsdorf, *Les études Jaina*, Paris 1965, 5-6; Akira Yuyama, Supplementary Remarks, etc., *IIJ* **IX** (1966) 100-101; Edward Conze, *Materials for a Dictionary of the Prajñāpāramitā Literature*, Tokyo 1967, p. 189; Ernst Waldschmidt, *Sanskrithandschriften aus den Turfanfunden*, II, Wiesbaden 1968, p. 26; F. Bernhard, *Udānavarga*, Band II, Göttingen 1968, p. 55b; Gustav Roth, ' "A Saint like that" and "A saviour" in Prakrit, Sanskrit, Pali and Tibetan Literature', *The Shri Mahavira Jaina Vidyalaya Golden Jubilee Volume*, Part 1, Bombay 1968, pp. 46-62.

See also the Pāli dictionaries (Childers, Kern's *Toevoegselen*, PTS), Schmidt's *Nachträge*, Wogihara's *Sanskrit-Japanese Dictionary*, Wogihara's edition of the *Mahāvyutpatti*, Tokyo 1915, part II notes p. 2, Mayrhofer's *Etymological Dictionary*.

Charles S. Prebish, *Buddhist Monastic Discipline: The Sanskrit Prātimokṣa Sūtras of the Mahāsāṃghikas and Mūlasarvāstivādins*. University Park and London, The Pennsylvania State University Press, 1975. VI, 156.

Prebish's book consists of three chapters. The first, entitled 'The Rise of Buddhist Monasticism: An Overview' describes the historical background, summarizes the contents of the Prātimokṣa-sūtra and explains what the author calls the 'Ritualization of the Prātimokṣa'. In the last section of this chapter the author begins by mentioning the etymologies of the word prātimokṣa proposed by Rhys Davids – Oldenberg, E. J. Thomas and Winternitz. The following passage deserves to be quoted: "And the derivations from *muc-* go on and on. Against this we find the evidence of the Pāli Mahāvagga, declaring Pātimokkha (the Pāli equivalent of Prātimokṣa) to be the face, the head of all good dharmas [mukhaṃ etaṃ, pamukhaṃ etaṃ kusalānaṃ dhammānaṃ]. With the exception of the Mahāvagga passage, each of our Western interpreters seems to commit one huge error in his interpretation of the term: etymological judgment was colored by the preconceived notion that Prātimokṣa, since it was a monastic code, had to be rendered accordingly" (pp. 17–18). It is difficult to understand how this Mahāvagga passage can be considered a Western interpreter. The etymology of *pātimokkha* in the Mahāvagga is of course impossible. Prebish is very much impressed by the etymological speculations of S. Dutt who explained *prātimokṣa* as something serving for a bond, the prefix *prati* meaning 'against' and the root *mokṣa* meaning 'scattering' (kṣepaṇe iti kavikalpadrumah). According to Prebish Dutt's bold statement abandoned the orthodoxy of the time. He fails to note that the meaning given to *prātimokṣa* by Dutt is not very different from the one at which E. J. Thomas arrived on the basis of a much sounder etymological explanation, i.e. 'that which binds, obligatory'. However, the boldness of Dutt seems to reside more in the fact that he assumed that the early Buddhist saṃgha had no special Vinaya of its own. According to Dutt: "very early in its history, the sect of the Buddha devised an external bond of union: it was called Pātimokkha." Prebish adheres to Dutt's views which he quotes at great length. He states that the Prātimokṣa text was flexible during its growth period and that this is attested by the inclusion of a substantial amount of late material in its final form. Prebish makes no mention of the fact that there is a very great

[13] Cf. *Ōtani Kanjur Catalogue* (Kyoto, 1930–1932), Nos. 734 and 112 (p. 36: No. 113 must be corrected into No. 112).

measure of agreement between the Prātimokṣas of the different schools. Lamotte remarked: "Chaque école bouddhique tint à dresser son propre Prātimokṣa, mais entre les diverses listes on ne constate que des différences minimes" (*Histoire du bouddhisme indien*, I, Louvain, 1958, p. 181). It is difficult to follow Prebish in his remarks on the ritualization of the Prātimokṣa and on the dates of the earliest Prātimokṣa and the Prātimokṣa in its final form. In the absence of reliable historical evidence any attempt to reconstruct the early history of the Prātimokṣa is pure speculation. In his conclusions Prebish refers to Bareau's *Les sectes bouddhiques du petit Véhicule* (Saïgon, 1955) and remarks that it is quite difficult to read Bareau without concluding that doctrinal matters were solely responsible for the sectarian movement. He quotes Banerjee on the importance of the Vinaya for the rise of the Buddhist schools. Prebish comments: "Banerjee overstates his case as severely as Bareau." This remark shows that he has very badly read Bareau's book. If he would have carefully studied the fourth chapter 'Les causes de division et les relations entre les sectes', he would not have made such a rash statement. Bareau concludes this chapter with the following words: "La division de la Communauté en de nombreuses sectes est ainsi due à des causes très diverses et complexes, que nous ne discernons pas toujours très bien, et qui ont pu varier au cours du temps."

In the second chapter Prebish describes the two texts which he has translated. He notes that Gustav Roth has pointed out editorial errors made by Pachow and Mishra in their edition of the Prātimokṣasūtra of the Mahāsāṃghikas. In his articles[1] Roth indicated only a few mistakes, but Pachow and Mishra's edition is so bad that in the notes to his edition of the Bhikṣuṇī-vinaya of the Mahāsāṃghikas (Patna, 1970) Roth was obliged to give a new edition of the many passages quoted by him from the Prātimokṣasūtra of the Mahāsāṃghikas. Roth's book seems to have remained entirely unknown to Prebish.

A translation of the Prātimokṣasūtra of the Mahāsāṃghikas will only be possible on the basis of a good critical edition of the text and by making use of the Chinese translation. A new edition by Dr. N. Tatia has been announced on the dust-cover of Roth's book.

Roth's articles have at least served to warn Prebish against putting too much confidence in the reliability of Pachow and Mishra's edition. However, he does not express any doubts as to the reliability of Anukul (spelled Ankul by Prebish throughout his book) Chandra Banerjee's edition of the Prātimokṣasūtra of the Mūlasarvāstivādin. Prebish remarks: "Banerjee's training and experience attest to his proficiency in working with Sanskrit materials. At the time of the publication of his manuscript, he was Lecturer in Pāli and Sanskrit at Calcutta University. In 1949 he edited 'Bhikṣukarmavākya', a manuscript also included in the Gilgit collection, affording him an opportunity to examine both the general character of the Gilgit Sanskrit manuscript and the style of the Mūlasarvāstivādin Vinaya texts." It is difficult to refrain from exclaiming 'Sancta simplicitas'. The quality of Banerjee's edition of the Prātimokṣasūtra would have become obvious to Prebish, if he had carefully compared Vidyabhusana's edition and translation of the Tibetan version with Banerjee's edition. Even more amazing is the fact that Prebish is completely unaware of the fact that the manuscript, used by Banerjee, was published in facsimile in 1959.[2] From the facsimiles it is easy to see that Banerjee not only misread innumerable passages but also completely failed to indicate correctly the missing parts in the manuscript. Moreover, Banerjee's restorations of missing words are in many cases far off the mark. The text as established by Banerjee often makes no sense at all. In order to substantiate these grave accusations I would like to examine in more detail the first ten introductory verses translated by Prebish on p. 43 of his book. To begin with I quote the text of the first two verses in Banerjee's edition, Prebish's translation, Vidyabhusana's edition of the Tibetan version (adding a numbering of the pādas) and Vidyabhusana's translation.

[1] 'Bhikṣuṇīvinaya and Bhikṣu-Prakīrṇaka and Notes on the Language', *JBRS*, LII (1966), pp. 29–51; 'Terminologisches aus dem Vinaya der Mahāsāṃghika-Lokottaravādin', *ZDMG*, 118 (1968), pp. 334–348.

praṇamya pūrvaṃ jagati pradhānaṃ
duḥkhālayottīrṇam anantapāram /
sarvajñaśikṣāpada[ratnakośa][1] –
m udghāṭayāmy āryagaṇasya madhye // 1 //
trailokyavikhyātayaśaḥpatākaṃ
saddharmanādoditasiṃhanādam /
sarvaṅkaṣā[2] sāditaratnakośaṃ
brahmāṇḍacūḍāmaṇighṛṣṭapādam // 2 //

1. Ms. *vuddha* . . . ; Tib. dkon mchog-snod.
2. Tib. thams-cad-mkhyen-pa = *sarvajñena* /

1–2. Having bowed down before the Chief One in the world, who crossed over the boundless attachment to suffering, who was a flag of glory celebrated in the three worlds, whose lion's roar made apparent the roar of the True Dharma, who reached the jeweled treasure of omniscience,[1] whose feet were rubbed by the crest-jewels of Brahmā's egg, I will explain the treasury of jewels, which is the moral precepts relating to omniscience, in the middle of the community of monks.[2]

1. Using the Tibetan text, which reads thams-cad-mkhyen-pa, Dr. Banerjee suggests sarvajñeya for sarvaṅkaṣa, providing a meaningful alternative to a thoroughly unusual, and perhaps untenable compound.
2. I have translated verses one and two of the Mūlasarvāstivādin text together, as seems appropriate for a proper understanding of the content. For a similar approach see S. C. Vidyabhusana, ed. and tr., 'So-sor-thar-pa, etc.', *JASB*, N.S., IX, 3–4 (1915), 37.

sñan-pa'i ba-dan 'jig-rten gsum-du grags / (1)
dam-pa'i chos sgra seṅ-ge'i sgra sgrags-pa / (2)
thams-cad mkhyen-pa dkon-mchog mdzod brñes-pa / (3)
źabs-la tshaṅs-dbaṅ gtsug-gi nor-bus gtugs / (4)
sdug-bsṅal rgya-mtsho gtiṅ-mtha'-med rgal-ba / (5)
'gro-ba'i gtso-la spyi-bos phyag 'tshal-lo // 1 (6)
thams-cad mkhyen-pa'i bslab-gźi dkon-mchog snod / (7)
'phags-pa'i tshogs-kyi dbus-su dbye-bar bya / (8)

I bow down my head to the Foremost of Beings who was a flag of glory renowned in the three worlds, who proclaimed in a lion's roar the message of the Sacred Faith, who obtained the precious treasure of omniscience, whose feet were touched by the crest gems of Brahmā and Indra and who crossed the bottomless and boundless ocean of miseries (1).

The So-sor-thar-pa is the basis of training in omniscience, it is a casket of jewels kept apart in the community of monks.

A comparison of Prebish's and Vidyabhusana's translations show clearly that the latter makes much better sense. Vidyabhusana misunderstood *dbye-bar bya* in line 8. This is due to the fact that the Tibetan translator rearranged the order of the pādas. The correspondence of the pādas is as follows: skt. 1a – tib. 6; 1b – 5; 1c – 7; 1d –8; 2a – 1; 2b – 2; 2c – 3; 2d – 4. Vidyabhusana's translation does not contain such nonsensical qualifications of the Buddha as 'who crossed over the boundless attachment to suffering' and 'whose feet were rubbed by the crest-jewels of Brahmā's egg'. According to the facsimiles the Sanskrit text is as follows:

[2] *Gilgit Buddhist Manuscripts*, part I [= *Śatapiṭaka*, vol. 10 (1)]. Edited by Prof. Dr. Raghu Vira and Dr. Lokesh Chandra. New Delhi, 1959. Cf. Oskar v. Hinüber, 'Eine Karmavācanā-Sammlung aus Gilgit', *ZDMG*, 119 (1969), pp. 102–103.

pranamya pūrvaṃ jagati pradhānaṃ
duḥkhārṇṇavottīrṇṇam anantapāram
sarvajñaśikṣāpada – – – – m
udghāṭayāmy āryagaṇasya madhye // 1 //
trailokyavikhyātayaśaḥpatākaṃ
saddharmmanādoditasiṃhanādam /
sarvajñam āsāditaratnakośaṃ
brahmendracūḍāmaṇighṛṣṭapadam // 2 //

Banerjee has read in 1c *vuddha* but I am unable to distinguish any akṣaras on the facsimile. Tib. *dkon-mchog snod* renders more probably *ratnapātram* than *ratnakośam*. The only difference between Skt. and Tib. is to be found in 1a where Tib. has 'with my head' and Skt. *pūrvaṃ*. In these two verses Banerjee has misread *duḥkhārnavo*°, *sarvajñam* and *brahmendra*. His emendation in 2c *sarvajñeya* makes no sense and is moreover metrically impossible. Prebish manages to translate *sarvajñeya* and *sarvajña* in 1c by 'omniscience'.

In verse 6 Banerjee's edition has: *eṣa kleśajayo mārgo nṛpater agra*[*nāyakaḥ*] // Prebish translates 'This is the foremost guide for a king', omitting entirely the words *kleśajayo mārgo*.

Banerjee points out that verse 9 has a parallel in the Dhammapada. His text has in b *sukhā dharmasya dhīṣaṇā*. Prebish translates 'happy is the knowledge of the Dharma.' However, the text of the Dhammapada has *sukhā saddhammadesanā* and the corresponding text of the Udānavarga (ed. F. Bernhard, XXX.22) which Prebish has failed to consult, *sukhaṃ dharmasya deśanā*. The text of the facsimile reads: *sukhā dharmmasya desanā*.

Verse 10 corresponds to Dhammapada 206. In b Banerjee reads *saṃvāso 'pi satā sukhaḥ*. Prebish translates: 'happy also is association with the truth'. The Pāli text has *sannivāso sadā sukhā* and in a note Prebish remarks that *saṃvāso* and *satā* are possibly corruptions for the Pāli *sannivāso* and *sadā*! The text of the facsimile reads *saṃvāso 'pi satāṃ sukham*. Tib. *dam-pa dag daṅ 'grogs-pa bde* suggests that *satā* is the correct reading. The meaning is, of course, 'happy also is the dwelling together with a good man'. Prebish's translation of *sat* by 'truth' is a blunder. The Udānavarga has *saṃvāso 'pi sadā sukham* and Bernhard does not indicate any variant. However, the corresponding verse in the Tibetan version of the Udānavarga is exactly the same as in the Tibetan translation of the Prātimokṣasūtra, cf. Udānavarga, ed. H. Beckh (Berlin, 1911), p. 116, 26c: *dam-pa dag daṅ 'grogs-pa bde*. Brough remarked that in Prākrit *satā* and *sadā* would be indistinguishable in form, cf. *The Gāndhārī Dharmapada* (London, 1962), p. 235.

It seems superfluous to examine any further Banerjee's edition and Prebish's translation. The mistakes made by both of them in editing and translating these verses, which are much easier to understand than the more technical passages of the Prātimokṣa text itself, show clearly that they were not equal to their task. Even when the text happens to be correct, Prebish manages to give an entirely wrong translation. For instance: *apramādena āyuṣmadbhir yogaḥ karaṇīyaḥ* is rendered by him as follows: "Yoga should be practiced by the Venerable Ones with diligence" (p. 47). If Prebish, who deems it necessary to point out in a note that the expression *kālaṃ karoti* is found in Monier-Williams's Dictionary (p. 122, n. 24), had taken the trouble to look up the word *yoga* in the same dictionary, he would have seen that *yoga* does not mean only Yoga!

As is the case with the Prātimokṣasūtra of the Mahāsāṃghikas, a new edition of the Prātimokṣa of the Mūlasarvāstivādin is required before a proper translation can be undertaken. Moreover, it will be necessary to compare carefully the Tibetan translation and the other Prātimokṣa texts. The Berlin collection of Sanskrit manuscripts contains many fragments of the Sarvāstivādin version of the Prātimokṣa. In her introduction to her study of the Vinayavibhaṅga on the Bhikṣuprātimokṣa of the Sarvāstivādin (Berlin, 1959, p. 13) Valentina Rosen announces a critical edition of all the manuscripts of the Prātimokṣasūtra in the Berlin collection. It is much to be hoped that this edition will appear in the near future.

Australian National University J. W. DE JONG

SHACKLETON BAILEY, D. R.: *The Śatapañcāśatka of Mātṛceṭa*. Sanskrit text, Tibetan translation & commentary and Chinese translation. Cambridge, University Press, 1951, XI+237 p.

Après avoir publié l'hymne en 400 strophes de Mātṛceṭa (BSOAS, XIII, 1950-1951, p. 671-701, 947-1003), M.S.B. donne une édition de l'hymne célèbre en 150 strophes. Longtemps connu par des fragments, publiés autrefois par Sylvain Lévi, La Vallée Poussin, Hoernle et M. F. W. Thomas, l'hymne entier fut publié en 1937 par K. P. Jayaswal et Rāhula Sāṃkṛtyāyana à l'aide d'une copie d'un MS trouvé par ce dernier au Tibet. En plus de ces éditions, M.S.B. a pu consulter un grand nombre de fragments, découverts en Asie Centrale par différentes expéditions allemandes et conservés à l'Académie de Berlin.

Dans son introduction, M.S.B. traite en détail du problème posé par l'identité de Mātṛceṭa, et reproduit in extenso les renseignements donnés sur lui par Yi-tsing, le *Mañjuśrīmūlakalpa*, Bu-ston et Tāranātha. Tous ces renseignements sont comparés et étudiés avec la plus grande compétence. Quant aux dates de Mātṛceṭa, M.S.B. arrive à la conclusion que le roi Kaniṣka à qui il a adressé une épître (éd. et tr. par M. F. W. Thomas, IA, 1903; éd. et tr. en japonais par Teramoto Enga 寺本婉雅 dans son *Chibetto-go-bumpō* 西藏語文法, p. 158-186, Tōkyō, 1922) n'est pas le monarque célèbre, mais Kaniṣka II. A ce propos, M.S.B. fait valoir aussi la tradition, conservée par Bu-ston et Tāranātha, d'après laquelle Mātṛceṭa aurait été converti par Āryadeva. Mais n'oublions pas que, d'une part, l'authenticité de l'épître n'est pas garantie par un témoignage indépendant — aux Indes la tradition associe souvent un docteur célèbre à un roi célèbre —, et que, d'autre part, la conversion par Āryadeva n'est attestée nulle part avant Bu-ston. Ces données ne sont donc valables qu'en l'absence d'autres données plus précises. Il est bien possible que Mātṛceṭa, en effet, ait vécu au deuxième siècle comme le suppose M.S.B. Mais l'absence de traductions de ses ouvrages en chinois avant Yi-tsing et le fait que seuls des ouvrages de date beaucoup plus récente le citent nous invitent à la prudence.

M.S.B. signale deux citations de Mātṛceṭa dans le commentaire de la *Nāmasaṃgīti* et dans l'*Abhidharmakośavyākhyā*. Dans ce dernier ouvrage (je n'ai pu consulter l'édition de Wogihara), une autre citation a été relevée par La Vallée Poussin (voir *Kośa*, IX, p. 230, n. 3). En outre, j'ai rencontré une citation de la troisième stance du *Śatapañcāśatka* dans un ouvrage, conservé seulement en chinois, le *Jou ta tch'eng louen* 入大乘論 (T. 1634, p. 37 a 13-16). Dès 1903 (BEFEO, III, p. 47) Sylvain Lévi a montré l'intérêt de ce texte qui contient toute une série de citations. Noël Peri a découvert dans ce même texte (p. 49 b 12 sq.) une citation du *Sūtrālaṃkāra* d'Asaṅga (BEFEO, 1911, p. 349). De ce fait, il est important de pouvoir déterminer la date de la traduction de ce texte. Pour autant que je sache, Ui est le seul qui ait fait une tentative dans cette direction (*Z.f. Indologie u. Iranistik*, VI, 1928, p. 218-9). Son raisonnement est le suivant. Tao-t'ai 道泰 a traduit avec Buddhavarman l'*A-p'i-t'an p'i-p'o-cha louen* 阿毘曇毘婆沙論 en 60 kiuan (T. 1546). Une préface à cet ouvrage par Tao-yen 道梴 a été conservée dans le *Tch'ou san tsang ki tsi* 出三藏記集. (T. 2145, k. 10, p. 73 c 28 — 74 b 23) et en tête et fin du T. 1546 lui-même. D'après cette préface, Tao-t'ai avait obtenu dans un voyage à l'ouest des monts Pamir des textes sanskrits, en tout plus de cent mille śloka. A l'invitation de Tao-t'ai, Buddhavarman traduisit le T. 1546. La traduction fut commencée en 425 (le texte dit plus précisément: la deuxième dizaine du quatrième mois de l'année yi-tch'eou 乙丑) et terminée en 427 (le texte: la première dizaine du septième mois de l'année ting-mao 丁卯). Comme, d'autre part, il est dit que le *Jou ta tch'eng louen* a été traduit entre 397 et 439 [1]), il est évident pour Ui que Tao-t'ai doit avoir traduit ce texte entre 427 et 439. Mais Ui ne signale nullement le fait que les dates données par la préface ne s'accordent pas du tout avec d'autres que nous trouvons ailleurs. Dans le même *Tch'ou san tsang ki tsi* (k. 2, p. 11 b 29 — c 5), il est dit que la traduction de l'*A-p'i-t'an p'i-p'o-cha* en 60 kiuan fut commencée au quatrième mois de l'année ting-tch'eou 丁丑

1) Ui indique les dates 397-437 (!) en se référant au catalogue de Nanjio p. 413, No. 71. Mais ici Nanjio ne donne aucune date, et c'est à la page 273, qu'il dit que le *Jou ta tch'eng louen* a été traduit sous les Leang septentrionaux, A.D. 397-439. Pour montrer l'exactitude de Ui citons la phrase suivante de son article: 'On his way back to the capital of the Liang dynasty (379(!)-439), he asked Buddhavarman to translate No. 1264 (T. 1546) and acted as assistant together with more than 300 other persons'. Mais la préface de Tao-yen que Ui résume ainsi dit clairement que Tao-t'ai n'adressa sa demande à Buddhavarman qu'une fois de retour au pays des Leang. En outre, la préface ne dit nulle part que Tao-t'ai ait collaboré à la traduction. Ce n'est que dans d'autres textes que l'on trouve ce renseignement.

(437) et terminée au septième mois de l'année ki-mao 己卯 (439). Ces mêmes dates sont données avec plus de précision dans la biographie de Buddhavarman du *Kao seng tchouan* 高僧傳 (T. 2059, k. 3, p. 339 a 14 — 28), suivant laquelle, après la mort de Mong-souen 蒙遜 (433) et pendant le règne de son fils Meou-k'ien 茂虔 (433-439) au huitième jour du quatrième mois de la cinquième année tch'eng 承 (erreur graphique pour yong 永)-ho 和, l'année ting-tch'eou 丁丑, c'est-à-dire la quatorzième année yuan-kia 元嘉 des Song 宋 (437), Tao-t'ai invita Buddhavarman à traduire le *P'i-p'o-cha*, et la traduction fut terminée deux ans plus tard (439). Les dates, données dans le deuxième kiuan du *Tch'ou san tsang ki tsi* et dans le *Kao seng tchouan*, s'accordent donc parfaitement. Ces deux ouvrages datent environ de la même époque. Le premier fut publié au premier quart du VIe siècle (cf. P. Demiéville, BEFEO, 1924, p. 4, n. 4) et le *Kao seng tchouan* en 519. Les autres catalogues aussi ont adopté ces mêmes dates, voir *Li tai san pao ki* 歷代三寶紀, compilé en 597 (T. 2034, k. 9, p. 84 c 20 — 85 a 6), *Ta T'ang nei tien lou* 大唐內典錄, compilé en 664 (T. 2149, k. 4, p. 256 b 11 — 21), *Kou kin yi king t'ou ki* 古今譯經圖紀, compilé en 664-665 (T. 2151, k. 3, p. 361 a 8 — 13; ici les signes cycliques yi-hai 乙亥 [435], donnés après yong-ho 永和 cinquième année, ont été substitués par erreur à ting-tch'eou 丁丑 [437]), et *K'ai-yuan che kiao lou* 開元釋教錄, compilé en 730 (T. 2154, k. 4. p. 521 b 4 — 21). Ce dernier ouvrage — travail excellent d'après l'opinion de juges qualifiés (cf. P. Demiéville, BEFEO, 1924, p. 19, n. 1) — copie presque textuellement la biographie de Buddhavarman dans le *Kao seng tchouan*, et signale que les dates de la préface ne s'accordent pas avec les données des catalogues: 與錄不同未詳何以. A la lumière de ce qui précède, il paraît très probable que, dans la préface, les signes cycliques yi-tch'eou 乙丑 (425) et ting-mao

丁卯 (427) ont été substitués aux signes cycliques ting-tch'eou 丁丑 (437) et ki-mao 己卯 (439) [1]).

Alors que le *Tch'ou san tsang ki tsi* et le *Kao seng tchouan* mentionnent l'*A-p'i-t'an p'i-p'o-cha louen* ils sont muets sur le *Jou ta tch'eng louen*. Dans le *Li tai san pao ki*, la traduction de ce texte n'est pas attribuée à Tao-t'ai, mais à T'an-yue 曇曜 (T. 2034, k. 9, p. 85 a 23 — b 6). Ceci est sans doute une erreur qui s'est glissée dans le texte car, d'après l'apparat critique du *Taishō shinshū daizōkyō*, cette attribution ne figure pas dans les éditions et les MSS les plus anciens du *Li tai san pao ki*. Le *Ta t'ang nei tien lou* (T. 2149, k. 3, p. 256 c 11-12), se référant au *T'ang kieou lou* 唐舊錄, affirme que Tao-t'ai a traduit le *Jou ta tch'eng louen* sous les Leang septentrionaux. Le *T'ang kieou lou* est le *T'ang tchong king mou lou* 唐衆經目錄, compilé par Hiuan-wan 玄琬 au début de la période tcheng-kouan 貞觀 (627-649) dans le monastère P'ou-kouang 普光 à Tch'ang-ngan (voir *K'ai-yuan che kia lou*, k. 10, p. 574 a 23-25). D'après la biographie de Hiuan-wan dans le *Siu kao seng tchouan* 續高僧傳 (k. 22, p. 616 a-617 c 12) il mourut le septième jour du douzième mois de la dixième année tcheng-kouan (le 8 Janvier 637)

1) T'ang Yong-t'ong 湯用彤 dans son *Han Wei leang Tsin nan pei tch'ao fo kiao che* 漢魏兩晉南北朝佛教史, 1939, p. 395, traitant de la date de la traduction du T. 1546, n'a guère eu la main plus heureuse que Ui. En effet, mentionnant d'après le *Tch'ou san tsang ki tsi*, k.2. et le *K'ai-yuan che kiao lou*, k.4, les signes cycliques ting-tch'eou 丁丑 (437), il les réduit à yuan-kia 元嘉 deuxième année (425)! Tokiwa Daijō 常盤大定 dans son *Go-Kan yori Sō Sei ni itaru yakugyō sōroku* 後漢より宋齊に到ろ譯經總錄, Tōkyō, 1938, p. 914-6, s'en tient aux dates données par la préface. Le seul fait qu'il ne mentionne même pas les données précises du *Kao seng tchouan* nous dispense de réfuter ici son raisonnement. Je n'ai pu consulter d'autres ouvrages japonais comme le *Bussho Kaisetsu Daijiten* 佛書解說大辭典, compilé par Ono Gemmyō 小野玄妙, Tōkyō, 1933-1936, et le *Kyōroku kenkyū* 經錄研究 par Hayashiya Tomojirō 林屋友次郎, Tōkyō, 1941.

et son catalogue a donc été compilé entre 627 et 637. Le *Kou kin yi king t'ou ki* (k. 3, p. 361 a 14) attribue aussi la traduction du *Jou ta tch'eng louen* à Tao-t'ai, mais sans en indiquer de date. De même le *K'ai-yuan che kiao lou*, qui se réfère au *T'ang kieou lou*, au *Ta T'ang nei tien lou* et au *Fan king t'ou* 翻經圖 (sans doute le *Kou kin yi king t'ou ki*). Nous voyons donc que l'attribution de la traduction à Tao-t'ai ne remonte qu'au *T'ang kieou lou*, et qu'avant ce catalogue (déjà perdu en 730 lors de la compilation du *K'ai-yuan che kiao lou*) cet ouvrage n'est mentionné nulle part. Il semble donc plus prudent de ne pas faire état du *Jou ta tch'eng louen* dans le problème d'Asaṅga, tant qu'un examen interne du texte n'aura pas livré des renseignements dignes de plus de confiance que ceux fournis par les catalogues.

En ce qui concerne Mātṛceṭa la date de la traduction du *Jou ta tch'eng louen* n'a guère d'importance. Toutefois la citation du *Śatapañcāśatka* nous apprend que le nom de Mātṛceṭa n'était pas entièrement inconnu en Chine avant Yi-tsing.

Tāranātha attribue à Mātṛceṭa toute une série d'autres noms parmi lesquels ceux de Śūra et d'Aśvaghoṣa. M.S.B. a étudié à nouveau cette identité surprenante qui a déjà fait couler tant d'encre. Par de bonnes raisons, il démontre l'impossibilité d'identifier Mātṛceṭa avec Aśvaghoṣa. Mais il n'exclut pas la possibilité que l'auteur du *Śatapañcāśatka* et celui de la *Jātakamālā* soient le même. Certes on ne peut nier les ressemblances en métrique, vocabulaire et phraséologie que M.S.B. fait ressortir, même si tous les exemples ne sont pas convaincants au même titre, p.ex. sauratya se trouve dans un grand nombre de textes; des expressions comme akāraṇavatsala, etc., se trouvent à plusieurs reprises dans la *Bodhicaryāvatārapañjikā* (p. 34, l. 14; p. 53, l. 5; p. 132, l. 10); la notion de pravivekasukha est courante. Il est même possible d'en ajouter en comparant le *Prajñāpāramitāsamāsa* dont l'attribution à Śūra paraît hors de doute: sarvābhiṣāreṇa (Śat. 1 et 31; PPS, VI, 28), bhujiṣyatā (Śat. 86; PPS, I, 25), prasvastha (Śat. 104; PPS, V, 19) et duṣkuha (Śat. 145; PPS. VI, 30). Mais ces ressemblances ne prouvent nécessairement ni l'identité des deux auteurs ni des emprunts de l'un à l'autre. Il est possible qu'ils aient puisé à une tradition commune [1]). Ne perdons pas de vue que très peu de textes bouddhiques ont été conservés en sanskrit et que, si l'on disposait de plus de textes, de telles ressemblances se retrouveraient peut-être chez d'autres auteurs. La recherche de l'originalité à tout prix n'est pas un trait propre au génie hindou! D'autre part les ouvrages attribués à Mātṛceṭa sont pour la plupart des stotra alors que les ouvrages attribués à Śūra sont d'un tout autre genre (voir sur ce point les remarques de Mlle Ferrari dans l'introduction de son édition du *Prajñāpāramitāsamāsa*, p. 12). Finalement il faut tenir compte du fait, démontré par Johnston (JRAS, 1929, p. 81-86), que l'auteur de la *Jātakamālā* fait clairement allusion à l'*Arthaśāstra* de Kauṭilya. Cela empêchera certainement beaucoup de savants de placer Śūra déjà au deuxième siècle.

Dans l'édition du texte, M.S.B. se montre un philologue averti qui est parfaitement à la hauteur de sa tâche [2]). Il n'est que peu d'éditions de textes bouddhiques qui aient été faites avec le même soin et la même compétence. L'Angleterre a trouvé en M.S.B. un digne successeur de feu Johnston. Dans l'établissement du texte et dans les notes à la traduction, il fait preuve de lectures étendues de la littérature bouddhique en sanskrit et en tibétain. Seules ses connaissances en chinois paraissent un peu moins solides.

Avec le texte sanskrit sont publiés la version tibétaine, la version

1) Ceci est aussi l'opinion de M. Tsuji Naoshirō 辻直四郎 qui a publié un long compte rendu de l'ouvrage de M.S.B. dans le *Tōyō gakuhō*, vol. XXXIII, p. 155-172. Sur ce point et sur d'autres encore, M. Tsuji fait des observations qui meritent l'attention.

2) Signalons que M.S.B. est en même temps un excellent latiniste. Voir son article: 'Echoes of Propertius', *Mnemosyne*, Ser. IV, vol. V, 4, p. 307-333, Leiden, 1953.

chinoise et le commentaire de Nandipriya qui n'est conservé qu'en tibétain. La publication du commentaire est la bienvenue. Dans les études bouddhiques, les commentaires conservés en tibétain seulement ont été trop négligés. A l'avenir, les bouddhisants seront bien obligés de se frayer un chemin dans ces textes. M.S.B. s'est efforcé de rendre le commentaire aisément accessible en indiquant dans des notes les mots sanskrits, expliqués dans celui-ci. Il serait à souhaiter que d'autres éditeurs suivent l'exemple de M.S.B.

Trois appendices contiennent: A. la transcription d'un fragment d'une traduction koutchéenne, B. le texte tibétain du *Miśrakastrotra*, attribué à Dignāga, dans lequel chaque vers du *Śatapañcāśatka* est suivi d'un vers complémentaire, et C. la traduction des histoires relatées par le commentaire. L'ouvrage se termine par un index tibétain-sanskrit-chinois, un index des noms propres tibétains cités dans le texte et le commentaire, et par un index général.

Pour conclure, qu'il me soit permis de faire quelques remarques de détail. Str. 3, comm.: l'histoire de Śāriputra et de Maudgalyāyana se trouve dans le *Kṣudrakavastu* du Vinaya des Mūlasarvāstivādin (tr. chin., kiuan 18). — Str. 5: aux références données dans l'introduction (p. 13) à propos de la parabole de la tortue, on peut ajouter: Harināth De, JPTS, 1906-7, p. 174-5; Col. Jacob, JRAS, 1909, p. 1120-1, *Third Handful*, ^{2}1911, p. 111-3; Winternitz, WZKM, 26, 1912, p. 43-47; *Bodhicaryāvatāra*, IV, 20; °*pañjikā* p. 9, l. 9; p. 263, l. 6; *Milindapañha*, p. 204. — Str. 62, comm.: pour l'histoire de Supriya voir Waldschmidt, *Mahāparinirvāṇasūtra*, Berlin, 1950-1, p. 459-469. — Str. 90: la traduction de M.S.B. me paraît fautive. D'après la traduction tibétaine la triple division est celle en arthacintā, bhāvanā et upāsanam. La même division se retrouve chez I-tsing qui traduit arthacintā par 思義, bhāvanā par 如實善修行 et upāsanam par 慧圓. Il ne peut être question ici de la division bien connue en śruta, cintā et bhāvanā comme le veulent M.S.B. et le commentateur Nandipriya. L'emploi par Mātṛceṭa d'une terminologie peu bouddhique s'explique peut-être par son éducation brahmanique. S'oppose-t-il ici à la quadruple division qui a fait fortune plus tard dans le Vedānta et qui se réclame de *Bṛhadāraṇyaka-Up.*, IV, 5, 6: „Ātmā vā are draṣṭavyaḥ śrotavyo mantavyo nididhyāsitavyaḥ"? — Str. 100: la lecture suratatvāt est adoptée bien que sūratatvāt se trouve dans deux MSS. M.S.B. considère la forme avec ū comme incorrecte mais n'oublie pas de remarquer qu'on la rencontre souvent. La forme avec ū paraît être tellement plus fréquente dans les textes bouddhiques que je l'aurais préférée ici (M. Edgerton dans son dictionnaire ne cite pour surata que le *Mahāvastu* et le *Sukhāvatīvyūha*). — Fautes d'impression, etc.: p. 50, l. 2: lire ṅes-pa au lieu de des-pa; p. 56, str. 30: lire sbyaṅs a.l.d. sbyans; p. 81. str. 63: écrire seṅgeḥi en deux syllabes seṅ-geḥi; p. 111, l. 9: lire gom-pa a.l.d. goms-pa; p. 177: dans la citation du *Kāśyapaparivarta* lire avec Weller arthaṃkara a.l.d. arthekara (cf. Weller, Index, s.v. byed-pa).

I. W. DE JONG

Heinz Zimmermann, *Die Subhāṣita-ratna-karaṇḍaka-kathā* (dem Āryaśūra zugeschrieben) und ihre tibetische Übersetzung. Ein Vergleich zur Darlegung der Irrtumsrisiken bei der Auswertung tibetischer Übersetzungen. [= *Freiburger Beiträge zur Indologie*, Band 8]. Wiesbaden, Otto Harrassowitz, 1975. VI + 273 pp.

The Subhāṣitaratnakaraṇḍakakathā (henceforth abbreviated SRKK) was mentioned for the first time by Sylvain Lévi in 1899. He stated that the SRKK consists of the verses which conclude the tales in the Dvāviṃśatyavadāna. The colophon attributes the SRKK to Āryaśūra. The SRKK was edited for the first time by A. C. Banerjee in 1959 in vol. 21 of the Buddhist Sanskrit Texts (pp. 275–307). This edition is based upon a Newari manuscript from the Durbar Library in Nepal in comparison with the Tibetan translation. Banerjee has not made use of the Dvāviṃśatyavadāna (henceforth abbreviated Dvāv.) and the text, established by him, is very unsatisfactory. Zimmermann's edition is based upon three manuscripts: a manuscript of the SRKK belonging to the Royal Asiatic Society in London (R) and two manuscripts of the Dvāv. (Bibliothèque Nationale: Pa; Cambridge University Library: Ca). The Tibetan version is to be found in two different places in the Tanjur. Zimmermann has made use of the two versions in the Peking and Narthang Tanjurs (P1, P2, N1, N2) and of one version in the Derge and Cone Tanjurs (D/Ce).

Zimmermann's study of the two manuscripts of the Dvāv. proves that Sylvain Lévi's assumption on the relationship between the SRKK and the Dvāv. is not correct. The Cambridge manuscript contains 97 verses of the SRKK and the Paris manuscript 107. The Paris manuscript does not give all the verses of the SRKK and, moreover, they are not always the concluding verses of the tales. Zimmermann shows that the text of the Paris manuscript is an expanded version as compared to the text of the Cambridge manuscript. He arrives at the conclusion that a critical edition of the Dvāv. on the basis of all the available manuscripts would be required in order to elucidate the composition and history of the Dvāv. and its relation to the SRKK. Zimmermann points out that our knowledge of the Dvāv. is due to three scholars: R. Mitra who described a manuscript of the Dvāv. in Calcutta,[1] R. Turner who has studied the language of the

[1] *The Sanskrit Buddhist Literature of Nepal* (Calcutta, 1882), pp. 85–89.

Dvāv.[2] and L. Feer who studied the relationship of the Dvāv. with other collections of Avadānas.[3] According to Zimmermann (p. 8, n. 1) reference is always made to one of these three scholars or to Sylvain Lévi in connection with the SRKK or the Dvāv. This is not quite correct with reference to Speyer who himself inspected the manuscript of the Dvāv. in Paris (cf. his introduction to his edition of the Avadānaśataka).

In his analysis of the SRKK Zimmermann shows that the text consists of two parts: chapters 1–22 which conclude with three *saṃgrahaśloka*-s, and chapters 23–27 which deal with five of the six *pāramitā*-s: *śīla*, *kṣānti*, *vīrya*, *dhyāna* and *prajñā*. The author of this supplement appears to have considered chapters 1–22 to be dealing only with the first of the *pāramitā*-s: *dāna*. Zimmermann remarks that although these 22 chapters have as a common theme *puṇya* in its manifold forms, many verses have no direct relation to the concept of *dāna*. According to him, however, even these 22 chapters do not constitute a unified whole. He considers chapters 1–4 to contain the oldest form of the SRKK. Consequently, Zimmermann is of the opinion that there must have been at least three different authors. He does not exclude the possibility that Āryaśūra was the author of the first four chapters even though four verses of the third chapter are to be found in the Bodhicaryāvatāra. Zimmermann points out that of these four verses a half-verse is also found in the Śatapañcāsatka (5b: *mahārṇavayugacchidrakūrmagrīvārpaṇopamam*). Zimmermann writes: "Dann wenn Śāntideva in diesem einen Falle als der Entleiher dasteht, so kann er sich auch den Rest der fraglichen Str. aus dem Schatz seiner bekanntlich ungewöhnlichen Literaturkenntnisse geholt haben." This argument has not much weight. D. R. Shackleton Bailey has rightly remarked that the simile of the tortoise and the yoke-hole was common property among Buddhist writers.[4] To the references, given by him, others can be added.[5] Recently this simile has been discussed by W. Bollée and K. R. Norman but without reference to the literature mentioned by Shackleton Bailey and myself.[6] The simile is also found in the Mahāyāna Mahāparinirvāṇasūtra.[7] There is no doubt that this half-verse was very popular and its occurrence in Śāntideva's Bodhicaryāvatāra does not prove anything with regard to his authorship of the other verses which are also found in the SRKK. There is therefore no conclusive argument to prove the existence of the SRKK before the time of Śāntideva. As to the *terminus ad quem*, Zimmermann mentions the ninth century since one of the two translators, the Tibetan monk Śākya 'od, is said to have lived in the ninth century. He refers for this date to W. Zinkgräf who stated that there have been two translators of the same name, an Indian and a Tibetan, but that both lived in the ninth century.[8] This is not correct. The Indian Śākya 'od (Śākyaprabha) is mentioned as one of the translators of the *Vinayasaṃgraha*.[9] One of the two other translators is Śīlendrabodhi who is well-known as one of the compilers of the Mahāvyutpatti in the first quarter of the ninth century. The Tibetan monk Śākya 'od, however, is a contemporary of Rin-chen bzaṅ-po (985–1055) as has been shown by Tucci.[10] He must have been active in the middle of the eleventh century as can be shown by an examination of the many colophons in

[2] 'Notes on the language of the Dvāviṃśatyavadānakathā', *JRAS* (1913), pp. 289–304.

[3] 'Le livre des cent légendes', *JA* (1879), II, pp. 293–297, 305–306; *Avadānaçataka* (Paris, 1891), Introduction; *Fragments extraits du Kandjour* (Paris, 1883), pp. 544–552.

[4] *The Śatapañcāsatka of Mātṛceṭa* (Cambridge, 1951), pp. 12–13.

[5] Compte rendu de *The Śatapañcāsatka of Mātṛceṭa*, *T'oung Pao*, 42 (1954), p. 404.

[6] Review of K. R. Norman, *The Elders' Verses II. Therigāthā* (London, 1971), *JAOS*, 93 (1973), p. 603; K. R. Norman, 'Middle Indo-Aryan Studies IX. The blind turtle and the hole in the yoke', *JOIBaroda*, XXI (1972), pp. 331–335.

[7] *The Mahāyāna Mahāparinirvāṇaśāstra*. Transl. by Kosho Yamamoto. Vol. I (The Karibunko, 1973), p. 34.

[8] *Vom Divyāvadāna zur Avadānakalpalatā* (Heidelberg, 1940), pp. 61–62.

[9] P. Cordier, *Catalogue du fonds tibétain de la Bibliothèque Nationale*. IIIe partie (Paris, 1915), p. 401.

[10] *Indo-Tibetica*, II (Roma, 1933), p. 50.

the Tanjur in which he is mentioned as translator.[11] The SRKK must therefore have been composed before the beginning of the eleventh century. It is quite possible that both the first part (chapters 1–22) and the second part (chapters 23–27) have come into existence in the period between Śāntideva and the eleventh century. Zimmermann refers to Bendall's introduction to the Śikṣāsamuccaya for Śāntideva's date (seventh century). It has to be pointed out, however, that this date is based entirely upon Tāranātha who wrote his history of Indian Buddhism in the beginning of the seventeenth century. Bendall draws attention to the fact that the Śikṣāsamuccaya was translated by Jīnamitra, Dānaśīla and Ye-śes-sde and that, consequently, 800 A.D. has to be admitted as the latest possible *terminus ad quem*. The dates of Śāntideva are as uncertain as those of Āryaśūra who is usually said to have lived in the third or fourth century. The translation into Chinese of a work by Āryaśūra in 434 A.D. seems to be the main reason for putting him in the third or fourth century. However, Lin Li-kouang has shown that this work, the *Fen-pieh ye-pao lüeh ching* (Taishō no. 723), is another recension of the *Fen-pieh shan-o so-ch'i ching* (Taishō no. 729) of which the translation is attributed to An Shih-kao (148–170 A.D.).[12] Both the attribution of this recension to An Shih-kao and the attribution of the work itself to Āryaśūra are very doubtful. The only reliable date in connection with Āryaśūra is furnished by the quotations of his Jātakamālā in the inscriptions in Ajaṇṭā. According to Lüders these inscriptions are from the sixth century.[13]

Zimmermann has found thirteen verses of the SRKK in other texts. The fact that out of 160 verses 13 are found elsewhere seems to indicate that the SRKK is a compilation largely based upon other texts. In an article which has escaped Zimmermann's notice V. V. Mirashi points out that verse 6 is quoted in two grants of the Maitraka-s of Valabhī, dated Gupta year 248 (A.D. 567–568) and Gupta year 269 (A.D. 588–589). According to Mirashi this proves that the SRKK was composed before A.D. 550.[14] He adds: "We know of no Buddhist writer named Āryaśūra who flourished before this date except the well-known author of the Jātakamālā. It is not therefore unlikely that the SRKK also was the work of Āryaśūra who flourished in the fourth century A.D." It is much more likely that this verse was well-known in the sixth century and that the SRKK was not the source of the quotations in the Valabhī grants.

Zimmermann's edition of the SRKK gives for each verse: 1. The text as published by Banerjee; 2. Variant readings from the manuscript used by Zimmermann; 3. Indication of the metre; 4. Translation of the verse; 5. Notes to the translation containing the readings proposed by the editor; 6. The Tibetan translation with indications of the corresponding parts of the Sanskrit verse; 7. Variant readings; 8. Translation of the Tibetan version containing comments on all points which require attention. His main object is to show that the Tibetan translation, though very imperfect and unsatisfactory, is based upon the same text. According to Zimmermann's English summary the frequent divergences between the Sanskrit and Tibetan versions are due to the following causes: 1. There were considerable deficiencies in the text used by the translators; 2. The Tibetan text is not free of corruptions. One may occasionally wonder whether that could not be the result of subsequent attempts at retouching, undertaken without help from the Sanskrit original; 3. The translators occasionally failed to understand the Sanskrit text. Zimmermann calls the risk which has its origin in the aforementioned discrepancies 'lexical risk'. The other uncertainty factor is, according to him, the 'syntactic risk' due to the fact that the Tibetan translators often stubbornly kept the order of words and/or lines of the Sanskrit version. Zimmermann points out that in several cases there would have been little chance of understanding the text correctly, had the Sanskrit text not been at hand.

[11] Marcelle Lalou, *Répertoire du Tanjur d'après le catalogue de P. Cordier* (Paris, 1933), p. 213.
[12] *L'aide-mémoire de la vraie loi* (Paris, 1949), pp. 102 and 313.
[13] 'Ārya-Śūras Jātakamālā und die Fresken von Ajaṇṭā', *Gött. Nachr. Phil.-Hist. Kl.* (1902), pp. 758–762 [= *Philologica Indica* (Göttingen, 1940), pp. 73–77].
[14] 'A note on the Subhāṣitaratna-karaṇḍakakathā of Āryaśūra', *Adyar Library Bulletin*, 25 (1961), pp. 304–307.

Zimmermann's exhaustive study of the Sanskrit and Tibetan versions of the SRKK is excellent from all points of view. The Sanskrit text, as established by him, leaves very few points in doubt. Banerjee's edition is very unsatisfactory. This is certainly partly due to the fact that he has used only one manuscript. It is, however, doubtful whether he has correctly reproduced the readings of his manuscript. His edition of the Prātimokṣa of the Mūlasarvāstivādin abounds in wrong readings of the Gilgit manuscript which forms the basis of his edition.[15] This is obvious if one takes the trouble to compare his edition with the facsimiles of the manuscript published by Raghu Vira and Lokesh Chandra.[16] It is a pity that Zimmermann has not been able to consult the Newari manuscript which has been used by Banerjee for his edition. He has also been unable to obtain a copy of the manuscript brought back by Sylvain Lévi. It is therefore not possible to know the relation of this manuscript with the Newari manuscript in the Durbar library. Nevertheless Zimmermann has been able to establish a text which leaves very little scope for uncertainties. It seems unlikely that the use of other manuscripts would result in more than some very minor changes in the text as established by him. The most important part of Zimmermann's work is undoubtedly his thorough examination of the Tibetan version which is probably one of the worst Tibetan translations in the whole of the Kanjur and Tanjur. The comments which Zimmermann has inserted in his translation of the Tibetan version constitute a kind of running commentary in which all peculiarities of the Tibetan translation are elucidated and, as far as possible, explained. The only work which can be compared to Zimmermann's study is Nils Simonsson's *Indo-tibetische Studien, Die Methoden der tibetischen Übersetzer, untersucht im Hinblick auf die Bedeutung ihrer Übersetzungen für die Sanskritphilologie* (Uppsala, 1957) which, as indicated by the subtitle, examines the methods of the Tibe'an translators with regard to the importance of their translations for Sanskrit philology. The Tibetan translations are of essential importance for Buddhist philology. Zimmermann has been successful in showing that even such a deplorable translation as that of the SRKK can be helpful in the study of the Sanskrit original if it is examined carefully pāda by pāda in order to explain all its imperfections.

Zimmermann's edition and translation of the Sanskrit and Tibetan versions are of such excellence that only on a few minor points is it possible to suggest other interpretations. Let me conclude this review by giving the notes which I have made while reading Zimmermann's work. All references are to the number of the verses.

47c: *rūpārūpyasamādhisaṃpadakhilaṃ bhuktvā ca sarvaṃ sukhaṃ*. Tr.: "Erfolgreich im Zustandebringen der formbehafteten und der formenfreien Versenkungsstufen, und nach dem Auskosten restlos aller Glückseligkeit." The translation is too free because *rūpārūpyasamādhi-saṃpadakhilam* refers to *sukham*: "a bliss which is complete through the attainment of concentrations endowed with form and without form".

67b: *kriyotthāpanam*. Tr.: "das Ausführen des Beschlusses". In a note Zimmermann remarks that perhaps one must understand "Bewerkstelligung der Ausführung". *Kriyā* has here undoubtedly the meaning 'rite'. The verse concerns the construction of a *maṇḍala*.

105: Zimmermann has omitted the translation of line 3 of the Tibetan version: *dbyaṅs sñan rol mo daṅ mgrin 'debs*. Four of the six Tibetan versions have *bsdebs* 'joined with'. The meaning of this pāda probably is "having joined together sweet sounding music and song" (cf. *mgrin gcig-tu* "with one voice").

116: *yadgarbhe paripuṣṭim eti śucibhiḥ pronnīyamāno rasaiḥ / bālye yan madhusarpiṣī ca pibati kṣīraṃ ca kāle punaḥ*. Tib. tr.: *gaṅ źig mṅal du rdsogs par ni / gtsaṅ źiṅ yid 'oṅ ro myaṅ la / mar daṅ sbraṅ rtsi stobs daṅ ni / gaṅ źig 'o ma 'thuṅ thse yaṅ*. Zimmermann corrects the reading of the Tibetan versions *stobs* into *stob* and translates: "Wer, im Mutterleib gedeihend, (sich von) reinem Ghee und Honig von angenehmem Geschmack nährt; wer andrerseits zur Zeit Milch

[15] 'The Prātimokṣa-Sūtra', *IHQ*, 29 (1953), pp. 162–174, 266–275, 363–377.

[16] Raghu Vira and Lokesh Chandra, *Gilgit Buddhist Manuscripts*, part 1 [= *Śatapiṭaka*, vol. 10(1)], New Delhi, 1959.

trinkt." Tib. *stob-pa* is 'to feed' and not 'to nourish oneself'. I would prefer to read with two Tibetan translations *myoṅ* instead of *myaṅ* and to translate as follows: "He who, developing in the womb, enjoys pure and pleasant juices and, in his youth, ghee and honey." The position of *thse* is parallel to that of *stobs* which represents Skt. *bālye* confounded with *bale*. It seems difficult to take *ro myaṅ* as rendering 'taste' and to connect *gtsaṅ źiṅ yid 'oṅ ro myaṅ* with *mar daṅ sbran rtsi* in the following line.

146c: *saṃpūjanāṃ sa labhate bahuratnajāto* (MS. *-jātaṃ*). Tr.: "Der gewinnt hienieden, als Besitzer vieler Juwelen, immer hohe Ehrung." Zimmermann translates *-jāto* als 'Besitzer' which seems not possible in this context. It is preferable to read with Banerjee *bahuratnajātair* 'with masses of many jewels'. The Tibetan translation has: *rin chen maṅ daṅ bźon pas phyug*. Probably the Tibetan translators rendered *bahuratnayānair*.

155a: *dagdhasthūṇāsamucchrayāḥ*. Tr. "mit Körpern wie flammende Säulen". *Dagdhasthūṇā* is 'a burnt wooden post'. It is used in Buddhist texts to describe a *pretī*, cf. Avadānaśataka (ed. Speyer, vol. I, p. 253.13): *pretīm adrākṣaṃ dagdhasthūṇāsadṛśīṃ*; Ratnamālāvadāna (ed. K. Takahata, p. 53.19): *pretīm . . . dagdhasthūṇāmahākṛtiṃ*.

155c: *dūropadrutasārameyanivahā vyāvṛtya tiṣṭhanty api*. Tr.: "und (dass sie, wie) ein von ferne angegriffenes Rudel von Hunden, auseinanderstieben und (wieder) stehen bleiben". The Tibetan translation has: *khyi daṅ 'dra bar riṅ na gnas / kun tu rgyug* (all versions: *'jug*) *ciṅ sloṅ ba la phyir ldog*. Tr.: "wie ein Hund fernab stehenbleibt und, (wenn man) von überall her (auf ihn los-)rennt und (ihn) aufscheucht, wieder zurückkehrt". Tib. *sloṅ-ba* does not mean 'verscheuchen'. According to Jäschke's dictionary it is used in the meaning 'to excite, cause, inspire (compassion, fear, passion)'. This meaning is derived from the primary meaning 'to cause to rise'. However, the Tibetan translators used here the verb *sloṅ-ba* 'to ask, to beg': "as dogs they remain at a distance, run in every direction, beg, and turn back". The Tibetan translation has *gaṅ-źig* but this can be used also for a plural. Undoubtedly the Tibetan translators made no effort to render the rather complicated Sanskrit compound *dūropadrutasārameyanivahā* and gave a very free rendering.

190cd: *jñātvā naraḥ svahitasādhanatatparasyām* (MS. *-paraḥ syāṃ*) / *kuryān na kaḥ satatam āśu dṛḍhaṃ prayatnam*. The first half of the verse mentions the six *pāramitā*-s. Zimmermann proposed to read *tatparasyām* and supposes that it refers to *pāramitā* as a unit comprising the six *pāramitā*-s. It is difficult to see why, in that case, he does not read *tatparāyām*. Probably one must read *-tatparās tāḥ / kuryān na kaḥ satatam āsu dṛḍhaṃ prayatnam*. The Tibetan translators have read *āśu* (*myur-du*) but the confusion of *s* and *ś* is a normal phenomenon.

Australian National University J. W. DE JONG

Yutaka Iwamoto, *Bukkyō setsuwa kenkyū josetsu* (= *Bukkyō setsuwa kenkyū*, I). Kyōto, Hōzōkan, 1967. 300 pp., 1 frontisp. Yen 4200.

Professor Iwamoto (2.3.1910-) has been studying the *avadāna* literature for many years. He has written a series of articles (listed on page 18 of the *Bukkyō setsuwa kenkyū josetsu*) and two short books: *Indo no setsuwa* [Indian tales] (Tōkyō, 1963); *Bukkyō setsuwa* [Buddhist tales] (Tōkyō, 1964).[1] Moreover he has published a revised version of the Sanskrit text of the *Sumāgadhāvadāna* (Tōkyō, 1959), which was first published by Tokiwai Gyōyū (1872-1951) in 1918, and an edition of the Tibetan version (*Acta Asiatica*, 7, 1964, pp. 1-19). *Bukkyō setsuwa kenkyū josetsu* [Introduction to the study of Buddhist tales], which appears as volume I of *Bukkyō setsuwa kenkyū* [Studies in Buddhist tales], constitutes a general introduction to the *avadāna* literature. In the past much work has been done in this field by Léon Feer (1830-1902), Sergej Ol'denburg (1863-1934) and J. S. Speyer (1849-1913). The last comprehensive survey of *avadāna* literature was given in 1909 by Speyer in the preface to his edition of the *Avādanaśataka* (*Bibliotheca Buddhica*, III, pp. I-CX).

The introduction (pp. 9-47) deals with a survey of editions and publications relating to *avadāna* literature, problems in the study of *avadānas*, the nature of *avadāna* and the change in the meaning of the word *avadāna*. Speyer (*op. cit.*, p. XIV) divided the *avadāna* texts into three classes. Professor Iwamoto points out that this division does

[1] Both volumes contain a wealth of interesting material. *Indo no setsuwa* contains an introduction, dealing with Indian story-literature, and two main parts. The first studies Indian tales in Japan, special attention being given to the *Konjaku monogatari* in which many Indian elements are to be found. The second part deals with Indian stories in Europe, and discusses, among others, the story of Barlaam and Josaphat, Shakespeare's *Merchant of Venice*, and Nathaniel Hawthorne's story "Rappacini's Daughter". In *Bukkyō setsuwa* Professor Iwamoto studies in detail the different versions of the following ten stories: Aṅgulimāla, Devadatta, Koṭikarṇa, Kuṇāla, King Candraprabha, Maitrakanyaka, Prince Kalyāṇakārin, Prince Kuśa, Ṛṣyaśṛṅga and Siṃhala.

not take into account the distinction between *avadāna* stories and *avadāna* literature. A text such as the *Avadānaśataka* belongs to the *avadāna* literature yet contains not only *avadāna* stories but also *vyākaraṇas* and *jātakas*. As characteristic of *avadāna* stories Iwamoto indicates the fact that they consist of a story of the present and a story of the past. The Buddha identifies the chief actor of the first story with the chief actor of the second story. *Avadāna* stories contain in general the following five elements: 1. Story of the present; 2. Verses praising the power of *karman*; 3. Story of the past; 4. Appearance on the scene of a Buddha of the past; 5. Teaching relating to *karman*. With the nature of the *avadāna* stories thus determined, Iwamoto studies the divisions of the Buddhist teaching in nine and twelve *aṅgas*, and remarks that to *itivuttaka*, in the group of the nine *aṅgas*, correspond the following four, *vyākaraṇa*, *nidāna*, *avadāna* and *itivṛttaka* in the group of the twelve *aṅgas*. Iwamoto attempts to determine the original meaning of these *aṅgas* and the classes of texts to which they relate. There are many problems connected with these two divisions into nine and twelve *aṅgas*, and Japanese scholars in particular have studied the relevant passages in Buddhist texts exhaustively. Among the most recent has been Professor Egaku Maeda who has devoted a large section of his *Genshi Bukkyō seiten no seiritsu kenkyū* (English title: A History of the Formation of original Buddhist texts) (Tōkyō, 1964) to a very thorough study of the nine and twelve *aṅgas* (see pp. 181-547). It seems to me, however, that no definite conclusions can be reached from the available evidence. Most of the materials come from a period when the division into nine and twelve *aṅgas* had lost any significance if it ever had any! The explanations of the meaning of the *aṅgas* given in Buddhist texts are of great interest because they reflect opinions and theories prevalent at the time when these texts were written. But, it is dangerous to accept these explanations as relevant to a much earlier period. It is even doubtful if the Buddhist texts were ever divided into nine or twelve classes corresponding to the nine and twelve *aṅgas*. In these circumstances one can only speculate, and the few pages devoted to the *aṅgas* by Iwamoto (pp. 32-36) must therefore be regarded as largely hypothetical. In order to make a critical examination of the theory advanced by Iwamoto, one would have to consider not only Maeda's book but also the third chapter of Professor Hirakawa Akira's *Ritsuzō no kenkyū* [A Study of the Vinaya-piṭaka] (Tokyo, 1960) in which much useful material on *avadāna* is to be found (see pp. 291-415).

Of great interest is the last part of the introduction in which Iwamoto studies the change of meaning of the word *avadāna* which, in the course of time, is applied to parables and examples and, finally, is used as synonymous with the word *kathā*.

In his introduction Iwamoto points out the necessity for careful study of the history of the *avadānas* which are to be found in the *avadāna* literature. The first chapter deals with the history of one story, the *Sumāgadhāvadāna*, which, according to Iwamoto, deserves to be studied for five reasons enumerated on pages 22-23. The *Sumāgadhāvadāna* is the legend of Sumāgadhā, the daughter of Anāthapiṇḍada. She marries a Jain merchant from Puṇḍravardhana, by the name of Vṛsabhadatta. She alienates him from the Jain monks, and then invites the Buddha who duly appears from the sky and converts Vṛsabhadatta's family and the whole town. The Buddha tells that in a former existence she was Kāñcanamālā, the daughter of King Kṛkin who dreamed ten strange dreams. Kāñcanamālā advised her father to ask the Buddha Kāśyapa for the explanation of these dreams. After having told the story of Kāñcanamālā the Buddha explains that in a former life Kāñcanamālā was a poor woman who dedicated a wreath of *palāla*-flowers to the *caitya* of a Pratyekabuddha. Through the merit of this act she was reborn with a golden garland on her head as a daughter of King Kṛkin. This is a brief outline of the story as given in the Sanskrit text edited by Iwamoto. In this edition Iwamoto remarks that the story is divided into two parts: an account of Sumāgadhā's present life and the story of her former existence as a daughter of King Kṛkin. However, the legend contains a third part: the story of Kāñcanamālā's former existence as a poor woman so that, properly speaking, the Sanskrit text presents an *avadāna* in the second degree as it relates the story of Sumāgadhā and two of her former existences; the first as Kāñcanamālā, the daughter of King Kṛkin, and the second as a poor woman. If one divides the legend in this way into three parts, it becomes evident that parts two and three constitute a regular *avadāna*. Part two relates Kāñcanamālā's existence as the daughter of King Kṛkin and part three how she earned in an earlier existence the merit which brought about her rebirth as daughter of King Kṛkin. Parts one and two do not constitute an *avadāna* because, although part two tells how Kāñcanamālā believes in the Buddha and provides him with everything he needs, there is no mention of a particular meritorious deed as is usually told in the stories of the past. It should also be noted that in part two Kāñcanamālā, as daughter of a king, has a higher position than Sumāgadhā, the daughter of a merchant. For these reasons it is obvious that the Sanskrit text consists of two heterogeneous stories (part 1; parts 2 and 3) which have been clumsily put together. Iwamoto has failed to draw attention to this fact which is fully confirmed by the comparison of the different versions of the legend.

The Sanskrit text of the legend is transmitted in eight manuscripts of which Iwamoto has been able to use seven. MS B, which dates from the thirteenth century, is, in several respects, different from the six others which descend from a sub-archetype β. The Sumāgadhā legend is also to be found in Kṣemendra's *Avadānakalpalatā* Nr. 93. This text has been re-edited by Iwamoto on the basis of two manuscripts in the Cambridge collection as an appendix to his edition of the Sanskrit text of the *Sumāgadhāvadāna*. The Tibetan *Kanjur* contains a version of the legend, and the Chinese canon five different versions, of which the oldest was translated A.D. 230 and the latest after A.D. 980. Iwamoto carefully studies all the versions which he summarizes and compares with each other. In the sixth section of this chapter, the author sketches the development of the legend and distinguishes five different stadia: A, B, C, D and E. Moreover, he tries to date these stadia and to establish their connections with Buddhist schools. Iwamoto's conclusions here are not always acceptable. Regarding the story of the poor woman MS B relates that as recompense for the dedication of a garland of *palāla*-flowers she was reborn as Kāñcanamālā (§§ 265-266 of Iwamoto's edition). The story of the past ends here but the Sanskrit manuscripts add another passage which varies according to the manuscripts. MS B has the following text: *praṇidhānacittayā śuddhayā śuddhavastuyā āryasaṃghāya dattaṃ. tenāḍhyeṣu kuleṣu pratyājātā praṇidhānavasāc ceti. yā Kāñcanamālā sā Sumāgadhā.* In the other manuscripts the following text is to be found: *paṇadvayaṃ ca tayā paṭāntāvabaddhaṃ vimucyāryasaṅghāya dattaṃ. tenāḍhyeṣu kuleṣu jātā praṇidhānavasāc ceti.* There is nothing corresponding to this passage in the Tibetan version or in Kṣemendra's *Sumāgadhāvadāna*. Only in the Chinese version, translated after A.D. 980, is there a similar passage: "O monks. Therefore, at present, this Sumāgadhā on account of her past root of merit and the power of her great vow has now obtained to be born in the very rich family of Anāthapiṇḍada. By her excellent guidance and by gifts she has done her duty in regard to the Buddha" (*Taishō*, II, p. 854a 7-9). It is easy to understand why this passage was added to the Indian text underlying this Chinese version. Once the *Sumāgadhāvadāna* was formed by joining together two different stories, comprising the three parts mentioned above, it became necessary to explain the relation of part three, dealing with the poor woman, to part one, the story of Sumāgadhā. This passage, which is absent from all the older versions, is differently worded in the three versions in which it is to be found. In the Chinese version it clearly answers its purpose, but in the versions represented by MS B and by β it contradicts what has been said before. According to MS B she has given gifts to the *saṃgha*. The other manuscripts specify that her gift consisted of two small coins. It is evident that in all the Sanskrit manuscripts the text has been corrupted in the course of transmission. MS B, dating from the thirteenth century, has a text which is slightly more satisfactory than that represented by the other manuscripts which probably belong all to a much later period.[2]

The gift of the two coins by the poor woman clearly alludes to the famous story 22 of the *Sūtrālaṃkāra*, which, following the translation by Huber in 1908, widely attracted the attention of the scholarly world with its parallel to the story of the "widow's mite" in the New Testament (see the literature quoted by Winternitz, *A History of Indian Literature*, II, pp. 408-409). The same story occurs in the *Kalpanāmaṇḍitikā* of Kumāralāta (ed. H. Lüders, Leipzig, 1926, p. 149). Iwamoto assumes that the *Sūtrālaṃkāra* was written by Aśvaghoṣa during the reign of Kaniṣka in the second half of the second century, and the *Kalpanāmaṇḍitikā* or *Dṛṣṭāntapaṅkti* by the Sautrāntika patriarch Kumāralāta at the end of the second century or in the beginning of the third century. As this story does not seem to occur elsewhere in the Buddhist literature Iwamoto concludes that it must have been borrowed by the author of the sub-archetype β shortly after Kumāralāta, probably in the middle of the third century A.D. or at the latest in the second half of the third century. This conclusion seems to me unacceptable. In the first place, the author of β could very well have found this story somewhere else, for the surviving Buddhist literature represents only a part of the literature which once existed. But a more serious objection lies in the fact that the gift of two coins is not mentioned in the Tibetan version, in Kṣemendra's version, in the Chinese version, discussed above, and in MS B, but is found only in recent manuscripts. For the same reasons it is impossible to accept Iwamoto's view that the author of β belongs to the Sautrāntika school, or that stadium E (which precedes β) constitutes the transitional stage between the Sarvāstivādin and Sautrāntika schools.

Another difference between MS B and β is the fact that the former one contains a comparison of the Buddha to gold. This comparison is absent in β. Iwamoto points out that in early times the Buddha is compared to gold and that later in Mahāyāna texts the Buddha is said to be ornated by light, or, to consist of light. Iwamoto regards it of great importance that this comparison is omitted from stadium E, but he does not explain why. Possible his idea is that such a Mahāyāna elements was still admissible in stadium D, belonging to the Sarvāstivādin school, but not anymore in stadium E which marks the transition to the Sautrāntika school. However this may be, I do not believe that the presence or absence of this comparison carries much weight from a doctrinal point of view. A few pages later Iwamoto quotes a story from the *Mahīśāsaka vinaya*.[3] In it the Buddha is compared to a mountain of gold (p. 96, l. 15). According to the Buddhist traditions the Mahīśāsaka descend from the Sarvāstivādin as do the Sautrāntikas.

Using quotations in the texts Iwamoto tries to show that stadia A, B, C and D all belong to the Sarvāstivādin school, though in a note he adds that stadium B′ belongs to the Dharmaguptaka school because it occurs in the *Ekottarāgāma*. This does not conflict with his theory because the Dharmaguptaka school descends from the Sarvāstivādin school. However, there is no agreement between scholars that this *āgama* belongs to the Dharmaguptaka school. Some have even maintained that it belongs to the Mahāsāṃghika school. This would seriously conflict with Iwamoto's view (see Maeda, *op. cit.*, pp. 671-672). Since most of the quotations relate to stereotyped ex-

[2] Iwamoto does not give a detailed palaeographic description of the manuscripts. According to Bendall's catalogue (pp. 129-133) MS C dates from the seventeenth century. Iwamoto shows that MSS C' and P are copies of this manuscript. However, no information is given about the date of the three other manuscripts of which two belong to Kyoto University and one to Tokyo University.

[3] Cf. Éd. Chavannes, *Cinq cents contes et apologues*, II (Paris, 1910), pp. 343-349; André Bareau, "La construction et le culte des stūpa d'après les *Vinayapiṭaka*", *BEFEO*, 50 (1962), pp. 265-267.

pressions, they prove little. The fact that the dreams of King Kṛkin are quoted by Vasubandhu and Yaśomitra in no way proves a doctrinal relation with the Sarvāstivādin school. More important is the invitation of Piṇḍola which is mentioned in the oldest Chinese translation dating from A.D. 230. The invitation of Piṇḍola by Sumāgadhā is mentioned in three versions of the Aśoka legend: the *Kuṇālāvadāna* of the *Divyāvadāna*; the *A-yü wang chuan* and the *A-yü wang ching* (Iwamoto, pp. 84-85). In *La Légende de l'empereur Açoka* (Paris, 1923) Przyluski has connected the Aśoka legend with the Sarvāstivādin school of Mathurā. However, the connection of the oldest Chinese version of the Sumāgadhā legend with the Sarvāstivādin school is not proved by a reference in the Aśoka legend to the invitation of Piṇḍola by Sumāgadhā. The author of the Aśoka legend quotes from the Sumāgadhā legend and not vice versa. It is interesting to note that the author of the Aśoka legend has known the Sumāgadhā legend, which guarantees a considerable antiquity for the legend. In the Sumāgadhā legend the invitation of Piṇḍola is not an integral part, as has already been shown by S. Lévi and Éd. Chavannes in their detailed study of Piṇḍola (*JA*, Juillet-Août et Septembre-Octobre 1916; see p. 127 of the offprint). In this study, to which Iwamoto does not refer, Lévi and Chavannes proved that Piṇḍola's flying through the air with a rock is an essential element of the Piṇḍola legend and is to be found in several texts. For this reason the mention of Piṇḍola in a version of the Sumāgadhā legend does not at all prove its connection with a particular Buddhist school.

I believe that it is generally very difficult to prove that a story belongs to a particular Buddhist school. There are several Indian stories of which Hindu, Buddhist and Jain versions are known. A story can very well have been adopted by different schools. Probably, at most, one can show that a certain version of a story, but not the story itself, belongs to a particular school. As Iwamoto himself remarks there is a parallel story in the *Mahāvastu* (vol. I, pp. 301-307) which certainly has no relations with the Sarvāstivādin school (cf. Iwamoto, pp. 99-100 and p. 111, n. 42). Already the existence of this parallel makes it difficult to attribute this legend entirely to the Sarvāstivādin school.

In the last section of Chapter I Iwamoto draws the attention to three parallel legends in the *Dhammapadaṭṭhakathā* and the *Manorathapūraṇī*. In these legends, though the names are different the story is quite similar to the story of Sumāgadhā. Much less similar is the story of Visākhā in the *Dhammapadaṭṭhakathā*. Visākhā is the daughter of Dhanañjaya, a treasurer (not a rich merchant as stated by Iwamoto in his summary) of the city of Bhaddiya. Dhanañjaya settles in Saketā, not far from Sāvatthī. Visākhā marries Puṇṇavaddhana, son of the treasurer Migāra in Sāvatthī. Migāra is a supporter of the Jain order. Visākhā invites the Buddha who converts Migāra and his wife. Apart from the fact that the husband of Visākhā is called Puṇṇavaddhana, which in the Sumāgadhā legend is the name of a king or of a city, only the general theme is similar to that of the Sumāgadhā legend. A daughter of a wealthy merchant or a treasurer marries an adherent of the Jains in a distant place; she invites the Buddha who converts her parents-in-law. According to Iwamoto this legend is very old because it relates to a period when Śrāvastī was not yet converted to Buddhism. He believes that this legend is based upon a historical fact because in later times Visākhā was a famous patron of Buddhism in Śrāvastī. Therefore he assumes that the oldest form of the Sumāgadhā legend is represented by the Visākhā story. Later, when Anāthapiṇḍada became famous as a protector of Buddhism in Śrāvastī, Sumāgadhā was substituted to Visākhā. It seems to me difficult to admit these conclusions. The stories of Visākhā and Sumāgadhā are variants of the same general theme. In some way or the other the name Puṇṇavaddhana was connected with this theme. Moreover, there is not the slightest proof as to the historical background of the story of Visākhā. Iwamoto has done well in drawing attention to this story, but I am afraid that it is impossible to regard the stories of Visākhā and Sumāgadhā as reflecting respectively a historical fact and a later legendary transformation of this fact due to historical developments.

Burnouf was the first scholar who studied the legend of Sumāgadhā, comparing the Sanskrit text with the Tibetan version (*Introduction à l'histoire du buddhisme indien*, Paris, 1844, p. 566; see also L. Feer, *Papiers d'Eugène Burnouf*, Paris, 1899, p. 65). Feer had prepared a translation and edition of both the Sanskrit and Tibetan versions but his work has remained unpublished (see *Bibliographie bouddhique*, II, Paris, 1931, p. 15). Professor Iwamoto has rendered a great service to Buddhist studies by publishing a critical edition of the Sanskrit text (Tokiwai's edition is based on only one manuscript), an edition of the Tibetan version and a detailed study of all the versions of the legend and of parallel stories. Although it is not always possible to accept his conclusions, he has brought to light a lot of interesting material. One can add to these materials a passage of Tāranātha's *History of Buddhism* which was first noticed by Minayeff (*Recherches sur le Bouddhisme*, Paris, 1894, p. 89) *de'i-tshe śar-phyogs-nas 'phags-pa rTsibs-logs ces bya-ba dgra-bcom-pa maṅ-du thos-pa'i mthar-phyin-pa cig byuṅ-ste / des gnas-brtan maṅ-du thos-pa 'ga'- las gSer-'phreṅ-can-gyi rtogs-brjod ces bya-ba rgyal-po Kri-ki'i rmi-lam luṅ-bstan-pa'i mdo-la sogs-pa mdo śin-tu dkon-pa dag kyaṅ 'don-par byed-do // de rgyal-po Ka-ni-ṣkas thos nas /* ...: "At that time in the East there was the Arhat Pārśva who was extremely learned. He recited the *Kāñcanamālāvadāna*, in which the dreams of King Kṛkin are explained, and other very rare sūtras [which he had obtained] from some learned *sthaviras*. When King Kaniṣka heard this ..." (see Schiefner's edition, p. 47.13-19, and his translation, p. 59.16-23). Tāranātha's source for this tradition concerning the relation of Pārśva with the *Kāñcanamālāvadāna* is not clear. gŹon-nu-dpal, who wrote his "Blue Annals" from 1476 to 1478, quotes the *Sumāgadhāvadāna* but is silent about Pārśva in this connection (see George N. Roerich, *The Blue Annals*, I, Calcutta, 1949, pp. 25-27). Perhaps a thorough investigation of the Tibetan literature may lead to the discovery of Tāranātha's source. In any case, one must be cautious as to how much importance to attach to this tradition, even if it can be proved to have been known in Tibet long before Tāranātha wrote his *History of Buddhism* in 1608.

Chapter Two deals with the *Avadānaśataka*. This text consists of ten groups of ten stories. Later metrical paraphrases as the *Kalpadrumāvadānamālā*, the *Ratnāvadānamāla* and the *Aśokāvadānamālā* seem not to have known the fourth group, although this already existed in the Chinese translation with a rather different arrangement of the stories. There are a few problems connected with this translation which are not mentioned by Iwamoto. The translation is attributed to Chih Ch'ien who translated many texts between 220 and 253 (see E. Zürcher, *The Buddhist Conquest of China*, Leiden, 1959, pp. 335-336, n. 136). However, his translation of the *Avadānaśataka* is not mentioned in the oldest catalogues nor in his biography, but seems to be recorded for the first time in the *Ta-T'ang nei-tien-lu* (*Taishō*, vol. LV, p. 227c19) which dates from A.D. 664. The same information is to be found in the *K'ai-yüan shih-chiao lu* (*Taishō*, vol. LV, p. 488c7; see also Tokiwa Daijō, *Yakkyō sōroku*, Tōkyō, 1938, pp. 558 and 564). One would have to compare the translation of the *Avadānaśataka* with other translations which can be attributed to Chih Ch'ien without any doubt, before accepting as a fact that this translation is really his. Another matter which calls for fuller investigation is the indication, given in *Taishō* edition, that the arrangement of the chapters is different in the *Shōgo-zō*.

Iwamoto points out that the construction of stories 1-40 is different from the stories 41-100. One confirmation of this difference, in Iwamoto's view, is the presence of a colophon after story 40 which is absent after other stories. However, a similar colophon is to be found after the stories 50, 60, 70, 80, 90 and 100. Much more striking is the fact that both story 40 and story 100 contain long quotations from the *Mahāparinirvāṇasūtra*. In this connection Iwamoto would have done well to have referred to two important articles: Jean Przyluski, "Le Parinirvāṇa et les funérailles du Buddha" (*JA*, 1918-1920; offprint, Paris, 1920, 216 pp.) and Charlotte Vaudeville, "La Légende de Sundara et les funérailles du Buddha dans l'Avadānaśataka" (*BEFEO*, LII, 1964, pp. 73-91). Przyluski has pointed out that story 100 can only have been composed in Gandhāra or Kaśmīr (p. 7 of the offprint; Iwamoto, p. 134). Iwamoto compares the Chinese version of story 100 with the Sanskrit text and concludes that the original text underlying the Chinese version of the *Avadānaśataka* is a product of the Sarvāstivādin school in Mathurā. It seems doubtful whether a conclusion based on comparison of different versions of a single story can legitimately be extended to the whole of the *Avadānaśataka*.

In the third chapter, Iwamoto studies the *Divyāvadāna* and related texts. A section of this chapter is devoted to the Kyōto manuscript of the *Divyāvadānamālā*. Cowell and Neil's edition of the *Divyāvadāna* is entirely based on manuscripts which go back to one source, a manuscript of the seventeenth century. It is therefore important to note that there are other materials consisting of two *Divyāvadāna* manuscripts in Tokyo, and three *Divyāvadānamāla* manuscripts in Paris, Calcutta and Kyōto. Iwamoto gives a very useful synopsis of these manuscripts (pp. 144-147). It is to be hoped that a thorough study of these materials will shed light on the formation of the text of the *Divyāvadāna*. In this respect I should like to draw attention to the fact that the text of the *Divyāvadāna* contains several verses identical to verses in Kṣemendra's *Avadānakalpalatā*. In the Kuṇāla legend one verse and a half is the same in the *Divyāvadāna* and the *Avadānakalpalatā* (*Div*. p. 417. 22-27; *Av*. 59.160cd, 161). Bongard-Levin and Volkova assume that later copyists or editors of the *Divyāvadāna* have taken this verse and a half from the *Avadānakalpalatā* (*Legenda o Kunale*, Moskva, 1963, p. 90; see also *IIJ*, VIII, 1965, p. 238). Recently Dr. P. S. Jaini has found six verses which are identical in the *Divyāvadāna* and the *Avadānakalpalatā* ("The story of Sudhana and Manoharā", *BSOAS*, XXIX, 1966, p. 541, n. 41; p. 545, n. 53). These verses are not to be found in the Gilgit MS of the *Bhaiṣajyavastu* nor in the Tibetan and Chinese versions. It would be of some importance to examine whether these verses are to be found in the manuscripts of the *Divyāvadāna* and *Divyāvadānamālā* mentioned by Iwamoto.

The fourth chapter deals with later *avadāna* literature: the *Kalpadrumāvadāṇamālā* (*Kv*.), the *Ratnāvadānamālā* (*Rv*.), the *Aśokāvadānamālā*, the *Vicitrakarṇikāvadāna*, the *Vicitrakarṇikāvadānamālā* and the *Vratāvadānamālā*. This chapter contains a lot of interesting information which makes it difficult to summarise. A few remarks must suffice. Both Speyer and Takahata have tried to show the influence of Mahāyāna concepts on the *avadānamālās*. Iwamoto remarks that although *Kv*. and *Rv*. contain Mahāyāna expressions, it does not follow that they are products of Mahāyāna Buddhism. In this context he draws attention to the *Kuo-ch'ü hsien-tsai yin-kuo ching* (*Taishō*, nr. 189) and to the fact that there are already Mahāyāna elements in the Sarvāstivādin school. I do not find these arguments entirely relevant. Speyer writes: "The authors of the *avadānamālās* were adherents of the Mahāyāna. They told the stories over with *mahāyāna* colours and imbued them with *mahāyāna* concepts" (Preface, p. XXVI). The second part of this statement is undoubtedly correct. It is difficult to prove that the authors were really Mahāyāna Buddhists but it seems even more difficult to prove that they were Hīnayānists. The presence of Mahāyāna expressions and concepts makes Speyer's conclusion more likely than Iwamoto's opinion to the contrary. In any case, his remarks are hardly sufficient proof that the *avadānamālās* (or at least *Kv*. and *Rv*. to which Speyer refers) belong to Hīnayāna Buddhism.

Iwamoto quotes a passage from the Subhūti story in the *Kv*. which was published by Speyer in his preface (pp. XXXVII-XCI). As was already indicated by the editor, the author of this text quotes many verses from the *Vajrasūci* which tradition attributes to Aśvaghoṣa. For Iwamoto this fact provides a motive for arguing that the *Vajrasūcī* can well have been written by Aśvaghoṣa and that the *Kv.* was composed in the third century. The metrical paraphrases of the *Avadānaśataka* seem not to have known the fourth *varga*. From this Iwamoto concludes that the prototype of the *Kv.* is earlier than the Chinese translation which dates from the middle of the third century. Whilst this is quite possible, it does not imply that the *Kv.* in its present form is very old. The authors of the metrical paraphrases can very well have known, at a much later period, a different version of the *Avadānaśataka* or simply a manuscript lacking the fourth *varga*. Even if the *Vajrasūcī* was written by Aśvaghoṣa, the *Kv.* could still have been composed many centuries later, and indeed the style points to a much later date than the third century. I must confess that I am unable to understand fully Iwamoto's argumentation concerning the authorship of the *Vajrasūcī*. It is difficult to follow Iwamoto's reasoning that because, first, the prototype of the *Kv.* precedes the Chinese version of the *Avadānaśataka* and, second, because the text underlying this Chinese version was translated by a Tokharian from Central Asia, where from the third century onwards the Sarvāstivādin school spread itself, therefore it should be possible that the *Vajrasūcī* could have been written by Aśvaghoṣa. Neither the prototype of the *Kv.* nor the text translated by Chih Ch'ien (if he is really the translator!) can have contained lengthy extracts from the *Vajrasūcī*.

In a short concluding chapter Iwamoto studies the classification and the development of the *avadāna* literature. He classifies the *avadāna* literature into four groups: 1. *Avadānaśataka* and its metrical paraphrases: *Kalpadrumāvadānamālā* and *Ratnāvadānamālā*; 2. *Divyāvadāna* and *Divyāvadānamālā*; 3. *Aśokāvadānamālā* and some *avadāna* texts which are similar in arrangement; 4. *Vratāvadānamālā*. For all four groups he establishes connections with the Sarvāstivādin and Mūlasarvāstivādin schools. In this connection Iwamoto remarks that some *avadāna* texts are in the form of conversations between Aśoka and Upagupta (*Kv.* and *Rv.*) but others are told by Jayaśrī who relates the stories which Upagupta tells to Aśoka. He places Jayaśrī as appearing in the transitional period from the Sarvāstivādin school to the Mūlasarvāstivādin school. Jayaśrī appears on the stage in the *Aśokāvadānamālā*, the *Guṇakāraṇḍavyūha*, the *Vicitrakarṇikāvadānamālā*, the *Bhadrakalpāvadāna* (see S. Ol'denburg, *Buddijskija legendy*, Sanktpeterburg, 1894, p. 1) and in the *Suvarṇavarṇāvadāna*. From the materials available it is difficult to see why these texts would be doctrinally different from texts such as the *Kalpadrumāvadānamālā*, the *Ratnāvadānamālā* and the *Dvaviṃśatyavadāna*.

In regard to the development of the *avadāna* literature Iwamoto distinguishes four periods: 1. The period of the formation of *avadāna* stories; 2. The period of old prose *avadāna* literature; 3. The period of metrical *avadāna* literature; 4. The period of late prose *avadāna* literature. He subdivides the third period into two: the first including the *avadānamalas* in the form of conversations between Aśoka and Upagupta; the second including the *avadanamālās* told by Jayaśrī. In dating these periods he places the second period in the second and third centuries and period 3a from the third century onward. He claims the third century was the great period of the development of the *avadāna* literature. This is certainly too early. Speyer has drawn attention to the fact that the *Kalpadrumāvadānamālā* quotes the *Jātakamālā* (Preface, p. XXXVI). One would have to study the texts quoted in the *avadānamālās* very closely, and to distinguish the different styles in which they are written, before making any definite statement about their date. Iwamoto relates the four periods to the specimens of styles, given by Professor John Brough (*BSOAS*, XVI, 1954, pp. 369-374), but I am afraid that much more research is needed to obtain a satisfactory classification of the *avadāna* literature according to the styles used by their authors.

An appendix contains three specimens of *avadāna* literature: the *Bhavaśarmāvadāna* (*Aśokāvadānamālā*, nr. 24), the *Kavikumārāvadāna* and the *Siṃhalasārthavāhoddhāraṇa* (*Guṇakāraṇḍavyūha*, nr. 16).

On p. 61 Iwamoto quotes a passage of the Tibetan translation of the *Sumāgadhāvadāna*. In lines 2 and 5 *ches sruṅ* and *pos sruṅ* must be corrected into *che sa sruṅ* and *po sa sruṅ*. In the quotation on page 62 of § 68 of the Sanskrit text *Sumerubhṛguṇaparivestitaṇ* is incomprehensible. MS B has *bhrigune*. Perhaps one must read °*triguṇa*°.

Professor Iwamoto's book contains a wealth of material. His knowledge of Sanskrit, Tibetan and Chinese enables him to make a much more comprehensive study of the *avadāna* literature than his western predecessors. One may expect that his future publications will bring many new results in this field which has been neglected since the days of Feer and Speyer. If Professor Iwamoto can restrain a certain tendency to draw conclusions which are not fully warranted by the available materials, one may look forward to very valuable contributions to the study of the *avadāna* literature from him. Above all, I hope that he will give us editions of unpublished texts. Many *avadāna* texts have been known for a long time from catalogues and brief mentions, but very little has been published, especially from the later *avadāna* literature. The most important of these texts must be published first. Only then can we hope to obtain a better insight into the development of this important branch of Buddhist literature.

A.N.U., Canberra J. W. de Jong

REVIEWS

Johannes Nobel, *Udrāyaṇa, König von Roruka.* Eine buddhistische Erzählung. Die tibetische Übersetzung des Sanskrittextes, Wiesbaden, 1955. I. Text, deutsche Übersetzung und Anmerkungen, xxvii + 113 pp.; II. Wörterbuch, vii + 87 pp. DM 28.—.

L'histoire d'Udrāyaṇa, roi de Roruka (*Divy.* p. 544–586), a été étudiée à plusieurs reprises mais sans tenir compte des versions tibétaine et chinoise. Dans deux volumes, édités de manière excellente par Harrassowitz, M. Nobel nous livre le résultat de ses études de la version tibétaine. Le premier volume contient une introduction, le texte tibétain édité d'apès les Kanjurs de Pékin, Lhasa, Narthang et le Kanjur manuscrit de Berlin, et une traduction annotée du texte tibétain; le deuxième volume un dictionnaire tibétain-sanskrit-allemand. Dans l'introduction l'auteur met en lumière l'importance de la version tibétaine pour établir un meilleur texte sanskrit, et donne un résumé de l'histoire. Ensuite il soumet à l'examen les données géographiques en indiquant les variations dans la version de Yi-tsing et s'occupe spécialement de la localisation de Roruka, identifié à tort par Huber et Lévi au Roruka près de Khotan que mentionne Hiuan-tsang. M. N. souligne que, déjà en 1915, Lulius van Goor dans son travail *De buddhistische non* a démontré l'impossibilité de cette identification. Finalement M. N. étudie d'autres recensions de la légende et des représentations sur des reliefs du Borobudur et sur une peinture dans les grottes de Qyzil près de Koutcha.

Le texte tibétain a été édité d'après les quatre éditions mentionnées ci-dessus. On remarquera l'absence des Kanjurs de Derge et de Cone. La préface n'explique pas si le choix des éditions a été déterminé par des raisons d'ordre pratique ou, ce qui ne paraît guère probable, par une préférence basée sur leur supériorité aux deux autres. A un endroit une correction du texte s'impose: p. 28, l. 31: *'jigs-pai chos-can yin-no //* correspond au sanskrit *bhaṅguram* (*Divy.* p. 567, l. 1); la confusion de *'jigs* et *'jig* est fréquente dans les xylographes, et il est évident qu'il faut lire ici *'jig* et qu'il n'est nullement nécessaire de supposer que les traducteurs ont lu *bhayadhārmikam* ou *bhayadharmam*. A la page 5, l. 17 *'on-cig* (skt. *ānaya*) est probablement une erreur pour *thon-cig*.

M. Shackleton Bailey a constaté (*JRAS*, 1950, 166–167) que plusieurs avadāna du Divyāvadāna sont des abrégés des histoires du Vinaya et que d'autres ne montrent que quelques omissions. Une comparaison de la version tibétaine de l'histoire de Roruka avec le texte sanskrit du Divyāvadāna montre que celui-ci comporte d'assez nombreuses omissions. A quelques endroits elles portent sur des clichés, et dans ces cas on peut renvoyer à des passages parallèles. Par exemple, après *cākirṇabahujanamanuṣyaṃ ca* (p. 545, l. 2) suit en tibétain un passage que l'on retrouve *Divy.* p. 435, l. 7–9: *śāntakalikalahaḍimbaḍamaraṃ taskaradurbhikṣarogāpagataṃ śālikṣugomahiṣīsaṃpannam | dhārmiko dharmarājo dharmeṇa rājyaṃ kārayati |* (l'édition de Cowell et Neil lit *°ḍamarataskara°* ce qui doit être changé comme ci-dessus d'après la version tibétaine); après *mārgaśobhā kṛtā* (p. 548, l. 14) il faut lire probablement: *Raurukaṃ nagaram apy apagatapāṣāṇaśarkarakaṭhallaṃ vyavasthāpitaṃ candanavārisiktam surabhidhūpaghaṭikopanibaddham āmuktapaṭṭadāmakalāpaṃ samucchritacchatradhvajaṃ nānāpuṣpābhikirṇaṃ ramaṇīyaṃ devodyānaṃ Nandanavanam iva*, voir *Divy.* p. 45, l. 10–, p. 441, l. 12–, p. 460, l. 16–, p. 576, l. 8–, *Mahāvastu*, III, p. 141, l. 15– et

Mahāvyutpatti 6058, 6059 et 6120. Ce dernier cliché ne se rencontre à aucun des endroits cités sous la même forme (signalons les variantes suivantes: *vyavasthitam* [une corruption évidente] au lieu de *vyavasthāpitam*, *pariṣiktam* au lieu de *siktam*, *samalaṃkṛtam* au lieu d'*upanibaddham*, *avasakta* au lieu d'*āmukta*, *ucchrita* au lieu de *samucchrita*, *avakīrṇa* au lieu d'*abhikīrṇa* sans mentionner les omissions et additions), et les mots *devodyānaṃ Nandanavanam iva* même manquent partout. Du seul passage parallèle (*Divy.* p. 45, l. 10–) dont j'ai pu consulter la version tibétaine, le texte est aussi différent: *rdo-ba daṅ gseg-ma daṅ gyo-mo rnams sel-du bcug-ste / tsan-dan-gyi chus chag-chag btab dri žim-poi bog-phor sna-thsogs bśams / dar-gyi chun'phyaṅ maṅ-po dpyaṅs / me-tog sna-thsogs chal-bar bkram-ste dga'-dga'-ltar byas-te* (édition Cone, *'Dul-ba.* vol. Ka, p. 310b, 1–2). C'est une preuve de plus que même un cliché peut rarement être reconstruit en sanskrit s'il n'est pas très fréquent. Cet exemple confirme bien les remarques judicieuses de M. N. sur la fidélité des retraductions en sanskrit.

Dans les notes de la traduction M. N. signale les différences entre les textes sanskrit et tibétain qui, le plus souvent, sont dues à des corruptions du premier. L'auteur suggère de nombreuses corrections, et, à part quelques passages désespérés, réussit à établir un texte très satisfaisant. Chemin faisant il apporte plusieurs corrections bienvenues au dictionnaire d'Edgerton, et montre ainsi en même temps la grande utilité de ce dictionnaire et la nécessité de vérifications à la lumière des versions tibétaines. Qu'il me soit permis d'ajouter une petite pierre au travail de construction d'un texte sanskrit plus correct en proposant quelques conjectures supplémentaires:

p. 546, l. 13 le texte skt. lit: *prātisīmaiḥ kīdṛśaṃ rājabhiḥ sārdhaṃ* alors que le texte tib. a: *ñe-'khor-gyi mkhar-gyi rgyal-po-rnams daṅ-lhan-cig*; probablement il faut corriger *kīdṛśaṃ rājabhiḥ* en *koṭṭarājabhiḥ*. La Mahāvyutpatti traduit *koṭṭa* par *mkhar* (5495) et par *khams* (3677); *khams* paraît suspect et est peut-être une erreur pour *mkhar*.

p. 568, l. 3 M. N. corrige *dharmavinaṣṭatvād* en *karma°*. Le tib. (*las-kyis non-pas*) correspond mieux à *karmāvaṣṭabdhatvād*.

p. 576, l. 30 le texte skt.: *pāṃśubhir anavikṛtā* mais le tib.: *sas phyed-tsam gaṅ-bar gyur-nas*. Lire *pāṃśubhir ardhāvakīrṇā* ou *pāṃśunārdhāvakīrṇā*?

C'est surtout dans les strophes que l'on trouve des corruptions irrémédiables. Sur quelques passages M. N. a demandé l'opinion de Helmer Smith, mais pour ingénieuses que soient ses suggestions, elles n'emportent pas la conviction. L'état corrompu de certaines strophes n'est certainement pas seulement dû au fait qu'elles ont été transmises d'abord en moyen-indien. Les Bouddhistes, en émaillant leurs contes de strophes, ont puisé dans le trésor inépuisable de strophes gnomiques qui présentent d'innombrables variations. C'est pourquoi il est intéressant d'essayer de rechercher ces strophes ailleurs dans la littérature bouddhique et brahmanique. Ce sera une tâche réservée à l'avenir d'étudier ainsi l'ensemble des strophes gnomiques qui figurent dans les textes bouddhiques. Ce travail a été amorcé par R. Otto Franke ("Jātaka-Mahābhārata-Parallelen", *WZKM*, 20, 1906, 317–372) et mérite d'être repris pour la lumière qu'il pourrait jeter sur le procès de formation de la littérature bouddhique. Pour apporter une petite contribution à cette recherche je signale quelques parallèles que j'ai notées en lisant l'histoire de Roruka:

p. 561, l. 1–4 cf. Dhammapada 128; Udānavarga I, 25 (éd. Chakravarti, p. 6).

p. 561, l. 5–7 cf. Dhammapada 127; Udānavarga IX, 5 (éd. Chakravarti, p. 98).

p. 561, l. 8–9 cf. Udānavarga I, 3 (éd. Beckh, p. 2); Gāthāsaṃgraha 21 (éd. Schiefner, *Mélanges asiatiques*, VIII, 565).

p. 563, l. 1–2 cf. Pañcatantra I, 67 (éd. Edgerton, p. 85 où sont indiquées toutes les variantes des différentes recensions du Pañcatantra): *viṣadigdhasya bhaktasya dantasya calitasya ca | amātyasya ca duṣṭasya mūlād uddharaṇaṃ sukham |*; il est intéressant de constater que Yi-tsing lui aussi parle de nourriture empoisonnée alors que dans la version tibétaine et dans le texte sanskrit il n'est question que de mauvaise nourriture.

Faut-il supposer que Yi-tsing a eu à sa disposition un texte moins corrompu que celui utilisé par les traducteurs tibétains?

p. 565, l. 2–3 cf. Pañcatantra I, 173 (éd. Edgerton, p. 179), Mahābhārata XII, 138,47 (Crit. Ed., p. 758) et I, App. I (81), 104–105 (Crit. Ed., p. 932).

Pour terminer quelques petites remarques:

p. 547, l. 10 *bhojayed* a été rendu en tib. par *gdugs-thsod gsol*. C'est l'équivalent de *spyan-draṅs-te* (skt. *upanimantrya*) qui manque.

p. 551, l. 1 M. N. traduit *mahāviśeṣo'dhigataḥ* par "die grosse Vorzüglichkeit (der Lehre) klar erkannten"; je crois qu'ici comme dans l'expression *guṇagaṇo'dhigataḥ* (voir Nobel, I, p. 111, n. 7) *adhigata* signifie "obtenu": "ils obtenaient une grande supériorité (en devenant śrota-āpanna, etc.)".

p. 551, l. 19 l'expression *avidyāvidāritāṇḍakośa* donne des difficultés. M. N. traduit par "spalteten die Eierschalen des Nichtwissens" mais cela serait en skt.: *vidāritāvidyāṇḍakośa*. Le tib. a *rig-pas* et dans l'Avadānaśataka Speyer a partout lu *vidyāvidāritāṇḍakośa* mais, dans l'introduction (p. lxxiii, n. 127), il propose de lire *avidyā*°. Dans les manuscrits de Gilgit, vol. III, part 2, p. 131, l. 3, le MS. a *vidyā*° mais la version tibétaine *ma-rig-pa*. D'autre part, dans des textes pālis anciens, on trouve *avijj'aṇḍakosa* (*Vin*. III, 4, 1; *AN*, IV, 176, 16; *Nett*. 61, 9). On se demande s'il ne faut pas corriger en *vidyāvidāritāvidyāṇḍakośa* ou s'il faut lire partout *vidyāvidāritāṇḍakośa*, *aṇḍakośa* étant identique à *avidyāṇḍakośa*, comme l'avait déjà suggéré Bloomfield (*JAOS*, 40, 1920, p. 340 qui y traite aussi d'autres épithètes de l'Arhat).

p. 62, n. 4 M. N. propose de corriger *svayam abhijñāya* (*Divy*. p. 618, l. 7) en *svayam abhijñayā*. Mais malgré le tib. *raṅ-gi mṅon-par śes-pas* et *Avadānaśataka* II, 195, 11 (où le MS a *abhijñāyā*) cette correction ne s'impose pas car, en pāli, il y a un absolutif (*sayaṃ abhiññā sacchikatvā*), voir CPD, p. 343b, de même que dans les MSS de Gilgit (vol. III, part 1, p. 48, l. 16: *svayam abhijñāya sākṣātkṛtvā*; mais étant donné les imperfections de cette édition il faudrait pouvoir consulter le MS pour être sûr de la lecture).

p. 94, l. 9 les mots "Bei meinem Anblick" ont été ajoutés par M. N. car ils manquent en tib. et en skt.

p. 97, n. 2 dans la troisième ligne il faut ajouter *saṃprayata* avant *samucchinna*.

p. 100, n. 4 et n. 5 ces corrections ont déjà été proposées par Bloomfield, *JAOS*, 40 (1920), 352.

p. 103 le thème de l'immobilité de l'ombre d'un arbre se retrouve dans la littérature indienne, voir J. J. Meyer, *Hindu Tales* (London, 1909), p. 212, n. 2 qui donne des références et V. Raghavan, Raghuvaṁśa XII, 21 (*Annals of Oriental Research*, XIII, 1957, Sanskrit part, p. 82–85) qui ignore le travail de Meyer.

Fautes d'impression: p. 53, n. 4 lire *yasya* au lieu de *yasga*; p. 105, n. 1 lire *saṃjñā* au lieu de *saṃjūā*.

Dans le dictionnaire il manque le mot *skar-khuṅ* (skt. *vātāyana*); s.v. *snod* ajouter une référence à p. 7, l. 1 où *snod* = skt. *ghaṭikā* et s.v. *len-pa* lire *abhyupapatti* au lieu d'*abhyutsāhanā*.

Le travail de M. Nobel est extrêmement soigné et témoigne de sa grande compétence dans le domaine des études bouddhiques. Plus de cent-dix ans après la publication par Burnouf de plusieurs contes du Divyāvadāna en traduction française dans son *Introduction à l'histoire du Buddhisme indien* (Paris, 1844), M. N. est le premier à nous présenter le texte tibétain d'un des contes, accompagné d'une traduction annotée et d'un dictionnaire. Espérons que son exemple incitera d'autres savants à se consacrer à l'étude de la version tibétaine des contes du Divyāvadāna.

Leiden J. W. de Jong

Sujitkumar Mukhopādhyāya, *The Aśokāvadāna. Sanskrit text compared with Chinese versions*. Edited, annotated and partly translated. New Delhi, Sahitya Akademi, 1963. lxxiii + 183 pp. Rs. 18 / 36 sh.

Le *Divyāvadāna* contient quatre chapitres relatifs à la légende d'Aśoka: 26. Pāṃśupradānāvadāna (éd. Cowell et Neil, pp. 348.4-382.3); 27. Kunālāvadāna (pp. 382.4-419.13); 28. Vītaśokāvadāna (pp. 419.14-429.5); 29. Aśokāvadāna (pp. 429.6-434). Burnouf en a traduit une grande partie (pp. 369.8-434) en lui donnant le titre d'*Aśokāvadāna* (*Introduction à l'histoire du Buddhisme indien*, Paris, 1844, pp. 358-432).[1] En réalité, le titre *Aśokāvadāna* ne se trouve dans les manuscrits qu'à la fin du chapitre 29. Puisque le texte de ces chapitres se retrouve presque en entier dans l' *A-yu wang tchouan* (*Taishō* No. 2042) et l'*A-yu wang king* (*Taishō* No. 2043), deux traductions chinoises d'un *Aśokāvadāna* indien, l'emploi du titre *Aśokāvadāna* n'est pas sans fondement. Toutefois, on aurait tort d'admettre que le *Divyāvadāna* a conservé fidèlement une recension authentique de l'*Aśokāvadāna* car une comparaison avec les textes chinois, mentionnés ci-dessus, montre que le *Divyāvadanā* ne contient que des fragments d'un ancien *Aśokāvadāna*. Dans sa nouvelle édition du texte de l'*Aśokāvadāna* Monsieur Sujitkumar Mukhopādhyāya ne suit pas l'ordre du *Divyāvadāna* en ce qui concerne l'arrangement des chapitres. Après le Pāṃśupradānāvadāna (pp. 1-55) suivent le Vītaśokāvadāna (pp. 56-70), le Kunālāvadāna (pp. 71-125) et le Aśokāvadāna (pp. 126-135). M. Mukhopādhyāya justifie cet ordre en se référant aux deux traductions chinoises (Introduction, p. lxx). Si l'on voulait suivre de plus près les textes chinois, il faudrait adopter l'ordre suivant : 1. La deuxième partie du Pāṃśupradānāvadāna (*Divy.* pp. 364.14-382.3); 2. La première partie du Kunālāvadāna à l'exception du début (pp. 384.28-405.15); 3. Le Vītaśokāvadāna (pp. 419.14-429.5); 4. La deuxième partie du Kunālāvadāna (pp. 405.16-419.13); 5. L' Aśokāvadāna (pp. 429.6-434); 6. La première partie du Pāṃsupradānāvadāna à l'exception des premières et dernières lignes (pp. 348.19-364.10); 7. Le début du Kunālāvadāna (pp. 382.4-383.3). La dernière section ne se retrouve que dans l'*A-yu wang tchouan* (k. 7, pp. 129c22-130a9) et n'est qu'une partie d'un conte qu'Édouard Huber a retrouvé dans le *Sūtrālaṃkāra* d'Aśvaghoṣa ("Trois contes du Sūtrālaṃkāra d'Açvaghoṣa conservés dans le Divyāvadāna", *BEFEO*, IV, 1904, pp. 719-723), cf. *Taishō* No. 201, k.3, pp. 274a13-275a27 = *Divy.* pp. 382.4-384.27. En plus de ce conte intitulé "Aśoka et Yaśas" par Huber, deux autres ont été identifiés par lui avec des contes du *Sūtrālaṃkāra*: 1. "Upagupta et Māra"

[6] For example, in Huang Wên-pi, *T'a-li-mu p'ên-ti k'ao-ku-chi* there are facsimiles of 1 palmleaf and 4 paper fragments of Sanskrit texts in Brāhmī script (Plates LXXVI-LXXVII, illustrations Nos. 8-11 and 13), obtained at a temple site near Qarašähr (Map No. 3, photo No. 1) [at this site 6 paper fragments were unearthed in all; see p. 128], and facsimiles of 4 pages of paper documents in Brāhmī script (Plates LXXIII-LXXIV, illustrations No. 6; see p. 134), obtained at an ancient tomb site near Maralbaši. They were all discovered during the 1928-1929 Chinese expedition to the Tarim Basin (see p. 97). In his *T'u-lu-fan k'ao-ku-chi*, however, Huang Wên-pi does not say anything about Sanskrit texts obtained during the 1928 and 1930 expeditions to Turfan.

[1] En outre Burnouf a traduit quelques pages (pp. 352.28-354.25) du chapitre 26 (*op. cit.*, pp. 146-148).

(*Divy.* pp. 357.18-363.6; *Taishō* No. 201, k.9, pp. 307c1-309b22); 2. "Le don de la moitié de la mangue" (*Divy.* pp. 430.25-432.25; *Taishō* No. 201, k.5, pp. 283a29-284b25), cf. *op. cit*, pp. 713-719 et 723-726. La comparaison du texte de l'Aśokāvadāna du *Divyāvadāna* avec les traductions chinoises a été avancée beaucoup par Jean Przyluski ("Le Nord-Ouest de l'Inde dans le Vinaya des Mūla-Sarvāstivādin et les textes apparentés", *JA*, 1914, II, pp. 493-568; *La légende de l'empereur Açoka*, Paris, 1923). On trouvera une mise au point dans le premier volume de l'*Histoire du bouddhisme indien* par M. Étienne Lamotte (Louvain, 1958), pp. 261-272 et 226-232.

Selon M. Mukhopādhyāya l'*Aśokāvadāna* a été écrit aux environs du deuxième siècle de notre ère. Un de ses arguments est que l'auteur a emprunté trois passages au *Sūtrālaṃkāra* d'Aśvaghoṣa. Depuis la publication de fragments de la *Kalpanāmaṇḍitikā* de Kumāralāta par Heinrich Lüders (*Bruchstrücke der Kalpanāmaṇḍitikā des Kumāralāta*, Leipzig, 1926) la paternité et le titre du *Sūtrālaṃkāra* ont été discutés par de nombreux savants. Les problèmes sont loin d'être définitivement résolus comme le relève à juste titre M. Yamada Ryūjō (*Hongo butten no shobunken*, Kyoto, 1959, p. 72). On trouvera dans le livre de M. Yamada une énumération des nombreux travaux d'auteurs occidentaux et japonais sur cette question. On peut y ajouter les articles suivants: Jean Przyluski, "Dārṣṭāntika, Sautrāntika and Sarvāstivādin", *IHQ*, XVI, 1940, pp. 246-254 et D. R. Shackleton Bailey, "Mecaka et le Sūtrālaṃkāra", *JA*, 1952, pp. 71-73. A ma connaissance l'ouvrage japonais le plus récent qu'il faut signaler est le livre de M. Kanakura Enshō: *Mamyō no kenkyū* [Studies on Aśvaghoṣa] (Kyoto, 1966). En tout cas, il ne suffit pas de renvoyer à deux articles de Sylvain Lévi, publiés respectivement en 1908 et 1928, pour prouver la paternité d'Aśvaghoṣa comme le fait M. Mukhopādhyāya. L'emploi du mot *dīnāra* dans deux passages du texte (*Divy.* pp. 427.13 et 434.12) ne prouve pas que l'*Aśokāvadāna* original n'ait été rédigé qu'après l'introduction des deniers romains dans l'Inde (cf. Przyluski, *Légende*, p. XIV). M. Mukhopādhyāya a le tort de ne pas tenir compte du fait que le *Divyāvadāna* et les traductions chinoises nous font connaître plusieurs recensions de l'*Aśokāvadāna*. En plus de l'*A-yu wang tchouan* et l'*A-yu wang king* des fragments d'un *Aśokāvadāna* ont été conservés dans le *Samyuktāgama* chinois (*Taishō* No. 99). M. Mukhopādhyāya affirme que cet ouvrage contient tous les chapitres de l'*Aśokāvadāna* à l'exception du Vītaśokāvadāna (Introduction, p. lix). Il a omis d'indiquer l'absence de la deuxième partie du Kunālāvadāna du *Divyāvadāna* (pp. 405-419) qui constitue le Kunālāvadāna proprement dit car la première partie contient l'avadāna du roi Aśoka (cf. Przyluski, *Légende*, pp. 55-56; Lamotte, *op. cit.*, p. 265). Que l'on accepte ou non l'hypothèse d'un *Aśokasūtra* primitif, rédigé entre 150 et 50 avant notre ère (cf. Przyluski, *Légende*, pp. 67 et 93), il n'y a pas de doute que la légende d'Aśoka ait dû se développer et s'accroître au cours des siècles. Quant au texte de l'Aśokāvadāna du *Divyāvadāna*, il a dû subir des remaniements et altérations jusqu'à une époque récente car on y trouve même une strophe et demie empruntée à l'*Avadānakalpalatā* de Kṣemendra (cf. G. M. Bongard-Levin et O. F. Volkova, *Legenda o Kunala*, Moskva, 1963, p. 90; *IIJ*, VIII, 1965, p. 238).

Pour sa nouvelle édition de l'*Aśokāvadāna* M. Mukhopādhyāya a consulté deux manuscrits de l'Asiatic Society of Bengal dont l'un contient le Pāṃśupradānāvadāna et l'autre le Vītaśokāvadāna et l'Aśokāvadāna (G 9982A et A 8)[2] mais ces manuscrits ne semblent contenir que rarement des leçons qui diffèrent de celles que donnent les manuscrits utilisés par les éditeurs du *Divyāvadāna*. Toutefois, il y a d'autres manuscrits du *Divyāvadāna* et de la *Divyāvadānamālā* que M. Iwamoto Yutaka a signalés dans un

[2] Le premier manuscrit a été décrit par Mahāmahopādhyāya Hara Prasad dans *A Descriptive Catalogue of Sanskrit Manuscripts in the Government Collection under the care of the Asiatic Society of Bengal*, vol. 1 (Calcutta, 1917), p. 23, no. 22. Toutefois le manuscrit y est numeroté 9882A. Pour le deuxième manuscrit voir Rājendralāla Mitra, *The Sanskrit Buddhist Literature of Nepal* (Calcutta, 1882), pp. 304-316.

ouvrage récent (*Bukkyō setsuwa kenkyū josetsu*, Kyoto, 1966, p. 138). En outre, l'*Aśokāvadānamālā* a emprunté beaucoup au *Divyāvadāna* comme l'ont prouvé M. Bongard-Levin et Melle Volkova dans leur édition du Kuṇālāvadāna. Ce chapitre de l'Aśokāvadānamālā contient 33 strophes empruntées au *Divyāvadāna*. Il y a lieu de supposer que les autres chapitres de cet ouvrage, relatifs à la légende d'Aśoka, ont également puisé largement dans le *Divyāvadāna* (cf. Przyluski, *Légende*, pp. xiv-xv). C'est surtout des traductions chinoises que M. Mukhopādhyāya dit avoir tiré profit pour corriger des leçons obscures (Introduction, p. lvii). M. Mukhopādhyāya semble avoir utilisé surtout (ou exclusivement) la traduction française de l'*A-yu wang tchouan* par Przyluski. Ce choix a été probablement déterminé par le seul fait que cette recension peut être lue dans l'excellente traduction faite par Przyluski, car, comme le relève Przyluski et après lui M. Mukhopādhyāya, c'est l'*A-yu wang king* qui est plus proche du texte du *Divyāvadāna* (Przyluski, *Légende*, p. xiii). Pour les trois contes qui se retrouvent dans le *Sūtrālaṃkāra* d'Aśvaghoṣa M. Mukhopādhyāya aurait dû consulter l'article d'Édouard Huber, cité ci-dessus, dans lequel Huber suggère plusieurs corrections du texte sanskrit basées sur la traduction chinoise (la plupart des ces corrections sont dues à Louis Finot). Bien que M. Mukhopādhyāya cite la traduction du *Sūtrālaṃkāra* par Huber, il ne semble pas avoir pris connaissance de cet article. Des fragments du texte sanskrit de ces trois contes ont été édités par Lüders qui a aussi donné un texte corrigé des passages suivants du *Divy.*: 382.4-383.23, 363.23-26, 430.25-431.16, 433.9-12, 431.17-432.23, 358.3-363.6 (*op. cit.*, pp. 145-150, 166-171; pour des corrections de *Divy.* pp. 356-358, 434 et 429-430 voir pp. 84 et 99-100). Enfin, pour le début de l'Aśokāvadāna (pp. 348.19-364.10) il y a, en plus des deux recencions de l'Aśokāvadāna, plusieurs autres textes parallèles que l'on trouvera énumérés dans l' *Histoire du bouddhisme indien* de M. Ét. Lamotte (p. 226).

Probablement toutes ces traductions chinoises ne seraient pas d'une grande aide pour l'établissement d'un texte plus correct. En effet, on ne voit pas que l'*A-yu wang tchouan* ait rendu beaucoup de services à M. Mukhopādhyāya sauf pour signaler en bas de page des différences de cette recension avec le texte du *Divyāvadāna*. Plus utile serait probablement la traduction tibétaine du Kunālāvadāna qui représente une recension élargie du Kunālāvadāna du *Divyāvadāna*. Malheureusement, bien que M. Mukhopādhyāya signale cette traduction, il ne s'en est pas servi du tout (pour le Kunālāvadāna tibétain voir aussi *IIJ*, VIII, 1965, pp. 238-239). En fin de compte, la plupart des corrections, proposées par M. Mukhopādhyāya, ne reposent pas sur des passages parallèles dans d'autres recensions. L'éditeur s'est surtout efforcé d'éloigner toutes les irrégularités grammaticales et métriques que présente le texte du *Divyāvadāna* dans l'édition de Cowell et Neil qui, délibérément, avaient choisi de garder le plus possible les leçons des manuscrits même si elles n'étaient pas d'accord avec les normes du sanskrit classique (preface, p. viii). On peut se demander si M. Mukhopādhyāya s'est rendu compte du fait que la langue du *Divyāvadāna* présente beaucoup de caractéristiques propres au 'Buddhist Hybrid Sanskrit'. Dans l'appendix C (explanations, textual criticism and references) on ne trouvera aucune référence au *Buddhist Hybrid Sanskrit Grammar and Dictionary* d'Edgerton. C'est uniquement en faisant appel au Pāli que des mots et des formes qui ne se rencontrent pas en sanskrit classique sont expliqués. En procédant ainsi, M. Mukhopādhyāya n'a pas évité des erreurs. Pour ne citer qu'un seul exemple. Le sens de *vicchandayati* a été bien interprété par Edgerton dans son dictionnaire où il cite *Divy.* 383.5-6: *yasmāt tvaṃ bhikṣucaraṇapraṇāmaṃ māṃ vicchandayitum icchasi*, "*since you wish to dissuade me* (against, from) *bowing at the feet of monks* (or is this acc. a Bhvr. adj., *me characterized by bowing* etc. ?)." M. Mukhopādhyāya traduit *vicchandayitum* par 'to interrupt, to prevent', renvoyant au Pāli *vicchindati*. Edgerton a bien montré qu'il ne faut pas confondre *vi-chand-* et *vi-chind-* comme le font parfois les manuscrits.

Il est hors de doute que le texte de l'*Aśokāvadāna* a été mal transmis. Même en gardant les particularités du Buddhist Hybrid Sanskrit que présente le texte, il y a de nombreux endroits qui se prêtent au jeu des conjectures. Depuis Burnouf qui déjà a proposé des corrections dans les leçons des manuscrits beaucoup de savants se sont penchés sur le texte de l'*Aśokāvadāna*. Il est surprenant que leurs travaux semblent être restés inconnus à M. Mukhopādhyāya à l'exception de la traduction du *Sūtrālaṃkāra* par Huber et celle de l'*A-yu wang tchouan* par Przyluski. *Divy*. pp. 356.14-364.3 a été étudié et traduit par Ernst Windisch (*Māra und Buddha*, Leipzig, 1895, pp. 163-176). On y trouvera de nombreuses corrections dont plusieurs sont dues à Böhtlingk. En 1902 J. S. Speyer a publié des "Critical Remarks on the text of the Divyāvadāna" (*WZKM*, 16, 1902, pp. 103-130; 340-361). Des corrections, proposées par Huber et Finot, se trouvent dans l'article que Huber a publié en 1904 ("Trois contes du Sutrālaṃkāra d'Açvaghoṣa conservés dans le Divyāvadāna", *BEFEO*, IV, 1904, pp. 709-726). Une partie du Kunālāvadāna (pp. 405.16-418.2) a été traduite par Johannes Hertel en 1908 (*Ausgewählte Erzählungen aus Hēmacandras Pariśiṣṭaparvan*, Leipzig, 1908, pp. 250-265). L'influence d'Aśvaghoṣa sur l'*Aśokāvadāna* a été étudiée par Andrzej Gawronski ("The epical poems of Aśvaghoṣa and the Divyāvadāna", *Studies about the Sanskrit Buddhist Literature*, Krakowie, 1919, pp. 49-56). Ici M. Mukhopādhyāya aurait pu trouver des arguments plus solides pour placer l'*Aśokāvadāna* après Aśvaghoṣa (cf. aussi E.J. Johnston, *The Buddhacarita*, Part II, Calcutta, 1936, p. xxv). Quelques corrections, relatives à l'*Aśokāvadāna*, se trouvent dans les "Notes on the Divyāvadāna" par Maurice Bloomfield (*JAOS*, 40, 1920, pp. 336-352). L'histoire d'Upagupta (pp. 348.19-356.5) a été traduite par Heinrich Zimmer (*Karman, ein buddhistischer Legendenkranz*, München, 1925, pp. 175-194). A ces travaux il faut ajouter ceux que j'ai déjà mentionnés ci-dessus tels que le dictionnaire et la grammaire du Buddhist Hybrid Sanskrit par Franklin Edgerton (New Haven, 1953) et l'étude de M. Bongard-Levin et Melle Volkova sur le Kuṇālāvadāna.[3]

En éditant de nouveau un texte, étudié si souvent, M. Mukhopādhyāya aurait dû être au courant des efforts déjà faits pour améliorer le texte de l'*Aśokāvadāna*. Plusieurs fois il propose des corrections qui ont été signalées il y a longtemps. Par exemple il corrige *Divy*. p. 359.19 *raviṃ maṇḍalinā* en *ravim añjalinā*, correction déjà suggérée par Böhtlingk (cf. Windisch, *Māra und Buddha*, p. 169, n. 1.). Huber avait remarqué que le traducteur chinois donne raison à Böhtlingk (*BEFEO*, IV, 1904, p. 716, n.1.). La même correction a été aussi proposée par Helmer Smith qui ne semble pas avoir connu les travaux de Windisch et Huber ("En marge du vocabulaire sanskrit des bouddhistes", *Orientalia suecana*, II, 1953, p. 120).[4] Comme on voit, M. Mukhopādhyāya n'est pas le seul à avoir négligé les travaux de ses devanciers. Un autre exemple est le mot *aṇḍakāṣṭha* qui a causé des difficultés à Edgerton (cf. *BHS Dictionary*, *aṇḍakāṣṭha* et *hirodaka*). Dans *Divy*. p. 384.19-20 Finot avait proposé de lire: *Aśoko rājā hirodakasikatāpiṇḍairaṇḍakāṣṭhebhyo'pi asārataratvaṃ kāyasyāvetya*, "Le roi A., ayant reconnu que le corps était moins durable que la foudre, l'eau, une boule de sable, une tige d'*eraṇḍa*, etc.", en se rapprochant de la traduction chinoise (*Taishō* No. 201, k.3. p. 275a23-24) que Huber a rendue ainsi: "Ce corps passe rapide comme un éclair, comme une bulle d'eau, comme morceau de sable; comme un bananier, il n'a pas de noyau solide" (*BEFEO*, IV, 1904, p. 722, n. 1.). L'*eraṇḍa* (Ricinus communis) est connu dans la littérature bouddhique comme causant la folie et la mort et répandant une mauvaise odeur (cf. le passage du *Buddhānusmṛtisamādhisāgarasūtra*, *Taishō* no. 643, k.1, p. 646a21sq., cité par Mochizuki, *Bukkyōdaijiten*, pp. 197-198). L'*eraṇḍa* est souvent comparé au bois de santal (cf. le passage, cité ci-dessus et *Sūtrālaṃkāra* d'Aśvaghoṣa, *Taishō* no. 201, k.7, p. 297a6sq).[5] Finot a eu certainement raison de lire °*piṇḍairaṇḍa*-

[3] Cf. aussi J. Brough, "The Language of the Buddhist Sanskrit Texts", *BSOAS*, XVI, 1954, p. 374 pour une correction de *Divy*. p. 405.6-9.

[4] V. S. Agrawala ne semble pas avoir connu cette correction car il a proposé de traduire *maṇḍalin* par "ring-well" (*JAOS*, 79, 1959, p. 30; 86, 1966, p. 74).

kāṣṭhebhyo et d'eliminer ainsi 'les coquilles d'œufs' de Burnouf qui traduit: "Le roi Açoka ayant ainsi reconnu que le corps avait moins de valeur que des coquilles d'œufs pleines de boules de sable faites avec les larmes de serpent". Sa correction de *hirodaka* en *hirodaka* est plus incertaine. D'après Monier-Williams les lexiques contiennent un mot *hīra* 'thunderbolt' (ce sens n'est pas donné dans les dictionnaires de Pétersbourg). Il faut remarquer que le texte chinois est assez différent du texte sanskrit, car on n'y retrouve que le morceau de sable. Probablement le traducteur chinois a remplacé les comparaisons du texte sanskrit avec d'autres plus courantes. La bulle d'eau (*budbuda*) et le tronc de bananier (*kadalīskandha*) sont souvent mentionnés dans les textes bouddhiques. Notons aussi que la tige d'*eraṇḍa* n'est pas non plus mentionnée dans la traduction chinoise. On aurait tort de suivre de trop près la traduction chinoise qui – ajoutons-le – est probablement attribuée à tort au célèbre Kumārajīva. Cowell et Neil ont voulu expliquer *hirodaka* comme "vein-water, i.e. blood" (p. 709). Cette explication invraisemblable a été acceptée par Monier-Williams. Edgerton rapproche *hirā* d'un mot *hilā* 'sand' ce qui n'est guère plus probable. M. Mukhopādhyāya corrige hardiment *hirodaka* en *hi kṣodaka* sans expliquer ce dernier mot qu'il considère probablement comme identique à *kṣoda* (cf. *Divy.* p. 383.29: *ikṣukṣodavad*). V. S. Agrawala a suggéré de lire *himodaka* ce qui n'est pas impossible (*Vāk*, 5, 1957, p. 153). En tout cas, cet exemple, auquel je me suis arrêté un peu longuement, montre bien la difficulté de corriger un endroit corrompu à l'aide d'une traduction chinoise. C'est peut-être seulement en trouvant dans un texte les mêmes comparaisons pour des choses d'aucune valeur[6] que l'on pourra rétablir ici un texte satisfaisant.

Il n'est guère possible d'étudier ici toutes les corrections apportées par M. Mukhopādhyāya dans son édition du texte. Remarquons toutefois qu'il faut absolument rejeter celles qui sont basées uniquement sur l'*A-yu wang tchouan*. En incorporant dans le texte des mots qui ne se trouvent que dans cette traduction chinoise M. Mukhopādhyāya semble la considérer comme un manuscrit sanskrit dont on peut adopter les leçons. Heureusement, M. Mukhopādhyāya s'est borné le plus souvent à signaler les particularités de cette recension en bas de page, en rendant le texte chinois (ou plutôt la version française de Przyluski) en anglais ou en sanskrit. A quelques endroits M. Mukhopādhyāya apporte des changements qui sont contredits par le texte de l'*A-yu wang king*. Citons par exemple: *Divy.* p. 385.28: *Upaguptaṃ nāma – Upaguptam āryaṃ*; *nāma* est confirmé par la traduction chinoise, cf. *Taishō* no. 2043, k.2, p. 135c10. *Divy.* 409.28 *pīṣayitvā* est confirmé par l'*A-yu wang king* (k.4, p. 145a25) et M. Mukhopādhyāya a tort de lire *peṣayitvā* (cf. aussi *BHS Dictionary* s.v. *pīṣati, pīṣayati, pīṣeti*). Faute d'avoir étudié le Buddhist Hybrid Sanskrit, M. Mukhopādhyāya change souvent des mots qu'il aurait pu trouver dans le dictionnaire d'Edgerton, par exemple: *Divy.* 393.18: *adhimuktam* (*adhiyuktam*); p. 393.21: *Ṛṣivadanam* (*Ṛṣipatanam*); p. 397.27: *śuṣkitum* (*śoṣṭum*); p. 403.21: *vikurvate* (*vikurute*), etc. Toutefois, je n'aimerais pas terminer ce compte rendu sur un ton entièrement négatif. M. Mukhopādhyāya connaît très bien le sanskrit et le pāli. A plusieurs endroits il a adopté des corrections qui méritent d'être sérieusement prises en considération par un futur éditeur de l'*Aśokāvadāna*. C'est surtout le cas en ce qui concerne les strophes. L'auteur de l'*Aśokāvadāna* a employé une grande variété de mètres. L'édition de Cowell et Neil contient beaucoup de strophes incorrectes dont M. Mukhopādhyāya a essayé de rétablir le mètre.[7] Malheureusement, souvent les

---

[5] Cf. *Majjhimanikāya*, vol. II, pp. 183-184 pour l'emploi de l'*elaṇḍakaṭṭha* comme bois à brûler.

[6] La traduction que Burnouf donne d'*asārataratvam* ('moins de valeur') est préférable à celle de Finot ('plus instable').

[7] Dans l'appendice (pp. 159-177) M. Mukhopādhyāya indique les mètres qui se rencontrent dans l'*Aśokāvadāna*. Un aperçu systématique des mètres des textes en

corrections proposées s'écartent trop des leçons des manuscrits. D'autre part, M. Mukhopādhyāya n'a pas tenu compte du fait que les strophes ont dû être sanskritisées comme l'avait déjà relevé Speyer qui parlait même d'une traduction du prākrit en sanskrit: "Likewise, the narrations concerning Aśoka, especially the ns. XXVI and XXVII contain sundry instances of what we may call metaphrastical Sanskrit" (*WZKM*, 16, 1902, p. 104). Dans beaucoup de cas il faudra rétablir les formes du Buddhist Hybrid Sanskrit pour arriver à des strophes correctes.

Australian National University J. W. de Jong

G. M. Bongard-Levin, O. F. Volkova, *Legenda o Kunale* (*Kuṇālāvadāna iz neopublikovannoj rukopisi Aśokāvadānamālā*), Moskva, 1963, 120 pp.

Dans son *Introduction à l'histoire du buddhisme indien* (Paris, 1844, p. 358) Burnouf mentionne l'*Aśokāvadānamālā* qu'il caractérise comme une sorte de *Purāṇa*. Après lui, Rājendralāla Mitra et Bendall ont étudié des MSS. de l'*Aś.* (= *Aśokāvadānamālā*) dans les collections de Calcutta et de Cambridge et ont publié un résumé du contenu.[1] A propos de l'*Avadānaśataka* Feer et Speyer ont eu l'occasion de s'occuper de l'*Aś.*[2] Enfin, Serge Oldenbourg a fait quelques remarques sur l'*Aś.* dans la préface à la première partie de ses *Légendes bouddhiques*.[3] Il y annonce une deuxième partie, consacrée à l'*Aś.* et au *Vicitrakarṇikāvadāna*, mais elle n'a jamais paru. Dans son livre sur *La légende de l'empereur Açoka* (Paris, 1923) Jean Przyluski ne mentionne que très brièvement l'*Aś.* (pp. xiv-xv) et ne semble pas avoir consulté des manuscrits.

Deux jeunes indianistes russes, M. G. M. Bongard-Levin et Mlle O. F. Volkova, ont entrepris d'éditer et de traduire le texte entier de l'*Aś.*[4] L'édition et la traduction du *Kuṇālāvadāna* est le début de ce travail de longue haleine. Les éditeurs ont utilisé un manuscrit de 332 ff. qui appartient à la collection de manuscrits de l'Institut des Peuples de l'Asie à Leningrad. Les feuillets 90b-105b contiennent le texte du *Kuṇālāvadāna*. Ils n'ont pas eu recours à d'autres manuscrits qui, pourtant, sont assez nombreux. En plus des manuscrits décrits par Rājendralāla Mitra[5] et Bendall, il y a six manuscrits complets dans la Bir Library à Kathmandu et un manuscrit complet et plusieurs manuscrits partiels dans la Tokyo University Library.[6] Un manuscrit qui

[1] Rājendralāla Mitra, *The Sanskrit Buddhist Literature of Nepal* (Calcutta, 1882), 6-17; Cecil Bendall, *Catalogue of the Buddhist Sanskrit Manuscripts in the University Library, Cambridge* (Cambridge, 1883), 110-114.

[2] Léon Feer, *Avadâna-çataka. Cent légendes* (*bouddhiques*) (Paris, 1891), Introduction, xviii-xix; J. S. Speyer, *Avadānaçataka* (= *Bibliotheca Buddhica*, III) (1902-1909), Preface.

[3] *Buddijskija legendy. Čast' pervaja. Bhadrakalpāvadāna. Jātakamālā.* (Sanktpeterburg, 1894).

[4] M. Bongard-Levin a publié des travaux sur l'archéologie, voir en dernier lieu un aperçu historico-archéologique des cultures anciennes de l'Inde et du Pakistan dans *Narody Južnoj Azii* [Les Peuples de l'Asie du Sud] (Moscou, 1963), 51-101, sur l'épigraphie de l'époque des Maurya: "L'inscription d'Aśoka à Taxila", *Sov. Vost.*, 1956/1, 121-128; "L'inscription prākrite des Maurya à Mahāsthān", *Wiss. Z. d. Martin-Luther-Un. Halle-Wittenberg*, X/6, 1399-1405; "Āhāle d'après les données de l'épigraphie des Maurya", *Kr. Soobšč. INA*, 57, 1961, 10-20, et surtout sur l'histoire des Maurya: "La guerre de Kaliṅga et sa signification dans l'histoire du règne d'Aśoka", *VDI*, 1958/3, 33-41; "La *rājasabhā* et la *pariṣad* de l'Inde ancienne d'après l'Indica de Mégasthène", *Probl. Vost.*, 1959/2, 158-161; "Megasthenes' 'Indica' and the Inscriptions of Aśoka", *XXV Int. Congress of Or.*, Moscow, 1960; "Agrames-Ugrasena-Nanda et l'insurrection de Candragupta", *VDI*, 1962/4, 3-20; "Les fondements historiques des avadāna de l'Inde ancienne (la légende de la privation du pouvoir d'Aśoka et 'L'édit de la reine')", *Narody Azii i Afriki*, 1963/1, 106-116; "Quelques particularités de l'organisation politique de l'empire des Maurya", *Istorija i kultura drevnej Indii* [Histoire et culture de l'Inde ancienne] (Moscou, 1963), 15-67. Mlle Volkova a édité la traduction de la *Jātakamālā* par A. P. Barannikov et a traduit les chapitres qu'il n'avait pas traduits: *Ar'ja Šura. Girljanda džatak* (Moscou, 1962).

[5] Cf. aussi le manuscrit décrit par Hara Prasad Shāstri: *A descriptive catalogue of Sanskrit Manuscripts in the Government Collection* Vol. I, *Buddhist Manuscripts* (Calcutta, 1917), 24-25.

[6] *Taisho Daigaku Kenkyukiyo*, 40 (Tokyo, 1955), 57-58.

a appartenu à la Société Asiatique y manque depuis 1900, date à laquelle il fut prêté à Oldenbourg.[7] A moins que tous ces manuscrits ne soient des copies parfaitement identiques d'un même original, la collation de plusieurs d'entre eux serait souhaitable car le manuscrit de Leningrad ne suffit pas pour établir partout un texte satisfaisant.

Le compilateur du *Kuṇālāvadāna* a emprunté beaucoup de strophes au 59e pallava de l'*Avadānakalpalatā* de Kṣemendra et au 27e chapitre du *Divyāvadāna* qui, tous les deux, sont consacrés à la légende de Kuṇāla. Des 328 strophes du *Kuṇālāvadāna* 160 se retrouvent dans l'*Av.* (= *Avadānakalpalatā*) et 33 dans le *Di.* (= *Divyāvadāna*). Le manuscrit de l'*AŚ.* contient des variantes pour les textes de l'*Av.* et du *Di.* et, à quelques endroits, les éditeurs ont pu corriger des passages corrompus qui se trouvent dans ces deux textes. Malheureusement, en ce qui concerne le *Di.* le compilateur du *Kuṇālāvadāna* n'a pas eu à sa disposition un texte qui diffère essentiellement de celui qui est transmis par les manuscrits du *Di.*. Le texte de l'*Av.* a été beaucoup mieux conservé mais l'édition de Sarat Chandra Das et Vidyabhusana n'est pas très satisfaisante. La tâche des éditeurs du *Kuṇālāvadāna* était donc loin d'être facile. Il y a des endroits où l'on pourrait suggérer d'autres leçons comme dans les strophes suivantes:

9. *Kaṃdarpamuktālatikopamānāḥ*, MS. °*tikāyamānāḥ*. Les éditeurs rejettent la leçon du MS., en se référant à T. (= traduction tibétaine de l'*Av.*) mais celle-ci confirme le MS.: *'dod-pa'i mu-tig 'khri-śiṅ lta-bu byin*, "(Leurs filles) arrivées comme un collier de perles du dieu de l'amour." Le traducteur a employé *byin* "arrivé" pour rendre *-āyamāna*; *muktālatikāyate* est un dénominatif en *-āyate*, cf. L. Renou, *Grammaire sanscrite* (Paris, 1930), § 360b.

17. *tatheti kṛtvā manasi prapanne kṛtapraṇāmaḥ svapadaṃ jagāma*. Il faut corriger *manasi prapanne* en *manasi prasanne*, cf. T. *rab-daṅ yid-la*.

35. *sā … svedāmbunaśyattilakādhikāraṃ* (MS. °*tilakāvikāraṃ*) *smaropadiṣṭaṃ prakaṭaṃ babhāra*. Il faut garder la leçon du MS., en séparant °*tilakā* et *vikāraṃ*, cf. T. *rṅul-chu'i mtshon-ris ñams-byas rnam-'gyur ni | 'dod-pas ñer-bstan rab-tshugs la-bar bzuṅ ||*.

44. *mohāndhakūpa(sya) janasya nāntar dharmopadeśārkakarā viśanti*. Lire *jalasya nāntar*, cf. T. *chu naṅ-du*.

78. *tena kumāreṇa mahātmanā | ekaratham abhyāruhya* (MS. *ekarathemahāruhya*). Lire *ekarathe sahāruhya*.

93. *vyādhir babhūvodarabaddhaśūlaḥ*, *Av.* °*baddhamūtrah*, T. °*baddhamūlaḥ*. Il paraît préférable de suivre T. qui donne un bon sens: "une maladie qui s'est enracinée dans le ventre", voir Böhtlingk und Roth, s.v. *baddhamūla*.

111. *Mithovivādaiḥ śrutagarvavādais tajjāpavādair abudhānuvādaiḥ*. Les éditeurs traduisent *tajjāpavādair* par "avec des chuchotements", en interprétant *jāpa* comme *japa*. T. permet d'établir un bon texte: *de-ñid-śes smod* = *tajjñāpavādair*. Ces deux pāda contiennent donc respectivement les mots *vivāda*, *vāda*, *apavāda* et *anuvāda*.

115. *Krurāśayā kruradhiyaiva*. Il faut lire, comme l'exige le mètre, *krūrāśayā krūradhiyaiva*.

145. *taralendujālam*. Lire *taralendrajālaṃ* comme dans l'*Av.*, cf. T. *rab-g.yo mig-'phrul*.

164. *nirviṣayasvatantraṃ* (dit de l'œil). Le MS. a *nirviṣam asvatantraṃ* comme le *Di.* Les éditeurs veulent que *nir-* porte sur le composé *viṣayasvatantraṃ* et ils traduisent: "Tu dépends des objets des sens." Cela est inacceptable. Il vaut mieux garder les leçons du MS. d'autant plus que, dans le passage correspondant de l'*A-yu-wang king* (*Taishō*, vol. L, p. 146 a 12), on lit: "Tu es sans force, sans indépendance."

170. *prajñācakṣuḥ*, MS. *prajñakṣaṇaṃ*. Lire *prajñekṣaṇaṃ* qui rétablit le mètre.

200. *vibaddham āndhyaṃ vidadhe janasya*. Au lieu de *vibaddham* le MS. a *vivarddham* et T. *rnam-par rgyas-pa* "augmenté". Lire *vivṛddham*.

[7] *JA*, 1941-1942, p. 12. Est-ce le manuscrit qui se trouve actuellement à Leningrad?

213. °*śalyopamānair*, MS. °*śalyāyamānair*. Il faut garder la leçon du MS. qui est confirmée par T. *zug-rṅu ltar spyod-pas* "se comportant comme la douleur". *śalyāyate* est un dénominatif comme ci-dessus *muktālatikāyate*.

232. *rājāśokaḥ samāhitaḥ*, MS. *samohitaḥ*. Lire *sa mohitaḥ*.

246. *jalena himacchaṭāśikarasaurabhena* (*Av*. °*śikaradantureṇa*). La leçon de l'*Av*. est incompréhensible, celle du MS. paraît invraisemblable car "parfumé" n'est pas une qualité de l'eau glacée. T. a *'dra* "semblable". Lire °*śīkarasaṃnibhena*?

327. *śrutvā te yatayas tatheti ca sāṅgikṛtya saṃvedire*. D'après les éditeurs deux longues manquent au début de ce pāda mais c'est après *tatheti ca* qu'une brève manque. Le MS. a *tathetivacasāṅgikṛbhya*. Lire *tatheti vacasāṅgikṛtya*.

Les éditeurs ont gardé un nombre de formes incorrectes qui peuvent être corrigées sans changer trop au texte: 67. *mahāpuri* – lire *mahāpurī*; 97. *nispanda*° – *niṣpanda*°; 130. *atmanas* – *ātmanas*; 135 in fine °*atyarthanā*° – °*abhyarthanā*° (le MS. a souvent *atya* au lieu de *abhya*, cf. notes 73, 90, 94, 101, 105, 106, etc.); 164. *pravitsyanti* – *pravikṣanti*; 169. *prāgṛhya* – *pragṛhya*; 176. *premnā* – *premṇā*; 210. *niśaktair* – *niṣaktair*; 231. *hastiśālāśṛto* – *hastiśālāśrito*; 269. *sutikṣṇair* – *sutīkṣṇair*; 279. *nṛpas sukho*° – *nṛpaḥ sukho*°; 284. *avāpyata* – *avāpyate* (le MS. a *avāpyate* que les éditeurs ont changé en *avāpyata*); 287. *kruro* – *krūro*; 288. *prāgṛhīt* – *prāgrahīt*; 290. *nitva* – *nītva*; 304. *purā yadā* – *purā tadā*; 310. *viśīrṇakāṣṭhaśeṣitaṃ* – *viśīrṇaṃ kāṣṭhaśeṣitaṃ*.

Les fautes d'impression sont assez nombreuses: 13. *tavāpata*° – lire *tavāpāta*°; 16. °*tṛṣṇa*° – °*tṛṣṇā*°; 19. *sindura*° – *sindūra*°; 24. *pinaṃśaṃ* – *pināṃśaṃ*; 25. *locanā*° – *locana*°; 33. *stāna*° – *stana*°; °*śobha*° – °*śobhā*°; 39. °*śubhraṃ* – °*śubhrāṃ*; 43. *mataś* – *mātaś*; 45. *sa* – *sā*; 55. °*śosair* – °*śoṣair*; 56. *tam* – *tām*; 58. *prahartysahyaṃ* – *praharaty asahyaṃ*; 64. *mṛ* – *me*; 66. *chidrānveṣinī* – *chidrānveṣiṇī*; 70. *Takṣaśilalokā* – *Takṣaśilālokā*; 90. °*tapino* – °*tāpino*; *nirārthaṃ* – *nirarthaṃ*; 97. *vilokyomānaḥ* – *vilokyamānaḥ*; 115. °*vihinā* – °*vihīnā*; 117. *kṣarair* – *kṣārair*; 122. *vadanān* – *radanān*; 133. *vigatānuragaḥ* – *vigatānurāgaḥ*; 135. prose °*vasareśvaraḥ* – °*vāsareśvaraḥ*; *yatha* – *yathā*; 138. *susadhoḥ* – *susādhoḥ*; 141. °*manyoh* – °*manyoḥ*; 143. °*janma* – °*janmā*; 157. *anityatam* – *anityatām*; 163. *pura* – *purā*; 166. *tatas* – *tataś*; 177. *sheha*° – *sneha*°; 183. (*pituḥ*) – (*patiḥ*;) 187. *purvam* – *pūrvam*; 191. °*vidyt*° – °*vidyut*°; 193. *śītātapapita*° – *śītātapāpīta*°; *vikṣya* – *vīkṣya*; 195. *hastiśalāṃ* – *hastiśālāṃ*; 199. *ghanāśalolāḥ* – *ghanāśālolāḥ*; 200. °*bhutaṃ* – °*bhūtaṃ*; 206. °*mayuka*° – °*mayūka*°; 210. *niśaktair* – *niṣaktair*; (*aghrataraktair*) – (*āghrātaraktair*); 214. °*anilodvelad*° – °*anilodvellad*°; 220. *saṅkākalaṅkair* – *śaṅkākalaṅkair*; 223. *idam* – *idaṃ*; 238. *rājasau* – *rājāsau*; 246. *himacchata*° – *himacchaṭā*°; 248. *kuṇālaprarime* – *kuṇālapratime*; 250. *sa* – *sā*; 251. *andhyaṃ* – *āndhyaṃ*; 260. *karmāny* – *karmāṇy*; 274. *ānāryāṃ* – *anāryāṃ*; 282. *paprachir* – *papracchur*; 291. *andhibhuto* – *andhībhūto*; 294. *duḥkam* – *duḥkham*; 300. *guruṇa* – *guruṇā*; 306. °*garbitaṃ* – °*garbhitaṃ*; 312. *sokaṃ* – *śokaṃ*; 317. *sādhu* – *sādhuḥ*; 326. *vairagyo*° – *vairāgyo*°.

Enfin, il faut signaler quelques passages très corrompus, des mots et des formes inconnus et d'autres particularités que les éditeurs ont passés sous silence: 5. *abhiṣekitaḥ*; 19. *pūrāyita*; 117. *palāṇḍunā khaṇḍitakaṇṭhalena*; les éditeurs traduisent "un oignon coupé en tranches". *kaṇṭhala* manque aux dictionnaires. Faut-il lire *khaṇḍala* qui ne se trouve que dans les kośa?; 121. *parirukṣa* et *virukṣa* (id. 166; 231. *virūkṣa*) manquent aux dictionnaires; 131. *sarvā digāsthā api devatās*?; 148. ici *vipāka* est neutre comme 312 *śoka*; 172 *aiśvaryakulovihino* – le mètre ne permet pas de lire °*kula*°; 192. *paiṇḍilyavṛttiḥ* dont le sens est bien établi (T. *sloṅ-źiṅ 'tsho-ba* "vivre en quémandant") doit être rapproché de *paiṇḍilika* (*Śikṣāsamuccaya* 150.18) que Edgerton (*BHSDict*, s.v.) propose de changer en *paiṇḍinyika*. *paiṇḍilya* n'est pas mentionné par lui; 229. *vinayann evam abravīt*? Les éditeurs traduisent *vinayann* par "humblement"!; 239. *dharmarājasya putro 'haṃ buddhasya sāṃprataṃ bhave*; *bhave* paraît suspect et n'est pas traduit par les éditeurs: "Maintenant je suis le fils du seigneur du Dharma-Buddha"; 260. *Labdhāphalasthāś ca pṛthagjanāś ca kṛtāni karmāṇy aśubhāni dehināṃ*? Les éditeurs traduisent: "Des gens simples n'échappent pas à la rétribution. Les hommes accomplissent des mauvais actes."; 265. *nivṛttavṛtteṣv api.* Les éditeurs traduisent: "à l'égard de lui qui commet un mauvais acte". C'est ce que l'on trouve dans T. *spyod-ṅan spyod-pa rnams-la'aṅ = durvṛttavṛtteṣv api*; 310. *samudvignāḥ śocitvā saṃvipetire* (MS. *saṃviṣetire*). *saṃvipetire* ne peut guère se défendre. Faut-il lire *saṃviṣedire* bien que *saṃvi-sad-* manque aux dictionnaires?; 311. *tāṃl lokāñ cātitān dṛṣṭvā*? Les éditeurs traduisent: "voyant les gens qui se sont rassemblés"; 312. *vaktavyaṃ cetad*? Les éditeurs traduisent: "Si on peut raconter cela"; 314. *viśīrṇita*; 327. *subhajin*; *saṃvedire*, metri causa pour *saṃvidire*?; 328. *subhadritāṃśā(ḥ)*.

Les éditeurs ont discuté des passages difficiles dans un commentaire du texte. Plusieurs d'entre eux ont été déjà mentionnés ci-dessus. Quelques remarques à propos des notes, relatives aux strophes 79, 84, 261 et 270, peuvent trouver une place ici. 79. Les éditeurs remarquent que le mètre est corrompu et proposent de lire *evaṃ cābravīt* au lieu de *evam abravīt* mais le 4e pāda de ce śloka est parfaitement correct: *prarudann evam abravīt*; 84d. *cirāc chanaiḥ svaṃ padam ājagāma.* Les éditeurs remarquent que le mètre *upajāti* est corrompu et qu'on peut le rétablir en lisant *svapadaṃ jagāma* mais il est parfaitement correct. 261ab. *na śastravajrāgniviṣāṇi pannagāḥ kurvanti pīḍāṃ nabhaso 'vikāriṇaḥ.* Les éditeurs citent la traduction de Burnouf ("Le glaive, la foudre, le feu, le poison, les oiseaux, rien ne blesse l'éther, qui est inaltérable de sa nature") et remarquent que Burnouf a compris *nabhaso 'vikāriṇaḥ* comme un accusatif du pluriel. C'est évidemment un génitif du singulier. 270. *Kṣareṇa jihvām atha kartayāmi viṣeṇa vāgnau paridāhayāmi.* Edgerton traduit *kṣara* par "rasoir". Les éditeurs mentionnent la possibilité de lire *kṣāreṇa* et de le prendre comme adjectif chez *viṣeṇa*: "Je détruis ta langue avec un poison caustique" et citent à l'appui de leur raisonnement l'*A-yu-wang tchouan* mais, aussi bien dans ce texte que dans l'*A-yu-wang king* (*Taishō*, vol. L, p. 147a25), on lit: "Avec un couteau je te couperai la langue." Le *Kuṇālāvadāna* tibétain traduit *kṣara* par *spu-gri* "rasoir".

Les éditeurs ont bien fait d'ajouter une traduction complète du texte car elle seule permet de voir comment ils interprètent le texte qu'ils éditent. Nous discuterons ci-dessous quelques passages qui pourraient être traduits de manière différente, en demandant l'indulgence des éditeurs, si, par manque de connaissance des idiotismes de la langue russe, nous n'avons pas toujours bien compris leur traduction.

8. *tārādhipotsaṅgamṛgopamasya*, "il rappela le lapin dans les bras du seigneur des étoiles." Bien que la lune soit nommée *śaśāṅka*, comme le dit une note explicative, on ne peut pas traduire *mṛga* par "lapin". La lune s'appelle aussi *mṛgāṅka* dans lequel *mṛga* signifie "daim".

9. *samastadigdvīpadharādhināthāḥ* ne signifie pas "les Souverains de tous les pays du monde, des îles et des terres" mais "les souverains (*dharādhinātha*) des continents dans toutes les directions de l'espace".

13. *idaṃ tavāpātanimittabhūtaṃ paśyāmi cittaṃ vibhavābhibhūtaṃ*, "tes pensées sont absorbées par ta haute situation... mais je vois des présages de malheur." Ici *nimitta* a le sens de "cible, but" et *nimittabhūta* se rapporte à *cetas*: "Je vois que ton âme, écrasée par ta fortune, sera la cible d'événements subits."

19. Les éditeurs traduisent *kiṃśuka* par "vêtements". L'ont-ils confondu avec *aṃśuka*?

32. *Nirlajjataiṣā paramārthaniyā yad arthayante svayam eva nāryaḥ*, "Certainement, c'est la plus grande impudence quand la femme elle-même demande." Cette strophe perd beaucoup de sa force par le fait qu'*arthaniyā* n'est pas traduit.

48. *Nāsty eva taptāṃ abalāṃ dāyaloḥ saṃrakṣatas te yadi ko'pi dharmaḥ / tat sādhubhir darśitagauravasya tasyābhāve katham asty adharmaḥ //*, "Toi, plein de miséricorde, tu ne suis pas le devoir moral – soutenir une femme souffrante, mais est-ce immoralité l'absence du dharma auquel les hommes intègres attachent tant d'importance (?)." Il nous semble qu'il faut interpréter cette strophe autrement. Tiṣyarakṣyā s'adresse à Kuṇāla qui a rejeté ses avances et elle dit: "Si, en protégeant par pitié une

femme souffrante, tu (n'accomplis pas un acte de) dharma, comment, même en l'absence de ce (dharma) dont les hommes vertueux ont montré l'importance, (un tel acte) pourra-t-il être contraire au dharma?"

49. *saṃtāpitānāṃ vyasanāturānāṃ niṣiddhakāryeṣv api ko vicaraḥ*, "Mais comment peut-on même penser retenir celles qui sont enflammées et frappées par la passion!" Plutôt: "Comment celles qui sont enflammées et souffrent par la passion peuvent-elles hésiter même à l'égard d'actes défendus!"

107. *paśyāmi tasmiṃ vimale suvṛtte sankrāntam adyaiva kṛtaṃ svarājyaṃ*, "Je (veux) le voir! Aujourd'hui même mon règne sera transmis à lui qui est pur et dont la conduite est sans tache." Plutôt: "Je veux voir qu'aujourd'hui même mon règne soit transmis à lui, le pur à la bonne conduite!"

174. *Ciraṃ sukhaṃ saiva ca Tiṣyarakṣyā āyur balaṃ palāyate sudīrghaṃ | saṃpreṣito 'yaṃ hi yayā yasyānubhāvena kṛtaḥ svakārthaḥ ||*, "Puisse Tiṣyarakṣyā prospérer pendant longtemps et heureusement, elle qui a arrangé cette intrigue grâce à laquelle elle a obtenu son but." *svakārthaḥ* se réfère ici à Kuṇāla qui prononce cette strophe: "grâce à laquelle j'ai obtenu mon propre but" car il doit l'obtention de l'œil de sagesse à Tiṣyarakṣyā qui l'a privé des yeux de chair.

198. *saṃvāhayantī caraṇau priyasya*, "tombant aux pieds de son époux". Plutôt: "caressant les pieds de son époux".

200. *Tataḥ sarāgā capalābhipatya doṣonmukhī dveṣavatīva saṃdhyā | hṛtvā raviṃ* ..., "Là parut la déesse du crépuscule, inconstante et passionnée, aspirante à l'obscurité de la nuit et comme si elle était dominée par la haine, elle ravit le soleil." Cette strophe contient un śleṣa car *sarāgā*, *capalā* et *doṣonmukhī* se rapportent à *saṃdhyā* aussi bien qu'à *dveṣavatī*: "Ensuite le crépuscule, rouge, instable et dans l'attente de l'obscurité ravit le soleil comme une femme haineuse qui est passionnée, capricieuse et à l'affût de fautes."

225-226. *tad anenāsmi śabdena dhairyād ākampito bhṛśaṃ | kalabhasyeva naṣṭasya premānubandhitaḥ karī*, "Je suis très excité par ces sons, comme un éléphant, dominé par l'amour, lors de la perte d'un jeune éléphant." Le génitif *kalabhasya* dépend de *śabdena*: "Je suis très ébranlé par cette voix comme l'est un éléphant affectionné par la voix du jeune éléphant perdu."

252. *kulānurūpā tava niścaleyaṃ | ekaiva patnī parivāraśeṣaḥ kṛcchre'pi sādhor iva dhairyavṛttiḥ ||*, "De tout l'entourage seulement une femme, digne de sa famille, n'a pas changé, en gardant même dans le malheur la fermeté d'une conduite sainte." Plutôt: "De ta suite il ne te reste que ta femme seule qui, conforme à sa famille, n'a pas changé comme, même dans la détresse, un homme noble (ne perd pas) sa conduite ferme."

254. *nāgavimuktavajra*, "les foudres émises par le nuage". Le sens de "nuage" pour *nāga* ne se trouve que dans les kośa. Il vaut mieux suivre Burnouf qui traduit: "la foudre lancée par les Nâgas".

273. *Evaṃ sa proktvā vipulāpakāre tasmin pratikārasamudyataṃ | avārayad duḥsahaduḥkhayogaṃ svakarmapākena vadan kumāraḥ ||*, "Parlant ainsi au roi, prêt à se venger pour un si grand crîme, le prince commença à le retenir d'un acte qui s'accompagne de souffrances insupportables, en expliquant ce qui s'était passé comme le résultat de son propre karma." Plutôt: "... il le retenait, en disant qu'il s'attirerait des souffrances insupportables comme résultat de son acte."

275. *yasyāpakāre 'sti na roṣaleśas tasyopakāre'pi kathaṃ prasādaḥ*, "Comment se fier même à celui qui a rendu service, s'il n'éprouve aucune colère à l'égard d'un crîme perpétré." Plutôt: "Celui qui n'est aucunement fâché d'un méfait, comment pourra-t-il se montrer reconnaissant même pour un service rendu?"

280. *Ghorāpacāre sadṛśaṃ vidhāya patnyāḥ pratikāram atha kṣitīśaḥ | krodhānalaṃ Takṣaśilādhipe'pi tanmarṣaṇād duḥsaham utsasarja ||*, "Ensuite le roi, après avoir préparé pour sa femme une vengeance, égale à son crîme terrible, éteigna le feu in-

supportable de sa colère contre elle et aussi contre le seigneur de Takṣaśilā et leur pardonna." La strophe ne dit certainement pas que le roi pardonne à sa femme. Il se montre plus clément à l'égard du seigneur de Takṣaśilā qui ne subit que le feu de sa colère: "Ensuite le roi, après avoir puni sa femme de son crime terrible conformément (à son crime), envoya au roi de Taksaśilā le feu de sa colère qui était difficile à supporter en raison de sa clémence." Il nous semble que *tanmarṣaṇād* veut dire que le roi manifesta sa colère au roi de Takṣaśilā mais finit par lui pardonner. Dans le *Divyāvadāna* Takṣaśilā est brûlée et les habitants sont tués.

Dans un chapitre, consacré à la légende de Kuṇāla, les auteurs examinent et comparent différentes recensions de la légende d'après les sources suivantes: *Divyāvadāna*, *Avadānakalpalatā*, l'*A-yu-wang tchouan* (trad. par J. Przyluski, *op. cit.*, 223-427), *Hiuan-tsang* (S. Beal, *Buddhist Records of the Western World*, vol II, London, 139-140), l'*Histoire du Bouddhisme* de Tāranātha et le *Pariśiṣṭaparvan* de Hemacandra (éd. H. Jacobi, *Bibliotheca Indica*, 1883-1891; 2e éd., 1932). Ils attirent l'attention sur l'identité d'une strophe et demie dans le *Divyāvadāna* et l'*Avadānakalpalatā* (*Di.* p. 417. 22-27; *Av.* 59. 160cd, 161). Ce passage parle de la restitution de la vue à Kuṇāla. Ceci ne se trouve pas dans les formes anciennes de la légende. D'autre part, aucun manuscrit du *Divyāvadāna* n'est antérieur au 17e siècle. Pour ces raisons les auteurs supposent que ce passage a été emprunté à l'*Av.* par les scribes ou les rédacteurs des manuscrits du *Di.* Cette conclusion paraît pleinement justifiée. L'importance en est considérable car il s'en suit que le texte des quatre chapitres du *Di.* qui contiennent la légende d'Aśoka a été altéré entre le 11e et le 17e siècle. A maints endroits, le texte est devenu si corrompu qu'il est souvent impossible de le comprendre. Il faut donc avoir recours aux traductions chinoises de l'*Aśokāvadāna*, l'*A-yu-wang king* et l'*A-yu-wang tchouan.* Przyluski (*op. cit.*, p. xiii) a affirmé que le premier est plus proche du *Divyāvadāna* que le deuxième. Plus important encore pour l'étude du texte du 27e chapitre du *Divyāvadāna* est un ouvrage qui n'est mentionné ni par Przyluski ni par les éditeurs du *Kuṇālāvadāna.* C'est la traduction tibétaine du *Kuṇālāvadāna* qui se trouve dans le *bsTan-'gyur* (éd. de Pékin, réimpression photomécanique, vol. 127, 294d1-302a6). Quand on compare *Di.* pp. 405.14-419.12 avec le *Kuṇālāvadāna* tibétain, il est évident que, malgré quelques différences mineures, c'est essentiellement le même texte. Les différences s'expliquent probablement dans la plupart des cas par des altérations que le texte du *Di.* a subies au cours de sa transmission. A titre d'exemple, examinons deux passages de l'*Aśokāvadānamālā* qui ont été empruntés au *Divyāvadāna.*

I. *Kuṇālāvadāna* 164ab (= *Di.* p. 412.11-12): *sāmagrajaṃ budbudasaṃnikāśaṃ sudurlabhaṃ nirviṣayasvatantraṃ.* Ci-dessus nous avons discuté ce passage et nous avons défendu la leçon *nirviṣam asvatantraṃ.* Néanmoins, il reste des difficultés car *nirviṣam* ne s'applique pas très bien à l'œil. Dans le *Kuṇālāvadāna* tibétain (p. 298d1) nous lisons: *dbu-ba 'dra-źiṅ chu-bur-dag daṅ mtshuṅs // śin-tu ñams-chuṅ gnod-byed raṅ-dbaṅ-med //* ce qu'on pourrait restaurer tentativement ainsi: *pheṇopamaṃ budbudasaṃnikāśaṃ sudurbalaṃ hiṃsakam asvatantraṃ.* Le passage correspondant de l'*A-yu-wang king* (*Taishō*, vol. L, p. 146a11-12) a: "Maintenant, on voit que tu n'es pas réel, que tu es faux à l'instar de l'écume, vide sans réalité, que tu es sans force, sans indépendance" (pour le passage correspondant de l'*A-yu-wang tchouan*, voir Przyluski, *op. cit.*, p. 289). Ces versions sont très proches l'une de l'autre et donnent un texte beaucoup plus acceptable.

II. *Kuṇālāvadāna* 269-270 (= *Di.* p. 417.6-11): *utpāṭya netre pravighāṭayāmi gātraṃ sutīkṣṇair musalaiś ca kiṃ te / jīvantīṃ śūlām avarohayiṣye kṣatsyāmi nāsām asinā śitena // Kṣareṇa jihvām atha kartayāmi viṣeṇa vāgnau paridāhayāmi /.* *Kuṇālāvadāna* tibétain (p. 300e2-5):

'di'i mig dbyuṅ-ṅam 'on-te 'di-yi lus //
sen-mo śin-tu rno-bas dral-ba'am //
yaṅ-na gson-por bdun-rtser skyon-pa'am //
'di'i-lus sogs-les rnam-par dgas-par-bya //

yaṅ-na lce ni spu-gris gtub-bya-źiṅ //
dgra-stas bsnun-pas mgo-bo bcad-par-bya //
yaṅ-na bskal-pa'i me-'drar gźug-bya-źiṅ //
'on-te dug-gis (Pékin: *gi*) *lus-'di dgaṅ-bar-bya* //

"Faut-il lui arracher l'œil ou lui déchirer
le corps avec des ongles très pointus?
Ou faut-il l'empaler vivante sur un (? *bdun-rtse*),
ou faut-il briser son corps en morceaux avec une scie?

Ou faut-il couper sa langue en pièces avec un rasoir,
ou faut-il lui trancher la tête avec une hache?
Ou faut-il la jeter dans un feu semblable au feu à la fin d'un kalpa,
ou faut-il remplir son corps de poison?"

L'*A-yu-wang king* (p. 147a24-28) a: "Maintenant, je veux arracher son œil, je veux avec une scie couper son corps en morceaux, avec un axe détruire son corps, avec un couteau couper la langue, avec un couteau trancher le cou, brûler le corps dans le feu, lui faire boire du poison pour lui ôter la vie."

On ne peut pas ici étudier en détail toutes les différences entre l'*Aś.*, le *Di.*, le *Kuṇālāvadāna* tibétain et l'*A-yu-wang king* (pour l'*A-yu-wang tchouan*, voir Przyluski, *op. cit.*, p. 293) mais il faut attirer l'attention sur deux faits importants. D'abord, dans le *Kuṇālāvadāna* tibétain et dans l'*A-yu-wang king*, il y a deux strophes dont le *Di.* et l'*Aś.* n'ont gardé qu'une et demie. Ensuite, aux endroits où le *Di.* et l'*Aś.* ont des leçons différentes le *Kuṇālāvadāna* tibétain s'accorde avec le *Di.*: *musalaiś*, *Di. nakharaiḥ* = tib. *sen-mo*; *asinā*, *Di. krakacena* = tib. *sogs-les*.

Ces deux exemples montrent bien l'importance des deux traductions chinoises et du *Kuṇālāvadāna* tibétain pour l'étude du texte du *Kuṇālāvadāna* dans le *Divyāvadāna*.

La légende de Kuṇāla se trouve encore dans d'autres textes chinois bouddhiques: I. Conte no. 30 du *Lieou tou tsi king*, T. 152 (*Taishō*, vol. III, 17c-18b). Traduction française: Éd. Chavannes, *Cinq cents contes et apologues*, Tome I (Paris, 1910), 106-111. – II. *Fou Fa-tsang yin-yuan tchouan*, T. 2058 (*Taishō*, vol. L, 309a-c). Résumé par Chavannes, *op. cit.*, Tome IV (Paris, 1935), p. 104. – III. *A-yu-wang si houai mou yin-yuan king*, T. 2045 (Cf. Przyluski, *op. cit.*, 106-108). – IV. *King liu yi siang*, T. 2121 (*Taishō*, vol. LIII, 180b-183c). Le texte de cette dernière recension est presqu'entièrement identique à celui de l'*A-yu-wang king* qui est reproduit littéralement, en omettant plusieurs passages. L'intérêt de ces recensions réside dans le fait que leur terminus ante quem est connu car il dépend de la date des traductions. Ce serait nécessaire de les comparer avec les autres recensions mentionnées par les auteurs.

La deuxième partie du chapitre consacré à la légende de Kuṇāla en étudie la valeur historique. Les auteurs y montrent l'importance de la légende au point de vue de l'histoire de l'époque d'Aśoka.

Le livre se termine par une reproduction photographique des feuillets 90b-105b du manuscrit. La qualité de la reproduction est excellente et permet au lecteur de vérifier les leçons adoptées par les éditeurs. C'est un exemple qui mérite d'être suivi par les éditeurs de textes.

Arrivés au bout de ce long compte rendu qui est inspiré par l'intérêt que nous avons pris à cette édition du *Kuṇālāvadāna*, nous exprimons l'espoir de voir bientôt l'édition d'autres chapitres de l'*Aśokāvadānamālā*.

Leiden J. W. de Jong

Ratna Handurukande, *Maṇicūḍāvadāna being a Translation and Edition and Lokānanda, a Transliteration and Synopsis* (= *Sacred Books of the Buddhists*, vol. XXIV). London, Luzac & Company Ltd. 1967. IV, 300 pp. £ 4.15 s.

Volume 24 of the *Sacred Books of the Buddhists* contains an edition and translation of a prose text of the *Maṇicūḍāvadāna*, an edition of a metrical version of the same text, and a transliteration and synopsis of the drama *Lokānanda* which has been preserved in a Tibetan translation. We must be grateful to the Pali Text Society for including in this series, in which translations of the *Jātakamālā* and the *Mahāvastu* had already appeared, Sanskrit and even Tibetan texts. Let us hope that by pursuing this course the Pali Text Society will increasingly become a Buddhist Text Society!

In collections of Buddhist Sanskrit manuscripts there is a great number of metrical and prose avadānas of which, to date, only very few have been published. The prose text of the *Maṇicūḍāvadāna* is to be found both as a separate text and as a chapter of the *Divyāvadānamālā*. Dr. Handurukande has used five manuscripts of the *Maṇicūḍāvadāna* and two manuscripts of the *Divyāvadānamālā*. In his recent book on the avadāna literature Iwamoto enumerates twelve manuscripts of the *Maṇicūḍāvadāna* (*Bukkyō setsuwa kenkyū josetsu*, Kyoto, 1967, pp. 142 and 162). Among these twelve manuscripts are three belonging to the Tokyo University Library: Nos. 277, 278 and 279 (see Seiren Matsunami, *A Catalogue of the Sanskrit Manuscripts in the Tokyo University Library*, Tokyo, 1965, pp. 103 and 235). Matsunami notes that in the colophons of No. 277 and No. 278 it is stated that this avadāna is the 31st chapter and that consequently this avadāna may be part of some avadāna collection. In a manuscript of the *Divyāvadānamālā*, belonging to the Kyoto University, the *Maṇicūḍāvadāna* is also the 31st chapter (see Iwamoto, *op.cit.*, pp. 141 and 147). However, in two other manuscripts of the *Divyāvadānamālā* (in Paris and Calcutta) it is respectively the 7th and 16th chapter (Iwamoto, *op.cit.*, p. 147).

The introduction deals in detail with the manuscripts, their mutual relation, and the linguistic characteristics of the text (pp. ix-xxvi). Handurukande shows clearly that all manuscripts go back to a common archetype which is not free from errors. According to the introduction, the *Maṇicūḍāvadāna* falls into the third group in Edgerton's classification of Buddhist Sanskrit texts, in which non-sanskritic forms are not common while the vocabulary is the clearest evidence that they belong to the BHS (= Buddhist Hybrid Sanskrit) tradition. In establishing the text Handurukande has tried to retain grammatical forms proper to BHS as far as the manuscripts show evidence of them. Although she has been aware of the danger of applying too mechanically Edgerton's principles, one cannot escape the impression that too many BHS forms have been introduced into the text. On pages xv-xvi the editor lists some of the grammatical features of BHS which are to be found in the *Maṇicūḍāvadāna*. Many of these features hardly occur in texts of Edgerton's third group. However, manuscript evidence does not always support the readings selected by the editor. For the use of an adjective in the accusative plural qualifying a noun in the accusative singular the reader is referred to p. 5.2: *prāpnoti tuṣṭiṃ paramāṃ yaśas ca.*[1] It is of course not necessary to relate *paramaṃ* to *yaśas* instead of to *tuṣṭiṃ*. Four features (use of a past passive participle with active meaning; transfer of a masculine ending to a feminine noun; use of a masculine modifier with a feminine noun; accusative plural endings in āṃ) occur in a single sentence p. 4.15-16: *Tatas sā Bodhisatvasyānubhāvenāśrutapūrvām imāṃ gāthāṃ pratibhāṣitā.* As is obvious from the variant readings, one has to read: *Tayā* ... °*pūrvā imā gāthāḥ pratibhāṣitāḥ* (*tatas sā*; A *tata tasyā* corrected to *tatas sā*, B C *tasyā*, D *tatasyā*, E *tatasmā*, F *tataḥ sā* – *imāṃ gāthāṃ*; A B *imāṃ gāthā*, C D E *imā gāthā* – *pratibhāṣitā*, C F °*bhāṣitāḥ*, D °*bhāvitā*, G *pratibhākhito*). Perhaps one must read *pūrvā-m-imā* with *-m-* as 'hiatus-bridger' (F °*pūrvām*; A B C D E G °*pūrvam*); *pūrvām* can easily have been corrupted to *pūrvam*. The reference given to Edgerton's *Grammar* 10.51 for the use of an accusative singular ending in *ī* (see p. 14.4-5: *Tvayaiṣām agramahiṣī sthāpayitvā* ...) is clearly wrong for here Edgerton is discussing occurrences of an accusative singular in *-i*. Moreover, he only deals with occurrences of this form in verses belonging to the first and second groups in his classification. As to the use of a neuter modifier with a masculine noun (Edgerton 6.14) the editor has failed to see that in *kiṃvikāro 'yam*

[1] The author refers to the sections into which she has divided the text. Some sections comprise more than two pages. For this reason I think it more convenient to refer to page and line. It is a pity that in the editions of the Pāli Text Society the lines are not numbered in the margin by adding the figures 5, 10, 15 etc. as has been done in the edition of the Pāli Jātakas from volume 2 onwards.

udāro 'vabhāṣo bhaviṣyati kimanuśaṃsa (p. 22.5-6) *kim* is part of a compound (see Speyer, *Sanskrit Syntax*, §408, Rem.), though her translation is correct.

Apart from the examples mentioned above, the text is very well edited. In a few places another reading could be suggested: p. 2.12 – read °*ḍamaraṃ taskara*° (cf. *IIJ*, I, 1957, p. 312); p. 16.7 *iṣṭopacāyakāḥ*?; – read *iṣṭopacārakāḥ*? p. 18.3 and p. 25.2 read *dhanajātaṃ* instead of *dhanaṃ jātaṃ*; p. 36.8 *karuṇāyamānam uvāca* – read *karuṇāyamāna* (sic MSS. CDEG) or *karuṇāyamāna-m- uvāca*; p. 39.9 *dhairyaṃ samuttamaṃ* – read *dhairyam anuttamam*?; p. 48.4 *abhiṣiktvā* – read *abhiṣiktā* (*ahaṃ* in 48.3 is probably a scribal error for *mayā*); p. 53.13-14 *parṣatmaṇḍalam ānayantī taṃ* – read *parṣanmaṇḍalamadhyapatitaṃ*? p. 75.3 *maitriṃ paribhāvitasya* – read *maitrīparibhāvitasya*; p. 75.8 °*upasargotsṛṣṭe* – read °*upasargopasṛṣṭe* (cf. p. 76.15); p. 85.11 °*balena vivārya* – read °*balenādhivāsya*? (cf. 82.11); p. 98.1 *kāyeṣu kāmacchandaṃ prahāya tad bahuyatnavihārī* – read *kāmeṣu kāmacchandaṃ prahāya tadbahulavihārī* (cf. *Divy.* p. 225,28: *kāmeṣu kāmacchandaṃ vyapahāya tadbahulavihāriṇo*). I have noted the following printing errors: p. 13.7 read *atikrāntā* for *atikrānta*; p. 15.13 read *paripācanārthaṃ* for *paripāraṇārtham*; p. 74.5 read *vākyasākhilyena* for *vāka*°; p. 102.2 read *tathāgataguṇān anusmṛtya* for *tathāgataguṇānusmṛtya*. I do not understand p. 34.13 *ākārayām āsa* (translated as 'he took') and p. 42.13 *samākārayām āsa* ('he appeared').

The translation which follows the text is excellent apart from a few minor points. P. 14.7: *na hi puṇyam apuṇyaṃ vā parasaṃtānaṃ saṃkrāmati*, "neither merit nor demerit finds continuance in others" – rather: "neither merit nor demerit passes over to an other series (i.e. individual; see Edgerton's Dictionary s.v. *saṃtati* and *saṃtāna*)"; p. 39.8: *kṛtsnaṃ jagat paritrātum udyatasyādya te kṣamaṃ*, "It is possible for you to save the whole world now, for which you are ready..." – "It is now proper for you, who are ready to save the whole world..."; p. 42.15 *vṛkkaṃ vā hṛdayamāṃsamedomastiṣkaṃ vā*, "the heart or the flesh and fat of the heart" – "the kidneys or the heart, the flesh and the fat" (there is no justification for giving the meaning 'heart' to *vṛkkam* as is done in p. 42, n. 32); p. 59.11: *smṛtyapramoṣe*, "mindfulness, abstinence from theft" – "non-loss of memory" (see *BHS Dictionary* s.v. *asaṃpramoṣaṇa*); p. 59.15: *samāsān*, "on occasions" – "concisely"; p. 63.6: *sukhasaṃjñāṃ tu mā kārṣīḥ kadā cid gṛhacārake*, "Do not ever designate the word 'happiness' in relation to one who leads a household life" – "...in relation to the prison of the house". This verse of the *Jatakamālā* is translated in the same way by all translators: Speyer "one who lives in the house"; Barannikov (1962) "o žizni v dome" ['life in the house']; Gnoli (1964) "uno che vive la vita di casa". In classical Sanskrit (*Kauṭ. Arth.* and *Daśak.*) and in Buddhist Sanskrit *cāraka* often occurs in the meaning 'prison'[2] (see *BHS Dictionary* s.v. *cāra*; *Lalitavistara*, ed. S. Lefmann, p. 204.9; *Divyāvadāna*, pp. 365.4; 377.16, 23: *Dharmasamuccaya* IV, 4a); p. 66.7: *hartum*, "to kill" – "to take away"; p. 82.10: *kamavairāgyāt parihiṇaḥ*, "disregarded (the pain), through (the power of) his detachment from sensuality" – "deprived of his detachment from pleasures"; p. 89.4-5: *'pidāniṃ satvāḥ svakam api bāhuṃ gṛhitaṃ na paśyanti*, "people could not see others, even those who held their own arms" "People could not even see their own arms which they grasped".

In the second part of the introduction (pp. xxxiii-xlv) the editor studies a metrical version of the Maṇicūḍa story which is contained in the fourth chapter of the *Svāyambhuvamahāpurāṇa*, of which the only known manuscript is in the Bibliothèque Nationale. This version has been analysed and studied by de La Vallée Poussin ("Maṇicūḍāvadāna, as related in the fourth chapter of the Svayambhūpurāṇa [Paris, dev. 78]", *JRAS*, 1894, pp. 297-319). It is surprising that this article is not mentioned in the introduction although references in notes show that it was known to the editor.[3] This

[2] The Tibetan translator renders *cāraka* by *btson-ra* 'prison', cf. *Tanjur* (Peking edition), Mdo-'grel, XCI, p. 68a5: *btson-ra 'dra-ba'i khyim-la / nams-yaṅ bde-bar ma sems-śig*.

metrical version of the *Maṇicūḍāvadāna* comprises 473 verses, and, inserted between verses 78 and 79, a very corrupt prose section of which a translation is given in the introduction (pp. xxxv-xxxix). This version contains a few sections which have no parallels in the prose avadāna. For establishing the text the editor has been able to use only one manuscript. In several places the text is incomprehensible, which is probably due not only to the corruption of the manuscript but also to the fact that some parts were written by an author who did not know Sanskrit very well. Nevertheless, in quite a few places the text can be emended without too many difficulties. In the following remarks I refer to the verses by their number and to the prose section by page and line. 2d: *dātāvadātāśayaḥ* – *dānāvadātā°*; 25b: *°dānagamyābhisaṃgame* – *°dānāgamyābhisaṃgamaṃ*; 63d: *vicerur* – *virecur* (cf. 149d); p. 154.17: *sarvaṃ darśayāmi* – *sarvadarśinī* (MS. *sarvadarśimī*); p. 155.10: *mahimām* – *mahimānam* (sic MS.): p. 155.24: *aprabādhito* – *aprabodhito*; p. 155.26: *bhavad aśrayāt* (MS. *ātrayāt*) – *bhavadāśrame*?; p. 156.22: *jvara-uddhareṇa kāmukām* – *jagaduddharaṇakāmuka* (MS. *jagaduddhareṇakāmukā*); 80a: *svāṃ śiṣyāṃ* – *svāśiṣā* (MS. *svāśiśyā*); 149a: *purodhasā* – *purodhaso*: 152c: *mukhair* – *makhe* (MS. *makhai*); 188a: *āśayāṃ* – *āśayā* (sic MS. cf. 193b: *nairāśaṃ*); 221a: *ghorāṃ* – *ghoro* (MS. *ghorā*); 224cd: *avijñāya jijñāsitaṃ* – *abhijñāya jijñāsituṃ*?; 228c: *kṣudhārtāyāpyalaṃ* – *kṣudhārtāyāparaṃ* (MS. *°tāyāpalaṃ*); 260d: *vā salilaṃ vodadhiṃ tathā* – *vā salilam vā dariṃ* (sic MS.) *tathā*; 312d: *bhūmikaṃ panaḥ* – *bhūmikampanam*; 335d: *gamanam* – *gaganam*; 345c: *°samāsinā* – *°samāsino*; 380c: *preritaṃ* – *parito* (MS. *peritoṃ*).

The third text published in this book is the Tibetan text of the drama *Lokānanda* which is based on the Maṇicūḍa legend. One must be grateful to the editor for having published the text of this drama together with a detailed introduction and a synopsis. She stresses the desirability of a reconstruction of the Sanskrit original (p. 203). An English translation would probably be more useful, and one must hope that the editor, who has taken such pains in studying this text, will herself undertake its translation. I have not been able to compare the text, which was transliterated from the Peking and Narthang editions, with one or more editions of the *Tanjur*. However, a quick look at the text shows that quite a few misprints and erroneous readings have to be corrected, for instance, p. 210.12: *mk'a* – *mk'as*; p. 210.23: *becas* – *bcas*; p. 213.21: *mt'oṅ bdul-ba'i* – *mt'oṅ-ba dul-ba'i*; p. 225.13, 17: *bkra-śes* – *bkra-śis*; p. 227.7: *btuṅ* – *btud*; p. 229.9: *spoṅ* – *gtoṅ* (PN *stoṅ*), etc.

Australian National University J. W. de Jong

The *Bodhisattvāvadānakalpalatā* and the *Ṣaḍdantāvadāna*

J. W. de Jong

THE *Bodhisattvāvadānakalpalatā*[1] was published in the *Bibliotheca Indica* in two volumes. Sarat Chandra Das and Paṇḍit Hari Mohan Vidyābhūshaṇa edited the first five fascicles of Volume 1 (Calcutta, 1888-1895, pp. xlii + 1-442) and the first five fascicles of Volume 2 (Calcutta, 1890-1897, pp. 1-480). After a long interval, publication was resumed by Das in 1906, and with Satis Chandra Vidyābhūṣaṇa he edited the remaining fascicles of both volumes (Vol. I, Fascicles 6-13, pp. 443-1171, Calcutta, 1906-1913; Vol. II, Fascicles 6-11, pp. 481-1093 +13 pp., Calcutta, 1910-1913). In 1959 P. L. Vaidya reprinted the Sanskrit text in Volumes 22 and 23 of *The Buddhist Sanskrit Texts*.

Das's edition is based upon a Tibetan blockprint which contains both the Sanskrit text in Tibetan transliteration and the Tibetan translation. According to him this blockprint consists of 620 folios and was printed in 1662-1663.[2] In editing the *Bodhisattvāvadāna-kalpalatā*, Das has done some rearrangement of the text. In the Peking edition of the Tanjur the *Bodhisattvāvadānakalpalatā* occupies Vol. 93 of the *Mdo-'grel*.[3] Story 107 ends on page 346a1. Then follows Somendra's introduction to the last tale composed by himself: 346a1-347b2 (=Das Vol. 2, pp. 1008-1015). This tale occupies ff. 347b2–357a7 (=Das Vol. 2, pp. 1016–1087). Then follows Somadeva's introduction to the *Bodhisattvāvadānakalpalatā*: ff. 357a8–358a6. This introduction has been published by Das on pp. xxiv–xxix of his introduction. The table of contents of the *Bodhisattvāvadānakalpalatā* occupies ff. 358a6–360a5 (cf. Das, Introduction, pp. xxx–xli). This table contains 42 verses and not 43. The 43d verse in Das's edition is the first of the four verses of the colophon for which see Das, Vol. 2, pp. 1088–1091 (=Tibetan translation, ff. 360a5–360b3). This colophon is followed in the Peking edition of the Tibetan translation by the colophon of the translation, ff. 360b4–361a8). The first lines of this colophon (ff. 360b4–6) are also found in the colophon of the blockprint used by Das (cf. Vol. 2, p. 1092, lines 1–7 of the Tibetan text). The same blockprint also contains a lengthy text edited with separate pagination (pp. 1–13) by Das at the beginning of Fascicle 11 of Volume 2. According to Das this text contains the "concluding remarks of the last Tibetan editor."

In the Tibetan translation the tenth *pallava* is called *Mngal-las 'byung-ba*. However, the Tibetan blockprint used by Das does not contain the Sanskrit text of this *pallava*. For this reason Das has relegated it to the end of Volume 1 (pp. 1165–1171). Moreover, Das has changed the numbers of *Pallavas* 11–49 to 10–48. Consequently, there is no *Pallava* 49 in his edition. This rearrangement of the *pallavas* agrees with the table of contents, which lists as the tenth *pallava* the story of Sundarīnanda. According to this table the forty-ninth story is the *Ṣaḍdantāvadāna*, text and translation, which are lacking in the Tibetan blockprint and in the Peking edition of the Tibetan translation. It is obvious that in the text used by the Tibetan translators one story was missing. According to Satis Chandra Vidyābhūṣaṇa (Vol. 1, p. 1171, footnote) the *Mngal-las 'byung-ba* was evidently an interpolation introduced to make up the auspicious total of 108 *pallavas*. Tucci speculates that the forty-ninth *pallava*, the *Ṣaḍdantāvadāna*, was lacking in the text on which the Tibetan translation was based and that, for this reason, the editors of the Tibetan translation compiled the *Mngal-las 'byung-ba*.[4] Tucci does not explain why the editors have filled the gap caused by the absence of the forty-ninth story by adding a story after the ninth with the consequence that Stories 10–48 had to be renumbered 11–49.

The *Mngal-las 'byung-ba*, 'The coming forth from the womb', is a sermon preached by the Buddha to Ānanda near Campā on conception, birth, and the miseries of human life. Vidyābhūṣaṇa reconstructs the Sanskrit title as *Garbhakrāntyavadāna*, but Tucci prefers *Garbhāvakrānti*. A *Garbhāvakrānti-sūtra* is quoted in the *Abhidharmakośabhāṣya* and the *Yogācārabhūmi* (ed. V. Bhattacharya, Calcutta, 1957, p. 27.5). The *Abhidharmakośavyākhyā* (ed. U. Wogihara, Tokyo, 1932–1936, p. 67.1) refers to the *Garbhāvakrānti-sūtra*, but the *Abhidharmakośabhāṣya* omits the word *sūtra*. Cf. *Abhidharmakośabhāsya* (ed. P. Pradhan, Patna, 1967, p. 24.10): *ṣaḍdhātur iyaṃ puruṣa iti garbhāvakrāntau*. The Tibetan translation of the *bhāṣya* renders *Garbhāvakrānti* with *Mngal-du 'jug-pa*. The *Mngal-du 'byung-ba* is not identical with the text quoted in the *Abhidharmakośabhāṣya* and other texts. A reconstructed Sanskrit title would not be *Garbhāvakrānti* but *Garbhotpatti*. As to the *Garbhāvakrānti-sūtra*, La Vallée Poussin refers to Chapter 11 of the *Vinayasaṃyuktakavastu* (Nanjio 1121, Taishō 1451), to Chapter 14 of the *Ratnakūṭa* (Nanjio 23.14, Taishō 310.14), and to the *Dhātuvibhaṅgasutta* in the *Majjhima-nikāya* (No. 140).[5] Moreover, he adds that the *Garbhāvakrāntisūtra* is one of the sources of the *Pitāputrasamāgama* which is quoted in the *Śikṣāsamuccaya*, the *Bodhicaryāvatāra*, and the *Madhyamakāvatāra*. However, he has not checked whether the quotations of the *Garbhāvakrāntisūtra* in the *Abhidharmakośabhāṣya* can be traced in the texts mentioned by him. He mentions only Chapter 14 of the *Ratnakūṭa*, but both the Chinese and Tibetan translations of the *Ratnakūṭa* contain two texts, entitled *Garbhāvakrāntinirdeśa*. According to the Peking edition of the Kanjur, the full Sanskrit titles are *Āyuṣmannandagarbhāvakrāntinirdeśa* and *Nandagarbhāvakrāntinirdeśa*.[6]

Pelliot has pointed out that the Chinese translation of the *Ratnakūṭa* contains two translations (Taishō 310.13 and 310.14) which correspond to Sūtras 13 and 14 of the Tibetan version of the *Ratnakūṭa*.[7] However, in Taishō 310.13 the Buddha is questioned by Ānanda; in the corresponding Tibetan text the Buddha addresses himself not to Ānanda but to Nanda. Pelliot remarks that in an older Chinese translation by Dharmarakṣa (Taishō 317) Nanda figures in the beginning but is later replaced by Ānanda. Marcelle Lalou has pointed out that the Tibetan text was translated by Chos-grub from the Chinese translation by Bodhiruci (Taishō 310.13).[8] Pelliot had already advanced the hypothesis that this text was translated from the Chinese and that the translator had substituted the name Nanda for Ānanda.[9] A careful comparison of both texts will be required in order to show whether this is the only substantial difference between the two texts.

As concerns Sūtra 14 of *Ratnakūṭa*, the situation is more complicated. Pelliot had pointed out that Chapters 11 and 12 of the Vinaya of the Mūlasarvāstivādin[10] are absolutely identical with Chapter 14 of the Chinese *Ratnakūṭa*. The *Vinayakṣudrakavastu* was translated by I-tsing, and in compiling the Chinese *Ratnakūṭa* Bodhiruci therefore must have made use of I-tsing's translation of Chapters 11 and 12. The Tibetan translation of the *Vinayakṣudrakavastu* contains, according to Csoma's analysis (folios 202–248 of Volume 10 of the Narthang edition of the *Vinaya*) instructions to Nanda on the conditions of existence in the womb and on the gradual formation of the human body.[11] Pelliot concluded that probably this sūtra too had been translated from the Chinese. Sakurabe Bunkyō arrived at the same conclusion in his study of the *Ratnakūṭa*.[12]

Marcelle Lalou, however, compared the Tibetan translation of Chapters 11 and 12 of the *Vinayakṣudrakavastu* with *Sūtras* 13 and 14 of the Tibetan *Ratnakūṭa* and showed that the text of *Sūtra* 13 is different from that of *Sūtra* 14 and that the latter is not identical with the text of the *Vinayakṣudrakavastu*. This conclusion, though, does not exclude the possibility that *Sūtra* 14 of the Tibetan *Ratnakūṭa* was translated from I-tsing's version of Chapters 11 and 12 of the *Vinayakṣudrakavastu*. It is quite possible that I-tsing's translation of these two chapters is not completely identical with the Tibetan translation of the same chapters. A final solution will require a close comparison of the Chinese and Tibetan versions of Sūtras 13 and 14 of the *Ratnakūṭa* with the Chinese and Tibetan versions of Chapters 11 and 12 of the *Vinayakṣudrakavastu*.

In *Sūtra* 14 of the Tibetan *Ratnakūṭa*, Buddha is first at Kapilavastu and then goes to Śrāvasti. From Śrāvasti he goes to Campā, and it is here on the banks of the pond of the *ṛṣi* Garga that he teaches Nanda the *Garbhāvakrāntisūtra*. In Chapter 11 of the *Vinayakṣu-*

drakavastu Buddha teaches the *Garbhāvakrāntisūtra* to Nanda at exactly the same place.[13] The *Vinaya* of the Mūlasarvāstivādin was well-known to the Tibetans. The fact that Buddha taught a *Garbhāvakrāntisūtra* to Nanda on the banks of the Pond of Garga[14] must have been in the minds of the compilers of the *Mngal-las 'byung-ba*, which is also set on the banks of a lotus-pond near Campā. Although they substituted Ānanda for Nanda they must have been aware of the fact that a *Garbhāvakrāntisūtra* is found in the Buddhist canon in connection with the story of Nanda. This is certainly the reason why the *Mngal-las 'byung-ba* is placed in the Tibetan translation of the *Bodhisattvāvadānakalpalatā* before the story of Nanda, which is No. 11 in the Tibetan translation and No. 10 in Das's edition.

In the Sanskrit text of the table of contents of the *Bodhisattvāvadānakalpalatā* no mention is made of the *Mngal-las 'byung-ba*. However, in the Peking and Cone editions of the Tibetan translation the title of this text has been mentioned in an additional *pāda* of Verse 4: *gang-zhig dpal-sbas la bstan dang / / me-skyes skal-ldan du* (Peking: *dus*) *gsung dang / / mngal-nas 'byung-ba bstan-pa dang / / gang-zhig dga'-bo'i mdzes-ma la / / chags-pa dag ni 'bad-pas bsal* (Peking: *gsal*) / /. It is obvious that this *pāda* has been added later in order to account for the presence of the *Mngal-las 'byung-ba*.

The *Ṣaḍdantāvadāna* is mentioned in both the Sanskrit text and the Tibetan translation of the table of contents. In his detailed bibliography on the *Ṣaḍdantajātaka*, Lamotte indicates that the *Ṣaḍdantāvadāna* is not found in the Paris manuscripts of the *Bodhisattvāvadānakalpalatā*. However, he points out that the two Cambridge manuscripts, Add. 1306 and Add. 913, contain this *avadāna*.[15] Add. 1306 is a manuscript written in A.D. 1302.[16] According to Somendra's introduction the *Bodhisattvāvadānakalpalatā* was completed in the twenty-seventh year, i.e., 1051-1052. The Cambridge manuscript is therefore written 250 years after the completion of the work. Bendall has described the manuscript in detail.[17] Leaves 1-174 are missing, and the manuscript begins with the last word, *sahiṣṇavaḥ*, of Verse 7 of Tale 42, *Paṇḍitāvadāna*. Bendall remarks that in the manuscript Tales 41-48 are numbered 42-49. He has changed the numbering according to the metrical table of contents. However, the numbering of the manuscripts agrees entirely with that of the Tibetan translation of the *Bodhisattvāvadānakalpalatā* in which Tale 42 is the *Paṇḍitāvadāna*. In Das's edition this is Tale 41, wrongly called *Kapilāvadāna*. The table of contents also gives the name *Paṇḍita*. If we keep the numbering of the tales as found in Add. 1306, Tale 49 (*Hastakāvadāna*) ends on f. 198b. Tale 50 (*Daśakarmaplutyavadāna*) begins on f. 199b: *namo buddhāya / ye helocchita-*.

However, this manuscript contains seven extra leaves numbered 199-205. Bendall has given them the numbers 199*-205*. The *Ṣaḍdantāvadāna* begins on the last line of f. 198b and occupies the leaves 199*-205*. It is obvious that the scribe completed the first part of the *Bodhisattvāvadānakalpalatā* (Tales 1-49) on f. 198b and continued with the second part on f. 199b. According to Bendall the scribe had by accident omitted this tale and copied it in afterwards. Bendall's conclusion was certainly justified because the table of contents lists the *Ṣaḍdantāvadāna* as the Tale 49. However, with the publication of Das's edition it has become evident that the *Ṣaḍdantāvadāna* was missing in the Sanskrit text translated in Tibet. It must also have been missing in the manuscript used by the scribe of Add. 1306, Mañjuśrībhadrasudhi. When copying the table of contents Mañjuśrībhadrasudhi must have made the same discovery as Bendall, i.e., that the *Ṣaḍdantāvadāna* is listed as Tale 49.

In order to supply this missing tale the scribe made use of another collection of tales which contains a recension of the *Ṣaḍdantāvadāna*: the *Kalpadrumāvadānamālā*. Both the Paris and Cambridge manuscripts contain the text of the *Ṣaḍdantāvadāna*.[18] In the *Kalpadrumāvadānamālā* the tale is comprised of 198 verses. They are followed by several additional verses of a moralistic nature which do not belong to the story itself, and which need not be considered. The scribe of the *Bodhisattvāvadānakalpalatā* did not use all 198 verses. He reproduced 110 verses without any alteration and added eight others, most of which were made from *pādas* of verses of the *Kalpadrumāvadānamālā* recension of the story.

Feer[19] has studied the *Kalpadrumāvadānamālā* recension of the *Ṣaḍdanta* story together with other recensions. However, in order to show how the scribe of the *Bodhisattvāvadānakalpalatā* made use of the *Kalpadrumāvadānamālā* recension, it is necessary to give a summary and to indicate the *Kalpadrumāvadānamālā* verse-numbers.

Verses 1-4: Introduction. Aśoka asks Upagupta to tell another tale.

5: A good man is purified by the fire of a bad man (*durjanāgni*) just as a jewel shines after having been polished by a whetstone.

6-11: Buddha teaches the law at the Garga Pond near Campā.

12-31: Devadatta warns the *kṣapaṇakas* against the Buddha.

32-37: His words provoke different reactions among them.

38-58: A *kṣapaṇaka* says that he knows a way to destroy the reputation of the Buddha. He asks Cañāmānavikā to simulate pregnancy and to accuse the Buddha of having made her pregnant. She fastens a wooden bowl under her garment.

59-88: Cañcāmānavikā goes to the Buddha and accuses him of having made her pregnant and of having abandoned her. The Buddha is unperturbed but the gods are greatly upset. Śakra creates two rats who cut the cord which holds the wooden bowl. Crying "I am burnt," Cañcāmānavikā disappears in the flames of Hell.

89-94: The Buddha explains that she has been guilty of a grave sin in a previous existence.

95-123: The Elephant King Ṣaḍdanta lived happily in the Himālayas with his two wives, Bhadrā and Subhadrā. Once he played with Subhadrā in the lotus pond Mandākinī. Bhadrā became jealous and decided to take revenge. She went to the forest where the *muni*s live and took upon herself a fast in eight parts. She expressed the wish to be reborn as a queen and to obtain a seat of pleasure (*krīḍāsana*) made from the tusks of Ṣaḍdanta. She killed herself by throwing herself from a mountain, and was reborn as the daughter of the minister Khaṇḍita (mistake for Paṇḍita ?) of King Brahmadatta in Kāśi.

The king married her. She asked him for a seat made from the tusks of Ṣaḍdanta. The king summoned an old hunter, who tried to dissuade him from killing Ṣaḍdanta because he was a Bodhisattva.

124–143: The old hunter persuaded the king, but Bhadrā insisted on her wish. The king summoned another hunter, who declared himself willing to kill Ṣaḍdanta.

144–161: Dressed in a yellow robe, the hunter was seen by Subhadrā. She told the king [Ṣaḍdanta] that she was frightened, but the king explained that she had nothing to fear from someone who wears a yellow robe. He had just spoken these words when the hunter pierced him with a poisoned arrow. Subhadrā fainted, but Ṣaḍdanta consoled her and asked the hunter why he wanted to kill him.

162–165: The hunter explained that Queen Bhadrā desired a seat made from his tusks.

166–184: Ṣaḍdanta arrived at the conclusion that he must give his tusks to the hunter, because it was impossible to disappoint someone who came with a request. He broke off his tusks against a mountain. Five hundred elephants arrived, but Ṣaḍdanta protected the hunter with his chest and sent him back with his tusks.

185–189: The hunter brought the tusks to the king, who recompensed him with gold. He sent him back to his own house. Suddenly both his hands were cut off and fell on the ground.

190: Bhadrā mounted the seat made from the tusks. Saying "I am burnt," she fell into Hell.

191–192: Brahmadatta's kingdom was destroyed by terrible plagues.

193–198: The *dramatis personnae* are identified. Ṣaḍdanta = the Buddha; Bhadrā = Cañcāmāṇavikā; the hunter = Devadatta' the other elephants = monks. There are two verses on the evil behaviour of women. In the last verse the Buddha proclaims that one must speak the truth, refrain from inflicting injuries, and concentrate on śānti.

The scribe of the *Bodhisattvāvadānakalpalatā* took from the *Kalpadrumāvadānamālā* recension the following verses: 5, 59-123, 144-161, 166-184, 190, and 193-198. In order to fill the lacunae he added five verses (A-E) between Verse 5 and Verse 59, one verse (F) between Verses 123 and 144, one verse (G) between Verses 161 and 166, and one verse (H) between Verses 190 and 193. A-B: The Buddha preaches the law at the Garga Pond near Campā. C-E: The jealous *kṣapaṇaka*s say, "You must destroy the lustre (*dīpti*) of the Buddha by saying that you have been made pregnant by him." The young woman simulates a pregnancy by means of a wooden bowl. F: A second hunter declares himself willing to kill Ṣaḍdanta. G: The hunter says that Queen Bhadrā wants to have a seat made from Ṣaḍdanta's tusks. H: The hunter loses his hands, and Brahmadatta's kingdom is destroyed by excessive rains.

It is obvious that the scribe of the *Bodhisattvāvadānakalpalatā* was more interested in the story of the past concerning Ṣaḍdanta than in the story of the present relating to Cañcāmānavikā. Through the omission of Verses 6-58, nothing is said of the role played by Devadatta, although identification of Devadatta with the hunter (Verse 194) has been maintained. Moreover, verses C-E do not explain why the *kṣapaṇaka*s are jealous nor the identity of the young woman whom they ask to simulate pregnancy. It is equally obvious that the scribe of the *Bodhisattvāvadānakalpalatā* has made use of the *Kalpadrumāvadānamālā*. In a long note added to the English translation of his article on the *Ṣaḍdanta-jātaka*, "*Essai de classement chronologique des diverses versions du Ṣaḍdanta-jâtaka*" (*Mélanges d'Indianisme*, Paris, 1911, pp. 231-248) Foucher writes that "The author of the latter collection [*Kalpadrumāvadānamālā*] restricted himself to reproducing, without however (in any way) informing the reader of the fact, the work of Kshemendra, except that on two points he has lengthened the narrative of his predecessor, which in his opinion was too much abbreviated."[20]

I hope to be able to publish shortly the text of the *Kalpadrumāvadānamālā* recension of the *Ṣaḍdantāvadāna* including the eight verses added by the scribe of the *Bodhisattvāvadānakalpalatā*. It will then become absolutely clear that Foucher was wrong in assuming that the *Kalpadrumāvadānamālā* recension is based upon the

Bodhisattvāvadānakalpalatā recension. It is not possible to prove that the scribe of Manuscript Add. 1306, Mañjuśrībhadrasudhi, himself took the *Ṣaḍdantāvadāna* from a manuscript of the *Kalpadrumāvadānamālā*, but the similarity of the script in the *Ṣaḍdantāvadāna* to that in other parts of the manuscript of the *Bodhisattvāvadānakalpalatā* makes this supposition highly probable.

The fact that the *Ṣaḍdantāvadāna* is listed in the table of contents as the forty-ninth *avadāna* obliges us to assume that originally the text contained this story. It was, however, already missing in the copy which was translated in Tibet in the second half of the thirteenth century.[21] It is difficult to find a satisfactory explanation for the disappearance of the *Ṣaḍdantāvadāna*. This is not the only problem connected with the *Bodhisattvāvadānakalpalatā*. It was completed by Kṣemendra in 1052, but he did not compose Tale 108. This is surprising in view of the fact that he was still living in 1066 (when he wrote the *Daśāvatāracarita*).[22] Somendra does not explain why his father, after having composed 107 tales, did not complete his work by writing the 108th. If it had been Kṣemendra's wish that his son fulfill this task, one would expect Somendra to have mentioned this.

NOTES

1. The *Bodhisattvāvadānakalpalatā* is often referred to as *Avadānakalpalatā*. However, according to all the colophons and the Tibetan translation the title is *Bodhisattvāvadānakalpalatā*.

2. A copy of the same blockprint edition is listed in *A Catalogue of the Tohoku University Collection of Tibetan Works on Buddhism* (Sendai, 1953), p. 521, No. 7034, but I have not been able to consult it. In the Cone Tanjur the *Bodhisattvāvadānakalpalatā* occupies two volumes (Vols. 91-92: *Khri-shing*). The Cone edition contains both the Sanskrit text and the Tibetan translation. I have not been able to consult the Derge edition, but it also probably contains the Sanskrit text, though this is not mentioned in the catalogue of the Tohoku University: *A Complete Catalogue of the Tibetan Buddhist Canons* (Sendai, 1934), pp. 633-634, No. 4155. In the Narthang Tanjur the *Bodhisattvāvadānakalpalatā* occupies only one volume. Cf. Mibu Taishun, *A Comparative List of the Tibetan Tripiṭaka of the Narthang Edition* (Tokyo, 1967), p. 98, No. 3646, Vol. Ge, ff. 1-328. It would appear that the Peking and Narthang editions contain only the Tibetan translation, while the Derge and Cone editions contain both text and translation.

3. Cf. P. Cordier, *Catalogue du fonds tibétain de la Bibliothèque Nationale*, Troisième Partie (Paris, 1915), pp. 419-421.

4. *Tibetan Painted Scrolls*, Vol. 2 (Rome, 1949), p. 613, n. 118.

5. *L'Abhidharmakośa de Vasubandhu*, Vol. 1 (Paris-Louvain, 1923), p. 49, n. 2.

6. *A Comparative Analytical Catalogue of the Kanjur Division of the Tibetan Tripiṭaka* (Kyoto, 1930-1932), p. 238.

7. "Notes à propos d'un catalogue du *Kanjur*," in *Journal Asiatique*, 1914, Vol. 2, p. 123.

8. "La version tibétaine du *Ratnakūṭa*", in *Journal Asiatique*, 1927, Vol. 2, pp. 240, 245.

9. *Op. cit.*, p. 126, No. 1.

10. Pelliot refers to Chapters 11 and 12 of the *Vinayakṣudrakavastu*, the same text which La Vallée Poussin refers to as the *Vinayasamyuktakavastu*. Cf. Taishō, Vol. 24, No. 1451, pp. 251a-263a.

11. Pelliot, *op. cit.*, p. 125.

12. "Chibetto-yaku Daihōshakukyō no kenkyū," *Ōtani Gakuhō*, Vol. 11 (1930), p. 550. In his analysis of this article Serge Elisséef says wrongly that Sakurabe tried to prove that the whole Tibetan *Ratnakūṭa* had been translated from the Chinese. See *Bibliographie Bouddhique*, Vol. 2 (Paris, 1931), p. 37, No. 110). Sakurabe observed that Chapters 7, 13, and 40 were translated from the Chinese by Chos-grub and suggested that Chapters 11, 14, 17, and 20 must also have been translated from the Chinese.

13. For the Tibetan version see Lalou, *op. cit.*, p. 242. For the Chinese version see Taishō, Vol. 24, No. 1451, p. 253a17-21.

14. In the Sanskrit text of the *Mūlasarvāstivādavinaya* the name of the pond is Gargā. Cf. Edgerton, *Buddhist Hybrid Sanskrit Dictionary*, p. 210. In Pāli texts the Gaggarā Pond is named after Queen Gaggarā.

15. Ét. Lamotte, *Le Traité de la Grande Vertu de Sagesse*, Tome 2 (Louvain, 1949), p. 716, n. 1. According to Bendall Add. 913 is a copy of a copy, more or less direct, of Add. 1306.

16. According to Petech the date mentioned in the colophon is Sunday, April 8th, 1302. Cf. L. Petech, *Mediaeval History of Nepal* (Roma, 1958), p. 98.

17. C. Bendall, *Catalogue of the Buddhist Sanskrit Manuscripts in the University Library, Cambridge* (Cambridge, 1883), pp. 41-43.

18. Cf. Bendall, *op. cit.*, p. 131, Add. 1590; also J. Filliozat, *Catalogue du fonds sanscrit*, Fascicule 1 (Paris, 1941), pp. 14-15. For other manuscripts see Seiren Matsunami, *A Catalogue of the Sanskrit Manuscripts in the Tokyo University Library* (Tokyo, 1965), pp. 230-231.

19. "Le Chaddanta-Jātaka," *Journal Asiatique*, 1895, Part 1, pp. 31-85 and 189-223.

20. A. Foucher, "The Six-Tusked Elephant," *Beginnings of Buddhist Art* (Paris-London, 1917), p. 204, n. 1.

21. The *Bodhisattvāvadānakalpalatā* was translated by Lakṣmīkara and the Master fron Shong rDo-rje rgyal-mtshan, at the instigation of 'Phags-pa and the Regent Śākya bzang-po. According to Cordier (*op. cit.*, p. 420) the translation was probably made in the year 1272 A.D. The colophon of the Peking edition does not mention a date, and it is not clear from which source Cordier took the date 1272. From the names mentioned in the colophon it is possible to deduce that the translation was made in the period 1260 to 1280.

22. Cf. Oscar Botto, *Il Poeta Kṣemendra e il suo Daśāvatāracarita* (Torino, 1951), p. 9.

V
Mahāyāna Sūtra Literature

J.W. de JONG

NOTES ON PRAJÑĀPĀRAMITĀ TEXTS

1. *Conze's translation of the Aṣṭasāhasrikā-prajñāpāramitā-sūtra.*

Edward Conze's translation of the Aṣṭasāhasrikā was first published in 1958 as Work Number 284 (Issue Number 1578) of the *Bibliotheca Indica.* According to Conze's preface the new edition of his translation (*The Perfection of Wisdom in Eight Thousand Lines & Its Verse Summary,* Four Seasons Foundation, Bolinas, 1973) contains numerous corrections.

Bibliographical information on editions, translations, etc. of the A [=Aṣṭasāhasrikā] is to be found in Conze's *The Prajñāpāramitā Literature* ('s-Gravenhage, 1960), pp. 51-52. A useful supplement to Conze's book on the Prajñāpāramitā literature is Hanayama Shōyū's article on Japanese studies: A Summary of Various Research on the Prajñāpāramitā Literature by Japanese Scholars, *Acta Asiatica,* 10 (Tokyo, 1966), pp. 16-93.

Conze's translation of A does not contain any notes and for his interpretation of the vocabulary of A and other Prajñāpāramitā texts it is necessary to consult his *Materials for a Dictionary of the Prajñāpāramitā Literature* (Tokyo, 1967) [1]. Very useful for the elucidation of difficult places in A is Haribhadra's commentary, the Abhisamayālaṃkārālokā, edited by U. Wogihara (Tokyo, 1932-1935; reprinted in 1973). Wogihara's edition contains the complete text of A and gives page references to Mitra's edition. Haribhadra's commentary dates from the eighth century. According to Mano Ryūkai Haribhadra lived roughly from 730 to 795 [2]. Of a much later date is another commentary, which has been preserved in Sanskrit, the Sāratamā (or Sārottamā) of Ratnākaraśānti who, according to P.S. Jaini,

1. For a supplement see Edward Conze (ed., tr.), *The Gilgit Manuscript of the Aṣṭādaśasāhasrikāprajñāpāramitā.* Chapters 70-82 corresponding to the 6th, 7th and 8th abhisamayas (*Serie Orientale Roma,* XLVI, 1974), pp. 245-254.

2. Cf. Mano Ryūkai, *Genkan shōgonron no kenkyū* (Tōkyō, 1972), p. 17.

lived in the first half of the eleventh century. We must await Jaini's edition of this text in order to know how much help it offers for a better understanding of A [3].

To the translation, mentioned by Conze in his book on Prajñāpāramitā literature, one must add two translations into Japanese, which have been published recently: a translation of chapters 1, 2, 3 and 30 by Hirakawa Akira (Nakamura Hajime ed., *Butten* vol. II Tōkyō, 1965, pp. 305-358) and the first volume (chapters 1-11)of a complete translation by Kajiyama Yūichi (Nagao Gajin ed., *Daijō butten* vol. 2; Hassenjuhannyakyō I, Tōkyō, 1974). Kajiyama's translation reached me after I had written the following notes on Conze's translation. Therefore it was not possible for me to study it in detail. However, I have been able to quote a few passages from it.

Buddhist scholars owe a great debt of gratitude to Edward Conze for his work on the Prajñāpāramitā literature. In the West the Prajñāpāramitā texts have been rather neglected in the past. It is the great merit of Edward Conze to have realized the importance of these texts and to have contributed much to a better knowledge of them by his numerous editions, translations and studies. His work has laid a solid foundation for further research in this field. It is generally acknowledged that, among the Prajñāpāramitā texts, A occupies a very important place. For this reason the new edition of Conze's translation is a very welcome opportunity to make some notes on his translation as a small contribution to the study of the Prajñāpāramitā literature. The notes follow the order of the text, referring first to the pages of Conze's translation and, between parentheses, to the pages of Wogihara's edition (the page references to Mitra's edition are taken from Wogihara's edition). The problems, discussed in these notes, are of a different order. Some point out obvious mistakes or omissions in Conze's translation. Others discuss in more detail difficult expressions or passages without an attempt to suggest a definitive solution. Finally, I would like to draw attention to the fact that the publication of these notes is entirely due to the insistence of Edward Conze himself who prompted me to publish them instead of communicating them to him by letter.

Sigla and abbreviations

A = Aṣṭasāhasrikā-prajñāpāramitā-sūtra.

AA = Abhisamayālaṃkārālokā

BHSD = Franklin Edgerton, *Buddhist Hybrid Sanskrit Dictionary*. New Haven, 1953.

3. Cf. Padmanabh S. Jaini, The *Ālokā* of Haribhadra and the *Sāratamā* of Ratnākaraśānti: a comparative study of the two commentaries of the *Aṣṭasāhasrikā*, *BSOAS*, 35 (1972), pp. 271-284.

BHSG = Franklin Edgerton, *Buddhist Hybrid Sanskrit Grammar*. New Haven, 1953.
C = Conze's translation of A.
H = Haribhadra.
Kajiyama = Kajiyama's translation of A, vol. I (chapters 1-11). Tōkyō, 1974.
M = Edward Conze, *Materials for a Dictionary of the Prajñāpāramitā Literature*. Tokyo, 1967.
Mi. = R. Mitra's edition of A. Calcutta, 1888.
MW = M. Monier-Williams, *A Sanskrit-English Dictionary*. Oxford, 1899.
P = Pañcaviṃśatisāhasrikā-prajñāpāramitā-sūtra.
PW = Petersburger Wörterbuch, 1855-1875.
T = Tibetan translation, Lhasa Kanjur.
TD = *Taishō daizōkyō*. Tōkyō, 1924-1934.
W = Wogihara's edition of the Abhisamayālaṃkārālokā.
Wall. = M. Walleser's partial translation of A. *Prajñāpāramitā. Die Vollkommenheit der Erkenntnis*. Göttingen-Leipzig, 1914.

P. 85 (W 44; Mi. 7): *etad eva Bhagavan kaukṛtyaṃ syāt yo 'haṃ vastv avidann anupalabhamāno 'samanupaśyan nāmadheyamātreṇ' āyavyayaṃ kuryāṃ yad uta bodhisattva iti* — C « It would surely be regrettable if I, unable to find the thing itself, should merely in words cause a Bodhisattva to arise and to pass away ». H explains *āya* and *vyaya* by *vidhi* « affirmation » and *niṣedha* « denial ». The same explanation is given by H in his Sphuṭārthā in explaining *āya-vyaya* in AA, 28 [4], cf. E. Obermiller, *Analysis of the Abhisamayālaṃkāra*, Fasc. I (London, 1933), p. 65, n. 3; Mano Ryūkai, *op. cit.*, p. 110. Obermiller remarks that Tsoṅ-kha-pa explains *āya-vyaya* (*'du-'god*) as « appearing and disappearing »: *'du-'god skye-'jig daṅ bral-ba'i gzugs-sogs*. The Laṅkāvatāra interprets *āya* and *vyaya* as « origination » and « destruction » (*vināśa*), cf. p. 175. 16-18 and BHSD s.v. *āya*. Vimuktisena, too, in commenting on a passage of P: *rūpasyāhaṃ Bhagavann āyaṃ* [5] *ca vyayaṃ ca nopalabhe na samanupaśyāmi* (ed N. Dutt p. 124. 6) gives the same explanation: *tatrāyam utpādo, vyayo nirodhaḥ* (Abhisamayālaṃkāravṛtti, ed. C. Pensa, Roma, 1967, p. 57. 16-17). Haribhadra's explanation seems not to be supported by other texts or commentaries. Kumārajīva translates *āya-vyaya* in A 7 by « coming and going » (TD 227, p. 537 b 28). Kajiyama (p.12) translates *āya-vyaya* with « origination and destruction », but adds in parentheses: « i.e. affirmation and denial ».

4. In M s.v. *āya* read AA i 28 for AA i 18.
5. In Pensa's edition of the Abhisamayālaṃkāravṛtti (p. 57.5) read *Bhagavann āyaṃ* for *Bhagavan nāyaṃ*.

P. 96 (W 131; Mi. 33): *baddhasīmāno hi te saṃsārasrotasaḥ* — C « The flood of birth-and-death hems them in ». The Arhats are incapable of rebirth because « they have put a limit to the stream of transmigration ». H explains *srotasaḥ* as an abl.: *saṃsārasrotaso janmapravāhād baddhasīmāno 'nutpattidharmatayā kṛtamāryādāḥ*. T translates *srotasaḥ* as an abl.: *de-dag-gis 'khor-ba'i rgyun-las mtshams bcad-pas* (29 b 7). However, *srotasaḥ* is undoubtedly a gen. and not an abl. Kumārajīva translates: « because they have made a dam in birth and death » (TD 227, 540 a 19), Hsüan-tsang « because they made a boundary partition in the stream of birth and death » (TD 220, 769 c 20). Conze's translation is probably due to a misunderstanding of *baddha* which, of course, has an active sense as in *baddhavaira*, etc. See also Suvikrāntavikrāmi-paripṛcchā (ed. R. Hikata, Fukuoka, 1958), p. 58.3-4: *kṛtaparyantāś ca saṃsāraśrotasaḥ* (T *'khor-ba'i rgyud mthar byas-pa*) « they have put an end to the stream of transmigration ».

P. 99 (W 163; Mi. 41): *atha khalu Śakro devānāṃ indras tasyāṃ velāyāṃ puṣpāṇy abhinirmāy' āyuṣmantaṃ Subhūtim abhyavākirat / atha khalv āyuṣmataḥ Subhūteḥ sthavirasya Śakraṃ devānām indram anu vyāharaṇāyaitad abhūt.* — C « Sakra then conjured up flowers, and scattered them over the Venerable Subhuti. The Venerable Subhuti thought to himself by way of reply ». Conze seems to read *anuvyāharaṇāya*, cf. M s.v. *vy-ā-harati*: *anu-vyāharaṇa*, reply, A ii 41. T also has read *anuvyāharaṇāya* (*brgya-byin-la rjes-su brjod-pa'i phyir*). However, it is obvious from Haribhadra's commentary that he considers *anu* to be a postposition: *Indram anu vyāharaṇāyeti anuśabdo lakṣaṇārthe* (cf. Pāṇini I.4.84: *anur lakṣaṇe*). The only meaning given by PW for *anuvyāharaṇa* is « repeatedly stating » (das wiederholte Hersagen). It seems better to separate *anu* and *vyāharaṇāya* as has been done by W in his edition and to translate *vyāharaṇa* by « utterance » and not by « answer ». It is not easy to understand the exact meaning of *Indram anu*. Probably one must understand that *Indram* implies the magical creation of the flowers by Indra: « Then Subhūti conceived the following thought in conformity with [the action of] Indra ». According to H Subhūti uses the explanation of the true nature of the magically created flowers as a pretext for teaching the essence of the substratum: *nirmitapuṣpatattvakathanavyājen' ādhārasvarūpasya pratipādanāyaitad vakṣyamāṇārthānukāri cittam abhūd iti.*

P. 107 (W 216; Mi. 61): *iyam eva prajñāpāramitā sukham abhīkṣṇaṃ śrotavyā* — C « he should indefatigably and continually hear ... this very perfection of wisdom ». H explains correctly that *sukham* here means « without effort » (*anāyāsam*).

P. 107 (W 216; Mi. 61): *tiṣṭhato vā Kauśika parinirvṛtasya vā Tathāgatasya* — C « when the Tathagata has disappeared into final Nirvana ». Conze omits *tiṣṭhato vā*: « Whether the Tathāgata remains or has entered into final Nirvāṇa ».

P. 110 (W 242; Mi. 77-78): *nāhaṃ Śāriputra teṣām anyatīrthyānāṃ parivrājakānām ekasyāpi śuklaṃ dharmaṃ samanupaśyāmi* — C « Because I saw not even one pure dharma in those Wanderers ». — « Because I saw no pure dharma in even one of those Wanderers ».

P. 112 (W 252; Mi. 84): *mā khalu māṃ kaścit paryanuyuñjītopārambhābhiprāya iti* — C « They will have no fear of being plied with questions by hostile persons ». A few lines further Conze translates *paryanuyoga* with « censure » (p. 113, l.1) cf. also M s.v. *paryanuyoga.* H (p. 40.3; 252.23) glosses *paryanuyoga* with *codyam* « objection ». The meaning « censure » is given by PW with reference to Halāyudha and the Mitākṣarā but in Buddhist texts *paryanuyoga* seems to have always the meaning « questioning, raising objections », cf. Abhidharmakośa (ed. P. Pradhan) p. 471.10: *paudgalikas tu paryanuyojyaḥ* (T *rgal-zhiṅ brtag-par bya*), tr. L. de La Vallée Poussin (IX, p. 269): « Interrogeons à notre tour le partisan du moi ». The same Tibetan equivalent (*brgal-zhiṅ brtag-pa*) is given in the Mahāvyutpatti for *paryanuyoga* (No. 7197). In Vimuktisena's Abhisamayālaṃkāravṛtti (p. 56.19) *paryānuyoga* is a misprint for *paryanuyoga.*

P. 118 (W 276; Mi. 98): *evam eva Bhagavan prajñāpāramitāyā ete guṇāḥ sarvajñajñānasya ca* — C « O Lord, the qualities of the cognition of the all-knowing are derived from the perfection of wisdom ». — « Such are those qualities of the perfection of wisdom and of the knowledge of the all-knowing one ».

P. 118 (W 277; Mi. 98-99): *yathā ca Bhagavan rājapuruṣo rājānubhavāt mahato janakāyasyākutobhayaḥ pūjyaḥ* — C « As a king should be worshipped, because his royal might gives courage to a great body of people ». — « As a servant of the king fears nothing on account of the power of the king and is honoured by a great body of people ». Just as the *rājapuruṣa* is honoured on account of the king, the preacher of the *dharma* is honoured on account of the *dharmakāya.*

P. 121 (W 298; Mi. 112): *mā praṇaṃkṣīt* — C « should beware of making obeisance to it ». Cf. Edgerton BHSG 32.83: AsP 112.17 (prose) has *pranaṅkṣīt*, from *naś* 'perish', wich has no s-aorist in Skt.; H: *mā vinaṣṭo bhaviṣyati.*

P. 130 (W 358; Mi. 153-154) *tryadhvatraidhātukāparyāpannatvāt tathaiva pariṇāmo 'py aparyāpannaḥ* — C « For everything that is in the three periods of time or in the triple world is unincluded [in ultimate reality]. In consequence the turning over is also unincluded ». The preceding passage explains that one should turn over with the understanding that morality, etc. are unincluded in the triple world and in the three periods of time: « because [all that, i.e. morality, etc.] is unincluded in the three periods of time and in the triple world the turning over is also unincluded ». Hsüan-tsang translates: « because these dharmas (*śīla*, etc.) are *svabhāvaśūnya*, therefore they are unincluded in the triple world and in the three periods of time. The turning over is also of such nature ». (TD 220, p. 795 a 13-14). *Traidhātuka* is « the triple world », not that which is in the triple world (cf. BHSD s.v.). Conze's explanation of *traidhātuka* in M has to be corrected accordingly. Conze's translation is probably influenced by H: *tryadhvatraidhātukasya tattvenānutpādād aparyāpannatve katham tatra sthitaḥ pariṇāma iti* « because in reality the triple world does not originate [everything] is unincluded in it. How then can the turning over repose in it »? This interpretation corresponds to H's commentary on the preceding passage: *traidhātukāparyāpannapariṇāmamanaskāraṃ pratipādayann āha* (p. 358.13). See also Kajiyama (p. 186): « For (morality, etc., which are *svabhāvaśūnya)* are not included in the three periods of time and in the triple world ».

P. 130 (W 359; Mi. 154): *atha taṃ pariṇāmayati niviśate* — C « when he settles down in what he turns over ». The text must be corrected: *atha taṃ pariṇāmam abhiniviśate* (T *de-ste yoṅs-su bsṅo-ba de-la mṅon-par chags-śiṅ*) « when he settles down in the turning over », cf. H: *aparyāpanna ity abhiniveśo.*

P. 140 (W 398; Mi. 181): *ye kecid imāṃ gambhīrāṃ prajñāpāramitāṃ .... pratibādhitavyāṃ maṃsyante .... nāhaṃ Śāriputraivaṃrūpāṇāṃ pudgalānāṃ darśanam apy abhyanujānāmi / kutas taiḥ saha saṃvāsaṃ kuto vā lābhasatkāraṃ kutaḥ sthānaṃ* — C « All those who oppose this perfection of wisdom and dissuade others from it are persons to whom I do not grant any vision. How can one become intimate with them, how can they gain wealth, honour and position »? — « As to those who oppose this perfection of wisdom and dissuade others from it, I do not allow you even to see such persons, how much less to dwell together with them, how much less [to give them] wealth and honour, how much less [to give them] high positions ». Kajiyama (p. 218) translates *taiḥ saha saṃvāsaṃ* with « to become intimate with them » and *sthānaṃ* with « to dwell together ». However, his rendering of *sthānaṃ* does not seem appropriate.

P. 140 (W 399; Mi. 182): *Śāriputra āha / na bhagavatā tasya pudgalasya tatropapannasya mahānirayagatasy' ātmabhāvasya pramāṇam ākhyātaṃ / Bhagavān āha / tiṣṭhatu Śāriputra tasya pudgalasya tatropapannasya mahānirayagatasy' ātmabhāvasya pramāṇaṃ / tat kasya hetoḥ / mā tathārūpasya pudgalasya tad ātmabhāvasya pramāṇaṃ śrutvā uṣṇaṃ rudhiraṃ mukhād āgacchet ... maiva mahāpratibhayaṃ tasy' ātmabhāvasya pramāṇam aśrauṣīt yasyeme doṣāḥ samvidyante* — C « *Sariputra:* the Lord has not told us about the length of time such a person must spend in the great hells. *The Lord:* Leave that alone, Sariputra. If this were announced those who hear it would have to beware lest hot blood spurt out of their mouths ... lest they be overpowered by a great fright ». — « ..... *The Lord*: Leave that alone, Śāriputra. Why? Lest hot blood spurt from the mouth of such a person after hearing the length of time (he has to spend in the great hells). ..... Lest he who is guilty of these sins, hear that frightful length of time ».

P. 151 (W 445; Mi. 204-205): *asatpāramiteyaṃ Bhagavann ākāśa-asattām* (W *sattām* but T *nam-mkha' ma mchis-pa;* H *ākāśasyeva nityarūpeṇāsattām) upādāya.* — C « This is a perfection of what is not, because space is not something that is ». H explains that the *prajñāpāramitā* is an *asatprajñāpāramitā* because its non-existence is similar to that of space. Cf. Wall.: « Dieses ist die Vollkommenheit eines Nichtseienden mit Hinsicht auf das Nichtsein des Weltraums » (p. 78).

P. 151 (W 446; Mi. 205): *asaṃhāryapāramiteyaṃ* — C « One cannot partake of this perfection » — One cannot take away this perfection » Conze has translated *asaṃhārya* in many different ways cf. M s.v. *asaṃhārya*. However, in all the passages, quoted by him, *asaṃhārya* has no meanings other than « cannot be taken away, cannot be overwhelmed ». This becomes clear by examining the following passages of A. P. 184 (W 583; Mi. 285): *yena bodhisattvena ... prajñāpāramitā ...· paripraśnīkṛtā ca bhavaty ekaṃ vā dinaṃ dve vā trīṇi vā catvāri vā pañca vā dināni tasya tāvatkālikī śraddhā bhavati saṃhriyate ca punar evāsaṃhāryā ca bhavati paripṛcchayā* — C « Another Bodhisattva, again, has asked questions about this perfection of wisdom, for one, two, three, four or five days, and now only for a certain time he has faith in it, but afterwards it is withdrawn again and he no longer feels like asking questions about it ». — « ... and his faith remains only for such a time and then it is withdrawn but by questioning it becomes again a faith which cannot be taken away » P. 202 (W 675; Mi. 329): *bhikṣuḥ kṣīṇāsravo na parasya śraddhayā gacchati dharmatāyāṃ pratyakṣakārī asaṃhāryo bhavati Māreṇa pāpīyasā* — C « a monk whose outflows are dried up, does not go by someone else whom he puts his trust in, but he has placed the nature of dharma (read *dharmatāṃ* for *dharmatāyāṃ*?) directly before his own eyes, and Mara has no access to him ». — « ... and Māra cannot overwhelm him » (cf. W 762; Mi. 380: *te bodhisattvā mahāsattvā asaṃhāryāḥ sadevamānuṣāsureṇa lokena)*. H glosses: *anapaharaṇīyatvād asaṃhāryaḥ*. P. 209 (W 695; Mi. 341): *anantam aparyantaṃ jñānaṃ pratilabdham asaṃhāryaṃ sarvaśrāvakapratyekabuddhaiḥ* — C « he has gained a cognition which is endless and boundless, and to which Disciples and Pratyekabuddhas have no claim ». — « ... and which cannot be taken away by Disciples and Pratyekabuddhas ». (H *sarvalokākampyatvenāsaṃhāryaṃ*). In PW *saṃhārya* is translated as « dem man Etwas zukommen lassen muss, Ansprüche habend auf » with a reference to Mahābhārata 13,2538: *bhūyo bhūyo 'pi saṃhāryaḥ pitṛvittāt*, but the Poona edition reads: *bhūyo 'pi bhūyasā hāryaṃ pitṛvittāt* (13.47.38).

P. 152 (W 450; Mi. 206): *asambhinnapāramiteyaṃ Bhagavan sarvadharmāsambhedanatām upādāya* — C « This perfection is undifferentiated, because all dharmas are ». — « ... because all dharmas are undifferentiated ».

P. 156 (W 474; Mi. 217): *tenaiva pūrvakeṇa kuśalamūlenopanāmiteyaṃ tasmai gambhīrā prajñāpāramitā* — C « It is just because of the existence of these wholesome roots in him that this deep perfection of wisdom has bent over to him ». — « These wholesome roots, acquired in the past, have brought this deep perfection of wisdom to him ». See also M s.vv. *upanāmita* and *upa-nāmayati*.

P. 157 (W 475; Mi. 218): *śṛṇvataś caināṃ* [i.e. *prajñāpāramitāṃ*] *ramate cittam asyām prajñāpāramitāyām arthikatayā cotpadyate* — C « when he hears it, his thought delights in it, and he becomes desirous of it ». Cf. M s.v. *arthikatā: arthikatayā utpadyate* « becomes desirous ». One must certainly read *arthikaṃ tayā*, cf. T *ñan-pa na de-la dga'-zhiṅ śes-rab-kyi pha-rol-tu phyin-pa la don-du gñer-ba'i sems bskyed-pa* (194 b 6).

P. 160 (W 490; Mi. 227): *yad utemām evānuttarāṃ samyaksambodhim ārabhya* — C « i.e. starting from just this my supreme enlightenment ». A few lines further on Conze translates *yad uta* ... *ārabhya* correctly by « i.e. concerning ».

P. 160 (W 491; Mi. 227): *asyāṃ prajñāpāramitāyāṃ Māreṇāpi te na śakyā bhedayituṃ kutaḥ punar anyaiḥ sattvaiḥ yad uta cchandato vā mantrato vā* — C « They cannot be diverted from it even by Mara, how much less by other beings, whether they use willpower or mantras ». H explains that *chanda* and *mantra* can refer to the Bodhisattvas or to Māra. In the first case *chanda* is explained as the *sūtrāntamahāyānābhilāṣa*, in the second as *oṣadhi*. Conze adopts the second alternative, but translates *chanda* by « willpower ». The Śabdakalpadruma indicates that the meaning « poison (*viṣa*) for *chanda* is found in a lexicon, the Śabdacandrikā (cf. Th. Zachariae, *Die indischen Wörterbücher*, Strassburg, 1897, p. 39). If one accepts the second alternative, *yad uta* has the normal meaning « namely, to wit », but the first alternative is only possible if *yad uta* has the meaning « because » for which Edgerton adduces one example from the Saddharmapuṇḍarīka (cf. BHSD s.v. *yad uta* 2).

P. 162 (W 502; Mi. 233): *prajñāpāramitāṃ sarvajñajñānasyāhārikāṃ* — C « this perfection of wisdom which nourishes the cognition of the all-knowing ». *Āhārika* means « bringing about », cf. H. *utpādika*. Conze seems to derive *āhārika* from *āhāra* « food » and not from *āhāra* « bringing near, procuring », cf. M s.v. *āhārika*. The correct meaning is to be found in BHSD s.v. *āhārika* « bringer, that which brings ».

P. 163 (W 504; Mi. 235): *so 'ndhakāre hastinaṃ labdhvā yena prakāśaṃ tenopanidhyāyeta, tenopanidhyāyan hastipadaṃ paryeṣitavyaṃ manyeta* — C « In the darkness he would touch and examine the foot of the elephant ». — « Having found an elephant in the darkness, he would examine it where there is light, but examining it there, he would think it fit to examine the footprint of the elephant ». *Pada* means here the footprint (T *rjes*, 207 b 4). Both Kumārajīva (TD 227, p. 556 a 18) and Hsüan-tsang (TD 220, p. 810 c 16) have understood *pada* in this sense. It is normal practice to judge the size of an elephant from his footprint, cf. for instance Majjhimanikāya I, pp. 175-176: *Seyyathā pi bho kusalo nāgavaniko nāgavanaṃ paviseyya, so passeyya nāgavane mahantaṃ hatthipadaṃ dīghato ca āyataṃ tiriyaṃ ca vitthataṃ, so niṭṭhaṃ gaccheya: mahā vata bho nāgo ti.*

P. 166 (W 511; Mi. 241): *gulmasthāna* — C « bathing places ». Conze follows H: *gulmasthānaṃ ghaṭṭasthānaṃ*. A little further on the word *gulmadarśana* occurs (W 512; Mi. 242). Conze translates it as « troops of soldiers ». A variant reads *gulmākṣadarśana* which is confirmed by T (*la-gcan-gyi cho-lo lta-ba*, 213 a 3) and by H: *gulmākṣadarśanaṃ ghaṭṭasthāne pāśakādidarśanaṃ*. The meaning of *gulma* is not well established, cf. BHSD *gulma* « a kind of fee, perhaps transit fee, fee for pass ». In Divyāvadāna 4.12 *gulma* is translated in Tibetan by *bsel-pa'i rṅan-pa* « charge for escort » (cf. D.R. Shackleton Bailey, « Notes on the Divyāvadāna », *JRAS*, 1950, p. 168). In translating Divyāvadāna p. 34.13 and p. 501.23 the Tibetan translation uses the expression *la-gcan* « duties on a ghat or a pass » (cf. H.A. Jäschke, *Tibetan-English Dictionary*, p. 539 a). The same equivalent was used by the translators of A, cf. M s.v. *gulmadarśana*. *Gulmākṣadarśana* is mentioned in A after *rāja, kumāra, hasti, aśva* and *ratha*. W reads *gulmadarśanamanasikārāḥ* but variants read *gulmamanasikārāḥ* and *gulmākṣadarśanamanasikārāḥ*. It is possible that *gulmākṣa* is a corruption for *gulmaka* « division of an army (cf. Edgerton s.v.) but *darśana* is difficult to explain. On *gulma* see also V.S. Agrawala *Vāk* 5 (1957), p. 158.

P. 173 (W 539-540; Mi. 257): *saṃkṣiptāni cittāni, vikṣiptāni cittāni* — C « collected thoughts, distracted thoughts ». In Lalitavistara p. 151.15 *saṃkṣipa* and *vikṣipa* are two adjectives qualifying the thoughts of the beings. Edgerton (BHSD s.v. *saṃkṣipa-vikṣipa*) interprets them as meaning « narrow, limited » and « wide, extensive ». In the Daśabhūmikasūtra *saṃkṣipta* is applied twice to the *lokadhātu* (ed. J. Rahder, p. 15.13: *-lokadhātuvipulasaṃkṣipta-*; p. 90.21-22: *saṃkṣiptāyā lokadhātor vistīrṇatām adhitiṣṭhati)*. In another passage which closely resembles A pp. 257-258 the mind is said to be *saṃkṣiptaṃ / vikṣiptaṃ / samāhitam / asamāhitam* (ed. R. Kondō p. 57.12). Moreover, *saṃkṣipta* is rendered in Tibetan by *dog-pa* « narrow » and in Chinese by « narrow, small », cf. J. Rahder, *Glossary of the Daśabhumika-sūtra* (Paris, 1928), s.v. *saṃkṣipta*. The use of *saṃkṣipta* in this text confirms the interpretation given by Edgerton.

P. 174 (W 543; Mi. 260): *tāni cittāni asatsaṃkalpāni* — C « they [i.e. those thoughts] are just a false representation of what is not ». Both H (*asattātulyāni*) and T (*med-pa daṅ 'dra-ba yin-te*) understand *saṃkalpa* in the sense of *kalpa* « like, similar ». *Saṃkalpa* cannot be amended to *kalpa* because Hsüan-tsang (TD 220, p. 815 a 23) has « without discrimination » and therefore it seems better to assume that *saṃkalpa* here is used in the sense of *kalpa*.

P. 175 (W 549; Mi. 264): *samadarśanāni ... tāni cittāni* — *C* « those thoughts look at the same thing ». Both PW and MW indicate that *samadarśana* has the meaning « of similar appearance, like » only at the end of a compound. However, it is the only meaning which fits this place cf. T *mñam-par bstan-pa* (232 a 7).

P. 175 (W 550; Mi. 265): *tāni cittāni śūnyāny ārambaṇavaśikāni* — C « those thoughts are empty, devoid of objective support ». Conze's translation is probably based upon the Tibetan which has a negation: *mi-dmigs-pa'i dbaṅ-du gyur-pa'o* (233 a 2). Hsüan-tsang confirms T: « not master over objects » (TD 220, 815 c 25-26). However, H has not read a negation and is therefore obliged to add the word *saṃvṛtyā: ālambanavaśikāni saṃvṛty' ālambanaparatantrāṇi*. It would be better to render *vaśika* as « depending on ».

P. 182 (W 579; Mi. 282); C « Bodhisattvas who resolutely believe ... ». Bodhisattvas should be corrected to « beings » (*sattva*).

P. 186 (W 587; Mi. 288): *tasyānyena bhaṇḍaṃ bhaviṣyati anyena sā naur vipatsyate iti* — C « When his ship has burst asunder ». — « His goods will be at one place and his ship will perish somewhere else ». Hsüan-tsang (TD 220, p. 820 b 1-2) translates: « men, ship and goods will all be scattered in different places ».

P. 190 (W 606; Mi. 299): *vainayikaviviktasvabhāvās te ... bodhisattvā* — C « Their own-being is isolated from the need for discipline ». H gives a very far-fetched explanation, cf. M s.v. *vainayikaviviktasvabhāva*. It seems preferable to translate: « their own-being is disciplined and detached », cf. Hsüan-tsang's translation (TD 220, p. 822 a 19-20): « their own-being is discipline and separation ». T renders *vainayika* by « deriving from discipline » (*'dul-ba las byuṅ-ba*, 264 a 7) = *vinayaprabhava*. The expression *vainayikaviviktatā* occurs in chapter 27 (C 259; W 847: Mi. 445) but here T translates *vainayika* by « one to be disciplined » (cf. M s.v.) and Conze translates accordingly *vainayikaviviktatā* by « the isolatedness of those who should be disciplined ».

P. 194 (W 642; Mi. 309): *iyaṃ mahāpṛthivī ... ṣaḍvikāram aṣṭādaśamahānimittam akampat* — C « the great earth shook in six ways ». Conze does not translate *aṣṭādaśamahānimittam*. According to H these eighteen great signs refer to the division of the six ways of trembling in weak, medium and strong: *aṣṭādaśa mahānimittāni punar eṣām eva ṣaṇṇāṃ vikārāṇāṃ mṛdumadhyādhimātrakriyābhedenākampat*. I have not seen this mentioned anywhere else.

P. 201 (W 668; Mi. 325): *daśa kuśalān karmapathān nādhyāpadyate* — C « He never commits offences against those ten precepts ». Edgerton (BHSD s.v. *adhyāpadyate*) reads *daśākuśalān* and translates *adhyāpadyate* with « commits (a sin) ». Both T (284 b 6) and Hsüan-tsang (TD 220, p. 826 a 21) translate *daśākuśalān*. See also H: *nādhyāpadyeta na kuryāt*; A 390 (W 777) *āpattim adhyāpadya*; E. Conze, *The Gilgit Manuscript of the Aṣṭādaśasāhasrikāprajñāpāramitā*. Chapters 70-82 (Roma, 1974), p. 108.3-4: *daśākuśalān* [ed. *daśāku(śa)lāḥ*] *karmapathān adhyāpadyeta*. Read *daśākuśalān*.

P. 201 (W 673; Mi. 327): *na ca kaṃcid dharmaṃ samanupaśyati yaṃ na dharmadhātunā yojayati sarvam eva ca taṃ prayujyamānaṃ samanupaśyati* — C « There is not any dharma which he does not see as yoked to the nature of dharmas, and each dharma he sees simply as engaged in that effort ». T translates *sarvam eva ca taṃ prayujyamānaṃ samanupaśyati* with *thams-cad kyaṅ de-daṅ ldan-par yaṅ-dag-par mthoṅ-ṅo* (286 b 3-4). According to M s.v. *prayujyamāna* T does not translate *prayujyamāna*. However, *daṅ-ldan-par* certainly corresponds to *prayujyamānaṃ*. Probably one must read *tatprayujyamānaṃ* « being yoked to that ». *Prayukta* is used as an equivalent of *saṃprayukta*, cf. M. s.v. *prayukta* and Suvarṇabhāsottamasūtra p. 74.10 (ed. J. Nobel). For this reason I suggest the following translation: « He does not see any dharma which he does not yoke to the nature of dharmas and he sees everything as being yoked to it ».

P. 204 (W 679; Mi. 331): *ko 'trāñjāsyati* — C « Who can anoint himself for it » — One must read *ko 'trājñāsyati*, cf. T *su-zhig de-la śes-par 'gyur* (290 a 4).

P 204 (W 679; Mi. 331): *nirarthakaṃ tvaṃ vihanyase* — C « it is useless for you to resist». *Vihanyate* has here the normal meaning «to suffer, to be distressed, to exert oneself in vain », cf. T *ñon-moṅs-so*. The same meaning applies to A 403 (W 793; C 239): *sattvān* ... *vihanyamānāṃś ca* « beings who suffer ». Conze translates: « beings who are doomed to be killed ».

P. 204 (W 680; Mi. 332): *vivecanatā* — C « critical examination ». See BHSD s.v. *vivecayati* « causes (one) to abandon, dissuades »: T *'bral-bar byed-pa*.

P. 205 (W 686; Mi. 335): *abhedavarṇavādinaś* — C « They praise without causing dissension » — « They praise the absence of dissension ».

P. 209 (W 696; Mi. 341): *sādhu sādhu Subhūte / yas tvaṃ gambhīrāṇi gambhīrāṇi sthānāny ārabhya nigamayitukāmaḥ* — C « Well said, Subhuti. You obviously bring up the very deep positions because you want me to change the subject ». The meaning of *nigamayati* is made clear by H (*pratipādayitukāmaḥ*) and by T: *śes-par bya-bar 'dod-pa* (297 b 5): « You desire to be instructed ». Cf. Wall.: « Gut, Gut, Subhūti, der du die überaus tiefen Örter zu Grunde legend ergründen willst ». (p. 106); M. Winternitz, *Der Mahāyāna-Buddhismus* (Tübingen, 1930): « Gut, gut, Subhūti, dass du in bezug auf die unergründlichen Tiefen etwas zu lernen wünschest » (p. 67).

P. 209 (W 698; Mi. 342): *āścaryaṃ Bhagavan yāvat sūkṣmeṇopāyena rūpataś ca nivārito nirvāṇaṃ ca sūcitaṃ* — C « It is wonderful, O Lord, how a subtle device has opened up [or: impeded] form, etc., and indicated Nirvana at the same time». Cf. T *gzugs-las kyaṅ bzlog-la mya-ṅan-las-'das-pa'aṅ bstan-pa* (298 b 2). H also understands *nivārito* in the sense of « kept off from »: *tathatāyāṃ rūpādipratiṣedhād rūpādau pravṛttinirākaraṇāya nivāritaḥ*. Hsüan-tsang (TD 220, p. 829 b 2-3) translates: « It is wonderful how a subtle device has removed the forms and revealed Nirvāṇa ». It is difficult to understand m.sg. *nivārito* instead of n.sg. A similar case occurs in A 422 (W 813): *na mayā 'dhyāśayato vikopayitavyaḥ yena* ... See below sub P. 247.

P. 211 (W 705-706; Mi. 346): *abhisaṃskāro, puṇyābhisaṃskāro* — C « accumulation, accumulation of merit ». Also Edgerton proposes this translation but, as indicated by H (*abhisaṃskāraś cittābhogo*), *abhisaṃskāra* signifies « performance, accomplishment » and *puṇyābhisaṃskāra* is the performance of a meritorious deed. It seems better to reserve the translation « accumulation » for *saṃcaya*.

P. 215 (W 729; Mi. 357): *asya prajñāpāramitābhyāsataḥ svapnāntaragatasyāpi* — C « He also in his dreams remains quite close to perfect wisdom ». *Prajñāpāramitābhyāsataḥ* is « because of the cultivation of perfect wisdom », cf. T *goms-pa'i* (310 a 1).

P. 222 (W 749; Mi. 370): *tathā ca pratyavekṣitavyam avikṣiptayā cittasaṃtatyā yathā pratyavekṣamāṇo rūpam iti tāṃ dharmatāṃ dharmatayā na samanupaśyet* — C «But he should contemplate that with an undisturbed series of thoughts in such a way, that when he contemplates the fact that « form, etc. is empty », he does not regard that true nature of dharmas [i.e. emptiness] as something which, as a result of its own true nature [i.e. emptiness] is a real entity ». Conze's translation is based upon Haribhadra's commentary: *tāṃ dharmatāṃ śūnyatāṃ dharmatayā śūnyatayā rūpaṃ vastv iti pratyavekṣamāṇo yathā na samanupaśyet*. Probably *dharmatayā* has to be translated as a predicative instrumental: « He does not regard that true nature of dharmas as a [really existing] true nature of dharmas ». T translates: *chos-ñid de-la chos-ñid-kyi raṅ-bzhin yod-pa yin-no / zhes yaṅ-dag-par rjes-su mi mthoṅ-ba* (320 a 3) which corresponds to the following passage in H: *śūnyatāṃ śūnyatāsvabhāvenāstīti yathā nopalabheta* (T *na samanupaśyati* cf. W note 3) « he does not consider that emptiness exists in its own nature of emptiness » (*śūnyatā* replaces here *dharmatā*). The Tibetan translators seem to have made use of Haribhadra's commentary or some other commentary which gives the same explanation.

P. 231 (W 774; Mi. 387): *apagatapādamrakṣaṇo* — C « frugal ». Conze translates the commentary and not the text, cf. H: *alpecchatvād apagatapādamrakṣaṇaḥ*.

P. 246 (W 812; Mi. 419): *aniṣṭatvāya* (W has *anirdiṣṭatvāya* but see H p. 814.23) — C « conditions which are unserviceable ». — « Conditions which are undesirable ».

P. 247 (W 813; Mi. 422): *na mayā 'dhyāśayato vikopayitavyaḥ* — C « For I, since I am earnestly intent [on full enlightenment], should not do harm to others ». T *bdag-gis lhag-pa'i bsam-pa 'khrug-par bya-ba ma yin-no* (362 b 5): « I must not disturb my earnest intention ». T seems to have read *adhyāśayo* instead of *adhyāśayato*. If one keeps the reading *adhyāśayato*, one is forced to consider *vikopayitavyaḥ* as an error for *vikopayitavyaṃ*: « I must not let myself be distracted from my earnest intention ». Cf. E. Conze, *The Gilgit Manuscript of the Aṣṭādaśasāhasrikāprajñāpāramitā*. Chapters 55 to 70 corresponding to the 5th abhisamaya (Roma, 1962) p. 37, lines 2-3: *(adhyāśaya)ś ca me na vikopitavyaḥ*.

P. 275 (W 912; Mi. 479): *rūpaṃ kuśalākuśaladharmasaṃcayavigatam* — C « it [i.e. form] has no definite boundary like the collection of all wholesome and unwholesome dharmas ». Conze adds *aparyantasamam* which occurs before. However, it is better to adhere to the text: « Form is free from the accumulation of wholesome and unwholesome dharmas».

P. 278 (W 930; Mi. 483: *asti hi...Māraḥ pāpiyān dharmabhāṇakasya... rūpaśabdagandharasasparśān upasaṃharati sevituṃ* — C « For there is always Mara, the Evil One, who may suggest that your teacher tends ... things that can be seen, heard, smelled, tasted or touched ». *Upasaṃharati* has here the meaning « brings together, provides for someone » (cf. BHSD s.v.). For *asti* see PW p. 535. « It happens that Māra, the Evil One, presents to the teacher things to be seen, etc. in order to make use of them ».

P. 279 (W 932; Mi. 485-486): *teṣāṃ ca saptaratnamayānāṃ prākārāṇāṃ Jāmbūnadasya suvarṇasya khoḍakasīrṣāṇi pramāṇavanty upodgatāni* — C « The walls all round that town are made of the seven precious substances. Their well-founded copings slope into the golden river Jambu ». *Jāmbūnadasya suvarṇasya* is a genitive of matter: « copings made of gold from the Jāmbū river ». See also A 488 (W 934: C 280): *Jāmbūnadasya suvarṇasya kadalīvṛkṣo.*

P. 280 (W 935; Mi. 488-489): *ye 'pi te sattvās tatra Gandhavatyāṃ nagaryāṃ vāstavyās te 'pi madhye nagarasṛṅgāṭakasya Dharmodgatasya bodhisattvasya mahāsattvasy' āsanaṃ prajñapayanti suvarṇapādakaṃ ... cailavitānaṃ muktāvicitritaṃ, samaṃ sahitā niratāḥ kiṃ ayaṃ saṃsthita iti susaṃsthitavicitravipākatayā dhārayanti, samantāc ca taṃ pṛthivīpradeśaṃ pañcavarṇikaiḥ kusumair abhyavakiranti* — C « And the citizens of that town built a pulpit for the Bodhisattva Dharmodgata in the central square of the town. It has a golden base ... there is an awning shining with pearls, even and firm. All round that pulpit flowers of the five colours are strewed ». — « ... there is an awning shining with pearls. [The citizens wondering whether the pulpit] was well established, hold it up, in like manner united and rejoicing, through the well-established ripening of their various deeds, and they strewed all round that place flowers of the five colours ». See T (which omits *niratāḥ*): *ci 'di legs-par gnas-sam sñam-pa / legs-par gnas-pa sna-tshogs-pa rnam-par smin-pas lhan-cig-tu mñam-par rab-tu 'dzin-par byed-ciṅ* (418 b 5-6).

P. 285 (W 947; Mi. 498) *kāraṇāṃ*; P. 286 (W 949; Mi. 500); P. 287 (W 952; Mi. 504): *kāraṇāṃ* — C « treatment ». Better « torture, torment », cf. BHSD s.v. For this meaning PW quotes one passage from the Daśakumāracaritam (= ed. M.R. Kale, Delhi, 1966, p. 92.4-5): *drakṣyasi pāram aṣṭādaśānāṃ kāraṇānām.* See also p. 174.4-5: *yad eṣa narakākaḥ kāraṇānāṃ nārakīṇāṃ rasajñānāya nītaḥ.*

Tirage à part du T'OUNG PAO, Vol. XLII, Livr. 3-4, 1953
E. J. Brill — Leiden

YAMADA Ryūjō 山田龍城 *Hannyakyōtenrui no keisei sareta jidai no haikei* 般若經典類の形成された時代の皆景 l'arrière-plan de la période de formation de la littérature des Prajñāpāramitāsūtra, Tōhoku Daigaku bungakubu-kenkyūnempō 東北大學文學部研究年報, (titre anglais:) The Annual Reports of the Faculty of Arts and Letters Tohoku University, vol. II, p. 1-41, Sendai, Japon, 1951.

Dans les *Prajñāpāramitāsūtra* se trouve une prédiction, relative à la diffusion de la Prajñāpāramitā (en abrégé P.P.), qui a donné lieu à des interprétations différentes. Dans la plupart des textes l'itinéraire de la P.P. commence au Sud. Plusieurs auteurs, parmi lesquels La Vallée Poussin et M. Tucci, ont considéré cela comme une indication de l'origine méridionale des sūtra de la P.P.

M. Lamotte s'est opposé à ces théories dans une longue note aux pages 25 et 26 de son *Traité de la Grande Vertu de Sagesse* (vol. I, Louvain, 1944). Il montre qu'il y a des versions différentes de cet itinéraire dans les textes de la P.P. Citant un passage du *Ta tche tou louen* qui compare la diffusion de la P.P. à la marche du soleil, de la lune, des cinq étoiles et des constellations, et rappelant la marche de la roue du roi Sudarśana dans les quatre directions de l'espace, M.L. considère ce prétendu itinéraire comme le symbole de la diffusion universelle de la P.P.

M. Yamada n'est pas de cet avis. Dans une longue étude il s'efforce de déceler dans les différentes versions de cet itinéraire le reflet d'événements historiques. Considérant l'itinéraire Sud-Ouest-Nord que l'on trouve dans le T. 224 (VIII, p. 446b), le T. 227 (VIII, p. 555a), le T. 223 (VIII, p. 317b) et le T. 228 (VIII, p. 623b) comme le plus ancien et le plus authentique, M.Y. consacre la plus grande partie de son article à une vue d'ensemble de l'histoire de l'Inde du deuxième siècle avant J.C. au deuxième siècle après J.C. et met en lumière la prépondérance successive du royaume Andhra dans le Sud, des Scythes et des Parthes dans l'Ouest et finalement des Koushans dans le Nord. Ainsi l'histoire se laisserait accorder assez bien avec ces textes. Mais dans le T. 225 (VIII, p. 490a) l'itinéraire est le suivant: pays des Śākya — pays Vartani — pays Uttaravatī. Ici les explications de M.Y. deviennent moins satisfaisantes. Etant donné que dans le texte sanskrit de la P.P. en huit mille (éd. Mitra, p. 225; éd. Wogihara, p. 487) l'itinéraire est: Sud-Est-Nord, le pays des Śākya doit, d'après M.Y., indiquer la région méridionale puisque, dans cette région, la doctrine du sage des Śākya a le mieux fleuri! En outre, la mention de l'Est au lieu de l'Ouest indiquerait qu'à une autre époque de la tradition bouddhique l'Inde orientale remplaça l'Inde occidentale dans l'intérêt de la communauté bouddhique. Ce n'est qu'à l'époque de Hiuan-tsang que l'itinéraire serait composé de manière mécanique, en énumérant successivement le Sud-Est, le Sud, le Sud-Ouest, le Nord-Ouest, le Nord et le Nord-Est (T. 220, VII, p. 212c-213c, p. 594a-b et p. 808b-c), à l'exception toutefois d'un passage (T. 220, VII, p. 889c-890a) où l'itinéraire va du Sud au Nord et de là au Nord-Est, reflétant ainsi l'importance de Nālandā comme centre du bouddhisme.

Cette analyse sommaire, qui ne fait pas justice à maint détail intéressant du travail de M.Y., montre à quelles constructions forcées il faut avoir recours pour tirer des renseignements historiques de cet itinéraire de la P.P. Néanmoins, il me paraît difficile d'adopter entièrement l'opinion de M. Lamotte. Si cet itinéraire relevait d'un bout à l'autre de l'allégorie, on s'attendrait plutôt à une énumération systématique, et identique dans tous les textes, des quatre régions de l'espace, comme c'est le cas pour la roue du roi Sudarśana. Pour ma part, je crois que nous avons à faire ici, comme si souvent dans les traditions bouddhiques, à une tradition appartenant en même temps à l'histoire et à l'allégorie, et que nous manquons de données positives pour faire le départ entre ces deux sphères.

J. W. de Jong

Notes on Prajñāpāramitā texts:
2. The *Suvikrāntavikrāmiparipṛcchā*

J. W. de Jong

The Sanskrit text of the ***Suvikrāntavikrāmiparipṛcchā*** (abbr. *Su.*) was published in 1956 by Matsumoto and in 1958 by Hikata. Conze has given a summary of the contents in ***The Prajñāpāramitā Literature*** ('s-Gravenhage, 1960, pp. 60–62). The vocabulary has been carefully studied by him in his ***Materials for a Dictionary of the Prajñāpāramitā Literature*** (Tokyo, 1967). Recently two translations have been published. Conze's translation is to be found in ***The Short Prajñāpāramitā Texts*** (London, 1973, pp. 1–78) and a Japanese translation by Tosaki Hiromasa in ***Daijō butten***, vol. 1 (Tōkyō, 1973, p. 73–296, 304–316, 325–329).

According to Conze the *Su.* is the latest in time of the full-scale Prajñāpāramitā texts and must be earlier than A.D. 625 since Candrakīrti quotes it in his ***Madhyamakāvatāra***.[1] Hikata puts the *terminus ante quem* in the beginning of the sixth century because Bhāvaviveka (c. 490–570) quotes it in his ***Prajñāpradīpa-Mūlamadhyamakavṛtti*** (cf. Hikata pp. lxxvi and lxxxii). However, all passages quoted by Bhāvaviveka are from one chapter only (chapter III) and it is therefore not possible to maintain that the entire text existed already in the beginning of the sixth century.

The editions of the Sanskrit text are based upon a single manuscript from the Cambridge University Library. According to Bendall the manuscript was written in the 12–13th centuries. It is therefore much later than the Chinese translation (660-663, cf. T. 2154, ch. 8, p. 555b) and the Tibetan translation by Śīlendrabodhi, Jinamitra and Ye-śes-sde (c. 800–825). The Sanskrit text is much closer to the Tibetan translation than to the Chinese translation. This is partly due to the fact that Hsüan-tsang has not always translated the text literally; in many instances he has given a paraphrase in order to bring out more clearly the meaning of the text. Moreover, Hsüan-tsang's translation is influenced by the rhythm of the Chinese sentence which consists of groups of four characters. On the other hand it is obvious that the Sanskrit text, as represented by the Cambridge manuscript, has been subjected to changes and corruptions. A great number of these must have been in existence already in the manuscript used by the Tibetan translators in the beginning of the ninth century. Finally, the Tibetan translation seems not to have been made with the same care as translations of other P.P. texts.

In several places the divergences between the three recensions are so great that it is very difficult to arrive at the meaning of the original text. In these cases it is impossible to establish the exact wording by emendations of the Sanskrit text. This is true for instance of pp. 7.9–8.16 (all references are to page and line of Hikata's edition). Tosaki translates the Sanskrit text but adds in a note a translation of both the Tibetan and the Chinese versions. However, even when the Sanskrit text agrees with the Tibetan translation and not with the Chinese translation, it is not always possible to assume that the text is correctly transmitted. For example, in chapter 4 there occurs the following passage: *Ataḥ Śāradvatīputra durlabhatamās te satvāḥ, ye gambhīrān dharmān śrutvā 'nuttarāyāṃ samyaksambodhau cittam utpādayanti cchandaṃ ca janayanti, mahākuśalamūlasamanvāgatāḥ. Nâhaṃ Śāradvatīputra tān satvān mahāsaṃsārasamprasthitān iti vadāmi, yeṣām ayaṃ prajñāpāramitānirdeśaḥ śravaṇapatham apy āgamiṣyati* (Hikata: *yanti*), *śrutvā ca paṭhiṣyanti, adhimokṣayiṣyanti, udāraṃ ca prītisaumanasyaṃ janayiṣyanti, eṣu dharmeṣu cchandaṃ janayiṣyanti, punaḥ punaḥ śravaṇāyâpi. Kaḥ punar vādaḥ uddeṣṭuṃ vā svādhyātuṃ vā parebhyo deśayituṃ vā* (p. 59.11–18). The Tibetan translation agrees with the Sanskrit text apart from two minor differences:

1. *mahākuśalamūlasamanvāgatāḥ*, T. *dge-ba chen-po daṅ-ldan-pa* = *mahākuśalasamanvāgatāḥ*; 2. *ayaṃ prajñāpāramitānirdeśaḥ*, T. *śes-rab-kyi pha-rol-pa 'di* = *iyaṃ prajñāpāramitā*. The Chinese translation agrees with the first sentence up to *mahākuśalamūlasamanvāgatāḥ* and continues as follows: "I say that they possess great wholesome roots, are provided with great equipment (*mahāsambhāra*) and are armed with the great armour (*mahāsannāhasannaddha*). Quickly they will realize the supreme and correct awakening (*anuttarasamyaksambodhi*). When these beings hear the exposition of this profound Prajñāpāramitā, they will rejoice and desire to hear it again and again. The merit reaped by them is without measure and without end. How much more (will be their merit) when they will be able to bear it in mind, to recite it and to teach it to others." The Chinese translation has certainly preserved the original text much better than the Sanskrit manuscript. The Sanskrit text makes a very clumsy impression and gives a distorted idea of the original version.

Probably *mahāsaṃsāra* is the result of a corruption of *mahāsambhāra*.

The editors and translators of the *Su.* have made many useful suggestions for emending the Sanskrit text, but many problems still remain.[2] In quite a few places the Chinese translation is based upon a much more reliable text. However, Hsüang-tsang's method of translating makes it difficult to make use of it for textual emendations. Nevertheless, it is certainly necessary to quote it each time when it seems to have preserved better the original sense of the text. A complete translation of Hsüang-tsang's version would be highly welcome. The following notes are limited to the discussion of a few passages only. For the Tibetan translation I have made use of the two editions at my disposal: the Peking and Lhasa editions of the Kanjur and for the Chinese translation I have used volume 7 of the Taishō edition (pp. 1065–1110). As the text is relatively short and moreover divided into seven chapters, I have refrained from giving references to page and line of the Tibetan and Chinese translations.

Su. 5.6: *nânapatrapānāṃ*. Ti *ṅo-tsha ma-'tshal-ciṅ khrel ma-mchis-pa rnams-kyi* = *nâhrīkānām anapatrapānāṃ*. C. agrees with Ti. Conze translates: "who discredit the doctrine by their deeds" and adds in a note: "Ch: who lack any shame and are without dread of blame". In MDPL Conze translates *an-apatrapa* by "one who discredits the doctrine by his deeds", but *apatrāpya* by "dread of blame".

Su. 5.19: *-vṛṣabhopamānāṃ bodhisatvānāṃ mahāsatvānām ābrīḍhaśalyānāṃ*. Ti does not have *bodhisatvānāṃ mahāsatvānām*. These two words are to be found in line 22 and have to be omitted in line 19.

Su. 5.22–6.5: *Ye dharmam api nopalabhante nâbhiniviśante, kutaḥ punar adharmaṃ, teṣāṃ vayaṃ Bhagavann arthāya Tathāgataṃ paripṛcchāmo bodhisatvānāṃ mahāsatvānām āśayaśuddhānām . . . . . . saṃśayacchedanakuśalānāṃ, [teṣāṃ] vayaṃ Bhagavan satvānāṃ kṛtaśas Tathāgataṃ paripṛcchāmo bodhisatvānāṃ mahāsatvānām.* Hikata adds *teṣāṃ* which is not in Ms. and in Ti. However, according to Ti one must put a full stop before *āśayaśuddhānām* and omit *teṣāṃ*: *bodhisatvānāṃ mahāsatvānām. Āśayaśuddhānām . . . . saṃśayacchedanakuśalānāṃ vayaṃ Bhagavan satvānāṃ kṛtaśas Tathāgataṃ paripṛcchāmo bodhisatvānāṃ mahāsatvānām.*

Su. 7.10: *Apāramitaiṣā Suvikrāntavikrāmin sarvadharmāṇāṃ, tenocyate prajñāpāramiteti.* According to Hikata's note C. and Ti have *pāramitaiṣā*. However, C. does not translate *pāramitā* with the usual equivalent but gives a free rendering: "Wisdom is able to penetrate far into the true nature of the dharmas". It seems preferable to read *pāramitā*, as in p. 27.3 where C. renders *pāramitā* in the same way (Hikata corrects the manuscript reading *ā pāramitā* to *pāramitā*. Conze reads *ā-pāram-itā* and refers to Ti *tshu-rol rtogs-pa ste*. However, *tshu-rol* corresponds to *āra* and not to *pāra*). In the following passage Conze corrects the readings of the manuscript: *ajñā* and *ajānanā* to *ājñā* and *ājānanā*. It is impossible to determine the original readings, but C. and Ti show clearly that the negative prefix *a* is incorrect.

Su. 7.17–18: *yatha satva ajānanas, tenocyate prajñeti.* Ti *ji-ltar sems-can rnams-kyis śes-par 'gyur-ba de-ltar śes-rab ces bya'o.* Cf. p. 27.4–5: *yathā punar yuṣmākam ājānanā* (Ms. *ajānanā*) *bhaviṣyanti*, Ti *ji-ltar khyed śes-par 'gyur-ba.* It is impossible to reconstruct the original readings.

Su. 8.1–3: [*Na*] *jñānagocara eṣa Suvikrāntavikrāmin nâjñānagocaraḥ, nâjñānaviṣayo nâpi jñānaviṣayaḥ; aviṣayo hi jñānaṃ; saced ajñānaviṣayaḥ syād, ajñānaṃ syāt.* Hikata adds *na* which is found in Ti but not in C. Ti inverts the order of *jñānagocara* and *ajñānagocara*. According to Hikata Ti and C. do not have *saced ajñānaviṣayaḥ syād* but correspond to: *sacej jñāne viṣayaḥ syād.* However, C. translates: *sacej jñānaṃ viṣayaḥ syād.* This follows logically after *aviṣayo hi jñānam*: "Knowledge is not the object (of knowledge); if it were the object (of knowledge), it would be non-knowledge." *Eṣa* refers to *prajñā*. Conze translates *prajñā* by 'wisdom' and *jñāna* by 'cognition'. His translation of this passage is as follows: "It [i.e. *prajñā*] is not the range of non-cognition, not the sphere of non-cognition, nor also the sphere of cognition; for it is a cognition without an (objective) sphere. If there were an objective sphere in non-cognition, that would be a non-cognition." However, this passage only makes sense by assuming that *prajñā* and *jñāna* are used without making a distinction between the two: "It is not the domain of knowledge, nor the domain of non-knowledge, nor the object of knowledge, nor the object of non-knowledge. For knowledge [i.e. *prajñā*] is not the object (of knowledge). If knowledge were the object of knowledge (*sacej jñānaṃ viṣayo syād*), it would be non-knowledge."

Su. 8.4–5: *nâjñānena jñānam ity ucyate, nâpi jñānena jñānam ity ucyate.* Ti *ye-śes-kyis ye-śes śes bya'o // ye-śes-kyis mi-śes-pa źes mi-bya'o // = jñānena jñānam ity ucyate, na jñānenâjñānam ity ucyate*, C. *nâjñānena jñānam ity ucyate, nâpi jñānenâjñānam ity ucyate, nâpi jñānena jñānam ity ucyate.*

Su. 8.6: *na tu tatra kiṃcid ajñānam, yac chakyam ādarśayitum; idaṃ taj jñānam . . .* Read with Ti and C. *kiṃcij jñānam.*

Su. 8.7–8: *Tena taj jñānaṃ jñānatvena na saṃvidyate, nâpi taj jñānaṃ tatvenâvasthitam.* C. translates: "Therefore in knowledge there is no property of true knowledge and neither does true knowledge reside in the property of knowledge" (*tena jñāne jñānatvaṃ na saṃvidyate, nâpi jñānaṃ jñānatve 'vasthitam* ?). Ti *de'i-phyir ye-śes de-ni/ye-śes-ñid-kyis med-do // ye-śes kyaṅ ye-śes-su mi-gnas-te = tena taj jñānaṃ jñānatvena na saṃvidyate, nâpi jñānaṃ jñānenâvasthitam.* The instrumentals *jñānatvena* and *tatvena* or *jñānena* are predicate instrumentals[3]: "Therefore that knowledge does not exist as (true) knowledge, that knowledge is not established as (true) knowledge."

Su. 8.11: *jñānâjñānaṃ yathābhūtaparijñā.* Read *jñānâjñānayor yathābhūtaparijñā*, cf. Ti *ye-śes daṅ mi-śes-pa yaṅ-dag-pa ji-lta-ba bźin-du yoṅs-su śes-pa.* C.: "true and complete knowledge of knowledge and non-knowledge."

Su. 8.12–14: *Na hi jñānaṃ vacanīyaṃ nâpi jñānaṃ kasyacid viṣayaḥ sarvaviṣayavyatikrāntaṃ hi jñānaṃ, na ca jñānaṃ viṣayam, ayaṃ Suvikrāntavikrāmiñ jñānanirdeśaḥ. Adeśo 'pradeśaḥ, yena jñānenâsau jñānināṃ jñānīti saṃkhyāṃ gacchati, yaivaṃ* . . . Hikata's punctuation is not correct because a full stop must be placed between *viṣayam* (read *viṣayaḥ*) and *ayaṃ*, and the full stop between *jñānanirdeśaḥ* and *adeśo* must be omitted. *Na ca jñānaṃ viṣayaḥ.* Ti *ye-śes-kyi yul yaṅ gaṅ-yaṅ ma yin-no = na câsti kaścij jñānaviṣayaḥ.* C.: "It can not be said that knowledge is the object of non-knowledge" (*na ca jñānam ajñānaviṣayaḥ*). Hikata remarks that for *jñānināṃ jñānīti* Ti has *jñānyajñānīti.* However, even with these changes Ti does not correspond to the Sanskrit text: *phyogs kyaṅ ma yin-pa 'di gaṅ-gis śes-pa de ni / ye-śes-can nam / ye-śes-can ma yin-pa źes-bya-ba'i graṅs-su mi 'gro'o //.* Perhaps the original text read: *yena jñānena nâsau jñānyajñānīti saṃkhyāṃ gacchati.*

Su. 9.14–15: *nirvidhyati nirvedhikā prajñety ucyate, nirvidhyati.* Ti seems to have read: . . . *prajñā nordhvaṃ nirvidhyati*, cf. Ti *steṅ ma rtogs-te.* C. is more detailed: "This penetrating wisdom does not exist at all, not above, not below; it is not slow, not quick; it does not progress nor regress; it neither goes nor comes".

Su. 10.9: *saṃsārātyantavihārī.* Ti *drug-la rtag-tu gnas* "always remaining in the six"; C. "possessing the six permanent states". Read *ṣaṭsātatyavihārī*? Cf. ***Abhidharmakośa*** p. 150.4: *ṣaṭ sātatā vihārā* and the references given by La Vallée Poussin ***L'Abhidharmakośa,*** III (Paris-Louvain, 1926), p. 114, n. 3.

Su. 10.13: *vajropamasamādhir nairvedhikyā prajñayā parigṛhītaṃ yatra sthāpayati*. Read: *vajropamaṃ samādhiṃ* (Ms. *vajropamaṃ samādhir*). Conze's translation has to be corrected, for *samādhiṃ* is the object of *sthāpayati* and *pracārayati*: "wherever he fixes his concentration and to which objects he directs it".

Su. 10.19: *tantraupayikayā* (Ms. *tatraupayikayā*) *mīmāṃsayā*. Read *tatropayikayā*, cf. Pāli *tatr'upāyāya vīmaṃsāya samannāgata* (***Vinaya*** I. 70, 71; IV. 211; Aṅg. Nik. II. 35; III. 37, 113; IV. 265, 286, 332; V. 24, 27, 90, 338). Cf. ***Daśabhūmikasūtra*** (ed. J. Rahder), p. 61.15: *tatropagatayā mīmāṃsayā samanvāgato*; ***Ratnagotravibhāga*** (ed. Johnston), p. 23.7: *tatropagamikayā mīmāṃsayā samanvāgataḥ* (see *IIJ*, XI, 1968, p. 44).

Su. 11.13–14: *na tasya, yaḥ svabhāvaḥ sa svayaṃsaṃbhavaḥ*. Ti *de'i raṅ-bźin de ni / raṅ-gi ṅaṅ-gis 'jig-ciṅ*. Tosani reads: *tasya yaḥ svabhāvaḥ sa svayamvibhavaḥ*, but *yaḥ* is not represented in Ti. C. has: "In this way the *svabhāva* is destroyed by itself."

Su. 11.14: *samudayânantaranirodhaḥ*. Hikata remarks: "Ms. is not clear but looks like to be *-nuttara°*; acc. to Tib. also *-nuttara°*; but Ch. *anantara*; from the context of this paragraph, it should be *-ânantara°*". *Samudaya* is absent in both Ti and C. Ti: *mñam* (L. *sñam*)*-pa ni / bla-na med-pa'i 'gog-pa ste;* C. "it is immediate destruction".

Su. 12.1: *Anirodho nirodhaḥ pratītyasamutpādasyâvabodhaḥ*. Ti *'gog-pa daṅ mi-'gal-ba; avirodho nirodhaḥ*. C.: *avirodho virodhaḥ*. Instead of *avabodhaḥ* Ti has read *anirodhaḥ* (*'gog-pa med-pa*) and C. *anubodha*. Cf. p. 13.14.

Su. 12.15–16: *Na kiṃcid anyad upalabhyate, idaṃ taj jñānavigama iti*. Instead of *idaṃ taj jñānavigama iti* Ti has: "apart from the *ajñānavigama* and the *jñānavigama*" (*mi-śes-pa daṅ bral-ba daṅ / śes-pa daṅ-bral-ba 'di-las*). C. translates: "Because one knows in this way cognition and non-cognition and nothing else is apprehended, therefore it is called *ajñānavigama*".

Su. 13.22–23: *na ca punar dharmâdharmasvabhāvena saṃvidyate*. Hikata remarks that C. agrees with S., but that Ti has *dharmo dharmasvabhāvena* (*chos ni chos-kyi ṅo-bo ñid-kyis*). Tosani follows Ti. Conze reads *dharmo 'dharmasvabhāvena*. C. has "Moreover, both dharma and adharma are without *svabhāva*".

Su. 15.1: *dhātuḥ saṃketena*. *Dhātuḥ* is not found in Ti and C.

Su. 15.9: *sarvadharmânubodha*. Both Ti and C. have read *buddhadharmânubodha*.

Su. 15.12: *apūrṇatvaṃ tad apariniṣpattiyogena*. Read with Ti and C.

apūrṇatvam aparinispattiyogena.

Su. 15.15–16: *Tena tad.* Tosaki suggests reading *Naitad* but according to Ti one must read *te na* (*de ni . . . . . . ma yin-no*). Instead of *te* C. has 'the Buddhadharmas'.

Su. 16.17: *viparyantāḥ* is obviously an error for *viparyastāḥ.*

Su. 17.2: *Sarvā manyanā 'sārambaṇā.* Conze translates *sārambaṇā.* Tosaki corrects *manyanā* to *'manyanā.* Ti: *sarvā 'manyanā 'sārambaṇā* (*thams-cad rloms-sems med-la dmigs-pa daṅ bcas-pa ma-yin-pa*), but C. seems to have read: *sarvā manyanā 'nārambaṇā.*

Su. 17.8–9: *vibhāvavitā hi tena satvāḥ sarva[saṃ]jñāḥ.* Hikata remarks that according to C. and Ti it should be *sarva[saṃ]jñāḥ* but Ti has *sattvasaṃjñā* (*sems-can-du 'du-śes-pa*) and C. *sarvasaṃjñā.* Read: *vibhāvitā hi tena satvasaṃjñā.*

Su. 18.1–2: *yasyāś caryā 'vabodhād.* Read *caryāyā 'vabodhād,* cf. Ti *spyod-pa gaṅ khoṅ-du chud-pas.*

Su. 19.7–8: *Nâtra bodhir na ca cittaṃ, na ca bodhir upalabdhā, notpādo nânutpādas, tena sa bodhisattva.* Ti *de-la ni byaṅ-chub kyaṅ-med / sems kyaṅ med-do // gaṅ-gis sems-ñid daṅ / byaṅ-chub daṅ / skye-ba daṅ / mi-skye-ba yaṅ mi-dmigs-pa de byaṅ-chub sems-dpa' = nâtra ca bodhir na ca cittaṃ, yena na ca cittaṃ, na ca bodhir upalabdhā, notpādo nânutpādaḥ, sa bodhisattva.* C. agrees with Ti, but does not translate *nâtra bodhir na ca cittaṃ.*

Su. 19.18: *sarvaṃ jñānaṃ.* Ti *thams-cad mkhyen-pa'i ye-śes = sarvajñajñānam.* C. can correspond both to *sarvajñā and to sarvajñajñāna,* cf. Nakamura Hajime, *Bukkyōgo daijiten* (Tōkyō, 1975), s.v. *issaiichi* (p. 60).

Su. 20.1: *cittaprakṛtiṃ ca prajānanti.* Ti *sems-kyi raṅ-bźin yaṅ rab-tu mi-śes = na ca cittaprakṛtiṃ prajānanti.* C. agrees with S.

Su. 20.3: *bodhiprakṛtiṃ ca prajānanti.* Ti *byaṅ-chub-kyi raṅ-bźin yaṅ rab-tu mi-śes-te = na ca bodhiprakṛtiṃ prajānanti.* C. agrees with S.

Su. 20.3: *te nâjñātacittena bodhiṃ ca paśyanti.* C. corresponds to: *te 'nena jñānena citte bodhiṃ na paśyanti.* C. does not translate *na bodhau cittaṃ paśyanti, na citte bodhiṃ paśyanti* (p. 20. 4–5).

Su. 20.6: *te bhāvanām api nopalabhante.* Ti *de rnam-par 'jig-par byed-pa de yaṅ mi-dmigs-śiṅ = te vibhāvanām api nopalabhante* C.: *te bhāvanāṃ ca vibhāvanāṃ ca nopalabhante.*

Su. 20.16: *Ye punaḥ Suvikrāntavikrāmin bodher nâpi dūre nâbhyāsanne samanupaśyanti.* According to C. *bodher* must be corrected to *bodhim.*

Su. 20.25: *yo hi naiv'âram upalabhate.* Ti *gaṅ pha-rol ñid kyaṅ mi-dmigs.* Tosaki reads: *yo hi naiva pāram.* This is confirmed by C.

Su. 22.20: *anulomaṃ ca saṃdhayanti.* Conze translates: "they explain (their secret intent) in agreement with just the fact". However, neither Ti nor C. support this explanation. Ti *rjes-su mthun-par smra-bar byed-do*; C. "they harmonize this and that so that there is no mutual opposition". Probably one must read *saṃdhāyanti* as has been proposed by Matsumoto. According to Edgerton *dhāyati* and *dhāyate* (from *dhā-*) occur chiefly in comp. with *antara-*. C. is correct in translating *saṃdhāyati* by 'to harmonize, to make agree'.

Su. 23.3–4: *na ca kaṃcid anurakṣyaṃ dharmaṃ deśayati.* Conze puts a question mark after his translation: "Although he does not demonstrate any dharma which can be preserved". Ti has read also *anurakṣyaṃ* (*rjes-su sruṅ-ba'i chos*), but according to C. one must read *kiṃcid anurakṣya*: "he teaches the dharma without holding back anything".

Su. 25.1: *ratnānām api.* Read *ratnānāṃ nāmāpi*, cf. Ti *rin-po-che rnams-kyi miṅ yaṅ.* C. agrees with Ti.

Su. 29.18: *Na hi Suvikrāntavikrāmin rūpaṃ rūpasvabhāvaṃ jahāti.* Ti translates *jānāti* (*śes-so*), but C. agrees with S. Also in line 19 Ti has *jānāti* but C. *jahāti.*

Su. 37.16: *nirvṛttir nânirvṛttiḥ.* According to Hikata C. has *nirvṛti* and *anirvṛti* but Ti agrees with S. However, Ti has *nivṛtti* (*ldog-pa*) and *anivṛtti* (*mi-ldog-pa*). In 41.5 Ti translates *nirvṛtti* with *grub-pa.*

Su. 41.16–17: *na ca svapnasvabhāvanirdeśaḥ kaścit saṃvidyate.* Ti agrees with S. but according to C. one must read: *na ca svapnasvabhāvaḥ kaścit saṃvidyate.*

Su. 42.3: *svabhāvanirdeśaḥ.* Read *svabhāvaḥ* (see Hikata note 1).

Su. 42.4: *māyāsvabhāvanirdeśasya svabhāvo.* Read with C. *māyāsvabhāvanirdeśo.*

Su. 42.19: *marīcinirdeśasvabhāvo.* Read with C. *marīcisvabhāvanirdeśo.*

Su. 43.2: *prajñāpāramitānirdeśapadaṃ câdhigacchati śravaṇāya.* According to C. one must read: *prajñāpāramitā nirdeśapadaṃ câdhigacchati śravaṇāya.*

Su. 43.2–3: *na ca kasyacid dharmasya nirdeśaśravaṇāya gacchati.* Conze translates: "it is not the exposition of any dharma which reaches the hearing". Obviously, Conze reads: *nirdeśaḥ śravaṇāya.* Ti *chos gaṅ bstan-pa thos-par 'gyur-ba med-do.* However, C. has: "The dharma which is heard is entirely without *svabhāva*": *na ca kasyacid dharmasya svabhāvaḥ śravaṇāya gacchati.*

Su. 43.7–8: *kutaḥ punas tannirdeśasvabhāvopalabdhir bhaviṣyati.* C.: "Why? The mass of foam does not exist, Suvikrāntavikrāmin. How much less will there be an exposition of its *svabhāva*": *Tat kasmād dhetoḥ! Phenapiṇḍa eva na saṃvidyate, kutaḥ punas tatsvabhavānirdeśo bhaviṣyati.*

Su. 43.24: *prajñāpāramitāyā nirdeśaḥ kāryaṃ ca karoti.* C.: *tasyā nirdeśena kāryaṃ ca karoti.*

Su. 45.10: C. adds *jantu* between *jīva* and *poṣa*, cf. ***Kāśyapaparivarta*** § 142. Likewise p. 47. 8–9.

Su. 47.1–2: *nâsyāṃ kaścid upalabhyate yo 'bhisambuddhaḥ.* (Ms. (*'bhisambuddhā*). Read with C. *'bhisaṃboddhā.* Ti has *nâsyāṃ kaścit pariniṣpanno dharma upalabhyate yo 'bhisambuddhaḥ: gaṅ mṅon-par rdzogs-par rtogs-pa yoṅs-su grub-pa'i chos gaṅ-yaṅ mi dmigs-so.*

Su. 47.21–22: *Paramārthajñānadarśanasaṃvṛtyasvabhāvato.* C. adds *jñānadarśana* between *saṃvṛti* and *asvabhāvato.*

Su. 52.22–23: *na kaṃcid dharmam upalabhate, na samanupaśyati, yaṃ dharmaṃ jānīyād yasya vā dharmasya jñāpayitrā vā bhavet.* Ti *chos gaṅ śes-pa 'am / chos gaṅ śes-par byed-par 'gyur-ba'i chos gaṅ-yaṅ mi dmigs-so = na kaṃcid dharmam upalabhate yaṃ dharmaṃ jānīyād yasya vā dharmasya jñāpayitā vā bhavet.* C. agrees with Ti.

Su. 58.6–7: *ca yeṣāṃ parijānante, te tathārūpāḥ satpuruṣāḥ.* Ti *gaṅ-gi* (L,T.T. *gis*) *yoṅs-su śes-pa de daṅ de-dag ni = ca yeṣāṃ parijñanaṃ, te te.* In the following lines read:, *te te* instead of *te, te.*

Su. 61.2: *pariniṣpattir darśanenopayātaḥ.* Read: *pariniṣpattidarśanam upayātaḥ,* cf. Ti *yoṅs-su grub-par mthoṅ-bar ñe-bar 'gro-ba ma yin-no.* See also p. 61.3, 8, 9, 13 and 14 where the same emendation has to be made. Probably the instrumentals have crept into the text under the influence of the instrumentals in the preceding passage.

Su. 62.24–25: *Asaṅgalakṣaṇ*[*eṣu*] *hi Śāradvatīputra* [*sajanti*] *sarvabālapṛthagjanāḥ.* Ms. *Asaṅgalakṣaṇā.* Read *Asaṅgasaṅgā* [or *asaṅgasaktā*] *hi Śāradvatīputra sarvabālapṛthagjanāḥ,* cf. Ti *byis-pa so-so'i skye-bo thams-cad ni / chags-pa med-pa la chags-so //.* C. agrees with Ti.

Su. 68.12–14: *yā 'pi sā "yuṣmañ Śāradvatīputra prajñā lokottarā nirvedhagāminī, tasyā api prajñāpāramitānidarśanaṃ nopaiti.* Tosaki separates correctly *prajñāpāramitā* and *nidarśanam.* Conze omits *tasyā* in his translation: "It is because this is a wisdom which is supramundane and which leads to penetration that the perfection of wisdom does not lend itself to explanation". *Tasyā* refers to *prajñā.* "As to *prajñā*, the perfection of wisdom does not envisage the explanation of it (i.e. *prajñā*)" ("does not envisage the explanation" is Conze's rendering of *nidarśanam upaiti* in the preceding passage).

Su. 68.14–16: *Tad yathā "yuṣmañ Śāradvatīputra dharmo nidarśanaṃ nopaiti kasyacid dharmasya, kathaṃ tasyaivodāhāranirdeśo* (Hikata *tasya evo-*, but Ms. *tasyaivo-*) *bhaviṣyati.* Tosaki omits *dharmo* but this is found both in Ti and in C., cf. Ti *chos gaṅ ṅes-par bstan-par yaṅ ñe-bar mi-'gro-ba'i chos de ji-ltar brjod-ciṅ ṅes-par bstan-par 'gyur.*

Su. 71.12–13: *na tathā yais te, te dharmā ye ca na tathā* (Ms. *'vitathā*) *yathā gṛhītās.* Ti: *chos de ni / ji-lta-ba bźin-du ma yin-no // gaṅ-dag ji-ltar bzuṅ-ba de-bźin-du ma yin-pa.* C.: "Such dharmas are not so. As they are seized, not such are their marks." Read: *na tathā yathā te te dharmā, ye ca na tathā yathā gṛhītās* (?).

Su. 72.4: *Sarvaiṣāṃ* (Ms. *sarveṣāṃ*) *Suvikrāntavikrāmin vikalpacaryā.* Ti. *rab-kyi rtsal-gyis rnam-par gnon-pa / 'di* (T.T. *de*)*-dag thams-cad ni / rnam-par rtog-pa la spyod-pa'o* = *sarvaiṣā* . . . .

Su. 72.5: *sarvavikalpaprahīṇā.* Tosaki emends to *sarvakalpaprahīṇā* in accordance with Ti. However, C. has *sarvakalpavikalpaprahīṇā.*

Su. 72.5–6: *kalpa iti Suvikrāntavikrāmin vikalpanaiṣā sarvadharmāṇām.* C.: *kalpa iti kalpasvabhāvaḥ sarvadharmāṇām, vikalpa iti kalpaviśeṣaḥ sarvadharmāṇām.*

Su. 73.7: *yato.* Read *yad* (Ti *gaṅ*).

Su. 73.11: *nocyeta.* C. adds: *viparyāsa iti.*

Su. 73.13: *Jñāto* (Ms. *jñātaṃ*) *hi tena viparyāso 'bhūta iti.* The reading of the manuscript *jñātaṃ* must be kept.

Su. 73.19: *tena sārdham* [*a*]*viparyāsaḥ sthita.* Ti *de'i phyir de phyin-ci-log med-par gnas-pa* = *tena sa 'viparyāsasthita.*

Su. 73.19: *caryāyāṃ* (Ms. *caryā*) *na vikalpayati.* Read *caryāṃ na vikalpayati.*

Su. 74.24: *tena ca caryā-'pagatā.* Ti *de spyod-pa med-pa ste* = *te caryā-'pagatās.*

Su. 78.18–19: *parijñātā hi ten' ātmasatvārambaṇaprakṛtipariśuddhā* (Ms. . . . *-ārambaṇaparijñā*). Read: *prakṛtipariśuddhaṃ hi ten' ātmasatvārambaṇaṃ parijñātam.*

Su. 84.5–6: *prajñāpāramitācaryā cittajanikā, tenocyate 'cintyateti.* Ti *sems-kyis bskyed-pa* (T.T. *sems-kyi skyed-pa*) *ma yin-pa'i phyir-te / de'i phyir bsam-gyis mi khyab-pa źes bya'o* = *cittajanitā, tenocyate 'cintyeti.* C. agrees with Ti but adds: *na ca cittajanikā, tenocyate 'cintyeti.*

Su. 84.7–8: *cittaṃ cittajam iti Suvikrāntavikrāmiṃś cetasaḥ pratiṣed-*

ha eṣaḥ. Ti *sems źes bya-ba de ni / sems rab-tu rtog-pa'o* (T.T. *gtogs-pa'o*) = *cittam iti. Suvikrāntavikrāmiṃś cetasaḥ prativedha eṣaḥ.* C.: "Non-production of mind also is perverted view. If one understands that both thought and mental elements (*caitasika*) do not exist, then there is absence of perverted view."

Su. 87.1: *Sarvalokābhyudayacaryeyaṃ.* Ti *'jig-rten thams-cad las mṅon-par 'phags-pa* = *sarvalokābhyudgateyam.* For *sarvalokābhyudgata* see p. 122.7; ***Lalitavistara*** (ed. S. Lefmann) p. 60. 14; ***Suvarṇabhāsottamasūtra*** (ed. J. Nobel), p. 206.6.

Su. 87.16–17: *Vaiśāradyabhūmir iyaṃ Suvikrāntavikrāmin dharmaṇeyaṃ* (Ms. *dharmaneyaṃ*) *prajñāpāramitācaryā. Dharmaneyaṃ* is missing in both Ti and C. and has to be omitted.

Su. 88.10: *na kaṃcid dharmaṃ, yat prajñāpāramitāyāṃ na yojayati.* Read: *na kaścid dharmaḥ, yaṃ* . . . . .

Su. 92.16–17: *phenapiṇḍopamā hi sarvadharmā avimardanakṣamatvāt.* Ti translates *avimardanakṣamatvāt* with *mñe* (L. *mi-ñe*) *mi-bzod-pa'i phyir* = *vimardana-a-kṣamatvāt.* C. has: "because they can not be picked up and rubbed". *A-vimardanakṣamatvāt* means: "because they do not withstand crushing". Conze translates: "because they are easily crushed".

Su. 96.12–13: *tām api nirālambanavaśikatāṃ na manyate.* Ti *dmigs-pa med-pa daṅ / dmigs-pa ya-ma-brla de-dag la yaṅ rlom-sems-su mi byed-do* = *tān api nirālambanān ālambanavaśikān na manyate.* C. agrees with Ti. For *ārambaṇavaśika* see ***Aṣṭasāhasrikā*** p. 265. According to Haribhadra *ālambana-vaśika* means 'depending on an *ālambana*' (*ālambana-paratantra*). Conze translates 'devoid of objective support' (***The Perfection of Wisdom***, p. 175) but *vaśika* cannot have the meaning 'empty' as second member of a compound.

Su. 98.20–22: *Yāvat kalpanā tāvad vikalpanā, nāsty atra vikalpanāsamucchedaḥ. Yatra punaḥ Suvikrāntavikrāmin na kalpanā na vikalpanā, tatra kalpasamucchedaḥ.* Tosani emends *vikalpanāsamucchedaḥ* to *kalpanā-*. Ti has *mi-rtog-pa* which corresponds to *vikalpanā.* For both *vikalpanāsamucchedaḥ* and *kalpasamucchedaḥ* C. has *kalpanāvikalpanāsamucchedaḥ* which is certainly the original reading.

Su. 99.1: *anto hi Suvikrāntavikrāmin kalpo vikalpo* (Ms. *'vikalpaḥ*) *viparyāsasamutthitas.* Ti *rtog-pa daṅ / mi-rtog-pa ni / phyin-ci log-pa las byuṅ-bas med-pa'i phyir-ro* = *asanto hi Suvikrāntavikrāmin kalpo vikalpaś ca viparyāsasamutthitās.* Tosaki changes *anto* to *asan* but it is more likely that *anto* is the result of a corruption of *asanto*.

Su. 100.7–8: *dharmadānaṃ.* Ti *chos-kyi sbyin-pa la* = *dharmadāne.*

Su. 101.20: *duḥkhito vedanāttamanā.* Hikata explains *vedanāttamanā* by Skt. *vedanārtamanā* and Pāli *vedanāṭṭamanā.* However, neither Ti nor C. translates *vedanāttamanā* and it is probably a corruption for *'nattamanā.*

Su. 106.15: *kāṅkṣāyitatvaṃ vā bandhāyitatvaṃ vā.* For *bandhāyitatvaṃ* read *dhandhāyitatvaṃ,* cf. p. 22.17 and Edgerton, BHSD s.v. *dhandhāyati.*

Su. 114.10–11: *āsanno bhavaty anavalokitamūrdhatāyāḥ.* Conze reads *avalokita-* with a reference to Edgerton, BHSD *avalokitamūrdhitā.* Edgerton quotes only one place: ***Gaṇḍavyūha*** 65.18. The text of the ***Gaṇḍavyūha*** is incorrect and *avalokitamūrdhitām* must be corrected to *anavalokitamūrdhitām.* The Chinese translations of the ***Gaṇḍavyūha*** have a negation. See further *Daizōkyō sakuin,* vol. 5: *kegon-bu* (Tōkyō, 1963), p. 326c *mukenchō, mukenchōsō*; Nakamura Hajime, *Bukkyōgo daijiten* (Tōkyō, 1975), p. 1321c *mukenchōsō*; ***Bodhisattvabhūmi*** (ed. Wogihara), p. 381.3; (ed. Dutt), p. 263.3–4.

Su. 116.24: *mahāsatvenârthaṃ.* Read *mahāsatvena sarvasatvānām arthaṃ,* cf. Ti *sems-dpa' chen-po sems-can thams-cad-kyi don.* C. agrees with Ti.

Su. 117.21–24: *Nâhaṃ Suvikrāntavikrāmin bodhisatvasya kaṃcid dharmam evaṃ kṣipraṃ paripūrikaraṃ samanupaśyāmi sarvadharmāṇām* [*an*]*yatheha prajñāpāramitāyāṃ yathā nirdiṣṭāyām abhiyogaḥ.* Hikata changes *yatheha* to *anyatheha.* However, *aparaṃ* has to be added between *kaṃcid* and *dharmaṃ* and *sarvadharmāṇām* has to be emended to *sarvabuddhadharmāṇāṃ,* cf. Ti *saṅs-rgyas-kyi chos thams-cad myur-du yoṅs-su rdzogs-par byed-pa de-lta-bu byaṅ-chub sems-dpa'i* (T.T. *dpa'*) *chos gźan gaṅ-yaṅ ṅas ma mthoṅ-ṅo; kaṃcid aparaṃ dharmam . . . . . sarvabuddhadharmāṇāṃ yatheha prajñāpāramitāyāṃ yathānirdiṣṭāyām* . . . . . C. agrees with Ti.

Su. 120.7–9: *iyaṃ mahāpṛthivī, meghān pratītya snigdhā bhavati, anupūrveṇa ca pravarṣati, devenâbhiṣyandamānā upary upary udakaṃ pravarṣanti, yenotsadhiṃ* (Ms. *utsāhaṃ*) *bahavo 'nugacchanti.* Read: . . . *bhavati, anupūrveṇa ca pravarṣatā devenābhiṣyandamānā,* [*meghā*] *upary upary udakaṃ pravarṣanti, yenotsā bahavo 'nugacchanti* (?). Ti *char mthar-gyis bab-pas baṅs-nas chu 'byuṅ-ste gaṅ-du* (L. *gaṅ*) *chu-mig maṅ-po 'byuṅ-ba.*

Su. 121.17: *sarvā diśaḥ prabhā dhyāmīkaroti. Diśaḥ* is not translated by Ti and C. Read: *sarvāḥ prabhā.*

Su. 123.17–18: *asaṅgo 'saṅgatayā, saṅgo 'saṅgabhūtatayā.* Ms. *asaṅgā asaṅgatayā, saṅgāsaṅgabhūtatayā.* Tosaki reads: *saṅgāsaṅgatayā, saṅgāsaṅgabhūtatayā.* Ti *chags-pa med-pa la chags-pa yaṅ-dag-pa ma yin-pa'i phyir* = *asaṅgasaṅgābhūtatayā.* C. reads: *saṅgāsaṅgatayā saṅgābhūtatayā.* For 124.1 *bandhâbhūtatayā* C. has *bandhābandhatayā bandhābhūtatayā.*

Su. 123.20: *Abaddha iti.* Ti *rtogs-pa med-pa* translates probably *avedha* but according to the context and C. the correct reading must be *abandha* and not *abaddha. Abandha* corresponds to *asaṅga* (123.18). Moreover, a corruption from *abandha* to *avedha* is more likely than from *abaddha* to *avedha.*

Su. 126.9–10: *Teṣāṃ kulaputrāṇāṃ kuladuhitṝṇāṃ ca bhūyo mārebhyaḥ pāpīyobhyaḥ* (sic!) *'bhayam* (Ms. *mārāḥ pāpīyāṃso bhayaṃ*) *pratikāṃkṣitavyam.* Read: *na ca bhūyo mārāt pāpīyaso bhayaṃ*, cf. Ti *bdud sdig-can-gyis 'jigs-so sñam-du dogs-par mi bgyi'o.* A corruption of *mārāt* to *mārāḥ* has led to the change of *pāpīyaso* to *pāpīyāṃsò.*

Su. 126.17: *Baddhasīmā Suvikrāntavikrāmin mārāṇāṃ pāpīyasām.* Read: *baddhā sīmā*, cf. Ti *bdud sdig-can rnams-kyi mtshams bcad-do.*

Su. 128.4–5: *vaistārikaṃ ca kariṣyanti,* [*te te manuṣye*]*ndrā manuṣy'-ājāneyāḥ, parigṛhītās te.* Read: *kariṣyanti. Ye manuṣyendrā manuṣy'-ājāneyāḥ, parigṛhītās te.*

NOTES

[1] ***The Short Prajñāpāramitā Texts***, p. i,

[2] Several passages have been discussed by Conze in his reviews of the editions of the *Su.* by Matsumoto (*IIJ.* 2, 1958, pp. 316–318) and Hikata (*IIJ.* 3, 1959, pp. 232–234). His translation does not always follow Hikata's text. Tosani gives a list of corrections (pp. 316–315).

[3] Cf. H. Jacobi, "Über den nominalen Stil des wissenschaftlichen Sanskrits", *IF*, 14 (1903), p. 239 [= *Kleine Schriften*, Wiesbaden, p. 9]: "Es kann nämlich bei gewissen Verben allgemeiner Bedeutung das Prädikatsnomen durch den Instrumentalis seines Abstraktums wiedergegeben werden, wo wir im Deutschen gewöhnlich 'als' zu dem Prädikatsnomen setzen." See also L. Renou, ***Grammaire sanscrite*** (Paris, 1930), p. 293.

R. O. Meisezahl, *Tibetische Prajñāpāramitā-Texte im Bernischen Historischen Museum*. Kopenhagen, Munksgaard, 1964. 42 pp. (Sonderdruck aus der Zeitschrift *Libri*, Band 13, No. 3-4, 1964).

Le Musée historique de Berne possède 21 textes tibétains et 61 textes mongols qui proviennent d'un monastère en Mongolie du Sud (cf. W. Heissig, "Eine kleine mongolische Klosterbibliothek in Tsakhar", *Jahrbuch des Bernischen Historischen Museums*, XLI/XLII, 1961/1962). M. R. O. Meisezahl à qui nous devons déjà des catalogues des collections tibétaines du Musée Linden à Stuttgart et du Musée Reiss à Mannheim[1] a décrit en détail les 21 volumes. Il s'agit de la traduction tibétaine de trois *Prajñāpāramitāsūtra*: la *Śatasāhasrikā* (vols. 1-16), la *Pañcaviṃśatisāhasrikā* (vols. 1-4) et l'*Aṣṭasāhasrikā* (un volume). Ce sont des textes bien connus qui se trouvent dans toutes les éditions du *Kanjur*. L'intérêt du travail de M. Meisezahl réside dans le fait qu'il ne s'est pas contenté de l'identification des textes, mais a comparé les données des dKarchag dont l'étude n'est pas encore bien avancée.

Au Tibet les *Prajñāpāramitāsūtra* sont connus sous le nom de Yum. Selon l'auteur (note 18) ce nom doit être de date récente car il n'est pas mentionné dans le *Chos-'byuṅ chen-mo* de Bu-ston. Je ne sais pas quand Yum a été employé pour la première fois mais je suppose que ce nom doit être fort ancien. En tout cas, il ne correspond pas à *mātṛkā*, comme le suppose l'auteur, car ce mot, dans le sens d'Abhidharma primitif, est rendu par *ma-mo* (cf. *Mahāvyutpatti* No. 5143: *mātṛkādharaḥ*; *ma-mo 'dzin-pa*. Dans *Divyāvadāna* p. 18.6 *mātṛkā* est aussi traduite par *ma-mo*). Probablement Yum correspond à Bhagavatī, le nom employé par Candrakīrti dans la *Prasannapadā* et par Śāntideva dans le *Śikṣāsamuccaya* pour désigner les *Prajñāpāramitāsūtra* qu'ils citent.

L'auteur mentionne le *Kanjur* de Kumbum qu'il met avec le *Kanjur* de Narthang dans un groupe intitulé "sNar-thaṅ Redaktion". Les références à ce *Kanjur* ont rapport au travail suivant: *Index du Gandjour imprimé dans le Couvent de Goumboum dans le Tübet. Composé par le Baron Schilling de Canstadt* (Kiakhta, 1831). Malheureusement, l'auteur ne donne pas d'autres détails sur ce travail ou sur le *Kanjur* de Kumbum. Probablement, il s'est servi d'une copie qui se trouve à la Bibliothèque Nationale (fonds tibétain, n. 471). Mlle Lalou l'a utilisée dans ses travaux sur la version tibétaine du *Ratnakūṭa* et des *Prajñāpāramitā* (*JA*, 1927, I, 233-259; 1929, I, 87-102), et l'a identifiée avec l'index publié par I. J. Schmidt en 1845[2] (*JA*, 1927, I, p. 234). Ce dernier index n'a rien à faire avec l'index du *Kanjur* de Kumbum. D'après Haarh (*AM*, IX, 1963, p. 179, n. 2), c'est la reproduction d'un index du *Kanjur* de Derge. Quant à

[1] Cf. *IIJ*, III (1959), pp. 75-78 et VI (1962), pp. 76-77.

[2] *Bkaḥ-ḥgyur-gyi-dkar-chag oder Der Index des Kanjur*. Herausgegeben von der Kaiserlichen Akademie der Wissenschaften und bevorwortet von I. J. Schmidt (St. Petersburg, 1845). M. Meisezahl cite cet index à propos du *Kanjur* d'Urga. Faut-il en déduire que le *Kanjur* d'Urga est basé sur celui de Derge?

l'index du *Kanjur* de Kumbum, il ressort des travaux de Mlle Lalou et de celui de M. Meisezahl que cet index s'accorde avec le *Kanjur* de Narthang.[3] Faut-il en conclure que le *Kanjur* de Kumbum est basé sur le *Kanjur* de Narthang? Je pense plutôt qu'il n'y a pas du tout de *Kanjur* imprimé à Kumbum. Aucun voyageur en parle et la seule indication, relative à l'existence d'un *Kanjur* de Kumbum, est le titre de l'index de Schilling von Canstadt. Dans les années 1830-1831 des lamas bouriates ont composé pour Schilling von Canstadt plusieurs index du *Kanjur* et *Tanjur* qui sont mentionnés dans le catalogue de Schmidt et Boehtlingk (*Bull. de la Cl. Hist.-Phil. de l'Acad. des Sc. de St.-P.*, Tome IV, Nos 6, 7, 8, 1846, pp. 81-125), Nos. 262-284.[4] On y trouve un index du *Tanjur* du Potala (no. 275) mais le titre tibétain *Bstan-bcos 'gyur-ro-cog gsuṅ-bar bsgrubs-pa'i dkar-chag tshaṅs-pa'i dbyaṅs źes-bya-ba* montre qu'il s'agit du *Tanjur* de Narthang (cf. Kenneth K. S. Ch'en, *HJAS*, IX, 1946, p. 56). Cet exemple montre le peu de confiance qu'on peut avoir dans les titres de ces index.[5]

Comme la plupart des éditions du *Kanjur*, le xylographe décrit n'indique pas les traducteurs de la *Śatasāhasrikā*. Seuls les *Kanjurs* de Narthang et de Lhasa l'attribuent à Jinamitra, Surendrabodhi et Ye-śes-sde. M.R.O.M. attire l'attention sur le fait que Bu-ston nomme comme traducteurs Go-cha, Vairocana, Khyi-'brug et Ye-śes-sde. Mlle Lalou a signalé que, dans des manuscrits de Touen-houang, avec Śākyaprabha et Surendrabodhi Vairocana et Ye-śes-sde sont nommés comme traducteurs de la *Śatasāhasrikā*.[6] Une traduction due à Vairocana est aussi mentionnée dans le colophon de *Mdo-'grel* X,2 (*RO*, XXI, p. 151). A propos d'un *Kanjur* manuscrit en 114 volumes dans la collection Kawaguchi, Mibu Taishun note que, dans ce *Kanjur*, la traduction de l'*Astadaśasāhasrikā* est attribuée à Jinamitra, Surendrabodhi et Ye-śes-sde alors que les éditions imprimées du même texte ne mentionnent pas de noms de traducteurs.[7] Ces exemples prouvent que l'on ne peut guère se fier aux indications des dKar-chag des *Kanjur*. Il sera nécessaire de les confronter avec les renseignements que fournissent les manuscrits de Touen-houang, les travaux de Bu-ston et d'autres savants tibétains et les éditions séparées des textes canoniques. Les éditions séparées des *Prajñāpāramitāsūtra* sont nombreuses car ces textes ont joui d'une grande vénération au Tibet.

Le colophon de la traduction tibétaine de l'*Aṣṭasāhasrikā* ajoute des renseignements qui ne se trouvent pas dans les éditions du *Kanjur*. Il faut noter que le colophon de l'édition de Narthang, reproduit par Mlle Lalou (*JA*, 1929, II, 92-93) contient deux lacunes après *Rin-čhen-bzaṅ-pos* (p. 93, l. 3) et *rgya-bod-kyi dpe* (ibid., l. 10).[8] Le

[3] Déjà, J. Bacot a indiqué ce fait, en confondant, lui aussi, l'index du *Kanjur* du Kumbum avec celui publié par Schmidt, *JA*, 1924, II, p. 322, n. 2. M. Bacot signale qu'au Musée Asiatique se trouve un catalogue manuscrit du *Tandjur* qui fait suite à l'index du *Kanjur* de Kumbum. Je crois me rappeler qu'il y a une copie de ce catalogue dans le fonds tibétain de la Bibliothèque Nationale. On aimerait bien savoir à quelle édition du *Tandjur* se réfère ce catalogue.

[4] Cf. A. I. Vostrikov, *Tibetskaja istoričeskaja literatura* (Moskva, 1962), p. 315, n. 603.

[5] Schilling von Canstadt a écrit un article sur le *Kanjur* de Narthang que je n'ai pas pu consulter: "Bibliothèque Bouddhique ou Index du Gandjour de Nartang composé sous la direction du Baron Schilling de Canstadt", *Bull. de la Cl. Hist.-Phil. de l'Acad. des Sc. de St.-P.*, Tome IV, Nos. 21-22 (1847), pp. 321-339.

[6] "Les manuscrits tibétains des grandes *Prajñā pāramitā* trouvés à Touen-houang", *Silver Jubilee Volume of the Zinbun-Kagaku-Kenkyusyo, Kyoto University* (1954), pp. 257-261; "Les plus anciens rouleaux tibétains trouvés à Touen-houang", *Rocznik Orientalistyczny*, XXI (1957), pp. 149-152; *Inventaire des manuscrits tibétains de Touen-houang conservés à la Bibliothèque Nationale (Fonds Pelliot tibétain)*, Tome III, nos 1283-2216 (Paris, 1961); "Manuscrits tibétains de la *Śatasāhasrikā-Prajñāpāramitā* cachés à Touen-houang", *JA*, 1964, pp. 479-486.

[7] "Kawaguchi korekushon ni tsuite", *Nihon Chibetto gakkai kaihō*, 2 (1955), p. 2.

[8] Il faut corriger *laṅ* (p. 93, 1.4) en *yaṅ* et *bstan* (*ibid.*, l. 11) en *bstun*.

colophon de l'exemplaire de Berne mentionne une révision avec l'aide de deux manuscrits sanskrits et des livres tibétains imprimés. Le colophon est suivi d'un hymne et d'un autre colophon. L'hymne dit que le texte a été collationné avec des textes de plusieurs endroits tels que bKra-śis lhun-po, Li-thaṅ et Pékin (*bkras lhun li thaṅ rgyal khab chen po sogs || yul gru du ma'i dpe daṅ bstun byas nas*) et non qu'il a été comparé dans la résidence bKras lhun Li thaṅ et à d'autres endroits avec des manuscrits d'origine différente comme le dit M. R.O.M. Aussi son interprétation du colophon ne me paraît pas correcte. Selon lui, on y mentionne comme copiste Tshul khrims chos 'phel qui fait partie de la suite de Ṅag dbaṅ Chos grags. Le colophon dit: ... *gu śrī dge sloṅ śes rab rgya mtshos par du sgrub pa'i tshe || par byaṅ 'di lta bu źig dgos źes bskul ba'i ṅor*[9] *|| rnam g.yeṅ daṅ chos brgyad kyi bran du gyur pa sku skyes ṅag dbaṅ chos grags kyis sbyar ba'i yi ge*[10] *ni rnam dpyod daṅ ldan pa tshul khrims chos 'phel gyis bgyis pa dge legs su gyur cig ||* "Quand le Gu-śrī dge-sloṅ Śes-rab-rgya-mtsho fit imprimer ce livre, il insista sur la nécessité d'une postface. Celle-ci fut écrite par l'incarné Ṅag-dbaṅ Chos-grags, esclave de la distraction (skt. *vikṣepa*) et des huit dharma (possession, non-possession, gloire, non-gloire, blâme, louange, plaisir, souffrance, cf. *Mahāvyutpatti* nos 2342-2348), et le scribe fut le savant Tshul-khrims chos-'phel. Qu'il soit béni!" Dans son livre sur les xylographes mongols, imprimés à Pékin, M. W. Heissig donne des renseignements sur Urad-un güüsi Bilig-ün dalai.[11] Il fut professeur à l'école tibétaine de Pékin (*op. cit.*, p. 65) et est l'auteur de nombreuses traductions mongoles. Selon M. Heissig, il est mentionné pour la première fois en 1717-1720 parmi les collaborateurs au *Kanjur* mongol et est, probablement, mort au milieu du 18e siècle (*op. cit.*, pp. 66 et 111). On lui doit une traduction mongole de l'*Aṣṭasāhasrikā* (*op. cit.*, p. 110).[12] C'est donc bien possible de lui attribuer également l'édition de la traduction tibétaine de l'*Aṣṭasāhasrikā*.

Pour terminer je signale quelques points de détail. p. 18: lire *ma phyi* au lieu de *ma phye*; p. 19: corriger *Bre brag tu* en *Bye brag tu*; p. 27: une traduction complète de l'*Aṣṭasāhasrikā* par Dr. Edward Conze fut publiée en 1958: *Aṣṭasāhasrikā Prajñāpāramitā*. Translated into English by Edward Conze (= *Bibliotheca Indica*, Work Number 284, Issue Number 1578) (Calcutta, The Asiatic Society). Voir aussi du même auteur: *The Prajñāparamitā Literature* (= *Indo-Iranian Monographs*, VI) ('s-Gravenhage, Mouton & Co., 1960); p. 31, l. 2: lire *gnad* au lieu de *gnaṅ*, l. 5: lire *legs* au lieu de *lags*; l. 20, lire *ṅed* au lieu de *ded*; p. 33: les mDo-maṅ ne sont pas identiques aux gZuṅs-bsdus car les derniers ne contiennent pas de sūtra. Récemment un Mdo-maṅ a été catalogué par M. P. Aalto: "Le Mdo-maṅ conservé à la Bibliothèque Universitaire de Helsinki", *Publications of the University at Helsinki*, XXIII: *Miscellanea bibliographica*, VI (Helsinki, 1952), pp. 27-47 (cf. *Bibliographie Bouddhique*, XXIV-XXVII, no. 315 où il faut corriger l'indication *Eripainos*).

Il faut espérer que M. Meisezahl continuera ses études des dKar-chag. Il reste encore beaucoup à faire dans ce domaine. Par exemple, on aimerait en apprendre davantage

[9] M. R.O.M. écrit *dor* qu'il faut corriger en *ṅor* (cf. aussi *IIJ*, VI, p. 77, l. 12). Dans les colophons on trouve souvent les expressions *bskul-ba'i ṅor* et *bskul-ba ltar* dont le sens est le même.

[10] Probablement il faut corriger *yi-ge* en *yi-ge-pa*. La formule pour indiquer le scribe est d'habitude: *yi-ge-pa ni* N.N. *-gyis bgyis-pa*, cf. J. Bacot, "Textes et colophons d'ouvrages non canoniques tibétains", *BEFEO*, XLIV (1954), 275-337.

[11] *Die Pekinger lamaistischen Blockdrucke in mongolischer Sprache* (Wiesbaden, 1954). Cf. l'index (p. 202) s.v. *Bilig-ün dalai*.

[12] M. Heissig cite deux lignes du colophon (p. 111, n. 3) et corrige *kičeči* en *bičeči* > *bičigeči* puisque l'équivalent tibétain est *gleg-bam-gyi bar-byad* "des Buches Ausführender". Il faut lire *gleg-bam-gyi par-byaṅ* "le colophon du livre". Je ne vois pas pourquoi cette expression correspondrait à *kičeči*. Il serait utile d'avoir le texte complet du colophon.

sur le *Kanjur* du Šel-dkar mi-'gyur rdo-rje'i rdzoṅ que M. Meisezahl mentionne (p. 20; aussi *Libri*, vol. 10, no. 4, 1960, p. 302).

A.N.U., Canberra J. W. de Jong

JACOB ENSINK. *The Question of Rāṣṭrapāla, translated and annotated.* — Zwolle, Holland, 1952; XXIII + 140 pages.

Le travail de M. Ensink, thèse soutenue à l'université d'Utrecht, contient la traduction (p. 1-59) et le texte tibétain (p. 60-125) de la *Rāṣṭrapālaparipṛcchā*, publiée par Finot en 1901 (Bibl. Budd., vol 2). En appendice, M. E. donne le texte tibétain (p. 126-132) et la traduction (p. 133-138) d'un petit texte de même titre qui ne fait pas partie du *Ratnakūṭa* mais se trouve dans la section *Mdo* (cf. *Otani Kanjur Catalogue*, n° 833). Les textes tibétains sont édités d'après les éditions de Sde-dge, Snar-thaṅ, Lhasa et Pékin.

M. E. ne s'est pas contenté du texte tel qu'il est établi par Finot d'après un manuscrit unique de Cambridge, mais a vérifié l'édition de Finot à l'aide d'une photocopie du manuscrit. Ainsi plusieurs lectures ont pu être corrigées. En outre, M. E. s'est servi des deux traductions chinoises dues à Jñānagupta et à Che-hou. Malheureusement, une troisième traduction lui est restée inconnue. C'est le Taishō, n° 170, intitulé *Tö kouang t'ai tseu king* «Sūtra du prince Puṇyaraśmi», traduit par Dharmarakṣa en 270 d'après le *Tch'ou san tsang ki tsi* (Taishō, n° 2145, k. 2, p. 7*c*) qui indique également comme autre titre *Rāṣṭrapālaparipṛcchā*. La traduction de Dharmarakṣa est antérieure de trois siècles à celle de Jñānagupta et permet donc de reculer considérablement la date de la composition de la *RP*. Mais l'intérêt principal de cette traduction est qu'elle nous fait connaître un état beaucoup moins développé du texte. Elle correspond aux passages suivants du texte sanskrit : p. 1, l. 6-7; 4, 20-5, 5; 8, 7-10, 9; 11, 3-5; 11, 18-12, 3; 12, 16-13, 3; 13, 16-14, 1; 14, 13-16; 15, 9-17, 6; 18, 1-5; 19, 16-20; 20, 11-15; 34, 1-37, 12; 39, 8-50, 6; 54, 1-11; 56, 3-60, 4. Il paraît donc évident que des passages comme l'énumération des *jataka* et la prophétie de la future décadence de l'église

IMPRIMERIE NATIONALE

furent ajoutés plus tard. Il est intéressant de noter que, dans la liste des qualités, ce sont les strophes qui manquent sauf une fois (p. 15, 14-17, 2). Ceci réfute l'opinion de Finot qui considérait les sommaires en prose comme postérieurs aux strophes. Pour l'étude de l'histoire de la *RP* la traduction de Dharmarakṣa est donc d'une grande importance. D'autre part, elle s'ajoute aux nombreuses traductions que Dharmarakṣa a faites de textes appartenant au *Ratnakūṭa* et que les éditeurs du *Taishō shinshū Daizōkyō* ont publiées dans les volumes XI et XII.

Dans les parties versifiées, le texte sanskrit se trouve dans un état très corrompu. Finot n'a suggéré que peu de conjectures en vue d'améliorer le texte. Sans l'aide de la traduction tibétaine il aurait aussi été difficile pour lui d'aller plus loin dans cette voie. Mais, en utilisant la traduction tibétaine, M. E. aurait dû être plus audacieux. Ce n'est que très rarement qu'il se sert de cette traduction pour corriger le texte. Même s'il avait voulu s'abstenir de faire des conjectures, les divergences entre le texte sanskrit et la traduction tibétaine, tout au moins, auraient dû être signalées de manière systématique. Il ne faut pas perdre de vue que le texte sanskrit tel qu'il a été transmis dans un manuscrit du XVIIe siècle mérite beaucoup moins notre confiance que la traduction tibétaine qui date du premier tiers du IXe siècle. Dans la plupart des divergences, la traduction tibétaine paraît bien devoir être préférée au texte sanskrit. Si, en outre, une des traductions chinoises vient la confirmer, le doute n'est plus permis. Tenant compte ainsi d'un côté des traductions et de l'autre des exigences de la métrique, M. E. aurait pu établir un texte plus correct, ou, au moins, mettre en évidence les passages corrompus. Sans aborder l'examen systématique de tous les passages difficiles qui abondent dans la *RP*, nous nous bornerons ici à présenter quelques remarques de détail.

P. IX-X : ajouter aux indications bibliographiques sur Rāṣṭrapāla : Sylvain Lévi, *JA*, 1928, II, p. 199-204; Vidhushekara Bhattacharya, *A New Drama of Aśvaghoṣa*, dans *Journal of the Greater India Society*, vol. V, 1938, p. 51-53; E. H. Johnston, *The Rāṣṭrapālanāṭaka of Aśvaghoṣa*, *ibid.*, p. 151-153; Bhaiṣajyavastu (*Gilgit Manuscripts*, vol. III, part I, 1947, p. 200-202; Taishō, n° 1448, k. 17, p. 84 *b* 22 *c*-26) et les textes chinois cités par Mochizuki (*Bukkyōdaijiten*, p. 4945 *c*-4946 *a*) et par Akanuma (*Indo bukkyō koyūmeiji jiten*, Nagoya, 1931, p. 544).

P. 1, l. 2-5 : ces lignes font défaut dans toutes les traductions; l. 2 : au lieu de *spaṣṭamā viśvakāra* lire avec La Vallée Poussin *spaṣṭam āviścakāra* (il est très regrettable que M. E. n'ait pas consulté le compte rendu de l'édition de Finot par La Vallée Poussin dans *Muséon*, N. S., vol. IV, 1903, p. 306-312).

P. 2, l. 20 : au lieu de *meruteja* la traduction tibétaine (en abrégé : tib.) a *gzi yaṅs* (éclat large); ceci est confirmé par la traduction chinoise de Jñānagupta (en abrégé : J). En lisant *urutejā* on rétablit aussi le mètre.

P. 4, l. 7 : *rūpasāgarabuddhiṃ* est énigmatique; tib. n'a pas *sāgara* (*rgya-mtsho*) mais «étendu» (*rgya-chen*).

P. 5, l. 18 et p. 10, l. 16 : *gatiṃ gata* (lire *gatiṃgata*) ne signifie pas «who has gone his way» mais «qui a parfaitement compris» (cf. *Saddharmapuṇḍarīka,* p. 26, 5; 131, 3; 186, 10; 200, 10; 202, 10; 204, 11; 205, 12; *Mahāvastu,* III, p. 386, 10 et 419, 2 : *Lalitavistara,* p. 179, 15; *Laṅkāvatāra,* p. 2, 2; *Mahāvyutpatti,* 356, 866, 2888; les traducteurs tibétains ne s'y sont pas trompés (cf. Nobel, *Suvarṇaprabhāsottamasūtra,* Wörterbuch, s. v. *rtogs-pa*).

P. 6, l. 7 : *kṣetraśuddhir api cāpi saṃbhavo* est intraduisible; tib. : *dag-pa'i źiṅ daṅ phun-sum-tshogs 'khor daṅ* comme p. 9, l. 3 où le texte sanskrit : *kṣetraśuddhiparivārasaṃpadaṃ* correspond exactement au tibétain.

P. 9, l. 4 : *sattvakāraṇakathā* ne signifie pas «you who tell the origin of being» mais «celui qui parle dans l'intérêt des êtres» (tib. : *sems-can ched kyi bka'-mchid*); p. 5, l. 13 : sattvakāraṇam (tib. : *sems-can kyi ched-du*) est traduit correctement par «for the sake of the beings».

P. 9. l. 5 : *mārabhañjana... vimuktisparśanā* sont des vocatifs.

P. 9, l. 6 : au lieu de *ayi* il faut lire avec La Vallée Poussin *api* (tib. : *yaṅ*).

P. 9, l. 7 : *toṣaṇī* n'est pas nominatif de *toṣaṇin-,* mais un nominatif féminin qui dépend de *vāk* (voir aussi texte sanskrit p. 47, l. 2).

P. 9, l. 10 : au lieu de *dharmakāma parṣatsamāgatā,* il faut lire *dharmakāmaparṣatsamāgatā;* tib. : *chos 'tshal gyur-pa'i 'khor rnams lhags lags kyis;* confirmé par J.

P. 13, l. 4 : au lieu de *cintānapekṣā,* tib. a *vittānapekṣā* (*nor mi-blta*).

P. 13, l. 17 : ms. *araṇyavāsānutsyajanatā* (Finot : *araṇyavāsākutsyajanatā*) mais tib. : *dgon-pa la gnas-pa mi gtoṅ-ba* (*araṇyavāsānutsarjanatā*).

P. 14, l. 14 : *nirāmiṣasevanatā* ne signifie pas «frequenting people who are free from desire», mais «docilité exempte de tout égoïsme» comme l'a traduit La Vallée Poussin.

P. 16, l. 4 : au lieu de *viharati siṃha ivottrasañjitāriṃ,* lire *viharati siṃha ivātrasañjitāriḥ?*

P. 16, l. 13 : *vicarati* ne signifie pas ici «goes through» mais «considère».

P. 19, l. 6 : *jīvapoṣe* ne signifie pas «the maintaining of their life»; *poṣa* équivaut au pāli *posa,* skt. *puruṣa* (cf. *Śikṣāsamuccaya,* p. 199, l. 8 et p. 236, l. 15; Wogihara et Bendall, *Muséon,* N. S., vol. V, 1904, p. 211; *Mahāvyutpatti,* 4672; *Mahāparinirvāṇasūtra,* éd. Waldschmidt, p. 154 et Edgerton, *JAOS,* 72, 1952, p. 192).

P. 20, l. 13 : *anigṛhitacittasya,* tib. : *kun- 'dzin-pa'i sems* (*āgṛhitacittasya*); voir p. 21, l. 1 où il faut lire *sadāgrahacittaḥ* au lieu de *sadā grahacittaḥ* (tib. : *kun-'dzin sems*). Pour *āgṛhita* et *āgraha* voir *Avadānaśataka,* index.

P. 20, l. 17 : au lieu de *dṛṣtiśatebhiḥ* tib. : *dṛṣṭigatebhiḥ* (*lta-gyur 'di -dag-gis*).

P. 21, l. 4 : *avamanyanamanyana* ne signifie pas «contempt of others»; lire *avamanyana* et *manyana* (voir La Vallée Poussin, *op. cit.,* p. 312; *Mahāvyutpatti,* 7082; *Saddharmapuṇḍarīka,* p. 282, l. 1); tib. : *bṅas-par byed daṅ rloṁ-sems.* [Je n'ai vu la grammaire et le dictionnaire du sanskrit bouddhique par M. Edgerton qu'après avoir écrit ce compte rendu. Dans la grammaire (21.43) il explique *anyana* comme équivalent à *anyeṣām, anyana* étant employé *metri causa* pour *anyāna*, et celui-ci, à son tour, *metri causa* pour *anyānām*. Mais le seul exemple cité pour la forme *anyana* est justement *RP*, p. 21, 4 (heureusement, dans le dictionnaire s.v. *avamanyanā* et *manyanā*, M. Edgerton donne de ce passage une explication correcte). Pour employer l'expression de M. Edgerton lui-même (*Grammar*, p. 6, note) : «This case shows how even the greatest of scholars may go astray on an individual case»].

P. 21, l. 11 : tib. a lu *śodhita āśaya* (*bsam-pa rnam-par sbyaṅs*) au lieu de *śoṣita āśrayu*; mais J. confirme le texte sanskrit.

P. 24, l. 14 : tib. *phyogs-kyi tog* ne correspond pas ici à Deśaketu mais à Āśaketu (confirmé par J.).

P. 25, l. 5 : M. E. traduit : «When I was prince Vikṛtajña and I rescued an ungrateful man out of the ocean» en se référant à la traduction tibétaine; mais la traduction de celle-ci est : «Quand j'étais prince Reconnaissant j'ai sauvé de la mer un homme ingrat»; il en est de même d'après J.

P. 28, l. 9 : *sa śāmitaguṇaughaḥ*; tib. : *de ni dpag-med yon-tan chuṅ* (erreur pour *chu?*) qui correspond à *sa sāmitaguṇaughaḥ*; il se peut que le *ś* provienne d'une fausse sanskritisation.

P. 29, l. 7 : *naiṣām anāryam api vācyam* ne signifie pas «nothing vulgar is blamable to them»; les traductions de Finot «pour eux il n'est pas de parole déshonorante» et de M. E. J. Thomas «for them no speech is ignoble», *The Perfection of Wisdom*, London, 1952, p. 68 (dans ce dernier ouvrage, p. 27, 11-32, 4 de la *RP* sont traduites) sont correctes.

P. 32, l. 17 : après *dūra*, une syllabe manque; tib. : *des-pa* qui traduit *surata* (p. 10, 14; 13, 5; 37, 17); J. : l'esprit dompté.

P. 33, l. 3 : *hi duram*; tib. : *'jig-par 'gyur* (*bhiduram*).

P. 34, l. 17 : au lieu de *bahumānyatā*, les trois traductions chinoises et la traduction tibétaine (*nan man-ba* doit évidemment être corrigé en *nad maṅ-ba*) ont «beaucoup de maladies» (*bahuglānyatā*).

P. 35, l. 14 : M. E. traduit ici *saṃgati* par «the way to favourable existences» alors que p. 32, l. 7, il traduit : «go»; il est préférable de lire avec le tib. (*bzaṅ-'gro*) *sadgati* «bonne destinée».

P. 36, l. 8 : *dṛḍhaḥ sa lepena kṛtaḥ kapirvā* ne signifie pas «as when a monkey has become violent by attachment», mais «comme un singe attaché avec de la colle» (même traduction chez J.); cette comparaison s'applique à celui qui, en s'imaginant avoir obtenu la délivrance, s'arrête et n'avance plus dans la voie du salut.

P. 40, l. 14 : Finot a eu tort de corriger *puṣkiriṇi* en *puṣkariṇī* (voir *Divyāvadāna*, index; *Mahāvastu*, III, p. 288, 7 et 438, 14 et 20; *ibid.*, p. 508 la note de Senart; *Avadānaśataka*, vol. II, p. 201, l. 12).

P. 42, l. 17 : au lieu de *svarangarucirāḥ*, tib. : *svarāṅgarucirāḥ* (*dbyaṅs kyi yan-lag sñan*).

P. 47, l. 7 : au lieu de *bodhani*, tib. : *śodhani* (*sbyoṅ-ba*); de même J.

P. 48, l. 1 : au lieu de *viṣaya*, lire avec La Vallée Poussin *viṣama* (tib. : *ya-na ba*); p. 48, l. 2, *viṣama* est traduit par *ya-na ba*.

P. 53, l. 5 : au lieu de *puṇyādhikasya*, tib. : *puṇyārthikasya* (*bsod-nams don gñer-ba'i*) ; confirmé par J. et la citation dans le *Śikṣāsamuccaya*.

P. 57, l. 12 : *antaśaḥ* ne signifie pas «at the end» (voir *Avadānaśataka*, vol. I, p. 314, l. 6 ; *Divyāvadāna*, p. 161, 24 ; *Śikṣāsamuccaya*, p. 42, 5 et 56, 10-11 ; *Saddharmapuṇḍarīka*, p. 108, 3 ; 224, 6 ; 224, 9 ; 227, 2 ; l'édition de Kern de *Saddharma°*, p. 225, 4 et 225, 9 a *antaśa* alors que les fragments publiés par Hoernle sont *antamaśa*, *JRAS*, 1916, p. 271-272 ; *Critical Pāli Dictionary*, s. v. *antamaso* ; Nobel, *op. cit.*, s. v. *tha-na*).

P. 58, l. 13 : au lieu de *daśabalacalite*, tib. : *daśabalacarite* (*stobs bcu mṅa' ba'i spyod-pa*) ; dans les mss népalais l'erreur de *l* pour *r* est fréquente.

P. 59, 6 : M. E. traduit *guṇamaṇḍa* par «the circle of virtues» en expliquant *maṇḍa* comme une forme alternative pour *maṇḍala*. Mais ni ici ni en *bodhimaṇḍa* ces deux mots ne sont confondus (voir Nobel, *op. cit.*, s. v. *sñiṅ-po* où le sens figuré de *maṇḍa* est bien expliqué : *sñiṅ-po, maṇḍa*, eig. Rahm, übertragen Essenz, *byaṅ-chub kyi sñiṅ-po, bodhimaṇḍa*).

Dans le texte tibétain il faut corriger *ston-par* en *stoṅ-par* (p. 61, 10), *tshig* en *tshigs* (p. 61, 28), *rton* en *rten* (p. 74, 28), *yaṅ* en *yaṅs* (p. 78, 15), *brten* en *brtan* (p. 81, 16), *źiṅ* en *ciṅ* (p. 83, 19), *thab* en *'thab* (p. 92, 9), *naṅ* en *nad* (p. 93, 5), *'or* en *bor* (p. 93, 10), *naṅ* en *nad* (p. 94, 27), *stobs* en *stabs* (p. 109, 25), *rṅul* en *rdul* (p. 113, 3 ; 116, 4), *ciṅ* en *źiṅ* (p. 116, 10). Partout *'am* et *'aṅ* sont écrits comme des syllabes séparées.

P. 128, l. 26 : *dge-sloṅ bdag-ñid-la ṅa'o sñam-du 'dzin-te* est traduit «the bhikṣu considers himself to be for himself» ; plutôt : «le moine s'attache à l'idée de moi à l'égard de lui-même».

P. 131, l. 5-8 : *dge-sloṅ rnams-kyis bud-med rnams || blta-bar mi bya rdzogs-saṅs gsuṅ || de-la śes-ldan su-źig rton || de ni bdud-kyi spyod-yul yin ||* au lieu de : «Bhikṣus must not regard women, the Buddha said ; therefore confide in men who know ; those others are the domain of Māra», il faut traduire : «le complètement éveillé a dit : les moines ne doivent pas regarder les femmes ; quel homme sage a confiance en elles ? Elles sont le domaine de Māra (*Māragocara*)».

A bien des égards le travail de M. Ensink mérite notre estime. Il a soigneusement analysé les traits frappants du sanskrit hybride du texte (voir Introduction, p. xiii-xix). D'autre part, écrite dans un anglais limpide et plein d'aisance, sa traduction est agréable à lire. Les termes techniques ont été partout relevés et expliqués en note. Si M. Ensink fait suivre sa traduction d'un index tibétain-sanskrit, tous les étudiants du bouddhisme lui seront obligés.

J. W. de Jong.

J. W. DE JONG

REMARKS ON THE TEXT OF THE *RĀṢṬRAPĀLAPARIPṚCCHĀ*

THE *RP* (= *Rāṣṭrapālaparipṛcchā*) was published in 1901 by L. Finot as volume two of the Bibliotheca Buddhica. This edition was based upon a single manuscript dating from A.D. 1661.[1] The *RP* has been translated three times into Chinese. The first translation was made by Dharmarakṣa in A.D. 270,[2] the second at the end of the sixth century by Jñānagupta (Taishō no. 310, chapters 80 and 81), and the third in A.D. 994[3] by Shih-hu (Taishō no. 321). The Tibetan translation, which is to be found in the Kanjur, is due to Jinamitra, Dānaśīla, Munivarma, and Ye-śes-sde, who translated many texts in the beginning of the ninth century. Finot made some use of the Chinese translations by Jñānagupta and Shih-hu, which had been compared for him by Pelliot, but did not consult the Tibetan translation. In a long review L. de La Vallée Poussin proposed several emendations of the text (*Muséon*, N.S. vol. 4, 1903, pp. 306-12).

[1] Cf. Cecil Bendall, *Catalogue of the Buddhist Sanskrit Manuscripts in the University Library, Cambridge* (Cambridge, 1883), p. 130 and pp. 206-7.

[2] Cf. *Journal asiatique*, 1953, p. 545. One must add 18. 17-19. 3 to the list of passages of the Sanskrit text corresponding to Dharmarakṣa's translation.

[3] Cf. Mochizuki Shinkō, *Bukkyō Daijiten*, vol. 8 (Tokyo, 1958), p. 262.

In 1952 Professor J. Ensink published an English translation (*The Question of Rāṣṭrapāla*, Zwolle) in which he made a number of emendations based upon a collation of Finot's edition with the Cambridge manuscript, and upon the Chinese translations by Jñānagupta and Shih-hu and the Tibetan translation. Ensink also added to his translation a careful edition of the Tibetan translation on the basis of the Derge, Narthang, Peking and Lhasa editions of the Kanjur. Ensink's work provoked new interest in the *RP* and several reviewers discussed both Ensink's translation and Finot's edition. Especially important is a review by Dr. D. R. Shackleton Bailey (*JRAS*, 1954, pp. 79-82) in which he suggested many new emendations. Other emendations are to be found in Edgerton's *Buddhist Hybrid Sanskrit Dictionary* (New Haven, 1953) which appeared shortly after Ensink's work.

In 1957 a photomechanical reprint of Finot's edition was published as *Indo-Iranian Reprints*, vol. II, 's-Gravenhage. An appendix to this lists the corrections and emendations suggested by Finot (p. xviii of his edition); by La Vallée Poussin (in the abovementioned review); by Ensink (op. cit.); by Shackleton Bailey (in his review), and by J. W. de Jong (*JA*, 1953, pp. 545-9).[1]

[1] The following corrections have to be made in this appendix. After 25.13 read *gajavaśagatena; rājavaśagatena* MS. (E). Add 25.14 *gajā; gajo* MS. (E). After 34.12 read *ricitvā* instead of *racitvā*. Shackleton Bailey (op. cit., p. 80) proposed *rahitvā*, but Edgerton (*Buddhist Hybrid Sanskrit Grammar*, p. 227a) *riñcitvā*. Tibetan has

Many of the proposed emendations help in establishing a much more satisfactory text. However, not all problems have been solved and some emendations are less convincing than others. New manuscript material would be highly desirable. Finot mentioned a manuscript belonging to the Bibliothèque Nationale in Paris,[1] which, according to him, is a copy of the Cambridge manuscript. For this reason he took no account of it. The Tokyo University possesses another manuscript of the *RP*.[2] I have been able to obtain a microfilm of this manuscript, and for this I express my sincere thanks to the authorities concerned.

However, I am afraid that this manuscript does not give any new readings.[3] In all the passages (about 60) in which I compared it with the text of Finot's edition, there is not a single variant. Probably the Tokyo manuscript is another copy of the Cambridge

bor-nas. After 40.9 read *aśvarathagodhanaṃ* instead of *aśvarathagodanaṃ*. Add 59.18 *anutpadanta pūrvāṇy*, *anutpādantapūrvāṇy* MS. (E) and expunge 59.19 *anupādāyāśravebhyaś*, etc.

[1] Cf. Jean Filliozat, *Catalogue du fonds sanskrit*, Fascicule 1 (Paris, 1941), p. 75.

[2] Cf. Seiren Matsunami, *A Catalogue of the Sanskrit Manuscripts in the Tokyo University Library* (Tokyo, 1965), p. 116.

[3] In his *Bongo butten no shobunken* (Kyoto, 1959, p. 93) Professor Yamada Ryūjō indicates that this manuscript has been collated by Itō Shinkai for his edition and translation of the verses of the *RP*: 'Bonbun Rāṣṭrapālaparipṛcchā gemon no kenkyū', *Taishō daigaku gakuhō*, vols. 28, 30-1 (Tokyo, 1938 and 1940). According to Yamada the edition and the translation are incomplete. To my regret I have not been able to consult Itō's article.

manuscript, made in Nepal before the latter was brought to Cambridge.

In the present circumstances a new examination of the text can only be made on the basis of the existing materials. The following remarks mainly refer to the Tibetan translation which, as usual, is more useful for textual studies than the Chinese translations which do not give a literal rendering of the Sanskrit text. All references are to page and line of Finot's edition. First Finot's text is quoted. This is followed by the Tibetan translation of the passage quoted and the emendation based upon the latter. In general I have refrained from making any comments. A question-mark indicates that the emendation proposed is even more hypothetical than is ordinarily the case. It is unnecessary to say that no emendation can be absolutely sure. I only hope that my remarks may help in again drawing attention to the *RP* and to the problems connected with the establishment of a correct text. At the same time I would like to express in this way a small tribute to Dr. V. Raghavan who, apart from his numerous other contributions to Sanskrit studies, has done such excellent work in emending corrupt Sanskrit texts.

1.10 *sarvaguṇavarṇaparyādattaiḥ. T. yon-tan-gyi tshogs thams-cad zad mi-śes-pa = sarvaguṇagaṇaparyādattaiḥ.*

2.12 *āśuviniścitārthaḥ.* T. *don śin-tu rnam-par ṅes-pa = suviniścitārthaḥ.*

3.13 *prabhāsati satvān.* T. *kun snaṅ = prabhāsati sarvam.*

6.12 *sarvadharmanayayuktamānasā.* T. *chos-rnams kun-la thugs ni chags mi-mṅa'* = *sarvadharma na p(r)ayuktamānasā?*

8.11 *satvakauśalyatāṃ.* T. *sems-can-gyi khams-la mkhas-pa* = *satvadhātukauśalyatāṃ.*

9.11 *dharma chanda vihito na yujyate.* T. *chos-la 'dun-pa bzlog-pa mi rigs-te* = *dharma chanda vihato na yujyate.*

14.6 *tṛṇakāṣṭhakothasama.* MS. *kutha* instead of *kotha.* T. *rtsva daṅ śiṅ daṅ rtsig pa 'dra-bar* = *tṛṇakāṣṭhakuḍyasama.* Cf. Edgerton's *Dictionary:* (?) *kotha.*

14.14 *nirāmiṣasevanatayā.* T. *zaṅ-ziṅ med-pa'i sems-kyis bsteṅ-pa* = *nirāmiṣacittasevanatayā.*

22.15 *kṛtsnam upārjitam āpya bhiṣagbhir bhaiṣajam apratimaṃ mama pūrvam.* T. *sman-pa mchog-gis ṅa-yi ched-du ni // mtshuṅs-med sman-rnams ma-lus sbyar-ba yaṅ* = *kṛtsnam upārjitam agryabhiṣagbhir . . .*

24.9 *hitvā svam asthi ca śarīrād.* T. *ṅa-yis lus-las rus-pa phyuṅ-nas ni* = *hṛtvā svam. . . .*

25.3 *ratnam anekavastrarathayānān.* T. *rin-chen du-ma gos daṅ śiṅ-rta bźon* = *ratnam aneka vastrarathayānān.*

25.16 *puruṣa-vadhaku tena ma prayukto.* T. *de-yis gsod-pa ṅa-la btaṅ-byas kyaṅ* = ... *tena ma pramukto.*

28.15 *pāpamataiḥ kutīrthakamataiś ca.* T. *sdig-pa'i blo daṅ mu-stegs ṅan mtshuṅs-pas* = ... *kutīrthakasamaiś ca.*

34.5 *te ajñānino jñānanimittātmānaṃ pratijñāsyanti.* T. *de-dag mi-śes bźin-du . . . bdag śes-pa daṅ-ldan-par khas 'che-bar 'gyur* = *te ajñānino jñāninam ātmānaṃ pratijñāsyanti.*

35.15 *daridrabhūtāś ca hi pravrajitvā dāridryamuktāṃ samavāpya pūjām.* T. *dbul-por gyur-pas rab-tu byuṅ gyur-te // mchod-pa rñed-nas dbul-las grol-bar 'gyur* = ... *dāridryamuktā samavāpya pūjām.*

39.2 *buddhamārgam imam eva suśrutam.* T. *saṅs-rgyas lam 'di-ñid-la gnas-par gyis* = *buddhamārgam imam eva saṃśraya.* Cf. 38.6 *saṃśrayasva vanam eva nispṛhaḥ,* T. *'dod-pa med-par dgon-par gnas-par gyis.*

39.13 *bhavābhiṣṭaṃ śamatṛptaṃ pṛthagjanatvaṃ.* T. *srid-pa la mṅon-par dga'-bas chog mi-śes-pa daṅ / so-so'i skye-bo ñid* = *bhavābhiratam atṛptaṃ pṛthagjanatvaṃ.*

41.5 *muktājālavitataṃ.* T. *mu-tig daṅ / nor-bu'i dra-bas bres-so* = *muktāmaṇijālavitataṃ.*

41.11 *sarvākārasaṃpannāni.* T. *ro'i rnam-pa thams-cad phun-sum tshogs-pa* = *sarvākārarasasaṃpannāni.*

41.20 *ekāntam anāmayacāriṇyaḥ.* T. *śin-tu yid-du 'oṅ-ba'i tshul daṅ-ldan-pa* = *ekāntamanāpacāriṇyaḥ.*

44.5 *tṛṣṇāpravṛttiniratāḥ.* T. *sred-pa rab-tu 'phel-la dga'-bas* = *tṛṣṇāpravṛddhiniratāḥ.*

44.10 *dhik kaṇḍitasya tribhave nṛpa kāmarāgaḥ.* T. *rgyal-po mkhas-la srid-gsum 'dod-la chags-pa ṅan* = *dhik paṇḍitasya....* Cf. *Lalitavistara* (ed. S. Lefmann), p. 191.5: *dhik paṇḍitasya puruṣasya ratiprasaṅgaiḥ.*

44.16 *oghe 'tiruhyati.* T. *chu-bo rnams-kyis bdas-na* = *oghebhir uhyati.* According to Shackleton Bailey (op. cit., p. 80) *atiruhyati* = *ati-r-uhyati* is a case of ' hiatus-bridging '.

45.12 *meruprayātam api sāgaram utsaheyaṃ.* T. *lhun-po'i rtse-nas rgya-mtsho'i naṅ-du mchoṅ spro-yi* = *meruprapātam api. . .* Cf. Kenneth Ch'en, *HJAS,*

17 (1954), p. 278 for translations of the Tibetan version and Shih-hu's Chinese version.

47.9 *kamburucira grīvā śāntasaṃvṛtta skandhaḥ*. T. *ston-pa'i mgul mdzes duṅ daṅ 'dra-źiṅ dpuṅ-mgo zlum* = *kamburucira grīvā śāstu saṃvṛtta skandhaḥ*. For *śāstu* see Edgerton's *Grammar*, 13.39.

48.5 *yathānāsvādaṃ ṣaḍāyatanaṃ*. T. *ji-ltar skye-mched drug dbugs-'byin-pa med-pa* = *yathānāsvāsaṃ ṣaḍāyatanaṃ*. Cf. 39.12 *asāram itvaraṃ ca lokam anāśvasan*, MS. *anāsvāsaṃ* (cf. Ensink, p. 37, n. 195). Edgerton (*Dictionary* s.v. *anāśvāsa*) proposes *anāśvāsam*. In both places the MS. has a dental *s*. For this reason *anāsvāsam* seems preferable.

58.9 *buddhajñānavirahitāḥ*. T. *saṅs-rgyas-kyi theg-pa daṅ bral-ba* = *buddhayānavirahitāḥ*.

59.9 *dharma yujyata tīvra gauravaṃ janayitvā*. T. *gus-pa drag-po bskyed-nas chos-la brtson-par gyis* = *dharme* . . . .

APPENDICE

Il nous a paru utile de joindre à cette réimpression un appendice qui énumère les fautes d'impression, les conjectures proposées dans le travail de M. Ensink et dans quelques comptes rendus et, finalement, les lectures du MS relevées par M. Ensink. Nous avons ajouté deux corrections (25.13 ; 41.6) et deux conjectures (39.13 ; 44.1). Cinq passages de la *Rāṣṭrapālaparipṛcchā* sont cités dans le *Śikṣāsamuccaya:*

13.4–9	–	*Śikṣāsamuccaya*	196.1–6
18.15–16	–	„	203.9–10
20.5–8	–	„	54.17–55.2
35.19–20	–	„	153.2–5
50.9–53.18	–	„	318.5–322.4

Abréviations:

F – L. Finot, Corrections, *Rāṣṭrapālaparipṛcchā*, p. XVIII.
L – La Vallée Poussin, *Muséon*, N.S., IV (1903), pp. 306–312.
E – J. Ensink, *The Question of Rāṣṭrapāla* (Zwolle, 1952).
S – D. R. Shackleton Bailey, *JRAS*, 1954, pp. 79–82.
J – J. W. de Jong, *JA*, 1953, pp. 545–549.
T – traduction tibétaine.
m.c. – metri causa
n.sg. – nominatif singulier.

1.2 *spaṣṭamāṃ viśvakārāṃ; spaṣṭam āviścakāra* (L)
2.13 *svarthaṃ suvyañjanaṃ; sārthaṃ savyañjanaṃ* (L) mais T confirme la lecture du MS
2.20 *merutejā; uru-* ou *pṛthutejā* (S), *urutejā* (J)
3.7 *anubhāsan; anuśāsan* (S)
3.14 *maharṣiḥ; maharṣeḥ* (S)
4.5 *bhāsayate; bhāsayato* n.sg. (S)
4.7 *rūpasāgarabuddhiṃ; kṛpasāgarabuddhiṃ* ? (S)
5.9 *varṇanāyakāḥ; varṇa nāyakāḥ* (E)
5.16 *prajñupāya sada pāramiṃ;* T *prajñupāyavaśipāramiṃ* (S)
5.18 *gatiṃ gataṃ; gatiṃgataṃ* (J)

6.7 *kṣetraśuddhir api cāpi saṃbhavo; kṣetraśuddhiparivārasaṃpado* (S, J)
6.7 *°gaṇāḥ; °gaṇa* m.c. (E)
6.15 *rūpyam; rūpam* (S)
6.16 *virājite; virājire* (L)
7.7 *tāmra nakha jāla citritaṃ; tāmranakha jālacitritaṃ* (E)
7.12 *jagadharmacaryayā; jaga dharmacaryayā* (E)
8.11 *bhūtasaṃghāyavacanaṃ; bhūtasaṃdhāyavacanaṃ* (L), ainsi MS (E)
8.14 *sabhavaḥ; saṃbhavaḥ* (F, E)
8.17 *parāyaṇa; parāyaṇaṃ* MS (E)
8.18 *jñānalotu; jñānalobhu* (L), *jñānalābhu* (E)
8.19 *prajñāsāgara; prajñasāgara* m.c. (E)
9.6 *dharmanetri rayina; dharmanetrir api na* (L, S, J)
9.6 *pramuhyata; pramuhyate* MS (E)
9.10 *dharmakāma parṣatsamāgatā; dharmakāmaparṣat samāgatā* (J)
10.7 *yadu tārāyādhāśaya°; yadutāsayādhyāsaya°* MS (E)
10.13 *bhavato; bhavasārato* (S)
10.16 *gatiṃ gata; gatiṃgata* (J)
10.17 *abudho; abudhā* MS (E)
11.8 *sati; mati* (E)
12.11 *satvadharma; sarvadharma* (S)
12.13 *yācakamupāgatam; yācakaṃ upāgataṃ* MS (E)
13.4 *cintānapekṣā; vittānapekṣā* (S, J)
13.8 *harṣitamanọ; harṣita mano* (E)
13.17 *araṇyavāsākutsyajanatā; araṇyavāsānutsarjanatā* (S, J)
14.3 *anuśīla susaṃyato; aha śīlasusaṃyato* (E), *aha śīli susaṃyato* (S)
14.6 *satvarūpaṃ; sarvarūpaṃ* (S)
14.10 *sa tārayanti; saṃtārayanti* MS (E)
15.3 *guruṣu; gurūṣu* MS (E)
15.5 *mahāśayānāṃ; mahāyaśānāṃ* MS (E)
15.6 *samādayanti; samānayanti* ? (L)
15.9 *°pāriśodhakā; °pariśodhakā* (L)
15.10 *kuhanalepana°; kuhanalapana°* MS (E)
16.4 *siṃha ivottrasañjitāriṃ; siṃha ivātrasañ jitāriḥ* ? (J)
16.8 *pajūnena; pūjanena* (F)
16.11 *smitābhilāṣī; smitābhilāpī* (S)
16.15 *prativadasi; pratipadati* (E)
16.16 *duḥkha satāṃ; duḥkhasatāṃ* (E)
17.8 *mātṛpitṛṣu; mātṛpitṝṣu* m.c. (E)

17.13 *śravaṇā; śramaṇaguṇā* (S)
17.15 *te'antara hāpayiṣyanti; te'ntardhāpayiṣyanti* (E)
17.15 *ma dharmaṃ; (i)mu dharmaṃ* (S)
19.11 *agnikhadhāṃ; agnikhadāṃ* MS (E)
20.2 *tāniājñaḥ; tān yadi ajñaḥ* ? (S)
20.3 *viṣameṇa sa deśati; viṣameṇa sa-d-eṣati* (E)
20.7 *cyuto hi; cyuta hī* m.c. (E)
20.8 *tiryaggatiṣu pretagatiṣu; tiryagatīṣu pretagatīṣu* MS (E)
20.12 *bhāvanatāprayoganimittasaṃjñā; bhāvanatāprayoga nimittasaṃjñā* (S)
20.13 *anigṛhītacittasya; āgṛhītacittasya* (J)
20.17 *dṛṣṭiśatebhiḥ; dṛṣṭigatebhiḥ* (J)
21.1 *sadā grahacittaḥ; sadāgrahacittaḥ* (J)
21.2 *ayuktacāribhiḥ; ayuktacarībhiḥ* m.c. (E)
21.6 *tyakta; tyaktva* (S)
21.6 *vikalmaṣadhīrāḥ; vikalmaṣa dhīrāḥ* (S)
21.12 *saṃsṛtu; sraṃsitu* ? (S)
21.13 *bhavacārake jagati; bhavacāraki jāgati* m.c. (E)
21.14 *bodhi balāj; bodhivarā* (S)
22.2 *dṛḍhavāṇahatana; dṛḍhavānahatena* MS (E), *dṛḍhavānahato 'ha* (S)
22.16 *kesarirāja; keśarirāja* MS (E)
22.17 *pativrata; patiṃvrata* MS (E)
22.18 *asaṃgha; asaṃga* MS (E)
22.20 *arthadhanaśriyo;* T *tyaktadhanaśriyo* (S)
23.9 *kāñcanamuktikāpravaraśrīmān; kāñcanabhūṣita pravaraśrīmān* (S)
23.11 *°padmapantau°* MS (F); *°padmapatra°* MS (E)
23.15 *bāli sa rākṣasī pramadasaṃjñā; bālisa rākṣasīpramadasaṃjñā* (E)
24.13 *paṇiyuga; pāṇiyuga* (F)
24.16 *sphītanarair; sphīta narair* (S)
25.5 *yadakṛtajñaḥ; yada kṛtajñaḥ* (F)
25.13 *gajavaśagatena; gajo rājavaśagatena* MS (E), rayer *gajo* (J)
25.13 *jagat; gajaṃ* (S)
25.18 *sa viṣeṇa; saviṣeṇa* (E)
26.2 *samito 'gniṃ; śamito 'gnir* (S)
26.9 *bhaiṣajabhūtasamucchraya; bhaiṣajabhūta samucchraya* (E)
27.6 *kṛpārtha tu; kṛpārthatu* (L)
27.7 *dadāmi; dadāmi hi* ou *dadāmy ahu* (S)
27.7 *sarvajanasya; sarvajagasya* (S)
27.11 *duṣkarakṛtāni; duṣkaraśatāni* (S)

28.2 *imāścaryam; ima caryam* (S)
28.4 *śatakāṅkṣāḥ; śaṭhadhvāṅkṣāḥ* (E)
28.9 *śāmitaguṇaughaḥ; amitaguṇaughaḥ* (S)
29.5 *°paśudānātsaṃbhavate hi dāsya pi; °paśudāsa saṃbhavate dāsya api* (S)
29.11 *gṛhīṇa; gṛhī na* MS (E)
29.12 *gṛhisamānam; gṛhisamānaṃ* MS (E)
30.4 *cala sidhya; ca labhiṣya* (S)
30.8 *narakeṣu; nara teṣu* (S)
30.14 *prapatitānāṃ; pratapitānāṃ* (S)
31.3 *na ca karmiko; navakarmiko* (S)
31.14 *vacanaṃ na caite; vacanaṃ ca te* (E)
31.15 *upekṣya; upeṣya* (S)
32.5 *sughoraḥ; sughore* (E)
32.7 *saṃgatiḥ; sadgatiḥ* (S)
32.16 *kṣuttṛṣṇayena; kṣuttṛṣṇabhayena* ou *kṣutṭṛdbhayena* m.c. (S)
32.17 *dūra; dūrata* (S), *sūrata* (J)
32.18 *paścāta; paścāt* (E)
33.3 *hi duram; bhiduram* (S, J)
34.3 *adhyavasāne bahulāḥ; adhyavasānabahulāḥ* (S)
34.8 *kuśīdājñānā navakalpanabahulāḥ; kuśīdā jñānānavakalpanabahulāḥ* (E)
34.9 *āparipṛcchanaśīlāḥ; aparipṛcchanaśīlāḥ* (E)
34.11 *samānālābha°; samānā lābha°* (L)
34.12 *rạcitvā; rahitvā* (S)
34.17 *bahumānyatā; bahumanyanā* (L), *bahumāndyatā* (S), *bahuglānyatā* (J)
34.17 *viṣamā parihāreṇa; viṣamāparihāreṇa* (E)
35.3 *duṣprajña°; duṣprajñā°* (L)
35.6 *na gauravasya; nāgauravasya* (E)
35.7 *dharmaveṣṭiṃ;* T *dharmaparyeṣṭiṃ, dharmagaveṣṭiṃ* ? (S)
35.14 *saṃgatiḥ; sadgatiḥ* (S, J)
35.20 *mānava śenamūdhāḥ; māṇavaśena mūdhāḥ* (F)
36.5 *boddharaḥ; coddhurāḥ* MS (E)
36.10 *śāsanam; śāsanāt* ou *śāsanena* (S)
36.14 *pakāśanam; prakāśanam* MS (E)
37.2 *rājārciṣman; rājārciṣmān* (F)
37.14 *karmakriyoddhareṇa; karmakriyoddhureṇa* MS (E)
37.19 *prameya°; 'prameya°* (L, E)

37.19 *atītāḥ; atītakāḥ* m.c. ? (E)
38.2 *dattaṃ; datta* m.c. (E)
38.9 *yatamāna; patamāna* (E)
38.10 *anuyānti; anuyāti* (S)
39.10 *gītābhilāṣyābhūt; gītābhilāṣyo'bhut* MS ? (E)
39.11 *sarvavasuṣu; sarvavastuṣu* (S)
39.12 *anāśvasan; anāsvāsaṃ* MS (E)
39.13 *vimoghadharmaṃ; vimoṣadharmaṃ* (J)
39.13 *śamatṛptaṃ;* T *atṛptaṃ, aśamaṁ atṛptaṃ* ? (S)
39.16 *ratipradānaṃ; ratipradhānaṃ* (F)
39.20 *yaṣṭiratna°; yaṣṭīratna°* MS, *ṣaṣṭī ratna°* (E)
40.6 *satvasyāpanāyaṃ; satvasyāmanāpaṃ* (S)
40.9 *aśvaśo dhanaṃ; aśvarathagoḍanaṃ* (S)
40.14 *puṣkariṇī; puṣkiriṇī* (J)
41.2 et 41.3 *dūṣya; duṣya* (E)
41.6 *aśītisahasrapralambitaṃ; aśītisahasraratnajālapralambitaṃ* (E), plutôt *aśītiratnajālasahasrapralambitaṃ* (J)
41.18 *vṛddhyaḥ; mṛdvaṅgyaḥ* (S)
42.1 *vadhyaḥ puruṣo dṛṣṭvā; vadhyaḥ puruṣo vadhakaṃ dṛṣṭvā* (S)
42.8 *tenopasaṃkramyāśrumukhaḥ; tenopasaṃkrāmanupasaṃkramyāśrumukhaḥ* (E)
42.11 *kṣayānte; kṣayāṃ te* (S)
42.16 *anyaiś; adya* (S)
42.17 *svaraṅga°; svarāṅga°* (S, J)
43.6 *varāsṛtāni; varāstṛtāni* MS (E)
43.8 *kriyānte; kriyante* MS (E)
43.10 *krīḍā sakhāya; krīḍāsakhāya* (S)
44.1 *svapnāya mābhiratayo; svapnāsamābhiratayo* (E), *svapnopamābhiratayo* (J)
44.6 *ahamaprakampyaḥ; iha aprakampyaḥ* (E)
44.10 *tribhave; tṛbhave* (E)
45.3 *andhe cakṣurapi; andhe ca cakṣurapi* ? (E)
45.11 *anusrota sarvajagatī pratisrotā; anuśrota sarvajagatī pratiśrota* MS (E)
45.13 *pārthiva varasvajanena; pārthivavara svajanena* (S)
46.4 *karuṇā; karuṇa* m.c. (E)
46.4 *evabhipṛcche; evābhipṛcche* MS (E)
46.5 *gacchetātrāntarikṣe; gacchethātrāntarikṣe* MS, *gacchathātrāntarikṣe* (E)

46.14 *śūnyo; sūryo* (E)
46.16 *sahasraṃ vai; sa hasan vai* ? (S)
46.17 *citrasuśuklā; citrāsuśuklā* MS (E)
46.18 *jinavarapravarasya; jinavarapravarasyā* m.c. (E)
47.4 *amararucisvarā; amararucirasvarā* MS, *amararutisvarā* (E)
47.7 *bodhanī;* T *śodhanī* (J)
47.11 *pariṇatāśca; pariṇatāścā* m.c. (E)
47.12 *uru; ūru* m.c. (E)
48.1 *viṣaya°; viṣama°* (L)
49.4 *cirādadya; cirāndhena* (S)
49.6 *devatātyaḥ; devatābhyaḥ* (L, E)
49.11 *vimati; vimatī* m.c. (E)
51.3 *bhagavanna samā; bhagavann asama* (E)
51.18 *°yuktiśaitar°; °yuktiśatair°* (F)
52.3 *°parivedaśataiḥ; °paridevaśataiḥ* (F)
52.4 *parimocayan; parimocayaṃ* MS (E)
52.6 *mārgam; mārgaṃ* MS, *mārgavaraṃ* (E)
52.9 *hyakarṣaya; hyakarkaśa* (S)
52.11 *satyārjavakṣayam; satyārjavākṣayam* MS (E)
52.15 *balacakra vartyapi; balacakravartyapi* (F)
53.5 *puṇyādhikasya; puṇyārthikasya* (S, J)
53.6 *bodhicarām; bodhivarāṃ* (E)
53.11 *kīrti; kīrtī* m.c. (E)
53.15 *labdhvā; labdhā* MS (E)
53.18 *yadārcitam; yadarjitam* (E)
54.9 *prāṇa°; prāṇi°* (S)
54.18 *yaṣṭyā; yaṣṭvā* MS ? (E)
54.20 *candrārka°; candrakānta°* (S)
55.5 *śikṣāṃ; śikṣāṃś* MS, *śikṣaṃś* (E)
55.14 *varṇanāyakā; varṇa nāyakā* (E)
55.16 *sati; muni* (S)
56.12 *niryatayati; niryātayati* (L)
57.18 *bhikṣuṇā buddhasahasrasya; bhikṣuṇā parigṛhītaḥ. etenopāyena caturnavatīnāṃ buddhakoṭiniyutānāṃ buddhasahasrasya* MS (E)
58.13 *aprameye; aprāmeye* m.c. (E)
58.13 *daśabalacalite;* T *daśabalacarite* (S, J)
58.15 *kṣetrārthaṃ; jñātrārthaṃ* (S)
58.19 *priyavadatāṃ; priyavad etāṃ* MS (E)
59.4 *ridhyate; sidhyate* (S)

59.7 *paṭapaṃśī; parapaṃśi* MS (E)
59.11 *bhevitāraḥ; bhavitāraḥ* (F)
59.13 *rāṣṭrapālabodhisatvaḥ; rāṣṭrapāla bodhisatvaḥ* (L)
59.14 *saṃcare; saṃvare* (E)
59.16 *śaṇanāmapi; gaṇanāmapi* (L), ainsi MS (E)
59.17 *sadevamānuṣāsurā yāśca; sadevamānuṣāsurāyāśca* (E)
59.19 *anupādāyāśravebhyaś; anutpādantapurvāṇy āśravebhyaś* MS (E)
59.20 *khalu; khalv* (E)

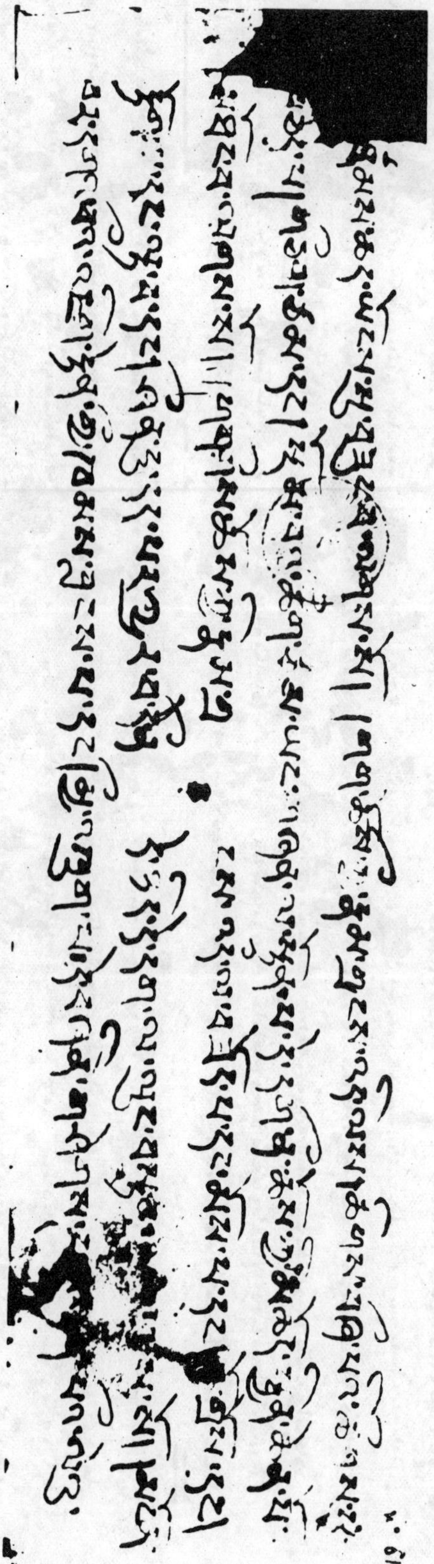

No. 611, Recto

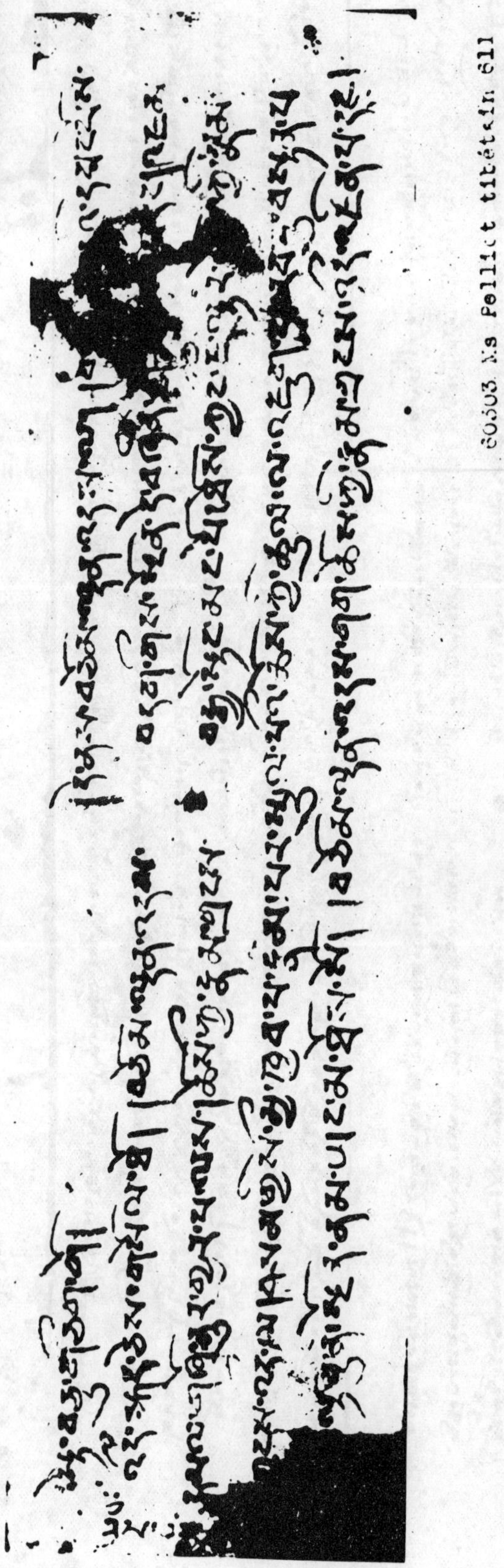

No. 611, Verso

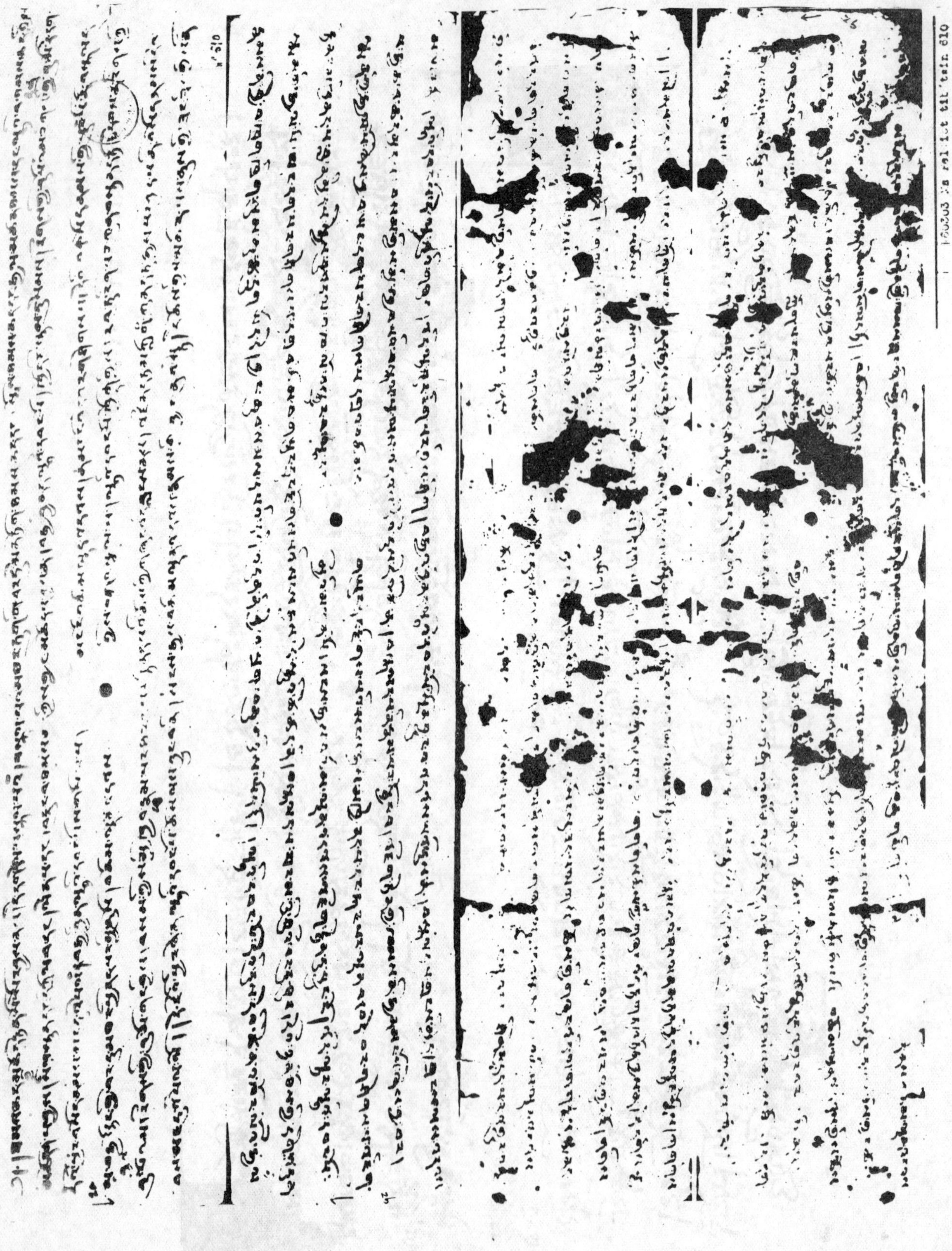

No. 610, f. 2, Recto   No. 610, f. 2, Verso   No. 610, f. 1, Recto   No. 610, f. 1, Verso

FONDS PELLIOT TIBÉTAIN N^{OS} 610 ET 611

par

J. W. de JONG

Sinologisch Instituut, Leiden

Parmi les manuscrits tibétains de Touen-houang conservés à la Bibliothèque Nationale de Paris trois ont été identifiés par Melle Lalou comme appartenant au Vimalakīrtinirdeśasūtra (*Inventaire des manuscrits tibétains de Touen-houang*, vol. I, Paris, 1939, N°s 610, 611 et 613). Comme la publication du dernier qui comprend 19 feuillets, occuperait trop de place, seuls les N°s 610 et 611 seront traités ici.

Le premier des deux feuillets du N° 610 contient la fin du onzième et le début du douzième chapitre et correspond à la fin du douzième et au début du treizième chapitre des traductions de Kumārajīva et de Hiuan-tsang (T. XIV, p. 555c^{21} -556a^{9} ; p. 585b^{27} -585c^{21}). Bien que ce feuillet soit assez abîmé, la confrontation avec le passage correspondant de la version tibétaine du Vimala° dans le Kandjour permet de reconstituer avec une assez grande vraisemblance les mots et les lettres qui manquent. Tout ce qui a été ainsi reconstitué est mis entre crochets [ ]. Des parenthèses ( ) enferment des lettres qui ne sont que partiellement lisibles mais dont la lecture est certaine. Les lettres dont la lecture est incertaine sont écrites en italique. Des points · indiquent le nombre approximatif des lettres qui manquent sans tenir compte des voyelles et des consonnes suscrites ou souscrites. Les lettres, biffées par le scribe, ont été marquées par un astérisque*. Pour le texte du Kandjour je me suis servi de l'édition de Narthang (N) conservée à la Bibliothèque Nationale de Paris et de l'édition de Lhasa (L) que j'ai pu consulter grâce à l'amabilité de M. G. Tucci (dans cette dernière édition le Vimala° se trouve dans la section mDo, vol. Pha, ff. 270b^{1} -376b^{3}). Je tiens à avertir le lecteur que je n'avais à ma disposition qu'une copie faite à la main de toute la version tibétaine du Vimala° il y a déjà plusieurs années, et que je n'ai pu consulter de nouveau les xylographes mêmes. Pour cette raison je n'ai pas hésité à changer à quelques endroits le texte de ma copie, en indiquant entre parenthèses ce que j'avais noté. Finalement je signale que la division en paragraphes a été établie afin de faciliter la comparaison des textes.

texte du Kandjour	N⁰ 610, feuillet 1
A. gaṅ dag thos nas mos pa daṅ/ yid ches pa daṅ/'dzin pa daṅ/'chaṅ ba daṅ/klog pa daṅ/kun chub par bgyid pa daṅ/mos nas ston pa daṅ/ rab tu 'don pa daṅ/gźan dag la 'aṅ 'chad pa daṅ/sgom pa'i rnal 'byor la rjes su sbyor ba rnams la lta soms kyaṅ ci 'tshal/	(Recto, l. 1) len pa daṅ ['dz] i (n) d pa daṅ/ klog pa da(ṅ) [ku] ndu rgyas par byed pa daṅ/śind tu dad pa la ston(d) pa da(ṅ)/sgyur ba daṅ gźan la yaṅ ston pa daṅ/sgom ba'i thub la nan tan byed pa·lta ji smos/
B. cḥos kyi rnam graṅs 'di gaṅ dag gi sug par thob par gyur pa de dag kyaṅ chos rin po che'i gter rñed par 'gyur ro//	gag gis (l. 2) chos gyi gźuṅ 'di lag tu 'oṅ · · de *la* chos · · · *m* · chog gi gter rab [t] u [th] ob pa l [ag] so /
C. gaṅ dag chos kyi rnam graṅs 'di kha ton du bgyid pa de dag kyaṅ de bźin (N 372b) gśegs pa'i grogs su gyur pa lags so//	de dag y [aṅ da] g pa(r) [g] śegs pa'i grogsu ' [gy] uro/gag gis chos gyi gźuṅ 'di rtag tu kha ton byas na/
D. gaṅ dag chos 'di la mos pa rnams la rim gro (L 367b) daṅ bsñen bkur bgyid pa de dag ni chos yaṅ dag par sruṅ ba lags so//	de dagis yaṅ (l. 3) [da] g par chos bsru[ṅ]bar 'g(yu)ro/gag gis · chos 'di n* a* la śi(n)[d tu dad pa d]e rnam · · g-yog · kun du spy [od pa] byas na
E. gaṅ dag chos kyi rnam graṅs 'di legs par bris te 'chaṅ ba daṅ ri mor bgyid pa de dag gi khyim na de bźin gśegs pa bźugs par 'gyur ro //	de dag gi khyim na yaṅ dag par gs-egs pa bźugs par 'gyur ro/gagis (l. 4) chos gyi gźuṅ ['d] i leg [s] par byas śi · · par byas te 'ch [aṅ bar] byed pa
F. gaṅ dag chos kyi rnam graṅs 'di la (LN las) rjes su yi raṅ ba de dag ni bsod nams thams cad yoṅs su bzuṅ (LN bsruṅ ?) ba lags so//	de [da]g ni bsod (n)[ams] tham[s cha]d yoṅsu zad pa lagso/chos gyi gźuṅ 'di la gag rjesu [s] mond (l. 5) pa
G. gaṅ dag chos kyi rnam graṅs 'di las tha na tshig bźi pa'i tshigs su bcad pa gcig tsam daṅ/sdom pa'i tshig tsam yaṅ gźan dag la ston pa de dag ni chos kyi mchod sbyin chen	'di dag gis ni cho [s gy] i sbyin ba chen [po] byin par 'gyuro/gagis chos [gyi gźuṅ 'di] · · · ṅ du na tshig bźi pa'i le'u gchig g · · la sdom źiṅ gźan la [yaṅ] bstand na/

po bgyidpa lags so//

H. gaṅ dag chos kyi rnam graṅs 'di la bzod pa daṅ/'dun pa daṅ/blo gros daṅ/rtogs pa daṅ/lta ba daṅ/mos pa dag ni de ñid de dag la luṅ bstan pa lags so//

bchom ldan 'da 's (l. 6) gyis rigs g[yi] bu po'am [ri]gs gyi bu m[o] de dag la luṅ bstan pa · · [ga]g [g]i[s] chos gyi gźuṅ 'di la [bz]o[d] pa da[ṅ] mos pa daṅ dga' ba daṅ · · · lta ba daṅ śin du dad par 'gyur ba [ya]ṅ (Verso, l. 1) d[e] bźin no/

I. 'jig rten gyi khams mṅon par dga' ba blaṅs pa daṅ/de bźin gśegs pa mi 'khrugs pa bstan pa'i le'u ste bcu gcig pa'o//

mṅon du dga['] ba'[i] ' [ji] g rten gyi khams blaṅ źin myi g-yos (p) a [']i [yaṅ] dag par gśegs pa kun gyis mtho(ṅ) [ba]'i le'u bchu gchig go//

Chapitre XII

J. de nas bcom ldan 'das la lha'i dbaṅ po brgya byin gyis 'di skad ces gsol to//

de nas bchom ldan 'da's (l. 2) la brgya' by[i]n (l)ha'[i] d [baṅ pos'] di skad ches gsold to //

K. bcom ldan 'das bdag gis sṅon de bźin gśegs pa daṅ/'jam dpal gźon nur gyur pa las chos kyi rnam graṅs (N 373a) brgya stoṅ maṅ po thos kyaṅ ji ltar chos kyi rnam graṅs 'di la (L las) rnam par sprul pa bsam gyis mi khyab pa'i tshul la 'jug pa rab tu bstan pa 'di lta bu ni sṅon nam yaṅ ma thos (L 368a) lags so//

bchom ldan 'da['s] bdag gi[s ya] ṅ dag [p]ar gśeg(s pa) daṅ/'jam d [pal] gźo nur gyur pa las chos gyi gźuṅ brgya' stoṅ du mar thos gyaṅ cho [s] (l.3) gyi gźuṅ [']di [lta] bur b[sta] n chin/bsam gyis myi khyab par chos gyi tshu [l] · · rnam [par sprul]d pas 'jug pa 'di lta bu (n)i sṅon ch* a*d* yoṅ th*o*s* ma b*m*y*o* thos so/

L. bcom ladn 'das sems can gaṅ dag chos kyi rnam graṅs 'di 'dzin pa daṅ/'chaṅ ba daṅ/klog pa daṅ/kun chub par bgyid pa de dag kyaṅ the tshom ma mchis par 'di lta bu'i chos kyi snod du 'gyur na/

bchom ldan 'da's gyis chos (l. 4) [gyi] gźuṅ 'di bla[ṅ]s pa [daṅ '] dz[i]nd pa (d)aṅ/klog pa daṅ kun la rgya [s] (p) ar bgyid pa (ni) gdon [mi] 'tsha' bar s [e] ms chan de dag/chos 'di 'dra ba'i snod du 'gyur bar mchi na'/

M. gaṅ dag bsgom pa'i rnal 'byor la rjes su sbyor ba rnams la smos kyaṅ ci 'tshal te/

(l. 5) [ga] gis bsgom ba'i sbyor ba · · · nan tan du '[g]yu[r] ba lta (ji) smo ste/

N. de dag gis ṅan soṅ thams cad ṇi bcad/

de dag gis [ṅan] s(o)[ṅ] thams chad ni [b](ch)ad/

O. de dag gis bde 'gro'i lam thams cad ni phye/	de dagi[s] bde bar 'gro ba'i laṃ ni 'pye'o
P. de dag saṅs rgyas thams cad kyis ni gzigs/	de dag gi(s) '* saṅs rgyas thams chad mtho[ṅ] /
Q. de dag gis phas kyi rgol ba thams cad ni bcom/	de dag (l. 6) (g)is smra [ba] thams [chad] gnod pa'o/
R. de dag gis bdud thams cad ni śin tu pham par bgyis/	de dag [g]i(s) bdud thams chad śin du btuld/
S. de dag gis byaṅ chub sems dpa'i lam ni rnam par sbyaṅs/	de dagis [byaṅ] chu[b] (s)em[s] dpa'i lam ni rnam par sbyaṅso/
T. de dag byaṅ chub kyi sñiṅ po la ni gnas/	de dag ni bya[ṅ] chub gyi dkyi(l) ['](kh)or

Avant de reproduire le texte du deuxième feuillet du N⁰ 610 il me paraît préférable de donner d'abord le texte du N⁰ 611 puisque l'unique feuillet de ce numéro correspond à la partie de milieu du feuillet précédent, en commençant par les mots *thams cad* du paragraphe F et terminant par les mots *'dzin pa daṅ* du paragraphe L.

N⁰ 611

F. (recto, l. 1) thams chad yoṅs su bzuṅ ba lags so //

G. gag chos kyi rnam graṅs 'di las tshigs bźi pa'i tshigs su (l. 2) bcad pa / gcig tsam daṅ/sdom ba'i tshig tsam yaṅ gźan la ston pa de dag ni chos kyi mchod sbyin chen po (l. 3) mthoṅ ba lags so //

H. gag gis chos kyi rnam graṅs 'di la bzod pa daṅ mos pa daṅ/blo gros daṅ / (l. 4) rtog (pa) daṅ lta ba daṅ 'śin du dad par gyur ba de ni de ñid de dag la luṅ bstan [pa] l[ag]s so //

I. mṅon (l. 5) bar dga' ba'i 'jig rten gyi khams blaṅs pa daṅ/myi 'khrug pa de bźin gśegs pa [bs] tan pa'i le'u (Verso, l. 1) ste bcu gcig go //

Chapitre XII

J. de nas bcom ldan 'das la // brgya (b)y[i](n) lha'i dbaṅ pos (l. 2) 'di skad ces gsol tho //

K. bcom ldan 'das bdag gis sṅon de bźin g[śegs] pa daṅ/'jam (l. 3) dpal gźo nur gyur pa las / chos kyi rnam graṅs brgya stoṅ maṅ po thos kyaṅ ji ltar chos kyi rnam (l. 4) g [r] aṅs 'di la/bsam gyis myi khyab pa rnam par sprul pa'i chos kyi tshul la 'jug pa rab du bstan pa (l. 5) ['di] lta bu ni sṅon nam yaṅ ma thos so //

L. bcom ldan 'das gag chos kyi rnam graṅs 'di 'dzin pa daṅ /

Le deuxième feuillet du N⁰ 610 contient un fragment du douzième chapitre et correspond à une partie du treizième chapitre des traductions de Kumārajīva et de Hiuan-tsang (T. XIV, p. $556a^{22}$-$556b^{7}$; p. $556a^{14}$-$586b^{5}$). Entre le premier et le deuxième feuillet du N⁰ 610 il ne doit en manquer qu'un seul comme la comparaison avec le texte du Kandjour et les traductions chinoises le fait ressortir.

texte du Kandjour	N⁰ 610, feuillet 2
A. de bźin gśegs pa thams cad kyi mchod rten so sor byas nas des de la bskal pa 'am/bskal pa las lhag par me tog thams cad daṅ/spos thams cad daṅ/rgyal mtshan thams cad daṅ/ba dan thams cad kyis mchod pa byas śiṅ (LN źiṅ) rṅa daṅ sil sñan rnams brduṅs te mchod na/lha'i dbaṅ po 'di ji sñam du sems/rigs kyi bu 'am/ rigs kyi bu mo de dag de'i gźi las bsod nams (N 374b) maṅ bu bskyed dam/	(Recto, l. 1) thams chad gyi mchod rten so sor byas nas/de dag de la bskal pa'aṃ/bskal pa'i mthar tug gi bar du men tog thams chad daṅ/spos thams chad daṅ rgyal mtshan thams daṅ lha'i ba dan thams chad gyis (l. 2) mchodn pa byas/sil sñan daṅ dkrol ba daṅ/len pa daṅ/brduṅ ba thams chad gyis gyaṅ mchod pa byas na/brgya byind lha'i dbaṅ po/khyod ji sñam du sems/rigs. gyi bu po'am rigs gyi bu mo de dag (l. 3) de'i pyir bsod nams maṅ du 'pelaṃd* /
B. gsol pa/bcom ldan 'das maṅ lags so//bde bar gśegs pa maṅ lags te/bskal pa bye ba brgya stoṅ gis kyaṅ bsod nams kyi phuṅ po de'i mthar phyin par mi nus lags so //	brgya byin lha'i dbaṅ pos gsol pa / maṅ ṅo bchom ldan 'da's/n*a* maṅ ṅo bde bar gśegs pa / de'i bch* sod nams gyi puṅ po ni bskald (l. 4) pa bye ba brgya stoṅ gyi bar du mthar pyind par myi nuso/
C. bcom ldan 'das kyis bka' stsal pa / lha'i dbaṅ po / khyod mos par bya'o//khyod kyis khoṅ du chud par (L 369b) bya'o//gaṅ rnam par thar	bchom ldan 'da's gyis bka' stsal pa / lha'i dbaṅ po khyog*d gyis/rab tu rig par kun bstand to/de bas na rigs gyi (l. 5) bu po'am/rigs gyi bu mo

pa bsam gyis mi khyab pa bstan pa'i
chos kyi rnam graṅs 'di 'dzin tam /
/ klog gam / kun chub par byed pa'i
rigs kyi bu pho 'am / rigs kyi bu mo
bsod nams śin tu maṅ du bskyed
do//

gaṅ gyis / bsam gyis myi khyab pa
rnam par thard₄par stoṅd pa'i chos
gyi gźuṅ 'di blaṅs nas / 'dzind tam
klogaṃ kuṅd tu rgyas par byed pa
ni bsod nams de'i (l. 6) bas maṅ du
'pel lo//

D.   de ci'i phyir źe na / lha'i dbaṅ
po / saṅs rgyas bcom ldan 'das rnams
kyi byaṅ chub ni chos las byuṅ ste /
de chos kyis (LN kyi) mchod par nus
kyi zaṅ ziṅ gis ni ma yin pa'i phyir
ro // lha'i dbaṅ po khyed kyis rnam
graṅs 'di (LN 'dis). kyaṅ 'di ltar rig
par bya ste /

de ji'i pyir źe na lha'i dbaṅ po chos
las byuṅ ba ni / saṅs rgyas bchom ldan
'da's rnams gyi byaṅ chub ste / de chos
gyis mchod pas nus gyi zaṅ ziṅ gyis
ni (Verso, l.1) ma yin no / lha'i dbaṅ
po de lta bu'i gźuṅ / 'di lta bur rig
par gyis śig /

E.   lha'i dbaṅ po / sṅon byuṅ ba
'das pa'i dus na bskal pa graṅs med
pa'i yaṅ ches graṅs med pa / rgya che
ba / tshad med pa / bsam gyis mi khyab
par gyur pa de'i dus de'i tshe na
bskal pa rnam par sbyoṅ ba la 'jig
rten gyi khams cher bkod par de
bźin gśegs pa / dgra bcom pa / yaṅ dag
par rdzogs pa'i saṅs rgyas / rig pa daṅ
źabs su ldan pa / bde bar gśegs pa /
'jig rten mkhyen pa / (N 375a) skyes
bu 'dul ba'i kha lo sgyur ba / bla na
med pa / lha daṅ mi rnams kyi stoṇ
pa / saṅs rgyas bcom ldan 'das sman
gyi rgyal po źes bya ba 'jig rten du
byuṅ ste //

brgya' byiṇd lha'i dbaṅ po sṅon byuṅ
ba 'da's pa'i dus n*a* / bskald pa
graṅs myed / graṅs las 'da's (l. 2) pa
rgya che ba tshad myed pa / bsam
gyis myi khyab pa'i bskal pa las 'da's
de'i dus de'i tshe na / bskald pa ni
rnam par sbyoṅ ba / 'jig rten gyi khams ni rgyan maṅ po źes bya bar / (l.
3) sman gyi rgyal po źes bya ba yaṅ
dag par gśegs pa dgra' bchom ba /
g-yuṅ druṅ rdzogs pa'i saṅs rgyas
mkhyend pa daṅ rkaṅ par ldan ba /
bde bar gśegs pa 'jig (l. 4) rtend
mkhyend pa bla na myed pa skyes
bu 'dul ba kha lo bsgyur ba lha daṅ
/ myi'i mkhan po / saṅs rgyas bchom
ldan 'da's 'jig rten du byuṅ ṅo /

F.   de bźin gśegs pa dgra bcom pa
yaṅ dag par rdzogs pa'i saṅs rgyas
sman gyi rgyal po de'i tshe'i tshad
ni bar gyi bskal pa ñi śur gyur to //

'di ltar lha'i dbaṅ po (l. 5) sman gyi
rgyal po / yaṅ dag par gśegs pa dgra
bchom ba g-yuṅ druṅ rdzogs pa'i
saṅs rgyas / de sku'i tshe tshad ni /
bskald pa bar ma ñi śu'i bar du
thub /

G.   de' i ñan thos kyi dge 'dun ni
bye ba khrag khrig phrag sum cu
rtsa drug yod do /

de'i ñan thos gyi dge 'dun (l. 6) rnams
ni bye ba khrag khrig sum chu rtsha
drug yod de /

H. byaṅ chub sems dpa'i dge 'dun ni (L 370a) bye ba khrag khrig phrag bcu gñis yod do //	byaṅ chub sems dpa'i dge 'dun ni bye ba prag bchu gñis yod do //
I. lha'i dbaṅ po de'i tshe de'i dus na 'khor los sgyur (L bsgyur) ba'i rgyal po	lha'i dbaṅ po de'i dus de'i tshe na 'khor lo'i rgyal

Quelle est la relation de ces textes de Touen-houang au texte du Kandjour? Si l'on compare le texte du N⁰ 611 à ce dernier, la ressemblance ressort clairement. Du point de vue orthographique il n'y a que de petites différences: *chad* au lieu de *cad* (F) ; *tshigs* a. l. d. *tshig* (G) ; *sdom-ba'i* a. l. d. *sdom-pa'i* (G) ; *rtog-pa* a. l. d. *rtogs-pa* (H) ; *mṅon-bar* a. l. d. *mṅon-par* (I) ; *myi-'khrug-pa* a. l. d. *mi-'khrugs-pa* (I) ; *tho* a. l. d. *to* (J) ; *gźo* a. l. d. *gźon* (K) ; *myi-khyab-pa* a. l. d. *mi-khyab-pa* (K). Quelques mots diffèrent: *mthoṅ-ba* a. l. d. *bgyid-pa* (G) ; *mos-pa* a. l. d. *'dun-pa* (H) ; *śin-du dad-par gyur-ba* a. l. d. *mos-pa* (H) ; *de* a. l. d. *dag* (H). En ce qui concerne la syntaxe il faut relever *gag-gis* a. l. d. *gaṅ-dag* (H); ordre différent des parties de la phrase (I) ; interversion de *brgya-byin* et *lha'i dbaṅ-po* (J) ; interversion de *bsam-gyis myi-khyab-pa* et *rnam-par sprul-pa* (K). Enfin il faut noter l'absence de *tha-na* entre *las* et *tshigs* (G) ; de *dag* entre *gźan* et *la* (G) ; de *lags* entre *thos* et *so* (K) et de *sems-can* entre *bcom-ldan-'das* et *gag* (L).

Tout autre est le résultat de la comparaison du texte du N⁰ 610 avec le texte du Kandjour. La divergence entre ces deux textes est considérable. Il est impossible de signaler ici toutes les différences orthographiques, grammaticales et lexicographiques. A titre d'exemple comparons la liste des épithètes du Buddha Bhaiṣajyarāja (610, f. 2, E): à *de-bźin-gśegs-pa* (tathāgata) correspond *yaṅ-dag-par gśegs-pa*, à *yaṅ-dag-par rdzogs-pa'i saṅs rgyas* (samyaksaṃbuddha) *g-yuṅ-druṅ rdzogs-pa'i saṅs-rgyas*, à *rig-pa daṅ źabs-su ldan-pa* (vidyācaraṇasaṃpanna) *mkhyend-pa daṅ rkaṅ-par ldan-ba*, à *lha daṅ mi-rnams-kyi ston-pa* (śāstṛ devānāṃ ca manuṣyānām) *lha daṅ myi'i mkhan-po*. Du point de vue syntactique il faut relever la construction de la phrase dans les paragraphes C-H du premier feuillet; la proposition principale précède la proposition relative, ce qui est entièrement contraire à la syntaxe du tibétain classique.

Le texte du Kandjour a été traduit par Dharmatāśila, un des compilateurs de la Mahāvyutpatti, et doit donc probablement dater du premier quart du neuvième siècle (sur la date de la compilation de la Mahāvyutpatti voir *Asiatica, Festschrift Friedrich Weller*, Leipzig, 1954, p. 312, n. 1). Déjà dans le plus ancien catalogue des traductions, celui du Palais de Ldan-kar, une traduction du Vimala° est mentionnée, intitulée *'Phags-pa dri-ma-med-par grags-pa bstan-pa*, en 1.800 śloka et 6 bam-po (cf. M. Lalou: Les textes bouddhiques au temps du roi Khri-sroṅ-lde-bcan, *Journal asiatique*, 1953, p. 322) qui ne peut guère être que celle due à Dharmatāśīla. Il n'est pas possible de savoir positivement si la traduction de Dharmatāśīla était connue à Touen-houang. Des traductions dues à ses contemporains Śīlendrabodhi, Dānaśīla et Ye-śes-sde (tous collaborateurs à la Mahāvyutpatti) se trouvent parmi les manuscrits de Touen-houang (cf. *Inventaire*, vol. 1. N°s 24, 51, 78, 99, 417, 551, 552 et 797). Certes, il est hors de doute que le scribe du N^0 610 n'a connu ni la traduction de Dharmatāśīla ni la Mahāvyutpatti. Les gaucheries du style rendent vraisemblable l'hypothèse que ce fragment fait partie d'une traduction établie à Touen-houang au début du travail de traduction à cet endroit. Or, les manuscrits tibétains de Touen-houang datent en gros de 800 à 1035 (cf. *Inventaire*, vol. 1. p. V) et il faudra donc placer cette traduction dans la première moitié du neuvième siècle. Mais, au contraire, le fragment N^0 611 ne peut être indépendant de la traduction de Dharmatāśīla. Quoique des différences entre ces deux textes existent, elles ne sont pas d'une telle grandeur qu'il faille admettre deux traductions distinctes. Il ne faut pas perdre de vue que la traduction de Dharmatāśīla ne nous est transmise que par des éditions du Kandjour, imprimées plusieurs siècles plus tard. Pendant cette période les traductions ont été soumises à un travail continu de révision et de correction. Si donc le fragment N^0 611 s'écarte sur plusieurs points de la traduction de Dharmatāśīla telle que les éditions imprimées la font connaître, cela peut très bien s'expliquer par des retouches ultérieures. Il n'est donc nullement exclu que le N°611 soit un fragment d'une copie de la traduction de Dharmatāśīla, établie soit au Tibet central soit à Touen-houang même. L'existence, parmi les fragments de Touen-houang, de deux traductions du Vimala°, l'une venue de Tibet central et l'autre faite sur place, est d'autant plus vraisemblable qu'il en est de même pour les grands Prajñāpāramitāsūtra comme Mlle Lalou l'a montré dans un article récent (Les manuscrits tibétains des grandes Prajñāpāramitā trouvés à Touen-houang, *Silver Jubilee Volume of the Zinbun-Kagaku-Kenkyusyo, Kyoto University*, 1954, p. 257-261).

Si importants que soient ces fragments de Touen-houang pour l'histoire des traductions tibétaines du Vimala°, ils ne livrent pas de nouveaux matériaux sur le texte original. Car si l'on compare le texte du N^0 610 avec celui du Kandjour, il paraît évident que les divergences sont dues aux traducteurs et non à différentes recensions du texte traduit. Il suffit de comparer les versions tibétaines de la fin du douzième chapitre avec le passage correspondant des traductions de Kumārajīva et de Hiuan-tsang pour voir à quel point ces deux traductions chinoises divergent entre elles et avec les versions tibétaines. Celles-ci reposent sur un même texte original qui doit s'écarter considérablement aussi bien du texte à la base de la traduction de Kumārajīva que de celui à la base de la traduction de Hiuan-tsang.

ENCORE UNE FOIS LE FONDS PELLIOT TIBÉTAIN NO. 610

par
J. W. DE JONG
A.N.U., Canberra

Parmi les textes tibétains de Touen-houang à Paris il y a plusieurs manuscrits fragmentaires de traductions tibétaines du *Vimalakīrtinirdeśasūtra.* Dans un article, intitulé "Fonds Pelliot Tibétain Nos. 610 et 611" (*Studies in Indology and Buddhology presented in Honour of Professor Susumu Yamaguchi on the Occasion of his Sixtieth Birthday*, Kyoto, 1955, pp. 60-67), j'ai édité deux de ces manuscrits Fonds Pelliot tibétain nos. 610 et 611 en les comparant avec le texte de la traduction tibétaine du *Vimalakīrtinirdeśasūtra* (abrégé: *V.*) dans le *Kanjur* (abrégé: *Kj.*) d'après les éditions de Narthang et de Lhasa. Récemment, M. Roy Andrew Miller a étudié de nouveau le manuscrit no. 610 et a proposé une reconstitution d'une partie du texte de ce manuscrit.[1]

Le manuscrit no. 610 comprend deux feuillets. Le premier contient la fin du chapitre XI et le début du chapitre XII. Pour faciliter la comparaison de ce feuillet avec le texte du *Kanjur* j'avais découpé le texte du *Kanjur* en paragraphes indiqués par les lettres A, B, C, etc. La fin du chapitre XI comprend les paragraphes A-I, le début du chapitre XII les paragraphes J-K. En comparant pour la fin du chapitre XII le texte du *Tanjur*, les manuscrits No. 610 et 611 et les versions chinoises de Kumārajīva et de Hiuan-tsang j'étais arrivé à la conclusion suivante:

> il suffit de comparer les versions tibétaines de la fin du douzième chapitre avec le passage correspondant des traductions de Kumārajīva et de Hiuan-tsang pour voir à quel point ces deux traductions chinoises divergent entre elles et avec les versions tibétaines. Celles-ci reposent sur un même texte original qui doit s'écarter considérablement aussi bien du texte à la base de la traduction de Kumārajīva que de celui à la base de la traduction de Hiuan-tsang.

Cette conclusion qui est citée par M. Miller (p. 45) ne pourrait pas être

[1] "Apropos of the Fonds Pelliot Tibétain No. 610 Fragment of the Tibetan *Vimalakīrtinirdeśasūtra*", *CAJ*, X, 1965, pp. 44-54.

maintenue si la reconstitution de la fin du chapitre XI dans le manuscrit No. 160, proposée par lui, était acceptable. Car le texte reconstitué des paragraphes C-H ne correspond plus du tout aux paragraphes correspondants du texte du *Kj.*

Dans mon article, cité ci-dessus, j'avais constaté que, en comparant le texte des paragraphes C-H du No. 610 et du *Kj.*, la construction de la phrase dans No. 610 est surprenante car la proposition principale y précède la proposition relative. A ce propos M. Miller remarque:

> This would indeed be a significant linguistic feature, and any anomaly of this proportion and category would be a valuable clue to the development of "Classical Tibetan", so that the passages concerned certainly merit a second look. (p. 45)

Sans aucun doute, ces passages méritent d'être étudiés de près. Il faut savoir gré à M. Miller de les avoir examinés si minutieusement. Toutefois, il faut observer d'abord que la remarque de M. Miller dépasse beaucoup la portée de mes observations qui étaient limitées à constater par une comparaison du no. 610 et du *Kj.* la correspondance des deux textes et le fait de l'ordre anormal de la proposition principale et de la proposition relative dans le no. 610. Je n'avais pas du tout expliqué cette anomalie par une particularité linguistique du tibétain pré-classique comme l'implique la remarque de M. Miller. On pourrait aussi bien expliquer cette anomalie par une inadvertence du scribe qui, en copiant un autre manuscrit, aurait inversé les propositions principales et relatives. Le but de mon article était purement philologique et ne consistait qu'en une comparaison de deux manuscrits de Touen-houang avec le texte du *Kj.*

En lisant l'article de M. Miller on a l'impression qu'il a été frappé par cette anomalie syntactique. Ensuite il a entrepris de l'éloigner en proposant une reconstitution du texte dont j'avais simplement reproduit les leçons du manuscrit. Si, du point de vue linguistique, M. Miller arrive à des conclusions différentes des miennes établies du point de vue philologiques, il faudra reconsidérer le problème des deux points de vue. Bien que M. Miller souligne lui-même l'importance d'un examen "both from the philological and the linguistic standpoints" (p. 45), c'est certainement le point de vue linguistique qui domine dans son travail. Dans un travail excellent auquel se réfère M. Miller M. Nils Simonsson a soigneusement comparé deux versions tibétaines du *Saddharmapuṇḍarīka*, l'une en tibétain pré-classique, l'autre en tibétain classique.[2] Comme le relève

[2] *Indo-tibetische Studien. Die Methoden der tibetischen Übersetzer, untersucht im Hinblick auf die Bedeutung ihrer Übersetzungen für die Sanskritphilologie*, I (Uppsala 1957).

M. Miller, M. Simonsson a trouvé très peu d'exemples qui attestent des changements radicaux dans la langue tibétaine. Dans le cas qui nous concerne il s'agit d'un passage en prose. M. Miller remarque très justement que:

... since Simonsson is almost solely concerned with metrical texts where the 'pāda-pāda-Regel' of word-for-word and line-for-line translation severely restricts the scope of syntactic possibilities open to the translators, the number of extra-linguistic considerations which may well have influenced the choice of a syntactic pattern in his material in any given instance is unfortunately a matter for serious concern. (p. 47)[3]

A vrai dire, je ne crois pas que, du point de vue linguistique, on ait comparé en détail des versions de textes en prose en tibétain préclassique et en tibétain classique. L'étude des textes de Touen-houang s'est concentrée surtout sur les textes non-traduits. Pour autant que l'on ait étudié les textes traduits, c'est surtout du point de vue philologique qu'on s'en est occupé. Il faudra espérer que l'exemple de M. Simonsson inspirera d'autres travaux dans ce domaine.

Dans no. 610 la proposition relative commence partout avec le mot *gag*. Selon M. Miller:

Simonsson has examined in detail a considerable number of cases in which there appear to be greater or lesser differences in syntactic usage between later texts and the Tun-huang manuscripts; in these *gañ* and *dag* interestingly enough generally appear in what later became the unknown sandhi-forms *gag* and *dañ* before velars including *ḥ* thus **gañ > gag gis*, **gañ > gag gnas*, and *de *dag > dañ ḥgros*. (p. 47)

Il faut évidemment corriger *ḥgros* en *ḥgrogs*. M. J. Bacot[4] et M. Simonsson qui le cite (p. 20) admettent que *gag* représente *gaṅ*. Toutefois, si l'on regarde de près les exemples de *gag* dans le livre de Simonsson, on verra que partout *gag* ne représente pas *gaṅ* mais *gaṅ-dag*, cf. p. 29 *ye ʾnuśikṣā sahāyakāḥ — slob paʼi grogs po gag yin baʼo*; p. 82: dans la stance 29 *gag gis* (skt. *ye*) correspond à *de dag* (skt. *te*) dans la stance 28 (ici la version tibétaine suit le texte sanskrit en mettant la proposition principale devant la proposition relative!); p. 103: *gag* (skt. *ye*) correspond à *de dag gi* (skt. *teṣām*); p. 109: *gag* traduit skt. *ye*. Dans tous ces cas *gag* est une contraction de *gaṅ-dag*. Il est donc incorrect de dire que *gag* est une

[3] Dans la référence au travail de Simonsson corriger p. 16 en p. 26 (*CAJ*, X, p. 47, n. 16).

[4] J. Bacot, F. W. Thomas, Ch. Toussaint, *Documents de Touen-houang relatifs à l'histoire du Tibet* (Paris, 1940-1946), p. 192: *gag* = *gaṅ*, quel.

forme de sandhi pour *gaṅ* devant vélaires inclus *ḥ*.[5] En ce qui concerne *daṅ* je ne crois pas que M. Simonsson (ou un autre tibétologue) ait affirmé l'équivalence de *daṅ* avec *dag*. Dans les deux exemples, cités par M. Miller, *daṅ* sert à rendre le sociatif du sanskrit: *saṃstavaṃ tair vivarjayet* — *de daṅ 'grogs pa rnam par spaṅ*; *varjayet tehi saṃstavam* — *de daṅ 'grogs pa spaṅ par bya'* (Simonsson, pp. 47 et 48). Dans le *Kanjur* on trouve: *de dag 'dris byed rnam par spaṅ*; *de dag rnams daṅ 'dris byed spaṅ*.[6] Dans le premier cas il y a *de dag* au lieu de *de daṅ*. Le même phénomème s'observe dans la stance 8 (Simonsson, p. 42): *de daṅ 'grogs pa rnam par spaṅ*; *Kanjur*: *de dag 'dris byed rnam par spaṅ*. Ici M. Simonsson suppose que, probablement, *de dag* a été employé pour indiquer clairement qu'il s'agit d'un pluriel. Il est évident que *de dag 'bris byed* équivaut à *de dag daṅ 'bris byed* puisque, dans les stances, ce *daṅ* sociatif peut être omis. M. Simonsson n'a pas jugé nécessaire d'attirer l'attention sur ce fait qui est généralement connu. Si M. Miller avait consulté le texte sanskrit ou avait eu quelque expérience de textes métriques, il n'aurait pas proposé une telle interprétation aberrante de *daṅ*.

Si, en suivant l'exemple de M. Miller, on indique dans les paragraphes B-H la proposition relative par **a**. et la proposition principale par **b**., les textes du No. 610 et du *Kj*. pourront être comparés de la manière suivante:

No. 610	*Kj.*
B a-b	B a-b
C b-a	C a-b
D b-a	D a-b
E b-a	E a-b
F b-a	F a-b
G b-a	G a-b
H b-a	H a-b

Pour éloigner l'anomalie dans l'ordre de **b**. et **a**. dans les paragraphes C-H M. Miller propose deux remèdes. Le premier est de supposer que C. **b**. a été précédé d'une proposition relative qui manque dans le manuscrit. Le deuxième est de diviser H. **a**. en une proposition relative et une proposition principale H". **a**. et H". **b**. M. Miller remarque que, dans le

[5] Pour *gag* = *gaṅ-dag* voir aussi mon compte rendu de L. de La Vallée Poussin, *Catalogue of the Tibetan Manuscripts from Tun-huang in the India Office Library* (Oxford, 1962), *IIJ*, X, 1966, p. 308. On ne peut pas dire que, dans les textes de Touen-houang, *gag* ne soit jamais employé pour *gaṅ* car il faudrait d'abord étudier tous les exemples de *gag*. Les textes cités qu'on pourrait facilement multiplier (cf. aussi No. 611 G, H et L) suggèrent que, en règle générale, *gag* doit être interprété comme équivalent à *gaṅ-dag*.

[6] M. Miller ne semble pas avoir remarqué que, dans cet exemple, le *Kanjur* a conservé *daṅ* et que *de dag rnams daṅ* correspond à *de daṅ*.

No. 610, H est: "suspiciously longer than the Kanjur equivalent text with which it has been aligned" (p. 48). Regardons de près ces deux textes en les juxtaposant comme l'a fait M. Miller:

H.	H.
bchom ldan ḥdaḥs (l. 6) gyis rigs g[yi] bu poḥam [ri]gs gyi bu m[o] de dag la luṅ bstan pa ... [ga]g [g]i[s] chos gyi gźuṅ ḥdi la [bz]o[d] pa da[ṅ] mos pa daṅ dgaḥ ba daṅ ... lta ba daṅ śin du dad par ḥgyur ba [ya]ṅ (Verso, l. 1) d[e] bzin no/[7]	**a**. gaṅ dag chos kyi rnam graṅs ḥdi la bzod pa daṅ/ḥdun pa daṅ/blo gros daṅ/rtogs pa daṅ/lta ba daṅ/mos pa **b**. dag ni de ñid de dag la luṅ bstan pa lags so//

Remarquons tout d'abord qu'il est étrange de voir commencer la proposition principale de H. *Kj.* après *mos pa*. If faut supposer qu'il s'agit d'une faute d'impression et que la proposition principale commence après *dag ni*. En comparant les textes du No. 610 et du *Kj*., il est évident que la plus grande longueur du No. 610 est causée par les mots *bchom ldan ḥdaḥs gyis rigs g[yi] bu poḥam [ri]gs gyi bu mo* qui n'ajoutent rien d'essentiel. Si l'on ôte ces mots la différence de plus de deux lignes ("a good two full lines longer", p. 48) disparaîtra tout de suite. Tout cela est passé sous silence par M. Miller qui arrive à couper H en trois propositions: une proposition principale, une proposition relative et une proposition principale, **b**. - **a**. - **b**. de la manière suivante:

H". **b**. bchom ldan ḥdaḥs gyis rigs [gy]i bu poḥam [ri]gs gyi bu m[o] de dag la luṅ bstan pa ⟨lags so/⟩
H". **a**. [ga]g gis chos gyi bźuṅ ḥdi la [bz]o[d] pa da[ṅ] mos pa daṅ dgaḥ ba daṅ ⟨rtogs pa *? or* ḥdun pa *?* da⟩ṅ lta ba daṅ
H". **b**. śin du dad par ḥgyur ba [ya]ṅ (Verso, l. 1) d[e] bźin no/

On ne comprend pas comment M. Miller peut proposer H" **ab** comme une phrase normale puisque **a**. se termine par *daṅ* et **b**. ne contient aucun élément qui correspond à *gag gis* dans **a**. Du point de vue linguistique une telle reconstitution est inacceptable aussi longtemps que M. Miller n'arrive pas à prouver que de telles phrases sont normales dans le tibétain pré-classique.

Du point de vue philologique la reconstitution, proposée par M.

[7] Sur plusieurs points M. Miller critique mon édition de ce passage. Ma transcription fut établie à Paris sur la base du manuscrit original. Je ne dispose que d'une photocopie qui ne permet pas d'étudier tous les détails relevés par M. Miller. Il n'est pas nécessaire de discuter les leçons proposées car elles ne changent rien aux objections que soulève la reconstitution du texte du No. 610.

Miller, est encore moins défendable. Comparons ce texte reconstitué avec le texte du *Kanjur*:

Texte reconstitué	*Kanjur*
B a-b	B a - b
C a [manquant]-b	O - C b
D a-b	C a - D b
E a-b	D a - E b
F a-b	E a - F b
G a-b	F a - G b
H' a-b	G a - H b
H" a-b	H a - O

La comparaison de ces deux textes montre que le texte reconstitué contient une proposition relative (C. **a**.) et une proposition principale (H"**b**.) qui n'ont pas de contrepartie dans le texte du *Kanjur*. Aux phrases D-H' correspondent des phrases dans le texte du *Kanjur* à condition que l'on les réarrange complètement. On constate que, dans le texte reconstitué, D. **a**. correspond à C. **a**. et D. **b**. à D. **b**. et ainsi de suite. Dans tous ces cas la proposition relative du texte reconstitué ne correspond pas à celle que précède la proposition principale dans le texte du *Kanjur* mais à la proposition relative de la phrase précédente. Ces différences considérables entre le texte reconstitué et le texte du *Kanjur* appellent une explication que M. Miller n'essaie pas de nous fournir. Seulement à propos de la proposition relative C. **a**. manquante il suggère la possibilité d'une "well-understandable contamination with the contents of the Urtext represented for us in CH 5. **a**, CK 2. **a**. Ch 3. **a**, and TxKdeJ C. **a**" (CH = la traduction de Hiuan-tsang, CK = celle de Kumārajīva, TxKdeJ = mon édition du texte du Kanjur) (p. 51).

Si l'on compare les traductions de Hiuan-tsang et de Kumārajīva avec le texte complet (et non seulement avec une partie du premier feuillet) du No. 610 et le texte correspondant du *Kanjur*, il est évident que, exception faite pour l'inversion des propositions dans les paragraphes C-H du premier feuillet, il y a trois recensions différentes: (A) la recension représentée par la traduction de Kumārajiva; (B) la recension représentée par la traduction de Hiuan-tsang; (C) la recension représentée par le No. 610 et le *Kanjur* (auquel on peut ajouter le No. 611). Il ne me paraît pas nécessaire de reproduire in extenso les textes en question que l'on trouvera facilement dans mon article, l'article de M. Miller, la traduction du *V*. par M. Lamotte, *L'enseignement de Vimalakīrti* (Louvain, 1962), pp. 367-376 et dans *Taishō* nos. 475 et 476. Les textes du No. 610 et du *Kanjur* ne se différencient que par quelques petits détails comme l'addition des mots "par le Bhagavat" et "le fils de famille ou la fille de famille" dans H comme il est indiqué ci-dessus. Ces différences ne proviennent pas d'une recension différente comme c'est le cas pour les textes traduits par Kumārajīva et Hiuan-tsang. Le texte du *Kanjur* a été traduit au Tibet même par Dharmatāśīla, un des compilateurs de la *Mahāvyutpatti.* Le no. 610 n'utilise pas le vocabulaire de la *Mahāvyutpatti.* Il est possible qu'il s'agit d'une recension primitive de la traduction de Dharmatāśīla revue plus tard après la compilation de la *Mahāvyutpatti.* Il se peut aussi que le No. 610 ait été traduit à Touen-houang où il fut trouvé. Dans ce dernier cas, le texte à la base aurait pu être une traduction chinoise. Dans le *Descriptive Catalogue of the Chinese Manuscripts from Tunhuang in the British Museum* (London, 1957) on trouvera plus de 230 manuscrits de traductions chinoises du *V.* (Nos. 3281-3514). Lionel Giles les rattache tous à la traduction de Kumārajīva. Les indications trop brèves du catalogue ne permettent pas de vérifier cette affirmation, mais nous savons que la traduction du *V.* par Kumārajīva a été extrêmement populaire comme la plupart de ses autres traductions. Si l'on avait trouvé une traduction tibétaine basée sur celle de Kumārajīva, cela n'aurait eu rien de surprenant. Cependant le No. 610 s'écarte essentiellement de la traduction de Kumārajīva comme de celle de Hiuan-tsang. Il n'est pas raisonnable de supposer que le no. 610 soit traduit sur une recension chinoise inconnue. Une contamination avec le texte du *Kanjur* et les traductions de Kumārajīva et de Hiuan-tsang comme le suppose M. Miller est difficile à imaginer. On ne voit pas bien comment et où elle aurait pu être réalisée et, par quel chemin, elle aurait pu résulter dans le texte du No. 610. Aucun exemple d'une telle contamination n'a été signalée jusqu'à maintenant. Il faudra certainement séparer nettement le No. 610 et le texte du *Kj.* des traductions chinoises. C'est la relation entre les deux traductions tibétaines qui pose un problème. Les textes correspondent étroitement même dans les paragraphes C-H où l'on retrouve les mêmes éléments mais dans un ordre différent. On peut faire toutes sortes de suppositions. Il ne paraît guère possible d'admettre que, dans le texte sanskrit des paragraphes C-H, la proposition principale, précédait la proposition relative car, dans un texte en prose, cela n'arrive presque jamais. S'agit-il d'une faute de traduction par le traducteur du No. 610 ou d'une erreur du scribe? Il vaut mieux, je crois, ne pas s'adonner au jeu des suppositions mais se borner à constater l'anomalie syntactique du No. 610 et réserver un essai d'explication au moment où les particularités des traductions en tibétain pré-classique seront mieux étudiées.

Lamotte, Étienne: **La concentration de la marche heroïque** (Śūraṃgamasamādhisūtra). Traduit et annoté. Bruxelles: Institut belge des Hautes Etudes chinoises 1965. XIII, 308 S. und 17 S. chines. Text. gr. 8⁰ = Mélanges chinois et bouddhiques, XIII, bfr. 650. – Bespr. von J. W. de Jong, Canberra, A. C. T.

Professor Lamotte's translation of the Chinese version of the Śūraṃgamasamādhisūtra adds another important work to his numerous contributions to Buddhist studies during the last three decades. His main publications include: "Saṃdhinirmocanasūtra" (1935), "Le traité de l'acte de Vasubandhu: Karmasiddhiprakaraṇa" (MCB, IV, 1936, pp. 151–288), "La somme du grand véhicule" (1938–1939), "Le traité de la grande vertu de sagesse" (1944–1949), "Histoire du bouddhisme indien. I" (1958), "Mañjuśrī" (TP, 48, 1961, pp. 1–96) and "L'enseignement de Vimalakīrti" (1962)[1]. The eminent qualities of his work are well-known to every student of Buddhism. Professor Lamotte has a profound knowledge of Buddhist literature in Sanskrit, Pāli, Tibetan and Chinese. He always returns to the original sources which are profusely quoted in the numerous and extensive notes accompanying his translations. A detailed index of all his publications would make it possible to obtain easy access to the encyclopaedic wealth of information provided on almost any aspect of Buddhism in India.

Professor Lamotte's translation of the Śgs. (= Śūraṃgamasamādhisūtra) shows again the astonishing range of his learning. The first chapter of the introduction (pp. 1–62) deals with the contents of the Śgs., the samādhi in the vehicles of the Śrāvakas and the Bodhisattvas, the place of the Śgs. in the literature of the Mahāyāna, and the sources of the Śgs. The second chapter studies in great detail the Chinese and Tibetan versions (pp. 63–112). The translation itself is furnished with no less than 357 notes several of which are in fact brief monographs on particular subjects.

The reader's attention is drawn to the following notes: 112 on the *bhūmis* (pp. 155–158), 119 on *kṣānti* (pp. 160–162), 138 on the wives of Śākyamuni (pp. 172 – 173)[2], 202 on the *vyākaraṇas* (pp. 202–205), 209 on

[1] An article, entitled "Vajrapāṇi en Inde", is announced in a note (p. 139, n. 79).

[2] This note expands a note of the "Traité" (vol. II, pp. 1001–1002, n. 1). As has been remarked by Demiéville in his review of volume II of the "Traité" (JA, 1950, p. 380, n. 1), this problem was earlier studied by Noël Peri: Les femmes de Çākyamuni, BEFEO, XVIII (1918), 2, pp. 1–35.

the *avaivartika* (pp. 208–210), 266 on *puṇyakṣetra* (pp. 231–233), 278 on the *bahuśruta* (pp. 236–237) and 299 on the *bhūmis* common to the Śrāvakas and the Bodhisattvas (pp. 246–251).

Extremely welcome are the detailed index, in which each Sanskrit term is translated, and the list of formulae and stereotyped phrases (pp. 277–302, 303–304).

In the following notes I would like to indicate a few points of detail relating to the chapter dealing with the Chinese and Tibetan versions, and to discuss some problems arising from Professor Lamotte's translation of Kumārajīva's version. These remarks, which may seem unduly critical, are in no way a reflection on Professor Lamotte's scholarship for which I have the highest regard. However, it seems to me that in the interest of the future development of Buddhist studies it is necessary to try to explain why, in some respects, this excellent work by an eminent scholar is not completely satisfactory. Such an explanation, if correct, may point to new methods to be elaborated and applied in the study of Chinese Buddhist texts.

L.'s study of the Chinese version of the Śgs. is an important contribution not only to the history of the Śgs. in China but also to that of Chinese Buddhism. L. lists all the indications of the Chinese catalogues concerning the Śgs., and presents a complete translation of the biographies of Chih Ch'an 支讖, Chih Ch'ien 支謙, Chu Fa-hu 竺法護 and Chu Shu-lan 竺叔蘭 in chapters 7 and 13 of the Ch'u san-tsang chi chi 出三藏記集 (T 2145) and of two important documents from chapter 7 of the same work: the notice of Chih Min-tu 支愍度 on the combined Śgs.s and an anonymous colophon of the translation of the Śgs. by Chang T'ien-hsi 張天錫, Chih Shih-lun 支施崙 and Po Yen 帛延[1]. These texts have been rendered with great precision and clarity. It is certainly no small merit for a scholar of Buddhism to have succeeded so well in the translation of texts which present great difficulties even to experienced Sinologists.

L.s notes on the Chinese catalogues (pp. 63–64) lean heavily on Demiéville's publications[2]. He has also adopted the latter's translation of the title of the Ch'u san-tsang chi chi as "Recueil de notes extraites des Trois Corbeilles" (cf. L'Inde classique, II, 1953 p. 459). In the Chinese catalogues and similar works the verb *ch'u* 出, when used in regard to texts, can often be rendered by "translate"[3]. This has been discussed at length apropos of Ware's and Hurvitz' translations of the Shih-lao-chih 釋老志 of the Wei Shou 魏書, cf. Chou I-liang 周一良, Shih-hsüeh nien-pao 史學年報 II, 4 (1937), pp. 183–184; Lien-sheng Yang, HJAS, 20 (1957), pp. 367 and 373. In his translation of the same text Tsukamoto Zenryū 塚本善隆 renders *ch'u* by *yakushutsu* 譯出 "translation" (Gi-sho Shaku-Rō-shi no kenkyū 魏書釋老志の研究, Kyōto, 1961, pp. 195 and 198). Zürcher, to whom I pointed out the remarks by Chou and Yang, accordingly translated Ch'u san-tsang chi chi as "Collection of notes concerning the translation of the Tripiṭaka" (The Buddhist Conquest of China, Leiden, 1959, p. 10)[1]. In support of this interpretation one may point to the fact that the position of *ch'u* before the word depending on it has become fixed, cf. for instance the expression *i-ch'u ching* 異出經 "differently translated sūtras", i. e. different Chinese versions of the same Indian original (T 2145, p. 13 c 22, cf. Demiéville, BEFEO, XXIV, 1924, p. 5, n. 1); T 2145, p. 62 b 24: 尋出經時 "When one studies the time of the translation of the sūtra".

The catalogues do not agree as to the number of translations of the Śgs. The Ch'u san-tsang chi chi (L. p. 64) enumerates seven translations, but the K'ai-yüan shih-chiao lu 開元釋教錄[2] (T 2153) lists nine (L. pp. 64–65)[3]. After enumerating the eight lost translations the author of the latter catalogue remarks 右八經同本前後九譯 "The preceding eight sūtras are based on the same original. There were altogether (litt. "before and after") nine translations". L. has misunderstood this sentence: Ces huit sūtra représentent un même original. Il y eut ensuite une neuvième traduction: [celle de Kumārajīva]. The difference between the two catalogues is due to the fact that the first does not mention the Hou-ch'u Shou-leng-yen ching 後出首楞嚴經 and the translation by Chang T'ien-shi and others[4]. Without stating his reasons, L. counts in all eight translations, taking the Shu Shou-leng-yen ching 蜀首楞嚴經 and the Hou-ch'u Shou-leng-yen ching as one translation (p. 104). According to the catalogues these two translations were made during the Ts'ao Wei (220–265). They are described as 曹魏失譯 "lost translations of the Ts'ao Wei". L. wrongly translates: traduction perdue sous les Ts'ao Wei (p. 65); Sous les Ts'ao Wei (220–265), on perdit la traduction (p. 73).

Tao-an 道安, however, seems to have known at least ten translations (a total which, of course, does not include Kumārajīva's). L. quotes from Tao-an's preface to his 合放光光讚略解 "Brief explication of the combined Fang kuang (T 221) and Kuang tsan (T 222)" (T 2145, p. 47 c 29–48 b 21) a passage in which Tao-an relates how he obtained from Liang-chou a copy of Dharmarakṣa's Kuang-tsan ching and made use of it for his commentary: 輒記其所長爲略解如左

[1] Hayashiya Tomojirō 林屋友次郎 attributes this colophon to Tao-an, cf. Iyaku kyōrui no kenkyū 異譯經の研究 (Tōkyō, 1945), p. 89.

[2] BEFEO, XXIV (1924), pp. 4–20; L'Inde classique, II (Paris-Hanoi, 1953), pp. 455, 459–460. There is no reference to these publications. The "Abréviations et éditions utilisées" (pp. VII–XII), which reproduce with only minor changes a similar list in "L'enseignement de Vimalakīrti" (pp. VII–XII), is a bibliography of Indian Buddhist texts rather than a list of texts and publications referred to explicitly or implicitly.

[3] L. reproduces a notice, translated by Maspero (JA, 1934, II, p. 94), in which he renders *ch'u* as "récita" (L. p. 67). L. seems to propose as an alternative the translation "transmet oralement" (p. 70). In other notices L. always renders *ch'u* as "traduire, publier". For the meaning of *ch'u* see also Richard H. Robinson, Early Mādhyamika in India and China (Madison, 1967), p. 298; Zürcher, op. cit., p. 202. A detailed study of the meaning of this word in Chinese Buddhist texts would be very welcome.

[1] Lien-sheng Yang pointed out that already in 1883 Nanjio Bunyiu had correctly translated this title as "A Collection of the Records of Translations of the Tripiṭaka" (Catalogue of the Chinese Translations of Buddhist Tripiṭaka, Oxford, 1883, p. 327), cf. HJAS, 17, 1954, p. 482.

[2] Not K'ai-yuan che-kiao mou-lou as given by L. (p. 64) who probably repeats an error to be found in the "Tables du Taishō Issaikyō" (Tōkyō, 1931), p. 123.

[3] L. quotes the lists of translations of the Śgs. which occur in the Ch'u san-tsang chi chi, the Li-tai san-pao chi (T 2034) and the K'ai-yüan shih-chiao lu. Similar lists are to be found in the Chung-ching mu-lu (T 2146, p. 119 c 1–10) and the Ta T'ang nei tien lu (T 2149, p. 252 c 23–24). The latter list is identical with the one in the Li-tai san-pao chi.

[4] Hayashiya (op. cit., pp. 86–94) has tried to explain the reasons for this omission. According to him the alleged translation of the Śgs., attributed to Po Yen 白延 of the Wei, never existed. The translation by Chang T'ien-hsi, Chih Shih-lun and Po Yen was wrongly attributed by the Pieh-lu 別錄 to Po Yen of the Wei. L. (p. 81) mentions the possibility of a confusion between Po Yen of the Wei and Po Yen of the Ch'ien Liang, but apparently is unaware that this problem had been thoroughly studied by Hayashiya.

"Immediately I noted down its excellent points and I composed this Brief Explication". L. translates: Aussitôt, j'en ai pris note et je l'ai largement utilisé dans la présente "Explication sommaire" (p. 100). The arrival of the Kuang-tsan ching in Hsiang-yang 襄陽 is recounted in more detail in a long letter concerning the Daśabhūmikasūtra (T 2145, p. 62 a 3–c 21). T'ang Yung-t'ung 湯用彤 (Han Wei liang-Chin nan-pei ch'ao fo-chiao shih 漢魏兩晉南北朝佛教史, Shanghai, 1938, p. 198), Hayashiya Tomojirō (op. cit., pp. 88–89) and Zürcher (op. cit., p. 196 and p. 392, n. 81) ascribe this letter to Tao-an. In it he relates how he obtained from Liang-chou the translation of the Śgs. by Chang T'ien-hsi[1]. Apropos of this new translation he declares: 首楞嚴經事事多於先者。非第一第二第九 "This Shou-leng-yen ching is in every respect more extensive than the preceding [translations] with the exception of the first, the second and the ninth". L. translates: Ce Cheou-leng-yen king, sur tous les points, est plus abondant que les traductions précédentes: ce qui n'est pas le cas pour les première, deuxième et neuvième (p. 101). L.'s translation implies that the first, second and ninth translations are not more extensive than the preceding ones. This clearly makes no sense. In any event, the passage seems to indicate that Tao-an was acquainted with at least nine translations before obtaining the new translation from Liang-chou in 376. However, as mentioned above, only seven translations are listed in the Ch'u san-tsang chi-chi which made great use of Tao-an's catalogue compiled in Hsiang-yang in 374. Of these seven translations one is Kumārajīva's version and another, the Shu Shou-leng-yen ching, is mentioned with a reference to the Chiu-lu 舊錄, a catalogue probably compiled after 435, cf. Demiéville, BEFEO, XXIV, 1924, p. 6. Only the five remaining translations can have been taken from Tao-an's catalogue. We know that already before receiving the new translation of the Śgs. from Liang-chou, Tao-an had carefully studied the existing translations. This is clear from a remark in his catalogue about Chih Ch'an's translation: 支讖所出其經首略如是我聞唯稱佛在王舍城靈鳥頂山中 (T 2145, p. 49a 14–15) "At the beginning of Chih Ch'an's translation the words 'Thus have I heard' are omitted. It is only said that 'The Buddha was in Rājagṛha on the Gṛdhrakūṭa mountain'". L. translates: Le sūtra traduit par Tche Tch'an ... débute en disant: "C'est ainsi que j'ai entendu: le Buddha se trouvait à Rājagṛha, sur le Gṛdhrakūṭaparvata" (p. 68).

It seems difficult to admit that Tao-an had known at least ten translations without any mention of this fact in the Chinese catalogues. I do not believe that we can deny Tao-an's authorship of this letter on this account. It may be that the remark about the first, second and ninth translations was added later by somebody who knew of the existence of nine translations. Or possibly the text originally contained another numeral instead of nine. No hypothesis is entirely satisfactory in helping us establish the number of translations known to Tao-an. Most of the translations seem to have been lost rather early. The author of the K'ai-yüan shih-chiao lu, which dates from 730, states expressly that of all nine translations only Kumārajīva's translation remains (L. p. 65). According to L. (p. 104) the seven translations previous to Kumārajīva's had already disappeared by the beginning of the 6th century, and Seng-yu in the Ch'u san-tsang chi chi is cited as authority for this fact. Unfortunately, L. gives no reference, and I have been unable to find any statement to this effect in Seng-yu's catalogue.

L. mentions three commentaries on the Śgs.: one by Po Yüan 帛遠, composed between 291 and 306; the second by Hsieh Fu 謝敷; and the third by Shih Hung-ch'ung 釋弘充, composed in 458. The Ch'u san-tsang chi chi (T 2145, p. 48 c 17–49 a 14) contains an anonymous preface to a commentary on the Śgs. The author is an unknown disciple of Chih Tao-lin 支道林 or Chih Tun 支遁 (314–366), cf. Zürcher, op. cit., p. 140. In this preface the author states that he has received oral explanations from Chih Tun. It is possible that Hsieh Fu, who belonged to the circle of Chih Tun, is the author of this preface[1]. However, in the absence of more definite evidence it seems more prudent to consider this commentary as different from the one written by Hsieh Fu. It is a pity that L. has not translated this preface which, indeed, he does not mention.

Of all the translations of the Śgs. and commentaries on it only Kumārajīva's translation has survived. This translation is mentioned in all the catalogues, and while none of them is in any doubt as to assigning this translation to Kumārajīva, they do not agree on the number of chüan. According to the older catalogues the work consists of two chüan (T 2145, p. 10 c 25, 14 a 16; T 2146, p. 119 c 7; T 2034, p. 78 a 12; T 2149, p. 252 c 23; T 2151, p. 359 a 26–27). The first catalogue to indicate three chapters is the Ta Chou k'an-ting chung-ching mu-lu 大周刊定衆經目錄 compiled in 695 (T 2153, p. 398 a 11). The same number it mentioned in two later catalogues (T 2154, p. 512 c 18; T 2157, p. 809 c 7). Both catalogues indicate that it is sometimes divided in two chüan. This indication seems to be taken from the Ch'u san-tsang chi chi to which both catalogues refer. However, the K'ai-yüan shih-chiao lu lioh-ch'u 開元釋教錄略出 (T 2155, p. 731 c 4) mentions only a version in three chüan. This shows that in the older editions of the Buddhist canon, based on this catalogue, Kumārajīva's translation was indeed divided into three chüan. This is confirmed by the fact that Hui-lin 慧琳 in his I-ch'ieh-ching yin-i 一切經音義 (T 2128, p. 515 c 8–516 a 4) also refers to an edition in three chüan. Hui-lin wrote his work probably between 783 and 817, cf. Demiéville, BEFEO, XXIV (1924), p. 2, n. 2. There seem to be only very few manuscripts of the Śgs. among Tun-huang collections. In his Tun-huang i-shu tsung-mo so-yin 敦煌遺書總目索引 (Shanghai, 1962) Wang Chung-min 王重民 mentions only two manuscripts. This, incidentally, also proves that interest in China in the Śgs. was much less after Kumārajīva than it had been in the preceding period. The first manuscript is described by Ch'en Yüan 陳垣 in his Tun-huang chieh-yü lu 敦煌劫餘錄 (Peiping, 1931, fasc. I, p. 31). The second is from the private collection of Takakusu Junjirō and is listed in the Shōwa Hōbō sōmokuroku 昭和法寶總目錄 vol. I (Tōkyō, 1929), p. 1065 b. This manuscript is a fragment of the middle chüan and thus also belongs to a text divided into three chüan. It is possible that a careful study of the list of Chinese Buddhist texts brought back by Japanese pilgrims, and of the catalogues of Japanese collections, will bring to light more information about the existence of old manuscripts and blockprints, but the relevant publications are not at my disposal.

The division into three chüan is maintained in the Chi-sha edition (fascicule 173, Shanghai, 1934, pp. 37 – 60)[2] and in the "Three editions" of the Taishō edition. However, the Korean edition of the 13th century now in course of being printed from the original blocks, divided the text in two chüan. According to the colophon the Śgs. was engraved in the year *jen-yin* 壬寅 which must correspond to the year 1242.

---

[1] Chang T'ien-hsi's name as translator of this new version of the Śgs. is mentioned in a passage not translated by L. (T 2145, p. 62 b 4–5). Here also the author of the letter remarks that this new translation is more detailed than the preceding ones.

[1] Tokiwa Daijō 常盤大定 has already mentioned this possibility, cf. Yakkyō sōroku 譯經總錄 (Tōkyō, 1938), p. 593. On Hsieh Fu, see Zürcher, op. cit., pp. 136–137; p. 358, n. 168.

[2] For this edition see P. Demiéville in P. Pelliot's "Les débuts de l'imprimerie en Chine" (Paris, 1953), pp. 134–135, 138, n. 4; Hu Shih, "The Gest Oriental Library at Princeton University", The Princeton University Library Chronicle, 15, 3 (1954), pp. 129–134; Mochizuki Shinkō, Bukkyō Daijiten, VIII (Tōkyō, 1958): Sekisaban daizōkyō, pp. 152 b–154 a.

The Taishō edition is clearly based upon the Korean edition, and variants of the Sung, Yüan and Ming editions are indicated in the notes. It is not in the strict sense of the word a critical edition. No manuscripts are mentioned and, of course, no use could be made of the Chi-sha edition. It is impossible to know if Kumārajīva's translation has been transmitted faithfully throughout the centuries. As L. indicates (p. 62) the Śgs. is quoted eight times in Kumārajīva's translation of the Mahāprajñāpāramitopadeśa. Nowhere does one find exactly the same wording, and there are even two major differences. In the Śgs, there is reference to a Buddha, named Lung-chung shang 龍種上, in Tibetan Klu'i-rigs mchog, whose name is reconstructed by L. as Nāgavaṃśāgra (p. 260). In the Upadeśa (T 1509, p. 134b 19 = Traité, I, p. 602) he is called Lung-chung tsun 龍種尊 which, incidentally, does not confirm L's reconstruction, for it is unlikely that *tsun* renders Sanskrit *agra*. Both *vara* and *uttama* would correspond better to the two Chinese renderings and to Tibetan *mchog*. Perhaps Buddha Nāgakulottama, who is mentioned in the Mahāvastu (III, 232. 20), is meant here. In the Śgs. Mañjuśrī tells how during 36.000.000 existences he was a Pratyekabuddha (p. 245). This is actually quoted three times in the Upadeśa (L. p. 62), but each time, instead of 36.000.000, the number given is 7.200.000. However, these differences have little evidential force. Kumārajīva may very well have translated the same name a little differently in two texts. The other variations in wording, and in the number of existences of Mañjuśrī as Pratyekabuddha, must in all probability be imputed to the author of the Upadeśa. Much more serious is the problem presented by a quotation of the Vimalakīrtinirdeśasūtra in the Upadeśa. This quotation seems to belong to a recension different from the one translated by Kumārajīva himself, cf. Lamotte, Vk. (= L'enseignement de Vimalakīrti), pp. 186–187, n. 82[1]. Although there exists neither a critical study of the information in the catalogues regarding the texts translated by Kumārajīva, nor a critical edition of his translation of the Śgs., there is no compelling reason for doubting Kumārajīva's authorship of this translation, or for supposing that the text has undergone major changes during its transmission. An entirely different problem, to which we shall have to return later, is the question of the extent to which Kumārajīva faithfully rendered the Indian original of the Śgs.

The Tibetan translation is due to Śākyaprabha and Ratnarakṣita. Ratnarakṣita is named among the scholars who compiled the Mahāvyutpatti and revised the texts already translated. In his "Indo-tibetische Studien. I" (Uppsala, 1957) Nils Simonsson has carefully studied the problems connected with this revision which is first mentioned in the introduction to the Sgra sbyor. Earlier scholars have referred to this text as the colophon of the Mahāvyutpatti (cf. Simonsson, op. cit., p. 214. n. 4; p. 238, n. 2). In his work, which L. seems not to have used, Simonsson gives a new and very careful translation of this text which has been copied or summarized by later authors such as Bu ston, Padma dkar po and the Fifth Dalai Lama. L. gives a new translation of the relevant passage of Bu ston which was previously translated by Obermiller and Ferrari. L.'s translation would have profited considerably from a study of Simonsson's work. For example, the expression *miṅ-du btags-pa dag* is translated by L. as "les [équivalents tibétains] attachés aux termes [sanskrits]". The same expression was rendered as "titles" by Obermiller and as "espressioni usate" by Ferrari; but more correctly by Simonsson as "als Termini festgelegte [Ausdrücke]". Jäschke (Tibetan-English Dictionary, London, 1881, p. 280a) renders *miṅ 'dogs-pa* as "to give a name" and in the Nyāyabindu (ed. Stcherbatsky, Petrograd, 1918, p. 62. 11) *saṃjñākaraṇa* is rendered in Tibetan as *miṅ btags-pa*. It seems to me that *miṅ-du btags-pa* simply means "technical term". Concerning the revision of the texts, a matter studied at length by Simonsson, it is important to point out that the colophon of the Śgs. indicates that the text has been revised; *skad gsar chad kyis kyaṅ bcos la gso* (cf. Simonsson, op. cit., pp. 222–232 for a discussion of the terms used in this phrase).

According to L. the Tibetan version contains two long and partly versified passages which are absent from the Chinese version (p. 108). As L.'s translation is based upon the Chinese version, these passages have not been translated by him. It would have been interesting to see the nature of these passages and to determine, if possible, their sources. L. has very conveniently divided the texts in 178 small sections. A concordance enables the reader to find quickly corresponding passages in the Chinese version and the Tibetan version for which L. has used the Japanese photomechanical reprint of the Peking edition.

In his introduction L. remarks that Kumārajīva's translation are rigorously precise (rigoureusement exactes) but that he is not always consistent in his renderings of technical terms, and that he generally abridges stereotyped phrases and passages. L. adds that the Tibetan version makes it possible to restore the technical terms and the few phrases omitted by Kumārajīva. I fear the difficulties are much greater than these remarks would lead us to suppose. In many instances Kumārajīva's version differs from the Tibetan version. In general, L. faithfully translates the Chinese version, but he sometimes follows the Tibetan without always indicating that he is doing so. In a number of cases where it is clear that Kumārajīva misunderstood the Indian original L. allows the passage to pass without comment. He also frequently adds Sanskrit equivalents between brackets. There is much to be said for this practice as long as the two versions agree, and as long as the Sanskrit term is well attested. However, in many instances, these Sanskrit equivalents are exclusively based upon the Chinese version and could never have been reconstructed from the corresponding passages in the Tibetan version. The result is that too often the translation reflects neither the Chinese version nor the Tibetan, not to speak of the presumed Indian original. In the case of the Vimalakīrtinirdeśasūtra L. decided to translate the Tibetan version. This time he has preferred the Chinese version, though without indicating the reasons for his choice. There would, of course, be no objection to a translation of the Chinese version provided it was consistently translated from beginning to end. But then one would have to be extremely careful in suggesting Sanskrit equivalents as they can only rarely be reconstructed with any degree of certainty from Kumārajīva's version. Divergences between the Tibetan and Chinese versions could be indicated in notes. In the case of the Śgs, however, these divergences are so considerable that it would be preferable to

[1] L. suggests the possibility that one of the two translations is not by Kumārajīva but there is too much evidence to the contrary to permit any serious doubt regarding the attribution of both translations to Kumārajīva.

give in addition a complete translation from the Tibetan. In that case one could be considerably more free in indicating Sanskrit equivalents which, as a rule, are more accurately rendered in the Tibetan version.

To substantiate these general remarks it will be necessary to examine more closely several passages in L.'s translation. Reference will be made to the relevant sections of the translation. As the Chinese version is easily available, and moreover has been added to this publication, it seems unnecessary to reproduce the Chinese text, though it will probably be useful to quote rather fully the Tibetan version.

§ 2. (L. p. 117): Ceux-ci [i. e. the Bodhisattvas] étaient universellement connus (*abhijñānābhijñāta*). – The translation is based upon K. (= Kumārajīva) but one wonders from where the Sanskrit equivalent is taken. T. (= Tibetan version) reads: *mṅon-par śes-pa'i ye-śes thob-pa = abhijñājñānapratilabdha*. In Vk. p. 98 one finds: universellement connus (*abhijñānābhijñāta*). Here, indeed, T. has: *mṅon-par śes-pa mṅon-par śes-pa* but "universellement connus" renders the Chinese versions by K. and Hsüan-tsang, but not T., upon which L.'s translation of the Vk. is based. In a note L. remarks that the epithet *abhijñānābhijñāta* is generally applied to Śrāvakas and not to Bodhisattvas, and he refers to Saddharmapuṇḍarīka p. 1.9 (Vk. p. 98, n. 1). In Edgerton's BHSD (= Buddhist Hybrid Sanskrit Dictionary, New Haven, 1953) this is the only reference given for *abhijñānābhijñāta*, which he renders as "renowned for knowledge" (or, with v. l. "for the abhijñā", *abhijñābhijñāta*, cf. Burnouf, note p. 291). However, L. seems to be convinced that "universellement connu" is the correct translation of the original Indian term for we find in the index of the Śgs.: *abhijñānābhijñāta* (pour *abhijanābhijñāta*?), universellement connu, 117, 119. One must remark that on p. 119 K. has indeed "universellement connu", but T. is entirely different: *gzi-brjid che-ba/gzi-brjid che-ba che-źiṅ che-ba 'oṅs-śiṅ lhags-pa*. To sum up: in three places L. translates "universellement connus (*abhijñānābhijñāta*)". In the first (Vk. p. 98) T. corresponds to *abhijñānābhijñāta*, which can only have the meaning given it by Edgerton. In the second and third (Śgs. pp. 117 and 119) K. has been rendered correctly, but the Sanskrit equivalent corresponds neither to K. nor to T. which, in both instances, is different. L. cites one example in which *abhijñānabhijñāta* is applied to Śrāvakas. In the Vk. it is applied to Bodhisattvas, and in K.'s version of the Śgs. it once applies to Bodhisattvas and once to Śakra, Brahmā, etc. However, it does not occur at all in the Tibetan version of Śgs. Finally L. seems to believe that "universellement connu" is the meaning of the original term and proposes to read *abhijanābhijñāta*, a term which is not attested and which could only mean "renowned for their noble descent".

L. seems not to have consulted Kumārajīva's glosses on the Vk., which are to be found in a collective commentary on the Vk. (T 1775), on which see Demiéville, Vk., p. 445. In this work one finds a gloss, attributed to K., on the meaning of the term "universellement connu" (T 1775, p. 328c 1–3): K. says: "The Sanskrit text reads 'much learning, much knowledge' (*to chih to shih* 多知多識)". This gloss clearly points to a Sanskrit original *abhijñānābhijñāta*. However, it is evident from Kern-Nanjio's edition that this reading is not absolutely sure since the manuscripts present a great variety of readings: *abhijñābhijñāta*, *abhijñātābhijñāta*, *abhijñānābhijñāna* and *abhijñānābhijñāta* which has been adopted by the editors. It must be left to future research to determine the exact reading, and also the categories of persons to which this epithet applies in different groups of texts[1].

§ 10. (L. p. 125): Ils . . . s'abstiennent des œuvres des cruels Māra (mārakarman); – The text has 而不依猗魔所行事 L. corrects *i* 猗 into *meng* 猛 but this breaks the rhythm of the phrase which is divided into groups of four characters. A possible but unnecessary correction would be to read *i* 倚. The translation remains the same: They do not rely upon the deeds of the Māras. This agrees with T.: *bdud-kyi las-la gnas-pa yaṅ ma-yin*, also they do not reside in the deeds of the Māras.

§ 10. (L. p. 125): Ils énoncent (*vyākurvanti*) habilement toutes les phrases de la Loi (*dharmapada*). – L. here translates *chieh-shuo* 解說 as "énoncent", but elsewhere (630 b 7) as "explication" which is certainly preferable. T. is quite different: *chos-kyi tshig rab-tu dbye-ba thams-cad kyaṅ ston*, they also point out all the divisions of the words of the Law. Although M. (= Mahāvyutpatti) indicates as equivalent for *rab-tu dbye-ba vibhajana* (5174), here it probably corresponds to *prabheda*, see the passage of the Bodhisattvabhūmi quoted by L. de La Vallée Poussin (Kośa, VII, p. 90, n. 1b): *yat punaḥ sarvadharmāṇām eva sarvaprakārapadaprabhedeṣu . . .iyam eṣām pratibhānasaṃvit* (Wogihara's edition is not at my disposal); Lalitavistara (ed. S. Lefmann, p. 8. 12): *sarvapadaprabhedanirdeśāsaṅgapratisaṃvidavatārajñānakuśalasya*. See also § 21 (L. p. 136, nr. 54) where T. reads: *chos-kyi tshig rab-tu dbye-ba thams-cad bstan-pa la mkhas-pa śes pa*, to know well to point out all the divisions of the words of the Law.

§ 13. (L. p. 127): This section describes the throne (*siṃhāsana*) of the Tathāgata. In his translation L. mixes elements taken from K. and T. For example: jonché d'étoffes précieuses et innombrables (*apramāṇaratnavastrāstirṇa*), couvert au sommet de tentures (*vitāna*), de bannières (*dhvaja*) et de merveilleux parasols précieux (*ratnacchattra*). K. has: innumerable precious fabrics are spread on it (*ch'i shang* 其上 does not mean "au sommet"); it is entirely covered with a multitude of wonderful and precious parasols. T reads: *ras bcos-ma brgya-stoṅ-du btiṅ-ba / steṅ-gi bar-snaṅ-las rin-po-che'i gdugs daṅ / rgyal-mtshan daṅ / dra-bas g.yogs-pa*, fabrics (*duṣya*, M. 5876) are spread over it by the hundred thousand; above in the air (*upary antarīkṣe*, cf. J. Nobel, Suvarṇaprabhāsottamasūtra. Wörterbuch. Leiden, 1950, p. 85) it is covered with parasols (*chattra*, M. 6108), banners (*dhvaja*, M. 6109) and nets (*jāla*, M. 6125). Further on L. translates: [planté] à gauche et à droite d'innombrables arbres précieux (*ratnavṛkṣa*) aux branches et aux feuilles desquels des rangées de perles (*muktāvali*) étaient savamment disposées. K. has: At the left and the right of the throne were innumerable precious trees, intermingled with branches and leaves, and appropriately disposed in a row. T. reads: *g.yas-g.yon-du rin-po-che'i śiṅ-ljon du-mas / brgyan-pa / dar-gyi lda-ldi bres-pa mu-tig-gi phreṅ-ba spyaṅs-pa /*, at the left and the right adorned by several precious trees; silken cords are stretched over it (*paṭṭadāmavitata*, M. 6119, 6126) and rows of pearls hung on it.

§ 18. (L. p. 129): ils [i. e. les dharma] sont inactifs (*niśceṣṭa*). – K. has: the dharmas are without doer. T. reads: the dharmas are without master (*bdag-po med-pa = asvāmika*, cf. T. Hirano, An Index to the Bodhicaryāvatārapañjikā, chapter IX, Tōkyō, 1966, p. 41).

§ 21. (L. p. 134, nr. 25): Avoir des attitudes et une démarche excluant toute bizarrerie. – "Excluant toute bizarrerie" translates 未曾有異 "wonderful and extraordinary" which would correspond to Sanskrit *ā-*

[1] In the Samādhirājasūtra (ed. N. Dutt, I, p. 7.2) *abhijñābhijñāta* is applied to Bodhisattvas. In the Larger Sukhāvatīvyūha (ed. Takakusu, Max Müller, Kawaguchi, Wogihara, Tōkyō, 1931, p. 6.1 and 6.13) *abhijñānābhijña* applies to Śrāvakas. In the Smaller Sukhāvatīvyūha (ibid., p. 194.3) occurs *abhijñātābhijñāta* which is also applied to Śrāvakas. Max Müller changed this to *abhijñānābhijñāta* (ibid., p. 446, n. 2). In the same note he remarked that in the Larger Sukhāvatīvyūha *abhijñātābhijña* occurs also but I have been unable to find it. For a discussion of the Chinese renderings of *abhijñānābhijñāta* see Watanabe Shōkō, Shōkai Shinyaku Hokekyō (III), Daihōrin (March, 1966), pp. 50–51.

śćaryādbhuta but T. is different: *spyod-lam ma-brtags-pa*, their behaviour is not feigned (*akalpita*). In § 3 (L. p. 118, ll. 4–5) T. reads: *spyod-lam thams-cad yoṅs-su brtags-pa ma-yin-pa*, their entire behaviour is not feigned (*aparikalpita*), see Kāśyapaparivarta § 123.

§ 21. (L. p. 138, nr. 81): Après l'avoir trouvée, échapper aux existences originelles [conditionnées] par les actes antérieurs (*pūrvakarman*). L. adds in a note: phrase obscure, sans correspondant en tibétain. – K. has: he has already obtained (*i te* 已得) the separation from his original body [produced by] his former acts. "Après l'avoir trouvée" would be *te i* 得已. Tokiwa Daijō, who published in 1934 a Japanese translation of the Śgs. in the Kokuyaku Issaikyō (Kyōshū-bu, vol. 6, pp. 1–61), has correctly translated this phrase. It is always useful to consult Japanese translations, especially when they are from the hand of such an eminent scholar as Tokiwa. For an appraisal of his work see A. F. Wright, FEQ, X (1950), pp. 75–79.

§ 48. (L. p. 159): il peut alors parfaire les six perfections. – T. has: he is perfectly skilled (*tshar phyin-pa* = *niryāta*, M. 360, 2544) in the six perfections.

§ 64. (L. p. 180): en effet sa sagesse (*prajñā*), son éloquence (*pratibhāna*) et ses pénétrations sans obstacle (*apratihatābhijñā*) sont si grandes – In K. *wu ai* 無礙 "without obstacle" relates to the knowledge and the eloquence; *wu ai* is often placed after the word to which it relates, see the examples given by Mochizuki, Bukkyō daijiten, s. v. *muge*. Although T. is slightly different, it confirms this interpretation: *'di'i spobs-pa ji-lta-ba daṅ / de'i ye-śes thogs-pa ma-mchis-par 'chad-pa ji-lta-ba*, as his eloquence and as his wisdom explain without obstacle. I do not believe that *apratihata* is used as an attribute of *abhijñā*. In § 133 (L. p. 234, nr. 6), § 136 (L. p. 238) and § 149 (L. p. 252, nr. 8) *wu ai* qualifies *pratibhāna*. L. translates respectively: éloquence intarissable (*anācchedyapratibhāna*); éloquence sans obstacle (*apratihatapratibhāna*); éloquence sans obstacle (*anācchedyapratibhāna*). If one does not take T. into account, everywhere one ought to translate as "unobstructed eloquence". T. reads respectively: *spobs-pa thogs-pa med-pa*, unobstructed eloquence; *spobs-pa zad mi-śes-pa*, inexhaustible eloquence; *spobs-pa rgyun mi-chad-pa*, *anācchedyapratibhāna* (M. 851). T. *thogs-pa med-pa* can correspond to *apratihata* or to *asaṅga*; *asaṅgapratibhāna* occurs several times, cf. BHSD s. v.

§ 65. (L. p. 181): se livrant au plaisir dans le Jardin de la joie (*nandavane paricārayamāna*). – This charming detail is L.'s invention for K. and T. have nothing of this kind.

§ 67. (L. p. 183): Ces hommes sont tout proches de l'état de Buddha. L. adds in a note: *kieou king fo tao* 究竟佛道 correspond ici au tib. *de bźin gśegs pa'i 'gros su mchi ba lags*, ce qui donne en sanskrit *tathāgatagatiṃgata*. – However, *gatiṃgata* is usually rendered in Tibetan by *rtogs-par khoṅ-du chud-pa* (M. 356, 866, 2888) and its meaning is rather different, cf. BHSD s. v.; JA, 1953, pp. 546–547. T. means: they go the way of the Tathāgata.

§ 71. (L. p. 186): il n'y a pour le Tathāgata aucune naissance réelle . . . il n'y a pour le Tathāgata aucune destruction réelle. – K. does not have *ju-lai* 如來 but twice has *ju-lai hsiang* 如來相 to which in T. correspond respectively *de-bźin gśegs-pa'i chos-ñid* (*tathāgata-dharmatā*) and *de-bźin gśegs-pa'i de-bźin-ñid* (*tathāgatatathatā*). Elsewhere L. has been more accurate, cf. p. 217, n. 237 and n. 238.

§ 116. (L. p. 218): Alors Ānanda dit au Buddha Bhagavat, on a offert au Buddha le terrain où il prêche le Śgs., et on a lui a offert le repas (*bhojana*) qu'il mangea avant d'atteindre la grande illumination (*abhisaṃbodhi*). De quelle grandeur sont les mérites (*puṇya*) gagnés par les deux maîtres du don (*dānapati*) qui lui ont fait ces offrandes? In a note L. remarks: La version tibétaine diffère et demande quels furent les mérites respectifs des deux *dānapati* qui offrirent à Śākyamuni le vihāra où il prêcha le Śgs. et le repas qu'il prit avant de prêcher ce même sūtra. – L. has misunderstood T.: *gaṅ-gi gtsug-lag-khaṅ na de-bźin gśegs-pa bźugs-śiṅ dpa'-bar 'gro-ba'i tiṅ-ṅe-'dzin 'di 'chad-par mdzad / ston-par mdzad-pa daṅ / gaṅ-gis bśos gsol-te dpa'-bar 'gro-ba'i tiṅ-ṅe-'dzin 'di 'chad-par mdzad-pa'i sbyin-pa-po sbyin-bdag gtsug-lag-khaṅ-gi bdag-po'i bsod-nams ji-tsam-du gyur*, how great is the merit of the giver, the master of the gift, the master of the monastery in whose monastery the Buddha resided and explained and preached the Śgs. and from whom he received food before explaining the Śgs . . . T. mentions only one *dānapati*, the *vihārasvāmin*, in whose monastery the Buddha preached and from whom he received food. K. seems to have misunderstood this phrase which must have required two relatives (*yasya*; *yena*) in its original form. Although he mentions two *dānapatis*, he does not say that the place where the Buddha preached was given to him: On the place where the Buddha resides he has preached the Śgs.; after food was given to him, the Buddha obtained the *abhisaṃbodhi*.

§ 120. (L. p. 221–222). According to L.'s translation two monasteries were given to the Buddha. However, K. says only that there are two monasteries. He continues: 此二施處其福不異 translated by L. as follows: Eh bien, les mérites résultant de ces deux dons de monastères ne diffèrent pas entre eux. Only in this place we find in Chinese a word for "to give". T. reads: *gtsug-lag-khaṅ de-dag la tha-dad-pa cuṅ-zad kyaṅ med-do*, there is not the slightest difference between these monasteries. Instead of *shih* 施 the "Three editions" have *fu* 福 which is also to be found in the Chi-sha edition. Only the Korean edition seems to have *shih*. Adopting the variant *fu* makes the sentence better Chinese, and also gives a better parallel to T. K. has then to be translated as follows: there is no difference in merit between these two meritorious places. Perhaps the editors of the Korean edition, or of the editions used by them, objected to the repetition of the same character in such a short phrase.

§ 122. (L. p. 223). This section describes how the Buddha, when residing in the Śgs., manifests himself simultaneously in all the Jambudvīpas and Caturdvīpakas of the *trisāhasramāhasāhasralokadhātu*. From K. and L.'s translation one obtains the impression that the manifestations of the Buddha take place successively in our Jambudvīpa: Dṛdhamati, tout en demeurant en Śgs., je suis dans le *trisāhasramahāsāhasralokadhātu* et, éventuellement, en Jambudvīpa, je pratique selon le cas les perfections (*pāramitā*) du don (*dāna*), de la moralité (*śīla*), etc. However, T. clearly describes the simultaneous manifestation of the Buddha in many Jambudvīpas: *byaṅ-chub sems-dpa' sems-dpa' chen-po dpa'-bar 'gro-ba'i tiṅ-ṅe-'dzin la gnas-te stoṅ-gsum-gyi stoṅ chen-po'i 'jig-rten 'dir 'dzam-bu'i gliṅ la-lar ni sbyin-pa'i pha-rol-tu phyin-pa spyod-do // 'dzam-bu'i gliṅ la-lar ni tshul-khrims-kyi pha-rol-tu phyin-pa spyod*. In this *trisāhasramāhasāhasralokadhātu* the Bodhisattva, the Mahāsattva, who resides in Śgs., exercises in one Jambudvīpa (*kasmiṃścid Jambudvīpe*) the perfection of the gift, in another Jambudvīpa he exercises the perfection of virtue, etc. This passage is alluded to in the Mahāparinirvāṇasūtra (T 374, p. 388 b 22; T 375, p. 628 b 25).

§ 140. (L. p. 241): voulut les détourner de leur résolution. – K. has: he desired that they would arise again [from their faint-heartedness].

§ 142. (L. p. 243): jamais il ne trompe le monde avec ses dieux et ses hommes (*sadevamanuṣyaloka*). – K. has: of the gods and men in the world nobody can deceive him. See also T.: *de ni lha-daṅ-bcas-pa'i 'jig-rten-gyis bslu-bar mi-nus-te*, he cannot be deceived by the world with its gods.

§ 152. (L. p. 255, nr. 8): la patience et la gentillesse (*kṣāntisauratya*). – Both K. and T. (*bzod-pa*) mention only *kṣānti*.

§ 158. (L. p. 260): qu'il a enseigné les êtres et qu'il est entré dans le grand Nirvāṇa. – K. has: he has manifested to the beings his entrance in the great Nirvāṇa. See also Tokiwa's translation, p. 56, and T.: *sṅon yoṅs-su mya-ṅan las-'das-pa bstan-pa*, formerly he has manifested his Parinirvāṇa.

§ 163. (L. p. 263, nrs. 5–6): Instead of *bodhivṛkṣagamana* and *bodhimaṇḍaniṣīdana* T. has only *bodhimaṇḍagamana* (*byaṅ-chub-kyi sñiṅ-por 'gro-ba*).

§ 174. (L. p. 272): This section deals with twenty inconceivable qualities but K. enumerates twenty-one qualities. The second (l'inconcevable savoir) does not occur in T. The third (l'inconcevable sagesse) is the second in T. This quality was split into two by K. in his translation.

In the present state of knowledge it is not an easy task to translate Kumārajīva's versions although, in general, they are written in a clear and comprehensible Chinese. One of the difficulties resides in the fact that it is not clear in how far these versions reflect faithfully the Indian originals. This can only be determined through a detailed examination of Kumārajīva's vocabulary based upon comparative studies of his versions and the corresponding Sanskrit texts and Tibetan versions. On the other hand it will be necessary to study carefully the Chinese catalogues, in which the number of translations attributed to Kumārajīva varies greatly. Only by combining both methods will it become possible to obtain a better foundation for the study of Kumārajīva's versions. The fact that even an eminent scholar has not been able to avoid several pitfalls may serve as a warning that the interpretation of Kumārajīva's versions, and of Chinese Buddhist texts in general, poses problems which are not to be underrated. Much work has still to be done in regard to the study of the vocabulary used by the translators, and also on the truthworthiness of the attributions made by the catalogues. Hayashiya Tomojirō (1886–1953) is one of the few scholars who have done excellent work in this respect, but his example does not seem to have inspired many scholars in Japan or elsewhere. Until more preliminary studies have been made it might be advisable not to undertake complete translations of Chinese Buddhist texts, but rather to make detailed analyses. It will be difficult to find a better example of the latter than the excellent analysis of Saṅgharakṣa's Yogācārabhūmi by Professor Demiéville (BEFEO, XLIV, 1954, pp. 339–436).

Addendum

The article, referred to in p. 72, note 1, appeared in the Mélanges de Sinologie offerts à Monsieur Paul Demiéville (vol. I, Paris, 1966), pp. 113–159. For the meaning of the word *ch'u* (p. 73, note 3) see also: Biographies des moines éminents (*Kao seng tchouan*) de Houei-kiao. Traduites et annotées par Robert Shih (Louvain, 1968), pp. 167–168.

R. E. Emmerick, *The Khotanese Śūraṅgamasamādhisūtra* (London Oriental Series, Vol. 23), xxiii + 133 pp. + 20 pl. London, Oxford University Press, 1970. £5.

A rather large portion of the Khotanese Ś[ūraṅ]g[ama]s[amādhisūtra] has been preserved. The remaining folios belong to three groups which were identified by Dr. Emmerick, E. Leumann and H. W. Bailey. They correspond to the following sections of Lamotte's translation of Kumārajīva's Chinese version: §§ 3–4, 125–52. Dr. Emmerick gives a literal translation of the Tibetan version wherever the Khotanese is missing. The passages translated from the Khotanese are in italics. The Tibetan text is critically edited on the basis of the four following editions: Derge, Lhasa, Narthang, and Peking. A Tibetan index discusses a few words of special interest. All Khotanese words are listed in the glossary. It gives all references for all words and, where possible, the Tibetan equivalent for each Khotanese form. The translation is followed by a detailed commentary. The introduction deals with such matters as the date of the Khotanese manuscript and of the Khotanese translation, the title of the Śgs., Khotanese fragments with Śgs. associations, archaic orthography, the two manuscripts to which the folios and fragments belong, and with the Tibetan translation.

It must be left to specialists to discuss the new readings and interpretations of the Khotanese text proposed by Dr. Emmerick. The interest of this publication is not limited to the field of Khotanese studies. The Khotanese version of the Śgs. is also important from the point of view of the history of the Śgs. The Chinese translation dates from the beginning of the fifth century, the Tibetan one from the ninth century. Dr. Emmerick remarks in his introduction that the Śgs. may have been translated into Khotanese before the earliest extant Chinese translation, that made by Kumārajīva c. A.D. 400. Dr. Emmerick has indicated in the commentary where the Khotanese agrees with the Chinese against the Tibetan. The comparison of the Khotanese and Chinese versions is hampered by the fact that both versions do not attain the same degree of literalness as shown by the Tibetan version. When comparing the Khotanese version with the two others, we must bear in mind the following four possibilities: the Khotanese version agrees (1) with the Chinese, (2) with the Tibetan, (3) with both, and (4) with neither of them. In quite a few cases the Khotanese agrees with the Chinese, but in others it agrees with the Tibetan. This may suggest that the Khotanese version has to be placed somewhere between the Chinese and Tibetan versions, perhaps closer to the first than to the second. If the Khotanese version of the Śgs. is one of the oldest Khotanese translations, as may be suggested by the archaic features of the orthography (cf. Intr. pp. xix–xxi), it would mean that the existing manuscripts are not much younger than the translations themselves and that both manuscripts and translations would have to be put in the second half of the first millennium A.D. Of course, a comparative study of other Khotanese versions and corresponding Chinese and Tibetan versions is necessary in order to corroborate this hypothesis.

The Khotanese version often helps us greatly in restoring the original Sanskrit text. In § 3 the Khotanese contains the names Mahāratnaketu and Prabhāketu. In both names *ketu* corresponds exactly to Tibetan *tog*, whereas the Chinese version has *hsiang* 相 rendered by Lamotte as *lakṣaṇa*. In this case it is obvious that the Sanskrit text must have had *ketu* and not *lakṣaṇa*. In the same section the name Sāgaraguṇaratnavyūhamati is reconstructed by the editor on the basis of Sāgaraguṇara- in the Khotanese manuscript and the corresponding versions. Lamotte reconstructs this name as Guṇaratnavyūhasamudramati (cf. Tib. yon-tan rin-po-che bkod-pa rgya-mtsho'i blo-gros). However, the Chinese text has 海德寶嚴淨意 which corresponds exactly to Sāgaraguṇaratnavyūhamati. In § 133 Lamotte translates *fu-t'ien* 福田 with *puṇyakṣetra* but the Khotanese version has *dakṣiṇīya* which agrees with Tibetan *sbyin-pa'i gnas* (see also Leumann, *Buddhistische Literatur, nordarich und deutsch*, I. Teil: Nebenstücke, Leipzig, 1920, p. 100). In § 138 Khotanese Sarvaratnapra- has enabled Dr. Emmerick to reconstruct Sarvaratnapratyupta as the name of the buddhakṣetra. Here Lamotte has Sarvaratnaracitā. According to the Khotanese version the name of the bodhisattva in §§ 136–8 is Saśivimalagarbha (cf. Daśabhūmika, p. 2.7) and not Vimalacandragarbha as given by Lamotte.

On page 11 Dr. Emmerick translates Tibetan *bdud daṅ phyir rgol-ba bcom-pa* with "they have conquered Māra and the adversaries", cf. also Lamotte, p. 227: "vainqueurs de Māra et des adversaires (*nihatamārapratyarthika*)". I believe that Ensink's translation of this expression is to be preferred: "having destroyed Māra, the adversary" (*The Question of Rāṣṭrapāla*, Zwolle, 1952, p. 1). The same expression occurs in the Saddharmapuṇḍarīka (Bibl. Buddh. p. 430.1), the Karuṇāpuṇḍarīka (ed. I. Yamada, p. 78.7) and the Lalitavistara (ed. S. Lefmann, p. 8.16–17: *nihatamānapratyarthikasya*, read *nihatamāra°*). The text of the following passage is almost entirely missing in the Khotanese manuscripts. Dr. Emmerick suggests that the Khotanese may have read "well-closed for them the paths to the Apāyas" (cf. p. 63). Lamotte translates Chinese 斷諸惡趣 as "libérés des destinées mauvaises (*kṣīṇāpāya*)". According to Dr. Emmerick Tibetan has *ltuṅ-ba bcad-pa* "they have cut off Apāya". I believe that both renderings are open to objections. Chin. *tuan* 斷 does not correspond to *kṣīṇa*, and the expression *kṣīṇāpāya* is not attested elsewhere. Tibetan *ltuṅ-ba* renders *āpatti*, *patana*, etc. but never *apāya*. Dr. Emmerick quotes Suvarṇabhāsottama 62.1: *pithitāni me trīṇy apāyapathāni*. Chinese *tuan* 斷 and Tibetan *bcad-pa* both probably correspond to *pithita* (cf. Lalitavistara, p. 46.7 *pithituṃ apāyapatha*; Tibetan *ṅan-soṅ rnams-kyi lam gcod-ciṅ*). If Tibetan *ltuṅ-ba* is an error for *ṅan-soṅ*, both the Chinese and Tibetan versions correspond to *pithitāny apāyāni*. I have not been able to find this expression in the texts which seem to expand this expression. For instance Vimalakīrtinirdeśasūtra, ch. 12: *de-dag-gis ṅan-soṅ thams-cad ni bcad* which Lamotte translates as follows: "ceux-ci barreront toutes les mauvaises destinées (*durgati*)". Hsüan-tsang seems to have read *apāyapathāni* (cf. Lamotte, *l'Enseignement de Vimalakīrti*, Louvain, 1962 p. 371). However, Kumārajīva's translation agrees with the Tibetan. In other places, *dvāra*, *patha* or *mārga* is added after *apāya*, cf. Divyāvadāna, p. 554.26 *pihitāny apāyadvārāṇi*, p. 554.28 *pihitaḥ sughoro hy apāyamargo*. Lalitavistara p. 46.7, p. 117.9 *apāyapatha*. Elsewhere both *sarva* and *dvāra* are added, cf. Pañcaviṃśatisāhasrikāprajñāpāramitā ed. N. Dutt, p. 75.15 *sarvāṇy apāyadvārāṇi pithitāni*. This example shows that a well-known cliché can occur in many different forms. This is of importance for the reconstruction of defective passages. In the Khotanese passage only *-ndā* remains. Both Leumann and Bailey have read *śandā*. According to Dr. Emmerick *śandā* "earth" does not seem required here. However, the expression *apāyabhūmi* is not unknown, cf. Suvarṇabhāsottama, p. 23.11; Lalitavistara, p. 178.7, 9. In this case, the presence of a well-known cliché is not of great help in reconstructing the Khotanese text. The many variants of this cliché make it impossible to reconstruct the original Sanskrit text and, consequently, the Khotanese text.

Another cliché is to be found on the same page (p. 11; 2.4 v 3–4). Dr. Emmerick remarks that the Chinese has here the cliché: *śrutvādhimokṣyanty udgrahīṣyanti dhārayiṣyanti vācayiṣyanti paryavāpsyanty adhimucya deśayiṣyanty upadekṣyanti parebhya uddekṣyanti bhāvanākāreṇa prayokṣyante* (p. 64; cf. Lamotte, p. 227). The same cliché occurs in § 11 of the Śgs. where we find: *adhimucya, udgṛhṇāti, dhārayati vācayati, parebhyaḥ saṃprakāśayati, bhāvanāyogena prayunakti* (Lamotte, p. 126). This reconstruction follows closely Kumārajīva's Chinese version (630 b 11–12). In § 129 Kumārajīva's translation is almost the same (641 a 15) and it is difficult to understand why the Sanskrit text here would be much more expanded. In both cases the cliché ends with the following passage: 如說修行."in accordance to what has been preached he applies himself to it". According to Lamotte this corresponds to Sanskrit *bhāvanākāreṇa prayunakti.* On page 126, note 28 he refers to his translation of the Vimalakīrtinirdeśasūtra, page 368, note 16, where references are given to several texts in which this cliché is to be found. The Tibetan translation has here: *sgom-pa'i rnal-'byor-la rjes-su sbyor-ba rnams* (same translation in ch. XII.2, Lamotte, p. 371). This does not correspond to *bhāvanākāreṇa prayunakti.* In only one of the passages, referred to by Lamotte, is this expression found: Daśabhūmika, p. 98.23 *bhāvanākāreṇa prayokṣyante*, but, according to Rahder's Glossary, the Tibetan translation corresponds exactly to the Sanskrit text. The Sanskrit equivalent of the Tibetan expression, quoted above, is to be found in Lamotte's reconstruction of the Sanskrit text of § 175 of the Śgs., cf. Lamotte p. 273, *bhāvanāyogam anuyuktaḥ.* In § 129 of the Śgs. the Tibetan translation has only *mos-pa.* In such cases it is difficult to know whether the original text is abridged or the translation. In any case, Kumārajīva's Chinese translation does not warrant the reconstructions given by Lamotte (p. 227) and by Dr. Emmerick (p. 64). Dr. Emmerick supplies *ays*[mū]*na* [byāta yanda] "remembers it with his mind". This reminds us of one of the variants of the cliché, not listed by Lamotte, in which the word *manasikariṣyanti* is to be found: Saddharmapuṇḍarīkasūtra p. 478.7. (cf. also *id.*, p. 226.5 *anusmaret*).

In some places the Khotanese translation seems to have misunderstood the text. Page 11 (2.4 r 5) aväṣkälsta-usā[v]*ä* "of indestructible endurance". Both Tibetan and Chinese have read *kṣānti* and *utsāha* seems here out of place. Page 41 (3.11 r 4) *duṣkarūṇa amāñandūna salāva* "extraordinary, unprecedented words". The use of *duṣkarūṇa-* "difficult" (cf. glossary) is strange. Tibetan has *ṅo-mtshar* which usually corresponds to *āścarya.* On page 29 (3.5 r 4) Dr. Emmerick translates *jsei'ṇu vätä* as "quickly" (I have quickly expounded the merits of Nirvāṇa), referring to *KT* 6.92. Here *jseiṇa-* is rendered as "small (fine, short)". Would it not be possible to interpret *jsei'ṇu vätä* as "in detail"?

In the Tibetan index Dr. Emmerick discusses the meaning of Tibetan *bla-dvags* in *tshig bla-dvags.* He quotes Chos-grags' explanation *miṅ-gi tha-sñad btags-pa* "to etymologize a word". I do not believe that this translation is correct. It is of course difficult to know exactly what is meant by *miṅ-gi tha-sñad*, but it does not seem to mean something different from *miṅ* alone, cf. Chos-grags: *tha-sñad btags-pa – miṅ-du btags-pa.* Another Tibetan dictionary (*Dag-yig thon-mi'i dgoṅs-rgyan*, Vol. 2, Mtsho-sṅon, 1957, p. 237) explains *bla-dvags* as follows: *bla-dvags ni – 'phral-du sbyar-ba'i miṅ-ste chog-pa'am ruṅ-bar btags-pa źes Gleṅ-'bum brda-bkrol-du bśad* "a word which is immediately attached as being suitable or fit; this is the explanation given in the Gleṅ-'bum." Finally, one must point out that *tshig bla-dvags* regularly translates *adhivacana* a term which occurs quite often in Prajñāpāramitā texts (cf. Edward Conze, *Materials for a Dictionary of the Prajñāpāramitā Literature*, Tōkyō, 1967, p. 16: *adhivacana – tshig bla-dgas – synonym*). One has to correct here *dgas* in *dags.* Usually this word is written *dvags* in which case the *va-zur* serves to distinguish in writing *dags* and *dgas*. Edgerton renders *adhivacana* as "designation, appellation, name, term".

May we conclude by expressing the wish that Dr. Emmerick will edit and translate in the same way other Khotanese versions of Buddhist texts. Khotanese Buddhist texts are not only important to the few specialists in Khotanese studies but to all those who are interested in the history of the transmission of Buddhist texts.

Additional note. H. W. Bailey points out that *jseiṇa-* 'small' refers to size. There is no case so far found where reference to time is certain.

Khotanese Texts III 60, l.35 ttu sūttri birāśąmī jsiṃṇä '(as to) this sūtra, we will expound it in *jseiṇa-* fashion' – 'briefly' or 'in detail' or 'in its small points'.

Ibid. l.43 ttye sūttri vīra vistārī dā ṣṭi u miri haṃbistä hvīṃde 'in this sūtra the dharma is vast and here it is taught in compact form'.

Ibid. l.57 ṣị buri hve śāstārä haṃbistäna sūtträ 'this so great a teacher taught in compact form the sūtra'.

J. W. de Jong

L'ÉPISODE D'ASITA DANS LE LALITAVISTARA

Par J. W. de Jong, Leiden

La visite d'Asita au roi Śuddhodana est racontée dans le septième chapitre du *Lalitavistara* (en abrégé LV). Nous y trouvons deux versions de cet épisode, l'une en prose (éd. Lefmann, Halle 1902, p. 100, l. 20—108, l. 8) et l'autre en vers (p. 108, l. 10—112, l. 2). Nous nous proposons d'étudier cet épisode à la lumière des deux traductions chinoises du LV qui ont été conservées. La première de celles-ci est la traduction de Dharmarakṣa (Tchou Fa-hou 竺法護), datée de 308 d'après le *Tch'ou san tsang ki tsi* (T. 2145, k. 7, p. 48b 29) et la deuxième celle de Divākara (Ti-p'o-ho-lo 地婆訶羅), datée de 683 d'après le *K'ai-yuan che kiao lou* (T. 2154, k. 9, p. 563c 12—13). Elles sont donc de beaucoup antérieures à la traduction tibétaine qui date vraisemblablement du premier quart du neuvième siècle[1]. Pour l'étude de l'histoire du texte sanskrit, celle-ci n'offre que peu d'intérêt. Les petites différences qu'elle montre avec le texte sanskrit, ne sont sans doute dues qu'au mauvais état dans lequel celui-ci nous a été transmis. Mais d'un tout autre ordre sont les divergences des traductions chinoises entre elles et avec le texte sanskrit. Afin de faciliter la comparaison de ces textes nous donnons, en appendice, une traduction de l'épisode d'Asita dans les deux versions chinoises. La première de celles-ci, le *P'ou yao king* (T. 186, k. 2, p. 495b 4—496b 15), débute par un court passage en prose dont le commencement correspond au texte sanskrit (p. 100,

[1] La détermination de la date de la traduction tibétaine n'est pas aisée. Les traducteurs étaient Jinamitra, Dānaśīla, Munivarma et Ye-śes-sde (Cf. *Otani Kanjur Catalogue*, No. 763). A l'exception de Munivarma, tous ont participé à la compilation de la *Mahāvyutpatti*, qui, d'après le colophon, eut lieu dans l'année du cheval pendant le règne du roi Khri lde sroṅ btsan (cf. le texte et la traduction du colophon dans l'ouvrage de Mademoiselle A. Ferrari: *Arthaviniścaya*, Atti della Reale Accademia d'Italia, Memorie, Classi di scienzi morali e storichi, Serie VII, Vol. IV, fasc. 13, Roma, 1944, p. 538—9 et p. 540—1). Mademoiselle Ferrari identifie ce roi au roi Ral pa can qu'elle fait régner de 817 à 836. Mais cette identification est rejetée par M. Tucci (*The tombs of the Tibetan kings*, Roma, 1950, p. 14ff.) qui est d'avis que Khri lde sroṅ btsan est le père de Ral pa can et qu'il a dû régner de 798 ou 799 à 817 (op. cit., p. 19—30). Toujours d'après M. Tucci l'année du cheval peut être l'année 802 ou 814. Cette dernière date lui semble préférable. Néanmoins il est possible que Khri lde sroṅ btsan mourût déjà en 804 comme semblent l'indiquer les sources chinoises (cf. P. Demiéville, Le concile de Lhasa, vol. I, Paris, 1952, p. 232, n. 1; la note 1 à la page 13 est à rectifier). Dans ce cas la compilation de la *Mahāvyutpatti* aurait eu lieu en 802. Signalons toutefois que la dernière discussion des dates de Khri lde sroṅ btsan que nous avons vue, place son règne de 800 à 815 (H. E. Richardson, JRAS, 1952, p. 150). Il ne nous appartient pas de choisir entre ces diverses dates. La chose qui paraît à peu près sûre, est que Jinamitra, etc. ont travaillé dans le premier quart du neuvième siècle.

l. 20—22). Suivent douze strophes qui, sans être littéralement identiques aux douze strophes formant le début de la version poétique du texte sanskrit (p. 108, l. 10—p. 110, l. 14), relatent toutefois les mêmes événements. Ici s'arrête la correspondance. Alors que, dans le texte sanskrit, l'épisode d'Asita se termine par huit strophes (p. 110, l. 15—p. 112, l. 2), la traduction chinoise contient une série de dix-neuf strophes, se rapportant au sommeil du Buddha, et, pour finir, un long passage en prose qui paraît être emprunté, presque textuellement, à une autre biographie du Buddha, le *T'ai tseu jouei ying pen k'i king* (T. 185, k. 1, p. 474a). — La traduction de Divākara, le *Fang kouang ta tchouang yen king*, correspond, à quelques petites différences près, à la version en prose du texte sanskrit (p. 100, l. 20—p. 108, l. 8); mais la fin du chapitre sept (p. 108, l. 9—p. 117, l. 14) y fait entièrement défaut. — Nous pouvons donc distinguer dans le LV sanskrit trois morceaux différents dont le premier (p. 100, l. 20—p. 108, l. 8) correspond à la traduction de Divākara et le deuxième (p. 108, l. 10—p. 110, l. 14) à une partie de la traduction de Dharmarakṣa; le troisième (p. 110, l. 15—p. 112, l. 2) ne se trouve que dans le texte sanskrit. Ceci prouve que non seulement Dharmarakṣa en 308 mais même encore Divākara en 683 ont connu le LV dans une recension qui diffère considérablement de celle que nous révèlent la traduction tibétaine et le texte sanskrit transmis. Il n'est pas probable que si, au temps de Divākara, le LV avait déjà atteint sa forme actuelle, Divākara eût ignoré cette recension. Car nous savons par Fa-tsang 法藏 (cf. le *Houa yen king tchouan ki*, T. 2073, k. 1, p. 154c 11) que Divākara a séjourné dans les monastères de la Mahābodhi (à Bodhgayā) et de Nālandā. Dans ces centres importants du bouddhisme une telle recension n'aurait pu être inconnue. D'après toute vraisemblance le texte sanskrit de l'épisode d'Asita et, à plus forte raison, du LV entier, a donc dû se constituer après l'époque de Divākara mais avant la traduction tibétaine au premier quart du neuvième siècle. Le compilateur du texte sanskrit a dû se servir d'une recension, apparentée à celle traduite par Divākara. Nous l'y retrouvons presque entièrement à l'exception de quelques passages dont le plus important est celui qui relate la conversion des trois frères Kāśyapa, l'entretien avec Bimbisāra, la conversion de Śāriputra et Maudgalyāyana et la visite du Buddha à Kapilavastu (T. 187, chap. 26b). Mais, d'autre part, nous découvrons aussi dans le texte sanskrit beaucoup de passages qui font défaut dans la traduction de Divākara mais correspondent à des passages de la traduction de Dharmarakṣa. Un texte, apparenté à celui traduit par Dharmarakṣa, a donc dû exister à l'époque de l'établissement de notre texte sanskrit. Mais dans ces passages correspondants il y a souvent des divergences entre le texte sanskrit et la traduction de Dharmarakṣa. Tantôt c'est le texte sanskrit qui est le plus développé tantôt la traduction de Dharmarakṣa. Evidemment cela peut être dû, aussi bien aux vicissitudes subies par le texte, traduit par Dharmarakṣa, qu'aux remaniements effectués par le compilateur. Avant de se prononcer sur ce point, il faudrait tout d'abord comparer d'un bout à l'autre la traduction de Dharmarakṣa au texte sanskrit. Signalons au moins ici un fait qui n'est pas dénué d'intérêt. Dans l'épisode d'Asita nous avons constaté que la traduction de Dharmarakṣa contient dix-neuf strophes, se rapportant au sommeil du Buddha, qui manquent entièrement dans le texte sanskrit. Or, ces strophes sont remplies de termes propres au Mahāyāna. — En tout cas l'analyse de l'épisode d'Asita montre déjà clairement que le texte sanskrit repose sur des matériaux de provenance diverse. Ainsi donc l'étude des traductions chinoises, en révélant le caractère composite du texte sanskrit du LV, confirme pleinement les résultats de l'analyse linguistique, faite par M. Hiän-lin Dschi (*Die Umwandlung der Endung -am in -o und -u im Mittelindischen*, NGGW, phil.-Hist. Kl., 1944, p. 138 et *Die Verwendung des Aorists als Kriterium für Alter und Ursprung buddhistischer Texte*, ibid., 1949, p. 263—266).

Dans l'épisode d'Asita la différence la plus notable entre les deux traductions chinoises est l'absence totale de Naradatta, le neveu d'Asita, dans la traduction la plus ancienne. Comment faut-il expliquer ce silence sur Naradatta alors que, dans l'autre traduction, Naradatta est mentionné dès le début de l'épisode ? Pour savoir, si, sur ce point, la traduction de Dharmarakṣa atteste un état plus ancien de la légende, force nous est de consulter les autres textes parlant d'Asita. Dans le canon chinois bouddhique l'épisode d'Asita se trouve dans huit "biographies" du Buddha: le *Sieou hing pen k'i king* (T. 184, k. 1, p. 464a 28—465a 11), le *T'ai tseu jouei ying pen k'i king* (T. 185, k. 1, p. 474a 4—25), le *Yi tch'ou p'ou sa pen k'i king* (T. 188, p. 618a 26—b 6), le *Kouo k'iu hien tsai yin kouo king* (T. 189, k. 1, p. 626c 12—627c 3), le *Fo pen hing tsi king* (T. 190, k. 9—10, p. 693b 23—701a 19), le *Tchong hiu mo ho ti king* (T. 191, k. 3, p. 939c 12—941c 10), le *Fo so hing tsan* (T. 192, k. 1, p. 2c 2—3c 1), le *Fo pen hing king* (T. 193, k. 1, p. 60b 12—61c 16), ensuite dans le *Saṃghabhedavastu* du *Mūlasarvāstivādavinaya* (T. 1450, k. 2—3, p. 108a 18—110b 8), le *Kṣudrakavastu* (T. 1451, k. 20, p. 298a 18—299c 7), le *Ta tche tou louen* (T. 1509, k. 29, p. 274b), et dans les deux traductions complètes du *Mahāparinirvāṇasūtra* (T. 374, k. 27, p. 528b; T. 375, k. 26, p. 773a). De ces treize textes, quatre (T. 190, T. 191, T. 1450, T. 1451) mentionnent Naradatta. Des neuf autres traductions la plus récente est celle due à Guṇabhadra, le T. 189. D'après sa biographie dans le *Tch'ou san tsang ki tsi* (T. 2145, k. 14, p. 105c 16—18) cette traduction fut faite à King tcheou 荆州 où il résida de 446 à 455 (cf. P. Demiéville, BEFEO, 1924, p. 11). Des quatre traductions mentionnant Naradatta la plus ancienne est le T. 190, traduit par Jñānagupta. D'après le *Li tai san pao ki* (T. 2034, k. 12, p. 103b 20—21) celle-ci fut traduite entre 587 et 591 (ou 592). Les mêmes dates sont données dans le *Ta t'ang nei tien lou* (T. 2149, k. 5, p. 276a 4) et dans le *K'ai-yuan che kiao lou* (T. 2154, k. 7, p. 549a 18—19). Le résultat de l'examen des traductions chinoises est donc le suivant: absence de Naradatta dans tous les textes traduits avant 450, et mention de Naradatta dans tous les autres textes traduits après 580. Ceci mérite d'autant plus d'attirer notre attention que, sans exception, les textes sanskrits et palis mentionnent Naradatta (*Buddhacarita*, I, 81; *Mahāvastu*, vol. II, p. 30, l. 7—45, l. 3; le *Nālakasutta* du *Suttanipāta*, 679—723, et la *Nidānakathā*, p. 54, l. 14—55, l. 29). Mais Johnston a déjà rejeté le vers *Buddhac.* I, 81 comme inauthentique puisque ce vers manque dans la traduction chinoise (T. 192), et M. Lamotte a fait remarquer que le *Mahāvagga* dont le *Nālakasutta* fait partie n'offre pas de garanties d'ancienneté (cf. Revue de l'histoire des religions, Tome CXXXIV, 1948, p. 69—69). Que le Mahāvastu et la Nidānakathā sont des textes assez récents, est un fait admis depuis longtemps. Il paraît donc être bien évident qu'à l'origine Naradatta ne figurait pas dans l'épisode d'Asita.

Asita et Naradatta n'appartiennent pas à la seule tradition bouddhique. Au contraire ils sont mentionnés dans les textes védiques longtemps déjà avant le bouddhisme (cf. Macdonell and Keith, *Vedic Index*, s. v. Asita et Nārada; Caland, *Jaiminīya-Brāhmaṇa*, s. v. Asita Daivala). Mais alors que dans les textes védiques aucun texte n'associe étroitement Asita et Naradatta, le *Mahābhārata* contient un passage qui nous intéresse ici particulièrement. Dans le Mokṣadharma (Mhbh., XII, 267; éd. de Poona, 1952, p. 1460—1) un entretien entre Asita et Nārada est relaté. Au début se trouvent les deux strophes suivantes:

Atraivodāharantīmam itihāsaṃ purātanam
Nāradasya ca saṃvādaṃ Devalasyāsitasya ca. I.
āsīnaṃ Devalaṃ vṛddhaṃ buddhvā buddhimatāṃ varaḥ
Nāradaḥ paripapraccha bhūtānāṃ prabhavāpyayam. 2.

Le même sujet est l'objet de la conversation d'Asita et de Naradatta selon le *Kṣudrakavastu* (T. 1451, k. 20, p. 289a 23—24): «Le ṛṣi Asita s'entretenait avec lui de la naissance et de la destruction dans le monde» (cf. aussi le *Saṃghabhedavastu*, T. 1450, k. 2, p. 108a 26—28). Il paraît vraisemblable que la tradition d'un entretien d'Asita et de Naradatta sur la naissance et la destruction des choses a pris origine dans un milieu non-bouddhique. En introduisant Naradatta dans l'épisode d'Asita, les bouddhistes ont adopté cette tradition. Mais cela n'était pas suffisant pour intégrer vraiment Naradatta à la tradition bouddhique. Les bouddhistes l'ont pour ainsi dire «bouddhisé», en l'identifiant au célèbre Mahākātyāyana. Cette identification se trouve à la fin de l'épisode d'Asita dans le T. 191, le T. 1450, le T. 1451 et le *Mahāvastu*, et sans lien avec elle dans le *Mahāvastu* (vol. III, p. 382, l. 8—389, l. 11), le T. 190 (k. 37—8, p. 825a 18—831b 9) et le T. 1451 (p. 303a 6—305a 17)[2]. Mentionnons en passant que, dans le *Mahāvastu* (vol. III, p. 386, l. 18—389, l. 11) et dans le T. 190 (k. 38, p. 830a 22—c 16) nous retrouvons la deuxième partie du *Nālakasutta*, vers 699—723 du *Suttanipāta*. Mais l'identification de Naradatta à Mahākātyāyana a eu pour suite un autre changement dans l'épisode d'Asita. Alors que, d'après l'ancienne tradition, Asita réside ou dans l'Himālaya ou dans le royaume du roi Śuddhodana, Mahākātyāyana est originaire de l'Avanti d'après la tradition bouddhique qui semble s'être établie de bonne heure puisque, d'après les *Nikāya* et les *Āgama*, Mahākātyāyana réside souvent dans l'Avanti (cf. S. Mochizuki, *Bukkyōdaijiten*, p. 4722b—c). C'est ce fait même qui fut la cause du changement du lieu de résidence d'Asita. Nous voyons, en effet, que, dans le *Mahāvastu* (vol. II, p. 30, l. 7—8) et dans le T. 190 (k. 9, p. 693c 16—19), Asita vit dans les montagnes Vindhya près d'Ujjayinī. Dans d'autres textes il est question d'une montagne qu'il est difficile de situer. Elle est nommée Kin-che-ki-t'o 緊使吉陀 (T. 191, p. 939c 12) ou Ki-si-ki-mi 吉悉枳迷 (T. 1450, p. 108a 25).[3] Au début de l'épisode d'Asita dans le T. 1451 (p. 298a 21) il est dit simplement: «Dans le Sud sur une grande montagne», alors que, dans le passage tibétain correspondant, une montagne Kishkindha est nommée d'après Schiefner (op. cit., p. 1). Notons encore qu'Asita, après sa visite à Kapilavastu, se rend à une montagne, nommée Ki-sö-ki-t'o 枳瑟計馱 dans le

[2] Ce même passage a été traduit du tibétain par A. Schiefner, *Mahā-Kātjājana und König Tshaṇḍa-Pradjota*, St.-Pétersbourg, 1875, p. 11—14.

[3] Le texte tibétain ici a, d'après Rockhill (*Life of the Buddha*, London, 1907, p. 17—18), *kun-'dzin*. Mademoiselle Lalou a eu l'obligeance de bien vouloir vérifier pour nous cette lecture dans les éditions de Pékin et de Narthang, et celles-ci portent, en effet, toutes les deux *kun-'dzin*.

T. 191 et Sin-t'o 莘陀 dans le T. 1450 (k. 3, p. 110 a 11) mais que le *Saṃghabhedavastu* (k. 20, p. 299b 18—19) dit qu'il revient vers sa montagne (pen chan 本山). Avant tout il faudrait ici pouvoir consulter le texte tibétain du *Saṃghabhedavastu* et du *Kṣudrakavastu* pour savoir comment chaque fois ces noms ont été traduits ou transcrits en tibétain. Ne disposant pas d'un Kandjour à Leiden, nous devrons nous contenter d'avoir signalé ce petit problème. — Deux textes (de ceux qui mentionnent Naradatta) ne l'identifient pas à Mahākātyāyana, et situent Asita dans l'Himālaya ou dans le royaume du roi Śuddhodana. Ce sont la version en prose du LV et la Nidānakathā. Néanmoins la tradition méridionale n'est pas inconnue dans les Jātaka car, d'après les Nos. 423 et 522, Kāḷadevala réside dans l'Avanti. Dans le LV la vieille tradition a dû sur ce point prévaloir. — Il nous a paru intéressant d'attirer l'attention sur ces changements de résidence d'Asita. Mais il nous paraît pour le moment impossible d'en donner une explication satisfaisante. Nous ne savons que trop peu de la géographie des traditions et des textes, et nous ignorons quelles traditions locales ont pu ici jouer un rôle.

Pour terminer, revenons encore une fois au texte sanskrit de la version poétique de l'épisode d'Asita. Il y a ici un point de divergence entre le texte sanskrit et la traduction de Dharmarakṣa qui doit être signalé. Dans la septième strophe (p. 109, l. 13) de cette version poétique le texte sanskrit porte: *cāsau* (i. e. Asita) *svaśiṣyānvitaḥ*. Ici donc le texte sanskrit mentionne Naradatta bien qu'il ne soit pas du tout mentionné dans le passage correspondant de la traduction. Il nous paraît très probable que le compilateur du texte sanskrit (ou déjà avant lui l'auteur d'une version développée de la recension traduite par Dharmarakṣa) a voulu mentionner dans les strophes Naradatta puisqu'il figurait dans la version en prose. L'absence de Naradatta au début de cette version poétique et dans tous les textes anciens nous empêche de considérer cette mention comme authentique. Que, d'autre part, il soit mentionné dans les huit strophes finales (p. 110, l. 15—112, l. 2) qui n'ont pas de contrepartie dans le texte sanskrit, n'a rien de surprenant.

APPENDICE

Fo chouo p'ou yao king 佛說普曜經, T. 186 k. 2, p. 495b 4—496b 15[4].

Le roi rassembla le clan des Śākya, et, désireux de les interroger, il demanda: «Le prince sera-t-il maître du royaume ou sortira-t-il de la maison?[5] Je désire trancher ce doute.»

Les Śākya dirent: «Nous avons entendu que, dans les montagnes neigeuses, vit un ṛṣi, un brahmacārin, nommé Asita[6], qui est vieux et savant et qui excelle dans l'art des marques.»

Le roi se réjouit beaucoup et il fit atteler ensuite un éléphant blanc. Il désirait se rendre auprès du religieux. Des dieux, des nāga et des etrês divins se transformèrent en nombre incalculable et formèrent sa suite et sa garde.

[4] Nous tenons à exprimer ici notre gratitude à Monsieur A. F. P. Hulsewé qui a bien voulu relire notre traduction et suggérer des corrections.

[5] Cf. LV, texte sanskrit, p. 100, l. 20—22.

[6] *A-yi-t'eou* 阿夷頭.

A ce moment Asita vit les transformations miraculeuses, et il sut qu'au roi Śuddhodana[7] était né un fils saint dont l'éclat de majesté surpassait [celui des] dieux et des hommes. Le cœur rempli de joie, il désira lui rendre visite.

Alors le Bhagavat dit de nouveau en gāthā à l'assemblée:

1. Le ṛṣi, le brahmacārin Asita vit dans le ciel voler des dieux dont le corps avait la couleur de l'or rouge. Ayant vu cela, il se réjouit beaucoup.
2. «Est-ce un dieu, un asura ou un garuḍa ?», ayant eu cette pensée (*cintā*)[8], [il entendit:] «C'est le Buddha». Quand il eut entendu ce mot cardinal, il se réjouit, et, avec son œil divin, il regarda dans les dix directions.
3. Sa renommée est grande, sa vertu élevée comme une montagne, et semblable aux fleurs et aux fruits doux des arbres. Il est vénéré dans les trois mondes où il demeure.
4. Toute la terre est unie comme la paume de la main. Ainsi que les dieux se réjouissent sans erreur, et que le roi de la mer possède des joyaux, ainsi se manifeste le chemin de la loi.
5. Ainsi que le mal est détruit, et qu'il y a absence de souffrance, que les dieux vont et viennent dans l'air, et que j'ai entendu une voix céleste et douce, [ainsi] c'est le signe qu'un joyau est apparu dans les trois mondes.
6. Asita[9] regarda le monde, et, portant ses regards sur le roi Śuddhodana[10] à Kapilavastu[11], il vit que l'enfant, qui lui était né, possédait les marques et les marques secondaires, [signes] du puṇya[12]. Ayant vu cela, plein de joie, il y alla.
7. Se trouvant devant la porte du palais royal, il vit une foule d'incalculables koṭi [d'hommes]. Apercevant un serviteur, il demanda: «Comme la résidence du roi est belle!
8. Je désire entrer et avoir une audience du roi du pays.» Quand le portier eut vu le vieux ṛṣi, il fut rempli de joie et entra pour rapporter [cela au roi]. Le roi ordonna à un serviteur de le faire introduire.
9. Il fit préparer un siège, et, avec empressement, il le reçut. Entendant [les paroles du roi], Asita se réjouit. Dans son cœur il ressentit le vide de la faim[13]. Il demanda où se trouvait le Vénérable.
10. [Il dit:] «Je suis âgé, et je ne me montrerai plus souvent.» Le roi l'invita ā prendre place, et lui demanda: «Pourquoi vous êtes-vous donné la peine [de venir]?» «C'est parce que j'ai vu toutes ces transformations miraculeuses que je suis venu.
11. J'ai entendu qu'un fils vous est né, qu'il est le premier [parmi les hommes] et que son corps est pourvu des trente-deux marques. Je désire voir Sarvasiddhārtha[14]. Pour cette raison je suis venu.»

---

[7] *Po-tsing* 白淨.
[8] *tchen t'o* 眞陀
[9] *A-yi* 阿夷
[10] *Po* 白
[11] *Kia-yi* 迦夷
[12] Mérite; traduit en chinois par *fou* 福. Equivalence qui se retrouve souvent. cf. p. ex. Demiéville, BEFEO, XXIV, 1924, p. 90, n. 3.
[13] Tant était intense son désir de voir le Buddha.
[14] *P'ou-ki-yi* 普吉義

12. «Vous êtes le bienvenu. Je me réjouis de [votre visite]. Mais, en ce moment, il dort tranquillement. Attendez un instant son réveil. [Alors] vous le verrez, lui. merveilleux comme la pleine lune.»[15]

Alors Asita, alarmé en son cœur, répondit au roi en gāthā:

1. Depuis des kalpa innombrables il a accumulé avec énergie (*vīrya*) des actions vertueuses. Depuis la bodhi beaucoup de temps s'est écoulé. Comment pourrait-il dormir ?
2. De vie en vie il a pratiqué l'aumône, plein de compassion pour les misérables et sans avarice à l'égard de ses biens. Comment pourrait-il dormir ?
3. Il a observé la pureté, la discipline (*saṃvara*) et la moralité (*śīla*). Il a respecté la loi sans l'enfreindre. Il désire sauver avec compassion tous les êtres. Comment pourrait-il dormir ?
4. Il a toujours été patient, et plein d'amour. Son cœur ne connaît pas la haine. Il considère son esprit à l'égal d'une motte de terre (*samacittaloṣṭa*). Comment pourrait-il dormir ?
5. Son énergie est pareille à celle de la lune à son début. Son œil regarde sans être oisif. Il va partout pour contempler les Buddha dans les dix directions. Comment pourrait-il dormir ?
6. L'esprit concentré, il médite toujours sans jamais avoir de pensées distraites. Son esprit est ferme comme une grande montagne. Comment pourrait-il dormir ?
7. Il n'est rien que son intelligence ne pénètre. Sa sainte illumination surpasse l'éclat du soleil. Il n'est rien qu'il ne comprenne. Comment pourrait-il dormir ?
8. Il pratique toujours les quatre [exercices] illimités (*apramāṇa*). Il exerce la bienveillance, la compassion, la joie et l'équanimité. Comme Brahmā il est sans négligence. Comment pourrait-il dormir ?
9. Il applique les quatre conduites d'affection (*saṃgrahavastu*): le don et l'amour[16], le service des hommes et l'impartialité. Comment pourrait-il dormir ?
10. Il cultive les trente-sept rubriques (*bodhipakṣa*): les aide-mémoires, les abandons, les puissances, les forces, les pouvoirs miraculeux, [les constituants de] l'éveil et l'octuple chemin. Comment pourrait-il dormir ?
11. Il applique toujours les moyens [adoptés] aux circonstances. Au moment propice il convertit. En tout lieu il sauve tous les êtres. Comment pourrait-il dormir ?
12. Son cœur est toujours calme. L'esprit ferme et sans négligence (*pramāda*), il entre dans ce samādhi profond. Comment pourrait-il dormir ?
13. Il examine l'autrui et le moi, l'essentiel et le secondaire. Il regarde les Buddha dans les dix directions. Il comprend que tout, en réalité, n'existe pas. Comment pourrait-il dormir ?
14. Il applique toujours les trois moyens de délivrance (*vimokṣamukha*): le moyen du vide, du sans-marque, et du sans-désir[17]. Etre ou non-être, il ne s'attache à rien. Comment pourrait-il dormir ?

---

[15] Ces douze strophes correspondent au texte sanskrit p. 108, l. 10—110, l. 14.

[16] *dāna* et *priyavadya(tā)*; nous retrouvons la même traduction de ces deux mots dans la traduction du *Daśabhūmikasūtra*, due à Dharmarakṣa, cf. J. Rahder: *Glossary of the Daśabhūmika-sūtra*, Paris, 1928, s. v. *dāna* et *priyavadyatā*.

[17] Nous traduisons comme s'il y avait *wou-yuan* 無願 dans le texte au lieu de *tchou-yuan* 諸願.

15. Sa grande pitié exerce sa compassion sans obstacle. Le vaisseau de la Loi navigue dans les trois mondes pour délivrer de la naissance et de la mort. Comment pourrait-il dormir ?
16. Le chemin est comme le vide. Pour les hommes il descend lui-même. Par là il convertit [les êtres] des trois véhicules. Comment pourrait-il dormir ?
17. Il peut mesurer même le vide, savoir le nombre des gouttes d'eau dans l'eau de la mer, et compter toutes les herbes et tous les arbres. Comment pourrait-il dormir ?
18. Je vous prie, roi, d'écouter mes paroles. La vertu de votre enfant est inconcevable. Sa sagesse surpasse le nombre des grains de poussière. Comment pourrait-il dormir ?
19. Depuis qu'il a fait descendre son être divin dans le ventre de sa mère, [le nombre des êtres] qu'il sauvera ne peut être calculé, et ne peut être atteint par un homme insignifiant. Comment pourrait-il dormir ?

A ce moment le Bodhisattva s'éveilla de son sommeil. Mahāprajāpatī[18] l'enveloppa dans du coton blanc, le prit dans ses bras et se rendit auprès du roi. Le roi présenta au religieux de l'or jaune et de l'argent blanc, de chacun un sac. Le religieux n'accepta pas. Il défit le coton blanc pour étudier les marques du prince. Il vit les trente-deux marques. Son corps avait la couleur de l'or. Sur son crâne il y avait une protubérance charnue. Ses cheveux étaient bleus-violets. Entre ses sourcils se trouvait du duvet blanc. Sa nuque répandait l'éclat du soleil. Ses cils étaient de couleur violette, et clignèrent à la fois en haut et en bas. Sa bouche contenait quarante dents. Ses dents étaient blanches et unies. Sa mâchoire était carrée. Sa langue était large et longue. Les sept jonctions[19] étaient pleines. Il avait la poitrine du lion. Son corps était carré, droit et grand. Ses bras et doigts étaient longs. Le talon de ses pieds était plein, bien planté, uni et droit. A l'intérieur et à l'extérieur ses mains étaient recouvertes d'un filet de soie. Dans les paumes de ses mains et sur ses pieds il y avait une roue à mille rayons. L'organe de la reproduction était caché comme chez le cheval. Il avait les mollets de la biche. Ses os étaient comme des crochets et des chaînes. Les poils tournaient à droite. Dans chaque pore il y avait un seul poil. Les poils de la peau étaient fins et doux et ne retenaient pas la poussière ni l'eau. Sur sa poitrine il y avait le signe 卍. Quand Asita eut vu cela il poussa de grands soupirs, versa des larmes, et, plein de tristesse, il ne put parler. Le roi et Mahāprajāpatī furent effrayés dans leur cœur, levèrent les mains et lui demandèrent: «Y a-t-il quelque chose de néfaste ? Nous vous prions d'expliquer la raison de [votre conduite].» [Asita] leva les mains, et dit: «Il n'y a que du bonheur et rien de défavorable. Je me permets de vous adresser mes félicitations, grand roi, pour la naissance de ce fils divin. Hier soir, le grand tremblement du ciel et de la terre fut causé par ce fait même. L'art des marques, tel que je le connais, dit: Si l'enfant qui est né à un roi et possède les trente-deux marques, demeure dans le royaume, il sera un roi auguste, qui tourne la roue; les sept joyaux se présenteront spontanément; il aura mille fils et règnera sur les quatre continents en gouvernant selon la vraie loi. S'il abandonne le royaume et sort de la maison, il sera un Buddha spontané (*svayaṃbhū*) qui sauvera tous les êtres. Hélas, ma vie est déjà sur le déclin. J'irai dans l'autre monde sans avoir vu

[18] *Ta-ngai-tao* 太愛道
[19] *ho* 合

l'apparition du Buddha et sans avoir entendu ses sūtra. C'est pour cette raison que, moi-même, je suis triste.»

Sachant très bien qu' [Asita] était versé dans [la science] des marques, le roi fit construire des palais pour [le prince]. Il fit construire des résidences pour les trois saisons, chacune d'elles en un endroit différent: un palais d'automne pour y passer la saison fraîche, un palais frais pour y passer la saison chaude et un palais chaud pour y passer la saison du froid et de la neige. Il choisit cinq cents chanteuses, sélectionnant des filles droites, pas grasses, pas maigres, pas grandes, pas petites, pas blanches, pas noires et disposant de talents excellents. Chacune d'elles connaissait à la fois plusieurs arts. Toutes portaient sur le corps des colliers de perles blanches et de joyaux célèbres. Cent hommes se relayaient à tour de rôle pour le garder la nuit. Devant le palais il fit planter en rangées des arbres aux fruits doux. Entre les arbres [il fit creuser] des étangs pour se baigner. Dans ces étangs se trouvaient des fleurs miraculeuses. Il y avait plusieurs centaines de milliers de sortes d'oiseaux d'espèces variées. L'éclat de cette magnificence réjouissait le cœur du prince. [Le roi fit tout cela] dans le dessein que le prince n'eût pas envie de s'appliquer à l'éveil. Les enceintes du palais étaient solides. Quand on ouvrait et fermait les portes le bruit se faisait entendre à une distance de quarante lieues[20].

Fang kouang ta tchouang yen king 方廣太莊嚴經, T. 187, k. 3, p. 556 b 12—557 c 22.

Le Buddha dit aux moines: En ce temps le roi Śuddhodana[21] délibérait avec le clan des Śākya, [disant:] «Le prince, mon fils, sera-t-il un roi auguste, qui tourne la roue, ou sortira-t-il de la maison pour obtenir l'éveil de Buddha ?"

A cette époque un ṛṣi, doué des cinq pouvoirs surnaturels et nommé Asita[22] vivait avec son neveu, le māṇavaka[23] Nara[24], dans les montagnes neigeuses. Au moment de la naissance du Bodhisattva il vit d'innombrables signes merveilleux; il entendit les dieux dans l'air chanter des louanges et dire: «Un Buddha est apparu dans le monde»; et il vit tomber du ciel une pluie de toute sorte de fleurs odorantes et de toute sorte de vêtements, et il vit des hommes et des dieux aller et venir et exulter de joie. Alors, avec son œil divin, il regarda partout et il vit que, dans la ville de Kapilavastu[25], l'éclat du puṇya[26] du prince, [fils] du roi Śuddhodana, illuminait le monde, et qu'il possédait les trente-deux marques du grand homme. Quand il eut vu cela, il dit au māṇavaka Nara: «Sachez que, dans le Jambudvīpa à Kapilavastu, l'éclat du puṇya du prince, fils du roi Śuddhodana, brille partout dans les dix directions. Dans le monde il est le grand joyau. Les trente-deux marques ornent son corps. S'il reste dans la maison, il sera un roi auguste, qui tourne la roue de la loi; il règnera sur les quatre continents, il possèdera les sept joyaux, et il aura mille fils; il gouvernera la grande terre entièrement jusqu'à sa limite, l'océan; il règnera selon la loi sans se servir d'armes ni de soldats; spontanément tous lui seront soumis. S'il sort de la

[20] Ce qui suit dans la traduction de Dharmarakṣa correspond au texte sanskrit, p. 112, l. 3 ff.
[21] *Chou-t'an* 輸檀
[22] *A-sseu-t'o* 阿斯陀
[23] *t'ong tseu* 童子, garçon.
[24] *Na-lo* 那羅
[25] *Kia-p'i-lo* 迦毗羅
[26] *fou tō* 福德, bonheur-vertu.

maison, il sera le Buddha, et arrivera à l'éveil sans être guidé; il sera le maître des dieux et des hommes; sa renommée sera entendue en tous lieux, et il fera du bien à tous les êtres. Maintenant, vous et moi, nous devons aller le vénérer.»

Puis le ṛṣi Asita et le māṇavaka Nara s'y rendirent en volant par l'air comme des rois d'oies. Ils serrèrent leur pouvoir miraculeux, et à pied ils entrèrent dans la ville royale. Arrivés au palais du roi Śuddhodana, ils s'arrêtèrent devant la porte et dirent à la sentinelle: «Veuillez aller annoncer qu'Asita est venu visiter le roi.» La sentinelle se rendit auprès du roi, et il dit au roi: «Grand roi, devant la porte il y a un ṛṣi, nommé Asita, qui désire obtenir la permission de vous voir.» Quand le roi eut entendu cela, il fit nettoyer les salles du palais, préparer des sièges excellents, et fit introduire le ṛṣi dans le palais. Le ṛṣi entra et adressa des vœux de bonheur au roi, en disant: «Salut à Votre Majesté. Je vous souhaite une longue vie et un règne selon la loi.» Puis le roi offrit toute sorte de fleurs odorantes au ṛṣi, et il l'invita à s'asseoir sur un siège. Quand le ṛṣi se fut assis, le roi dit: «Grand ṛṣi, bien que j'aie sans cesse pensé à vous rendre hommage, je n'ai pas encore réalisé ce désir. Je ne sais pas pourquoi vous êtes venu aujourd'hui.» Le ṛṣi dit: «Grand roi, j'ai appris que vous avez un fils divin. Je désire le voir. C'est pour cela que je suis venu ici.» Le roi dit: «En ce moment mon fils dort. Je vous prie d'attendre un instant.» Le ṛṣi dit: «De tels grands êtres[27] sont éveillés de nature, et, en réalité, ne dorment pas.»

Moines, sachez qu'en ce moment le Bodhisattva eut pitié du ṛṣi et s'éveilla de son sommeil. Le roi lui-même le prit dans ses bras et le remit au ṛṣi. Agenouillé, le ṛṣi le reçut dans ses bras et l'examina complètement. Il vit que le corps du Bodhisattva était pourvu des marques et des marques secondaires et surpassait le roi Brahmā, Śakra Devendra et les quatre rois, Protecteurs du Monde, et que son éclat l'emportait sur cent mille soleils. Quand il eut vu cela, il se leva, joignit les mains, respectueusement le vénéra, et le loua de diverses manières, [disant] avec un soupir: «C'est un miracle[28] que l'apparition de ce grand homme dans le monde.» En lui présentant sa droite, il tourna trois fois autour de lui. Puis tenant le Bodhisattva dans ses bras, il eut cette pensée: «Maintenant un Buddha paraîtra dans le monde. Je suis désolé d'être faible et vieux, car je ne rencontrerai pas le Tathāgata. Je resterai toujours et pendant longtemps, et pour toujours je serai égaré de la vraie loi.» Alors, rempli de tristesse, il pleura, s'affligea, sanglota et fut suffoqué par des larmes. Quand le roi Śuddhodana vit que le ṛṣi Asita était tellement triste et qu'il ne pouvait se maîtriser, il fondit en larmes ainsi que la tante [du prince] et tous les parents. Il dit au ṛṣi: «Immédiatement après la naissance de mon fils, j'ai fait venir des connaisseurs de marques pour faire des prognostics. Je leur ai demandé si [les marques] étaient favorables ou non. Ils étaient tous très joyeux, et le considéraient comme [un être] miraculeux. Mais aujourd'hui, grand ṛṣi, vous pleurez si tristement que nous, les parents, avons le cœur rempli de doute: aura-t-il du bonheur ou du malheur? Je vous prie de nous le dire.» Alors le ṛṣi Asita essuya ses larmes et dit: «Mon seul désir est que le roi ne se livre pas à des idées tristes. Ma tristesse actuelle ne provient pas d'autres sentiments que de mon regret d'être vieux. L'heure de la

[27] *mahāsattva*; rendu par *tcheng che* 正士

[28] *adbhuta*. La traduction chinoise: *wei ts'eng yeou* 未曾有 repose sur une analyse du mot *adbhuta* en *a-bhūta*. Nous retrouvons cette même analyse aux Indes, cf. *Critical Pāli Dictionary*, s. v. *abbhuta*.

mort arrivera sans que j'aie entendu la vraie loi et que j'aie vu le Buddha paraître. Grand roi, sachez que d'innombrables êtres sont brûlés par le feu des passions, et que le Buddha sera capable de répandre la pluie de la loi ambrosiaque *(amṛtadharma)* pour l'éteindre. D'innombrables êtres errent dans le désert des vues perverses; le Buddha sera capable de leur montrer le chemin du Nirvāṇa et de la pureté. D'innombrables êtres sont enchaînés dans la prison des passions; le Buddha sera capable de leur pardonner et de leur faire obtenir la délivrance. D'innombrables êtres sont enfermés dans la transmigration et n'en peuvent sortir d'eux-mêmes; le Buddha sera capable de leur ouvrir la porte des moyens. D'innombrables êtres sont blessés par la flêche des passions; le Buddha sera capable de l'extraire pour les délivrer de cette douleur. Grand roi, ainsi qu'au cours des siècles les fleurs de l'udumbara ne paraissent qu'une seule fois, ainsi les Buddha, les Tathāgata, paraissent dans ce monde. Maintenant je regrette de ne pas devoir voir ce moment. Je suis triste pour la seule raison que je serai privé de sa protection. Grand roi, sachez que, si un homme rencontre le Buddha, assis sur le bodhimaṇḍa, soumettant l'ennemi Māra ou tournant la roue de la loi, cet homme obtiendra assurément un fruit excellent. Grand roi, d'innombrables êtres rencontreront le Buddha lors de son apparition dans le monde, observeront son enseignement vrai et obtiendront l'état d'arhat. Je regrette de ne pouvoir à ce moment prendre part à cela. C'est pour cette raison que je suis triste.

Grand roi, d'après ce qui est déclaré dans les traités védiques, le prince, fils du roi, ne sera certainement pas un roi auguste, qui tourne la roue. Pourquoi ? Parce que les trente-deux marques du grand homme sont extrêmement distinctes.»

Le roi dit: «Qu'est ce que vous nommez les trente-deux marques?» Le ṛṣi dit: «Voici les trente-deux marques:

1. Sur son crâne il y a une protubérance charnue.
2. Ses cheveux sont enroulés vers la droite en forme de conque. Leur couleur est bleue-violette.
3. Son front est large, plat et droit.
4. Entre ses sourcils il y a du duvet blanc comme la coquille k'o[29] et la neige.
5. Ses cils sont comme ceux du roi des bœufs.
6. Ses yeux sont de la couleur bleue-violette.
7. Il a quarante dents, égales et étincelantes.
8. Ses dents sont rapprochées et ne sont pas séparées.
9. Ses dents sont blanches comme la fleur du kiun t'ou[30] *(kunda)*.
10. Il a la voix brahmique.
11. Il obtient la meilleure saveur parmi les saveurs.
12. Sa langue est douce et mince.
13. Sa mâchoire est celle du lion.
14. Ses deux épaules sont pleines.
15. Son corps mesure sept coudées.
16. La partie antérieure de son corps est comme la poitrine du roi des lions.
17. Ses quatre canines sont étincelantes.
18. Sa peau et son corps sont doux et lisses et ont la couleur de l'or rouge pulvérisé.

[29] 珂 cf. Hōbōgirin, p. 221b.

[30] 軍圖

19. Son corps est droit.
20. Quand il laisse pendre ses mains, elles dépassent ses genoux.
21. Les parties de son corps sont pleines comme chez l'arbre nyagrodha.
22. Dans chaque pore il n'y a qu'un seul poil.
23. Les poils de son corps sont tournés vers la droite et fins au bout.
24. L'organe de reproduction est caché.
25. Ses cuisses sont droites et longues.
26. Ses mollets sont comme chez la biche (*eṇī*) [31] et le roi des animaux (*mṛgarāja*) [32].
27. Son talon est rond et droit.
28. Son cou-de-pied est saillant.
29. Ses mains et ses pieds sont doux et lisses.
30. Les doigts de ses mains et de ses pieds sont couverts d'un filet.
31. Sur la plante de ses pieds et dans la paume de ses mains il y a la marque de la roue, complète avec moyeux et jantes, pourvue de mille rayons, et étincelante d'un éclat de lumière.
32. La plante de ses pieds est plate, droite et partout bien plantée par terre.

Grand roi, ces trente-deux marques du grand homme que possède votre fils divin sont distinctes et évidentes. Seuls les Buddha portent ainsi les marques et non les rois de la roue. Grand roi, en outre votre fils divin possède les quatre-vingt marques secondaires. A cause de cela il ne restera pas dans la maison pour devenir un roi, qui tourne la roue, mais certainement il sortira de la maison pour obtenir l'éveil de Buddha.»

Le roi dit: «Grand ṛṣi, qu'est-ce que vous nommez les quatre-vingt marques secondaires?» Le ṛṣi dit: «Voici les quatre-vingt marques secondaires:

1. Les ongles des doigts de la main et du pied sont bombés.
2. Les ongles des doigts sont comme du cuivre rouge.
3. Les ongles des doigts sont lisses.
4. Les lignes de la main sont lisses.
5. Les lignes de la main sont profondes.
6. Les lignes de la main sont distinctes et évidentes.
7. Les lignes de la main sont droites et fines.
8. Les mains et les pieds ne sont pas courbés.
9. Les doigts de la main sont fins et longs.
10. Les doigts de la main sont pleins.
11. La pointe des doigts de la main s'affine graduellement.
12. Les doigts de la main ne sont pas courbés.
13. Les muscles et les veines ne sont pas visibles.
14. La cheville n'est pas visible.
15. La plante des pieds est plate.
16. Les talons sont ronds et droits.
17. Les lèvres sont de couleur rouge comme le fruit du bimba.
18. Sa voix n'est pas rude.
19. La langue est douce et a la couleur du cuivre rouge.

---

[31] *yi-ni* 伊尼
[32] *lou-wang* 鹿王

21*

20. Sa voix est comme le bruit du tonnerre, clair et agréable.
21. Ses organes sont complets.
22. Ses bras sont fins et longs.
23. Son corps est pur et beau.
24. Son corps est doux.
25. Son corps est uni et droit.
26. Son corps est sans lacune.
27. Son corps graduellement s'affine et est droit.
28. Son corps est inamovible.
29. Les parties du corps s'équilibrent.
30. Le cercle des genoux est plein.
31. Son corps est léger et merveilleux.
32. Son corps répand un éclat de lumière.
33. Son corps n'est pas incliné.
34. Le nombril est profond.
35. Le nombril n'est pas incliné.
36. Le nombril est au bon endroit.
37. Le nombril est pur.
38. Son corps est droit et beau.
39. Son corps est très pur et répand partout un éclat de lumière qui dissipe l'obscurité.
40. Sa démarche est celle du roi des éléphants.
41. Sa démarche est celle du roi des lions.
42. Sa démarche est celle du roi des bœufs.
43. Sa démarche est celle du roi des oies.
44. Sa démarche tourne vers la droite.
45. Son ventre est plein.
46. Son ventre est merveilleux et beau.
47. Son ventre n'est pas incliné.
48. Les marques de son ventre ne sont pas visibles.
49. Son corps n'a pas de taches noires.
50. Ses canines sont rondes et droites.
51. Ses dents incisives sont blanches, unies et rapprochées.
52. Ses quatre canines sont égales.
53. Son nez est haut, long et droit.
54. Ses yeux sont clairs.
55. Ses yeux sont sans souillure.
56. Ses yeux sont beaux et merveilleux.
57. Ses yeux sont longs et larges.
58. Le bord des yeux est droit.
59. Ses yeux sont comme le lotus bleu.
60. Ses sourcils sont fins et longs.
61. Tous ceux qui les voient se réjouissent.
62. La couleur des sourcils est bleue-violette.
63. Ses sourcils sont droits et s'affinent graduellement.
64. Les pointes des sourcils sont fines et liées ensemble.

65. Les joues sont unies et pleines.
66. Les joues sont sans lacune.
67. Les joues sont sans imperfection.
68. Son corps est sans lacune, et n'a rien de répréhensible ou de répugnant.
69. Ses organes des sens sont calmes.
70. Entre ses sourcils il y a un duvet à l'éclat blanc et étincelant.
71. Son front est large, plat et droit.
72. Le sommet de la tête est plein.
73. Ses cheveux sont beaux et noirs.
74. Ses cheveux sont fins.
75. Ses cheveux ne sont pas en désordre.
76. L'odeur de ses cheveux est pure.
77. Ses cheveux sont lisses.
78. Sur ses cheveux il y a le signe dix-mille.
79. Ses cheveux sont brillants et tournés en forme de conque.
80. Sur ses cheveux il y a les marques du Nandyāvarta[33], de la roue du bonheur[34] et du poisson[35].

Grand roi, telles sont les quatre-vingt marques secondaires de votre fils saint. Quand un homme possède ainsi les quatre-vingt marques secondaires, il ne peut pas rester dans la maison et certainement il en sortira pour obtenir l'éveil correct sans supérieur.»

Quand le roi Śuddhodana eut entendu ces paroles du ṛṣi Asita, dans son corps et son esprit il fut réjoui et il exulta de joie. Il se leva de son siège, s'inclina devant le Bodhisattva et prononça les gāthā suivantes:

«Toi qui es respecté et vénéré par Śakra et par tous les dieux et tous les hommes,
toi que tous les saints ṛṣi viennent honorer et vénérer,
toi, temple du monde, je m'incline devant toi, Seigneur[36], Roi.»

Moines, le roi Śuddhodana donna au ṛṣi Asita et au māṇavaka Nara toutes sortes de nourritures et de vêtements excellents et merveilleux, tourna autour d'eux, en leur présentant le côté droit, et s'inclina devant eux. Puis le ṛṣi Asita posa sa main sur l'épaule gauche du māṇavaka Nara et s'en alla par les airs. Alors le ṛṣi dit au māṇavaka: «Bientôt le Buddha paraîtra dans le monde. Vous devrez vous rendre auprès de lui pour demander sa permission de sortir de la maison. Pour une longue période[37] vous obtiendrez de grands profits et avantages.»

---

[33] *nan t'o yue to* 難陀越多
[34] *ki louen* 吉輪
[35] *yu* 魚
[36] *iśvara*; *tseu tsai* 自在
[37] *dīrgharātra*; *tch'ang ye* 長夜

P. S. Nous exprimons notre gratitude à Monsieur P. Demiéville qui a eu l'obligeance de lire une épreuve et de nous faire profiter de ses observations.

Karuṇāpuṇḍarika. Edited with Introduction and Notes by Isshi Yamada. Two volumes. London, School of Oriental and African Studies, 1968. 287 pp.; 420 + 22 pp. £ 6.6.—. [Sole distributing agents: Luzac & Company, London.]

The Sanskrit text of the *Karuṇapuṇḍarika* was first published in 1898 by the Buddhist Text Society of India (cf. Emeneau, *Union List*, No. 3718). This edition which I have not been able to consult seems to be very unsatisfactory. Sylvain Lévi has remarked that it contains many mistakes.[1] Apart from Sylvain Lévi, few scholars appear to have made use of it. Edgerton does not even mention it in his Grammar and Dictionary of Buddhist Hybrid Sanskrit. According to Dr. Yamada the edition of the Buddhist Text Society of India is based upon a single manuscript belonging to the Asiatic Society of Bengal (Ms. D of Yamada's edition).

[1] "Une légende du Karuṇā-Puṇḍarīka en langue tokharienne", *Mémorial Sylvain Lévi* (Paris, 1937), p. 276 (first published in the *Festschrift V.Thomsen*, Leipzig, 1912, pp.155-165).

The present edition is based upon six Sanskrit manuscripts, two versions of the Tibetan translation (Peking and Narthang) and two Chinese translations. Moreover, the editor has added a long introduction which occupies the greater part of volume one (pp. 7-250). Undoubtedly, this edition marks a great progress upon the editio princeps, but I am afraid that it is not free from imperfections. As long as no other manuscript materials become available, it will probably be impossible to establish an entirely satisfactory Sanskrit text. Nevertheless, with the help of the materials at present available, a better text could have been established. The main reason for the defects of this edition must be sought in the fact that the editor has not sufficiently taken into account the grammatical particularities of the text. He devotes a section of his introduction to the "Method of presentation of the text" (pp. 33-58) and discusses in it peculiarities of the spelling of words in manuscripts and differences between the Sanskrit text and the Tibetan and Chinese versions, especially as regards proper names, but little is said about the grammatical features of the text. The editor merely observes that on account of the flexibility of Buddhist Sanskrit grammar, he has refrained from correcting any grammatical peculiarities in the Sanskrit manuscripts. As examples he quotes *abhisaṃskārsīt* instead of *abhisamaskārṣit* (!), *samanupaśyāmaḥ* instead of *samanupaśyāvaḥ*, *pradakṣiṇikṛtvā*, *sajjikṛtvā* and irregularities of saṃdhi before initial *r*. This statement and the editorial practice of the editor make it clear that, in his opinion, a text, written in Buddhist Hybrid Sanskrit, may show almost any grammatical or lexicographical irregularity. Especially since the publication of Edgerton's Grammar and Dictionary of Buddhist Hybrid Sanskrit, there is often a tendency to select the most aberrant readings of the manuscripts and to justify them with references to Edgerton's work.[2] Dr. Yamada does not refer to Edgerton, but his edition shows clearly his conviction that any anomaly, described in Edgerton's Grammar, is admissible in the *Karuṇāpuṇḍarika*. Insufficient attention is being paid to Edgerton's classification of BHS (= Buddhist Hybrid Sanskrit Grammar) into three classes. Each editor of a BHS text has to determine to which of the three classes his text belongs. In an important article on "The language of the Buddhist Sanskrit texts" (*BSOAS*, xvi, 1954, pp. 351-371) John Brough has declared that the immediate task for the future is the closer delineation of the various forms and styles of Buddhist writings in Sanskrit, and a detailed grammatical analysis of each type. In his article he presents specimens of nine distinct styles. For the time being, it will perhaps be better to adhere to the three classes set up by Edgerton. The *Karuṇāpuṇḍarika* clearly falls within the second class in which the verses are hybridized, but the prose has relatively few signs of Middle Indian phonology and morphology. The prose of the *KP* (= *Karuṇāpuṇḍarika*) is very rich in BHS words. Although most of them have been recorded in Edgerton's dictionary, it would have been the task of the editor to give an index of BHS words. Below I list a number of BHS words with references to the text without trying to be complete with regard to the words selected and to the references given. A second list contains words, which are absent from Edgerton's Dictionary and a few others worthy of note.

The Sanskrit text of the *KP* has been badly transmitted. This is especially true of the first part. All six manuscripts used by the editor are recent Nepalese manuscripts, written by scribes who had only a vague knowledge of Sanskrit. They are certainly responsible for such anomalies as confusions of number, gender and case. The prose of the *KP* is written in a fairly correct Sanskrit as is obvious from the passages which have suffered less in the course of transmission. Undoubtedly, in many places it is impossible to establish a correct text, because the manuscripts are too corrupt. However, in other cases it is quite well possible to correct the readings of the manuscripts with the help of the Tibetan and Chinese translations. The editor shows an exaggerated confidence in the correctness of the manuscripts. Even when the manuscripts omit an

2 Cf. my review of Ratna Handurukande's edition of the *Maṇicūḍāvadāna*, *IIJ*, XII, p. 140-143.

anusvāra, he does not correct them. It is clear that all six manuscripts go back to a fairly recent archetype which is full of scribal errors. In these circumstances, it is the task of the editor to correct the text wherever possible with the help of the Tibetan and Chinese translations. In places where the manuscripts are too corrupt, it is necessary to indicate in the notes the text on which the translations are based. Dr. Yamada could have made much more use of the translations. Often he does not indicate differences between the Sanskrit text and the translations, although he is aware that these differences exist. In his introduction Dr. Yamada even states that they indicate the fact that there were many versions of the *KP* in the past (p. 43). The examples which he gives only concern the omission or addition of words. However, in some passages there are more considerable differences between the Sanskrit text and the translations (cf. introduction pp. 24-26; cf. also Vol. I, notes pp. 251-287). In view of the fact that the Sanskrit text has been so badly transmitted, more importance must be attached to the places where differences exist between the Tibetan translation, on the one hand, and the Chinese translation on the other.[3] These differences are not such that they point to the existence of many versions in the past. In a few places, the Tibetan translation is based upon a text which is slightly expanded or altered. Most of the differences between the Tibetan translation and the Chinese translations are of a very minor nature, as can be expected in the course of several centuries of transmission. In some cases it is evident that the Tibetan translation is based upon a manuscript which contained corrupt readings. Other differences are caused by wrong interpretations due to the translators of the Sanskrit text into Tibetan. In his notes the editor often merely reproduces the text of the Tibetan and Chinese translations and leaves it to the reader to draw his own conclusions.

The introduction is divided into two parts. The first deals with the materials and the text (pp. 8-62). It is a pity that the English text has not been corrected as carefully as one might expect in a publication of the School of Oriental and African Studies. According to the editor his edition is based upon six manuscripts, but I have failed to discover in the notes any reference to the manuscript of the Kyoto University Library (MS. F). For the Tibetan translation the editor has used the Peking and Narthang editions.[4] A long passage is repeated twice in the Narthang edition as is pointed out by the editor. For the history of the Kanjur editions, it would be interesting to know whether this repetition also occurs in other editions.

The beginning of the Sanskrit text (1.4-7.15) is quite different from the Chinese and Tibetan versions. The editor remarks that it is very similar to the beginning of the *Saddharmapuṇḍarīka*, but that it is not a simple quotation from it, for there are passages which are not found in it (*KP* 6.7-7.15). In this connection the editor raises a series of questions: "Was this alteration made on purpose, or by accident? If it were the former, what was the reformer's intention to change the introductory part following the fashion of that in the SP? What was the relationship between our text and the SP? Was it the reformer of the Sanskrit version of the KP who added the new sentences, after quoting the SP, in order to expound the idea? Did a certain recension of the SP exist, which

[3] According to the editor the two manuscripts used by the two Chinese translators are fundamentally similar and belong to the same transmission (cf. p.16).

[4] Winternitz (*A History of Indian Literature*, Vol. II, Calcutta, 1933, p. 313, n. 2) states that Feer translated the introduction to the Tibetan version. However, Feer translated the first chapter of the *Mahākaruṇāpuṇḍarīka* which is an entirely different text (cf. *Bibliographie bouddhique*, II, Paris, 1931, p. 6 no. 27 and p. 7 no. 33). Feer translated also a passage of the same text relating to the compilation of the Canon (*Annales du Musée Guimet*, Vol. V, 1883, pp. 78-80). The Tibetan text was edited by him in 1865 (cf. *Bibliographie bouddhique*, II, p. 3 no. 6). The same text was translated from the Chinese version by Jean Przyluski (*Le concile de Rājagṛha*, Paris, 1926-1928, pp. 122-124).

was different from the recensions we have today and possessing all passages quoted by the KP, and which was also lost in the course of transmission? Was there a certain sūtra from which both the writer of the SP and the reformer of the KP quoted the opening passages?" He concludes with saying: "Although these are such questions that cannot be answered from the existing materials in our hands, new discoveries of materials in future and investigations on this matter may give us certain clues one day to advance the morphological studies on these Mahāyāna texts." I have not quoted these two passages in order to give a specimen of the style of the editor. It would have been the task of the Publications Committee to make the necessary corrections. However, they show with how little care the editor has studied his text. It is obvious that pp. 1.4-6.7 have been copied from the beginning of the *Saddharmapuṇḍarika*.[5] The following passage (6.9-7.3) is clearly based upon *Lalitavistara* pp. 51.19-52.15 (ed. S. Lefmann). The remaining passage (7.4-7.15) is a fragment of the original text (cf. the Tibetan translation, Vol. I, 255.6-10; 256.22-24; 257.7-13). Only one small passage (7.8-10), a well-known cliché, is not found in the Tibetan translation. The only reason for quoting the *Saddharmapuṇḍarika* and the *Lalitavistara* as a substitute for the original text of the beginning is to be sought in the fact that often the first leaves of a manuscript are lost. It is not surprising to see that the Nepalese scribe of the archetype of the six manuscripts has used two texts of which many manuscripts existed in Nepal in order to fill the gap. This, incidentally, furnishes another argument for assuming that the archetype has been written at a fairly recent date.

The second part of the introduction contains a summary of the text (pp. 63-120) and a study of its contents (pp. 121-250). Especially this last section is a very valuable contribution to the study of Buddhist literature. Dr. Yamada examines the development of the concept of many Buddhas, the texts relating to *vyākaraṇa* and *praṇidhāna*, the formation of the *Karuṇāpuṇḍarika* and its relations with the Amithābha literature. He quotes a wide range of Chinese Buddhist texts as perhaps only a Japanese scholar is able to do.

As far as I know no other scholar has made such an exhaustive study of the *KP*. Dr. Yamada does not refer to any Japanese studies. Therefore it is perhaps useful to list the publications dealing with the *KP*, which have come to my notice (an asterisk indicates publications which I have not been able to consult).

- * Ono Gemmyō, "Hikekyō no ni-honshōdan", *Shūkyō Kai*, III,5 (1907).
- * Katō Chigaku, "Muryōjukyō to Hikekyō no taishō", *Mujintō*, XXIV, 11 (cf. *IBK*, III, 1, p. 187).
- * Mochizuki Shinkō, "Hikekyō no Mida honjō setsuwa ni tsuite", *Bukkyōgaku zasshi*, III,7 (1922).
- Mochizuki Shinkō, *Jōdokyō no kigen oyobi sono hattatsu* (Tokyo, 1930), pp. 336-345.
- * Nishio Kyōo, "Hikekyō no seiritsu oyobi sono busshinkan", *Ōtani Gakuhō*, XII, 2 (1931), pp. 44-62 (cf. *Bibliographie bouddhique*, III, No. 250).
- Mochizuki Shinkō, *Bukkyō daijiten*, vol. V (Tokyo, 1933), pp. 4294c-4296b.
- Mochizuki Shinkō, *Bukkyō kyōten seiritsu shiron* (Kyoto, 1946), pp. 236-246.
- Ujitani Yūken, "Karuṇāpuṇḍarīka no Amidabutsu inganmon ni tsuite", *IBK*, III,1 (1954), pp. 186-190.
- Sanada Ariyoshi, "Hikekyō ni tsuite", *Nihon bukkyō gakkai nenpō*, 21 (1955), pp. 1-14.
- * Sanada Ariyoshi, "Hikekyō no betsushutsukyō ni tsuite", *Ryūkoku daigaku ronshū*, 354 (1957), pp. 1-23 (cf. *Bibliographie bouddhique*, XXVIII-XXXI, No. 568).
- * Ujitani Yūken, "Hikekyō" no Amidabutsu hongan kō", *Dōhō gakuhō*, IV (1957), pp. 41-95 (cf. *Bibliographie bouddhique*, XXVIII-XXXI, No. 570).
- Ujitani Yūken, "Karuṇāpuṇḍarīka ni okeru ichini no mondai", *IBK*, X, 1 (1962), pp. 108-113.

[5] With the exception of 5.7-13 for which passage see *LV*, p. 51.10-16.

Ujitani Yūken, "Bonzō taishō ni yoru Hikekyō shosetsu no Muryōjubutsu honganmon ni tsuite", *IBK*, XIII,1 (1965), pp. 221-226.
* Ujitani Yūken, "Hikekyō ni okeru shobutsu honnen to Muryōjubutsu honganmon", *Shinshū Kenkyū*, vol. X (cf. *IBK*, XV,2, p. 510).
Ujitani Yūken, "Hikekyō no Bayuhichū 'Vāyuviçṇu' to Daihi biku", *IBK*, XV,2 (1967), pp. 506-511.

While reading the text of the *KP* I have made a number of notes. In several places I have consulted the Tibetan translation but I have only rarely made use of the Chinese translation. The *Karuṇāpuṇḍarika* is a very long text. To compare it from the beginning to the end with the Tibetan translation and the two Chinese translations is a task which can only be undertaken by the future editor of a new edition of the Sanskrit text. It is difficult to know whether the manuscripts contain readings worthy of note which have not been recorded by Dr. Yamada. According to his introduction he has only noted the variant readings which effect (sic!) the meaning of the passage or have some grammatical significance (Vol. I, p. 33). A future editor would have to take much more account of parallel passages to be found in the text itself or in other texts. As remarked above, not sufficient use has been made of the Tibetan and Chinese translations. On account of its literalness, the Tibetan translation will generally be more useful. However, where both Chinese translations are clearly based upon a text different from the one used by the Tibetan translation, an attempt must be made to establish a text which corresponds with the text underlying the Chinese translations, provided that the context shows the latter to be more acceptable. The following notes contain a number of emendations. Others have been mentioned in the indices. These notes are only meant to provide an indication of the work which will have to be done for the establishment of a better text.

It is easier in a review to point out the defects of a book rather than its merits. I am afraid that the above remarks have created the mistaken impression that Dr. Yamada's work is without any merit. This is undoubtedly not the case. It is obvious from the notes to the text that Dr. Yamada has an excellent knowledge of Tibetan and Chinese. Often his suggestions are extremely useful. My main objection concerns the principles which have guided him in the establishment of the text.

In the following notes and indices Y. indicates Dr. Yamada's readings. For the Tibetan translation I refer to the Peking edition. *BHSD* = Edgerton's *Buddhist Hybrid Sanskrit Dictionary*; *CPD* = *A Critical Pāli Dictionary*. Texts are referred to by the abbreviations used in these two dictionaries.

1.10 °*vaśi*° – *SP* 1.8 °*vaśitā*°.
2.3 *Mahāsthāmnā* – *SP* 1.10 *mahanāmnā*.
5.3 *samādhānamukhanirdeśaṃ caryāvaiśāradyaṃ* Cf. 287.11-12, etc. (see below Index I *samādhāna*).
5.10 *nābhipatato* – *nābhitapato*.
5.11 *bāhuprasāritaṃ* – *bāhuṃ pra*°.
7.8 *avacot* – *avocat*.
8.20 *padmaṃ* – *padma*. Both *padma* n. and *padma* m. are used, cf. 9.19, 66.10, 68.3, etc.
12.6 *mukhān nir*°. Dr. Yamada adds in a note: "Read *mukhāt* (abl)!
15, n.11 Ch ins *arajocittāḥ*. More probably *amalacittāḥ*.
16.4-5 '*sārabhinnāccālanabalino* – °*bhinnoccālana*°, cf. T. *goṅ-du skyod-par byed-pa* = *uccālana*.
17.9 *tārakārūpā*; note 5: New comp. for constellation. – See *PTSD tārakā*.
20.11 *daśābhyantarakalpān* – *daśāniarakalpān* (same correction in 21.4). Cf. 31.10
29.19 T. adds *dharmabhāṇakasya* (160b7).
30. n.5 *snobs pa* – *spobs pa*.

32.6 *tasyām eva rātryām atyayena* – *tasyā eva rātryā atyayena*. The frequent use of the *m* as saṃdhi-consonant in the *Karuṇāpuṇḍarikā* is due to the tendency of the scribes to avoid hiatuses. In 70.2 all MSS. read *tasyā eva rātryā*. Elsewhere the *m* is to be found, cf. 34.1, 119.4,20, 120.1 etc.

38.3-4 *vacasā ... suprativídhāḥ* – °*viddhāḥ*, cf. *Mvy* 2411,2415,2416; *BHSD paricita*.

39.3 *utsārayitavyāḥ* – *uccārayitavyāḥ*. Cf. 73.4 *uccārayiṣyanti*.

41.15 *Santāraṇa* – The Chinese versions read *Santīraṇa* (cf. p. 52, n. 7) but the Tibetan version *Santāraṇa* (*yaṅ-dag-par sgrol-ba*) or *Santiraṇa* (*yaṅ-dag rtog*), cf. 116.11, 220.13, 285.18, 288.5, 290.12, 291.8, 295.4, 297.14, 300.9 and *Utpalasaṃtīraṇa* 181.3, 183.13. See also Yamada, Vol. I, p. 79. The original reading must have been *Saṃtīraṇa*.

43.2 *Maitreyāśāparipūrṇāśaktas* – *Maitreyāśā paripurṇā, śaktas*. This is one of the cases in which the editor had failed to separate the words correctly.

47.14 *tataḥ parṣadam* – according to T. one must read *tasyāṃ parṣadi tādṛśam*, cf. 80.7.

49.7 *buddhadarśanāt sukhā priṇitagātrā* – T. *saṅs-rgyas mthoṅ-ba'i bde-bas lus tshim-par gyur-nas* = *buddhadarśanasukhena priṇitagātrā*.

51, n. 2 *bsṅus pa* – *bsdus pa*.

62.17 °*bhṛṅgārāma*° – °*bhṛṅgārārāma*°, cf. 60.12

67.5 *bhakṣayante* – *bhakṣayantaṃ*. cf. T. 177a7.

68.9 *saṃvicintayamāna* – *svapnaṃ vicintayamāna*, cf. p. 68, n. 2 for T.

68.15 *adhatriyāṃ varṣaśatāṃ* – *ardhatṛtiyāṃ* ... Also 71.4

69.2-3 *strī*° ... *yācayitvā* not in T. (178a3-4).

75.16,17 *duḥkhotpattibhūtaṃ* – T. *duḥkhotpattihetubhūtaṃ* (*sdug-bsṅal 'byuṅ-ba'i rgyu*).

79.11 *katame sattvā bhagavatā vinītāḥ sad ekasattvasyāpi* – ... *vinītāḥ yad* ...

80.8 *tadĀdarśavyūhaṃ* – *yathādarśavyūhaṃ* (MSS. *yadā*-).

90.4-6 *gacchata rājānaḥ svakasvakāṃ devaparṣadāṃ sannipātayata Jambūdvipe, bhagavantaṃ darśanāyopasaṃkrāmata* – *gacchata rājānaḥ, svakasvakāṃ devaparṣadāṃ sannipātayata, Jambūdvīpe bhagavantaṃ darśanāyopasaṃkrāmata*.

98.2 *āsanasthā*, n. 1: T. *adūrasthāyino* – T. *āsannasthā*.

102.7 *samāptā* – *samāpto*.

117.3 *vellitavasumatīsaśailā* – *calitavasumatī saśailā*. Cf. 120.12, 123.15, 134.16. MSS. BE *calita*°.

124.20 *sattvānām āśayapariśodhayamānaḥ* – ... *āśayaṃ pari*°.

125.19 *nāsmākaṃ pratirūpaṃ*, n. 7: read *pratibhāgam* – T. *cha* renders Sanskrit *pratirūpa*, cf. Jäschke, *Tibetan-English Dictionary*, p. 151a: *cha ma yin-pa* "unfit, improper, unbecoming", *Divy* 127.11 *na mama pratirūpaṃ* = T. *bdag-gi cha ma yin-te*.

130, n. 7 *dril* – *dri la*.

132, n. 2 *dur smrig* – *ṅur smrig*.

133.7 *nāmaṃ* – *nāma*.

145.13 *śarīraṃ sādhayeyuḥ* – *śarīraṃ dhyāyeyuḥ* (T. *sregs-par gyur-nas*), cf. *BHSD* **dhyāyati*.

153.9 *anuttarais tavais taveyaṃ* – *anuttaraiḥ stavaiḥ staveyaṃ* (T. *bla-na ma mchis-pa dag-gis bstod-pa gyur-cig* 218b8).

159.15 *Māravinarditaḥ* – T. *Mānavinarditaḥ* (*ṅa-rgyal sgrogs*), Ch. 1 "destroying king Māra" (193b4): *Māravimarditaḥ*?

163.7 *upasthiteyaṃ* – *upasthiheyaṃ* (MSS. ACDE: *upasthiheyaṃ*), cf. *adhiṣṭhiheyaṃ* 245.3, *upasthiheyaṃ* 314.5.

168.18-19 *na dvijihve nerṣyāmātsaryaparicite* – *na dvijihvo nerṣyāmātsaryaparito* (T. *dkris-pa* = *parīta*, cf. *Mvy* 2443; 149.6 *parītās*, T. *dkris-pa*). Same correction 419.2 *mithyādharmaparicitānāṃ*, read °*parītānāṃ* (T. *yoṅs-du dkris-pa*).

170.2,6 *karmakṛtam* – *karma kṛtam*.

170.7-8 *nityagarbhavāsena pratyājāyeyur duḥkhaṃ pratyanubhavitavyaṃ bhavet* T. – *mṅal-na gnas-pa'i sdug-bsṅal ñams-su myoṅ-bar gyur-pa* (227a2) = *garbhavāsaduḥ*-

khaṃ pratyanubhavitavyaṃ bhavet.

170.11 *garbhavāsena ca pratyājāyeyus – garbhavāse na ca* ... (T. *mṅal-na gnas-par skye-bar ma gyur-cig* 227a4). Yamada, Vol. I, p. 270: *na garbha-vāsena – garbhavāse na.*

170.12 *karmaparikṣayaṃ – karma parikṣayaṃ.*

181.4 *Baliṣṭhā – Variṣṭhā* (MSS. *cariṣṭhā*; T. *mchog*).

188.7 *sarvaparigrahāvasaraṇatāyai – °vasarjanatāyai*? (T. *spoṅ-par byed-par 'gyur-ro*).

197.7 *abhiśaya – atiśaya* (T. *khyad-'phags*).

197.10 *naramanu – naravaru* (T. *mi-yi dam-pa*), cf. 199.13.

204.16 *manāthā – manāpā*? (T. *yid-du mchi*).

206.1 *bhavacārake pratibhayaṃ – ... °bhaye.*

214.7 *ratnavṛṣṭiḥ pravarṣān ni° – ... pravarṣen* ... (MS. C *°varṣon*; MS. D.*°varṣen*).

215.9 *śrotrapatheṣu – śrotrapuṭeṣu* (MS. A *°puteṣu*, MSS BCDE *°puṭeṣu*), cf. 419.9 *karṇapuṭeṣu* (T. *rna lam-du* 336b5). The Tibetan translator has wrongly translated *patha* instead of *puṭa*.

219.10-11 *mahākaruṇāṃ sarjayeyuḥ – mahākaruṇāṃ saṃjanayeyuḥ.*

219.14 *sattvān pratyuhyamānān – sattvān uhyamānān* (MSS. ABE *satvāny ujyamānāny*).

219.17 *praṇidhānaṃ sarjayitvā – praṇidhānaṃ saṃjanayitvā.*

224.6 *tad api – tathāpi* (T. *'on-kyaṅ* 251a4).

224.13 *saṃpratipannāḥ daśasu kuśaleṣu karmapatheṣu – ... daśasv akuśaleṣu karmapatheṣu.* However, the Chinese and Tibetan versions of this passage (224.11-18) are different from the Sanskrit text. The Tibetan translator has failed to see that *anarthikās* (224.11) relates not only to *triṣu sucariteṣu* but also to *devamānuṣikābhiḥ śrisaṃpattibhir* (cf. 230.6, 234.10).

230.4-5 *riktamuṣṭisadṛśasantānāṃ – riktamuṣṭisadṛśadagdhasantānān.* T. *chaṅ-pa* (not *chad-pa* as in 230, n. 2, cf. *Mvy* 2813, Jäschke, *'chaṅs-pa*) *stoṅ-pa lta-bu daṅ sems-can rgyud tshig* (Peking *cig* must be corrected into *tshig* as is obvious from the Chinese versions) *-gi.*

235.3-4 *pañcakāmaguṇāgṛddhacittā – °guṇagṛddha°* (T. *'dod-pa'i yon-tan lṅa-la 'chums-pa'i sems* 256b2).

235, n. 7: Ch T ins. *mātsaryacittāḥ – kadaryacittāḥ*, cf. *Mvy* 2485; 238.3 *kadaryāḥ*, T. *'juṅs-pa.*

237.14 *paruṣadaṃśamaśakāśīviṣa° – paruṣa* not in T.

246.12 *pūrvaṃ vaireṇa – pūrvavaireṇa* (T. *sṅon-gyi 'khon-gyis* 262a4), cf. BR *pūrvavairin.*

246.18 *āpatyāṃ – āyatyāṃ* (T. *slan-chad* 262a7).

248.12 *mā cāhaṃ śakyaṃ – mā cāhaṃ śaknuyāṃ* (MSS. ABE *satkuryā*; MSS. CD *satkuryāṃ*)

250.10 *°śrutadhāraṇīvipraṇāśa° – °śrutadharāvipraṇāśa°.*

255.3 *pūrvabuddhāsukṛtādhikāriṇāṃ* T. has translated *pūrvabuddheṣu kṛtādhikārāṇāṃ* but the Chinese versions have rendered *pūrvabuddheṣv akṛtādhikārāṇāṃ.*

263.11 *°rocamahārocamānapūrṇācandravimalā°* – Ch. 2 seems to have read *rocamahāroca* (*māna* is a mistake for *mahā*)*-sthalamahāsthalacakravimala.* Cf. *Mvy* 6183-6192.

265.16 *akalahābandhanavigrahāḥ* – T. has read *akalikalahabandhanavigrahāḥ* (*thab-mo daṅ / 'thab-pa daṅ / rtsod-pa daṅ / 'chiṅ-ba dag ma mchis-pa* 271a1), cf. *Mvy* 5229.

266.15 *śarīrās tṛkāryaṃ – śarīrāḥ śāstṛkāryaṃ* (T. *ston-pa'i mdzad-pa*), cf. 313.17

268.5 *nirvarte tu gaticakre – nivartite gaticakre* (T. *'gro-ba'i 'khor-lo zlog-ciṅ* 272a5). Cf. 313.2 *vivartitagaticakraḥ*, read *nivartita°.*

270.3 *tīvrakleśe raṇakaṣāye kaliyuge – tīvrakleśaraṇakaṣāye kaliyuge* T. *ñon-moṅs-pa daṅ / thab-mo daṅ / sñigs-ma bdo-źiṅ rtsod-pa'i dus-la* 273a5), cf. 287.18, 297.8-9.

270.7 *na ca visarāmi bodhau praṇidhānaṃ – na ca visṛjāmi* (T. *spaṅ-bar mi bgyi-źiṅ* 273a8)

291.2 *bhagavataḥ sakāśāt parivartitvā – ... parāvṛtya* (T. *phyir-phyogs-te*), cf. 301.4.

296.10-11 *tena bhagavatā tathārūpaṃ smitaṃ prāviṣkṛtaṃ yadā* – ... *prāviṣkṛtaṃ yathā* (T. *'di-lta-ste* 282a7).

305.3 *te puṣpā visaritā* – ... *vikasitā* (T. *kha-bye-źiṅ* 286b6).

306.9 *śrāvakapratyekabuddhavarjitā* – °*varjita*.

315.4 *Saurabhyākiṃśukā* – *Sauratyākiṃśukā* (T. *des-pa* ...), cf. 345.3, 347.7.

336.11-12 *nirodhavidhapraśamena samādhinā* – The Chinese versions translate *anurodhavirodha*°, but T. *nirodhavirodha*°, cf. *Mvy* 606 *sarvanirodhavirodhasaṃpraśamano nāma samādhiḥ*.

337.8 *araṇena samādhinā* – T. *araṇasaraṇasarvasamavasaraṇena samādhinā*, cf. *Mvy* 618.

337.9 *anilaniketena samādhinā* – Ch. 2 *aniketaniratena samādhinā*? Cf. *Mvy* 619 *anilambhaniketanirato nāma samādhiḥ*; *Pañcaviṃśatisāhasrikā Prajñāpāramitā* (ed. N. Dutt), p. 203.14: *anilāniketo nāma samādhiḥ*; *BHSD a-nilambha*.

339.9 *vivaraṇaprahāṇāya* – *nivaraṇa*° (T. *sgrib-pa* 301b7).

340.4 *sarvakleśān avamardanatayā* – *sarvakleśāvamardanatāyai* (T. *ñon-moṅs-pa thams-cad 'joms-par byed-par 'gyur-ro* 302a5), cf. 189.4-5.

340.8 *akuśaladharmāpasaraṇa*° – *akuśaladharmāvasarjana*°? See above 188.7

351.14 *netrāv utpādya* – ... *utpāṭya*, id. 380.2

360, n. 14 *spos* (311a5) is to be corrected into *spyos*.

362.11 °*saṃkṣobhavividam* – ... *vivādam* (T. *rtsod-pa* 312a1).

367.10 *mārabalaparāśayaśabdaṃ* – °*parājayaśabdaṃ*. See Yamada, vol I, p. 39 for a strange attempt to justify the reading *parāśaya*.

376.9 *saṃśrayase mahākalpe* – *saśreyase* (T. *legs-bcas*) *mahākalpe*.

397.9 *adhiṣṭhavān* – *adhiṣṭavān*.

406.4 *Dharmaveśapradīpaḥ* – *Dharmavegapradīpaḥ*, cf. T. (*chos-kyi śugs-kyi sgron-ma*) and Ch. 1.

407.2 *Vigatasaṃtāpodbhava*° – *Vigatasaṃtāpobhyudgata*°, cf. the Chinese and Tibetan translations and 407, n. 15.

415.3 *avikṣiptam* – T. *anutkṣiptam aprakṣiptam*, cf. *Mvy* 6357.

Index I.

a-kṣūṇa – *akṣūṇavyākaraṇā* 258.15-259.1

adhitiṣṭhati – *vajramayam ātmabhāvam adhitiṣṭhati* 33.6-7; *sāvaśeṣakarmaphalaṃ cādhiṣṭhiheyaṃ* 245.3-4; *evaṃrūpāṃ karmaphalān aparikṣiṇān adhiṣṭhihitvā* 246.10; *sarvatathāgatādhiṣṭhitatvāt* 78.11; *sarvasaṃyojanādhiṣṭhitacittāḥ* 235.11-12.

adhyavasita – *asakto 'gṛddho 'grathito 'mūrcchito 'nadhyavasito* (Y. *'navadhyavasito*) *'nadhyavasānam āpannaḥ* 35.13-14 (cf. *Divy* 534.18-20; *Mvy* 2191-2197); *anadhyavasitacittāḥ* (Y. *anavasthitacittāḥ*) 235.6-7.

Anaṅgaṇa – *rājaputram Anaṅgaṇaṃ nāmāmantrayati* 135.2.

anarthika – see *arthika*.

an-upacchedana-tā – *triratnavaṃśānupacchedanatāyai* (Y. °*tayā*) *saṃvartate* 341.2

anubudhyana-tā – *arthagatyanubudhyanatāyai* 188.13-14.

anuśāsanī – *anuśāsaniprātihāryālaṅkṛtā yathāvadanuśāsanipradāyakā* 259.1-2.

anusaṃdhi – *tathāgatasyānusaṃdhau* 196.11-12, 196.16-17; *tasyānusaṃdhau* (Y.°*dheḥ*) 209.15, 210.1.

antara-kalpa – 201.4, 211.16, 266.4 *śastrāntarakalpa*; 212.3, 266.11-12 *durbhikṣāntarakalpa*; 212.8, 266.14 *rogāntarakalpa*.

a-paryādinna – *aparyādinnavyāhāreṇa* (Y. *aparyādinavavyāhāreṇa*) 256.2.

abhinirmāti – *ātmānam abhinirmāya* 11.6; *yakṣarūpam ātmānam abhinirmāya* 384.11-12.

abhiṣyanda – *puṇyābhiṣyandaḥ* (Y.°*syandaḥ*) *kuśalābhiṣyando* (T. *rgyun rgyas*) 85.9; *puṇyābhiṣyandena* (Y.°*syandena*) (T. *rgyu mthun-pa*) 140.20 Cf. Pāli *kammābhisanda*, *kusalā*°, *puññā*°; *Mv* ii.276.10 *puṇyābhisyandaḥ kuśalābhiṣyandaḥ*; *Sanskrithand-*

schriften aus den Turfanfunden, Teil II (Wiesbaden, 1968), p. 19 (*BHSD* has only *abhiṣyanda* "flux, ulceration of the teeth" but see *abhiṣyaṇṇa* and *abhiṣyandati*).

abhisaṃskāra – 11.5, 12.12, 13.4, 47.14, 51.2, 80.7, 396.6 *ṛddhyabhisaṃskāra*.

a-manyana – sarvadharmāmanyane samādhau 330.2-3.

a-manyana-tā – tyāgasyāmanyanatāṃ (Y. °*tā*) *careyaṃ* ... *kṣāntyamanyanatāṃ* (Y. *kṣāntyāmanyanatā*) ... *careyaṃ* 229.8-10; *sarvasamādhaya udayavyayāmanyanatāṃ gacchanti* 330.3.

artha-vaśa – kim-arthavaśaṃ samanupaśyamāno 193.9-10; *kaṃ arthavaśaṃ sampaśyamānaḥ* 268.9.

arthika – in comp.: 163.9, 268.7,11,14, 269.2,6 *bodhyarthika*; *puṇyārthī* 85.16; *annārthikā yāvad ratnārthikā* 350.11; with loc.: *saṃbodhāv arthikā* 84.15, *'narthikās* (Y. *'nāthakās*) *triṣu sucariteṣu* 224.11; with instr.: *kuśalamūlenārthikaḥ* 85.15 *svakāyajīvitenāpy anarthikāḥ* 144.18, *anarthikās* (Y. °*kāḥ*) *tribhir yānair anarthikā devamānuṣikābhiḥ saṃpattibhir anarthikāḥ kuśalaparyeṣṭyā* 149.3-5, *anarthikās tribhiḥ puṇyakriyāvastubhir* 200.9, *anarthikās tribhir yānair* 200.11-12, *anarthiko* (Y. *anārthako*) *divyasukhopapattibhiḥ* 230.6, *anarthikās tribhir yānair* 234.3, *anarthikā devamanuṣyaśrīsaṃpattibhir* 234.10.

avabhāsa – teṣāṃ na Sumerur avabhāsam āgacchati 11.10-11, *na ca Sumeruś cakṣuṣo 'vabhāsam āgacchati* 99.11, *na ca teṣāṃ Sumeruś* ... 100.11-12; *buddhakṣetrānavabhāsagatānāṃ sattvānāṃ* 252.1, *sarvabuddhakṣetrāvabhāsagatā* 258.14-15.

avarupta – 31.17-18, 79.9, 115.12, 133.5, 151.14, 170.14, 224.2, 225.6, 305.19, 310.12,14 *avaruptakuśalamūla*; 79.13, 170.15, 208.10, 240.2, 260.9 *anavaruptakuśalamūla*; *śrāvakayāne bījam avaruptaṃ syāt* 242.17; *lakṣaṇānuvyañjanānavaruptabījānām* 253.7-8.

avaropayati – kuśalamūlāny avaropayitvā 32.10-11; *kuśalamūlāny avaropya* 42.8-9; *kuśalamūlāny avaropitavān* 34.9; *bhagavataḥ śāsane 'varopitakuśalamūlas* 76.16-17, *avaropitanirvāṇabījasantatīnāṃ sattvānāṃ* 240.3-4, *śrāvakayāne bījāny avaropitāni* 244.8; *agramārgabījam avaropayeyaṃ* 239.4.

avahoṭimaka – durvarṇā avahoṭimakā ahrikā 234.17; *durvarṇā avahoṭimakā* (? MSS. *drohoḍimakā, prohoḍimakā*; T. *mi sdug-pa* as in 234.17) 307.6.

avinipāta-dharman – avinipātadharmāṇo yāvad bodhiparyantāt 15.9-10.

asaṅga-pratibhāna-tā – bodhisattvo mahāsattvaḥ asaṅgapratibhānatāṃ pratilabhate 30.11

āgṛhīta – svaśarīre 'py anāgṛhītamānasāḥ 107.7; *āgṛhītasantānāḥ* 260.1, *āgṛhītasantānānāṃ sattvānām* 261.11.

āgraha – āgrahaparigrahaśabdo 236.11.

ājaneya – dhyānasaṃbhāro bodhisattvānām ājāneyacittatāyai saṃvartate 187.8-9, id. 338.11-12 (Y. °*tayā*).

ātmabhāva – body of a *tathāgata*: *tathāgatasyātmabhāvaṃ* 11.16-17, *vajramayam ātmabhāvam adhitiṣṭhati* (Candrottamas *tathāgataḥ*) 33.6-7; great body seen by Samudrareṇu (= Śākyamuni): *sahasrayojanapramāṇam ātmabhāvaṃ samanupaśyati* 66.15-16, *mahān ātmabhāvo dṛṣṭaḥ* 69.13, *yat tvaṃ brāhmaṇādrākṣīt mahāntam ātmabhāvaṃ* 72.7-8; body magically created by Samudrareṇu: *nairayikam ātmabhāvam abhinirmiṇitvā* 153.15-16, *tathārūpam ātmabhāvaṃ nirmiṇitvā* 154.11; enormous body obtained by Durdhana (= Śākyamuni): *parvatapramāṇam ātmabhāvaḥ samvṛttaḥ* 364.4, *evaṃrūpo mamātmabhāvaḥ prādurabhavat* 366.9-10, *evaṃrūpeṇātmabhāvena* ... *sattvāṃ saṃtarpayeyaṃ* 367.2-4 (cf. 367.16,19); enormous body of Śākyamuni: *yojanapramāṇamātram ātmabhāvaḥ saṃsthitaḥ* 411.9-10; attainment of a body by ordinary beings: *yathārūpeṣu ca bhagavan sattvāḥ kuleṣūpapadyante, yathārūpaś ca teṣām ātmabhāvapratilābhaḥ* 154.6-8.

ādīnava – ādīnavadarśī 35.14.

ādeya-vākya – dharmadeśakaḥ ādeyavākyaḥ 162.16-17.

ābhāsa – naiva tasmin samaye SumeruCakravāḍaMahācakravāḍāḥ (Y. °*ḍaḥ*) *cakṣuṣa ābhāsam āgacchanti* 26.9-10 (cf. 411.16); *pṛthivī cakṣuṣo nābhāsam āgacchati*

(Y. °*nti*) 412.2; *yeṣāṃ ca sattvānāṃ mama kāyo lakṣaṇālaṅkṛtaś cakṣurindriyasyābhāsam āgacchet* 131.10-11; *teṣāṃ sarveṣāṃ śrotrendriyeṣv ayaṃ dharmaparyāya* (Y. °*yam*) *ābhāsam āgacchatu* 164.8-9 (cf. 164.19-165.1).
āya-dvāra – *kalyāṇamitrasaṃbhāro bodhisattvānāṃ sarvaguṇāyadvāratāyai* (Y. *sarvaguṇāya dvāratayā*) *saṃvartate* 340.11-12; *yathānye kuṭumbino dadanty āyadvāraṃ* (T. *'du-ba'i sgo*) *ye devasya nagaragrāmajanapadakarvaṭeṣu prativasanti* 368.17-369.1.
ārāgayati – *dharmavinayam ārāgayeyuḥ* 271.10; *sarve ca te sattvā buddhān* (Y. *buddhā*) *bhagavanta ārāgayeyuḥ* 272.12-13 (*ārādhayati*: 215.7, 361.12).
āryavaṃśa – *iha bodhisattvo mahāsattvaś caturṣv āryavaṃśeṣu vyavasthito bhavati* 35.7-8.
āsphānaka – *tathārūpam aham āsphānakaṃ dhyānaṃ dhyāyeyaṃ* 242.9-10.
utkūla – *parvatotkūlā ca dharaṇī bhaviṣyati* 237.13.
uttāraṇa-tā – *prayogālaṅkṛtāḥ pratijñottāraṇatāyai* (Y. °*tayā*) 257.8-9, *prayogasaṃbhāro bodhisattvānāṃ sarvasaṃbhārottāraṇatāyai* (Y. °*taraṇatayā*) *saṃvartate* 340.14-15 (confusion between *saṃsārottaraṇa* and *saṃbhārottāraṇa*: 187.3, 189.8, 189.11).
utsada – *notsadaśarkarakaṭhallakaṇṭakagahanā* (T. *utsada* = *mtho-dman*) 142.6-7; *puṇyotsadavyāhāreṇa* (T. *utsada* = *che-ba*) 254.9.
upadhāna – *parameṇa ca sukhopadhānena samarpitāḥ* 169.16-17.
ekajātipratibaddha – 107.16, 129.14,20, 230.6-7, 244.9.
kālānusāri – *kālānusārigandhaṃ* 167.15; *gośīrṣoragasārakālānusārigandhavṛṣṭiḥ* (Y. °*sārī gandhavṛṣṭiḥ*) 214.9-10.
kuhaka – *akuhakaś ca bhavaty alapako* 38.14.
khaṭuṅka – *krūrakhaṭuṅkasantānā* (MSS. *khadvaṅka*, *khadvaṃka*, *khadvaka*; T. *dmu-rgod* = *khaṭuṅka Mvy* 2450) 260.1.
citrikāra – *tīvrapremaprasādagurugauravacitrīkārajātāḥ* 398.1-2.
jātīya – *aviheṭhanajātīyo* 38.12, *ṛjukajātīyāś* 256.9, *yādṛgjātīyāṃ buddhakṣetraguṇavyūhān ākāṅkṣeyuḥ tādṛgjātīyān buddhakṣetraguṇavyūhāṃs* (Y. °*hāḥ*) *teṣu ratnavṛkṣeṣu paśyeyuḥ* 108.19-109.1, *yathādhimuktā bodhisattvās tādṛgjātīyāṃ śabdāṃ śṛṇuyuḥ* 128.18.
tāttaka – *yāttakaṃ* (Y. *yāntakaṃ*) *teṣām ekonāśītināṃ buddhānāṃ āyuḥpramāṇaṃ tāttakaṃ* (Y. *tāntakaṃ*) 184.2-3, *tāttakaṃ* (Y. *tāntakam*) *mama bodhiprāptasya dīrgham āyur bhavet* 212.18-19, *na kevalaṃ tāttakā nirdeśayanti yāttakā devasya yācanakāḥ* 377.5-6.
dakṣiṇīya – *adakṣiṇīyacittāḥ* 235.10.
dhāraka – *saddharmadhārako babhūva* 347.1.
nidhyapti – *nidhyaptibalinaḥ* 16.5, *nidhyapticittatā* 342.6.
nirhāra – *Nirhārapatiṃ nāma samādhiṃ* 102.1.
netrī – 219.8, 295.13 *praṇidhānanetrī*; 288.19, 298.8 *praṇidhānanetrīdhvaja*; 227.16 *parityāganetrīguṇa*; 229.4 *netrīguṇa*; 211.14-15, 212.15, 321.15, 321.18, *saddharmanetrī*.
naiṣadyika – *traicīvarikaḥ vṛkṣamūlikaḥ naiṣadyikaḥ āraṇyakaḥ* 162.14-15.
paricita – *dharmā bahavaḥ śrutā bhavanti dhṛtā vacasā paricitā* 38.2-3.
paripūri – 94.18-19, 118.11, 133.10-11, 138.11-12 *āśāparipūri*; 343.5 *lakṣaṇaparipūri*; *śīlasaṃbhāro bodhisattvānāṃ praṇidhānaparipūryai* (Y. °*dhānapūryai*) *saṃvartate* 187.5-6; *kṣāntisaṃbhāro bodhisattvānāṃ lakṣaṇānuvyañjanaparipūryai saṃvartate* 187.6-7; *indriyasaṃbhāro bodhisattvānāṃ saṃvaraparipūryai saṃvartate* 189.3-4; *indriyasaṃbhāro bodhisattvānāṃ sarvasattvendriyaparipūryai* (Y.°*yā*) *saṃvartate* 340.2-3; *upāyakauśalyasaṃbhāro bodhisattvānāṃ sarvajñajñānaparipūryai* (Y.°*yā*) *saṃvartate* 341.4-5; *kathaṃ ca punaḥ kṣāntiparipūrir* (Y. *kṣāntyā paripūrir*; T. *bzod-pa yoṅs-su 'rdzogs-par 'gyur*; cf. 341.12) *bhavati* 341.18; *naivaṃrūpā* (Y. °*paṃ*) *ca me praṇidhānaparipūriḥ* (Y. °*naṃ paripūri*) *syād* 367.14; *daśatathāgatabalapariniṣpādanasannāhaḥ sarvapāramitāparipūryai* (Y. °*yā*) 414.13-14.
paribhāvita – °*darśanaparibhāvitā amī mantrapadāḥ* 46.16; *mahākaruṇāparibhāvitā vāg*

bhāṣitā (Y. *vāgbhāṣitā*) 286.6-7; *mahākaruṇāparibhāvitā vācā bhāṣitā* 295.11.
pariṣkāra – 36.1, 54.14-15, 64.3, 65.5,9, 322.4-5 *glānapratyayabhaiṣajyapariṣkāra*; *dharmagurukā na pariṣkāragurukā* 173.1; *vividhapariṣkāraparihiṇāś ca te sattvā* 249.2.
paryāpanna – *aviciparyāpanno* 215.10, *caturyoniparyāpannāṃ* 240.9, *sarve devā ye Sahe buddhakṣetre paryāpannās* 242.14-15.
paryeṣṭi – *sarvakuśaladharmaparyeṣṭicittā* 15.16, *kuśalaparyeṣṭyā* 149.5, *dharmaparyeṣṭiparā* 167.1-2, *kuśalaparyeṣṭicittānāṃ* 190.20, *adharmabhogaparyeṣṭino* 233.18-19, *śāntanirvāṇāparyeṣṭicittā* 235.9, *akuśalaparyeṣṭicaryāṃ* 384.10.
pithati – *apāyapathāḥ pithitāḥ* 374.11.
paudgalika – *paudgalikam* (Y. °*kaṃ*) *upabhogaparibhogopasthānaparicaryāntaḥpuraṃ* 55.8-9; *paudgalikaparigṛahe* 322.5-6 (MSS. *yophalika, yoddhalika, pīdbhalika*; T. *gaṅ-zag-gir*). Read °*pariṣkāraṃ vācchindyā paudgalikaṃ parigṛhya*? Cf. *Bbh* 166.26.
pratikruṣṭa – *pratikruṣṭe* (Y. *pratikaṣṭe*) *pañcakaṣāye buddhakṣetra upapannaḥ* 52.5; *pratikruṣṭe pañcakaṣāye buddhakṣetre* 310.1-2.
pratijāgrati – *āhāraṃ pratijāgrati* 58.14.
pratiprasrambhayati – *vimuktiprītisukhaṃ pratiprasrabhya* 9.8, *ṛddhyabhisaṃskāraṃ pratiprasrabhya* 13.4; *jihvendriyarddhyabhisaṃskāraṃ* (Y. °*driyam ṛddhyabhisaṃskāreṇa*) *pratiprasrambhayitvā* 12.12, *tām ṛddhiṃ pratiprasrambhayitvā* 413.4-5; *svarddhyabhisaṃskāre pratiprasraṃbhite* 51.2.
pratisaṃlayana – *ekākinaḥ pratisaṃlayananiṣaṇṇā* (Y. °*ṣaṇṇaṃ*) 101.8; *pratisaṃlayanād vyutthāya* 101.15; *pratisaṃlayanaśabdaḥ* 264.7.
pratisaṃlāna – *pratisaṃlānasaṃbhāro bodhisattvānāṃ yathāśrutadharmapratipatyai* (Y. °*tyā*) *saṃvartate* 340.16-17.
pratyājāyate – °*yeyuḥ* (-*us*, -*ur*) 109.5, 130.4, 143.3, 169.17, 170.8,11,13,14,15, 259.17; *pratyājātāḥ pratyājāyiṣyanti* 15.7-8, 16.12,15, 18.5-6, 19.10-11; °*jātā* 147.16, 238.17, 239.15; °*yiṣyanti* 237.9-10.
prabhedana-tā – *matisaṃbhāro bodhisattvānāṃ buddhiprabhedanatāyai saṃvartate* 188.12-13, id. (Y. °*tayā*) 339.13-14.
praśrabdha – *praśrabdhakāyasaṃskāraḥ praśrabdhavākṣaṃskāraḥ* 243.9-10.
praśrabdhi – *Ākāśasphuraṇadharmāvacchedapraśrabdhiṃ samādhiṃ* (Y. °*raṇaṃ dhar*° ... *śrabdhisamādhiṃ*) 412.4-5.
bhūyasyā – *bhūyasyā mātrayā* 238.2-3, 328.2, 361.5-6.
yathā-paurāṇa – *Sālaguhā yathāpaurāṇā* (Y. °*paurvāṇāṃ*) *saṃsthitā* 396.18-19.
yadbhūyasā – *saṃchāditā yadbhūyasānantaryakārakā* (Y. *saṃcchāditāya bhūyas ān*°) 274.13 (T. *phal-cher*).
yāttaka – see *tāttaka*.
raṇaṃjaha – *raṇaṃjahena samādhinā* 330.8.
riñcati – *akuśalaṃ riñcitvā* 201.5; *riñcitāḥ sarvapaṇḍitaiḥ* 224.14; *antaśa ekasattvam api riṃceyāṃ* (Y. *riṃceyur*) 323.16.
luḍita – *askhalitāluḍitacittānāṃ* 190.17.
lūha – *vividhalūhatapovratābhiyuktā* (Y. °*tapavrata*) 238.8, *lūhatapovrataduṣkaracārikāṃ* (Y. *lūhatapo vrata*°) 243.6.
vitihāraka – *padavitihārakam api* 162.10.
vaimātra – *na ca tatra sattvā vaimātrā bhaveyuḥ* (T. *rim-pa ma mchis-pa*) 166.16-17.
vaiyāvṛtya – *vaiyāvṛtyakarmāṇi* 262.1; *vaiyāvṛtyaśabdo* (Y. °*vṛttiśabdo*) 264.6-7.
vairamaṇa – *prāṇātipātavairamaṇe* (Y. °*viramaṇe*) 350.4.
vairamaṇī – *prāṇātipātavairamaṇyāṃ pratiṣṭhāpayeyaṃ* 211.17, *prāṇātipātavairamaṇyāṃ* (Y. *prāṇā*°) *vyavasthāpayeyaṃ* 260.12; with *adattādāna* etc. 260.13,14,15, 261.1-2,3.
vairamaṇya – *mithyādṛṣṭivairamaṇye samādāpitāḥ* 350.5-6, *prāṇātipātavairamaṇye samādāpitā* 354.12-13.
vyantī-karoti – *mama cātra parikṣiṇaṃ karmaphalaṃ kṣiṇaṃ vyantikṛtaṃ bhavet* (Y. ... *cātrāparikṣiṇakarmaphalakṣiṇavyantikṛtaṃ* ...) 247.2-3.
vyavasthāna – *triyānavyavasthānena* (Y. *triyānena vya*°) *dharmaṃ deśayeyaṃ* 245.13-14.

śraddhā-deya – *tad api dānapratigrāhakasya śraddhādeyavinipātanaṃ* 318.2, *na ca yuṣmākaṃ śraddhādeyaṃ bhaviṣyati* 364.18-19.
śrutādhāra – *bahuśruto bhavati śrutādhāraḥ śrutasannicayaḥ* 37.18.
samaṅgi-bhūta – *pañcabhiḥ kāmaguṇaiḥ samarpitāḥ samaṅgibhūtā vihareyus* 304.17-18.
samanvāharati – *bhagavāṃś caināṃ samanvāharatu* 101.14; "*agrato Ratnagarbhas tathāgato niṣaṇṇo 'ham*" *sarvacetasā samanvāharanti* 302.16-17; *tad yuṣmābhiḥ sarvacetasā samanvāhartavyaṃ* (Y. °*yāḥ*) 413.16; *saṃprajānantaḥ* (Y. *saṃprajānaṃ tataḥ*) *sattvāḥ samanvāharata* 413.7.
samavasaraṇa – *Vaiśāradyasamavasaraṇaṃ nāma bodhisattvam* 46.12-13, *Sarvapuṇyasamavasaraṇaṃ nāma samādhiṃ* 47.16; *samavasaraṇaḥ sa mārgaḥ cintanāya* 77.13-14; *vajrāsanaṃ syāt, Praśamakṣamasuvicitrajñānagandhasamavasaraṇaṃ nāma bhavec* 130.15-16; *sarvadharmasamavasaraṇasāgaramudre samādhau* 329.18-330.1.
samādāpanā – *cittam utpādayata Samudrareṇor brāhmaṇasya samādāpanāyai* (Y. °*nayā*) 90.16-17.
samādhāna – *samādhānabalinaḥ* 16.5-6; *nirodhasamādhānena* 34.5; *samādhānabalena* 20.19, 226.6, 262.6; *vividhasamādhānabalena* 300.17; *Darśanavyūhasamādhānabalena* 155.15; *samādhānāṅkuraṃ ropayeyaṃ* 240.11; *dṛḍhavīryasamādhāno* 356.11-12; *dṛḍhavīryasamādhāna* 276.6 (vs); *jñānaśīlasamādhānaḥ* 279.8 (vs); 5.3, 287.11-12, 288.8, 290.5, 296.19, 299.19, 327.5-6,8,10,14, 344.3-4, 13-14 *samādhānamukhanirdeśa*.
samudānana – *sarvasaṃyojanabandhanasamudānanacittā* 235.10.
samudānana-tā – *atīrṇasattvottāraṇatāyai* (Y. °*tayā*) *mahānāvasamudānanatā* 414.6-7.
samudānaya-tā – *pariśeṣā dharmāḥ prajñājñānopāyasaṃbhārasamudānayatāyai paryeṣṭavyāḥ* 189.17-190.2.
samudānayati – *catvāra ime māṇavaka* (Y.°*kā*) *bodhimārgapratipannena bodhisattvenākṣayakośāḥ samudānayitavyāḥ* 186.13-15; *tribhiḥ puṇyakriyāvastubhiḥ samudānītakuśalamūlānāṃ* 191.1-2, *aviciparāyaṇāni karmāṇi samudānītāni syur* 272.6-7.
samudānayana – *sarvadharmasamudānayanasaṃbhāraḥ* 187.1.
sarvāvant – 12.13, 43.8, 81.7 etc.
sārāyaṇīya – *ṣaṭsārāyaṇīyasaṃbhāro* (Y. *ṣaṭparā*°; T. *sñiṅ-por byed-pa drug-gi tshogs*) 189.6, *sattvāṃ ṣaṭsārāyaṇīyeṣu* (Y. *ṣaṭparā*°) *samādāpayeyaṃ* 212.8-9, *ṣaṭsārāyaṇīyadharmaparivarjitānāṃ* (Y. *ṣaṭparā*°) 255.6-7, *tvam api sattvāṃ ṣaṭsārāyaṇīyadharmaiḥ* (Y. *ṣaṭparā*°) *saṃtarpayiṣyasi* 319.8-9.
sukhasaṃsparśa – *śītalā vāyavaḥ sugandhikā mṛdukāḥ sukhasaṃsparśacalitāḥ* (?) *pravāyante* 9.5-6, *sukhasaṃsparśā vāyavaḥ pravāyanti* 14.13.
heṣṭima – *ūrdhvaṃ yāvad akaniṣṭhabhavanaparyantaṃ heṣṭimena ca yāvat kāñcanacakraparyantaṃ* 239.12-14; *dakṣiṇapaścimottaraheṣṭimopariṣu dikṣu* 388.11-12.
heṣṭhā – *heṣṭhā* (Y. *heṣṭhaṃ*) *yāvat kāñcanacakraparyantam* 238.15.

Index II.

a-kṣaṇyana-tā – *yā viṣayeṣv akṣaṇyanatā ātmapratyavekṣaṇā iyaṃ kṣāntipāramitā* 228.2-4 (T. *mi bzod-pa ma mchis-pa* "absence of impatience"! The Chinese versions are quite different).
an-āyūhana-tā – *vīrye 'nāyūhanatāṃ* (Y. °*tā*) 229.9. Cf. *BHSD an-āyūha*.
apratisaṃdhinirodha – "destruction without rebirth" 347.12 (T. *mtshams-med-pa'i 'gog-pa*; *mtshams sbyor-ba* = *pratisaṃdhi*). Cf. *CPD a-ppaṭisandhiya* : *appaṭisandhika-nirodha Ud-a* 434.1.
abhisaṃbudhyana – °*bodhyabhisaṃbudhyana*° 249.7; *bodhipakṣābhisaṃbudhyanakaro* 418.12.
avabudhyana-tā – *kugatyavabudhyanatayā* 257.7; *sarvadharmāvabudhyanatayā* 414.11.
a-sajjana – "unimpeded", *tasya ca samādheḥ pratilābhād asajjanā daśasu dikṣv*

aprameyeṣv anyeṣu buddhakṣetreṣu gaccheyuḥ 126.7-8. Cf. *CPD asajja(t), asajjamāna*. T. *thogs-pa ma mchis-par* "without impediment".
ārambha – *parasparasārambhacittāḥ* (T. *phan-tshun noṅs-pa rtsom-pa'i sems*) 235.7; *dharmeṣu sārambhacittā* (T. *chos-rnams la noṅs-par brtson-pa'i sems*) 235.8-9. Cf. *CPD ārambha* (*d*) "evil act, offence, injury".
utsoḍha – *utsoḍhaḥ sa mārgaḥ* 78.11 Cf. *BHSD utsoḍhi*.
ullaṅghana – *ullaṅghanavacanena* 317.10. T. *brñas-pa'i tshig* "despising words".
ullaṅghya – *ullaṅghyavacanena* 318.9. T. *brñas-tshig* "despising words".
kāṣāyakaṇṭha – *sahadarśanena sattvāḥ kāṣāyakaṇṭhās tribhir yānair avaivartikā bhaveyur* 324.2-3. T. *ṅur-smrig 'gul-na thogs-par 'gyur-ba* "wearing the yellow robe on the neck". Cf. *RP* 29.2: *kāṣāyakaṇṭha vicarantā grāmakuleṣu madyamadamattāḥ*.
gāḍhakarma – *sarvāṇi gāḍhakarmāṇi niravaśeṣaṃ kṣapayati* 29.2-3. T. *las daṅ-po rnams* "the first acts" (?). Read *las ṅan-pa rnams* "bad acts"? See *pragāḍha*.
cāraka – "prison", *saṃsāracārake* 202.4,15; *bhavacārake* 206.1 (vs); *bhavacārake* 224.14-15; *haḍinigaḍabandhanacārakaśabdo* 236.6: *saṃsārabhavacārakeṣu* 207.5 (vs). Cf. *IIJ*, XIII, p. 142.
dakaprasāda – 377.16, 382.16. Cf. *BHSD udakaprasāda*.
dagdhasantāna – *dagdhasantānānāṃ kuśalamūlaparihīnānām* 231.8-9, *dagdhasantānā akuśalamūlasamādhānāḥ* 231.19-232.1, *mūlāpattim āpannāḥ dagdhasantānāḥ śubhamārgapraṇaṣṭāḥ* 247.14-15, *mūlāpattisāparādhikā dagdhasantānāḥ* 259.14-15, *gṛhītā dagdhasantānā(ḥ)* 278.9 (vs), 278.14 (vs), 279.5,10 (vs), 280.4,9 (vs), *dagdhasantānāḥ sattvā akuśalamūlasamavadhānagatā* 233.6-7, *dagdhasantānā akuśalasamavadhānagatā* 268.1-2, *akuśalamūlasamavadhānagatā dagdhasantānā(ḥ)* 286.14-15, 288.1-2, 296.1-2, 297.10, 308.15-16. T. *sems-kyi rgyud tshig* "of burnt continuity of mind". Cf. *BHSD saṃtāna*. See also above 230.4-5.
pragāḍhakarma – *pragāḍhakarmapratyayena* (T. *las-kyi rkyen rab-tu dam-pos*) *te sattvās tasmin samaye Bhadrakalpe viṃśottaravarṣaśatāyuṣkeṣu pratyājāyiṣyanti* 237.8-10. The Chinese versions translate *pragāḍha* and *gāḍha* as "weighty, heavy" (Ch. 1-207a6; Ch. 2-266c26). T. *rab-tu dam-po* "very strong". Cf. *BHSD āgāḍhatara*.
prajñapana – *divyāsanāni divyāni prajñapanāni* 88.10-11, *pīṭhaṃ sthāpayitvā śatasahasramūlyena prajñapanena prajñapya* 198.2-3, *kṛtsnaṃ Sahaṃ buddhakṣetraṃ prajñapanapramāṇaṃ* (Y. *prajñāpana*°) *me tatra svacarma parityaktaṃ* 365.17-18. Probably meaning "carpet". In 365.7-18 the text seems to be in disorder.
praśrambhayati – *teṣāṃ ca tṛṣṇāsaṃyojanaratikrīḍāsaumanasyābhiratāṃś cittacaitasikāṃ sarvān praśrambhayeyuḥ* 265.5-7. Cf *BHSD praśrabhyate*.
vinipātana – *tad api dānapratigrāhakasya śraddhādeyavinipātanaṃ* 318.2. Cf. *BHSD śraddhā-deya*.
vimārgita – *brahmavihāravimārgitānāṃ* 254.3. Cf. 254, notes 2 and 3.
saṃkhyāta – *yathā na pūrvaṃ kenacit sattvasaṃkhyātena anyatīrthikena vā śrāvakayānikena vā* 244.16-18. T. *sems-can du bgraṅ-ba* "counted as living being".
samavadhāna – 108.13-14, 145.8-9 (Y. *samavadhānakuśalamūla*), 269.13 *kuśalamūlasamavadhāna*; 224.17-18 (Y. *sakuśala*°; T. *mi-dge-ba'i...*), 233.7, 268.1-2, 306.9-10, 307.6-7 *akuśalamūlasamavadhānagata*; 306.16 *kuśalamūlasamavadhānagata*; 231.19-232.1 (Y. °*mūlasamādhānāḥ*; T. ... *daṅ 'grogs-pa*), 259.17, 348.10-11 *akuśalamūlasamavadhāna*; *ānantaryakārakā yāvad akuśalamūlasamavadhānagatā* 274.13-14, 286.14-15, 288.1-2, 297.9-10, 308.15, 310.8-9, 312.4; *ānantaryakārakānāṃ yāvad akuśalamūlasamavadhānagatānāṃ* 310.3.

Australian National University J. W. de Jong

R. E. Emmerick, *The Sūtra of Golden Light. Being a Translation of the Suvarṇabhāsottamasūtra* (= *Sacred Books of the Buddhists*, vol. XXVII). London, Luzac & Company Ltd., 1970. xiii + 108 pp. £ 3.—

R. E. Emmerick's translation of the *Suvarṇabhāsottamasūtra* is based upon Nobel's edition (Leipzig, 1937). Nobel used seven manuscripts, six of which are written on paper and one (G) on palmleaf. According to Nobel all six paper manuscripts derive from a common archetype. The text is much better preserved in the palmleaf MS. However, Nobel points out that of the 76 folios of this MS. 28 (1-7, 12-13, 16, 22,

27-34, 37, 41-43, 46-47, 49-50, 52) are missing. The writing has been obliterated in five of these folios (15, 18, 19, 23, 60) and subsequent retracing has resulted in wrong readings. The existing folios correspond to the following pages of Nobel's edition: 8-11 = 25.1-42.17; 14 = 52.1-56.12; 15+ (+ = writing obliterated and retraced) = 56.12-62.5; 17 = 65.10-67.13; 18+-19+ = 67.13-72.12; 20-21 = 72.12-77.9; 23+ = 79.11-81.10; 24-26 = 81.10-89.3; 35-36 = 106.14-113.3; 38-40 = 116.6-124.7; 44-45 = 130.16-138.10; 48 = 146.7-151.7; 51 = 158.10-162.6; 53-59 = 165.6-188.9; 60+ = 188.9-192.4; 61-72 = 192.4-251. Even MS. G is not free from corruptions: especially in the verses, it is often almost impossible to arrive at a satisfactory text. Edgerton has severely criticized Nobel for inconsistencies in his treatment of Buddhist Hybrid forms (cf. *JAOS*, 77, 1957, pp. 184-188). However, Edgerton's criticisms hardly ever affect the meaning of the text as established by Nobel. Wherever the Sanskrit text is hopelessly corrupt, the Tibetan and Chinese versions are of great assistance. Therefore Emmerick is right in maintaining that it is quite possible to render the text adequately into a modern European language even though the words 'verderbt', 'dunkel' and 'unsicher' and the like are alarmingly frequent in the apparatus of Nobel's edition.

In the critical apparatus of his edition of the Tibetan version (Leiden, 1944) Nobel has made a number of corrections in the Sanskrit text. They have been listed by Emmerick in his notes. Moreover, Emmerick himself suggests some emendations based upon the manuscripts, and also on the Tibetan and Khotanese versions. Although the text as established by Nobel and corrected by himself and Emmerick is infinitely superior to that of the two preceding editions,[1] there is still room for improvement quite apart from the inconsistencies pointed out by Edgerton. Emmerick has compared the Khotanese versions and an appendix lists the fragments previously identified and those which he himself has been able to identify. One would have expected the study of these Khotanese fragments to be helpful in suggesting emendations in the Sanskrit text, but in his preface Emmerick remarks that they require further study. Apparently it was his intention to translate the Sanskrit text first, before undertaking an exhaustive study of the Khotanese fragments.

Two chapters of the text have been separately studied by Nobel: chapter 7, cf. "Das Zauberbad der Göttin Sarasvatī" (*Festschrift Schubring*, Hamburg, 1951, pp. 123-239) and chapter 16, cf. *Ein alter medizinischer Sanskrit-Text und seine Deutung* (Supplement to *JAOS*, no. 11, 1951). Passages from chapters 6 and 12 have been translated by A. L. Basham, cf. Th. de Bary, ed., *Sources of Indian Tradition* (New York, 1958), pp. 181-185. This translation is not free from errors. To quote a single example: Nobel p. 74.10-75.1: *ahorātraṃ grahanakṣatracandrasūryāś ca samyak vahiṣyanti* has been rendered as follows: "Planets and stars, moon and sun, will duly bring on the days and nights" (*op. cit.*, p. 182). Emmerick translates: "Day and night, planets, asterisms, moon and sun, will move properly" (p. 28). The intransitive meaning of *vah-* has been rendered correctly by the Tibetan translators: *gza daṅ rgya-skar daṅ zla-ba daṅ ñi-ma yaṅ ñin-mts'an-du legs-par rgyu-bar 'gyur* (p. 56.11-12). Emmerick has carefully compared the Tibetan translation which is of great help even in places more obscure than the one just mentioned. His translation is excellent and only very few improvements can be suggested. The following notes point out a number of passages or words which can be rendered in a different way. In a few passages the

[1] The partial edition by Çarat Chandra Dās and Çarat Chandra Çāstri (Fasc. 1, Calcutta, 1898) and the edition by Bunyiu Nanjio and Hokei Idzumi (Kyoto, 1931) have been reviewed by Nobel (*OLZ*, 1933, Sp. 572-575). The recent edition of the text by S. Bagchi in the *Buddhist Sanskrit Texts* (no. 8, Darbhanga, 1967) is based upon the edition by Nanjio and Idzumi but a 15 page appendix, entitled *Errata* and *Variae Lectiones*, lists different readings from Nobel's edition!

text has to be corrected before a satisfactory sense can be obtained. All references are to page and line of Nobel's edition.

P. 3.9: *gaṇeśvara* – rather 'army chief' than 'chief servant'.

P. 5.4: *uttapta* – 'ripened'; 'purified' as on p. 159.5 (Emmerick, p. 67.7).

P. 24.11: *nistrāṇa* – 'without deliverance'; 'without protection', cf. p. 53.1, 4 (Emmerick, p. 19) and Nobel, *Wörterbuch Tibetisch-Deutsch-Sanskrit* (Leiden, 1950), s.v. *skyob-pa*.

P. 29.2: *karmāvaraṇa* – 'acts (and) hindrances'; 'obstruction due to past actions', cf. Edgerton, *BHSD* (= *Buddhist Hybrid Sanskrit Dictionary*), s.v.

P. 38.10: *nistrāṇa* – 'without salvation'; cf. above p. 24.11.

P. 38.15: *te sarvi sattva vyaṣanāgataduḥkhitāni* 'all those beings who are oppressed by the advent of trouble'; read *vyasanāgataduḥkhitā hi* with MSS. ABCDEF and *Ś* (= *Śikṣāsamuccaya*): 'all those beings who are oppressed and suffering'.

P. 44.5: *imāya pariṇāmanavarṇitāya* – 'by means of this (Confession), which is praised (as a cause of) ripening'; Edgerton, *BHSD*, p. 323b '*with this* (sc. deśanā) *which is praised as a cause of ripening*'. In his article on *pariṇāmana* Edgerton does not give the meaning 'transfer of merit', for which see L. de La Vallée Poussin, *Bouddhisme, études et matériaux* (London, 1898), p. 108 n. 1; id., *JA*, 1903, II, p. 439sq.; Pelliot, *JA*, 1914, II, p. 135; Har Dayal, *The Bodhisattva Doctrine in Buddhist Sanskrit Literature* (London, 1932), pp. 188-193; Nobel, *Wörterbuch*, s.v. *sṅo-ba*.

P. 48.7: *sugataśaśāṇkasuvimalavaktraṃ* – 'He has the face of one who has attained bliss, pure as the moon'; read *saumyaśaśāṅka°* with MSS. ABCDE as against MS. F and Tib. *bde-gśegs*. Dharmakṣema translates: "He has a face pure as the moon which is full" (*Taishō*, no. 663, p. 339b2).

P. 48.9: *taruṇaruhāṅga* – 'the members of a newly-born'; *taruṇaruha* can hardly mean 'newly-born', although Tib. has *gźon-nu btsas*, cf. Nobel's note, p. 48 n. 9.

P. 63.3: *uttamāṅga* – 'the supreme member'; 'the head' (also p. 170.4).

P. 65.2: *sarvabhayaprabandhacchedakaḥ* – 'destroys the continuity of all fears'; Nobel remarks: "unsicher, die Korrektur würde dem Tib. *'jigs-pa thams-cad-kyi rgyun gcog-pa* entsprechen. ABDE *sarvabhayapratiśamanaḥ*; C *°bhayapratisrambhena*; F *°bhayaprasastena*." Read *sarvabhayapratiprasrambhaṇaḥ* 'allays all fears', cf. Edgerton, *BHSD*, s.v. *pratipraśrambhaṇa* and Mahāvyutpatti nos. 845 and 1383: *rgyun bcad-pa = pratiprasrabdha*.

P. 72.17-73.4: *sādhu sādhu mahārājānaḥ ... yad yūyam ... svastyayanaṃ kariṣyatha* – "Bravo, bravo great kings! ... If you ... give welfare"; "Bravo, bravo, great kings! ... since you ... will give welfare", cf. 88.14-89.3: *sādhu sādhu satpuruṣa ... yat tvam ... saṃprakāśayitukāmaḥ* – 'Bravo, bravo good fellow! ... since you are desirous of making known' (Emmerick, p. 35).

P. 80.18-81.1: *mahārājaguṇānuśaṃsāni* – 'great blessings resulting from royal virtues'; read *mahārājā guṇā°*, cf. 79.10 (ABDE *mahārājāḥ*), Tib. *rgyal-po chen-po dag yon-tan-gyi* ... Dharmakṣema 'O, you, four great kings' (p. 342b12).

P. 84.2-3: *kiyanmātraṃ kuśalaṃ pratyaṃśaṃ* – 'whatever was his share of merit'; 'only a small share of merit'.

P. 98.9: *etāś ca mahārājānaḥ sūtrendradhārakā* – 'And these great kings will sustain those monks'; 'And, O great kings, they will sustain those monks', cf. Tib. *rgyal-po chen-po-dag ... mdo-sdei dbaṅ-poi rgyal-po 'dzin-pa de-dag kyaṅ*.

P. 100.15: *yasya cāsti narapater viṣaye priyatā* – 'by that king of men in whose region there is affection (for it)'; 'by that king of men who has affection for his domain', cf. 77.12-13: *ātmanaś ca sarvaviṣayam ārakṣitukāmo bhavet*.

P. 120.9: *bodhayati* – 'understands'; 'explains'.

P. 138.4: *śastreṇa nāśa adharmaś ca viṣaye tu bhaviṣyati* – Emmerick n. 62: "Instead of *tu* read *yatra* with MSS. ABCDE, supported by Khotanese *kāmiña*"; *yatra* is not supported by MS. G, Tib. and Dharmakṣema and does not give a good sense.

P. 140.2: *maram* – 'defilement', n. 63: "Read *malam* with MSS. BDE(F), supported by Khotanese *ächei* 'disease'"; Dharmakṣema 'epidemic' (p. 347c2) and Tib. *'chi* 'death' probably render *māri, mārī* or *māra*.

P. 164.4: *purastāt* – 'formerly'; Tib. *'og-tu* = *adhastāt*, cf. 164.5 *ūrdhvaṃ*.

P. 166.3: *jāmbūnadasuvarṇasya vimānāntarasaṃsthitaḥ* – 'residing in his orb of Jambudvīpa gold'; 'residing in a palace of Jāmbūnada gold'.

P. 180.13-14: *tenaivaṃrūpena naimittikena dhātukauśalyena paripṛṣṭena* – 'as soon as ... had inquired about such skill in the elements', n. 91: "Read *mātrakeṇa* (cf. MS. G) for *naimittikena* with Nobel, Tib. p. 141 n. 119"; read *tanmātrakeṇa* (Tib. *de tsam-źig*) – 'having inquired about so little skill in the elements'.

P. 185.6: *tatrādrākṣid vṛkṣād ardhakāyena devatāṃ niṣkramantīm* – 'He saw there a goddess, with half a body, coming out of a tree'; 'He saw there a goddess coming out of a tree with half her body only', cf. Tib. *lus-phyed tsam* 'only half the body'.

P. 196.11: *gaṇaka* – 'treasurer'; 'astrologer'.

P. 206.3: *āvarjitamanasas* – 'with humble heart'; 'with converted minds', cf. Edgerton, *BHSD*, s.v. *āvarjayati*.

P. 212.1-2: *tayor vikṣepaṃ cakāra* – 'he reproached those two'; cf. Edgerton, *BHSD*, s.v. *vikṣepa*; here probably 'he distracted them'.

P. 216.7: *bhrātṛka* – 'mother'; 'brother'.

P. 233.8: *tiṣṭhanti te putra manāpāḥ* – 'Your sons are delightful'; 'Your charming sons are alive', cf. Tib. *mchis* 'exist' and Dharmakṣema 'your sons still exist' (p. 356a27).

P. 249.9: *trātaṃ* – 'delivered'; 'protected'.

Australian National University J. W. de Jong

Fujita Kōtatsu 藤田宏達, *Genshi jōdo shisō no kenkyū* 原始浄土思想の研究. 2ème éd., Tōkyō, Iwanami Shoten, 1970, xviii + 630 + 48 pp.

Les trois textes fondamentaux de l'école de la Terre Pure sont le grand *Sukhāvatīvyūha*, le petit *Sukhāvatīvyūha* et le *Kuan-wu-liang-shou ching* 觀無量壽經. Le texte sanskrit du s. (= petit *Sukhāvatīvyūha*) fut publié pour la première fois par Max Müller en 1880 (*JRAS*, 1880, pp. 153-188); celui du S. (= grand *Sukhāvatīvyūha*) par le même en 1883. Le troisième texte n'existe qu'en chinois (T. 365). La traduction en est attribuée à Kālayaśas mais, aujourd'hui, beaucoup de savants japonais pensent que ce texte ne vient pas de l'Inde, mais qu'il a été composé soit en Asie Centrale, soit en Chine. Au Japon, ce ne sont pas les textes sanskrits du S. et du s., mais les traductions chinoises qui sont vénérées par les adeptes des écoles Jōdō-shū et Jōdo-shin-shū. Traditionnellement les savants japonais ont étudié l'histoire et la pensée de l'école de la Terre Pure sur la base des traductions chinoises. Dans le grand travail que M. Fujita vient de publier sur la pensée de la Terre Pure, l'accent est mis sur les origines indiennes de l'école. Il rejette catégoriquement les interprétations traditionnelles qui ont cours au Japon et fait appel aux méthodes historiques et philologiques. M. Fujita est un représentant de la nouvelle vague des bouddhisants japonais. Ces savants ont l'esprit critique et étudient de préférence les textes sanskrits et les traductions tibétaines, ces dernières étant jugées plus dignes de confiance que les traductions chinoises. Alors que les savants d'autrefois s'intéressaient surtout aux développements doctrinaux sans s'occuper du milieu historique qui en forme l'arrière-plan, ceux d'aujourd'hui sont avant tout des historiens et des philologues. À cet égard ils ont subi l'influence des grands maîtres des études bouddhiques en Occident, dont les travaux leur sont bien connus. Évidemment, il ne faut pas faire une séparation trop nette entre la génération ancienne et la nouvelle vague, car celle-ci doit beaucoup aux travaux de tous les érudits japonais qui, depuis la fin du siècle passé, se sont mis à l'étude du sanskrit et du tibétain et qui ont appliqué des méthodes historiques et philologiques à l'étude du bouddhisme.

Le livre de M. Fujita se signale par son style lucide qui en facilite la lecture, même quand il s'agit de problèmes fort compliqués. Il exprime son opinion sans aucune ambiguïté et n'hésite pas à rejeter les théories de savants japonais renommés. Pour chaque problème, il analyse soigneusement les données connues ainsi que les théories proposées par d'autres avant d'exposer son propre point de vue. Toutefois, M. Fujita ne perd pas son temps à discuter en détail des théories qui ne sont pas suffisamment fondées, et il ne les mentionne que pour mémoire.

Le lecteur occidental saura gré à M. Fujita d'avoir ajouté à son livre une traduction anglaise de la table des matières (pp. 3-8) et un résumé détaillé en anglais (pp. 9-21), qui permettent de s'orienter rapidement sur le contenu de ce livre de 630 pages. Les savants japonais qui ont l'habitude d'écrire de gros livres nous obligeraient beaucoup s'ils suivaient l'exemple de M. Fujita, car il n'est pas toujours facile de trouver son chemin dans leurs travaux. Cela est encore plus nécessaire quand il s'agit du bouddhisme indien qui, en Occident, est étudié par des savants ayant rarement eu l'occasion et le temps d'apprendre à fond le japonais.

Le livre de M. Fujita comprend six grands chapitres qui traitent des sujets suivants: I. Les textes fondamentaux de la Terre Pure et les matériaux qui s'y rapportent; II. La formation de la pensée de la Terre Pure dans sa première période; III. L'origine d'Amitābha et d'Amitāyus; IV. La structure des vœux d'Amitābha; V. L'idée de la Terre Pure Sukhāvatī; VI. Problèmes relatifs à la pratique religieuse. Le résumé anglais, mentionné ci-dessus, m'exempte de la nécessité d'énumérer les nombreuses questions abordées par M. Fujita; il ne me serait guère possible, au reste, de les examiner de manière exhaustive. M. Fujita se réfère à de nombreux textes bouddhiques en pāli, sanskrit et chinois. En outre, il cite un grand nombre de travaux japonais que je n'ai pu consulter et qui, probablement, ne se trouvent réunis dans aucune bibliothèque européenne ou américaine. Je me contenterai de faire quelques remarques que m'ont suggérées la lecture de ce livre. Il va de soi qu'elles ne peuvent guère donner une idée des richesses qu'il contient.

Dans le premier chapitre, M. Fujita étudie les textes sanskrits et tibétains du S. et du s., le problème de la composition du *Kuan-wu-liang-shou ching*, et il énumère les textes chinois et sanskrits qui mentionnent Amitābha, Amitāyus et Sukhāvatī. En ce qui concerne le texte sanskrit du S., M. Fujita énumère 23 manuscrits et cinq éditions; les trois éditions les plus importantes sont celles de Max Müller (1883), de Wogihara Unrai (1931) et d'Ashikaga Atsuuji (1965), mais aucune n'est satisfaisante. Il faut espérer que M. Fujita publiera une édition qui les remplace. Malgré l'abondance des manuscrits et l'aide fournie par les traductions tibétaines et chinoises, ce ne sera pas chose aisée, car le texte sanskrit a été mal transmis dans les manuscrits népalais. Le plus ancien des manuscrits datés porte la date de 1699. Selon M. Ashikaga, le manuscrit qu'il a utilisé pour établir son édition date du 14ème ou du 15ème siècle, mais son affirmation ne s'appuie pas sur un examen paléographique approfondi.

En ce qui concerne les traductions chinoises, les savants japonais ont beaucoup étudié les problèmes que posent les indications fournies par les catalogues chinois. M. Fujita reprend la question à fond. Ses arguments sont presque toujours convaincants. Sur un seul point nous sommes enclins à adopter un autre point de vue. Les catalogues mentionnent deux Po Yen 白延 (ou 帛延) dont le premier aurait traduit des textes à la fin des Ts'ao Wei (220-265), le deuxième à la fin des Chang Liang 張涼 (Liang Antérieurs 前涼, 302-376). Aux deux Po Yen les catalogues attribuent une traduction du *Śūraṃgamasamādhisūtra* et de la *Surataparipṛcchā*. On trouvera les données des catalogues réunies dans l'introduction à *La concentration de la marche héroïque* de M. Ét. Lamotte (Bruxelles, 1965, pp. 79-81 et 98-101). Le *Ch'u san-tsang chi-chi* reproduit le colophon de la traduction du *Śūraṃgamasamādhisūtra* due à l'upāsaka Chih Shih-lun 支施崙 et à Po Yen (cf. Lamotte, pp. 98-99). Les données de ce colophon sont confirmées par une lettre concernant le *Chien-pei ching* 漸備經 ou *Daśabhūmikasūtra* (cf. Lamotte, pp. 100-101). Le colophon et la lettre sont tous deux anonymes, mais Hayashiya Tomojirō 林屋友次郎 a avancé de bonnes raisons pour supposer que Tao-an 道安 en est l'auteur (*Iyaku kyōrui no kenkyū* 異譯經類の研究, Tōkyō, 1945, pp. 86-89). M. E. Zürcher attribue également la lettre à Tao-an (cf. *The Buddhist Conquest of China*, Leiden, 1959, p. 392, n. 81). Même si ces deux documents ne sont pas de la main de Tao-an, l'auteur s'en montre si bien renseigné sur les traductions faites par Po Yen, que l'on ne peut ne pas lui faire confiance. Ses renseignements paraissent plus dignes de foi que les maigres données fournies par le *Kao-seng chuan* et le *Ch'u san-tsang chi-chi* sur Po Yen des Ts'ao Wei. C'est pourquoi Ono Gemmyō 小野玄妙, Tokiwa Daijō 常盤大定 et Hayashiya Tomojirō sont d'avis que ce dernier n'a jamais existé et que c'est Po Yen des Chang Liang qui a traduit le *Śūraṃgamasamādhisūtra* et la *Surataparipṛcchā*. Un des arguments avancés contre l'existence d'une traduction du *Śūraṃgama* par Po Yen des Ts'ao Wei, est le fait que celle-ci est passée sous silence par Chih Min-tu 支敏度 dans sa notice sur son édition synoptique du *Śūraṃgama* (cf. Lamotte, pp. 92-93). M. Fujita avance comme contre-argument le fait que Chih Min-tu ne mentionne pas non plus deux traductions faites sous les Ts'ao Wei (cf. Lamotte, pp. 72-74). Cet argument n'est pas très convaincant car ces traductions, dont l'une aurait été faite au Szu-ch'uan, n'ont pas été entre les mains des auteurs des catalogues. M. Fujita n'est pas non plus enclin à attribuer à Seng-yu 僧祐 la confusion des deux Po Yen; mais on ne peut avoir une confiance absolue dans le bon jugement de Seng-yu quand il s'agit de textes qu'il n'a pu consulter lui-même. Plus compliqué est le problème de l'existence de deux traductions de la *Surataparipṛcchā* dont la première est attribuée à Po Yen (T. 328) et la deuxième à Chih Shih-lun (T. 329). Selon Hayashiya, la première traduction serait de la main de Chu Fa-hu 竺法護 (*op. cit.*, p. 111). Hayashiya a des doutes concernant l'attribution du T. 329 à Chih Shih-lun, mais cela provient surtout d'une interprétation erronée d'un passage de la lettre mentionnée ci-dessus. Selon cette interprétation, Tao-an n'aurait pas reçu la traduction de la *Surataparipṛcchā*. Toutefois, ce n'est pas la *Surataparipṛcchā* qui n'est pas arrivée à Hsiang-yang, mais un texte de vinaya intitulé ,,Les cinq cents défenses'' (cf. Fujita, p. 48, n. 27). Il est donc bien possible d'admettre que le T. 329 est en effet la traduction faite autour de l'an 373 à Liang-chou par Po Yen et Chih Shih-lun. Malheureusement, le colophon et la lettre ne font pas mention d'une traduction du S. par Po Yen. Cette attribution se trouve pour la première fois dans le *Kao-seng chuan*, et ensuite dans le *Chung-ching mu-lu* (cf. Fujita, pp. 41-42). Dans ces deux sources, le titre correspond à celui du T. 361. Le *Kao-seng chuan* et le *Chung-ching mu-lu* attribuent cette traduction au Po Yen des Ts'ao Wei. M. Fujita accepte cette attribution comme correcte. Toutefois, d'autres savants ont attribué cette traduction à Chu Fa-hu. Ils ont signalé une grande ressemblance de la terminologie de ce texte avec celle de Chu Fa-hu; mais M. Fujita remarque que Chu Fa-hu ne peut pas avoir traduit Amitābha ou Amitāyus par *Wu-liang ch'ing-ching* 無量清淨. Si, toutefois, le T. 361 n'a pas été traduit par Chu Fa-hu mais par Po Yen, s'agit-il du Po Yen des Ts'ao Wei ou de celui des Chang Liang? Le premier a vécu avant Chu Fa-hu et ne peut pas avoir connu ses traductions. Mais, en ce qui concerne les deux traductions de la *Surataparipṛcchā*, Hayashiya est arrivé à la conclusion que la première (T. 328) serait de la main de Chu Fa-hu et que la deuxième, celle de Chih Shih-lun, le co-traducteur de Po Yen, serait basée sur la première (*op. cit.*, pp. 111-112). Il me semble qu'il faudrait donc, en premier lieu, comparer soigneusement la terminologie de ces deux traductions attribuées à Po Yen et Chih Shih-lun (T. 361, T. 329). M. Fujita, qui admet l'existence d'un Po Yen des Ts'ao Wei et d'un Po Yen des Chang Liang, n'a pas entrepris cette comparaison. Il a probablement estimé superflu de comparer un texte traduit par Po Yen des Ts'ao Wei avec un autre traduit par Chih Shih-lun, le co-traducteur de Po Yen des Chang Liang.

Dans le livre de M. Fujita, l'examen du problème de l'identité du traducteur du T. 361 occupe seize pages. Je n'ai pas relevé un par un tous les arguments avancés par M. Fujita pour ou contre telle ou telle thèse. Toutefois, il y a une remarque de M. Fujita sur laquelle il faut s'attarder. À propos de la différence d'opinion entre, d'une part, Mochizuki Shinkō 望月信亨 et Kitagawa Kenjō 北川賢淨 et, d'autre part, Ōno Hōdō 大野法道, sur la ressemblance de la terminologie de Chu Fa-hu avec celle du traducteur du T. 362, M. Fujita remarque que l'étude comparative de la terminologie des traducteurs comporte un élément subjectif qui dépend du point de vue adopté. Il me semble que M. Fujita sous-estime quelque peu l'importance de l'étude de la terminologie employée par les traducteurs. En étudiant les traductions chinoises, on dispose de données externes et de données internes. Les savants japonais ont davantage étudié les premières, c'est-à-dire les indications fournies par les catalogues, par les biographies, etc. Mais ce n'est que par l'étude approfondie des traductions ou translitérations des termes techniques et des noms propres, et par celle du style des traductions, que l'on arrivera à plus de certitude à l'égard de leur attribution. Cela vaut surtout pour la période la plus ancienne du bouddhisme chinois, de la fin des Han jusqu'à la fin des Tsin Orientaux. Les textes traduits pendant cette période ont subi les vicissitudes historiques des Dynasties du Sud et du Nord. Au début du sixième siècle, Seng-yu n'a pas toujours pu obtenir des renseignements dignes de foi sur des traductions faites longtemps avant son époque dans le Nord de la Chine. Il a pu se servir de catalogues antérieurs, et avant tout de celui de Tao-an qui date de 374; mais beaucoup de traductions lui étaient inaccessibles. L'importance de l'étude de la terminologie et du style des traductions a été bien mise en lumière par Hayashiya (*op. cit.*, pp. 47-52). Cette étude comporte certes un élément subjectif si l'on ne s'appuie que sur un choix limité d'exemples comme cela se fait d'habitude. Il faudrait procéder à un examen systématique, en commençant par des traducteurs bien connus, en premier lieu An Shih-kao 安世高. Hayashiya avait annoncé une étude systématique de la terminologie de trois grands traducteurs de l'époque des Han Postérieurs aux Tsin Occidentaux mais, pour autant que je sache, ce travail n'a jamais paru (*op. cit.*, p. 52). Il est à espérer que les savants japonais continueront les travaux de Hayashiya et entreprendront des travaux systématiques au lieu d'étudier isolément telle ou telle traduction.

Dans son deuxième chapitre, M. Fujita compare les différentes versions du grand et du petit *Sukhāvatīvyūha*. En ce qui concerne le premier il distingue deux groupes de textes, l'un comprenant les traductions de Chih-ch'ien 支謙 (T. 362) et de Po Yen (T. 361), l'autre les trois traductions chinoises T. 360, 310. 5 et 363, le texte sanskrit et la traduction tibétaine. Ces deux groupes reflètent un développement du texte qui se manifeste clairement dans l'accroissement du nombre des vœux, vingt-quatre dans le premier groupe et quarante-sept, quarante-huit ou quarante-neuf dans le deuxième. Le T. 363 ne contient que trente-six vœux, mais ce texte, traduit en 991 par Fa-hsien 法賢, ne représente pas un stage intermédiaire entre les deux groupes, comme le montre plus loin l'auteur (pp. 386-388). M. Fujita affirme que, pour reconstruire l'état primitif du texte, on ne peut pas se servir uniquement des deux traductions chinoises les plus anciennes. Pour déterminer l'état ancien du texte, il adopte les quatre méthodes suivantes. I. En comparant toutes les recensions, il en isole les parties communes. II. Dans les autres parties du texte des deux traductions chinoises anciennes (T. 361, 362), il écarte tous les éléments ajoutés par les traducteurs chinois. III. Les parties ainsi distinguées par ces deux méthodes sont examinées avant tout sur la base du texte sanskrit et de la traduction tibétaine. Quand, dans le texte sanskrit, il n'y a pas de passage correspondant, il essaie de déterminer autant que possible quel était le texte sanskrit original. IV. En ce qui concerne les textes du deuxième groupe, les parties communes sont étudiées avant tout sur la base du texte sanskrit. Ces parties ne sauraient être considérées comme faisant partie du texte ancien, mais elles fournissent des matériaux importants pour retrouver l'état primitif qui s'y trouve augmenté et développé. Ces quatre méthodes sont systématiquement appliquées par M. Fujita au cours de son travail. Il va de soi que, pour retrouver la forme primitive du texte, il est de première importance d'écarter les éléments ajoutés par les traducteurs chinois. M. Fujita montre que ces éléments se trouvent dans les trois premières traductions (T. 360-362). C'est la première de celles-ci, le T. 360, qui est le texte de base au Japon. M. Fujita signale des retouches confucianistes et taoïstes dans cette traduction et, reprenant une formule appliquée par M. Nakamura Hajime 中村元 au bouddhisme chinois, il constate que l'amidisme japonais est un amidisme *plus* un peu de confucianisme et de taoïsme. M. Fujita a raison de faire confiance à la recension sanskrite plus qu'aux traductions chinoises. Il me semble, toutefois, que l'on ne saurait toujours donner la préférence à la recension sanskrite. Laissons de côté le fait que celle-ci nous est connue seulement par des manuscrits assez récents; la traduction tibétaine, qui date du début du neuvième siècle, s'accorde assez bien avec le texte sanskrit. Plus grave est le fait que le texte sanskrit utilisé par les traducteurs tibétains s'éloigne beaucoup du texte primitif qui, selon M. Fujita, date d'environ l'an cent de notre ère. Prenons à titre d'exemple un passage étudié par M. Fujita pour montrer la supériorité du texte sanskrit (pp. 178-180).

Dans ce passage tous les textes, après avoir mentionné le vœu de Dharmākara, décrivent sa conduite de bodhisattva (*bodhisattvacaryā*). Dans les textes du premier groupe le texte est concis; dans ceux du deuxième groupe, plus développé. Selon ceux-ci, Dharmākara passe par de nombreuses existences. Au cours de ces existences, dans lesquelles il renaît d'abord comme *śreṣṭhin*, ensuite comme *gṛhapati* et finalement comme le dieu Brahmā, il vénère les Buddha. Le texte sanskrit et la traduction tibétaine racontent que Dharmākara fait renaître d'innombrables êtres comme *śreṣṭhin*, etc.: "It is not easy to know the limit by pointing it out in words, as to how many beings were established by him in the noble families of brāhmaṇas, kṣatriyas, ministers, householders and merchants. In the same manner they were established in the sovereignty of Jambudvīpa (India), and they were established in the character of Cakravartins, Lokapālas, Śakras, Suyāmas, Sutuṣitas, Sunirmitas, Vaśavartins, Devarājas, and Mahābrahmans" (trad. Max Müller, *S. B. of the East*, XLIX, 1894, part II, p. 26). M. Fujita n'hésite pas à dire que le texte sanskrit reproduit plus fidèlement le texte original que les traductions chinoises. Mais cela me paraît très douteux. Il y a de nombreux textes qui racontent comment des bodhisattva, renaissant d'existence en existence, établissent les hommes dans l'*anuttarā samyaksaṃbodhi*. Par contre, pour autant que je sache, on ne trouvera pas beaucoup de textes qui racontent qu'un bodhisattva établit les hommes dans l'état de *śreṣṭhin*, etc. Au lieu de supposer que toutes les traductions chinoises du deuxième groupe aient mal lu ou mal traduit le texte sanskrit original, il est plus vraisemblable que le texte sanskrit a été modifié [1]). Cette modification avait probablement pour motif la glorification de Dharmākara. Celui qui a modifié le texte dans ce sens a voulu exalter la gloire et le pouvoir de Dharmākara, le futur Amitābha; il lui paraissait impossible que Dharmākara ait dû passer par de nombreuses existences en tant qu'être humain et être divin. Cette explication n'est évidemment qu'une hypothèse, mais elle paraît plus conforme à l'esprit des textes du Mahāyāna que l'explication proposée par M. Fujita. Il faudra étudier les textes du Mahāyāna pour voir s'ils contiennent des passages exprimant des idées comparables à celle qui se reflète dans le texte sanskrit cité ci-dessus. Il faudra voir aussi si ces passages représentent un état primitif ou un état modifié des textes originaux. En tout cas, il est dangereux de supposer qu'au cours des siècles les textes sanskrits bouddhiques ne se soient développés qu'en ajoutant des éléments nouveaux sans modification aucune des parties plus anciennes.

Dans une autre section du deuxième chapitre, M. Fujita compare quelques passages du texte sanskrit du S. avec des passages parallèles dans les écritures pālies (pp. 181-194). Dans un article récent M. Fujita a discuté en détail 33 passages parallèles en pāli (Sukhāvatīvyūha to Pāli seiten, *Hokkaidō-daigaku-bungakubu-kiyō*, 24, 1970, pp. 1-45). Ici il n'en étudie que trois à titre d'exemples [2]). La comparaison de passages parallèles est d'une grande importance pour l'histoire des textes, mais il faut se garder de trop s'y fier

[1]) M. Fujita cite en note la traduction du texte chinois (T. 360) de ce passage par M. Hayashima Kyōshō qui traduit ce texte à la lumière du texte sanskrit (p. 181, n. 19). Cette traduction fait violence au texte chinois et ne mérite pas d'être prise en considération.

[2]) À propos de *samatitthika* et *samatittika*, M. Fujita remarque que *samatittika* ne peut pas être une corruption pour *samatitthika* et il cite à cet égard l'étymologie de T. W. Rhys Davids: *tittika* <*tṛptika* (p. 210, n. 12). Il faut certainement lire partout *samatitthika*. Le fait que, par extension, ce mot ait été appliqué au *piṇḍapāta* et même au *gūthakūpa* (AN, III, p. 403, 21) ne peut servir d'argument contre l'explication de *samatitthika* comme 'level with the banks' (*sama* + *tīrtha*, cf. H. Kern, *Toevoegselen*, II, 1916, pp. 55-56; Ernst Leumann, *Maitreya-samiti*, 1919, p. 197; Franklin Edgerton, *Buddhist Hybrid Sanskrit Dictionary* s.v. *sama-tīrthika*).

pour l'établissement des textes sanskrits. Par exemple, M. Fujita corrige *abhijñānābhijñātaiḥ* (éd. Ashikaga, p. 1, l. 19) en *abhijñātābhijñātaiḥ* à la lumière du pāli *abhiññātā abhiññātā*. Les manuscrits du S. ont *abhijñānābhijñaiḥ* ou *abhijñānābhijñātaiḥ*, mais au début du s. les textes transmis au Japon ont tous *abhijñātābhājñātaiḥ*. Déjà Bendall avait signalé à l'attention de Max Müller l'expression pālie *abhiññātā-abhiññātā* dans *Vinaya-piṭaka*, I, p. 43, l. 13 (cf. *Sacred Books of the East*, vol. XLIX part II, p. 90, note). En pāli cette expression s'applique à plusieurs catégories de personnes, y compris les *thera* (cf. *Critical Pāli Dictionary* et *Pāli Tipiṭakaṁ Concordance*, s.v.). L'expression se rencontre plusieurs fois dans les textes sanskrits bouddhiques où elle s'applique aussi bien à des śrāvaka qu'à des bodhisattva (cf. *OLZ*, 65, 1970, col. 79); mais les manuscrits offrent beaucoup de variantes. Les traductions chinoises ainsi que les traductions tibétaines rendent cette expression de manières différentes. Il faut se demander si l'on est en droit d'adopter partout la leçon *abhijñātābhijñāta*, car il se peut qu'en sanskrit bouddhique la forme primitive ait été réinterprétée et altérée. Ce problème ne pourra être résolu qu'après une étude exhaustive de l'emploi de cette expression dans les textes pālis et sanskrits d'une part, et dans les versions chinoises et tibétaines correspondantes de l'autre. Si une conclusion nette ne se dégage pas d'un tel examen, il faudra, en chaque cas, établir le texte en tenant compte des leçons des manuscrits et des versions chinoises et tibétaines. Au cours des siècles, les textes sanskrits bouddhiques ont subi des remaniements. Les manuscrits et les versions chinoises et tibétaines ne fournissent que des renseignements incomplets sur ce procès. Dans beaucoup de cas, on ne pourra faire autre chose que d'essayer de fixer l'état du texte tel qu'il a dû être à un certain stade de son histoire. C'est seulement si l'on dispose de manuscrits anciens et de versions fidèles qu'on pourra remonter plus loin.

M. Fujita ne consacre que quelques passages à l'aspect linguistique des textes (pp. 239-247). Il signale l'emploi de la terminaison *-u* pour *am* (nom. sg. nt.; acc. sg. nt.) et pour *-as* (nom. sg. masc.), de *ahu* pour *aham*, de *ayu* pour *ayam* dans les *gāthā* du S. Il pense que c'est un phénomène propre au prākrit du Nord-Ouest pour lequel M. H. W. Bailey a proposé le nom de Gāndhārī. Dans le *Dharmapada* en Gandhārī on trouve *-o*, *-u*, et *-a* pour la terminaison *-am* (cf. J. Brough, *The Gāndhārī Dharmapada*, London, 1952, p. 113) et au lieu de *ayu* ce texte a *a'i*. La substitution de *-u* pour

-am et *-as* n'est pas confinée à la Gāndhārī, cf. F. Edgerton, *Buddhist Hybrid Sanskrit Grammar*, §§ 1.95 et 1.96. Plus importantes, pour déterminer l'origine des anciennes traductions, sont les transcriptions citées par M. Fujita: Suhamadi pour Sukhāvatī, Divagara pour Dīpaṃkara, tadhagada pour tathāgata, Ayita pour Ajita et Mahācunna pour Mahācunda. J'exclus ṣamaṇa pour śramaṇa car *sha-men* 沙門 ne peut pas être cité pour prouver l'origine d'un texte déterminé (cf. J. Brough, *op. cit.*, p. 53). M. Fujita étudie aussi les traductions de trois noms propres. M. Brough a démontré que les traductions employées dans le T. 360 reposent sur les formes prākrites suivantes: Ko(ṃ)diñña pour Kauṇḍinya, Aśśayi pour Aśvajit et Baṣa ou Bhaṣa pour Bāṣpa (Comments on third-century Shan-shan and the history of Buddhism, *BSOAS*, XVIII, 1965, p. 610). M. Fujita hésite à accepter entièrement les conclusions de M. Brough, mais ses arguments ne sont pas toujours bien fondés. Le fait que les versions chinoises du *Laṅkāvatāra* sont postérieures au T. 360 n'a aucune importance. M. Brough ne cite leurs traductions de *koṭi* et *pūrva-koṭi* par *chi* 際 et *pen-chi* 本際 qu'à titre d'exemple pour montrer que ces traductions n'ont rien de surprenant. L'addition de *cheng* 正 pour traduire Aśśayi (正願) et B(h)aṣa (正語) s'explique tout naturellement par la tendance à créer des noms faits de deux caractères. Sur un seul point on pourrait partager les hésitations de M. Fujita. M. Brough suppose que *liao pen-chi* 了本際 et *chih pen-chi* 知本際 correspondent à *Ko(ṃ)diñña* et que les anciennes traductions du S. n'ont pas contenu une forme correspondante au sanskrit Ājñāta-Kauṇḍinya. On peut, comme l'a déjà suggéré M. Lamotte, supposer que *liao* et *chi* rendent Ājñāta, mais cela ne change rien au fait que *pen-chi* doit reposer sur une forme Gāndhārī *Ko(ṃ)di* (cf. Brough, *op. cit.*, p. 610, n. 98). En tout cas, il faudra examiner de plus près les transcriptions et les traductions de noms propres et de termes techniques dans les versions chinoises si l'on veut essayer d'établir le caractère linguistique des textes indiens originaux. Un tel examen aidera aussi à élucider les relations de ces traductions entre elles. Par exemple, M. Fujita remarque en passant que la traduction de (Ājñāta)-Kauṇḍinya par *liao pen-chi* dans le T. 360 repose sur la traduction par *chih pen-chi* que l'on trouve dans le T. 361. On se demande pourquoi M. Fujita n'a pas comparé systématiquement les termes techniques employés dans les trois plus anciennes traductions (T. 360-362).

Je me suis attardé ci-dessus assez longuement sur des problèmes textuels. Le livre de M. Fujita contient des matériaux importants pour l'étude des problèmes que pose l'histoire du texte du *Sukhāvatīvyūha* [1]): j'ai voulu indiquer les directions dans lesquelles ses recherches pourraient être prolongées et approfondies. La philologie bouddhique n'en est encore qu'à ses débuts. Quand on compare le travail fait dans ce domaine aux travaux consacrés par des générations de philologues aux textes classiques et à la Bible, on peut avoir une idée de ce qui reste encore à faire. Il faut espérer que nos confrères japonais y contribueront largement.

Les origines d'Amitābha, d'Amitāyus et du paradis Sukhāvatī ont été étudiées par de nombreux savants. Beaucoup d'entre eux les ont cherchées en Iran, d'autres en Inde, soit dans le védisme et l'hindouisme, soit dans le bouddhisme primitif. M. Fujita énumère toutes les opinions émises, même les plus aberrantes comme, par exemple, celle de Beal qui avait trouvé la Sukhāvatī dans l'île Socotra et celle d'Iwamoto qui l'a rapprochée du paradis judéo-chrétien. Il ne mentionne que brièvement les théories selon lesquelles ces origines doivent être cherchées hors de l'Inde, remarquant avec raison que la plupart des auteurs se bornent à mentionner cette possibilité sans apporter de preuves solides. M. Fujita montre clairement qu'il faut chercher les origines d'Amitābha avant tout dans la conception du Buddha telle qu'elle s'est développée dans l'évolution du bouddhisme. En ce qui concerne la Sukhāvatī, il en cherche les origines aussi bien dans le bouddhisme que dans l'hindouisme. Dans le chapitre consacré aux vœux, l'auteur montre que la notion de vœu existe déjà dans le bouddhisme primitif et se développe dans les écoles du Petit Véhicule. Le chapitre final, enfin, étudie la doctrine de la renaissance dans la Terre Pure, la commémoration du Buddha, la vision du Buddha et le caractère de la foi dans le bouddhisme primitif et dans l'amidisme. Tous ces problèmes sont étudiés par l'auteur avec une grande perspicacité et de manière méthodique et systématique. Il analyse soigneusement le sens des termes sanskrits et leurs traductions chinoises et tibétaines. Il cite une masse abondante de textes bouddhiques et indiens et fait preuve d'une vaste lecture des nombreux travaux occidentaux et japonais consacrés à ces problèmes. On ne peut

[1]) M. Fujita aurait facilité la lecture de son ouvrage s'il avait indiqué quels passages des trois traductions chinoises anciennes correspondent à des passages du texte sanskrit. Une édition synoptique de toutes les versions du *Sukhāvatīvyūha*, à l'instar de celle du *Kāśyapaparivarta* publiée par von Staël-Holstein, serait la bienvenue.

entreprendre ici l'analyse de ces chapitres pour lesquels on doit renvoyer le lecteur, ignorant du japonais, au résumé anglais qui, évidemment, ne peut remplacer la lecture de l'ouvrage même. Je me bornerai à faire des remarques sur quelques points.

Le problème de l'origine d'Amitābha et de l'amidisme ne peut pas être séparé de celui du lieu de provenance du *Sukhāvatīvyūha* primitif. Comme je l'ai mentionné ci-dessus, quelques transcriptions et traductions semblent indiquer que le texte primitif fut écrit en Gāndhārī. L'auteur tente de démontrer que le contenu du texte reflète la situation historique de l'Inde du Nord-Ouest à l'époque des Kuṣāṇa. Par exemple, il mentionne le fait que le texte sanskrit énumère des *grāma*, *nagara*, etc.: *grāmanagaranigamajanapadarāṣṭrarājadhānīṣu* (éd. Ashikaga, p. 24, ll. 18-19). Déjà dans les textes pālis on trouve mentionnés ensemble *gāma*, *nigama* et *rājadhānī* (cf. *Pāli Tipiṭakaṁ Concordance* s.v. *gāmo*). On ne voit pas pourquoi l'élargissement de ce cliché avec *nagara*, *janapada* et *rāṣṭra* ne pourrait s'être fait que dans le royaume des Kuṣāṇa. L'auteur semble se contredire quelque peu quand il dit que la mention d'arbres secoués par le vent ne peut avoir pris origine que dans un pays de chaleur tropicale (p. 256). Dans l'Inde du Nord-Ouest, le froid est bien connu: le fait que le *Kuan wu-liang-shou ching* parle de glace ne saurait non plus être invoqué comme preuve que ce texte ne peut pas avoir été écrit dans l'Inde (cf. p. 133, n. 5). La description de la Sukhāvatī contient des clichés que l'on retrouve ailleurs, comme le montre M. Fujita lui-même. M. Fujita cite aussi comme preuve de la composition du *Sukhāvatīvyūha* dans le royaume des Kuṣāṇa le fait que les trois traductions chinoises les plus anciennes racontent que Dharmākara, avant de devenir moine, était un roi (p. 349-350). Le texte sanskrit n'en fait pas mention mais, même si cela se trouvait dans le texte original, on ne pourrait guère y voir le reflet d'une situation historique déterminée. Non seulement il est dangereux de vouloir tirer trop de conclusions d'indications de ce genre, mais on peut même se demander si le texte primitif du *Sukhāvatīvyūha* provient vraiment de l'Inde du Nord-Ouest. Il ne faut pas perdre de vue le fait que les moines étrangers qui se sont rendus en Chine sont venus d'abord principalement des Contrées occidentales (Sérinde) et ensuite de l'Inde du Nord-Ouest. C'est seulement après 479 que l'on trouvera en Chine des moines venus de tout le continent indien (cf. *Buddha's Word in China*, Canberra, 1968, p. 6). Il n'y a donc rien de surprenant à ce que les Chinois aient connu d'abord les textes bouddhiques indiens dans une recension établie dans l'Inde du Nord-Ouest. Cela n'exclut nullement la possibilité que nombre de ces textes aient été d'abord composés dans d'autres parties de l'Inde et dans d'autres dialectes.

En énumérant les savants occidentaux qui ont cherché l'origine d'Amitābha dans l'Iran, l'auteur mentionne M. André Bareau et La Vallée Poussin (p. 264). Il ne donne pas de références en ce qui concerne l'opinion de M. Bareau; il s'agit probablement de son article sur „Der indische Buddhismus", paru dans *Die Religionen Indiens* III (Stuttgart, 1964, pp. 1-215). En parlant d'Amitābha, M. Bareau dit expressément: „Wie bei vielen dieser legendären Helden des Mahāyāna hat man an iranischen Ursprung gedacht, und zwar seiner glänzenden Gestalt und seiner Ewigkeit wegen; es gibt jedoch auch frühere rein indische und sogar buddhistische Beispiele dieser Art" (p. 151). En ce qui concerne La Vallée Poussin, il est vrai qu'il n'a pas exclu une influence iranienne; mais l'auteur lui fait tort quand il le cite de travers et ajoute de manière désobligeante: „Même Poussin qui se targue de méthodes strictement scientifiques . . ." (*gemmitsu-na gakufū o hokoru Poussin de sae mo*, cf. p. 268). La Vallée Poussin a écrit: „Il est presque trop facile de démontrer que le plus notable des Bouddhas du Grand Véhicule, l'actuel grand dieu, l'actuel Dieu du bouddhisme sino-japonais, Amitābha, 'Lumière infinie', 'd'éclat infini', est un dieu solaire, et par conséquent, iranien" (*Dynasties et Histoire de l'Inde depuis Kanishka*, 1935, p. 353). M. Fujita lit: „Il est facile de démontrer . . ." (*yōi-ni shōmei dekiru*), et oublie de mentionner que, quelques lignes plus loin, La Vallée Poussin écrit: „L'Inde ne manque pas de dieux lumineux depuis le Veda et le Mahābhārata. Le paradis d'Amitābha est bien hindou" (cf. aussi *La Siddhi de Hiuan-tsang*, II, 1929, p. 812). M. Fujita a aussi mal lu le *Hôbôgirin* quand il soutient que cet ouvrage explique Amita par *amṛta* comme l'a fait Wogihara Unrai (p. 291, n. 5). On y trouve le passage suivant: „Un autre nom d'Amida dans l'És. [= Ésotérisme] est Amṛta, de sorte que les Charmes d'Amṛta, comme Tt. 1316 et 1317, s'emploient pour Amida" (p. 25a).

Le texte sanskrit du *Sukhāvatīvyūha* ne nous renseigne pas sur la vie de Dharmākara avant qu'il ne fût devenu moine. D'autres textes le mentionnent à peine, mais racontent de manières fort différentes la vie antérieure d'Amitābha et celle d'Amitāyus. L'auteur l'explique par le fait qu'un seul et même Buddha était connu sous deux noms différents: Amitābha et Amitāyus (p. 344).

Cette explication n'est pas très satisfaisante, car on ne voit pas du tout comment les quinze *jātaka* énumérés par l'auteur se seraient développés à partir de l'existence de ces deux noms. Ne faudrait-il pas plutôt supposer que, comme c'est souvent le cas, des histoires existantes auraient été transformées en *jātaka* de façon plus ou moins arbitraire?

On sait l'importance de la commémoration du Buddha, la *buddhānusmṛti*, dans les textes amidistes. M. Paul Demiéville a étudié un grand nombre de textes amidistes qui s'y rapportent dans un travail qui a échappé à la vigilance de l'auteur (Sur la pensée unique, *BÉFEO*, XXIV, 1924, pp. 231-246). Selon les traductions chinoises, la commémoration du Buddha est une oraison mentale; ce n'est que dans le *Kuan wu-liang-shou ching* et dans l'exégèse des patriarches chinois de l'école de la Terre Pure que l'on trouve nettement l'idée d'invocations vocales (cf. Demiéville, pp. 236 et 238; Fujita, p. 547). M. Fujita remarque que le texte sanskrit emploie deux verbes pour exprimer la commémoration du Buddha: *(sam)anu-smṛ-* et *manasi-kṛ-* (p. 545). Ces deux verbes semblent exprimer l'idée d'une oraison mentale. Il faut, toutefois, signaler un autre texte dans lequel *anusmārayati* s'emploie pour exprimer une invocation vocale. Le *Kāraṇḍavyūha* raconte que le bodhisattva Avalokiteśvara voit des centaines de milliers de vers et leur enseigne l'invocation des Trois Joyaux: *tad eṣāṃ śabdaṃ niścārayati—namo buddhāya, namo dharmāya, namaḥ saṃghāya iti/tac chrutvā te ca sarve prāṇakāḥ namo buddhāya namo dharmāya namaḥ saṃghāyeti nāmam anusmārayanti* (éd. P. L. Vaidya, *Mahāyānasūtrasaṃgraha*, I, Darbhanga, 1961, p. 281, ll. 27-29). Ici *anusmārayanti* doit désigner une invocation vocale, et c'est aussi ainsi que l'a compris la version chinoise qui le rend par *ch'eng nien* 稱念 (T. 1050, vol. XX, p. 55a20). Il n'est donc pas exclu que dans l'Inde déjà, la *buddhānusmṛti* ait pu être une invocation et pas seulement une oraison mentale. Dans les textes pālis, l'invocation du Buddha n'est pas une *anusmṛti* mais un *udāna* (cf. MN, I, p. 112, l. 5: *tikkhattuṃ udānaṃ udānesi*: *Namo tassa Bhagavato arahato sammāsambuddhassa*). Un *udāna* est de nature vocale. Il est bien possible que la *buddhānusmṛti* ait hérité de ce caractère vocal de l'*udāna*. Dans ce cas, les exégètes chinois n'auraient pas eu tort en expliquant la *buddhānusmṛti* comme une invocation vocale. Il faudra examiner les textes du Mahāyāna sur ce point; on ne peut se fier à l'explication d'*anusmṛti* donnée par les dictionnaires. En pratique, l'*anusmṛti* peut bien avoir été une invocation. Il ne faut pas oublier que la lecture silencieuse est étrangère à l'Inde. Quand on lit un livre, on le fait à voix haute ou à voix basse. D'autre part, l'invocation *namo 'mitābhāya samyaksaṃbuddhāya* se rencontre déjà, comme l'indique M. Fujita, dans les deux traductions chinoises les plus anciennes (T. 362, XII, p. 316b27-28; T. 361, XII, p. 298c 2); elle était donc connue en Chine dès le troisième siècle de notre ère (cf. p. 547).

Le grand travail de M. Fujita ne contient qu'une partie de la thèse qu'il a soumise à l'Université de Tōkyō en janvier 1967. Toute une section, relative au bouddhisme primitif, a été omise dans le présent livre. C'est un des grands mérites de ce livre que d'être basé sur une connaissance approfondie du bouddhisme primitif. Il faut mentionner plus spécialement à cet égard les belles pages qu'il consacre à la foi dans le bouddhisme primitif et à ses relations avec l'amidisme (pp. 603-618) [1]. Comme l'indique le titre, l'auteur a concentré ses recherches sur la période ancienne de l'amidisme. Une postface esquisse les tâches qui restent à accomplir pour l'étude de la période postérieure et pour celle des rapports des textes amidistes avec les sūtra du Grand Véhicule. On peut être sûr que M. Fujita s'en acquittera de la façon la plus honorable. On attendra donc avec impatience la parution d'un deuxième volume; il parachèvera un ouvrage qui promet de faire époque dans l'histoire des études bouddhiques.

J. W. de Jong.

N. H. Samtani (ed.), *The Arthaviniścaya-sūtra and Its Commentary* (*Nibandhana*). Critically edited and annotated for the first time with Introduction and several Indices (*Tibetan Sanskrit Works Series*, Vol. XIII). Patna, K. P. Jayaswal Research Institute, 1971, xxxi + 186 + 413 pp. Rs. 25/–.

An incomplete text of the Arthaviniścaya was published in 1944 by Alfonsa Ferrari on the basis of two Nepalese manuscripts.[1] In 1961 P. L. Vaidya published a complete text on the basis of a Nepalese manuscript in the Oriental Institute, Baroda (*Buddhist Sanskrit Texts*, No. 17, Mahāyānasūtrasaṃgrahaḥ I, Darbhanga, 1961, pp. 309–328). Dr. N. H. Samtani's edition contains both the text and the commentary by Vīryaśrīdatta, which had already been briefly mentioned by Alfonsa Ferrari who had made use of a photocopy of an incomplete manuscript made by Professor Tucci in the Ṅor monastery (cf. *op. cit.*, pp. 552 and 617). Samtani has been able to consult other manuscripts both of the text and the commentary. His edition of the text is based upon a photocopy of a manuscript, dated 1199 A.D., from the Ṅor monastery, three Nepalese manuscripts and Ferrari's edition. Moreover, he has consulted the Tibetan translation which dates from the beginning of the ninth century[2] and two Chinese versions (Taishō nos. 762 and 763). The first Chinese version was translated by Fa-hsien. According to Nanjio he changed his name in 982 from Fa-t'ien to Fa-hsien but this is not correct. His original name was T'ien-hsi-tsai. In 987 his name was changed to Fa-hsien. He died in 1000.[3]

[1] Alfonsa Ferrari, *Arthaviniścaya* (Testo e versione), *Atti delle Reale Accademia d'Italia*, Memorie, Classe di scienze morali e storiche, Serie VII, Volume IV, Fascicolo 13 (Roma, 1944), pp. 534–625.

[2] According to the catalogue of the Derge edition the translators were Jinamitra, Prajñāvarma and Ye-śes-sde. The catalogue of the Peking edition does not mention the names of the translators.

[3] Jan Yün-hua, 'Buddhist Relations Between India and Sung China', *History of Religions*, VI (1966), 34–36.

According to the Ta-chung-hsiang-fu fa-pao-lu (chüan 10), a catalogue, a copy of which was discovered in 1933, the text was translated in 998 from a Sanskrit manuscript which had been brought to China from Central India.[4] The catalogue describes the text as a Hīnayāna sūtra. The second Chinese version was translated by Chin-tsung-chih during the period 1111–1117 (cf. *Hôbôgirin*, fascicule annexe, p. 143). The edition of the Nibandhana is based upon photocopies of two manuscripts from the Ṅor monastery and one Nepalese manuscript. The Nibandhana does not seem to have been translated into Chinese or Tibetan. The Tibetan Tanjur contains a different commentary which occupies 221 folios in the Peking edition (cf. P. Cordier, *Catalogue du fonds tibétain*, 3e partie, Paris, 1915, p. 493). According to Alfonsa Ferrari this commentary is very long but rather pedestrian. The names of the author and the translator are unknown (*op. cit.*, p. 551).

The Arthaviniścaya is divided into 27 sections (26 in the Nepalese manuscript and in the Tibetan version; 21 in Fa-hsien's version). Some sections contain only lists of technical terms but others add explanations. It is possible that the original text did not contain any explanations. Samtani discusses briefly the problem of the original text of the Arthaviniścaya and points out that interpolations and amplifications have crept into the text in the course of time (pp. 155–156). The manuscripts, the translations and the commentary represent different recensions. Strictly speaking one can distinguish six different recensions: (1) the Ṅor manuscript; (2) the Nepalese manuscripts; (3) the first Chinese translation; (4) the second Chinese translation; (5) the Tibetan translation; (6) the text on which the commentary is based.[5] Only a synoptic edition would make it possible to see the differences between the recensions. However, the Sanskrit manuscripts and the Tibetan translation seem to belong to the same tradition. As to the Chinese versions it is difficult to know whether their divergences from the other texts are due to the translators or to the original text on which they are based. Samtani remarks that in the second Chinese version there are references to *dharmaśūnyatā* in the section on the five *samādhi*. This section describes meditation on the impermanence of the body (T. 763, p. 655a 26–b19). It does not give five different kinds of meditation. The number five refers to the five members (*aṅga*) of the body. One wonders whether the author of this passage has not replaced the five *skandha* by the five *aṅga*. In any case, there is no trace of Mahāyāna in this section. Alfonsa Ferrari wrote that the second Chinese version often refers to the *dharmaśūnyata* but she does not single out this section (p. 551). A quick perusal of the text did not reveal any occurrence of the term *dharmaśūnyatā*.

Samtani's introduction (pp. 1–172) deals exhaustively with all problems connected with the Arthaviniścaya and the commentary. I would like to draw attention to a few points. The date of the commentary can be determined within narrow limits because the colophon states that the work was written by Vīryaśrīdatta in the monastery of Nālandā during the reign of king Dharmapāla. Hence it must have been written in the second half of the eighth century. In this connection Samtani discusses the date of Yaśomitra, the author of the Abhidharmakośavyākhyā. He criticizes Alfonsa Ferrari for placing him in the eighth century. Alfonsa Ferrari pointed out that dPal-brtsegs, the translator of the Vyākhyā, worked during the last part of the eighth century and in the beginning of the ninth century and that, consequently, Yaśomitra must have lived at least several decennia before dPal-britsegs, but she did not exclude the possibility that he may have lived in an earlier period ('Ora, anche ammettendo che il commentatore di Vasubandhu sia vissuto nell' VIII secolo e non prima', p. 547). As to the *terminus a quo* the only indication I have found is the fact that Yaśomitra quotes the commentaries on the Kośa by Guṇamati and his pupil Vasumitra (cf. Burnouf, *Introduction à l'étude du buddhisme indien*, Paris, 1844, p. 566). According to Noël Peri, Guṇamati must have lived in the beginning of the sixth century ('A propos de la date de Vasubandhu'. *BEFEO*, **11**, 1911, p. 387). Both the Chinese and the Tibetan tradition tell us that

[4] The *Ta-chung-hsiang-fu fa-pao-la* was completed in 1013 (cf. Jan Yün-hua, *op. cit.*, p. 27), 15 years after the translation of the Arthaviniścaya by Fa-hsien.

[5] If the commentary in the Tanjur is based upon still another recension, one would arrive at seven different recensions.

Guṇamati was the master of Sthiramati (cf. Peri, *op. cit.*, pp. 354 and 379). The date given for Guṇamati by Peri agrees with the opinions of Frauwallner and Kajiyama, according to whom Sthiramati has lived from 510 to 570 (cf. Yuichi Kajiyama, 'Bhāvaviveka, Sthiramati and Dharmapāla', *WZKSOA*, XII–XIII, 1968–69, 200). Therefore Yaśomitra has lived between 550 and 750. One must add that neither Hsüan-tsang nor I-ching make any mention of Yaśomitra. One cannot rely too much on an *argumentum e silentio* but it is at least an indication which favours placing Yaśomitra more towards the end of the period 550–750 than at the beginning. It is possible that Vīryaśrīdatta has known Yaśomitra's Vyākhyā. Samtani is very positive on this point (cf. p. 135), but I have failed to find any definite evidence that Vīryaśrīdatta has quoted the Vyākhyā. Vīryaśrīdatta has undoubtedly made much use of the Kośabhāṣya and, as Yaśomitra comments on the Bhāṣya, the same matters are obviously discussed by him. In the footnotes to the commentary Samtani quotes many passages from the Vyākhyā but, as far as I have been able to see, one does not find in the commentary any passage which cannot be but a quotation from the Vyākhyā.

Samtani gives a detailed analysis of the commentary. Two errors have to be corrected. On p. 108 he writes: "By *bhujiṣya-śīla*, the Comr. means even freedom from (cultivating) *śīlavipattipratipakṣas* (opponents of moral turpitude) which are given as *pratisaṃkhyānabala* and *bhāvanābala* (powers of careful consideration and meditation)." However, the text clearly states that one is free through the possession of these *pratipakṣa: bhujiṣyaiḥ* (i.e. *śīlaiḥ*) *śīlavipattipratipakṣaparigraheṇa svatantratvāt* (p. 256.8–9). On p. 118 Samtani speaks of "impurities (*kleśopakleśas*) born of physical and vocal depravities (*kāyavāgdauṣṭhalyajanakānāṃ*)". One must correct 'born of' to 'giving rise to'.

Both the Arthaviniścaya and the commentary have been very carefully edited by Samtani. The annotation contains not only many passages from the Kośabhāṣya and the Vyākhyā but also from Pāli commentaries. Very useful are also the detailed indices which the editor has provided. Samtani has done everything possible to make this edition as useful as possible. I think there is no better way to show one's appreciation for the excellent work done by the editor than to list a few minor points noted while reading the text.

Section 5 of the text (pp. 5–14) seems to be an expanded version of the Pratītyasamutpādavibhaṅganirdeśa (*Epigraphia Indica*, XXI, 1931–2, 193–204).[6] The commentary quotes from the same text, cf. p. 118. 10–12: *yathā nāmarūpavibhaṅge nāma vistareṇoktam: – 'rūpaṃ katamat? yat kiñcid rūpaṃ sarvaṃ tac catvāri mahābhūtāni, catvāri ca mahābhūtāny upādāya' hi.* – P. 23.3: *bhikṣur aṇyagato* – read *araṇyagato* (also 25.8, 15). – P. 24.4: *yadbhūtam* – read *yathābhūtaṃ* (cf. 23.5). – P. 24, n. 2: the word *sbyaṅ* is recorded in Sumatiratna's *Tibetan-Mongolian Dictionary*, II, (Ulanbator, 1959), p. 357: rtsva daṅ 'bru-la sogs-pa 'jog-pa'i gnas-te sgo daṅ skar-khuṅ med-pa/yaṅ baṅ-ba 'am rdzaṅ yaṅ źes-pa sbyaṅ "a place without doors and windows where herbs and grains are stored; also a store-room or a box". – P. 46.1: *dharmopacchedaḥ* – one finds also *dharmopaccheda* in the Mahāvastu (ed. Senart III.200.11) but the Pāli texts have *vaṭṭūpaccheda* (cf. Critical Pāli Dictionary s.v. *ālaya-samugghāta*) and the Tibetan translator seems to have rendered *vartmopaccheda* (lam-gyi rgyun-bcad-pa). – P. 61, n. 2: T has also *pradakṣiṇagrāhitayā* and not *anukūlagrahaṇatayā*, cf. Śikṣāsamuccaya (ed. C. Bendall), p. 286, n. 6. – P. 72.5: *ādau vācāṃ prayojanam* – read with N. *ādau vācyaṃ prayojanam*. – P. 73.5: *samāropāya vādaparihārārtham* – read *samāropāpavāda-parihārārtham*. – P. 91.2: *tadupabhogād* – read with MSS. *tadupayogād*. P. 99.11: *vedanāvāsanāc* – read with Kośabhāṣya *vedanāvaśāc*. – P. 203.1: *mutodīti* – to the texts, listed by Edgerton s.v. *mūtodī*, add Pañcaviṃśatisāhasrikā Prajñāpāramitā (ed. N. Dutt), p. 205.20 – P. 210.3, 6: *ko 'bhiśayaḥ* – read *ko 'tiśayaḥ* ("What is added by mentioning *adhyātma* and *bahirdhā* together and by twice mentioning *kāya*?"). – P. 257, n. 1: Samtani is quite right in supposing that one must read *'bhujiṣyo* in Divyāvadāna p. 302.26; this has been overlooked by Edgerton. For *bhujiṣya* see also Mātṛceṭa's Śatapañcāśatka (ed. by D. R. Shackleton Bailey) verse 86 and Pāramitāsamāsa (ed.

[6] For more bibliographical information see *IIJ* X (1967), 198. The article announced therein 'A propos du Nidānasaṃyukta' has been published in 1975.

Alfonsa Ferrari), I.25. – P. 280.3: *utpattyagamanam* – read *utpatya gamanam*. For the story of Madhuvāsiṣṭha who was a monkey in his former life see Ét. Lamotte, *Le Traité de la grande vertu de sagesse*, T. III (Louvain, 1970), p. 1659, n. 3; for that of Pilindavatsa Lamotte, *op. cit.*, T. I (Louvain, 1944), pp. 121–122 and T. III, p. 1661.

Australian National University J. W. DE JONG

SANSKRIT FRAGMENTS OF THE KĀŚYAPAPARIVARTA

by J. W. DE JONG, Canberra

In 1938 Kuno Hōryū edited two fragments of a manuscript of the Kāśyapaparivarta[1]. They had been sent to Hoernle by P. J. Miles in 1903. According to Hoernle the fragments had been found in Khadalik. The two fragments (Hoernle No. 143 S.B. 38 and No. 143 S.B. 39) are at present in the India Office Library to which institution I am obliged for having put at my disposal excellent photocopies. Kuno had no difficulty in showing that they belong to one and the same leaf. The text corresponds to sections 128–136 of the edition of the Kāśyapaparivarta published by A. von Staël-Holstein (Shanghai, 1926). In von Staël-Holstein's edition each of the sections 128–133 consists of a prose part and a verse part, but in the fragments the verses are missing. However, the fragments do contain the first words of section 136: *atha khalu bhagavāṃ tasyā[ṃ] velā(y)[ām imāṃ gāthām abhāṣata].* Kuno pointed out that of the four Chinese versions the two versions dating from the periods of the Chin and Ch'in dynasties, correspond more closely to the Sanskrit text of the fragments. He concluded that this text must have been in existence in the 3rd–5th centuries A.D. Comparing the fragments with the corresponding prose parts in von Staël-Holstein's edition, Kuno tried to reconstruct the missing parts of the entire leaf. His readings of the manuscript are not always correct and his reconstruction does not take into account the exact extent of the missing portions. Even more important is the fact that Kuno was not aware of the fact that a fragment of the same leaf was edited twenty years before by J. N. Reuter[2]. The fragments, published by Reuter, were brought back from his expedition to Central Asia and North China in 1906–1908 by Colonel Baron Gustav Mannerheim. The third fragment contains a passage of the Kāśyapaparivarta corresponding to sections 130–135. It exactly fills one gap in the leaf, edited by Kuno, between lines 3 to 8 of the recto and lines 1 to 6 of the verso. The following edition of the three fragments of this leaf is based upon a photocopy of the two fragments in the India Office Library and a photocopy of the Manner-

[1] 'Saiiki shutsudo bukkyō bonpon to sono seiten shiron-jo chii (jō). Daihōshakkyō to Zōagonkyō no genten, I. Uten shutsudo Daihōshakkyō bonpon to sono kachi', *Bukkyō kenkyū*, II,3 (1938), pp. 71–110.

[2] J. N. REUTER, *'Some Buddhist Fragments from Chinese Turkestan in Sanskrit and "Khotanese"'*, Journal de la société finno-ougrienne, 30 (1913–1918), pp. 1–37 [Reprinted in: C. G. Mannerheim, *Across Asia from West to East in 1906–1908*, vol. II, Helsinki, 1940].

heim fragment which Professor Pentti Aalto has been so kind as to send me at my request. (M) indicates the beginning and end of the Mannerheim fragment. Missing syllables are indicated with – and missing letters with .. As in von Staël-Holstein's edition a single oblique stroke represents a dot, a pair of oblique strokes two upright strokes. Moreover, a colon stands for a colon in the manuscript, a punctuation mark which was not recognized as such by von Staël-Holstein[3]. Akṣaras which can only be read partially are put between round brackets and restored akṣaras between square brackets. ○ is used to indicate the circle round the hole in the right half of the leaf.

RECTO

1. m eva kāśyapaikatyā śramaṇabrāhmaṇā bahūmn darmāṃ paryāpya na rāg . – – – – – – – – – – – – – m(o) hatṛṣṇā vinodayaṃti / tte dharmārṇavānohya-mānne : klaiśa(tṛ)ṣṇayā kā(la) – – – –
2. ·tigāmino bhavaṃti // tadyathā kāśyapa vaidya auṣa(da)bhrastā gṛhi(t) – – – – – – – – – – – – – – utpadyeta / na ca taṃ vyādhi / śaknuyā cikitsittu / evam eva kāśyapa bahuśrutasya – – – –
3. draṣṭavyaḥ yaḥs tena śrutenna na knoty ātmānaṃ klaiśavyādhiṃ citsi – irarthakaṃ (tasya) taṃ śruttaṃ·bhavatt(i) (M) // tadya[thā kā](śyapa) glānapu[ru]ṣ[o] r (M) ājārhaṃ bhaiṣajyaṃm upayujyattāsaṃvatsareṇa kālaṃ – –
4. evam eva kāśyapa bahuśrutasya klaiśavyādhi draṣṭa – yaḥs tenāsaṃvat-sareṇa kā (M) laṃ karotti // tadyathā kāśyapa maṇ[i] (M) ratnaṃ ucāre patita akāryopagaṃ bhavaty evam e(va) – –
5. pa bahuśrutasya lābhasatkāro(cārapa) – ○ – – ṣṭavyaḥ niṣkiṃcana devaman(u) . . e (M) . yaṣu // tadyathā kāśyapa mṛtasya mālā (M) / evam eva kāśyapa duśīlasya kāṣ(ā)ya(ndra) –
6. vyaḥ // tadyathā kāśyapa susnātasya suvili – (sya) – – innakeśana-khasyāvadā(ta) (M) vastraprāvṛtasya pravaracandanānuliptasya śre (M) ṣṭiputrasya śirṣe caṇpakamālā evam eva kāśya – – –
7. lavato (ba)huśrutasya kāṣāya(dhā)ra – – – – // catvāraḥ ime (M) kāśyapa duśīlā śīlavapratirūpakāḥ kata (M) m(e) catvāra iha kāśya – – katyo bhikṣu – –
8. mok(ṣa)saṃ – – – – rto bhavati / ācā – – – – – – – aṇ – (M) treṣv api vadyeṣu bhayadarśī samādāya (śi)kṣa (M) ti śikṣāpa(de) – – – (iśuddha) – – – – – –

[3] F. WELLER, *Zum Kāśyapaparivarta*. Heft 2. Verdeutschung des sanskrit-tibetischen Textes (Berlin, 1965), p. 63, n. 3.

VERSO

1. – – – – ga(t)o (v)iharati pa(ri)śu – – – – – – – – – – – – (M) yaṃ kāśyapa prathamo duśīla śīlavapratirūpakaḥ // (M) (p)unar apa(ra)ṃ kāś(ya) – (i)haikatyo bhikṣu vvina(ya) – –
2. – vati pravṛta – nayo v(i)naya – pto – – – – (ya)dṛṣṭim cāsy(a)nuca (M) litaṃ bhavati : ayaṃ kāśyapa dvitīyo duśīla śīla (M) vaprattirūpakaḥ // puna paraṃ kāśyapa (i)haikat – –
3. kṣu maitrāvihārī bhavati / satvārambaṇa – – – – – – manvāgatto bhavati / (a) (M) jātiṃ ca sarvvasaṃskārāṇāṃ śrutvā : utrasati saṃ (M) trasati saṃtrāsam āpadyate / ayaṃ kāśyapa tṛtī – –
4. śīlaḥ śīlavapratirūpakaḥ // pu(na)r apara(ṃ) ○ kāśyapa ihaikatyo bhikṣuḥ dv (M) ādaśa dhuttaguṇān samā – ya varttatte / (M) upalaṃbhadṛṣṭikaś ca bhavati / ahaṃkāramamaṃkāra – – –
5. ayaṃ kāśyapa caturtho duśīlaḥ śīlavapra ○ tirūpakaḥ // ime kāśyapa ca (M) tvāro duśīla śīlavapratirūpakā (M) śīlaṃ śīlam itti kāśyapa ucyate / yatra nātmā (n) – –
6. yaṃ : na kriyā nākriyā / na karaṇaṃ nākaraṇaṃ : na cāro nācāro na pracār. (M) na nāmarūpam / na nimittaṃ : na śamo (M) na praśamaḥ na graho notsargaḥ na grāhyaṃ : na satvo na – – – –
7. ptiḥ na vā na vāprajñaptiḥ na citaṃ na citaprajñapti / na lo(k)o nālokaḥ na niś(ra)yo nān(i)śrayaḥ nātmaś – – tka . (ṣa) – – parākarmmaśīlyapaṃnsanā : na śīlamannyanā / na śi – – – –
8. nā : na saṃkalpanā : idam ucyate kāśyapa aryāṇāṃ śīlaṃm / a – – – – – – – – – – – – āpagatam // sarvvaniśrayavigatam // atha khalu bhagavāṃ tasyā velā(y)

In line 5 of the recto the word *devamanuṣyeṣu* has to be read. Fragment 143 S.B. 38 has *devaman* and the vowel *e*. M contains the subscript *y* and the syllable *ṣu*. Reuter read *xyanu*, *x* indicating a deleted consonant. In line 7 of the verso Reuter read only the word [*du*](*śīle*). It is possible to read *ilo – r – : ā*. The fragment 143 S.B. 39 has *ātmaś – – tka . – . ā* (*ṣa*) – . It is therefore possible to reconstruct the word *ātmaśīlotkarṣaṇā*. The scribe has the habit of doubling the *t* and the *n*, cf. recto (1) *tte*, *-ohyamānne*; (2) *cikisittu*; (3) *śrutenna*, *śruttaṃ*, etc. Several syllables have been omitted by him, cf. recto (3) *knoty* for *śaknoty*; (4) *citsi* — for *cikitsi* —; verso (2) *puna paraṃ* for *punar aparaṃ*. In recto (3) and (4) the scribe wrote *asaṃvatsareṇa* which must be a mistake for *asaṃvareṇa*, cf. Weller's translation of the corresponding passage in the Chin version: "Gerade wie wenn ein kranker Mensch die wunderbare Arznei eines Königs einnimmt, sein Ende erreicht, (da er) *sich nicht an die Regel hält*, so, Kāśyapa, verhält es sich wiederum auch (damit) so, daß es vielfach Śramaṇa, Brahmanen gibt, (die) *das der Lehre nicht Gemäße ausführen*, (sondern) alle Krankheiten der Bindungen aufkommen lassen, (und sie nach ihrem) Ende auf dem schlimmen Wegen (wieder) geboren werden[4]." It is difficult to know how far the scribe has correctly reproduced the language of the text. In saṃdhi between vowels, a hiatus usually occurs, but in the first line of recto the scribe wrote *kāśyapaikatyā*. In reconstructing the text of the leaf I have normalized the spellings and the saṃdhi, although I am aware of the fact that the language of the original may have been more irregular. Apart from this aspect, it does not seem too difficult to reconstruct the text of the leaf. It is possible that the original had *na pracāro nāpracāraḥ* instead of *na pracāraḥ* and *na nāma na rūpaṃ* instead of *na nāmarūpaṃ* (cf. § 135).

RECONSTRUCTED TEXT OF THE LEAF

128. evam eva kāśyapaikatyāḥ śramaṇabrāhmaṇā bahūn dharmān paryāpya na rāgatṛṣṇāṃ vinodayanti / na dveṣatṛṣṇāṃ na mohatṛṣṇāṃ vinodayanti / te dharmārṇavenohyamānāḥ kleśatṛṣṇayā kālagatā durgatigāmino bhavanti /

129. tadyathā kāśyapa vaidya auṣadhabhastrāṃ gṛhītvānuvicaret / tasya kaścid eva vyādhir utpadyeta / na ca taṃ vyādhiṃ śaknuyāc cikitsitum / evam eva kāśyapa bahuśrutasya kleśavyādhir draṣṭavyo yas tena śrutena na śaknoty ātmanaḥ kleśavyādhiṃ cikitsitum / nirarthakaṃ tasya tac chrutaṃ bhavati /

130. tadyathā kāśyapa glānaḥ puruṣo rājārhaṃ bhaiṣajyam upayujyāsaṃvareṇa kālaṃ kuryāt / evam eva kāśyapa bahuśrutasya kleśavyādhir draṣṭavyo yas tenāsaṃvareṇa kālaṃ karoti /

131. tadyathā kāśyapa maṇiratnam uccāre patitam akāryopagaṃ bhavaty evam eva kāśyapa bahuśrutasya lābhasatkāroccārapatanaṃ draṣṭavyam / niṣkiṃcana devamanuṣyeṣu /

132. tadyathā kāśyapa mṛtasya mālā / evam eva kāśyapa duḥśīlasya kāṣāyam draṣṭavyaṃ /

133. tadyathā kāśyapa susnātasya suviliptasya suchinnakeśanakhasyāvadātavastraprāvṛtasya pravaracandanānuliptasya śreṣṭhiputrasya śīrṣe campakamālā evam eva kāśyapa duḥśīlavato bahuśrutasya kāṣāyadhāraṇaṃ draṣṭavyam /

134. catvāra ime kāśyapa duḥśīlāḥ śīlavatpratirūpakāḥ / katame catvāraḥ / iha kāśyapaikatyo bhikṣuḥ prātimokṣasamvarasaṃvṛto bhavati / ācāragocarasaṃpanna aṇumātreṣv api vadyeṣu bhayadarśī samādāya śikṣate śikṣāpadeṣu pariśuddhakāyavāṅmanaskarmaṇā samanvāgato viharati pariśuddhajīvaḥ sa ca bhavaty ātmavādī / ayaṃ kāśyapa prathamo duḥśīlaḥ śīlavatpratirūpakaḥ //

[4] '*Kāśyapaparivarta nach der Djin-Fassung verdeutscht*', MIO, XII (1966), p. 419.

punar aparaṃ kāśyapehaikatyo bhikṣur vinayadharo bhavati pravṛtavinayo vinayaguptau sthitaḥ[a] satkāyadṛṣṭiś cāsyānucalitā bhavati / ayaṃ kāśyapa dvitīyo duḥśīlaḥ śīlavatpratirūpakaḥ //
punar aparaṃ kāśyapehaikatyo bhikṣur maitrāvihārī bhavati / sattvāraṃbaṇayā karuṇayā samanvāgato bhavati / ajātiṃ ca sarvasaṃskārāṇāṃ śrutvā / uttrasati saṃtrasati saṃtrāsam āpadyate / ayaṃ kāśyapa tṛtīyo duḥśīlaḥ śīlavatpratirūpakaḥ //
punar aparaṃ kāśyapehaikatyo bhikṣur dvādaśa dhutaguṇān samādāya vartate / upalaṃbhadṛṣṭikaś ca bhavati / ahaṃkāramamakārasthitaḥ / ayaṃ kāśyapa caturtho duḥśīlaḥ śīlavatpratirūpakaḥ //
ime kāśyapa catvāro duḥśīlāḥ śīlavatpratirūpakāḥ //

135. śīlaṃ śīlaṃ iti kāśyapocyate / yatra nātmā nātmīyam / na kriyā nākriyā / na karaṇaṃ nākaraṇam / na cāro nācāro na pracāraḥ / na nāmarūpaṃ na nimittam / na śamo na praśamaḥ / na grāho notsargaḥ / na grāhyaṃ na sattvo na sattvaprajñaptiḥ / na vāṅ na vākprajñaptiḥ / na cittaṃ na cittaprajñaptiḥ / na loko nālokaḥ / na niśrayo nāniśrayaḥ / nātmaśīlotkarṣaṇā na paraśīlapaṃsanā / na śīlamanyanā / na śīlavikalpanā (?) / na saṃkalpanā / idam ucyate kāśyapāryāṇāṃ śīlam anāsravam aparyāpannaṃ traidhātukāpagataṃ sarvaniśrayavigatam //

136. atha khalu bhagavāṃs tasyāṃ velāyām

[a] Cf. Tib. *'dul-ba'i tshul-la gnas-pa* and the Iṅdikaṭusāya copper plaque no. 67: *vanaya-gupto sthitaḥ* (S. Paranavitana, 'A Note on the Iṅdikaṭusāya copper plaques', *Epigraphica Zeylanica*, vol. IV, pt. 5, 1939, p. 241). Thanks are due to Mr. G. Schopen for drawing my attention to this article.

In 1957 V.S. Vorob'ev-Desjatovskij published two fragments of Sanskrit manuscripts of the Kāśyapaparivarta[5]. The first fragment is an almost complete leaf. It carries the number three and forms part of the manuscript published by von Staël-Holstein. Weller is of the opinion that this leaf does not agree in all details with the manuscript published by von Staël-Holstein[6]. As his only reason Weller adduces the fact that this leaf contains the words: *idam uvāca bhagavāṃs* which are absent in the Tibetan version. This only proves that the Sanskrit original on which the Tibetan version is based is different. Vorob'ev-Desjatovskij points out that the dimensions of the leaf are the same as those of the other leafs of the manuscript. His conclusion that this leaf is the formerly unknown third leaf of the manuscript is undoubtedly

[5] *'Vnov' najdennye listy rukopisej Kāśyapaparivarty'*, Rocznik Orientalistyczny, 21 (1957), pp. 491–500.
[6] *Zum Kāśyapaparivarta*, p. 63, n. 3.

correct. The Institute of Oriental Studies has kindly put at my disposal a photocopy. Vorob'ev-Desjatovskij's transliteration has to be corrected in the following points: recto (3) *vākṣyaparamaḥ*; read: *vākyaparamaḥ*; verso (2) *dhāritvā*; read: *dhāritva*; (3) *taparo*; read: *ca taparo*; (4) *vartate*; read: *vartaṃte*; (5) *-visaṁvādanataya*; read: *-visaṁvādanatayā*. Recto (1) Vorob'ev-Desjatovskij reads *ādīptaśiras ce [la . . śru]* and adds in a note that he is unable to restore the missing word. The Tibetan version has *mgo-'am-gos-la me 'bar-ba bźin* which renders *ādiptaśiraścelopama*, cf. Edgerton, *Buddhist Hybrid Sanskrit Dictionary* s.v. *ādīptaśiraścailopama*. Recto (2) *śrutaś* for *śrutāś* and verso (2) *pratipattiya* for *pratipattiyā* are misprints as is obvious from Vorob'ev-Desjatovskij's notes. At the beginning of verso (1) Vorob'ev-Desjatovskij reads . . *y* . . . *taḥ*. I fail to see any trace of a *y* on the photocopy. Also the photocopy does not show the syllable *ka* which Vorob'ev-Desjatovskij adds at the end of recto (5): *lābhasatkāraśiloka*.

The second fragment corresponds to sections 14—19. The text does not contain the verses which are to be found in von Staël-Holstein's text. The Institute of Oriental Studies has kindly given me a photocopy of this fragment also. In recto (6) read *bh[ūtagu]ṇāḥ* for *bh[uta gu]ṇaḥ*; (7) read *cābhiśraddhadāti* for *cābhiśraddadhāti*; verso (2) read *ṣaṭpāramitā-* for *ṣaṭpāramita-*, (2—3) read *dharmabhāṇakadar[śa]* (b3) *naṁm for dharmābhāṇakadar[śa]* (b3) *nāṁ*; (4—5) read *sarvvadṛṣṭikr[tānā]* (b5) *m* for *sarvvadṛṣṭikṛta[na]* (b5) *m*; (6) read *niṣkuhakasy[āra]ṇyavāsaḥ* for *niṣkuhasy[āra]ṇyavāsaḥ*, *pratikārāpratikaṁkṣinaś* for *pratikārakratikaṁkṣinaś*; (7) read *saddharmaparyeṣṭim* for *saddharmamaryaṣṭim*.

Weller is of the opinion that this fragment does not entirely agree with the Chinese Chin version, as Vorob'ev-Desjatovskij had maintained[7]. This is not quite correct because Vorob'ev-Desjatovskij said only that "of all Chinese versions only the Chin version reproduces exactly *mārasamatikramaṇā dharmāḥ* in section 18 and that this represents a distinctive peculiarity of this version" (p. 498).

Although Weller agrees with him on this point, I fail to see in what way the Chin version is any closer to the Sanskrit text of the fragment than the Han and Ch'in versions. None of the three versions translates only the word *māra*. According to Weller's translations of the three versions, the Han version has "die Welt Māras", the Chin version "alle māra" und the Ch'in version "māras Angelegenheiten"[8].

[7] *Op. cit.*, p. 10.

[8] *'Kāśyapaparivarta nach der Han-Fassung verdeutscht*, Buddhist Yearly 1968/69 (Halle, 1970), p. 114; *'Kāśyapaparivarta nach der Djin-Fassung verdeutscht'*, MIO, XII (1966), p. 394; *'Kāśyapaparivarta nach der Tjin-Übersetzung verdeutscht'*, Wiss. Z. der Karl-Marx-Universität Leipzig, 13 (1964), Gesellschafts- und Sprachw. Reihe, Heft 4, p. 775.

Again according to Weller, the fragment agrees with the Chin version in section 19: *śrutārthātṛptatā sarvvakuśalamūlasamudānayan[āya]*[9]. The Chin version has: "Die Lehre zu suchen gibt es (für ihn) keinen Überdruß (und kein) Genügen, weil (er) jedwede Wurzel des Heilsamen aufsammelt." However, "die Lehre zu suchen" does not correspond to *śrutārtha* but to *saddharmaparyeṣṭim ārabhya* which belongs to the third category in this section. It is interesting to note that in this instance the text of the fragment corresponds better to the Sung version and the Tibetan version than the text of von Staël-Holstein's manuscript. The latter has *atṛptitā* as against *śrutārthātṛptatā* which is confirmed by the Tibetan version: *thos-pa daṅ don-gyis ṅoms mi-myoṅ źiṅ* and the Sung version: "Der Sinn (der Lehre) zu hören findet er kein Genügen"[10]. Another example is *niṣkuhakasyāraṇyavāsaḥ* in section 19. In this case the fragment agrees with the Tibetan version (*tshul-'chos-pa med-par dgon-pa na gnas-pa*) and von Staël-Holstein's manuscript (*niṣkuhakasyāraṇyavāsābhiratiḥ*) with the Sung version: "Er freut sich, im Walde zu weilen, (ist) völlig still und zurückgezogen"[11]. In section 14 von Staël-Holstein's manuscript has *bhūtakalyāṇamitrāṇi* as against *kalyāṇamitrāṇi* in the fragment and in the Tibetan version (*dge-ba'i bśes-gñen*). Von Staël-Holstein's manuscript adds after each category the word *saṃvartate* which is missing in the fragment and in the Tibetan version.

The oldest Chinese version does not contain any verses in sections 136–137. In spite of this, it is not certain that the Sanskrit original, on which this version is based, was written in prose. The Chinese version is very primitive and it is possible that the translator rendered the original Sanskrit verses into prose. It is noteworthy that section 136 in the Han translation begins with a solemn statement which is not found anywhere else in the text: "At that time the Buddha spoke, saying". As to the date and the author of this translation, both Pelliot and Ōno Hōdō have drawn attention to the fact that, although the oldest extant Chinese catalogue, the *Ch'u san-tsang chi-chi* (about 515 A.D.), states that the text was translated in 179 A.D. by Lou-chia-ch'an (Taishō no. 2145, p. 6b17), this is very doubtful[12] Pelliot supposes that Lou-chia-ch'an's translation of the Aṣṭasāhasrikāprajñāpāramitāsūtra was confused with the translation of the Kāśyapaparivarta. However, Pelliot points out that the translation judging by its archaic aspect could well have been made in the Han period. Ōno declared peremptorily that the language of the text proves that it was translated during the Eastern Chin. It is impossible to adhere to his point of view.

[9] *Zum Kāśyapaparivarta*, p. 10.

[10] *'Die Sung-Fassung des Kāśyapaparivarta'*, Monumenta Serica, 25 (1966), p. 240.

[11] *Ibid.*, p. 239.

[12] P. Pelliot, Compte rendu de *The Kāçyapaparivarta*, etc., T'oung Pao, 32 (1936), pp. 68–76; Ōno Hōdō, *Daijō kaikyō no kenkyū* (Tōkyō, 1954), pp. 98, 101–102. Cf. also Taishō no. 2145, pp. 19b19 and 29c17.

Already von Staël-Holstein remarked that the translation uses the same equivalent for *bhagavat* as Lou-chia-ch'an's translation of the *A-ch'u fo-kuo ching* (Taishō no. 313). The transliterations of *cakravartin*, *upāyakauśalya* and *abhijñā* are the same as those found in Lou-chia-ch'an's translation of the Aṣṭasāhasrikāprajñāpāramitāsūtra[13]. It is therefore probable that this translation of the Kāśyapaparivarta is indeed due to Lou-chia-ch'an.

According to von Staël-Holstein the manuscript edited by him was probably written in the ninth and tenth centuries. His main argument seems to be the agreement of the text with the Chinese Sung version. This version was made in the year 986[14]. Whatever the date of the manuscript may be, the text must already have been more or less the same at the time of the Tibetan translation, which dates from the beginning of the ninth century. It is possible to push the *terminus ad quem* even further back. The Kāśyapaparivarta is quoted in many texts. Von Staël-Holstein listed quotations in the Śikṣāsamuccaya, the Mahāyānasūtrālaṃkāra and the Bodhicaryāvatārapañjikā. Japanese scholars have pointed out quotations in the Prasannapadā, the Madhyāntavibhāgaṭīkā, the Laṅkāvatārasūtra and the Ratnagotravibhāga and in texts, preserved only in Chinese and/or Tibetan translation, such as the Mahāyānasaṃgraha, the Daśabhūmivibhāṣā (Taishō no. 1522), the Prajñāpāramitopadeśa (Taishō no. 1509), the Mahāyānāvatāra (Taishō no. 1634), the Fo-hsing lun (Taishō no. 1610), the Chi chu-fa-pao tsui-shang-i lun (Taishō no. 1638), the Anuttarāśrayasūtra (Taishō no. 669) and the Mahāparinirvāṇasūtra (Taishō nos. 374–377)[15]. Tsukinowa drew attention to the fact that the four verses of section 71 are quoted in the Prasannapadā pp. 156–157[16]. As Sthiramati, the commentator of the Kāśyapaparivarta, did not yet know a text which contained verses apart from those in section 136–137, he concluded that the text, as transmitted in von Staël-Holstein's manuscript, the Tibetan version and the Sung version, was established in the period

[13] Cf. F. Weller, Buddhist Yearly 1968/69, pp. 91, 85 and 75; L. R. Lancaster, *An Analysis of the Aṣṭasāhasrikāprajñāpāramitāsūtra from the Chinese Translations* (The University of Wisconsin, Ph. D. 1968), pp. 393, no. 198, p. 388 no. 144 and p. 392, no. 185. Cf. also Paul Pelliot, *Pāpiyān > Po-siun*', T'oung Pao, 30 (1933), p. 92.

[14] Cf. Mochizuki Shinkō, *Bukkyō daijiten*, vol. 8 (Tōkyō, 1958), p. 259.

[15] Shiomi Tetsudō, '*Ryūju shoin no Daijō kyōten no ni-san ni tsuite*', Shūkyō kenkyū, N.S. IX, 6 (1932), pp. 1031–1044; Tsukinowa Kenryū, '*Kohon Daihōshakkyō ni tsuite*', Bukkyōgaku no shomondai (Tōkyō, 1935), pp. 849–869 [= Butten no hihanteki kenkyū (Kyōto, 1971), pp. 393–407]; Kuno, *op. cit.*; Ōno, *op. cit.*; Haseoka Kazuya, '*Jūjūji-basharon ni okeru Kāçyapaparivarta no inyō ni tsuite*', Indogaku Bukkyōgaku kenkyū, 2 (1954), pp. 553–556; Amano Hirofusa, '*Hōchōkyō ni tsuite*', ibid., 4 (1956), pp. 464–465; Hachiriki Hiroki, '*Purasannapadā no inyō kyōten (2). Ratnakūṭasūtra no inyō ni tsuite*', ibid., 15 (1967), pp. 720–723.

[16] *Op. cit.*, p. 863.

between Sthiramati and Candrakīrti. This is certainly possible, although it must be pointed out that other quotations in the Prasannapadā do not entirely agree with the text of von Staël-Holstein's manuscript. This, however, is only to be expected in the case of a text which has been transmitted over centuries and which has been continually expanded. In any case, the quotations of the Kāśyapaparivarta are capable of throwing much light on the history of the text. For instance, it is very interesting to see that the comparison of the *bodhisattva* with the *kalaviṅka* in section 84 is absent in the Chin and Ch'in versions, but is already quoted in the Prajñāpāramitopadeśa which was translated about 404 A.D.[17]. It is interesting to note that this comparison is also absent in Sthiramati's commentary which was translated into Chinese in the period 508—535, and in a hitherto unnoticed Chinese version of the Kāśyapaparivarta, chapter 7 of the Ratnameghasūtra (Taishō no. 659, vol. XVI, pp. 276—283). This latter version was recently discovered almost simultaneously by Takasaki Jikidō[18] and by Nagao Gajin[19]. Nagao shows that this version is closely related to the Ch'in version. According to him the translator of it was not Man t'o lo hsien from Funan, but Subodhi from Funan who worked as translator during the Ch'en dynasty (557—589).

The Sanskrit fragments in London, Helsinki and Leningrad confirm the evidence which can be gained from the Chinese versions and the quotations of the Kāśyapaparivarta in other texts. The Kāśyapaparivarta, in which the verse parts are later than the prose parts, offers an interesting example of a text in which the verses, written in Buddhist Hybrid Sanskrit, are definitely later than the prose parts, the language of which is much closer to standard Sanskrit.

[17] Taishō no. 1599, p. 266c. Cf. KUNO, *op. cit.*, p. 92. The same comparison is already found in the Ratnakaraṇḍasūtra, cf. Śikṣāsamuccaya (ed. CECIL BENDALL, Bibliotheca Buddhica, vol. 1, 1897—1902), p. 6.11—15; Taishō no. 461, p. 454c5—9, no. 462, p. 468b25—29. Taishō no. 461 was translated by Chu Fa-hu in 289, cf. Taishō no. 2145, p. 7c.

[18] Cf. *Nyoraizō shisō no keijō* (Tōkyō, 1974), p. 449.

[19] '*"Kashōhon no shohon" to "Daihōshakkyō" seiritsu no mondai*', Suzuki gakujutsu kenkyū nenpō, 10 (1973) [published in 1974], pp. 13—25.

Pierre Python, *Vinaya-viniścaya-Upāli-paripṛcchā* [= *Collection Jean Przyluski*, tome V]. Paris, Adrien-Maisonneuve, 1973. XXIII, 223 pp. 6 ill.

La Vinaya-viniścaya-Upāli-paripṛcchā est un des textes les plus importants pour l'étude de la discipline des bodhisattva. On en trouve des citations dans le Śikṣāsamuccaya, la Bodhicaryāvatāra-pañjikā et la Prasannapadā. Cecil Bendall, l'éditeur du Śikṣāsamuccaya, avait retrouvé un passage, cité dans le Śikṣāsamuccaya (p. 178.9–16), dans un texte, intitulé Bodhisattvaprātimokṣa, dont il avait obtenu un manuscrit en 1899.[1] Le manuscrit fut édité en 1931 par N. Dutt (*IHQ*, 7, 1931, pp. 259–286). M. Python a reproduit les feuillets 5–10 du manuscrit qui contiennent la première partie du deuxième chapitre.

D'après la numérotation des feuillets, donnée par M. Python, le texte commence à la ligne 3 du feuillet 5b. Je pense que M. Python s'est trompé dans la numérotation des feuillets. Ceux-ci portent leur numéro d'ordre au verso, coutume commune aux manuscrits du Nord selon M. J. Filliozat.[2] Il faut donc corriger 5b en 5a, etc. Le texte commence au feuillet 5a, ligne 3 et se termine au feuillet 10a, ligne 1.[3]

L'ouvrage de M. Python contient une édition de la version tibétaine d'après les Kanjur de Narthang et de Pékin et, en bas de page, le texte sanskrit des citations et du fragment tiré du manuscrit rapporté par Bendall. M. Python a donné une nouvelle édition de ce fragment que Dutt avait édité sans consulter la version tibétaine. En outre, le livre contient une reproduction photomécanique de deux versions chinoises: Taishô no. 325 (Ch1), Taishô no. 310, 24e sūtra (Ch2), et de la version chinoise du passage sur la confession: Taishô no. 326.(Ch3). En outre, une grande partie du texte a été traduite par Guṇavarman: Taishô 1582, I (Ch4). On trouvera une reproduction du texte et une traduction dans l'appendice I (pp. 137–153). Un deuxième appendice donne le texte tibétain et la traduction française du Sugatapañcatriṃsatstotra de Mātṛceṭa, un hymne aux trente-cinq Sugata qui, selon M. Python, s'inspire de la liste des trente-cinq Buddha de l'Upālipariprcchā. Le troisième appendice donne les listes des bodhisattva, des samādhi et des buddha qui sont énumérés dans le texte (§§ 3–14, § 29, § 23). Le livre se termine par un index sanscrit-tibétain-chinois-français et un index tibétain-sanscrit.

L'introduction nous renseigne sur les sources et sur la doctrine. Une concordance des traductions chinoises facilite beaucoup leur utilisation, d'autant plus que M. Python a divisé le texte en 94 paragraphes et qu'il donne une concordance détaillée pour les paragraphes 1–14. Il est intéressant de constater que la traduction de Dharmarakṣa (Ch1) s'accorde avec la version tibétaine alors que la traduction de Bodhiruci semble avoir réarrangé le texte des paragraphes 1–14.

La traduction du texte est faite d'après la version tibétaine et le texte sanskrit. M. Python indique en bas de page les différences que présentent les versions chinoises. La traduction est accompagnée de notes copieuses qui ne renseignent pas seulement sur les problèmes d'ordre textuel mais aussi sur des points de doctrine. L'étude d'un texte tel que l'Upālipariprcchā demande de solides connaissances en sanskrit, tibétain et chinois. En outre, il faut être bien versé dans la littérature et la doctrine bouddhiques. L'auteur s'est montré pleinement à la hauteur de sa tâche difficile. Nous devons lui être reconnaissants d'avoir étudié de manière approfondie un texte dont l'importance avait été reconnue depuis longtemps.

L'interprétation du texte n'est pas toujours facile surtout dans les parties pour lesquelles il n'y a pas de texte sanskrit. C'est pourquoi il m'a paru utile de signaler quelques passages qui peuvent être traduits de façon différente ou qui présentent des difficultés que M. Python n'a pas toujours signalées. Les abréviations dont je me sers sont les mêmes que celles employées par M. Python, notamment ch1, ch2, ch3 et ch4, voir ci-dessus, tib. – traduction tibétaine, S – Śikṣāsamuccaya, skt. – texte sanskrit.

[1] Cf. Śikṣāsamuccaya p. 408. M. Python a oublié de signaler cette citation dans son introduction (p. 1) mais il s'en est servi dans l'édition du texte sanskrit (cf. p. 44, n. 2).

[2] *L'Inde classique*, tome II (Paris-Hanoi, 1953), p. 712.

[3] Il faut ajouter le numéro 10a dans la dernière ligne de la page 52 entre *upā* et *dāya*.

P. 22, § 2: *glaṅ-po-čhe'i lta-staṅs*. M. Python renvoie à la Mahāvyutpatti pour l'équivalent sanskrit *nāga-vilokitena*, mais, dans les textes, on trouve toujours *nāgāvalokitena*, cf. Edgerton, *Dict.* s.v. – *byaṅ-čhub 'di yaṅ-dag-par bzuṅ-ba daṅ / sems-čan rnams yoṅs-su smin-par bya ba'i phyir / thabs daṅ chul daṅ bsam-pa sna-chogs-kyis yoṅs-su bskyaṅ-bar* (Python: *par*) *su spro*. M. Python traduit: "Qui serait capable de se fixer sur ce (parfait et complet) Éveil, et de veiller à faire mûrir les êtres par des moyens très variés, par la prudence et par les bonnes dispositions?" Dans le paragraphe suivant M. Python traduit *yaṅ-dag-par 'jin-pa* par 'atteindre' qui est certes préférable à 'se fixer sur'. En traduisant *yoṅs-su bskyaṅ-ba* par 'veiller à' M. Python escamote les difficultés de ce passage. *Yoṅs-su skyoṅ-ba* signifie 'garder, protéger' (*paripālayati*, *paritrāti*, cf. Lokesh Chandra, *Tibetan-Sanskrit Dictionary*, Kyoto, 1971, s.v.). Ici probablement *yoṅs-su bskyaṅ-ba* se rapporte à la *bodhi*: "Qui serait capable d'obtenir l'éveil et de le maintenir pour faire mûrir les êtres?" En ce qui concerne la triade *thabs*, *chul* et *bsam-pa* le mot *sna-chogs* se rapporte à tous les trois. Dans une note (p. 84, n. 1) M. Python fait remarquer que cette triade n'est pas courante mais, malheureusement, il ne cite aucun texte où elle se rencontre. Il traduit *naya* par 'prudence de conduite' mais, dans les textes bouddhiques, *naya* signifie d'habitude 'système, méthode'. On a l'impression que le texte tibétain de ce passage a été altéré. Les traductions chinoises ne nous aident pas car elles n'ont rien qui correspondrait à *chul* et *bsam-pa*. M. Python dit que ch1 a: 'qui serait capable de protéger la bonne Loi et de faire mûrir les êtres par tous les moyens?' et que ch2 a 'par des moyens secrets (*guhya*).' Toutefois, ch2 ne dit pas 'de faire mûrir les êtres par des moyens secrets' comme le ferait penser la note de M. Python mais 'bien établi dans le secret, de faire mûrir les êtres par toutes sortes de moyens.' Je me suis arrêté sur ce passage pour montrer les difficultés qui se présentent quand les trois versions montrent de telles divergences. Dans ces cas, il serait probablement préférable de traduire les trois versions.

P. 23, § 4: *bdag ni sems-čan rnams ṅan-soṅ-du mčhis-pa* (N *mčhi ba*) *las yoṅs-su thar-par bgyid-par spro lags-so*. M. Python traduit: "Je serai capable d'arracher, pour leur délivrance, les êtres aux mauvaises destinées." Ici, aussi, le texte tibétain n'est pas facile à comprendre. Peut-être *ṅan-soṅ-du mčhi-ba* rend sanskrit *apāyagati*: "Je serai capable de délivrer les êtres des mauvaises destinées." La traduction de M. Python semble avoir été influencée par ch2: "Je serai capable de délivrer les êtres dans les mauvaises destinées pour qu'ils obtiennent la délivrance."

P. 23, § 4: *bdag ni sems-čan rnams-kyi* (Python: *kyis*; P *kyi*) *gaṅ-zag-gi bsam-pa yoṅs-su rjogs-par bgyid par spro lags*. Python: "Je serai capable de veiller à l'accomplissement par les êtres de leurs dispositions individuelles (*pudgalāśaya*)." M. Python remarque que cette phrase n'a pas de correspondant chinois mais elle se trouve bel et bien dans ch1 et ch4. Il ne donne aucun commentaire sur l'expression *pudgalāśaya* dont le sens n'est pas bien établi. Il aurait été utile de rappeler l'expression *pudgalādhyāśaya* que l'on rencontre dans le Mahāvastu dans une énumération de vingt *adhyāśaya* dans la deuxième *bhūmi* (Vol. I, pp. 85–89), cf. Edgerton, *Dict.* s.v. *pudgala*. Selon Senart, *pudgala* est ici la personnalité par excellence, celle du Buddha, et il traduit '(inclinations) tournées vers la grande personnalité'. De même Jones dans sa traduction 'intent on the Foremost Man'.[4] Edgerton préfère une autre explication: 'rather = Skt. *ātma-*, *with self-determined (-directed, -controlled?) dispositions*.' Ajoutons que l'expression *pudgalādhyāśaya* fait défaut dans le Daśabhūmikasūtra mais nous y trouvons *māhātmyāśayatā* (éd. Rahder p. 23.2). Le sens exact de *pudgalāśaya* et de *pudgalādhyāśaya* ne pourra se déterminer qu'à la lumière d'autres textes mais, en tout cas, il semble peu probable que l'on puisse rendre *pudgala* ici par 'individu.' Je pense que, dans cette expression, *pudgala* n'est pas le *pudgala* par excellence, le Buddha mais l'*āryapudgala* qui s'est engagé sur le chemin qui mène à la délivrance.

P. 23, § 5: *bdag ni miṅ 'bras-bu mčhis-par sgrog-pas sems-čan rnams yoṅs-su smin-par bgyid-par spro lags-so*. Python: "Je serai capable d'amener les êtres à maturité en prêchant des paroles efficaces (*amogha*)." Curieusement M. Python remarque dans une note que ch2 a 'en prêchant

[4] Ernst Leumann traduit 'eine Persönlichkeits-Anlage haben', cf. *Mahavastu*, ein buddhistischer Sanskrittext. Heft II übersetzt von Prof. Dr. Ernst Leumann – Shindo Shiraishi, *Proceedings of the Faculty of Liberal Arts and Education*, No. 2 (Yamanashi University Japan, 1957), p. 39.

mon nom efficace' car c'est exactement ce que l'on trouve dans la traduction tibétaine alors que ch2 a: "Je serai capable d'effectuer que les êtres, après avoir entendu mon nom, seront tous immanquablement mûris."

P. 23, § 6: *bdag ni bde-ba'i yo-byad thams-čad-kyis sems-čan rnams rab-tu 'god-par spro lags-so*. Python: "Je serai capable d'assurer aux êtres l'accès à ce qui est le fondement du bonheur (*sukhopadhāna*)." La traduction de M. Python est basée sur celle donnée par Edgerton pour Saddharmapuṇḍarīka 284.10 *evaṃ* (or *etad*) *mamo sarvasukhopadhānaṃ saddharma* . . . the Good Law which is the basis of all happiness. Toutefois, il faut lire *yaṃ dharma* . . . avec les manuscrits de Gilgit et la traduction tibétaine.[5] *Sarvasukhopadhāna* est une expression courante pour désigner 'toutes sortes de choses agréables.' *Rab-tu 'god-pa* est normalement l'équivalent de *pratiṣṭhāpayati* 'établir dans', cf. l'index du Daśabhūmikasūtra. Faut-il comprendre ici 'supporter les êtres par toutes sortes de choses agréables'? On peut se demander s'il n'y a pas une lacune dans la traduction tibétaine quand on compare Saddharmapuṇḍarīka (éd. Kern-Nanjio), p. 348.6: *sarvasattvānāṃ sarvasukhopadhānaiḥ paripūryārhattve pratiṣṭhāpya*.

P. 25, § 9: *bdag ni sems-čan mos-pa sna-chogs daṅ-ldan-pa rnams mos-pa ǰi-lta-ba bźin-du yoṅs-su smin-par bgyid-par spro lags-so*. Python: "Je serai capable de faire mûrir les êtres dans la ligne de leurs divers attachements." Dans une note M. Python donne comme équivalent sanskrit: *nānādhimuktikasattvānāṃ yathādhimuktyā*. Ce serait plutôt: *nānādhimuktikān sattvān yathādhimuktyā*. La même expression se trouve quelques lignes plus loin avec le verbe *yaṅ-dag-par ston-pa*. Ici M. Python traduit: "Je serai capable, tout en restant conforme à la vérité, d'adapter mon message aux croyances des êtres selon leur foi respective." A d'autres endroits M. Python traduit *adhimukti* (tib. *mos-pa*) par 'conviction' (p. 104, l. 12) et par 'attrait' (p. 106, l. 7). Ainsi nous trouvons cinq traductions différentes pour le même mot: attachement, croyance, foi, conviction et attrait. Il ne paraît guère justifié de traduire *yaṅ-dag-par* comme le fait M. Python ('tout en restant conforme à la vérité'), car *yaṅ-dag-par* souvent représente skt. *sam-*. *Yaṅ-dag-par ston-pa* traduit probablement *saṃprakāśayati*, cf. l'index du Suvarṇaprabhāsasūtra de Nobel.

P. 26, § 10: *bdag ni yaṅ-dag-pa'i smon-lam-gyis sems-čan rnams 'dren-par spro lags-so*. Python: "Je serai capable de diriger les êtres dans l'accomplissement de leur juste résolution." Il faut évidemment traduire 'grâce à ma juste résolution' comme dans § 5: *smon-lam rgya-čhen-pos* que M. Python traduit correctement par 'grâce à la vaste résolution.'

P. 27, § 13: *čhos-kyi phyogs*. M. Python traduit 'toutes les parties de la Loi' (*dharmadiś*). *Phyogs* représente plutôt skt. *pakṣa* mais l'expression *dharmapakṣa* m'est inconnue.

P. 32, ligne 18: *dpal-dgyes* correspond à skt. Vīranandin. Lire *dpa'-dgyes*? De même p. 33, ligne 6 *dpal-byin* correspond à Śūradatta. Lire *dpas byin*, cf. p. 157, ligne 5 d'en bas où M. Python lit *d(pal s)byin* (?).

P. 37, § 27: *iti hi śāriputra bodhisattvenemān pañcatriṃśato buddhān pramukhān kṛtvā sarvatathāgatānugatair manasikāraiḥ pāpaśuddhiḥ kāryā*. Python: "De cette façon doit s'opérer, Śāriputra, la purification des fautes pour l'Être à Éveil qui s'est mis en présence physique de ces trente-cinq Buddha bienheureux, et en rapport mental avec tous les Tathāgata." Bendall et Rouse traduisent: "Thus, Śāriputra, the Bodhisattva must purge his sins, putting first those thirty-five Buddhas, with earnest attention paid to all Tathāgatas." Bendall et Rouse suivent tib. qui rend *pramukhān kṛtvā* avec *sogs-pa*. Je traduirais: "C'est ainsi que le bodhisattva doit se purifier de ces fautes en dirigeant son attention vers tous les Tathāgata à commencer par les trente-cinq Buddha." La traduction de M. Python est peut-être influencée par ch1: "C'est ainsi que le bodhisattva en contemplant ces trente-cinq Buddha comme s'ils se trouvent devant ses yeux." Le traducteur chinois semble avoir confondu *saṃmukha* avec *pramukha*. Voir aussi p. 34, § 24: *evaṃpramukhā yāvantaḥ sarvalokadhātuṣu tathāgatārhantaḥ*.

P. 38, § 30: *byaṅ-čhub sems-dpa' ni . . . gzugs rnam-pa sna-chogs ñe-bar ston-par byed-kyaṅ /*

[5] Cf. *Saddharmapuṇḍarīka Manuscripts found in Gilgit*. Edited and annotated by Shoko Watanabe. Part Two (Tokyo, 1975), p. 256.

de-la bdag-tu dmigs-pa yaṅ med / sems-čan-du dmigs-pa yaṅ med-la / sems-čan rnams la 'gro-ba sna-chogs-kyi gzugs ñe-bar ston-par yaṅ byed-pa'i phyir-ro. Python: "Quoique les Êtres à Éveil montrent des formes aux aspects variés (*nānākāra*) de différents vivants (*nānajagad-rūpa*) à des êtres dont le moi et l'essence sont sans réalité (*ātmānupalambha, sattvānupalambha*)." Je comprends: "Quoique les bodhisattva montrent ces formes différentes (*nānāvidha*), c'est sans notion de moi ou de notion d'être qu'ils montrent aux êtres la variété du monde (*jagadvaicitryarūpam*)." Pour l'expression *jagadvaicitrya* voir Bodhicaryāvatārapañjikā (éd. L. de La Vallée Poussin), p. 559.14, 560.1.

P. 39, § 32: *byaṅ-čhub sems-dpa' rnams-kyis sems-dpa'-ba daṅ / dge-ba'i rca-ba'i stobs bskyed-pa las byuṅ-žiṅ / śes-pa las ṅes* (N *rnam*)-*par byuṅ-ba'i ñes-pa gaṅ yin-pa daṅ / ñes-pa 'gyod-pa'i gnas saṅs-rgyas mthoṅ-ba'i tiṅ-ṅe-'jin la sñoms-par 'jug-pa thob-pas / rnam-par sbyoṅ-ba gaṅ yin-pa.* Python: "Quelles que soient les fautes dues à la perte du savoir et quel que soit l'état de remords dû au péché, les Êtres à Éveil s'en purifient grâce à la possession des pouvoirs des racines de bien et d'un esprit vigoureux (*vīracitta*) et en obtenant le recueillement où ils jouissent de la vision des Buddha." La construction de cette phrase est difficile mais je ne vois pas comment M. Python arrive à la traduction 'la perte du savoir'. Je pense que *byuṅ-žiṅ* et *ṅes-par byuṅ-ba'i* se rapportent à la purification (*viśodhana*) qui découle, d'une part, de l'esprit vigoureux et de la production des pouvoirs des *kuśalamūla*, et, de l'autre, du savoir. Ici aussi la traduction tibétaine semble être défectueuse.

Pp. 44–45, § 39: les leçons de S *pūrvāhṇakālasamaye* et *madhyāhnakālasamaye* sont confirmées par tib. *dus-kyi che.*

P. 48, § 41: M. Python a mal rendu *ekānta* dans *ekāntanirvinnena* 'chez qui un seul mouvement de dégoût est noté'. Il faut traduire 'qui est complètement dégoûté.' De même plus loin *ekāntavirāga* et *ekāntasaṃvega.*

P. 51, § 43: *tatropāle yo dhandhavirāgo 'lpasāvadyaḥ saṃkleśaḥ sa* (*na dṛ*) (9b: Python 10a) *śyo bodhisattvasya / yaḥ kṣipravirāgo mahāsāvadyaḥ kleśaḥ sa bodhisattvasya svapnāntaragasyāpi naiva yuktaḥ /.* Les photographies du manuscrit ne sont pas aisées à déchiffrer mais il n'y a aucun doute que le manuscrit au début de la première ligne du feuillet 9b a *vyo* et non *śyo.* C'est pourquoi je propose de lire *sa kleśaḥ na draṣṭavyo*, cf. tib.: *de ni . . . ñoṅ-moṅs-pa ma yin-par blta'o.* Au lieu de *naiva yuktaḥ* je lis *naiveṣṭavyaḥ.* D'après l'édition de M. Python tib. a *'don-bar* (sic) *mi bya'o* mais l'édition de Lhasa a *'dod-par mi bya'o.*

P. 54, § 48: *gal-te śes-rab-kyi pha-rol-tu phyin-pa la ṅes-par 'byuṅ-ba yin-par sems-te.* Python: "S'il pense: Le salut est dans la Perfection de sagesse." *Ṅes-par 'byuṅ-ba* rend skt. *niryāta* 'adept, perfected, perfectly skilled', cf. Edgerton, *Dict.* s.v. *niryāta* (2). Je traduis: "S'il pense: Je suis versé dans la Perfection de sagesse." Le texte tibétain ne répète pas le mot *bdag* (*aham*) qui est mentionné au début de ce paragraphe.

P. 55, § 48: *gal-te myur-du bla-na med-pa yaṅ-dag-par rjogs-pa'i byaṅ-čhub-tu mṅon-par rjogs-par 'chaṅ rgya-bar bya'o.* Python: "S'il pense: Est-ce rapidement qu'on arrive à la compréhension totale du parfait et complet Éveil qui surpasse tout (*anuttarāyāṃ samyaksaṃbodhau abhisaṃbudhyate*)?" Tib. *bya* sert souvent à rendre le futur, cf. F. Weller, *Tibetisch-sanskritischer Index zum Bodhicaryāvatāra*, I–II (Berlin, 1952–1955), p. 349b: "mittels *bya* wird fut. act. übersetzt: VI 8 b *rnam-par gžom-par bya vighātayiṣyāmi*, etc." Il faut traduire: "S'il pense: J'atteindrai rapidement le suprême et parfait Éveil (*anuttarāṃ samyaksaṃbodhim abhisaṃbhotsyāmi* or *abhisaṃbhotsye*)."

P. 59, § 66: *rab-dben čhog-śes sbyaṅs la dga'-gyis śes // dka'-thub ṅan-pa* (N *pa'i*) *'jig-rten ṅas bśad kyaṅ //.* Python: "J'enseigne aux gens gâtés la voie de l'ascèse: Que la solitude soit votre satisfaction, et votre plaisir, les austérités." Je comprends: "J'enseigne l'ascèse pénible aux gens: réjouissez-vous dans la solitude, le contentement (*saṃtoṣa*) et les austérités."

P. 64, § 94: *chigs-su bcad-pa bsgrub-pa* correspond au skt. *gāthābhinirhāra*, cf. Edgerton, *Dict.* s.v. *abhinirhāra*; *gāthābhi*° *production (= recitation) of verses* SP 329.9.

Dans la traduction du Sugatapañcatriṃśatstotra il faut corriger la traduction de 9b: *'dom-gaṅ 'od-kyis sa-le yaṅ*, 'émettant la lumière de l'arc-en-ciel'. *'Dom-gaṅ 'od* traduit *vyāmaprabhā*, cf.

Edgerton, *Dict.* s.v. M. Python traduit 14c: *chaṅs-pas 'khor-lo bskor-bar bskul* par 'tu as mis en mouvement la roue divine.' Je comprends: 'Brahmā t'a incité à tourner la roue.' 27c: *gaṅ-gis khyod dran 'phoṅs sel-bas*. Python: 'Tu remédies à toute faiblesse de la mémoire.' Je traduirais: 'Celui qui pense à toi écarte la pauvreté.' 30a: *dṅos-por grags-pa'i rtog-ge*. Python: 'Les célèbres dialecticiens de l'existence.' Je comprends: 'La doctrine qui admet l'existence (*bhāva-prasiddhatarka*?).'.

Les textes, traduits par M. Python, semblent à première vue ne pas être très difficiles, mais, comme il ressort des remarques faites ci-dessus, leur interprétation est loin d'être aisée. M. Python nous a donné un très bon travail qui est une contribution de premier ordre aux études de la littérature du Mahāyāna. Il annonce une édition et traduction du Triskandhakasūtra (Kanjur de Pékin no. 950). L'excellence de son travail sur l'Upālipariprcchā est telle que nous attendons avec impatience la parution de cet ouvrage.

Australian National University J. W. DE JONG

Nils Simonsson, *Indo-tibetische Studien. Die Methoden der tibetischen Übersetzer, untersucht im Hinblick auf die Bedeutung ihrer Übersetzungen für die Sanskritphilologie*, I. Uppsala, 1957. 291 pp.

En 1933 un membre de l'expédition Sven Hedin 1927–1933 a acheté à Khotan un manuscrit composé de quatre liasses de feuillets. Le manuscrit qui est incomplet contient une traduction tibétaine du *Saddharmapuṇḍarikasūtra*. Le texte correspond aux pages suivantes de l'édition du texte sanskrit par Kern et Nanjio: 277, 4–314,6; 328,13–329,6; 354,9–394,8; 402,11–481,8. Comparée avec la traduction du même texte dans le Kandjour, cette version est nettement plus archaïque. Dans les parties versifiées elle traduit le texte sanskrit *pāda* par *pāda* sans tenir compte des exigences de la syntaxe tibétaine. La traduction des termes bouddhiques s'écarte souvent de celle fixée par la *Mahāvyutpatti*. Constatant de telles différences entre cette version et la version canonique, M. Simonsson a essayé d'en trouver l'explication par une étude des méthodes de traduction qu'ont appliquées les auteurs des deux versions. Dans ce but M. S. compare, de manière minutieuse, 84 stances du manuscrit Hedin (Tm) avec le texte correspondant de la traduction canonique (Tx) pour laquelle il s'est servi de l'édition de Narthang et d'un xylographe imprimé à Pékin. En outre, pour 32 stances du chapitre XXIV du texte il a pu consulter un fragment provenant de Touen-houang (Th). De cet examen M. S. dégage les conclusions suivantes: il faut admettre l'existence d'une version intermédiaire (X) entre Tm et Tx; cette version ne peut être identique à Th car, à plusieurs endroits, Tm et Tx s'accordent alors que Th s'écarte de ces deux versions; Tx et Th doivent donc remonter toutes les deux à la version intermédiaire; en ce qui concerne la technique de traduction X, Tx et Th forment un groupe de caractère plus moderne par rapport à Tm.

En comparant les différentes versions tibétaines des stances du *Saddharmapuṇḍarīkasūtra* M. S. fait preuve d'une excellente connaissance du tibétain. Dans des analyses pénétrantes il montre dans chaque cas comment la version archaïque, en adhérant servilement au texte sanskrit, a violé la syntaxe tibétaine. Etudiant les modifications que les reviseurs ont apportées à cette version afin de la rendre plus conforme aux règles de la syntaxe tibétaine, M. S. essaie d'expliquer les raisons qui les ont guidés dans leur travail. Dans cet examen il n'esquive aucune difficulté – quelquefois même il les multiplie à volonté – et réussit à tirer de cette confrontation des différentes versions un maximum d'enseignement.

Bien que le travail de M. S. ait pour principal but l'étude des traductions tibétaines, il a été obligé de prendre en considération également les problèmes que pose le texte sanskrit. Il le reproduit d'après l'édition Kern-Nanjio en y ajoutant les principales variantes de cette édition, des éditions de Wogihara-Tsuchida et de Nalinaksha Dutt et du manuscrit népalais rapporté du Tibet par Kawaguchi (Kaw).[1] Il est très à regretter que Baruch n'ait jamais pu publier son édition pour laquelle il avait collationné quatorze manuscrits népalais, sept feuillets trouvés à Gilgit et le fragment Stein F XII, 7 et comparé la traduction tibétaine et les traductions chinoises.[2] Probablement cette édition aurait donné, à de nombreux endroits, de meilleures lectures et ainsi épargné à M. S. plusieurs difficultés dans l'interprétation du texte sanskrit. Mais même si, à l'avenir, une nouvelle édition critique du *Saddharmapuṇḍarīkasūtra* entraînait ici et là quelques changements dans les analyses de M. S., la valeur de son travail ne s'en

[1] A la suite de M. Edgerton (*Buddhist Hybrid Grammar*, p. XXVII) M. S. remarque que Wogihara et Tsuchida ont souvent mal déchiffré le manuscrit de Kawaguchi. Dans l'ensemble, les lectures données par M. S. sont correctes mais il nous semble que, à quelques endroits, une autre lecture s'impose: Str. 4 *adhimānīn*, Kaw *adhimānī*; Str. 6 *tābhiḥ*, Kaw *tābhir*; Str. 8 *tair*, Kaw aussi *tair* non *tai*; Str. 9 *saṃstavaṃ*, Kaw *saṃstavan*; Str. 12 *parivarjayet*, Kaw *parivarttayet*; Str. 13 *yadā*, Kaw *sadā*; *deśeyā*, Kaw *deseyā*; Str. 15 *viharanti*, Kaw *vaharanti*; Str. 17 *paśyati*, Kaw *paśyarti*; Str. 24 *śaṅkha°*, Kaw *śaṃkha°*; *vividhāṃś*, Kaw *vividhaś*; Str. 26 *deśayī*, Kaw *desayī*; Str. 30 *kuto*, Kaw *bhūto*; Str. 32 *vijñinaḥ*, Kaw *vijñāno*; Str. 33 *gaṅgā°*, Kaw *gaṃgā°*; *kalpān*, Kaw *kalpāṃ*; Str. 34 *nāma*, Kaw *nāmaṃ*; Str. 42 *aśvāna*, Kaw *asvāna*; Str. 43 *rutāni*, Kaw *rutāna*; *dārakāṇām*, Kaw *dārakānāṃm*; Str. 53 Kaw *°diśāva* non *°diśava*; Str. 63 Kaw *nāśakā* non *nāsakā*; Str. 66 *śikhi*, Kaw *sikhi*; Str. 67 *sa*, Kaw *su*.

[2] Malheureusement Baruch n'a jamais réussi à obtenir une photocopie des manuscrits Petrovskij. Récemment Kiyoda Jikuun a reçu un microfilm de ces manuscrits et en a signalé quelques particularités (*Indogaku Bukkyōgaku Kenkyū*, 5, 1957, pp. 188–191). Espérons qu'enfin ils seront publiés ainsi que les nombreux feuillets trouvés à Gilgit qui sont actuellement conservés aux Archives Nationales de New Delhi. Aux renseignements bibliographiques relatifs aux éditions de fragments du *Saddharmapuṇḍarīka* (Simonsson, p. 15 note 2) ajoutons les titres de deux ouvrages japonais dont le premier contient des fac-similés de nombreux fragments et le deuxième des renseignements sur des travaux japonais: G. Honda and J. Deguchi, *Sanskrit Manuscripts of Saddharmapuṇḍarīka* (Kyoto, 1949) (cf. *Bibliographie bouddhique*, XXI-XXIII, No. 105); Yamada Ryūjō, *Bongo butten no bunkengaku josetsu* [Introduction to the Bibliography of Buddhist Sanskrit Literature] (Sendai, 1957), pp. 91–94.

trouverait nullement diminuée car, dans le cadre de ses recherches, l'incertitude à l'égard de telle ou telle lecture du texte sanskrit n'a qu'une portée secondaire. En raison de l'insuffisance des éditions dont on dispose M. S. s'est abstenu aussi, avec raison, de spéculations sur les relations des traductions tibétaines avec les différents manuscrits du texte sanskrit. Il se contente de signaler le fait intéressant qu'aucune des versions tibétaines ne s'accorde avec la recension représentée par les manuscrits Petrovskij trouvés à Kashgar.

Dans le deuxième chapitre M. S. étudie quatorze stances et deux passages en prose d'une traduction du *Suvarṇaprabhāsasūtra* dont des fragments ont été trouvés à Touen-houang. M. S. montre que, dans cette traduction, l'on retrouve les traits caractéristiques du manuscrit Hedin. Aussi, dans ce cas, la traduction canonique est le produit d'une revision complète d'une traduction de caractère archaïque. Le chapitre se termine par des remarques sur les relations entre les différentes versions tibétaines, la traduction de Yi-tsing et les recensions du texte sanskrit. Le problème est très compliqué, et M. S. se borne à émettre des hypothèses, en soulignant la nécessité de recherches plus détaillées.

Après avoir montré ainsi, à l'aide de deux exemples, comment d'anciennes traductions tibétaines ont été soumises à une revision M. S. examine ensuite les colophons des traductions canoniques du *Saddharmapuṇḍarikasūtra* et du *Suvarṇaprabhāsasūtra* dont l'interprétation se heurte à des difficultés. Au cours de cet examen M. S. traite plusieurs questions comme, par exemple, celle de la date du *dkar-chag* publié par Melle Lalou (*JA*, 1953, pp. 313-354).[3] Mais surtout il essaie de déterminer le sens exact de l'expression *skad gsar bcad kyis kyaṅ bcos nas* qui figure dans plusieurs colophons. M. S. arrive à la conclusion que cette expression se réfère à la grande revision du début du neuvième siècle. Il identifie *skad gsar bcad* avec les trois *bkas bcad* que mentionne Bu ston et traduit cette expression par "Instruktion über die neue Sprache". Cette instruction se rapporte aux trois *Vyutpatti:* la *Mahāvyutpatti*, la *Madhyavyutpatti* (c'est-à-dire le *Sgra sbyor*) et la *Kṣudravyutpatti*, texte qui n'existe plus mais est mentionné dans le colophon du *Sgra sbyor*. M. S. attire l'attention sur un passage du *dkar-chag* du Kandjour de Narthang qui fait mention des *skad gsar bcad che 'briṅ chuṅ gsum* et confirme ainsi son interprétation.[4]

Il nous semble que l'opinion de M. S. sur le caractère de la grande revision et sa codification par les trois *Vyutpatti* est pleinement justifiée. Il est peut-être intéressant de signaler ici trois colophons reproduits dans l'Index de Schmidt. Cet index, qui doit se fonder sur l'édition de Dergué, mentionne trois textes qui, d'après leur colophon, n'ont pas été revisés: p. 40, *Saddharmarājasūtra: sṅon rgya las 'gyur ba'i rñiṅ pa skad gsar*

---

[3] M. Simonsson montre que le *dkar-chag* ne peut dater de l'époque du roi Khri-sroṅ lde-btsan (mort en 797). D'autres savants partagent son opinion. M. Sh. Yoshimura, qui publiait une édition du *dkar-chag* en 1950, opte pour 824, M. Frauwallner pour 800 (*WZKSOA*, 1, 1957, p. 103) et M. Tucci pour 812 (*Minor Buddhist Texts*, II, Roma, 1958, p. 48).

[4] Dans un article récent ("Shoki Chibetto bukkyō ni okeru honyaku keisei", *Indogaku Bukkyōgaku Kenkyū*, 6, 1958, p. 506) M. Yoshimura Shūki cite un passage du *dkar-chag 'phaṅ-thaṅ-ma* reproduit par Bu ston dans son *chos-'byuṅ* (f. 186–188): *lo-pan maṅ-pos mdzad-pa'i bkas-bcad che-'briṅ-chuṅ gsum*. Cette citation fournit une autre preuve à l'appui de la thèse de M. S. Dans le même article M. Yoshimura essaie de dater le *Sgra sbyor*. Pour l'année du cheval mentionnée dans l'introduction de ce texte, il arrive à la même date (814) que M. Tucci (*Tombs of the Tibetan Kings*, Roma, 1950, p. 18). Signalons enfin que M. Sakai Shirō a également consacré un article au *Sgra sbyor* ("Honyaku-myōgidaishū no nangoshaku – Pañjikā-madhyavyutpatti ni tsuite", *Mikkyō Bunka*, 29–30, 1955, pp. 66–57) dans lequel il en décrit en détail le contenu.

gyis mi bcos snaṅ; p. 49, *Āyuḥpattiyathākāraparipṛcchāsūtra: bstan pa sṅa dar ba'i tshe 'gyur ba las skad gsar chad kyis kyaṅ ma bcos* (Schmidt lit *mcos*) *pa'o*; p. 53, *rGyal bu don grub kyi mdo: sṅon rgya las 'gyur ba'i brda rñiṅ par 'dug*. Si les indications des colophons sont correctes, ces trois textes devraient ressembler aux traductions archaïques du *Saddharmapuṇḍarīkasūtra* et du *Suvarṇaprabhāsasūtra*. Il faut d'ailleurs se méfier des indications fournies par les colophons. Une étude comparative des colophons et des *dkar-chag* des différentes éditions du Kandjour et du Tandjour est d'abord nécessaire car il y a des contradictions entre les colophons et les *dkar-chag*. Par exemple, d'après les colophons, les deux traductions tibétaines du *Laṅkāvatārasūtra* seraient traduites du chinois par Chos-grub (cf. Simonsson, p. 258). Mais une note du catalogue de l'université Ōtani nous apprend que, d'après le *dkar-chag* de Dergué (f.124a), la première version est traduite de l'indien par un traducteur inconnu. Cette version s'accordant parfaitement avec le texte sanskrit, cela paraît, en effet, beaucoup plus probable. Aussi pour mieux connaître, dans l'ensemble, l'histoire de la formation du Kandjour et du Tandjour, il faudrait étudier la partie historique des *dkar-chag* ainsi que les travaux des savants tibétains comme, par exemple, la dernière partie du *chos-'byuṅ* de Bu ston qui, malheureusement, n'a pas été traduite par Obermiller. Ce n'est qu'au bout de recherches de ce genre que l'on pourrait évaluer à leur juste valeur les colophons et comparer leur enseignement avec ce que les textes mêmes nous apprennent.

Dans deux des colophons cités ci-dessus se rencontre le mot *rgya*. En parlant des textes traduits du chinois M. S. cite le colophon suivant: *rgya las 'gyur ba skad gsar chad kyis gtan la phab pa'o* (p. 233). Il semble admettre que *rgya* doit obligatoirement se référer au chinois. Nous nous demandons si cette interprétation est toujours correcte car on rencontre aussi bien *rgya nag* que *rgya* dans les colophons du Kandjour de Dergué. Mais, même en dehors de cette question, il nous paraît que M. S. fait fausse route en supposant que ce colophon, s'il est authentique, infirme son raisonnement. Bien que la *Mahāvyutpatti* et le *Sgra sbyor* servent à traduire des termes bouddhiques du sanskrit en tibétain, il est évident que la terminologie, telle qu'elle a été fixée par ces ouvrages, a dû être appliquée également lors de la revision des textes traduits du chinois.

Le quatrième et dernier chapitre est consacré à une étude du *Sgra sbyor*. M. S. traduit l'introduction, qui contient le récit le plus ancien de la revision, et le colophon. Une partie de l'introduction avait déjà été traduite par Alfonsa Ferrari[5] mais la traduction de M. S. marque un grand progrès. Le *Sgra sbyor* peut être considéré comme un commentaire de la *Mahāvyutpatti*. A titre d'exemple M. S. traduit 17 paragraphes en y ajoutant un commentaire très instructif. L'ouvrage entier contient environ 450 paragraphes consacrées à l'explication des traductions de termes figurant dans la *Mahāvyutpatti*. M. S. se propose d'en donner ultérieurement une édition complète.

Pour terminer signalons quelques points de détail: p. 115, corriger *dban-po* en *dbaṅ-po*; p. 257, à la place de *sko-loṅ* l'édition de Narthang a *ko-loṅ* que Jäschke traduit par "disdain" et Desgodins par "mépris"; p. 272, lire *mṅon-par sdud-pa* au lieu de *sṅon-par sdud-pa*; p. 280, corriger *yons-(su) 'dus-brtol* en *yoṅs-(su) 'dus-brtol*.

Nous nous sommes arrêtés assez longuement sur le travail de M. S. et nous espérons en avoir montré les grands mérites. Ses recherches sont de la plus haute importance pour l'étude des traductions tibétaines. Même si l'on ne peut toujours accepter ses conclusions, il faut reconnaître l'excellence de son travail qui témoigne d'une grande originalité.

Leiden J. W. de Jong

[5] Arthaviniścaya, *Atti della Reale Accademia d'Italia. Memorie. Classe di scienze morali e storiche*, Serie VII, Vol. IV, Fasc. 13 (Roma, 1944), pp. 540–541.

VI
Sāstra Literature

Candrakīrti, Prasannapadā madhyamakavṛtti. Douze chapitres traduits du sanscrit et du tibétain, accompagnés d'une introduction, de notes et d'une édition critique de la version tibétaine par Jacques May (= *Collection Jean Przyluski*, II). Paris, 1959. iv + 539 pp.

Après la publication du texte sanskrit de la Prasannapadā par La Vallée Poussin (*Bibliotheca Buddhica*, IV, St.-Pétersbourg, 1903-1913) une traduction de cet ouvrage important s'imposait. C'est un travail qui n'a avancé que lentement et seulement grâce au concours de cinq traducteurs: Stcherbatsky (chapitres I et XXV, 1927), Schayer (chapitres, V, X, XII-XVI, 1930–1931), M. Ét. Lamotte (chapitre XVII, 1936), de Jong (chapitres XVIII-XXII, 1949) et maintenant M. Jacques May (chapitres II-IV, VI-IX, XXIII-XXIV, XXVI-XXVII, 1959). On peut certes regretter le fait que nous ne disposons pas d'une traduction complète faite par un seul auteur. Néanmoins, nous sommes d'opinion que cette "higgledy-piggledy way of dealing with a great classic" pour citer M. E. Conze (*The Middle Way*, XXXIV, 1960, p. 148) n'a pas eu que des désavantages. Il est extrêmement instructif de comparer les traductions de cinq auteurs qui diffèrent non seulement dans leurs méthodes de traduction mais aussi dans leur interprétation du texte même. Un ouvrage difficile comme la Prasannapadā ne peut être traduit, d'un seul coup, de manière satisfaisante. Après Stcherbatsky chaque traducteur a dû se confronter avec son ou ses prédécesseurs et a ainsi apporté sa contribution à l'étude de cet ouvrage. Comme le dit avec raison M. J. M. dans son introduction, il est à souhaiter que, maintenant, une traduction intégrale et homogène vienne remplacer ces traductions fragmentaires et souvent imparfaites (l'auteur de ce compte rendu, pour sa part, sait très bien que sa traduction des chapitres XVIII-XXII est loin d'être impeccable). Nous ajoutons que, d'après notre opinion, M. J. M. lui-même est éminemment qualifié pour exécuter ce travail de longue haleine. Sa traduction de ces douze chapitres est, à tous les points de vue, excellente. L'auteur qui a eu le grand avantage sur Stcherbatsky, Schayer et de Jong de pouvoir se servir de sa langue maternelle, a rédigé sa traduction dans une langue claire et précise. Sa double compétence de philologue et de philosophe lui a permis de donner une traduction dont chaque mot a été soigneusement pesé avant d'être adopté définitivement. Les notes qui accompagnent la traduction (au nombre de 1096!) témoignent de l'effort de l'auteur pour ne laisser aucune difficulté dans l'ombre ainsi que de sa grande connaissance de la littérature relative aux problèmes traités. L'édition du texte tibétain selon les Tanjurs de Pékin et de Narthang est établie avec le même soin que la traduction. Les divergences de la traduction tibétaine avec le texte sanskrit ont été scrupuleusement relevées. Enfin, un index sanskrit-tibétain-français des termes techniques (pp.493–531) rendra de grands services comme répertoire des termes techniques du Madhyamaka car il porte non seulement sur les chapitres traduits par l'auteur mais aussi sur les notes qui contiennent un grand nombre de références aux autres chapitres de la Prasannapadā ainsi qu'à de nombreux autres textes.

L'introduction est divisée en trois parties. La première est consacrée aux éditions et traductions des stances de Nāgārjuna et de la Prasannapadā. Ajoutons aux indications bibliographiques qu'une partie du chapitre II (éd. La Vallée Poussin, pp. 92–101.8) a été traduite avec quelques omissions par M. G. Tucci (*Il Buddhismo*, Foligno, 1926, pp. 234–246) et que les chapitres XII-XVII (le dernier jusqu'à la page 334 de l'édition du texte) ont été traduits par Wogihara Unrai (*Wogihara Unrai Bunshū*, Tōkyō, 1938, pp. 560–628). La deuxième partie traite des divisions et de la composition de la Prasannapadā alors que la troisième partie contient un aperçu doctrinal sur lequel nous aimerions nous arrêter un peu plus longuement.

L'interprétation du système Madhyamaka est un des problèmes les plus difficiles dans le domaine des études bouddhiques. Pendant longtemps on considérait généralement Nāgārjuna comme un nihiliste absolu. Stcherbatsky s'est élevé le premier contre cette opinion dans "The Conception of Buddhist Nirvāṇa" (Leningrad, 1927). Il y soulignait avec force que le Madhyamaka reconnaît un Absolu qui n'est accessible qu'à l'intuition mystique. L'interprétation de Stcherbatsky a été acceptée par plusieurs savants bien qu'il y ait renoncé lui-même par la suite (*RO*, X, 1934, pp. 1-37; *Madhyāntavibhāga*, Bibliotheca Buddhica, vol. XXX, Leningrad, 1936, pp. vi-vii). Non seulement Schayer (*Ausgewählte Kapitel aus der Prasannapadā*, Krakow, 1931: *OLZ*, 38, 1935, Sp. 401-415) et Tuxen (*Indledende Bemærkninger til buddhistisk Relativisme*, København, 1936) ont accepté et développé cette interprétation mais aussi La Vallée Poussin a fini par y souscrire dans sa dernière publication: "J'ai longtemps cru (divers articles de l'*Encyclopédie de Hastings, Nirvâṇa, Dogme et philosophie*) que le Madhyamaka était "nihiliste", niait l'Absolu, la chose en soi. Dans un mémoire "Madhyamaka" (*Mélanges chinois et bouddhiques* 2), je glisse vers une solution moins catégorique. Enfin, dans la présente note, je me dispose à admettre que le Madhyamaka reconnaît un Absolu (*HJAS*, III, 1938, p. 148)." On constate donc dans l'interprétation du Madhyamaka une tendance de plus en plus marquée à mettre en lumière son caractère mystique. Il nous semble que la pensée de M. J. M. s'est développée dans un sens contraire. Dans son premier article sur le Madhyamaka (Recherches sur un système de philosophie bouddhique, *Bulletin annuel de la fondation suisse*, III, 1954, pp. 21-33) il distingue un aspect dialectique et un aspect mystique de l'absolu mais, dans l'aperçu doctrinal, il met en garde contre une séparation trop radicale entre l'aspect mystique et l'approche intellectuelle. Selon lui, la *prajñā*, qui est une faculté de nature intellectuelle, permet de connaître la réalité absolue et lui est homogène. Elle opère aux deux niveaux de réalité, *saṃvṛti* et *paramārtha*; elle assure le passage de l'un à l'autre; au fur et à mesure qu'elle s'épure, elle se ramasse en une intuition intellectuelle qui contracte en une saisie globale, fulgurante, instantanée, intemporelle, les termes du rapport analysé ci-dessus. Assurément, elle ne connaît la réalité absolue qu'à la limite de sa portée, et par sa propre annulation, selon la loi de la dialectique Mādhyamika. Mais il n'y a pas rupture. – M. J. M. a précisé sa pensée dans deux articles (Kant et le Mādhyamika, *IIJ*, III, 1959, pp. 102–111; La philosophie bouddhique de la vacuité, *Studia philosophica*, XVIII, 1958, pp. 123-137). Dans le dernier article, il s'oppose encore davantage à l'interprétation du Madhyamaka dans un sens mystique. En se référant à la préface de nos *Cinq Chapitres de la Prasannapadā*, M. J. M. reproche aux exégètes actuels de soutenir la thèse d'un mysticisme irrationaliste: "Sans doute elle [la *prajñā*] est, à son plus haut degré, connaissance par identification; mais loin d'être irrationnelle, elle retient en elle, intrinsèquement, toutes les démarches rationnelles et discursives préalablement accomplies, à titre de moment dépassé ou supprimé certes, mais bien présentes, et présentes en tant que telles: "aufgehoben", pour reprendre le terme hégélien qui convient bien ici: à la fois exaltées à la limite de leurs possibilités, et par là même supprimées ... cette opération, que l'on peut certes appeler intuitive, contracte-t-elle en une appréhension globale, fulgurante, instantanée, intemporelle, des moments de connaissance que le processus discursif étalait dans le temps. C'est une intuition intellectuelle.'

Il nous semble que l'emploi de l'expression "mysticisme irrationaliste" – que nous n'avons rencontrée nulle part chez les exégètes actuels – provient d'une interprétation erronée des idées de Stcherbatsky, Schayer, Tuxen[1] et La Vallée Poussin sur le caractère mystique de l'absolu du Madhyamaka. Le Mādhyamika n'est pas un mystique qui s'enivre du sentiment d'unité avec l'univers. Cette forme de mystique sentimentale

[1] L'étude pénétrante de Tuxen, citée ci-dessus, est mentionnée dans la bibliographie de M. J.M. mais n'est citée nulle part au cours de son ouvrage alors qu'il note toujours soigneusement dans les notes tous les passages traduits ou discutés par d'autres savants. Tuxen n'était pas seulement un des meilleurs connaisseurs de la philosophie indienne mais s'était aussi beaucoup occupé de l'étude du bouddhisme qu'il connaissait,

lui est foncièrement étrangère. Sa mystique n'est pas irrationaliste car, pour lui, l'obtention de la délivrance implique la connaissance de l'absolu. Mais cette connaissance n'est pas une connaissance d'ordre rationnel car celle-ci fait partie du domaine de la *saṃvṛti* dans laquelle on n'échappe pas à l'opposition du sujet et de l'objet et à l'expression verbale. Le problème de la connaissance de l'absolu ne se pose pas, pour la première fois, dans le Madhyamaka. Nous le retrouvons déjà dans les Upaniṣad qui affirment en même temps la possibilité et l'impossibilité de la connaissance de l'absolu (voir Hermann Oldenberg, *Die Lehre der Upanishaden*, 2e éd., Göttingen, 1923, pp. 114-116). Oldenberg a très bien vu que la solution dernière de ce problème ne se trouve que dans une mystique du silence: "Die eigenste Sprache dieser Mystik wie aller Mystik ist Schweigen ... Nicht das Schweigen des Nichtwissens, sondern des Wissens jenseits vom Wissen, der höchsten Fülle des Schauens und inneren Erlebens. (*op. cit.*, p. 116)." Aussi pour le Mādhyamika le silence est le but ultime de son itinéraire spirituel. Une "intuition intellectuelle" ne pourrait guère satisfaire ses aspirations profondes car il n'est pas un philosophe allemand de l'école idéaliste mais un bouddhiste qui, avant tout, cherche à obtenir la délivrance de la transmigration. Par l'expérience mystique il arrive finalement à connaître l'absolu en se l'appropriant. C'est dans ce sens seulement que l'on peut parler d'une connaissance de l'absolu dans le Madhyamaka.

Quant à la conception dialectique d'une *prajñā* qui assure le passage de la *saṃvṛti* au *paramārtha*, elle ne nous paraît attestée ni dans les *kārikā* de Nāgārjuna ni dans la *vṛtti* de Candrakīrti. Pour comprendre comment M. J.M. est arrivé à cette conception il faut renvoyer à un passage de son article "Kant et le Mādhyamika" (*IIJ*, III, 1959, p. 109) où il cite la "Central Conception of Buddhism" de Stcherbatsky. Ce dernier avait relevé que le système de l'Abhidharmakośa connaît une *prajñā sāsravā* qui est une fonction de l'esprit empirique et une *prajñā anāsravā* ou *amalā*. Il paraît difficile de déduire de ce seul fait que le Madhyamaka a transformé ces deux *prajñā* dans une *prajñā* qui fonctionne de la manière hégélienne décrite par M. J.M. Tout d'abord, la conception abhidharmique de la *prajñā* n'est pas aussi facile à comprendre que pourrait le faire supposer la lecture de l'analyse sommaire de l'Abhidharmakośa par Stcherbatsky. La Vallée Poussin s'est occupé à plusieurs reprises de ce problème (voir les notes de sa traduction du Kośa, notamment VII, p.l, n. 2; *La morale bouddhique*, Paris, 1927, pp. 101-107; Musīla et Nārada, *MCB*, V, 1937, pp. 189-222). La Vyākhyā de Yaśomitra qui systématise l'enseignement du Kośa énumère quatre *prajñā*: *upapattipratilambhikā*, *śrutamayī*, *cintāmayī* et *bhāvanāmayī* (p. 9.15-18). La *bhāvanāmayī prajñā* qui conduit au *satyābhisamaya* est loin d'être une faculté intellectuelle car celle-ci ne pourrait avoir pour résultat la possession du Nirvāṇa. Même dans l'Abhidharma, où le caractère mystique du Bouddhisme est peut-être le moins évident, la délivrance reste un fait d'ordre mystique.

Le rôle de la *prajñā* dans le Bouddhisme est d'une telle importance qu'il faudrait l'étudier séparément, dans le Bouddhisme primitif, dans les écoles de l'Abhidharma, dans les Prajñāpāramitāsūtra, dans le Madhyamaka et dans le Yogācāra. A l'étude de la *prajñā* dans le Bouddhisme primitif, celui des *nikāya* et des *āgama*, M. Nishi Yoshio a consacré déjà un livre volumineux (*Genshi Bukkyō ni okeru hannya no kenkyū*, Yokohama, 1953). En ce qui concerne le Madhyamaka il faudrait certes tenir compte de différents stades dans le développement de ce système. Par exemple, chez Nāgārjuna on ne voit guère trace d'un chemin qui mène progressivement à la délivrance, et on peut se demander s'il n'était pas le premier "subitiste" dans l'histoire du Bouddhisme. Plus tard, on trouvera le système des dix *bhūmi* pleinement développé dans le

---

de première main, grâce à un séjour au Siam à la suite duquel il publia un livre excellent qui, malheureusement, semble être inconnu aux spécialistes: *Buddha. Hans Lære, dens Overlevering og dens Liv i Nutiden* (København, 1928).

Madhyamakāvatāra de Candrakīrti. Enfin, les conceptions de l'Abhidharma paraissent être incorporées au système du Madhyamaka par Prajñākaramati qui s'y réfère souvent dans sa Bodhicaryāvatārapañjikā, et surtout dans son commentaire du 9e chapitre (voir, par exemple, p. 349.9 sq. à propos de la distinction de deux *prajñā*). Dans le domaine de l'étude du Madhyamaka il y a encore beaucoup de problèmes à résoudre. Nous espérons que M. J.M. continuera à se consacrer à leur étude.

Pour terminer quelques remarques de détail à propos de la traduction:

p. 96.11 M. J.M. suit le texte tel qu'il a été établi par La Vallée Poussin: *yadāyaṃ devadattaḥ sthitaḥ sa na[nu] bhāṣate [nanu] paśyati / na[nu] tadaik-* (Mss.... *sthitaḥ sa na bhāṣate paśyati na tadaiko*). Il faudrait mieux garder les lectures des Mss. en corrigeant seulement *sa na* en *san*. Les Mss. omettent souvent le *virāma*. La traduction tibétaine rend *sthitaḥ san* par *'dug bźin-du*.

p. 144.1 Dans note 254 la suggestion de corriger la lecture des Mss. *teṣāmāśu* en *teṣāṃ hi* ne tient pas compte du fait que *teṣām* est le dernier mot de *c* (143.12); La Vallée Poussin a cité la fin de *c* et le début de *d*. D'ailleurs, on pourrait difficilement avoir *teṣām* en *c* et en *d*. M. J.M. remarque, que, dans la graphie népalaise, les groupes °*āśu* et *hi* ne se distinguent guère que par l'absence ou la présence de la crosse du *i*. Cela revient à dire qu'il n'y a presque pas de différence entre *śu* et *ha*. Or, dans les Mss. népalais que nous avons vus, cette différence est toujours très nette.

p. 154.1 M. J.M. traduit *viṣayādigrahaṇam* par "concevoir un objet, etc". Nous préférerions traduire par "saisir un objet, etc." car le sens du passage en question est que, sujet et objet étant identiques, il n'y a pas un sujet qui saisisse un objet.

p. 156.9 Il faudrait probablement interpréter *manyati* comme l'a fait le traducteur tibétain en rendant *na ca kiṃ ca manyati* par *rlom-sems ci-yaṅ med*; *manyati* signifie "s'imaginer, être fier" aussi bien en pāli qu'en sanskrit bouddhique (voir Prajñāpāramitāratnaguṇasaṃcayagāthā, *Indo-Iranian Reprints*, V, 1960, index p. 149b).

p. 166.10 *Saṃcayagāthā* ne signifie pas "Stances colligées" mais "Stances sur l'accumulation". Pour ces deux citations voir *Prajñāpāramitāratnaguṇasaṃcayagāthā*, XX. 5 et II. 3d.

p. 190.10 Les lectures adoptées par La Vallée Poussin ne donnent pas un sens satisfaisant. Au lieu d'*adhigatatvād* les Mss. ont *api gatatvāt* et la traduction tibétaine *don rtogs-zin-pa'i p'yir*. D'après la trad. tib. on doit lire *upādānaṃ* au lieu de *upādānopādānaṃ*. Il faudrait donc lire: *nanu ca śeṣān bhāvān vibhāvayed ity anenaivopādānopādātror adhigatārthatvād upādānaṃ punar ayuktaṃ* (Puisque par le *pāda*: "On reconnaîtra les autres essences" on a compris aussi l'appropriation et son agent, n'est-il pas illogique de les mentionner de nouveau?).

p. 468.6 *Yasyāpi* est certainement à rejeter mais, malgré la trad. tib., il faut garder *tasya* qui se réfère à *viparyāsacatuṣṭaya*: "même s'il est admis que les quatre méprises existent en quelque manière, il est impossible d'affirmer qu'elles ont une nature-de-méprise."

p. 489.1 M. J.M. corrige Madhyoddeśika en Madhyadeśika et remarque que le tibétain a *madhyapāṭhaka* mais *bar-ma 'don-par byed-pa* rend très bien Madhyoddeśika.

p. 491.19 Nous préférerions traduire °*aviparītasatyadvayavibhāga* par "la distinction correcte entre les deux vérités" au lieu de par "l'infaillible principe des deux vérités". Voir aussi 499.3 (*satyadvayāviparītavyavasthā*) où M. J.M. traduit *vyavasthā*, qui est synonyme de *vibhāga*, par "principe" alors que 499.8 (*satyadvayavyavasthā*) il rend *vyavasthā* par "définition" (pour *vyavasthā* = *vibhāga* voir, par exemple, Sāṃkhyapravacanabhāṣya, éd. R. Garbe, *HOS*, 2, 1895, p. 67.10).

p. 554.7 Tib. rend *viṣayānubhavo vedanaṃ vittir vedanety ucyate* par *yul-gyi myoṅ-ba rig-pas-na / ts'or-ba yin-pa ni ts'or-ba źes-bya-ste /*. Dans note 945 M. J.M. remarque que *yul-gyi myoṅ-ba rig-pas-na* = *viṣayānubhavavidyeti* mais *rig-pa* doit rendre *vitti* (voir Mahāvyutpatti, No. 7646) et le traducteur tibétain n'a pas traduit un seul composé mais deux mots: *viṣayānubhava* et *vitti*. Probablement le traducteur tibétain a inverti *vedanam* et *vitti* parce que le seul mot *ts'or-ba* devait servir à rendre *vedanam* et *vedanā*. En outre, ... *pas-na* ne rend pas toujours skt. *iti*. Dans des définitions *iti* manque d'habitude dans le texte sanskrit, voir 457.3, 4, 5: *rañjanaṃ rāgo*, tib. *dga'-bas-na 'dod-c'ags-te*, *dūṣaṇaṃ doṣaḥ*, tib. *sun-'byin-na źe-sdaṅ-ste*, *mohanaṃ mohaḥ*, tib. *gti-mug-pas-na gti-mug-ste*, et 557.1 (dans la note 951 M. J.M. rétablit à tort *iti* d'après tib. ... *bas-na*). Ces exemples montrent comment la structure différente du tibétain oblige le traducteur à s'écarter d'une traduction mot-à-mot.

p. 574.6 M. J.M. a oublié de signaler que tib. a rendu Māndhātṛ par *Maṅ-pos bkur-ba*, Mahāsaṃmata.

p. 585.11 D'après La Vallée Poussin et M. J.M. le texte sanskrit ne s'accorde pas avec la traduction tibétaine mais il faut certes admettre que *kiṃcit* ne signifie pas ici "quelque chose" mais "quelque part": "Il faudrait que quelque [être] *(kaścit)*, arrivé *(āgataḥ)* quelque part *(kiṃcid)* de quelque part *(kutaścid)*, repartît *(gacchet punaḥ)* quelque part *(kva cit)*..." Dans la note 1055 il faudra corriger partout *kva cid* en *kiṃcid* car *gatyantaram āgamanaṃ* glose *kiṃcid gamanaṃ*. Ensuite seulement le commentaire explique *gacchet punaḥ kva cit*: *tataś ca gatyantarāt punaḥ kva cid gamanaṃ syāt*. C'est certainement *metri causa* que la kārikā a *kiṃcid*.

Leiden J. W. de Jong

La Madhyamakaśāstrastuti de Candrakīrti

Par **J. W. de Jong**

(Leiden)

L'édition de la Prasannapadā par La Vallee Poussin *(Bibliotheca Buddhica,* IV, St.-Pétersbourg, 1903—1913) se termine par un colophon final (p. 594. 9—10) qui manque dans la version tibétaine. Par contre, celle-ci contient quatorze stances qui ne figurent pas dans les trois manuscrits utilisés par La Vallée Poussin: un manuscrit de Cambridge (C. Bendall, *Catalogue of the Buddhist Sanskrit Manuscripts in the University Library, Cambridge,* Cambridge, 1883, pp. 114—117, Add. 1483), un manuscrit de Paris (J. Filliozat, «Catalogue des manuscrits sanskrits et tibétains de la Société Asiatique», *JA* 1941—1942, pp. 12—13, No. 8) et un manuscrit de Calcutta (R. Mitra, *The Sanskrit Buddhist Literature of Nepal,* Calcutta, 1882, pp. 169—172, B 2). Bendall et Mitra reproduisent le colophon du 27e chapitre[1] et le colophon final alors que M. Filliozat se contente d'un renvoi à l'édition de La Vallée Poussin. Dans la version tibétaine le colophon final se trouve après les quatorze stances. Le texte en est: *bstan-bcos dbu-ma rtsa-ba'i 'grel-pa ts'ig-gsal-ba źes-bya-ba / slob-dpon zla-ba grags-pa t'eg-pa mc'og-la t'ugs-gźol-ba // mi-'p'rogs-pa'i mk'yen-rab daṅ t'ugs-rje mṅa'-ba // ri-mor bris-pa'i ba-drus-ma las 'o-ma bźos-pas bden-par źen-pa bzlog-par mdzad-pas sbyar-ba yoṅs-su rdzogs-so //.*

Les quatorze stances se trouvent dans un manuscrit découvert par M. G. Tucci. Nous lui sommes profondément reconnaissants d'avoir gracieusement mis d'excellentes photographies de ce manuscrit à notre disposition. Le manuscrit qui n'est pas daté est écrit en écriture népâlaise tardive. Selon M.J. Filliozat *(L'Inde classique,* tome II, Paris, 1953, p. 679), cette écriture s'est fixée environ au XVIIe siècle. Bien que ce soit donc un manuscrit relativement moderne, les lectures en sont souvent supérieures à celles des manuscrits de Paris, de Cambridge et de Calcutta que La Vallée Poussin caractérise comme des «copies médiocres d'un original qui ne paraît pas avoir été irréprochable». D'autre part, le manuscrit de M. G. Tucci (désigné par R) a des erreurs en commun avec l'original des trois manuscrits (désigné par O) et contient aussi des erreurs qui ne figurent pas dans les trois

[1] Dans l'édition de La Vallee Poussin le colophon du 27e chapitre se termine par le mot *samāptaṃ* (p. 594.8) qui ne figure que dans le texte reproduit par Mitra; *samāptaṃ* manque dans le colophon du manuscrit de Cambridge, dans les colophons de tous les autres chapitres et dans la version tibétaine.

manuscrits. R et O remontent donc à un archétype dont O est plus éloigné que R:

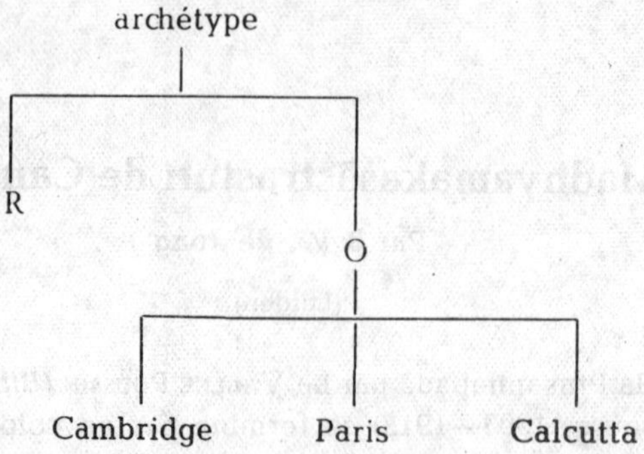

Après le colophon du 27e chapitre R contient le colophon final (éd. La Vallée Poussin, p. 594.9—10) qui manque dans la version tibétaine. Suivent les quatorze stances en mètre *śārdulavikrīḍita*. Après les stances R contient encore quelques lignes qui manquent dans la version tibétaine. Le texte en est le suivant: *ācāryacandrakīrtipādoparacitā sakalapravacanārthasaṃgranthanamadhyamakaśāstrastutiḥ parisamāptā // ye dharmā . . . // śubham astu sarvajagatāṃ //*. Ces lignes sont probablement dûes à un copiste. Nous nous sommes permis de lui emprunter l'expression Madhyamakaśāstrastuti pour désigner les stances de Candrakīrti mais ajoutons tout de suite qu'il n'y a aucune indication qui permette d'affirmer que ces stances ont été connues sous un titre quel qu'il soit. Ainsi, dans le *Lam-rim c'en-mo*[2], Tsoṅ-k'a-pa cite les stances 1 et 2 en se référant à la Prasannapadā.

Le contenu des stances n'appelle que quelques remarques. Les stances 7 et 8 déplorent la décadence de la Loi du Buddha. C'est un thème que l'on rencontre si souvent dans les textes bouddhiques qu'on peut se demander si ce n'est pas plutôt un cliché littéraire que la description d'une réalité historique. La stance 10 énumère les ouvrages de Nāgārjuna étudiés par Candrakīrti: le Sūtrasamuccaya[3], la Ratnāvalī, les Louanges, les Versets du Traité du Milieu, la Yuktiṣaṣṭikā, la Vidalā, la Śūnyatāsaptati et la Vigrahavyāvartanī. C'est une pièce à joindre au dossier concernant l'authenticité des ouvrages attribués à Nāgārjuna. Dans la stance 11 nous rencontrons le nom de Bhavya sous la forme de Bhāvin[4]. C'est la troisième forme sous laquelle son nom est attesté dans des textes sanskrits. La Prasannapadā a partout Bhāvaviveka et la Mahāvyutpatti (éd. Sakaki, no.

---

[2] Voir Nagao Gajin Masato, *Chibetto Bukkyō Kenkyū*, Tōkyō 1954, p. 206 et p. 424, note 160 où, probablement par erreur, il est fait mention de quinze stances que contiendrait la version tibétaine, éd. de sDe-dge ff. 198b—199a; nous n'avons pu consulter l'édition de sDe-dge mais le manuscrit aussi bien que les éditions de Pékin et de Co-ne ne contiennent que quatorze stances.

[3] Pour le Sūtrasamuccaya voir A. C. Banerjee, *IHQ* XVII, 1941, pp. 121—126.

[4] Pour les différentes formes du nom de Bhavya voir La Vallee Poussin, *MCB* II. 1933, pp. 60—61 et V. V. Gokhale, *Indo-Iranian Journal* II, 1958, pp. 165— 166 n. 1.

3495) Bhavya (tib. *sKal-ldan)*. La version tibétaine de la stance 11 a *Legs-ldan byed* qui correspond à Bhavyaviveka si l'on corrige *byed* en *'byed.*

En corrigeant le manuscrit nous avons respecté les irrégularités grammaticales telles que *sa* dans 3d et *amum* dans 14d. Nous n'avons pas réussi à établir un texte satisfaisant pour 9c et nous nous sommes contentés de reproduire le texte du manuscrit. Pour l'édition du texte de la version tibétaine les éditions de Pékin et de Co-ne ont été utilisées *(bsTan-'gyur, mDo-'grel,* vol. 23, éd. de Pékin ff. 224a—225b; éd. de Co-ne ff. 195b—197a). M. F. B. J. Kuiper a bien voulu lire l'édition du texte sanskrit et la traduction. Nous lui sommes très reconnaissants pour ses remarques critiques.

yad buddhair iha śāsanaṃ navavidhaṃ sūtrādi saṃkīrtitaṃ
lokānāṃ caritānurodhanipuṇaṃ[5] satyadvayāpāśrayaṃ[6] /
tasmin[7] rāganirākṛtau na hi kathā doṣakṣaye jāyate
dveṣasyāpi nirākṛtau na hi kathā rāgakṣaye jāyate // 1

mānāder api yat[8] kṣayāya vacanaṃ nānyaṃ malaṃ hanti tat
tasmād vyāpitaraṃ na tatra ca punas tās tā 'mahārthāḥ[9] kathāḥ[10] /
yā mohasya parikṣayāya tu kathā kleśān aśeṣān asau
hanyān mohasamāśritā hi sakalāḥ kleśā jinair bhāṣitāḥ // 2

mohasyāsya[11] parikṣayāya[12] ca yato dṛṣṭāḥ pratītyādayas
tattvaṃ tat pratipac ca saiva sugataiḥ saṃkīrtitā madhyamā[13] /
kāyo dharmamayo muneḥ sa ca yataḥ sā śūnyatety ucyate
buddhānāṃ hṛdayaṃ sa cāpi mahatī vidyeti saṃkīrtyate[14] // 3

yasmāt[15] sarvaguṇākaro 'yam udito buddhair atas tatkathā
śāstre madhyamake 'tha[16] vistaratarā mukhyātmanā varṇitā /
kāruṇyadrutacetasā pravacanaṃ buddhvā yathāvasthitaṃ
buddhānāṃ tanayena tena sudhiyā nāgārjunenādarāt // 4

---

[5] Version tibétaine (dorénavant désignée par T) °*vipulaṃ (rgya-c'er).*
[6] R *satyadvayapāśrayaṃ.*
[7] R *tasmiṃ.*
[8] R *yata;* T *yataḥ (gaṅ-p'yir).*
[9] Ainsi T *(don-c'en min).*
[10] R *kathā.*
[11] R *mohasthāsya;* T *mohasyāsya (gti-mug de).*
[12] R *parīkṣayāya.*
[13] R *madhyamāḥ.*
[14] R *saṃkirttyate.*
[15] R *tasmāt;* T *yasmāt (gaṅ-p'yir).*
[16] R *śa.*

gambhīraṃ jinaśāsanāṃ na hi jano yo vetti tatsaṃvide
maunīndrād vacasaḥ pṛthaṅ[17] nigadituṃ[18] vāñchanti tattvaṃ ca ye /
anye ye 'pi kubuddhayaḥ pravacanaṃ vyācakṣate cānyathā
teṣāṃ cāpi nirākṛtau kṛtam idaṃ śāstraṃ hatāntadvayaṃ[19] // 5

spaṣṭaṃ rāhulabhadrapādasahito nāgārjuno tan[20] mataṃ
devenāpy[21] anugamyamānavacanaḥ kālaṃ ciraṃ diṣṭavān /
tacchāstrapravivekaniścitadhiyas tīrthyān vijityākhilāṃs
tacchiṣyā api śāsanaṃ munivarasyādiṣṭavantaś ciraṃ // 6

āyātāya śiro 'rthine karuṇayā protkṛtya dattvā śiraḥ
saṃyāte tu sukhāvatīṃ jinasute nāgārjune tatkṛtāḥ /
granthāḥ śiṣyagaṇāś ca te 'pi bahunā kālena nāśaṃ gatās
tattvārke 'stamite 'dhunā na hi mataṃ spaṣṭaṃ tad asti kvacit // 7

utprekṣāracitārthamātranipuṇe dūraṃgate satpathād
unmatte[22] 'tha nipīya tarkamadirāṃ loke 'dhunā bhūyasā /
sarvajñoditatattvabodharahite bauddhe[23] mate vyākule[24]
dhanyo 'sau kṣaṇam apy apāsya vimatiṃ yaḥ śūnyatāṃ gāhate // 8

bhītyā[25] vastunibandhanoparacitair yaḥ śāstrapāśair[26] vṛtaś
chittvotplutya[27] ca yāti vastuparikhāṃ cheko[28] mṛgo 'sau mahān /
taṃ praty adya na[29] cintayā mama gunaś chekas[30] tu yo nādhunā[31]
taṃ[32] praty eva tadanyaśāstramathanī vṛttiḥ[33] kṛteyaṃ[34] mayā // 9

---

[17] R *pṛthag.*

[18] R *nigaditaṃ;* T *nigadituṃ vāñchanti (bstan-par 'dod-pa).*

[19] R *hatāntardvayaṃ.*

[20] R *yaṃ;* T *tanmataṃ (de-yi ts'ul-lugs).*

[21] R *devyenāpy.*

[22] R *unmate.*

[23] R *bauddha.*

[24] R *vyākulaṃ.*

[25] R *bhītyo.*

[26] R *°pāṇair.*

[27] R *citvotplutya.*

[28] R *ccheko.*

[29] *adya na* est certainement corrompu mais la version tibétaine n'aide pas à établir une lecture satisfaisante. Les autres mots de ce pāda se retrouvent dans la version tibétaine. La traduction de *cintayā* par *brtsams-pas* est assez surprenante mais, dans la version tibétaine du Bodhicaryāvatāra, il y a un autre exemple de l'emploi de *rtsom-pa* pour rendre *cintay-* (voir F. Weller, *Tibetisch-Sanskritischer Index zum Bodhicaryāvatāra,* Heft II, Berlin, 1955, p. 414 b).

[30] R *guṇa cchekas?*

[31] Avant *nādhunā* R a *dhā* qui est rayé.

[32] R *ta.*

[33] R *vṛtti.*

[34] R *kṛtyeyaṃ.*

dṛṣṭvā sūtrasamuccayaṃ parikathāṃ ratnāvalīṃ[35] saṃstutīr
abhyasyāticiraṃ ca śāstragaditās tāḥ kārikā[36] yatnataḥ /
yuktyākhyām atha ṣaṣṭikāṃ savidalāṃ tāṃ śūnyatāsaptatiṃ[37]
yā cāsāv atha vigrahasya racitā vyāvartanī tām api // 10

dṛṣṭvā tac chatakādikaṃ bahuvidhaṃ sūtraṃ gabhīraṃ tathā
vṛttiṃ[38] cāpy atha buddhapālitakṛtāṃ śūkṣmaṃ ca yad bhāvinā
pāramparyasamāgataṃ pravicayāc cāsāditaṃ[39] yan mayā
piṇḍīkṛtya tad etad unnatadhiyāṃ tuṣṭau samāveditaṃ // 11

cintāmaṇḍala eṣa tarkamathanaḥ[40] sākṣād ihāvasthitān
arthān samyag anākulān paṭudhiyāṃ[41] vāgaṃśubhir bhāsayan /
vṛttiṃ spaṣṭatarām imāṃ ca vidadhac candro 'dhunā[42] kīrtimān
lokānām udito[43] nihanti[44] vimatīḥ sāndrāndhakāraiḥ saha // 12

kṛtvā vṛttim imām anākulapadāṃ satprakriyām ādarāt
śrāddhānāṃ sudhiyāṃ ca niścayavidhau yuktyāgamāpāśrayāṃ /
yat puṇyaṃ mama śūnyateva[45] vipulaṃ tenaiva loko 'khilas[46]
tyaktvā dṛṣṭigaṇam prayātu padavīṃ sarvaprapañcacchidāṃ // 13

śāstāraṃ praṇipatya gautamam ahaṃ taddharmatāvasthitān[47]
saṃbuddhān sakalaṃ jinātmajagaṇaṃ dharmaṃ ca tair bhāṣitaṃ /
cakṣurbhūtam anantabuddhavacanasyālocane dehināṃ
yo 'muṃ madhyamakaṃ cakāra kṛpayā nāgārjunas taṃ name // 14

saṅs-rgyas rnams-kyi mdo-sde la-sogs bden-pa gñis-brten bstan-pa rnam-pa dgu //
'jig-rten rnams-kyi spyod-ṅor[48] rgya-c'er gaṅ-źig 'dir ni yaṅ-dag bsgrags gyur-pa //

---

35 R *ratnāvalīsaṃ.*
36 R *kāritā.*
37 R *śūnyatāṃ saptatiṃ.*
38 R *vṛtti.*
39 R *pravicayāv āsāditaṃ.*
40 R *tarṣa°.*
41 R *paṭudhiyā.*
42 R *candrādhunā.*
43 R *uditā.*
44 R *nidanti.*
45 R *śūnyataiva;* T *śūnyateva (stoṅ-pa ñid-ltar).*
46 R *lokhā khilaṃs.*
47 R *saddhar°;* T *taddhar° (de'i-c'os).*
48 Dans la version tibétaine du Mahāyānasūtrālaṁkāra il y a deux exemples de l'emploi de *ṅor* pour rendre *anurodha* (voir Gajin M. Nagao, *Index to the Mahāyāna-sūtrālaṁkāra,* Part One, Tōkyō, 1958, p. 18).

der ni 'dod-c'ags bsal-bar bya-p'yir gsuṅs-pas że-sdaṅ zad-par byed mi-'gyur //
że-sdaṅ bsal-bar bya-p'yir gsuṅs-pas kyaṅ ni 'dod-c'ags zad-par byed 'gyur-min // 1

gaṅ-p'yir ṅa-rgyal sogs zad-bya-p'yir gsuṅs-pa des kyaṅ dri-ma gźan mi-'joms //
de-p'yir de ni[49] c'es-k'yab ma-yin gsuṅs de-dag daṅ de-dag[50] don-c'en min //
gti-mug zad-par bya-p'yir gsuṅs-pa gaṅ-yin des ni ñon-moṅs ma-lus 'joms //
ñon-moṅs mt'a'-dag gti-mug la ni yaṅ-dag brten-par rgyal-ba rnams-kyis bśad // 2

gaṅ-p'yir rten-'byuṅ gti-mug de zad byed-par[51] mt'oṅ-ste de ni de-ñid yin //
de-ñid bde-bar gśegs-pa rnams-kyis dbu ma'i lam-du yaṅ-dag bsgrags-par gyur //
de ni t'ub-pa-i c'os-kyi raṅ-bźin skur 'dod de ni stoṅ-pa ñid-du brjod //
saṅs-rgyas rnams-kyi t'ugs yin de ni rig-pa c'en-po yin-no żes kyaṅ bsgrags // 3

gaṅ-p'yir yon-tan kun-gyi 'byuṅ-gnas 'di ni saṅs-rgyas rnams-kyis bstan gyur-pa //
de-p'yir de'i-gtam śin-tu rgyas daṅ-bcas[52]-par t'ugs-rjes brlan-pa'i t'ugs mṅa -żiṅ //
saṅs-rgyas rnams-kyi sras-po blo-bzaṅ klu-sgrub de-yis[53] gsuṅ-rab ji-lta-bar //
gnas-pa bźin-du mk'yen-nas gus-pas bstan-bcos dbu-mar gtso-bo'i ṅo-bor bstan // 4

skye-bo gaṅ-gis rgyal-ba'i bstan-pa zab-mo ma-rtogs[54]-pa des rtogs-p'yir daṅ //
gaṅ-dag t'ub-pa'i dbaṅ-po'i gsuṅ-las gźan-du de-ñid bstan-par 'dod-pa daṅ //
blo-gros ṅan-pa gźan gaṅ gsuṅ-rab rnam-pa gźan-du 'c'ad-par byed gyur-pa //
de-dag kyaṅ ni bzlog-par bya-p'yir mt'a'-gñis sel-ba'i bstan-bcos 'di mdzad-do // 5

---

[49] *de-na* (skt. *tatra*) serait plus conforme au texte sanskrit mais contraire à la construction de la phrase tibétaine.
[50] *de-dag* manque dans l'édition de Pékin (dorénavant désignée par P).
[51] P *pa na.*
[52] *daṅ-bcas* manque dans l'édition de Co-ne (dorénavant désignée par C).
[53] C *de-yi.*
[54] P *gñogs.*

klu-sgrub sgra-gcan-'dzin ni bzaṅ-po'i źal-sṅa daṅ [55]-bcas lhas kyaṅ gsuṅ
rjes-su //
'braṅs-pas de-yi ts'ul-lugs dus ni yun-riṅ źig-tu gsal-bar bstan-par
mdzad //
de-yi slob-ma bstan-bcos de-la rnam-par 'byed-pas rnam-ṅes blo-
ldan-pa //
rnams-kyis kyaṅ ni mu-stegs ma-lus p'aṃ-byas t'ub-mc'og bstan-pa
yun-riṅ bśad // 6

dbu ni don-du gñer-ba 'oṅs-la t'ugs-rjes dbu ni bcad-de stsal mdzad-nas //
bde-ba can-du rgyal-ba'i sras-po klu-sgrub gśegs-par gyur-pa des
mdzad-pa'i //
gźuṅ-rnams daṅ ni slob-ma'i [56] ts'ogs de-dag kyaṅ dus-maṅ źig-na ñams-
par gyur //
de-ñid ñi-ma nub-pas deṅ-saṅ gźuṅ-lugs gsal-po de ni gaṅ-na'aṅ
med // 7

da-ltar 'jig-rten p'al-c'er rtogs-pas sbyar-ba'i don-tsam-la ni mk'as
gyur-la //
dam-pa'i lam-las riṅ-źiṅ [57] rtog-ge'i c'aṅ 't'uṅs-pa-yis myos-pa daṅ [58] //
saṅs-rgyas gźuṅ-lugs t'ams-cad mk'yen-pas gsuṅs-pa'i de [59]-ñid bral-źiṅ
'k'rugs-pa-i ts'e //
gaṅ-źig skad-cig tsam-yaṅ yid-gñis bsal-nas stoṅ-ñid rtogs-te skal-bar
ldan // 8

dṅos-po'i 'c'iṅ-bas ñer-sbyar bstan-bcos źags-pas dkris-śiṅ 'jigs-pas bcad
byas-nas //
dṅos-po'i ra-ba mc'oṅs-te 'gro-ba'i ri-dags mk'as-gaṅ de ni c'en-po ste //
de-bltos brtsams-pas bdag-la yon-tan 'di med deṅ-saṅ mi-mk'as gaṅ
yin-pa //
de-c'ed k'o-nar de-las gźan-pa'i bstan-bcos 'joms-pa'i 'grel 'di bdag-gis
byas // 9

mdo-sde kun-las btus daṅ gtam-bya rin-c'en-p'reṅ daṅ yaṅ-dag bstod-pa
daṅ //
'bad-pas śin-tu yun-riṅ 'p'ags-pa'i bstan-bcos-las bstan ts'ig-le'ur-byas
de daṅ //
rigs-pa drug-cu źes-bya rnam-par-'t'ag bcas [60] stoṅ-ñid bdun-cu-pa de
daṅ //
gaṅ yaṅ rtsod-pa rnam-par bzlog-pa bkod-pa de-dag kyaṅ ni mt'oṅ
gyur-źiṅ // 10

---

[55] C nas.
[56] C de-yi slob-ma'i.
[57] P źig.
[58] Ligne de quinze syllabes.
[59] P don.
[60] P byas.

brgya-pa la-sogs de-dag daṅ ni de-bźin mdo-sde zab-mo rnam[61]-maṅ daṅ //
saṅs-rgyas bskyaṅs-kyis mdzad-pa'i 'grel-pa mt'oṅ-nas legs-ldan byed-kyis legs-bśad gaṅ //
gcig-nas gcig-tu brgyud-las 'oṅs daṅ bdag-gis rnam-par p'ye[62]-las rñed-pa gaṅ //
de-dag bsdoms-te blo-c'en ldan-rnams mgu-bar bya-p'yir yaṅ-dag bstan-pa yin // 11

dpyod-pa'i dkyil-'k'or daṅ-ldan rtog-ge 'joms-byed blo-gsal rnams-la ts'ig-gi ni //
'od-zer dag-gis 'di-na gnas don yaṅ-dag ma-dkrugs dṅos-su gsal byed-ciṅ //
'grel-pa c'es-gsal 'di yaṅ byed-pa'i zla-ba grags-ldan 'di deṅ śar-ba-yis //
'jig-rten rnams-kyi yid-gñis mun-pa stug-po-dag daṅ-lhan-cig sel-ba yin // 12

luṅ daṅ rigs-pa la-brten 'grel-pa sdeb-legs ma-dkrugs ts'ig daṅ-ldan-pa 'di //
blo-bzaṅ dad-ldan rnams-la ṅes-par bsgrub-par bya-p'yir gus-par byas-nas ni //
bdag-gis bsod-nams stoṅ-pa ñid-ltar yaṅs-par gyur-pa gaṅ-źig bsags-pa des //
'jig-rten ma-lus lta-ts'ogs spaṅs-nas spros-kun c'ad-pa'i go-'p'aṅ bgrod-par śog // 13

ston-pa gau-tam daṅ ni de'i c'os-la źugs rdzogs-pa'i saṅs-rgyas mt'a'-dag daṅ //
rgyal-ba'i sras-po'i ts'ogs daṅ de-dag-gis gsuṅs c'os-la p'yag 'ts'al-nas[63] //
saṅs-rgyas gsuṅ mt'a'-yas-la blta-p'yir lus-can rnams-kyi mig-gyur dbu-ma ni //
gaṅ-gis t'ugs-rje'i sgo-nas mdzad-pa'i klu-sgrub de-la bdag ni p'yag 'ts'al-lo // 14

1. Les Buddha ont prêché ici un enseignement nonuple, fait de sūtra, etc., habile à s'adapter au comportement des hommes et reposant sur les deux vérités. Dans cet (enseignement) les discours qui mettent fin à la passion ne détruisent pas la haine et les discours qui mettent fin à la haine ne détruisent pas la passion.
2. De même les discours qui détruisent l'orgueil, etc. n'effacent pas d'autres impuretés. C'est pourquoi (la portée de ces discours) est limitée et que, tous, ils sont insignifiants. Mais le discours qui détruit l'erreur abolira toutes les passions car les Jina ont déclaré: «Toutes les passions reposent sur l'erreur.»

---

[61] P *rnams*.
[62] P *p'yi*.
[63] Ligne de quinze syllabes.

3. Parce que (les doctrines de la production) en dépendance, etc. se sont montrées capables de détruire cette erreur, les Sugata ont déclaré qu'elles sont la Vérité et le Chemin du Milieu. C'est pourquoi elles sont aussi nommées Corps de la Loi du Muni, Vacuité, Cœur des Buddha et Grande Sagesse.

4. Les Buddha ont dit qu'elles sont la source de tous les mérites. C'est pourquoi, l'esprit trempé de miséricorde, ce fils des Buddha, le sage Nāgārjuna, après avoir compris le vrai sens des paroles du Buddha, a pieusement exposé (ces doctrines), en détail et selon leur sens essentiel, dans le Traité du Milieu.

5. Ce Traité qui détruit les deux extrêmes a été composé pour instruire les hommes qui ne comprennent pas l'enseignement profond du Jina et pour confondre ceux qui veulent proclamer une vérité sans lien avec la parole du Seigneur des Muni et aussi ces autres hommes de mauvaise intelligence qui, de manière erronée, expliquent la parole du Buddha.

6. Pendant longtemps Nāgārjuna et Rāhulabhadra ont clairement enseigné ces doctrines et leurs paroles ont été suivies par Deva. Par l'étude pénétrante de son Traité la certitude est née dans l'esprit de ses disciples. Eux aussi ont vaincu tous les hérétiques et ont exposé pendant longtemps l'enseignement du Muni excellent.

7. Mais Nāgārjuna, le fils des Jina, après avoir coupé sa tête et l'avoir donné, par pitié, à l'homme qui est venu la lui demander, est allé au paradis Sukhāvatī. Depuis longtemps les livres qu'il a composés et aussi la foule de ses disciples ont disparu. Maintenant que le soleil de la Vérité s'est couché, sa doctrine n'est nullement claire.

8. Aujourd'hui la plupart des hommes n'excellent qu'à saisir le sens établi par des métaphores. Ils se sont éloignés du bon chemin et se sont intoxiqués en buvant le vin du raisonnement. La doctrine du Buddha est troublée car l'intelligence de la Vérité proclamée par l'Omniscient fait défaut. Béni soit celui qui rejette le doute — ne fût-ce qu'un instant — et pénètre dans la Vacuité.

9. Celui-là est un animal adroit qui, enveloppé par les lacets des traités — lacets faits des liens de la réalité —, sous l'effet de la peur, coupe (ces liens) et saute par-dessus le fossé de la réalité. J'ai écrit ce commentaire qui détruit les autres traités pour celui qui, maintenant, n'est pas adroit . . .

10. Après avoir lu le Sūtrasamuccaya, le discours Ratnāvalī, les Louanges, et après avoir étudié pendant très longtemps et avec application les Versets proclamés par le Traité, la Yuktiṣaṣṭikā, la Vidalā, la Śūnya tāsaptati et la Vigrahavyāvartanī,

11. Et après avoir lu également ces nombreux sūtra profonds tels que le Śataka ainsi que le commentaire de Buddhapālita et l'ouvrage subtil de Bhāvin, j'ai résumé l'enseignement de la tradition et ce que j'ai appris par des études pénétrantes et j'en ai fait part pour satisfaire aux hommes de haute intelligence

12. Cette lune, pourvue de gloire, (Candrakīrti) dont le cercle est fait de réflexion, détruit le raisonnement et, pour les hommes de vive intelligence, éclaire, par les rayons de ses paroles, correctement et sans confusion, les sens (des paroles du Traité) et les rend ici manifestes.

Par la composition de ce commentaire très clair elle s'est levée et a dissipé les doutes des hommes en même temps que les obscurités épaisses.

13. En écrivant pieusement ce commentaire, dont les mots sont bien ordonnés et les explications correctes et qui s'appuie sur la logique et les textes sacrés, afin de créer la certitude chez les hommes croyants et intelligents, j'ai obtenu un mérite étendu à l'égal de la Vacuité. Que, par ce mérite, le monde entier abandonne la multitude des vues fausses et s'engage sur le chemin de ceux qui abolissent toute multiplicité.

14. Après m'être incliné devant le Maître Gautama, devant les Complètement Éveillés qui se tiennent dans sa doctrine, devant la foule entière des fils des Jina et devant la doctrine qu'ils ont proclamée, je vénère Nāgārjuna, l'œil avec lequel les hommes contemplent les paroles infinies du Buddha, celui qui, par pitié, a écrit ce Traité du Milieu.

VITARATI

vitarati se rencontre dans un passage du Dhyāyitamuṣṭisūtra qui est cité deux fois dans la Prasannapadā (éd. L. de La Vallée Poussin, *Bibl. B*, IV, St.-Pétersbourg, 1903–1913): p. 297, l. 2 *sa ebhyo dharmebhya ātīryate jehrīyate vitarati vijugupsate* (p. 516, l. 21 *sa sarvadharmebhya* . . .). La traduction tibétaine, qui manque la première fois, confirme la lecture *ebhyo dharmebhya: c'os 'di dag gis ñen par 'gyur | c'es ṅo ts'a bar 'gyur | mi dga' bar 'gyur | smod par 'gyur.* Elle rend *vitarati* par "ne pas se réjouir". L'article de M. Edgerton sur *ar*(*t*)*tiyati* dans son *Buddhist Hybrid Sanskrit Dictionary* (p. 66) permet de découvrir un autre exemple de l'emploi de *vitarati* en combinaison avec les mêmes trois verbes. Dans le Mahākarmavibhaṅga (éd. Sylvain Lévi, Paris, 1932), p. 47, l. 26, on lit: *āstīryati jihreti vigarhati vijugupsati* mais, selon l'apparat critique,

Ms. A omet *vigarhati* alors que Ms. B omet *āstīryati* mais a *vitarati* au lieu de *vigarhati*; p. 49, l. 2 *nāstīryati na jihrīyati na vigarhati na jugupsati*, Ms. A *nāstīryati naiva hriyati na vijugupsati*, Ms. B *nāstīryati na jihrīyati na vitarati na jugupsate*; p. 49, l. 9 *nāstīryati na jihrīyati na vigarhati na jugupsate*, Ms. A *nāstīryati na jihrīyati na vijugupsati*, Ms. B *nāstīryati na jihrīyati na vitarati na jugupsate*; p. 49, l. 16 *āstīryati jihrīyati vigarhati vijugupsati*, Ms. A *āstīryati jihrīyate vijugupsati*, Ms. B pas de variantes. Il s'en suit donc que, trois fois sur quatre, Ms. B a *vitarati* au lieu de *vigarhati* alors que *vitarati* ou *vigarhati* manque dans Ms. A. La version tibétaine[1] contient partout trois verbes, le premier signifiant "avoir honte" (*ṅo ts'a bar 'dzin pa*, *ṅo ts'ar 'dzem*, *'dzem pa*, *ṅo ts'a bar 'dzin*) et le troisième "blâmer" (partout *smod pa*). Il n'y a pas de doute que le premier verbe traduise *jihrīyati* et le troisième *vijugupsati* ou *jugupsate*.[2] Dans trois cas le deuxième verbe tibétain est *'gyod pa* "se repentir", une seule fois on rencontre *'dog pa* dont le sens est incertain mais qui est probablement identique à *dogs pa* "craindre". A une exception près nous trouvons donc dans la traduction tibétaine trois verbes signifiant "avoir honte", "se repentir" et "blâmer". Il paraît probable que le traducteur tibétain ait lu dans son texte: *jihrīyati vitarati vijugupsati* (ou *jugupsate*). Comme il a été indiqué ci-dessus Ms. A omet toujours *vitarati* alors que, à l'exception du premier exemple, Ms. B contient les quatre verbes tels qu'on les trouve dans la citation du Dhyāyitamuṣṭisūtra. Sans aucun doute, il faut préférer les lectures du Ms. B. La traduction tibétaine doit remonter à un manuscrit qui a omis *āstīryati*, mot assez rare et donc facilement omis. Par contre, dans la tradition que représente le Ms. A, c'est le mot *vitarati* qui a été omis probablement aussi parce que l'on ne l'a plus compris.[3]

Les exemples cités ci-dessus permettent de suggérer une autre lecture pour un feuillet des manuscrits Pelliot provenant de l'ancien temple de Douldour-âqour à Koutcha (cote 496,9) et publié par L. Finot (*JA*, 1913, II, p. 554–555). Ce feuillet appartient au Vinaya des Sarvāstivādin, et raconte l'histoire du Nāga qui prend la forme humaine pour se faire recevoir moine (Mahāvagga, I, 63; Sarvāstivādavinaya, T. XXIII,

[1] Les deux traductions chinoises du Mahākarmavibhaṅga sont trop libres pour qu'il soit utile de les citer ici.

[2] P. 47, n. 8, Sylvain Lévi défend la lecture *vigarhati* en disant: "A om. *vigarhati* (B écrit par erreur *vitarati*); mais T a *smod pa* "il blâme"." Mais, dans ce cas, *vijugupsati* n'est pas représenté dans la traduction tibétaine. Ne doutant pas de la nécessité de changer *vitarati* en *vigarhati*, Sylvain Lévi ne s'est pas aperçu de cet obstacle à sa conjecture.

[3] Ms. A est la copie d'un manuscrit daté de 1410–1411 J.-C. Du Ms. B Sylvain Lévi dit (p. 2): "Le texte est en général plus correct que celui de A et il en est indépendant."

154a27–b16). On y lit: *sa svakena nāgabhogena ṛtīyate jehṛyate vicarati vijugupsate*. La correction de *vicarati* en *vitarati* paraît évidente. Evidemment il faudrait consulter de nouveau le manuscrit mais, en tout cas, dans l'écriture des Mss. sanskrits de Koutcha *ca* et *ta* peuvent se confondre assez facilement.[4] Si cette correction est bonne, ce dernier exemple est le plus intéressant de tous. Non seulement le Ms. de Koutcha est beaucoup plus ancien[5] que les Mss. de la Prasannapadā et du Mahākarmavibhaṅga mais aussi nous disposons ici d'une version pālie de la même histoire. On n'y rencontre pas un parallèle exact mais tout au début nous lisons: *aññataro nāgo nāgayoniyā aṭṭiyati harāyati jigucchati*. Selon le *Critical Pāli Dictionary* (p. 63) *aṭṭiyati* est "generally followed by *harāyati, jigucchati*". Comme le Ms. A du Mahākarmavibhaṅga les textes pālis ont éliminé *vitarati*. Est-il trop téméraire de supposer que cela représente une innovation par rapport à l'ancienne tradition?

Puissent ces quelques exemples, qu'une lecture attentive des textes sanskrit bouddhiques permettra sans doute de multiplier, suffire pour signaler cet emploi de *vitarati* à l'attention des linguistes à qui il appartient d'en fournir une explication.

Leiden J. W. de Jong

Étienne Lamotte, *Le Traité de la Grande Vertu de Sagesse de Nāgārjuna* (*Mahāprajñāpāramitāśāstra*), avec une nouvelle Introduction. Tome III, chapitres XXXI–XLII. Publié avec le concours de la Fondation Francqui. Publications de l'Institut Orientaliste de Louvain, Vol. II, pp. lxviii+1119–1733. Louvain, Institut Orientaliste, 1970. Fr. 1100.

In 1944 Professor Lamotte published the first volume of his translation of the *Ta-chih-tu-lun* (Taishō 1509) followed in 1949 by a second volume (*cf.* W. Baruch, *AM*, III, 1952–3, pp. 109–12). The third volume contains the translation of chapters 31–42 (chüan 19–26 and the beginning of 27). In the Taishō edition the *Ta-chih-tu-lun* occupies about 700 pages of which 200 have been translated by Professor Lamotte in these three volumes. One cannot possibly expect L. to translate the entire work. However, the most important part is the first 34 chüan which, according to the colophon, contain a complete translation of the first *parivarta* of the Sanskrit text. The other *parivarta* have been abridged by the translator (*cf.* P. Demiéville, *JA*, 1950, p. 388). It is to be hoped that L. will publish a fourth volume containing a translation of the final part of Kumārajīva's translation of the first *parivarta* (the remainder of chüan 27 and chüan 28–34). On completion of these four volumes only one desideratum would remain: a detailed index which would make this translation one of the most important reference works available to students of Buddhism and India.

The third volume is preceded by a long introduction (pp. v–lx) in which L. deals with several problems relating to the author and the sources of the *Ta-chih-tu-lun*. In his review of Volume II Demiéville had suggested that the original title must have been *Mahāprajñāpāramitā-upadeśa* (*JA*, 1950, p. 375, n. 1). In his subsequent publications L. has used this title but without discussing the arguments advanced by Demiéville. On pp. vii–viii he states his reason for assuming that the title must have been *Prajñāpāramitopadeśa* or *Mahāprajñāpāramitāsūtropadeśa* (*cf.* also his note in Jaçques May's review of K. V. Ramanan's *Nāgārjuna's Philosophy*, *TP*, LIV, 1968, pp. 334–5). Demiéville quoted a biography of Nāgārjuna which is traditionally attributed to Kumārajīva: *Lung-shu p'u-sa chuan* (Taishō 2047). According to L., Kumārajīva is not the author of this biography (*cf.* pp. liv–lv). Already in his *L'Enseignement de Vimalakīrti* (henceforth: Vk.), Lamotte mentions the "rocambolesque Biographie de Nāgārjuna (*Long-chou p'ou-sa tchouan*, T 2047), attribuée abusivement à Kumārajīva" (p. 71). In his *Early Mādhyamika in India and China*,[1] Richard H. Robinson believes that "In so far as it is genuine, this *Biography* must consist of Kumārajīva's oral account as worded by his disciples" (p. 25; *cf.* also pp. 21, 22). This conclusion agrees with Demiéville's description of the biography as belonging to "les biographies chinoises de Nāgārjuna, qui doivent émaner de Kumārajīva" (*op. cit.*, p. 375, n. 1). The authorship of the biography is not without importance, because it says at the end that one hundred years have lapsed since Nāgārjuna's death. If this statement is due to Kumārajīva himself, it would indicate that Kumārajīva believed Nāgārjuna to have lived in the third century. However, even in this case it seems difficult to consider it as a decisive argument for

[1] Lamotte does not refer to Robinson's book; neither is it mentioned in the "Supplément à la bibliographie" (pp. lxi–lxviii), although this lists many publications to which no reference is made in the text.

determining the date of Nāgārjuna. Rather surprisingly, L. quotes this statement, although he attaches no value to the biography (*cf.* Vk., p. 76).[2]

The *Upadeśa* has traditionally been attributed to Nāgārjuna (*cf.* Demiéville, *op. cit.*, p. 381, n. 1). In his preface to the first volume L. wrote as follows: "Il [=Nāgārjuna] vécut probablement au IIe siècle de notre ère et joua un rôle de premier plan dans la formation du bouddhisme du Grand Véhicule. Originaire du Sud (pays d'Andhra), il étendit son influence jusqu'au Nord-Ouest de l'Inde" (p. x). In an article, published in 1954: "Sur la formation du Mahāyāna" (*Asiatica*, Leipzig, 1954, pp. 377–96), L. had changed his point of view and wrote: "La critique moderne y va de sa légende à elle et propose de chercher les origines du Mahāyāna dans l'Inde du Sud, en pays Andhra" (p. 386). Nāgārjuna exercised his activity in the north-west of India and his role in the formation of Mahāyāna Buddhism is not primordial: "Nāgārjuna est bien postérieur à l'éclosion des Mahāyānasūtra, car on trouve dans ses œuvres et notamment dans son *Upadeśa* (T 1509) et sa *Daśabhūmivibhāṣā* (T 1522) des références et des citations empruntées à une bonne cinquantaine de sûtra et śâstra mahâyânistes" (p. 391). L.'s change of opinion, which was characterized by Demiéville as a "volte-face" (*OLZ*, 1959, Sp. 248), is carried to a logical conclusion in his most recent discussion of the problem of the authorship. Whereas in 1954 he still considered Nāgārjuna to be the author of the *Upadeśa*, in the introduction to Volume III of this translation (henceforth: III, Intr.) the author is said to have lived after the first Mādhyamika: Nāgārjuna, Āryadeva and Rāhulabhadra, probably in the beginning of the fourth century (p. xl). L. even sketches in some detail the spiritual development of the author as a sarvāstivādin converted to the Madhyamaka (*cf.* also Demiéville, *JA*, 1950, p. 382). The date of the author depends on two lines of argument. The first shows that Nāgārjuna lived between A.D. 243 and 300. The second that the author of the *Upadeśa* quotes not only Nāgārjuna's works, but also those of his pupil, Āryadeva, and of his contemporary, Rāhulabhadra. The date of Nāgārjuna has been studied by L. in his Vk. (pp. 70–7). In III, Intr. L. quotes the same texts but the argumentation is not entirely the same (pp. li–lv). The texts, quoted by him, are well known (*cf.* Mochizuki, *op. cit.*, p. 4996a–b). According to Tao-an of the Later Chou Kumārajīva adopted 637 B.C. as the date of Buddha's Nirvāṇa (Vk. p. 73; III, Intr. p. li). Robinson rightly queries the authenticity of this passage which was written in A.D. 568, a century and a half after Kumārajīva (*op. cit.*, p. 23). In the second place L. quotes a preface to the *Satyasiddhiśāstra*, written by Seng-jui, a disciple of Kumārajīva. This preface is lost, but is quoted by Chi-tsang in his commentaries. According to this quotation Aśvaghoṣa was born 350 years after the Nirvāṇa of the Buddha and Nāgārjuna in the year 530. L. explains that this can be understood in two ways: (1) Aśvaghoṣa and Nāgārjuna were born, respectively, 350 and 530 years after the Nirvāṇa; (2) Aśvaghoṣa was born 350 years after the Nirvāṇa and Nāgārjuna 530 years after Aśvaghoṣa. L. tries to prove that the second alternative has to be preferred. However, Mochizuki has already pointed out two other quotations of the same preface, in which the addition of *hou* 後 or *ch'i hou* 其後 clearly indicates that 530 years after Aśvaghoṣa are meant.[3] Consequently Nāgārjuna was born 880 years after the Nirvāṇa of the Buddha (637 B.C.) = A.D. 243. L. arrives at the date of A.D. 300 for his death by referring to the *Lung-shu p'u-sa chuan*, as mentioned above, and to the *Tibetische Lebensbeschreibung Śākyamuni's* (tr. A. Schiefner, St. Petersburg, 1848, p. 310) according to which Nāgārjuna lived 60 years. Schiefner's work is an abridged translation of a text written in 1734 (*cf.* *T'oung Pao*, XLIII, 1955, pp. 317–18). Moreover, L. quotes as "un indice, permettant de contrôler l'exactitude de la date 243 p.C. proposée pour la naissance de Nāgārjuna" the fact that

[2] Thomas Watters already referred to the Biography: "If we regard his Life as having been composed by Kumārajīva, its professed translator, he lived in the latter part of the 3rd century of our era" (*On Yuan Chwang's travels in India*, Vol. II, 1905, p. 204). *Cf.* also Mochizuki Shinkō's *Bukkyōdaijiten*, Vol. V, 1933, p. 4996b; Robinson, *op. cit.*, p. 25.

[3] *Op cit.*, p. 4996b1–2. Mochizuki refers to Taishō 1855 (p. 119a21 ff.) and to Hui-ying's commentary on the Upadeśa (*Dainihon bukkyō zensho*, Vol. XCIV, p. 110b).

according to two Chinese catalogues Dharmarakṣa translated between 265 and 313 a work described as an extract of the *Daśabhūmikaśāstra* (*cf.* Vk., p. 76). It is difficult to see how this information, even assuming that it is correct and that Nāgārjuna is indeed the author of the *Daśabhūmikaśāstra*, can confirm 243 as the date of birth of Nāgārjuna. Hikata, from whom L. has taken this indication, argues that the *Daśabhūmika* must have reached Tun-huang before 265 (the date of Dharmarakṣa's departure from Tun-huang) and that the text must have come into existence by 250 at the latest. In that case Nāgārjuna would have written the text at the age of seven at the latest! In III, Intr. L. does not refer any more to the *Lung-shu p'u-sa chuan*, the *Tibetische Lebensbeschreibung Śākyamuni's* and Dharmarakṣa's translation of an extract of the *Daśabhūmika*, but he still seems to consider Tao-an's information concerning the date of Nirvāṇa, accepted by Kumārajīva, and Seng-jui's preface to the *Satyasiddhiśāstra*, as indications sufficient to determine which dates Kumārajīva and his disciples adopted for the Nirvāṇa of the Buddha and the lives of Āśvaghoṣa and Nāgārjuna. However, one must remark that Tao-an wrote in 568 and that Seng-jui's preface is only known from quotations. Even admitting that this information is reliable and that it originated in Kashmir where Kumārajīva studied in his youth, it is still difficult to attach much value to it. L. himself points out that the period of more than 500 years ("près de 500 ans" is probably a slip of the pen for "plus de 500 ans") between Aśvaghoṣa and Nāgārjuna is not acceptable. He continues: "On n'échappe pas à l'impression que toutes ces datations relèvent de vues théoriques sur les étapes successives de la Bonne Loi et que, en chronologie absolue, leur valeur est plutôt faible" (p. liii).

Much more important is the internal evidence which can be gained from the *Upadeśa* itself. On p. 1370 occurs the following passage: "Tous les dharma dépendent des causes et conditions: dépendant des causes et conditions, ils ne sont pas autonomes; puisqu'ils ne sont pas autonomes, il n'y a pas de Moi, et le caractère du Moi est inexistant, ainsi qu'il est dit dans le *P'o-wo-p'in* (Ātmapratiṣedhaprakaraṇa) 'Chapitre de la réfutation du Moi'." This passage is followed by a long note (pp. 1370–5) in which L. maintains that *P'o-wo-p'in* 破我品 refers to the tenth chapter of Āryadeva's *Catuḥśataka*: "Le Traité ne se réfère pas davantage ici à un chapitre des *Mūlamadhyamakakārikā* (ou *Madhyamakaśāstra*) de Nāgārjuna car le chapitre XVIII qui y traite de l'Ātman est intitulé 'Examen de l'Ātman' (*Ātmaparīkṣā* en sanskrit, *Bdag brtag pa* en tibétain, *Kouan-wo* en chinois). Le seul chapitre entrant ici en ligne de compte est l'*Ātmapratiṣedhaprakaraṇa* du Catuḥśataka d'Āryadeva." L. continues: "Cette citation est d'importance car elle prouve que les premiers auteurs Mādhyamika (Nāgārjuna, Āryadeva, Rāhulabhadra) étaient connus de l'auteur du *Traité* et que par conséquent ce dernier leur est postérieur." There is not the slightest doubt that the author of the *Upadeśa* quotes Nāgārjuna's *Mūlamadhyamakakārikā* and Rāhulabhadra's *Prajñāpāramitāstotra* (*cf.* pp. 1060–5).[4] However, this fact in itself does not prove that Nāgārjuna cannot have been the author of the *Upadeśa*. He may well have quoted his own work. As to Rāhulabhadra, his relation to Nāgārjuna is not well established. The Indian tradition seems to consider him as Nāgārjuna's teacher (*cf.* Lamotte, "Sur la formation du Mahāyāna", p. 391; *Upadeśa* pp. 1373–4). This is followed by the Tibetan tradition (*cf.* Bu-ston's *History of Buddhism*, tr. E. Obermiller, II, Heidelberg, 1932, p. 123; *The Blue Annals*, tr. George N. Roerich, I, Calcutta, 1949, p. 35). L. quotes two Chinese texts to prove that Rāhulabhadra was a contemporary of Nāgārjuna and a commentator of his works (*ibid.*), but not much value can be attached to texts written in China in the seventh and eighth centuries.[5] In any case, there is not enough evidence to

[4] On this stotra see Ui Hakuju, *Indo tetsugaku kenkyū*, I, Tōkyō, 1924, pp. 339–54 (first published in 1920–1 in the *Tetsugaku zasshi*); W. Baruch, *Asia Major*, III, 1952, p. 112; Edward Conze (ed.), *Buddhist Texts through the Ages* (Oxford, 1954), pp. 147–9. Rāhulabhadra is also the author of 20 ślokas in honour of the *Saddharmapuṇḍarīka*. The text of these verses has been published in the edition of the SP by Wogihara and Tsuchida (Tōkyō, 1934–5, pp. 37–9).

[5] Chi-tsang's *Chung-kuan-lun shu* (Taishō, 1824) was probably written in 602, *cf.* Satō Tatsugen, "Kichizō no senjutsusho ni tsuite," *Indogaku bukkyōgaku kenkyū*, X, 1962, p. 566.

consider Rāhulabhadra "un successeur proche ou lointain" of Nāgārjuna. For this reason, the quotation from Āryadeva is much more important because in India, China and Tibet Āryadeva is unanimously considered to be a disciple of Nāgārjuna. However, does *P'o-wo-p'in* really refer to the tenth chapter of the *Catuḥśataka*? The *Upadeśa* contains a long passage on the ātman (pp. 734–40). L. remarks in a note (p. 734, n. 1): "Il est à remarquer que le Mppś [= *Upadeśa*], attribué à tort ou à raison à Nāgārjuna, ne manifeste, dans sa réfutation de l'Ātman, aucune ressemblance spéciale avec les Madh. kārikā de Nāgārjuna, et, pour tout dire, semble les avoir négligées, alors qu'en d'autres endroits il y a eu fréquemment recours." This passage it not based on the eighteenth chapter of the *Mūlamadhyamakakārikā*, nor is it based on the tenth chapter of the *Catuḥśataka*. The passage, quoted on p. 1370, is too short to enable us to determine its source, but I have not found any evidence in the tenth chapter of the *Catuḥśataka* to prove that it has been used by the author of the *Upadeśa*. L.'s only argument seems to be the title of the tenth chapter of the *Catuḥśataka* in the Chinese translations (Taishō 1570–1). However, both translations were made by Hsüan-tsang in 650–1 (*cf.* p. 1371). The name of the Sanskrit version has not been handed down; that of the Tibetan version is **Ātmapratiṣedhabhāvanāsaṃdarśana* (*Bdag dgag-pa bsgom-pa bstan-pa*).[6] There is no evidence that the author of the *Upadeśa* was able to use a text of this chapter bearing the name **Ātmapratiṣedhaprakaraṇa*. Therefore, neither the contents of the tenth chapter of the Catuḥśataka nor its name confirm L.'s hypothesis.

On the other hand, the possibility is not to be ruled out that *P'o-wo-p'in* refers to the eighteenth chapter of Nāgārjuna's *Mūlamadhyamakakārikā*. In Sanskrit this text is transmitted together with Candrakīrti's commentary, the *Prasannapadā*. According to this commentary the title of the eighteenth chapter is *Ātmaparīkṣā* (in Tibetan: *Bdag brtag-pa*). Nāgārjuna's *Mūlamadhyamakakārikā* are transmitted separately in a Tibetan translation, but this version has been corrected with the help of the Tibetan translation of Candrakīrti's commentary (*cf.* P. Cordier, *Catalogue du fonds tibétain de la bibliothèque nationale.* III, Paris, 1915, pp. 290–1: Mdo-'grel, XVII, 1). Therefore the fact that, in this version, the name of the eighteenth chapter is **Ātmaparīkṣā* does not prove that this was the original name of this chapter. The Tibetan Tanjur contains three other commentaries on the *Mūlamadhyamakakārikā*: the *Akutobhayā* (Peking edn. No. 5229; Cordier, *op. cit.*, XVII, 6), Buddhapālita's commentary (Peking edn. No. 5242; Cordier, *op. cit.*, XVII, 20) and Bhāvaviveka's *Prajñāpradīpa* (Peking edn. No. 5253; Cordier, *op. cit.*, XVIII, 8). Both Buddhapālita's and Bhāvaviveka's commentaries are quoted by Candrakīrti. In all these three commentaries the name of the eighteenth chapter is **Ātmadharmaparīkṣā* (Tib. *Bdag daṅ chos brtag-pa*). According to the Chinese versions of the commentary ascribed to Pin-lo-chieh (Taishō 1564) and of Bhāvaviveka's commentary (Taishō 1566) the name of this chapter is **Dharmaparīkṣā* (*kuan-fa p'in* 觀法品). Therefore, only Candrakīrti's commentary and the revised Tibetan version of the *Mūlamadhyamakakārikā* give the name *Ātmaparīkṣā* to the eighteenth chapter. According to the other commentaries the title is either **Ātmadharmaparīkṣā* or **Dharmaparīkṣā*. It is impossible to decide whether the original title was *Ātmaparīkṣā*, *Ātmadharmaparīkṣā* or *Dharmaparīkṣā*. The chapter itself contains a refutation of the Ātman. It is quite possible that the author of the *Upadeśa* has referred to it by the name **Ātmapratiṣedhaprakaraṇa*, even though the real name is probably different. Another possibility is that Kumārajīva translated **Ātmaparīkṣāprakaraṇa* as *P'o-wo-p'in*. For a similar instance one may compare the Chinese translation of Pin-lo-chieh's commentary (Taishō 1564), in which the names of chapters three and five are **Ṣaḍindriyaparīkṣā* and **Ṣaḍdhātuparīkṣā* (*Kuan-liu-ch'ing p'in* 觀六情品; *Kuan liu-chung p'in* 觀六種品). However, the text itself refers to these two chapters as **Indriyapratiṣedhaprakaraṇa* (*P'o-ken p'in* 破根品, p. 24b24) and **Ṣaḍdhātupratiṣedhaprakaraṇa* (*P'o liu-chung p'in* 破六種品, p. 24a26). In this case, too, it is impossible to know

[6] The fragments of the Sanskrit text, published by Haraprasad Sastri, do not contain the name of this chapter. The name *Ātmaśuddhyupāyasaṃdarśana*, which is mentioned by L., is a rather fanciful reconstruction from the Tibetan by P. L. Vaidya. Probably Vaidya has misread *dag-pa* for *dgag-pa*.

if this is due to the author or to the translator.[7] Therefore, it is certainly possible that *P'o-wo p'in* refers to the eighteenth chapter of the *Mūlamadhyamakakārikā*.

There is not enough evidence to support L.'s supposition that the *Upadeśa* was written in the beginning of the fourth century in north-western India. According to Kumārajīva's biography, he studied in Kashmir between the age of nine and twelve (*cf.* Robert Shih, *Biographies des Moines éminents*, Louvain, 1968, pp. 62–3). Whichever dates we adopt for his life (344–413 or 350–409),[8] Kumārajīva must have lived in Kashmir in the beginning of the second half of the fourth century, about half a century after the composition of the *Upadeśa*. It seems difficult to admit with L. that Kumārajīva did obtain reliable information on the dates of Nāgārjuna but not on the authorship of the *Upadeśa*. If this work had really been written in the beginning of the fourth century in north-western India, Kumārajīva would almost certainly have met younger contemporaries of the author. For this reason, it seems preferable not to attach too much value both to the computation of the dates of Nāgārjuna and to the attribution of the authorship of the *Upadeśa* to him by Kumārajīva. From the *Upadeśa* itself it is obvious that the author was well-versed in the Abhidharma literature of the *Sarvāstivādin* and that he lived in north-western India. It does not seem necessary to assume that he was a former Sarvāstivādin converted to the Madhyamaka. As L. indicates (III, Intr. p. xlii), even for a Mādhyamika the Abhidharma remained important as belonging to the *samvṛtisatya*.

The author of the *Upadeśa* often quotes the *Mūlamadhyamakakārikā* but, to my knowledge, he does not seem to refer to any of the other works attributed to Nāgārjuna. It is difficult to give a satisfactory explanation of this fact for it seems probable that Nāgārjuna is the author of several works. Some information about the works attributed to Nāgārjuna can be obtained from Candrakīrti's *Madhyamakaśāstrastuti* to which L. refers twice (III, Intr. pp. xliii–xliv; pp. 1373–4). Candrakīrti lived several centuries after Nāgārjuna, but if we compare the list of eight works mentioned by him to the long lists of works enumerated as Nāgārjuna's works by Tibetan and Chinese catalogues, it makes a much more reliable impression. It is not an exhaustive list of the works attributed to Nāgārjuna by Candrakīrti. Recently, Uryūzu Ryūshin has shown that, in his commentary on the *Catuḥśataka*, Candrakīrti refers twice to the *Bodhisaṃbhāra* (Taishō 1660), a work also mentioned by Bu-ston (*op. cit.*, II, p. 126 where *Bodhigaṇa* must be corrected to *Bodhisaṃbhāra*).[9] Bu-ston attributes six works to Nāgārjuna (*op. cit.*, I, p. 51) as mentioned by L., but attention must be drawn to the fact that Bu-ston considers these six to be his logical works. Among other works of Nāgārjuna he enumerates the *Ratnāvalī*, stotras, works dedicated to the practical side of the doctrine: the *Sūtrasamuccaya*, the *Svapnacintāmaṇiparikathā* and works on the conduct of householders and of monks: *Suhṛllekha* and *Bodhisaṃbhāra* (*op. cit.*, II, pp. 125–6). The authorship of the *Akutobhayā* is disputed among the Tibetans. Obermiller refers to Mkhas-grub's discussion of the fact that the *Akutobhayā* quotes from the *Catuḥśataka* with the words: "It has thus been said by the venerable Āryadeva" (*Acta Orientalia*, XI, 1933, p. 4, n. 9). Walleser has already observed that the same quotation occurs at the same place in Pin-lo-chieh's commentary (tr. Walleser, Heidelberg, 1912, p. 189). L. considers Pin-lo-chieh's work to belong to the authentic works of Āryadeva (*cf.* p. 1373), but it seems more likely that both the *Akutobhayā* and the commentary attributed to Pin-lo-chieh have been written by authors who knew Āryadeva's works.[10]

---

[7] According to Seng-jui, Kumārajīva has taken great liberties with the text (*cf.* Robinson, *op. cit.*, p. 29).

[8] The dates 350–409 have recently been proposed by Tsukamoto Zenryū, *cf.* Robinson, *op. cit.*, pp. 244–7. Robinson discusses in detail Tsukamoto's arguments.

[9] Uryūzu Ryūshin, "*Bodaishiryōron* no Ryūju shinsen ni tsuite", *Indogaku bukkyōgaku kenkyū*, XVII, 1969, pp. 513–19.

[10] On Pin-lo-chieh and his commentary (Taishō 1564) see Mochizuki, *op. cit.*, III, pp. 2793b–4a; Robinson, *op. cit.*, pp. 28–30. On the relation between chapters XXIII–XXVII of the *Akutobhayā* and the corresponding chapters of Buddhapālita's commentary,

—Continued on following page

The authenticity of Āryadeva's *Śatakaśāstra* (Taishō 1569) is also open to grave doubts. Ui listed 17 quotations from Āryadeva in Chinese Buddhist texts. He was able to identify 9 with verses of the *Catuḥśataka*, but did not discover a single quotation from the *Śatakaśāstra* (*op. cit.*, pp. 277–81). The fact that Candrakīrti often quotes the *Catuḥśataka* by the name *Śataka* seems also to indicate that Āryadeva did not write both a *Catuḥśataka* and a *Śataka*.[11]

The uncertainty regarding the authenticity of the works attributed to Nāgārjuna makes it difficult to form a reliable picture of his philosophical and religious ideas. In his review of Frederick J. Streng's *Emptiness, A Study in Religious Meaning* (Nashville, New York, 1967) Jacques May rightly remarks that Nāgārjuna has been studied until now chiefly as a philosopher or as a logician (*Asiatische Studien/Études Asiatiques*, XXIV, 1970, p. 69). The interpretation of the *śūnyatā* concept has given rise to many discussions among scholars. Perhaps it is necessary to study not only the *Mūlamadhyamakakārikā*, but also the other works, attributed by Candrakīrti to Nāgārjuna, in order to determine the place of this concept in Nāgārjuna's thought. In any case, one is rather surprised to see L. describe the *śūnyatā* as "rien que ce soit (*akiṃcid*), 'une simple inexistence' (*abhāvamātra*)" (III, Intr. p. xxxi). L. does not give any references to texts and, as far as I have been able to ascertain, the *Mūlamadhyamakakārikā* do not use these terms to characterize *śūnyatā*.[12] On page 1229 L. quotes a verse from Śāntideva's *Bodhicaryāvatāra* in which the words *kiṃcin nāstīti* are to be found; however, they do not describe the *śūnyatā*. As the commentary explains, the practice of meditating on the idea that "nothing exists" brings about the cessation of all ideas of voidness and existence (*cf. Bodhicaryāvatārapañjikā*, ed. L. de La Vallée Poussin, Calcutta, 1901–14, p. 414). As to the expression *abhāvamātra*, this has been discussed by L. in his introduction to his translation of the *Vimalakīrtinirdeśasūtra* (p. 57; *cf.* J. May, *T'oung Pao*, LI, 1964, p. 95), but the *cittam acittam* of the *Prajñāpāramitāsūtra* is not identical with the *śūnyatā* of the Madhyamaka.

It is impossible to discuss fully the many topics treated by L. in his introduction. Two points of minor importance have to be mentioned. On p. xiii L. states that the name Mahāyāna never occurs in inscriptions, but one finds the expression *mahāyānika-Śākyabhikṣu-ācāryya* in an inscription from East Bengal dated A.D. 507–8 and inscriptions of the Pāla period mention *mahāyāna-anuyāyin* "followers of Mahāyāna" (*cf.* Shizutani Masao, *Gupta jidai bukkyō himei mokuroku*, Kyōto, 1968, pp. 12–13, where further bibliographical references are given). On pp. xxxviii–xxxix L. translates a

---

Continued from previous page—
see Hirano Takashi, "Muichū to Butsugo-chū to no idō ni tsuite", *Indogaku bukkyōgaku kenkyū*, III, 1954, pp. 236–8. The biography of Nāgārjuna, attributed to Kumārajīva, attributes to him an *Akutobhayaśāstra* in 100,000 verses (*cf.* M. Walleser, "The Life of Nāgārjuna from Tibetan and Chinese Sources", *Hirth Anniversary Volume*, p. 447). L. does not believe that this work is identical with the *Akutobhayā* (III, Intr. p. lv), but the similarity in name and the fact that this work is said to contain the *Chung-lun* 中論 rather suggest a connexion between the two works. Walleser mentioned the possibility that Pin-lo-chieh's commentary was based upon the *Akutobhayā*, but ruled it out because, in that case, Kumārajīva would not have mentioned the *Akutobhayaśāstra* in the way he did in his biography of Nāgārjuna. However, if this biography is not written by Kumārajīva, but reproduces information obtained from Kumārajīva, the mention of an *Akutobhayaśāstra* may well indicate a connexion between Pin-lo-chieh's commentary and the *Akutobhayā* (*cf.* Walleser, *Die Mittlere Lehre des Nāgārjuna*, Heidelberg, 1912, pp. ix–x).

[11] Richard R. Gard's discussion of the authenticity of the *Śatakaśāstra* is conducted along different lines: "On the authenticity of the *Pai-lun* and *Shih-erh-mên-lun*", *Indogaku bukkyōgaku kenkyū*, II, 1954, pp. 751–42.

[12] Candrakīrti rejects nihilistic interpretations of *śūnya*, *cf. Prasannapadā*, p. 495. 12–13: yadi tāvat sarvam idaṃ śūnyaṃ sarvaṃ nāstīti parikalpayet tadāsya mithyādṛṣṭir āpadyate; tr. J. May, p. 231: s'il suppose que "le donné empirique tout entier est vide" veut dire "tout est non-être", il tombe dans la vue fausse par excellence.

passage from the *Hsi-yü-chih* as quoted in the *Fa-yüan-chu-lin* (Taishō 2122). According to L. this passage is taken from Tao-an's *Hsi-yü-chih* and contains the oldest mention of Nāgārjuna. The same passage is quoted in Mochizuki (*op. cit.*, p. 4996a), but he does not attribute this *Hsi-yü-chih* to Tao-an, because it is well known that the *Hsi-yü-chih*, quoted in the *Fa-yüan-chu-lin*, has nothing to do with Tao-an's *Hsi-yü-chih*. Sylvain Lévi, who translated several passages of the *Hsi-yü-chih* from the *Fa-yüan-chu-lin*, has given the following information on this work: "Les mémoires de Wang Hiuen-ts'e et de Hiouen-tsang servirent de base à une compilation officielle, le *Si-iu-tchi* (appelé aussi *Si-kouo-tchi*) en cent chapitres, soixante de textes, quarante de cartes et dessins, qui fut exécutée en 666" (*JA*, 1900, I, p. 298).

In this third volume of his translation of the *Upadeśa* L. shows his great knowledge of the Abhidharma literature. As shown in the table on pp. lxvi–lxvii, chapters XXXI–XLII deal with the *dharmas* of the Way of Nirvāṇa and with the attributes of the Buddha. The systematic nature of these chapters have made it possible for L. to add preliminary notes, in which useful information is given on the *dharmas*, their treatment in canonical literature, Abhidharma texts and Mahāyāna texts. One must admire L.'s extensive knowledge of the Buddhist literature in Pāli, Sanskrit, Tibetan and Chinese. L. gives numerous references to the original sources but mentions only rarely secondary sources in Western languages. It is only by consulting these works that one realizes to what extent L.'s knowledge surpasses that of his predecessors. However, one cannot but regret the fact that L. does not seem to have made great use of the works of Japanese scholars apart from reference works. To mention only one example: chapter XLI of the *Upadeśa* treats in great detail of the eighteen *āveṇikadharma* of the Buddhas. L. mentions that the wording of these *dharmas* is not always the same and that their order varies according to the texts. He refers to many texts but does not indicate in which order they are listed in them (*cf.* pp. 1626–7). This problem has been examined very carefully by Mizuno Kōgen in his study on the classification of the eighteen *āveṇikadharma* (*cf.* Miyamoto Shōson, ed., *Daijō bukkyō no seiritsushiteki kenkyū*, Tōkyō, 1954, pp. 292–302).[13] Mizuno points out, for instance, that the same list of *dharmas* is to be found in two biographies of the Buddha (Taishō 184, p. 472a1–10; Taishō 185, p. 478b16–25) and in Dharmarakṣa's version of the *Lalitavistara* (*cf.* Lamotte, p. 1627). He demonstrates that this list was copied from Taishō 184 by the translator of Taishō 185 which, in its turn, is the source for the list in Dharmarakṣa's translation. In such and similar instances references to Japanese publications would have been very welcome. There is much to be learned from the excellent work done by Japanese scholars, just as Japanese scholars can derive much profit from studying the work of Western scholars. Probably, Japanese scholars could considerably facilitate the access to their publications, which are widely scattered in innumerable periodicals, by publishing regularly annotated bibliographies in a Western language.

L.'s translation of this volume is superior even to that of the two preceding ones. Only rarely would one like to suggest a different rendering, as, for instance, in the following passages:

P. 1140: Les êtres sont dignes de pitié; je dois les sauver et les attacher au séjour inconditionné (*asaṃskṛtapada*) 衆生可愍. 我當拔出著無爲處 (p. 197c14–15). The beings are to be pitied. I must extirpate my attachment to the unconditioned place. Similar instances of the use of *chu* 著 can be found in Gadjin M. Nagao's *Index to the Mahāyāna-sūtrālaṃkāra* (Tōkyō, 1961), Vol. II, p. 232b: 著財 bhoga-sakti; 著諸有 bhavâbhirāma.

P. 1144: les choses qu'ils aiment ou dont ils se détachent sont multiples 所樂所解法亦種種 (198a14). The things which they like and which they understand are manifold.

P. 1211: caravanier (*sārthavāha*) 御者 (206a16). Charioteer (*sārathi*).

[13] One must add to Mizuno's references to Pāli texts the recently published *Vimuttimagga* (Colombo, 1963, p. 17), a text closely related to Upatiṣya's *Chieh t'o tao lun* (Taishō 1648). Some information on this text, mainly on the basis of the Sinhalese introduction, can be found in Mori Sodō, "Shin-shiryō Vimuttimagga", *Indogaku bukkyōgaku kenkyū*, XVII, 1968, pp. 132–3.

P. 1263: Le bonheur (*sukha*) aimé par tous les êtres est important (*guru*) 樂是一切衆生所愛重 (211a13). Happiness is liked and esteemed by all beings.

P. 1377: Supposons un homme chaussant des sandales: si celles-ci étaient neuves dès le premier jour, elles ne vieilliraient jamais; après coup, elles seraient toujours neuves et n'auraient pas de vieillissement. 如人著履. 若初日新而無有故. 後應常新不應有故 (222c10–12). Suppose that a man puts on sandals. If, on the first day, they were new and without aging, then later they would be always new and would not become old.—This is explained in the preceding passage: "tout dharma dont on constate après coup le caractère de destruction doit évidemment posséder dès sa naissance ce caractère de destruction".

P. 1511: qui n'a pas encore détruit les impuretés 未斷結使 (235b8). Who has not yet cut off his bonds (*saṃyojana*).

P. 1601: le Buddha qui a atteint les félicités du Sommet de l'existence (*bhavāgra*) y a renoncé 佛乃至有頂樂已離 (245a16). The Buddha has given up even the joys of the Summit of existence.—The expression *nai chih* 乃至 has presented difficulties to the translator, *cf.* p. 1691: le présent qui ne dure qu'un instant 現在乃至一念中無住時 (254c12). The present does not possess duration even during one moment (Vasumitra admits that *saṃskāras* possess duration during one instant but not the Sautrāntikas, *cf.* L. de La Vallée Poussin, *Mélanges chinois et bouddhiques*, V, 1937, p. 155); p. 1694: Ainsi des saints comme Avalokiteśvara 乃至觀世音 (255a29). Even saints such as Avalokiteśvara.

P. 1692: Dès qu'il se trouverait dans des dispositions mauvaises (*duṣṭacitta*) et transgresserait ses engagements (*śīla*) antérieurs, ce religieux ne serait plus un bhikṣu. 若現在惡心中住. 過去復無戒. 是爲非比丘 (255a6–7). If at the present moment [the monk] were in an evil disposition, in the past, too, he would be without morality. He could not be a monk [at all].—The Sarvāstivādin argues that, if past and future were non-existent, all three times would be identical. Therefore, if somebody is sinful at the present moment, he is also sinful in the past. Consequently, it is impossible to be a monk.

P. 1709: qu'est-ce que la petite bienveillance et la petite compassion? Après ces petites, pourquoi parler des grandes? 何等是小慈小悲. 因此小而名爲大. (256b18). What are the small benevolence and the small compassion by reason of the smallness of which [the great benevolence and the great compassion] are called great?

The *Upadeśa* contains the following quotation from the *Kāśyapaparipṛcchā*: "L'Ātman est un extrême, l'Anātman est un autre extrême: éviter ces deux extrêmes est nommé le Chemin du milieu" (p. 1684). In a note L. refers to *Kāśyapaparivarta* §56 but he has overlooked §57: ātmeti kāśyapa ayam eko ntaḥ nairātmyam ity ayaṃ dvitīyo ntaḥ yad ātmanerātmyayor madhyaṃ tad . . . iyam ucyate kāśyapa madhyamā pratipad dharmāṇāṃ bhūtapratyavekṣā. L. believes that the *Upadeśa* quotes the *Sūtra of Kātyāyana*. The *Upadeśa* contains also a long quotation from *Kāśyapaparivarta* §§82–4 (266c28–267a15). Kuno Hōryū has drawn attention to the interesting fact that the quotation in the *Upadeśa* contains the beginning of §84, a passage which is missing in the three oldest Chinese translations of the *Kāśyapaparivarta* (*Bukkyō kenkyū*, II, 3, 1938, p. 95).

The publication of the third volume of the translation of the *Upadeśa* is an important milestone in the history of Buddhist studies. To conclude we express the wish that Professor Lamotte may find the courage and energy to continue his admirable work on this important text!

J. W. DE JONG

Jikido Takasaki, *A Study on the Ratnagotravibhāga* (*Uttaratantra*). *Being a Treatise on the Tathāgatagarbha Theory of Mahāyāna Buddhism* (= *Serie Orientale Roma*, XXXIII). Roma, 1966, xiii + 439 pp. L. 16.000.

For several reasons the *Ratnagotravibhāga* deserves our attention. It is the only text on the *tathāgatagarbha* which has been preserved in Sanskrit. There are many problems connected with its place in the history of Mahāyāna philosophy and with its authorship.

The Tibetan tradition attributes the verses to Maitreya and the prose commentary to Asaṅga. This text is held in high regard as one of the five treatises composed by Maitreya. However, the Chinese tradition attributes the whole work to Sāramati. This tradition is mentioned by Yüan-ts'e (613-696) in his commentary on the *Saṃdhinirmocanasūtra*[1] and by Fa-tsang (643-712) in his commentary on the *Dharmadhātvaviśeṣaśāstra*[2]. Probably the earliest reference to Sāramati as author of the *Ratnagotravibhāga* is to be found in Chih-i's *Mo-ho chih-kuan* (*Taishō*, Vol. XLVI, Nr. 1911, p. 31b18-26) which has been dictated by him in 594 (cf. p. 125 of Tsukinowa's article mentioned in note 8). The identity of Sāramati raises many problems. Some scholars have identified him with Sthiramati,[3] others have distinguished two Sāramati's.[4] There are also many obscurities in the Chinese traditions concerning the translator of the Chinese version. Chinese catalogues mention two translations, one by Ratnamati and the other by Bodhiruci.

In 1931 E. Obermiller published a translation of the *Ratnagotravibhāga* from the Tibetan: "The Sublime Science of the Great Vehicle to Salvation", *Acta Orientalia*, Vol. IX, Part II.III, pp. 81-306.[5] His interpretation of the text is based upon a commentary by Tsoṅ-kha-pa's pupil and successor rGyal-tshab Dar-ma rin-chen (1364-1432).[6] The Sanskrit text has been edited by E. H. Johnston and published by T. Chowdhury: *The Ratnagotravibhāga Mahāyānottaratantraśāstra* (Patna, 1950). This edition is based upon two manuscripts found in Tibet by Rāhula Sāṁkṛtyāyana. The edition of the Sanskrit text has given a new impulse to the study of the *Ratnagotravibhāga*. Several passages of the *Ratnagotravibhāga* have been translated by E. Conze (*Buddhist Texts through the Ages*, Oxford, 1954, pp. 130-131, 181-184 and 216-217). In *Die Philosophie des Buddhismus* (Berlin, 1956, pp. 255-264) E. Frauwallner has

[1] P. Demiéville, *BEFEO*, XXIV, 1-2 (1924), p. 53.

[2] N. Peri, *BEFEO*, XI (1911), p. 350; Takasaki, p. 9.

[3] Cf. H. W. Bailey and E. H. Johnston, "A Fragment of the Uttaratantra in Sanskrit", *BSOS*, VIII (1935), pp. 77-89 (esp. p. 81) and Johnston's foreword to his edition of the Sanskrit text, pp. x-xii. To this Sthiramati the Tibetan tradition attributes a commentary on the *Kāśyapaparivarta*. The Chinese translation (*Taishō*, 1523) is due to Bodhiruci. According to Chinese catalogues this commentary, just as the *Ratnagotravibhāga*, has been translated by both Bodhiruci and Ratnamati. Cf. A. Staël-Holstein's edition (*A Commentary of the Kāśyapaparivarta*, Peking, 1933) and P. Pelliot's review, *TP*, XXXII (1936), pp. 75-76. According to Chinese traditions both Bodhiruci and Ratnamati have translated also the *Daśabhūmikasūtraśāstra* (*Taishō*, No. 1522), cf. Noël Peri, "A propos de la date de Vasubandhu", *BEFEO*, XI (1911), pp. 352-353; Stanley Weinstein, "The concept of *ālaya-vijñāna* in pre-T'ang Chinese Buddhism". *Essays on the History of Buddhist Thought. Presented to Professor Reimon Yūki* (Tōkyō, 1964), pp. 34-35. On the relations between Bodhiruci and Ratnamati see P. Demiéville, "Sur l'authenticité du *Ta tch'eng k'i sin louen*", *Bulletin de la Maison Franco-Japonaise*, II, 2 (Tōkyō, 1929), pp. 30ff.

[4] See the references given by Ét. Lamotte, *L'Enseignement de Vimalakīrti* (Louvain, 1962), pp. 92-93, n. 2. According to Hattori Masaaki, there is only one Sāramati who lived between Nāgārjuna and Asaṅga-Vasubandhu.

[5] Cf. La Vallée Poussin's interesting review, *MCB*, I (1931-1932), pp. 406-409.

[6] Cf. G. Tucci, *Tibetan Painted Scrolls*, I (Roma, 1949), p. 119: A *Catalogue of the Tohoku University Collection of Tibetan Works on Buddhism* (Sendai, 1953), No. 5434. Ogawa Ichijō, "Butsu (Nyorai) to Busshō (Nyoraizō) — Darumarinchen-zō Hōshōron Shakuso o shoe to shite", *IBK*, XIII (1965), pp. 247-250. Id.: "Indo Daijō Bukkyō ni okeru Nyoraizō-Busshō-shisō ni tsuite — Darumarinchen-zō Hōshōron Shakuso no kaidoku o kokoromite —", *Tōhōgaku*, 30 (1965), pp. 102-116. A complete translation of this commentary would be very welcome.

given a summary of the ideas contained in this text and a translation of several verses.[7] In 1959 Ui Hakuju published a detailed study on the *Ratnagotravibhāga* (*Hōshōron Kenkyū*) which contains a complete translation (pp. 471-648), together with a Sanskrit-Japanese glossary (pp. 1-60 with separate pagination).[8] Professor Takasaki's translation was undertaken during his stay in India (1954-1957) and continued afterwards. Apart from this book he has published between 1958 and 1964 ten articles relating to the *Ratnagotravibhāga* (a list is given on pp. xii-xiii).[9]

The translation is preceded by a long introduction (pp. 5-62) and a synopsis (pp. 63-133) which indicates the divisions of the chapters, the main topics, the numbers of the verses, the page numbers in Sanskrit, Tibetan (Derge edition) and in Chinese, quotations and comparisons with passages in the *Buddhagotraśāstra* (*Taishō*, No. 1610), the *Mahāyānadharmadhātvaviśeṣaśāstra* (*Taishō*, No. 1626-1627) and the *Anuttarāśrayasūtra* (*Taishō*, No. 669).

The introduction deals briefly with the Tibetan and Chinese traditions concerning the authorship of the *Ratnagotravibhāga*, but refrains from discussing the theories of modern scholars. The latest discussion of the problems connected with Sāramati is to be found in Ui's book (pp. 89-97), in which the author acrimoniously attacks Johnston's hypothesis of an older Sthiramati, to whom are due the *Ratnagotravibhāga*, the commentary on the *Kāśyapaparivarta*, the *Dharmadhātvaviśeṣaśāstra*, and possibly the *Mahāyānāvatāra* (*Taishō*, No. 1634).[10] In the second section of the introduction Professor Takasaki studies the structure of the text and tries to reconstruct the original text which, according to him, consists of 27 verses of chapter I (cf. pp.

[7] According to Frauwallner Sāramati lived about 250 A.D.

[8] For completeness' sake mention must be made of a synoptic edition of the Sanskrit text in Roman letters and the Chinese translation by Nakamura Zuiryū: *The Ratnagotravibhāga-Mahāyānottaratantra-çāstra. Compared with Sanskrit and Chinese. with introduction and Notes* (Tokyo, 1961) (published originally in *Ōsaki Gakuhō*, 103-110, 1955-1959). More important are the following articles: Tsukinowa Kenryū, "Kukyōichijōhōshōron ni tsuite", *Nihon Bukkyō Kyōkai Nenpō*, VII (1935) pp. 121-139; Takata Ninkaku, "Kukyōichijōhōshōron no johon ni tsuite", *Mikkyō Bunka*, 31 (1955) pp. 9-37; Hattori Masaaki, "'Busshōron' no ichi kōsatsu", *Bukkyō Shigaku*, IV, 3-4 (1955), pp. 16-36 (I have not been able to consult the last two articles); Takata Ninkaku, "Hōshōron ni okeru tenne (āśrayaparivṛtti) ni tsuite", *IBK*, VI (1958), pp. 501-504; Ogawa Ichijō, "'Busshō' to 'buddhatva'", *IBK*, XI (1963), pp. 544-545.

[9] Not mentioned are two articles published in 1953: "Hōshōron ni okeru nyoraizō no igi", *IBK*, I, pp. 368-369; "Nyoraizō to engi — Hōshōron o tegakari to shite —", *IBK*, II, pp. 244-247.

[10] Ui dwells at great length on the fact that Johnston gives the Chinese translation of Sāramati's name as Chien I and not as Chien Hui, and insists that Hui and I must be sharply distinguished. However, Tsukinowa quoted as early as 1934 a passage of Chih-i's *Mo-ho chih-kuan* (see above, p. 37) where Sāramati is translated by Chien-i. As far as I can see Ui does not mention anywhere either this passage or Tsukinowa's article. In general, he is very sparing with references to other scholars. Ui's bitter attack on Johnston culminates in the remark that Johnston treats Chinese Buddhism and the history of Chinese Buddhism with too much ease. He adds that without knowledge of Chinese Buddhism, it is impossible to understand Indian Buddhism and Buddhism in general. One could make a similar remark about Ui in respect of Tibetan Buddhism. Although Ui states that the translation of *sāra* by *chien* is quite usual and not limited to personal names, nevertheless Johnston is quite right in remarking that Sāramati is a somewhat unusual form. Usually, personal names ending in *-mati* have as first element an adjective or a participle. The name Sāramati does not seem to occur anywhere else.

393-395 which give the text of these verses). Ui has reconstructed a basic text in 187 verses which he gives in Japanese translation (pp. 38-81). The form of the *Ratnagotravibhāga* is, as Johnston remarks, somewhat unusual. It consists of verses and prose but only part of the verses are *kārikās*. The remaining verses either explain the *kārikās* or illustrate them by similes. Moreover, the Chinese translation consists of two parts. The first contains only verses with occasional captions (*Taishō*, vol. XXXI, pp. 813-820) and the second agrees on the whole with the Sanskrit text but omits many verses which occur in the first part (pp. 820-848). There is a number of omissions and additions in the Sanskrit as compared to the Chinese translation. The main differences between the two texts are listed on page 19 of the introduction and the less important ones are pointed out in the notes to the translation, but not exhaustively (cf. for instance, my remark below apropos of p. 50. 13-15). It would have been helpful to have a synopsis of the two parts of the Chinese translation with the Sanskrit text. In view of the form of the Sanskrit text and the complicated hybrid structure of the Chinese translation, attempts to reconstruct an original text are quite justified, however hypothetical they will always be. Both Ui and Professor Takasaki rely exclusively on internal evidence. For a more reliable reconstruction this should be combined with a detailed comparison of the *Ratnagotravibhāga* with related texts.

Section III of the introduction is devoted to an exposition of the main doctrines of the text and section IV to the genealogy of the *tathāgatagarbha* theory, in which Professor Takasaki discusses the main texts quoted in the *Ratnagotravibhāga*.[11] In the following section it is proved that the *Mahāyānadharmadhātvaviśeṣaśāstra*, the *Buddhagotraśāstra* and the *Anuttarāśrayasūtra* depend on the *Ratnagotravibhāga*.[12] In the last section Professor Takasaki considers the place of the *Ratnagotravibhāga* in Mahāyāna Buddhism. As to the date and the authorship he arrives at the following conclusions: (1) The original verses were composed before Asaṅga. Most probably they are to be attributed to Maitreya. (2) The present form of the text dates from the early 5th century A. D. and after Asaṅga and Vasubandhu. Sāramati is the author of the commentary and the systematizer of the *garbha* theory.

Many problems relating to the *Ratnagotravibhāga* are also discussed in the articles mentioned above. These articles as well as the introduction and the notes to the text contain a wealth of information. We may expect that they form the prelude to a systematic treatment of the *garbha* theory and its history. With his profound knowledge of the Sanskrit, Chinese and Tibetan texts and of the results of Japanese scholarship, Professor Takasaki is eminently qualified to give us an exhaustive study of this important chapter of Mahāyāna philosophy.

The translation of the *Ratnagotravibhāga* by Professor Takasaki is the first to be based on the Sanskrit text and the Chinese and Tibetan translations. Obermiller utilized only the Tibetan version and his translation, excellent as it is, contains a number of mistakes which are obvious in the light of the Sanskrit text. Ui utilized both the Sanskrit text and the Chinese translation, but he was unable to consult the Tibetan translation directly. His knowledge of it was based upon a Japanese translation, made for him by Tada Tōkan, and upon Obermiller's English translation. It is clear from many indications that the Chinese translation is closer to the original than both the Sanskrit text and the Tibetan translation. However, as concerns the interpretation of the text, the Chinese translation is now always a reliable guide. There

[11] Ui has studied in great detail the texts quoted (pp. 272-353) and has devoted a special chapter to the *Śrīmālādevīsiṃhanādasūtra* (pp. 435-469).

[12] In chapter four of his book entitled "The relations with other sūtras and śāstras" (pp. 354-429) Ui has examined the *Anuttarāśrayasūtra* (pp. 354-366), the *Buddhagotraśāstra* (pp. 366-389), the *Mahāyānadharmadhātvaviśeṣaśāstra* (pp. 389-407) and the *Mahāyānāvatāra* (pp. 407-423).

are several places where Professor Takasaki has been too much influenced by it but in general he indicates very well the wrong interpretations which are to be found in the Chinese translation. For the Tibetan translation Professor Takasaki has consulted only the Derge edition. A comparison of the passages quoted in the notes with the corresponding passages in the Peking edition (the only one at my disposal) shows that the Derge edition does not always give a satisfactory text. An edition of the Tibetan translation based on the Derge, Peking and Narthang editons would be highly desirable. In view of the importance of the vocabulary of the *Ratnagotravibhāga* for both Buddhist Sanskrit and Mahāyāna terminology, it would also be very useful to have indexes on the lines of those compiled by Professor Nagao for the *Mahāyānasūtrālaṃkāra*.

The *Ratnagotravibhāga* is not always easy to interpret. While reading the translation, I have made a number of notes with regard to the interpretation, the edition of the text and similar matters. I venture to publish them in the conviction that any contribution, however, insignificant, may be of some help in the study of this very important text. At the same time my remarks are meant as a tribute to Professor Takasaki's scholarship for which I have the greatest respect. I have used the following abbreviations: T. = Tibetan translation (my quotations of T. are taken from the Peking edition. Whenever necessary, I refer to the Derge, Peking and Narthang editions by the initials D., P. and N.); J. = Johnston's edition of the Sanskrit text; O. = Obermiller's translation of the Tibetan translation: *BHSD* = Edgerton's *Buddhist Hybrid Sanskrit Dictionary* (New Haven, 1953); *CPD* = *A Critical Pāli Dictionary* (Copenhagen, 1924-1965).

2.8-10 *sarvaśrāvakapratyekabuddhair api tāvac chāriputrāyam artho na śakyaḥ samyak svaprajñayā jñātuṃ vā drașṭuṃ vā pratyavekșituṃ vā / prāg eva bālapṛthagjanair anyatra tathāgataśraddhāgamanataḥ* / Tak. "This meaning, O Śāriputra, can neither be known nor be seen, nor be examined correctly through the knowledge of the Śrāvakas and the Pratyekabuddhas. Needless to say, this applies to the case of ignorant and ordinary beings, except when they have faith in the Tathāgata." Tak. has followed the punctuation of the Sanskrit text which is wrong. The *daṇḍa* after *vā* must be deleted, because those who are able to understand through faith (*śraddhāgamana*; T. *dad-pas rtogs-pa*) in the Tathāgata are to be found among the Śrāvakas and Pratyekabuddhas, cf. 22.3-4: *śeṣāṇāṃ devi sarvaśrāvakapratyekabuddhānāṃ tathāgataśraddhāgamanīyāv evaitau dharmāv iti.* The Tibetan translation puts a double stroke (*ñis-śad*) before *sarvaśrāvaka*° and after *tathāgataśraddhāgamanataḥ*. Ui is right in translating *anyatra* ... as a new sentence, cf. p. 484: *shikashi, nyorai ni taisuru shin ni yotte nomi tsūzuru koto o nozoku.*

4.3 *indriyaparamapāramitāprāptaḥ*; Tak. "brings all faculties [of living beings] to the highest perfection"; T. *dbaṅ-po mchog-gi pha-rol-tu phyin-pa.* See Edgerton, *BHSD* s.v. *pāramitā* (1). It is not possible to give a causative meaning to *prāpta*. One must translate: "has obtained the supreme perfection of [his] faculties", cf. 31.14 *sarvadharmanairātmyaparapāramiprāptaḥ* (°*parapāram abhiprāptaḥ* has been corrected on p. xvi; T. *dam-pa'i pha-rol-tu phyin-pa brñes*); Tak. "has attained the highest supremacy, [knowing] non-substantiality of all the phenomena"; 87.3-4 *gunaiḥ / viśuddhipāramīprāptair*; 115.18 *divyabrahmavihārapāramigataḥ*: Tak. "having been transferred to the abode of Brahman in heaven"; T. *lha tshaṅs-gnas mthar-soṅ*. This passage deals with meditation (115.17 *dhyāyed dhyānam* ...) and must be translated accordingly: "who has arrived at mastery in the divine brahmic states", cf. Ui. p. 643: *Tenteki no shibonjū no higan ni tōtatsu-shi.*

4.5-6 *anābhogabuddhakāryāpratipraśrabdho*; Tak. "calmed in the Buddha's effortless acts uninterruptedly". Edgerton gives a more understandable translation, cf. *BHSD* s.v. *apratipraśrabdha*: "unceasing in the effortless activities of a Buddha". This passage must be added to those quoted by Edgerton.

5.6-7 *imaṃ cārthavaśam upādāya*; Tak. "and because of the effect of this meaning". See Edgerton, *BHSD* s.v. *artha-vaśa* and Ui, p. 488: *soshite, kakaru riyū ni motozuite.*

7.2 *saṃghe garbho jñānadhātvāptiniṣṭhaḥ*; Tak. "In the Community exists the Matrix, which is The element of Wisdom, aiming at its acquisition". Both T. (*tshogs-las*) and C. have read *saṃghād*. Johnston prefers the MS. reading *saṃghe* "as the Tathāgatagarbha is in each member of the community and by its working leads to the acquisition of knowledge and realisation of the *dhātu*". Ui remarks that the *tathāgatagarbha* exists in all men and is not restricted to the *saṃgha*. I believe that the reading *saṃghād* is preferable also, because it corresponds to the ablatives in the first pāda: *buddhād dharmo dharmataś cāryasaṃghaḥ*. According to Tak. *taj* in the third pāda (*tajjñānāptiś cāgrabodhir*) refers to *garbha* in the second pāda: "Its acquisition of the Wisdom is the Supreme Enlightenment". T. (*ye-śes de thob byaṅ-chub mchog*) does not bear out this interpretation. I suggest that these two pādas be translated as follows: "From the Community comes the Matrix which culminates in the obtaining of the Element of Wisdom. The obtaining of that Wisdom is the Supreme Awakening", see Ui's translation, p. 490: *sō kara zō ga ari, chiekai no shōtoku o kukyō to shi, soshite, sono chie no shōtoku wa saijō bodai de ari.*

8.2 *iti smṛtam*; Tak. "Thus remembered by tradition". Better "thus it is taught (or declared)".

8.10 *udayo 'trābhisaṃbodho 'bhipretotpādaḥ*; "Here the word '*udaya*' means 'perfect enlightenment' (*abhisaṃbodha*), in which the sense 'origination' is implied". T. (P.; D. is quoted by Tak., p. 157, n. 17) *o-ta-ya ni 'dir mṅon-par rtogs-pa la 'dod-kyi skye-ba ni ma yin-no*; O. "Here the word '*udaya*' is to be understood in the sense of 'thorough cognition', but not in that of 'origination'". One must certainly correct the Sanskrit text according to T., which has been misunderstood by Johnston, and add the syllable *no*: *'bhipreto notpādaḥ*; *no* and *to* are almost similar in the script used in the MS. B, so that the omission of *no* is practically a case of haplology. That Ui follows Johnston's text is certainly due to his ignorance of Tibetan, p. 493: *kokoni kaku o eta to yū no wa, shōgaku shita koto de atte, nozomareta mono o eta koto de aru.*

8.18-19 *tatra duḥkhamūlaṃ samāsato yā kācid bhaveṣu nāmarūpābhinirvṛttiḥ*; Tak. "Of these, the root of Suffering is, in short, one kind of origination of Individuality (*nāmarūpa*) on the [three] existences"; *yā kācid* means "any whatsoever", cf. Ui's translation, p. 494: *issai.*

10.7-8 *vikrīḍitā vividhā sampannavinayopāyamukheṣu supraviṣṭatvāt*; Tak. "[The Compassion is 'named] mastery (*vikrīḍitā*)', because it enters well into the gates of accomplished means of training in various ways (*vividhā*)". Ui also translates *vividhā* as an adverb: p. 496: *shuju ni*, but no such adverb exists. As Johnston remarks, T. corresponds to *vividheṣu sampannavineyopāyamukheṣu* (p. 10, n. 2). The simplest solution would be to read *vividhasampanna°*.

10.9 *svadharmatādhigamasamprāpaṇāśayatvāt*; Tak. "because [the Buddha] ... has the intention to lead [the living beings] to the acquisition of their own nature". In note 50 Tak. remarks "it seems C. takes '*svadharmatā*' as 'Buddha's own nature'". Here *svadharmatā* has indeed the same meaning as in 10.4: *svadharmatāprakṛtinirviśiṣṭatathāgatagarbham* and in verse 100 (60.16-17) *vilokya tadvat sugataḥ svadharmatām avīcisaṃstheṣv api buddhacakṣuṣā*. Ui gives the same interpretation, p. 496: *jiko no hosshō no shōtoku ni tasseshimen to yū igyō taru ga yue de aru.*

10.12-13 *api khalu jñānena paramanityopaśāntipadasvābhisaṃbodhisthānaguṇāt svārthasampat paridīpitā*; Tak. "Besides [there is another meaning]. By the word 'Wisdom', the fulfilment of self-benefit is designated, in so far as the highest, eternal and quiescent place has the character of being the basis of his own perfect enlightenment". T. *yaṅ-na ye-śes-kyis ni mchog-tu rtag-pa daṅ / ñe-bar źi-ba'i gnas raṅ-ñid mṅon-par byaṅ-chub-la gnas-pa'i yon-tan-gyis na raṅ-gi-don phun-sum-tshogs-pa bstan-pa.* T. suggests the following translation of the Sanskrit text; "On the other hand, 'Wisdom' elucidates the accomplishment of one's own purpose, because it has the property of being the basis for the self-realisation of the supreme and eternal place of Quiescence".

12.4 *dvayavikalpāsamudācārayogena*. Tak. translates *samudācāra* by 'origination' just as *samudaya* in 12.3 Elsewhere he translates *samudācāra* by 'takes place' (13.6), 'produce' (13.9) and 'arising' (33.8). Better is the translation 'manifestation' in 50.12. Everywhere T. has *kun-tu spyod-pa* and Ui, p. 499, etc.: *gengyō*. In 13.9 T. (*kun-'byuṅ-ba las*) and the context (*ayoniśomanasikārasamudācārāt kleśasamudayaḥ / kleśasamudayāt karmasamudayaḥ*) suggest a reading °*samudayāt*.

13.1-4 *vibandhaḥ punar abhūtavastunimittārambaṇamanasikārapūrvikā rāgadveṣamohotpattir anuśayaparyutthānayogāt / anuśayato hi bālānām abhūtam atatsvabhāvaṃ vastu śubhākāreṇa vā nimittaṃ bhavati rāgotpattitaḥ / pratighākāreṇa vā dveṣotpattitaḥ / avidyākāreṇa vā mohotpattitaḥ*; Tak. "And 'bondage' (*vibandha*) means the origination of Desire, Hatred and Ignorance preceded by the thought which takes its basis of cognition upon the characteristic of unreal things. It is due to the union of the state of tendency (*anuśaya*) with manifested state (*paryutthāna*) [of defilement]. Indeed, people regard the unreal, i.e. 'not of its nature (*atatsvabhāva*)' thing as the [real] characteristic because of its desirable looks (*śubhākāra*) when Desire comes forth from its state of tendency; when Hatred comes forth [from its state of tendency], [they regard the unreal thing as the real characteristic] because of its detestable looks (*pratighākāreṇa*); and when Ignorance comes forth, then it is the same because of its obscure looks (*avidyākāreṇa*)". This difficult passage becomes clearer when compared with chapter XXIII of the *Prasannapadā* which is devoted to the *viparyāsas*, see kārikā 1: *saṃkalpaprabhavo rāgo dveṣo mohaś ca kathyate / śubhāśubhaviparyāsān saṃbhavanti pratītya hi /* and the commentary (p. 452.4-5): *tatra hi śubham ākāraṃ pratītya rāga utpadyate / aśubhaṃ pratītya dveṣaḥ / viparyāsān pratītya moha utpadyate / saṃkalpas tv eṣāṃ trayāṇām api sādhāraṇakāraṇam utpattau /*. The commentary explains that the beautiful aspect (*śubhākāra*), the ugly aspect (*aśubhākāra*), the permanent, the self etc. (*nityātmādi*) have been superimposed (*adhyāropa*), see p. 457.6-8. The *Ratnagotravibhāga* explains that an unreal object (*abhūtaṃ vastu*) becomes something which appears (*nimitta*) as having a beautiful, repulsive or wrongly understood aspect, although it has not the nature of those [three characteristics] because desire, repulsion or delusion arise out of their latent state. For *nimitta* see *BHSD nimitta* (I): "external aspect or feature, appearance"; Jacques May, *Candrakīrti, Prasannapadā madhyamakavṛtti* (Paris, 1959), p. 510: "indice de détermination, détermination, cause déterminante", and Haribhadra's *Abhisamayālaṃkārālokā* (Wogihara's ed.), p. 333: *sāmānyarūpaparicchedān nimittikuryāt* (transl. by Edward Conze, *Oriens Extremus*, IX, 1962, p. 36, n. 15 by "[treat as a sign] by defining their general marks"). Tak. has wrongly rendered *atatsvabhāvam* at other places too, see 31.12: *sarve hy anyatīrthyā rūpādikam atatsvabhāvaṃ vastv ātmety upagatāḥ*; Tak. "Indeed, all the other Heretics consider the things consisting of form, etc. as the Ego though they are of the unreal nature". One must understand: "For all other heretics consider the object, consisting of matter, etc. as the Self, although it has not the nature of it." See also 86.5-6 (verse 40 c-d): *kriyāsu cintāmaṇirājaratnavad vicitrabhāvo na ca tatsvabhāvavān*; Tak. "He has a resemblance, in his acts, to the king of wish-fulfilling gems, appearing in various forms, which, however, have not their own substance." This passage refers to the *saṃbhogakāya* which appears as different beings but without possessing the nature of those [different beings] (T. *sna-tshogs-dṅos daṅ de-yi raṅ-bźin min*). In the verses 51 and 52 (87.11-14) which explain verse 40 *atatsvabhāva* occurs once and *atadbhāva* twice: *deśane darśane kṛtyāsraṃsane 'nabhisaṃskṛtau / atatsvabhāvākhyāne ca citratoktā ca pañcadhā / (51) raṅgapratyayavaicitryād atadbhāvo yathā maṇeḥ / sattvapratyayavaicitryād atadbhāvas tathā vibhoḥ / (52)*; Tak. "In teaching, in the visible form, in acting ceaselessly, and acting with no artificial effort, and in its appearance of illusion, the variety of [its manifestation] is said to be five-fold (51). Just as a gem, being dyed with various colours, does not make manifest its real essence; similarly, the Lord never shows its real nature, though it appears in various forms, according to the conditions of the living beings (52)". Here *atatsvabhāvākhyāne* means "in the manifestation of what is not its nature" (T. *de-yi ṅo-bo mi-ston-la* = "in the non-manifestation of its nature"). See also Nyāyabindu (ed. Stcherbatsky), 27.3: *yady atatsvabhāve 'nutpādake ca kaścit pratibaddhasvabhāvo*; Stcherbatsky, *Buddhist Logic*, II, p. 75: "If the existence of something could be necessarily conditioned by something else, something that would neither be its cause, not essentially the same reality." Tak.'s translation of *anuśayaparyutthānayogāt* (13.2) has to be corrected; *yogāt* (T. *daṅ-ldan-pas*) does not indicate the union of *anuśaya* with *paryutthāna*, but the union with both.

13.15-17 *ya evam asataś ca nimittārambaṇasyādarśanāt sataś ca yathābhūtasya paramārthasatyasya darśanāt tadubhayor anutkṣepāprakṣepasamatājñānena sarvadharmasamatābhisambodhaḥ*: Tak. "And thus, this realization of all natures by Wisdom, as being equal without any addition nor diminution because of these two facts, i.e. because we cannot see any characteristic nor basis of non-being, and we can see the real character of being as the absolute truth." This passage explains that the realization of the sameness of all dharmas is due to the knowledge of the sameness which does neither reject (*utkṣepa*, T. *bsal-ba*) the non-existing support of the appearance (*asan nimittārambaṇam*) nor establish (*prakṣepa*, T. *bźag-pa*) the existing absolute in its true reality (*sad yathābhūtaṃ paramārthasatyam*) because the first is not seen and the second is seen.

15.1-2 *anāsrave dhātau kuśalākuśalayoś cittayor ekacaratvād dvitīyacittānabhisaṃdhānayogena*; Tak. "In the immaculate sphere there is no succession of a second mind because both minds, good and bad, act together as one and the same." T. *dge-ba daṅ mi-dge-ba'i sems-dag las gcig rgyu-bas sems-gñis-pa mtshams-sbyor-ba med-pa'i tshul-gyi*. O. "when one of the two forms of the Spirit, either the defiled or the undefiled, manifests itself, it has no (real) contact with the other (its counterpart)." Tak. understands *ekacara* as "acting together", T. as "acting of one". The usual meaning, however, of *ekacara* is "wandering or living alone". In the immaculate sphere the good and bad thoughts are isolated from each other and therefore there is no relation of a second thought with a first thought, i.e. a bad thought cannot arise from a good thought and vice versa. Ui seems to understand it in this way: p. 503: *muro no kai ni oitewa, zen to fuzen to wa tandoku no mono de aru kara, dainishin to no ketsugō ni tekishinai node.*

16.17 and 17.2 °*avabhāsapratyupasthitam*; Tak. "standing in the illumination"; *pratyupasthita* means here "engaged in", cf. *BHSD* s.v. *pratyupasthāna, pratyupasthita*. In 36.3 Tak. has misunderstood *pratyupasthāpanam*: *buddhadhātuviśuddhigotraṃ ... dvividhakāryapratyupasthāpanaṃ bhavati*; Tak. "the Essence of the Buddha, the perfectly pure Germ, ... has the two kinds of foundation of its actions." The meaning is: "The Germ brings about two kinds of effect", cf. *Daśabhūmika* 49.18: *avidyā dvividhakāryapratyupasthānā* which is quoted by Edgerton.

17.4 *ananyapoṣigaṇyam ... āryaśrāvakam*; Tak. "the holy Śrāvakas ... indifferent to the nourishment of others"; J. notes that *poṣin* is recorded by the *PW* only from the *Kathāsaritsāgara* and Tak. that C. probably has misread *poṣa* for *poṣin*. There is no doubt about the meaning of *ananyapoṣin*, cf. Pāli *anaññaposin*, *CPD*: "not supporting others, said of the houseless ascetic, who maintains no family and fosters no passion"; °*gaṇya* probably has to be interpreted as "belonging to a class" but T. (*gźan rgyas-par byed-pa mi-ldan-pa* according to D.; P. ... *daṅ-ldan-pa*, which is certainly wrong) has no word corresponding to it.

20.17 *sarvajagadāśayaśobhānimittatvāt*; Tak. "because they are the cause of beauty intended by the whole world." T. *'gro-ba thams-cad-kyi bsam-pa dge-ba'i rgyu yin-pa'i phyir*, O. "as they are the cause of the virtuous thoughts of all living beings." The interpretation given by the Tibetan translator is correct; *āśayaśobhā* is litterally "the splendour of the thoughts", cf. also Ui's translation, p. 512: *issai seken no kesshutsuseru igyō no in taru ga yue de aru.*

21.11-12 *teṣām eva daśabalādīnāṃ buddhadharmāṇāṃ pratisvam anuttaraṃ karma*: Tak. "the automatic, highest act of these Qualities of the Buddha — 10 Powers, etc." The meaning of *pratisvam* is "one by one", not "automatic" as given by Tak. in accordance with C. One must translate: "the single supreme acts of these qualities of the Buddhas as the ten powers, etc", cf. Ui's translation, p. 513: *sorera jūriki-tō no buppō no ichi-ichi no mujō no gō de atte.*

23.7 *tatropagamikayā mīmāṃsayā samanvāgataḥ*: Tak. "possessed of the skill to approach there (i.e. to the big cloth)." Here *upagamika* has the same meaning as *-upaga* and *-upaka* in Buddhist Hybrid Sanskrit, cf. *BHSD* s.v. *-upaka*: "pertaining, belonging to; suitable, appropriate". The same expression occurs in the *Daśabhūmikasūtra* (p. 61.15) which has *upagatayā* instead of *upagamikayā*: *tatropagatayā mīmāṃsayā samanvāgato*. In *Vinaya* IV.211: *tatrupāyāya vīmaṃsāya samannāgatā* (quoted by The Pali Text Society's *Pali-English Dictionary* s.v. *tatra*) one must probably read *tatrupayāya*. Kern's explanation has to be rejected (*Toevoegselen op 't woordenboek van Childers*. II, Amsterdam, 1916, p. 90: *tatrupāya* = *tadūpiya*, suitable, corresponding, SVibh.II,211. Misschien vervorming van *tadrūpiya*).

26.10-11 *pūrvataraṃ tu yenārthena sarvatrāviśeṣeṇa pravacane sarvākāraṃ tadarthasūcanaṃ bhavati tad apy adhikṛtya nirdekṣyāmi*. Tak. notes that T. reads *pravacana* (*gsuṅ-rab*) as the subject. However, T. has *gsuṅ* (omitted by P.) *-rab thams-cad-du* which corresponds to *sarvatra pravacane*, O. "throughout the whole of Scripture". I do not believe that Tak.'s translation and explanation (p. 198, n. 13) of this sentence are correct, but the text (26.1-11) is clearly in disorder as noted by J. and Tak.

28.10-11 *śūnyatādṛṣṭayaś cābhimānikā yeṣām iha tadvimokṣamukhe 'pi śūnyatāyāṃ mādyamānānāṃ śūnyataiva dṛṣṭir bhavati*; T. *mṅon-pa'i ṅa-rgyal-can stoṅ-pa-ñid-du lta-ba ste / 'di-lą stoṅ-pa ñid-du lta-ba gaṅ-dag de'i rnam-par thar-pa'i sgo-la yaṅ stoṅ-pa-ñid-du lta-ba 'gyur-ba*. Probably the text at the basis of T. had *śunyatādṛṣṭīnāṃ* instead of *śūnyatāyāṃ mādyamānānāṃ* which is not represented in C., too.

32.10 *ākāśopamasattvabhājanalokanairātmyaniṣṭhāgamanād*; Tak. "[the Tathāgata] has realized perfectly the non-substantiality of living beings and of the material world, just as the sky [reaches up to the limit of the world]." In a note Tak. remarks that *akāśopama* (T. *nam-mkha' ltar*) is relating to *niṣṭhāgamana*. However, T. relates it to *nairātmya*: *sems-can daṅ snod-kyi 'jig-rten nam-mkha'-ltar bdag-med-pa'i mthar-thug-pa ñid-du rtogs-pa'i phyir* = "because the Tathāgata has realized completely the sky-like non-substantiality of the world of the living beings and the material world." This interpretation seems more obvious, although Tak's interpretation is not precluded. Ui's translation is ambiguous, p. 530: *kokū no gotoki, shujō-seken to kiseken to no muga no kukyō ni tasshita kara to.*

32.15 *vaśitāprāptānāṃ ca bodhisattvānām*. In note 109 Tak. remarks that it is not necessary to limit this qualification to those Bodhisattvas who abide on the 10th *bhūmi* as mentioned in the Tibetan commentary and that we can regard this '*vaśitāprāpta*' as an epithet for Bodhisattvas in general. Tak. refers to *Laṅkāvatāra*, p. 274.21: *sarvabodhisattvabhūmiṣu vaśitāprāptaḥ*, but this quotation is from the *Lalitavistara*. The Tibetan commentary (O., p. 170, n. 1) does not limit this qualification to bodhisattvas on the 10th *bhūmi*, but to bodhisattvas who abide in the last three *bhūmis*. The ten *vaśitās* are obtained on the 8th *bhūmi*, cf. *Daśabhūmikasūtra* (ed. J. Rahder), p. 70 and *Mahāyānasūtrālaṃkāra* 26.2-3: *daśavaśitālābhāt / yathā daśabhūmike 'ṣṭamyāṃ bhūmau nirdiṣṭāḥ.*

33.5-6 *sarvakleśamaladaurgandhyavāsanāpakarṣaparyantaśubhapāramitāṃ*; J. notes: "Text as in A; °*vāsanāprakarṣa*°, B, which does not make sense; T. seems to have read °*vāsanāyogāt* (*bag-chags ... daṅ-ldan-pa'i phyir*), which would bring the sentence into the same form as the following ones." According to Tak. (p. 216, n. 122) both T and C. take '*paryanta*' as '*atyanta*' and attach it to *śubhāpāramitā* as an attribute and instead of *apakarṣa* T. has *daṅ-ldan-pa'i phyir*. However, *prakarṣa* makes good sense and corresponds to T. *rab*; T. *mthar-thug-pa* corresponds to *paryanta* and not to *atyanta* which is rendered in T. by *śin-tu* (cf. 32.9, 33.8,9). T. *ñon-moṅs-pa'i dri-ma dri-ṅa-ba'i bag-chags thams-cad daṅ-ldan-pa'i phyir gtsaṅ* (P. *gsaṅ*) *-ba'i pha-rol-tu phyin-pa rab-kyi mthar-thug-pa = sarvakleśamaladaurgandhyavāsanāyogāt prakarṣaparyantaśubhapāramitām* / T. confirms the reading of MS. B, but adds *yogāt*. Tak. translates *kleśamaladaurgandhyavāsanā* by the "dusts of defilements with their bad-smelling impressions". In this case, too, the Tibetan interpretation is to be preferred: "the traces of the bad smell of the impurities of the defilements".

34.18-19 *anityasaṃsārānapakarṣaṇataś cocchedāntāpatanān nityanirvāṇāsamāropaṇataś ca śāśvatāntāpatanāt*; Tak. "Because he does not fall into the Nihilistic Extremity through his not diminishing, neglecting the non-eternal Phenomenal Life; nor does he fall into the Eternalistic Extremity through his not intensifying the eternal Nirvāṇa." In T. (P., D. and N.) *apakarṣaṇa* is rendered by *'brid-pa* which has misled both J. and Tak.; it must be corrected into *'bri-ba* which corresponds exactly to *apakarṣaṇa*. The terms *apakarṣaṇa* and *samāropaṇa* are synonymous with the more usual terms *apavāda* and *samāropa*, cf. 76.11. *Samāropa* is the superimposition of non-existing ideas and entities upon the absolute reality; *apavāda* is the opposite of it. For these two terms see Jacques May, *op.cit.*, p. 187, n. 609.

36.13-15 *na ca bhavati tāvad yāvad āgantukamalaviśuddhigotraṃ trayāṇām anyatamadharmādhimuktiṃ na sa samudānayati satpuruṣasaṃsargādicatuḥśuklasamavadhānayogena*; Tak. "Really, it cannot take place unless they bring about the Germ which is purified from accidental pollutions and the faith in any one of three Vehicles through being endowed with the four kinds of good actions, beginning with having contact with a personage of high virtue." The subject is the *gotra* which brings about the *adhimukti* by means of the *catuḥśukla*. The preceding lines explain that without the *gotra* the *duḥkhadoṣadarśanam* and the *sukhānusaṃśadarśanam* are impossible. T. *ji-srid-du blo-bur-gyi dri-ma rnam-par dag-pa'i rigs skyes-bu dam-pa la brten-pa la sogs-pa 'khor-lo bźi yaṅ-dag-par 'byor-ba'i tsul-gyis / gsum-las gaṅ-yaṅ-ruṅ-ba'i chos-la mos-pa / skyed-par byed-par ma-yin-pa de-srid-du ni 'gyur-ba yaṅ ma-yin-no /*.

38.5-7 *bodhisattvakaruṇābhāvanāyā vārisādharmyaṃ tasyāḥ sarvajagati paramasnigdhabhāvaikarasalakṣaṇaprayogād iti*; J. remarks: "T. om. *laksaṇapra*; C either as in text or reading *°lakṣaṇayogad*, which is perhaps preferable." Both Tak. (p. 226, n. 203) and Ui (p. 538, n. 2) point out that C. corresponds to *°lakṣaṇaprayogād*. T. *de ni' gro-ba thams-cad-la mchog-tu brlan-pa'i raṅ-bźin-gyi ro-gcig-pa daṅ-ldan-pa'i phyir-ro*. Tak. renders T. as follows: "its nature of the highest moisture in all the world is endowed with one taste", but the meaning is: "because it [*bodhisattvakaruṇābhāvanā*] possesses the unique savour of extreme moisture in regard to all living beings."

39.2 *prabhāsvaras tadubhayāgantukatāprakṛtitaḥ*: Tak. "It (*āśrayakṣaya*) is 'radiant' by nature because these two Obstructions are merely of an occasional nature." In note 214 Tak. remarks: "T. reads as '*tad-ubhaya-āgantukatā-aprakṛtitaḥ*' (*glo-bur-pa-ñid-kyi raṅ-bźin ma yin-pa'i phyir-ro*, being *āgantukatā*, they are not the innate character)." The Sanskrit text must be interpreted in conformity with the Tibetan translation: "It is radiant because these two, being accidental, do not constitute its nature." The compound *āgantukatāprakṛtitaḥ* is analysed by T. as *āgantukatayā-aprakṛtitaḥ*, cf. P. *'od-gsal-ba ni de gñi-ga glo-bur-ba ñid-kyis raṅ-bźin ma-yin-pa'i phyir-ro* (P. adds *raṅ-ñid-kyis* after *ñid-kyis*). See Ui's translation, p. 539: *myōjō towa kono ryōsha no kyakujin taru mono o jishō to nasanai kara de aru.*

50.13-15 *sā punar āsravakṣayābhijñābhimukhyasaṅgaprajñāpāramitābhāvanayā mahākaruṇābhāvanayā ca sarvasattvadhātuparitrāṇāya tadasākṣātkaraṇād abhimukhyām bodhisattvabhūmau pradhānyena vyavasthāpyate*; Tak. "And this state is predominantly established in the 6th stage of Bodhisattva called Abhimukhī. Because, [in this Stage], the Bodhisattva, facing the acquisition of the Extinction of Evil Influences through his practices of unobstructed Highest Intellect and Great Compassion, still does never realize that acquisition in order to protect all living beings." Tak. has omitted the word *abhijñā*, which is missing in C., although both T. and S. give it. I would prefer to follow T. and S. The MS. B has the reading *āsravakṣayābhijñābhimukhyāṁ asaṅga°* which seems preferable: "And this [pure and impure state (*śuddhāśuddhāvasthā*)] is mainly established on the Stage of the Bodhisattva, called Abhimukhī, which approaches the superknowledge of the extinction of the defilements on account of the practice of the unobstructed perfection of wisdom [but does not obtain it] because [the Bodhisattva] on account of the practice of the great compassion has not realized it in order to protect all living beings." T. gives no clue which would allow to choose between the readings of the MSS. A and B but palaeographically it is more likely that the reading of MS. A is corrupt as against that of MS. B. It is necessary to connect *asaṅgaprajñāpāramitābhāvanayā* with *āsravakṣayābhijñābhimukhyām* and *mahākaruṇābhāvanayā* with *asākṣātkaraṇād*, see the commentary (50.16-51.9) which explains that on the sixth stage the Bodhisattva approaches the extinction of the defilements because he has produced the unobstructed wisdom, but that, out of compassion, he is born in the Kāmadhatu, thus being at the same time in the pure and impure state. In his translation Tak. has followed T., whereas C. gives the right interpretation (Tak., p. 251, n. 395). In the Chinese translation the passage between *sarvasattvaparitrāṇāya* (50.19) and *ṣaṣṭhyām* (51.1) is missing. In its place there is a different passage (834c27-835a3) which has been translated by Ui (pp. 554-555) who combines both S. and C.

51.5-7 *śamasukhānāsvādanatayā tadupāyakṛtaparijayasya saṃsārābhimukhasattvāpekṣayā nirvāṇavimukhasya bodhyaṅgaparipūraṇāya dhyānair vihṛtya punaḥ kāmadhātau saṃcintyopapattiparigrahaṇato*; Tak. "While cultivating the means for the bliss of the Quiescence, but not in order to taste it [by himself] he turns his face away from Nirvāṇa, for the sake of the living beings who are facing the world of transmigration. Though abiding [in the desireless World of Form] with [4 kinds of] contemplations in order to accomplish the factors for the acquisition of Enlightenment, he voluntarily assumes again existence in the World of Desire." Instead of *nirvāṇavimukhasya* both T. and C. have *nirvāṇābhimukhasya* (Tak., p. 252, n. 407). This reading is to be preferred: "Although he has cultivated the means for the bliss of Quiescence without tasting it, [nevertheless] for the sake of the living beings who are turned towards transmigration, he, who is turned towards Nirvāṇa, after having dwelt in meditations in order to obtain fully the factors of Awakening, again voluntarily assumes existence in the sphere of desire." T. *ži-ba'i bde-ba'i ro mi-myaṅ-bar-de'i thabs-la byaṅ-bar byas-pa'i 'khor-ba-la mṅon-du phyogs-pa'i sems-can-la bltos-te / mya-ṅan-las-'das-pa la mṅon-du phyogs-pa / byaṅ-chub-kyi yan-lag yoṅs-su rdzogs-par bya-ba'i phyir bsam-gtan dag-gi gnas-nas slar 'dod-pa'i khams-su bsams-bžin-du skye-ba yoṅs-su 'dzin-pas /*. It is exactly the opposition between *saṃsārābhimukhasattva* and *nirvāṇābhimukha-[bodhisattva]* which brings fully into relief the great compassion of the Bodhisattva.

51.13-14 *ata eva jagadbandhor upāyakaruṇe pare / yad āryagotraprāpto dṛśyate bālagocare // (70)*; Tak. "Having attained the position of the Saints, he is nevertheless seen amongst ordinary beings; therefore, he is, for the friends of all the world, the Highest means and Compassion." Tak. had misunderstood *jagadbandhu* "the friend of mankind", i.e. the bodhisattva. 70a-b = "therefore the means and the compassion of the friend of mankind are supreme". T. *de-ñid-phyir ni 'gro-ba-yi // gñen-gyi thabs daṅ sñiṅ-rje mchog //*. Ui's translation is correct, p. 555: *seken no shitashiki mono no, saikō no hōben to daihi to no ni o.*

52 8 *jagaty ākāśaparyante*; Tak. "among the world, limitless like the sky". In note

421 Tak. remarks that for *paryanta* T. has *mtha'-klas* (*ananta*) but *mtha'-klas-pa* occurs more often for *paryanta* and *paryavasāna*, cf. G. M. Nagao, *Index to the Mahāyāna-sūtrālaṃkāra*, part I (Tokyo, 1958), p. 150 (*samudraparyantamahāpṛthivī*), Friedrich Weller, *Tibetisch-sanskritischer Index zum Bodhicaryāvatāra*, I (Berlin, 1952), p. 182 (*aśeṣākāśaparyantavāsināṃ kimu dehināṃ*), *Mahāvyutpatti*, No. 371: *ākāśadhātuparyavasānaḥ*. H. A. Jäschke has already noted a case in which *mthas-klas* corresponds to *paryanta*, cf. A *Tibetan-English Dictionary* (London, 1881), p. 240b. Therefore one must translate "in the world bounded by the sky", cf. Ui, p. 556: *kokū o henzai to suru seken ni oite*.

60.20 *jalaruhaṃ saṃmiñjitaṃ*; Tak. "a faded ... lotus flower"; T. *padma zum*; O. "a lotus flower with folded leaves". Tak. 's wrong translation is due to the fact that the lotus is described above (60.12) as *vivarṇa*.

61.4-9 *yathā madhu prāṇigaṇopagūḍhaṃ vilokya vidvān puruṣas tadarthī* / *samantataḥ prāṇigaṇasya tasmād upāyato 'pakramaṇaṃ prakuryāt* // (102) *sarvajñacakṣurviditaṃ maharṣir madhūpamaṃ dhātum imaṃ vilokya* / Tak. "Suppose a clever person, having seen honey surrounded by cloudy bees, and wishing to get it, with skillful means, would deprive the bees completely of it; — (102) Similarly, the Great Sage, possessed of the eyes of the Omniscience, perceiving this Essence known as akin to honey." T. ... *de-daṅ thabs-kyis srog-chags tshogs* (P. *sogs*) // *kun-nas bral-bar rab-tu byed-pa bźin* // (102) *draṅ-sroṅ chen-pos kun-mkhyen-spyan-gyis ni* // *rigs khams sbraṅ-rtsi daṅ-'dra 'di gzigs-nas* // = "with the help of a strategem he would completely remove the swarm of bees from it. (102). The Great Seer, having seen that this Essence, which he has perceived with his omniscient eye, is like honey ..."

61.13-14 *madhvā ... kuryāt kāryam*; J. notes: "*kuryāt tatvam*, A and B (reading doubtful in both); *bya byed-pa* T." Perhaps one must read *kuryāt kṛtyam*.

61.19 *bhavanti ye 'nnādibhir arthinas tu*: Tak. "Those who wish to utilize it as food and the like." In a note Tak. remarks that *annādibhir* (instr.) is grammatically peculiar (usually in loc.). However, in classical Sanskrit the instrumental is normal and in Buddhist Hybrid Sanskrit *arthika* also is constructed with the instrumental, cf. *BHSD* s.v. The meaning of this *pāda* is: "those who want food, etc."; T. *zas-sogs don-du gñer-ba gaṅ yin-pa*.

69.4 *kāmasevānimittatvāt paryutthānāny amedhyavat* / Tak. "Being characterized as devoted to [such] Passion, the outburst of Passions is repulsive like impurities." Tak.'s translation is based upon C. which has misunderstood *nimitta*. T. *'dod-pa bsten-pa'i rgyu yin-phyir* // *kun-nas ldaṅ-pa mi-gtsaṅ 'dra* // ; O. "The outburst of their passions, being the cause for giving way to the desires, is abhorrent like impurities." See also Ui's translation, p. 580: *yoku ni fukeru koto o in to nasu node, ten wa fun no gotoku de aru*.

69.12 *vikośagarbhavaj jñānam avikalpaṃ vipākavat*; Tak. "And the non-discriminative Wisdom has a resemblance to the matured form of an embryo delivered from its covering." It is impossible to relate *vipākavat* to *vikośagarbha*. Ui (p. 580: *mufunbetsu no chi wa taizō o hanareta mono no gotoku, jukushita mono no gotoku de aru*) takes both *vikośagarbhavat* and *vipākavat* as comparisons. The same interpretation is given by T.: *mṅal-sbubs bral-'dra mi-rtog-pa'i* // *ye-śes rnam-par smin-pa bźin* /, but this does not make sense. One has to take *vipākavat* as a possessive adjective relating to *jñāna* "the ripened knowledge", i.e. the knowledge obtained in the last three stages of the bodhisattva.

71.3 *rūpagateṣu sarvagaṃ*; Tak. remarks that *Mahāyānasūtrālaṃkāra* IX, 15, the source of this quotation, has *rūpagaṇeṣu* instead of *rūpagateṣu*. One must certainly correct *rūpagaṇeṣu* into *rūpagateṣu*; T. has *gzugs-gyur kun-tu*, cf. Nagao, *op.cit.*, I, p. 208. This correction is not listed in Nagao's corrigenda to Lévi's edition. Ui (p. 582) has changed the reading of the *Ratnagotravibhāga* according to the *Mahāyānasūtrālaṃkāra*!

73.10 *sattvadhātāv iti*; Johnston's correction of the reading of the MS. (*saṁrvadyatanatija*) is based upon C. However, T. has *yod-do || źes-bya ba'i bar ni |* = *saṃvidyata iti yāvat*.

73.12-14 *yaiva cāsau dharmatā saivātra yuktir yoga upāyaḥ paryāyaḥ | evam eva tat syāt | anyathā naiva tat syād iti |*. J. remarks: "Reading uncertain. *paryāya eva vai tat syāt*, B." and Tak. notes that both T. and C. do not translate *paryāya*. T. *chos-ñid gaṅ-yin-pa de-ñid ni 'dir gaṅ-gis de-lta-bu kho-nar 'gyur-gyi gźan-du mi 'gyur-ro źes-bya-ba'i rigs-pa daṅ sbyor-ba daṅ thabs yin-te |* = *yaiva cāsau dharmatā saivatra yuktir yoga upāyaḥ | yayaivam eva tat syāt | anyathā naiva tat syād iti |*.

74.10 *nedaṃ sthānaṃ vidyate*; Tak. "There is [absolutely] no room for it." The meaning is: "This is impossible", cf. *BHSD* s.v. *sthāna* (5).

75.14-15 *sata eva dharmasyottārakālam ucchedo vināśaḥ parinirvāṇam iti*; Tak. "thinking that the perfect Nirvāṇa means the Extinction, i.e. the destruction of the elements [for the Phenomenal Existence] in future." Tak. has omitted *sata eva*, T. *yod-pa'i*; O. "... the destruction of elements which did really exist." Cf. Ui, p. 588: *jitsuu no hō ga goji ni danmetsu-shi metsue-suru no ga sunawachi nehan de aru to kangaeru mono*.

77.18 *ātmasnehaś cādhikaḥ*; Tak. "and besides, affection for one's self." T. *bdag-chags lhag-pa['i]* = "excessive self-love." The Tibetan translation is correct. See Ui's translation, p. 591: *tsuyoi jitsuga no aijaku ga*.

78.1 *viviktaṃ saṃskṛtaṃ sarvaprakāraṃ bhūtakoṭiṣu*; Tak. "all kinds of phenomena, made by causes and conditions ... are ... deprived of reality." In Mahāyāna philosophy *vivikta*, litt. "separated, free from", means "without substance", cf. *Prasannapadā*, p. 349,4: *skandha sabhāvatu śūnya vivikta*. Therefore the translation is as follows: "In the absolute reality everything which is produced by causes is isolated (without substance)." See Ui's translation, p. 591: *shinjitsuzai ni oitewa, issai no shurui no ui wa onri-serarete iru*.

78.9 *bodhicittodaye 'py asya*; Tak. remarks that T. has *bodhicittodaye yasya* and relates *yasya* to *tasya* in the next verse, but he prefers the reading of the MSS. because in relation to the preceding verse *api* is quite necessary. I am not convinced by this argument and would prefer to follow T.

78.21-22 *tathāgatagarbhādhikāraḥ prathamaḥ paricchedaḥ ślokārthasaṃgrahavyākhyānataḥ samāptaḥ*; T. *de-bźin-gśegs-pa'i sñiṅ-po'i skabs-te tshigs-su bcad-pa daṅ-po'i don-gyi bsdus-pa'i bśad-pa rdzogs-so ||* = *tathāgatagarbhādhikāraḥ prathamaślokārthasaṃgrahavyākhyānaṃ samāptam*. MS. B has °*ādhikāraprathamaśloka*°. Chapter II ends with *bodhyadhikāro nāma dvitīyaḥ paricchedaḥ* which corresponds to T. *byaṅ-chub-kyi skabs źes-bya-ba ste le'u gñis-pa'o*, chapter III with *guṇādhikāro nāma tritīyaḥ paricchedaḥ*; T. omits *nāma*: *yon-tan-gyi skabs-te le'u gsum-pa'o*. Chapter IV ends with *tathāgatakṛtyakriyādhikāraś caturthaḥ paricchedaḥ ślokārthasaṃgrahavyākhyānataḥ samāptaḥ*; T. *de-bźin-gśegs-pa'i phrin-las mdzad-pa'i skabs-te le'u bźi-pa'o || || tshigs-su bcad-pa'i don-gyi bśad-pa rdzogs-so ||* = ... *caturthaḥ paricchedaḥ | ślokārthasaṃgrahavyākhyānaṃ samāptam*. Finally, chapter V ends with *anuśaṃsādhikāro nāma pañcamaḥ paricchedaḥ ślokārthasaṃgrahavyākhyānataḥ samāptaḥ*; T. *phan-yon-gyi le'u-ste lṅa-pa'o || || tshigs-su bcad-pa'i don-gyi bsdus-pa'i bśad-pa rdzogs-so ||* = ... *pañcamaḥ paricchedaḥ | ślokārthasaṃgrahavyākhyānaṃ samāptam*.

80.5 *dharmāṇāṃ tad akalpanapravicayajñānāśrayād āpyate*; Tak. "and is attained when the elements [of existence] take resort to the non-discriminative and Analytical Wisdom." Tak. considers the reading *dharmāṇāṃ* as doubtful because both T. and C. connect *dharma* with *avikalpa*. However, T. corresponds quite well to S.: *de ni chos-la mi-rtog rnam-'byed ye-śes-la brten-nas 'thob* = "it (Buddhahood) is obtained by having recourse to non-discriminative and analytical knowledge in regard to the dharmas." See Ui's translation, p. 595: *shohō ni taisuru mufunbetsu to kenchaku to no chi ni eshi-suru koto ni yotte, tasserareru no de aru*.

85.14 *tatprayatnāḥ*: T. *de rtogs-pa* = *tatprapannāḥ*?

88.11 *bālasārthātivāhanāt*: Tak. "toiling excessively for the company of ordinary beings." It is better to render *ativāhana* by "leading, guiding", cf. *BHSD* s.v. *ativāha*. Ui's translation is too literal and he has gone wrong in his interpretation of *sārtha*, p. 606: *bonbu o mokuteki kansei ni hakobu ga yue ni*.

89.13 *nityam aśaraṇānāṃ ca śaraṇābhyupapattitaḥ*; Tak. "and he gives a refuge for those who have no shelter, because of these [10] points, he is 'eternal'." Ui interprets *nityam* in the same way, cf. p. 607: *soshite kiesho no nai hito-bito ni kie o keiyo-suru kara, butsu wa jōjū de aru*. It seems to me impossible to relate *nityam* n. to *lokanāthaḥ* in verse 62 (89.2). The eternity of the Buddha is explained by verse 68 (89.14-15). Both C. and T. relate *nityaṃ* to *aśaraṇānām*, etc. T. *rtag-pa skyabs-med rnams-kyi ni // skyabs-la sogs-pa 'thad phyir-ro /*.

89.19 *upamānivṛttitaḥ*: T. has read *upamātivṛttitaḥ* (*dpe-las 'das-pa'i phyir*). This reading seems preferable.

92.11 *jñeye vastuni sarvathātmaparayor jñānāt svayaṃ jñāpanād*; Tak. "He himself knows and causes others to know all the things cognizable in all their forms." Tak. seems to relate *ātman* to *jñāna* and *para* to *jñāpana*. Also Ui has the same interpretation, p. 613: *ji to ta to no ni oite, mizukara shiru kara, ta ni shirashimeru kara*. However, T. relates *ātmaparayor* to *jñeye vastuni*: *bdag-gźan śes-bya'i dṅos-po rnam-kun śes daṅ śes-mdzad phyir*. Obermiller's translation ("He knows himself and makes known to others all the things cognizable in their forms") is improbable on account of the position of *bdag-gźan*. It is impossible to translate the Sanskrit text in this way because *svayaṃ* would duplicate *ātman*. Moreover, the caesura after *ātmaparayor* shows also that it is related to *jñeye vastuni*: "In regard to the things to be known completely by himself and others he himself knows and causes others to know."

93.6 *nopekṣāpratisaṃkhyāya*; Tak. "He is not indifferent, nor without consideration." Of course, one must understand: "He has no *apratisaṃkhyāyopekṣā*", cf. T *ma-brtags btaṅ-sñoms mi-mṅa'-ste*. *Apratisaṃkhyāya* is a gerund and not a BHS form for *-yāyām* (fem-loc.) as stated by Tak. See Ui's note (p. 615, n. 1) and his translation p. 615: *shichaku-sezu shite no sha no nai to*.

93.11 *svarasādhyupekṣaṇam*; Tak. "indifference to one's own taste". *Svarasādhyupekṣaṇam* (T. *ṅaṅ-gis gtaṅ-sñoms*), litterally "natural indifference", is a synonym of *apratisaṃkhyāyopekṣā*. See Ui's note (p. 615, n. 2) and his translation p. 615: *jinen no sha*. Tak.'s renderings of *svarasa* are not very adequate, cf. 44.13 *svarasayogena*, T. *raṅ-gi ṅaṅ-gis*, Tak. "with its own essence"; 58.1 °*svarasavāhimārgajñāna*° (*svarasavāhin*, T. *raṅ-gi ṅaṅ-gis 'jug-pa*). Tak. "the knowledge of the Path ... bearing its own taste". In both places C. translates well by "natural" (*tzŭ-jan*). *Svarasayogena* means "in its nature" and *svarasavāhimārgajñāna* "the knowledge of the path which proceeds naturally".

93.13 *muktijñānanidarśanāc ca*; Tak. "of the intuition of freedom". In a note Tak. remarks that T. om. *nidarśana* of *muktijñānanidarśana* (reading apparently '*vimuktijñānadarśanāt*'). However, T. has *grol-ba'i ye-śes las* (*muktijñānāt*). Both the Sanskrit text and the Tibetan translation are imperfect renderings of *vimuktijñānadarśanāt* (cf. 93.7) Metrical exigencies made it impossible for the Sanskrit text to repeat *vimuktijñānadarśanāt* and for T. to translate *darśana*. As one of the *āveṇikabuddhadharmas* '*nāsti vimuktijñānadarśanaparihāṇiḥ*' is mentioned in the *Dharmasaṃgraha*. However, it does not occur in other lists, cf. *Mahāvyutpatti*, 136-153; *Mahāyānasūtrālaṃkāra*, pp. 187-188. Its authencity is guaranteed by the fact that it is listed in the *Daśasāhasrikā Prajñāpāramitā*, cf. Sten Konow, *The two first chapters of the Daśasāhasrikā Prajñāpāramitā* (Oslo, 1941), p. 43. As far as I know, there is no detailed study of these lists. References are given by L. de La Vallée Poussin, *L'Abhidharmakośa de Vasubandhu*, VII (Paris-Louvain, 1923), p. 67; Har Dayal, *The Bodhisattva Doctrine in Buddhist Sanskrit Literature* (London, 1932), p. 326, n. 81; Ét. Lamotte, *La somme* *du grand Véhicule*, Tome II (Louvain, 1939), p. 61*; *BHSD* s.v. *āveṇika*; *Mochizuki Shinkō's Bukkyō daijiten*, s.v. *jūhachi fuguhō*, pp. 2361c-2366a.

97.11 *dvātriṃśal lakṣaṇāḥ kāye darśanāhlādakā guṇāḥ*; Tak. "the 32 marks are the properties, visible and causing delight in the body." T. *mthoṅ-na tshim-byed yon-tan gaṅ || sum-cu-rtsa-gñis źes bya-ba ||* O. "The other 32 distinctive features, which, being perceived, arouse delight." T. 's translation of *darśanāhlādaka* is correct. See also Ui's translation, p. 619: *shin ni sonsuru sanjūnisō wa, kore o mireba kangi o ataeru shokudoku de atte*.

98.8-10 *kṛtsnaṃ niṣpādya yānaṃ pravaraguṇagaṇajñānaratnasvagarbhaṃ puṇyajñānārkaraśmipravisṛtavipulānantamadhyāmbarābham | buddhatvaṃ ... vilokya*; Tak. "Having completely established the Vehicle, the ocean of knowledge filled with the multitudes of the excellent virtues and endowed with the rays of the sun of Merit and Knowledge, and having perceived that Buddhahood, like space, pervading extensively and of neither limit nor middle ..." Tak. follows T. in making a break after °*raśmi* and in relating *puṇyajñānārkaraśmi* to *yānaṃ* and *pravisṛta*° to *buddhatvaṃ*. T. *yon-tan rin-chen mchog tshogs daṅ-ldan ye-śes chu-mtsho bsod-nams ye-śes ñi-'od can || theg-pa ma-lus ṅes-par bsgrubs-te mtha'-daṅ-dbus med rgya-chen nam-mkha' ltar khyab-pa || saṅs-rgyas-ñid* ... C. relates *puṇya*°...°*bham* to *buddhatvaṃ*. I prefer to follow this interpretation and to translate: "Buddhahood, which is like the sky without end and middle and pervaded by the rays of the sun of merit and knowledge." Ui, also, does not split up *puṇya*°...°*bham* but relates it to *yānaṃ* p. 620: *fukutoku to chie to no hi no hikari o sosogi, kōdai de, hen mo chū mo naki kokū no gotoki jō no subete o jōju-shita no de*, ... The impossibility of this interpretation is clearly shown by 99.9 *vipulānantamadhyatvād bodhir ākāśadhātuvat*. A break after °*raśmi* is impossible because the rays of the sun of merit and wisdom cannot illuminate the Vehicle which is compared to an ocean but only the Buddhahood which is likened to the sky.

101.7-8 *svacittapratibhāso 'yam iti naivaṃ pṛthagjanāḥ | jānanty atha ca tat teṣām avandhyaṃ bimbadarśanam ||* Tak. "Ordinary people do not notice that this is merely a reflection of their mind; still this manifestation of the Buddha's features is useful for fulfilling their aim." A preceding verse (100.16-17) explains that one sees the Buddha appear in one's own mind (*svacetasi*) when it is pure through faith etc. (*śraddhādivimale*) and developed by the virtues of faith, etc. (*śraddhādiguṇabhāvite*). [Tak.'s translation of this verse is rather too free.] Therefore, I think that it is better to translate *svacittapratibhāsa* by "an appearance in their own mind" and *bimdadarśanam* by "the vision of the image (of the Buddha)". *Bimba* refers to the *nirmāṇakāya*, cf. 86.9.

101.17-18 *vaiḍūryasvacchabhūte manasi munipaticchāyādhigamane, citrāṇy utpādayanti pramuditamanasas tadvaj jinasutāḥ ||* Tak. "Similarly, for obtaining the shadow of the Lord of Sages on their mind which is radiant like the Vaiḍūrya stone, the sons of the Buddha, with minds full of delight, produce various pictures showing the Buddha's life, etc." The reading *citrāṇy utpādayanti* gives no good sense. T. has *sems rab-skyed-par byed* (D.; P. *gśegs* instead of *sems*, a mistake due to the preceding *de-bźin*) and C. "they make vows to carry out different acts." Johnston himself had read *cittān vyutpādayanti* which was "corrected" by T. Chowdhury (p. ii). I propose to read *cittāny utpādayanti* which corresponds well to both C. and T.

102.6 *pūrvaśuklānubhāvataḥ*; Tak. "owing to the previous, virtuous experiences". Here as well as in 107.10 (*śubhānubhāvāt*; Tak. "of the pure experiences") Tak. has mistaken *anubhāva* for *anubhava*.

102.7 *yatnasthānamanorūpavikalparahitā sati*; Tak. "[the divine drum], being apart from efforts, from a particular place, from forms of mind, and from thought-constructions." Tak.'s translation is probably the result of the wrong interpretation by T.: *'bad daṅ gnas daṅ yid-gzugs daṅ || rnam-par rtog-pa med*. It is clear from 102.14 (*yatnasthānaśarīracittarahitaḥ śabdaḥ*; P. *'bad gnas lus daṅ sems bral-ba'i || sgra*) that one has to translate as follows: "[the divine drum] which is free from thought-constructions as to effort, place, mind and matter". Tak. equates *manorūpa* and *vikalpa* in 102.7 with *śarīra* and *citta* in 102.14, but *manas* and *rūpa* correspond to *citta* and *śarīra*. Perhaps one must translate *sthāna* by "pitch, tone"; C. (818b29) has "use, function" (*yung*).

102.10-11 *vyāpya buddhasvareṇaivaṃ vibhur jagad aśeṣataḥ / dharmaṃ diśati bhavyebhyo yatnādirahito 'pi san //* Tak. "Similarly in this world, the Buddha who is all-pervading and free from effort and the rest, reaches the Doctrine by his voice towards the worthy without exceptions." I prefer T.'s interpretation: *de-bźin khyab-bdag 'bad-sogs-daṅ // bral-daṅ 'gro-ba ma-lus-pa // saṅs-rgyas gsuṅ-gis khyab-mdzad-de // skal-ldan rnams-la chos ston-to //* = "In the same way, the Lord who pervades the world entirely with his Buddha-voice teaches without effort etc. the Law to the worthy." See Ui's translation, p. 626: *butsu no koe no hibiki mo, hiroku, amasu tokoro mo naku, seken ni shūhen-shite, doryoku-nado o hanarete itemo, butsu ni narubeki mono-tō ni hō o shisetsu-suru no de aru.*

103.4 *asurādiparacakra*°; Tak. "the invasion of Asuras and others." One must follow T.: *lha-ma-yin la-sogs-pa pha-rol-ghi tshogs*, O. "the Asuras and the other hosts of adversaries." Ui translates *cakra* with "weapon" which is possible but less probable, p. 627: *ashura-tō no teki no buki.*

103.5 *asatkāmaratisukhavivecanatayā*; Tak. "owing to its distinguishing bliss from the pleasure caused by evil enjoyment." See *BHSD* s.v. *vivecayati*: "causes to abandon, dissuades from". See Ui's translation, p. 627: *fujitsunaru gokan no yokubō kiraku no raku kara hanareshimeru koto ni yori.*

104.2 *samādhicittārpaṇabhāvavācakam*: T. *tiṅ-'dzin sems-gtod bsam-pa skul-byed ñid //* = *samādhicittārpaṇabhāvacodakam.* This latter reading seems preferable.

104.3-6 *samāsato yat sukhakāraṇaṃ divi kṣitāv anantāsv api lokadhātuṣu / aśeṣalokaspharaṇāvabhāsanaṃ praghoṣam āgamya tad apy udāhṛtam //* Tak. "In short, that which is the cause of bliss, in heaven, on earth, as well as in all the other numberless worlds, is the voice [of the Buddha] which manifests pervadingly in the world leaving no residue; and in respect to those points, thus it is illustrated." T. *mdor-na ma-lus 'jig-rten khams-su yaṅ // lha daṅ sa-gnas bde-ba'i rgyu gaṅ-yin // de ni ma-lus 'jig-rten khyab snaṅ-ba // dbyaṅs-ñid la ni rab-tu brten-par brjod //*; O. "In short, that which is the cause of bliss, in all the regions of the world, the celestial and the earthly is said to have its foundation in the unique voice which pervades the whole of the world without exception." Obermiller's translation corresponds well to the Sanskrit text. For *āgamya* see *BHSD* s.v.: "with reference to, owing to, because of, on account of, thanks to", "that which is the cause of bliss is said to be due to the voice [of the Buddha]".

104.10 *aparicchinna*°; Tak. "without interruption"; rather "without limitation".

106.14 °*śraddhānumānyād*; Tak. "because of their following the faith". Tak.'s translation corresponds to T.: *dad-pa'i rjes-'braṅs-nas.* Perhaps one must read °*śraddhānusārād.*

108.15-16 *sadā sarvatra visṛte dharmadhātunabhastale / buddhasūrye vineyādritannipāto yathārhataḥ //* Tak. remarks: "The readings '*visṛte*' and '*buddhasūrye*' are to be corrected into '*visṛto*' and '*buddhasūryo*', respectively. Also '*vineyādri*' should be changed into '*vineyādrau*' (loc.) and be separated from '*tannipāto*'. So T., C. omit this verse." There is no need to change this verse in this drastic way. T. corresponds to S.: *rtag-tu thams-cad-la khyab-pa // chos-dbyiṅs nam-mkha'i dkyil-du ni // saṅs-rgyas ñi-ma gdul-bya-yi // ri-la ji-ltar 'os-par 'bab //* The fact that T. does not render the locative absolute and has *ri-la* does not mean that the Tibetan translator has made use of a different Sanskrit text.

109.15-16 *yugapad gocarasthānāṃ sarvābhiprāyapūraṇam / kurute nirvikalpo 'pi pṛthak cintāmaṇir yathā //* Tak. "Just as the wishfulfilling gem, though itself is of no thought-construction, fulfills all desires of those living in the same region, separately".

Tak. considers *yugapadgocarastha* as a compound. It seems preferable to relate *yugapad* to *kurute*: "Just as the wishing gem, without discriminations, fulfills simultaneously and separately the wishes of all who are in its reach". T. *ji-ltar yid-bźin nor-bu ni // rtog-pa med-kyaṅ cig-car-du // spyod-yul-gnas-pa rnams-kyi ni // bsam-kun so-sor rdzogs-byed ltar //.*

115.9 *maṇisaṃskṛtāni kanakakṣetrāṇi*; Tak. "golden lands, constructed by jewels"; preferable "adorned with jewels". T. renders *saṃskṛta* by *spras-pa*, not *spros-pa* as given by Tak. See Ui's translation, p. 642: *manishu ni kazarareta ōgon no kokudo o.*

116.10-11 *asty asau viṣayo 'cintyaḥ śakyaḥ prāptuṃ sa mādṛśaiḥ / prāpta evaṃgunaś cāsāv iti śraddhādhimuktitaḥ //* Tak. "Indeed, as he is full of devotion and faith that there 'exists' this inconceivable sphere, that it 'can' be realized by one like him, and this sphere, 'endowed with such virtues', has been attained." The context shows that it is impossible to translate *prāpta* by 'has been attained'. I suggest to translate:"that it (this sphere), when attained, has such good qualities." This interpretation agrees with C: "that it has such good qualities." T. *bsam mi-khyab-pa'i yul 'di ni // yod-pa* (P. *yon-tan*) *bdag-'dras thob* (P. *thos*)*-nus daṅ // thob-pa 'di-'dra'i yon-tan daṅ // ldan żes dad-pas mos-pa'i phyir //* O. "Indeed, he is full of devotion and faith that this inconceivable sphere exists that one like himself can realize it, and, having once attained it, becomes endowed with such properties." Also Ui relates *prāpta* to the wise man mentioned in the preceding verse; cf. p. 643: *soshite tasshita toki ni wa, kare wa kakuno gotoki moromoro no kudoku o uru to.* This translation is not possible because *asau* (which is not rendered in T.) can only refer to *viṣaya.*

117.7-8 *dhiyādhimuktyā kuśalopasaṃpadā samanvitā ye* ...; Tak. "Those intelligent people who are endowed with faith and accomplishment of virtues." Tak.'s interpretation corresponds to C. and T.: *gaṅ-dag mos dge phun-sum-tshogs ldan blo //* but, nevertheless, one must understand *dhiyā-adhimuktyā*: "Those who are endowed with intelligence, faith and the attainment of virtue." See Ui's translation, p. 645: *chi to shinge to o gushi, shuzen bugyō o guseru mono.*

117.18 *śāstaram ekaṃ jinam uddiśadbhiḥ*. Tak. "who refer to the Lord as only Preceptor." See *BHSD* s.v. *uddiśyati*: "*uddiśyati* (= *uddiśati*; not recorded in this sense), recognizes: *Divy.* 191.3 (*māṃ* ...) *śāstaram uddiśyadbhir* ..., those who recognize me as teacher ..."

118.5 *yat svayam eva nītam ṛṣiṇā sūtraṃ vicālyaṃ na tat*; Tak. "the Scripture should not be interpolated, which is discoursed by the Sage himself." *Vi-cal-* means "to depart or deviate from". Therefore, it would be better to translate: "One must not deviate from the discourse taught as final doctrine by the Sage himself."

118.9 *tasmān nābhiniveśadṛṣṭimaline tasmin niveśyā matiḥ*; Tak. "Therefore, your mind should not be attached to the dirt of the prejudiced conception." More precisely: "to that which is soiled by a prejudiced conception".

118.13 *lobhagredhatayā*; Tak. notes that T. has *lābhagredhatayā* (P. *rñed-la brkam*). This reading must be adopted.

In the notes there are many references to the Tibetan text. Tak. has used only the Derge edition. In several cases P. gives a better reading. In some cases the interpretation of the Tibetan translation is not correct. Also quite a few misprints must be corrected. P. 146, n. 27: "For '*svalakṣaṇenānugatāni*', T. as if '*svalakṣaṇasyānugatāni*'". P. *raṅ-mtshan-ñid-kyis rjes-'brel-ba* corresponds to S. p. 148, n. 51: correct *yoṇs-su* to *yoṅs-su*. P. 149, n. 59: correct *ne-bar* to *ñe-bar*. P. 151, n. 74: correct *lal* to *bal*. P. 158. n. 25: correct *śen* to *żen*. P. 166, n. 15: correct *ṅe-tshig* to *ṅes-tshig*. P. 168, n. 29: correct *brol* to *bral*. P. 170, n. 43: correct *mtshan-par* to *mtshan-mar*. P. 176, n. 25: correct *cig-śes* to *cig-śos*. P. 179, n. 49: correct *gzugs-brñen* to *gzugs-brñan*. P. 183, n. 28: correct *gśad* to *gśed*. P. 184, n. 33: correct *thung* to *thug*. P. 185, n. 49: correct *bsñan to brñan*. P. 203, n. 31: read with P. *mun-pa bas kyaṅ ches mun-pa /*

mun-pa nas mun-pa chen-por instead of *mun-pa-las kyaṅ ches, mun-pa chen-por*. P. 209, n. 78: read with P. *gźuṅ* instead of *bźuṅ*; n. 82: correct *ston* to *stoṅ*. P. 216, n. 123: correct *drir* to *dri-ṅa*. P. 221, n. 162: *pratyupasthāpana* (not *pratyupasthāna*) corresponds exactly to T. *ñe-bar gnas-par byed-de*. P. 229, n. 225: read with P. *sgo-nas* instead of *sgo-la*. P. 241, n. 310: read with P. *'go-nad* instead of *mgo'i nad*. P. 254, n. 420: correct *sbyod* to *spyod*. P. 264, n. 491: T. does not omit *ākāra*; P. has *de-rnams* which has to be corrected to *de-rnam*. P. 270, n. 21: read with P. *zum* instead of *thum*. P. 272, n. 40: P. has *kun-tu dag-par*. P. 283, n. 115: correct *sniṅ* to *sñiṅ*. P. 294, n. 4: correct *tshas* to *tshad*. P. 295, n. 12: read with P. *ṅes-par* instead of *ñe-bar*. P. 299, n. 42: *ñe-bar bźag* (D. *gźags)-pa* corresponds to *upasthāpita*, not to *upasthita*. P. 302, n. 63: correct *'phrol* to *'phro-la*. P. 304, n. 76: P. has *mthoṅs*. P. 305, n. 4: correct *lam* to *lan*. P. 306, n. 12.: correct *bgag-cag* to *bdag-chags*; n. 17: correct *spral-ba* to *sprul-pa*. P. 318, n. 35: correct *rjas* to *rdzas*. P. 319, n. 49: read with P. *dam-pa* instead of *dag-pa*. P. 322, n. 65: correct *bstan* to *brtan*. P. 326, n. 102: correct *gzugz* to *gzugs*. P. 328, n. 120: correct *stoṅ* to *ston*. P. 329, n. 133: read with P. *'khor dgyes-rol-pa* instead of *'khor-gyis dkyes-rol*. P. 339, n. 18: delete *go-cha*. P. 341, n. 36: correct *nams* to *ñams*. P. 344, n. 69: read with P. *ni* instead of *riṅ*. P. 346, n. 95: correct *sphu* to *spu*; n; 96: correct *mthor* to *mthon*. P. 357, n. 17: *sgom-pa* renders *bhāvita* P. 358, n. 30: read with P. *lha-bdag* instead of *lha-dag*; T. does not omit *marutām* which is rendered by *lha'i*. P. 362, n. 70: correct *gtoṅ* to *gtod*. P. 363, n. 77: correct *rtogs* to *gtogs*. P. 366, n. 110: read with P. *rdo-tshan* instead of *rdo-than*; n. 111: read with P. *sul* instead of *yul* (cf. Mahāvyutpatti 5260). P. 381, n. 8: read with P. *spras* instead of *spros*; n. 13: *bsgoms* renders *dhyāyed* (115.17). P. 384, n. 33: correct *rje* to *rjes*. P. 386, n. 46: read with P. *rgyal-ba ston-pa* instead of *rgyal-pa'i bstan-pa*. P. 387, n. 63: correct *brtam* to *brkam*. P. 388, n. 71: correct *ṅams* to *ñams* (so P.); n. 76: *bya-ba min* renders *acaraṇa*; *vadhācaraṇa* "the bad act of killing".

Due to a slip of the pen is the remark that *abudha* is Buddhist Hybrid Sanskrit for Sanskrit *abuddha* (p. 155, n. 5; p. 158, n. 20). In note 417 (p. 254) *Catuḥśubha* must be corrected to *Catuḥstava* and *Minor Buddhist Works*, II, etc. to *Minor Buddhist Texts*, II, pp. 235-246, Roma, 1956. Misprints are rather numerous, especially in Sanskrit words. They will give no difficulties to specialists and it is superfluous to list them here.

The translation does not indicate the pages of the Sanskrit text. For this reason a concordance of the page numbers of the text and the translation may be helpful. The first number refers to the text, the second to the translation.

1 – 141	18 – 180	35 – 219	52 – 253	69 – 282
2 – 142	19 – 182	36 – 221	53 – 255	70 – 284
3 – 144	20 – 183	37 – 224	54 – 257	71 – 286
4 – 147	21 – 186	38 – 226	55 – 258	72 – 288
5 – 149	22 – 188	39 – 228	56 – 261	73 – 291
6 – 151	23 – 190	40 – 230	57 – 262	74 – 296
7 – 153	24 – 191	41 – 232	58 – 264	75 – 298
8 – 156	25 – 193	42 – 234	59 – 266	76 – 300
9 – 158	26 197	43 – 237	60 – 269	77 – 303
10 – 160	27 – 200	44 – 238	61 – 270	78 – 306
11 – 163	28 – 202	45 – 240	62 – 271	79 – 310
12 – 166	29 – 205	46 – 242	63 – 272	80 – 314
13 – 169	30 – 207	47 – 244	64 – 273	81 – 316
14 – 172	31 – 209	48 – 246	65 – 274	82 – 318
15 – 174	32 – 212	49 – 248	66 – 276	83 – 320
16 – 176	33 – 215	50 – 249	67 – 277	84 – 321
17 – 178	34 – 217	51 – 252	68 – 280	85 – 323

86 – 325	93 – 341	100 – 356	107 – 368	114 – 379
87 – 327	94 – 342	101 – 357	108 – 369	115 – 380
88 – 329	95 – 345	102 – 359	109 – 370	116 – 381
89 – 332	96 – 347	103 – 361	110 – 372	117 – 383
90 – 334	97 – 347	104 – 362	111 – 374	118 – 386
91 – 336	98 – 351	105 – 364	112 – 375	119 – 388
92 – 339	99 – 353	106 – 366	113 – 377	

A. N. U., Canberra J. W. de Jong

Takasaki Jikidō, *Nyoraizō shisō no keisei* [The formation of the tathāgatagarbha theory]. Tōkyō, Shunjūsha, 1974. xxii + 779 + 106 pp. Yen 9.000.

In 1966 Takasaki published a translation of the *Ratnagotravibhāga* together with a lengthy introduction: *A Study of the Ratnagotravibhāga* (*Uttaratantra*). In a review we expressed the wish that Takasaki would undertake a systematic treatment of the *tathāgatagarbha* theory and its history (*IIJ*, XI, p. 39). His voluminous book is not a complete history of the *tathāgatagarbha* theory in India. According to the English subtitle it is a study on the historical background of the *tathāgatagarbha* theory based upon the scriptures preceding the *Ratnagotravibhāga*.

Takasaki's book contains a detailed table of contents, an English translation of which is given on pp. 3–7. Moreover, the author has added a summary in English (pp. 9–14) which will be very helpful for Western readers. The same section of the book contains five indices: I. Sino-Japanese (pp. 16–41); II. Sanskrit-Pāli (pp. 42–58); III. Tibetan (pp. 59–69); IV. Texts quoted (pp. 70–72); V. Names of scholars quoted (pp. 73–74). The bibliography is divided into a Japanese section (pp. 76–97) and a Western section (pp. 98–106). In the preface the author lists his own contributions to the study of the *tathāgatagarbha* theory: *A Study of the Ratnagotravibhāga* (Roma, 1966) and twenty-seven articles published during a period of twenty years (1953–1972).

Takasaki's book is based upon a careful study of Sanskrit, Pāli, Chinese and Tibetan sources. As is obvious from the extensive bibliography, the number of scholarly publications in Western languages and in Japanese consulted by the author is very considerable. Within the limited scope of a review it is clearly impossible to examine all the problems discussed by the author. We can only attempt to indicate the way in which the author has undertaken his task.

In his introduction Takasaki points out that in the past Japanese studies of the *tathāgatagarbha* theory were not based on the *Ratnagotravibhāga*, although this text was known in Chinese translation, but on such texts as the *Fo-hsing lun* (T. no. 1610), attributed to Vasubandhu and translated by Paramārtha, and the *Ta-ch'eng ch'i-hsin lun* (T. nos. 1666–1667), attributed to Aśvaghoṣa and translated by Paramārtha and Śikṣānanda. Already sixty years ago Mochizuki Shinkō had tried to show that the *Ta-ch'eng ch'i-hsin lun* was not translated from an Indian text but had been compiled in China. Mochizuki's thesis has given rise to a heated controversy among Japanese scholars. In an article, published in 1929, Demiéville defended the authenticity of the text but in a note, added to a reprint of this article, he states without any hesitation that the text has been composed in China.[1] Demiéville lists the

[1] "Sur l'authenticité du *Ta tch'eng k'i sin louen*", *BMFJ*, II, 2 (Tokyo, 1929), pp. 1–78; *Choix d'études bouddhiques* (Leiden, 1973), p. XXXIII. Walter Liebenthal has arrived at the same conclusion, cf.'New light on the Mahāyāna-śraddhotpāda Śāstra', *T'oung Pao* 46 (1958), 155–216.

Japanese studies on this problem published before 1929. Japanese scholars have continued the discussion without coming to any agreement.[2] In a note Takasaki raises doubts about the Indian origin of the text but adds that the apocryphal nature of the text has still to be proved (p. 774, n. 4). As to the *Fo-hsing lun* Hattori Masaaki has demonstrated that it was compiled by Paramārtha on the basis of the *Ratnagotravibhāga* and the *Yogācārabhūmi*.[3] In India and Tibet the Mādhyamika and the Yogācāra are considered the only Mahāyāna schools. Fa-tsang (643–711), the third patriarch of the Hua-yen school, recognized a third Mahāyāna school: the *ju-lai-tsang yüan-ch'i tsung* 'the school of dependent origination based on the *tathāgatagarbha*' but Fa-tsang's concept of this school is based upon texts such as the *Laṅkāvatārasūtra* and the *Ta-ch'eng ch'i-hsin lun* which combine the *garbha* theory with the Vijñānavāda theory of the *ālayavijñāna*. It is therefore not surprising that Japanese scholars, who follow the Sino-Japanese tradition and the traditional exegesis of the Sino-Japanese schools, were not able to form an adequate picture of the *garbha* theory as it existed in India.

Obermiller's translation of the *Ratnagotravibhāga* from the Tibetan (*Acta Orientalia*, IX, 1931, pp. 81–306) stimulated new studies on the *garbha* theory in Japan. Ui reexamined the Chinese materials and Tsukinowa Kenryū (1888–1969) compared Chinese and Tibetan texts.[4] It also became more and more apparent that Paramārtha (500–569) had played an important role in introducing the *garbha* theory in China. Paramārtha combined the *garbha* theory with Vijñānavāda doctrines and composed texts (*Anuttarāśrayasūtra* and the *Fo-hsing lun*) with the intention of giving authority to his theories. Moreover, he incorporated the *garbha* in his translation of Vasubandhu's *Mahāyānasaṃgrahabhāṣya*. Takasaki explains that Paramārtha by making use of the name of Vasubandhu, author of the *Mahāyānasaṃgrahabhāṣya* and alleged author of the *Fo-hsing lun*, has deluded contemporary scholars.

The publication of the Sanskrit text of the *Ratnagotravibhāga* in 1950 gave increased impetus to the study of the *garbha* theory. In Japan Nakamura Zuiryū published in 1961 a synoptic edition of the Sanskrit text and the Chinese translation and in 1967 an edition of the Tibetan text together with a Japanese translation, a Sanskrit-Tibetan-Chinese index and a Tibetan-Sanskrit index. Ui's study and translation of the *Ratnagotravibhāga* appeared in 1959 and Takasaki's English translation in 1966. Sanskrit and Tibetan materials have been studied in Seyfort Ruegg's magnum opus: *La théorie du Tathāgatagarbha et du Gotra* (Paris, 1969). Recently Lambert Schmithausen has published two important articles on the text of the *Ratnagotravibhāga* and Takasaki's translation and on Ruegg's book.[5] Numerous articles have been written in Japanese by Japanese scholars in recent years (cf. Takasaki's bibliography).

Takasaki defines the *tathāgatagarbha* theory as the theory which is propounded by the *Ratnagotravibhāga*. In the first place it is necessary to understand the structure of the

[2] Takasaki points out that Ui Hakuju has defended the authenticity of the text. In an article in a recently published bibliographical dictionary Tamaki Koshirō says that the authenticity is defended by Tokiwa Daijō, Sakaino Kōyō, Hatani Ryōtai, Matsumoto Bunzaburō and Hayashiya Tomojirō. As only supporter of Mochizuki's thesis, he mentions Murakami Senshō (*Shin Butten kaidai jiṭen*, Tōkyō, 1966, p. 158a). For a recent bibliography of the *Ta-ch'eng ch'i-hsin lun* (editions and studies) see Kashiwagi Hiroo's bibliographical appendix to Hirakawa Akira's *Daijōkishiron* (*Butten Kōza*, Vol. 22, Tokyo, 1973), pp. 390–413.

[3] 'Busshōron no ichi kōsatsu', *Bukkyō shigaku* 4 (1955), 160–174 (cf. *Revue Bibliographique de Sinologie*, 2, 1956, no. 584). Cf. also Takasaki's article in the volume in honour of Yūki Reimon: *Bukkyō shisōshi ronshū* (Tōkyō, 1964), pp. 241–264.

[4] Ui Hakuju, *Indo tetsugakushi* (Tōkyō, 1932), pp. 317–322, 407–416 and 418–433. Tsukinowa Kenryū, 'Kukyōichijōhōshōron ni tsuite', *Nihon bukkyō kyōkai nenpō* 7 (1935), 121–139 = *Butten no hihan-teki kenkyū* (Tōkyō, 1972), pp. 364–381.

[5] 'Philologische Bemerkungen zum Ratnagotravibhāga', *WZKSA* **15** (1971), 123–177; 'Zu D. Seyfort Rueggs Buch "La Théorie du Tathāgatagarbha et du Gotra" (Besprechungsaufsatz)", *WZKSA* **18** (1973), 123–160.

Ratnagotravibhāga and the essence of its doctrine. Takasaki explains that the *tathāgatagarbha* theory is based upon the doctrines of several sūtras just as the Mādhyamika doctrine is based on the *Prajñāpāramitāsūtras*, the Yogācāra doctrine on the *Saṃdhinirmocanasūtra* and other texts. The germ of the *tathāgatagarbha* doctrine can be seen in the concept of the original luminosity of the mind.

In China and Japan the most common synonym of *tathāgatagarbha* is the 'Buddha-nature' (*fo-hsing*; Jap. *busshō*). The Sanskrit terms which correspond to *fo-hsing* are according to the *Ratnagotravibhāga buddhadhātu* and *buddhagotra*. The first term is of special importance because it is used in the *Mahāparinirvāṇasūtra*. Nevertheless, the author prefers the term *tathāgatagarbha* because it is found in the colophon of the *Mahāparinirvāṇasūtra* (*kevala-tathāgatagarbhanirdeśasūtra*) and because the *Laṅkāvatārasūtra* uses the term *tathāgatagarbhavāda*. Moreover, the term *buddhadhātu* is not found in either the *Śrīmālāsūtra* or the *Laṅkāvatārasūtra*. Finally, the *Tathāgatagarbhasūtra* is one of the most important sources for the *tathāgatagarbha* doctrine in the *Mahāparinirvāṇasūtra* and the *Ratnagotravibhāga*. The fundamental idea of the *Tathāgatagarbhasūtra* is expressed in the formula: *sarvasattvās tathāgatagarbhāḥ* which Takasaki translates "all beings possess the *tathāgatagarbha*".[6]

Takasaki formulates as working hypotheses: 1. The *tathāgatagarbha* theory has been systematized in the *Ratnagotravibhāga*. 2. The *tathāgatagarbha* theory teaches that in all beings the *tathāgatagarbha*, i.e. the cause of potential Buddhahood is present. 3. It is necessary to trace the formation of this theory and of this theory only. 4. In Mahāyāna Buddhism the possibility for the beings to become Buddha is widely recognized but the *tathāgatagarbha* theory has arisen in opposition to the Śūnyavāda.

The method adopted by the author consists of three parts: 1. Examination of the texts (*sūtras* and *śāstras*) which are quoted in the *Ratnagotravibhāga* and which teach the *tathāgatagarbha* doctrine. Study of their doctrinal content, the place of the *tathāgatagarbha* theory in them and their relation to other texts. 2. Examination of texts which are not quoted in the *Ratnagotravibhāga* but which proclaim the *tathāgatagarbha* theory. In the case of these texts it is necessary to investigate whether they are earlier or later than the *Ratnagotravibhāga*. 3. Examination of texts, quoted or not in the *Ratnagotravibhāga* and which do not make use of the term *tathāgatagarbha* but which have nevertheless fulfilled an important function with regard to the formation of the *tathāgatagarbha* theory.

The first part of the book dealing with the formation of the *tathāgatagarbha* theory examines the texts in groups one and two. The study of the texts in the third group forms the second part dealing with the pre-history of the *tathāgatagarbha* theory. The first part is divided into four chapters. Chapter one deals with the three scriptures which are of fundamental importance for the formation of the *tathāgatagarbha* theory: the *Tathāgatagarbhasūtra*, the *Anūnatvāpūrṇatvanirdeśa* and the *Śrīmālāsūtra*. The second chapter studies the *Mahāparinirvāṇasūtra* and related texts which use both the terms *buddhadhātu* and *tathāgatagarbha*. Chapter three is devoted to a study of the *gotra* theory in the *Mahāmeghasūtra* and the *Mahāyānadaśadharmaka*. Chapter four deals briefly with the identification of the *tathāgatagarbha* with the *ālayavijñāna*. However, Takasaki points out that this topic does not belong to the first period in the history of the *tathāgatagarbha* theory from the beginning up to and including the *Ratnagotravibhāga* but to the second period which will be studied by the author in a forthcoming publication. The two appendices to this chapter deal with the chapter on the three *kāyas* in the *Suvarṇaprabhāsottamasūtra*, and with the relation between the *Śrīmālāsūtra* and the *Vijñānavāda*.

[6] Seyfort Ruegg has pointed out that in the texts the compound *tathāgatagarbha* is understood mostly as a *tatpuruṣa* but sometimes also as a *bahuvrīhi* (op. cit., pp. 507–513). Takasaki remarks that in the *Ratnagotravibhāga* it is analysed as (1) a *tatpuruṣa* (*tathāgatasyeme garbhāḥ sarvasattvāḥ*), (2) a *karmadhāraya* (*tathāgatas tathataiṣāṃ garbhaḥ sarvasattvānām*) and as (3) a *bahuvrīhi* (*tathāgatadhātur eṣāṃ garbhaḥ sarvasattvānām*), cf. p. 21. Seyfort Ruegg considers rightly (2) as a *bahuvrīhi*.

The second part of the book deals with the pre-history of the *tathāgatagarbha* theory and investigates a great number of *Mahāyānasūtras* which contain concepts which are of essential importance for the formation of the *tathāgatagarbha* theory, such as *gotra*, *dhātu* and *cittaprakṛti* or concepts related to it such as *dharmakāya*, *dharmatā*, *tathatā*, *tathāgata*, *ekayāna*, etc. Among the sūtras studied are the *Prajñāpāramitāsūtras*, the *Saddharmapuṇḍarīka*, the *Kāśyapaparivarta*, the *Vimalakīrtinirdeśasūtra*, the *Śūraṃgamasamādhisūtra*, texts belonging to the *Buddhāvataṃsaka*, the *Jñānālokālaṃkārasūtra*, the *Dhāraṇīśvararājasūtra* and texts belonging to the *Mahāsannipātasūtra*.

A concluding chapter deals with three topics: 1. The history of the Chinese translations of texts relating to the *tathāgatagarbha* theory. The author distinguishes three periods: 1. The stage of the sūtras translated by Buddhabhadra, Guṇabhadra and Dharmakṣema. 2. The stage of the śāstras translated by Bodhiruci, Ratnamati, Paramārtha, Hsüan-tsang and I-tsing. 3. The stage of the tantric texts beginning immediately after Hsüan-tsang. The first stage is the period of the formation of the sūtras which expound the *tathāgatagarbha* theory. The second is the period of the śāstras which combine the *tathāgatagarbha* with the *ālayavijñāna*. The third is the period in which the *tathāgatagarbha* theory is combined with tantric ideas. The translations belonging to these three stages were made in 1. the fifth century; 2. the sixth and the first half of the seventh century; 3. from the middle of the seventh century onward. Takasaki adds that the original Indian texts were composed roughly a century earlier but that some texts must have been translated almost immediately after they had been composed. A table clearly illustrates the history of the Chinese translations. A second table illustrates the development of the basic concepts connected with the *tathāgatagarbha* theory: 1. *gotra* (*vaṃśa*, *kula*, *buddhaputra*, etc.); 2. *citta* (*cittaprakṛtiprabhāsvaratā*); 3. *tathāgatagarbha*; 4. *dhātu* (*sattvadhātu*, *buddha* – and *dharma*-); 5. *dharmakāya* (*tathāgata* and *dharmakāya*); 6. other items (*guhya*, *saṃdhāvacana*, *uttaratantra*). The historical development of these concepts with the exception of the *tathāgatagarbha* itself is briefly outlined by the author (pp. 751–771). The same section contains also a table illustrating the relations between the sūtras and śāstras which propound the *tathāgatagarbha* theory or which have fulfilled an important function in its formation (p. 769). The final section of this chapter is entitled "Remaining problems". Takasaki points out that his book deals mainly with the first period in the history of the *tathāgatagarbha* theory which concludes with the composition of the *Ratnagotravibhāga* in the beginning of the fifth century. The next task which lies ahead is the history of the *tathāgatagarbha* theory in the second period in which the *tathāgatagarbha* doctrine is combined with *Vijñānavāda* doctrines. The author remarks that this second period is important not only in itself, but also because it has exercised its influence in four directions. I. The *tathāgatagarbha* theory was completely absorbed by the *Vijñānavāda* and the existence of the *Ratnagotravibhāga* was almost entirely forgotten. After this period which is dominated by disputes between the Mādhyamika and Yogācāra schools, the tradition of the *Ratnagotravibhāga* was revived and both the *Abhisamalālaṃkāra* and the *Ratnagotravibhāga* are numbered among the five texts of Maitreya. II. The revival of the *Ratnagotravibhāga* and the formation of a group of five texts attributed to Maitreya must have taken place in recent times because both phenomena are unknown in China. However, they are of the greatest importance for the history of the exegesis of the *tathāgatagarbha* theory in Tibet. III. In China the idea that "All beings possess the Buddha-nature" has had an enormous influence since the beginning of the fifth century at which time two recensions of the *Mahāparinirvāṇasūtra* were translated by Fa-hsien (T. no. 376) and by Dharmakṣema (T. no. 374). A striking feature of the history of the *tathāgatagarbha* theory in China is the popularity of texts the Indian origin of which is doubtful: the second part of Dharmakṣema's translation of the *Mahāparinirvāṇasūtra*, the *Fo-hsing lun*, the *Ta-ch'eng ch'i-hsin lun* and the *Vajrasamādhisūtra*.[7] IV. The *tathāgatagarbha* theory is mentioned in tantric texts such as the

[7] For this text see P. Demiéville, *Le concile de Lhasa* (Paris, 1952), pp. 54–58; Walter Liebenthal, 'Notes on the "Vajrasamādhi"', *T'oung Pao* **44** (1956), 347–386.

Prajñāpāramitānayaśatapañcaśatikā.[8] Takasaki points out that this theory has also influenced tantric theories in many respects as can be shown by tracing the history of the idea of the *bodhicitta*.

We hope that we have been able to give at least an idea of the scope of Takasaki's magnum opus. His main purpose has been to trace the formation of the *tathāgatagarbha* theory and its prehistory. According to Takasaki the first period in the history of this theory ends with its definite formulation in the *Ratnagotravibhāga* in the beginning of the fifth century. Takasaki's book has given the *tathāgatagarbhavāda* its proper place as the third Mahāyāna school. However, its importance is not limited to the early history of the *tathāgatagarbha* theory in India. This theory is so closely interrelated with the philosophical ideas expressed in many Mahāyānasūtras that it is no exaggeration to say that Takasaki's book is at the same time of fundamental importance for the history of Mahāyāna philosophy in general.

Canberra J. W. DE JONG

NOTES ON THE SECOND CHAPTER OF THE MADHYĀNTAVIBHĀGAṬĪKĀ

by
J. W. DE JONG
Canberra

In 1928 Sylvain Lévi obtained in Kathmandu a copy of an incomplete manuscript of Sthiramati's Madhyāntavibhāgaṭīkā, a commentary on Vasubandhu's Madhyāntavibhāgabhāṣya which explains the *kārikā*-s written by Maitreya. Sylvain Lévi entrusted the edition of the text to Yamaguchi Susumu who first edited the Sanskrit text of the first two chapters in several issues of the Ōtani Gakuhō in the years 1930–1932.[1] In 1934 Yamaguchi published an edition of the complete text in which the missing parts were restored with the help of the Tibetan translation.[2] In 1930 Tucci announced an edition with a complete restoration into Sanskrit from the Tibetan of all missing passages, by himself and Vidhuśekhara Bhaṭṭācārya.[3] The first and only chapter of this edition appeared in 1932.[4] Yamaguchi published a complete Japanese translation of the Madhyāntavibhāgaṭīkā in 1935.[5] The first chapter was rendered into English simultaneously by Th. Stcherbatsky and D. L. Friedmann.[6]

---

[1] Vol. XI (1930), pp. 576–602; Vol. XII (1931), pp. 24–67; 307–335; 719–775; Vol. XIII (1932), pp. 59–99. Cf. L. de La Vallée Poussin, *Mélanges chinois et bouddhiques*, I (1932), pp. 400–403 (on p. 400 correct Shukyokenkyu to Ōtani Gakuhō).

[2] Sthiramati, Madhyāntavibhāgaṭīkā. Exposition systématique du Yogācāravijñaptivāda. Tome I. Texte. Nagoya, Hajinkaku, 1934. Reprinted by the Suzuki Research Foundation, Tokyo in 1966.

[3] 'Animadversiones Indicae', *JASB*, 26 (1930), pp. 195–196.

[4] Madhyāntavibhāgasūtrabhāṣyaṭīkā of Sthiramati, being a subcommentary on Vasubandhu's Bhāṣya on the Madhyāntavibhāgasūtra of Maitreyanātha. Part I, 1932 (Calcutta, Oriental Series, no. 24). Cf. Obermiller's review, *IHQ*, IX (1933), pp. 1019–1030.

[5] Anne ashariya zō Chūbenfunbetsuron shakusho. Nagoya, Hajinkaku, 1935. Reprinted by The Suzuki Research Foundation, Tokyo in 1966.

[6] Th. Stcherbatsky, Madhyāntavibhaṅga. Discourse on Discrimination between Middle and Extremes ascribed to Maitreya and commented by Vasubandhu and Sthiramati. Moscow–Leningrad, 1936 (*Bibliotheca Buddhica*, XXX). Cf. L. de La Vallée Poussin, *Mélanges chinois et bouddhiques*, V (1937),

In 1937 Yamaguchi published a synoptic edition of the Tibetan translation and the two Chinese translations by Paramārtha and Hsüan-tsang of Vasubandhu's *bhāṣya*.[7] A translation of the third chapter of the *bhāṣya* was published by Paul Wilfred O'Brien S. J. in 1953–1954.[8] In 1934 Rahula Sankrityāyana discovered a manuscript of the *bhāṣya* in the Ṅor Monastery in Tibet. The text was published by Gadjin M. Nagao in 1964.[9] Nagao also translated chapters 1 and 3 of the *bhāṣya*[10] and a complete translation is due to appear in vol. 15 of the Daijō butten. Another edition of the *bhāṣya* appeared in 1967.[11] Vasubandhu's *bhāṣya* contains the complete text of the *kārikā*-s. Parts of both the *kārikā*-s and the *bhāṣya* are quoted in Sthiramati's *ṭīkā*. The publication of the text of the *kārikā*-s and the *bhāṣya* makes it possible to correct the text of the quotations in the *ṭīkā*. This is of course especially important for the quotations which have been restored from the Tibetan by the editors of the *ṭīkā*.

The restoration of a Sanskrit text from the Tibetan is a difficult undertaking. I believe that in the case of a philosophical text such as the Madhyāntavibhāgaṭīkā, which has been carefully translated into Tibetan, it is justified to attempt to reconstruct at least the technical terms. With the help of parallel passages it is also sometimes possible to restore the original Sanskrit text. However, it is certainly impossible to reconstruct the original text in its entirety. La Vallée Poussin, quoting Tucci's words: "by the combined efforts of myself and of Vidhuśekhara Śāstri, it is hoped to be restored completely in its Sanskrit original form", comments as follows: "Magnanime pensée! Car il est rare qu'on puisse restituer avec confiance ne fût-ce qu'une strophe estropiée ou lacuneuse."[12] How different the results of attempted restorations can be is clearly

pp. 271–273. D. L. Friedmann, Sthiramati, Madhyantavibhāgaṭīkā. Analysis of the Middle Path and the Extremes. Utrecht, Utr. Typ. Ass., 1937.

7 Kanzō taishō Benchūbenron. Nagoya, Hajinkaku, 1939. Reprinted by the Suzuki Research Foundation, Tokyo in 1966.

8 'A Chapter on Reality from the Madhyântavibhâgaçâstra', *Monumenta Nipponica*, 9 (1953), pp. 277–303; 10 (1954), pp. 227–269.

9 Madhyāntavibhāga-bhāṣya. A Buddhist Philosophical Treatise Edited for the first time from a Sanskrit Manuscript. Tokyo, Suzuki Research Foundation, 1964.

10 Sekai no meicho, vol. 2: Daijō butten (Tōkyō, 1967), pp. 397–426.

11 Madhyānta-vibhāga-bhāṣya. Deciphered & Edited by Nathmal Tatia & Anantalal Thakur. Patna, K. P. Jayaswal Research Institute, 1967 (*Tibetan Sanskrit Works Series*, vol. X).

12 *Mélanges chinois et bouddhiques*, V (1937), p. 401.

shown by the two editions of the first chapter and Stcherbatsky's translation of the same chapter in which many passages have been restored in the notes. Until recently the only text available for chapters 2 to 5 of Sthiramati's *ṭīkā* was that published by Yamaguchi in 1934. Yamaguchi's restorations are based upon a careful study of the Sanskrit text of the *ṭīkā* and the Tibetan and Chinese translations of the *kārikā*-s, the *bhāṣya* and the *ṭīkā*. However, Yamaguchi's restorations are not always acceptable and, in several cases, the restored text is written in unidiomatic or even incorrect Sanskrit. In 1971 Ramchandra Pandeya published the Sanskrit text of the *kārikā*-s, the *bhāṣya* and the *ṭīkā*.[13] According to the preface his edition corrects the text of the missing parts of the *ṭīkā* with the help of the Tibetan version and the text of the *bhāṣya*. Pandeya has noted the readings of the *bhāṣya*, but his claim to have made use of the Tibetan translation of the *ṭīkā* is not borne out by an examination of several passages of the second chapter. He seems to have done nothing more than to correct Yamaguchi's restorations according to his own light without any recourse to the Tibetan version.

In the following notes all references are to page and line of Yamaguchi's edition. P = the Peking edition of the Tibetan translation of the *ṭīkā* in volume 109 of the Japanese reprint. R.P. = Ramchandra Pandeya's edition. Sanskrit words which have been restored by Yamaguchi are printed in italics.

P. 67.28–68.1: yaṅ-na ji-ltar Dkon-mchog-brtsegs-pa chen-po-las / de'i bsam-pa mya-ṅan-las 'das-pa yaṅ gnas-la / 'khor-ba-na yaṅ sbyor-bar gnas-pa źes bstan-pa lta-bu ste. Yamaguchi's restoration: atha vā yathoktaṃ Mahāratnakūṭe / tasyāśayaś nirvāṇe ca tiṣṭhati saṃsāre caprayogena tiṣṭhatīti (p. 267.4–6). In his translation Yamaguchi refers to von Staël-Holstein's preface to his edition of the Kāśyapaparivarta (Shanghai, 1926), p. XV: "The assumption that Sthiramati himself regarded Ratnakūṭa as the title of the work he had commented upon seems also to be supported by the concluding verse of the commentary." Yamaguchi adds that he has not been able to trace the quotation in the Chinese translations of the Kāśyapaparivarta. However, it is to be found in section 16 of the Sanskrit text: nirvāṇagataś cāsyāśayaḥ saṃsāragataś ca prayo-

[13] Madhyānta-vibhāga-śāstra. Containing the Kārikā-s of Maitreya, Bhāṣya of Vasubandhu and Ṭīkā by Sthiramati. Critically Edited by Ramchandra Pandeya. Delhi-Varanasi-Patna, Motilal Banarsidass, 1971.

gaḥ. The Tibetan translation of the Kāśyapaparivarta has: de'i bsam-pa mya-ṅan-las 'das-pa la yaṅ gnas-la sbyor-ba 'khor-ba-na yaṅ gnas-pa. R. P.: sa āśayena nirvāṇe tiṣṭhati, saṃsāre ca prayogeṇa tiṣṭhatīti.

P. 72.7: ātmā*tmaśūnyatāyāḥ* P.: bdag daṅ bdag-gir (P. gis) stoṅ-pa-ñid. Read: ātmātmīyaśūnyatāyāḥ. Cf. p. 72.16: tatra satkāyadṛṣṭiḥ pañcasūpādānaskandheṣv ātmata ātmīyato (Yamaguchi -ta) veti *darśanam*. R. P. ātmany ātmaśūnyatāyāḥ.

P. 73.21: *sarvaguṇadoṣasya prakṛṣṭāpanītasya paryantāśrayatvena buddharatne parijñānam*. P. saṅs-rgyas dkon-mchog-la yon-tan daṅ ñes-pa thams-cad phul-du phyin-pa daṅ / bsal-ba'i mthar-thug-pa'i gnas-su yoṅs-su śes-pa'o. Cf. p. 189.22: sarvaguṇadoṣaprakarṣāpakarṣaniṣṭhādhiṣṭhānatvād buddhasya, P.: yon-tan daṅ ñes-pa thams-cad phul-du phyin-pa daṅ bsal (P. brtsal)-ba'i mthar-phyin-pas-na saṅs-rgyas-su grub-pa ste. Read: sarvaguṇadoṣaprakarṣāpakarṣaniṣṭhādhiṣṭhānatvena buddharatne parijñānam. R. P. prakarṣeṇā'panītasarvaguṇadoṣasya paryantāśrayatvena buddharatne parijñānam.

P. 79.16: kujano hi pratipattiyuktam api bodhisattvopamitaṃ na jānīte. P.: skye-bo ṅan-pa ni sgrub-pa daṅ-ldan-pa'i byaṅ-chub sems-dpa' la 'di'o źes mi śes-pa'o. Read: kujano hi pratipattiyuktam api bodhisattvo 'yam iti na jānīte. R. P. has the same text as Yamaguchi.

P. 80.1: sarvatragadharmadhātubodhapratibaddhasya. Read: -pratibandhasya. P.: chos-kyi dbyiṅs thams-cad-du 'gro-bar khoṅ-du chud-par bya-ba'i bgegs-su gyur-pa. R. P. has the same text as Yamaguchi.

P. 85.12: bodheḥ sthitiviyātaṃ kurvantīti. P.: byaṅ-chub-kyi gnas-pa-la gnod-pa byed-pa'i phyir. Read: bodheḥ sthitivighātaṃ kurvantīti. R. P.: bodheḥ sthitiṃ kurvantīti.

P. 89.17: tatra sādhāraṇaṃ bodhipakṣāḥ śrāvakabodhisattvayor aviśeṣeṇa tatrāvikārāt. P.: der gtogs-pas ñan-thos daṅ byaṅ-chub sems-dpa' gñi-ga'i bya-ba bye-brag med-pa'i phyir de-la byaṅ-chub-kyi phyogs ni thun-moṅ-ba'o. Read: tatrādhikārāt. In the Tibetan translation of the Triṃśikā gtogs-pa is used to translate adhikāra (ed. Sylvain Lévi p. 29.18), cf. Nagasawa Jitsudō, 'Bonzōkan taishō Yuishiki sanjūjushaku goi', *Taishō daigaku kenkyū kiyō*, 40 (1955), p. 17. R. P. has the same text as Yamaguchi.

P. 91.22: *aparipūrṇena cchandavīryacittamīmāṃsānām anyatama*-vaikalyād [vikala]bhāvanayā ca prahāṇasaṃskāravaikalyād iti. P.:

'dun-pa daṅ brtson-'grus daṅ sems daṅ / dpyod-pa rnams las gaṅ-yaṅ ruṅ-ba źig ma-tshaṅ-ba yoṅs-su rdzogs-pa daṅ / spoṅ-ba'i 'du-byed bsgom-pa ma-tshaṅ-bas źes-bya-ba. This passage is a quotation from the *bhāṣya*, cf. Nagao's edition p. 33.10: paripūryā ca cchandavīryacittamīmānsānām anyatamavaikalyāt / bhāvanayā ca prahāṇasaṃskāravaikalyāt. The Tibetan translation of the *bhāṣya* has: 'dun-pa daṅ / brtson-'grus daṅ sems daṅ / dpyod-rnams las gaṅ-yaṅ ruṅ-ba źig ma-tshaṅ-bas yoṅs-su rdzogs-pa daṅ / spoṅ-ba'i 'du-byed bsgom-pa ma-tshaṅ-bas (Yamaguchi's edition, p. 35.7). Sthiramati's *ṭīkā* explains that samādhi can have two deficiencies (p. 91.21: samādher dvayahīnatā āvaraṇam uktam): 1. Lack of completeness because of the absence of chanda, vīrya, citta or mīmāṃsā (p. 92.1: tatra paripūrihīnatā tāsāṃ chandavīryacittamīmāṃsānām anyatamavaikalyāt). 2. Absence of bhāvanā because of the absence of one of the eight prahāṇasaṃskāra (p. 92.2: bhāvanā hīyata *ity aṣṭaprahāṇasaṃskārāṇām anyatamavaikalyāt*). R. P. reads aparipūryā instead of paripūryā. The edition of the *Madhyāntavibhāgabhāṣya* by Nathmal Tatia and Anantalal Thakur has apāripūryā. The instrumentals paripūryā and bhāvanayā depend on the preceding word in the *bhāṣya:* dvayahīnatā. In his edition Nagao adds a daṇḍa between hīnatā and paripūryā. This daṇḍa is not to be found in the manuscript and has to be omitted.[14]

P. 95.16: *upaśāntyā gaurava utpadyamāne sattvāḥ saṃja*lparddhyaprayatnena śāsanaṃ pratipadyante. P.: ñe-bar źi-bas gus-pa skye-ste sems-can kun-brjod-pa daṅ rdzu-'phrul-gyis (P. gyi) bsgrim mi-dgos-par bstan-pa rtogs-par byed-do. Tibetan kun-brjod-pa translates ādeśanā, cf. Abhidharmakośabhāṣya (ed. P. Pradhan), p. 424.10; ṛddhicetaḥparyāyāsravakṣayābhijñās trīṇi prātihāryāṇi yathākramam ṛddhyādeśanānuśāsanaprātihāryāṇi. Read: ādeśanayārddhyā cāyatnena ? MS. . . . rādyāvāyatnena. R. P.: sañjalparddhyā'prayatnena.

P. 96.22: *yathābhūtaśrutārtha*vicāraṇā. P.: thos-pa'i don-la sgra

[14] In an article in Japanese, 'Some Problems in the Madhyāntavibhāgabhāṣya', *Journal of Indian and Buddhist Studies*, XXII (1974), pp. 402–406, which came to my notice after having written these notes, Funahashi Naoya discusses this passage. I am glad to see that he has arrived at the same solution. Funahashi has also written two articles on the *bhāṣya* in Japanese: 'Some Problems in the Madhyāntavibhāga-bhāṣya – with special reference to the three chapters: lakṣaṇa-pariccheda, āvaraṇa-pariccheda and tattva-pariccheda'. *Ōtani Gakuhō*, LII, 3 (1973), pp. 50–66; 'Japanese translation and study of the Madhyāntavibhāga-bhāṣya (āvaraṇa-pariccheda)', *Bukkyōgaku Seminā*, vols. 18–19. I have not yet been able to see the second article.

ji-bźin-du spyod-pa. Yamaguchi indicates that yathābhūtaśrutārtha is quoted from the *bhāṣya*, cf. Nagao's edition p. 34.17: ayathārutaśrutārthāvabodhāt. Read: yathārutaśrutārthavicāraṇā. R. P. has the same text as Yamaguchi.

P. 101.9: viśiṣṭārthaprārthanayā sutarām ātmamātrīkaraṇāt. P.: khyad-par-du 'phags-pa'i don-la smos-pas bdag śin-tu snod-du byed-pa'i phyir-ro. Read: ātmapātrikaraṇāt. R. P. has the same text as Yamaguchi.

P. 102.11: śrutārthaṃ sarvakleśasahanādibhir *apy abhedyāt*. P.: thos-pa'i ched-du ñon-moṅs-pa thams-cad la yaṅ mi 'byid-pa'i phyir-ro. Yamaguchi adds in a note that sahana is not rendered into Tibetan. His restoration is clearly based upon a misreading: mi-'byed-pa'i instead of mi-'byid-pa'i. The Tibetan translation has translated sarvakleśasahanāt rather freely: "because he does not slip in all impurities". Read: sarvakleśasahanād iti. R. P.: sarvakleśasahanādibhir apy abhedyatvāt.

P. 107.3: samādhisamāpattyādikam uttarottarabhūmiviśiṣṭaṃ sarvākāraṃ nānāvasānaṃ phalaṃ. P.: tiṅ-ṅe-'dzin brgya-la sñoms-par 'jug-pa la sogs-pa sa goṅ-nas goṅ-du khyad-du 'phags-pa rnchog-rnams-kyi ye-śes-kyi mthar-thug-pa'i 'bras-bu. Read: sarvākārajñānāvasānaṃ. R. P. has the same text as Yamaguchi.

It would certainly be possible to propose a different text for other passages restored by Yamaguchi, but there is not much to be gained by correcting Yamaguchi's restorations unless they can be shown to be wrong or improved by making use of parallel passages. From the examples given above it is obvious that Ramchandra Pandeya has not made any contribution towards the establishment of a more correct Sanskrit text on the basis of the Tibetan translation. In his introduction he accuses Yamaguchi of having failed to read the MS. correctly and of possessing insufficient familiarity with the complicated grammar of Sanskrit.[15] Elsewhere in his preface he states that "many scholars, like Yamaguchi, have committed serious mistakes because of their preference for Tibetan or Chinese versions over original Sanskrit". Pandeya adds that "when the original Sanskrit is available, not much reliance should be placed on Tibetan

[15] Pandeya does not seem to have had access to the manuscript used by Yamaguchi. For a well-founded opinion of Pandeya's carefulness in reading manuscripts see Wezler's remarks in his article: 'Some Observations on the Yuktidīpikā', *Supplement II. XVIII. Deutscher Orientalistentag.* Vorträge herausgegeben von Wolfgang Voigt. Wiesbaden, 1974, pp. 434–455.

or Chinese translations", but he seems to be unaware of the fact that a single manuscript (in this case a recent copy of a manuscript) does not represent the original Sanskrit text and that its value can only be judged with the help of Tibetan and Chinese translations. If Pandeya had carefully studied the Tibetan translation of Sthiramati's *ṭīkā*, his edition would have been welcome. In the study of Buddhist Sanskrit texts the Tibetan translations cannot be neglected without harmful consequences.

Karunesha Shukla (ed.), *Śrāvakabhūmi of Ācārya Asaṅga* [= *Tibetan Sanskrit Works Series* vol. XIV]. Patna, K. P. Jayaswal Research Institute, 1973. CV + 511 pp. Rs. 45.00.

In 1961 Alex Wayman published an *Analysis of the Śrāvakabhūmi Manuscript* in which he edited and translated many passages of the text. The first three chapters of Wayman's work deal

[4] Shinichi Tsuda, *The Saṁvarodaya-tantra. Selected Chapters* (Tokyo, 1974), p. 124 (= Ch. XVII, 43).

[5] Gli otto cimiteri nella letteratura liturgica.

with paleography, literary history and the language of the Śrāvakabhūmi manuscript. Karunesha Shukla's edition contains the text of the Śrāvakabhūmi and a long introduction. According to the editor a second volume will contain four appendices: 1. The lost portions of the text reconstructed from the Tibetan version; 2. A list of verses occurring in the text; 3. The text of Asaṅga's views on Hetuvidyā from the Cintamayībhūmi; 4. The text of the various *gāthāvyavasthānas*.

Shukla's edition is based on a unique manuscript and it is of course not possible to know how far the editor has correctly reproduced the readings of his manuscript. A request for photocopies of the manuscript (letter 15 May 1974) remained unanswered. However, it is possible to compare some passages, edited by Wayman, with the corresponding passages of Shukla's edition. Both Wayman and Shukla have pointed out that the photocopies of the manuscript are often difficult to read. Wayman has carefully compared the Tibetan translation which assisted him greatly in deciphering the readings of the manuscript. In his preface Shukla remarks that there are three translations of the Śrāvakabhūmi into Tibetan. Shukla adds that "Prof. V. Bhattacharya informs us that Jinamitra also translated the work into Tibetan. We had, however; an access only to the portions of the version as preserved in the Tibetan Tripiṭaka (Tanjour, Vol. 110) through secondary sources". (p. xxii). It is obvious from the above remarks that the editor himself has not been able to use the Tibetan translation (not to mention the four translations invented by him!). In his foreword he expresses his thanks to Shri L. Jamspal for his help in reading the Tibetan version. Shri L. Jamspal's help seems to have been of little avail to the editor as will be shown below on the basis of some selected passages.

On the first page of his book Wayman quoted Johnston's words: "No Buddhist text in Sanskrit can be satisfactorily edited without detailed comparison with such Chinese and Tibetan versions as exist". Scholars such as Vidhusekhara Bhattacharya have been fully aware of the importance of the Tibetan versions of Buddhist texts and Bhattacharya's edition of the first five bhūmis of the *Bahubhūmikavastu* of the *Yogācārābhūmi* is based upon a careful comparison of the manuscript with the Tibetan version. Bhattacharya had an excellent knowledge of Tibetan and he was not obliged to rely on the help of a Tibetan scholar. It is a great pity that his example seems to have had little impact in India.

In discussing a few passages of the text of the *Śrāvakabhūmi* the following abbreviations have been used: T. = Tibetan translation (Peking edition, Mdo-'grel, vol. L); C. = Chinese translation (references are given to page, column and line of the Taishō edition, vol. 30, No. 1579, pp. 395–477); W. = Wayman's *Analysis of the Śrāvakabhūmi Manuscript*; S. = Shukla's edition.

S. p. 9.18–19: *teṣāṃ saṃvarāya pratipadyate* [/] *sa śrotreṇa śabdāṃ* (*bdān*); W. p. 61: *teṣāṃ saṃvarāya pratipadyate rakṣati mana-indriyaṃ sa śrotreṇa śabdān*. The words *rakṣati mana-indriyaṃ*, which are found in Wayman's edition, are absent from Shukla's edition. From the Tibetan translation it is clear that the text of the manuscript is corrupt. T. 6a5–6: *de-dag bsdam-par bya-ba'i phyir sgrub-par byed-ciṅ / mig-gi dbaṅ-po yaṅ sruṅ-bar byed-la / mig-gi dbaṅ-pos kyaṅ sdom-pa sgrub-par byed-pa daṅ / de rna-bas sgra-dag* = *teṣāṃ saṃvarāya pratipadyate / rakṣati cakṣurindriyam / cakṣurindriyeṇa saṃvaram āpadyate / sa śrotreṇa śabdān*. C. (397a24–25) agrees with T. The corruption of the manuscript is probably due to the fact that the scribe read the words *rakṣati mana-indriyam* in the following line of the manuscript (cf. S. p. 10.2), substituted them for *rakṣati cakṣurindriyam* and then omitted the words *cakṣurindriyeṇa saṃvaram āpadyate*. Of course, this conclusion can be substantiated only if the manuscript does, in fact, contain the words *rakṣati mana-indriyam* as indicated by Wayman. Neither Wayman nor Shukla have indicated here any disagreement of the text of the manuscript with either the Tibetan or the Chinese version.

S. pp. 10.11–11.5: *jāgarikānuyogaḥ katamaḥ* / [*sa divā caṃkramaniṣadyābhyām āvaraṇīyebhyo dharmebhyaś cittaṃ pari*] *śodhayati / sa divā caṃkramaniṣadyābhyām āvaraṇīyebhyo dharmebhyaś cittam pariśodhya, tato vihārān nirgamya, bahir vihārasya pādau prakṣālya, dakṣiṇena pārśvena siṃhaśayyāṃ kalpayaty ālokasaṃjñī*. W. p. 62: *jāgarikānuyogaḥ katamaḥ* / [In the following, I have had to correct the partially illegible manuscript and fill it in by means of the later extended treatment of the same subject.] [*sa*(*s*). . .] *divā caṅkrama-niṣadyābhyām āvaraṇīyebhyo dharmebhyaś cittaṃ pariśodhayati / rātryāḥ prathame yāme caṅkrama-niṣadyābhyām āvaraṇīyebhyo dharmebhyaś cittaṃ pariśodhayati / pariśodhya tato vihārān nirgamya bahir vihārasya pādau prakṣālya vihāraṃ praviśya dakṣiṇena pārśvena śayyāṃ kalpayati / pāde pādam ādhāyālokasaṃjñī*. I have quoted a large part of this passage because it shows clearly the importance of a comparison of the manuscript with the Tibetan translation. Shukla remarks: "MS. leaf blurred with ink, photo indistinct and illegible, construed from the text that follows (sic)". T. 6b3-5: *nam-gyi cha-stod daṅ nam-gyi cha-smad-la mi-ñal-bar sbyor-ba'i rjes-su brtson-pa ñid gaṅ-że-na / de-ltar zas-kyi tshod rig-par gyur-pa de ñin-mo 'chag-pa daṅ 'dug-pa dag-gis sgrib-par 'gyur-ba'i chos-rnams las sems yoṅs-su sbyoṅ-bar byed-ciṅ mtshan-mo'i thun daṅ-po la yaṅ 'chag-pa daṅ 'dug-pa dag-gis sgrib-par 'gyur-ba'i chos-rnams las sems yoṅs-su sbyoṅ-bar byed-la / yoṅs-su sbyaṅs-nas de'i-'og-tu gtsug-lag-khaṅ nas phyir-byuṅ-ste gtsug-lag-khaṅ-gi phyi-rol-tu rkaṅ-pa bkrus-nas gtsug-lag-khaṅ-gi naṅ-du źugs-te / glo g.yas-pas phab-nas rkaṅ-pa rkaṅ-pa'i steṅ-du gźag-ste / snaṅ-ba'i 'du-śes*. Wayman's edition agrees completely with T. apart from the beginning: *pūrvarātrāpararātraṃ jāgarikānuyuktatā katamā / sa tathā bhojane mātrajño divā caṅkrama-niṣadyābhām . . .* Shukla's edition, however, differs greatly. Shukla points out in his notes that after [*cittaṃ pari*] *śodhayati* Wayman reads: *rātryāḥ prathame yāme caṃkramaniṣadyābhyām āvaraṇīyebhyo dharmebhyaś cittaṃ pariśodhayati / pariśodhya tato vihārān nirgamya*. He also points out that after *pādau prakṣālya* Wayman adds: *vihāraṃ praviśya* and that Wayman omits *siṃha* in *siṃhaśayyām*. Shukla omits to mention that Wayman adds after *śayyāṃ kalpayati* the words *pāde pādam ādhāya*. Shukla seems to have been guided in his readings by a parallel passage from the Vibhaṅga quoted by him.[1] This passage contains the expression *sīhaseyyaṃ*. However, it contains also several expressions not found in Shukla's edition: *rattiyā paṭhamaṃ yāmaṃ*; *pādena pādaṃ accādhāya*. C. agrees with T. and W. but omits the words *vihāraṃ praviśya* (397b12). It would be important to know whether or not these two words are found in the Sanskrit manuscript.

S. p. 19.11–12: *akṣaṇopannaḥ / apramattaḥ*. W. p. 64: *akṣaṇopapannaḥ kṣaṇopannaḥ / pramattaḥ apramattaḥ*. T. (9b7–8) agrees with W.: *mi-khom-par skyes-pa daṅ / khom-par skyes-pa daṅ / bag med-pa daṅ ldan-pa*. C. (398c1–2) also agrees with W.

S. p. 35.8–10: *sa tathādarśī tadbahulavihārī satkāyavairāgyam anuprāpnoti / prathamañca dhyānaṃ samāpadyate / evaṃ sarvvadhyānād ūrdhvam*. W. pp. 66–67: *sa tathā-darśī tadbahulavihāri samāno* [MS.: *satkāma*] *vairāgyam anuprāpnoti / prathamaṃ ca dhyānaṃ samāpadyate / evaṃ prathamadhyānād ūrdhvaṃ*. T. 17b7–8: *de de-ltar lta-źiṅ de-la lan maṅ-du gnas-pa na 'dod-pa la 'dod-chags daṅ bral-ba thob-ciṅ / bsam-gtan daṅ-po la yaṅ sñoms-par 'jug-par 'gyur-ro // de-bźin-du bsam-gtan daṅ-po'i goṅ-ma dag-nas*. Wayman corrects *satkāmavairāgyam* to *samāno vairāgyam*. It seems more likely that the original reading is: *san kāmavairāgyam*. The only difference between C. and T. is that C. has *kāmadhātuvairāgyam* for *kāmavairāgyam* (401c21). However, neither in T. nor in C. is there the slightest reference to *satkāyavairāgyam*. It is also difficult to imagine that the manuscript read *sarvadhyānād* for *prathamadhyānād*.

It is undoubtedly superfluous to examine any other passages. The differences between the readings given by Wayman and Shukla are so considerable that it seems as if they had consulted two different manuscripts instead of one and the same. It is, of course, theoretically possible that in each case Shukla's readings are based on the manuscript and those given by Wayman, on the Tibetan translation. Granted this most unlikely supposition, one would be obliged to conclude that Shukla was not aware of the fact that his manuscript contained some very

[1] Shukla refers to Vbh. pp. 299–300. The abbreviation Vbh. is not found in his bibliography. The passage, referred to by Shukla, occurs in the edition of the Pāli Text Society on p. 249.22–32. One wonders whether Shukla quotes correctly from the edition used by him. For example, the P.T.S. edition has: *uṭṭhānasaññaṃ manasikaritvā* but Shukla quotes: *uṭṭhānasa manasikaritvā*.

incorrect readings which ought to have been checked against the Tibetan translation. However, I have not the slightest doubt that wherever Wayman's readings agree with the Tibetan version the manuscript has been correctly deciphered by him. The conclusion forces itself upon the reader that Shukla's edition is without any value for the following reasons: 1) It does not adequately reproduce the readings of his manuscript. 2) It is not based on a systematic and careful comparison with the Tibetan version.

For the edition of a Sanskrit Buddhist text the Tibetan version is of the greatest importance. This is a fact well-known to every serious student of Buddhism. However, Chinese versions cannot be entirely overlooked, even if, in general, they are much less literal. Hsüan-tsang, the translator of the Śrāvakabhūmi, had an excellent knowledge of Sanskrit and his interpretation, even if it does not adhere literally to the original text, can be quite helpful in understanding a difficult passage. An interesting example is to be found on p. 144.1–5 of Wayman's book where we read: *tvag-māṃsa-śoṇitam asmākam anuprayacchanti / yad utānukampās upādāya viśeṣaphalārthinaḥ tasyāsmākaṃ tathā pratilabdhasya piṇḍapātasyāyam evaṃrūpa ta rūpaḥ paribhogaḥ syād yad ahaṃ tathā paribhūtam ātmānaṃ / sthāpayitvā paribhumjīya yathā teṣāṃ kārāḥ kṛtā* . . . Wayman italicizes the words *ayam evaṃrūpa . . . paribhumjīya* and adds in a note that this phrase is an intrusion. Wayman finds this phrase further on in the Tibetan version: *de-ltar bdag-ñid bźag-ste / yoṅs-su loṅs-spyod-par byed-na / de-ltar yoṅs-su loṅs-spyod-par byed-pa de ni / bdag-gi tshul daṅ mthun-pa yin-te.* However, Wayman's hypothesis is proved wrong by the Chinese version which contains a passage corresponding to the phrase italicized by Wayman: (409a25–27) "After having obtained this food I must enjoy it in the following way (by making use of) an expedient (*upāya*). I must put myself in the proper way, enjoy it not wrongly and recompense the kindness of the giver so that he reaps a very excellent and great fruit . . . ." The Tibetan version agrees both with the Sanskrit text and the Chinese version but the Tibetan translator has put the phrase, mentioned above, at the very end of the entire passage (Wayman's edition p. 144.5–20 = T. 39a3–39b3). For *utānukampās* read *utānukampām*, for *ta rūpaḥ* read *'nurūpaḥ* (cf. Shukla p. 82.14 and 16), for *paribhūtaṃ paribhuñjānaṃ*, and add a *daṇḍa* after *viśeṣaphalārthinaḥ*.

A photocopy of the manuscript is available in Göttingen and we can only hope that a German scholar will prepare a proper edition of this important text.

The Australian National University J. W. DE JONG

Le compendium de la super-doctrine (*philosophie*) (*Abhidharmasamuccaya*) *d'Asaṅga*. Traduit et annoté par Walpola RAHULA. Publications de l'École française d'Extrême-Orient, Vol. LXXVIII. Paris, 1971, XXI + 236 pp.

L'Abhidharmasamuccaya est un des textes les plus importants de l'école Yogācāra. En Chine et au Japon il jouit d'une grande autorité comme un des onze śāstra cités dans la *Siddhi* (Taishō, no. 1585), l'ouvrage fondamental de l'école Fa-hsiang [1]). Au Tibet aussi une grande importance était attachée au Samuccaya. Selon Bu-ston ce texte contient un sommaire de la doctrine commune aux trois Véhicules [2]). Bu-ston et Rgyal-tshab dar-ma rin-chen (1364-1432), un des principaux disciples de Tsoṅ-kha-pa, ont écrit des commentaires détaillés de cet ouvrage [3]). Alors que le Mahāyānasaṃgraha est un compendium des doctrines spécifiquement mahāyāniques de l'école Yogācāra, le Samuccaya est un guide systématique de la partie Abhidharma du système doctrinal de ladite école.

Des fragments du texte sanskrit qui contiennent environ deux-cinquièmes de l'ouvrage entier furent découverts en 1934 par

[1]) On trouvera la liste des onze śāstra dans les *Notes sur la Siddhi* de K'uei-chi, Taishō No. 1830, ch. 1, p. 230a 1-3; cf. l'historique placé en tête de S. Lévi, *Matériaux pour l'étude du système Vijñaptimātra* (Paris, 1932), p. 33. Les citations de l'Abhidharmasamuccaya et de l'Abhidharmavyākhyā sont énumérées par Katsumata Shunkyō 勝又俊教, *Bukkyō ni okeru shinshikisetsu no kenkyū* (Tōkyō, 1961), pp. 139-143.

[2]) Bu-ston, *History of Buddhism*, I (Heidelberg, 1931), p. 56; II (Heidelberg, 1932), p. 140.

[3]) *A Catalogue of the Tohoku Collection of Tibetan Works on Buddhism* (Sendai, 1953), nos. 5183 et 5435.

Rāhula Sāṃkṛtyāyana. Ils furent publiés en 1947 par V. V. Gokhale ("Fragments from the Abhidharmasamuccaya of Asaṅga", *Journal of the Bombay Branch, Royal Asiatic Society*, N.S., Vol. 23, 1947, pp. 13-38). En 1950 Pralhad Pradhan publiait les mêmes fragments, mais en y ajoutant une restitution sanskrite des parties perdues basée sur les traductions chinoise (Taishō no. 1605) et tibétaine [1]). Le Tanjur tibétain contient également des traductions de l'Abhidharmasamuccayabhāṣya et de l'Abhidharmasamuccayavyākhyā [2]). Un manuscrit complet du texte sanskrit du Bhāṣya a été également découvert et photographié par Rāhula Sāṃkṛtyāyana. Selon M. Shinoda Masashige, une édition de ce texte sera publiée bientôt par le Jayaswal Research Institute à Patna [3]). Le Bhāṣya n'a pas été traduit en chinois, mais nous devons à Hsüan-tsang, le traducteur du Samuccaya, une traduction de la Vyākhyā (Taishō no. 1606). Nous ne sommes pas bien renseignés sur les auteurs du Bhāṣya et de la Vyākhyā. Le Tanjur tibétain les attribue tous les deux à Jinaputra (Rgyal-ba'i sras), alors que la tradition chinoise attribue à Sthiramati la compilation de la Vyākhyā. Selon K'uei-chi [4]) et Hui-ch'ao [5]), Sthiramati aurait combiné le Samuccaya et le commentaire de Chüeh Shih-tzu 覺師子 (Buddhasiṃha?). Un disciple d'Asaṅga qui porte ce nom est mentionné par Hsüan-tsang dans le Hsi-yü chi (Taishō no. 2087, ch. 5, p. 896c1-5; trad. Watters, I, p. 358). Récemment les problèmes relatifs à la date et à l'auteur du Bhāṣya ont été étudiés par Shinoda Masashige (cf. n. 3) et Takasaki Masayoshi [6]). Pradhan avait déjà signalé des passages correspondants dans le Samuccaya et le Triṃśikābhāṣya de Sthiramati. Les savants japonais, mentionnés ci-dessus, ont montré

[1]) Pradhan ne dit pas quelle édition du Tanjur il a utilisée, mais les références aux numéros des folios montrent qu'il s'agit de l'édition de Narthang. J'ai consulté la réimpression photomécanique de l'édition de Pékin, vol. 112 (Tōkyō-Kyōto, 1957), pp. 236-272 (Mdo-'grel Li 51a3-141b2).

[2]) Réimpression photomécanique, vol. 113 (Tōkyō-Kyōto, 1957), pp. 83-141 (Mdo-'grel Śi 1-143b2) et 141-229 (id. 143b2-362a8).

[3]) Shinoda Masashige 篠田正成, „Abhidharmasamuccayabhāṣya no seiritsu nendai", *IBK* (= Indogaku Bukkyōgaku kenkyū), XVIII, 1970, p. 878.

[4]) Cf. ses *Notes sur la Vyākhyā*, Zoku zōkyō, A LXXIV, 4, p. 302Bb11-14; Taishō No. 1700, p. 125b1-5 (cité par Noël Peri, *BÉFEO*, XI, 1911, p. 385, n. 1).

[5]) Taishō No. 1832, ch. 1, p. 666b2-4.

[6]) Takasaki Masayoshi 高崎正芳, „Daijō Abidatsumazōjūron no kan-zō densho ni tsuite", *IBK*, XIX, 1971, pp. 513-516.

que de nombreux passages de l'Abhidharmasamuccayabhāṣya se retrouvent dans le Triṃśikābhāṣya et d'autres commentaires de Sthiramati ainsi que dans d'autres ouvrages tels que l'Abhidharmakośabhāṣya, le Mahāyānasaṃgraha, le Sūtrālaṃkāra, etc. [1]) Shinoda croit que l'Abhidharmasamuccayabhāṣya a été composé avant Sthiramati et peu après Asaṅga et Vasubandhu. Selon lui, la tradition chinoise qui en attribue la composition à Buddhasiṃha, disciple d'Asaṅga, mérite d'être prise en considération. Toutefois, Takasaki préfère identifier l'auteur à Jinaputra, un des dix maîtres de la Siddhi et l'auteur d'un commentaire du Yogācārabhūmiśāstra (Taishō no. 1580) [2]). Peut-être la publication du texte sanskrit de l'Abhidharmasamuccayabhāṣya aidera-t-elle à clarifier cette question.

M. Rahula s'est acquitté admirablement de la tâche de traduire un texte qui contient un aussi grand nombre de termes techniques. On trouvera ces termes et leurs équivalents français dans les glossaires sanskrit-français et français-sanskrit (pp. 189-216). Heureusement, M. Rahula n'a pas suivi le système de traduction adopté par Sylvain Lévi et le Hōbōgirin. Le glossaire sanskrit-français pourrait bien former la base d'un dictionnaire des termes bouddhiques en langue française. Il faudrait y incorporer les équivalents que l'on trouve dans les ouvrages de La Vallée Poussin et de M. Lamotte. Si un tel dictionnaire donnait en même temps des références aux travaux de ces savants, en manière d'index général, on disposerait d'un instrument de travail d'une très grande utilité.

Les mérites du travail de M. Rahula sont indéniables. Le style est lucide et les nombreuses références aux sources pālies sont les bienvenues. La traduction d'un texte tel que le Samuccaya pose de grands problèmes. Pour les parties perdues du texte sanskrit, M. Rahula a suivi généralement la restitution de Pradhan. Il ne

[1]) Voir p. 340, notes 3 et 6, et aussi Takasaki Masayoshi, ,,Daijō Abidatsumashūron oyobi Zōjūron to Sanjūju Anneshaku-tō to no kanren ni tsuite", *IBK*, IV, 1956, pp. 116-117; ,,Mujaku-Abidatsumashūron ni tsuite", *Ōtani Gakuhō*, XXXVI, 2, 1956, pp. 33-46; ,,Abidatsumashūron ni tsuite", *Ōtani daigaku bukkyō gakkai kaihō*, vol. 8, pp. 1-13; ,,Zōjūron ni okeru zō-kan ryōshoden", *Zengaku kenkyū*, vol. 45, 1964, pp. 189-198 (je n'ai pu consulter les deux derniers articles); Shinoda Masashige, ,,Abidatsumazōjūron ni okeru roku haramitta shisō", *Nihon bukkyō gakkai nempō*, vol. 35, 1970, pp. 63-76.

[2]) K'uei-chi distingue nettement Buddhasiṃha et Jinaputra, cf. ses *Notes sur la Vyākhyā*, p. 307Ba11 (cité par Noël Peri, voir la note 4 de la page précédente).

s'en écarte qu'en peu de cas. Pradhan a eu l'avantage de pouvoir consulter le manuscrit du texte sanskrit du Bhāṣya. Toutefois, le Bhāṣya ne suffit pas pour pouvoir rétablir tous les termes techniques. En outre, il y a beaucoup de divergences entre la traduction tibétaine et la traduction chinoise. Pradhan en signale un grand nombre dans ses notes, mais sa restitution sanskrite est essentiellement basée sur la version chinoise, dont elle est une traduction. Il n'y a pas de doute que la version chinoise de Hsüan-tsang est beaucoup moins fidèle au texte original que la version tibétaine. Cela se voit déjà dans la division du texte en deux parties, comportant chacune quatre chapitres. Comme l'a déjà relevé Pradhan (Introduction, p. 10), le texte original ne contenait que cinq chapitres, un chapitre pour la première partie (Lakṣaṇasamuccaya) et quatre pour la deuxième partie (Viniścayasamuccaya): Satyaviniścaya, Dharmaviniścaya, Prāptiviniścaya et Sāṃkathyaviniścaya [1]).

La restitution sanskrite des parties perdues du texte par Pradhan, fondée sur la version de Hsüan-tsang, peut sans doute rendre des services, mais il faut la confronter soigneusement avec la version tibétaine du Samuccaya et avec celle de la Vyākhyā qui contient également le texte du Samuccaya. La version chinoise de Hsüan-tsang peut tout au plus aider à élucider des passages obscurs du texte tibétain. Toutefois, il ne faudrait pas imputer à Hsüan-tsang toutes les imperfections de la retraduction en sanskrit de Pradhan. Pour ne citer qu'un seul exemple, le troisième chapitre (chapitre II de la deuxième partie dans la traduction de Rahula) commence par une énumération et explication des douze membres de l'enseignement du Buddha. Cette division en douze membres est mentionnée dans de nombreux textes. M. Rahula se contente d'ajouter dans une note que les sources pālies ne mentionnent que neuf membres. Une explication des douze membres se trouve dans toute une série de textes, énumérés par M. Maeda Egaku qui a consacré une étude détaillée aux neuf et aux douze membres du Buddhavacana [2]). D'un intérêt particulier est à cet égard un passage de la Śrāvakabhūmi dont le texte sanskrit a été publié par M. Wayman (*Analysis of the Śrāvakabhūmi Manuscript*, Berkeley and Los Angeles, 1961, pp. 75-78). A propos de *geya*,

[1]) Voir aussi Takasaki Masayoshi, *Ōtani gakuhō*, XXXVI, 2, 1956, pp. 35-38.

[2]) Maeda Egaku 前田惠學, *Genshi bukkyō seiten no seiritsushi kenkyū* (Tokyo, 1961), pp. 181-549. Voir pp. 224-225.

le Samuccaya dit: *sūtreṣu anirūpito 'rtho vā yad vyākhyāte / ato geyam ity ucyate* (trad. Pradhan, p. 78), mais la Śrāvakabhūmi lit: *yat* (sic) *ca sūtraṃ neyārtham idam ucyate geyam* (Wayman, p. 76). Le texte de la traduction tibétaine du Samuccaya en est très proche: *yaṅ draṅ-ba don-gyi mdo-ste rtogs-par byed-pas dbyaṅs-kyis bsñad-pa'i sde'o*, ,,ou aussi ce qui explique un sūtra de sens à expliquer (*sūtraṃ neyārtham*) est le groupe du *geya*". Hsüan-tsang traduit: ,,ou c'est une explication en vers d'un sūtra de sens à expliquer. C'est pourquoi on l'appelle *geya*" (Taishō no. 1605, ch. 6, p. 686b3-4). De la même manière la deuxième explication de *vyākaraṇa* l'interprète comme un sūtra de sens explicite (*sūtraṃ nītārtham*; *ṅes-pa'i don-gyis mdo-ste*) [1]. Les termes *sūtraṃ neyārtham* et *sūtraṃ nītārtham* ont été bien rendus par Hsüan-tsang. Dans un autre passage, c'est Hsüan-tsang qui a induit M. Rahula en erreur. Le Samuccaya contient un passage sur l'*antarābhava* (Rahula pp. 68-69) que l'on retrouve presque littéralement dans la Yogācārabhūmi (éd. Vidhushekhara Bhattacharya, Calcutta, 1957, pp. 19-20). Le texte dit: ,,L'existence intermédiaire se déroule, devant celui qui a fait le mal, par exemple sous l'apparence d'un taureau (ou bouc) noir (*kṛṣṇa kutapa*); . . . devant une personne qui a fait le bien, sous l'apparence d'une étoffe blanche" (Rahula p. 68). Bhattacharya remarque dans une note que *kutapa* désigne ,,a sort of blanket (made of the hair of the Mountain goat)". Dans la Yogācārabhūmi, *kutapa* est rendu en tibétain par *phyar-ba* que Bhattacharya n'arrive pas à expliquer; mais *phyar-ba*, comme équivalent de *kutapa*, est donné dans la Mahāvyutpatti (éd. Sakaki no. 9563). La traduction de M. Rahula repose probablement sur la version de Hsüan-tsang qui traduit ,,l'éclat d'une chèvre ou d'un agneau noir" (ch. 3, p. 675c24). Parmi d'autres passages parallèles de la Yogācārabhumi, il faut signaler celui qui traite des synonymes de *kleśa* (pp. 166-168; Samuccaya, trad. Rahula, pp. 71-79). Le vingt-troisième synonyme est *vanasa* dans le manuscrit de la Yogācārabhūmi (cf. p. 167, n. 8). Bhattacharya l'a changé en *vanatha*, mais Pradhan a gardé *vanasa* dans sa traduction du Samuccaya. M. Rahula opte pour *vanatha* ou *gahana*. Il faut certainement garder *vanasa* car ce mot se retrouve aussi dans l'Udānavarga (cf. Udānavarga XXXII.78, éd. Bernard Pauly, *JA*, 1960, p. 251; éd. Franz Bernhard, Göttingen, 1965, p. 457).

[1]) Voir aussi L. de La Vallée Poussin, *La Siddhi de Hiuan-tsang*, II (Paris, 1929), p. 558.

En ce qui concerne les parties du texte conservées en sanskrit, M. Rahula a pu comparer les deux éditions, indépendantes l'une de l'autre, de Gokhale et de Pradhan. Toutefois, elles sont quelquefois toutes deux incorrectes. Ainsi on trouve dans l'édition de Gokhale *bodhisattvanyāsāvakrāntaḥ* alors que Pradhan lit *bodhim anavadyāṁ avakrāntaḥ* (cf. Rahula, p. 174, n. 1). Il faut évidemment lire *bodhisattvanyāmāvakrāntaḥ* (*byaṅ-chub sems-dpa'i skyon-med-pa la źugs*, p. 137a6-7). Le changement d'un *s* en un *m* n'est qu'une correction mineure du point de vue paléographique. On se demande comment Pradhan, en utilisant le même manuscrit que Gokhale, a pu lire *bodhim anavadyāṁ*. Il s'agit probablement d'une traduction erronée du texte tibétain. Les traducteurs tibétains traduisent régulièrement *nyāma* par *skyon-med* (cf. Edgerton, *Buddhist Hybrid Sanskrit Dictionary* s.v. *nyāma*).

Ces exemples montrent qu'en traduisant un texte comme l'Abhidharmasamuccaya il faut absolument avoir recours à la traduction tibétaine en premier lieu. En outre, il ne suffit pas de renvoyer à des textes pālis, en négligeant les textes du Mahāyāna et surtout ceux qui sont accessibles en sanskrit comme le début de la Yogācārabhūmi et les extraits de la Śrāvakabhūmi édités par Wayman. M. Rahula n'hésite même pas à préférer l'exégèse pālie à celle fournie par le Samuccayabhāṣya et la Samuccayavyākhyā. Ainsi le Samuccaya (trad. Rahula p. 184) cite un vers célèbre que l'on retrouve dans l'Udānavarga: *pha daṅ ma ni bsad byas-śiṅ / rgyal-po gtsaṅ-sbra-can gñis daṅ / yul-'khor 'khor daṅ-bcas bcom-na / mi ni dag-par 'gyur źes bya* (p. 140a2-3). Dans l'Udānavarga tibétain (éd. H. Beckh, Berlin, 1911, p. 107), ce vers porte le numéro XXIX.24. Le texte sanskrit peut être rétabli en combinant les trois premiers pāda du texte sanskrit d'Udānavarga XXIX.24 (ou XXXIII.61) et le dernier pāda d'Udānavarga XXXIII.62: *mātaraṃ pitaraṃ hatvā / rājānaṃ dvau ca śrotriyau / rāṣṭraṃ sānucaraṃ hatvā / śuddha ity ucyate naraḥ*. M. Rahula ne fait aucune mention de l'Udānavarga et ne cite que le texte du Dhammapada (294). Pour le sens caché de ce vers, M. Rahula suit la Dhammapada-aṭṭhakathā (vol. III, p. 454) sans la nommer. Bernhard qui a consacré une savante étude à l'interprétation de ce vers („Zur Textgeschichte und Interpretation der Strophen: Dhammapada 294, 295", *Festschrift für Wilhelm Eilers*, Wiesbaden, 1967, pp. 511-526) cite l'explication de ce vers par Kātyāyana dans l'Udānavargavivaraṇa de Prajñāvarman (p. 519). L'explication donnée par le Samuccayabhāṣya (p. 141b8-142a2) et la Samuccayavyākhyā (p. 359b8-360a2; T. 1606, ch. 16, p. 773b2-3), est presque identique: la mère est la soif (*tṛṣṇā*; *sred-pa*), le père le *karmabhava* (*las-kyi srid-pa*) [1]), le roi le *vijñāna* avec l'*upādāna* (*ñe-bar len-pa daṅ-bcas-pa'i rnam-par śes-pa*), les deux *śrotriya* le *dṛṣṭiparāmarśa* et le *śīlavrataparāmarśa*, le royaume les six *āyatana* (*skye-mched*) et les *anucara* leur domaine (*gocara*; *spyod-yul*). M. Rahula a eu tort de ne pas tenir compte de l'explication donnée par le Bhāṣya que, d'ailleurs, il ne semble avoir consulté que rarement (une seule référence explicite, p. 11, n. 1).

M. Rahula mérite notre gratitude pour l'excellente traduction de ce texte difficile. On n'y trouvera que rarement des erreurs évidentes, comme, par exemple, la traduction de *saṃśraya* (tib. *gnas-pa*) par „doute" (p. 14, l. 11) et la traduction d'*atītānāgatabhāvanimitta* par „le signe du passé et du futur" (p. 34, l. 18). Dans le manuscrit sanskrit une syllabe manque avant et après *bhāva*. Gokhale lit *atītānāgata(pra)bhāva(nā)nimitto*. Pradhan suggère *prabhāvana* et fait remarquer que le Bhāṣya a *prabhāva*. La traduction tibétaine a *rab-tu bźag-pa* (p. 71b1) ce qui confirme la correction de Gokhale (cf. Mahāvyutpatti no. 6917). Les remarques faites ci-dessus n'ont pour but que de montrer que son travail aurait gagné en valeur s'il avait comparé soigneusement la traduction de Pradhan avec la version tibétaine. D'autre part, on ne peut pas traduire un texte tel que le Samuccaya sans tenir compte des passages parallèles dans les textes du Mahāyāna et, avant tout, dans les ouvrages d'Asaṅga dont le texte sanskrit a été conservé.

L'introduction de M. Rahula ne donne que quelques renseignements sur la vie d'Asaṅga, d'après la vie de Vasubandhu par Paramārtha, et un aperçu du contenu du Samuccaya. M. Rahula ne dit rien de la relation du Samuccaya avec les textes d'Abhidharma de l'école Sarvāstivāda et d'autres écoles. C'est une question qui mériterait d'être étudiée en détail. Pour autant que je sache, les savants japonais ne s'en sont guère occupés. Ui Hakuju et Fukaura Seibun se contentent de remarquer que la structure du Samuccaya ressemble à celle du Prakaraṇapādaśāstra (Taishō

[1]) Bernhard traduit *zag-pa daṅ bcas-pa'i las daṅ srid-pa* par „das Werk, *karman*, mit dem (üblen) Einflüss(en), und das Werden, *bhava*". Le Samuccayabhāṣya a *las-kyi srid-pa* qui rend *karmabhava*, cf. Prahlad Pradhan, „A Note on Abhidharma-samuccaya-bhāṣya and its Author Sthiramati (?)", *J. Bihar Res. Society*, XXXV, 1949, p. 45. *Las daṅ srid-pa* doit aussi correspondre à *karmabhava* sur lequel voir L. de La Vallée Poussin, *Kośa*, vol. V, p. 1, n. 3.

nos. 1541-2) et du Śāriputrābhidharmaśāstra (Taishō no. 1548) [1]. D'autre part, il faudrait comparer le Samuccaya aux autres ouvrages d'Asaṅga, et, en premier lieu, au Yogācārabhūmiśāstra. M. Wayman a signalé déjà des différences considérables dans la terminologie logique entre une section du Yogācārabhūmiśāstra qui traite de la hetuvidyā et le Sāṃkathyaviniścaya [2]. On ne pourra arriver à plus de certitude dans cette question que par une étude comparative du Samuccaya et du Yogācārabhūmiśāstra. Espérons que la prochaine publication de l'Abhidharmasamuccayabhāṣya provoquera de nouvelles recherches sur la place qu'occupe l'Abhidharmasamuccaya dans le développement du Mahāyāna, et, en particulier, dans le système philosophique d'Asaṅga.

Australian National University, Canberra. J. W. de Jong.

Abhidharmadīpa with Vibhāṣāprabhāvṛtti, critically edited with notes and introduction by Padmanabh S. Jaini (=*Tibetan Sanskrit Works Series*, IV) (Patna, 1959), xii + 144 + 499 pp. Rs. 12/-

Le manuscrit de l'Abhidharmadīpa fut découvert au Tibet par Rāhula Sāṅkṛityāyana en 1937. Un grand nombre de feuillets manque et presque les deux tiers du texte sont perdus. Néanmoins, ce qui reste est d'un très grand intérêt car l'Abhidharmadīpa est une réplique de l'orthodoxie Vaibhāṣika à l'Abhidharmakośa du Sautrāntika Vasubandhu. L'ouvrage consiste en des kārikā, intitulées Abhidharmadīpa, et un commentaire en prose, la Vibhāṣāprabhāvṛtti. Très probablement l'auteur des kārikā a aussi écrit le commentaire comme c'est le cas pour le Kośa. Le nom de l'auteur n'est malheureusement mentionné nulle part dans l'ouvrage. Selon M. Jaini, il n'est pas probable que Saṃghabhadra, après avoir écrit deux ouvrages pour réfuter les opinions de Vasubandhu, ait écrit un troisième ouvrage. On peut ajouter que l'on constate de petites divergences entre les explications de Saṃghabhadra et celles de l'auteur du Dīpa, par exemple, en ce qui concerne l'explication du *sat* de *satkāyadṛṣṭi*. Selon Vasubandhu et l'auteur du Dīpa *sat* = *sīdati* (Dīpa, p. 229.12 et n. 6) alors que, selon Saṃghabhadra, *sat* parce qu'existant (cf. Kośa, trad. La Vallée Poussin, V, p. 16). Il faudrait comparer en détail les ouvrages de Saṃghabhadra avec le Dīpa pour voir s'il y a d'autres divergences. De cet examen résulteraient peut-être aussi des indices permettant de déterminer la relation entre Saṃghabhadra et l'auteur du Dīpa. M. Jaini mentionne la possibilité d'identifier l'auteur du Dīpa avec Vimalamitra dont Hiuantsang raconte la légende. Dans ce cas, on s'attendrait à trouver dans le Dīpa des références aux ouvrages de Saṃghabhadra mais aucun auteur, postérieur au Kośa, n'y est mentionné. Pour le moment, l'énigme que pose l'identité de l'auteur du Dīpa ne peut être résolue. Espérons que l'étude des ouvrages de Saṃghabhadra ou des commentaires du Kośa, conservés en traduction tibétaine, puisse apporter la solution.

Deux ouvrages de Saṃghabhadra sont conservés en traduction chinoise. Le Tandjour contient un ouvrage qui, d'après le catalogue de l'université Tōhoku (no. 4091), serait identique à Taishō no. 1563 connu sous le titre d'Abhidharmasamayapradīpikāśāstra que Takakusu lui a donné. Il est peu probable que cette identification soit correcte. Dans l'édition de sDe-dge l'Abhidharmakośabhāṣya comprend 328 feuillets et no. 4091 172 feuillets alors que, dans le Taishō, le Bhāṣya (T.1558) occupe 159 pages et no. 1563 201 pages. D'ailleurs, le nom de l'auteur de cet ouvrage ne semble pas être bien fixé car, d'après le catalogue de Cordier (vol. III, p. 395), celui-ci est écrit tantôt 'Dul-bzaṅ (Vinītabhadra) tantôt 'Dus-bzaṅ (Saṃgamabhadra, alias Saṃgamaśrībhadra, Saṃghabhadra, du Kaśmīr, élève de Vinītabhadra). En outre, la traduction correcte de Saṃghabhadra serait dGe-'dun bzaṅ et non 'Dus-bzaṅ.

Dans une longue introduction M. Jaini étudie l'origine de la controverse entre les Ābhidharmika et les Sautrāntika et les principales divergences de vue qui opposent l'auteur du Dīpa à Vasubandhu. Une partie de l'introduction a été publiée dans une série de cinq articles parus dans le *BSOAS* (vols. XXI–XXII, 1958–59). Enfin, pour le premier fascicule de l'*Encyclopaedia of Buddhism* (Colombo, 1961, pp. 55–57) M. Jaini a contribué un excellent article sur le Dīpa. Tous ces travaux font preuve d'une grande connaissance de l'Abhidharma et de la pénétration avec laquelle l'auteur a étudié ce domaine difficile.

L'éditeur du Dīpa n'avait à sa disposition qu'un seul manuscrit plein de lacunes. En outre, il n'existe aucune traduction en chinois ou en tibétain. Heureusement, M. Jaini a pu tirer grand profit de la traduction du Kośa par La Vallée Poussin et de l'édition de l'Abhidharmakośabhāṣya par M. Prahlad Pradhan. Les résultats d'une étude approfondie des textes d'Abhidharma, transmis en pāli et en sanskrit, se manifestent dans l'annotation abondante qui en contient de longs extraits et constitue une sorte de compendium de tous les problèmes d'Abhidharma discutés dans le texte. Ainsi cette édition est devenue un ouvrage indispensable pour l'étude de l'Abhidharma. Sans aucun doute, le travail de M. Jaini est la publication la plus importante dans ce domaine depuis la parution de la traduction du Kośa par La Vallée Poussin.

Pour terminer signalons quelques fautes d'impression et des passages où on peut suggérer une autre lecture.

P. 5 kārikā 4d: *dhuvatrayāḥ*; lire *dhruvatrayāḥ*.

P. 9. 10: *saṃgrahavastu* n'est pas le titre d'un texte, cf. Kośa, I, p. 34.

P. 10. 11: *-vayuktatvāc*; lire *-viyuktatvāc*.

P. 11 kārikā 12b: *matyāder*; lire *satyāder*.

Pp. 46.12 et 47.1: *ātmabhāvaparikarṣaṇe*; lire *ātmabhāvaparirakṣaṇe*? D'après p. 48, n.1 le Kośabhāṣya a aussi *-parikarṣaṇa*, mais le contexte exige *-parirakṣaṇa*, cf. Kośa, I, p. 104.

P. 47.6: MS *tadviyutavikalānāṃ*; l'éditeur lit *-vikalpānāṃ* conformément à la lecture du Kośabhāṣya citée dans note 1: *tadviprayuktavikalpānāṃ*, mais la Vyākhyā a *-vikalānāṃ*, cf. p. 94.15, 25.

P. 54.10: *santrasanti sattvā*; lecture incompréhensible, cf. Vyākhyā p. 104.4: *santi bhadanta sattvā*.

P. 64 kārikā 108ab: *aṣṭābhir daśabhiḥ sekair ārūpyāḥ svalpabhūmibhiḥ*; lire *saikair* (= *sa* + *ekair*) et *svalpabhūribhiḥ* car, au lieu de *bhūmibhiḥ*, un synonyme de *bahubhiḥ* est exigé par le commentaire p. 94.9.

P. 90.1: *vajahyāt*; lire *vijahyāt*.

P. 90.3: *avakrāmat*; lire *avakrāman*.

P. 115 kārikā 150c et p. 116.4: *samatvasya*; lire *sasattvasya*, cf. Kośa, III, kārikā 101c: *saha sattvena*.

P. 138.8: *apakṣālās*; lire *apakṣālāṃs*.

P. 139, n.4: Akb. III 54cd; lire Akb. II. 54cd.

P. 143.16: *ukṣanirmocana*; référence à l'histoire de l'eunuque de Kaniṣka et des taureaux? Cf. Kośa, Introduction, p. 148a. Pour le changement de sexe voir aussi P.V. Bapat, Change of Sex in Buddhist Literature, *Felicitation Volume presented to S.K. Belvalkar*, Banaras, 1957, pp. 209–15.

P. 145.3: *khalu vicāraṃ*; lire *khalv avicāraṃ*.

P. 146.16: *śuklaśabdaḥ*; lire *'śukla-*.

P. 175 kārikā 201cd: *-pāruṣyāṇy uṣanti*; lire *-pāruṣyāṇi santi*?

P. 178 kārikā 205b: MS *alpāyuṣṭvan tu*; l'éditeur lit *alpāyuṣyan tu* mais il faut garder la lecture du MS, cf. pāli *appāyutta*.

P. 178 kārikā 206c: *amalenāryaṃ*; lire *amale sārdhaṃ*?

P. 180.18: MS *tevedanāsravās*; l'éditeur lit *trivedanāsravās*; lire *te ced anāsravās*.

P. 199.8: *kiyato buddhānāṃ*; lire *kiyatāṃ buddhānāṃ*.

P. 211.3: *kāyavāṅganaḥ*; lire *kāyavāṅmanaḥ*.

P. 216.8: *mithyāhaṣṭyādibhir*; lire *mithyādṛṣṭyādibhir*.

P. 217.1: *tailam .... tanmayī*; lire *tailam .... tanmayi*.

P. 241 kārikā 283b: *mārgasthan navabhūmikaḥ*; lire *mārgaḥ ṣaṇṇavabhūmikaḥ*?

P. 243.6: *ye vatsarvatragāḥ*; lire *ye tv asarvatragāḥ*.

P. 253.3: *yathā prahīṇā*; lire *yatrāprahīṇā*, cf. kārikā 296c.

P. 256 kārikā 298c: *sadasaddhetuno*; lire *sadasaddhetutā*.

P. 265.8: *naihakatīyas*; lire *nehaikatīyas*.

P. 273.22: *mukhyasattāyā*; lire *mukhyasattāyāṃ*.

P. 274.6,20: *viprakṛta*; lire *viprakṛṣṭa*?

P. 281 kārikā 322b: MS *atītājānatā*; l'éditeur lit *atītānāgatā*; lire *atītājātatā*.

P. 294 kārikā 357b: *anugrāhekṣaṇaṃ*; lire *antagrāhekṣaṇaṃ*.

P. 295.4: MS *sattvavījapudgala-*; l'éditeur lit *sattvabījapudgala-*; lire *sattvajīvapudgala-*, cf. Kośa, IX, p. 245.

P. 308 kārikā 373a: *markṣyerṣyā-*; lire *mrakṣyerṣyā-*.

P. 308.4: *anubandhā 'dārḍhyān*; lire *anubandhādārḍhyān*.

P. 313.16: *nopekṣayā*; lire *copekṣayā*.

P. 321.16: *mūrdhānatasthaiva*; lire *mūrdhānas tathaiva*.

P. 332.1: *laukikāgradhirma-*; lire *laukikāgradharma-*.

P. 339.2: *dhyānavyavakaraṇaphalā*; lire *dhyānavyavakiraṇaphalā*.

P. 361.3: *kleśasaṃgrāmāvatīrṇaḥ*; lire *-tīrṇasya*?

P. 362.15: *parihāṇyābhāvān*; lire *parihāṇyabhāvān*.

P. 365 kārikā 458c: MS *apasaṃkalpā*; l'éditeur lit *apasaṃkalpād*; maintenir la lecture du MS, cf. L. Renou, *Grammaire sanscrite* §82 sur l'emploi de *apa* comme simple négation en composition.

Leiden J. W. de Jong

Paṇḍita Durveka Miśra's Dharmottarapradīpa [Being a sub-commentary on Dharmottara's Nyāyabinduṭīkā, a commentary on Dharmakīrti's Nyāyabindu]. Edited by Paṇḍita Dalsukhbai Malvania, *Tibetan Sanskrit Works Series*, vol. II (Patna, 1955). vii + 60 + 303 pp.

M. Malvania a rendu un grand service aux études bouddhiques par la publication d'un commentaire de la *Nyāyabinduṭīkā* de Dharmottara. Ce texte assez volumineux qui ne paraît pas avoir été traduit par les Tibétains a été découvert au Tibet par Rāhula Sāṅkṛityāyana. M. M. a joint à son édition une longue préface dans laquelle il donne des renseignements utiles sur le *Nyāyabindu*, ses commentaires et sous-commentaires. A quelques endroits ses indications relatives aux manuscrits et aux éditions peuvent être corrigées et complétées. C'est pourquoi il nous paraît utile de mentionner brièvement les principales publications relatives au *Nyāyabindu* et les manuscrits qu'elles ont utilisés.

Pour l'editio princeps[1] du *Nyāyabindu* et de la *ṭīkā* de Dharmottara P. Peterson s'est servi de deux manuscrits dont le premier[2] ne contenait que la *ṭīkā* et le deuxième[3] le *Nyāyabindu* et la *ṭīkā*. Dans un compte rendu[4] du *Third Report* de Peterson, Bühler avait supposé que la *Nyāyabinduṭīkā* était identique à un ouvrage intitulé *Dharmottaravṛtti*[5] qu'il avait découvert à Jesalmer, mais Peterson a montré qu'il s'agissait d'un commentaire de la *ṭīkā*.[6] Stcherbatsky l'a publié en 1909[7] en se servant d'une copie que Bühler avait fait établir. Le texte s'arrête avant la fin du premier *pariccheda* et le nom de l'auteur n'y est mentionné nulle part. Stcherbatsky l'avait attribué à Mallavādi, auteur

[1] Calcutta, 1889; Re-issue, Calcutta, 1929.

[2] MS appartenant au Śāntinātha Jain bhaṇḍār de Cambay. Voir P. Peterson, *A Third Report of Operations in Search of Sanskrit MSS. in the Bombay Circle* 1884–1886 (Bombay, 1887), p. 33 et appendix pp. 33–34, Nr. 215.

[3] Collection Bhao Daji, Bombay Branch of the Royal Asiatic Society.

[4] *WZKM*, I (1887), p. 323.

[5] *IA*, 4 (1875), p. 82.

[6] Voir la préface de son édition du *Nyāyabindu* (pp. VIII–IX) et *JBBrRAS*, XVII, part II (1887–1889), pp. 47–52.

[7] *Nyāyabinduṭīkāṭippaṇī*, (= *Bibliotheca Buddhica*, XI) (St.-Pétersbourg, 1909).

d'une *Dharmottaraṭippaṇī* découverte par Bhandarkar[8] à Jesalmer. Stcherbatsky a ignoré apparemment l'existence d'un deuxième MS de la *Dharmottaraṭippaṇī* de Mallavādi signalé déjà en 1892 par Peterson[9] qui l'avait découvert à Patan. Plus tard Stcherbatsky a dû se procurer une copie de ce texte car dans *Buddhist Logic* il distingue la *Nyāyabinduṭīkāṭippaṇī* de Mallavādi de la *Nyāyabinduṭīkāṭippaṇī* d'un auteur inconnu. L'ouvrage de Mallavādi n'a jamais été publié.

Les imperfections de l'editio princeps n'ont pas effrayé Stcherbatsky qui, dès 1903, fit paraître une traduction russe du *Nyāyabindu* et de la *ṭīkā*. Six ans plus tard il publia une étude systématique de la philosophie de Dharmakīrti.[10] Une nouvelle édition du *Nyāyabindu* et de la *ṭīkā* fut publiée par lui en 1918.[11] En plus des deux manuscrits qu'avait utilisés Peterson, Stcherbatsky avait recours à un troisième manuscrit[12] (de la seule *ṭīkā*) qu'il avait découvert en 1910 dans la bibliothèque de l'Asiatic Society of Bengal. D'une grande utilité lui fut la traduction tibétaine dont il avait déjà publié le texte en 1904.[13] Se basant sur ces éditions Obermiller compilait des index sanskrit-tibétain et tibétain-sanskrit[14] qui remplaçaient l'index fait par Vidyabhusana[15] en se servant de l'édition de Peterson. Reprenant ses travaux russes parus en 1903 et 1909 Stcherbatsky fit paraître en 1930 une nouvelle traduction du *Nyāyabindu* et de la *ṭīkā* et en 1932 la somme de ses connaissances sur la philosophie de Dharmakīrti.[16] Ajoutons à ces indications bibliographiques que M. M. mentionne deux éditions indiennes du *Nyāyabindu* et de la *ṭīkā* qui paraissent se baser principalement sur l'édition de Stcherbatsky. Finalement, M. Yamada nous renseigne sur l'existence d'une traduction

---

8 *Report of a Second Tour in Search of Sanscrit Manuscripts, made in Rajputana and Central India in* 1904–1905 *and* 1905–1906 (Bombay, 1907), p. 27.

9 *A Fourth Report of Operations in Search of Sanskrit MSS. in the Bombay Circle* 1886–1892 (Bombay, 1892), pp. 3–4; voir aussi P, Peterson, *A Fifth Report of Operations in Search of Sanscrit MSS. in the Bombay Circle* 1892–1895 (Bombay, 1896), p. li et p. 3, nr. 1.

10 Ѳ. И. Щербатской, Теорія познанія и логика по ученію позднѣйшихъ буддистовъ. Ч. I, Учебник логики Дармакирти съ толкованіемъ на него Дармоттары; Ч. II, Ученіе о воспріятіи и умозаключеніи (Изд. Фак. Вост. Яз., No. XIV). Le deuxième volume a été traduit par Otto Strauss, *Erkenntnislehre und Logik nach der Lehre der späteren Buddhisten* (München-Neubiberg, 1924) et par Mme. I de Manziarly et Paul Masson-Oursel, *La théorie de la connaissance et la logique chez les Bouddhistes tardifs* (Paris, 1926).

11 Fascicule I, (= *Bibliotheca Buddhica*, VII) (Petrograd, 1918). Un deuxième fascicule qui devait contenir une introduction, une description détaillée des MSS et probablement des notes, ne fut jamais publié. *Buddhist Logic*, vol. II, contient trois pages de corrections aux textes du *Nyāyabindu*, de la *ṭīkā* et de la *ṭippaṇī* (pp. 435–437). M. M. ne paraît pas en avoir tenu compte dans ses références à l'édition de Stcherbatsky.

12 Voir Hara Prasad Shāstri, *A Descriptive Catalogue of Sanscrit Manuscripts in the Government Collection, under the care of the Asiatic Society of Bengal*, vol. I, Buddhist Manuscripts (Calcutta, 1917), Nr 33A, MS 4771. M. M. se trompe en disant que ce manuscrit appartient à Denison Ross. C'est par l'intermédiaire de celui-ci que Stcherbatsky a pu consulter le manuscrit à Leningrad, voir *Bibl. Buddh.*, vol. VII, p. II.

13 Fascicules I–II (= *Bibliotheca Buddhica*, VIII) (Sanktpeterburg, 1904). Un troisième fascicule annoncé n'a jamais paru. Quelques années plus tard Louis de La Vallée Poussin publia le texte de la traduction tibétaine du commentaire du *Nyāyabindu* par Vinītadeva (Calcutta, 1908–1913).

14 *Bibliotheca Buddhica*, XXIV–XXV (Leningrad, 1927–1928).

15 *A bilingual Index of Nyāyabindu* (Calcutta, 1917).

16 *Buddhist Logic*, II, pp. 1–253; *Buddhist Logic*, I (= *Bibliotheca Buddhica*, XXVI) (Leningrad, 1930–1932; reprint, 's-Gravenhage, 1958).

japonaise incomplète qui s'arrête au milieu du troisième *pariccheda* dûe à M. Watanabe Shōkō.[17]

L'introduction de M. M. nous apprend la découverte de deux nouveaux manuscrits qui contiennent le texte du *Nyāyabindu* et de la *ṭīkā*. Ainsi on dispose donc actuellement de cinq manuscrits.[18] Deux ne contiennent que la *ṭīkā* et trois le *Nyāyabindu* et la *ṭīkā*. En ontre, M. M. signale un manuscrit d'un commentaire, inconnu jusqu'alors, de la *ṭīkā*, le *Tātparyanibandhanaṭippana* d'un auteur inconnu. Dans ses notes il s'en est servi ainsi que de la *ṭippaṇī* de Mallavādi.

N'ayant à sa disposition qu'un seul manuscrit[19] M. M. s'est efforcé de le reproduire le plus fidèlement possible. Pour le texte de la *Nyāyabinduṭīkā* il a donné la préférence aux lectures corroborées par le *Dharmottarapradīpa*. M. M. a joint à son édition des notes qui se réfèrent aux autres ouvrages de Dharmakīrti, aux trois autres commentaires de la *ṭīkā* et à quelques autres textes. Sept index contiennent les termes techniques, les noms propres et les citations qui se rencontrent dans le *Nyāyabindu*, la *ṭīkā* et le *Dharmottarapradīpa*. Il faut savoir gré à M. M. d'avoir édité, d'une manière si soignée, l'ouvrage de Durveka Miśra[20] dont on ne connaissait que depuis 1949 le *Hetubinduṭīkāloka*. Nous espérons qu'il publiera également les deux autres commentaires de la *ṭīkā*: la *ṭippaṇī* de Mallavādi et le *Tātparyanibandhanaṭippana*.

Leiden J. W. de Jong

VII
Tantric Literature

J. W. DE JONG

NOTES ON THE SOURCES AND THE TEXT OF THE SANG HYANG KAMAHĀYĀNAN MANTRANAYA

For Dr. C. Hooykaas, on the occasion of his seventieth birthday, in fulfilment of an old promise.

In 1910 J. Kats published the text of the Sang hyang Kamahāyānan Mantranaya [1] in his book *Sang hyang Kamahâyânikam* (pp. 17-30). The text consists of 42 Sanskrit verses together with an Old-Javanese commentary. A footnote (p. 12; n. 1) informs the reader that H. Kern had corrected the Sanskrit verses in accordance with the Old-Javanese translation. Kats does not indicate the readings of his manuscript. In 1913 J. S. Speyer published a new edition of the verses together with textual notes and a translation: "Ein altjavanischer mahāyānistischer Katechismus", *ZDMG*, 67, 1913, pp. 347-362. Speyer consulted the manuscript which had been the basis of Kats's edition (cod. 5068; MS. A in Kats's edition). Speyer's edition does not give the exact readings of the manuscript: "Ich habe die oft fehlerhafte Orthographie korrigiert und die Textverderbnisse stillschweigend verbessert, insoweit die Emendierung sicher ist; wo nicht, so gebe ich die handschriftliche Lesung, mit Vorsetzung eines Sternchens, eventuell mit Verbesserungsvorschlägen" (p. 354).[2] Kats's translation was severely criticized by K. Wulff who published a new translation in 1935: *Sang hyang Kamahāyānan Mantrānaya. Ansprache bei der Weihe buddhistischer Mönche aus dem altjavanischen übersetzt und sprachlich erläutert* (København, 1935). Wulff made several corrections in the Sanskrit text of the verses, mainly basing himself on the paraphrase given in the commentary. Apropos of Wulff's edition H. von Glasenapp published two articles: "Ein Initiations-Ritus im buddhistischen Java", *OLZ*, 39, 1936, Sp. 483-489; "Noch einmal: "Ein Initiations-Ritus im buddhistischen Java" ", *OLZ*,

[1] Abridged: SHKM.

[2] Speyer probably did not omit any significant manuscript readings. Unfortunately Speyer has not edited the verses of the Sang Hyang Kamahāyānikan (Kats, pp. 31-70). It is not clear how far Kern has also emended the text of these verses. A critical edition of these Sanskrit verses would be of importance for the study of Javanese Tantrism.

41, 1938, Sp. 201-204. In these articles von Glasenapp tried to explain the meaning of the initiation rite described in the text. With regard to the text of the verses, von Glasenapp pointed out that several verses are also to be found in a text published by Louis Finot in his "Manuscrits sanskrits de sādhana's retrouvés en Chine" (*JA*, 1934, II, pp. 1-85). This text, called Hevajrasekaprakriyā, contains the following verses of the SHKM: 1, 4, 5ab, 6, 13, 17, 31 and 41. However, these verses are not free from corruptions and they are of no help in establishing a more correct text. Finally, in 1952, von Glasenapp published a third article on the SHKM: "Ein buddhistischer Initiationsritus des javanischen Mittelalters", *Tribus, Jahrbuch des Linden-Museums Stuttgart,* N.F. 2/3, 1952/53, pp. 259-274. Apart from an introduction based on his abovementioned articles it contains a metrical translation of the 42 verses.

The publications by Kats, Speyer, Wulff and von Glasenapp have made the SHKM widely known outside the small circle of specialists in Old-Javanese literature. However, none of these scholars have tried to trace the sources of the Sanskrit verses. Speyer assumed that they were not composed in Java but in India. His opinion was shared by von Glasenapp who discovered that several of the verses were also to be found in the Hevajrasekaprakriyā: "Das Auftreten so vieler auch anderwärts belegter Strophen im M [= SHKM] (sie machen fast ein Fünftel des ganzen Textes aus!) legt die Vermutung nahe, dass alle Strophen nicht in Java selbst gedichtet worden sind, sondern aus Indien stammen. Wahrscheinlich haben M und H [= Hevajrasekaprakriyā], beide unabhängig voneinander aus älteren tantrischen Ritualwerken geschöpft." (Ein buddhistischer Initiationsritus des javanischen Mittelalters, p. 263). He was unaware that two Japanese scholars had been able to identify most of the verses of the SHKM in two tantric texts preserved in Chinese and Tibetan translations. In 1915 Wogihara Unrai [3] published an article entitled: "Jawa ni oite hakken-sararetaru

[3] Wogihara Unrai (1869-1937) studied from 1899 to 1905 in Strassburg with Ernst Leumann. He obtained his doctorate in 1905 with a dissertation on Asaṅga's Bodhisattvabhūmi (Leipzig, 1908). Wogihara has edited several important Buddhist Sanskrit texts: Bodhisvattvabhūmi (Tokyo, 1930-1936), Haribhadra's Abhisamayālaṃkārālokā (Tokyo, 1932-1935), Yaśomitra's Abhidharmakośavyākhyā (Tokyo, 1932-1936) and the Saddharmapuṇḍarīka (with C. Tsuchida, Tokyo, 1935). A great number of his articles and translations have been brought together in his *Bunshū* (Tokyo, 1938) which also contains a reprint of his article on the SHKM (pp. 737-746). Wogihara has left a comprehensive Sanskrit-Japanese dictionary, six fascicles of which were published from 1940-1943. It is being published by the Suzuki Foundation (fascicles 7-15, Tokyo, 1964-1972). It will be complete in 16 fascicles of about 100 pages each.

mikkyō yōmon [An important tantric text discovered in Java]", *Mikkyō*, Vol. V, No. 2. Reading Speyer's edition of the text, Wogihara noticed that several of the verses (1-5ab, 6-9, 16, 17-18, 20-22) occurred in the Chinese version of the Mahāvairocanasūtra, one of the most sacred texts of the Shingon sect. Wogihara translated Speyer's introduction and gave a Japanese translation of the 42 verses, comparing the Chinese version of the above-mentioned verses and adding textual notes. Further progress in the identification of the verses of the SHKM was made in an article published in 1950 by Sakai Shirō[4]: "Jaba hakken mikkyō yōmon no issetsu ni tsuite [On a section of an important tantric text discovered in Java]", *Mikkyō bunka*, 8, 1950, pp. 38-46. Sakai traced the last 17 verses (26-42) to a tantric text which exists both in Chinese and Tibetan translation. The Chinese version of this text is known under the Sanskrit title Adhyardhaśatikā prajñāpāramitā-sūtra. The Tibetan version has the title Śrīparamādyamantrakalpakhaṇḍa. Sakai reproduced the text of these 17 verses according to Speyer's edition, adding a Japanese translation, the text of the Tibetan version in the Derge edition of the Kanjur and the text of the Chinese version. Sakai did not add any textual notes but his article contains a short introduction on the importance of the text from the point of view of tantric studies.

The verses identified by Wogihara are to be found in the second chapter of the Mahāvairocanasūtra. A short summary of this chapter is given by R. Tajima in his *Étude sur le Mahāvairocana-sūtra* (Paris, 1936, pp. 111-115). According to the Tibetan version its title is "The treasury of the mantras which are to be placed in the maṇḍala" (*dkyil-'khor-du dgod-pa'i gsaṅ-sṅags-kyi mdzod*). It deals with the preparations for the construction of the maṇḍala and the performance of the abhiṣeka rite. The tantric texts are divided into four groups: *kriyā, caryā, yoga* and *anuttarayoga*. According to Sakai four kinds of abhiṣeka are mentioned in the *anuttarayoga* texts: 1. The Jar-consecration (*Kalaśābhiṣeka*); 2. The Secret Consecration (*Guhyābhiṣeka*); 3. The consecration in the knowledge of Wisdom (*Prajñājñānābhiṣeka*); and 4. The Fourth consecration (*Caturthābhiṣeka*). The Jar-consecration is again subdivided into six consecrations: those of water (*udaka*), crown (*mukuṭa*),

---

4 Sakai Shirō (1908-), professor at the University of Kōyasan, is a specialist in tantric studies. He has published a great number of articles and two books: *Chibetto mikkyō kyōri no kenkyū* [A study of the doctrines of Tibetan Tantrism] (Kōyasan, 1956) and *Dainichikyō no seiritsu ni kan-suru kenkyū* [A study on the formation of the Mahāvairocanasūtra] (Kōyasan, 1962). Sakai has devoted much attention to Tibetan versions of Indian tantric texts, many of which have never been translated into Chinese.

vajra, bell (*ghaṇṭā*), name (*nāma*), and master (*ācārya*).[5] The last of these six consecrations, the master-consecration, is described in the SHKM.[6] According to Sakai the Jar-consecration is described in texts belonging to the *caryā* and *yoga* groups, but the other three only in *anuttarayoga* texts. The Mahāvairocanasūtra, which belongs to the *caryā* group, described the Jar-consecration only in brief, whereas the Adhyardhaśatikā prajñāpāramitā does so in detail. Sakai remarks that Tibetan commentaries place this latter text in the *yoga* group but that it can also be considered as an *anuttarayoga* text because it is one of the principal texts dealing with the idea of 'Great Bliss' (*mahāsukha*).

The emendations, proposed by Kern (in Kats's edition of the SHKM), Speyer, Wulff and Wogihara, have done much for the establishment of a more satisfactory text. However, only Wogihara was able to compare the Sanskrit text of some of the verses with a different version. Wogihara did not compare the Tibetan version which is much closer to the Sanskrit text. Although he compared both the Chinese and Tibetan versions of 17 verses, Sakai did not propose any emendations. For this reason it is not superfluous to compare the verses identified by Wogihara and Sakai with the Tibetan and Chinese versions. For the Chinese versions of the Mahāvairocanasūtra and the Adhyardhaśatikā prajñāpāramitā I have used the so-called Taishō edition of the Chinese Buddhist canon; and for the Tibetan versions the photomechanic reprint of the Peking edition of the Kanjur [= P.].[7] For verses 26-42 Sakai gives the text of the Derge edition [= D.] which I have adopted in a few places. The following tables indicate the numbers of the verses in the SHKM and their locations in the Tibetan and Chinese versions:

[5] For a brief description of the abhiṣeka according to the *anuttarayoga* texts, see Sakai's *Chibetto mikkyō kyōri no kenkyū*, pp. 166-176. Sakai refers to Advayavajra's Sekatānvayasaṃgraha (Advayavajrasamgraha, *Gaekwad Or.Ser.* 40, Baroda, 1927, pp. 36-39) which gives the Sanskrit technical terms.

[6] According to Sakai the ācāryābhiṣeka consists of eight parts. The SHMK describes the eighth. The Sanskrit names are: vajrasamaya, ghaṇṭāsamaya, mudrāsamaya, bhavyatā, anujñā, vrata, vyākaraṇa and āśvāsa, see Advayavajrasamgraha p. 38. 10-11.

[7] In the Taishō edition the Mahāvairocanasūtra is No. 848. It is to be found in vol. XVIII (Tokyo, 1928, pp. 1-55). The Adhyardhaśatikā Prajñāpāramitā is No. 244 (vol. VIII, Tokyo, 1928, pp. 786-824). The Tibetan version of the Mahāvairocanasūtra is No. 126 in the Peking Kanjur (cf. *A comparative analytical catalogue of the Kanjur division of the Tibetan Tripitaka*, Kyoto, 1930-1932, pp. 45-48), vol. Tha ff. 115b-225b (*Chibetto daizōkyō*, vol. 5, Tokyo-Kyoto, 1957, pp. 240-284). The Śrīparamādyamantrakalpakhaṇḍa is No. 120 (*A comparative analytical catalogue*, etc. p. 43), vol. Ta ff. 178a-277b (*Chibetto daizōkyō*, vol. 5, pp. 133-173).

A. Mahāvairocanasūtra

SHKM	Tib. version (Peking ed.)	Chinese version
1-5ab	Tha f. 125a3-5	XVIII, p. 4b7-16
6-9	128a3-6	6a17-24
16	138a3-4	12a13-14
17-18	138a4-5	12a17-20
20-22	138a6-8	12a23-28

B. Adhyardhaśatikā prajñāpāramitā (= Ch. version); Śrīparamādya-mantrakalpakhaṇḍa (= Tib. version)

26-41	Ta ff. 239b4-240a8	VIII, p. 815b13-c3
42	241a6	815c14-16

The verses 26-41 are not arranged in the same order in the Tibetan and Chinese translations as in the SHKM. The order of the verses in the Tibetan version is: 26, 27, A, 28, 29, 30, 31, 32, 33, B, 34, C, 37, 38, 35, 36, 39, 40, 41. The verses marked A, B and C, are missing in the SHKM. The Chinese version of the Adhyardhaśatikā Prajñāpāramitā does not correspond very well to the Sanskrit text and it is not always easy to find the corresponding Chinese text. In several places it would be possible to arrange the corresponding Chinese text differently from the way done by Sakai. In any case, the order of the verses is the same in the Chinese translation as in the Tibetan translation, but 31 is missing.

1. ehi vatsa mahāyānaṃ mantravāryanayaṃ [1] vidhim
deśayiṣyāmi te samyak bhājanas tvaṃ mahānaye

khyod ni tshul-chen snod-yin-gyis
bu tshur theg-pa chen-po-yis
gsaṅ-sṅags spyod-tshul cho-ga ni
khyod-la yaṅ-dag bstan-par bya //

1) Kern *mantracārya*°. Speyer hesitated between *mantracaryā*° and *mantrācārya*° which is to be found in verse 21. Wulff *mantracaryā*° which is confirmed by Ch. [= Chinese version], T. [= Tibetan version] and Finot's MS. (p. 20.20).

2-3. atītā ye hi sambuddhāḥ tathā caivāpy anāgatāḥ
pratyutpannāś ca ye nāthāḥ tiṣṭhanti ca jagaddhitāḥ
taiś ca sarvair imaṃ vajraṃ [1] jñātvā mantravidhiṃ param
prāptā sarvajñatā vīraiḥ bodhimūle hy alakṣaṇa.[2]

2. rdzogs-pa'i saṅs-rgyas gaṅ 'das daṅ
de-bẓin yaṅ-dag ma-byon daṅ
da-ltar byuṅ-ba'i mgon-po rnams
'gro-la phan-phyir ẓugs-pa dag //

3. de-dag kun-gyis gsaṅ-sṅags-kyi
cho-ga mchog-bzaṅ 'di mkhyen daṅ
dpa'-bos byaṅ-chub śiṅ druṅ-du
thams-cad mkhyen-pa mtshan-med brñes //

1) According to Wogihara Ch. has *dharmaṃ* instead of *vajraṃ* but Ch. *fa* renders *vidhiṃ*. Ch. and T. do not translate *vajraṃ*. 2) Speyer and Wulff *alakṣaṇā* which is confirmed by Ch. and T.

4. mantraprayogam atulaṃ yena bhagnaṃ mahābalam
Mārasainyaṃ mahāghoraṃ Śākyasiṃhena tāyinā

gsaṅ-sṅags sbyor-ba mñam-med de
śā-kya seṅ-ge skyob-pa-yis
bdud-sde śin-tu mi bzad (P. zad)-pa
dpuṅ-chen dag kyaṅ de-yis bcom //

5ab. tasmān matiṃ imāṃ varya [1] kuru sarvajñatāptaye
de-bas kun-mkhyen thob-bya'i phyir
bu-yis blo-gros 'di gyis-śig

1) Speyer *vatsa*. This is confirmed by T. *bu* which renders *vatsa* in 1a. Finot's MS. also has *vatsa* (p. 21.15).

6. eṣa mārgavaraḥ śrīmān mahāyānamahodayaḥ
yena yūyaṃ gamiṣyanto bhaviṣyatha tathāgatāḥ
7ab. svayambhuvo mahābhāgāḥ [1] sarvalokasya yetiyāḥ [2]

6. theg-pa chen-po cher 'byuṅ-ba'i
lam-mchog 'di ni dpal-daṅ-ldan
khyed-rnams der ni doṅ-bas-na
raṅ-byuṅ skal-ba chen-po-pa //

7ab. 'jig-rten thams-cad mkhyen-pa-yi
de-bẓin gśegs-pa rnams-su 'gyur

1) Wogihara remarks that Ch. has *mahānāgāḥ* instead of *mahābhāgāḥ*. T. translates *mahābhāgāḥ*, but it is possible that *mahānāgāḥ* was the original reading. However, *mahānāga* is an epithet of śrāvakas and not of tathāgatas (cf. Edgerton, *Buddhist Hybrid Sanskrit Dictionary*; Lamotte, *Le traité de la grande vertu de sagesse,* I, Louvain, 1944,

p. 212). [2]) Kern *yajñīyāḥ*; Speyer *ye priyāḥ*. Wogihara has found the correct solution by emending it to *cetiyāḥ*. One finds *sarvalokasya cetiyo* in the Mahāvastu (cf. Edgerton, *op. cit.* s.v. *cetiya*). Ch. renders *cetiya* by "honoured as a caitya". T. has "known", deriving *cetiya* from the verb *cit-*.

7cd. astināstivyatikrāntam ākāśam iva nirmalam
8. gambhīraṃ sarvatarkebhir apy atarkyam [1] anāvilam [2]
sarvaprapañcarahitaṃ prapañcebhiḥ prapañcitam
9. karmakriyāvirahitaṃ [3] satyadvayam anāśrayam [4]
idaṃ yānavaraṃ śreṣṭhaṃ labhiṣyatha naye sthitāḥ

7cd. yod daṅ med las rnam-par 'das
nam-mkha' bẓin-du dri-ma med //

8. zab-mo rtog-ge thams-cad-kyis
rab-tu mi-rtogs gnas med-pa
spros-pa kun daṅ bral-ba ste
spros-pa rnams-kyis rnam-par spros //

9. las daṅ bya-ba la-sogs bral
bden-pa gñis-la phan gnas-pa'i
theg-pa rab-kyi mchog 'di ni
tshul-la gnas-na thob-par 'gyur //

1) Wogihara's emendation of *apy atarkyam* to *apratarkyam* is confirmed by T. 2) Wogihara *anālayam*. This, too, is confirmed by T. 3) T. has read *karmakriyādirahitaṃ*. The literal translation of Ch. is "action and act are excellent and incomparable". 4) Wogihara *satyadvayasamāśrayam*. T. (P.) is not clear but, in any case, it does not render the negation in *anāśrayam*. Instead of *phan gnas-pa'i* the Lhasa edition has *gnas-pa yis* which corresponds to *samāśrayam*.

11ab. vajraṃ ghaṇṭāṃ ca mudrāṃ ca adya maṇḍalino [1] vadet

1) Speyer *nādyāmaṇḍalino*; Wogihara *na hy amaṇḍalino*.

16. ajñānapaṭalaṃ vatsa punitaṃ jinanes [1] tava
śalākair vaidyarājendraiḥ yathālokasya [2] taimiram

sṅon-gyi mig-mkhan rgyal-po-yis
'jig-rten liṅ-tog bsal-ba bẓin
bu khyod-kyis ni mi śes-pa'i
liṅ-tog rgyal-ba rnams-kyis bsal //

1) Speyer *apanītaṃ jinais*. T. "removed by Jinas". 2) Read *yathā lokasya*. So T.

17. pratibimbasamā dharmā acchāḥ śuddhā anāvilāḥ
agrāhyā abhilāpyāś [1] ca hetukarmasamudbhavāḥ
18. evaṃ jñātvā imān dharmān nissvabhāvān anāvilān [2]
kuru satvārthaṃ atulaṃ jāto 'sy urasi tāyinām

17. chos-rnams gzugs-brñan lta-bu ste
daṅ-ẓiṅ dag-la rñog-pa med
gzuṅ-du med-ciṅ brjod-du med
rgyu-daṅ-las las byuṅ-ba ste //

18. ṅo-bo ñid-med gnas med-pa
de-ltar chos 'di śes-nas-su
sems-can don ni mñam-med byos
'on-kyaṅ saṅs-rgyas sras-su skyes //

1) Speyer *agrāhyānabhilāpyāś* which is confirmed by Ch. and T. 2) T. has *anālayān* but Ch. confirms *anāvilān*.

20. adyaprabhṛti lokasya cakraṃ vartaya tāyinām
sarvatra pūrya [1] vimalaṃ dharmaśaṅkham anuttaram

chos-kyi duṅ ni bla-med-pa
kun-tu rgyas-par bus-nas-su
de-riṅ phan-chad 'jig-rten-la
skyob-pa rnams-kyi 'khor-lo bskor //

1) Wogihara remarks that *pūrya* is an incorrect form. He quotes from I-hsing's commentary (see below) the pāda *āpurayan samantād vai*. T. seems to have read the same text.

21. na te 'tra vimatiḥ kāryā nirviśaṅkena cetasā
prakāśaya mahātulaṃ [1] mantrācāryanayaṃ [2] param

som-ñi yid-gñis mi bya-ẓiṅ
dogs-pa med-pa'i sems-kyis khyod
gsaṅ-sṅags spyod (P. spyad)-pa'i tshul-gyi mchog
'jig-rten 'di-la rab-tu śod //

1) Both Ch. and T. have "proclaim in this world". Wogihara *prakāśayasva loke 'smin*. 2) Ch. and T. have *mantracaryānayam*, cf. 1b.

22. evaṃ kṛtajño buddhānām upakārīti gīyate [1]
te ca vajradharāḥ sarve rakṣanti tava sarvaśaḥ

de-ltar byas-na saṅs-rgyas-la
phan-dogs byas-pa bzo ẓes bya

rdo-rje 'dzin-pa de kun yaṅ
khyod-la rnam-pa kun-tu bsruṅ //

[1]) Wogihara quotes *gīyase* from I-hsing's commentary. This is not found in Ch. and T., but is required by the context.

26. dṛṣṭaṃ praviṣṭaṃ paramaṃ rahasyātkhama maṇḍalam [1]
sarvapāpair vinirmuktaḥ [2] bhavanto 'dyaiva [3] śuddhitāḥ [4]

gsaṅ-ba'i dkyil-'khor dam-pa ni
mthoṅ-ba daṅ ni ẓugs-pas kyaṅ
sdig-pa kun-las ṅes-grol-ẓiṅ
khyed-rnams der-ñid legs-par gnas //

[1]) Speyer *rahasyottamamaṇḍalam* which is confirmed by T. [2]) Speyer *vinirmuktā.* [3]) T. has *atraiva* but, by making a slight change, one can read *deṅ-ñid* (*adyaiva*) for *der-ñid* (*atraiva*). [4]) T. *susthitāḥ* which is preferable.

27. na bhūyo ramanaṃ bhosti [1] yānād asmān mahāsukhāt
avṛṣyāś [2] cāpy avandyāś [3] ca ramadhvam akutobhayāḥ

bde-chen theg (P. thob)-pa 'di-las ni
slar 'chi-ba ni yod min-te
mi tshugs-pa daṅ mi sod-pas
cis-kyaṅ mi-'jigs rol-par-gyis //

[1]) Speyer *bhramaṇaṃ bhoti,* Wulff *ramaṇam bho 'sti.* T. has read *maraṇaṃ bhoti.* Probably one must read *ramaṇaṃ bhoti.* [2]) Speyer's emendation *adhṛṣyāś* is confirmed by T. and Ch. The latter has confused *adhṛṣya* and *adṛśya.* [3]) Speyer and Wulff *cānavadyāś* but T. *cāpy avadhyāś* which must be the correct reading.

28. ayaṃ vaḥ satataṃ rakṣyaḥ siddhasamayasaṃvaraḥ
sarvabuddhasamaṃ proktaḥ [1] ajñāparamaṃśāsvati [2]

dam-tshig sdom-pa grub-pa 'di
khyod-kyis rtag-tu bsruṅ-bar bya
saṅs-rgyas kun-gyis mthun-par gsuṅs
dam-pa rtag-pa'i bka' yin-no //

[1]) Wulff ingeniously proposes *sarvabuddhasamāḥ proktāḥ*. However, T. and Ch. seem to have read *sarvabuddhaiḥ samaṃ proktaḥ.* [2]) Speyer's emendation *ājñā paramaśāśvatī* is confirmed by T.

29. bodhicittaṃ tavātyājyaṃ [1] yad vajram iti mudrayā
yasyotpādaikamātreṇa [2] buddha eva na saṃśayaḥ

gaṅ-ẓig skyed-pa tsam-gyis ni
saṅs-rgyas ñid-du dogs med-pa'i
byaṅ-chub-sems ni gtaṅ mi-bya
phyag-rgya rdo-rje gaṅ yin-pa //

1) Wulff changed *tavā°* to *tvayā°* without indicating the MS reading. His emendation is unnecessary. 2) T. does not translate *eka*. Perhaps one must read *yasyotpādanamātreṇa*.

30. saddharmo na pratikṣepyaḥ na tyājyaś ca kadācana
ajñānād atha mohād vā na vai vivṛṇuyāt [1] sa tu

dam-pa'i chos ni mi smod-ciṅ
nam-yaṅ btaṅ-bar mi-bya'o
mi śes-pa 'am rmoṅs-pa yis
des ni smad-par mi-bya'o //

1) T. and Ch. have read *vivarṇayet* which is preferable. For *vivarṇayati* see Edgerton, *op. cit.*

31. svam ātmānaṃ parityajya tapobhir ṇnaḥtha [1] pīḍayet
yathāsukhaṃ sukhaṃ dhāryaṃ sambuddho 'yam anāgataḥ

raṅ-gi bdag-ñid yoṅs-spaṅs-nas
dka'-thub rnams-kyi gduṅ mi-bya
ci bde-bar ni bde-bar gzuṅ
'di ni ma-byon rdzogs saṅs-rgyas //

1) Three different emendations have been proposed: Kern *nāti-*, Speyer *na tu,* Wulff *nātha*. T. is of no help. Kern's emendation is very attractive. Speyer's translation is not correct: "Wiewohl man sein Selbst preiszugeben hat, soll man es doch nicht durch *tapas*-Arten quälen." The meaning is: "One must not give up one's self and harm it by mortifications." Finot's MS is different: [ā]tmanam na vai tyājyaṃ tapobhir na ca pīḍayet (p. 27.3).

32. vajraṃ ghaṇṭāñ ca mudrāñ ca na saṃtyajya kadācana
ācāryo nāvamantavyaḥ sarvabuddhasamo hy asau

rdo-rje dril-bu phyag-rgyas rnams
nam-yaṅ yoṅs-su spaṅ mi-bya
slob-dpon smad-par mi bya-ste
'di ni saṅs-rgyas kun daṅ-'dra //

33. yaś cāvamanyed ācāryaṃ sarvabuddhasamaṃ gurum
sarvabuddhāvamānena nityaṃ duhkham avāpnuyāt

34. tasmāt sarvaprayatnena vajrācāryaṃ mahāgurum [1]
pracchannavarakalyāṇaṃ nāvamanyet kadācana

33. saṅs-rgyas kun mtshuṅs bla-ma yis
slob-dpon la ni gaṅ smad-pa
de (P. des) ni saṅs-rgyas kun smad-pas
rtag-tu sdug-bsṅal thob 'gyur-pa //

34. de-bas 'bad-pa thams-cad-kyis
rdo-rje slob-dpon blo-gros-che
dge-ba rab-tu mi spyoms-pa
nam-yaṅ smad-par mi-bya'o //

1) T. has read *mahāmatim* but *mahāgurum* is confirmed by Ch.

35. nityaṃ svasamayaḥ sādhyo nityaṃ pūjyas tathāgataḥ [1]
nityañ ca guruvedeyaṃ [2] sarvabuddhasamo hy asau

rtag-tu raṅ-gi dam-tshig bsruṅ
rtag-tu de-bẓin-gśegs-pa mchod //
rtag-tu bla-ma la yaṅ dbul (P. 'bul)
'di ni saṅs-rgyas kun daṅ-'dra

1) Speyer *pūjyās tathāgatāḥ*. T. has no plural particle but this is often omitted. 2) Speyer *guruvaidheyyaṃ*. T. has *gurave deyaṃ* which is undoubtedly the correct reading.

36. datte 'smin sarvabuddhebhyo dattaṃ bhavati cākṣayam
taddānāt puṇyasambhāraḥ sambhārāt siddhir uttamā

de-byin saṅs-rgyas thams-cad la
rtag-tu sbyin-pa ñid-du 'gyur
de-byin bsod-nams tshogs yin-te
tshogs-las dṅos-grub mchog-tu 'gyur //

37. nityaṃ svasamayācāryaṃ prāṇair api nijair bhajet
adeyaiḥ putradārair vā kiṃ punar vibhavaiś calaiḥ

38. yasmāt sudurlabhaṃ nityaṃ kalpāsaṃkhyeyakoṭibhiḥ
buddhatvam udyogavate dadatīhaiva janmani

37. raṅ-gi dam-tshig slob-dpon ni
sbyin-min bu daṅ chuṅ-ma daṅ
raṅ-srog-gis rtag bsten byas-na
loṅs-spyod g.yo-ba smos ci-dgos //

38. gaṅ-gis bskal-pa bye-bar ni
graṅs-med-par ni ñed dka'-ba'i
saṅs-rgyas-ñid kyaṅ brtson-ldan la
tshe 'di-ñid la ster-bar byed //

39. adya vaḥ saphalaṃ janma yad asmin supratiṣṭhitaḥ [1]
samaḥ samāya devānām [2] adya jātāḥ svayambhavaḥ [3]

de-phyir 'di ni legs gnas-pas
deṅ khyod skye-ba 'bras-bur bcas
raṅ-byuṅ dam-tshig lha daṅ-mñam
deṅ khyod gyur-bar the-tshom med //

1) Speyer *supratiṣṭhitāḥ*. 2) Speyer *samasamā ye devānām*. T. has read *samāḥ samayadevānām*, which is metrically preferable to Speyer's reading. However, I have not been able to trace the expression *samaya-deva*. Perhaps one must keep the MS readings *supratiṣṭhitaḥ* and *samaḥ* in spite of the grammatical incorrectness of the singular. 3) Speyer *svayambhuvaḥ*.

40. adyābhiṣiktāyuṣmantaḥ sarvabuddhaiḥ savajribhiḥ
traidhātukamahārājye rājādhipatayaḥ sthitāḥ

saṅs-rgyas rdo-rje-'dzin bcas-par
kun-gyi deṅ khyod dbaṅ-bskur-bas
khams-gsum-gyi ni rgyal-po che
rgyal-po'i bdag-por bstan-pa yin //

41. adya Māraṃ vinirjitya praviṣṭāḥ paramaṃ puram
prāptam adyaiva buddhatvaṃ bhavadbhir nātra saṃśayaḥ

deṅ (P. D. de) ni bdud-las rnam-rgyal te
groṅ-khyer mchog-tu rab-tu ẓugs
khyed-rnams kyi ni saṅs-rgyas ñid
deṅ 'dir thob-par the-tshom med //

42. iti kuruta manaḥ prasādavajraṃ
svasamayam akṣayasaukhyadaṃ bhajadhvam
jagati laghusukhe 'dya sarvabuddha- [1]
pratisamaśāśvatitāṃ gatā bhavantaḥ

de-ltar yid ni rab-daṅ rdo-rje ñid-du gyis
raṅ-gi dam-tshig mi-zad bde-ster (P. gter) bsten-par gyis
deṅ (P. D. de) ni 'gro-la myur-bde rdo-rje sems-dpa' daṅ
rab-tu mñam-ẓiṅ rtag-tu ñid-du rtogs-par gyis //

1) T. and Ch. have read *vajrasattva*.

In his introduction Wulff has briefly summarized the opinions of scholars on the date of the (Old-Javanese) text of the SHKM. Opinions vary from the 14th or 15th century to before the first half of the 10th century (*op. cit.*, p. 9).[8] It is obvious that the verses must have existed in Java before the commentary was written. With regard to the verses the problem is twofold: the date of their original composition and the date of their arrival in Java. The identification of the majority of the verses of the SHKM makes it possible to give some indications on these two points. In order to do so it is necessary to consider briefly the date and the history of the two tantric texts to which most of the verses of the SHKM have been traced back. This is not an easy task because Tantrism, especially Indian and Tibetan Tantrism, is still largely a terra incognita. Most Sanskrit manuscripts are still as yet unedited. Of the Sanskrit Tantras which have been published only a very few have been critically edited. Japanese scholars have studied Tantrism for many centuries but until recently their studies were based entirely on Sino-Japanese materials. In the last fifty years, however, they have made many contributions to the study of Tibetan translations of tantric texts. These Tibetan translations are of great importance because they are in general much more faithful to the original Indian text than the Chinese translations. Moreover, many more tantric texts were translated into Tibetan than into Chinese. The catalogue of the Derge edition of the Kanjur and Tanjur (*A complete catalogue of the Tibetan Buddhist canons*, Sendai, 1934) lists 4569 texts. Of these, the texts numbered 360-3785 belong to the Tantra sections of these two collections. In the Taishō edition of the Chinese Buddhist canon the tantric texts have been published in volumes XVIII-XXI (nos. 848-1420). As against more than 3400 texts in the Tibetan Buddhist canon there are less than 600 texts in the Chinese Buddhist canon. Tibetan scholars have also written many more commentaries and original works than their Chinese counterparts. Only when at least the most important of these texts have been translated and studied, will it become possible to obtain a better knowledge of the history of Indian Tantrism and its later developments in Tibet. For this reason it would at present be impossible to arrive at any definite conclusions even if one had read the already extensive literature on Tantrism in Western languages and in Japanese.

---

8 Tenth century according to Iwamoto Yutaka, "Jaba bukkyō bunken ni tsuite [On the Buddhist literature of Java]", *Indogaku Bukkyōgaku kenkyū*, II, 1953, p. 236.

The Mahāvairocanasūtra was translated into Chinese in 724-725 by Śubhakara in collaboration with two Chinese scholars, Pao-yüeh and I-hsing.[9] As was the custom in China, Śubhakara, while translating the text, added explanations which were noted down by I-hsing (683-727). These notes formed the basis of his own commentary on the Mahāvairocanasūtra (Taishō no. 1796). In it, I-hsing quotes the Sanskrit text of several verses of the Mahāvairocanasūtra, which he had transliterated into Chinese characters.[10] These verses were studied by a Japanese scholar, Jiun Sonja (1718-1804), who tried to reconstruct the Sanskrit text, using the Siddham script.[11] On the basis of Jiun's reconstruction, Ashikaga Atsuuji has published a romanized text of these verses: "A propos de certaines gāthās remontant au *Mahāvairocanasūtra*", *Studies in Indology and Buddhology presented in honour of Professor Susumu Yamaguchi* (Kyoto, 1955, pp. 106-121). Several of these verses occur also in the SHKM: 4cd, 6-9, 16-18, 20-22. The text of these verses, as transliterated by I-hsing, differs greatly in several places from the text of the corresponding verses of the SHKM. The main variants are the following:

7a. mahānāgāḥ instead of mahābhāgāḥ; 8. gambhīraṃ sarvadharmebhir apratarkyam anālayam / sarvaprapañcarahitaṃ prapañcair [12] aprapañcitam; 9ab. sarvakriyābhir atulaṃ satyadvaye samāśrayam; 16b. apanītaṃ jinais tava; 17a. pratibimbamayā instead of pratibimbasamā; 18d. buddhānāṃ jātas tvam aurasaḥ [13]; 20c. āpūrayan [14] samantād vai; 21c. prakāśayasva loke'smin; 22b. gīyase instead of gīyate.

---

[9] Cf. Tajima, *op. cit.*, p. 35. Śubhakara (or Śubhakarasiṃha) arrived in Ch'ang-an in 716. He died in 735. For a translation of his biography see Chou Yi--liang, "Tantrism in China", *HJAS*, 8, 1945, pp. 251-272.

[10] In his textual notes, Wogihara quoted variant readings from I-hsing's transliteration. Jiun's work must have been unknown to him as it was only published in 1953.

[11] For the Siddham script see R. H. van Gulik, *Siddham*, Nagpur, 1956.

[12] Ashikaga reconstructs *sarvaprapañca(bhi)r*. One must correct Jiun's °*pañcer* to °*pañcair*.

[13] This pāda contains nine syllables. The text of the SHKM has: jāto 'sy urasi tāyinām. Ch. has: "You are born from the heart of Buddhas." T. has: "For you are born as the son of Buddhas." It is difficult to know whether Ch. and T. had read *Buddha* or *tāyin* because they may well have rendered *tāyin* by the equivalent of *Buddha*.

[14] Ashikaga reads *āpūrayet* which does not makes good sense (*cakraṃ vartaya ... āpūrayet ... dharmaśaṅkham*). Jiun has clearly read *āpūrayaṃ* which I have changed to *āpūrayan*. The Chinese character which transliterates *-yaṃ* has been used by I-hsing for transliterating *-yaṃ* in *jayaṃ*. Probably the Sanskrit text had *āpūraya*.

If one compares the four versions of these verses: SHKM, Ch (Mahāvairocanasūtra, Chinese tr.), T (id., Tib. tr.) and IH (I-hsing's transliteration), it becomes clear that in several instances SHKM and T go together as opposed to Ch and IH:

7a.	mahānāgāḥ	Ch - IH
	mahābhāgāḥ	SHKM - T
8a.	gambhīraṃ sarvadharmebhir	Ch - IH
	gambhīraṃ sarvatarkebhir	SHKM - T
8d.	prapañcair aprapañcitam	Ch - IH
	prapañcebhiḥ prapañcitam	SHKM - T
9a.	sarvakriyābhir atulaṃ	Ch (see above 9, n. 3) - IH
	sarvakriyāvirahitaṃ	SHKM; sarvakriyādirahitaṃ T

In other instances SHKM is isolated and the other three versions are essentially the same. In these cases there seems to be no doubt that the text of the SHKM is corrupt:

8b.	apratarkyam anālayam	Ch - IH - T
	apy atarkyam anāvilam	SHKM
9b.	satyadvaye samāśrayam	Ch - IH - T
	satyadvayam anāśrayam	SHKM
16b.	apanītaṃ jinais	Ch - IH - T
	punitaṃ jinanes	SHKM
20c.	āpūrayan samantād vai	Ch - IH - T
	sarvatra pūrya vimalaṃ	SHKM
21c.	prakāśayasva loke'smin	Ch - IH - T
	prakāśaya mahātulaṃ	SHKM

It is obvious that there are two recensions of the Sanskrit text of the Mahāvairocanasūtra. The first is the text translated into Chinese by Śubhakara and transliterated by I-hsing. According to Chinese tradition the manuscript translated by Śubhakara was obtained in India by Wu-hsing, who died in North India just as he was about to return to China. The manuscripts which he collected were brought to the Chinese capital and placed in the Hua-yen Temple.[15] A Japanese scholar, Osabe Kazuo, has put this tradition in doubt. According to him two manuscripts of the Mahāvairocanasūtra were brought to China: Wu-hsing's manuscript which arrived in China some time after his death and a manuscript brought by Śubhakara himself. Both manuscripts were

[15] Tajima, *op. cit.*, p. 35.

translated into Chinese by Śubhakara, the first by Imperial order in 717, the second in 724-725. The translation which is preserved is the second one.[16] Osabe's arguments are not very convincing.[17] There are, however, other arguments which can be adduced in support of the hypothesis of the existence of more than one manuscript of the Mahāvairocanasūtra in China at the beginning of the eighth century. Recently, a Japanese scholar, Kiyota Jakuun, has drawn attention to differences in the text of several mantras of the Mahāvairocanasūtra.[18] Kiyota has consulted Sanskrit manuscripts of these mantras and their Chinese and Tibetan transliterations. He points out differences between Śubhakara's translation of the Mahāvairocanasūtra and I-hsing's transliterations in his commentary. He refers to Osabe's theory and advances the hypothesis that these differences may be explained by the fact that Śubhakara's translation was based on the manuscript obtained by Wu-hsing, and I-hsing's commentary on the manuscript brought to China by Śubhakara. However, it is not possible to attach much importance to the very minor differences which Kiyota has pointed out in the text of mantras in Śubhakara's translation and in I-hsing's commentary. They do not warrant the supposition that two different manuscripts were used by Śubhakara and I-hsing. One must not forget the fact that the texts were orally translated and explained. Under these circumstances slight variations in the text of mantras in Śubhakara's translation and I-hsing's commentary are no matter for surprise. In the absence of more conclusive evidence there seems to be no valid reason to doubt the tradition that the Sanskrit manuscript translated by Śubhakara and commented upon by I-hsing was the one obtained by Wu-hsing. This is not without importance for the history of Tantrism in Indonesia because Wu-hsing had been in Śrīvijaya and Malāyu, as we know from his biography by I-ching.[19] The date of his stay there is not known. I-ching saw Wu-hsing for the last time in Nālandā in 685. Wu-hsing was then 56 years old.

---

[16] Osabe Kazuo, "Ichigyō zenji no kenkyū", *Mikkyō kenkyū,* 87, 1944, pp. 13-17.

[17] The information given by the *K'ai-yüan shih-chiao lu* (cf. Tajima, *loc. cit.*) is more reliable than that found in later sources. The *K'ai-yüan shih-chiao lu* was compiled in 730, six years after the completion of Śubhakara's translation, when Śubhakara was still alive. The *K'ai-yüan shih-chiao lu* is considered to be a very reliable source, cf. P. Demiéville, "Les versions chinoises du Milindapañha", *BEFEO,* 24, 1924, p. 19, n. 1.

[18] Kiyota Jakuun, "Dainichikyō shingon no genmon ni tsuite", *Indogaku Bukkyōgaku kenkyū,* VIII, 1960, pp. 276-279.

[19] Cf. Éd. Chavannes, *Mémoire composé à l'époque de la grande dynastie T'ang sur les religieux éminents qui allèrent chercher la loi dans les pays d'Occident,* Paris, 1894, pp. 138-157 et p. 10.

He must have been in Śrīvijaya some time between 650 and 680. His biography does not tell us whether Wu-hsing collected manuscripts in Śrīvijaya, but this is not impossible. I-ching, who sojourned in Śrīvijaya in 672 and again from 685 to 695, translated several texts during his stay there.

The second recension of the Sanskrit text is represented by the Tibetan translation and the SHKM. The Tibetan translation was made in the beginning of the ninth century.[20] Nothing is known about the origin of the manuscript used. It may of course have been written long before the ninth century, because the work of translating texts began in Tibet only in the second half of the eighth century. Wu-hsing's manuscript probably dates from the second half of the seventh century. The manuscript used in Tibet may have been written in the eighth century.

The Adhyardhaśatikā Prajñāpāramitā was translated into Chinese and Tibetan much later than was the Mahāvairocanasūtra. The Chinese translation was made in 999 by Fa-hsien.[21] According to Chinese sources his original name was T'ien-hsi-tsai. He was a monk from Kashmir and arrived in China in 980 with Sanskrit manuscripts. In 987 his name was altered to Fa-hsien. He died in 1000.[22] The Tibetan version (Śrīparamādyamantrakalpakhaṇḍa) was translated by the Indian Mantrakalaśa and the Tibetans Lha btsan-po and Ẓi-ba'i od at Tho-ling[23] in the Sutlej river valley about 40 miles southwest of Gartok.[24] The translation was revised by Rin-chen bzaṅ-po who died in 1055. The original Adhyardhaśatikā prajñāpāramitāsūtra was a short text. An incomplete Sanskrit text from the Petrovsky collection was published by Leumann in 1910. Leumann also edited and translated an incomplete Khotanese translation.[25] The text translated by Fa-hsien

[20] Cf. Tajima, *op. cit.*, p. 36. This translation is already mentioned in the Ldan-dkar catalogue, cf. Marcelle Lalou, "Les textes bouddhiques au temps du roi Khri-sroṅ-lde-bcan"; *JA,* 1953, p. 326, no. 321. According to G. Tucci, the Ldan-dkar catalogue was compiled in 812, cf. *Minor Buddhist Texts,* II, Roma, 1958, p. 48.

[21] Cf. Mochizuki Shinkō, *Bukkyō daijiten,* VIII, 1958, p. 264.

[22] On Fa-hsien, see Jan Yün-hua, "Buddhist relations between India and Sung China", *History of Religions,* VI, 1966, pp. 34-37 and 147-151.

[23] Cf. F. A. Bischoff, *Der Kanjur und seine Kolophone,* I, Bloomington, 1968, p. 79.

[24] Cf. T. V. Wylie, *The geography of Tibet according to the 'Dzam-gling-rgyas-bshad,* Roma, 1962, p. 125, n. 96.

[25] For bibliographical information on this text see Yamada Ryūjō, *Bongo butten no shobunken,* Kyoto, 1958, pp. 88-89, 165 and 205; Edward Conze, *The Prajñāpāramitā Literature,* 's-Gravenhage, 1960, pp. 79-80. See also P.

is a greatly expanded version which seems to have been unknown to previous Chinese translators. For this reason it is not likely that the text is much older than the tenth century.

Although the sources of the SHKM are known, it is not possible to know where the text was compiled. Sakai has tried to find a corresponding text in the Tibetan Buddhist canon, but in vain. However, it is not impossible that the text was compiled in India but not transmitted to Tibet and China. Neither should the possibility be excluded that the Sanskrit verses of the SHKM existed already in India before they were later incorporated into the Mahāvairocanasūtra and the Adhyardhaśatikā Prajñāparamitā. Some of the verses are also found in other texts, for instance verse 17 in the Kriyāsamuccaya and 35cd in the Ādikarmapradīpa.[26] However, these texts are probably rather late. It seems much more probable that the verses of the SHKM were taken from these two famous tantras in order to serve as a short ritual text to be used during the ācāryābhiṣeka. The text may have been compiled in India or outside India, but it is unlikely that this took place before the tenth century.

Addendum

In 1966 Matsunaga Yūkei published an article on Sanskrit fragments of the Mahāvairocanasūtra in which he compared the Sanskrit text of the verses, quoted in the SHKM, with the Chinese and Tibetan versions: "Dainichikyō no bonbun danpen ni tsuite [Sanskrit fragments of the Mahāvairocanasūtra]", *Indogaku bukkyōgaku kenkyū*, XIV (1966), pp. 858 (139) - 856 (141). Unfortunately, this article had escaped my notice. Matsunaga suggests that in 3a *vajraṃ* be corrected to *bhadraṃ* (cf. T. *bzaṅ*).

Demiéville's detailed summary of Toganoo Shōun's *Rishukyō no kenkyū*: *Bibliographie bouddhique*, IV-V, Paris, 1934, pp. 96-98. Most of the Japanese publications are not at my disposal.

26 Cf. L. de La Vallée Poussin, *Bouddhisme, Études et matériaux*, London, 1898, p. 209, n. 5 et pp. 194-195.

F. A. Bischoff, *Contribution à l'étude des divinités mineures du Bouddhisme tantrique*. Ārya Mahābala-nāma-mahāyānasūtra. Tibétain (MSS. de Touen-houang) et chinois (*Buddhica, documents et travaux pour l'étude du bouddhisme*, première série: mémoires, tome X). Paris, 1956. xii + 126 pp., 4 pl. fr. 2.800.

La littérature tantrique est encore peu explorée malgré l'existence d'une grande masse de textes sanskrits, tibétains et chinois dans les bibliothèques. C'est pourquoi on accueille avec joie chaque travail qui apporte de la lumière dans ce domaine en majeure partie inconnu. M. Bischoff s'est consacré à l'étude d'un petit texte tantrique, le Mahābalasūtra, dont la popularité à Touen-houang est bien attestée par le fait qu'il en a pu retrouver 15 manuscrits fragmentaires dans les manuscrits tibétains rapportés de Touen-houang par Paul Pelliot. Peut-être en existe-t-il d'autres à Londres mais l'auteur ne semble pas s'en être enquis. Il ne nous renseigne pas non plus sur l'existence de fragments chinois dans les collections de Paris et de Londres.

Dans l'introduction M. B. décrit les manuscrits et les textes qu'il a utilisés et donne quelques brefs renseignements sur des textes apparentés. A propos du système de translittération de l'époque des Song il ne cite que deux articles de Staël-Holstein mais non son édition de la Gaṇḍīstotragāthā, du Saptajinastava et de l'Āryamañjuśrīnāmāṣṭaśataka (*Bibl.B.*, vol. XV, St. P., 1913). Le premier de ces textes a été examiné de nouveau par Johnston (*IA*, 62, 1933, 61–70) et le dernier par R. Kambayashi (*Journal of the Taisho University*, vol. VI–VII, part II, 1930, 243–297). Les premiers travaux de ce genre sont dus à Sylvain Lévi: "Une poésie inconnue du roi Harṣa Çilâditya", *Actes du Xe Congrès Or.*, 1895, vol. 2, 189–203 (réimprimé dans le *Mémorial Sylvain Lévi*, Paris, 1937, 244–256), et la reconstruction du Trikāyastava (*RHR*, xxiv, 1896, 17–21; à la bibliographie, relative à ce stava, donnée par L. de La Vallée Poussin, *Siddhi*, 763 et *Hōbōgirin*, 184 il faut ajouter maintenant Sekoddeśaṭīkā, *GOS*, XC, Baroda, 1941, 57–58 et G. N. Roerich, *The Blue Annals*, I, Calcutta, 1949, p. 1–2). D'après M. B. les mantra ne sont pas rédigés en sanskrit classique or, ni dans la version tibétaine dans laquelle ils sont en partie traduits et en partie translittérés ni dans la version chinoise dans laquelle ils sont entièrement translittérés on ne rencontre des formes prākrites. Evidemment on y voit beaucoup de mots et formules incompréhensibles mais c'est le cas pour presque tous les mantra. En chinois les mantra sont plus étendus qu'en tibétain mais il y a beaucoup de parties qui se recouvrent et il aurait été intéressant d'essayer d'en reconstruire le texte sanskrit original en comparant ces deux versions. M. B. a publié en caractères chinois les mantra de la version chinoise, accompagnés d'une re-translittération en sanskrit et d'une traduction. Dans un appendix il donne une liste des caractères ayant servi à la translittération des mantra. Il aurait été préférable de suivre l'exemple de Staël-Holstein (*op. laud.*) qui a numéroté les caractères et qui a indiqué où et avec quelle valeur ils figurent dans les textes.

Aussi bien l'introduction que les notes de la traduction sont assez succinctes et le rôle et l'iconographie de Mahābala et d'Ucchuṣmakrodha restent à déterminer plus exactement. L'intérêt principal de ce travail réside dans l'édition de la version tibétaine, let dans la traduction de celle-ci et de la version chinoise. L'édition de la version tibétaine a l'air d'être bien faite autant que l'on puisse en juger sans avoir recours aux manuscrits, et l'on se demande seulement pourquoi l'auteur n'a pas consulté également l'édition de Narthang, d'habitude bien supérieure à celle de Pékin. Malheureusement on ne peut pas en dire autant de la traduction de la version tibétaine. Alors que la traduction de la version chinoise est excellente celle de la version tibétaine est remplie d'erreurs et de méprises. En outre, on y trouve des formes sanskrites assez curieuses (*sarvārthadatta* et même *sarvārtha-īpsudatta*) et des équivalents sanskrits erronés (*kapāṭa* pour verrou), or, ils manquent dans la traduction de la version chinoise. Puisqu'il n'est guère probable que quelqu'un reprenne la traduction de M.B., il m'a paru utile d'énumérer ci-dessous un nombre de corrections que j'aimerais proposer.

p. 50, l. 9 *dbugs 'byin čhiṅ*: "consolant" (skt. *samāśvāsayan*, cf. Nobel, *Udrāyaṇa*, II, p. 56 s.v. *'byin-pa*), non "faisant respirer".

p. 50, l. 17 d'après Mvy. 4328 *gnod mjes* est en skt. Śumbha. Il faut donc lire en tib. *rgyal po* au lieu de *rgyai mo*. Dans la version chinoise (en abrégé: C) il y a à la place de Śumbha Trailokyavijaya que la Sādhanamālā (nr. 262) identifie à Śumbha.

p. 50, l. 22 au lieu de Vajrāṅkuśa il faut lire Vajrāṅkuśī, cf. Mvy. 4284 et l'index de la Sādhanamālā; à la ligne suivante Vajraśr̥ṅkhalā au lieu de Vajraśr̥ṅkhala, voir Sādhanamālā Nrs. 207–209.

p. 51, l. 29 M. B. rend *lus 'jigs byed* par "qui rend le corps infirme" alors que, dans le mot précédent, il rend *'jigs byed* par *bhairava*. C a *kataṃkaṭabhairava*. Tib. *lus* peut correspondre au skt. *kaṭa*, voir Mvy. 4759. On pourrait donc reconstruire Kaṭaṃkaṭabhairava mais cette reconstruction reste hypothétique tant que l'on ne retrouve pas ce nom dans un texte sanskrit. Kaṭaṃkaṭa est employé comme un nom de Śiva (*Mahābhārata*, XII, App. 1, No. 28,193 et 219, Crit. Ed. p. 2060 et 2061). P. 52, l. 30 dans un mantra il y a / *kaṭa kaṭa kaṭa* / *mahakaṭa* / (C seulement *kaṭakaṭa*). M. B. traduit *kaṭa* par "tresse". Pourquoi? On trouve encore *kaṭaṅkata* dans une série de vocatifs: "O *Kaṭaṅkata*, O *Jaya*, O *Vijaya*, O *Ajita*, O *Aparājita*." (p. 63, l. 2).

p. 51, l. 31 verrou est en skt. *argala* non *kapāṭa*, cf. Mvy. 5581. En C *vajrārgala* et *vajrāṅga* ont été invertis. Le premier a été translittéré comme *vajradgala* et le deuxième comme *vajradbhala*; *dbh* au lieu de *ṅg* se trouve aussi dans le Gaṇḍīstotra (*op. laud.*, p. 5).

p. 51, l. 32 corriger Tapadhara en Tapodhara.

p. 51, l. 33–34 M. B. traduit tib. *mdog dkar ba* deux fois; par *karkarava* et par la couleur blanche (*śvetavarṇa*). C n'a que *śvetavarṇa* comme le tib.

p. 51, l. 35 *sṅo bsaṅs* correspond au skt. *śyāma*, cf. Mvy. 2088. C translittère *śyāma* par deux caractères dont le premier rend *śyā*, cf. Staël-Holstein, *op. laud.*, p. 180, nr. 189.

p. 52, l. 27 corriger Samyakpratigata en Samyaggata, cf. Mahāmāyūrī, éd. Oldenburg, *Zap. Vost. otd. Russk. arxeol. obšč.*, 11, 1899, p. 244, l. 20.

p. 53, l. 33 après "avec sa suite" il y a en tib. un passage non-traduit par l'auteur: *bdag la gsaṅ sṅags kyi gži 'di rnams grub par gyur čig* //. C: *sidhyatu* (à corriger en *sidhyantu*) *mantrapadāni*; *dhya* est rendu par une combinaison de deux caractères qui se rencontre aussi dans le Saptajinastava, cf. Staël-Holstein, *op. laud.*, p. 185, nr. 226.

p. 53, l. 36 corriger trois mille grands chiliocosmes en trichiliomégachiliocosme (consistant de 1.000.000.000 mondes), cf. L. de La Vallée Poussin, l'*Abhidharmakośa*, III, p. 170.

p. 54, l. 10 *mi bzod pa*: "terrible" ou "irrésistible", non "piaffant"; p. 58, l. 2 l'auteur le rend par "irrésistible".

p. 54, l. 17 *srog la mi lta ba*: "il était indifférent (*anapekṣa*) à l'égard de la vie" non "il n'avait plus l'air en vie".

p. 54, l. 31 M. B. traduit *'čhaṅ ba* par "porter" en justifiant sa traduction par la note 27. Mais il s'agit ici d'un cliché bien connu de la littérature bouddhique, voir par exemple Vajracchedikā Prajñāpāramitā (en abrégé: Vajr.) § 15a: *kaḥ punar vādo yo likhitvodgr̥hṇīyād dhārayed vācayet paryavāpnuyāt parebhyaś ca vistareṇa samprakāśayet*. M. Conze (*Vajr.*, Roma, 1957, p. 79) traduit: "What then should we say of him who, after writing it, would learn it, bear it in mind, recite it, and illuminate it in full detail for others?". Ici *paryavāpnuyāt* manque mais la suite logique des idées montre bien qu'il est impossible de traduire *dhārayet* par "porter".

p. 54, l. 35 M. B. traduit *gsaṅ sṅags kyi gži* par "la base de la formule secrète" (*guhyamantravastu*) mais l'équivalent sanskrit est *mantrapada* (voir ci-dessus la note à la page 53, l. 33) que l'on rencontre souvent dans des textes de ce genre (par exemple, Mahāmāyūrī, p. 219, l. 25).

p. 55, l. 26 *gaṅ mdo sde 'di rab tu ston pa de mčhod par bgyi daṅ // phyag bgyi ba daṅ // rim gro bgyi ba daṅ // bskor bar bgyi ba'i 'os su 'gyur ba lags so //*: "Celui qui expliquera ce *sūtra*, deviendra digne d'honneur (*pūjanīya*), d'hommage (*vandanīya*), de respect (*mānanīya*) et de circumambulation (*pradakṣiṇīya*)", cf. Vajr. § 15c, non "Celui qui honorera l'explication de ce *sūtra*, qui lui rendra hommage, qui lui vouera un culte, qui l'entourera [en faisant *pradakṣiṇa*], deviendra digne de respect".

p. 57, l. 28 cette phrase est difficile, et je ne vois pas d'autre solution que de supprimer *daṅ* après *smyo byed, skems byed* et *gtan pa* et de lire: *smyo byed skrod pa daṅ / skems byed gsod pa daṅ / sgo glegs daṅ / 'khrul 'khor daṅ / gtan pa rdo rje s rnam par 'joms pa //*: "Elle chasse les unmāda, tue les Skanda (cf. Mvy. 4761) et détruit par le vajra les portes (*dvārakapāṭa*, cf. Mvy., 5567), les serrures et les verrous (*argala*)".

p. 57, l. 33 *thams čad daṅ ldan ba'i 'khor* rend skt. *sarvāvati parṣad*; ce n'est pas "l'Assemblée des assistants"; quelques lignes plus loin M. B. le traduit correctement.

p. 58, l. 5 *kun tu ston pa*: "celui qui montre", non "Maître absolu".

p. 58, l. 11 *dṅom bag čan du rdo rje sbar the*: "majestueusement il saisit le *vajra*", non "il saisit le *vajra* magnifique".

p. 58, l. 14 *tiṅ ṅe 'jin sñoms par žugs so*: "il entra dans le *samādhi*" (*sñoms par 'jug* rend skt. *samapadyate*), non "il entra indolemment dans le *samādhi*".

p. 58, l. 16 *sñoms par žugs ma tag tu khro bo čhol pas // bgegs bye ba brgya stoṅ phrag du ma 'dar te / gzir par bdag ñid kyis mthoṅ ṅo //* "dès qu'il y fut entré, il (Vajrapāṇi) vit lui-même qu'à cause d'Ucchuṣmakrodha des centaines de milliers de *koṭi* de démons tremblaient et étaient oppressés", non "Dès qu'il y fut indolemment entré, Ucchuṣmakrodha vit des centaines de milliers de *koṭi* de démons tremblants, par lui-même tourmentés".

p. 58, l. 38 *de la nad daṅ / bgegs daṅ / log 'dren gyis glags rñed par myi 'gyur ro //* "la maladie, les Vighna et les Vināyaka n'obtiendront pas d'occasion de lui [faire mal]" (*avatāraṃ lapsyante*, cf. *BHS Dictionary* s.v. *avatāra*), non "Il n'aura pas l'occasion d'être tourmenté par la maladie, les démons-obstacle (*Vighna*) et les log-'dren (*Vināyaka*)".

p. 59, l. 8 *byas pa bzo ba*: "reconnaissant" (*kṛtajña*, cf. Mvy. 2357), non "a fait ce qui est à faire (*ābhoga*)".

p. 59, l. 13 *gaṅ bdud thams čad daṅ sdaṅ ba'i sems rnam par 'jigs par byed pa // rig sṅags kyi rgyal po / stobs po čhe žes bya ba 'di / 'čaṅ ba daṅ / klog pa de / bdud daṅ / dgra thams čad gyis myi chugs par 'gyur ro //* "Celui qui retient et lit ce *vidyārāja* Mahābala qui détruit tous les Māra et les pensées de haine (p. 33, l. 35 il y a *sdaṅ ba'i sems čan*; on s'attendrait ici à la même lecture), il ne sera pas maltraité par tous les Māra et ennemis", non "Celui qui porte et lit ce *vidyārāja* nommé Mahābala détruit les pensées de haine et tous les Māra, il ne sera pas maltraité par tous les ennemis et Māra".

p. 59, l. 19 *gsad* pa: "amputation", non "maladie chronique".

p. 59, l. 38 *g-yul ṅor soṅ na*: "quand il est allé à la bataille", non "quoi qu'il arrive dans la bataille".

p. 60, l. 3 après "*pradakṣiṇa*" ajouter "autour de Bhagavat".

p. 60, l. 9 *dge bsñen gyi yan lag bzuṅ bar bgyi'o*; cette formule ne se rencontre pas dans les différentes versions de la prise des vœux par l'*upāsaka*, étudiées par M. Lamotte (*Le traité de la grande vertu de sagesse*, II, Louvain, 1949, p. 829–830). M. B. traduit: "Je m'estime membre des fidèles laïcs" mais *yan lag* (skt. *aṅga*) ne peut être employé ainsi; *'jin pa* comme *'čhaṅ ba* traduit *dhārayati* (dans le cliché traité ci-dessus, voir ci-dessus la note à la page 54, l. 31, *'jin pa* traduit *udgṛhṇāti*; mais les tibétains traduisent *udgṛhṇāti* par *'jin pa* et *len pa*, et *dhārayati* par *'jin pa* et *'čhaṅ ba*) et ne signifie pas "estimer" comme M. B. le traduit ici et p. 60, l. 16 et l. 30, et p. 61, l. 23. (Pour ce dernier passage voir Vajr. § 13a: *ko nāma-ayaṃ Bhagavan dharma-paryāyaḥ, kathaṃ cainaṃ dhārayāmi*; trad. Conze, p. 74: "What then, O Lord, is (this) discourse on dharma, and how should I bear it in mind?"). Je traduirais donc ainsi: "Je retiendrai les vœux d'*upāsaka*", cf. *PTS Dictionary*, s.v. *anga*: *uposathanga*, the vows of the fast.

p. 60, l. 13 *bde daṅ thard daṅ mtho ris daṅ / mkhas pa dag daṅ sems čan ni / dam pa kun la phan ba'i phyir // stobs po čhe ni gzuṅ bar bgyi //* M. B. traduit: "O joie (*sukha*)! O Délivrance (*mokṣa*)! O paradis (*svarga*)! Les êtres sagaces, pour le bénéfice de tous les saints, estimeront Mahābala". *Bde, thard* et *mtho ris* ne peuvent être des vocatifs et doivent dépendre de *phyir* bien que cette construction de la phrase ne soit pas très élégante. Je traduirais donc: "Pour [obtenir] la joie, la délivrance et le paradis et pour le bénéfice des sages et de tous les êtres excellents je retiendrai [le *sūtra* de] Mahābala".

p. 60, l. 21 *bskald pa mtha' yas par*: "pendant un *kalpa* infini", non "A la fin de (ces) *kalpa*".

p. 61, l. 35 *mdo sde 'di . . . . . yi ger 'drir 'Jug pa*: "Qui fera écrire (*likhāpayiṣyati*, cf. Aparamitāyur-jñāna-nāma-mahāyāna-sūtram, éd. Walleser, Heidelberg, 1916, p. 23) ce *sūtra*", non "qui pénètre ce *sūtra* dans le tracé de chaque syllabe".

p. 63, l. 11 *stan las laṅs te // bla gos phrag pa gčig la bzar nas bus mo g-yas pa'i lha ṅa sa la bcugs te / bčom ldan 'das ga la ba der logs su thal mo sbyar ba btud nas bčom ldan 'das la 'di skad čes gsol to //*. Un des clichés les plus fréquents de la littérature bouddhique, en skt.: *utthāya-āsanād, ekāṃsam uttarāsaṅgaṃ kṛtvā, dakṣiṇaṃ jānu-maṇḍalaṃ pṛthivyāṃ pratiṣṭhāpya, yena Bhagavāṃs tena-añjaliṃ praṇamya Bhagavan-tam etad avocat* (Vajr. § 2). M. B. traduit: "se levant de sa natte, rejetant son manteau sur une épaule, s'agenouillant sur son genou droit à côté de Bhagavat, incliné, les mains jointes, dit à Bhagavat".

p. 64, l. 14 *mdo sde 'di 'cho žiṅ sdod na*: "Quand ce *sūtra* vit et dure", non "Si on désire ce *sūtra* vivant".

p. 65, l. 1 ces strophes sont assez obscures et je ne puis en donner une traduction satisfaisante; d'après P. le texte en est:

saṅs rgyas 'khor ba bgrod dkar sems čan gyi //
srid pa'i phur pa 'byin čiṅ šes rab kyis //
srid phur sems kluṅ 'Joms šiṅ thub pa yi //
čhos bstan pas ni sdig 'Joms čhos legs spyod (je corrige *sbyod*) *//*

M. B. traduit: "Difficile est pour les êtres la marche [vers l'état de] Buddha, extirpant, grâce à la *prajñā*, la taie (*phur ba*) malsaine; dominant, grâce à la doctrine du Muni, le flot des pensées mauvaises, le mal est vaincu et la bonne Loi pratiquée" sans donner aucune explication. *Bgrod dka' ba* rend skt. *durga* (cf. le dictionnaire tibétain-sanscrit, publié par Bacot) et *phur pa* (le texte a *ba*; mais *pa* et *ba* se confondent aisément dans les xylographes) skt. *kīla*, cheville. Le début peut donc se traduire ainsi: "Le Buddha ôte la cheville de l'existence (*bhavakīla*) pour les êtres dans la forteresse de la transmigration (*saṃsāradurga*)". Mais comment traduire *srid phur sems kluṅ*? Faut-il comprendre: "Grâce à sa sagesse il détruit la cheville de l'existence et le courant des pensées"? La fin ne donne pas de difficultés.

p. 65, l. 18 *dge ba'i rca ba de dag kyaṅ / bla na myed pa yaṅ dag par rjogs pa'i byaṅ čhub tu yoṅs su sṅo bar byed do //* "Il appliquera (skt. *pariṇāmayiṣyati*) les racines de bien aussi à [l'acquisition de] l'*anuttarasamyaksaṃbodhi*", non "Et toutes ces racines de bien verdoieront entièrement dans l'*anuttarasamyaksaṃbodhi*".

Leiden J. W. de Jong

D. L. Snellgrove, *The Hevajra Tantra. A Critical Study.* Part I, Introduction and Translation, xv+149 pp.; Part II, Sanskrit and Tibetan Texts, xi+ 188 pp. (= *London Oriental Series*, volume 6.) London, Oxford University Press, 1959. 105/–.

Dans l'histoir du bouddhisme indien la période tantrique est encore toujours la moins connue. Les manuscrits ne manquent pourtant pas et le nombre des textes traduits en chinois et tibétain est énorme mais très peu de savants ont été attirés par l'étude de cette littérature. A la fin du siècle dernier, La Vallée Poussin avait commencé l'étude de ce domaine, et son *Bouddhisme, Etudes et matériaux* reste un ouvrage de grande valeur. Mais il n'a pas pu réussir à dissiper les préjugés contre le tantrisme qui fut considéré "a very unpleasant subject" comme disait E. J. Rapson dans un compte rendu célèbre (*JRAS*, 1898, p. 914). Se tournant ensuite vers les grands ouvrages de Candrakīrti et de Śāntideva, La Vallée Poussin n'a pas continué l'étude des tantra. Néanmoins, depuis 1898 le tantrisme n'a pas été négligé et surtout, des points de vue archéologique et iconographique, beaucoup de progrès ont été faits. Aussi plusieurs textes furent publiés mais la plupart de ces éditions reposent uniquement sur des manuscrits récents sans qu'on eût tiré profit des traductions tibétaines qui remontent à une époque beaucoup plus ancienne. C'est pourquoi on accueille avec joie le travail de M. D. Snellgrove sur le *Hevajratantra.* Il y met en juste lumière la grande importance, non seulement de la traduction tibétaine, mais aussi des commentaires, pour une compréhension correcte du tantra. Le premier volume de son travail contient une traduction pourvue de longues notes explicatives dans lesquelles les commentaires sont abondamment cités. Le deuxième volume donne le texte sanskrit avec, en regard, la traduction tibétaine (pp. 2–101) et le texte sanskrit du commentaire de Kāṇha intitulé *Yogaratnamālā* (pp. 103–159). M.D.S. n'a épargné aucun effort pour faciliter la compréhension du texte. On trouvera ainsi dans le premier volume des appendices très utiles tels qu'un résumé du contenu, des diagrammes et un index. Le deuxième volume contient des vocabulaires tibétain-sanskrit-anglais et sanskrit-tibétain qui pourront aussi rendre de grands services dans l'étude d'autres textes tantriques.

Dans une longue introduction à sa traduction M. D.S. explique très clairement les idées fondamentales qui sont à la base du *Hevajratantra.* Il y fait aussi plusieurs remarques relatives au tantrisme en général qui méritent d'être relevées car elles permettent de voir quelle place M. D.S. attribue au tantrisme dans l'histoire du bouddhisme. Selon lui, il y a une continuité dans le développement du bouddhisme. Le but ultime, l'expérience mystique, est toujours resté le même mais les moyens, employés pour arriver à ce but, ont varié au cours des siècles. La base philosophique des tantra est le *madhyamaka* qui proclame l'unité fondamentale du *nirvāṇa* et du *saṃsāra*. Quant aux rites prescrits par les tantra, ils reposent largement sur des pratiques en usage depuis longtemps chez les bouddhistes. Les éléments nouveaux des tantra ne représentent pas une rupture dans le développement du bouddhisme, et loin d'être des facteurs de dégénération, ils ont, au contraire, contribué à rajeunir le bouddhisme. Le déclin et la disparution du bouddhisme dans l'Inde ne sont pas dus aux doctrines tantriques mais à la destruction des centres intellectuels et à l'absence du support royal. Il y a, certes, un côté dangereux à l'enseignement tantrique pour autant qu'il remplace des symboles par des actes rituels. Si l'on perd de vue le sens symbolique des rites, ils risqueront d'être mal appliqués et l'identification du *saṃsāra* et du *nirvāṇa* pourra mener à la fausse conclusion qu'on soit libre de faire ce que bon nous semble. Néanmoins, les commentateurs s'efforcent toujours de souligner le sens symbolique des tantra. Sur ce point, on peut constater un désaccord entre les tantra et les commentaires car, à beaucoup d'endroits, il n'est guère possible d'interpréter les tantra dans un sens symbolique. – En résumant ici les idées de M. D.S., que l'on trouve dans son introduction, nous espérons les avoir reproduites assez fidèlement pour qu'il soit permis de s'y arrêter un moment. Indubitablement, sur beaucoup de points, on doit être pleinement d'accord avec M. D.S. Avec raison, M. D.S. proteste contre l'idée d'un bouddhisme pur qui ne serait qu'un système de notions philosophiques et éthiques. De tout temps, l'expérience mystique et les techniques du yoga ont été d'une importance primordiale pour les bouddhistes. Il est peut-être aussi vrai de dire que 99 pour-cent des bouddhistes ont été des gens ordinaires pour qui les invocations, attitudes des mains et circumambulations étaient très importantes. Mais tout cela ne permet pas de conclure que le tantrisme, en construisant des systèmes de symboles et de rites qui servent pour réaliser le *nirvāṇa* dans l'état de *saṃsāra*, ne s'éloigne pas essentiellement du bouddhisme ancien. Il nous semble qu'il faut tenir compte de la nette distinction entre religieux et laïcs que l'on peut constater dans le bouddhisme ancien. Les pages, consacrées par M. Et. Lamotte dans son *Histoire du bouddhisme indien* à la confrérie des laïcs, font nettement ressortir le fait que, pour le laïc, le but ultime n'était pas l'expérience mystique poursuivie par les religieux. Il aspirait surtout à une bonne renaissance par la pratique de la foi, de la moralité et de la générosité. Le culte et l'adoration sont le domaine du laïc et ce n'est donc pas surprenant que les rites aient joué un grand rôle pour lui. Pour les religieux le bouddhisme est un chemin de délivrance. Ils sont avant tout des *yogin* mais il ne faut pas perdre de vue que la réflexion n'est pas étrangère au yoga bouddhique. Il y a dans "chemin de délivrance" les deux termes "chemin" et "délivrance". Cela explique que l'on voit se profiler deux types de religieux. Il y a d'abord les "philosophes" qui se consacrent à l'analyse du chemin. Leur analyse conduira plus tard à la construction des grands systèmes d'*abhidharma* dans plusieurs sectes du Hīnayāna et dans l'école Yogācāra. Ce ne sont certes pas des philosophes "purs" car la réflexion est un exercice de yoga et n'est valable que parce que la bonne pensée est indispensable pour arriver à la délivrance. Ils sont pareils à tant de mystiques, qui, tout en aspirant uniquement à l'ineffable, n'ont pas tari sur la *via mystica*. D'autre part, il y a les mystiques pour qui rien ne compte hors l'obtention de la délivrance par les techniques du yoga. Mais, philosophe ou mystique, le religieux se distingue nettement du laïc et, au moins dans le bouddhisme ancien, c'est lui qui incarne par excellence le bouddhisme. Au cours des siècles, l'influence croissante des laïcs a lentement transformé le bouddhisme et, sur ce point, le tantrisme n'est que le point d'aboutissement d'un long procès pendant lequel le bouddhisme change profondément de caractère. Au début, ce sont les religieux qui donnent le ton et les laïcs n'occupent qu'une place secondaire. Dans le bouddhisme tardif et peut-être déjà dans le Mahāyāna, l'impulsion décisive est donnée par les laïcs et les religieux subissent leur influence. C'est ainsi que le rite, qui, au début, n'était important que pour le laïc, devient de plus en plus prépondérant. Certes, le tantrisme conserve l'armature philosophique du *madhyamaka* mais, dans les textes, on n'en entend guère plus que quelques faibles échos presqu'entièrement étouffés par la prolifération du rituel. On aurait pourtant tort de considérer le bouddhisme tantrique comme une dégénération du message du Bouddha. Comme toute religion vivante, le bouddhisme s'est transformé pendant sa longue histoire sur le sol indien, et chacune de ses manifestations possède sa propre valeur.

En établissant le texte, M. D.S. a essayé d'abord d'en déterminer le sens avant de choisir entre les lectures des manuscrits. Dans ce genre de textes, écrits dans un sanskrit abominable, un autre procédé aurait certainement été impossible. Fort heureusement, la traduction tibétaine et les commentaires aident beaucoup à comprendre le texte et à corriger les fautes des manuscrits népalais. M. D.S. n'a consulté que rarement la traduction chinoise en raison de son obscurité. Il est vrai qu'elle est très mauvaise. En outre, tous les passages relatifs aux rites sexuels ont été passés sous silence. Néanmoins, il aurait été utile de la consulter plus souvent car, comme représentant indépendant de la transmission du texte sanskrit, elle peut confirmer le choix d'une lecture. Plus d'une fois, en étudiant le texte, nous nous en sommes servis et nous avons signalé ci-dessous plusieurs passages où M. D.S. aurait pu tirer profit de cette version. L'apparat critique ne donne pas toutes les variantes des manuscrits. Evidemment, un tel choix reste toujours subjectif, car c'est difficile de savoir ce qu'il faut rejeter ou garder. M. D.S. aurait pu aussi citer plus souvent les lectures de la traduction tibétaine et du commentaire de Kāṇha qui s'écartent de celles adoptées dans le texte. Ces deux sources sont d'une telle importance qu'il faut signaler certainement tous les cas où leur témoignage a été écarté.

De tous les points de vue, la traduction est excellente. Il en ressort clairement comment M. D.S. a compris le texte, et on ne peut qu'en admirer la clarté et la précision. Cela vaut aussi pour la traduction des extraits des commentaires. La lecture de tous ces commentaires a dû demander beaucoup de temps et d'énergie. Mais, grâce à ce travail, M. D.S. est le premier savant à avoir montré clairement les grands services que ces commentaires peuvent rendre pour la compréhension d'un tantra.

Félicitons M. D.S. de ce beau travail qui, espérons-le, inaugurera une exploration systématique de la littérature tantrique. Avec son édition et traduction du *Hevajratantra* il nous a donné la meilleure contribution, dans ce domaine, depuis le vieux *Bouddhisme* de la Vallée Poussin. S'il continue dans cette voie, l'avenir des études tantriques sera assuré.

Pour terminer qu'il nous soit permis de reproduire ci-dessous des notes marginales faites au cours de la lecture. Peut-être le lecteur de l'ouvrage y trouvera des suggestions à retenir ou – à rejeter. Nous avons également signalé quelques fautes d'impression qui pourraient gêner la lecture.

Part I.

I.ii.22 – n. 5 (p. 53) *'di ni 'p'ral-du yid-c'es-par byed pa'o*, "He then exercises faith so that these are severed." Cette traduction est erronée. On peut, avec assez de vraisemblance, reconstruire l'original sanskrit comme suit: *ayam* (c'est-à-dire le *vidhi*) *sadyaḥpratyayakārī*, cf. II.ii.10: *vidyā sadyaḥpratyayakāriṇī*. Pour l'équivalence *pratyaya*, T *yid-c'es* cf. II.ii.40.

I.ii.28 – *prabhātakāle*, traduit erronément par "at night".

I.iii.1 – n. 1 corriger *skyabs-su 'dro-ba'i* en *skyabs-su 'gro-ba'i*; plus loin rayer le premier *la* dans *dgra-bo-rnams la p'a-rol-pa la*?

I.v.1 – *caittika* n'est pas "thinker" mais "élément mental".

I.v.3 – n.1 "so that no threefold dependence of sound" n'est pas très clair; il faut probablement comprendre "afin que l'on n'observe pas la triade (agent, acte et objet) à l'égard du son", cf. K p. 117, ll. 32–33.

I.vii.5 – la traduction de *cakra* par "mouth" n'est pas évidente. T traduit en effet par *k'a* mais Ch par "roue" et K glosse *cakra* par *dharmacakra*. Faut-il lire *vaktra* comme dans I.viii.10 où T *źal* s'oppose à Ch "roue"?

I.vii.7 – *kautuka* est traduit dans T par *ldo* mais dans le commentaire de V on trouve *lto*. Ni l'un ni l'autre s'explique facilement.

I.vii.22 – la traduction de *duṣṭāvatāraṇe* . . . n'est pas très claire. Selon K *duṣṭāvatāraṇa* signifie "introduire les méchants dans le *mantrayāna*". Ne peut-on pas accepter cette explication?

I.vii.27 – une note, expliquant la traduction de *vyūha* par "discriminating thought", aurait été souhaitable.

II.ii.1 – corriger "goad" en "gourd" (skt. *tumbikā*).

II.ii.39 – "endowed with good qualities". Le texte a *sugaṇair yutaḥ* qui est confirmé par T; dans K on lit *śiṣyaguṇayuktaḥ* (p. 139, 1.31) mais on s'attend à lire *śiṣyagaṇayuktaḥ*; seul Ch a lu *guṇa*; comme *vyākhyātā* s'oppose à *dharmaḥ*, *śrotā* doit s'opposer à *sugaṇair yutaḥ*; dans 39d *loka* et *laukiko* ne correspondent pas à T et à Ch "supramondain et mondain"; probablement il faut lire *'loka* au lieu de *loka*.

II.iii.10 – n. 1, l.10 "The Secret Consecration is so called, because it is a secret from the *śrāvakas, pratyekabuddhas* and all those below them". Dans le texte tibétain *ñan-t'os daṅ raṅ-saṅs-rgyas rnal-'byor-gyi rgyud man-c'ad-la gsaṅ-bas* fait difficulté et "all those below them" peut difficilement traduire correctement *rnal-'byor-gyi rgyud man-c'ad* "à partir des (ou jusqu'aux) Yogatantra". La construction de la phrase nous échappe. M. D.S. traduit la fin de la citation *bskur-ba'i rdzas ni slob-dpon la-la-dag ni rten-can-du yaṅ 'dod-do / bla-ma'i gźuṅ-gis ni rdzas mi 'dod-do* par "As for the agent of consecration, one requires to have some guru as one's support, and with his inner power one needs no (other) agent." Il nous semble qu'il faut traduire plutôt comme suit: "Quant à l'instrument de la consécration, quelques maîtres pensent que (cette consécration) aussi est pourvue de support, mais, selon le livre de notre guru, un instrument est exclu."

II.iv.8 – n.2 *vājjai* = skt. *vādyati*.

II.v.36 – M. D.S., traduit *karcūra* par "golden" mais il vaut mieux considérer *karcūra* comme une variante de *karbura* conformément à T et à Ch "pourvu de différentes couleurs".

Part II.

I.ii.20 – *'dhyātmakrūracetasā*; les MSS suggèrent plutôt *'bhyantarakrūra°*, de même II.ix.2.

I.ii.22 – *vatikāṃ*; identique à *vartikāṃ*?

I.ii.22 – *tāṃ sādhyakamaṇḍalugrīvāṃ veṣṭayet*, "He should then wrap round the neck upon which the ritual is being practised". Lire *tāṃ sādhya kamaṇḍalu°*, cf. T *de bsgrubs-la*, Ch "après avoir accompli"; *tāṃ* renvoit à *pūrvasevā*.

I.iii.3 – *nābhau*; C et T *ravau*; Ch "disque du soleil".

I.iii.7 – *dveṣātmakaṃ*; C *dveṣātmanaṃ*, K *dveṣātmānaṃ*.

I.iii.9 – corriger *Caurī* en *Gaurī* et *Gaurī* en *Caurī*.

I.iii.18 – corriger *nagnoḥ* en *nagnaḥ*.

I.v.16 – T corriger *śes brjod-par-bya* en *źes brjod-par-bya*.

I.vi.6 – *ramye*; Ch s'accorde avec B, T et la traduction de M. D.S. "at night".

I.vi.19 – au lieu de *bhāgābhāga°* K lit *bhāgyābhāgya°* qui est préférable.

I.vi.23 – T corriger *'dras* en *'bras*.

I.vii.9 – T corriger *gtaṅ* en *gtad*.

I.vii.17 – corriger *grāmantaṣṭham* en *grāmāntaṣṭhaṃ*.

I.viii.3 – *dvipuṭaṃ‹hi›*; tous les MSS ont *śuddhaṃ* au lieu de *hi*, de même Ch "pur et frais" et T (*dag* qui n'est pas ici signe du pluriel), cf. aussi I.x.28 où *'p'ar-ma gñis bzaṅ* rend *śuddhaṃ dvipuṭam*.

I.viii.8 – *ākārān bhāvayet pañcavidhānaiḥ kathitair budhaḥ*; d'après T et Ch (il faut concevoir ces cinq sagesses comme il a été dit) *pañca* se réfère à *ākārān* que K explique par *ādarśādīn*. Il faut donc lire *pañca vidhānaiḥ* en deux mots et changer la traduction de M. D.S. qui traduit *ākāra* par "phenomenal form".

I.viii.49 – corriger *sopāyanvitaṃ* en *sopāyānvitaṃ*.

I.ix.2 – n.2 corriger *kleśajñānāvaraṇaṃ* en *kleśajñeyāvaraṇaṃ*.

I.ix.3 – corriger *nānaśuddhyā* en *nānyaśuddhyā*.

I.x.17 – *bodhir*; les MSS lisent *sambodhir*, de même K et Ch "éveil correct".

I.x.19 – T corriger *byed-par* en *p'yed-par*.

I.x.24 – T corriger *ts'aṅ-mar* en *ts'ad-mar*.

I.x.33 – *na charda na moha*; il vaut mieux suivre les MSS et lire *na ca ghṛṇamoha* qui correspond à *skyug-bro rmoṅs med* car *ghṛṇā* signifie aussi "aversion, écœurement.". Cf. *Saundarananda*, II, 64; VIII, 21, 52, 53; XIII, 52 (et la note de Johnston dans son édition); XVII, 35.

II.i.6 – *caturasvaṃ*; lire *caturaśraṃ* ou *caturasraṃ*.

II.ii.7 – T corriger *'dug* en *gdug*.

II.ii.8 – T corriger *'jigs* en *'jig*.

II.ii.17 – T corriger *don kyis* en *don gyis*.

II.ii.18 – *tasyām*; lire *tasyā*.

II.ii.19 – T *dam-ts'ig sems daṅ gcig-pa ñid*; lire *dam-ts'ig daṅ sems gcig-pa ñid*?

II.ii.22 – *vācalaṃ*; lire *vā calaṃ*.

II.ii.23 – corriger *dhvābhyāṃ* en *dvābhyāṃ*.

II.ii.41 – corriger *śukranāmna* en *śukranāmnā*.

II.iii – première ligne corriger *nāmopayaṃ* en *nāmopāyaṃ*.

II.iii.27 – *malanaṃ*; il faut probablement lire *milanaṃ* qui est aussi confirmé par Ch "réunion". Dans I.v.19 *maṇḍala* est expliqué par *pādalekha* et *malana* cadre avec cette explication; ici *maṇḍala* est expliqué, de la manière traditionnelle, comme *maṇḍa* et *lā* (= *ādāne*) et *malana* est hors de propos; cette dernière explication est tellement courante que K la donne aussi à propos de la stance I.v.19 et ne commente qu'ensuite l'explication toute différente que donne la stance.

II.iii.34 – *vijñānāntā*; A *saṃskārānta*, de même K et Ch "nature de *saṃskāra*"

II.iii.50 – T corriger *lṅar* en *sṅar*.

II.iii.51, 52a-b – ces lignes manquent dans Ch.

II.iii.55 – corriger *vaksyāmy* en *vakṣyāmy*.

II.iv.25 – T dans la ligne suivante corriger *p'yed* en *byed*.

II.iv.42 – T corriger *mya ṅan* en *myaṅ las*?

II.iv.75 – T corriger *bźan* en *gźan*.

II.iv.102 – lire *tadanu yāti* au lieu de *tad anuyāti*.

II.v.7 – corriger *madhe* en *madhye*.

II.v.20 – *suṇṇasamāhi* est traduit par T et Ch (nature du vide) comme s'ils avaient lu *suṇṇasabhāvaḍā* qu'on trouve dans II.v.21.

II.v.22 – *loa nimantia* représente peut-être *lokanimantrita* "invité par le monde."

II.v.22 – *uhami na dīsa* est confirmé par Ch (je ne vois pas les directions) et par K qui traduit *uhami* par *paśyāmi* conformément à l'explication donnée par *Deśināmamālā* I.98.

II.v.23 – *cheamaṇḍa*; M. D.S. et T traduisent "weak in mind" mais l'explication de K *nāgarikā* est conforme au sens de skt. *cheka*.

II.v.26 – corriger *karuṇādbhūta°* en *karuṇādbhuta°*; *ravanādyarasair* est inexplicable; d'après T et K il faut lire *navanāṭyarasair*.

II.v.34 – corriger *ūrdhvakeśaś* en *ūrdhvakeśāś*.

II.v.35 – T *btsod* ne correspond pas à *mārtaṇḍa* mais à *mañjiṣṭhā*, cf. Ch "rouge".

II.v.38 – *bhūṣayitvā*; d'après T il faut lire *cūṣayitvā*, cf. aussi II.v.62.

II.v.46 – *adhyānta°* est incompréhensible; la transcription chinoise suggère *ādhmāta°*.

II.v.58 – T corriger *do śad* en *do śal*.

II.vi.10 – T corriger *'p'ags* en *'bags*, cf. aussi part II, p. 115, n. 1.

II.vii.7 – *prānte*; A, B *samudānte*; T et Ch (rivage de la grande mer) ont certainement lu *samudrānte*.

II.x.3, 4 – T corriger *bśad* en *bsad*.

II.xi.8 – *nābhimantavyā*; *nāvamantavyā* correspond mieux à T et aux lectures des MSS.

II.xi.10 – T corriger *mñas nes* en *mñes nas*.

II.xi.13 – *madanāṅga°*; il faut probablement lire *madanāṅka°*, cf. T et K qui explique bien qu'il s'agit de marques faites par les ongles. Dans K il faut certainement lire *aṅka* et non *aṅga*.

p.104, 1.21 corriger *deśaṇā* en *deśanā*; p. 105, 1.3 corriger *°lakṣanaṃ* en *°lakṣaṇaṃ*; p. 105, 1.30 *iha guhyamantramahāyāne*, MS *iha hi manta°*; T *t'eg-pa c'en-po gsaṅ-sṅags 'dir*; lire *iha hi mantra°* car *mantra* est souvent traduit par *gsaṅ-sṅags*; p.106, 1.20 *anāvasrava°*, lire *anāśrava°* ?; p.107, 1.9 corriger *°apatejo°* en *°aptejo°*; p.107, 1.28 lire *yoginītantra ārād* au lieu de *yoginītantre arad* ?; p.108, 1.3 corriger *yoginītantra* en *yoginītantre*; p.111, 1.20 corriger *sadarpa°* en *sarpa°* ?; p.113, 1.21 lire *divyasukhāvicchedopanayākārāṃ* au lieu de *°vicchedaniyamākārāṃ*, cf. 1.19; p.113, n.2 corriger *'c'ed* en *'c'ad*; p.115, 1.25 corriger *°niriitety* en *°nirjitety*; p.129, 1.33 corriger *ṛgvajuḥ* en *ṛgyajuḥ*; p.130, 1.4 lire *sūcitasya* au lieu de *sucitrasya* ?; p.130, 1.8 lire *dīpaśikhā* au lieu de *dīpaśekhā* ?; p.131, 1.31 corriger *aṅguṣṭhayādhikam* en *aṅguṣṭhatrayādhikam*; p.131, 1.34 corriger *yauvanapradhārāḥ* en *yauvanapradhānāḥ*; p.132, 1.15 corriger *pratiṣādayan* en *pratipādayan*; p.133, 1.33 corriger *upadeśeṇa* en *upadeśena*; p.134, 1.27 K explique *vicitra* comme absence (*vi-*) de différenciation; M. D.S. a eu tort de lire *vicitro* et *avicitram* au lieu de *citro* et *vicitram*. Dans le texte T a rendu *vicitra* par *sna-ts'ogs* mais M. D.S. suit K en traduisant par "undifferentiated"; p.139, 1.32 corriger *varṇataḥ* en *varṇitaḥ*; p.140, 1.12 corriger *sākṣeyaṃ* en *sāpekṣaṃ* ?; p.146, 1.29 corriger *aṅgaṃ* en *aṅkaṃ*; p. 147, n.5 MS *saṃsarattaḥ*, lire *saṃsārasthaḥ*; p.151, 1.26 corriger *nāyeti* en *'nayeti* ?; p.155, n.3 corriger *mts'an* en *mc'an*; p.158, 1.17 *meghopari*; MS? *medropari*; lire *meḍhropari* ?

Leiden J. W. de Jong

Errata

Number of Bibliography:		
92	p.58	1.11 — hānam. Read — ṭhānam
		1.17 — thāna. Read — ṭhāna
		1.22 — kāmādhātu. Read — kāmadhātu
	p.61	1.4 from below — Sachayer. Read — Schayer
	p.63	1.8 — abhisambujjhat. Read — abhisambujjhati
		1.9 — etasimiṁ. Read — etasmiṁ
		1.15 — samyakasaṁbodhim. Read — samyaksaṁbodhim
200	p.3	1.2 from below — that what. Read — that which
223	p.401	1.9 — baigner. Read — baigner dans
	p.403	1.9 — excursus. Read — excursis
145	p.3	1.5 — De not go alone, go together. Read — Let not two go together (*ekena* is explained as *ekena maggena* by Buddhaghosa but the Chinese versions show that it has to be interpreted as 'together', cf. I.B. Horner, *The Book of the Discipline*, vol. IV, London, 1951, p.28, n.4; André Bareau, *Recherches sur la biographie du Buddha dans les Sūtrapiṭaka et les Vinayapiṭaka anciens*, Paris, 1963, p.243;

Number of Bibliography:		
		Taishō vol. II, p.288b4; XXII, p.108a5, p. 793a7; XXIV, p.130b14).
	p.4	1.15 — east to west. Read — west to east
	p.7	1.8 — for *chu* (Mathews no.1374 read *chu* (Mathews no.1346)
202	p.101	1.1 from below — the en. Read — the end
	p.102	1.15 — princpail. Read — principal.
	p.105	n.15 refers to Pao-lin chüan [XX], not Hung-tsan fa-hua chuan [XXI]
	p.105	n.18 — .fJaCn. Read — Cf. Jan
262	p.174	1.3 — II. Read — III
97	p.171	1.12 — facon. Read — façon
204	p.511	1.4 — certainemant. Read — certainement
	p.512	1.4 from below—Srījñānātkara. Read — Srījñanākara
	p.516	1.11 — Indrabhuti. Read — Indrabhūti
	p.533	1.10 from below — Maghā. Read — Māgha
	p.544	1.9 from below — burqan-a. Read — burqan-u
	p.555	1.2 from below — Źi-ba 'od 'od. Read — Źi-ba'i 'od
250	p.146	1.8 — ldam. Read — ldan
	p.146	1.8 from below—re-na. Read — źe-na
124	p.17	n.2.8 — Abhidharama°. Read — Abhidharma°
	p.24	1.4 — aksaṇa. Read — akṣaṇa
258	Sp.80	1.5 — untertook. Read — undertook
284	p.274	1.23 — aprés. Read — après
	p.275	1.6 from below — avaitattiré. Read — avait attiré n.2, 1.1 — Verbindung met. Read — Verbindung mit

Number of
Bibliography:

251	p.65	1.3 — of this chinese passage. Read — Chinese passage 1.4 — XLII. Read — XLIII
	p.69	n.6, 1.2 — 1926–1938. Read — 1926–1928
	p.70	1.22 — 1943–1956 p.72.2. Read — 1953–1956, p.76.2
302	p.316	1.11 from below — (D,c). Read — (D,C).
173	p.57	1.9 — Tokiwai's. Read — Tokiwa's
35	p.312	1.28 — *'on-cig (ānaya)* is found also in Divy. p.522, 1.13. It was omitted by Nobel in his dictionary. The reading *'on* is correct, cf. Jäschke's Dictionary p.503a.
	p.314	1.23 — II, 195, 11. Read — II, 195, 1.1
263	p.108	1.4 — translation. Read — translations
	p.109	1.20 from below — *avidann.* Read — *avidvann*
	p.109	1.15 from below — in AA, 28^4. To be deleted
	p.114	1.20 — "poison. Read — "poison"
13	p.345	1.3 for *chieh* (Mathews no.620). Read — *pei* (Mathews no. 4989).
148b	p.73	1.31 25.13 *gajavaśagatena; gajo rājavaśagatena* MS (E), rayer *gajo* (J). Read — *gajavaśagatena; rājavaśagatena* MS (E); 25.14 *gajā; gajo* MS (E).
	p.74	1.25 34.12 *racitvā*. Read — *ricitva.*
	p.75	1.13 40.9 *aśvarathagodanaṃ*. Read — *aśvarathagodhanaṃ*
	p.77	1.7 59.19 *anupādāyāśravebhyaś; anutpādantapūrvāṇy āśravebhyaś* ME (E). Read — 59.18 *anutpadanta pūrvāṇy; anutpādantapūrvāṇy* MS (E)

Number of Bibliography		
177	p.270	l.21 — Mamyō. Read — Memyō
310	p.28	l.13 from below — the *Ṣaḍdantāvadāna*, text and translation, which are. Read — the *Ṣaḍdantāvadāna* which is
	p.33	l.13 — Cañāmānavikā. Read — Cañcāmānavikā
	p.37	l.12 — p.126, No. 1. Read — p.126, n.1
146	p.1	l.11 from below — Tanjur. Read — Kanjur
	p.2	l.2 — No. 160. Read — 610
179	p.78	l.24 — translation. Read — translations
	p.83	l.14 from below — truthworthiness. Read — trustworthiness
11	p.316	l.28 — dans le texte sanskrit. Read — dans la traduction de Dharmarakṣa
206	p.304	l.7 from below — Amithāba. Read — Amitābha
277	p.116	l.6 from below — secclo. Read — secolo
	p.117	l.9 — has. Read — had
	p.117	l.36 — *upādāya 'hi*. Read — *upādāya' iti*
	p.117	l.49 — *mutoḍiti*. Read *mutoḍiti*
	p.117	l.50 *muṭodī*. Read — *mūṭodī*
71	p.65	l.3 — *ātīryate*. Read — *ārtīyate*
185	p.106	l.14 — (T.1522). Read — (T.1521)
161	p.39	last line — now. Read — not
	p.49	l.22 from below — litterally. Read — literally
	p.51	l.7 — reaches. Read — teaches
45	p.159	l.24 — *RHR*, xxiv. Read — *RHR*, xxxiv
	p.159	l.3 from below — let. Read — et.
80	p.198	l.1 — histoir. Read — histoire

Index

For Chinese texts published in the Taisho edition (= T.), the number is given in parentheses after the title. At the end of both items nos. 204 and 206 will be found a separate index as it appeared in the original publication.

J.W. de Jong

Bibliography 1949-1977

Department of South Asian & Buddhist Studies
Faculty of Asian Studies
Australian National University
Canberra.

ABBREVIATIONS

ALB	=	Bulletin of the Adyar Library
AM	=	Asia Major
Bespr.	=	Besprechung
BSOAS	=	Bulletin of the School of Oriental and African Studies (University of London)
CAJ	=	Central Asiatic Journal
CR	=	Compte rendu de
FEQ	=	Far Eastern Quarterly
HJAS	=	Harvard Journal of Asiatic Studies
IBK	=	Indogaku Bukkyōgaku Kenkyū (Journal of Indian and Buddhist Studies)
IIJ	=	Indo-Iranian Journal
JA	=	Journal Asiatique
JAOS	=	Journal of the American Oriental Society
JIP	=	Journal of Indian Philosophy
OLZ	=	Orientalistische Literaturzeitung
TP	=	T'oung Pao
ZAS	=	Zentralasiatische Studien
ZDMG	=	Zeitschrift der deutschen morgenländischen Gesellschaft.

1949

1. *Cinq chapitres de la Prasannapadā (= Buddhica. Documents et Travaux pour l'étude du Bouddhisme*. Collection fondée par Jean Przyluski, publiée sous la direction de Marcelle Lalou, première série: *Mémoires*, tome IX). Paris: Paul Geuthner, 1949, [printed in The Netherlands by E.J. Brill, Leiden], XVI + 167 pp. (Ph.D. thesis, University of Leiden).
2. Contributions à *Bibliographie bouddhique,* IX-XX, Paris, 1949.

1950

3. Le problème de l'absolu dans l'école Madhyamaka, *Revue philosophique de la France et de l'étranger*, Paris, 1950, pp. 322–327. [Cf. No. 200].

1951

4. Suggestions for a Polyglot Buddhist Dictionary, *Vāk*, I. Poona, Dec. 1951, pp. 5–7.
5. Review of L. Petech, *China and Tibet in the early 18th century,* Leiden,1950.
   ——— *FEQ*, XI (1951), pp. 114–116.

1952

6. Contributions à *Bibliographie bouddhique,* XXI-XXIII, Paris, 1952.
7. CR de J. Nobel, *Suvarṇaprabhāsottamasūtra,* Bd. II, Leiden, 1950.
   ——— *TP,* XLI (1952), pp. 247–250.

1953

8. CR de J. Ensink, *The Question of Rāṣṭrapāla*, Zwolle, 1952.
——— *JA*, 241 (1953), pp. 545–549.
9. CR de P. Hacker, *Untersuchungen über Texte des frühen Advaitavāda*, I, Wiesbaden, 1951.
——— *Museum*, LVIII (1953), cols. 3–4.
10. CR de E. Waldschmidt, *Das Mahāparinirvāṇasūtra*, Berlin, 1950–1951.
——— *OLZ*, 48 (1953), Sp. 178–180.

1954

11. L'épisode d'Asita dans le Lalitavistara, *Asiatica. Festschrift F. Weller*, Leipzig, O. Harrassowitz, 1954, pp. 312–325.
12. Three Notes on the Vasudevahiṇḍi, *Saṃjñāvyākaraṇam. Studia Indologica Internationalia*, I (1954), Centre for International Indological Research, Poona and Paris, 12 pp.
13. CR de R. Yamada, "Hannyakyōtenrui no keiseisareta jidai no haikei", *Tōhoku Daigaku bungakubukenkyūnempō*, II, Sendai, 1951.
——— *TP*, XLII (1954), pp. 345–347.
14. CR de D.R. Shackleton Bailey, *The Śatapañcāśatka of Mātṛceṭa*, Cambridge, 1951.
——— *ibid.*, pp. 397–405.
15. CR de Y. Kanakura et al., *A Catalogue of the Tohoku University Collection of Tibetan Works on Buddhism*, Sendai, 1953.

——— *TP*, XLIII (1954), pp. 121–125.

16. CR de L. Petech, *I Missionari Italiani nel Tibet e nel Nepal*, I-IV, Rome, 1952–1953.
——— *ibid*., pp. 125–129.

17. CR de F. Weller, *Tibetisch-Sanskritischer Index zum Bodhicaryāvatāra*, Heft I, Berlin, 1952.
——— *ibid*., pp. 129–132.

1955

18. Fonds Pelliot tibétain Nos. 610 et 611, *Studies in Indology and Buddhology*, presented to S. Yamaguchi, Kyōto, Hōzōkan, 1955, pp. 58–67.

19. CR de E. Conze, *Abhisamayālaṅkāra*, Rome, 1954.
——— *Muséon*, LXVIII (1955), pp. 394–397.

20. CR de H. Lüders, *Beobachtungen über die Sprache des buddhistischen Urkanons*. Aus dem Nachlass hrsg. von E. Waldschmidt, Berlin, 1954.
——— *Museum*, LX (1955), cols. 144–147.

21. CR de F. Weller, *Zwei zentralasiatische Fragmente des Buddhacarita*, Berlin, 1953.
——— *OLZ*, 50 (1955), Sp. 404–406.

22. CR de *Bibliographie bouddhique*, XXI-XXIII, Paris, 1952.
——— *TP*, XLIII (1955), p. 297.

23. CR de T. Schmid, *The Cotton-clad Mila*, Stockholm, 1952.
——— *ibid*., pp. 298–301.

24. CR de W. Heissig, *Die Pekinger lamaistischen Blockdrucke in mongolischer Sprache*, Wiesbaden, 1954.
——— *ibid*., pp. 301–318.

25. CR de R. Shafer, *Ethnography of Ancient India*,

Wiesbaden, 1954.

——— *ibid.*, pp. 318–320.

26. CR de Dawa-Samdup, *Tibet's Great Yogī Milarepa*, London, 1951.

——— *ibid.*, pp. 320–324.

1956

27. *De Studie van het Boeddhisme. Problemen en Perspectieven* (Rede, Leiden, 28 Sept. 1956), The Hague, Mouton & Co., 1956, 25 pp.

28. CR de E. Frauwallner, *Geschichte der indischen Philosophie,* I, Salzburg, 1953.

——— *Museum*, LXI (1956), cols. 84–85.

29. CR de E.O. Reischauer, *Ennin's Diary*, New York, 1955, *Ennin's Travels in T'ang China*, New York, 1955.

——— *OLZ*, 51 (1956), Sp. 461–463.

1957

30. Sanskrit Studies in the Netherlands, *Indo-Asian Culture,* V, 4, New Delhi, April 1957, pp. 421–427. [Cf. Nos. 31 and 107.]

31. Sanskrit Studies in the Netherlands, *A.I.R. Selections. A quarterly journal consisting of important talks broadcast from the various stations of All India Radio,* New Delhi, Government of India, Dec. 1957, pp. 45–48 and 64. [Cf. Nos. 30 and 107.]

32. De Buddha Jayanti-vieringen in India, *Mens en Kosmos*, XIII, Deventer, 1957, pp. 149–157.

33. Contributions à *Revue bibliographique de sinologie,*

1, Paris-La Haye, 1957.

34. CR de H. Hoffmann, *Die Religionen Tibets*, Freiburg-München, 1956.
——— *CAJ*, III (1957), pp. 79–80.

35. CR de J. Nobel (ed. and tr.), *Udrāyaṇa, König von Roruka*, 2 Bde., Wiesbaden, 1955.
——— *IIJ*, I (1957), pp. 312–314.

36. CR de H. Siiger, *From the Third Danish Expedition to Central Asia*, Copenhagen, 1956.
——— *Museum*, LXII (1957), col. 189.

37. CR de D. Schlingloff, *Buddhistische Stotras aus ostturkistanischen Sanskrittexten*, Berlin, 1955.
——— *OLZ*, 52 (1957), Sp. 73–74.

38. CR de R. Robinson, *Chinese Buddhist Verse*, London, 1954.
——— *ibid.*, Sp. 175–176.

39. CR de R. A. Stein, *L'épopée tibétaine de Gesar*, Paris, 1956.
——— *TP*, XLV (1957), pp. 270–272.

40. CR de Mgr. Giraudeau et R.P. Francis Goré, *Dictionnaire français-tibétain*, Paris, 1956.
——— *ibid.*, pp. 272–274.

1958

41. Contributions à *Bibliographie bouddhique*, XXIV-XXVII, Paris, 1958.

42. CR de R. Shafer (ed.), *Bibliography of Sino-Tibetan Languages*, Wiesbaden, 1957.
——— *IIJ*, II (1958), pp. 74–77.

43. CR de *Dans les pas du Bouddha*. Présentation de J. Filliozat, Introd., notices et photogr. de Louis-

Frédéric, Paris, 1957.
——— *ibid.*, p. 77.
44. CR de E. Bryner, *Thirteen Tibetan Tankas*, Indian Hills, 1956.
——— *ibid.*, pp. 77–79.
45. CR de F. A. Bischoff, *Contribution à l'étude des divinités mineures du Bouddhisme tantrique*. Ārya Mahābalanāma-mahāyānasūtra, Paris, 1956.
——— *ibid.*, pp. 159–162.
46. CR de F. Kern, *Aśoka, Kaiser und Missionar*, Bern, 1956.
——— *Museum*, LXIII (1958), cols. 210–212.

1959

47. *Mi la ras pa'i rnam thar. Texte tibétain de la vie de Milarépa*, The Hague, Mouton & Co., 1959, 218 pp.
48. René Mario von Nebesky-Wojkowitz, †, 29. VI. 1923–9. VII. 1959, *IIJ*, III (1959), pp. 306–309.
49. Contributions à *Revue bibliographique de sinologie*, 2, Paris-La Haye, 1959.
50. Review of L. Giles, *Descriptive Catalogue of the Chinese Manuscripts from Tunhuang in the British Museum*, London, 1957.
——— *AM*, VII (1959), pp. 228–230.
51. CR de *Tribus*, No. 7, Stuttgart, 1957.
——— *IIJ*, III (1959), pp. 75–78.
52. CR de M. Monier Williams, *A Dictionary English and Sanskrit*, Delhi-Varanasi-Patna, 1956.
——— *ibid.*, p. 78.
53. CR de *Paṇḍita Durveka Miśra's Dharmottarapradīpa*, ed. by Paṇḍita D. Malvania, Patna, 1955.

——— *ibid.*, pp. 151–153.

54. CR de C.E. Godakumbura, *Sinhalese Literature*, Colombo, 1955.

——— *ibid.*, pp. 153–154.

55. CR de J. J. Poortman, *Ochêma. Geschiedenis en zin van het Hylisch Pluralisme*, II, Assen, 1958.

——— *ibid.*, pp. 154–155.

56. CR de N. Simonsson, *Indo-tibetische Studien*, I, Uppsala, 1957.

——— *ibid.*, pp. 216–219.

57. CR de A. Ferrari, *Mk'yen brtse's Guide to the Holy Places of Central Tibet*, compl. and ed. by L. Petech with the coll. of H. Richardson, Rome, 1958.

——— *ibid.*, pp. 220–221.

58. CR de D. Snellgrove, *Buddhist Himālaya*, Oxford, 1957.

——— *ibid.*, pp. 221–223.

59. CR de W.Y. Evans-Wentz (ed.), *Tibetan Yoga and Secret Doctrines*, 2nd ed., London-New York-Toronto, 1958.

——— *ibid.*, pp. 223–225.

60. CR de L. Petech, *Mediaeval History of Nepal*, Rome, 1958.

——— *ibid.*, pp. 225–226.

61. CR de G. Tucci, *Storia della filosofia indiana*, Bari, 1957.

——— *ibid.*, pp. 226–227.

62. CR de Yamada Ryūjō, *Bongo butten no bunkengaku josetsu*, Sendai, 1957, pp. 222–410.

——— *ibid.*, pp. 227–228.

63. CR de K.E. Neumann, *Die Reden Gotamo Buddhos*, 3 Bde., Zürich-Wien, 1957.

——— *ibid.*, pp. 229–230.
64. CR de L. Sternbach, *Cāṇakya's Aphorisms in the Hitopadeśa* (I-IV); *A New Cāṇakya-rāja-nīti-śāstra Manuscript*, Bombay, 1958.
——— *ibid.*, pp. 230–232.
65. CR de D. Schlingloff, *Chandoviciti*, Berlin, 1958.
——— *OLZ*, 54 (1959), Sp. 619–620.
66. CR de *Contributions to Ethnography, Linguistics and History of Religion*, Stockholm, 1954.
——— *TP*, XLVII (1959), pp. 146–154.
67. CR de W. Pachow, *A Comparative Study of the Prātimokṣa*, Santiniketan, 1955.
——— *ibid.*, pp. 155–157.
68. CR de R.J. Miller, *Monasteries and Culture Change in Inner Mongolia*, Wiesbaden, 1959.
——— *ibid.*, pp. 157–160.
69. CR de W. Kirfel, *Symbolik des Hinduismus und des Jinismus; Symbolik des Buddhismus*, Stuttgart, 1959.
——— *ibid.*, pp. 160–162.
70. CR de W. Heissig, *Die Familien- und Kirchengeschichtsschreibung der Mongolen*, I, Wiesbaden, 1959.
——— *ibid.*, pp. 162–167.

1960

71. Vitarati, *IIJ*, IV (1960), pp. 65–67.
72. CR de M. Hermanns, *Die Familie der Amdo-Tibeter*, Freiburg-München, 1959.
——— *CAJ*, V (1960), p. 330.
73. CR de Lokesh Chandra, *Tibetan-Sanskrit Dictionary*, 1, *Ka*, New Delhi, 1958.
——— *IIJ*, IV (1960), pp. 73–74.

74. CR de E. Conze (ed. and tr.), *Vajracchedikā Prajñāpāramitā*, Rome, 1957.
——— *ibid.*, p. 75, with corrigenda by E. Conze himself, pp. 75–76.

75. CR de E. Conze, *Buddhist Wisdom Books*, London, 1958.
——— *ibid.*, pp. 76–77.

76. CR de T. Schmid, *The Eighty-five Siddhas*, Stockholm, 1958.
——— *ibid.*, pp. 191–193.

77. CR de G. de Roerich, *Le parler de l'Amdo*, Rome, 1959.
——— *ibid.*, pp. 194–195.

78. CR de A. Thakur (ed.), *Ratnakīrtinibandhāvalī*, Patna, 1957.
——— *ibid.*, pp. 196–197.

79. CR de H.V. Guenther (tr.), *Sgam. po. pa. The Jewel Ornament of Liberation*, London, 1959.
——— *ibid.*, pp. 197–198.

80. CR de D.L. Snellgrove, *The Hevajra Tantra*, London, 1959.
——— *ibid.*, pp. 198–203.

81. CR de J. Bacot, *Zugiñima, texte et traduction*, Paris, 1957.
——— *ibid.*, pp. 203–207.

82. CR de S. Śrīrāma Śāstrī and S. R. Krishnamurthi Śāstrī (eds.), *Pañcapādikā of Śrī Padmapādācārya with Prabodhapariśodhinī of Ātmasvarūpa and Tātparyārthadyotinī of Vijñānātman and Pañcapādikāvivaraṇa of Śrī Prakāśātman with Tatparyadīpikā of Citsukhācārya and Bhāvaprakāśikā of Nṛsiṁhāśrama*, Madras, 1958.
——— *ibid.*, pp. 208–209.

1961

83. Contributions à *Bibliographie bouddhique*, XXVIII-XXXI, Paris, 1961.
84. George N. de Roerich, †, 1902-1960, *IIJ*, V (1961), pp. 146-152.
85. CR de J. May, *Candrakīrti, Prasannapadā madhyamakavṛtti*, Paris, 1959.
——— *ibid.*, pp. 161–165.
86. Review of L. Silburn (tr.), *Vātūlanātha Sūtra avec le commentaire d'Anantaśaktipāda*, Paris, 1959.
——— *JAOS*, LXXXI (1961), pp. 159–161.
87. CR de F. D. Lessing (gen. ed.), *Mongolian-English Dictionary*, Berkeley-Los Angeles, 1960.
——— *TP*, XLIX (1961–62), pp. 105–109.
88. CR de H. Clarke, *The Message of Milarepa*, London, 1958.
——— *ibid.*, pp. 109–112.
89. CR de A. K. Gordon, *The Hundred Thousand Songs*, Rutland-Tokyo, 1961.
——— *ibid.*, pp. 113–114.
90. CR de W. Heissig. *Mongolische Handschriften-Blockdrucke-Landkarten*, Wiesbaden, 1961.
——— *ibid.*, pp. 217–220.

1962

91. La Madhyamakaśāstrastuti de Candrakīrti, *Oriens Extremus*, IX (1962), pp. 47-56.
92. The Absolute in Buddhist Thought, *Essays in Philosophy*, presented to Dr. T. M. P. Mahadevan, Madras, Ganesh & Co., 1962, pp. 56–64.

93. Review of P.S. Jaini (ed.), *Milinda-ṭīkā*, PTS, 1961.
——*BSOAS*, XXV (1962), pp. 375–376.

94. Review of G.P. Malalasekera (ed.), *Encyclopaedia of Buddhism*, Fasc. *A-Aca*, Colombo, 1961.
—— *ibid.*, pp. 380–381.

95. CR de A. Thakur (ed.), *Jñānaśrīmitranibandhāvali*, Patna, 1959.
—— *IIJ*, VI (1962), pp. 75–76.

96. CR de R. O. Meisezahl, *Alttibetische Handschriften der Völkerkundlichen Sammlungen der Stadt Mannheim im Reiss-Museum*, Copenhagen, 1961. [Sonderdruck aus *Libri*, XI, 1, 48 pp., 33 ills.].
—— *ibid.*, pp. 76–77.

97. CR de *Biography of Dharmasvāmin (Chag lo-tsa-ba Chos-rje-dpal)*. Deciphered and tr. by G. Roerich, Patna, 1959.
—— *ibid.*, pp. 167–173.

98. CR de P. S. Jaini (ed.), *Abhidharmadīpa with Vibhāṣāprabhāvṛtti*, Patna, 1959.
—— *ibid.*, pp. 173–175.

99. CR de *Studia Sino-Altaica. Festschrift für E. Haenisch zum 80. Geburtstag*, Wiesbaden, 1961.
—— *TP*, XLIV (1962), pp. 431–433.

1963

100. CR de G. H. Sasaki, *Abidatsuma shisō kenkyū*, Tokyo, 1959.
—— *IIJ*, VI (1963), pp. 304–305.

101. CR de W. Geiger, *Culture of Ceylon in Mediaeval Times*, ed. by H. Bechert, Wiesbaden, 1960.
—— *ibid.*, pp. 305–306.

102. CR de A. F. Wright, *Buddhism in Chinese History*, Stanford-London, 1959.
——— *OLZ*, 58 (1963), Sp. 403–404.

103. CR de Walther Heissig, *Beiträge zur Übersetzungsgeschichte des mongolischen buddhistischen Kanons*, Göttingen, 1962.
——— *ZDMG*, 113, 1963, pp. 426–427.

1964

104. The Background of Early Buddhism *IBK*, XII, 1 (Jan. 1964), pp. 437–424. (English translation of (No. 105).

105. Het Ontstaan van het Boeddhisme in India, *Forum der Letteren*, V, 4 (Leiden, Nov. 1964), pp. 177–190. [Cf. Nos. 104 and 106.]

106. Podłoże wczesnego buddyzmu, *Euhemer. Przeglad Religioznawczy*, 1964, Nr. 2 (39), pp. 3–12. (Polish translation of No. 104).

107. Sanskrit Studies in the Netherlands, *Indian Studies Abroad*, ed. by the Indian Council for Cultural Relations, New Delhi, (Bombay, Asia Publishing House, 1964), pp. 60–64. Japanese translation with notes by A. Yuyama, J. W. de Jong-cho: Oranda no Indogaku Bukkyōgaku, *IBK*, XIV, 1 (Dec. 1965), pp. 382(73)–359(96).

108. Contributions à *Revue bibliographique de sinologie*, 4, Paris-La Haye, 1964.

109. Introduction to *Hiraṇyagarbha* (Volume in honour of F. D. K. Bosch), The Hague, 1964, p. 7 [With P. H. Pott and F. B. J. Kuiper.]

110. Voorwoord ad *Profiel van een Incarnatie. Het leven en*

de conflicten van een Tibetaanse geestelijke in Tibet en Europa, door F. Sierksma, Amsterdam, G. A. van Oorschot, 1964, pp. 5–6.

111. CR de H. Bechert, *Bruchstücke buddhistischer Verssammlungen aus zentralasiatischen Sanskrithandschriften*, I: *Die Anavataptagāthā und die Sthaviragāthā*, Berlin, 1961.
——— *IIJ*, VII (1964), pp. 232–235.

112. CR de H. Lüders, *Mathurā Inscriptions*, ed. by K. L. Janert, Göttingen, 1961.
——— *ibid.*, p. 236.

113. CR de J. F. Rock, *A* [1]*Na-*[2]*khi-English Encyclopedic Dictionary*, Part I, Rome, 1963.
——— *ibid.*, pp. 236–238.

114. CR de H. Scharfe, *Die Logik im Mahābhāṣya*, Berlin, 1961.
——— *ibid.*, pp. 330–331.

115. CR de R. Shafer (ed.), *Bibliography of Sino-Tibetan Languages*, II, Wiesbaden, 1963.
——— *IIJ*, VIII (1964), pp.154–155.

1965

116. Boeddhistische opvattingen van goed en kwaad, *Wijsgerig Perspectief op maatschappij en wetenschap*, Jaargang 5, No. 4 (Maart 1965), pp. 140–157.

117. Beknopte bibliografie van het Boeddhisme, *ibid.*, pp. 158–164.

118. CR de G. M. Bongard-Levin i O. F. Volkova, *Legenda o Kunale*, Moskva, 1963.
——— *IIJ*, VIII (1965), pp. 233–240.

119. CR de É. Chavannes, *Cinq cents contes et apologues*

extraits du Tripiṭaka chinois, Paris, 1962, 4 tomes.
——— *ibid.*, pp. 240–242.

120. CR de B. V. Semičov, et al., *Kratkij tibetsko-russkij slovar'*, Moskva, 1963.
——— *ibid.*, pp. 242–245. [Cf. No. 123.]

121. CR de S. Lienhard, *Maṇicūḍāvadānoddhṛta*, Stockholm-Göteborg-Uppsala, 1963.
——— *IIJ*, IX (1965), pp. 74–75.

122. CR de Th. Aufrecht, *Catalogus Catalogorum*, 2 Vols., Wiesbaden, 1962.
——— *ibid.*, p. 76.

123. CR de B. V. Semičov et al., *Kratkij tibetsko-russkij slovar'*, Moskva, 1963.
——— *Materialy po istorii i filologii central'noj Azii*, vyp. 2 (Ulan-Udè, 1965), pp. 255–257. [Russian translation of No. 120.]

1966

124. The Daśottarasūtra, *Kanakura Hakushi Koki Kinen: Indogaku Bukkyōgaku Ronshū*, Kyōto, Heirakuji Shoten, 1966, pp. 3–25.

125. CR de H. V. Guenther, *The Life and Teaching of Nāropa*, Oxford, 1963.
——— *IIJ*, IX (1966), pp. 161–163.

126. CR de J. K. Balbir, *L'histoire de Rāma en tibétain*, Paris, 1963.
——— *ibid.*, pp. 227–235.

127. CR de L. de La Vallée Poussin, *Catalogue of the Tibetan Manuscripts from Tun-huang in the India Office Library, O. U. P.,* 1962.
——— *ibid.*, pp. 308–309.

128. CR de U. Oppenberg, *Quellenstudien zu Friedrich Schlegels Übersetzungen aus dem Sanskrit*, Marburg, 1965.
——— *ibid.*, pp. 309–311.

129. CR de E. O. Reischauer, *Die Reisen des Mönchs Ennin*, Stuttgart, 1963.
——— *OLZ*, 61 (1966), Sp. 89.

1967

130. L'auteur de l'Abhidharmadīpa, *TP*, LII (1966), pp. 305–307.

131. Sum-pa mkhan-po (1704–1788) and his works, *HJAS*, XXVII (1967), pp. 208–217.

132. Review of S. Matsunami, *A Catalogue of the Sanskrit Manuscripts in the Tokyo University Library*, Tokyo, 1965.
——— *IIJ*, X (1967), pp. 191–192.

133. Review of F. Wilhelm, *Prüfung und Initiation im Buche Pausya und in der Biographie des Nāropa*, Wiesbaden, 1965.
——— *ibid.*, pp. 192–197.

134. CR de K. Mittal, *Dogmatische Begriffsreihen im älteren Buddhismus*, I: Fragmente des Daśottarasūtra aus zentral-asiatischen Sanskrit-Handschriften, Berlin, 1957; D. Schlingloff, *Dogmatische Begriffsreihen im älteren Buddhismus*, Ia: Daśottarasūtra IX-X, Berlin, 1962.
——— *ibid.*, pp. 197–198.

135. CR de Chandrabhāl Tripāṭhī, *Fünfundzwanzig Sūtras des Nidānasaṃyukta*, Berlin, 1962.
——— *ibid.*, pp. 198–199.

136. CR de J. Brough, *The Gāndhārī Dharmapada*, London, 1962.
——— *ibid.*, pp. 199–203.
137. Review of *Annual of Oriental and Religious Studies*, I, Tokyo, 1965.
——— *ibid.*, pp. 203–204.
138. Review of W. Rau, *Bilder hundert deutscher Indologen*, Wiesbaden, 1965.
——— *ibid.*, p. 204.
139. CR de Garma C. C. Chang (tr.), *The Hundred Thousand Songs of Milarepa*, New York, 1962.
——— *ibid.*, pp. 204–212.
140. CR de R. O. Meisezahl, *Tibetische Prajñāpāramitā-Texte im Bernischen Historischen Museum*, Kopenhagen, 1964.
——— *ibid.*, pp.212–215.
141. Review of E. Conze, *Buddhist Thought in India*, London, 1962.
——— *ibid.*, pp. 215–217.
142. Review of *Temenos. Studies in Comparative Religion presented by Scholars in Denmark, Finland, Norway and Sweden*, Vol. I, Helsinki, 1965.
——— *ibid.*, pp. 217–218.
143. CR de E. Waldschmidt, *Sanskrithandschriften aus den Turfanfunden*. Teil I, Wiesbaden, 1965.
——— *OLZ*, 62 (1967), Sp. 498–499.

1968

144. The Magic Wall of the Fortress of the Ogresses: Apropos of āsīyati (Mahāvastu III, 86.3), *Pratidānam. Indian, Iranian and Indo-European Studies presented*

to Franciscus Bernardus Kuiper on his Sixtieth Birthday, The Hague, 1968, pp. 484–487.

145. *Buddha's Word in China*. 28th George Ernest Morrison Lecture, Canberra, 1968, 26 pp.

146. Encore une fois le fonds Pelliot tibétain no. 610, *CAJ*, XII (1968), pp. 1–7.

147. Les Sūtrapiṭaka des Sarvāstivādin et des Mūlasarvāstivādin, *Mélanges d'indianisme à la mémoire de Louis Renou*, Paris, 1968, pp. 395–402.

148. Remarks on the text of the Rāṣṭrapālaparipṛcchā, *ALB*, 31–32 (1968), pp. 1–7.

149. Contributions à *Revue bibliographique de sinologie*, 7, Paris-La Haye, 1968.

150. Review of J. D. Pearson, *Oriental and Asian Bibliography*, Melbourne-Canberra-Sydney, 1966.
——— *IIJ*, X (1968), pp. 292–295.

151. CR de *Vāgbhaṭa's Aṣṭāṅgahṛdayasaṃhitā*. The first five chapters of its Tibetan version, ed. and rend. into Engl. with the orig. Sanskrit by C. Vogel, Wiesbaden, 1965.
——— *ibid.*, pp. 295–297.

152. CR de Biswadeb Mukherjee, *Die Überlieferung von Devadatta, dem Widersacher des Buddha in den kanonischen Schriften*, München, 1966.
——— *ibid.*, pp. 297–298.

153. Review of W. N. Brown (ed. & tr.), *The Mahimnastava or Praise of Shiva's Greatness*, Poona, 1965.
——— *ibid.*, pp. 299–300.

154. Review of K. L. Janert, *An Annotated Bibliography of the Catalogues of Indian Manuscripts*, Part 1, Wiesbaden, 1965.
——— *ibid.*, pp. 300–302.

155. CR de D. S. Ruegg, *The Life of Bu ston Rin po che*,

Roma, 1966.

——— *TP*, LIV (1968), pp. 168–172.

156. CR de Š. Bira, *O "Zolotoj knige" S. Damdina*, Ulan-Bator, 1964.

——— *ibid.*, pp. 173–189.

157. CR de D. A. Birman i G. G. Kotovskij, *Bibliografija Indii*, Moskva, 1965.

——— *IIJ*, XI (1968), p. 34.

158. Review of F. Kielhorn, *Grammatik der Sanskrit-Sprache*, aus d. Engl. übers. v. W. Solf, Wiesbaden, 1965.

——— *ibid.*, p. 35.

159. Review of L. Sternbach, *Supplement to O. Böhtlingk's Indische Sprüche*, Wiesbaden, 1965.

——— *ibid.*, pp. 35–36.

160. Review of R. Hauschild, *Register zur Altindischen Grammatik*, Bd. I-III, von J. Wackernagel und A. Debrunner, Göttingen, 1964.

——— *ibid.*, p. 36.

161. Review of J. Takasaki, *A Study on the Ratnagotravibhāga*, Roma, 1966.

——— *ibid.*, pp. 36–54.

162. Review of *Studies on Esoteric Buddhism and Tantrism*, Koyasan, 1965.

——— *ibid.*, pp. 54–56.

163. Review of *The Catalogue of the Tibetan Texts in the Bihar Research Society*, vol. I. Ed. by Prof. A. Jha. Comp. by Shri G. R. Choudhary, Patna, 1965.

——— *ibid.*, pp. 56–57.

1969

164. *Dharmasamuccaya. Compendium de la Loi.* 2e partie

(chapitres VI à XII). Texte sanskrit édité avec la version tibétaine et les versions chinoises et traduit en français par Lin Li-kouang. Révision de André Bareau, J. W. de Jong et Paul Demiéville. Avec des Appendices par J. W. de Jong, Paris, 1969, 416 + 27 pp.

165. Korea's Edition of the Chinese Buddhist Canon, *Hemisphere*, vol. 13, number 4 (April 1969), pp. 26–29.

166. Contributions à *Revue bibliographique de Sinologie*, 8, Paris-La Haye, 1969.

167. Review of G. Tucci, *Tibetan Folk Songs from Gyantse and Western Tibet*, 2nd rev. enl. ed., Ascona, 1966.
——— *IIJ*, XI (1969), pp. 151–153.

168. Review of O. Böhtlingk u. R. Roth, *Sanskrit Wörterbuch*. Neudruck d. Ausgabe St. Petersburg, 1855–1875. 7 vols.
——— *ibid.*, p. 212.

169. Review of *Panchadashi. A Treatise on Advaita metaphysics by Swami Vidyaranya*, tr. fr. the Sanskrit by H. P. Shastri. 2nd ed., London, 1966.
——— *ibid.*, p. 213.

170. Review of *Tattva-kaumudī. Vācaspati Miśra's Commentary on the Sāṁkhya-Kārikā*, tr. into Engl. by G. Jha. Rev. and reed. by Dr. M. M. Patkar. Poona, 1965.
——— *ibid.*, p. 308.

171. Review of J. F. Rock, *Na-khi Manuscripts*, ed. by K. L. Janert. Wiesbaden, 1965; J. F. Rock, *The Life and Culture of the Na-khi Tribe of the China-Tibet Borderland*. M. Harders-Steinhäuser und G. Jayme, *Untersuchung des Papiers acht verschiedener alter*

Na-Khi-Handschriften auf Rohstoff und Herstellungsweise. Wiesbaden, 1963.
——— *ibid.*, pp. 308–310.

172. Review of R. Shafer, *Introduction to Sino-Tibetan*, part I, Wiesbaden, 1966.
——— *ibid.*, pp. 310–311.

173. Review of Yutaka Iwamoto, *Bukkyō setsuwa kenkyū josetsu*, Kyōto, 1967.
——— *IIJ*. XII (1969), pp. 52–60.

174. Review of J. Przyluski, *The Legend of Emperor Aśoka in Indian and Chinese Texts*. Calcutta, 1967.
——— *JAOS*, 89 (1969), pp. 793–794.

1970

175. Review of R. Pischel, *Comparative Grammar of the Prākṛit Languages*. Tr. by Dr. S. Jhā. 2nd ed., Delhi-Varanasi-Patna, 1965.
——— *IIJ*, XII (1970), p. 144.

176. Review of Hermann Oldenberg, *Kleine Schriften*, Wiesbaden, 1967.
——— *ibid.*, pp. 224–226.

177. CR de Sujitkumar Mukhopādhyāya, *The Aśokāvadāna, Sanskrit text compared with Chinese versions*. New Delhi, 1963.
——— *ibid.*, pp. 269–274.

178. Review of J. Kolmaš, *A Genealogy of the Kings of Derge, Sde-dge'i rgyal-rabs. Tibetan Text edited with Historical Introduction*, Prague, 1968.
——— *ibid.*, pp. 274–275.

179. Review of É. Lamotte, *La concentration de la marche héroïque*. Bruxelles, 1965.

——— *OLZ*, 65 (1970), Sp. 72–83.

1971

180. Un fragment de l'histoire de Rāma en tibétain, *Études tibétaines dediées à la mémoire de Marcelle Lalou*, Paris, 1971, pp. 127–141.
181. Lhasa, *Grote Winkler Prins*, Zevende druk, deel 12, Amsterdam-Brussel, 1971, pp. 6–7.
182. Contributions à *Revue bibliographique de Sinologie*, 9, Paris-La Haye, 1971.
183. Review of R. E. Emmerick, *The Khotanese Śūraṅgamasamādhisūtra*, London, 1970.
——— *AM*, XVI, parts 1–2 (January 1971), pp. 207–210.
184. Review of W. Liebenthal, *Chao Lun. The Treatises of Seng-chao*, Hongkong, 1968.
——— *ibid.*, pp. 220–221.
185. Review of É. Lamotte, *Le Traité de la Grande Vertu de Sagesse de Nāgārjuna (Mahāprajñāpāramitāśāstra)*, Tome III, Louvain, 1970.
——— *AM*, XVII, part 1 (December 1971), pp. 105–112.
186. Review of *Festschrift für Wilhelm Eilers. Ein Dokument der internationalen Forschung zum 27. September 1966*, Wiesbaden, 1967; *Die Sprache, Zeitschrift für Sprachwissenschaft*, XII. Band, 2. Heft (1966): *Festgabe für Wilhelm Eilers*, Wiesbaden, Wien, 1966.
——— *IIJ*, XIII (1971), pp. 62–63.
187. Review of E. Waldschmidt, *Von Ceylon bis Turfan. Schriften zur Geschichte, Literatur, Religion und Kunst des indischen Kulturraumes. Festgabe zum 70. Geburtstag am*

15. Juli 1967. Göttingen, 1967.
——— *ibid.*, pp. 63–64.

188. Review of O. Zeller, *Problemgeschichte der vergleichenden (indogermanischen) Sprachwissenschaft*. Osnabrück, 1967.
——— *ibid.*, pp. 64–65.

189. Review of Ratna Handurukande, *Maṇicūḍāvadāna being a Translation and Edition and Lokānanda, a Transliteration and Synopsis*. London, 1967.
——— *ibid.*, pp. 140–143.

190. Review of E. Conze, *Thirty Years of Buddhist Studies*, Oxford, 1967.
——— *ibid.*, pp. 143–144.

191. Review of *Dvādaśāraṃ Nayacakraṃ* of Ācārya Śrī Mallavādi Kṣamāśramaṇa. With the Commentary *Nyāyāgamānusariṇī* of Srī Śiṃhasūri Gaṇi Vādi Kṣamāśramaṇa, Part I (1–4 Aras). Ed. with crit. notes by Muni Jambūvijayajī. Bhavnagar, 1966.
——— *ibid.*, pp. 144–150.

192. CR de L. Alsdorf, *Les études jaina. État présent et tâches futures*, Paris, 1965; L. Alsdorf, *Die Āryā-Strophen des Pāli-Kanons metrisch hergestellt und textgeschichtlich untersucht*, 1967.
——— *ibid.*, pp. 207–212.

193. Review of Lalmani Joshi, *Studies in the Buddhistic Culture of India* (During the 7th and 8th Centuries A.D.). Delhi-Patna-Varanasi, 1967.
——— *ibid.*, pp. 212–213.

194. Review of Tilak Raj Chopra, *The Kuśa-jātaka*. A crit. and compar. study, Hamburg, 1966.
——— *ibid.*, pp. 214–215.

195. CR de K. Sagaster, *Subud Erike. Ein Rosenkranz aus*

Perlen. Hrsg., übers. und komment. von K. S. Wiesbaden, 1967.
——— *ibid.*, pp. 215–220.

196. Review of D. L. Snellgrove, *The Nine Ways of Bon. Excerpts from gZi-brjid edited and translated.* London, 1967.
——— *ibid.*, pp. 220–222.

197. Review of R. E. Emmerick, *Tibetan Texts concerning Khotan.* London, 1967.
——— *ibid.*, pp. 222–225.

198. Review of *Buddhist Yearly 1966*. Jahrbuch für Buddhistische Forschungen. Halle, 1966; *Buddhist Yearly 1967*, Jahrbuch für Buddhistische Forschungen, ibid., 1967; *Bibliography of Literature on Buddhist topics published on the territory of the G.D.R. since 1945*; *Studia Asiae.* Festschrift für Johannes Schubert, Part I, ibid., 1969.
——— *ibid.*, p. 225.

199. CR de Tso Sze-bong, *Chung-kuo fo-chiao shih-chuan yü mu-lu yüan-ch'u lü-hsüeh sha-men chih t'an-t'ao.* (A study of Chinese Buddhist biographies and bibliographies derived from the Vinaya sect), *Hsin Ya hsüeh-pao,* VI, I (1964), pp. 415–486; VII, 1 (1965), pp. 305–361; VII, 2 (1966), pp. 79–155.
——— *TP*, 56 (1970), pp. 314–321.

1972

200. The Problem of the Absolute in the Madhyamaka School, *JIP*, II (1972), pp. 1–6. (English translation of No. 3).

201. Emptiness, *ibid.*, pp. 7–15.

202. A brief survey of Chinese Buddhist historiography, *Studies in Indo-Asian Art and Culture*, Vol. 1 (Commemoration Volume on the 69th birthday of Acharya Raghu Vira). New Delhi, 1972, pp. 101–108.

203. An Old Tibetan Version of the Rāmāyaṇa, *TP*, 58 (1972), pp. 190–202.

204. Notes à propos des colophons du Kanjur, *ZAS*, 6, (1972), pp. 505–559.

205. Review of *The Elders' Verses, I: Theragāthā*, Tr. w. an introd. and notes by K. R. Norman, London, 1969.
——— *IIJ*, XIII (1972), pp. 297–301.

206. Review of *Karuṇāpuṇḍarīka*. Ed. w. introd. and notes by Isshi Yamada, London, 1968.
——— *ibid.*, pp. 301–313.

207. CR de Saigusa Mitsuyoshi, *Studien zum Mahāprajñāpāramitā-(upadeśa)śāstra*, Tōkyō, 1969.
——— *ibid.*, pp. 314–315.

208. Review of *Lives of Eminent Korean Monks. The Haedong Kosŭng Chŏn*. Tr. w. an introd. by Peter H. Lee, Cambridge, Mass., 1969.
——— *ibid.*, pp. 315–317.

209. CR de L. Sander, *Paläographisches zu den Sanskrithandschriften der Berliner Turfansammlung*, Wiesbaden, 1968.
——— *ibid.*, pp. 317–318.

210. Review of *Beiträge zur Geistesgeschichte Indiens. Festschrift für Erich Frauwallner*. Hrsg. v. G. Oberhammer. Wien, 1968.
——— *IIJ*, XIV (1972), pp. 77–81.

211. Review of O. Botto (ed.), *Storia delle letterature d'Oriente*, Milano, 1969. 4 volumes.

——— *ibid.*, pp. 83–84.
212. Review of H. Jacobi, *Kleine Schriften*, hrsg. v. B. Kölver. 2 Teile. Wiesbaden, 1971.
——— *ibid.*, pp. 84–85.
213. Review of R. E. Emmerick, *The Sūtra of Golden Light*. Being a tr. of the Suvarṇabhāsottamasūtra. London, 1970.
——— *ibid.*, pp. 118–121.
214. Review of E. Frauwallner, *Materialien zur ältesten Erkenntnislehre der Karmamīmāṃsā*. Wien, 1968.
——— *ibid.*, pp. 122–123.
215. Review of F. Kielhorn, *Kleine Schriften mit einer Auswahl der epigraphischen Aufsätze*. 2 Teile. Hrsg. v. W. Rau. Wiesbaden, 1969.
——— *ibid.*, pp. 254–255.
216. Review of H. von Glasenapp, *Bibliographie*. Bearb. v. Zoltán Károlyi. Wiesbaden, 1968.
——— *ibid.*, pp. 255–256.
217. CR de L. Boulnois et H. Millot, *Bibliographie du Népal*, vol. 1: Sciences humaines. Paris, 1969.
——— *ibid.*, pp. 256–257.
218. Review of Tsuji Naoshirō, *Genson Yajuru-vēda bunken-Kodai Indo no saishiki ni kansuru konpon shiryō no bunkengakuteki kenkyū*. Tokyo, 1970.
H. S. Ananthanarayana, *Verb Forms of the Taittirīya Brāhmaṇa*. Poona, 1970.
Maitrāyaṇī Saṃhitā. Die Saṃhitā der Maitrāyaṇīya-Śākhā. Hrsg. v. L. von Schroeder. 1. und 2. Buch. Wiesbaden, 1970 und 1971.
Kāṭhaka. Die Saṃhitā der Kaṭha-Śākhā. Hrsg. v. L. von Schroeder, 1. und 2. Buch. Wiesbaden, 1970–71.
——— *ibid.*, pp. 260–262.
219. CR de L. Silburn, *Hymnes de Abhinavagupta*. Traduits

et commentés par L. S. Paris, 1970.
——— *ibid.*, pp. 262–264.

220. CR de F. Bourgeois, *Veṇīsaṃhāra*. Drame sanskrit. Paris, 1971.
——— *ibid.*, pp. 264–265.

221. Review of R. Hoernle (ed.), *Manuscript Remains of Buddhist Literature found in Eastern Turkestan*. Facs. w. transcripts, translations and notes. Vol. I, parts 1–2. Amsterdam, 1970.
——— *ibid.*, p. 265.

222. Review of B. Bergmann, *Nomadische Streifereien unter den Kalmüken in den Jahren 1802 und 1803*. Reprint. Mit einer Einführung von S. Hummel. New York, 1969.
——— *ibid.*, pp. 265–267.

223. Review of G. R. Welbon, *The Buddhist Nirvāṇa and its Western Interpreters*. The Univ. of Chicago Pr., 1968.
——— *JIP*, 1 (1972), pp. 396–403.

224. CR de Fujita Kōtatsu, *Genshi jōdo shisō no kenkyū*, 2ème éd., Tokyo, 1970.
——— *TP*, 58 (1972), pp. 352–366.

1973

225. *Dharmasamuccaya. Compendium de la Loi*. 3e partie (chapitres XIII à XXXVI). Texte sanskrit édité avec la version tibétaine et les versions chinoises et traduit en français par Lin Ḷi-kouang. Révision de André Bareau, J. W. de Jong et Paul Demiéville. Avec des Appendices par J. W. de Jong, Paris, 1973. VI + 567 + 48 pp.

226. An Old Tibetan Version of Ramayana. *Cultural*

Forum, XV, 2, Jan. 1973, pp. 22–32 [uncorrected and unauthorized reprint of No. 203.]

227. Tibetan *blag-pa* and *blags-pa*, *BSOAS*, 36, part 2 (1973) (volume in honour of Walter Simon), pp. 309–312.

228. The Discovery of India by the Greeks, *AS*, XXVII. 2, 1973, pp. 115–142.

229. Girisha-nin ni yoru Indo no hakken, Minoru Hara yaku. *Suzuki gakujutsu zaidan kenkyū nenpō*, 10, 1973 (Tokyo), pp. 59–76. [Japanese translation of No. 228.]

230. Contributions à *Revue bibliographique de Sinologie*, 10, Paris-La Haye, 1973.

231. Review of Samten G. Karmay (ed. and tr.), *The Treasury of Good Sayings: a Tibetan history of Boṅ*. London, 1972.
——— *BSOAS*. 36 (1973), pp. 488–489.

232. Review of Garma C. C. Chang, *The Buddhist Teachings of Totality*. London, 1972.
——— *AM*, XVIII (1973), pp. 118–119.

233. Review of K. L. Janert and N. Narasimhan Poti, *Indische und Nepalische Handschriften*. Teil 2. Wiesbaden, 1970.
——— *IIJ* 15 (1973), pp. 61–62.

234. Review of *Journal of Indian Philosophy*, ed. by B. K. Matilal, vol. 1, No. 1. Dordrecht, 1970.
——— *ibid.*, pp. 62–63.

235. CR de A. W. Macdonald et M. Lalou, *L'oeuvre de Jean Przyluski*. Paris, 1970.
——— *ibid.*, p. 63.

236. Review of O. von Hinüber, *Studien zur Kasussyntax des Pāli, besonders des Vinaya-piṭaka*, München, 1968.

——— *ibid.*, pp. 64–66.

237. Review of D. L. Snellgrove, *Four Lamas of Dolpo*. Oxford, 1967.
——— *ibid.*, pp. 68–74.

238. Review of D. N. MacKenzie (ed. and tr.), *The 'Sūtra of the Causes and Effects of Actions' in Sogdian*. London, 1970.
——— *ibid.*, pp. 74–75.

239. Review of A. J. Alston (tr.), *The Realization of the Absolute*. London, Shanti Sadan, 1971.
——— *ibid.*, pp. 233–236.

240. Review of P. Thieme, *Kleine Schriften*, Wiesbaden, 1971.
——— *JAOS*, 93 (1973), pp. 109–110.

241. Review of Madeleine Biardeau, *La philosophie de Maṇḍana Miśra vue à partir de la Brahmasiddhi*. École française d'Extrême Orient, Paris, 1969, and *Maṇḍanamiśra's Brahmasiddhih Brahmakāndam*. Übersetzung, Einleitung und Anmerkungen by Tilmann Vetter. Wien, 1969.
——— *Journal of the Oriental Society of Australia*, vol. 9, nos. 1 & 2, pp. 109–110.

242. Bespr. von L. Frédéric, *Südost-Asien*. Essen, 1968.
——— *OLZ*, 68 (1973), 93–94.

243. Bespr. von Lama Anagarika Govinda, *Der Weg der weissen Wolken*. Zürich und Stuttgart: Raschen 1969.
——— *ibid.*, Sp. 612–613.

244. CR de Walpola Rahula (tr.), *Le compendium de la super-doctrine (philosophie) (Abhidharmasamuccaya) d'Asaṅga*. Paris, 1971.
——— *TP*, LIX (1973), pp. 339–346.

1974

245. A Brief History of Buddhist Studies in Europe and America (Part I), *The Eastern Buddhist*, N. S., vol. VII, no. 1, May 1974, pp. 55–106.
246. *A Brief History of Buddhist Studies in Europe and America* (Part II), *ibid.*, no. 2, October 1974, pp. 49–82.
247. Chūgoku ni okeru Butsuda no kotoba, *Komazawa daigaku bukkyōgaku-bu kenkyū kiyō*, vol. 32 (1974), pp. 50–72.
[Japanese translation of No. 145 by Okabe Kazuo.]
248. Tibetaanse Literatuur, *Moderne Encyclopedie der Wereldliteratuur*, vol. 8, 's-Gravenhage, 1974, pp. 432b–437a.
249. Notes on the sources and the text of the Sang Hyang Kamahāyānan Mantranaya, *Bijdragen tot de taal-, land- en volkenkunde*, deel 130, 's-Gravenhage, 1974, pp. 465–482.
250. À propos du Nidānasaṃyukta, *Mélanges de Sinologie offerts à Monsieur Paul Demiéville*, II, Paris, 1974, pp. 137–149.
251. Notes on the Bhikṣuṇī-vinaya of the Mahāsāṃghikas, *Buddhist Studies in Honour of I. B. Horner*, Dordrecht, 1974, pp. 63–70.
252. The Study of Buddhism. Problems and Perspectives. *Studies in Indo-Asian Art and Culture*, vol. 4 (1974), (Acharya Raghu Vira Commemoration Volume), pp. 13–26.
[English translation of No. 27.]
253. Review of Karl H. Potter, *Bibliography of Indian Philosophies*. Delhi-Patna-Varanasi, Motilal Banarsidass, 1970.

——— *IIJ*, XVI, 2 (1974), pp. 145-47.

254. Review of A. K. Warder, *Outline of Indian Philosophy*. Delhi-Patna-Varanasi, Motilal Banarsidass, 1971.
——— *ibid.*, pp. 147-49.

255. Review of Gustav Roth (ed.), *Bhikṣuṇī-vinaya including Bhikṣuṇīprakīrṇaka and a summary of the Bhikṣuprakīrṇaka of the Ārya-Mahāsāṃghika-Lokottaravādin* (= *Tibetan Sanskrit Works Series*, vol. XII). Patna, K. P. Jayaswal Research Institute, 1970.
——— *ibid.*, pp. 149–150.

256. Review of B. Jinananda (ed.), *Abhisamācārikā* [*Bhikṣuprakīrṇaka*] (= *Tibetan Sanskrit Works Series*, vol. IX). Patna, K.P. Jayaswal Research Institute, 1969.
——— *ibid.*, pp. 150–152.

257. CR de E. Waldschmidt, *Sanskrithandschriften aus den Turfanfunden*, Teil II. Wiesbaden, 1968.
——— *OLZ* 69, 1/2 (1974), Sp. 74–75.

258. Review of V. Stache-Rosen, *Dogmatische Begriffsreihen im älteren Buddhismus*, II. Berlin, 1968.
———*ibid.*, Sp. 80–84.

259. Review of McDermott, A.C. Senape: *An Eleventh-Century Buddhist Logic of 'Exists'*. Dordrecht 1969.
——— *ibid.* 11/12 (1974), Sp. 587–589.

1975

260. *Bukkyō kenkyū no rekishi*. Tōkyō, Shunjūsha Press, 1975. 208 pp. [Japanese translation of nos. 201, 223, 245, 246 + bibliography of author 1949–1973.]

261. *Bukkyō Kenkyū. Mondai to Mitōshi, Hokke-Bunka Kenkyū* No. 1, Tōkyō, 1975, pp. 1–12.

[Japanese translation of no. 252.]

262. La Légende de Śāntideva, *IIJ*, XVI, 3, 1975, pp. 161–182.

263. Notes on Prajñāpāramitā Texts, *Indologica Taurinensia*, vol. II (1974), Torino, 1975, pp. 107–119.

264. Recent Russian Publications on the Indian Epic, *The Adyar Library Bulletin*, vol. 39 (1975), pp. 1–42.

265. Review of Bernhard Kölver, *Textkritische und philologische Untersuchungen zur Rājataraṅgiṇī des Kalhaṇa* (= *Verzeichnis der Orientalischen Handschriften in Deutschland*, Supplementband 12). Wiesbaden, 1969.
—— *IIJ* XVI (1975), pp. 225–227.

266. Review of J. F. Staal (ed.), *A Reader on the Sanskrit Grammarians*. Cambridge, Mass. and London, 1972.
—— *ibid.*, pp. 227–229.

267. Review of Herbert V. Guenther, *The Tantric View of Life*. Berkeley and London, 1972.
—— *ibid.*, pp. 229–231.

268. Review of G. M. Bongard-Levin, *Studies in Ancient India and Central Asia* (= *Soviet Indology Series* 7). Calcutta, 1971.
—— *ibid.*, pp. 231–232.

269. Review of T. Venkatacharya (ed.), *The Śrīharicaritamahākāvya of Śrīhari Padmanābhaśāstrin* (= *The Adyar Library Series* 102). Adyar, The Adyar Library and Research Centre, 1972.
—— *ibid.*, pp. 302–303.

270. Review of V. Raghavan, *Studies on Some Concepts of the Alaṃkāra Śāstra* (= *The Adyar Library Series* 33). Adyar, The Adyar Library and Research Centre, 1973. Revised edition.
—— *ibid.*, p. 303.

271. Review of Franz László, *Die Parallelversion der Manusmṛti im Bhaviṣyapurāṇa* (= *Abhandlungen für die Kunde des Morgenlandes*, XL, 2). Wiesbaden, 1971.
——— *ibid.*, pp. 307–308.

272. Review of Heinz Bechert, *Buddhismus. Staat und Gesellschaft in den Ländern des Theravāda-Buddhismus*, I: Grundlagen. Ceylon, Frankfurt am Main und Berlin, 1966, II: Birma, Kambodscha, Laos, Thailand (= *Schriften des Instituts für Asienkunde in Hamburg* XVII: 1–2). Wiesbaden, 1967.
——— *ibid.*, pp. 308–310.

273. Review of *The Vimalakīrti Nirdeśa Sūtra* (Wei Mo Chieh So Shuo Ching), transl. by Lu K'uan Yü (Charles Luk). Berkeley and London, 1972.
——— *ibid.*, pp. 310–311.

274. Review of Anne-Marie Blondeau, *Matériaux pour l'étude de l'hippologie et de l'hippiatrie tibétaines* (à partir des manuscrits de Touen-houang). Genève-Paris, 1972.
——— *ibid.*, pp. 311–313.

275. Review of Giuseppe Tucci, *Il libro tibetano dei morti* (Bardo Tödöl) (= *Classici delle religioni* N. 22. Sezione prima diretta da Oscar Botto; Le religioni orientali). Torino, 1972.
——— *ibid.*, pp. 314–316.

276. Review of *Myōhō-renge-kyō. The Sutra of the Lotus Flower of the Wonderful Law*. Transl. by Bunnō Katō. Rev. by W. E. Soothill and Wilhelm Schiffer, Risshō Kōsei-Kai, Tokyo, 1971.
The Sutra of the Lotus Flower of the Wonderful Law. Transl. by Senchu Murano. Nichiren Shu Headquarters, Tokyo, 1974.

——— *The Eastern Buddhist*, N. S., Vol. VIII no. 2, October, 1975, pp. 154–159.

277. Review of N. H. Samtani (ed.), *The Arthaviniścaya-sūtra and Its Commentary (Nibandhana)*. (= *Tibetan Sanskrit Works Series*, Vol. XIII). Patna, K. P. Jayaswal Research Institute, 1971.
——— *IIJ*, XVII (1975), pp. 115–118.

278. Review of *India Maior*. Congratulatory Volume presented to J. Gonda (ed. by J. Ensink and P. Gaeffke). Leiden, 1971.
——— *ibid.*, p. 118.

279. Review of *Maitrāyaṇī Saṃhitā. Die Saṃhitā der Maitrāyaṇīya-Śākhā*. Herausgeg. von Leopold von Schroeder. Vols. III and IV, Wiesbaden, 1972; *Kaṭhaka. Die Saṃhitā der Kaṭha-Śākhā*. Herausgeg. von Leopold von Schroeder. Vols. 3 and 4. Wiesbaden, 1972.
——— *ibid.*, p. 119.

280. Review of *Śaṅkara's Upadeśasāhasrī*. Critically ed. w. intr. by Sengaku Mayeda. Tokyo, 1973.
——— *ibid.*, XVII, pp. 261-262.

281. Review of Paul Martin-Dubost, *Çankara et le Vedānta* (= *Maîtres spirituels* No. 39). Paris, Editions du Seuil, 1973.
——— *ibid.*, p. 263.

282. Review of Giuseppe Tucci, *Opera minora*. Roma, 1971.
——— *ibid.*, pp. 263–264.

283. Review of Wilhelm Geiger, *Kleine Schriften zur Indologie und Buddhismuskunde*. Herausgeg. von Heinz Bechert (= *Glasenapp-Stiftung*, Band 6). Wiesbaden, 1973.

——— *ibid.*, pp. 264–265.

284. Review of *Sanskrit Wörterbuch der buddhistischen Texte aus den Turfan-Funden.* Begonnen von Ernst Waldschmidt. Herausgeg. von der Akademie der Wissenschaften in Göttingen unter der Leitung von Heinz Bechert. 1. Lieferung: *a-*, *an-/antar-vāsa.* Göttingen, 1973.

——— *ibid.*, pp. 273–276.

285. Review of *Sprachwissenschaftliche Ergebnisse der deutschen Turfan-Forschung*, 2 Bde. Leipzig, 1972.

——— *ibid.*, pp. 288–290.

286. Review of Michael Silverstein (ed.), *Whitney on Language, Selected Writings of William Dwight Whitney.* MIT Press, 1971.

——— *ibid.*, pp. 290–291.

1976

287. *A Brief History of Buddhist Studies in Europe and America.* Varanasi, Bharat-Bharati, 1976. 94 pp. [Reprint of Nos. 245 and 246 with the addition of two indices, pp. 89–94.]

288. Review of Waldschmidt, Ernst, Clawiter, Walter u. Lore Sander-Holzmann (Hrsg.): *Sanskrithandschriften aus den Turfanfunden.* 3: Die Katalognummers 802–1014. Wiesbaden, 1971.

——— *OLZ*, 71, 1/2 (1976), Sp. 75–76.

289. Review of Nakamura Hajime, *Bukkyō-go Daijiten.* Tokyo, 1975. Vols. I, II and index.

——— *The Eastern Buddhist*, N. S., vol. IV No. 1, May, 1976, pp. 131–135.

290. Review of *The Mahayana Mahaparinirvaṇa-Sūtra.*

A Complete Translation from the Classical Chinese Language in 3 volumes. Annotated and with Full Glossary, Index, and Concordance by Kosho Yamamoto. The Karin Buddhological Series No. 5. The Karinbunko, Oyama, Ono-ku, Ube City, Yamaguchi-ken.
——— *ibid.*, No. 2, October, 1976, pp. 134–136.

291. Review of L. Alsdorf, *Kleine Schriften* [= *Glasenapp-Stiftung*, Band 10]. Wiesbaden, 1974.
——— *IIJ*, XVIII (1976), pp. 297.

292. Review of R. Gnoli (tr.), *Luce delle Sacre Scriture* (Tantrāloka) di Abhinavagupta [= *Classici delle religioni* N. 25]. Torino, 1972.
——— *ibid.*, pp. 298–300.

293. Review of L. Sternbach, *Mahā-subhāṣita-saṁgraha.* Volume I: a° – anve° [= Vishveshvaranand Indological Series 64]. Hoshiarpur, 1974.
——— *ibid.*, pp. 300–302.

294. Review of Volker Moeller, *Symbolik des Hinduismus und des Jainismus*. Tafelband [= Symbolik der Religionen, Band XIX]. Stuttgart, 1974.
——— *ibid.*, p. 303.

295. Review of Esther A. Solomon (ed.), *Sāṁkhya-Saptati-Vṛtti* (V_1), Ahmedabad, 1973. And Esther A. Solomon (ed.), *Sāṁkhya-Vṛtti* (V_2), Ahmedabad, 1973.
——— *ibid.*, pp. 303–304.

296. Review of Jean Filliozat, *Laghu-prabandhāḥ*. Choix d'articles d'Indologie. Leiden, 1974.
——— *ibid.*, pp. 304–305.

297. Review of R. O. Meisezahl, 'Śmaśānavidhi des Lūyī. Textkritik nach der tibetischen Version des Kom-

mentars Lūyīpādābhisamayavṛtti Sambarodaya nāma von Tathāgatavajra', *Zentralasiatische Studien* 8 (1974), 9–127.

——— *ibid.*, pp. 305–307.

298. Review of Karunesha Shukla (ed.), *Śrāvakabhūmi of Ācārya Asaṅga* [= Tibetan Sanskrit Works Series, vol. XIV]. Patna, 1973.

——— *ibid.*, pp. 307–310.

299. Review of Robert Shafer, *Introduction to Sino-Tibetan*, Parts 3, 4, 5. Wiesbaden, 1968.

——— *ibid.*, pp. 310–311.

300. Review of Takasaki Jikidō, *Nyoraizō-shisō no keisei* [The formation of the tathāgatagarbha theory]. Tōkyō, 1974.

——— *ibid.*, pp. 311–315.

301. Review of Helmut Hoffmann, *Symbolik der tibetischen Religionen und des Schamanismus* [= Symbolik der Religionen, Band XII]. Stuttgart, 1967.

——— *ibid.*, pp. 315–316.

302. Review of Heinz Zimmermann, *Die Subhāṣita-ratnakaraṇḍaka-kathā* (dem Aryaśūra zugeschrieban) und ihre tibetische Übersetzung. [= Freiburger Beiträge zur Indologie, Band 8]. Wiesbaden, 1975.

——— *ibid.*, pp. 316–320.

303. Review of *Mikkyō jiten*. Sawa Ryūken hen. Kyōto, 1975.

——— *ibid.*, pp. 320–321.

304. Review of Ria Kloppenborg, *The Paccekabuddha*. A Buddhist Ascetic. A Study of the concept of the paccekabuddha in Pāli canonical and commentarial literature [= *Orientalia Rheno-Traiectina*, vol. 20]. Leiden, 1974.

——— *ibid.*, pp. 322–324.

305. Review of *The Sūtra on the Foundation of the Buddhist Order* (Catuṣpariṣatsūtra) transl. by Ria Kloppenborg [= Religious Texts Translation Series Nisaba, volume one]. Leiden, 1973.

——— *ibid.*, pp. 324–327.

306. F. B. J. Kuiper: Bibliography 1967–1976, *IIJ*, 19 (1977), pp. 1–4.

307. The Tun-huang Manuscripts of the Tibetan Rāmāyaṇa Story, *ibid.*, pp. 37–88.

308. Jātakamālā II. 17, *ibid.*, p. 97.

309. Yamaguchi Susumu 27.1.1895–21.10.1976, *ibid.*, pp. 99–103.

310. The Bodhisattvāvadānakalpalatā and the Ṣaḍdantāvadāna, *Buddhist Thought and Asian Civilisation.* Essays in Honor of Herbert V. Guenther on His Sixtieth Birthday, Emeryville, Cal., 1977, pp. 27–38.

311. Sanskrit Fragments of the Kāśyapaparivarta, *Beiträge zur Indien-Forschung* Ernst Waldschmidt zum 80. Geburtstag gewidmet. [Veröffentlichugen des Museums für Indische Kunst Berlin, Band 4], 1977, pp. 247–255,

312. Notes on the Second Chapter of the Madhyāntavibhāgaṭīkā, *CAJ* XXI, 2 [In honour of the 65th birthday of Professor Helmut Hoffmann], 1977, pp. 111–117.

313. Notes on Prajñāpāramitā Texts 2. The Suvikrāntavikrāmi-paripṛcchā, in L. Lancaster, ed., *Prajñāpāramitā and Related Systems,* Berkeley, Berkeley Buddhist Studies Series, 1979.

314. Review of Sonam Angdu (ed.), *Tibeto-Sanskrit Lexi-*

cographical Materials. The *Sgra sbyor bam po gñis pa*, the *Dag yig Za ma tog*, and the *Dag yig Li śi'i gur khaṅ* (= Tibeto-Sanskrit-Hindi Grammars and Dictionaries, vol. 1). Leh (Ladakh), Basgo Tongspon Publication, 1973.
——— *IIJ*, 19 (1977), pp. 120–121.

315. Review of Ngawang Gelek Demo (ed.), *The Collected Works of 'Jam-dbyaṅs bźad-pa'i rdo-rje* (= Gedan Sungrab Minyam Gyunphel Series, vols. 40–54). New Delhi, 1972–1974.
——— *ibid.*, pp. 124–125.

316. Review of Horiuchi Kanjin (ed.), *Bonzōkan taishō Shoe Kongōchōgyō no kenkyū*. Bonpon kōteihon (ge). Kōyasan, Mikkyō bunka kenkyūjo, 1974.
——— *ibid.*, pp. 125–127.

317. Review of Charles S. Prebish, *Buddhist Monastic Discipline: The Sanskrit Prātimokṣa Sūtras of the Mahāsāṃghikas and Mūlasarvāstivādins*, University Park and London, The Pennsylvania State University Press, 1975.
——— *ibid.*, pp. 127–130.

318. Review of Pierre Python, *Vinaya-viniścaya-Upāli-paripṛcchā* (= Collection Jean Przyluski, tome V). Paris, 1973.
——— *ibid.*, pp. 131–135.

Index of Books Reviewed

No. of Bibliography: